COLLINS

SPANISH★ENGLISH
ENGLISH★SPANISH
DICTIONARY

MIKE GONZALEZ

BERKLEY BOOKS, NEW YORK

General Editor
R. H. Thomas

The text of this dictionary has been
adapted from the Collins Gem
Spanish–English, English–Spanish
Dictionary

First published in this edition 1982

Contributors
Margaret Tejerizo, John Forry,
Carmen Billinghurst, Liam Kane, Pat Feehan

Editorial Staff
Irene Lakhani

This Berkley book contains the complete
text of the original edition.
It has been completely reset in a type face
designed for easy reading, and was printed
from new film.

COLLINS SPANISH/ENGLISH ENGLISH/SPANISH
DICTIONARY

A Berkley Book / published by arrangement with
Collins Publishers

PRINTING HISTORY
Collins Gem edition published 1982
Berkley edition / August 1982
Second printing / August 1983

ISBN: 0-425-05448-9

A BERKLEY BOOK ® TM 757,375
Berkley Books are published by The Berkley Publishing Group,
200 Madison Avenue, New York, New York 10016.
The name "BERKLEY" and the stylized "B" with design
are trademarks belonging to Berkley Publishing Corporation.
PRINTED IN THE UNITED STATES OF AMERICA

INTRODUCCIÓN

Quien desee leer y entender el inglés encontrará en este diccionario un extenso léxico moderno que abarca una amplia gama de locuciones de uso corriente. Igualmente encontrará, en su debido orden alfabético, las abreviaturas, las siglas, los nombres geográficos más conocidos y, además, las principales formas de verbo irregulares, donde se le referirá a las respectivas formas de base, hallándose allí la traducción.

Quien aspire comunicarse y expresarse en lengua extranjera, hallará aquí una clara y detallada explicación de las palabras básicas, empleándose un sistema de indicadores que le remitirán a la traducción más apta y le señalarán su correcto uso.

INTRODUCTION

The user whose aim is to read and understand Spanish will find a comprehensive and up-to-date wordlist including numerous phrases in current use. He will also find listed alphabetically the main irregular forms with a cross-reference to the basic form where a translation is given, as well as some of the most common abbreviations, acronyms and geographical names.

The user who wishes to communicate and to express himself in the foreign language will find clear and detailed treatment of all the basic words, with numerous indicators pointing to the appropriate translation, and helping him to use it correctly.

ABREVIATURAS

ABBREVIATIONS

adjetivo, locución adjetivo	**a**	adjective, adjectival phrase
abreviatura	**ab(b)r**	abbreviation
adverbio, locución adverbial	**ad**	adverb, adverbial phrase
administración, lengua administrativa	**ADMIN**	administration
agricultura	**AGR**	agriculture
América Latina	**AM**	Latin America
anatomía	**ANAT**	anatomy
arquitectura	**ARQ, ARCH**	architecture
astrología, astronomía	**ASTRO**	astrology, astronomy
el automóvil	**AUT(O)**	the motor car and motoring
aviación, viajes aéreos	**AVIAT**	flying, air travel
biología	**BIO(L)**	biology
botánica, flores	**BOT**	botany
inglés británico	**Brit**	British English
química	**CHEM**	chemistry
conjunción	**conj**	conjunction
lengua familiar	**col**	colloquial usage
comercio, finanzas, banca	**COM(M)**	commerce, finance, banking
construcción	**CONSTR**	building
compuesto	**cpd**	compound element
cocina	**CULIN**	cookery
determinante, artículo	**det**	determiner, article
economía	**ECON**	economics
electricidad, electrónica	**ELEC**	electricity, electronics
enseñanza, sistema escolar y universitario	**ESCOL**	schooling, schools and universities
especialmente	**esp**	especially
exclamación, interjección	**excl**	exclamation, interjection
femenino	**f**	feminine
lengua familiar	**fam**	colloquial usage
ferrocarril	**FERRO**	railways
uso figurado	**fig**	figurative use
fotografía	**FOTO**	photography
(verbo inglés) del cual la partícula es inseparable	**fus**	(phrasal verb) where the particle is inseparable
generalmente	**gen**	generally
geografía, geología	**GEO**	geography, geology
geometría	**GEOM**	geometry
invariable	**inv**	invariable
irregular	**irg**	irregular
lo jurídico	**JUR**	law
gramática, lingüística	**LING**	grammar, linguistics
masculino	**m**	masculine

matemáticas	**MAT(H)**	mathematics
medicina	**MED**	medical term, medicine
masculino/femenino	**m/f**	masculine/feminine
lo militar, ejército	**MIL**	military matters
música	**MUS**	music
sustantivo, nombre	**n**	noun
navegación, náutica	**NAUT**	sailing, navigation
sustantivo numérico	**num**	numeral noun
complemento	**obj**	(grammatical) object
	o.s.	oneself
peyorativo	**pey, pej**	derogatory, pejorative
fotografía	**PHOT**	photography
fisiología	**PHYSIOL**	physiology
plural	**pl**	plural
política	**POL**	politics
participio de pasado	**pp**	past participle
prefijo	**pref**	prefix
preposición	**prep**	preposition
pronombre	**pron**	pronoun
psicología, psiquiatría	**PSICO, PSYCH**	psychology, psychiatry
tiempo pasado	**pt**	past tense
sustantivo no empleado en el plural	**q**	collective (uncountable) noun, not used in plural
ferrocarril	**RAIL**	railways
religión, lo eclesiástico	**REL**	religion, church service
	sb	somebody
escolar, universitario	**SCOL**	schools, universities
singular	**sg**	singular
	sth	something
sujeto	**su(b)j**	(grammatical) subject
sufijo	**suff**	suffix
tauromaquia	**TAUR**	bullfighting
técnica, tecnología	**TEC(H)**	technical term, technology
telecomunicaciones	**TELEC, TEL**	telecommunications
televisión	**TV**	television
imprenta, tipografía	**TYP**	typography, printing
inglés norteamericano	**US**	American English
verbo	**vb**	verb
verbo intransitivo	**vi**	intransitive verb
verbo pronominal	**vr**	reflexive verb
verbo transitivo	**vt**	transitive verb
zoología, animales	**ZOOL**	zoology
marca registrada	**®**	registered trademark
indica un equivalente cultural	**≈**	introduces a cultural equivalent

SPANISH PRONUNCIATION

Consonants

c	[k]	caja	c before *a*, *o* or *u* is pronounced as in *c*at
ce, ci	[θe, θi]	cero cielo	c before *e* or *i* is pronounced as in *th*in
ch	[tʃ]	chiste	ch is pronounced as *ch* in *ch*air
d	[d, ð]	danés ciudad	at the beginning of a phrase or after *l* or *n*, d is pronounced as in English. In any other position it is pronounced like *th* in *th*e
g	[g, ɤ]	gafas paga	g before *a*, *o* or *u* is pronounced as in *g*ap, if at the beginning of a phrase or after *n*. In other positions the sound is softened
ge, gi	[xe, xi]	gente girar	g before *e* or *i* is pronounced similar to *ch* in Scottish lo*ch*
h		haber	h is always silent in Spanish
j	[x]	jugar	j is pronounced similar to *ch* in Scottish lo*ch*
ll	[ʎ]	talle	ll is pronounced like the *lli* in mi*lli*on
ñ	[ɲ]	niño	ñ is pronounced like the *ni* in o*ni*on
q	[k]	que	q is pronounced as *k* in *k*ing
r, rr	[r, rr]	quitar garra	r is always pronounced in Spanish, unlike the silent r in dance*r*. rr is trilled, like a Scottish r
s	[s]	quizás isla	s is usually pronounced as in pa*ss*, but before *b, d, g, l, m* or *n* it is pronounced as in ro*se*
v	[b, ß]	vía dividir	v is pronounced something like *b*. At the beginning of a phrase or after *m* or *n* it is pronounced as *b* in *b*oy. In any other position the sound is softened
z	[θ]	tenaz	z is pronounced as *th* in *th*in

b, f, k, l, m, n, p, t and x are pronounced as in English.

Vowels

[a]	p*a*ta	not as long as *a* in f*a*r. When followed by a consonant in the same syllable (i.e. in a closed syllable), as in am*a*nte, the *a* is short, as in b*a*t
[e]	m*e*	like *e* in th*ey*. In a closed syllable, as in g*e*nte, the *e* is short as in p*e*t
[i:]	p*i*no	as in m*ea*n or mach*i*ne
[o]	l*o*	as in l*o*cal. In a closed syllable, as in c*o*ntrol, the *o* is short as in c*o*t
[u:]	l*u*nes	as in r*u*le. It is silent after *q*, and in *gue, gui*, unless marked *güe, güi* e.g. anti*güe*dad

Diphthongs

ai, ay	b*ai*le	as *i* in r*i*de
au	*au*to	as *ou* in sh*ou*t
ei, ey	bu*ey*	as *ey* in gr*ey*
eu	d*eu*da	both elements pronounced independently [e] + [u:]
oi, oy	h*oy*	as *oy* in t*oy*

Stress

The rules of stress in Spanish are as follows:

(a) when a word ends in a vowel or in *n* or *s*, the second last syllable is stressed: pat*a*ta, pat*a*tas, c*o*me, c*o*men

(b) when a word ends in a consonant other than *n* or *s*, the stress falls on the last syllable: par*e*d, habl*a*r

(c) when the rules set out in a and b are not applied, an acute accent appears over the stressed vowel: com*ú*n, geograf*í*a, ingl*é*s

In the phonetic transcription, the symbol [ˈ] precedes the syllable on which the stress falls.

PRONUNCIACIÓN INGLESA

Vocales y diptongos

	Ejemplo inglés	*Ejemplo español/explicación*
ɑ:	f**a**ther	Entre *a* de *padre* y *o* de *noche*
ʌ	b**u**t, c**o**me	*a* muy breve
æ	m**a**n, c**a**t	Se mantienen los labios en la posición de *e* en *pena* y luego se pronuncia el sonido *a*
ə	fath**er**, **a**go	Sonido indistinto parecido a una *e* u *o* casi mudas
ə:	b**i**rd, h**ea**rd	Entre *e* abierta, y *o* cerrada, sonido alargado
ɛ	g**e**t, b**e**d	como en p**e**rro
ɪ	**i**t, b**i**g	Más breve que en s**í**
i:	t**ea**, s**ee**	Como en f**i**no
ɔ	h**o**t, w**a**sh	Como en t**o**rre
ɔ:	s**aw**, **a**ll	Como en p**o**r
u	p**u**t, b**oo**k	Sonido breve, más cerrado que en b**u**rro
u:	t**oo**, y**ou**	Sonido largo, como en **u**no
aɪ	fl**y**, h**i**gh	Como en fr**ai**le
au	h**ow**, h**ou**se	Como en p**au**sa
ɛə	th**ere**, b**ea**r	Casi como en v**ea**, pero el sonido *a* se mezcla con el indistinto [ə]
eɪ	d**ay**, ob**ey**	*e* cerrada seguida por una *i* débil
ɪə	h**ere**, h**ea**r	Como en man**ía**, mezclándose el sonido *a* con el indistinto [ə]
ɔu	g**o**, n**o**te	[ə] seguido por una breve *u*
ɔɪ	b**oy**, **oi**l	Como en v**oy**
uə	p**oo**r, s**u**re	*u* bastante larga más el sonido indistinto [ə]

Consonantes

	Ejemplo inglés	Ejemplo español/explicación
d	men*ded*	Como en con*d*e, an*d*ar
g	*g*o, *g*et, bi*g*	Como en *g*rande, *g*ol
dʒ	*g*in, ju*dge*	Como en la *ll* andaluza y en *G*eneralitat (catalán)
ŋ	si*ng*	Como en ví*n*culo
h	*h*ouse, *h*e	Como la jota hispanoamericana
j	*y*oung, *y*es	Como en *y*a
k	*c*ome, mo*ck*	Como en *c*aña, Es*c*ocia
r	*r*ed, t*r*ead	Se pronuncia con la punta de la lengua hacia atrás y sin hacerla vibrar
s	*s*and, ye*s*	Como en ca*s*a, *s*esión
z	ro*s*e, *z*ebra	Como en de*s*de, mi*s*mo
ʃ	*sh*e, ma*ch*ine	Como en *ch*ambre (francés), ro*x*o (portugués)
tʃ	*ch*in, ri*ch*	Como en *ch*ocolate
v	*v*alley	Como en f, pero se retiran los dientes superiores vibrándolos contra el labio inferior
w	*w*ater, *wh*ich	Como en la *u* de h*u*evo, p*u*ede
ʒ	vi*si*on	Como en *j*ournal (francés)
θ	*th*ink, my*th*	Como en re*c*eta, *z*apato
ð	*th*is, *th*e	Como en la *d* de habla*d*o, verda*d*

b, p, f, m, n, l, t iguales que en español
El signo * indica que la r final escrita apenas se pronuncia en inglés británico cuando la palabra siguiente empieza con vocal. El signo [´] indica la sílaba acentuada.

A

a [a] *prep* (*a* + *el* = *al*) (*lugar*) at, in, on; (*dirección*) to; (*destino*) to, towards; (*tiempo*) at; ~ **la derecha/ izquierda** on the right/left; **al lado de** beside, at the side of; **subir** ~ **un avión/tren** to get on *or* board a plane/train; **hablar** ~ **larga distancia** to speak long distance; ~ **las cuatro** at four o'clock; ¿~ **qué hora?** at what time?; ~ **los 30 años** at 30 years of age; **al día siguiente** the next day; ~ **eso de las cuatro** at about four o'clock; **al poco tiempo** a short time later; **al verlo yo** when I saw it; (*manera*): **hacerlo** ~ **la fuerza** to do it by force; **ir** ~ **caballo/pie** to go on horseback/foot; (*evaluación*): **poco** ~ **poco** little by little; **de dos** ~ **tres** from two to three; **ocho horas al día** eight hours a *or* per day; ~ **50 ptas el kilo** 50 pesetas a kilo; (*con verbo*): **empezó** ~ **llover** it started raining; **enseñar** ~ **leer** to teach to read; **voy** ~ **llevarlo** I am going to carry it; (*complemento de objeto*): **quiero** ~ **mis padres** (*not translated*) I love my parents; (*complemento circunstancial*): **cercano** ~ **near** (to); **por miedo** ~ **out** of fear of; (*frases elípticas*): ¡~ **comer!** let's eat!; ¿~ **qué viene eso?** what's the meaning of this?; ~ **ver** let's see.

abacero, a [aßa'θero, a] *nm/f* grocer.

abad, esa [a'ßað, 'ðesa] *nm/f* abbot/abbess; ~**ía** *nf* abbey.

abajo [a'ßaxo] *ad* (*situación*) down, below, underneath; (*en casa*) downstairs; (*dirección*) down, downwards; ~ **de** *prep* below, under; **el piso de** ~ the downstairs flat; **la parte de** ~ the lower part; ¡~ **el gobierno!** down with the government!; **cuesta/río** ~ downhill/downstream; **de arriba** ~ from top to bottom; **el** ~ **firmante** the undersigned; **más** ~ lower *or* further down; **echar** ~ to bring down.

abalanzar [aßalan'θar] *vt* to weigh; (*equilibrar*) to balance; (*arrojar*) to hurl; ~**se** *vr*: ~**se sobre** *o* **contra** to throw o.s. at.

abandonado, a [aßando'naðo, a] *a* derelict; (*desatendido*) abandoned; (*desierto*) deserted; (*descuidado*) neglected.

abandonar [aßando'nar] *vt* (*dejar*) to leave, abandon, desert; (*descuidar*) to neglect; (*ceder, dejar de*) to give up; ~**se** *vr*: ~**se a** to abandon o.s. to.

abandono [aßan'dono] *nm* (*acto*) desertion, abandonment; (*estado*) abandon, neglect; (*renuncia*) withdrawal, retirement; **perdió por** ~ he lost by default.

abanicar [aßani'kar] *vt* to fan; **abanico** *nm* fan; (*NAUT*) derrick.

abaratar [aßara'tar] *vt* to lower (the price of) // *vi*, ~**se** *vr* to go *or* come down in price.

abarcar [aßar'kar] *vt* to include, embrace; (*AM*) to monopolize.

abarrotar [aßarro'tar] *vt* to bar; (*NAUT*) to stow; (*fig*) to overstock.

abarrote [aßa'rrote] *nm* packing; ~**s** *nmpl* (*AM*) groceries, provisions; ~**ro, a** *nm/f* (*AM*) grocer.

abastecer [aßaste'θer] *vt* to supply; **abastecimiento** *nm* supply; (*suministrar*) supplying.

abasto [a'ßasto] *nm* supply; (*abundancia*) abundance; **dar** ~ **con** to manage to finish.

abatido, a [aßa'tiðo, a] *a* dejected, downcast.

abatimiento [aßati'mjento] *nm* (*acto*) demolition; (*moral*) dejection, depression.

abatir [aßa'tir] *vt* (*muro*) to demolish; (*pájaro*) to shoot, bring down; (*fig*) to depress; (*humillar*) to humiliate // *vi* to go off course; ~**se** *vr* to be depressed; ~**se sobre** to swoop *or* pounce on.

abdicación [aßðika'θjon] *nf* abdication; **abdicar** *vi* to abdicate.

abdomen [aß'ðomen] *nm* abdomen.

abecedario [aßeθe'ðarjo] *nm* alphabet; (*libro*) spelling book.

abedul [aße'ðul] *nm* birch.

abeja [a'ßexa] *nf* bee.

aberración [aßerra'θjon] *nf* aberration.

abertura [aßer'tura] *nf* opening, gap; (*fig*) openness.

abeto [a'ßeto] *nm* fir.

abierto, a [a'ßjerto, a] *pp de* **abrir** // *a* open; (*AM*) generous.

abigarrado, a [aßiɣa'rraðo, a] *a* multi-coloured.

abismar [aßis'mar] *vt* to humble, cast down; ~**se** *vr* to sink; ~**se en** (*fig*) to be plunged into.

abismo [a'ßismo] *nm* abyss.

abjurar [aßxu'rar] *vt*, *vi* to abjure, forswear.

ablandar [aßlan'dar] *vt* to soften up; (*AUTO*) to run in // *vi*, ~**se** *vr* to grow softer.

ablución [aßlu'θjon] *nf* ablution.

abnegación [aßneɣa'θjon] *nf* self-denial; **abnegarse** *vr* to act unselfishly.

abobado, a [aβo'βaðo, a] a silly.

abobar [aβo'βar] vt to daze.

abocar [aβo'kar] vt to seize in one's mouth; ~**se** vr to approach.

abochornar [aβotʃor'nar] vt to embarrass; ~**se** vr to get flustered; (BOT) to wilt.

abofetear [aβofete'ar] vt to slap (in the face).

abogacía [aβoxa'θia] nf legal profession; (ejercicio) practice of the law; **abogado** nm lawyer.

abogar [aβo'ɣar] vi: ~ **por** to plead for; (fig) to advocate.

abolengo [aβo'leŋgo] nm ancestry, lineage.

abolición [aβoli'θjon] nf abolition.

abolir [aβo'lir] vt to abolish; (cancelar) to cancel.

abolladura [aβoʎa'ðura] nf dent; (chichón, choque) bump; **abollar** vt to dent; to raise a bump on.

abominación [aβomina'θjon] nf abomination.

abonado, a [aβo'naðo, a] a (deuda) paid // nm/f subscriber.

abonar [aβo'nar] vt (deuda) to settle; (terreno) to fertilize; (idea) to endorse; ~**se** vr to subscribe; **abono** nm payment; fertilizer; subscription.

abordar [aβor'ðar] vt to board; (fig) to broach.

aborigen [aβo'rixen] nm aborigine.

aborrecer [aβorre'θer] vt to hate, loathe; **aborrecible** a hateful, loathsome.

abortar [aβor'tar] vi (malparir) to have a miscarriage; (deliberadamente) to have an abortion; **hacerse** ~ to have an abortion; **aborto** nm miscarriage; abortion.

abotonar [aβoto'nar] vt to button (up), do up // vi to bud.

abovedado, a [aβoβe'ðaðo, a] a vaulted, domed.

abrasar [aβra'sar] vt to burn (up); (AGR) to dry up, parch.

abrazar [aβra'θar] vt to embrace.

abrazo [a'βraθo] nm embrace, hug; **un** ~ (en carta) with best wishes.

abrelatas [aβre'latas] nm inv tin opener.

abreviar [aβre'βjar] vt to abbreviate; (texto) to abridge; (plazo) to reduce; **abreviatura** nf abbreviation.

abrigar [aβri'ɣar] vt (proteger) to shelter; (suj: ropa) to keep warm; (fig) to cherish; **abrigo** nm shelter; (apoyo) support; (prenda) coat, overcoat.

abril [a'βril] nm April.

abrir [a'βrir] vt to open (up) // vi to open; ~**se** vr to open (up); (extenderse) to open out; (cielo) to clear; ~**se paso** to find or force a way through.

abrochar [aβro'tʃar] vt (vestido) to button (up); (AM) to staple; (zapato) to buckle; (atar) to lace up.

abrumar [aβru'mar] vt to overwhelm; (sobrecargar) to weigh down; (agotar) to wear out; ~ **se** vr to become foggy.

abrupto, a [a'βrupto, a] a abrupt; (empinado) steep.

absceso [aβs'θeso] nm abscess.

absolución [aβsolu'θjon] nf (REL) absolution; (JUR) pardon; (: de acusado) acquittal.

absoluto, a [aβso'luto, a] a absolute; **en** ~ ad in no way, not at all.

absolver [aβsol'βer] vt to absolve; (JUR) to pardon; (: acusado) to acquit.

absorber [aβsor'βer] vt to absorb; (embeber) to soak up.

absorción [aβsor'θjon] nf absorption.

absorto, a [aβ'sorto, a] pp de **absorber** // a absorbed, engrossed.

abstemio, a [aβs'temjo, a] a teetotal.

abstención [aβsten'θjon] nf abstention; **abstenerse** vr: **abstenerse de** to abstain or refrain from.

abstinencia [aβsti'nenθja] nf abstinence; (ayuno) fasting.

abstracción [aβstrak'θjon] nf abstraction; (despiste) absent-mindedness; ~ **hecha de** leaving aside.

abstraer [aβstra'er] vt to abstract // vi: ~ **de** to leave aside; ~**se** vr to be/become absorbed.

abstraído, a [aβstra'iðo, a] a preoccupied; (despistado) absent-minded.

absuelto, a [aβ'swelto] pp de **absolver.**

absurdo, a [aβ'surðo, a] a absurd.

abuelo, a [a'βwelo, a] nm/f grandfather/mother.

abulia [a'βulja] nf spinelessness, weakness.

abultado, a [aβul'taðo, a] a bulky.

abultar [aβul'tar] vt to enlarge; (aumentar) to increase; (fig) to exaggerate // vi to be bulky.

abundancia [aβun'danθja] nf abundance, plenty; **abundante** a abundant, plentiful; **abundar** vi to abound, be plentiful.

aburrido, a [aβu'rriðo, a] a (hastiado) bored; (que aburre) boring; **aburrimiento** nm boredom, tedium; **aburrir** vt to bore; **aburrirse** vr to be bored, get bored.

abusar [aβu'sar] vi to go too far; ~ **de** to abuse; **abuso** nm imposition; abuse.

abyecto, a [aβ'jekto, a] a wretched, abject.

A.C. abr de **Año de Cristo** A.D. (Anno Domini).

a/c abr de **al cuidado de** c/o (care of).

acá [a'ka] ad (lugar) here; (tiempo) now.

acabado, a [aka'βaðo, a] a finished, complete; (perfecto) perfect; (agotado) worn out; (fig) masterly // nm finish.

acabar [aka'βar] vt (llevar a su fin) to finish, complete; (llegar al final de) to finish, conclude; (perfeccionar) to complete; (consumir) to use up; (rematar) to finish off // vi to finish, end, come to an end; ~ **con** to put an end to; ~ **de llegar** to have just arrived; ~ **por** to end (up) by; ~**se** vr to finish, stop; (terminarse) to be over; (agotarse) to run out; ¡**se acabó**! that's enough!; it's all over!

academia [aka'ðemja] *nf* academy; **académico, a** *a* academic.

acaecer [akae'θer] *vi* to happen, occur; **acaecimiento** *nm* occurrence, happening.

acalorar [akalo'rar] *vt* to heat; (*fig*) to inflame; ~ **se** *vr* (*fig*) to get heated.

acampar [akam'par] *vi* to camp.

acanalar [akana'lar] *vt* to groove; (*ondular*) to corrugate.

acantilado, a [akanti'laðo, a] *a* steep, sheer // *nm* cliff.

acaparar [akapa'rar] *vt* to monopolize; (*acumular*) to hoard.

acariciar [akari'θjar] *vt* to caress; (*fig*) to cherish.

acarrear [akarre'ar] *vt* to transport; (*fig*) to cause, result in; **acarreo** *nm* transport, haulage; (*precio*) carriage.

acaso [a'kaso] *ad* perhaps, maybe // *nm* chance; **por si** ~ just in case; **si** ~ in case; **al** ~ at random.

acatamiento [akata'mjento] *nm* respect; (*reverencia*) reverence; (*deferencia*) deference; **acatar** *vt* to respect; to revere; (*obedecer*) to obey.

acatarrarse [akata'rrarse] *vr* to catch a cold.

acaudalado, a [akauða'laðo, a] *a* well-off; **acaudalar** *vt* to accumulate.

acaudillar [akauði'λar] *vt* to lead, command.

acceder [akθe'ðer] *vi* to accede, agree.

accesible [akθe'siβle] *a* accessible.

acceso [ak'θeso] *nm* access, entry; (*camino*) access road; (*MED*) attack, fit.

accesorio, a [akθe'sorjo, a] *a, nm* accessory.

accidentado, a [akθiðen'taðo, a] *a* uneven; (*áspero*) rough; (*montañoso*) hilly; (*azaroso*) eventful // *nm/f* injured person.

accidental [akθiðen'tal] *a* accidental; **accidentarse** *vr* to have an accident.

accidente [akθi'ðente] *nm* accident; (*MED*) faint; ~ **s** *nmpl* unevenness *sg*, roughness *sg*.

acción [ak'θjon] *nf* action; (*acto*) action, act, deed; (*COM*) share; (*JUR*) action, lawsuit; ~ **ordinaria/preferente** ordinary/preference share; **accionar** *vt* to work, operate // *vi* to gesticulate.

accionista [akθjo'nista] *nm/f* shareholder.

acebo [a'θeβo] *nm* holly; (*árbol*) holly tree.

acechanza [aθe'tʃanθa] *nf* = **acecho**.

acechar [aθe'tʃar] *vt* to spy on; (*aguardar*) to lie in wait for; **acecho** *nm* spying, watching; ambush.

acedía [aθe'ðia] *nf* acidity; (*MED*) heartburn; (*fig*) sourness.

aceitar [aθei'tar] *vt* to oil, lubricate; **aceite** *nm* oil; (*de oliva*) olive oil; **aceitera** *nf* oilcan; **aceitoso, a** *a* oily.

aceituna [aθei'tuna] *nf* olive.

acelerar [aθele'rar] *vt* to accelerate.

acento [a'θento] *nm* accent; (*acentuación*)

stress; **acentuar** *vt* to accent; to stress; (*fig*) to accentuate.

acepción [aθep'θjon] *nf* meaning; (*preferencia*) preference.

acepillar [aθepi'λar] *vt* to brush; (*alisar*) to plane.

aceptación [aθepta'θjon] *nf* acceptance; (*aprobación*) approval; **aceptar** *vt* to accept; to approve.

acequia [a'θekja] *nf* irrigation ditch.

acera [a'θera] *nf* pavement.

acerado, a [aθe'raðo, a] *a* steel; (*afilado*) sharp; (*fig: duro*) steely; (: *mordaz*) biting.

acerbo, a [a'θerβo, a] *a* bitter; (*fig*) harsh.

acerca [a'θerka]: ~ **de** *ad* about, concerning.

acercar [aθer'kar] *vt* to bring or move nearer; ~ **se** *vr* to approach, come near.

acero [a'θero] *nm* steel.

acérrimo, a [a'θerrimo, a] *a* out-and-out, staunch.

acertado, a [aθer'taðo, a] *a* correct; (*apropiado*) apt; (*sensato*) sensible.

acertar [aθer'tar] *vt* (*dar en: el blanco*) to hit; (*llegar a encontrar*) to get right; (*adivinar*) to guess; (*alcanzar*) to achieve // *vi* to get it right, be right; ~ **a** to manage to; ~ **con** to happen on.

acertijo [aθer'tixo] *nm* riddle, puzzle.

acervo [a'θerβo] *nm* heap; ~ **común** undivided estate.

acicalar [aθika'lar] *vt* to polish; (*adornar*) to bedeck; ~ **se** *vr* to smarten o.s. up.

acicate [aθi'kate] *nm* spur.

acidez [aθi'ðeθ] *nf* acidity.

ácido, a [a'θiðo, a] *a* sour, acid // *nm* acid.

acierto [a'θjerto] *nm* success; (*buen paso*) wise move; (*solución*) solution; (*habilidad*) skill, ability.

aclamación [aklama'θjon] *nf* acclamation; (*aplausos*) applause; **aclamar** *vt* to acclaim; to applaud.

aclaración [aklara'θjon] *nf* rinsing, rinse; (*clasificación*) classification.

aclarar [akla'rar] *vt* to clarify, explain; (*ropa*) to rinse // *vi* to clear up; ~ **se** *vr*: ~ **se la garganta** to clear one's throat.

aclimatación [aklimata'θjon] *nf* acclimatization; **aclimatar** *vt* to acclimatize; **aclimatarse** *vr* to become acclimatized.

acobardar [akoβar'ðar] *vt* to daunt, intimidate.

acodarse [ako'ðarse] *vr*: ~ **en** to lean on.

acogedor, a [akoxe'ðor, a] *a* welcoming; (*hospitalario*) hospitable; **acoger** *vt* to welcome; (*abrigar*) to shelter; **acogerse** *vr* to take refuge; **acogida** *nf* reception; refuge.

acolchar [akol'tʃar] *vt* to pad; (*tapizar*) to upholster; (*fig*) to cushion.

acometer [akome'ter] *vt* to attack; (*emprender*) to undertake; **acometida** *nf* attack, assault.

acomodadizo, a [akomoða'ðiθo, a] *a* obliging, acquiescent.

acomodado, a [akomo'ðaðo, a] *a* suitable; (*precio*) moderate; (*persona*) well-to-do.

acomodador, a [akomoða'ðor, a] *nm/f* usher/ette.

acomodar [akomo'ðar] *vt* to adjust; (*alojar*) to accommodate; (*convenir*) to suit; (*reparar*) to repair; (*reconciliar*) to reconcile // *vi* to suit, be suitable; ~**se** *vr* to conform; (*instalarse*) to install o.s.; (*adaptarse*) to adapt o.s.

acomodo [ako'moðo] *nm* arrangement; (*puesto*) post.

acompañar [akompa'ɲar] *vt* to accompany; (*documentos*) to enclose.

acondicionar [akondiθjo'nar] *vt* to arrange, prepare; (*determinar*) to condition.

acongojar [akongo'xar] *vt* to distress, grieve.

aconsejar [akonse'xar] *vt* to advise, counsel; ~**se** *vr*: ~**se con** to consult.

acontecer [akonte'θer] *vi* to happen, occur; **acontecimiento** *nm* event.

acopio [a'kopjo] *nm* store, stock; (*asamblea*) gathering.

acoplamiento [akopla'mjento] *nm* coupling, joint; **acoplar** *vt* to fit, couple; (*unir*) to connect.

acorazado, a [akora'θaðo, a] *a* armour-plated, armoured // *nm* battleship.

acordar [akor'ðar] *vt* (*resolver*) to agree, resolve; (*recordar*) to remind; (*MUS*) to tune; ~**se** *vr* to agree; ~**se (de)** to remember; **acorde** *a* in agreement; (*MUS*) harmonious // *nm* chord.

acordeón [akorðe'on] *nm* accordion.

acordonado, a [akorðo'naðo, a] *a* cordoned-off.

acorralar [akorra'lar] *vt* to round up, corral.

acortar [akor'tar] *vt* to shorten; (*duración*) to cut short; (*cantidad*) to reduce; ~**se** *vr* to become shorter.

acosar [ako'sar] *vt* to pursue relentlessly; (*fig*) to hound, pester.

acostar [akos'tar] *vt* (*en cama*) to put to bed; (*en suelo*) to lay down; (*barco*) to bring alongside; ~**se** *vr* to go to bed; to lie down.

acostumbrar [akostum'brar] *vt*: ~ **a uno a** to accustom sb to // *vi*: ~ **a** to be used to; ~**se** *vr*: ~**se a** to get used to.

acotación [akota'θjon] *nf* marginal note; (*GEO*) elevation mark; (*de límite*) boundary mark; (*TEATRO*) stage direction.

acre ['akre] *a* sharp, bitter; (*fig*) biting // *nm* acre.

acrecentar [akreθen'tar] *vt* to increase, augment.

acreditar [akreði'tar] *vt* (*garantizar*) to vouch for, guarantee; (*autorizar*) to authorize; (*dar prueba de*) to prove; (*COM: abonar*) to credit; (*embajador*) to accredit; ~**se** *vr* to become famous.

acreedor, a [akree'ðor, a] *a*: ~ **a** worthy of // *nm/f* creditor.

acribillar [akriβi'ʎar] *vt*: ~ **a balazos** to riddle with bullets.

acrimonia [akri'monja], **acritud** [akri'tuð] *nf* acrimony.

acta ['akta] *nf* certificate; (*de comisión*) minutes *pl*, record; ~ **de nacimiento/matrimonio** birth/marriage certificate; ~ **notarial** affidavit.

actitud [akti'tuð] *nf* attitude; (*postura*) posture.

activar [akti'βar] *vt* to activate; (*acelerar*) to expedite.

actividad [aktiβi'ðað] *nf* activity.

activo, a [ak'tiβo, a] *a* active; (*vivo*) lively // *nm* assets *pl*.

acto ['akto] *nm* act, action; (*ceremonia*) ceremony; (*TEATRO*) act; **en el ~** immediately.

actor [ak'tor] *nm* actor; (*JUR*) plaintiff.

actora [ak'tora] *a*: **parte ~** prosecution; (*demandante*) plaintiff.

actriz [ak'triθ] *nf* actress.

actuación [aktwa'θjon] *nf* action; (*comportamiento*) conduct, behaviour; (*JUR*) proceedings *pl*; (*desempeño*) performance.

actual [ak'twal] *a* present(-day), current; ~**idad** *nf* present, present time; ~**idades** *nfpl* news *sg*; (*película, nodo*) newsreel *sg*; **en la ~idad** nowadays, at the present time.

actualizar [aktwali'θar] *vt* to update, modernize.

actualmente [aktwal'mente] *ad* now, nowadays, at present.

actuar [ak'twar] *vi* (*obrar*) to work, operate; (*actor*) to act, perform // *vt* to work, operate; ~ **de** to act as.

actuario [ak'twarjo] *nm* clerk; (*COM*) actuary.

acuarela [akwa'rela] *nf* watercolour.

acuario [a'kwarjo] *nm* aquarium; **A~** (*ASTRO*) Aquarius.

acuático, a [a'kwatiko, a] *a* aquatic.

acuciar [aku'θjar] *vt* to urge on.

acuclillarse [akukli'ʎarse] *vr* to crouch down.

acudir [aku'ðir] *vi* to come along, turn up; ~ **a** to turn to; ~ **en ayuda de** to go to the aid of.

acuerdo *etc vb ver* **acordar** // [a'kwerðo] *nm* agreement; **¡de ~!** I agreed!; **de ~ con** (*persona*) in agreement with; (*acción, documento*) in accordance with.

acumulador [akumula'ðor] *nm* storage battery; **acumular** *vt* to accumulate, collect.

acuñar [aku'ɲar] *vt* (*moneda*) to coin, mint; (*poner cuñas*) to wedge.

acuoso, a [a'kwoso, a] *a* watery.

acurrucarse [akurru'karse] *vr* to crouch; (*ovillarse*) to curl up.

acusación [akusa'θjon] *nf* accusation; **acusar** *vt* to accuse; (*revelar*) to reveal; (*denunciar*) to denounce.

acuse [a'kuse] *nm*: ~ **de recibo**

acknowledgement of receipt.
acústico, a [a'kustiko, a] *a* acoustic // *nm* hearing aid.
achacar [atʃa'kar] *vt* to attribute.
achacoso, a [atʃa'koso, a] *a* sickly.
achaque [a'tʃake] *nm* ailment.
achicar [atʃi'kar] *vt* to reduce; (*humillar*) to humiliate; (*NAUT*) to bale out.
achicoria [atʃi'korja] *nf* chicory.
achicharrar [atʃitʃa'rrar] *vt* to scorch, burn.
adagio [a'ðaxjo] *nm* adage; (*MUS*) adagio.
adaptación [aðapta'θjon] *nf* adaptation; **adaptar** *vt* to adapt; (*acomodar*) to fit.
a. de C. *abr* = **a. de J.C.**
A. de C. *abr* = **A.C.**
adecuado, a [aðe'kwaðo, a] *a* adequate; (*apto*) suitable; (*oportuno*) appropriate; **adecuar** *vt* to adapt; to make suitable.
a. de J.C. *abr de* **antes de Jesucristo** B.C. (before Christ).
adelantado, a [aðelan'taðo, a] *a* advanced; (*reloj*) fast; **pagar por ~** to pay in advance; **adelantamiento** *nm* advance, advancement; (*AUTO*) overtaking; (*progreso*) progress.
adelantar [aðelan'tar] *vt* to move forward; (*avanzar*) to advance; (*acelerar*) to speed up // *vi*, **~se** *vr* to go forward, advance; (*AUTO*) to overtake.
adelante [aðe'lante] *ad* forward(s), onward(s), ahead // *excl* come in!; **de hoy en ~** from now on; **más ~** later on; (*más allá*) further on.
adelanto [aðe'lanto] *nm* advance; (*mejora*) improvement; (*progreso*) progress.
adelgazar [aðelxa'θar] *vt* to thin (down); (*afilar*) to taper // *vi*, **~se** *vr* to grow thin.
ademán [aðe'man] *nm* gesture; **ademanes** *nmpl* manners; **en ~ de** as if to.
además [aðe'mas] *ad* besides; (*por otra parte*) moreover; (*también*) also; **~ de** besides, in addition to.
adentro [a'ðentro] *ad* inside, in; **mar ~** out at sea; **tierra ~** inland.
adepto [a'ðepto, a] *nm/f* supporter.
aderezar [aðere'θar] *vt* to prepare; (*persona, ensalada*) to dress; (*comida*) to season; **~se** *vr* to dress up; **aderezo** *nm* preparation; dressing; seasoning.
adeudar [aðeu'ðar] *vt* to owe // *vi* to become related by marriage; **~se** *vr* to run into debt.
adherirse [aðe'rirse] *vr*: **~ a** to adhere to.
adhesión [aðe'sjon] *nf* adhesion; (*fig*) adherence.
adición [aði'θjon] *nf* addition.
adicionar [aðiθjo'nar] *vt* to add.
adicto, a [a'ðikto, a] *a*: **~ a** given to; (*dedicado*) devoted to // *nm/f* supporter, follower.
adiestrar [aðjes'trar] *vt* to train, teach; (*conducir*) to guide, lead; **~se** *vr* to practise; (*enseñarse*) to train o.s.

adinerado, a [aðine'raðo, a] *a* wealthy.
adiós [a'ðjos] *excl* (*para despedirse*) goodbye!, cheerio!; (*para saludar*) hello!
aditivo [aði'tißo] *nm* additive.
adivinanza [aðißi'nanθa] *nf* riddle; **adivinar** *vt* to prophesy; (*conjeturar*) to guess; **adivino, a** *nm/f* fortune-teller.
adj *a abr de* **adjunto** encl. (enclosed).
adjetivo [aðxe'tißo] *nm* adjective.
adjudicación [aðxuðika'θjon] *nf* award; **adjudicar** *vt* to award; **adjudicarse** *vr*: **adjudicarse algo** to appropriate sth.
adjuntar [aðxun'tar] *vt* to attach, enclose; **adjunto, a** *a* attached, enclosed // *nm/f* assistant.
administración [aðministra'θjon] *nf* administration; (*dirección*) management; **administrador, a** *nm/f* administrator; manager/ess.
administrar [aðminis'trar] *vt* to administer; **administrativo, a** *a* administrative.
admirable [aðmi'raßle] *a* admirable; **admiración** *nf* admiration; (*asombro*) wonder; (*LING*) exclamation mark; **admirar** *vt* to admire; (*extrañar*) to surprise; **admirarse** *vr* to be surprised.
admisible [aðmi'sißle] *a* admissible.
admitir [aðmi'tir] *vt* to admit; (*aceptar*) to accept.
admonición [aðmoni'θjon] *nf* warning.
adobe [a'ðoße] *nm* adobe, sun-dried brick.
adolecer [aðole'θer] *vi* to be ill, fall ill; **~ de** to suffer from.
adolescente [aðoles'θente] *nm/f* adolescent.
adonde [a'ðonðe] *conj* (to) where.
adónde [a'ðonde] *ad* = **dónde.**
adopción [aðop'θjon] *nf* adoption.
adoptar [aðop'tar] *vt* to adopt.
adoquín [aðo'kin] *nm* paving stone.
adorar [aðo'rar] *vt* to adore.
adormecer [aðorme'θer] *vt* to put to sleep; **~se** *vr* to become sleepy, fall asleep.
adornar [aðor'nar] *vt* to adorn.
adorno [a'ðorno] *nm* adornment; (*decoración*) decoration.
adquiero *etc vb ver* **adquirir.**
adquirir [aðki'rir] *vt* to acquire, obtain.
adquisición [aðkisi'θjon] *nf* acquisition.
adrede [a'ðreðe] *ad* on purpose.
adscribir [aðskri'ßir] *vt* to appoint.
aduana [a'ðwana] *nf* customs *pl.*
aduanero, a [aðwa'nero, a] *a* customs *cpd* // *nm/f* customs officer.
aducir [aðu'θir] *vt* to adduce; (*dar como prueba*) to offer as proof.
adueñarse [aðwe'narse] *vr*: **~ de** to take possession of.
adulación [aðula'θjon] *nf* flattery.
adular [aðu'lar] *vt* to flatter.
adulterar [aðulte'rar] *vt* to adulterate // *vi* to commit adultery.
adulterio [aðul'terjo] *nm* adultery.
adulto, a [a'ðulto, a] *a, nm/f* adult.

adusto, a [a'ðusto, a] *a* stern; (*austero*) austere.

advenedizo, a [aðβene'ðiθo, a] *nm/f* upstart.

advenimiento [aðβeni'mjento] *nm* arrival; (*al trono*) accession.

adverbio [að'βerßjo] *nm* adverb.

adversario, a [aðβer'sarjo, a] *nm/f* adversary.

adversidad [aðβersi'ðað] *nf* adversity; (*contratiempo*) setback.

adverso, a [að'βerso, a] *a* adverse; (*opuesto*) opposite.

advertencia [aðβer'tenθja] *nf* warning; (*prefacio*) preface, foreword.

advertir [aðβer'tir] *vt* to notice; (*avisar*) to warn // *vi:* ~ **en** to notice.

Adviento [að'βjento] *nm* Advent.

adyacente [aðja'θente] *a* adjacent.

aéreo, a [a'ereo, a] *a* aerial.

aerodeslizador [aeroðesli'θaðor], **aerodeslizante** [aeroðesli'θante] *nm* hovercraft.

aeronáutica [aero'nautika] *nf* aeronautics *sg.*

aeropuerto [aero'pwerto] *nm* airport.

afabilidad [afaßili'ðað] *nf* friendliness; **afable** *a* affable.

afán [a'fan] *nm* hard work; (*deseo*) desire.

afanar [afa'nar] *vt* to harass; ~**se** *vr:* ~**se por** to strive for; **afanoso, a** *a* hard; (*trabajador*) industrious.

afear [afe'ar] *vt* to make ugly; (*mutilar*) to deface.

afección [afek'θjon] *nf* affection; (*MED*) disease.

afectación [afekta'θjon] *nf* affectation; **afectado, a** *a* affected; **afectar** *vt* to affect.

afectísimo, a [afek'tisimo, a] *a* affectionate; ~ **suyo** yours truly.

afecto, a [a'fekto, a] *a* affectionate // *nm* affection; ~ **a** fond of.

afectuoso, a [afek'twoso, a] *a* affectionate.

afeitar [afei'tar] *vt* to shave; ~**se** *vr* to shave.

afeminado, a [afemi'naðo, a] *a* effeminate.

aferrado, a [afe'rraðo, a] *a* stubborn.

aferrar [afe'rrar] *vt* to moor; (*fig*) to grasp // *vi* to moor.

afianzamiento [afjanθa'mjento] *nm* strengthening; (*garantía*) guarantee; (*COM*) security; **afianzar** *vt* to strengthen; to guarantee; to secure; **afianzarse** *vr* to become established.

afición [afi'θjon] *nf* fondness, liking; **la** ~ the fans *pl*; **pinto por** ~ I paint as a hobby; **aficionado, a** *a* keen, enthusiastic; amateur // *nm/f* enthusiast, fan; amateur.

aficionar [afiθjo'nar] *vt:* ~ **a uno a algo** to make sb like sth; ~**se** *vr:* ~**se a algo** to grow fond of sth.

afilado, a [afi'laðo, a] *a* sharp.

afilar [afi'lar] *vt* to sharpen.

afiliarse [afi'ljarse] *vr* to become affiliated to.

afín [a'fin] *a* bordering, adjacent; (*parecido*) similar; (*conexo*) related.

afinar [afi'nar] *vt* (*TEC*) to refine; (*MUS*) to tune // *vi* to play/sing in tune.

afinidad [afini'ðað] *nf* affinity; (*parentesco*) relationship; **por** ~ by marriage.

afirmación [afirma'θjon] *nf* affirmation; **afirmar** *vt* to affirm, state; (*sostener*) to strengthen; **afirmativo, a** *a* affirmative.

aflicción [aflik'θjon] *nf* affliction; (*dolor*) grief.

afligir [afli'xir] *vt* to afflict; (*apenar*) to distress; ~**se** *vr* to grieve.

aflojar [aflo'xar] *vt* to slacken; (*desatar*) to loosen, undo; (*relajar*) to relax // *vi* to drop; (*bajar*) to go down; ~**se** *vr* to relax.

afluente [aflu'ente] *a* flowing; (*elocuente*) eloquent // *nm* tributary.

afluir [aflu'ir] *vi* to flow.

afmo, a *abr de* **afectísimo(a) suyo(a)**.

afónico, a [a'foniko, a] *a* (*ronco*) hoarse; (*sin voz*) voiceless.

afortunado, a [afortu'naðo, a] *a* fortunate, lucky.

afrancesado, a [afranθe'saðo, a] *a* francophile; (*pey*) frenchified.

afrenta [a'frenta] *nf* affront, insult; (*deshonra*) dishonour, shame; **afrentar** *vt* to affront; to dishonour; **afrentarse** *vr* to be ashamed; **afrentoso, a** *a* insulting.

África ['afrika] *nf* Africa; ~ **del Sur** South Africa; **africano, a** *a*, *nm/f* African.

afrontar [afron'tar] *vt* to confront; (*poner cara a cara*) to bring face to face.

afuera [a'fwera] *ad* out, outside; ~**s** *nfpl* outskirts, suburbs.

agachar [aɣa'tʃar] *vt* to bend, bow; ~**se** *vr* to stoop, bend.

agalla [a'ɣaʎa] *nf* (*ZOOL*) gill; ~**s** *nfpl* (*MED*) tonsillitis *sg*; (*ANAT*) tonsils.

agarradera [aɣarra'ðera] *nf* (*AM*), **agarradero** [aɣarra'ðero] *nm* handle; ~**s** *npl* pull *sg*, influence *sg*.

agarrado, a [aɣa'rraðo, a] *a* mean, stingy.

agarrar [aɣa'rrar] *vt* to grasp, grab; (*AM*) to take, catch // *vi* (*planta*) to take root; ~**se** *vr* to hold on (tightly).

agarrotar [aɣarro'tar] *vt* (*llo*) to tie tightly; (*persona*) to squeeze tightly; (*reo*) to garrotte; ~**se** *vr* (*motor*) to seize up; (*MED*) to stiffen.

agasajar [aɣasa'xar] *vt* to treat well, fête; **agasajo** *nm* lavish hospitality.

agencia [a'xenθja] *nf* agency; ~ **de viajes/inmobiliaria** travel/estate agency.

agenda [a'xenda] *nf* diary.

agente [a'xente] *nm* agent; (*de policía*) policeman; ~ **femenino** policewoman.

ágil ['axil] *a* agile, nimble; **agilidad** *nf* agility, nimbleness.

agio ['axjo] *nm* speculation.

agiotista [axjo'tista] *nm* (stock)jobber; (*especulador*) speculator.

agitación [axita'θjon] *nf* shaking, waving, stirring; (*del mar*) roughness; (*fig*) agitation.

agitar [axi'tar] *vt* to wave, shake, stir; (*fig*) to stir up, excite; ~**se** *vr* to get excited.

aglomerar [axlome'rar] *vt*, ~**se** *vr* to agglomerate, crowd together.

agnóstico, a [ax'nostiko, a] *a, nm/f* agnostic.

agobiar [axo'βjar] *vt* to weigh down; (*oprimir*) to oppress; (*cargar*) to burden.

agolparse [axol'parse] *vr* to crowd together.

agonía [axo'nia] *nf* agony, anguish.

agonizante [axoni'θante] *a* dying.

agonizar [axoni'θar] *vi* (*también* **estar agonizando**) to be dying.

agosto [a'xosto] *nm* August.

agotado, a [axo'taðo, a] *a* exhausted; (*libros*) out of print; (*acabado*) finished; (*mercancías*) sold out; **agotamiento** *nm* exhaustion.

agotar [axo'tar] *vt* to exhaust; (*consumir*) to drain; (*recursos*) to use up, deplete; ~**se** *vr* to be exhausted; (*acabarse*) to run out; (*libro*) to go out of print.

agraciar [axra'θjar] *vt* (*JUR*) to pardon; (*con premio*) to reward.

agradable [axra'ðaβle] *a* pleasing, pleasant, nice.

agradar [axra'ðar] *vt, vi* to please.

agradecer [axraðe'θer] *vt* to thank; (*favor etc*) to be grateful for; **agradecimiento** *nm* thanks *pl*; gratitude.

agrado [a'xraðo] *nm* affability; (*gusto*) liking.

agrandar [axran'dar] *vt* to enlarge; (*fig*) to exaggerate; ~**se** *vr* to get bigger.

agrario, a [a'xrarjo, a] *a* agrarian.

agravar [axra'βar] *vt* to make heavier; (*irritar*) to aggravate; (*oprimir*) to oppress; ~**se** *vr* to worsen, get worse.

agraviar [axra'βjar] *vt* to offend; (*ser injusto con*) to wrong; ~**se** *vr* to take offence; **agravio** *nm* offence; wrong; (*ofensa*) grievance.

agregado [axre'xaðo] *nm* aggregate; (*persona*) attaché.

agregar [axre'xar] *vt* to gather; (*añadir*) to add; (*persona*) to appoint.

agresión [axre'sjon] *nf* aggression; **agresivo, a** *a* aggressive.

agriar [a'xrjar] *vt* to (turn) sour; ~**se** *vr* to turn sour.

agricultor, a [axrikul'tor, a] *nm/f* farmer; **agricultura** *nf* agriculture, farming.

agridulce [axri'ðulθe] *a* bittersweet.

agrietarse [axrje'tarse] *vr* to crack; (*la piel*) to chap.

agrio, a ['axrjo, a] *a* bitter.

agronomía [axrono'mia] *nf* agronomy, agriculture.

agrupación [axrupa'θjon] *nf* group; (*acto*) grouping.

agrupar [axru'par] *vt* to group.

agua ['axwa] *nf* water; (*lluvia*) rain; (*NAUT*) wake; (*ARQ*) slope of a roof; ~**s** *nfpl* (*de piedra*) water *sg*, sparkle *sg*; (*MED*) water *sg*, urine *sg*; (*NAUT*) waters; ~**s abajo/arriba** downstream/upstream; ~ **bendita/destilada/potable** holy/distilled/drinking water; ~ **corriente** running water; ~ **de colonia** eau de cologne; ~**s jurisdiccionales** territorial waters; ~**s mayores** excrement *sg*.

aguacate [axwa'kate] *nm* avocado pear.

aguacero [axwa'θero] *nm* (heavy) shower.

aguado, a [a'xwaðo, a] *a* watery, watered down // *nf* (*AGR*) watering place; (*NAUT*) water supply; (*ARTE*) water-colour.

aguafiestas [axwa'fjestas] *nm/f inv* spoilsport.

aguafuerte [axwa'fwerte] *nf* etching.

aguamar [axwa'mar] *nm* jellyfish.

aguantable [axwan'taβle] *a* bearable; **aguantar** *vt* to bear, put up with; (*contener*) to hold; (*sostener*) to hold up // *vi* to last; **aguantarse** *vr* to restrain o.s.

aguar [a'xwar] *vt* to water down.

aguardar [axwar'ðar] *vt* to wait for.

aguardiente [axwar'ðjente] *nm* brandy.

aguarrás [axwa'rras] *nm* turpentine.

agudeza [axu'ðeθa] *nf* sharpness; (*ingenio*) wit; **agudo, a** *a* sharp; (*voz*) high-pitched, piercing; (*dolor, enfermedad*) acute.

agüero [a'xwero] *nm* omen; (*pronóstico*) prediction.

aguijar [axi'xar] *vt* to goad; (*incitar*) to urge on // *vi* to hurry along.

aguijón [axi'xon] *nm* sting; (*BOT*) spine; (*estímulo, fig*) spur; **aguijonear** *vt* = **aguijar**.

águila ['axila] *nf* eagle; (*fig*) genius.

aguileño, a [axi'leɲo, a] *a* aquiline; (*facciones*) sharp-featured.

aguinaldo [axi'naldo] *nm* Christmas box.

aguja [a'xuxa] *nf* needle; (*de reloj*) hand; (*ARQ*) spire; (*TEC*) firing-pin; ~**s** *nfpl* (*ZOOL*) ribs; (*FERRO*) points.

agujerear [axuxere'ar] *vt* to make holes in; **agujero** *nm* hole.

agujetas [axu'xetas] *nfpl* stitch *sg*; (*rigidez*) stiffness *sg*.

aguzar [axu'θar] *vt* to sharpen; (*fig*) to incite.

ahí [a'i] *ad* there; **de** ~ **que** so that, with the result that; ~ **llega** here he comes; **por** ~ that way; (*allá*) over there.

ahijado, a [ai'xaðo, a] *nm/f* godson/daughter.

ahínco [a'iŋko] *nm* earnestness.

ahitar [ai'tar] *vt* to surfeit; ~**se** *vr* to stuff o.s.

ahíto, a [a'ito, a] *a*: **estoy** ~ I have indigestion // *nm* indigestion.

ahogar [ao'xar] *vt* to drown; (*asfixiar*) to suffocate, smother; (*fuego*) to put out; ~**se** *vr* (*en el agua*) to drown; (*suicidio*) to drown o.s.; (*por asfixia*) to suffocate.

ahogo [a'oxo] *nm* shortness of breath; (*fig*) financial difficulty.

ahondar [aon'dar] *vt* to deepen, make

deeper; (*fig*) to go deeply into // *vi*: ~ **en** to go deeply into.

ahora [aˈora] *ad* now; (*poco tiempo ha*) a moment ago, just now; (*dentro de poco*) in a moment // *conj* now; ~ **voy** I'm coming; ~ **mismo** right now; ~ **bien** now then; **por** ~ for the present.

ahorcar [aorˈkar] *vt* to hang; ~**se** *vr* to hang o.s.

ahorita [aoˈrita] *ad* (*fam*) right now.

ahorrar [aoˈrrar] *vt* (*dinero*) to save; (*esfuerzos*) to save, avoid; **ahorro** *nm* economy, saving; (*frugalidad*) thrift; **ahorros** *nmpl* savings.

ahuecar [aweˈkar] *vt* to hollow (out); (*voz*) to deepen; ~**se** *vr* to give o.s. airs.

ahumar [auˈmar] *vt* to smoke, cure; (*llenar de humo*) to fill with smoke // *vi* to smoke; ~**se** *vr* to fill with smoke.

ahuyentar [aujenˈtar] *vt* to drive off, frighten off; (*fig*) to dispel; ~**se** *vr* to run away.

airado, a [aiˈraðo, a] *a* angry; **airar** *vt* to anger; **airarse** *vr* to get angry.

aire [ˈaire] *nm* air; (*viento*) wind; (*corriente*) draught; (*MUS*) tune; ~**s** *nmpl*: **darse** ~**s** to give o.s. airs; **al** ~ **libre** in the open air; ~ **acondicionado** air conditioning; **airoso, a** a windy; draughty; (*fig*) graceful.

aislador [aislaˈðor] *nm* insulator; **aislar** *vt* to isolate; (*ELEC*) to insulate.

ajar [aˈxar] *vt* to spoil; (*fig*) to abuse.

ajedrez [axeˈðreθ] *nm* chess.

ajeno, a [aˈxeno, a] *a* (*que pertenece a otro*) somebody else's; (*impropio*) inappropriate; (*extraño*) alien, foreign; ~ **a** foreign to; ~ **de** free from, devoid of.

ajetreo [axeˈtreo] *nm* bustle.

ají [aˈxi] *nm* chili, red pepper; (*salsa*) chili sauce.

ajo [ˈaxo] *nm* garlic; ~ **porro** *o* **puerro** leek.

ajorca [aˈxorka] *nf* bracelet.

ajuar [aˈxwar] *nm* household furnishings *pl*; (*de novia*) trousseau; (*de niño*) layette.

ajustado, a [axusˈtaðo, a] *a* (*tornillo*) tight; (*cálculo*) right; (*ropa*) tight-fitting; (*DEPORTE: resultado*) close.

ajustar [axusˈtar] *vt* (*adaptar*) to adjust; (*encajar*) to fit; (*TEC*) to engage; (*contratar*) to hire; (*IMPRENTA*) to make up; (*apretar*) to tighten; (*concertar*) to agree (on); (*reconciliar*) to reconcile; (*cuenta*) to settle // *vi* to fit; ~**se** *vr* to come to an agreement.

ajuste [aˈxuste] *nm* adjustment; (*TEC costura*) fitting; (*acuerdo*) compromise; (*de cuenta*) settlement.

al [al] = **a** + **el**, *ver* **a**.

ala [ˈala] *nf* wing; (*de sombrero*) brim; (*futbolista*) winger.

alabanza [alaˈβanθa] *nf* praise.

alabar [alaˈβar] *vt* to praise; ~**se** *vr*: ~**se de** to boast of (being).

alabear [alaβeˈar] *vt*, ~**se** *vr* to warp.

alacena [alaˈθena] *nf* cupboard.

alacrán [alaˈkran] *nm* scorpion.

alambicado, a [alambiˈkaðo, a] *a* distilled; (*fig*) affected.

alambicar [alambiˈkar] *vt* to distil.

alambique [alamˈbike] *nm* still.

alambrado [alamˈbraðo] *nm* wire fence; (*red*) wire netting; **alambre** *nm* wire; **alambre de púas** barbed wire; **alambrista** *nm/f* tightrope walker.

alameda [alaˈmeða] *nf* (*plantío*) poplar grove; (*lugar de paseo*) avenue, tree-lined walk.

álamo [ˈalamo] *nm* poplar; ~ **temblón** aspen.

alano [aˈlano] *nm* mastiff.

alar [aˈlar] *nm* eaves *pl*.

alarde [aˈlarðe] *nm* (*MIL*) review; (*ostentación*) show, display; **hacer** ~ **de** to boast of.

alargar [alarˈxar] *vt* to lengthen, extend; (*paso*) to hasten; (*brazo*) to stretch out; (*cuerda*) to pay out; (*conversación*) to spin out; ~**se** *vr* to get longer; ~**se en** to enlarge upon; (*pey*) to drag out.

alarido [alaˈriðo] *nm* shriek.

alarma [aˈlarma] *nf* alarm.

alazán [alaˈθan] *nm* sorrel.

alba [ˈalβa] *nf* dawn.

albacea [alβaˈθea] *nm/f* executor/trix.

Albania [alˈβanja] *nf* Albania.

albañal [alβaˈɲal] *nm* drain, sewer.

albañil [alβaˈɲil] *nm* bricklayer; (*cantero*) mason.

albaricoque [alβariˈkoke] *nm* apricot.

albedrío [alβeˈðrio] *nm*: **libre** ~ free will.

alberca [alˈβerka] *nf* reservoir.

albergar [alβerˈxar] *vt*, ~**se** *vr* to shelter.

albergue [alˈβerxe] *nm* shelter, refuge; ~ **de juventud** youth hostel.

albóndiga [alˈβondixa] *nf* meatball.

albor [alˈβor] *nm* whiteness; (*amanecer*) dawn; ~**ada** *nf* dawn; (*diana*) reveille; ~**ear** *vi* to dawn.

albornoz [alβorˈnoθ] *nm* (*de los árabes*) burnous; (*para el baño*) bathrobe.

alborotar [alβoroˈtar] *vi* to make a row // *vt* to agitate, stir up; ~**se** *vr* to get excited; (*mar*) to get rough; **alboroto** *nm* row, uproar.

alborozar [alβoroˈθar] *vt* to gladden; ~**se** *vr* to rejoice.

alborozo [alβoˈroθo] *nm* joy.

albricias [alˈβriθjas] *nfpl* reward *sg* // *excl* good news!

álbum [ˈalβum] *nm* album.

albumen [alˈβumen] *nm* egg white.

alcachofa [alkaˈtʃofa] *nf* artichoke.

alcalde [alˈkalde] *nm* mayor.

alcaldía [alkalˈdia] *nf* mayoralty; (*lugar*) mayor's office.

alcance [alˈkanθe] *nm* reach; (*COM*) adverse balance; (*de periódico*) stop-press (news); **de pocos** ~ not very clever; ~ **de última hora** late postal collection.

alcancía [alkanˈθia] *nf* money box.

alcantarilla [alkantaˈriʎa] *nf* (*de aguas*

cloacales) sewer; (*en la calle*) gutter.

alcanzar [alkan'θar] *vt* (*algo: con la mano, el pie*) to reach; (*alguien en el camino*) to catch up with; (*autobús*) to catch; (*suj: bala*) to hit, strike // *vi*: ~ **a hacer** to manage to do.

alcatraz [alka'traθ] *nm* gannet.

alcázar [al'kaθar] *nm* fortress; (*palacio*) royal palace; (*NAUT*) quarter-deck.

alcoba [al'koβa] *nf* bedroom.

alcohol [al'kol] *nm* alcohol; **alcohólico, a** *a* alcoholic; ~ **ismo** *nm* alcoholism.

alcornoque [alkor'noke] *nm* cork tree.

aldaba [al'daβa] *nf* (door) knocker.

aldea [al'dea] *nf* village; ~ **no, a** *a* village *cpd* // *nm/f* villager.

aleación [alea'θjon] *nf* alloy.

aleccionar [alekθjo'nar] *vt* to instruct; (*adiestrar*) to train.

alegación [alexa'θjon] *nf* allegation;

alegar [ale'xar] *vt* to allege; (*JUR*) to plead; (*AM*) to dispute, argue.

alegato [ale'xato] *nm* (*JUR*) allegation; (*AM*) argument.

alegoría [alexo'ria] *nf* allegory.

alegrar [ale'xrar] *vt* (*causar alegría*) to cheer (up); (*fuego*) to poke; (*fiesta*) to liven up; ~ **se** *vr* to get merry or tight; ~ **se de** to be glad about.

alegre [a'lexre] *a* happy, cheerful; (*fam*) merry, tight; (*licencioso*) risqué, blue; **alegría** *nf* happiness; merriment.

alejamiento [alexa'mjento] *nm* removal; (*distancia*) remoteness.

alejar [ale'xar] *vt* to remove; (*fig*) to estrange; ~ **se** *vr* to move away.

aleluya [ale'luja] *nm* (*canto*) hallelujah; (*Pascuas*) Easter time // *nf* Easter print.

alemán, ana [ale'man, ana] *a, nm/f* German // *nm* (*lengua*) German.

Alemania [ale'manja] *nf*: ~ **Federal/Oriental** West/East Germany.

alentado, a [alen'taðo, a] *pp* de **alentar** // *a* brave; (*orgulloso*) proud; (*fuerte*) strong.

alentador, a [alenta'ðor, a] *a* encouraging.

alentar [alen'tar] *vt* to encourage; ~ **se** *vr* to cheer up.

alerce [a'lerθe] *nm* larch.

alergia [a'lerxja] *nf* allergy.

alero [a'lero] *nm* (*de tejado*) eaves *pl*; (*de carruaje*) mudguard.

alerta [a'lerta] *a, nm* alert.

aleta [a'leta] *nf* (*de pez*) fin; (*de ave*) wing; (*de coche*) mudguard.

aletargar [aletar'xar] *vt* to make drowsy; (*entumecer*) to make numb; ~ **se** *vr* to grow drowsy; to become numb.

aletazo [ale'taθo] *nm* wingbeat, flap of the wing.

aletear [alete'ar] *vi* to flutter.

aleve [a'leβe] *a* treacherous.

alevosía [aleβo'sia] *nf* treachery.

alfabeto [alfa'βeto] *nm* alphabet.

alfarería [alfare'ria] *nf* pottery; (*tienda*) pottery shop; **alfarero** *nm* potter.

alférez [al'fereθ] *nm* (*MIL*) second lieutenant; (*NAUT*) ensign.

alfiler [alfi'ler] *nm* pin; (*broche*) clip; ~ **de seguridad** safety pin.

alfombra [al'fombra] *nf* carpet; (*más pequeña*) rug; **alfombrar** *vt* to carpet; **alfombrilla** *nf* rug, mat; (*MED*) German measles.

alforja [al'forxa] *nf* saddlebag.

alforza [al'forθa] *nf* pleat.

alga ['alxa] *nf* seaweed, alga.

algarabía [alxara'βia] *nf* (*fam*) gibberish; (*BOT*) cornflower.

algarrobo [alxa'rroβo] *nm* carob tree.

algazara [alxa'θara] *nf* din, uproar.

álgebra ['alxeβra] *nf* algebra.

algo ['alxo] *pron* something; anything // *ad* somewhat, rather; **por** ~ **será** there must be some reason for it.

algodón [alxo'ðon] *nm* cotton; (*planta*) cotton plant; (*dulce*) candy floss; ~ **hidrófilo** cotton wool.

algodonero, a [alxoðo'nero, a] *a* cotton *cpd* // *nm/f* cotton grower // *nm* cotton plant.

alguacil [alxwa'θil] *nm* bailiff; (*TAUR*) mounted official.

alguien ['alxjen] *pron* someone, somebody, anybody.

alguno, a [al'xuno, a], **algún** [al'xun] *a* some, any // *pron* some; one; someone, somebody; ~ **que otro libro** some book or other; **algún día iré** I'll go one or some day; **sin interés** ~ without the slightest interest; ~ **que otro** an occasional one; ~ **s piensan** some (people) think.

alhaja [a'laxa] *nf* jewel; (*tesoro*) precious object, treasure; (*pey*) rogue.

aliado, a [a'ljaðo, a] *a* allied.

alianza [a'ljanθa] *nf* alliance.

aliar [a'ljar] *vt* to ally; ~ **se** *vr* to form an alliance.

alias ['aljas] *ad* alias.

alicantino, a [alikan'tino, a] *a* of or from Alicante.

alicates [ali'kates] *nmpl*: ~ **de uñas** nail clippers.

aliciente [ali'θjente] *nm* incentive; (*atracción*) attraction.

alienación [aljena'θjon] *nf* alienation.

aliento [a'ljento] *nm* breath; (*respiración*) breathing; **sin** ~ breathless.

aligerar [alixe'rar] *vt* to lighten; (*reducir*) to shorten; (*aliviar*) to alleviate; (*mitigar*) to ease.

alimaña [ali'maɲa] *nf* pest.

alimentación [alimenta'θjon] *nf* (*comida*) food; (*acción*) feeding; (*tienda*) grocer's (shop); **alimentar** *vt* to feed; (*nutrir*) to nourish; **alimentarse** *vr* to feed.

alimenticio, a [alimen'tiθjo, a] *a* nourishing.

alimento [ali'mento] *nm* food; (*nutrición*) nourishment; ~ **s** *nmpl* (*JUR*) alimony *sg*.

alinear [aline'ar] *vt* to align; ~ **se** *vr*: ~ **se en** to fall in with.

aliñar [ali'nar] *vt* to adorn; (*preparar*) to prepare; (*CULIN*) to season; **aliño** *nm* decoration; (*esmero*) neatness; (*CULIN*) dressing.

alisar [ali'sar] *vt* to smooth; (*pulir*) to polish.

aliso [a'liso] *nm* alder.

alistamiento [alista'mjento] *nm* recruitment; **alistar** *vt* to recruit; (*inscribir*) to enrol; **alistarse** *vr* to enlist; to enrol.

aliviar [ali'ßjar] *vt* (*carga*) to lighten; (*persona*) to relieve; (*dolor*) to alleviate; ~ **se** *vr*: ~**se de** to unburden o.s. of.

alivio [a'lißjo] *nm* alleviation, relief.

aljibe [al'xiße] *nm* cistern; (*AUTO*) oil tanker.

aljofaina [alxo'faina] *nf* = **jofaina.**

alma ['alma] *nf* soul; (*persona*) person; (*que anima*) life and soul; (*TEC*) core.

almacén [alma'θen] *nm* (*depósito*) warehouse, store; (*MIL*) magazine; (*AM*) shop; **almacenes** *nmpl* department store *sg*; **almacenaje** *nm* storage.

almacenar [almaθe'nar] *vt* to store, put in storage; (*proveerse*) to stock up (with); **almacenero** *nm* warehouseman.

almanaque [alma'nake] *nm* almanac.

almeja [al'mexa] *nf* shellfish, clam.

almendra [al'mendra] *nf* almond; **almendro** *nm* almond tree.

almiar [al'mjar] *nm* hayrick.

almíbar [al'mißar] *nm* syrup; **almibarado, a** *a* syrupy.

almidón [almi'ðon] *nm* starch; **almidonar** *vt* to starch.

almirantazgo [almiran'taθ\xo] *nm* admiralty; **almirante** *nm* admiral.

almohada [almo'aða] *nf* pillow; (*funda*) pillowcase; **almohadilla** *nf* cushion; (*TEC*) pad; (*AM*) pincushion.

almoneda [almo'neða] *nf* auction; (*liquidación*) clearance sale.

almorranas [almo'rranas] *nfpl* piles, haemorrhoids.

almorzar [almor'θar] *vt*: ~ **una tortilla** to have an omelette for lunch // *vi* to (have) lunch.

almuerzo [al'mwerθo] *nm* lunch.

alnado, a [al'naðo, a] *nm/f* stepson/daughter.

alocado, a [alo'kaðo, a] *a* crazy.

alojamiento [aloxa'mjento] *nf* lodging(s) (*pl*); (*viviendas*) housing.

alojar [alo'xar] *vt* to lodge; ~**se** *vr* to lodge, stay.

alondra [a'londra] *nf* lark, skylark.

alpargata [alpar'xata] *nf* rope-soled sandal; (*de lona*) canvass shoe.

Alpes ['alpes] *nmpl*: **los** ~ the Alps.

alpinismo [alpi'nismo] *nm* mountaineering, climbing; **alpinista** *nm/f* mountaineer, climber.

alquería [alke'ria] *nf* farmhouse.

alquilar [alki'lar] *vt* to rent (out), let, hire (out); (*de inquilino*) to rent, hire; **se alquilan casas** houses to let.

alquiler [alki'ler] *nm* renting, letting, hiring; (*arriendo*) rent, hire charge; **de** ~ for hire.

alquimia [al'kimja] *nf* alchemy.

alquitrán [alki'tran] *nm* tar.

alrededor [alreðe'ðor] *ad* around, about; ~**es** *nmpl* surroundings; ~ **de** *prep* around, about; **mirar a su** ~ to look (round) about one.

alta ['alta] *nf ver* **alto.**

altanería [altane'ria] *nf* haughtiness, arrogance; **altanero, a** *a* arrogant, haughty.

altar [al'tar] *nm* altar.

altavoz [alta'βoθ] *nm* loudspeaker; (*amplificador*) amplifier.

alteración [altera'θjon] *nf* alteration; (*alboroto*) disturbance; (*discusión*) quarrel; **alterar** *vt* to alter; to disturb; **alterarse** *vr* (*alimento etc*) to go bad or off; (*voz*) to falter; (*persona*) to get upset.

altercado [alter'kaðo] *nm* argument.

alternar [alter'nar] *vt* to alternate // *vi*, ~**se** *vr* to alternate; (*turnar*) to take turns; ~ **con** to mix with; **alternativo, a** *a* alternative; (*alterno*) alternating // *nf* alternative; (*elección*) choice; **alternativas** *nfpl* ups and downs.

alteza [al'teθa] *nf* (*tratamiento*) highness; (*altura*) height.

altibajos [alti'ßaxos] *nmpl* ups and downs.

altiplanicie [altipla'niθje] *nf*, **altiplano** [alti'plano] *nm* high plateau.

altisonante [altiso'nante] *a* high-flown.

altitud [alti'tuð] *nf* altitude.

altivez [alti'βeθ] *nf* haughtiness, arrogance; **altivo, a** *a* haughty, arrogant.

alto, a ['alto, a] *a* high; (*de tamaño*) tall; (*precio, importante*) high; (*sonido*) high, sharp; (*noble*) high, lofty // *nm* halt; (*MUS*) alto; (*GEO*) hill; (*AM*) pile // *ad* (*de sitio*) high; (*de sonido*) loud, loudly // *excl* halt!; **tiene 2 metros de** ~ he is 2 metres tall; **en** ~ **a mar** on the high seas; **en voz** ~**a** in a loud voice; **las** ~**as horas de la noche** the small hours; **en lo** ~ **de** at the top of; **pasar por** ~ to overlook; **dar de** ~**a** to discharge.

altoparlante [altopar'lante] *nm* (*AM*) loudspeaker.

altura [al'tura] *nf* height; (*NAUT*) depth; (*GEO*) latitude; **tiene 1.80 de** ~ he is 1 metre 80cm tall; **a esta** ~ **del año** at this time of the year.

alubia [a'lußja] *nf* French bean, kidney bean.

alucinación [aluθina'θjon] *nf* hallucination; **alucinar** *vi* to hallucinate // *vt* to deceive; (*fascinar*) to fascinate.

alud [a'luð] *nm* avalanche.

aludir [alu'ðir] *vi*: ~ **a** to allude to; **darse por** ~ to take the hint.

alumbrado [alum'braðo] *nm* lighting; **alumbramiento** *nm* lighting; (*MED*) childbirth, delivery.

alumbrar [alum'brar] *vt* to light (up); (*ciego*) to restore the sight of // *vi* to give birth.

aluminio [alu'minjo] *nm* aluminium.

alumno, a [a'lumno, a] *nm/f* pupil, student.

alunizar [aluni'θar] *vi* to land on the moon.

alusión [alu'sjon] *nf* allusion.

alusivo, a [alu'siβo, a] *a* allusive.

aluvión [alu'βjon] *nm* alluvium; (*fig*) flood.

alza ['alθa] *nf* rise; ~**s** *nfpl* sights.

alzada [al'θaða] *nf* (*de caballos*) height; (*JUR*) appeal.

alzamiento [alθa'mjento] *nm* (*aumento*) rise, increase; (*acción*) lifting, raising; (*mejor postura*) higher bid; (*rebelión*) rising; (*COM*) fraudulent bankruptcy.

alzar [al'θar] *vt* to lift (up); (*precio, muro*) to raise; (*cuello de abrigo*) to turn up; (*AGR*) to gather in; (*IMPRENTA*) to gather; ~**se** *vr* to get up, rise; (*rebelarse*) to revolt; (*COM*) to go fraudulently bankrupt; (*JUR*) to appeal.

allá [a'ʎa] *ad* (*lugar*) there; (*por ahí*) over there; (*tiempo*) then; ~ **abajo** down there; **más** ~ further on; **más** ~ **de** beyond; ¡~ **tu!** that's your problem!

allanar [aʎa'nar] *vt* to flatten, level (out); (*igualar*) to smooth (out); (*fig*) to subdue; (*JUR*) to burgle, break into; ~**se** *vr* to fall down; ~**se a** to submit to, accept.

allegado, a [aʎe'ɣaðo, a] *a* near, close // *nm/f* relation.

allegar [aʎe'ɣar] *vt* to gather (together); (*añadir*) to add; ~**se** *vr* to approach.

allí [a'ʎi] *ad* there; ~ **mismo** right there; **por** ~ over there; (*por ese camino*) that way.

ama ['ama] *nf* lady of the house; (*dueña*) owner; (*institutriz*) governess; (*madre adoptiva*) foster mother; ~ **de cría** *o* **de leche** wet-nurse; ~ **de llaves** housekeeper.

amabilidad [amaβili'ðað] *nf* kindness; (*simpatía*) niceness; **amable** *a* kind; nice.

amado, a [a'maðo, a] *nm/f* beloved, sweetheart.

amaestrar [amaes'trar] *vt* to train; (*preparar*) to coach.

amagar [ama'ɣar] *vt, vi* to threaten; **amago** *nm* threat; (*gesto*) threatening gesture; (*MED*) symptom.

amalgama [amal'ɣama] *nf* amalgam; **amalgamar** *vt* to amalgamate; (*combinar*) to combine, mix.

amamantar [amaman'tar] *vt* to suckle, nurse.

amanecer [amane'θer] *vi* to dawn // *nm* dawn; **el niño amaneció afiebrado** the child woke up with a fever.

amanerado, a [amane'raðo, a] *a* affected.

amansar [aman'sar] *vt* to tame; (*templar*) to subdue.

amante [a'mante] *a*: ~ **de** fond of // *nm/f* lover.

amapola [ama'pola] *nf* poppy.

amar [a'mar] *vt* to love.

amargado, a [amar'ɣaðo, a] *a* bitter; **amargar** *vt* to make bitter; (*fig*) to embitter; **amargarse** *vr* to get bitter.

amargo, a [a'marɣo, a] *a* bitter; **amargura** *nf* bitterness.

amarillento, a [amari'ʎento, a] *a* yellowish; (*tez*) sallow; **amarillo, a** *a*, *nm* yellow.

amarrar [ama'rrar] *vt* to moor; (*sujetar*) to tie up.

amartelar [amarte'lar] *vt* to make jealous; (*enamorar*) to win the heart of; ~**se** *vr*: ~**se de** to fall in love with.

amartillar [amarti'ʎar] *vt* = **martillar**.

amasar [ama'sar] *vt* to knead; (*mezclar*) to mix, prepare; (*MED*) to massage; (*confeccionar*) to concoct; **amasijo** *nm* kneading; mixing; (*masa*) dough; (*pasta*) paste; (*fig*) hotchpotch.

amateur ['amatur] *nm/f* amateur.

amatista [ama'tista] *nf* amethyst.

amazona [ama'θona] *nf* horsewoman; **A**~**s** *nm*: **el A**~**s** the Amazon.

ambages [am'baxes] *nmpl*: **sin** ~ in plain language.

ámbar ['ambar] *nm* amber.

ambición [ambi'θjon] *nf* ambition; **ambicionar** *vt* to aspire to; **ambicioso, a** *a* ambitious.

ambidextro, a [ambi'ðekstro, a] *a* ambidextrous.

ambiente [am'bjente] *nm* atmosphere; (*medio*) environment.

ambigüedad [ambiɣwe'ðað] *nf* ambiguity; **ambiguo, a** *a* ambiguous.

ámbito ['ambito] *nm* compass; (*campo*) field; (*límite*) boundary; (*fig*) scope.

ambos, as ['ambos, as] *apl, pron pl* both.

ambulancia [ambu'lanθja] *nf* ambulance.

ambulante [ambu'lante] *a* walking *cpd*, itinerant.

ambulatorio [ambula'torjo] *nm* national health clinic.

amedrentar [ameðren'tar] *vt* to scare.

amén [a'men] *excl* amen; ~ **de** except for.

amenaza [ame'naθa] *nf* threat; **amenazar** *vt, vi* to threaten.

amenguar [amen'ɣwar] *vt* to diminish; (*fig*) to dishonour.

amenidad [ameni'ðað] *nf* pleasantness.

ameno, a [a'meno, a] *a* pleasant.

América [a'merika] *nf* America; ~ **del Norte/del Sur** North/South America; ~ **Central/Latina** Central/Latin America; **americano, a** *a*, *nm/f* American // *nf* coat, jacket.

ametralladora [ametraʎa'ðora] *nf* machine gun.

amigable [ami'ɣaβle] *a* friendly.

amígdala [a'miɣðala] *nf* tonsil; **amigdalitis** *nf* tonsillitis.

amigo, a [a'miɣo, a] *a* friendly // *nm/f* friend.

amilanar [amila'nar] *vt* to scare.

aminorar [amino'rar] vt to diminish; (reducir) to reduce.

amistad [amis'taδ] nf friendship; ~es nfpl friends; **amistoso, a** a friendly.

amnesia [am'nesja] nf amnesia.

amnistía [amnis'tia] nf amnesty.

amo ['amo] nm owner; (dueño) boss; ~ **de casa** householder.

amodorrarse [amoδo'rrarse] vr to get sleepy.

amolar [amo'lar] vt to sharpen; (fig) to bore.

amoldar [amol'dar] vt to mould; (adaptar) to adapt.

amonestación [amonesta'θjon] nf warning; **amonestaciones** nfpl marriage banns; **amonestar** vt to warn; to publish the banns of.

amontonar [amonto'nar] vt to collect, pile up; ~**se** vr to crowd together; (acumularse) to pile up.

amor [a'mor] nm love; (amante) lover; **hacer el** ~ to make love; (cortejar) to court.

amoratado, a [amora'taδo, a] a purple, blue with cold.

amordazar [amorδa'θar] vt to muzzle; (fig) to gag.

amorío [amo'rio] nm (fam) love affair.

amoroso, a [amo'roso, a] a affectionate, loving.

amortajar [amorta'xar] vt to shroud.

amortiguador [amortigwa'δor] nm shock absorber; (parachoques) bumper; (silenciador) silencer; **amortiguar** vt to deaden; (ruido) to muffle; (color) to soften.

amortización [amortiθa'θjon] nf redemption, repayment.

amotinar [amoti'nar] vt to stir up, incite (to riot); ~**se** vr to mutiny.

amparar [ampa'rar] vt to protect; ~**se** vr to seek protection; (abrigar) to shelter; **amparo** nm help, protection.

ampliación [amplja'θjon] nf enlargement; (extensión) extension; **ampliar** vt to enlarge; to extend.

amplificación [amplifika'θjon] nf enlargement; **amplificador** nm amplifier; **amplificar** vt to amplify.

amplio, a ['ampljo, a] a spacious; (de falda etc) full; (extenso) extensive; (ancho) wide; **amplitud** nf spaciousness; extent; (fig) amplitude.

ampolla [am'poʎa] nf blister; (MED) ampoule.

amputar [ampu'tar] vt to cut off, amputate.

amueblar [amwe'βlar] vt to furnish.

amurallar [amura'ʎar] vt to wall up/in.

anacronismo [anakro'nismo] nm anachronism.

ánade ['anaδe] nm duck.

anadear [anaδe'ar] vi to waddle.

anales [a'nales] nmpl annals.

analfabetismo [analfaβe'tismo] nm illiteracy; **analfabeto, a** a illiterate.

análisis [a'nalisis] nm analysis.

analizar [anali'θar] vt to analyse.

analogía [analo'xia] nf analogy.

ananá(s) [ana'na(s)] nm pineapple.

anaquel [ana'kel] nm shelf.

anarquía [anar'kia] nf anarchy; **anarquismo** nm anarchism; **anarquista** nm/f anarchist.

anatomía [anato'mia] nf anatomy.

anciano, a [an'θjano, a] a old, aged // nm/f old man/woman // nm elder.

ancla ['ankla] nf anchor; ~**dero** nm anchorage; **anclar** vi to (drop) anchor.

ancho, a ['antʃo, a] a wide; (falda) full; (fig) liberal // nm width; (FERRO) gauge; **ponerse** ~ to get conceited; **estar a sus** ~**as** to be at one's ease.

anchoa [an'tʃoa] nf anchovy.

anchura [an'tʃura] nf width; (extensión) wideness; (fig) freedom.

andaderas [anda'δeras] nfpl baby walker sg.

andadura [anda'δura] nf gait, pace.

Andalucía [andalu'θia] nf Andalusia; **andaluz, a** a, nm/f Andalusian.

andamio [an'damjo], **andamiaje** [anda-'mjaxe] nm scaffold.

andar [an'dar] vt to go, cover, travel // vi to go, walk, travel; (funcionar) to go, work; (estar) to be // nm walk, gait, pace; ~**se** vr to go away; ~ **a pie/a caballo/en bicicleta** to go on foot/on horseback/by bicycle; ¡**anda!, ¡andando!** go on!; (vamos) come on!; (bien) well!; **anda en los 40** he's about 40.

andariego, a [anda'rjexo, a] a fond of travelling.

andén [an'den] nm (FERRO) platform; (NAUT) quayside; (AUTO) hard shoulder.

Andes ['andes] nmpl: **los** ~ the Andes.

Andorra [an'dorra] nf Andorra.

andrajo [an'draxo] nm rag; ~**so, a** a ragged.

andurriales [andu'rrjales] nmpl out-of-the-way place sg.

anduve etc vb ver **andar**.

anécdota [a'nekδota] nf anecdote, story.

anegar [ane'xar] vt to flood; (ahogar) to drown; ~**se** vr to drown; (hundirse) to sink.

anemia [a'nemja] nf anaemia.

anestésico [anes'tesiko] nm anaesthetic.

anexar [anek'sar] vt to annex; (documento) to attach; **anexo, a** a attached // nm annexe.

anfibio, a [an'fiβjo, a] a amphibious // nm amphibian.

anfiteatro [anfite'atro] nm amphitheatre; (TEATRO) dress circle.

anfitrión, ona [anfi'trjon, ona] nm/f host.

ángel ['anxel] nm angel; **angélico, a**, **angelical** a angelic(al).

angina [an'xina] nf (MED) inflammation of the throat; ~ **de pecho** angina (pectoris).

anglicano, a [angli'kano, a] a, nm/f Anglican.

angosto, a [an'gosto, a] *a* narrow.
angostura [angos'tura] *nf* narrowness; (*paso*) narrow passage.
anguila [an'gila] *nf* eel; ~s *nfpl* slipway *sg*.
ángulo ['angulo] *nm* angle; (*esquina*) corner; (*curva*) bend.
angustia [an'gustja] *nf* anguish; **angustiar** *vt* to distress, grieve.
anhelante [ane'lante] *a* eager; (*deseoso*) longing; **anhelar** *vt* to be eager for; to long for, desire // *vi* to pant, gasp; **anhelo** *nm* eagerness; desire.
anidar [ani'ðar] *vi* to nest.
anillo [a'niλo] *nm* ring; ~ **de boda** wedding ring.
ánima ['anima] *nf* soul; **las** ~s **the** Angelus (bell) *sg*.
animación [anima'θjon] *nf* liveliness; (*vitalidad*) life; (*actividad*) bustle; **animado, a** *a* lively; (*vivaz*) animated.
animadversión [animaðßer'sjon] *nf* ill-will, antagonism.
animal [ani'mal] *a* animal; (*fig*) stupid // *nm* animal; (*fig*) fool; (*bestia*) brute.
animar [ani'mar] *vt* (*BIO*) to animate, give life to; (*fig*) to liven up, brighten up, cheer up; (*estimular*) to stimulate; ~**se** *vr* to cheer up, feel encouraged; (*decidirse*) to make up one's mind.
ánimo ['animo] *nm* soul, mind; (*valentía*) courage // *excl* cheer up!
animosidad [animosi'ðað] *nf* animosity.
animoso, a [ani'moso, a] *a* brave; (*vivo*) lively.
aniquilar [aniki'lar] *vt* to annihilate, destroy; ~**se** *vr* to be wiped out, disappear; (*empeorarse*) to deteriorate.
anís [a'nis] *nm* aniseed.
aniversario [anißer'sarjo] *nm* anniversary.
anoche [a'notʃe] *ad* last night; **antes de** ~ the night before last.
anochecer [anotʃe'θer] *vi* to get dark // *nm* nightfall, dark.
anomalía [anoma'lia] *nf* anomaly.
anonadamiento [anonaða'mjento] *nm* annihilation; (*desaliento*) discouragement; **anonadar** *vt* to annihilate; to discourage; **anonadarse** *vr* to get discouraged.
anónimo, a [a'nonimo, a] *a* anonymous; (*COM*) limited // *nm* anonymity.
anormal [anor'mal] *a* abnormal.
anotación [anota'θjon] *nf* note.
anotar [ano'tar] *vt* to note down; (*comentar*) to annotate.
ansia ['ansja] *nf* anxiety; (*añoranza*) yearning; **ansiar** *vt* to long for.
ansiedad [ansje'ðað] *nf* anxiety.
ansioso, a [an'sjoso, a] *a* anxious; (*anhelante*) eager.
antagónico, a [anta'xoniko, a] *a* antagonistic; (*opuesto*) contrasting; **antagonista** *nm/f* antagonist.
antaño [an'taɲo] *ad* long ago.

Antártico [an'tartiko] *nm*: **el** ~ **the** Antarctic.
ante ['ante] *prep* before, in the presence of; (*encarado con*) faced with // *nm* suede, buckskin; ~ **todo** above all.
anteanoche [antea'notʃe] *ad* the night before last.
anteayer [antea'jer] *ad* the day before yesterday.
antebrazo [ante'ßraθo] *nm* forearm.
antecedente [anteθe'ðente] *a* previous // *nm* antecedent; ~**s** *nmpl* record *sg*, background *sg*.
anteceder [anteθe'ðer] *vt* to precede, go before.
antecesor, a [anteθe'sor, a] *nm/f* predecessor; (*antepasado*) ancestor.
antedicho, a [ante'ðitʃo, a] *a* aforementioned.
antelación [antela'θjon] *nf*: **con** ~ in advance.
antemano [ante'mano]: **de** ~ *ad* beforehand, in advance.
antena [an'tena] *nf* antenna; (*de televisión etc*) aerial.
anteojo [ante'oxo] *nm* eyeglass; ~**s** *nmpl* spectacles, glasses.
antepasados [antepa'saðos] *nmpl* ancestors.
antepecho [ante'petʃo] *nm* guardrail, parapet; (*repisa*) ledge, sill.
anteponer [antepo'ner] *vt* to place in front; (*fig*) to prefer; ~**se** *vr*: ~**se a** to overcome.
anteproyecto [antepro'jekto] *nm* preliminary sketch; (*fig*) blueprint.
anterior [ante'rjor] *a* preceding, previous; ~**idad** *nf*: **con** ~**idad a** a prior to, before.
antes ['antes] *ad* sooner; (*primero*) first; (*con prioridad*) before; (*hace tiempo*) previously, once; (*más bien*) rather // *prep*: ~ **de** before // *conj*: ~ **(de) que** before; ~ **bien** (but) rather; **dos días** ~ two days before *or* previously; ~ **muerto que esclavo** better dead than enslaved; **tomo el avión** ~ **que el barco** I take the plane rather than the boat; **cuanto** ~, **lo** ~ **posible** as soon as possible.
antesala [ante'sala] *nf* anteroom.
antibiótico [anti'ßjotiko] *nm* antibiotic.
anticipación [antiθipa'θjon] *nf* anticipation; (*COM*) advance; **con 10 minutos de** ~ 10 minutes early; **anticipado, a** *a* (in) advance.
anticipar [antiθi'par] *vt* to anticipate; (*adelantar*) to bring forward; (*COM*) to advance; ~**se** *vr*: ~**se a su época** to be ahead of one's time.
anticipo [anti'θipo] *nm* = **anticipación.**
anticonceptivo, a [antikonθep'tißo, a] *a*, *nm* contraceptive.
anticongelante [antikonxe'lante] *nm* antifreeze.
anticuado, a [anti'kwaðo, a] *a* out-of-date, old-fashioned; (*desusado*) obsolete.
anticuario [anti'kwarjo] *nm* antique dealer.

antídoto [an'tiðoto] *nm* antidote.

antifaz [anti'faθ] *nm* mask; (*velo*) veil.

antigualla [anti'xwaʎa] *nf* antique; (*reliquia*) relic.

antiguamente [antixwa'mente] *ad* formerly; (*hace mucho tiempo*) long ago.

antigüedad [antixwe'ðað] *nf* antiquity; (*artículo*) antique; (*rango*) seniority; **antiguo, a** *a* old, ancient; (*que fue*) former.

antílope [an'tilope] *nm* antelope.

antillano, a [anti'ʎano, a] *a, nm/f* West Indian.

Antillas [an'tiʎas] *nfpl*: **las ~** the West Indies.

antipara [anti'para] *nf* screen.

antipatía [antipa'tia] *nf* antipathy, dislike; **antipático, a** *a* disagreeable, unpleasant.

antisemita [antise'mita] *nm/f* antisemite.

antítesis [an'titesis] *nf* antithesis.

antojadizo, a [antoxa'ðiθo, a] *a* capricious.

antojarse [anto'xarse] *vr* (*desear*): **se me antoja comprarlo** I have a mind to buy it; (*pensar*): **se me antoja que** I have a feeling that.

antojo [an'toxo] *nm* caprice, whim; (*rosa*) birthmark; (*lunar*) mole.

antología [antolo'xia] *nf* anthology.

antorcha [an'tortʃa] *nf* torch.

antro ['antro] *nm* cavern.

antropófago, a [antro'pofaxo, a] *a, nm/f* cannibal.

antropología [antropolo'xia] *nf* anthropology.

anual [a'nwal] *a* annual.

anualidad [anwali'ðað] *nf* annuity.

anuario [a'nwarjo] *nm* yearbook.

anublar [anu'ßlar] *vt* to cloud; (*oscurecer*) to darken; **~se** *vr* to become cloudy, cloud over; (*bot*) to wither.

anudar [anu'ðar] *vt* to knot, tie; (*unir*) to join; **~se** *vr* to get tied up.

anulación [anula'θjon] *nf* annulment; (*cancelación*) cancellation; **anular** *vt* to annul; to cancel; (*revocar*) to revoke, repeal // *nm* ring finger.

anunciación [anunθja'θjon] *nf* announcement; **anunciar** *vt* to announce; (*proclamar*) to proclaim; (*com*) to advertise.

anuncio [a'nunθjo] *nm* announcement; (*señal*) sign; (*com*) advertisement; (*cartel*) poster.

anzuelo [an'θwelo] *nm* hook; (*para pescar*) fish hook.

añadidura [aɲaði'ðura] *nf* addition, extra; **por ~** besides, in addition.

añadir [aɲa'ðir] *vt* to add.

añejo, a [a'ɲexo, a] *a* old.

añicos [a'ɲikos] *nmpl*: **hacer ~** to smash, shatter.

año ['aɲo] *nm* year; **¡Feliz A~ Nuevo!** Happy New Year!; **tener 15 ~s** to be 15 (years old); **los ~s 60** the sixties; **~ bisiesto/escolar** leap/school year.

añoranza [aɲo'ranθa] *nf* nostalgia; (*anhelo*) longing.

apacentar [apaθen'tar] *vt* to pasture, graze.

apacible [apa'θißle] *a* gentle, mild.

apaciguar [apaθi'xwar] *vt* to pacify, calm (down).

apadrinar [apaðri'nar] *vt* to sponsor, support; (*rel*) to act as godfather to.

apagado, a [apa'xaðo, a] *a* out; (*volcán*) extinct; (*cal*) slaked; (*color*) dull; (*voz*) quiet, timid; (*sonido*) muted, muffled; (*apático*) listless.

apagar [apa'xar] *vt* to put out; (*sonido*) to silence, muffle; (*sed*) to quench; (*fig*) to kill.

apagón [apa'xon] *nm* blackout, power cut.

apalabrar [apala'ßrar] *vt* to agree to; (*obrero*) to engage.

apalear [apale'ar] *vt* to beat, thrash; (*agr*) to winnow.

apañar [apa'ɲar] *vt* to pick up; (*asir*) to take hold of, grasp; (*vestir*) to dress up; (*reparar*) to mend, patch up; **~se** *vr* to manage, get along.

aparador [apara'ðor] *nm* sideboard; (*escaparate*) shop window.

aparato [apa'rato] *nm* apparatus; (*máquina*) machine; (*doméstico*) appliance; (*boato*) ostentation; **~so, a** *a* showy, ostentatious.

aparcamiento [aparka'mjento] *nm* car park.

aparcar [apar'kar] *vt, vi* to park.

aparecer [apare'θer] *vi*, **~se** *vr* to appear.

aparejado, a [apare'xaðo, a] *a* a fit, suitable.

aparejar [apare'xar] *vt* to prepare; (*caballo*) to saddle, harness; (*naut*) to fit out, rig out; **aparejo** *nm* preparation; harness; rigging; (*de poleas*) block and tackle.

aparentar [aparen'tar] *vt* to feign; (*parecer*) to look, seem (to be).

aparente [apa'rente] *a* apparent; (*adecuado*) suitable.

aparición [apari'θjon] *nf* appearance; (*de libro*) publication.

apariencia [apa'rjenθja] *nf* (outward) appearance; **en ~** outwardly, seemingly.

apartado, a [apar'taðo, a] *a* separate; (*lejano*) remote // *nm* post office box; (*tipográfico*) paragraph.

apartamento [aparta'mento] *nm* apartment, flat.

apartamiento [aparta'mjento] *nm* separation; (*aislamiento*) remoteness; (*am*) apartment, flat.

apartar [apar'tar] *vt* to separate; (*quitar*) to remove; (*mineralogía*) to extract; **~se** *vr* to separate, part; (*irse*) to move away, keep away; **aparte** *ad* (*separadamente*) separately; (*además*) besides // *nm* aside; (*tipográfico*) new paragraph.

apasionado, a [apasjo'naðo, a] *a* passionate; biassed, prejudiced.

apasionar [apasjo'nar] vt to arouse passion in; ~se vr to get excited.
apatía [apa'tia] nf apathy.
apático, a [a'patiko, a] a apathetic.
apdo nm abr de apartado (de correos).
apeadero [apea'ðero] nm halt, wayside station.
apearse [apea'arse] vr to dismount; (bajarse) to get down/out.
apedrear [apeðre'ar] vt to stone.
apegarse [ape'xarse] vr: ~se a to become attached to; apego nm attachment, fondness.
apelación [apela'θjon] nf appeal.
apelante [ape'lante] nm/f appellant.
apelar [ape'lar] vi to appeal; ~ a to resort to.
apellidar [apeʎi'ðar] vt to call, name; ~se vr to be called; apellido nm surname, name.
apenar [ape'nar] vt to grieve, trouble; ~se vr to grieve.
apenas [a'penas] ad scarcely, hardly // conj as soon as, no sooner.
apéndice [a'pendiθe] nm appendix; apendicitis nf appendicitis.
apercibir [aperθi'βir] vt to prepare; (avisar) to warn; (JUR) to summon; (AM) to notice, see; ~se vr to get ready.
aperitivo [aperi'tiβo] nm aperitif.
apertura [aper'tura] nf opening.
apesadumbrar [apesaðum'brar] vt to grieve, sadden; ~se vr to distress o.s.
apestar [apes'tar] vt to infect // vi to stink.
apetecer [apete'θer] vt: ¿te apetece una tortilla? do you fancy an omelette?; apetecible a desirable; (llamativo) attractive.
apetito [ape'tito] nm appetite; ~so, a a appetizing; (fig) tempting.
apiadarse [apja'ðarse] vr: ~ de to take pity on.
ápice ['apiθe] nm apex; (fig) whit, iota.
apio ['apjo] nm celery.
aplacar [apla'kar] vt to placate; ~se vr to calm down.
aplanamiento [aplana'mjento] nm smoothing, levelling.
aplanar [apla'nar] vt to smooth, level; (allanar) to roll flat, flatten.
aplastar [aplas'tar] vt to squash (flat); (fig) to crush.
aplaudir [aplau'ðir] vt to applaud.
aplauso [a'plauso] nm applause; (fig) approval, acclaim.
aplazamiento [aplaθa'mjento] nm postponement, adjournment; aplazar vt to postpone, defer.
aplicación [aplika'θjon] nf application; (esfuerzo) effort.
aplicado, a [apli'kaðo, a] a diligent, hard-working.
aplicar [apli'kar] vt (ejecutar) to apply; ~se vr to apply o.s.

aplomo [a'plomo] nm aplomb, self-assurance.
apocado, a [apo'kaðo, a] a timid.
apocamiento [apoka'mjento] nm timidity; (depresión) depression.
apocar [apo'kar] vt to reduce; ~se vr to feel small, feel humiliated.
apodar [apo'ðar] vt to nickname.
apoderado [apoðe'raðo] nm agent, representative; apoderar vt to authorize, empower; (JUR) to grant (a) power of attorney to; apoderarse vr: apoderarse de to take possession of.
apodo [a'poðo] nm nickname.
apogeo [apo'xeo] nm peak, summit.
apología [apolo'xia] nf eulogy; (defensa) defence.
apoplejía [apople'xia] nf apoplexy, stroke.
aporrear [aporre'ar] vt to beat (up); aporreo nm beating.
aportar [apor'tar] vt to contribute // vi to reach port; ~se vr (AM) to arrive, come.
aposentar [aposen'tar] vt to lodge, put up; aposento nm lodging; (habitación) room.
apostar [apos'tar] vt to bet, stake; (destinar) to station, post // vi to bet.
apostilla [apos'tiʎa] nf note, comment.
apóstol [a'postol] nm apostle.
apóstrofe [a'postrofe] nm insult; (reprimenda) reprimand.
apóstrofo [a'postrofo] nm apostrophe.
apostura [apos'tura] nf neatness, elegance.
apoyar [apo'jar] vt to lean, rest; (fig) to support, back; ~se vr: ~se en to lean on; apoyo nm support, backing; (sostén) prop.
apreciable [apre'θjaβle] a considerable; (fig) esteemed.
apreciación [apreθja'θjon] nf appreciation; (COM) valuation; apreciar vt to evaluate, assess; (COM) to appreciate, value.
aprecio [a'preθjo] nm valuation, estimate; (fig) appreciation.
aprehender [apreen'der] vt to apprehend, seize; aprehensión nf detention, capture.
apremiante [apre'mjante] a urgent, pressing; apremiar vt to compel, force // vi to be urgent, press; apremio nm compulsion; urgency.
aprender [apren'der] vt, vi to learn.
aprendiz, a [apren'diθ, a] nm/f apprentice; (principiante) learner; ~aje nm apprenticeship.
aprensión [apren'sjon] nm apprehension, fear; (delicadeza) squeamishness; aprensivo, a a apprehensive; (nervioso) nervous, timid.
apresar [apre'sar] vt to seize; (capturar) to capture.
aprestar [apres'tar] vt to prepare, get ready; (TEC) to prime; size; ~se vr to get ready.
apresurado, a [apresu'raðo, a] a hurried,

hasty; **apresuramiento** *nm* hurry, haste.
apresurar [apresu'rar] *vt* to hurry,
accelerate; ~**se** *vr* to hurry, make haste.
apretado, a [apre'taðo, a] *a* tight;
(*escritura*) cramped; (*difícil*) difficult;
(*fam*) stingy.
apretar [apre'tar] *vt* to squeeze, press;
(*TEC*) to tighten; (*presionar*) to press
together, pack // *vi* to be too tight;
(*insistir*) to insist.
apretón [apre'ton] *nm* squeeze; (*abrazo*)
hug; (*aglomeración*) crush; (*dificultad*)
difficulty, jam; (*carrera*) dash, sprint; ~
de manos handshake; **apretura** *nf*
squeeze; hug; crush; difficulty, jam;
(*escasez*) scarcity.
aprieto [a'prjeto] *nm* squeeze, press;
(*dificultad*) difficulty, jam.
aprisionar [aprisjo'nar] *vt* to imprison.
aprobación [aproßa'θjon] *nf* approval; (*de
examen*) pass; (*nota*) pass mark; **aprobar**
vt to approve (of); to pass // *vi* to pass.
apropiación [apropja'θjon] *nf*
appropriation.
apropiado, a [apro'pjaðo, a] *a*
appropriate.
apropiar [apro'pjar] *vt* to adapt, make fit;
~**se** *vr*: ~**se de** to appropriate.
aprovechado, a [aproße't∫aðo, a] *a*
diligent, hardworking; (*económico*) thrifty;
(*pey*) unscrupulous, grasping; **apro-
vechamiento** *nm* use, exploitation.
aprovechar [aproße't∫ar] *vt* to use,
exploit, profit from; (*sacar partido de*) to
take advantage of // *vi* to progress,
improve; ~**se** *vr*: ~**se de** to make use of,
take advantage of; **¡que aproveche!**
enjoy your meal!
aproximación [aproksima'θjon] *nf*
approximation; (*cercanía*) nearness; (*de
lotería*) consolation prize; **aproximado, a**
a approximate; **aproximar** *vt* to bring
nearer; **aproximarse** *vr* to come near,
approach.
aptitud [apti'tuð] *nf* aptitude; (*idoneidad*)
suitability.
apto, a ['apto, a] *a* suitable.
apuesto, a [a'pwesto, a] *a* neat, elegant //
nf bet, wager.
apuntador [apunta'ðor] *nm* prompter.
apuntalar [apunta'lar] *vt* to prop up.
apuntar [apun'tar] *vt* (*con arma*) to aim
at; (*con dedo*) to point at or to; (*anotar*) to
note (down); (*TEATRO*) to prompt; (*dinero*)
to stake; ~**se** *vr* to score a point.
apunte [a'punte] *nm* note.
apuñalar [apuɲa'lar] *vt* to stab.
apurado, a [apu'raðo, a] *a* needy; (*difícil*)
difficult, dangerous; (*agotado*) exhausted;
(*AM*) hurried, rushed.
apurar [apu'rar] *vt* (*purificar*) to purify;
(*agotar*) to drain; (*recursos*) to use up;
(*molestar*) to annoy; ~**se** *vr* to worry;
(*AM*) to hurry.
apuro [a'puro] *nm* (*aprieto*) fix, jam;
(*escasez*) want, hardship; (*aflicción*)
distress; (*AM*) haste, urgency.

aquejar [ake'xar] *vt* to distress, grieve;
(*MED*) to afflict.
aquel, aquella, aquellos, as [a'kel,
a'keʎa, a'keʎos, as] *det* that; (*pl*) those.
aquél, aquélla, aquéllos, as [a'kel,
a'keʎa, a'keʎos, as] *pron* that (one); (*pl*)
those (ones).
aquello [a'keʎo] *pron* that, that business.
aquí [a'ki] *ad* (*lugar*) here; (*tiempo*) now;
~ **arriba** up here; ~ **mismo** right here;
~ **yace** here lies; **de** ~ **a siete días** a
week from now.
aquietar [akje'tar] *vt* to quieten (down),
calm (down).
árabe ['araße] *a* Arab, Arabian, Arabic //
nm/f Arab // *nm* (*lengua*) Arabic.
Arabia Saudita [araßjasau'ðita] *nf* Saudi
Arabia.
arado [a'raðo] *nm* plough.
aragonés, esa [araxo'nes, esa] *a*, *nm/f*
Aragonese.
arancel [aran'θel] *nm* tariff, duty; ~ **de
aduanas** customs duty.
araña [a'raɲa] *nf* (*ZOOL*) spider; (*de luces*)
chandelier.
arañar [ara'ɲar] *vt* to scratch.
arañazo [ara'ɲaθo] *nm* scratch.
arar [a'rar] *vt* to plough, till.
arbitrador, a [arßitra'ðor, a] *nm/f*
arbiter.
arbitraje [arßi'traxe] *nm* arbitration.
arbitrar [arßi'trar] *vt* to arbitrate in;
(*DEPORTE*) to referee // *vi* to arbitrate.
arbitrariedad [arßitrarje'ðað] *nf*
arbitrariness; (*acto*) arbitrary act;
arbitrario, a *a* arbitrary.
arbitrio [ar'ßitrjo] *nm* free will; (*JUR*)
adjudication, decision.
árbitro ['arßitro] *nm* arbitrator; (*DEPORTE*)
referee; (*TENIS*) umpire.
árbol ['arßol] *nm* (*BOT*) tree; (*NAUT*) mast;
(*TEC*) axle, shaft; **arbolado, a** *a* wooded,
tree-lined // *nm* woodland.
arboladura [arßola'ðura] *nf* rigging;
arbolar *vt* to hoist, raise; **arbolarse** *vr* to
rear up.
arboleda [arßo'leða] *nf* grove, plantation.
arbusto [ar'ßusto] *nm* bush, shrub.
arca ['arka] *nf* chest, box; (*caja fuerte*)
strongbox.
arcada [ar'kaða] *nf* arcade; (*de puente*)
arch, span; ~**s** *nfpl* retching *sg*.
arcaduz [arka'ðuz] *nm* pipe, conduit.
arcaico, a [ar'kaiko, a] *a* archaic.
arce ['arθe] *nm* maple tree.
arcediano [arθe'ðjano] *nm* archdeacon.
arcilla [ar'θiʎa] *nf* clay.
arco ['arko] *nm* arch; (*MAT*) arc; (*MIL*, *MUS*)
bow; ~ **iris** rainbow.
archipiélago [art∫i'pjelaxo] *nm*
archipelago.
archivar [art∫i'ßar] *vt* to file (away);
archivo *nm* archive(s) (*pl*).
arder [ar'ðer] *vi*, *vt* to burn.
ardid [ar'ðið] *nm* ruse.

ardiente [ar'ðjente] *a* burning; (*apasionado*) ardent.

ardilla [ar'ðiʎa] *nf* squirrel.

ardor [ar'ðor] *nm* (*calor*) heat, warmth; (*fig*) ardour; ~ **de estómago** heartburn; ~**oso, a** *a* = **ardiente**.

arduo, a ['arðwo, a] *a* arduous.

área ['area] *nf* area; (*DEPORTE*) penalty area.

arena [a'rena] *nf* sand; (*de una lucha*) arena; (*MED*) stone.

arenal [are'nal] *nm* sandy ground; (*arena movediza*) quicksand.

arengar [aren'gar] *vt* to harangue.

arenisco, a [are'nisko, a] *a* sandy // (*il* sandstone; (*cascajo*) grit.

arenoso, a [are'noso, a] *a* sandy.

arenque [a'renke] *nm* herring.

arete [a'rete] *nm* earring.

argamasa [arɣa'masa] *nf* mortar, plaster; **argamasar** *vt* to mortar, plaster.

Argel [ar'xel] *n* Algiers; ~**ia** *nf* Algeria; **argelino, a** *a, nm/f* Algerian.

argentino, a [arxen'tino, a] *a* Argentinian; (*de plata*) silvery // *nm/f* Argentinian // *nf*: **A** ~ **a** Argentina.

argolla [ar'xoʎa] *nf* (large) ring; (*juego*) croquet.

argot [ar'xo] *nm* slang.

argucia [ar'xuθja] *nf* subtlety, sophistry.

argüir [ar'ɣwir] *vt* to deduce; (*discutir*) to argue; (*indicar*) to indicate, imply; (*censurar*) to reproach // *vi* to argue.

argumentación [arxumenta'θjon] *nf* (line of) argument; **argumentar** *vt, vi* to argue.

argumento [arxu'mento] *nm* argument; (*de obra*) plot.

aria ['arja] *nf* aria.

aridez [ari'ðeθ] *nf* aridity, dryness.

árido, a [a'riðo, a] *a* arid, dry; ~**s** *nmpl* dry goods.

Aries ['arjes] *nm* Aries.

ariete [a'rjete] *nm* battering ram.

ario, a [a'rjo, a] *a* Aryan.

arisco, a [a'risko, a] *a* surly; (*insociable*) unsociable.

aristócrata [aris'tokrata] *nm/f* aristocrat.

aritmética [arit'metika] *nf* arithmetic.

arma ['arma] *nf* arm; ~**s** *nfpl* arms; ~ **blanca** blade, knife; (*espada*) sword; ~ **de fuego** firearm; ~**s cortas** small arms.

armadillo [arma'ðiʎo] *nm* armadillo.

armado, a [ar'maðo, a] *a* armed; (*TEC*) reinforced // *nf* armada; (*flota*) fleet.

armadura [arma'ðura] *nf* (*MIL*) armour; (*TEC*) framework; (*ZOOL*) skeleton; (*FÍSICA*) armature.

armamento [arma'mento] *nm* armament; (*NAUT*) fitting-out.

armar [ar'mar] *vt* (*soldado*) to arm; (*máquina*) to assemble; (*navío*) to fit out; ~ **la**, ~ **un lío** to start a row.

armario [ar'marjo] *nm* wardrobe.

armatoste [arma'toste] *nm* large useless object, contraption.

armazón [arma'θon] *nf* body, chassis; (*de*

mueble etc) frame; (*ARQ*) skeleton.

armería [arme'ria] *nf* (*museo*) military museum; (*tienda*) gunsmith's.

armiño [ar'miɲo] *nm* stoat; (*piel*) ermine.

armisticio [armis'tiθjo] *nm* armistice.

armonía [armo'nia] *nf* harmony.

armónica [ar'monika] *nf* harmonica.

armonioso, a [armo'njoso, a] *a* harmonious.

arnés [ar'nes] *nm* armour; **arneses** *nmpl* harness *sg*.

aro ['aro] *nm* ring; (*tejo*) quoit; (*pendiente*) earring.

aroma [a'roma] *nm* aroma.

aromático, a [aro'matiko, a] *a* aromatic.

arpa ['arpa] *nf* harp.

arpía [ar'pia] *nf* shrew.

arpista [ar'pista] *nm/f* harpist.

arpón [ar'pon] *nm* harpoon.

arquear [arke'ar] *vt* to arch, bend; ~**se** *vr* to arch, bend; **arqueo** *nm* (*gen*) arching, curve; (*de navío*) tonnage.

arqueología [arkeolo'xia] *nf* archaeology; **arqueólogo, a** *nm/f* archaeologist.

arquero [ar'kero] *nm* archer, bowman.

arquetipo [arke'tipo] *nm* archetype.

arquitecto [arki'tekto] *nm* architect; **arquitectura** *nf* architecture.

arrabal [arra'ßal] *nm* suburb; (*AM*) slum.

arraigado, a [arrai'xaðo, a] *a* deep-rooted; (*fig*) established.

arraigar [arrai'xar] *vt* to establish // *vi*, ~**se** *vr* to take root.

arrancar [arran'kar] *vt* (*sacar*) to pull up, extract, pull out; (*separar*) to snatch (away), wrest; (*fig*) to extract // *vi* to start, pull out.

arranque [a'rranke] *nm* sudden start; (*AUTO*) start; (*fig*) fit, outburst.

arras ['arras] *nfpl* pledge *sg*, security *sg*.

arrasar [arra'sar] *vt* (*aplanar*) to level, flatten; (*destruir*) to demolish; (*llenar*) to fill up // *vi* to clear.

arrastrado, a [arras'traðo, a] *a* poor, wretched; (*AM*) servile.

arrastrar [arras'trar] *vt* to drag (along); (*fig*) to drag down, degrade; (*suj: agua, viento*) to carry away // *vi* to drag, trail on the ground; ~**se** *vr* to crawl; (*fig*) to grovel; **llevar algo arrastrado** to drag sth along.

arrastre [a'rrastre] *nm* drag, dragging; (*DEPORTE*) crawl.

arrayán [arra'jan] *nm* myrtle.

arrear [arre'ar] *vt* to drive, urge on; (*enganchar*) to harness // *vi* to hurry along; **¡arrea(r)!** get up!, gee up!

arrebatado, a [arreßa'taðo, a] *a* rash, impetuous; (*repentino*) sudden, hasty.

arrebatar [arreßa'tar] *vt* to snatch (away), seize; (*fig*) to captivate; ~**se** *vr* to get carried away, get excited.

arrebato [arre'ßato] *nm* fit of rage, fury; (*éxtasis*) rapture.

arreglado, a [arre'xlaðo, a] *a* (*ordenado*)

neat, orderly; (*moderado*) moderate, reasonable.

arreglar [arre'xlar] *vt* (*poner orden*) to tidy up; (*algo roto*) to fix, repair; (*problema*) to solve; (*MUS*) to arrange; ~**se** *vr* to reach an understanding; **arreglárselas** (*fam*) to get by, manage.

arreglo [a'rreɣlo] *nm* settlement; (*orden*) order; (*acuerdo*) agreement; (*MUS*) arrangement, setting.

arremangar [arreman'gar] *vt* to roll up, turn up; ~**se** *vr* to roll up one's sleeves.

arremeter [arreme'ter] *vt* to attack, assault.

arrendador, a [arrenda'ðor, a] *nm/f* landlord/lady; (*inquilino*) tenant.

arrendamiento [arrenda'mjento] *nm* letting; (*alquilar*) hiring; (*contrato*) lease; (*alquiler*) rent; **arrendar** *vt* to let, lease; to rent; **arrendatario, a** *nm/f* tenant.

arreo [a'rreo] *nm* adornment; ~**s** *nmpl* harness *sg*, trappings.

arrepentimiento [arrepenti'mjento] *nm* regret, repentance.

arrepentirse [arrepen'tirse] *vr*: ~ **de** to regret, repent of.

arrestar [arres'tar] *vt* to arrest; (*encarcelar*) to imprison; **arresto** *nm* arrest; (*MIL*) detention; (*audacia*) boldness, daring; **arresto domiciliario** house arrest.

arriar [a'rrjar] *vt* (*velas, bandera*) to lower, strike; (*un cable*) to pay out; ~**se** *vr* to flood.

arriba [a'rriβa] *ad* (*posición*) above, overhead, on top; (*en casa*) upstairs; (*dirección*) up, upwards; ~ **de** above, higher (up) than; ~ **del todo** at the very top; **el piso de** ~ the flat upstairs; **de** ~ **abajo** from top to bottom; **calle** ~ up the street; **lo** ~ **mencionado** the aforementioned; ~ **de 20 pesetas** more than 20 pesetas; ¡~ **las manos!** hands up!

arribar [arri'βar] *vi* to put into port; (*llegar*) to arrive.

arribista [arri'βista] *nm/f* parvenu/e, upstart.

arriendo [a'rrjendo] *nm* = **arrendamiento**.

arriero [a'rrjero] *nm* muleteer.

arriesgado, a [arrjes'xaðo, a] *a* (*peligroso*) risky; (*audaz*) bold, daring; **arriesgar** *vt* to risk; (*poner en peligro*) to endanger; **arriesgarse** *vr* to take a risk.

arrimar [arri'mar] *vt* (*acercar*) to bring close; (*poner de lado*) to set aside; ~**se** *vr* to come close or closer; ~**se a** to lean on; **arrimo** *nm* approach; (*fig*) support.

arrinconado, a [arrinko'naðo, a] *a* forgotten, neglected; **arrinconar** *vt* to put in a corner; (*fig*) to put on one side; (*abandonar*) to push aside; **arrinconarse** *vr* to withdraw from the world.

arrodillarse [arroði'ʎarse] *vr* to kneel, kneel down.

arrogancia [arro'xanθja] *nf* arrogance; **arrogante** *a* arrogant.

arrojar [arro'xar] *vt* to throw, hurl; (*humo*) to emit, give out; (*COM*) to yield, produce; ~**se** *vr* to throw or hurl o.s.

arrojo [a'rroxo] *nm* daring.

arrollador, a [arroʎa'ðor, a] *a* crushing, overwhelming.

arropar [arro'par] *vt* to cover, wrap up; ~**se** *vr* to wrap o.s. up.

arrope [a'rrope] *nm* syrup.

arrostrar [arros'trar] *vt* to face (up to); ~**se** *vr* to rush into the fight.

arroyo [a'rrojo] *nm* stream; (*de la calle*) gutter.

arroz [a'rroθ] *nm* rice; ~ **con leche** rice pudding.

arruga [a'rruɣa] *nf* fold; (*de cara*) wrinkle; (*de vestido*) crease; **arrugar** *vt* to fold; to wrinkle; to crease; **arrugarse** *vr* to get creased.

arruinar [arrwi'nar] *vt* to ruin, wreck; ~**se** *vr* to be ruined.

arrullar [arru'ʎar] *vi* to coo // *vt* to lull to sleep.

arsenal [arse'nal] *nm* naval dockyard; (*MIL*) arsenal.

arsénico [ar'seniko] *nm* arsenic.

arte ['arte] *nm* (*gen m en sg y siempre f en pl*) art; (*maña*) skill, guile; ~**s** *nfpl* arts.

artefacto [arte'fakto] *nm* appliance; (*ARQUEOLOGÍA*) artefact.

artejo [ar'texo] *nm* knuckle.

arteria [ar'terja] *nf* artery.

artesanía [artesa'nia] *nf* craftsmanship; (*artículos*) handicrafts *pl*; **artesano** *nm* artisan, craftsman.

ártico, a ['artiko, a] *a* Arctic // *nm*: **el Á** ~ the Arctic.

articulación [artikula'θjon] *nf* articulation; (*MED, TEC*) joint; **articulado, a** *a* articulated; jointed; **articular** *vt* to articulate; to join together.

artículo [ar'tikulo] *nm* article; (*cosa*) thing, article; ~**s** *nmpl* goods.

artífice [ar'tifiθe] *nm* artist, craftsman; (*fig*) architect.

artificial [artifi'θjal] *a* artificial.

artificio [arti'fiθjo] *nm* art, skill; (*artesanía*) craftsmanship; (*astucia*) cunning; ~**so, a** *a* skilful, clever; cunning.

artillería [artiʎe'ria] *nf* artillery.

artillero [arti'ʎero] *nm* artilleryman, gunner.

artimaña [arti'maɲa] *nf* trap, snare; (*astucia*) cunning.

artista [ar'tista] *nm/f* (*pintor*) artist, painter; (*TEATRO*) artist, artiste; **artístico, a** *a* artistic.

artritis [ar'tritis] *nf* arthritis.

arzobispo [arθo'βispo] *nm* archbishop.

as [as] *nm* ace.

asa ['asa] *nf* handle; (*fig*) lever.

asado [a'saðo] *nm* roast (meat).

asador [asa'ðor] *nm* spit.

asalariado, a [asala'rjaðo, a] *a* paid, wage-earning // *nm/f* wage earner.

asaltabancos [asalta'bankos] *nm inv* bank robber.

asaltador, a [asalta'ðor, a], **asaltante** [asal'tante] *nm/f* assailant; **asaltar** *vt* to attack, assault; (*fig*) to assail; **asalto** *nm* attack, assault; (*DEPORTE*) round.

asamblea [asam'blea] *nf* assembly; (*reunión*) meeting.

asar [a'sar] *vt* to roast.

asbesto [as'ßesto] *nm* asbestos.

ascendencia [asθen'denθja] *nf* ancestry; (*AM*) ascendancy.

ascender [asθen'der] *vi* (*subir*) to ascend, rise; (*ser promovido*) to gain promotion // *vt* to promote; ~ **a** to amount to; **ascendiente** *nm* ascendency, influence // *nm/f* ancestor.

ascensión [asθen'sjon] *nf* ascent; **la A~** the Ascension.

ascensionista [asθensjo'nista] *nm/f* balloonist.

ascenso [as'θenso] *nm* ascent; (*promoción*) promotion.

ascensor [asθen'sor] *nm* lift, elevator.

ascético, a [as'θetiko, a] *a* ascetic.

asco ['asko] *nm* loathing, disgust; (*cosa*) loathsome thing; **el ajo me da** ~ I hate *or* loathe garlic.

ascua ['askwa] *nf* ember.

aseado, a [ase'aðo, a] *a* clean; (*arreglado*) tidy; (*pulcro*) smart; **asear** *vt* to clean, wash; to tidy (up); (*adornar*) to adorn.

asediar [ase'ðjar] *vt* to besiege, lay siege to; (*fig*) to chase, pester; **asedio** *nm* siege; (*COM*) run.

asegurado, a [asexu'raðo, a] *a* insured; **asegurador, a** *nm/f* insurer; underwriter.

asegurar [asexu'rar] *vt* (*consolidar*) to secure, fasten; (*dar garantía de*) to guarantee; (*preservar*) to safeguard; (*afirmar, dar por cierto*) to assure, affirm; (*tranquilizar*) to reassure; (*tomar un seguro*) to insure; ~ **se** *vr* to assure o.s., make sure.

asemejarse [aseme'xarse] *vr* to be alike; ~ **a** to be like, resemble.

asentado, a [asen'taðo, a] *a* established, settled.

asentar [asen'tar] *vt* (*sentar*) to seat, sit down; (*poner*) to place, establish; (*alisar*) to level, smooth down *or* out; (*anotar*) to note down; (*afirmar*) to affirm, assent; (*afinar*) to sharpen, hone // *vi* to be suitable, suit.

asentir [asen'tir] *vi* to assent, agree.

aseo [a'seo] *nm* cleanliness; ~**s** *nmpl* toilet *sg*, cloakroom *sg*.

asequible [ase'kißle] *a* attainable, available.

aserradero [aserra'ðero] *nm* sawmill; **aserrar** *vt* to saw.

aserrín [ase'rrin] *nm* sawdust.

asesinar [asesi'nar] *vt* to murder; (*POL*) to assassinate; (*fig*) to pester; **asesinato** *nm* murder; assassination.

asesino, a [ase'sino, a] *nm/f* murderer, killer; (*POL*) assassin.

asesor, a [ase'sor, a] *nm/f* adviser, consultant.

asfalto [as'falto] *nm* asphalt.

asfixia [as'fiksja] *nf* suffocation.

asfixiar [asfik'sjar] *vt*, ~**se** *vr* to asphyxiate, suffocate.

asgo *etc vb ver* **asir**.

así [a'si] *ad* (*de esta manera*) so, in this way, like this, thus; (*aunque*) although; (*tan luego como*) as soon as; ~ **que** so, therefore; ~ **como** as well as; ~ **y todo** even so; **¿no es** ~**?** isn't it?, didn't you? *etc.*

Asia ['asja] *nf* Asia; **asiático, a** *a* Asiatic, Asian.

asidero [asi'ðero] *nm* handle.

asiduidad [asiðwi'ðað] *nf* assiduousness; **asiduo, a** *a* assiduous; (*frecuente*) frequent // *nm/f* regular (customer).

asiento [a'sjento] *nm* (*mueble*) seat, chair; (*de coche, en tribunal etc*) seat; (*localidad*) seat, place; (*fundamento*) site; (*colocación*) establishment; (*depósito*) sediment; (*cordura*) good sense; ~ **delantero/trasero** front/back seat.

asignación [asixna'θjon] *nf* (*atribución*) assignment; (*reparto*) allocation; (*cita*) appointment; (*sueldo*) salary; **asignar** *vt* to assign, allocate.

asignatura [asixna'tura] *nf* subject.

asilo [a'silo] *nm* (*refugio*) asylum, refuge; (*establecimiento*) home, institution.

asimilación [asimila'θjon] *nf* assimilation.

asimilar [asimi'lar] *vt* to assimilate; ~**se** *vr*: ~**se a** to resemble; (*incorporarse*) to become assimilated to.

asimismo [asi'mismo] *ad* in the same way, likewise.

asir [a'sir] *vt* to seize, grasp.

asistencia [asis'tenθja] *nf* audience; (*MED*) attendance; (*ayuda*) assistance; **asistir** *vt* to assist // *vi* to attend, be present.

asma ['asma] *nf* asthma.

asno ['asno] *nm* donkey; (*fig*) ass.

asociación [asoθja'θjon] *nf* association; (*COM*) partnership; ~ **aduanera** customs union; **asociado, a** *a* associate // *nm/f* associate; partner.

asociar [aso'θjar] *vt* to combine.

asolear [asole'ar] *vt* to put in the sun; ~**se** *vr* to sunbathe.

asomar [aso'mar] *vt* to show, stick out // *vi* to appear; ~**se** *vr* to appear, show up; ~ **la cabeza por la ventana** to put one's head out of the window.

asombrar [asom'brar] *vt* (*causar admiración, sorpresa*) to amaze, astonish; (*asustar*) to frighten; (*dar sombra a*) to shade; ~**se** *vr* to be amazed; to be frightened; **asombro** *nm* amazement, astonishment; fright; **asombroso, a** *a* astonishing, amazing.

asomo [a'somo] *nm* hint, sign; (*apariencia*) appearance.

aspa ['aspa] *nf* (*cruz*) cross; (*de molino*) sail.

aspar [as'par] *vt* to reel, wind; (*fig*) to vex, annoy.

aspaviento [aspa'ßjento] *nm* exaggerated display of feeling; (*fam*) fuss.

aspecto [as'pekto] *nm* (*apariencia*) look, appearance; (*fig*) aspect.

aspereza [aspe're̱θa] *nf* roughness; (*agrura*) sourness; (*severidad*) harshness, surliness; **áspero, a** *a* rough; bitter, sour; harsh.

aspersión [asper'sjon] *nf* sprinkling.

áspid ['aspið] *nm* asp.

aspiración [aspira'θjon] *nf* breath, inhalation; (*MUS*) short pause; **aspiraciones** *nfpl* (*AM*) aspirations.

aspiradora [aspira'ðora] *nf* vacuum cleaner.

aspirar [aspi'rar] *vt* to breathe in // *vi*: ~ **a** to aspire to.

aspirina [aspi'rina] *nf* aspirin.

asquear [aske'ar] *vt* to sicken // *vi* to be sickening; ~**se** *vr* to feel disgusted; **asqueroso, a** *a* disgusting, sickening.

asta ['asta] *nf* lance; (*arpón*) spear; (*mango*) shaft, handle; (*ZOOL*) horn; **a media** ~ at half mast.

astilla [as'tiʎa] *nf* splinter; (*pedacito*) chip; ~**s** *nfpl* firewood *sg*.

astillero [asti'ʎero] *nm* shipyard.

astringente [astrin'xente] *a, nm* astringent.

astringir [astrin'xir] *vt* to bind.

astro ['astro] *nm* star.

astrología [astrolo'xia] *nf* astrology; **astrólogo, a** *nm/f* astrologer.

astronauta [astro'nauta] *nm/f* astronaut.

astronomía [astrono'mia] *nf* astronomy; **astrónomo** *nm* astronomer.

astucia [as'tuθja] *nf* astuteness; (*destreza*) clever trick; **astuto, a** *a* astute; (*taimado*) cunning.

asueto [a'sweto] *nm* holiday; (*tiempo libre*) time off *q*.

asumir [asu'mir] *vt* to assume.

asunción [asun'θjon] *nf* assumption.

asunto [a'sunto] *nm* (*tema*) matter, subject; (*negocio*) business.

asustar [asus'tar] *vt* to frighten; ~**se** *vr* to be/become frightened.

atacar [ata'kar] *vt* to attack.

atadura [ata'ðura] *nf* bond, tie.

atajo [a'taxo] *nm* short cut; (*DEPORTE*) tackle.

ataque [a'take] *nm* attack; ~ **cardíaco** heart attack.

atar [a'tar] *vt* to tie, tie up; ~**se** *vr* (*fig*) to be *or* get embarrassed.

atardecer [atarðe'θer] *vi* to get dark // *nm* evening; (*crepúsculo*) dusk.

atareado, a [atare'aðo, a] *a* busy.

atarear [atare'ar] *vt* to give a job to; ~**se** *vr* to be busy, keep busy.

atascamiento [ataska'mjento] *nm* = **atasco**.

atascar [atas'kar] *vt* to clog up; (*obstruir*) to jam; (*fig*) to hinder; ~**se** *vr* to stall; (*cañería*) to get clogged up; **atasco** *nm* obstruction; (*AUTO*) traffic jam.

ataúd [ata'uð] *nm* coffin.

ataviar [ata'ßjar] *vt* to deck, array; ~**se** *vr* to dress up.

atavío [ata'ßio] *nm* attire, dress; ~**s** *nmpl* finery *sg*.

atemorizar [atemori'θar] *vt* to frighten, scare; ~**se** *vr* to get scared.

Atenas [a'tenas] *n* Athens.

atención [aten'θjon] *nf* attention; (*bondad*) kindness; (*cortesía*) civility // *excl* (be) careful!, look out!

atender [aten'der] *vt* to attend to, look after // *vi* to pay attention.

atenerse [ate'nerse] *vr*: ~ **a** to abide by, adhere to.

atentado [aten'taðo] *nm* crime, illegal act; (*asalto*) assault; (*contra la vida de uno*) attempt on sb's life.

atentar [aten'tar] *vi*: ~ **a** *o* **contra** to commit an outrage against.

atento, a [a'tento, a] *a* attentive, observant; (*cortés*) polite, thoughtful.

atenuación [atenwa'θjon] *nf* attenuation, lessening; **atenuante** *a* attenuating, extenuating; **atenuar** *vt* to attenuate; (*disminuir*) to lessen, minimize.

ateo, a [a'teo, a] *a* atheistic // *nm/f* atheist.

aterrador, a [aterra'ðor, a] *a* frightening.

aterrar [ate'rrar] *vt* to pull down, demolish; (*AGR*) to cover with earth; (*espantar*) to frighten; ~**se** *vr* to be frightened.

aterrizar [aterri'θar] *vi* to land.

aterrorizar [aterrori'θar] *vt* to terrify; (*MIL*, *POL*) to terrorize.

atesorar [ateso'rar] *vt* to hoard, store up.

atestar [ates'tar] *vt* to pack, stuff; (*JUR*) to attest, testify to.

atestiguar [atesti'xwar] *vt* to testify to, bear witness to.

atiborrar [atißo'rrar] *vt* to fill, stuff; ~**se** *vr* to stuff o.s.

ático ['atiko] *nm* attic.

atildar [atil'dar] *vt* to criticize; ~**se** *vr* to spruce o.s. up.

atisbar [atis'ßar] *vt* to spy on; (*echar ojeada*) to peep at.

atizar [ati'θar] *vt* to poke; (*horno etc*) to stoke; (*fig*) to stir up, rouse.

atlántico, a [at'lantiko, a] *a* Atlantic // *nm*: **el (océano) A**~ the Atlantic (Ocean).

atlas ['atlas] *nm* atlas.

atleta [at'leta] *nm* athlete; **atlético, a** *a* athletic; **atletismo** *nm* athletics *sg*.

atmósfera [at'mosfera] *nf* atmosphere.

atolondramiento [atolondra'mjento] *nm* bewilderment; (*insensatez*) silliness.

atollar [ato'ʎar] *vi*, ~**se** *vr* to get stuck; (*fig*) to get into a jam.

atómico, a [a'tomiko, a] *a* atomic.

atomizador [atomiθa'ðor] *nm* atomizer.

átomo ['atomo] *nm* atom.

atónito, a [a'tonito, a] *a* astonished, amazed.

atontado, a [aton'taðo, a] *a* stunned; (*bobo*) silly, daft.

atontar [aton'tar] *vt* to stun; ~se *vr* to become bewildered.

atormentar [atormen'tar] *vt* to torture; (*molestar*) to torment; (*acosar*) to plague, harass.

atornillar [atorni'ʎar] *vt* to screw on *or* down.

atracar [atra'kar] *vt* (*NAUT*) to moor; (*robar*) to hold up, rob; (*fam*) to stuff (with food) // *vi* to moor.

atracción [atrak'θjon] *nf* attraction.

atraco [a'trako] *nm* holdup, robbery.

atractivo, a [atrak'tiβo, a] *a* attractive // *nm* attraction; (*belleza*) attractiveness.

atraer [atra'er] *vt* to attract.

atrancar [atran'kar] *vt* (*con tranca, barra*) to bar, bolt.

atrapar [atra'par] *vt* to trap; (*fig*) to take in, deceive.

atrás [a'tras] *ad* (*movimiento*) back, backwards; (*lugar*) behind; (*tiempo*) previously; **ir hacia** ~ to go back *or* backwards; to go to the rear; **estar** ~ to be behind *or* at the back.

atrasado, a [atra'saðo, a] *a* slow; (*pago*) overdue, late; (*país*) backward.

atrasar [atra'sar] *vi* to be slow; ~se *vr* to remain behind; (*llegar tarde*) to arrive late; **atraso** *nm* slowness; lateness, delay; (*de país*) backwardness; **atrasos** *nmpl* arrears.

atravesar [atraβe'sar] *vt* (*cruzar*) to cross (over); (*traspasar*) to pierce, go through; (*poner al través*) to lay *or* put across; ~se *vr* to come in between; (*intervenir*) to interfere.

atrayente [atra'jente] *a* attractive.

atreverse [atre'βerse] *vr* to dare; (*insolentarse*) to be insolent; **atrevido, a** *a* daring; insolent; **atrevimiento** *nm* daring; insolence.

atribuir [atriβu'ir] *vt* to attribute; (*funciones*) to confer.

atribular [atriβu'lar] *vt* to afflict, distress; ~se *vr* to grieve, be distressed.

atributo [atri'βuto] *nm* attribute.

atrocidad [atroθi'ðað] *nf* atrocity, outrage.

atropellar [atrope'ʎar] *vt* (*derribar*) to knock over, knock down; (*empujar*) to push (aside); (*pasar por encima de*) to run over, run down; (*agraviar*) to insult; ~se *vr* to act hastily; **atropello** *nm* accident; push; insult; (*agravio*) wrong; (*atrocidad*) outrage.

atroz [a'troθ] *a* atrocious, awful.

atto. a, *abr de* **atento**.

atuendo [a'twendo] *nm* dress.

atún [a'tun] *nm* tuna, tunny.

aturdir [atur'ðir] *vt* to stun; (*de ruido*) to deafen; (*fig*) to dumbfound, bewilder.

audacia [au'ðaθja] *nf* boldness, audacity; **audaz** *a* bold, audacious; (*descarado*) cheeky, impudent.

audible [au'ðiβle] *a* audible.

audición [auði'θjon] *nf* hearing; (*TEATRO*) audition.

audiencia [au'ðjenθja] *nf* audience; (*JUR*) high court.

auditor [auði'tor] *nm* (*JUR*) judge-advocate; (*COM*) auditor.

auditorio [auði'torjo] *nm* audience; (*sala*) auditorium.

auge ['auxe] *nm* boom; (*clímax*) climax.

augurar [auxu'rar] *vt* to predict; (*presagiar*) to portend; **augurio** *nm* omen; **augurios** *nmpl* good wishes.

aula ['aula] *nf* classroom.

aullar [au'ʎar] *vi* to howl, yell.

aullido [au'ʎiðo] *nm* howl, yell.

aumentar [aumen'tar] *vt* (*precios, sueldo*) to raise; (*producción*) to increase; (*con microscopio, anteojos*) to magnify // *vi*, ~se *vr* to increase; (*subirse*) to rise; (*multiplicarse*) to multiply; **aumento** *nm* increase; rise.

aun [a'un] *ad* even.

aún [a'un] *ad* still, yet.

aunque [a'unke] *conj* though, although, even though, even if.

aura ['aura] *nf* gentle breeze; (*fig*) popularity.

aureola [aure'ola] *nf* halo.

auricular [auriku'lar] *nm* (*dedo*) little finger; (*del teléfono*) earpiece, receiver; ~es *nmpl* headphones.

ausencia [au'senθja] *nf* absence.

ausentarse [ausen'tarse] *vr* to go/stay away, absent o.s.

ausente [au'sente] *a* absent.

auspicios [aus'piθjos] *nmpl* auspices; (*protección*) protection *sg*.

austeridad [austeri'ðað] *nf* austerity; **austero, a** *a* austere.

austral [aus'tral] *a* southern.

Australia [aus'tralja] *nf* Australia; **australiano, a** *a*, *nm/f* Australian.

Austria ['austrja] *nf* Austria; **austríaco, a** *a*, *nm/f* Austrian.

autenticar [autenti'kar] *vt* to authenticate; **auténtico, a** *a* authentic.

auto ['auto] *nm* (*JUR*) edict, decree; (*orden*) writ; (*fam*) car; ~s *nmpl* (*JUR*) proceedings; (: *acta*) court record *sg*.

autobiografía [autoβjoxra'fia] *nf* autobiography.

autobús [auto'βus] *nm* bus.

autocar [auto'kar] *nm* coach.

autócrata [au'tokrata] *nm/f* autocrat.

autóctono, a [au'toktono, a] *a* native, indigenous.

autodefensa [autoðe'fensa] *nf* self-defence.

autodeterminación [autoðetermina-'θjon] *nf* self-determination.

autoescuela [autoes'kwela] *nf* driving school.

autógrafo [au'toxrafo] *nm* autograph.

autómata [au'tomata] *nm* automaton.

automático, a [auto'matiko, a] *a* automatic.

automotor, triz [automo'tor, 'triz] *a* self-propelled // *nm* Diesel train.

automóvil [auto'moβil] *nm* (motor) car, automobile; **automovilístico, a** *a* driving *cpd*, motoring *cpd*.

autonomía [autono'mia] *nf* autonomy; **autónomo, a** *a* autonomous.

autopista [auto'pista] *nf* motorway.

autopsia [au'topsja] *nf* autopsy.

autor, a [au'tor, a] *nm/f* author.

autoridad [autori'ðað] *nf* authority; **autoritario, a** *a* authoritarian.

autorización [autoriθa'θjon] *nf* authorization; **autorizado, a** *a* authorized; (*aprobado*) approved; **autorizar** *vt* to authorize; to approve.

autorretrato [autorre'trato] *nm* self-portrait.

autoservicio [autoser'βiθjo] *nm* self-service restaurant.

autostop [auto'stop] *nm* hitch-hiking; **hacer el ~** to hitch-hike; **~ista** *nm/f* hitch-hiker.

autosuficiencia [autosufi'θjenθja] *nf* self-sufficiency.

auxiliar [auksi'ljar] *vt* to help // *nm/f* assistant; **auxilio** *nm* assistance, help; **primeros auxilios** first aid *sg*.

Av *abr de* **Avenida**.

aval [a'βal] *nm* guarantee; (*persona*) guarantor.

avalancha [aβa'lantʃa] *nf* avalanche.

avaluar [aβa'lwar] *vt* to value, appraise.

avance [a'βanθe] *nm* advance; (*pago*) advance payment.

avanzar [aβan'θar] *vt*, *vi*, **~se** *vr* to advance.

avaricia [aβa'riθja] *nf* avarice, greed; **avariento, a** *a* avaricious, greedy.

avaro, a [a'βaro, a] *a* miserly, mean // *nm/f* miser.

avasallar [aβasa'ʎar] *vt* to subdue, subjugate; **~se** *vr* to submit.

Avda *abr de* **Avenida**.

ave ['aβe] *nf* bird; **~ de rapiña** bird of prey.

avellana [aβe'ʎana] *nf* hazelnut; **avellano** *nm* hazel tree.

avemaría [aβema'ria] *nf* Hail Mary, Ave María.

avena [a'βena] *nf* oats *pl*.

avenencia [aβe'nenθja] *nf* agreement; (*COM*) bargain.

avenida [aβe'niða] *nf* (*calle*) avenue; (*de río*) flood, spate.

avenir [aβe'nir] *vt* to reconcile; **~se** *vr* to come to an agreement, reach a compromise.

aventajado, a [aβenta'xaðo, a] *a* outstanding; **aventajar** *vt* (*sobrepasar*) to surpass, outstrip; (*preferir*) to prefer; **aventajarse** *vr* to surpass *or* excel o.s.

aventar [aβen'tar] *vt* to fan, blow;

(*esparcir*) to scatter; (*grano*) to winnow; **~se** *vr* to fill with air.

aventura [aβen'tura] *nf* adventure; (*casualidad*) chance; **aventurado, a** *a* risky; **aventurero, a** *a* adventurous.

avergonzar [aβerɣon'θar] *vt* to shame; (*desconcertar*) to embarrass; **~se** *vr* to be ashamed; to be embarrassed.

avería [aβe'ria] *nf* damage; (*TEC*) breakdown, fault.

averiguación [aβeriɣwa'θjon] *nf* investigation; (*determinación*) ascertainment; **averiguar** *vt* to investigate; to find out, ascertain.

aversión [aβer'sjon] *nf* aversion, dislike.

avestruz [aβes'truθ] *nm* ostrich.

avezarse [aβe'θarse] *vr*: **~se a algo** to grow used to sth.

aviación [aβja'θjon] *nf* aviation *q*; (*fuerzas aéreas*) air fc ce.

aviador, a [aβja'ðor, a] *nm/f* aviator, airman/woman.

avicultura [aβikul'tura] *nf* poultry farming.

avidez [aβi'ðeθ] *nf* avidity, eagerness; **ávido, a** *a* avid, eager.

avinagrado, a [aβina'ɣraðo, a] *a* sour, acid; **avinagrarse** *vr* to turn sour.

avío [a'βio] *nm* preparation; **~s** *nmpl* gear *sg*, kit *sg*.

avión [a'βjon] *nm* aeroplane; (*ave*) martin; **~ de reacción** jet plane.

avisar [aβi'sar] *vt* (*advertir*) to warn, notify; (*informar*) to tell; (*aconsejar*) to advise, counsel; **aviso** *nm* warning; (*noticia*) notice; (*prudencia*) caution, discretion.

avispa [a'βispa] *nf* wasp.

avispado, a [aβis'paðo, a] *a* sharp, clever.

avispar [aβis'par] *vt* to spur (on); **~se** *vr* to fret, worry.

avispero [aβis'pero] *nm* wasp's nest.

avispón [aβis'pon] *nm* hornet.

avistar [aβis'tar] *vt* to sight, spot; **~se** *vr* to have an interview.

avituallar [aβitwa'ʎar] *vt* to supply with food.

avivar [aβi'βar] *vt* to strengthen, intensify; **~se** *vr* to revive, acquire new life.

avizorar [aβiθo'rar] *vt* to spy on.

axila [ak'sila] *nf* armpit.

axioma [ak'sjoma] *nm* axiom.

ay [ai] *excl* (*dolor*) ow!, ouch!; (*aflicción*) oh!, oh dear!; **¡~ de mí!** poor me!; **¡~ del que!** pity help *or* woe betide whoever!

aya ['aja] *nf* governess; (*niñera*) children's nurse.

ayer [a'jer] *ad*, *nm* yesterday; **antes de ~** the day before yesterday.

ayo ['ajo] *nm* tutor.

ayuda [a'juða] *nf* help, assistance; (*MED*) enema; (*AM*) laxative // *nm* page; **ayudante, a** *nm/f* assistant, helper; (*ESCOL*) assistant; (*MIL*) adjutant; **ayudar** *vt* to help, assist.

ayunar [aju'nar] *vi* to fast; **ayunas** *nfpl*: **estar en ayunas** (*no haber comido*) to be fasting; (*ignorante*) to be in the dark; **ayuno** *nm* fasting; ignorance.

ayuntamiento [ajunta'mjento] *nm* (*consejo*) council; (*edificio*) town hall; (*cópula*) sexual intercourse.

azabache [aθa'βatʃe] *nm* jet.

azada [a'θaða] *nf* hoe.

azafata [aθa'fata] *nf* air hostess.

azafrán [aθa'fran] *nm* saffron.

azahar [aθa'ar] *nm* orange/lemon blossom.

azar [a'θar] *nm* (*casualidad*) chance, fate; (*desgracia*) misfortune, accident; **por ~** by chance; **al ~** at random.

azarearse [aθare'arse] *vr* = **azorarse**.

azogue [a'θoxe] *nm* mercury.

azoramiento [aθora'mjento] *nm* alarm; (*confusión*) confusion.

azorar [aθo'rar] *vt* to alarm; **~se** *vr* to get alarmed.

Azores [a'θores] *nmpl*: **los ~** the Azores.

azótar [aθo'tar] *vt* to whip, beat; (*pegar*) to spank; **azote** *nm* (*látigo*) whip; (*latigazo*) lash, stroke; (*en las nalgas*) spank; (*calamidad*) calamity.

azotea [aθo'tea] *nf* terrace roof.

azteca [aθ'teka] *a, nm/f* Aztec.

azúcar [a'θukar] *nm* sugar; **azucarado, a** a sugary, sweet.

azucarero, a [aθuka'rero, a] *a* sugar *cpd* // *nm* sugar bowl.

azucena [aθu'θena] *nf* white lily.

azufre [a'θufre] *nm* sulphur.

azul [a'θul] *a, nm* blue.

azulejo [aθu'lexo] *nm* glazed tile.

azuzar [aθu'θar] *vt* to incite, egg on.

B

B.A. *abr de* **Buenos Aires.**

baba ['baβa] *nf* spittle, saliva; **babear** *vi* to drool, slaver.

babel [ba'βel] *nm o f* bedlam.

babero [ba'βero] *nm* bib.

babor [ba'βor] *nm* port (side).

babucha [ba'βutʃa] *nf* slipper.

bacalao [baka'lao] *nm* cod(fish).

bacía [ba'θia] *nf* basin, bowl.

bacín [ba'θin] *nm* chamber pot.

bacteria [bak'terja] *nf* bacterium, germ.

báculo ['bakulo] *nm* stick, staff.

bache ['batʃe] *nm* pothole, rut; (*fig*) bad patch.

bachillerato [batʃiʎe'rato] *nm* (*ESCOL*) school-leaving examination.

bagaje [ba'vaxe] *nm* baggage.

bagatela [baxa'tela] *nf* trinket, trifle.

bahía [ba'ia] *nf* bay.

bailar [bai'lar] *vt, vi* to dance; **~ín, ina** *nm/f* (*ballet*) dancer; **baile** *nm* dance; (*formal*) ball.

baja ['baxa] *nf ver* **bajo**.

bajada [ba'xaða] *nf* descent; (*camino*) slope; (*de aguas*) ebb.

bajamar [baxa'mar] *nf* low tide.

bajar [ba'xar] *vi* to go/come down; (*temperatura, precios*) to drop, fall; (*de coche*) to get out; (*de autobús*) to get off // *vt* (*cabeza*) to bow, bend; (*escalera*) to go/come down; (*precio, voz*) to lower; (*llevar abajo*) to take down; **~se** *vr* to bend down; to get out of; to get off; (*fig*) to humble o.s.

bajeza [ba'xeθa] *nf* baseness *q*; (*una ~*) vile deed.

bajío [ba'xio] *nm* shoal, sandbank; (*AM*) lowlands *pl*.

bajo, a ['baxo, a] *a* (*terreno*) low(-lying); (*mueble, número, precio*) low; (*piso*) ground; (*de estatura*) small, short; (*color*) pale; (*sonido*) faint, soft, low; (*voz: en tono*) deep; (*metal*) base; (*humilde*) low, humble // *ad* (*hablar*) low, quietly; (*volar*) low // *prep* under, below, underneath // *nm* (*MUS*) bass // *nf* drop, fall; (*MIL*) casualty; **~ la lluvia** in the rain; **dar de ~a** (*soldado*) to discharge; (*empleado*) to dismiss, sack.

bajón [ba'xon] *nm* (*MUS*) bassoon; (*baja*) decline, fall, drop.

bajorrelieve [baxorre'ljeβe] *nm* bas-relief.

bala ['bala] *nf* bullet.

baladí [bala'ði] *a* trivial.

baladrón, ona [bala'ðron, ona] *a* boastful.

bálago ['balaxo] *nm* thatch.

balance [ba'lanθe] *nm* (*balanceo*) oscillation, rocking; (*NAUT*) roll; (*COM*) balance; (: *libro*) balance sheet; (: *cuenta general*) stocktaking; **~ar** *vt* to balance // *vi*, **~arse** *vr* to swing (to and fro); (*vacilar*) to hesitate; **balanceo** *nm* swinging.

balanza [ba'lanθa] *nf* balance, scales *pl*; **~ comercial** balance of trade; **~ de pagos** balance of payments; (*ASTRO*): **B~** = **Libra.**

balar [ba'lar] *vi* to bleat.

balazo [ba'laθo] *nm* (*golpe*) shot; (*herida*) bullet wound.

balbucear [balβuθe'ar] *vi, vt* to stammer, stutter; **balbuceo** *nm* stammering, stuttering.

balbucir [balβu'θir] *vi, vt* to stammer, stutter.

balcón [bal'kon] *nm* balcony.

baldaquín [balda'kin], **baldaquino** [balda'kino] *nm* canopy.

baldar [bal'dar] *vt* to cripple.

balde ['balde] *nm* bucket, pail; **de ~** *ad* (for) free, for nothing; **en ~** *ad* in vain.

baldío, a [bal'dio, a] *a* uncultivated // *nm* waste land.

baldón [bal'don] *nm* (*injuria*) insult.

baldosa [bal'dosa] *nf* paving stone.

Baleares [bale'ares] *nfpl*: **las (Islas) ~** the Balearic Islands.

balido [ba'liðo] *nm* bleat, bleating.

balística [ba'listika] *nf* ballistics *pl*.

baliza [ba'liθa] *nf* (*AVIAT*) beacon; (*NAUT*) buoy.

balneario, a [balne'arjo, a] *a*: **estación**
~**a** bathing resort // *nm* spa, health
resort.

balón [ba'lon] *nm* ball.

baloncesto [balon'θesto] *nm* basketball.

balsa ['balsa] *nf* raft; (*BOT*) balsa wood.

bálsamo ['balsamo] *nm* balsam, balm.

baluarte [ba'lwarte] *nm* bastion, bulwark.

ballena [ba'ʎena] *nf* whale.

ballesta [ba'ʎesta] *nf* crossbow; (*AUTO*)
spring.

ballet [ba'le] *nm* ballet.

bambolear [bambole'ar] *vi*, ~**se** *vr* to
swing, sway; (*silla*) to wobble; **bamboleo**
nm swinging, swaying; wobbling.

bambú [bam'bu] *nm* bamboo.

banca ['banka] *nf* (*asiento*) bench; (*COM*)
banking; ~**da** *nf* (*banco*) stone bench;
(*TEC*) bench.

bancario, a [ban'karjo, a] *a* banking *cpd*,
bank *cpd*.

bancarrota [banka'rrota] *nf* (*esp*
fraudulent) bankruptcy.

banco ['banko] *nm* bench; (*ESCOL*) desk;
(*COM*) bank; (*GEO*) stratum; ~ **de
crédito/de ahorros** credit/ savings
bank; ~ **de arena** sandbank; ~ **de hielo**
iceberg.

banda ['banda] *nf* band; (*pandilla*) gang;
(*NAUT*) side, edge; **la B**~ **Oriental**
Uruguay; ~ **sonora** soundtrack.

bandada [ban'daða] *nf* (*de pájaros*) flock;
(*de peces*) shoal.

bandeja [ban'dexa] *nf* tray.

bandera [ban'dera] *nf* (*de tela*) flag;
(*estandarte*) banner.

banderilla [bande'riʎa] *nf* banderilla.

banderola [bande'rola] *nf* banderole,
pennant.

bandidaje [bandi'ðaxe] *nm* banditry;
bandido *nm* bandit.

bando ['bando] *nm* (*edicto*) edict,
proclamation; (*facción*) faction; **los** ~**s**
the banns.

bandolero [bando'lero] *nm* bandit,
brigand.

banquero [ban'kero] *nm* banker.

banqueta [ban'keta] *nf* (*asiento*) bench;
(*escabel*) stool.

banquete [ban'kete] *nm* banquet; (*para
convidados*) formal dinner.

banquillo [ban'kiʎo] *nm* (*JUR*) dock,
prisoner's bench; (*banco*) bench; (*para los
pies*) footstool.

bañador [baɲa'ðor] *nm* swimming
costume.

bañar [ba'ɲar] *vt* (*niño*) to bath, bathe;
(*objeto*) to dip; (*de barniz*) to coat; ~**se** *vr*
(*en el mar*) to bathe, swim; (*en la bañera*)
to bath, have a bath.

bañera [ba'ɲera] *nf* bath(tub).

bañero [ba'ɲero] *nm* lifeguard.

bañista [ba'ɲista] *nm/f* bather.

baño ['baɲo] *nm* (*en bañera*) bath; (*en río*)
dip, swim; (*cuarto*) bathroom; (*bañera*)
bath(tub); (*capa*) coating.

baptista [bap'tista] *nm/f* baptist.

baqueta [ba'keta] *nf* (*MUS*) drumstick.

bar [bar] *nm* bar.

barahúnda [bara'unda] *nf* uproar,
hubbub.

baraja [ba'raxa] *nf* pack (of cards);
barajar *vt* (*naipes*) to shuffle; (*fig*) to
jumble up.

baranda [ba'randa] *nf* rail, railing.

barandilla [baran'diʎa] *nf* rail, railing.

baratija [bara'tixa] *nf* trinket.

baratillo [bara'tiʎo] *nm* (*tienda*) junkshop;
(*subasta*) bargain sale; (*conjunto de cosas*)
secondhand goods *pl*.

barato, a [ba'rato, a] *a* cheap // *nm*
bargain sale // *ad* cheap, cheaply;
baratura *nf* cheapness.

baraúnda [bara'unda] *nf* = **barahúnda.**

barba ['barβa] *nf* (*ANAT*) chin; (*pelo*) beard,
whiskers *pl*.

barbacoa [barβa'koa] *nf* (*parrilla*)
barbecue; (*carne*) barbecued meat.

barbado, a [bar'βaðo, a] *a* bearded // *nm*
seedling.

barbaridad [barβari'ðað] *nf* barbarity;
(*acto*) barbarism; (*atrocidad*) outrage; **una**
~ (*fam*) a huge amount; **¡qué** ~**!** (*fam*)
how awful!

barbarie [bar'βarje] *nf*, **barbarismo**
[barβa'rismo] *nm* barbarism; (*crueldad*)
barbarity.

bárbaro, a ['barβaro, a] *a* barbarous,
cruel; (*grosero*) rough, uncouth // *nm/f*
barbarian // *ad*: **lo pasamos** ~ (*fam*) we
had a tremendous time; **¡qué** ~**!** (*fam*)
how marvellous!; **un éxito** ~ (*fam*) a
terrific success; **es un tipo** ~ (*fam*) he's
a splendid chap.

barbear [barβe'ar] *vt* (*AM*) to shave.

barbecho [bar'βetʃo] *nm* fallow land.

barbero [bar'βero] *nm* barber,
hairdresser.

barbilampiño [barβilam'piɲo] *a* smooth-
faced; (*fig*) inexperienced.

barbilla [bar'βiʎa] *nf* chin, tip of the chin.

barbotar [barβo'tar], **barbotear**
[barβote'ar] *vt, vi* to mutter, mumble.

barbudo, a [bar'βuðo, a] *a* bearded.

barca ['barka] *nf* (*small*) boat; ~ **de
pesca** fishing boat; ~ **de pasaje** ferry;
~**za** *nf* barge; ~**za de desembarco**
landing craft.

barcelonés, esa [barθelo'nes, esa] *a* of *or*
from Barcelona.

barco ['barko] *nm* boat; (*buque*) ship; ~
de carga cargo boat.

bardar [bar'ðar] *vt* to thatch.

barítono [ba'ritono] *nm* baritone.

barman ['barman] *nm* barman.

Barna *abr de* **Barcelona.**

barniz [bar'niθ] *nm* varnish; (*en la loza*)
glaze; (*fig*) veneer; ~ **para las uñas** nail
varnish; ~**ar** *vt* to varnish; (*loza*) to glaze.

barómetro [ba'rometro] *nm* barometer.

barquero [bar'kero] *nm* boatman.

barquillo [bar'kiʎo] *nm* cone, cornet.

barra ['barra] *nf* bar, rod; (*de un bar, café*) bar; (*de pan*) small loaf; (*palanca*) lever; ~ **de carmín** *o* **de labios** lipstick.

barraca [ba'rraka] *nf* hut, cabin.

barranca [ba'rranka] *nf* ravine, gully; **barranco** *nm* ravine; (*fig*) difficulty.

barrena [ba'rrena] *nf* drill; **barrenar** *vt* to drill (through), bore; **barreno** *nm* large drill, borer.

barrer [ba'rrer] *vt* to sweep; (*quitar*) to sweep away.

barrera [ba'rrera] *nf* barrier.

barriada [ba'rrjaða] *nf* quarter, district.

barricada [barri'kaða] *nf* barricade.

barrido [ba'rriðo] *nm*, **barrida** [ba'rriða] *nf* sweep, sweeping.

barriga [ba'rriva] *nf* belly; (*panza*) paunch; **barrigón, ona**, **barrigudo, a** *a* fat, potbellied.

barril [ba'rril] *nm* barrel, cask.

barrio ['barrjo] *nm* (*en el pueblo*) district, quarter; (*fuera del pueblo*) suburb.

barro ['barro] *nm* (*lodo*) mud; (*objetos*) earthenware; (*MED*) pimple.

barroco, a [ba'rroko, a] *a, nm* baroque.

barroso, a [ba'rroso, a] *a* (*lodoso*) muddy; (*MED*) pimply.

barruntar [barrun'tar] *vt* (*conjeturar*) to guess; (*presentir*) to suspect; **barrunto** *nm* guess; suspicion.

bartola [bar'tola]: **a la ~** *ad*: **tirarse a la ~** to take it easy, do nothing.

bártulos ['bartulos] *nmpl* things, belongings.

barullo [ba'ruʎo] *nm* row, uproar.

basa ['basa] *nf* base; (*fig*) basis; ~**mento** *nm* base, plinth.

basar [ba'sar] *vt* to base; ~**se** *vr*: ~**se en** to be based on.

basca ['baska] *nf* nausea.

báscula ['baskula] *nf* (*platform*) scales *pl*.

base ['base] *nf* base; **a ~ de** on the basis of.

básico, a ['basiko, a] *a* basic.

basílica [ba'silika] *nf* basilica.

bastante [bas'tante] *a* (*suficiente*) enough, sufficient; (*no poco(s)*) quite a lot of // *ad* (*suficientemente*) enough, sufficiently; (*muy*) quite, rather.

bastar [bas'tar] *vi* to be enough *or* sufficient; ~**se** *vr* to be self-sufficient; ~ **para** to be enough to; ¡**basta!** (that's) enough!

bastardilla [bastar'ðiʎa] *nf* italics *pl*.

bastardo, a [bas'tarðo, a] *a, nm/f* bastard.

bastidor [basti'ðor] *nm* frame; (*de coche*) chassis.

basto, a ['basto, a] *a* coarse, rough; ~**s** *nmpl* (*NAIPES*) clubs.

bastón [bas'ton] *nm* (*gen*) stick, staff; (*para el paseo*) walking stick.

basura [ba'sura] *nf* rubbish, refuse.

basurero [basu'rero] *nm* (*hombre*) dustman; (*lugar*) rubbish dump; (*cubo*) (rubbish) bin.

bata ['bata] *nf* (*salto de cama*) dressing gown, housecoat; (*de alumno etc*) smock, overall.

batalla [ba'taʎa] *nf* battle; **de ~** everyday, for everyday use.

batallar [bata'ʎar] *vi* to fight.

batallón [bata'ʎon] *nm* battalion.

bate ['bate] *nm* bat; ~**ador** *nm* batter, batsman.

batería [bate'ria] *nf* battery; (*MUS*) drums *pl*; ~ **de cocina** kitchen utensils *pl*.

batido, a [ba'tiðo, a] *a* (*camino*) beaten, well-trodden // *nm* (*CULIN*) batter; ~ **de leche** milk shake.

batidora [bati'ðora] *nf* beater, mixer.

batir [ba'tir] *vt* to beat, strike; (*vencer*) to beat, defeat; (*revolver*) to beat, mix; (*acuñar*) to strike, mint; (*pelo*) to comb; ~**se** *vr* to fight; ~ **palmas** to clap, applaud.

batuta [ba'tuta] *nf* baton.

baúl [ba'ul] *nm* trunk; (*AUTO*) boot.

bautismo [bau'tismo] *nm* baptism, christening.

bautizar [bauti'θar] *vt* to baptize, christen; (*fam*) to water down; **bautizo** *nm* baptism, christening.

bayo, a ['bajo, a] *a* bay // *nf* berry.

bayoneta [bajo'neta] *nf* bayonet.

baza ['baθa] *nf* trick.

bazar [ba'θar] *nm* bazaar.

bazofia [ba'θofja] *nf* left-overs *pl*.

beato, a [be'ato, a] *a* blessed; (*piadoso*) pious // *nm/f* lay brother/sister.

bebé [be'ße] *nm* baby.

bebedero, a [beße'ðero, a] *a* drinkable // *nm* (*para animales*) drinking trough; (*de vasija*) spout.

bebedizo, a [beße'ðiθo, a] *a* drinkable // *nm* potion.

bebedor, a [beße'ðor, a] *a* hard-drinking.

beber [be'ßer] *vt, vi* to drink.

bebida [be'ßiða] *nf* drink.

beca ['beka] *nf* grant, scholarship.

befa ['befa] *nf ver* **befo**.

befar [be'far] *vt* to scoff at.

befo, a ['befo, a] *a* thick-lipped // *nm* lip // *nf*: **hacer** ~**a de** to jeer, mock.

beldad [bel'dað] *nf* beauty.

belfo, a ['belfo, a] *a* = **befo**.

belga ['belxa] *a, nm/f* Belgian.

Bélgica ['belxika] *nf* Belgium.

bélico, a ['beliko, a] *a* warlike, martial; **belicoso, a** *a* (*guerrero*) warlike; (*agresivo*) aggressive, bellicose.

beligerante [belixe'rante] *a* belligerent.

bellaco, a [be'ʎako, a] *a* sly, cunning // *nm* villain, rogue; **bellaquería** *nf* (*acción*) dirty trick; (*calidad*) wickedness.

belleza [be'ʎeθa] *nf* beauty.

bello, a ['beʎo, a] *a* beautiful, lovely; ~**as artes** fine arts.

bellota [be'ʎota] *nf* acorn.

bemol [be'mol] *nm* (*MUS*) flat; **esto tiene** ~**es** (*fam*) this is a real problem.

bendecir [bende'θir] *vt* to bless.

bendición [bendi'θjon] *nf* blessing.

bendito, a [ben'dito, a] *pp de* **bendecir** // *a* holy; (*afortunado*) lucky; (*feliz*) happy; (*sencillo*) simple // *nm/f* simple soul.

benedictino, a [beneðik'tino, a] *a, nm* Benedictine.

beneficencia [benefi'θenθja] *nf* charity.

beneficiar [benefi'θjar] *vt* (*hacer bien a*) to benefit, be of benefit to; (*tierra*) to cultivate; (*mina*) to exploit; (*mineral*) to process, treat; ~**se** *vr* to benefit, profit; ~**io, a** *nm/f* beneficiary.

beneficio [bene'fiθjo] *nm* (*bien*) benefit, advantage; (*ganancia*) profit, gain; (*AGR*) cultivation; ~**so, a** *a* beneficial.

benéfico, a [be'nefiko, a] *a* beneficent, charitable.

beneplácito [bene'plaθito] *nm* approval, consent.

benevolencia [beneβo'lenθja] *nf* benevolence, kindness; **benévolo, a** *a* benevolent, kind.

benignidad [benixni'ðað] *nf* (*afabilidad*) kindness; (*suavidad*) mildness; **benigno, a** *a* kind; mild.

beodo, a [be'oðo, a] *a* drunk.

berenjena [beren'xena] *nf* aubergine, eggplant.

Berlín [ber'lin] *n* Berlin; **berlinés, esa** *a* of *or* from Berlin // *nm/f* Berliner.

bermejo, a [ber'mexo, a] *a* red.

Berna ['berna] *n* Berne.

berrear [berre'ar] *vi* to bellow, low.

berrido [be'rriðo] *nm* bellow, bellowing.

berrinche [be'rrintʃe] *nm* (*fam*) temper, tantrum.

berro ['berro] *nm* watercress.

berza ['berθa] *nf* cabbage.

besar [be'sar] *vt* to kiss; (*fig*) to graze; ~**se** *vr* to kiss (one another); **beso** *nm* kiss.

bestia ['bestja] *nf* beast, animal; (*fig*) idiot; ~ **de carga** beast of burden.

bestial [bes'tjal] *a* bestial; (*fam*) terrific; ~**idad** *nf* bestiality; (*fam*) stupidity.

besuquear [besuke'ar] *vt* to cover with kisses; ~**se** *vr* to kiss and cuddle.

betún [be'tun] *nm* bitumen, asphalt; (*para calzado*) shoe polish.

biberón [biβe'ron] *nm* feeding bottle.

Biblia ['biβlja] *nf* Bible.

bíblico, a ['biβliko, a] *a* biblical.

bibliografía [biβljoɣra'fia] *nf* bibliography.

biblioteca [biβljo'teka] *nf* library; (*mueble*) bookshelves *pl*; ~ **de consulta** reference library; ~**rio, a** *nm/f* librarian.

B.I.C. *nf abr de* **Brigada de Investigación Criminal** CID (Criminal Investigation Department); FBI (Federal Bureau of Investigation) (*US*).

bicarbonato [bikarβo'nato] *nm* bicarbonate.

bicicleta [biθi'kleta] *nf* bicycle, bike.

bicho ['bitʃo] *nm* (*animal*) small animal; (*sabandija*) bug, insect; (*TAUR*) bull.

bidé [bi'ðe] *nm* bidet.

bien [bjen] *nm* good; (*interés*) advantage, benefit // *ad* well; (*correctamente*) properly, right; (*oler*) nice; (*muy*) very; **más** ~ rather // *excl*: ¡(**muy**) ~! well done! // *conj*: **no** ~ **llovió, bajó la temperatura** no sooner had it rained than the temperature dropped; ~ **que** although; ~**es inmuebles/muebles** real estate *sg*/personal property *sg*; ~**es de consumo** consumer goods; ~**es raíces** real estate *sg*.

bienal [bje'nal] *a* biennial.

bienandanza [bjenan'danθa] *nf* happiness.

bienaventurado, a [bjenaßentu'raðo, a] *a* (*feliz*) happy, fortunate; (*sencillo*) simple, naïve.

bienestar [bjenes'tar] *nm* well-being.

bienhechor, a [bjene'tʃor, a] *a* beneficent.

bienvenida [bjenße'niða] *nf* welcome; **bienvenido** *excl* welcome!

biftec [bif'tek] *nm* (*beef*)steak.

bifurcación [bifurka'θjon] *nf* fork.

bigamia [bi'ɣamja] *nf* bigamy; **bígamo, a** *a* bigamous // *nm/f* bigamist.

bigote [bi'ɣote] *nm* moustache; **bigotudo, a** *a* moustached.

bilbaíno, a [bilßa'ino, a] *a* of *or* from Bilbao.

bilingüe [bi'lingwe] *a* bilingual.

billar [bi'ʎar] *nm* billiards *sg*; (*lugar*) billiard hall.

billete [bi'ʎete] *nm* ticket; (*de banco*) banknote; (*carta*) note; ~ **simple** single (ticket); ~ **de ida y vuelta** return (ticket); ~ **kilométrico** runabout ticket.

billetera [biʎe'tera] *nf*, **billetero** [biʎe'tero] *nm* wallet.

billón [bi'ʎon] *nm* billion.

bimensual [bimen'swal] *a* twice monthly.

bimotor [bimo'tor] *a* twin-engined // *nm* twin-engined plane.

binóculo [bi'nokulo] *nm* pince-nez.

biografía [bjoɣra'fia] *nf* biography; **biógrafo, a** *nm/f* biographer.

biología [bjolo'xia] *nf* biology; **biológico, a** *a* biological; **biólogo, a** *nm/f* biologist.

biombo ['bjombo] *nm* (*folding*) screen.

biopsia [bi'opsja] *nf* biopsy.

biplano [bi'plano] *nm* biplane.

birlar [bir'lar] *vt* (*derribar*) to knock down; (*matar*) to kill; (*fam*) to pinch.

bis [bis] *excl* encore! // *ad*: **viven en el 27** ~ they live at 27a.

bisabuelo, a [bisa'ßwelo, a] *nm/f* great-grandfather/mother.

bisagra [bi'saɣra] *nf* hinge.

bisbisar [bisßi'sar], **bisbisear** [bisßise-'ar] *vt* to mutter, mumble.

bisexual [bisek'swal] *a* bisexual.

bisiesto [bi'sjesto] *a*: **año** ~ leap year.

bisnieto, a [bis'njeto, a] *nm/f* great-grandson/daughter.

bisonte [bi'sonte] *nm* bison.

bisoño, a [bi'soɲo, a] *a* green, inexperienced.

bistec [bis'tek], **bisté** [bis'te] *nm* steak.
bisturí [bistu'ri] *nm* scalpel.
bisutería [bisute'ria] *nf* imitation *or* costume jewellery.
bizarría [biθa'rria] *nf* (*valor*) bravery; (*generosidad*) generosity; **bizarro, a** *a* brave; generous.
bizcar [biθ'kar] *vi* to squint; **bizco, a** *a* cross-eyed.
bizcocho [biθ'kotʃo] *nm* (*CULIN*) sponge cake.
bizquear [biθke'ar] *vi* to squint.
blanco, a ['blanko, a] *a* white // *nm/f* white man/woman, white // *nm* (*color*) white; (*intervalo*) space, interval; (*en texto*) blank; (*MIL, fig*) target // *nm* (*MUS*) minim; **en ~** blank; **noche en ~** sleepless night; **estar sin ~** to be broke.
blancura [blan'kura] *nf* whiteness.
blandir [blan'dir] *vt* to brandish.
blando, a ['blando, a] *a* soft; (*tierno*) tender, gentle; (*carácter*) mild; (*fam*) cowardly; **blandura** *nf* softness; tenderness; mildness.
blanquear [blanke'ar] *vt* to whiten; (*fachada*) to whitewash; (*paño*) to bleach // *vi* to turn white; **blanquecino, a** *a* whitish; **blanqueo** *nm* whitewashing; bleaching.
blanquillo, a [blan'kiʎo, a] *a* white.
blasfemar [blasfe'mar] *vi* to blaspheme, curse; **blasfemia** *nf* blasphemy.
blasón [bla'son] *nm* coat of arms; (*fig*) honour; **blasonar** *vt* to emblazon // *vi* to boast, brag.
bledo ['bleðo] *nm*: **(no) me importa un ~** I don't care two hoots.
blindaje [blin'daxe] *nm* armour, armour-plating; **blindar** *vt* to armour, armour-plate.
bloc [blok] *nm* writing pad.
bloque ['bloke] *nm* block; (*POL*) bloc; **~ de cilindros** cylinder block.
bloquear [bloke'ar] *vt* to blockade; **bloqueo** *nm* blockade; (*COM*) freezing, blocking.
bluejean ['bludʒin] *nm inv* jeans *pl.*
blusa ['blusa] *nf* (*de alumno*) smock; (*de mujer*) blouse.
boardilla [boar'ðiʎa] *nf* = **buhardilla**.
boato [bo'ato] *nm* show, ostentation.
bobada [bo'ßaða], **bobería** [boße'ria] *nf* foolish action/ statement.
bobina [bo'ßina] *nf* (*TEC*) bobbin; (*FOTO*) spool; (*ELEC*) coil; **bobinar** *vt* to wind.
bobo, a ['boßo, a] *a* (*tonto*) daft, silly; (*cándido*) naïve // *nm* (*TEATRO*) clown, funny man, fool.
boca ['boka] *nf* mouth; (*de crustáceo*) pincer; (*de cañón*) muzzle; (*de vino*) flavour, taste; (*entrada*) mouth, entrance; **~s** *nfpl* (*de río*) mouth *sg*; **~ abajo/arriba** face down/up; **a ~ de jarro** point-blank; **se me hace la ~ agua** my mouth is watering.
bocacalle [boka'kaʎe] *nf* entrance to a street.

bocadillo [boka'ðiʎo] *nm* (*emparedado*) sandwich; (*comida ligera*) snack.
bocado [bo'kaðo] *nm* mouthful, bite; (*de caballo*) bridle; **~ de Adán** Adam's apple.
bocanada [boka'naða] *nf* (*de vino*) mouthful, swallow; (*de aire*) gust, puff.
boceto [bo'θeto] *nm* sketch, outline.
bocina [bo'θina] *nf* (*MUS*) trumpet; (*AUTO*) horn; (*para hablar*) megaphone; (*para sordos*) ear trumpet.
bocha ['botʃa] *nf* bowl; **~s** *nfpl* bowls.
bochinche [bo'tʃintʃe] *nm* (*fam*) uproar.
bochorno [bo'tʃorno] *nm* (*calor*) sultry weather; (*vergüenza*) embarrassment; **~so, a** *a* sultry; embarrassing; (*sofocante*) stuffy.
boda ['boða] *nf* (*también* **~s** *nfpl*) wedding, marriage; (*fiesta*) wedding reception; **~s de plata/de oro** silver/golden wedding.
bodega [bo'ðexa] *nf* (*de vino*) (wine) cellar; (*depósito*) storeroom; (*de barco*) hold.
bodegón [boðe'xon] *nm* cheap restaurant; (*ARTE*) still life.
bofe ['bofe] *nm* (*también* **~s** *nmpl*) lung.
bofetada [bofe'taða] *nf* slap (in the face).
bofetón [bofe'ton] *nm* punch (in the face).
boga ['boxa] *nf* (*NAUT*) rowing; (*fig*) vogue, fashion // *nm/f* rower; **en ~** in vogue; **bogar** *vi* (*remar*) to row; (*navegar*) to sail.
Bogotá [boxo'ta] *n* Bogota; **bogotano, a** *a* of *or* from Bogota.
bohardilla [boar'ðiʎa] *nf* = **buhardilla**.
bohemio, a [bo'emjo, a] *a*, *nm/f* Bohemian.
boicot [boi'kot] *nm* boycott; **~ear** *vt* to boycott; **~eo** *nm* boycott.
boina ['boina] *nf* beret.
bola ['bola] *nf* (*gen*) ball; (*canica*) marble; (*NAIPES*) (grand) slam; (*betún*) shoe polish; **~ de billar** billiard ball; **~ de nieve** snowball.
bolchevique [boltʃe'ßike] *nm/f* Bolshevik.
boleadoras [bolea'ðoras] *nfpl* (*AM*) bolas.
bolera [bo'lera] *nf* skittle alley.
boleta [bo'leta] *nf* (*billete*) ticket; (*permiso*) pass, permit.
boletín [bole'tin] *nm* bulletin; (*periódico*) journal, review; (*billete*) ticket; **~ escolar** school report; **~ de noticias** news bulletin; **~ de pedido** application form; **~ de precios** price list; **~ de prensa** press release.
boleto [bo'leto] *nm* ticket.
boliche [bo'litʃe] *nm* (*bola*) jack; (*juego*) bowls *sg*; (*lugar*) bowling alley.
bolígrafo [bo'lixrafo] *nm* ball-point pen.
bolívar [bo'lißar] *nm* monetary unit of Venezuela.
Bolivia [bo'lißja] *nf* Bolivia; **boliviano, a** *a*, *nm/f* Bolivian.
bolo ['bolo] *nm* skittle; (*píldora*) (large) pill; (*juego de*) **~s** skittles *sg*.
bolsa ['bolsa] *nf* (*cartera*) purse; (*saco*) bag; (*ANAT*) cavity, sac; (*COM*) stock exchange; (*MINERÍA*) pocket; **~ de agua**

caliente hot water bottle; ~ **de aire** air pocket; ~ **de papel** paper bag.

bolsillo [bol'siʎo] *nm* pocket; (*cartera*) purse; **de** ~ pocket(-size).

bolsista [bol'sista] *nm/f* stockbroker.

bolso ['bolso] *nm* (*bolsa*) bag; (*de mujer*) handbag.

bollo ['boʎo] *nm* (*pan*) roll; (*bulto*) bump, lump; (*abolladura*) dent.

bomba ['bomba] *nf* (*MIL*) bomb; (*TEC*) pump // *a* (*fam*): **pasarlo** ~ to have a great time; ~ **atómica/de humo/de retardo** atomic/smoke/ time bomb; ~ **de gasolina** petrol pump; ~ **de mano** grenade; ~ **lacrimógena** tear gas bomb.

bombardear [bombarðe'ar] *vt* to bombard; (*MIL*) to bomb; **bombardeo** *nm* bombardment; bombing.

bombardero [bombar'ðero] *nm* bomber.

bombear [bombe'ar] *vt* (*agua*) to pump (out *or* up); (*MIL*) to bomb; ~**se** *vr* to warp.

bombero [bom'bero] *nm* fireman.

bombilla [bom'biʎa] *nf* bulb.

bombín [bom'bin] *nm* bowler hat.

bombo ['bombo] *nm* (*MUS*) bass drum; (*TEC*) drum.

bombón [bom'bon] *nm* chocolate.

bonachón, ona [bona'tʃon, ona] *a* good-natured, easy-going.

bonaerense [bonae'rense] *a* of *or* from Buenos Aires.

bonancible [bonan'θißle] *a* (*tiempo*) fair, calm.

bonanza [bo'nanθa] *nf* (*NAUT*) fair weather; (*fig*) bonanza; (*MINERÍA*) rich pocket *or* vein.

bondad [bon'dað] *nf* goodness, kindness; **tenga la** ~ **de** (please) be good enough to; ~**oso, a** *a* good, kind.

bonito, a [bo'nito, a] *a* (*lindo*) pretty; (*agradable*) nice.

bono ['bono] *nm* voucher; (*FIN*) bond.

boquear [boke'ar] *vi* to gasp.

boquerón [boke'ron] *nm* (*anchoa*) anchovy; (*agujero*) large hole.

boquete [bo'kete] *nm* gap, hole.

boquiabierto, a [bokia'ßjerto, a] *a* open-mouthed (in astonishment).

boquilla [bo'kiʎa] *nf* (*para riego*) nozzle; (*para cigarro*) cigarette holder; (*MUS*) mouthpiece.

borbollar [borßo'ʎar], **borbollear** [borßoʎe'ar], **borbotar** [borßo'tar] *vi* to bubble.

borbotón [borßo'ton] *nm* bubbling.

bordado [bor'ðaðo] *nm* embroidery.

bordar [bor'ðar] *vt* to embroider.

borde ['borðe] *nm* edge, border; (*de camino etc*) side; (*en la costura*) hem; **al** ~ **de** (*fig*) on the verge *or* brink of; ~**ar** *vt* to border.

bordo ['borðo] *nm* (*NAUT*) side; **a** ~ on board.

Borinquén [borin'ken] *nm* Puerto Rico;

borinqueño, a *a, nm/f* Puerto Rican.

borra ['borra] *nf* (*pelusa*) fluff; (*sedimento*) sediment.

borrachera [borra'tʃera] *nf* (*ebriedad*) drunkenness; (*orgía*) spree, binge.

borracho, a [bo'rratʃo, a] *a* drunk // *nm/f* (*que bebe mucho*) drunkard, drunk; (*temporalmente*) drunk, drunk man/woman.

borrador [borra'ðor] *nm* (*escritura*) first draft, rough sketch; (*cuaderno*) scribbling pad; (*goma*) rubber, eraser.

borrajear [borraxe'ar] *vt, vi* to scribble.

borrar [bo'rrar] *vt* to erase, rub out.

borrascoso, a [borras'koso, a] *a* stormy.

borrica [bo'rrika] *nf* she-donkey; (*fig*) stupid woman; ~**da** *nf* foolish action/statement.

borrico [bo'rriko] *nm* donkey; (*fig*) stupid man.

borrón [bo'rron] *nm* (*mancha*) stain; (*proyecto*) rough draft; (*de cuadro*) sketch.

borroso, a [bo'rroso, a] *a* vague, unclear; (*escritura*) illegible.

bosque ['boske] *nm* wood, forest.

bosquejar [boske'xar] *vt* to sketch; **bosquejo** *nm* sketch.

bosta ['bosta] *nf* dung, manure.

bostezar [boste'θar] *vi* to yawn; **bostezo** *nm* yawn.

bota ['bota] *nf* (*saco*) leather wine bottle; (*calzado*) boot.

botadura [bota'ðura] *nf* launching.

botánico, a [bo'taniko, a] *nm/f* botanist // *nf* botany.

botar [bo'tar] *vt* to throw, hurl; (*NAUT*) to launch; (*fam*) to throw out // *vi* to bounce.

bote ['bote] *nm* (*salto*) bounce; (*golpe*) thrust; (*vasija*) tin, can; (*embarcación*) boat; **de** ~ **en** ~ packed, jammed full; ~ **salvavidas** lifeboat.

botella [bo'teʎa] *nf* bottle.

botica [bo'tika] *nf* chemist's (shop), pharmacy; ~**rio, a** *nm/f* chemist, pharmacist.

botija [bo'tixa] *nf* (*earthenware*) jug; **botijo** *nm* (*earthenware*) jug; (*tren*) excursion train.

botín [bo'tin] *nm* (*calzado*) half boot; (*polaina*) spat; (*MIL*) booty.

botiquín [boti'kin] *nm* (*armario*) medicine cabinet; (*portátil*) first-aid kit.

botón [bo'ton] *nm* button; (*BOT*) bud; (*de florete*) tip; ~ **de oro** buttercup.

botones [bo'tones] *nm* buttons *sg*, bellboy.

bóveda [bo'ßeða] *nf* (*ARQ*) vault.

boxeador [boksea'ðor] *nm* boxer.

boxeo [bok'seo] *nm* boxing.

boya ['boja] *nf* (*NAUT*) buoy; (*flotador*) float.

bozal [bo'θal] *a* (*novato*) raw, green; (*tonto*) stupid; (*salvaje*) wild // *nm* (*de caballo*) halter; (*de perro*) muzzle.

bracear [braθe'ar] *vi* (*agitar los brazos*) to wave one's arms; (*nadar*) to swim (the crawl).

bracero [bra'θero] *nm* labourer; (*en el campo*) farmhand.

bracete [bra'θete]: **de** ~ *ad* arm in arm.
braga ['braxa] *nf* (*cuerda*) sling, rope; (*de bebé*) nappy; ~**s** *nfpl* (*de mujer*) panties.
bragueta [bra'xeta] *nf* fly, flies *pl*.
braille [breil] *nm* braille.
bramar [bra'mar] *vi* to bellow, roar; **bramido** *nm* bellow, roar.
brasa ['brasa] *nf* live coal.
brasero [bra'sero] *nm* brazier.
Brasil [bra'sil] *nm*: **el** ~ Brazil; **brasileño, a** *a, nm/f* Brazilian.
bravata [bra'βata] *nf* boast.
braveza [bra'βeθa] *nf* (*valor*) bravery; (*ferocidad*) ferocity.
bravío, a [bra'βio, a] *a* wild; (*feroz*) fierce.
bravo, a ['braβo, a] *a* (*valiente*) brave; (*bueno*) fine, splendid; (*feroz*) ferocious; (*salvaje*) wild // *excl* bravo!; **bravura** *nf* bravery; ferocity; (*pey*) boast.
braza ['braθa] *nf* fathom; **nadar a la** ~ to swim the breast-stroke.
brazada [bra'θaða] *nf* stroke.
brazado [bra'θaðo] *nm* armful.
brazalete [braθa'lete] *nm* (*pulsera*) bracelet; (*banda*) armband.
brazo ['braθo] *nm* arm; (*zool*) foreleg; (*bot*) limb, branch; **a** ~ **partido** hand-to-hand; **del** ~ arm in arm.
brea ['brea] *nf* pitch, tar.
brebaje [bre'βaxe] *nm* potion.
brecha ['bretʃa] *nf* breach, gap, opening.
brega ['breχa] *nf* (*lucha*) struggle; (*trabajo*) hard work.
breve ['breβe] *a* short, brief // *nf* breve; ~**dad** *nf* brevity, shortness.
brezal [bre'θal] *nm* moor(land), heath; **brezo** *nm* heather.
bribón, ona [bri'βon, ona] *a* idle, lazy // *nm/f* (*vagabundo*) vagabond; (*pícaro*) rascal, rogue.
bricolaje [briko'laxe] *nm* do-it-yourself, DIY.
brida ['briða] *nf* bridle, rein; (*tec*) clamp; **a toda** ~ at top speed.
bridge [britʃ] *nm* bridge.
brigada [bri'xaða] *nf* (*unidad*) brigade; (*trabajadores*) squad, gang // *nm* ≈ staffsergeant, sergeant-major.
brillante [bri'ʎante] *a* brilliant // *nm* diamond; **brillar** *vi* to shine.
brillo ['briʎo] *nm* shine; (*brillantez*) brilliance; (*fig*) splendour; **sacar** ~ **a** to polish.
brincar [brin'kar] *vi* to skip about, hop about, jump about; **está que brinca** he's hopping mad.
brinco ['brinko] *nm* hop, skip, jump.
brindar [brin'dar] *vi*: ~ **a** *o* **por** to drink (a toast) to // *vt* to offer, present.
brindis ['brindis] *nm* toast; (*taur*) (ceremony of) dedicating the bull.
brío ['brio] *nm* spirit, dash; **brioso, a** *a* spirited, dashing.
brisa ['brisa] *nf* breeze.
británico, a [bri'taniko, a] *a* British // *nm/f* Briton, British person.

brocal [bro'kal] *nm* rim.
brocha ['brotʃa] *nf* brush.
broche ['brotʃe] *nm* brooch; ~ **para papeles** (*am*) paper clip.
broma ['broma] *nf* (*bulla*) fun; (*chanza*) joke; **en** ~ in fun, as a joke; **bromear** *vi* to joke.
bromista [bro'mista] *a* fond of joking // *nm/f* joker, wag.
bronca ['bronka] *nf* row.
bronce ['bronθe] *nm* bronze; ~**ado, a** *a* bronze; (*por el sol*) tanned // *nm* (sun)tan; (*tec*) bronzing.
broncearse [bronθe'arse] *vr* to get a suntan.
bronco, a ['bronko, a] *a* (*superficie*) rough; (*manera*) rude, surly; (*voz*) harsh.
bronquitis [bron'kitis] *nf* bronchitis.
brotar [bro'tar] *vi* (*bot*) to sprout; (*aguas*) to gush (forth), flow; (*med*) to break out; **brote** *nm* (*bot*) shoot; (*med, fig*) outbreak.
bruces ['bruθes]: **de** ~ *ad*: **caer** *o* **dar de** ~ to fall headlong, fall flat; **estar de** ~ to lie face downwards.
bruja ['bruxa] *nf* witch; (*lechuza*) owl; **brujería** *nf* witchcraft.
brujo ['bruxo] *nm* wizard, magician.
brújula ['bruxula] *nf* compass.
bruma ['bruma] *nf* mist; **brumoso, a** *a* misty.
bruñido [bru'ɲiðo] *nm* polish; **bruñir** *vt* to polish.
brusco, a ['brusko, a] *a* (*súbito*) sudden; (*áspero*) brusque.
Bruselas [bru'selas] *n* Brussels.
brutal [bru'tal] *a* brutal; (*fig*) sudden; ~**idad** *nf* brutality.
bruto, a ['bruto, a] *a* (*idiota*) stupid; (*bestial*) brutish; (*peso*) gross; (*diamante etc*) raw, uncut; **en** ~ raw, unworked.
Bs.As. *abr de* **Buenos Aires.**
buba ['buβa] *nf* tumour.
bucal [bu'kal] *a*: **por vía** ~ by *or* through the mouth, orally.
bucear [buθe'ar] *vi* to dive // *vt* to explore; **buceo** *nm* diving; (*fig*) investigation.
bucle ['bukle] *nm* curl.
budismo [bu'ðismo] *nm* Buddhism.
buenamente [bwena'mente] *ad* (*fácilmente*) easily; (*voluntariamente*) willingly.
buenaventura [bwenaβen'tura] *nf* (*suerte*) good luck; (*adivinación*) fortune.
bueno, a ['bweno, a], **buen** [bwen] *a* (*amable*) kind; (*med*) well; (*guapo*) attractive; ~**as!** hello!; **buen día,** ~**as días** good morning!; good afternoon!; hello!; ~**as tardes** good afternoon!; good evening!; ~**as noches** good night!; **¡buen sinvergüenza resultó!** a fine rascal he turned out to be // *excl* right!, all right!; ~**, ¿y qué?** well, so what?
buey [bwei] *nm* ox.
búfalo ['bufalo] *nm* buffalo.
bufanda [bu'fanda] *nf* scarf, muffler.
bufar [bu'far] *vi* to snort.

bufete [bu'fete] *nm* (*mesa*) desk; (*de abogado*) lawyer's office.

bufo, a ['bufo, a] *a* comic.

bufón, oña [bu'fon, ona] *a* funny // *nm* clown.

buhardilla [buar'ðiʎa] *nf* (*ventana*) skylight; (*desván*) attic.

búho ['buo] *nm* owl; (*fig*) hermit, recluse.

buhonero [buo'nero] *nm* pedlar.

buitre ['bwitre] *nm* vulture.

bujía [bu'xia] *nf* (*vela*) candle; (*ELEC*) candle (power); (*AUTO*) spark plug.

bula ['bula] *nf* (*papal*) bull.

bulbo ['bulβo] *nm* bulb.

búlgaro, a ['bulxaro, a] *a, nm/f* Bulgarian.

bulto ['bulto] *nm* (*paquete*) package; (*fardo*) bundle; (*tamaño*) size, bulkiness; (*MED*) swelling, lump; (*silueta*) vague shape; (*estatua*) bust, statue; **de mucho/poco** ~ important/unimportant.

bulla ['buʎa] *nf* (*ruido*) uproar; (*de gente*) crowd.

bullicio [bu'ʎiθjo] *nm* (*ruido*) uproar; (*movimiento*) bustle.

bullir [bu'ʎir] *vi* (*hervir*) to boil; (*burbujear*) to bubble; (*mover*) to move, stir.

buñuelo [bu'ɲwelo] *nm* fritter.

buque ['buke] *nm* ship, vessel.

burbuja [bur'βuxa] *nf* bubble; **burbujear** *vi* to bubble.

burdel [bur'ðel] *nm* brothel.

burdo, a ['burðo, a] *a* coarse, rough.

burgués, esa [bur'xes, esa] *a* middle-class, bourgeois; **burguesía** *nf* middle class, bourgeoisie.

burla ['burla] *nf* (*mofa*) gibe; (*broma*) joke; (*engaño*) trick.

burladero [burla'ðero] *nm* (bullfighter's) refuge.

burlador, a [burla'ðor, a] *a* mocking // *nm* (*bromista*) joker; (*libertino*) seducer.

burlar [bur'lar] *vt* (*engañar*) to deceive; (*seducir*) to seduce // *vi*, ~**se** *vr* to joke; ~**se de** to make fun of.

burlesco, a [bur'lesko, a] *a* burlesque.

burlón, ona [bur'lon, ona] *a* mocking.

burocracia [buro'kraθja] *nf* civil service; (*pey*) bureaucracy.

burócrata [bu'rokrata] *nm/f* civil servant; (*pey*) bureaucrat.

burra ['burra] *nf* (she-)donkey; (*fig*) stupid woman.

burro ['burro] *nm* donkey; (*fig*) ass, idiot.

bursátil [bur'satil] *a* stock-exchange *cpd*.

busca ['buska] *nf* search, hunt; **en** ~ **de** in search of.

buscapleitos [buska'pleitos] *nm/f inv* troublemaker.

buscar [bus'kar] *vt* to look for, search for, seek // *vi* to look, search, seek; **se busca empleado** employee wanted.

buscón, ona [bus'kon, ona] *a* thieving // *nm* petty thief // *nf* whore.

busilis [bu'silis] *nm* (*fam*) snag.

busque *etc vb ver* **buscar.**

búsqueda ['buskeða] *nf* = **busca.**

busto ['busto] *nm* bust.

butaca [bu'taka] *nf* armchair; (*de cine, teatro*) stall, seat.

butano [bu'tano] *nm* butane.

buzo ['buθo] *nm* diver.

buzón [bu'θon] *nm* letter box; (*en la calle*) pillar box.

C

c. *abr de* **capítulo.**

C. *abr de* **centígrado; compañía.**

C/ *abr de* **calle.**

c.a. *abr de* **corriente alterna.**

cabal [ka'βal] *a* (*exacto*) exact; (*correcto*) right, proper; (*acabado*) finished, complete; ~**es** *nmpl*: **estar en sus** ~**es** to be in one's right mind.

cabalgadura [kaβalxa'ðura] *nf* mount, horse.

cabalgar [kaβal'xar] *vt, vi* to ride.

caballa [ka'βaʎa] *nf* mackerel.

caballeresco, a [kaβaʎe'resko, a] *a* noble, chivalrous.

caballería [kaβaʎe'ria] *nf* mount; (*MIL*) cavalry.

caballeriza [kaβaʎe'riθa] *nf* stable; **caballerizo** *nm* groom, stableman.

caballero [kaβa'ʎero] *nm* rider, horseman; (*hombre galante*) gentleman; (*de la orden de caballería*) knight; (*hidalgo*) noble(man); (*señor, término de cortesía*) sir.

caballerosidad [kaβaʎerosi'ðað] *nf* chivalry.

caballo [ka'βaʎo] *nm* horse; (*AJEDREZ*) knight; (*NAIPES*) queen; ~ **de vapor** *o* **de fuerza** horsepower.

cabaña [ka'βaɲa] *nf* (*casita*) hut, cabin; (*rebaño*) flock.

cabaré, cabaret (*pl* **cabarets**) [kaβa're] *nm* cabaret.

cabás [ka'βas] *nm* satchel.

cabecear [kaβeθe'ar] *vt* to head // *vi* to nod; (*negar*) to shake one's head.

cabecera [kaβe'θera] *nf* (*gen*) head; (*de distrito*) chief town; (*IMPRENTA*) headline.

cabecilla [kaβe'θiʎa] *nm/f* ringleader; (*fig: fam*) hothead.

cabellera [kaβe'ʎera] *nf* hair; (*de cometa*) tail.

cabello [ka'βeʎo] *nm* (*también* ~**s** *nmpl*) hair *sg*; **cabelludo, a** *a* hairy.

caber [ka'βer] *vi* (*entrar*) to fit, go; (*tener lugar*) to have enough room; **caben 3 más** there's room for 3 more.

cabestrillo [kaβes'triʎo] *nm* sling.

cabestro [ka'βestro] *nm* halter.

cabeza [ka'βeθa] *nf* head; (*POL*) chief, leader; ~**da** *nf* (*golpe*) butt; (*al dormirse*) nod.

cabezudo, a [kaβe'θuðo, a] *a* bigheaded; (*fig*) pigheaded.

cabida [ka'βiða] *nf* space.

cabildo [ka'βildo] *nm* (*de iglesia*) chapter; (*POL*) town council.

cabina [ka'ßina] *nf* booth; (*de camión*) cabin.

cabizbajo, a [kaßiθ'ßaxo, a] *a* crestfallen, dejected.

cable ['kaßle] *nm* cable; **~grama** *nm* cablegram.

cabo ['kaßo] *nm* (*de objeto*) end, extremity; (*de tiempo, proceso*) end; (*persona*) head, chief; (*MIL*) corporal; (*NAUT*) rope, cable; (*GEO*) cape; **al ~ de 3 días** after 3 days; **al fin y al ~** in the end.

cabra ['kaßra] *nf* (she-)goat, nanny goat.

cabré *etc vb ver* **caber.**

cabria ['kaßrja] *nf* hoist, derrick.

cabrío, a [ka'ßrio, a] *a* goatish; **macho ~** (he-)goat, billy goat.

cabriola [ka'ßrjola] *nf* caper.

cabritilla [kaßri'tiʎa] *nf* kid, kidskin.

cabrito [ka'ßrito] *nm* kid, goat.

cabrón [ka'ßron] *nm* cuckold; (*fig: fam*) bastard (*fam!*).

cacahuete [kaka'wete] *nm* peanut, monkey nut.

cacao [ka'kao] *nm* cocoa; (*BOT*) cacao.

cacarear [kakare'ar] *vi* (*persona*) to boast; (*gallo*) to cackle.

cacería [kaθe'ria] *nf* hunting, shooting.

cacerola [kaθe'rola] *nf* pan, saucepan.

cacique [ka'θike] *nm* chief, local ruler; (*POL*) local boss; **caciquismo** *nm* (system of) dominance by the local boss.

caco ['kako] *nm* pickpocket.

cacto ['kakto], **cactus** ['kaktus] *nm* cactus.

cacumen [ka'kumen] *nm* (*fig: fam*) acumen.

cachar [ka'tʃar] *vt* to smash, break.

cacharro [ka'tʃarro] *nm* earthenware pot.

cachear [katʃe'ar] *vt* to search, frisk.

cachemira [katʃe'mira] *nf* cashmere.

cacheo [ka'tʃeo] *nm* searching, frisking.

cachimba [ka'tʃimba] *nf*, **cachimbo** [ka'tʃimbo] *nm* pipe.

cachiporra [katʃi'porra] *nf* truncheon.

cachivache [katʃi'ßatʃe] *nm* pot; (*utensilio*) utensil; (*persona*) good-for-nothing.

cacho, a ['katʃo, a] *a* bent, crooked // *nm* (small) bit.

cachondeo [katʃon'deo] *nm* (*fam*) farce, joke.

cachondo, a [ka'tʃondo, a] *a* (*ZOOL*) on heat; (*vulg*) randy, sexy; (*gracioso*) funny.

cachorro, a [ka'tʃorro, a] *nm/f* (*perro*) pup, puppy; (*león*) cub.

cada ['kaða] *a inv* each; (*antes de número*) every; **~ día** each day, every day; **~ uno/a** each one, every one; **~ vez más** more and more; **uno de ~ diez** one out of every ten.

cadalso [ka'ðalso] *nm* scaffold.

cadáver [ka'ðaßer] *nm* (dead) body, corpse.

cadena [ka'ðena] *nf* chain; (*TV*) channel; **trabajo en ~** assembly line work.

cadencia [ka'ðenθja] *nf* cadence, rhythm.

cadera [ka'ðera] *nf* hip.

cadete [ka'ðete] *nm* cadet.

caducar [kaðu'kar] *vi* (*permiso, ley*) to lapse, expire; (*persona*) to become senile; **caduco, a** *a* expired; (*persona*) very old.

C.A.E. *abr de* **cóbrese al entregar** COD (cash on delivery).

caer [ka'er] *vi*, **~se** *vr* to fall (down); **~ bien/mal** to make a good/bad impression; **el pago cae mañana** the payment is due tomorrow; **~ en la cuenta** to catch on.

café [ka'fe] (*pl* **~s**) *nm* (*bebida, planta*) coffee; (*lugar*) café // *a* (*color*) brown; **cafetal** *nm* coffee plantation.

cafetero, a [kafe'tero, a] *a* coffee *cpd* // *nf* coffee pot.

cáfila ['kafila] *nf* (*de personas*) group; (*de ovejas*) flock.

caída [ka'iða] *nf* (*gen*) fall; (*declive*) slope; (*disminución*) fall, drop.

caigo *etc vb ver* **caer.**

caimán [kai'man] *nm* alligator.

caimiento [kai'mjento] *nm* fall, falling.

caja ['kaxa] *nf* box; (*para reloj*) case; (*de ascensor*) shaft; (*COM*) cashbox; (*donde se hacen los pagos*) cashdesk; **~ de ahorros** savings bank; **~ de cambios** gearbox; **~ fuerte, ~ de caudales** safe, strongbox.

cajero, a [ka'xero, a] *nm/f* cashier.

cajetilla [kaxe'tiʎa] *nf* small box; (*de cigarrillos*) packet.

cajón [ka'xon] *nm* big box; (*de mueble*) drawer.

cal [kal] *nf* lime.

cala ['kala] *nf* (*GEO*) cove, inlet; (*de barco*) hold; (*MED*) suppository.

calabaza [kala'ßaθa] *nf* (*BOT*) pumpkin.

calabozo [kala'ßoθo] *nm* prison (cell).

calamar [kala'mar] *nm* squid.

calambre [ka'lambre] *nm* cramp.

calamidad [kalami'ðað] *nf* calamity, disaster.

calamina [kala'mina] *nf* calamine.

calaña [ka'laɲa] *nf* model, pattern.

calar [ka'lar] *vt* to soak, drench; (*penetrar*) to pierce, penetrate; (*comprender*) to see through; (*vela, red*) to lower; **~se las gafas** to stick one's glasses on.

calavera [kala'ßera] *nf* skull.

calcañar [kalka'ɲar], **calcañal** [kalka'ɲal], **calcaño** [kal'kaɲo] *nm* heel.

calcar [kal'kar] *vt* (*reproducir*) to trace; (*imitar*) to copy.

calceta [kal'θeta] *nf* (knee-length) stocking; **hacer ~** to knit; **calcetín** *nm* sock.

calcina [kal'θina] *nf* concrete.

calcinar [kalθi'nar] *vt* to burn, blacken.

calcio ['kalθjo] *nm* calcium.

calco ['kalko] *nm* tracing.

calcomanía [kalkoma'nia] *nm* transfer.

calculadora [kalkula'ðora] *nf* calculator; **~ de bolsillo** pocket calculator.

calcular [kalku'lar] *vt* to calculate, compute; (*suponer, creer*) to reckon, expect; **cálculo** *nm* calculation; reckoning.

caldear [kalde'ar] *vt* to warm (up), heat (up); (*los metales*) to weld.

caldera [kal'dera] *nf* boiler.

calderilla [kalde'riʎa] *nf* (*REL*) vessel for holy water; (*moneda*) small change.

caldero [kal'dero] *nm* small boiler.

calderón [kalde'ron] *nm* cauldron.

caldo ['kaldo] *nm* stock; (*consomé*) consommé; (*para la ensalada*) dressing.

calefacción [kalefak'θjon] *nf* heating.

calendario [kalen'darjo] *nm* calendar.

calentador [kalenta'ðor] *nm* heater.

calentar [kalen'tar] *vt* to heat (up); ~**se** *vr* to heat up, warm up; (*fig*) to get heated.

calentura [kalen'tura] *nf* (*MED*) fever, (high) temperature; **calenturiento, a** *a* feverish.

calero, a [ka'lero, a] *a* lime *cpd*.

calibrar [kali'ßrar] *vt* to gauge, measure; **calibre** *nm* (*de cañón*) calibre, bore; (*diámetro*) diameter; (*fig*) calibre.

calidad [kali'ðað] *nf* quality; **en** ~ **de** in the capacity of.

cálido, a ['kaliðo, a] *a* hot; (*fig*) warm.

caliente [ka'ljente] *a* hot; (*sin exceso*) warm; (*fig*) fiery; (*disputa*) heated.

calificación [kalifika'θjon] *nf* qualification; (*de alumno*) grade, mark.

calificado, a [kalifi'kaðo, a] *a* qualified, competent; (*trabajador*) skilled.

calificar [kalifi'kar] *vt* to qualify; (*enaltecer*) to distinguish; (*alumno*) to grade, mark; (*determinar*) to describe.

calma ['kalma] *nf* calm; (*pachorra*) slowness.

calmante [kal'mante] *nm* sedative, tranquillizer.

calmar [kal'mar] *vt* to calm, calm down // *vi* (*tempestad*) to abate; (*mente etc*) to become calm.

calmoso, a [kal'moso, a], **calmudo, a** [kal'muðo, a] *a* calm, quiet.

calofrío [kalo'frio] *nm* = **escalofrío.**

calor [ka'lor] *nm* heat; (~ *agradable*) warmth.

caloría [kalo'ria] *nf* calorie.

calorífero, a [kalo'rifero, a] *a* heat-producing, heat-giving // *nm* heating system.

calumnia [ka'lumnja] *nf* calumny, slander; **calumnioso, a** *a* slanderous.

caluroso, a [kalu'roso, a] *a* hot; (*sin exceso*) warm; (*fig*) enthusiastic.

calva ['kalßa] *nf* bald patch; (*en bosque*) clearing.

calvario [kal'ßarjo] *nm* stations *pl* of the cross.

calvicie [kal'ßiθje] *nf* baldness.

calvo, a ['kalßo, a] *a* bald; (*terreno*) bare, barren; (*tejido*) threadbare.

calza ['kalθa] *nf* wedge, chock.

calzado, a [kal'θaðo, a] *a* shod // *nm* footwear // *nf* roadway, highway.

calzador [kalθa'ðor] *nm* shoehorn.

calzar [kal'θar] *vt* to put on; (*un mueble*) to put a wedge under; ~**se** *vr*: ~**se los zapatos** to put on one's shoes; ¿**qué (número) calza?** what size do you wear or take?

calzón [kal'θon] *nm* (*también* **calzones** *nmpl*) shorts *pl.*

calzoncillos [kalθon'θiʎos] *nmpl* underpants.

callado, a [ka'ʎaðo, a] *a* quiet.

callar [ka'ʎar] *vt* to keep quiet about, say nothing about // *vi*, ~**se** *vr* to keep quiet, be silent.

calle ['kaʎe] *nf* street; (*DEPORTE*) lane; ~ **arriba/abajo** up/down the street; ~ **de un solo sentido** one-way street.

calleja [ka'ʎexa] *nf* alley, narrow street; **callejear** *vi* to wander about the streets; **callejero, a** *a* street *cpd.*

callejón [kaʎe'xon] *nm* alley, passage; ~ **sin salida** one-way street.

callejuela [kaʎe'xwela] *nf* side-street, alley.

callista [ka'ʎista] *nm/f* chiropodist.

callo ['kaʎo] *nm* callus; (*en el pie*) corn; ~**s** *nmpl* tripe *sg*; ~**so, a** *a* horny, rough.

cama ['kama] *nf* bed; (*GEO*) stratum; ~ **de matrimonio** double bed.

camada [ka'maða] *nf* litter; (*de personas*) gang, band.

camafeo [kama'feo] *nm* cameo.

camandulear [kamandule'ar] *vi* to be a hypocrite.

cámara ['kamara] *nf* (*gen*) chamber; (*habitación*) room; (*sala*) hall; (*CINE*) cine camera; (*fotográfica*) camera; ~ **de aire** inner tube.

camarada [kama'raða] *nm* comrade, companion.

camarera [kama'rera] *nf* (*en restaurante*) waitress; (*en casa, hotel*) maid.

camarero [kama'rero] *nm* waiter.

camarilla [kama'riʎa] *nf* (*clan*) clique; (*POL*) lobby.

camarín [kama'rin] *nm* dressing room.

camarón [kama'ron] *nm* shrimp.

camarote [kama'rote] *nm* cabin.

cambiable [kam'bjaßle] *a* (*variable*) changeable, variable; (*intercambiable*) interchangeable.

cambiante [kam'bjante] *a* variable // *nm* moneychanger.

cambiar [kam'bjar] *vt* (*gen*) to change; (*de moneda*) to change; (*dinero*) to exchange // *vi* (*gen*) to change; ~**se** *vr* (*mudarse*) to move; (*de ropa*) to change; ~**(se) de...** to change one's ... .

cambio ['kambjo] *nm* change; (*trueque*) exchange; (*COM*) rate of exchange; (*oficina*) (foreign) exchange office; (*dinero menudo*) small change; **en** ~ **on the other hand; (*en lugar de eso*) instead; ~ **de velocidades** gear lever; ~ **de vía** points *pl.*

cambista [kam'bista] *nm* (*COM*) exchange broker; (*FERRO*) switchman.

camelar [kame'lar] *vt* (*galantear*) to flirt with; (*engañar*) to cajole.

camello [ka'meʎo] *nm* camel.

camilla [ka'miʎa] *nf* (*cama*) cot; (*MED*) stretcher.

caminante [kami'nante] *nm/f* traveller.

caminar [kami'nar] *vi* (*marchar*) to walk, go; (*viajar*) to travel, journey // *vt* (*recorrer*) to cover, travel.

caminata [kami'nata] *nf* long walk.

camino [ka'mino] *nm* (*gen*) way, road; (*senda*) track; **a medio** ~ halfway (there); **en el** ~ on the way, en route.

camión [ka'mjon] *nm* lorry, truck.

camisa [ka'misa] *nf* shirt; (*BOT*) skin; ~ **de dormir** nightdress; ~ **de fuerza** straitjacket; **camisería** *nf* outfitter's (shop).

camiseta [kami'seta] *nf* (*prenda*) vest; (*de deportista*) singlet.

camisón [kami'son] *nm* nightdress, nightgown.

campamento [kampa'mento] *nm* camp.

campana [kam'pana] *nf* bell; ~**da** *nf* peal; ~**rio** *nm* belfry.

campanilla [kampa'niʎa] *nf* (*campana*) small bell; (*burbuja*) bubble.

campaña [kam'paɲa] *nf* (*MIL*, *POL*) campaign; (*campo*) countryside.

campar [kam'par] *vi* to camp; (*sobresalir*) to excel, stand out.

campeón, ona [kampe'on, ona] *nm/f* champion; **campeonato** *nm* championship.

campesino, a [kampe'sino, a] *a* country *cpd*, rural // *nm/f* countryman/woman; (*agricultor*) farmer.

campestre [kam'pestre] *a* country *cpd*, rural.

camping ['kampin] *nm* camping; (*lugar*) campsite; **hacer** ~ to go camping.

campiña [kam'piɲa] *nf* countryside.

campo ['kampo] *nm* (*fuera de la ciudad*) country, countryside; (*AGR, ELEC*) field; (*de fútbol*) ground, pitch; (*de golf*) course; (*de tenis*) court; (*MIL*) camp.

camposanto [kampo'santo] *nm* cemetery.

camuflaje [kamu'flaxe] *nm* camouflage.

Canadá [kana'ða] *nm* Canada; **canadiense** *a, nm/f* Canadian // *nf* fur-lined jacket.

canal [ka'nal] *nm* canal; (*GEO*) channel, strait; (*de televisión*) channel; (*de tejado*) gutter; ~**izar** *vt* to channel.

canalón [kana'lon] *nm* (*conducto vertical*) drainpipe; (*del tejado*) gutter.

canalla [ka'naʎa] *nf* rabble, mob // *nm* swine, rotter.

canapé [kana'pe] (*pl* ~**s**) *nm* sofa, settee; (*CULIN*) canapé.

canario, a [ka'narjo, a] *a, nm/f* (native) of the Canary Isles // *nm* canary.

canasta [ka'nasta] *nf* (round) basket; **canasto** *nm* large basket.

cancelación [kanθela'θjon] *nf* cancellation.

cancelar [kanθe'lar] *vt* to cancel; (*una deuda*) to write off.

cáncer ['kanθer] *nm* (*MED*) cancer; **C**~ (*ASTRO*) Cancer.

canciller [kanθi'ʎer] *nm* chancellor.

canción [kan'θjon] *nf* song; ~ **de cuna** lullaby; **cancionero** *nm* song book.

candado [kan'daðo] *nm* padlock.

candela [kan'dela] *nf* candle.

candelero [kande'lero] *nm* (*para vela*) candlestick; (*de aceite*) oil lamp.

candente [kan'dente] *a* red-hot; (*fig*) burning.

candidato [kandi'ðato] *nm/f* candidate.

candidez [kandi'ðeθ] *nf* (*sencillez*) simplicity; (*simpleza*) naiveté; **cándido, a** *a* simple; naive.

candil [kan'dil] *nm* oil lamp; ~**eja** *nf* small oil lamp.

candor [kan'dor] *nm* (*sinceridad*) frankness; (*inocencia*) innocence.

canela [ka'nela] *nf* cinnamon.

canelón [kane'lon] *nm* (*canal*) drainpipe; (*carámbano*) icicle.

cangrejo [kan'grexo] *nm* crab.

canguro [kan'guro] *nm* kangaroo.

caníbal [ka'niβal] *a, nm/f* cannibal.

canica [ka'nika] *nf* marble.

canijo, a [ka'nixo, a] *a* frail, sickly.

canino, a [ka'nino, a] *a* canine // *nm* canine (tooth).

canjear [kanxe'ar] *vt* to exchange.

cano, a ['kano, a] *a* grey-haired, white-haired.

canoa [ka'noa] *nf* canoe.

canon ['kanon] *nm* canon; (*pensión*) rent; (*COM*) tax.

canónigo [ka'nonixo] *nm* canon.

canonizar [kanoni'θar] *vt* to canonize.

canoro, a [ka'noro, a] *a* melodious.

cansado, a [kan'saðo, a] *a* tired, weary; (*tedioso*) tedious, boring.

cansancio [kan'sanθjo] *nm* tiredness, fatigue.

cansar [kan'sar] *vt* (*fatigar*) to tire, tire out, weary; (*aburrir*) to bore; (*fastidiar*) to bother; ~**se** *vr* to tire, get tired; (*aburrirse*) to get bored.

cantante [kan'tante] *a* singing // *nm/f* singer.

cantar [kan'tar] *vt* to sing // *vi* (*gen*) to sing; (*insecto*) to chirp; (*rechinar*) to squeak // *nm* (*acción*) singing; (*canción*) song; (*poema*) poem.

cántara ['kantara] *nf* large pitcher.

cántaro ['kantaro] *nm* pitcher, jug.

cantatriz [kanta'triθ] *nf* singer.

cante ['kante] *nm*: ~ **jondo** flamenco singing.

cantera [kan'tera] *nf* quarry.

cantidad [kanti'ðað] *nf* quantity, amount.

cantilena [kanti'lena] *nf* = **cantinela**.

cantimplora [kantim'plora] *nf* (*frasco*) water bottle, canteen; (*sifón*) syphon.

cantina [kan'tina] *nf* canteen; (*de estación*) buffet; (*sótano*) wine cellar.

cantinela [kanti'nela] *nf* ballad, song.
canto ['kanto] *nm* (*gen*) singing; (*canción*) song; (*borde*) edge, rim; (*de un cuchillo*) back; ~ **rodado** boulder.
cantor, a [kan'tor, a] *nm/f* singer.
canturrear [kanture'ar], **canturriar** [kantu'rrjar] *vi* to sing softly.
caña ['kaɲa] *nf* (*BOT: tallo*) stem, stalk; (*carrizo*) reed; (*de cerveza*) glass; (*ANAT: del brazo*) long bone; (: *de la pierna*) shinbone; (*MINERÍA*) gallery; ~ **de azúcar** sugar cane.
cañada [ka'ɲaða] *nf* (*entre dos montañas*) gully, ravine; (*camino*) cattle track.
caño ['kaɲo] *nm* (*tubo*) tube, pipe; (*de aguas servidas*) sewer; (*MUS*) pipe; (*NAUT*) navigation channel; (*de fuente*) jet.
cañón [ka'ɲon] *nm* tube, pipe; (*MIL*) cannon; (*de fusil*) barrel; (*GEO*) canyon, gorge.
cañonero [kaɲo'nero] *nm* gunboat.
caoba [ka'oβa] *nf* mahogany.
caos ['kaos] *nm* chaos.
cap. *abr de* **capítulo.**
capa ['kapa] *nf* cloak, cape; (*GEO*) layer, stratum; (*pretexto*) pretence.
capacidad [kapaθi'ðað] *nf* (*medida*) capacity; (*aptitud*) capacity, ability.
capacitación [kapaθita'θjon] *nf* training.
capar [ka'par] *vt* to castrate, geld.
caparazón [kapara'θon] *nm* shell.
capataz [kapa'taθ] *nm* foreman.
capaz [ka'paθ] *a* able, capable; (*amplio*) capacious, roomy.
capcioso, a [kap'θjoso, a] *a* wily, deceitful.
capellán [kape'ʎan] *nm* chaplain; (*sacerdote*) priest.
caperuza [kape'ruθa] *nf* hood; **caperucita** *nf*: **Caperucita Roja** Little Red Riding Hood.
capilla [ka'piʎa] *nf* chapel; (*capucha*) hood, cowl.
capital [kapi'tal] *a* capital // *nm* (*COM*) capital // *nf* capital; ~ **social** share capital.
capitalismo [kapita'lismo] *nm* capitalism; **capitalista** *a, nm/f* capitalist.
capitalizar [kapitali'θar] *vt* to capitalize.
capitán [kapi'tan] *nm* captain.
capitana [kapi'tana] *nf* flagship.
capitanear [kapitane'ar] *vt* to captain.
capitolio [kapi'toljo] *nm* capitol.
capitoné [kapito'ne] *nm* removal van.
capitulación [kapitula'θjon] *nf* (*rendición*) capitulation, surrender; (*acuerdo*) agreement, pact.
capitular [kapitu'lar] *vi* to come to terms, make an agreement // *a* chapter *cpd*.
capítulo [ka'pitulo] *nm* chapter; ~**s** *nmpl*: ~**s matrimoniales** marriage contract *sg*.
capó [ka'po] *nm* bonnet.
caporal [kapo'ral] *nm* chief, leader.
capota [ka'pota] *nf* (*de mujer*) bonnet; (*de coche*) hood, roof.
capote [ka'pote] *nm* (*abrigo, de militar*)

greatcoat; (*de torero*) cloak; (*NAIPES*) slam.
Capricornio [kapri'kornjo] *nm* Capricorn.
capricho [ka'pritʃo] *nm* whim, caprice; ~**so, a** *a* capricious.
cápsula ['kapsula] *nf* capsule; (*de botella*) cap.
captar [kap'tar] *vt* to win (over).
captura [kap'tura] *nf* capture; (*JUR*) arrest; **capturar** *vt* to capture; to arrest.
capucha [ka'putʃa] *nf* hood, cowl.
cara ['kara] *nf* (*ANAT*) face; (*aspecto*) appearance; (*de moneda*) face; (*de disco*) side; (*fig*) boldness; ~ **a** *ad* facing; **de** ~ **opposite**, facing; **dar la** ~ to face the consequences; ¿~ **o cruz?** heads or tails?
carabina [kara'βina] *nf* carbine, rifle.
caracol [kara'kol] *nm* (*ZOOL*) snail; (*concha*) shell.
caracolear [karakole'ar] *vi* to prance about.
carácter [ka'rakter] (*pl* **caracteres**) *nm* character.
característico, a [karakte'ristiko, a] *a* characteristic // *nf* characteristic.
caracterizar [karakteri'θar] *vt* (*distinguir*) to characterize, typify; (*honrar*) to confer (a) distinction on.
caramba [ka'ramba] *excl* well!, good gracious!
carámbano [ka'rambano] *nm* icicle.
caramelo [kara'melo] *nm* (*dulce*) sweet; (*dulce de* ~) toffee; (*azúcar fundida*) caramel.
caramillo [kara'miʎo] *nm* (*flauta*) recorder; (*montón*) untidy heap; (*chisme, enredo*) bit of gossip.
carapacho [kara'patʃo] *nm* shell, carapace.
caraqueño, a [kara'keɲo, a] *a, nm/f* (*native*) of Caracas.
carátula [ka'ratula] *nf* (*careta, máscara*) mask; (*TEATRO*): **la** ~ the stage.
caravana [kara'βana] *nf* caravan; (*fig*) group; (*sucesión de autos*) stream; (*embotellamiento*) traffic jam.
carbón [kar'βon] *nm* coal; **papel** ~ carbon paper; **carbonero** *nm/f* coal merchant; **carbonilla** *nf* coal dust.
carbonizar [karβoni'θar] *vt* to carbonize; (*quemar*) to char.
carbono [kar'βono] *nm* carbon.
carburador [karβura'ðor] *nm* carburettor.
carcajada [karka'xaða] *nf* (*loud*) laugh, guffaw.
cárcel ['karθel] *nf* prison, jail; (*TEC*) clamp; **carcelero, a** *a* prison *cpd* // *nm/f* warder.
carcomer [karko'mer] *vt* to bore into, eat into; (*fig*) to undermine; ~**se** *vr* to become worm-eaten; (*fig*) to decay.
carcomido, a [karko'miðo, a] *a* worm-eaten; (*fig*) rotten.
cardenal [karðe'nal] *nm* (*REL*) cardinal; (*equimosis*) bruise.
cárdeno, a ['karðeno, a] *a* purple; (*lívido*) livid.

cardíaco, a [kar'ðiako, a] *a* cardiac, heart *cpd.*

cardinal [karði'nal] *a* cardinal.

cardo ['karðo] *nm* thistle.

cardumen [kar'ðumen] *nm* shoal.

carear [kare'ar] *vt* to bring face to face; (*comparar*) to compare; ~**se** *vr* to come face to face, meet.

carecer [kare'θer] *vi:* ~ **de** to lack, be in need of.

carencia [ka'renθja] *nf* lack; (*escasez*) shortage; (*MED*) deficiency.

carente [ka'rente] *a:* ~ **de** lacking, devoid of.

carestía [kares'tia] *nf* (*escasez*) scarcity, shortage; (*COM*) high cost.

careta [ka'reta] *nf* mask.

carga ['karɣa] *nf* (*peso, ELEC*) load; (*de barco*) cargo, freight; (*MIL*) charge; (*obligación, responsabilidad*) duty, obligation.

cargadero [karɣa'ðero] *nm* goods platform, loading bay.

cargado, a [kar'ɣaðo, a] *a* loaded; (*ELEC*) live; (*café, te*) strong; (*el cielo*) overcast.

cargamento [karɣa'mento] *nm* (*acción*) loading; (*mercancías*) load, cargo.

cargar [kar'ɣar] *vt* (*barco, arma*) to load; (*ELEC*) to charge; (*COM: algo en cuenta*) to charge, debit; (*MIL: enemigo*) to charge // *vi* to load (up); (*inclinarse*) to lean; ~ **con** to pick up, carry away.

cargo ['karɣo] *nm* (*puesto*) post, office; (*responsabilidad*) duty, obligation; (*fig*) weight, burden; (*JUR*) charge; **hacerse** ~ **del gobierno** to take charge of the government.

carguero [kar'ɣero] *nm* freighter, cargo boat; (*avión*) freight plane.

caribe [ka'riße] *a, nm/f* (native) of the Caribbean.

Caribe [ka'riße] *nm:* **el** ~ the Caribbean.

caricatura [karika'tura] *nf* caricature.

caricia [ka'riθja] *nf* caress.

caridad [kari'ðað] *nf* charity.

cariño [ka'riɲo] *nm* affection, love; (*caricia*) caress; (*en carta*) love...; ~**so, a** *a* affectionate.

caritativo, a [karita'tißo, a] *a* charitable.

carmesí [karme'si] *a, nm* crimson.

carnal [kar'nal] *a* carnal; **primo** ~ first cousin.

carnaval [karna'ßal] *nm* carnival.

carne ['karne] *nf* flesh; (*CULIN*) meat; **echar** ~**s** to put on weight.

carnero [kar'nero] *nm* sheep, ram; (*carne*) mutton.

carnet [kar'ne] *nm:* ~ **de conducir** driving licence.

carnicería [karniθe'ria] *nf* butcher's (shop); (*mercado*) meat market.

carnicero, a [karni'θero, a] *a* carnivorous // *nm/f* butcher // *nm* carnivore.

carnívoro, a [kar'nißoro, a] *a* carnivorous.

carnoso, a [kar'noso, a] *a* beefy, fat.

caro, a ['karo, a] *a* dear; (*COM*) dear, expensive // *ad* dear, dearly.

carpeta [kar'peta] *nf* table cover; (*para documentos*) folder, file.

carpintería [karpinte'ria] *nf* carpentry, joinery; **carpintero** *nm* carpenter.

carraspera [karras'pera] *nf* hoarseness.

carrera [ka'rrera] *nf* (*DEPORTE*) running; (*espacio recorrido*) run; (*certamen*) race; (*trayecto*) course; (*profesión*) career; (*ESCOL*) course.

carreta [ka'rreta] *nf* wagon, cart.

carrete [ka'rrete] *nm* reel, spool; (*TEC*) coil.

carretel [karre'tel] *nm* reel, spool.

carretera [karre'tera] *nf* (main) road, highway.

carretilla [karre'tiʎa] *nf* trolley; (*AGR*) (wheel)barrow.

carril [ka'rril] *nm* furrow; (*de autopista*) lane; (*FERRO*) rail.

carrillo [ka'rriʎo] *nm* (*ANAT*) cheek; (*TEC*) pulley.

carrizo [ka'rriθo] *nm* reed.

carro ['karro] *nm* cart, wagon; (*MIL*) tank; (*AM: coche*) car.

carrocería [karroθe'ria] *nf* bodywork, coachwork.

carta ['karta] *nf* letter; (*CULIN*) menu; (*naipe*) card; (*mapa*) map; (*JUR*) document; ~ **de crédito** credit card; ~ **certificada** registered letter.

cartel [kar'tel] *nm* (*anuncio*) poster, placard; (*alfabeto*) wall chart; (*COM*) cartel.

cartera [kar'tera] *nf* (*de bolsillo*) wallet; (*de colegial, cobrador*) satchel; (*de señora*) handbag; (*para documentos*) briefcase; (*COM, POL*) portfolio.

cartero [kar'tero] *nm* postman.

cartón [kar'ton] *nm* cardboard; (*ARTE*) cartoon.

cartucho [kar'tutʃo] *nm* (*MIL*) cartridge.

casa ['kasa] *nf* house; (*hogar*) home; (*edificio*) building; (*COM*) firm, company; (*de tablero de ajedrez*) square; ~ **consistorial** town hall; ~ **de huéspedes** boarding house; ~ **de socorro** first aid post; ~ **editorial** publishing house.

casamiento [kasa'mjento] *nm* marriage, wedding.

casar [ka'sar] *vt* to marry; (*JUR*) to quash, annul // *nm* hamlet; ~**se** *vr* to marry, get married.

cascada [kas'kaða] *nf* waterfall.

cascar [kas'kar] *vt,* ~**se** *vr* to crack, split, break (open).

cáscara ['kaskara] *nf* (*de huevo, fruta seca*) shell; (*de fruta*) skin; (*de limón*) peel.

casco ['kasko] *nm* (*de bombero, soldado*) helmet; (*cráneo*) skull; (*de botella, obús*) fragment; (*BOT: de cebolla*) skin; (*tonel*) cask, barrel; (*NAUT: de barco*) hull; (*ZOOL: de caballo*) hoof; (*botella*) empty bottle.

caserío [kase'rio] *nm* hamlet; (*casa*) country house.

casero, a [ka'sero, a] *a* domestic, household *cpd* // *nm/f* (*propietario*) landlord/lady; (*portero*) caretaker; (*COM*) house agent.

caseta [ka'seta] *nf* hut; (*para bañista*) cubicle; (*de feriantes*) stall.

casi ['kasi] *ad* almost; ~ **te caes** you almost fell.

casilla [ka'siʎa] *nf* (*casita*) hut, cabin; (*TEATRO*) box office; (*de ajedrez*) square.

casino [ka'sino] *nm* club.

caso ['kaso] *nm* case; **en** ~ **de...** in case of...; **el** ~ **es que** the fact is that; **hacer** ~ **a** to pay attention to; **hacer** *o* **venir al** ~ to be relevant.

caspa ['kaspa] *nf* dandruff.

cassette [ka'set] *nf* cassette.

casta ['kasta] *nf* caste; (*raza*) breed; (*linaje*) lineage.

castaña [kas'taɲa] *nf* chestnut.

castaño, a [kas'taɲo, a] *a* chestnut-brown // *nm* chestnut tree.

castañuela [kasta'ɲwela] *nf* castanet.

castellano, a [kaste'ʎano, a] *a* Castilian // *nm* (*lengua*) Castilian, Spanish.

castidad [kasti'ðað] *nf* chastity, purity.

castigar [kasti'xar] *vt* to punish; (*DEPORTE*) to penalize; (*afligir*) to afflict; **castigo** *nm* punishment; (*DEPORTE*) penalty.

castillo [kas'tiʎo] *nm* castle.

castizo, a [kas'tiθo, a] *a* (*LING*) pure; (*de buena casta*) purebred, pedigree.

casto, a ['kasto, a] *a* chaste, pure.

castor [kas'tor] *nm* beaver.

castrar [kas'trar] *vt* to castrate.

casual [ka'swal] *a* fortuitous, accidental; ~**idad** *nf* chance, accident; (*combinación de circunstancias*) coincidence.

cataclismo [kata'klismo] *nm* cataclysm.

catalán, ana [kata'lan, ana] *a, nm/f* Catalan, Catalonian.

catalizador [kataliθa'ðor] *nm* catalyst.

catálogo [ka'taloxo] *nm* catalogue.

Cataluña [kata'luɲa] *nf* Catalonia.

cataplasma [kata'plasma] *nf* poultice.

catar [ka'tar] *vt* to taste, sample.

catarata [kata'rata] *nf* (*GEO*) waterfall, falls *pl*; (*MED*) cataract.

catarro [ka'tarro] *nm* catarrh; (*constipado*) cold.

catástrofe [ka'tastrofe] *nf* catastrophe.

catedral [kate'ðral] *nf* cathedral.

catedrático, a [kate'ðratiko, a] *nm/f* professor.

categoría [katexo'ria] *nf* category; (*rango*) rank, standing; (*calidad*) quality.

categórico, a [kate'xoriko, a] *a* categorical.

catolicismo [katoli'θismo] *nm* Catholicism.

católico, a [ka'toliko, a] *a, nm/f* Catholic.

catorce [ka'torθe] *num* fourteen.

caución [kau'θjon] *nf* bail; **caucionar** *vt* to prevent, guard against; (*JUR*) to bail, go bail for.

caucho [kau'tʃo] *nm* rubber.

caudal [kau'ðal] *nm* (*de río*) volume, flow;

(*fortuna*) wealth; (*abundancia*) abundance; ~**oso, a** *a* (*río*) large; (*aguas*) copious; (*persona*) wealthy, rich.

caudillo [kau'ðiʎo] *nm* leader, chief.

causa ['kausa] *nf* cause; (*razón*) reason; (*JUR*) lawsuit, case; **causar** *vt* to cause.

cáustico, a [ka'ustiko, a] *a* caustic.

cautela [kau'tela] *nf* caution, cautiousness; **cauteloso, a** *a* cautious, wary, careful.

cautivar [kauti'βar] *vt* to capture; (*fig*) to captivate.

cautiverio [kauti'βerjo] *nm*, **cautividad** [kautiβi'ðað] *nf* captivity.

cautivo, a [kau'tiβo, a] *a, nm/f* captive.

cauto, a ['kauto, a] *a* cautious, careful.

cavar [ka'βar] *vt* to dig.

caverna [ka'βerna] *nf* cave, cavern.

cavidad [kaβi'ðað] *nf* cavity.

cavilar [kaβi'lar] *vt* to ponder.

cayado [ka'jaðo] *nm* (*de pastor*) staff, crook; (*de obispo*) crozier.

cayó *etc vb ver* **caer**.

caza ['kaθa] *nf* (*gen*) hunting, shooting; (*una* ~) hunt, chase; (*animales*) game // *nm* (*AVIAT*) fighter.

cazador [kaθa'ðor] *nm* hunter.

cazar [ka'θar] *vt* to hunt; (*perseguir*) to chase; (*coger*) to catch.

cazo ['kaθo] *nm* saucepan.

cazuela [ka'θwela] *nf* pan; (*guisado*) casserole.

cebada [θe'βaða] *nf* barley.

cebar [θe'βar] *vt* (*animal*) to fatten (up); (*anzuelo*) to bait; (*MIL, TEC*) to prime; (*pasión*) to nourish; (*ira*) to inflame.

cebo ['θeβo] *nm* (*para animales*) feed, food; (*para peces, fig*) bait; (*de arma*) charge.

cebolla [θe'βoʎa] *nf* onion.

cebra ['θeβra] *nf* zebra.

cecear [θeθe'ar] *vi* to lisp; **ceceo** *nm* lisp.

cedazo [θe'ðaθo] *nm* sieve.

ceder [θe'ðer] *vt* to hand over, give up, part with // *vi* (*renunciar*) to give in, yield; (*disminuir*) to diminish, decline; (*romperse*) to give way.

cedro ['θeðro] *nm* cedar.

cédula ['θeðula] *nf* certificate, document; ~ **de aduana** customs permit.

C.E.E. *nf abr de* **Comunidad Económica Europea** E.E.C. (European Economic Community).

cegar [θe'xar] *vt* to blind; (*fig: pozo*) to block up, fill up // *vi* to go blind; ~**se** *vr* to be blinded (*de* by).

ceguedad [θexe'ðað], **ceguera** [θe'xera] *nf* blindness.

ceja ['θexa] *nf* eyebrow.

cejar [θe'xar] *vi* to move back, go back; (*fig*) to back down.

cejijunto, a [θexi'xunto, a] *a* with bushy eyebrows; (*fig*) scowling.

celada [θe'laða] *nf* ambush, trap.

celador, a [θela'ðor, a] *nm/f* (*de edificio*) watchman; (*de museo etc*) attendant.

celar [θe'lar] *vt* (*vigilar*) to watch over; (*encubrir*) to conceal, hide.

celda ['θelda] nf cell.
celebración [θeleβra'θjon] nf celebration.
celebrar [θele'βrar] vt to celebrate; (alabar) to praise // vi to be glad; ~se vr to occur, take place.
célebre ['θelebre] a famous; (chistoso) witty, funny.
celebridad [θeleβri'ðað] nf (gen) fame; (persona) celebrity; (festividad) celebration(s) (pl).
celeste [θe'leste] a celestial, heavenly.
celestial [θeles'tjal] a celestial, heavenly.
celibato [θeli'βato] nm celibacy.
célibe ['θeliβe] a celibate // nm/f unmarried person.
celo ['θelo] nm zeal; (REL) fervour; (pey) envy; (de animales) rut, heat; ~s nmpl jealousy sg.
celofán [θelo'fan] nm cellophane.
celoso, a [θe'loso, a] a (envidioso) jealous; (trabajo) zealous; (desconfiado) suspicious.
celta ['θelta] nm/f Celt.
célula [θelula] nf cell.
cementar [θemen'tar] vt to cement.
cementerio [θemen'terjo] nm cemetery, graveyard.
cemento [θe'mento] nm cement; (hormigón) concrete.
cena ['θena] nf evening meal.
cenagal [θena'xal] nm bog, quagmire.
cenar [θe'nar] vt to have for supper // vi to dine.
cenicero [θeni'θero] nm ashtray.
cenit [θe'nit] nm zenith.
ceniza [θe'niθa] nf ash, ashes pl.
censo ['θenso] nm (empadronamiento) census; (JUR) tax; (renta) rent; (carga sobre una casa) mortgage.
censor [θen'sor] nm censor.
censura [θen'sura] nf (POL) censorship; (moral) censure, criticism.
censurar [θensu'rar] vt (idea) to censure; (cortar: película) to censor.
centella [θen'teʎa] nf spark.
centellar [θenteʎe'ar] vi (metal) to gleam; (estrella) to twinkle; (fig) to sparkle; **centelleo** nm gleam(ing); twinkling; sparkling.
centenar [θente'nar] nm hundred.
centenario, a [θente'narjo, a] a centenary.
centésimo, a [θen'tesimo, a] a hundredth.
centígrado, a [θen'tivraðo, a] a centigrade.
centímetro [θen'timetro] nm centimetre.
céntimo, a ['θentimo, a] a hundredth // nm cent.
centinela [θenti'nela] nm sentry, guard.
central [θen'tral] a central // nf head office; (TEC) plant; (TELEC) exchange.
centralización [θentraliθa'θjon] nf centralization.
centralizar [θentrali'θar] vt to centralize.
centrar [θen'trar] vt to centre.
céntrico, a ['θentriko, a] a centre.
centro ['θentro] nm centre.

centroamericano, a [θentroameri'kano, a] a, nm/f Central American.
ceñidor [θeɲi'ðor] nm sash.
ceñir [θe'ɲir] vt (rodear) to encircle, surround; (ajustar) to fit (tightly); (apretar) to tighten.
ceño ['θeɲo] nm frown, scowl; **fruncir el** ~ to frown, knit one's brow.
cepillar [θepi'ʎar] vt to brush; (madera) to plane (down); **cepillo** nm (gen) brush; (TEC) plane.
cera ['θera] nf wax.
cerámico, a [θe'ramiko, a] a ceramic // nf ceramics sg.
cerca ['θerka] nf fence // ad near, nearby, close; ~s nmpl foreground sg; ~ de prep near, close to.
cercanía [θerka'nia] nf nearness, closeness; ~s nfpl outskirts.
cercano, a [θer'kano, a] a close, near.
cercar [θer'kar] vt to fence in; (rodear) to surround.
cerciorar [θerθjo'rar] vt (informar) to inform; (asegurar) to assure; ~se vr (descubrir) to find out; (asegurarse) to make sure.
cerco ['θerko] nm (AGR) enclosure; (AM) fence; (MIL) siege.
cerdo ['θerðo] nm pig.
cereal [θere'al] nm cereal.
cerebro [θe'reβro] nm brain; (fig) brains pl.
ceremonia [θere'monja] nf ceremony; **ceremonial** a, nm ceremonial; **ceremonioso, a** a ceremonious; (cumplido) formal.
cereza [θe'reθa] nf cherry.
cerilla [θe'riʎa] nf (fósforo) match.
cerner [θer'ner] vt to sift, sieve; (fig) to scan, watch // vi to blossom; (lloviznar) to drizzle; ~se vr to hover.
cernidor [θerni'ðor] nm sieve.
cero ['θero] nm nothing, zero.
cerrado, a [θe'rraðo, a] a closed, shut; (con llave) locked; (tiempo) cloudy, overcast; (curva) sharp; (acento) thick, broad.
cerradura [θerra'ðura] nf (acción) closing; (mecanismo) lock.
cerraja [θe'rraxa] nf lock.
cerrar [θe'rrar] vt to close, shut; (paso, carretera) to close; (grifo) to turn off; (trato, cuenta, negocio) to close; ~ **con llave** to lock // vi to close, shut; (la noche) to come down; ~se vr to close, shut.
cerro ['θerro] nm hill.
cerrojo [θe'rroxo] nm (herramienta) bolt; (de puerta) latch.
certamen [θer'tamen] nm competition, contest.
certero, a [θer'tero, a] a accurate; (cierto) sure, certain.
certeza [θer'teθa], **certidumbre** [θerti'ðumbre] nf certainty.
certificado [θertifi'kaðo] nm certificate.
certificar [θertifi'kar] vt (asegurar,

atestar) to certify; (*carta*) to register.
cervato [θer'βato] *nm* fawn.
cervecería [θerβeθe'ria] *nf* (*fábrica*) brewery; (*tienda*) public house.
cerveza [θer'βeθa] *nf* beer.
cesación [θesa'θjon] *nf* cessation; (*suspensión*) suspension.
cesante [θe'sante] *a* out of a job.
cesar [θe'sar] *vi* to cease, stop.
cese ['θese] *nm* (*de trabajo*) dismissal; (*de pago*) suspension.
césped ['θespeð] *nm* grass, lawn.
cesta ['θesta] *nf* basket; **cesto** *nm* (large) basket, hamper.
ch... *ver bajo la letra CH, después de* C.
Cía *abr de* **compañía.**
cianuro [θja'nuro] *nm* cyanide.
ciar [θjar] *vi* to go backwards.
cicatriz [θika'triθ] *nf* scar.
ciclismo [θi'klismo] *nm* cycling.
ciclo ['θiklo] *nm* cycle.
ciclón [θi'klon] *nm* cyclone.
ciego, a ['θjeɣo, a] *a* blind // *nm/f* blind man/woman.
cielo ['θjelo] *nm* sky; (REL) heaven; ¡~s! good heavens!
ciempiés [θjem'pjes] *nm* centipede.
cien [θjen] *num ver* **ciento.**
ciénaga ['θjenaɣa] *nf* marsh, swamp.
ciencia ['θjenθja] *nf* science; ~-**ficción** *nf* science fiction.
cieno ['θjeno] *nm* mud, mire.
científico, a [θjen'tifiko, a] *a* scientific // *nm/f* scientist.
ciento ['θjento], **cien** *num* hundred; **pagar al 10 por** ~ to pay at 10 per cent.
cierne ['θjerne] *nm*: **en** ~ in blossom.
cierre ['θjerre] *nm* closing, shutting; (*con llave*) locking; ~ **a cremallera** zip fastener.
cierro *etc vb ver* **cerrar.**
cierto, a ['θjerto, a] *a* sure, certain; (*un tal*) a certain; (*correcto*) right, correct; ~ **hombre** a certain man; **sí, es** ~ yes, that's correct.
ciervo ['θjerβo] *nm* (*especie*) deer; (*macho*) stag.
cierzo ['θjerθo] *nm* north wind.
cifra ['θifra] *nf* number, numeral; (*cantidad*) number, quantity; (*secreta*) code; (*siglas*) abbreviation.
cifrar [θi'frar] *vt* to code, write in code; (*resumir*) to abridge.
cigarra [θi'ɣarra] *nf* cicada.
cigarrera [θiɣa'rrera] *nf* cigar case.
cigarrillo [θiɣa'rriʎo] *nm* cigarette.
cigarro [θi'ɣarro] *nm* cigarette; (*puro*) cigar.
cigüeña [θi'ɣweɲa] *nf* stork.
cilíndrico, a [θi'lindriko, a] *a* cylindrical.
cilindro [θi'lindro] *nm* cylinder; (*rodillo*) roller.
cima ['θima] *nf* (*de montaña*) top, peak; (*de árbol*) top; (*fig*) summit, height.
címbalo ['θimbalo] *nm* cymbal.
cimbrar [θim'brar], **cimbrear** [θimbre-

'ar] *vt* to brandish; ~**se** *vr* (*al viento*) to sway.
cimentar [θimen'tar] *vt* to lay the foundations of.
cimiento [θi'mjento] *nm* foundation.
cinc [θink] *nm* zinc.
cincel [θin'θel] *nm* chisel; ~**ar** *vt* to chisel.
cinco ['θinko] *num* five.
cincuenta [θin'kwenta] *num* fifty.
cincho ['θintʃo] *nm* sash, belt.
cine ['θine] *nm* cinema.
cinematográfico, a [θinemato'ɣrafiko, a] *a* cine-, film *cpd.*
cínico, a ['θiniko, a] *a* cynical // *nm/f* cynic.
cinismo [θi'nismo] *nm* cynicism.
cinta ['θinta] *nf* band, strip; (*de seda, lana, algodón*) ribbon, tape; (*película*) reel; (*máquina de escribir*) ribbon; (*métrica*) tape measure; (*magnetofónica*) tape; (*adhesiva*) adhesive tape.
cinto ['θinto] *nm* belt, girdle.
cintura [θin'tura] *nf* waist.
cinturón [θintu'ron] *nm* belt; ~ **de seguridad** safety belt.
ciprés [θi'pres] *nm* cypress (tree).
circo ['θirko] *nm* circus.
circuito [θir'kwito] *nm* circuit.
circulación [θirkula'θjon] *nf* circulation; (AUTO) traffic.
circular [θirku'lar] *a*, *nf* circular // *vi*, *vt* to circulate.
círculo ['θirkulo] *nm* circle.
circuncidar [θirkunθi'dar] *vt* to circumcise; **circuncisión** *nf* circumcision; **circunciso, a** *pp de* **circuncidar** // *a* circumcised.
circundar [θirkun'dar] *vt* to surround.
circunferencia [θirkunfe'renθja] *nf* circumference.
circunlocución [θirkunloku'θjon] *nf,* **circunloquio** [θirkun'lokjo] *nm* circumlocution.
circunscribir [θirkunskri'βir] *vt* to circumscribe; ~**se** *vr* to be limited.
circunscripción [θirkunskrip'θjon] *nf* division; (POL) constituency.
circunspección [θirkunspek'θjon] *nf* circumspection.
circunspecto, a [θirkuns'pekto, a] *a* circumspect, cautious.
circunstancia [θirkuns'tanθja] *nf* circumstance.
circunstante [θirkuns'tante] *nm/f* onlooker, bystander.
cirio ['θirjo] *nm* (wax) candle.
ciruela [θi'rwela] *nf* plum; ~ **pasa** prune.
cirugía [θiru'xia] *nf* surgery; ~ **estética** plastic surgery.
cirujano [θiru'xano] *nm* surgeon.
cisne ['θisne] *nm* swan.
cisterna [θis'terna] *nf* cistern.
cita ['θita] *nf* appointment, engagement; (*de novios*) date; (*referencia*) quotation.
citación [θita'θjon] *nf* (JUR) summons *sg*; (*referencia*) quotation.

citar [θi'tar] vt (gen) to make an appointment with; (JUR) to summons; (un autor, texto) to quote.

citrón [θi'tron] nm lemon.

ciudad [θju'ðað] nf town; (capital de país etc) city; ~ano, a nm/f citizen; ~ela nf citadel, fortress.

cívico, a ['θiβiko, a] a civic.

civil [θi'βil] a civil // nm (guardia) policeman; ~idad nf civility, courtesy.

civilización [θiβiliθa'θjon] nf civilization.

civilizar [θiβili'θar] vt to civilize.

civismo [θi'βismo] nm public spirit.

cizaña [θi'θaɲa] nf discord.

clamar [kla'mar] vt to clamour for // vi to cry out, clamour.

clamor [kla'mor] nm (grito) cry, shout; (gemido) whine; (de campana) knell; (fig) clamour, protest.

clamorear [klamore'ar] vt to clamour for // vi (campana) to toll; **clamoreo** nm clamour(ing).

clandestino, a [klandes'tino, a] a clandestine; (POL) underground.

clara ['klara] nf (de huevo) white of an egg; (del día) bright interval.

claraboya [klara'βoja] nf skylight.

clarear [klare'ar] vi (el día) to dawn; (el cielo) to clear up, brighten up; ~se vr to be transparent.

claridad [klari'ðað] nf (del día) brightness; (de estilo) clarity.

clarificar [klarifi'kar] vt to clarify.

clarín [kla'rin] nm bugle.

clarinete [klari'nete] nm clarinet.

clarividencia [klariβi'ðenθja] nf clairvoyance; (fig) far-sightedness.

claro, a ['klaro, a] a (gen) clear; (luminoso) bright; (poco subido) light; (evidente) clear, evident; (ralo) sparse; (poco espeso) thin // nm (en escritura) space; (en bosque) clearing // ad clearly // excl of course!

clase ['klase] nf class; ~ alta/media/obrera upper/middle/ working class.

clásico, a ['klasiko, a] a classical; (fig) classic.

clasificación [klasifika'θjon] nf classification; (DEPORTE) league.

clasificar [klasifi'kar] vt to classify.

claudicar [klauði'kar] vi to limp; (fig) to back down.

claustro ['klaustro] nm cloister.

cláusula ['klausula] nf clause.

clausura [klau'sura] nf closing, closure.

clavar [kla'βar] vt (clavo) to knock in, drive in; (cuchillo, tenedor) to stick, thrust; (mirada) to fix.

clave ['klaβe] nf key; (MUS) clef.

clavel [kla'βel] nm carnation.

clavícula [kla'βikula] nf collar bone.

clavija [kla'βixa] nf peg, dowel, pin; (ELEC) plug.

clavo ['klaβo] nm (de metal) nail; (BOT) clove; (callo) corn.

claxon ['klakson] nm horn.

clemencia [kle'menθja] nf mercy, clemency; **clemente** a merciful, clement.

cleptómano, a [klep'tomano, a] nm/f kleptomaniac.

clerical [kleri'kal] a clerical // nm clergyman.

clérigo ['klerixo] nm clergyman.

clero ['klero] nm clergy.

cliente ['kljente] nm/f client, customer.

clientela [kljen'tela] nf clientele, customers pl.

clima ['klima] nm climate.

clínica ['klinika] nf clinic; (particular) private hospital.

clip [klip] nm paper clip.

clorhídrico, a [klo'ridriko, a] a hydrochloric.

cloroformo [kloro'formo] nm chloroform.

club [klub] (pl ~s o ~es) nm club.

C.N.T. abr de **Confederación Nacional de Trabajo**.

coacción [koak'θjon] nf coercion, compulsion.

coalición [koali'θjon] nf coalition.

coartar [koar'tar] vt to limit, restrict.

cobarde [ko'βarðe] a cowardly // nm coward; **cobardía** nf cowardice.

cobertizo [koβer'tiθo] nm shelter.

cobertor [koβer'tor] nm bedspread.

cobertura [koβer'tura] nf cover.

cobija [ko'βixa] nf roof; **cobijar** vt (cubrir) to cover; (abrigar) to shelter.

cobra ['koβra] nf cobra.

cobrador [koβra'ðor] nm (de autobús) conductor; (de impuestos, gas) collector.

cobrar [ko'βrar] vt (cheque) to cash; (sueldo) to collect, draw; (objeto) to recover; (precio) to charge; (deuda) to collect // vi to draw one's pay; ~se vr to recover, get well; **cóbrese al entregar** cash on delivery (COD).

cobre ['koβre] nm copper; ~s nmpl brass instruments.

cobro ['koβro] nm recovery; (paga) payment.

cocaína [koka'ina] nf cocaine.

cocción [kok'θjon] nf cooking.

cocear [koθe'ar] vi to kick.

cocer [ko'θer] vt, vi to cook; (en agua) to boil; (en horno) to bake; ~se vr to suffer intensely.

cocido [ko'θiðo] nm stew.

cocina [ko'θina] nf kitchen; (aparato) cooker, stove; (acto) cookery; **cocinar** vt, vi to cook.

cocinero, a [koθi'nero, a] nm/f cook.

coco ['koko] nm (árbol) coconut palm; (fruto) coconut.

cocodrilo [koko'ðrilo] nm crocodile.

coche ['kotʃe] nm car, motorcar; (de tren, de caballos) coach, carriage; (fúnebre) hearse; (para niños) pram; ~ celular Black Maria, prison van.

coche-cama [kotʃekama] (pl coches-camas) nm sleeping car, sleeper.

cochera [ko'tʃera] *nf* garage.
cochero [ko'tʃero] *nm* coachman.
cochino, a [ko'tʃino, a] *a* filthy, dirty // *nm* pig.
codazo [ko'ðaθo] *nm* jab, poke (with the elbow).
codear [koðe'ar] *vi* to elbow, jostle; ~se *vr*: ~**se con** to rub shoulders with.
códice ['koðiθe] *nm* manuscript, codex.
codicia [ko'ðiθja] *nf* greed; (*fig*) lust; **codiciar** *vt* to covet; **codicioso, a** *a* covetous.
código ['koðixo] *nm* code; ~ **civil** common law.
codillo [ko'ðiʎo] *nm* (*ZOOL*) knee; (*TEC*) elbow (joint).
codo ['koðo] *nm* (*ANAT, de tubo*) elbow; (*ZOOL*) knee.
codorniz [koðor'niθ] *nf* quail.
coerción [koer'θjon] *nf* coercion.
coetáneo, a [koe'taneo, a] *a* contemporary.
coexistencia [koeksis'tenθja] *nf* coexistence; **coexistir** *vi* to coexist.
cofradía [kofra'ðia] *nf* brotherhood, fraternity.
cofre ['kofre] *nm* chest.
coger [ko'xer] *vt* (*gen*) to take (hold of); (*objeto caído*) to pick up; (*frutas*) to pick, harvest; (*resfriado, ladrón, pelota*) to catch // *vi*: ~ **por el buen camino** to take the right road; ~**se** *vr* to catch; (*robar*) to steal.
cogida [ko'xiða] *nf* gathering, harvesting; (*de peces*) catch.
cogote [ko'xote] *nm* back *or* nape of the neck.
cohabitar [koaβi'tar] *vi* to live together, cohabit.
cohechar [koe'tʃar] *vt* to bribe; **cohecho** *nm* (*acción*) bribery; (*soborno*) bribe.
coherente [koe'rente] *a* coherent.
cohesión [koe'sjon] *nm* cohesion.
cohete [ko'ete] *nm* rocket.
cohibición [koiβi'θjon] *nf* restraint, restriction.
cohibir [koi'βir] *vt* to restrain, restrict.
coincidencia [koinθi'ðenθja] *nf* coincidence; (*acuerdo*) agreement.
coincidir [koinθi'ðir] *vi* (*en idea*) to coincide, agree; (*en lugar*) to coincide.
coito ['koito] *nm* intercourse, coitus.
cojear [koxe'ar] *vi* (*persona*) to limp, hobble; (*mueble*) to wobble, rock.
cojera [ko'xera] *nf* lameness; (*andar cojo*) limp.
cojín [ko'xin] *nm* cushion; **cojinete** *nm* small cushion, pad; (*TEC*) ball bearing.
cojo, a ['koxo, a] *a* (*que no puede andar*) lame; (*manco*) crippled; (*mueble*) shaky // *nm/f* lame person; cripple.
col [kol] *nf* cabbage; ~ **de Bruselas** Brussels sprouts.
cola ['kola] *nf* (*gen*) tail; (*de gente*) queue; (*lugar*) end, last place; (*para pegar*) glue, gum; **hacer la** ~ to queue (up).

colaborador, a [kolaβora'ðor, a] *nm/f* collaborator.
colaborar [kolaβo'rar] *vi* to collaborate.
coladera [kola'ðera] *nf* strainer.
coladura [kola'ðura] *nf* (*filtración*) straining; (*residuo*) grounds *pl*, dregs *pl*.
colapso [ko'lapso] *nm* collapse; ~ **nervioso** nervous breakdown.
colar [ko'lar] *vt* (*líquido*) to strain off; (*ropa*) to bleach; (*metal*) to cast // *vi* to ooze, seep (through); ~**se** *vr* to slip in *or* past.
colateral [kolate'ral] *nm* collateral.
colcha ['koltʃa] *nf* bedspread.
colchón [kol'tʃon] *nm* mattress.
colear [kole'ar] *vi* to wag its tail.
colección [kolek'θjon] *nf* collection; **coleccionista** *nm/f* collector.
colecta [ko'lekta] *nf* collection.
colectar [kolek'tar] *vt* to collect.
colectivo, a [kolek'tiβo, a] *a* collective, joint.
colector [kolek'tor] *nm* collector; (*sumidero*) sewer.
colega [ko'leɣa] *nm/f* colleague.
colegio [ko'lexjo] *nm* (*gen*) college; (*escuela*) (*private*) school; (*de abogados etc*) association.
colegir [kole'xir] *vt* (*juntar, reunir*) to collect, gather; (*deducir*) to infer, conclude.
cólera ['kolera] *nf* (*ira*) anger; (*MED*) cholera.
colérico, a [ko'leriko, a] *a* angry, furious.
coleta [ko'leta] *nf* pigtail.
colgadero [kolɣa'ðero] *nm* (*gancho*) hook; (*percha*) hanger.
colgadura [kolɣa'ðura] *nf* hangings *pl*, drapery.
colgante [kol'ɣante] *a* hanging // *nm* drop earring.
colgar [kol'ɣar] *vt* to hang (up); (*ropa*) to hang (out); (*teléfono*) to hang up // *vi* to hang.
coliflor [koli'flor] *nf* cauliflower.
colilla [ko'liʎa] *nf* fag end, butt.
colina [ko'lina] *nf* hill.
colindante [kolin'dante] *a* adjacent, neighbouring.
colindar [kolin'dar] *vi* to adjoin, be adjacent.
colisión [koli'sjon] *nf* collision; (*choque*) crash.
colmado, a [kol'maðo, a] *a* abundant, copious; (*cuchara etc*) heaped.
colmar [kol'mar] *vt* to fill to the brim; (*fig*) to fulfil, realize.
colmena [kol'mena] *nf* beehive.
colmillo [kol'miʎo] *nm* (*diente*) eye tooth; (*de elefante*) tusk; (*de perro*) fang.
colmo ['kolmo] *nm* height, summit.
colocación [koloka'θjon] *nf* placing; (*empleo*) job, position; (*de mueble*) place, position.
colocar [kolo'kar] *vt* to place, put,

position; (*poner en empleo*) to find a job
for.

Colombia [ko'lombja] *nf* Colombia;
colombiano, a *a*, *nm/f* Colombian.

colon ['kolon] *nm* colon.

colonia [ko'lonja] *nf* colony; (*de casas*)
housing estate; (*agua de* ~) cologne.

colonización [koloniθa'θjon] *nf*
colonization.

colonizador, a [koloniθa'ðor, a] *a*
colonizing // *nm/f* colonist, settler.

colonizar [koloni'θar] *vt* to colonize.

coloquio [ko'lokjo] *nm* conversation;
(*congreso*) conference.

color [ko'lor] *nm* colour.

colorado, a [kolo'raðo, a] *a* (*que tiene
color*) coloured; (*rojo*) red.

colorar [kolo'rar] *vt* to colour; (*teñir*) to
dye.

colorear [kolore'ar] *vt* to colour // *vi* to
redden.

colorido [kolo'riðo] *nm* colouring.

colosal [kolo'sal] *a* colossal.

columbrar [kolum'brar] *vt* to glimpse,
spy.

columna [ko'lumna] *nf* column; (*pilar*)
pillar; (*apoyo*) support.

columpiar [kolum'pjar] *vt*, ~**se** *vr* to
swing; **columpio** *nm* swing.

collar [ko'ʎar] *nm* necklace; (*de perro*)
collar.

coma ['koma] *nf* comma // *nm* coma.

comadre [ko'maðre] *nf* (*partera*) midwife;
(*madrina*) godmother; (*vecina*) neighbour;
~**ar** *vi* to gossip.

comandancia [koman'danθja] *nf*
command.

comandante [koman'dante] *nm*
commandant.

comandar [koman'dar] *vt* to command.

comarca [ko'marka] *nf* region.

comarcar [komar'kar] *vi*: ~ **con** to
border on, be adjacent to.

combar [kom'bar] *vt* to bend, curve.

combate [kom'bate] *nm* fight; (*fig*) battle;
combatiente *nm* combatant.

combatir [komba'tir] *vt* to fight, combat.

combinación [kombina'θjon] *nf*
combination; (*QUÍMICA*) compound;
(*bebida*) cocktail; (*plan*) scheme, setup.

combinar [kombi'nar] *vt* to combine.

combustible [kombus'tiβle] *nm* fuel.

combustión [kombus'tjon] *nf* combustion.

comedia [ko'meðja] *nf* comedy; (*TEATRO*)
play, drama.

comediante [kome'ðjante] *nm/f* (comic)
actor/actress.

comedido, a [kome'ðiðo, a] *a* moderate;
(*cortés*) courteous.

comedirse [kome'ðirse] *vr* to behave
moderately; (*ser cortés*) to be courteous.

comedor, a [kome'ðor, a] *nm/f* (*persona*)
glutton // *nm* (*habitación*) dining room;
(*restaurante*) restaurant; (*cantina*)
canteen.

comentador, a [komenta'ðor, a] *nm/f* =
comentarista.

comentar [komen'tar] *vt* to comment on;
(*fam*) to discuss.

comentario [komen'tarjo] *nm* comment,
remark; (*literario*) commentary; ~**s** *nmpl*
gossip *sg*.

comentarista [komenta'rista] *nm/f*
commentator.

comento [ko'mento] *nm* = **comentario**.

comenzar [komen'θar] *vt*, *vi* to begin,
start, commence.

comer [ko'mer] *vt* (*gen*) to eat; (*DAMAS,
AJEDREZ*) to take, capture // *vi* to eat;
(*almorzar*) to have lunch; ~**se** *vr* to eat
up.

comercial [komer'θjal] *a* commercial;
(*relativo al negocio*) business *cpd*.

comerciante [komer'θjante] *nm/f* trader,
merchant.

comerciar [komer'θjar] *vi* to trade, do
business.

comercio [ko'merθjo] *nm* commerce;
(*tráfico*) trade; (*negocio*) business; (*fig*)
dealings *pl*.

comestible [komes'tiβle] *a* eatable,
edible // *nm* foodstuff.

cometa [ko'meta] *nm* comet // *nf* kite.

cometer [kome'ter] *vt* to commit.

cometido [kome'tiðo] *nm* (*misión*) task,
assignment; (*deber*) commitment.

comezón [kome'θon] *nf* itch, itching.

cómico, a ['komiko, a] *a* comic(al) // *nm/f*
comedian; (*de teatro*) (comic)
actor/actress.

comida [ko'miða] *nf* (*alimento*) food;
(*almuerzo, cena*) meal; (*de mediodía*) lunch.

comienzo [ko'mjenθo] *nm* beginning,
start.

comillas [ko'miʎas] *nfpl* inverted
commas.

comisario [komi'sarjo] *nm* commissary;
(*POL*) commissar.

comisión [komi'sjon] *nf* commission.

comité [komi'te] *nm* committee.

como ['komo] *ad* as; (*tal* ~) like; (*aproximadamente*) about, approximately // *conj*
(*ya que, puesto que*) as, since; (*en seguida
que*) as soon as; ¡~ **no!** of course!; ~ **no
lo haga hoy** unless he does it today; ~ **si**
as if; **es tan alto** ~ **ancho** it is as high as
it is wide.

cómo ['komo] *ad* how?, why? // *excl*
what?, I beg your pardon? // *nm*: **el** ~ **y
el porqué** the whys and wherefores.

comodidad [komoði'ðað] *nf* comfort;
venga a su ~ come at your convenience.

comodín [komo'ðin] *nm* joker.

cómodo, a ['komoðo, a] *a* comfortable;
(*práctico, de fácil uso*) convenient.

compacto, a [kom'pakto, a] *a* compact.

compadecer [kompaðe'θer] *vt* to pity, be
sorry for; ~**se** *vr*: ~**se de** to pity, be
sorry for.

compadre [kom'paðre] *nm* (*padrino*)
godfather; (*amigo*) friend, pal.

compañero, a [kompa'ɲero, a] *nm/f* companion; ~ **de clase** classmate.
compañía [kompa'ɲia] *nf* company.
comparación [kompara'θjon] *nf* comparison; **en ~ con** in comparison with.
comparar [kompa'rar] *vt* to compare.
comparativo, a [kompara'tiβo, a] *a* comparative.
comparecer [kompare'θer] *vi* to appear (in court).
compartimiento [komparti'mjento] *nm* division; (*distribución*) distribution; (*FERRO*) compartment.
compartir [kompar'tir] *vt* to divide (up), share (out).
compás [kom'pas] *nm* (*MUS*) beat, rhythm; (*MAT*) compasses *pl*; (*NAUT*) compass.
compasión [kompa'sjon] *nf* compassion, pity.
compasivo, a [kompa'siβo, a] *a* compassionate.
compatibilidad [kompatiβili'ðað] *nf* compatibility.
compatible [kompa'tiβle] *a* compatible.
compatriota [kompa'trjota] *nm/f* compatriot.
compeler [kompe'ler] *vt* to compel.
compendiar [kompen'djar] *vt* to summarize; (*libro*) to abridge; **compendio** *nm* summary; abridgement.
compensación [kompensa'θjon] *nf* compensation.
compensar [kompen'sar] *vt* to compensate.
competencia [kompe'tenθja] *nf* (*incumbencia*) domain, field; (*aptitud, idoneidad*) competence; (*rivalidad*) competition.
competente [kompe'tente] *a* (*persona, jurado, tribunal*) competent; (*conveniente*) fit, suitable.
competición [kompeti'θjon] *nf* competition.
competir [kompe'tir] *vi* to compete.
compilar [kompi'lar] *vt* to compile.
complacencia [kompla'θenθja] *nf* (*placer*) pleasure; (*satisfacción*) satisfaction; (*buena voluntad*) willingness.
complacer [kompla'θer] *vt* to please; ~**se** *vr* to be pleased.
complaciente [kompla'θjente] *a* kind, obliging, helpful.
complejo, a [kom'plexo, a] *a, nm* complex.
complementario, a [komplemen'tarjo, a] *a* complementary.
completar [komple'tar] *vt* to complete.
completo, a [kom'pleto, a] *a* complete; (*perfecto*) perfect; (*lleno*) full // *nm* full complement.
complicar [kompli'kar] *vt* to complicate.
cómplice ['kompliθe] *nm/f* accomplice.
complot [kom'plot] *nm* plot; (*conspiración*) conspiracy.
componenda [kompo'nenda] *nf*

compromise; (*pey*) shady deal.
componer [kompo'ner] *vt* to make up, put together; (*MUS, LITERATURA, IMPRENTA*) to compose; (*algo roto*) to mend, repair; (*adornar*) to adorn; (*arreglar*) to arrange; (*reconciliar*) to reconcile; ~**se** *vr*: ~**se de** to consist of.
comportamiento [komporta'mjento] *nm* behaviour, conduct.
comportarse [kompor'tarse] *vr* to behave.
composición [komposi'θjon] *nf* composition.
compositor, a [komposi'tor, a] *nm/f* composer.
compostura [kompos'tura] *nf* (*reparación*) mending, repair; (*arreglo*) arrangement; (*acuerdo*) agreement; (*actitud*) composure.
compra ['kompra] *nf* purchase; ~**s** *nfpl* purchases, shopping *sg*.
comprador, a [kompra'ðor, a] *nm/f* buyer, purchaser.
comprar [kom'prar] *vt* to buy, purchase.
comprender [kompren'der] *vt* to understand; (*incluir*) to comprise, include.
comprensión [kompren'sjon] *nf* understanding; (*totalidad*) comprehensiveness.
comprensivo, a [kompren'siβo, a] *a* comprehensive; (*actitud*) understanding.
compresión [kompre'sjon] *nf* compression.
comprimir [kompri'mir] *vt* to compress; (*fig*) to control.
comprobante [kompro'βante] *a* verifying, supporting // *nm*
comprobar [kompro'βar] *vt* to check; (*probar*) to prove; (*TEC*) to check, test.
comprometer [komprome'ter] *vt* to compromise; (*exponer*) to endanger; ~**se** *vr* to compromise o.s.; (*involucrarse*) to get involved.
compromiso [kompro'miso] *nm* (*obligación*) obligation; (*cometido*) commitment; (*convenio*) agreement; (*dificultad*) awkward situation.
compuesto, a [kom'pwesto, a] *a*: ~ **de** composed of, made up of // *nm* compound.
compulsión [kompul'sjon] *nf* compulsion.
compunción [kompun'θjon] *nf* compunction, regret.
computador [komputa'ðor] *nm*, **computadora** [komputa'ðora] *nf* computer.
comulgar [komul'xar] *vi* to receive communion.
común [ko'mun] *a* common // *nm*: **el ~** the community.
comunicación [komunika'θjon] *nf* communication; (*ponencia*) report.
comunicar [komuni'kar] *vt, vi,* ~**se** *vr* to communicate; **comunicativo, a** *a* communicative.
comunidad [komuni'ðað] *nf* community.
comunión [komu'njon] *nf* communion.
comunismo [komu'nismo] *nm*

communism; **comunista** a, nm/f communist.

con [kon] prep with; (a pesar de) in spite of; ~ **que** so, and so; ~ **apretar el botón** by pressing the button.

concebir [konθe'βir] vt, vi to conceive.

conceder [konθe'ðer] vt to concede.

concejo [kon'θexo] nm council.

concentración [konθentra'θjon] nf concentration.

concentrar [konθen'trar] vt, ~**se** vr to concentrate.

concepción [konθep'θjon] nf conception.

concepto [kon'θepto] nm concept.

concertar [konθer'tar] vt (MUS) to harmonize; (acordar: precio) to agree; (: tratado) to conclude; (trato) to arrange, fix up; (combinar: esfuerzos) to coordinate; (reconciliar: personas) to reconcile // vi to harmonize, be in tune.

concesión [konθe'sjon] nf concession.

conciencia [kon'θjenθja] nf conscience.

concienzudo, a [konθjen'θuðo, a] a conscientious.

concierto [kon'θjerto] nm concert; (obra) concerto.

conciliar [konθi'ljar] vt to reconcile.

concilio [kon'θiljo] nm council.

conciso, a [kon'θiso, a] a concise.

concluir [konklu'ir] vt, vi, ~**se** vr to conclude.

conclusión [konklu'sjon] nf conclusion.

concordar [konkor'ðar] vt to reconcile // vi to agree, tally; **concordia** nf concord, harmony.

concretar [konkre'tar] vt to make concrete, make more specific; ~**se** vr to become more definite.

concreto, a [kon'kreto, a] a, nm (AM) concrete; **en** ~ (en resumen) to sum up; (específicamente) specifically; **no hay nada en** ~ there's nothing definite.

concurrir [konku'rrir] vi (juntarse: ríos) to meet, come together; (: personas) to gather, meet; (ponerse de acuerdo, coincidir) to concur; (competir) to compete; (contribuir) to contribute.

concurso [kon'kurso] nm (de público) crowd; (ESCOL, DEPORTE, competencia) competition; (coincidencia) coincidence; (ayuda) help, cooperation.

concusión [konku'sjon] nf concussion.

concha ['kontʃa] nf shell.

conde ['konde] nm count.

condecorar [kondeko'rar] vt to decorate.

condena [kon'dena] nf sentence.

condenación [kondena'θjon] nf (gen) condemnation; (condena) sentence; (REL) damnation.

condenar [konde'nar] vt to condemn; (JUR) to convict; ~**se** vr (JUR) to confess (one's guilt); (REL) to be damned.

condensar [konden'sar] vt to condense.

condescender [kondesθen'der] vi to acquiesce, comply.

condición [kondi'θjon] nf condition;

condicionado, a a a conditioned.

condicional [kondiθjo'nal] a conditional.

condimento [kondi'mento] nm seasoning.

condolerse [kondo'lerse] vr to sympathize.

conducir [kondu'θir] vt to take, convey; (AUTO) to drive // vi to drive; (fig) to lead; ~**se** vr to behave.

conducta [kon'dukta] nf conduct, behaviour.

conducto [kon'dukto] nm pipe, tube; (fig) channel.

conductor, a [konduk'tor, a] a leading, guiding // nm (FÍSICA) conductor; (de vehículo) driver.

conduje etc vb ver **conducir**.

conduzco etc vb ver **conducir**.

conectar [konek'tar] vt to connect (up), plug in.

conejo [ko'nexo] nm rabbit.

conexión [konek'sjon] nf connection.

confeccionar [konfekθjo'nar] vt to make (up).

confederación [konfeðera'θjon] nf confederation.

conferencia [konfe'renθja] nf conference; (lección) lecture; (TELEC) call.

conferir [konfe'rir] vt to award.

confesar [konfe'sar] vt to confess, admit.

confesión [konfe'sjon] nf confession.

confesionario [konfesjo'narjo] nm confessional.

confiado, a [kon'fjaðo, a] a (crédulo) trusting; (presumido) confident; (pey) conceited, vain.

confianza [kon'fjanθa] nf trust; (aliento, confidencia) confidence; (familiaridad) intimacy, familiarity; (pey) vanity, conceit.

confiar [kon'fjar] vt to entrust // vi to trust.

confidencia [konfi'ðenθja] nf confidence.

confidencial [konfiðen'θjal] a confidential.

confidente [konfi'ðente] nm/f confidant/e; (policial) informer.

configurar [konfiɣu'rar] vt to shape, form.

confín [kon'fin] nm limit; ~**es** nmpl edges.

confinar [konfi'nar] vi to confine; (desterrar) to banish.

confirmar [konfir'mar] vt to confirm.

confiscar [konfis'kar] vt to confiscate.

confitería [konfite'ria] nf confectionery; (tienda) confectioner's (shop).

confitura [konfi'tura] nf jam.

conflicto [kon'flikto] nm conflict; (fig) clash.

conformar [konfor'mar] vt to shape, fashion // vi to agree; ~**se** vr to conform; (resignarse) to resign o.s.

conforme [kon'forme] a (gen) alike, similar; (de acuerdo) agreed, in agreement; (resignado) resigned // ad as // excl agreed! // nm agreement // prep: ~ a in accordance with.

conformidad [konformi'ðað] *nf* (*semejanza*) similarity; (*acuerdo*) agreement; (*resignación*) resignation.

confortable [konfor'taβle] *a* comfortable.

confortar [konfor'tar] *vt* to comfort.

confrontar [konfron'tar] *vt* to confront; (*dos personas*) to bring face to face; (*cotejar*) to compare // *vi* to border.

confundir [konfun'dir] *vt* to blur; (*equivocar*) to mistake, confuse; (*mezclar*) to mix; (*turbar*) to confuse; ~**se** *vr* to become blurred; (*turbarse*) to get confused; (*equivocarse*) to make a mistake; (*mezclarse*) to mix.

confusión [konfu'sjon] *nf* confusion.

confuso, a [kon'fuso, a] *a* confused.

congelar [konxe'lar] *vt* to freeze; ~**se** *vr* (*sangre, grasa*) to congeal.

congeniar [konxe'njar] *vi* to get on (well).

conglomeración [konglomera'θjon] *nf* conglomeration.

congoja [kon'goxa] *nf* distress, grief.

congratular [kongratu'lar] *vt* to congratulate.

congregación [kongreɣa'θjon] *nf* congregation.

congresista [kongre'sista] *nm/f* delegate, congressman/woman.

congreso [kon'greso] *nm* congress.

conjetura [konxe'tura] *nf* guess; **conjeturar** *vt* to guess.

conjugar [konxu'ɣar] *vt* to combine, fit together; (*un verbo*) to conjugate.

conjunción [konxun'θjon] *nf* conjunction.

conjunto, a [kon'xunto, a] *a* joint, united // *nm* whole; (*mus*) group; **en** ~ as a whole.

conmemoración [konmemora'θjon] *nf* commemoration.

conmemorar [konmemo'rar] *vt* to commemorate.

conmigo [kon'miɣo] *pron* with me; with myself.

conminar [konmi'nar] *vt* to threaten.

conmiseración [konmisera'θjon] *nf* pity, commiseration.

conmoción [konmo'θjon] *nf* shock; (*med*) concussion; (*fig*) upheaval.

conmovedor, a [konmoβe'ðor, a] *a* touching, moving; (*impresionante*) exciting.

conmover [konmo'βer] *vt* to shake, disturb; (*fig*) to move.

conmutador [konmuta'ðor] *nm* switch.

conocedor, a [konoθe'ðor, a] *a* expert, knowledgeable // *nm/f* expert.

conocer [kono'θer] *vt* (*gen*) to know; (*por primera vez*) to meet, get to know; (*entender*) to know about; (*reconocer*) to know, recognize; ~**se** *vr* (*una persona*) to know o.s.; (*dos personas*) to (get to) know each other.

conocido, a [kono'θiðo, a] *a* (well-)known // *nm/f* acquaintance.

conocimiento [konoθi'mjento] *nm* knowledge; (*med*) consciousness; ~**s** *nmpl*

(*personas*) acquaintances; (*ciencia*) knowledge *sg*.

conozco *etc vb ver* **conocer**.

conque ['konke] *conj* and so, so then.

conquista [kon'kista] *nf* conquest.

conquistador, a [konkista'ðor, a] *a* conquering // *nm* conqueror.

conquistar [konkis'tar] *vt* to conquer.

consagrar [konsa'ɣrar] *vt* (*rel*) to consecrate; (*fig*) to devote.

consciente [kons'θjente] *a* conscious.

consecución [konseku'θjon] *nf* acquisition; (*de fin*) attainment.

consecuencia [konse'kwenθja] *nf* consequence, outcome; (*firmeza*) consistency.

consecuente [konse'kwente] *a* consistent.

consecutivo, a [konseku'tiβo, a] *a* consecutive.

conseguir [konse'ɣir] *vt* to get, obtain; (*sus fines*) to attain.

consejero, a [konse'xero, a] *nm/f* adviser, consultant; (*pol*) councillor.

consejo [kon'sexo] *nm* advice; (*pol*) council.

consenso [kon'senso] *nm* consensus.

consentimiento [konsenti'mjento] *nm* consent.

consentir [konsen'tir] *vt* (*permitir, tolerar*) to consent to; (*mimar*) to pamper, spoil; (*admitir*) to admit // *vi* to agree, consent.

conserje [kon'serxe] *nm* caretaker; (*portero*) porter.

conserva [kon'serβa] *nf* (*acción*) preserving; (*alimento*) preserved food.

conservación [konserβa'θjon] *nf* conservation; (*de alimentos, vida*) preservation.

conservador, a [konserβa'ðor, a] *a* preservative; (*pol*) conservative // *nm/f* conservative; (*de museo*) keeper.

conservar [konser'βar] *vt* to conserve, keep; (*alimentos, vida*) to preserve; ~**se** *vr* to survive.

considerable [konsiðe'raβle] *a* considerable.

consideración [konsiðera'θjon] *nf* consideration; (*estimación*) respect.

considerado, a [konsiðe'raðo, a] *a* (*prudente, reflexivo*) considerate; (*respetado*) respected.

considerar [konsiðe'rar] *vt* to consider.

consigna [kon'siɣna] *nf* (*orden*) order, instruction; (*para equipajes*) left-luggage office.

consigo [kon'siɣo] *pron* (*m*) with him; (*f*) with her; (*Vd.*) with you; (*reflexivo*) with o.s.

consiguiente [konsi'ɣjente] *a* consequent; **por** ~ and so, therefore, consequently.

consistente [konsis'tente] *a* consistent; (*sólido*) solid, firm; (*válido*) sound.

consistir [konsis'tir] *vi*: ~ **en** (*componerse de*) to consist of; (*ser resultado de*) to be due to.

consolación [konsola'θjon] *nf* consolation.

consolar [konso'lar] *vt* to console.
consolidar [konsoli'ðar] *vt* to consolidate.
consomé [konso'me] *nm* consommé, clear soup.
consonante [konso'nante] *a* consonant, harmonious // *nf* consonant.
conspicuo, a [kons'pikwo, a] *a* conspicuous.
conspiración [konspira'θjon] *nf* conspiracy.
conspirador, a [konspira'ðor, a] *nm/f* conspirator.
conspirar [konspi'rar] *vi* to conspire.
constante [kons'tante] *a* constant.
constar [kons'tar] *vi* (*evidenciarse*) to be clear *or* evident; ~ **de** to consist of.
consternación [konsterna'θjon] *nf* consternation.
constipación [konstipa'θjon] *nf* = **constipado**.
constipado, a [konsti'paðo, a] *a*: **estar** ~ to have a cold // *nm* cold.
constitución [konstitu'θjon] *nf* constitution; **constitucional** *a* constitutional.
constituir [konstitu'ir] *vt* (*formar, componer*) to constitute, make up; (*fundar, erigir, ordenar*) to constitute, establish.
constitutivo, a [konstitu'tiβo, a] *a* constitutive, constituent.
constituyente [konstitu'jente] *a* constituent.
constreñir [konstre'ɲir] *vt* (*obligar*) to compel, oblige; (*restringir*) to restrict.
construcción [konstruk'θjon] *nf* construction, building.
constructor, a [konstruk'tor, a] *nm/f* builder.
construir [konstru'ir] *vt* to build, construct.
consuelo [kon'swelo] *nm* consolation, solace.
cónsul ['konsul] *nm* consul; **consulado** *nm* consulate.
consulta [kon'sulta] *nf* consultation.
consultar [konsul'tar] *vt* to consult.
consultorio [konsul'torjo] *nm* information bureau; (*MED*) surgery.
consumar [konsu'mar] *vt* to complete, carry out; (*crimen*) to commit; (*matrimonio*) to consummate.
consumición [konsumi'θjon] *nf* consumption; (*bebida*) drink; (*en restaurante*) meal.
consumidor, a [konsumi'ðor, a] *nm/f* consumer.
consumir [konsu'mir] *vt* to consume; ~**se** *vr* to be consumed; (*persona*) to waste away.
consumo [kon'sumo] *nm*, **consunción** [konsun'θjon] *nf* consumption.
contabilidad [kontaβili'ðað] *nf* accounting, book-keeping; (*profesión*) accountancy.
contacto [kon'takto] *nm* contact.
contado, a [kon'taðo, a] *a*: ~**s** (*escasos*)

numbered, scarce, few // *nm*: **al** ~ for cash.
contador [konta'ðor] *nm* (*aparato*) meter; (*COM*) accountant; (*de café*) counter.
contagiar [konta'xjar] *vt* (*enfermedad*) to pass on, transmit; (*persona*) to infect; ~**se** *vr* to become infected.
contagio [kon'taxjo] *nm* infection.
contagioso, a [konta'xjoso, a] *a* infectious; (*fig*) catching.
contaminación [kontamina'θjon] *nf* contamination.
contaminar [kontami'nar] *vt* to contaminate.
contar [kon'tar] *vt* (*páginas, dinero*) to count; (*anécdota*) to tell // *vi* to count; ~ **con** to rely on, count on.
contemplación [kontempla'θjon] *nf* contemplation.
contemplar [kontem'plar] *vt* to contemplate; (*mirar*) to look at.
contemporáneo, a [kontempo'raneo, a] *a*, *nm/f* contemporary.
contender [konten'der] *vi* (*gen*) to contend; (*en un concurso*) to compete.
contener [konte'ner] *vt* to contain, hold; (*retener*) to hold back, contain.
contenido, a [konte'niðo, a] *a* (*moderado*) restrained; (*reprimido*) suppressed // *nm* contents *pl*, content.
contentar [konten'tar] *vt* (*satisfacer*) to satisfy; (*complacer*) to please; ~**se** *vr* to be satisfied.
contento, a [kon'tento, a] *a* contented, content; (*alegre*) pleased; (*feliz*) happy // *nm* contentment; (*felicidad*) happiness.
contestación [kontesta'θjon] *nf* answer, reply.
contestar [kontes'tar] *vt* to answer, reply; (*JUR*) to corroborate, confirm.
contigo [kon'tixo] *pron* with you.
contiguo, a [kon'tixwo, a] *a* (*de al lado*) next; (*vecino*) adjacent, adjoining.
continental [kontinen'tal] *a* continental.
continente [konti'nente] *a*, *nm* continent.
contingencia [kontin'xenθja] *nf* contingency; (*riesgo*) risk; **contingente** *a*, *nm* contingent.
continuación [kontinwa'θjon] *nf* continuation; **a** ~ then, next.
continuar [konti'nwar] *vt* to continue, go on with // *vi* to continue, go on.
continuidad [kontinwi'ðað] *nf* continuity.
continuo, a [kon'tinwo, a] *a* (*sin interrupción*) continuous; (*acción perseverante*) continual.
contorno [kon'torno] *nm* outline; (*GEO*) contour; ~**s** *nmpl* neighbourhood *sg*, environs.
contorsión [kontor'sjon] *nf* contortion.
contra ['kontra] *prep*, *ad* against // *nm* con.
contraataque [kontraa'take] *nm* counter-attack.
contrabajo [kontra'βaxo] *nm* double bass.

contrabandista [kontraßan'dista] *nm/f* smuggler.

contrabando [kontra'ßando] *nm* (*acción*) smuggling; (*mercancías*) contraband.

contracción [kontrak'θjon] *nf* contraction; (*encogimiento*) shrinkage.

contracepción [kontraθep'θjon] *nf* contraception.

contraceptivo [kontraθep'tißo] *nm* contraceptive.

contradecir [kontraðe'θir] *vt* to contradict.

contradicción [kontraðik'θjon] *nf* contradiction.

contradictorio, a [kontraðik'torjo, a] *a* contradictory.

contraer [kontra'er] *vt* to contract; (*encoger*) to shrink; (*limitar*) to restrict; ∼**se** *vr* to contract; to shrink; (*limitarse*) to limit o.s.

contragolpe [kontra'xolpe] *nm* backlash.

contrahacer [kontraa'θer] *vt* to copy, imitate; (*falsificar*) to forge.

contramaestre [kontrama'estre] *nm* foreman.

contrapelo [kontra'pelo]: **a** ∼ *ad* the wrong way.

contrapesar [kontrape'sar] *vt* to counterbalance; (*fig*) to offset.

contrariar [kontra'rjar] *vt* (*oponerse*) to oppose; (*poner obstáculo*) to impede; (*enfadar*) to vex.

contrariedad [kontrarje'ðað] *nf* (*oposición*) opposition; (*obstáculo*) obstacle, setback; (*disgusto*) vexation, annoyance.

contrario, a [kon'trarjo, a] *a* contrary; (*de persona*) opposed; (*sentido, lado*) opposite // *nm/f* enemy, adversary; (*DEPORTE*) opponent; **de lo** ∼ otherwise.

contrarrestar [kontrarres'tar] *vt* to counteract; (*pelota*) to return.

contrastar [kontras'tar] *vt* to resist // *vi* to contrast.

contraste [kon'traste] *nm* contrast.

contratante [kontra'tante] *nm/f* contractor.

contratar [kontra'tar] *vt* (*firmar un acuerdo para*) to contract for; (*empleados, obreros*) to hire, engage; ∼**se** *vr* to sign on.

contratiempo [kontra'tjempo] *nm* setback.

contratista [kontra'tista] *nm/f* contractor.

contrato [kon'trato] *nm* contract.

contravención [kontraßen'θjon] *nf* contravention, violation.

contravenir [kontraße'nir] *vi*: ∼ **a** to contravene, violate.

contraventana [kontraßen'tana] *nf* shutter.

contribución [kontrißu'θjon] *nf* (*municipal etc*) tax; (*ayuda*) contribution.

contribuir [kontrißu'ir] *vt, vi* (*COM*) to pay (in taxes).

contribuyente [kontrißu'jente] *nm/f* (*COM*) taxpayer; (*que ayuda*) contributor.

control [kon'trol] *nm* control; (*inspección*) inspection, check; ∼**ar** *vt* to control; to inspect, check.

controversia [kontro'ßersja] *nf* controversy.

convalecencia [konßale'θenθja] *nf* convalescence.

convalecer [konßale'θer] *vi* to convalesce, get better.

convaleciente [konßale'θjente] *a, nm/f* convalescent.

convencer [konßen'θer] *vt* to convince; (*persuadir*) to persuade.

convencimiento [konßenθi'mjento] *nm* convincing; (*persuasión*) persuasion; (*certidumbre*) conviction.

convención [konßen'θjon] *nf* convention.

convencional [konßenθjo'nal] *a* conventional.

convenido, a [konße'niðo, a] *a* agreed.

conveniencia [konße'njenθja] *nf* suitability; (*conformidad*) agreement; (*utilidad, provecho*) usefulness; ∼**s** *nfpl* conventions; (*COM*) property *sg*.

conveniente [konße'njente] *a* suitable; (*útil*) useful.

convenio [kon'ßenjo] *nm* agreement, treaty.

convenir [konße'nir] *vi* (*estar de acuerdo*) to agree; (*ser conveniente*) to suit, be suitable; ∼**se** *vr* to agree.

convento [kon'ßento] *nm* monastery; (*de monjas*) convent.

converger [konßer'xer], **convergir** [konßer'xir] *vi* to converge.

conversación [konßersa'θjon] *nf* conversation.

conversar [konßer'sar] *vi* to talk, converse.

conversión [konßer'sjon] *nf* conversion.

convertir [konßer'tir] *vt* to convert.

convicción [konßik'θjon] *nf* conviction.

convicto, a [kon'ßikto, a] *a* convicted, found guilty; (*condenado*) condemned.

convidado, a [konßi'ðaðo, a] *nm/f* guest.

convidar [konßi'ðar] *vt* to invite.

convincente [konßin'θente] *a* convincing.

convite [kon'ßite] *nm* invitation; (*banquete*) banquet.

convivencia [konßi'ßenθja] *nf* coexistence, living together.

convocar [konßo'kar] *vt* to summon, call (together).

convulsión [konßul'sjon] *nf* convulsion.

conyugal [konju'yal] *a* conjugal.

coñac [ko'nak] *nm* cognac, brandy.

cooperación [koopera'θjon] *nf* cooperation.

cooperar [koope'rar] *vi* to cooperate.

cooperativo, a [koopera'tißo, a] *a* cooperative // *nf* cooperative.

coordinación [koorðina'θjon] *nf* coordination.

coordinar [koorði'nar] *vt* to coordinate.

copa ['kopa] nf cup; (vaso) glass; (de árbol) top; (de sombrero) crown; ~s nfpl (NAIPES) ≈ hearts.

copia ['kopja] nf copy; **copiar** vt to copy.

copioso, a [ko'pjoso, a] a copious, plentiful.

copita [ko'pita] nf (small) glass; (GOLF) tee.

copla ['kopla] nf verse; (canción) (popular) song.

coqueta [ko'keta] a flirtatious, coquettish; **coquetear** vi to flirt.

coraje [ko'raxe] nm courage; (ánimo) spirit; (ira) anger.

coral [ko'ral] a choral // nf choir.

corazón [kora'θon] nm heart.

corazonada [koraθo'naða] nf impulse; (presentimiento) presentiment, hunch.

corbata [kor'ßata] nf tie.

corcovado, a [korko'ßaðo, a] a hunchbacked.

corchete [kor'tʃete] nm catch, clasp.

corcho [kor'tʃo] nm cork; (PESCA) float

cordel [kor'ðel] nm cord, line.

cordero [kor'ðero] nm lamb.

cordial [kor'ðjal] a cordial; ~idad nf warmth, cordiality.

cordillera [korði'ʎera] nf range, chain (of mountains).

Córdoba ['korðoßa] n Cordoba; **cordobés, esa** a or from Cordoba.

cordón [kor'ðon] nm (cuerda) cord, string; (de zapatos) lace; (policía) cordon.

corneta [kor'neta] nf bugle.

coro ['koro] nm chorus; (conjunto de cantores) choir.

corolario [koro'larjo] nm corollary.

corona [ko'rona] nf crown; (de flores) garland; ~ción nf coronation; **coronar** vt to crown.

coronel [koro'nel] nm colonel.

coronilla [koro'niʎa] nf crown (of the head).

corporación [korpora'θjon] nf corporation.

corporal [korpo'ral] a corporal.

corpulento, a [korpu'lento a] a (árbol) stout; (persona) well-built.

corral [ko'rral] nm farmyard; ~illo nm playpen.

correa [ko'rrea] nf strap; (cinturón) belt.

corrección [korrek'θjon] nf correction; (represión) rebuke; **correccional** nm reformatory.

correcto, a [ko'rrekto, a] a correct; (persona) well-mannered.

corredor, a [korre'ðor, a] a running; (rápido) fast // nm (COM) agent, broker; (pasillo) corridor, passage; (DEPORTE) runner.

corregir [korre'xir] vt (error) to correct; (amonestar, reprender) to rebuke, reprimand; ~se vr to reform.

correo [ko'rreo] nm post, mail; (persona) courier; (cartero) postman; **C~** Post Office; ~ aéreo airmail.

correr [ko'rrer] vt to run; (viajar) to cover, travel; (cortinas) to draw; (cerrojo) to shoot // vi to run; (líquido) to run, flow; (moneda) to pass, be valid; ~se vr to slide, move; (colores) to run.

correspondencia [korrespon'denθja] nf correspondence; (FERRO) connection.

corresponder [korrespon'der] vi to correspond; (convenir) to be suitable; (pertenecer) to belong; (tocar) to concern; ~se vr (por escrito) to correspond; (amarse) to have mutual affection.

correspondiente [korrespon'djente] a corresponding // nm correspondent.

corrido, a [ko'rriðo, a] a (avergonzado) abashed; (fluido) fluent // nf run, dash; (de toros) bullfight; **3 noches ~as** 3 nights running; **un kilo ~** a good kilo.

corriente [ko'rrjente] a (agua) running; (fig) flowing; (dinero etc) current; (común) ordinary, normal // nf current // nm current month.

corrillo [ko'rriʎo] nm huddle; (fig) clique.

corro ['korro] nm ring, circle (of people).

corroborar [korroßo'rar] vt to corroborate.

corroer [korro'er] vt to corrode; (GEO) to erode.

corromper [korrom'per] vt (madera) to rot; (alimento) to turn bad; (fig) to corrupt.

corrosivo, a [korro'sißo, a] a corrosive.

corrupción [korrup'θjon] nf rot, decay; (fig) corruption.

corsé [kor'se] nm corset.

cortado, a [kor'taðo, a] a (con cuchillo) cut; (leche) sour; (confuso) confused; (disconcertado) embarrassed; (estilo) abrupt // nm white coffee (with just a little milk).

cortador, a [korta'ðor, a] a cutting // nf cutter, slicer.

cortadura [korta'ðura] nf cut.

cortar [kor'tar] vt to cut; (el agua) to cut off; (un pasaje) to cut out // vi to cut; ~se vr (turbarse) to become embarrassed; (leche) to turn, curdle; ~se el pelo to have one's hair cut.

corte ['korte] nm cut, cutting; (filo) edge; (de tela) piece, length; **las C~s** the Spanish Parliament.

cortedad [korte'ðað] nf shortness; (fig) bashfulness, timidity.

cortejar [korte'xar] vt to court.

cortejo [kor'texo] nm entourage; ~ **fúnebre** funeral procession.

cortés [kor'tes] a courteous, polite.

cortesía [korte'sia] nf courtesy.

corteza [kor'teθa] nf (de árbol) bark; (de pan) crust.

cortina [kor'tina] nf curtain.

corto, a ['korto, a] a (breve) short; (tímido) bashful; (poco inteligente) not very clever; ~ **de vista** short-sighted; **estar ~ de fondos** to be short of funds.

corvo, a [kor'ßo, a] a curved.

cosa ['kosa] nf thing; (asunto) affair; ~ **de** about; **eso es ~ mía** that's my affair.

cosecha [ko'setʃa] *nf* (*AGR*) harvest; (*de vino*) vintage.

cosechar [kose'tʃar] *vt* to harvest, gather (in).

coser [ko'ser] *vt* to sew.

cosmético, a [kos'metiko, a] *a, nm* cosmetic.

cosquillas [kos'kiʎas] *nfpl*: **hacer ~** to tickle; **tener ~** to be ticklish.

cosquilloso, a [koski'ʎoso, a] *a* ticklish; (*fig*) touchy.

costa ['kosta] *nf* (*gasto*) cost; (*GEO*) coast.

costado [kos'taðo] *nm* side.

costal [kos'tal] *nm* sack.

costar [kos'tar] *vt* (*valer*) to cost; (*necesitar*) to require, need; **me cuesta hacer** I find it hard to do.

Costa Rica [kosta'rika] *nf* Costa Rica; **costarricense, costarriqueño** *a, nm/f* Costa Rican.

coste ['koste] *nm* = **costo**.

costilla [kos'tiʎa] *nf* rib; (*CULIN*) chop.

costo ['kosto] *nm* cost, price; **~ de la vida** cost of living; **~so, a** *a* costly, expensive.

costra ['kostra] *nf* crust; (*MED*) scab.

costumbre [kos'tumbre] *nf* custom, habit.

costura [kos'tura] *nf* sewing, needlework; (*de medias*) seam.

costurera [kostu'rera] *nf* dressmaker.

costurero [kostu'rero] *nm* sewing box *or* case.

cotejar [kote'xar] *vt* to compare.

cotejo [ko'texo] *nm* comparison.

cotidiano, a [koti'ðjano, a] *a* daily, day to day.

cotización [kotiθa'θjon] *nf* (*COM*) quotation, price; (*cuota*) dues *pl*.

cotizar [koti'θar] *vt* (*COM*) to quote, price; **~se** *vr*: **~se a** to sell at, fetch.

coto ['koto] *nm* (*terreno cercado*) enclosure; (*de caza*) reserve.

coyote [ko'jote] *nm* coyote, prairie wolf.

coyuntura [kojun'tura] *nf* (*ANAT*) joint; (*oportunidad*) opportunity.

cráneo ['kraneo] *nm* skull, cranium.

cráter ['krater] *nm* crater.

creación [krea'θjon] *nf* creation.

creador, a [krea'ðor, a] *a* creative // *nm/f* creator.

crear [kre'ar] *vt* to create, make.

crecer [kre'θer] *vi* (*niño*) to grow; (*precio*) to rise; (*días*) to get longer; (*mar*) to swell.

crecido, a [kre'θiðo, a] *a* (*persona, planta*) full-grown; (*cantidad*) large; (*fig*) conceited.

creciente [kre'θjente] *a* (*persona*) growing; (*cantidad*) increasing; (*luna*) crescent // *nm* crescent // *nf* flood.

crecimiento [kreθi'mjento] *nm* growth; (*aumento*) increase.

credenciales [kreðen'θjales] *nfpl* credentials.

crédito ['kreðito] *nm* credit.

credo ['kreðo] *nm* creed.

crédulo, a ['kreðulo, a] *a* credulous.

creencia [kre'enθja] *nf* belief.

creer [kre'er] *vt, vi* to think, believe; **~se** *vr* to believe o.s. (to be); **¡ya lo creo!** I should think so!

creíble [kre'iβle] *a* credible, believable.

crema ['krema] *nf* cream; (*de huevo*) custard.

cremallera [krema'ʎera] *nf* zip (fastener).

crepúsculo [kre'puskulo] *nm* twilight, dusk.

crespón [kres'pon] *nm* crêpe.

creta ['kreta] *nf* chalk.

creyente [kre'jente] *nm/f* believer.

creyó *etc vb ver* **creer.**

cría ['kria] *nf* (*de animales*) rearing, breeding; (*animal*) baby animal; (*niño*) child.

criadero [kria'ðero] *nm* nursery; (*ZOOL*) breeding place.

criado, a [kri'aðo, a] *a* bred, reared // *nm* servant // *nf* servant, maid; **mal/bien ~** badly/well brought up.

criador [kria'ðor] *nm* breeder.

crianza [kri'anθa] *nf* rearing, breeding; (*fig*) breeding.

criar [kri'ar] *vt* to suckle, feed; (*educar*) to bring up; (*producir*) to grow, produce; (*animales*) to breed.

criatura [kria'tura] *nf* creature; (*niño*) baby, (small) child.

criba ['kriβa] *nf* sieve; **cribar** *vt* to sieve.

crimen ['krimen] *nm* crime.

criminal [krimi'nal] *a, nm/f* criminal.

crin [krin] *nf* (*también* **~es** *nfpl*) mane.

crisis ['krisis] *nf inv* crisis.

crispar [kris'par] *vt* (*músculo*) to make contract; (*nervios*) to set on edge.

cristal [kris'tal] *nm* crystal; (*de ventana*) glass, pane; (*lente*) lens; **~ino, a** *a* crystalline; (*fig*) clear // *nm* lens of the eye; **~izar** *vt, vi* to crystallize.

cristiandad [kristjan'daŏ] *nf* Christianity.

cristianismo [kristja'nismo] *nm* Christianity.

cristiano, a [kris'tjano, a] *a, nm/f* Christian.

Cristo ['kristo] *nm* (*dios*) Christ; (*crucifijo*) crucifix.

criterio [kri'terjo] *nm* criterion; (*juicio*) judgement.

criticar [kriti'kar] *vt* to criticize.

crítico, a ['kritiko, a] *a* critical // *nm* critic // *nf* criticism.

cromo ['kromo] *nm* chrome.

crónico, a ['kroniko, a] *a* chronic // *nf* chronicle, account.

cronista [kro'nista] *nm/f* chronicler.

cruce ['kruθe] *nm* crossing; (*de carreteras*) crossroads.

crucificar [kruθifi'kar] *vt* to crucify.

crucifijo [kruθi'fixo] *nm* crucifix.

crucigrama [kruθi'ɤrama] *nm* crossword (puzzle).

crudo, a ['kruðo, a] *a* raw; (*no maduro*) unripe; (*petróleo*) crude; (*rudo, cruel*) cruel.

cruel [krwel] a cruel.
crueldad [krwel'ðað] nf cruelty.
crujido [kru'xiðo] nm creak.
crujir [kru'xir] vi (madera) to creak; (dedos) to crack; (dientes) to grind; (nieve, arena) to crunch.
cruz [kruθ] nf cross; (de moneda) tails sg.
cruzado, a [kru'θaðo, a] a crossed // nm crusader // nf crusade.
cruzar [kru'θar] vt to cross; ~se vr to cross; (personas) to pass each other.
cuaderno [kwa'ðerno] nm notebook; (de escuela) exercise book; (NAUT) logbook.
cuadra ['kwaðra] nf (caballeriza) stable; (gran sala) hall.
cuadrado, a [kwa'ðraðo, a] a square // nm (MAT) square; (regla) ruler.
cuadrar [kwa'ðrar] vt to square // vi: ~ con to square with, tally with; ~se vr (soldado) to stand to attention.
cuadrilla [kwa'ðriʎa] nf party, group.
cuadro ['kwaðro] nm square; (de vidrio) frame; (PINTURA) painting; (TEATRO) scene.
cuádruplo, a ['kwaðruplo, a], **cuádruple** ['kwaðruple] a quadruple.
cuajar [kwa'xar] vt to thicken; (leche) to curdle; (sangre) to congeal; (adornar) to adorn; ~se vr to curdle; to congeal; (llenarse) to fill up.
cual [kwal] ad like, as // pron: **el** ~ etc which; (persona: sujeto) who; (: objeto) whom // a such as; **cada** ~ each one; ~ **más,** ~ **menos** some more, some less; **tal** ~ just as it is.
cuál [kwal] pron interr which (one).
cualesquier(a) [kwales'kjer(a)] pl de cualquier(a).
cualidad [kwali'ðað] nf quality.
cualquiera [kwal'kjera], **cualquier** [kwal'kjer] a any // pron anybody, anyone; (quienquiera) whoever; **en cualquier parte** anywhere; ~ **que sea** whichever it is; (persona) whoever it is.
cuando ['kwando] ad when; (aún si) if, even if // conj (puesto que) since // prep: **yo,** ~ **niño...** when I was a child...; ~ **no sea así** even if it is not so; ~ **más** the more; ~ **menos** the less; ~ **no** if not, otherwise; **de** ~ **en** ~ from time to time.
cuándo ['kwando] ad when; ¿desde ~?, ¿de ~ acá? since when?
cuanto, a ['kwanto, a] a all that, as much as // pron all that (which), as much as; **llévate todo** ~ **quieras** take as much as you like; **en** ~ (en seguida que) as soon as; (ya que) since, inasmuch as; **en** ~ **profesor** as a teacher; **en** ~ **a** as for; ~ **más difícil sea** the more difficult it is; ~ **más hace** (tanto) **menos avanza** the more he does, the less he progresses; ~ **antes** as soon as possible; **unos** ~**s libros** a few books.
cuánto, a ['kwanto, a] a what a lot of; (interr: sg) how much?; (: pl) how many? // pron, ad how; (interr: sg) how much?; (: pl) how many?; ¡~**a gente!** what a lot of people!; ¿ ~ **cuesta?** how much does it

cost?; ¿**a** ~**s estamos?** what's the date?; **Señor no sé** ~**s** Mr. So-and-So.
cuarenta [kwa'renta] num forty.
cuarentena [kwaren'tena] nf quarantine.
cuartear [kwarte'ar] vt to quarter; (dividir) to divide up; ~**se** vr to crack, split.
cuartel [kwar'tel] nm (de ciudad) quarter, district; (MIL) barracks pl; ~ **general** headquarters pl.
cuarteto [kwar'teto] nm quartet.
cuarto, a ['kwarto, a] a fourth // nm (MAT) quarter, fourth; (habitación) room // nf (MAT) quarter, fourth; (palmo) span; ~ **de baño** bathroom; ~ **de hora** quarter (of an) hour.
cuatro ['kwatro] num four.
cuba ['kuβa] nf cask, barrel; (fig) drunkard.
Cuba ['kuβa] nf Cuba; **cubano, a** a, nm/f Cuban.
cúbico, a ['kuβiko, a] a cubic.
cubierto, a [ku'βjerto, a] pp de **cubrir** // a covered // nm cover; (en la mesa) place; ~**s** nmpl cutlery sg // nf cover, covering; (neumático) tyre; (NAUT) deck; **a** ~ **de** covered with or in.
cubo ['kuβo] nm cube; (de madera) bucket, tub; (TEC) drum.
cubrir [ku'βrir] vt to cover; ~**se** vr (cielo) to become overcast.
cucaracha [kuka'ratʃa] nf cockroach.
cuchara [ku'tʃara] nf spoon; (TEC) scoop; ~ **da** nf spoonful; ~**dita** nf teaspoonful.
cucharita [kutʃa'rita] nf teaspoon.
cucharón [kutʃa'ron] nm ladle.
cuchichear [kutʃitʃe'ar] vi to whisper.
cuchilla [ku'tʃiʎa] nf (large) knife; (de arma blanca) blade.
cuchillo [ku'tʃiʎo] nm knife.
cuello ['kweʎo] nm (ANAT) neck; (de vestido, camisa) collar.
cuenca ['kwenka] nf (escudilla) hollow; (ANAT) eye socket; (GEO) bowl, deep valley.
cuenta ['kwenta] nf (cálculo) count, counting; (en café, restaurante) bill; (COM) account; (de collar) bead; (fig) account; **a fin de** ~**s** in the end; **caer en la** ~ to catch on; **darse** ~ **de** to realize; **tener en** ~ to bear in mind; **echar** ~**s** to take stock; ~ **corriente/de ahorros** current/savings account.
cuento etc vb ver **contar** // ['kwento] nm story.
cuerdo, a ['kwerðo, a] a sane; (prudente) wise, sensible // nf rope; (hilo) string; (de reloj) spring; **dar** ~**a a un reloj** to wind up a clock.
cuerno ['kwerno] nm horn.
cuero ['kwero] nm (ZOOL) skin, hide; (TEC) leather; **en** ~**s** stark naked; ~ **cabelludo** scalp.
cuerpo ['kwerpo] nm body.
cuesta ['kwesta] nf slope; (en camino etc) hill; ~ **arriba/abajo** uphill/downhill; **a** ~**s** on one's back.
cuestión [kwes'tjon] nf matter, question,

issue; (*riña*) quarrel, dispute.
cuesto *etc vb ver* **costar**.
cueva ['kweßa] *nf* cave; (*bodega*) cellar.
cuidado [kwi'ðaðo] *nm* care, carefulness; (*preocupación*) care, worry; *excl* careful!, look out!
cuidadoso, a [kwiða'ðoso, a] *a* careful; (*preocupado*) anxious.
cuidar [kwi'ðar] *vt* (MED) to care for; (*ocuparse de*) to take care of, look after // *vi*: ~ **de** to take care of, look after; ~**se** *vr* to look after o.s.; ~**se de hacer algo** to take care not to do something.
culebra [ku'leßra] *nf* snake.
culebrear [kuleßre'ar] *vi* to wriggle along; (*río*) to meander.
culinario, a [kuli'narjo, a] *a* culinary, cooking *cpd*.
culminación [kulmina'θjon] *nf* culmination.
culo ['kulo] *nm* bottom, backside.
culpa ['kulpa] *nf* fault; (JUR) guilt; **tener la** ~ **(de)** to be to blame (for).
culpabilidad [kulpaßili'ðað] *nf* guilt.
culpable [kul'paßle] *a* guilty // *nm/f* culprit.
culpar [kul'par] *vt* to blame; (*acusar*) to accuse.
cultivador, a [kultißa'ðor, a] *nm/f* farmer // *nf* cultivator.
cultivar [kulti'ßar] *vt* to cultivate.
cultivo [kul'tißo] *nm* cultivation; (*plantas*) crop.
culto, a ['kulto, a] *a* (*cultivado*) cultivated; (*que tiene cultura*) cultured // *nm* (*homenaje*) worship; (*religión*) cult.
cultura [kul'tura] *nf* culture.
cumbre ['kumbre] *nf* summit, top.
cumpleaños [kumple'aɲos] *nm* birthday.
cumplido, a [kum'pliðo, a] *a* complete, perfect; (*abundante*) plentiful; (*cortés*) courteous // *nm* compliment; (*cortesía*) courtesy.
cumplimentar [kumplimen'tar] *vt* to congratulate.
cumplimiento [kumpli'mjento] *nm* (*de un deber*) fulfilment; (*acabamiento*) completion; (*cumplido*) compliment.
cumplir [kum'plir] *vt* (*orden*) to carry out, obey; (*promesa*) to carry out, fulfil; (*condena*) to serve; (*años*) to reach, attain // *vi*: ~ **con** (*deberes*) to carry out, fulfil; ~**se** *vr* (*plazo*) to expire.
cuna ['kuna] *nf* cradle, cot.
cuñado, a [ku'ɲaðo, a] *nm/f* brother/sister-in-law.
cuota ['kwota] *nf* (*parte proporcional*) share; (*cotización*) fee, dues *pl*.
cupe *etc vb ver* **caber**.
cura ['kura] *nf* (*curación*) cure; (*método curativo*) treatment // *nm* priest.
curación [kura'θjon] *nf* cure; (*acción*) curing.
curar [ku'rar] *vt* (*herida*) to treat, dress; (*enfermo*) to cure; (*carne, pescado*) to cure,

salt; (*cuero*) to tan // *vi*, ~**se** *vr* to get well, recover.
curiosear [kurjose'ar] *vt* to glance at, look over // *vi* to look round, wander round.
curiosidad [kurjosi'ðað] *nf* curiosity.
curioso, a [ku'rjoso, a] *a* curious // *nm/f* bystander, onlooker.
cursi ['kursi] *a* (*fam*) in bad taste, vulgar.
cursivo, a [kur'sißo, a] *a* italic // *nf* italics *pl*.
curso ['kurso] *nm* course; **en** ~ (*año*) current; (*proceso*) going on, under way.
curvo, a [ku'rßo, a] *a* (*gen*) curved; (*torcido*) bent // *nf* (*gen*) curve, bend.
custodia [kus'toðja] *nf* care, safekeeping, custody.
custodiar [kusto'ðjar] *vt* (*guardar*) to keep, take care of; (*vigilar*) to guard, watch over.
custodio [kus'toðjo] *nm* guardian, keeper.
cutis ['kutis] *nm* skin, complexion.
cuyo, a ['kujo, a] *pron* (*de quien*) whose, of whom; (*de que*) of which.

CH

chabacano, a [tʃaßa'kano, a] *a* vulgar, coarse.
chacal [tʃa'kal] *nm* jackal.
chacota [tʃa'kota] *nf* fun (and games).
chal [tʃal] *nm* shawl.
chalán [tʃa'lan] *nm* (*pey*) shady dealer.
chaleco [tʃa'leko] *nm* waistcoat, vest (US); ~ **salvavidas** life jacket.
chalupa [tʃa'lupa] *nf* launch, boat.
champán [tʃam'pan] *nm*, **champaña** [tʃam'paɲa] *nf* champagne.
champiñón [tʃampi'ɲon] *nm* mushroom.
champú [tʃam'pu] *nm* shampoo.
chamuscar [tʃamus'kar] *vt* to scorch, sear, singe.
chantaje [tʃan'taxe] *nm* blackmail.
chapa ['tʃapa] *nf* (*de metal*) plate, sheet; (*de madera*) board, panel.
chaparrón [tʃapa'rron] *nm* downpour, cloudburst.
chapotear [tʃapote'ar] *vt* to sponge down // *vi* (*fam*) to splash about.
chapucero, a [tʃapu'θero, a] *a* rough, crude // *nm/f* bungler.
chapurrar [tʃapu'rrar], **chapurrear** [tʃapurre'ar] *vt* (*idioma*) to speak badly; (*bebidas*) to mix.
chapuzar [tʃapu'θar] *vi* to duck.
chaqueta [tʃa'keta] *nf* jacket.
charca ['tʃarka] *nf* pond, pool.
charco ['tʃarko] *nm* pool, puddle.
charla ['tʃarla] *nf* talk, chat; (*conferencia*) lecture.
charlar [tʃar'lar] *vi* to talk, chat.
charlatán, ana [tʃarla'tan, ana] *nm/f* chatterbox; (*embaidor*) trickster; (*curandero*) charlatan.
charol [tʃa'rol] *nm* varnish; (*cuero*) patent leather.

chascarrillo [tʃaska'rriʎo] *nm* (*fam*) funny story.

chasco ['tʃasko] *nm* (*broma*) trick, joke; (*desengaño*) disappointment.

chasquear [tʃaske'ar] *vt* (*engañar*) to disappoint; (*bromear*) to play a trick on; (*látigo*) to crack; (*lengua*) to click.

chasquido [tʃas'kiðo] *nm* (*de lengua*) click; (*de látigo*) crack.

chato, a ['tʃato, a] *a* flat // *excl* hey handsome/beautiful!

chaval, a [tʃa'βal, a] *nm/f* lad/girl.

checo(e)slovaco, a [tʃeko(e)slo'βako, a] *a, nm/f* Czech, Czechoslovak.

Checo(e)slovaquia [tʃeko(e)slo'βakja] *nf* Czechoslovakia.

cheque ['tʃeke] *nm* cheque.

chequeo [tʃe'keo] *nm* (*MED*) check-up; (*AUTO*) service.

chequera [tʃe'kera] *nf* cheque-book.

chico, a ['tʃiko, a] *a* small, little // *nm/f* (*niño, niña*) child; (*muchacho, muchacha*) boy/girl.

chicharrón [tʃitʃa'rron] *nm* crackling.

chichón [tʃi'tʃon] *nm* bump, hump.

chiflado, a [tʃi'flaðo, a] *a* daft, barmy.

chiflar [tʃi'flar] *vt* to hiss, boo; ~se *vr*: ~se por to be/go crazy about.

chile ['tʃile] *nm* chilli, red pepper.

Chile ['tʃile] *nm* Chile; **chileno, a** *a, nm/f* Chilean.

chillar [tʃi'ʎar] *vi* (*persona*) to yell, scream; (*animal salvaje*) to howl; (*cerdo*) to squeal; (*puerta*) to creak.

chillido [tʃi'ʎiðo] *nm* (*de persona*) yell, scream; (*de animal*) howl; (*de frenos*) screech(ing).

chillón, ona [tʃi'ʎon, ona] *a* (*niño*) noisy; (*color*) loud, gaudy.

chimenea [tʃime'nea] *nf* chimney; (*hogar*) fireplace.

China ['tʃina] *nf*: la ~ China.

chinche ['tʃintʃe] *nf* bug; (*TEC*) drawing pin // *nm/f* nuisance, pest.

chino, a ['tʃino, a] *a, nm/f* Chinese // (*lengua*) Chinese.

Chipre ['tʃipre] *nf* Cyprus; **chipriota, chipriote** *a, nm/f* Cypriot.

chiquito, a [tʃi'kito, a] *a* very small, tiny // *nm/f* kid.

chirle ['tʃirle] *a* watery, wishy-washy.

chirriar [tʃi'rrjar] *vi* (*goznes*) to creak, squeak; (*pájaros*) to chirp, sing.

chirrido [tʃi'rriðo] *nm* creak(ing), squeak(ing); (*de pájaro*) chirp(ing).

chis [tʃis] *excl* sh!

chisme ['tʃisme] *nm* (*habladurías*) piece of gossip; (*fam: objeto*) thing, thingummyjig.

chismoso, a [tʃis'moso, a] *a* gossiping // *nm/f* gossip.

chispa ['tʃispa] *nf* spark; (*fig*) sparkle; (*ingenio*) wit; (*fam*) drunkenness.

chispeante [tʃispe'ante] *a* sparkling, scintillating.

chispear [tʃispe'ar] *vi* to spark; (*lloviznar*) to drizzle.

chisporrotear [tʃisporrote'ar] *vi* (*fuego*) to throw out sparks; (*leña*) to crackle; (*aceite*) to hiss, splutter.

chiste ['tʃiste] *nm* joke, funny story.

chistoso, a [tʃis'toso, a] *a* (*gracioso*) funny, amusing; (*bromista*) witty.

chivo, a ['tʃiβo, a] *nm/f* (billy-) nanny-)goat.

chocante [tʃo'kante] *a* startling; (*extraño*) odd; (*ofensivo*) shocking; (*antipático*) annoying.

chocar [tʃo'kar] *vi* (*coches, trenes*) to collide, crash // *vt* to shock; (*sorprender*) to startle; ~ con to collide with; (*fig*) to run into *or* up against; ¡chócala! put it there!

chocolate [tʃoko'late] *a, nm* chocolate.

chochear [tʃotʃe'ar] *vi* to dodder, be senile.

chocho, a ['tʃotʃo, a] *a* a doddering, senile; (*fig*) soft, doting.

chollo ['tʃoʎo] *nm* (*fam*) bargain, snip.

choque ['tʃoke] *nm* (*impacto*) impact; (*golpe*) jolt; (*AUTO*) crash; (*ELEC, MED*) shock; (*MIL*) clash; (*fig*) conflict.

chorizo [tʃo'riθo] *nm* hard pork sausage, salami.

chorrear [tʃorre'ar] *vi* to gush, spout (out); (*gotear*) to drip, trickle.

chorro ['tʃorro] *nm* jet; (*fig*) stream.

choza ['tʃoθa] *nf* hut, shack.

chuleta [tʃu'leta] *nf* chop, cutlet.

chulo ['tʃulo] *nm* (*pícaro*) rascal; (*fam: joven lindo*) dandy.

chupado, a [tʃu'paðo, a] *a* (*delgado*) skinny, gaunt; (*ajustado*) tight.

chupar [tʃu'par] *vt* to suck; (*absorber*) to absorb; ~se *vr* to grow thin.

churro [a ['tʃurro, a] *a* coarse // *nm* fritter.

chuscada [tʃus'kaða] *nf* funny remark, joke.

chusco, a ['tʃusko, a] *a* funny; (*persona*) coarse but amusing.

chusma ['tʃusma] *nf* rabble, mob.

D

D. *abr de* **Don.**

Da. *abr de* **Doña.**

dactilógrafo, a [dakti'loɣrafo, a] *nm/f* typist.

dádiva ['daðiβa] *nf* (*donación*) donation; (*regalo*) gift.

dado, a ['daðo, a] *pp de* **dar** // *nm* die; ~s *nmpl* dice; ~ que *conj* given that.

dador, a [da'ðor, a] *nm/f* (*gen*) giver.

dama ['dama] *nf* (*gen*) lady; (*AJEDREZ*) queen; ~s *nfpl* draughts.

damasco [da'masko] *nm* (*tela*) damask.

damnificar [damnifi'kar] *vt* (*gen*) to harm; (*persona*) to injure.

danés, esa [da'nes, esa] *a* Danish // *nm/f* Dane.

danzar [dan'θar] *vt, vi* to dance.

dañar [da'nar] *vt* (*objeto*) to damage;

(*persona*) to hurt; ~**se** *vr* to get hurt.
dañino, a [da'ɲino, a] *a* harmful.
daño ['daɲo] *nm* (*a un objeto*) damage; (*a una persona*) harm, injury; ~**s y perjuicios** (*JUR*) damages; **hacer** ~ **a** to damage; to harm, injure.
dar [dar] *vt* (*gen*) to give; (*TEATRO*) to perform, put on; (*película*) to show; (*intereses*) to yield; (*naipes*) to deal; (*la hora*): ~ **las 3** to strike 3 // *vi*: ~ **a** to look out on(to), overlook; ~ **con** (*persona etc*) to meet, run into; (*idea*) to hit on; ~ **contra** to knock against, bang into; ~ **de cabeza** to fall on one's head; ~ **en** (*objeto*) to strike, hit; (*broma*) to catch on to; ~ **de sí** to give, stretch; ~**se** *vr* (*pasar*) to happen; (*presentarse*) to occur; ~**se a** to be given to; ~**se por** to consider o.s.; **dárselas de** to pose as; ~ **de comer/beber a uno** to give sb sth to eat/drink; **da lo mismo** *o* **qué más da** it's all the same; ~ **en el blanco** to hit the mark; **me da pena** it saddens me; ~**se prisa** to hurry (up).
dardo ['darðo] *nm* dart.
dársena ['darsena] *nf* dock.
datar [da'tar] *vi*: ~ **de** to date from.
dátil ['datil] *nm* date.
dato ['dato] *nm* fact, piece of information.
d. de J. C. *abr de* **después de Jesucristo** A.D. (Anno Domini).
de [de] *prep* of; from; **libro** ~ **cocina** cookery book; **el hombre** ~ **largos cabellos** the man with long hair; **guantes** ~ **cuero** leather gloves; **fue a Londres** ~ **profesor** he went to London as a teacher; **una** ~ **dos** one or the other; ~ **mañana** in the morning; **vestido** ~ **negro** dressed in black; **más/menos** ~ more/less than; ~ **cabeza** on one's head; ~ **cara** a facing.
deambular [deambu'lar] *vi* to stroll, wander.
debajo [de'βaxo] *ad* underneath; ~ **de** below, under; **por** ~ **de** beneath.
debate [de'βate] *nm* debate; **debatir** *vt* to debate.
deber [de'βer] *nm* duty // *vt* to owe // *vi*: **debe (de)** it must, it should; **debo hacerlo** I must do it; **debe de ir** he should go; ~**se** *vr*: ~**se a** to be owing *or* due to.
debido, a [de'βiðo, a] *a* proper, just; ~ **a** due to, because of.
débil ['deβil] *a* (*persona, carácter*) weak; (*luz*) dim; **debilidad** *nf* weakness; dimness; **debilidad senil** senility.
debilitar [deβili'tar] *vt* to weaken; ~**se** *vr* to grow weak.
débito ['deβito] *nm* debit.
década ['dekaða] *nf* decade.
decadencia [deka'ðenθja] *nf* decadence.
decaer [deka'er] *vi* (*declinar*) to decline; (*debilitarse*) to weaken.
decaimiento [dekai'mjento] *nm* (*declinación*) decline; (*desaliento*) discouragement; (*MED*: *empeoramiento*) weakening; (: *estado débil*) weakness.

decano, a [de'kano, a] *nm/f* dean.
decapitar [dekapi'tar] *vt* to behead.
decena [de'θena] *nf*: **una** ~ ten (or so).
decencia [de'θenθja] *nf* (*modestia*) modesty; (*honestidad*) respectability.
decente [de'θente] *a* (*correcto*) seemly, proper; (*honesto*) respectable.
decepción [deθep'θjon] *nf* disappointment; **decepcionar** *vt* to disappoint.
decidir [deθi'ðir] *vt* (*persuadir*) to convince, persuade; (*resolver*) to decide // *vi* to decide; ~**se** *vr*: ~**se a** to make up one's mind to.
décimo, a ['deθimo, a] *a* tenth // *nm* tenth.
decir [de'θir] *vt* (*expresar*) to say; (*contar*) to tell; (*hablar*) to speak // *nm* saying; ~**se** *vr*: **se dice que** it is said that; ~ **para/entre sí** to say to o.s.; **querer** ~ to mean.
decisión [deθi'sjon] *nf* (*resolución*) decision; (*firmeza*) decisiveness.
decisivo, a [deθi'siβo, a] *a* decisive.
declamar [dekla'mar] *vt, vi* to declaim.
declaración [deklara'θjon] *nf* (*manifestación*) statement; (*explicación*) explanation; **declarar** *vt* to declare, state; to explain // *vi* to declare; (*JUR*) to testify; **declararse** *vr* to propose.
declinar [dekli'nar] *vt* (*gen*) to decline; (*JUR*) to reject // *vi* (*el día*) to draw to a close; (*salud*) to deteriorate.
declive [de'kliβe] *nm* (*cuesta*) slope; (*inclinación*) incline.
decolorarse [dekolo'rarse] *vr* to become discoloured.
decoración [dekora'θjon] *nf* decoration.
decorado [deko'raðo] *nm* scenery, set.
decorar [deko'rar] *vt* to decorate; **decorativo, a** *a* ornamental, decorative.
decoro [de'koro] *nm* (*respeto*) respect; (*dignidad*) decency; (*recato*) decorum, propriety; ~**so, a** *a* (*decente*) decent; (*modesto*) modest; (*digno*) proper.
decrecer [dekre'θer] *vi* to decrease, diminish.
decrépito, a [de'krepito, a] *a* decrepit.
decretar [dekre'tar] *vt* to decree; **decreto** *nm* decree.
dedal [de'ðal] *nm* thimble.
dedicación [deðika'θjon] *nf* dedication; **dedicar** *vt* (*libro*) to dedicate; (*tiempo, dinero*) to devote; (*palabras*: *decir, consagrar*) to dedicate, devote; **dedicatoria** *nf* (*de libro*) dedication.
dedo ['deðo] *nm* finger; ~ (**del pie**) toe; ~ **pulgar** thumb; ~ **índice** index finger; ~ **mayor** *o* **cordial** middle finger; ~ **anular** ring finger; ~ **meñique** little finger.
deducción [deðuk'θjon] *nf* deduction.
deducir [deðu'θir] *vt* (*concluir*) to deduce, infer; (*COM*) to deduct.
defecto [de'fekto] *nm* defect, flaw; (*ELEC*) fault; **defectuoso, a** *a* defective, faulty.
defender [defen'der] *vt* to defend.
defensa [de'fensa] *nf* defence; (*DEPORTE*)

back; **defensivo, a** a defensive // nf: **a la defensiva** on the defensive.

defensor, a [defen'sor, a] a defending // nm/f (abogado) defending counsel; (protector) protector.

deficiencia [defi'θjenθja] nf deficiency; **deficiente** a (defectuoso) defective; (imperfecto) deficient, wanting.

déficit ['defiθit] nm deficit.

definición [defini'θjon] nf definition.

definir [defi'nir] vt (determinar) to determine, establish; (decidir) to define; (aclarar) to clarify; **definitivo, a** a definitive; **en definitiva** definitively.

deformación [deforma'θjon] nf (alteración) deformation; (distorsión) distortion.

deformar [defor'mar] vt (gen) to deform; ~**se** vr to become deformed; **deforme** a (informe) deformed; (feo) ugly; (mal hecho) misshapen.

defraudar [defrau'ðar] vt (decepcionar) to disappoint; (estafar) to cheat, defraud; (engañar) to deceive.

defunción [defun'θjon] nf decease, demise.

degeneración [dexenera'θjon] nf (de las células) degeneration; (moral) degeneracy; **degenerar** vi to degenerate.

degollar [dexo'ʎar] vt (animal) to slaughter; (decapitar) to behead, decapitate.

degradar [dexra'ðar] vt to debase, degrade; ~**se** vr to demean o.s.

degüello [de'sweʎo] nm: **entrar a** ~ **de** to slaughter, put to the sword.

degustación [dexusta'θjon] nf sampling, tasting.

deidad [dei'ðað] nf deity, divinity.

deificar [deifi'kar] vt (persona) to deify.

dejación [dexa'θjon] nf (abandono) abandonment.

dejadez [dexa'ðeθ] nf (negligencia) neglect; (descuido) untidiness, carelessness; **dejado, a** a (negligente) careless; (indolente) lazy.

dejar [de'xar] vt (gen) to leave; (permitir) to allow, let; (abandonar) to abandon, forsake; (beneficios) to produce, yield // vi: ~ **de** (parar) to stop; (no hacer) to fail to; ~ **a un lado** to leave or set aside.

dejo ['dexo] nm (LING) accent; (sabor fuerte) tang; (sabor que queda) aftertaste.

del [del] = **de + el**, ver **de.**

delantal [delan'tal] nm apron.

delante [de'lante] ad in front; (enfrente) opposite; (adelante) ahead; ~ **de** in front of, before.

delantero, a [delan'tero, a] a front // nm (DEPORTE) forward // nf (de vestido, casa) front part; (DEPORTE) forward line; **llevar la** ~ **a** a uno to be ahead of sb.

delatar [dela'tar] vt to inform on or against, betray; **delator, a** nm/f informer.

delegación [delexa'θjon] nf delegation; (COM) office, branch; ~ **de policía** police station; ~ **municipal** local government

office; **delegado, a** nm/f delegate; (COM) agent; **delegar** vt to delegate.

deleitar [delei'tar] vt to delight; ~**se** vr: ~**se con** o **en** to delight in, take pleasure in; **deleite** nm delight, pleasure.

deletrear [deletre'ar] vi to spell (out); (fig) to interpret, decipher; **deletreo** nm spelling; interpretation, decipherment.

deleznable [deleθ'naβle] a inv (frágil) fragile; (resbaloso) slippery; (fugaz) fleeting.

delfín [del'fin] nm dolphin.

delgadez [delxa'ðeθ] nf thinness, slimness; **delgado, a** a (gen) thin; (persona) slim, thin; (tierra) poor; (tela etc) light, delicate.

deliberación [deliβera'θjon] nf deliberation; **deliberar** vt to debate, discuss.

delicadeza [delika'ðeθa] nf (gen) delicacy; (refinamiento) sutileza) refinement.

delicado, a [deli'kaðo, a] a (gen) delicate; (sensible) sensitive; (quisquilloso) touchy.

delicia [de'liθja] nf delight.

delicioso, a [deli'θjoso, a] a (gracioso) delightful, agreeable; (placentero) pleasant; (exquisito) delicious.

delincuencia [delin'kwenθja] nf delinquency; **delincuente** nm/f delinquent, criminal.

delinquir [delin'kir] vi to commit an offence.

delirante [deli'rante] a delirious; **delirar** vi to be delirious, rave.

delirio [de'lirjo] nm (MED) delirium; (palabras insensatas) wanderings pl, ravings pl.

delito [de'lito] nm (infracción) offence; (crimen) crime; ~ **político/común** political/common crime.

demagogo [dema'soxo] nm demagogue.

demanda [de'manda] nf (pedido, COM) demand; (petición) request; (JUR) action, lawsuit; **demandante** nm/f claimant.

demandar [deman'dar] vt (gen) to demand; (JUR) to sue.

demarcación [demarka'θjon] nf (de terreno) demarcation; **demarcar** vt to demarcate.

demás [de'mas] a: **los** ~ **niños** the other children, the remaining children // pron: **los/las** ~ the others, the rest (of them); **lo** ~ the rest (of it) // ad besides.

demasía [dema'sia] nf (exceso) excess, surplus; (atrevimiento) boldness; (insolencia) outrage; **comer en** ~ to eat to excess.

demasiado, a [dema'sjaðo, a] a too, too much; ~**s** too many // ad too, too much; **¡es** ~**!** it's too much!

demencia [de'menθja] nf (locura) madness; **demente** nm/f lunatic // a mad, insane.

democracia [demo'kraθja] nf democracy.

demócrata [de'mokrata] nm/f democrat; **democrático, a** a democratic.

demoler [demoʻler] *vt* to demolish; **demolición** *nf* demolition.

demonio [deʻmonjo] *nm* devil, demon; ¡~s! hell!, confound it!; ¿cómo ~s? how the hell?

demora [deʻmora] *nf* delay; **demorar** *vt* (*retardar*) to delay, hold back; (*dilatar*) to hold up // *vi* to linger, stay on.

demostración [demostraʻθjon] *nf* (*de teorema*) demonstration; (*de afecto*) show, display.

demostrar [demosʻtrar] *vt* (*probar*) to prove; (*mostrar*) to show; (*manifestar*) to demonstrate; **demostrativo, a** *a* demonstrative.

denegar [deneʻxar] *vt* (*rechazar*) to refuse; (*JUR*) to reject.

denigrar [deniʻxrar] *vt* (*desacreditar, infamar*) to denigrate; (*injuriar*) to insult.

denominación [denominaʻθjon] *nf* (*nombramiento*) designation; (*clase*) denomination.

denotar [denoʻtar] *vt* (*indicar*) to indicate; (*significar*) to denote.

densidad [densiʻðað] *nf* (*FISICA*) density; (*fig*) thickness.

denso, a [ʻdenso, a] *a* (*apretado*) solid; (*espeso, pastoso*) thick; (*fig*) heavy.

dentadura [dentaʻðura] *nf* (set of) teeth *pl*; ~ **postiza** false teeth *pl*.

dentera [denʻtera] *nf* (*sensación desagradable*) the shivers *pl*, the shudders *pl*; (*envidia*) envy, jealousy; (*deseo*) desire.

dentista [denʻtista] *nm/f* dentist.

dentro [ʻdentro] *ad* inside // *prep*: ~ **de** in, inside, within; **vayamos a** ~ let's go inside; **mirar por** ~ to look inside; ~ **de tres meses** within three months.

denuedo [deʻnweðo] *nm* boldness, daring.

denuncia [deʻnunθja] *nf* (*delación*) denunciation; (*acusación*) accusation; (*de accidente*) report; **denunciar** *vt* to report; (*delatar*) to inform on or against.

departamento [departaʻmento] *nm* (*sección administrativa*) department, section; (*de caja, tren*) compartment; (*AM: piso*) apartment, flat.

dependencia [depenʻdenθja] *nf* dependence; (*POL*) dependency; (*COM*) office, section.

depender [depenʻder] *vi*: ~ **de** to depend on.

dependienta [depenʻdjenta] *nf* saleswoman, shop assistant; **dependiente** a dependent // *nm* salesman.

deplorable [deploʻraβle] *a* deplorable; **deplorar** *vt* to deplore.

deponer [depoʻner] *vt* to lay down // *vi* (*JUR*) to give evidence; (*declarar*) to testify.

deportar [deporʻtar] *vt* to deport.

deporte [deʻporte] *nm* sport; **deportista** *a* sports *cpd* // *nm/f* sportsman/woman.

depositante [depositante], **depositador, a** [deposi taʻðor, a] *nm/f* depositor.

depositar [depositar] *vt* (*dinero*) to deposit; (*mercaderías*) to put away, store;

(*AM: persona*) to confide; ~**se** *vr* to settle; ~**io, a** *nm/f* trustee.

depósito [deʻposito] *nm* (*gen*) deposit; (*de mercaderías*) warehouse, store; (*de agua, gasolina etc*) tank; ~ **de equipajes** cloakroom.

depravar [depraʻβar] *vt* to deprave; ~**se** *vr* to become depraved.

depreciar [depreʻθjar] *vt* to depreciate, reduce the value of; ~**se** *vr* to depreciate, lose value.

depredación [depreðaʻθjon] *nf* (*saqueo, pillaje*) pillage; (*malversación*) depredation.

depresión [depreʻsjon] *nf* depression.

deprimido, a [depriʻmiðo, a] *a* depressed.

deprimir [depriʻmir] *vt* to depress; ~**se** *vr* (*persona*) to become depressed.

depuración [depuraʻθjon] *nf* purification; (*POL*) purge; **depurar** *vt* to purify; (*purgar*) to purge.

derecha [deʻretʃa] *nf* right(-hand) side; (*POL*) right.

derechamente [deretʃaʻmente] *ad* (*dirección*) straight.

derecho, a [deʻretʃo, a] *a* right, right-hand // *nm* (*privilegio*) right; (*lado*) right(-hand) side; (*leyes*) law // *ad* straight, directly; ~**s** *nmpl* (*de aduana*) duty *sg*; (*de autor*) royalties; **tener** ~ **a** to have a right to.

deriva [deʻriβa] *nf*: **ir** o **estar a la** ~ to drift, be adrift.

derivación [deriβaʻθjon] *nf* derivation.

derivar [deriʻβar] *vt* (*gen*) to derive; (*desviar*) to drift; ~**se** *vr* to derive, be derived; to drift.

derramamiento [derramaʻmjento] *nm* (*de sangre*) shedding; (*dispersión*) spilling.

derramar [derraʻmar] *vt* to spill; (*echar*) to pour out; (*dispersar*) to scatter; ~**se** *vr* to pour out; ~ **lágrimas** to weep.

derrame [deʻrrame] *nm* (*de líquido*) spilling; (*de sangre*) shedding; (*de tubo etc*) overflow; (*perdida*) loss, leakage; (*MED*) discharge; (*declive*) slope.

derredor [derreʻðor] *ad*: **al** o **en** ~ **de** around, about.

derretido, a [derreʻtiðo, a] *a* melted, molten.

derretir [derreʻtir] *vt* (*gen*) to melt; (*nieve*) to thaw; (*fig*) to squander; ~**se** *vr* to melt.

derribar [derriʻβar] *vt* to knock down; (*construcción*) to demolish; (*persona, gobierno, político*) to bring down; ~**se** *vr* to fall down.

derrocar [derroʻkar] *vt* (*despeñar*) to demolish, knock down; (*gobierno*) to bring down, overthrow.

derrochar [derroʻtʃar] *vt* to squander; **derroche** *nm* (*despilfarro*) waste, squandering.

derrota [deʻrrota] *nf* (*camino, vereda*) road, route; (*NAUT*) course; (*MIL*) defeat, rout; (*fig*) disaster; **derrotar** *vt* (*gen*) to defeat; (*destruir*) to ruin; **derrotero** *nm* (*rumbo*) course.

derrumbar [derrum'bar] *vt* to throw down; ~**se** *vr* (*despeñarse*) to collapse; (*precipitarse*) to throw o.s. down.

desabotonar [desaβoto'nar] *vt* to unbutton, undo // *vi* to open out; ~**se** *vr* to come undone.

desabrido, a [desa'βriðo, a] *a* (*insípido, soso*) insipid, tasteless; (*persona*) rude, surly; (*respuesta*) sharp.

desabrochar [desaβro'tʃar] *vt* (*botones, broches*) to undo, unfasten; (*fig*) to expose; ~**se** *vr* to confide, unburden o.s.

desacato [desa'kato] *nm* (*falta de respeto*) disrespect; (*irreverencia*) insulting behaviour; (*JUR*) contempt.

desacertado, a [desaθer'taðo, a] *a* (*equivocado*) mistaken; (*inoportuno*) unwise.

desacertar [desaθer'tar] *vi* (*errar*) to be mistaken; (*desatinar*) to act unwisely.

desacierto [desa'θjerto] *nm* mistake, error.

desacomodar [desakomo'ðar] *vt* (*molestar*) to put out, inconvenience; **desacomodo** *nm* (*incomodidad*) inconvenience; (*molestia*) trouble.

desaconsejado, a [desakonse'xaðo, a] *a* ill-advised; **desaconsejar** *vt* to dissuade, advise against.

desacordarse [desakor'ðarse] *vr* (*MUS*) to get out of tune; **desacorde** *a inv* discordant.

desacreditar [desakreði'tar] *vt* (*desprestigiar*) to discredit, bring into disrepute; (*denigrar*) to run down.

desacuerdo [desa'kwerðo] *nm* (*conflicto*) discord, disagreement; (*error*) error, blunder.

desafecto, a [desa'fekto, a] *a* (*opuesto*) disaffected // *nm* (*hostilidad*) disaffection.

desafiar [desa'fjar] *vt* (*retar*) to challenge; (*enfrentarse a*) to defy.

desafilar [desafi'lar] *vt* to blunt; ~**se** *vr* to become blunt.

desafinado, a [desafi'naðo] *a*: **estar** ~ to be out of tune; **desafinarse** *vr* (*MUS*) to go out of tune.

desafío [desa'fio] *nm* (*reto*) challenge; (*combate*) duel; (*resistencia*) defiance; (*competencia*) competition.

desafortunado, a [desafortu'naðo, a] *a* (*desgraciado*) unfortunate, unlucky.

desagradable [desaxra'ðaβle] *a* (*fastidioso, enojoso*) unpleasant; (*irritante*) disagreeable.

desagradar [desaxra'ðar] *vi* (*disgustar*) to displease; (*molestar*) to bother; **desagradecido, a** *a* ungrateful.

desagrado [desa'xraðo] *nm* (*disgusto*) displeasure; (*contrariedad*) dissatisfaction.

desagraviar [desaxra'βjar] *vt* to make amends for; **desagravio** *nm* (*recompensa*) amends; (: *en efectivo*) compensation.

desaguadero [desaxwa'ðero] *nm* drain.

desagüe [des'axwe] *nm* (*de un líquido*) drainage; (*cañería*) drainpipe.

desaguisado, a [desaxi'saðo, a] *a* illegal // *nm* outrage.

desahogado, a [desao'xaðo, a] *a* (*descarado*) brazen, impudent; (*holgado*) comfortable; (*espacioso*) roomy.

desahogar [desao'xar] *vt* (*consolar*) to console; (*aliviar*) to ease, relieve; (*ira*) to vent; ~**se** *vr* (*distenderse*) to take it easy; (*desfogarse*) to let off steam.

desahogo [desa'oxo] *nm* (*alivio*) relief; (*comodidad*) comfort, ease; (*descaro*) impudence.

desahuciar [desau'θjar] *vt* (*enfermo*) to give up hope for; (*inquilino*) to evict; **desahucio** *nm* eviction.

desairado, a [desai'raðo, a] *a* (*menospreciado*) disregarded; (*desgarbado*) shabby.

desairar [desai'rar] *vt* (*menospreciar*) to slight, snub; (*ultrajar*) to dishonour.

desaire [des'aire] *nm* (*afrenta*) rebuff; (*menosprecio*) slight; (*falta de garbo*) unattractiveness, lack of charm.

desajustar [desaxus'tar] *vt* (*desarreglar*) to disarrange; (*desconcertar*) to throw off balance; ~**se** *vr* to get out of order; (*cintura*) to loosen.

desajuste [desa'xuste] *nm* (*de máquina*) disorder; (*situación*) imbalance.

desalentador, a [desalenta'ðor, a] *a* disheartening; **desalentar** *vt* (*desanimar*) to discourage; **desalentar a uno** to make sb breathless.

desaliento [desa'ljento] *nm* discouragement.

desalinear [desaline'ar] *vt* to throw out of the straight; ~**se** *vr* to go off the straight.

desaliño [desa'liɲo] *nm* (*negligencia*) slovenliness.

desalmado, a [desal'maðo, a] *a* (*cruel*) cruel, heartless.

desalojamiento [desaloxa'mjento] *nm* ousting; (*cambio de residencia*) removal; (: *forzado*) eviction.

desalojar [desalo'xar] *vt* (*expulsar, echar*) to eject; (*abandonar*) to abandon, evacuate // *vi* to move out.

desamarrar [desama'rrar] *vt* to untie; (*NAUT*) to cast off.

desamor [desa'mor] *nm* (*frialdad*) indifference; (*odio*) dislike; (*enemistad*) enmity.

desamparado, a [desampa'raðo, a] *a* (*persona*) helpless; (*lugar: expuesto*) exposed; (*desierto*) deserted.

desamparar [desampa'rar] *vt* (*abandonar*) to desert, abandon; (*JUR*) to leave defenceless; (*barco*) to abandon.

desandar [desan'dar] *vt*: ~ **lo andado** *o* **el camino** to retrace one's steps.

desanimado, a [desani'maðo, a] *a* (*persona*) downhearted; (*espectáculo, fiesta*) dull; **desanimar** *vt* (*desalentar*) to discourage; (*deprimir*) to depress.

desapacible [desapa'θiβle] *a* (*gen*) unpleasant; (*carácter*) disagreeable; (*voz*) harsh.

desaparecer [desapare'θer] vt (gen) to hide // vi (gen) to disappear; (el sol, la luz) to vanish; **desaparición** nf disappearance.

desapego [desa'peɣo] nm (frialdad) coolness; (distancia) detachment.

desapercibido, a [desaperθi'βiðo, a] a (desprevenido) unprepared; **pasar** ~ **to** go unnoticed.

desaplicación [desaplika'θjon] nf (negligencia) slackness; (ocio) laziness; **desaplicado, a** a slack; lazy.

desaprensivo, a [desapren'siβo, a] a unscrupulous.

desaprobar [desapro'βar] vt (reprobar) to disapprove of; (condenar) to condemn; (no consentir) to reject.

desaprovechado, a [desaproβe'tʃaðo, a] a (improductivo) unproductive; (atrasado) backward; **desaprovechar** vt to waste.

desarmar [desar'mar] vt (MIL, fig) to disarm; (TEC) to take apart, dismantle; **desarme** nm disarmament.

desarraigar [desarrai'xar] vt to uproot; **desarraigo** nm uprooting.

desarreglado, a [desarre'xlaðo, a] a (TEC) out of order; (desordenado) disorderly, untidy.

desarreglar [desarre'xlar] vt (desordenar) to disarrange; (mecánica) to put out of order; (trastocar) to upset, disturb.

desarreglo [desa'rrexlo] nm (de casa, persona) untidiness; (desorden) disorder.

desarrollar [desarro'ʎar] vt (gen) to develop; (extender) to unfold; ~**se** vr to develop; (extenderse) to open (out); (film) to develop; **desarrollo** nm development.

desarticular [desartiku'lar] vt (hueso) to put out; (objeto) to take apart; (fig) to break up.

desaseo [desa'seo] nm (suciedad) slovenliness; (desarreglo) untidiness.

desasir [desa'sir] vt to loosen; ~**se** vr to extricate o.s.; ~**se de** to let go, give up.

desasosegar [desasose'xar] vt (inquietar) to disturb; (afligir) to make uneasy; ~**se** vr to become uneasy.

desasosiego [desaso'sjexo] nm (intranquilidad) uneasiness; (aflicción) restlessness; (ansiedad) anxiety.

desastrado, a [desas'traðo, a] a (desaliñado) shabby; (sucio) dirty; (desgraciado, adverso) wretched.

desastre [de'sastre] nm disaster; **desastroso, a** a disastrous.

desatado, a [desa'taðo, a] a (desligado) untied; (violento) violent, wild.

desatar [desa'tar] vt (nudo) to untie; (paquete) to undo; (separar) to detach; ~**se** vr (zapatos) to come untied; (tormenta) to break.

desatender [desaten'der] vt (no prestar atención a) to disregard; (abandonar) to neglect; (invitado) to slight.

desatento, a [desa'tento, a] a (distraído) inattentive; (descortés) discourteous.

desatinado, a [desati'naðo, a] a (disparatado) wild, reckless; (absurdo) foolish, silly; **desatinar** vi (desvariar) to behave foolishly; **desatino** nm (idiotez) foolishness, folly; (error) blunder.

desautorizado, a [desautori'θaðo, a] a unauthorized; **desautorizar** vt (oficial) to deprive of authority; (informe) to deny.

desavenencia [desaβe'nenθja] nf (desacuerdo) disagreement; (discrepancia) rift, quarrel.

desaventajado, a [desaβenta'xaðo, a] a (inferior) inferior; (poco ventajoso) disadvantageous.

desayunar [desaju'nar] vi to have breakfast // vt to have for breakfast; **desayuno** nm breakfast.

desazón [desa'θon] nf (insipidez) tastelessness; (angustia) anxiety; (fig) annoyance.

desazonar [desaθo'nar] vt to make tasteless; (fig) to annoy, upset; ~**se** vr (enojarse) to be annoyed; (preocuparse) to worry, be anxious; (MED) to be off colour.

desbandarse [desβan'darse] vr (MIL) to disband; (fig) to flee in disorder.

desbarajuste [desβara'xuste] nm confusion, disorder.

desbaratar [desβara'tar] vt (deshacer, destruir) to ruin; (malgastar) to squander; (mecánica) to take apart.

desbordar [desβor'ðar] vt (sobrepasar) to go beyond; (exceder) to exceed // vi, ~**se** vr (río) to overflow; (entusiasmo) to erupt; (persona) to express one's feelings freely.

descabalgar [deskaβal'xar] vi to dismount.

descabellado, a [deskaβe'ʎaðo, a] a (disparatado) wild, crazy; (insensato) ridiculous.

descabellar [deskaβe'ʎar] vt to ruffle; (TAUR: toro) to give the coup de grace to.

descabezar [deskaβe'θar] vt (persona) to behead; (árbol) to lop; ~**se** vr (AGR) to shed the grain; (fig) to rack one's brains.

descafeinado [deskafei'naðo] nm decaffeinated coffee.

descalabro [deska'laβro] nm blow; (desgracia) misfortune.

descalzar [deskal'θar] vt (zapato) to take off; **descalzo, a** a barefoot(ed); (fig) destitute.

descaminado, a [deskami'naðo, a] a (equivocado) on the wrong road; (fig) misguided.

descaminar [deskami'nar] vt (alguien) to misdirect; (: fig) to lead astray; ~**se** vr (en la ruta) to go the wrong way; (fig) to go astray.

descansado, a [deskan'saðo, a] a (gen) rested; (que tranquiliza) restful; **descansar** vt (gen) to rest // vi to rest, have a rest; (echarse) to lie down.

descanso [des'kanso] nm (reposo) rest; (alivio) relief; (pausa) break; (DEPORTE) interval, half time.

descarado, a [deska'raðo, a] a (sin

vergüenza) shameless; (*insolente*) cheeky;
descararse *vr* to be insolent *or* cheeky.

descarga [des'karɣa] *nf* (ARQ, ELEC, MIL)
discharge; (NAUT) unloading.

descargadero [deskarɣa'ðero] *nm* wharf.

descargar [deskar'ɣar] *vt* to unload;
(*golpe*) to let fly; ~ **se** *vr* to unburden o.s.;
descargo *nm* unloading; (COM) receipt;
(JUR) evidence.

descarnado, a [deskar'naðo, a] *a*
scrawny; (*fig*) bare.

descaro [des'karo] *nm* (*atrevimiento*)
shamelessness, nerve; (*insolencia*) cheek.

descarriar [deska'rrjar] *vt* (*descaminar*)
to misdirect; (*fig*) to lead astray; ~ **se** *vr*
(*perderse*) to lose one's way; (*separarse*) to
stray; (*pervertirse*) to err, go astray.

descarrilamiento [deskarrila'mjento]
nm (*de tren*) derailment.

descartar [deskar'tar] *vt* (*rechazar*) to
reject; (*poner a un lado*) to set aside;
(*eliminar*) to rule out; ~ **se** *vr* (NAIPES) to
discard; ~ **se de** to shirk; **descartado, a** *a*
rejected; set aside, eliminated.

descendencia [desθen'denθja] *nf* (*origen*)
origin, descent; (*hijos*) offspring.

descender [desθen'der] *vt* (*bajar:
escalera*) to go down; (: *equipajes*) to take
down // *vi* to descend; (*temperatura, nivel*)
to fall, drop; ~ **de** to be descended from.

descendiente [desθen'djente] *nm/f*
descendant.

descenso [des'θenso] *nm* descent; (*de
temperatura*) drop.

descifrar [desθi'frar] *vt* to decipher.

descolgar [deskol'ɣar] *vt* (*bajar*) to take
down; (*teléfono*) to pick up; ~ **se** *vr* to let
o.s. down.

descolorir [deskolo'rir], **descolorar**
[deskolo'rar] *vt* = **decolorar**.

descomedido, a [deskome'ðiðo, a] *a*
(*descortés*) rude; (*excesivo*) excessive.

descompaginar [deskompaxi'nar] *vt*
(*desordenar*) to disarrange, mess up.

descompasado, a [deskompa'saðo, a] *a*
(*sin proporción*) out of all proportion; (*excesivo*) excessive.

descomponer [deskompo'ner] *vt*
(*desordenar*) to disarrange, disturb; (TEC)
to put out of order; (*dividir*) to break down
(into parts); (*fig*) to provoke; ~ **se** *vr*
(*corromperse*) to rot, decompose; (*el
tiempo*) to change (for the worse); (TEC) to
break down; (*irritarse*) to lose one's
temper.

descomposición [deskomposi'θjon] *nf*
(*gen*) breakdown; (*de fruta etc*)
decomposition.

descompostura [deskompos'tura] *nf*
(TEC) breakdown; (*desorganización*)
disorganization; (*desorden*) untidiness.

descompuesto, a [deskom'pwesto, a] *a*
(*corrompido*) decomposed; (*roto*) broken;
(*descarado*) brazen; (*furioso*) angry.

desconcertado, a [deskonθer'taðo, a] *a*
disconcerted, bewildered.

desconcertar [deskonθer'tar] *vt*

(*confundir*) to baffle; (*incomodar*) to upset,
put out; (TEC) to put out of order; (ANAT) to
dislocate; ~ **se** *vr* (*turbarse*) to be upset.

desconcierto [deskon'θjerto] *nm* (*gen*)
disorder; (*daño*) damage; (*desorientación*)
uncertainty; (*inquietud*) uneasiness.

desconectar [deskonek'tar] *vt* to
disconnect.

desconfianza [deskon'fjanθa] *nf* distrust;
desconfiar *vi* to be distrustful;
desconfiar de to distrust, suspect.

desconocer [deskono'θer] *vt* (*alguien*) to
ignore; (*ignorar*) not to know, be ignorant
of; (*no recordar*) to fail to remember; (*no
aceptar*) to deny; (*repudiar*) to disown.

desconocimiento [deskonoθi'mjento] *nm*
(*falta de conocimientos*) ignorance;
(*repudio*) disregard; (*ingratitud*)
ingratitude.

desconsiderado, a [deskonsiðe'raðo, a] *a*
(*descuidado*) inconsiderate; (*insensible*)
thoughtless.

desconsolar [deskonso'lar] *vt* to distress;
~ **se** *vr* to despair.

desconsuelo [deskon'swelo] *nm* (*tristeza*)
distress; (*desesperación*) despair.

descontar [deskon'tar] *vt* (*deducir*) to
take away, deduct; (*rebajar*) to discount;
(*predecir, dar por cierto*) to take for
granted.

descontento, a [deskon'tento, a] *a*
dissatisfied // *nm* dissatisfaction,
discontent.

descorazonar [deskoraθo'nar] *vt* to
discourage, dishearten.

descorchar [deskor't[ar] *vt* to uncork.

descortés [deskor'tes] *a* (*mal educado*)
discourteous; (*grosero*) rude.

descoser [desko'ser] *vt* to unstitch; ~ **se**
vr to come apart (at the seams).

descosido, a [desko'siðo, a] *a* (*costura*)
unstitched; (*indiscreto*) indiscreet; (*desordenado*) disjointed.

descoyuntar [deskojun'tar] *vt* (ANAT) to
dislocate.

descrédito [des'kreðito] *nm* discredit.

descreído, a [deskre'iðo, a] *a* (*incrédulo*)
incredulous; (*falto de fe*) unbelieving.

describir [deskri'ßir] *vt* to describe.

descripción [deskrip'θjon] *nf* description.

descrito [des'krito] *pp de* **describir**.

descuajar [deskwa'xar] *vt* (*disolver*) to
melt; (*planta*) to pull out by the roots.

descubierto, a [desku'ßjerto, a] *pp de*
descubrir // *a* uncovered, bare; (*persona*)
bareheaded; **al ~** in the open.

descubrimiento [deskußri'mjento] *nm*
(*hallazgo*) discovery; (*revelación*)
revelation.

descubrir [desku'ßrir] *vt* to discover, find;
(*inaugurar*) to unveil; (*vislumbrar*) to
detect; (*revelar*) to reveal, show; (*quitar la
tapa*) to uncover; ~ **se** *vr* to reveal o.s.;
(*quitarse sombrero*) to take off one's hat;
(*confesar*) to confess.

descuento [des'kwento] *nm* discount; ~
jubilatorio retirement pension.

descuidado, a [deskwi'ðaðo, a] *a* (*sin cuidado*) careless; (*desordenado*) untidy; (*olvidadizo*) forgetful; (*dejado*) neglected; (*desprevenido*) unprepared.

descuidar [deskwi'ðar] *vt* (*dejar*) to neglect; (*olvidar*) to overlook // *vi*, ~**se** *vr* (*distraerse*) to be careless; (*estar desaliñado*) to let o.s. go; (*desprevenirse*) to drop one's guard; ¡**descuida!** don't worry!; **descuido** *nm* (*dejadez*) carelessness; (*olvido*) negligence.

desde ['desðe] *ad* from; ~ **que** *conj* since; ~ **lejos** from afar; ~ **ahora en adelante** from now onwards; ~ **hace 3 días** for 3 days now; ~ **luego** of course.

desdecirse [desðe'θirse] *vr* (*de promesa*) to go back on one's word.

desdén [des'ðen] *nm* scorn.

desdeñar [desðe'nar] *vt* (*despreciar*) to scorn.

desdicha [des'ðitʃa] *nf* (*desgracia*) misfortune; (*infelicidad*) unhappiness; **desdichado, a** *a* (*sin suerte*) unlucky; (*infeliz*) unhappy.

desdoblar [desðo'ßlar] *vt* (*extender*) to spread out; (*desplegar*) to unfold; (*separar en dos*) to split.

desear [dese'ar] *vt* to want, desire, wish for.

desecar [dese'kar] *vt*, ~**se** *vr* to dry up.

desechar [dese'tʃar] *vt* (*basura*) to throw out *or* away; (*ideas*) to reject, discard; **desechos** *nmpl* rubbish *sg*, waste *sg*.

desembalar [desemba'lar] *vt* to unpack.

desembarazado, a [desembara'θaðo, a] *a* (*libre*) clear, free; (*desenvuelto*) free and easy.

desembarazar [desembara'θar] *vt* (*desocupar*) to clear; (*desenredar*) to free; ~**se** *vr*: ~**se de** to free o.s. of, get rid of.

desembarcar [desembar'kar] *vt, vi*, ~**se** *vr* to land.

desembocadura [desemboka'ðura] *nf* (*de río*) mouth; (*de calle*) opening.

desembocar [desembo'kar] *vi* to flow into; (*fig*) to result in.

desembolso [desem'bolso] *nm* payment; ~**s** *nmpl* expenses; ~ **inicial** deposit, down payment.

desemejante [deseme'xante] *a* dissimilar, unlike; **desemejanza** *nf* dissimilarity.

desempeñar [desempe'nar] *vt* (*cargo*) to hold; (*papel*) to perform; (*lo empeñado*) to redeem; ~**se** *vr* to get out of debt; ~ **un papel** (*fig*) to play (a role).

desempeño [desem'peno] *nm* redeeming; (*de cargo*) occupation; (*TEATRO*, *fig*) performance.

desempleado, a [desemple'aðo, a] *nm/f* unemployed person; **desempleo** *nm* unemployment.

desencadenar [desenkaðe'nar] *vt* to unchain; (*ira*) to unleash; ~**se** *vr* to break loose; (*tormenta*) to burst.

desencajar [desenka'xar] *vt* (*hueso*) to put out of joint; (*mandíbula*) to dislocate;

(*mecanismo, pieza*) to disconnect, disengage.

desencanto [desen'kanto] *nm* disillusionment.

desenfadado, a [desenfa'ðaðo, a] *a* (*desenvuelto*) uninhibited; (*descarado*) forward; **desenfado** *nm* (*libertad*) freedom; (*comportamiento*) free and easy manner; (*descaro*) forwardness.

desenfrenado, a [desenfre'naðo, a] *a* (*descontrolado*) uncontrolled; (*inmoderado*) unbridled; **desenfreno** *nm* (*vicio*) wildness; (*de las pasiones*) lack of self-control.

desengañar [desenga'nar] *vt* to disillusion; ~**se** *vr* to become disillusioned; **desengaño** *nm* disillusionment; (*decepción*) disappointment.

desenlace [desen'laθe] *nm* outcome.

desenmarañar [desenmara'nar] *vt* (*desenredar*) to disentangle; (*fig*) to unravel.

desenredar [desenre'ðar] *vt* to resolve; (*intriga*) to unravel; ~**se** *vr* to extricate o.s.

desentenderse [desenten'derse] *vr*: ~ **de** to pretend to be ignorant about; (*apartarse*) to have nothing to do with.

desenterrar [desente'rrar] *vt* to exhume; (*tesoro, fig*) to unearth, dig up.

desentrañar [desentra'nar] *vt* to disembowel; (*misterio*) to unravel.

desentumecer [desentume'θer] *vt* (*pierna etc*) to stretch; (*DEPORTE*) to loosen up.

desenvoltura [desenßol'tura] *nf* (*libertad, gracia*) ease; (*descaro*) free and easy manner; (*desvergüenza*) forwardness.

desenvolver [desenßol'ßer] *vt* (*paquete*) to unwrap; (*madeja*) to disentangle; (*fig*) to develop; ~**se** *vr* (*desarrollarse*) to unfold, develop; (*arreglárselas*) to extricate o.s.

deseo [de'seo] *nm* desire, wish; ~**so, a** *a*: **estar** ~**so de** to be anxious to.

desequilibrado, a [desekili'ßraðo, a] *a* unbalanced.

desertar [deser'tar] *vi* to desert.

desesperación [desespera'θjon] *nf* (*impaciencia*) desperation, despair; (*irritación*) fury.

desesperar [desespe'rar] *vt* to drive to despair; (*exasperar*) to drive to distraction // *vi*: ~ **de** to despair of; ~**se** *vr* to despair, lose hope.

desestimar [desesti'mar] *vt* (*menospreciar*) to have a low opinion of; (*rechazar*) to reject.

desfachatez [desfatʃa'teθ] *nf* (*insolencia*) impudence; (*descaro*) cheek.

desfalco [des'falko] *nm* embezzlement.

desfallecer [desfaʎe'θer] *vi* (*perder las fuerzas*) to become weak; (*desvanecerse*) to faint.

desfavorable [desfaßo'raßle] *a* unfavourable.

desfigurar [desfiɣu'rar] vt (cara) to disfigure; (cuerpo) to deform.

desfilar [desfi'lar] vi to parade; **desfile** nm procession.

desgaire [des'ɣaire] nm (desaliño, desgano) slovenliness; (menosprecio) disdain.

desgajar [desɣa'xar] vt (arrancar) to tear off; (romper) to break off; ~**se** vr to come off.

desgana [des'ɣana] nf (falta de apetito) loss of appetite; (renuencia) unwillingness; **desganarse** vr to lose one's appetite; (cansarse) to become bored.

desgarrar [desɣa'rrar] vt to tear (up); (fig) to shatter; **desgarro** nm (muscular) tear; (aflicción) grief; (descaro) impudence.

desgastar [desɣas'tar] vt (deteriorar) to wear away or down; (estropear) to spoil; ~**se** vr to get worn out; **desgaste** nm wear (and tear); (MED) weakening, decline.

desgracia [des'ɣraθja] nf misfortune; (accidente) accident; (vergüenza) disgrace; (contratiempo) setback; **por** ~ unfortunately.

desgraciado, a [desɣra'θjaðo, a] a (infortunado) unlucky, unfortunate; (miserable) wretched; (infeliz) miserable; (feo) ugly; (desagradable) unpleasant.

desgreñado, a [desɣre'ɲaðo, a] a dishevelled.

deshacer [desa'θer] vt (casa) to break up; (dañar) to damage; (TEC) to take apart; (enemigo) to defeat; (diluir) to melt; (contrato) to break; (intriga) to solve; ~**se** vr (disolverse) to melt; (despedazarse) to come apart or undone; ~**se de** to get rid of; ~**se en lágrimas** to burst into tears.

deshecho, a [des'etʃo, a] a undone.

deshelar [dese'lar] vt (cañería) to thaw; (heladera) to defrost.

desheredar [desere'ðar] vt to disinherit.

deshielo [des'jelo] nm (de cañería) thaw; (de heladera) defrosting.

deshilar [desi'lar] vt (tela) to unravel.

deshonesto, a [deso'nesto, a] a indecent.

deshonra [des'onra] nf (deshonor) dishonour; (vergüenza) shame; **deshonrar** vt to dishonour; (insultar) to insult.

deshora [des'ora]: **a** ~ ad at the wrong time.

desierto, a [de'sjerto, a] a (casa, calle, negocio) deserted // nm desert.

designar [desiɣ'nar] vt (nombrar) to designate; (indicar) to fix.

designio [de'siɣnjo] nm (proyecto) plan; (destino) fate.

desigual [desi'ɣwal] a (terreno) uneven; (lucha etc) unequal.

desilusión [desilu'sjon] nf disappointment, disillusionment; **desilusionar** vt to disappoint; **desilusionarse** vr to become disillusioned.

desinfectar [desinfek'tar] vt to disinfect.

desinflar [desin'flar] vt to deflate.

desintegración [desinteɣra'θjon] nf disintegration.

desinterés [desinte'res] nm (objetividad) disinterestedness; (altruismo) unselfishness.

desistir [desis'tir] vi (renunciar) to stop, desist.

desleal [desle'al] a (infiel) disloyal; ~**tad** nf disloyalty.

deslenguado, a [deslen'gwaðo, a] a (grosero) foul-mouthed.

desligar [desli'ɣar] vt (desatar) to untie, undo; (separar) to separate; ~**se** vr (dos personas) to break up, separate; (de un compromiso) to extricate o.s.

desliz [des'liθ] nm (de coche) skid; (de persona) slip, slide; (fig) lapse; ~**ar** vt to slip, slide; ~**arse** vr (escurrirse: persona) to slip, slide; (coche) to skid; (aguas mansas) to flow gently; (error) to slip in.

deslucido, a [deslu'θiðo, a] a (gen) dull; (torpe) awkward, graceless; (marchitado) tarnished.

deslumbrar [deslum'brar] vt to dazzle.

desmán [des'man] nm (exceso) outrage; (abuso de poder) abuse.

desmandarse [desman'darse] vr (abusarse) to behave badly; (excederse) to get out of hand; (caballo) to bolt.

desmantelar [desmante'lar] vt (deshacer) to dismantle; (casa) to strip.

desmayado, a [desma'jaðo, a] a (sin sentido) unconscious; (carácter) dull; (débil) faint, weak.

desmayar [desma'jar] vi to lose heart; ~**se** vr (MED) to faint; **desmayo** nm (desvanecimiento) faint; (sin conciencia) unconsciousness; (depresión) dejection.

desmedido, a [desme'ðiðo, a] a excessive; **desmedirse** vr to go too far, forget o.s.

desmejorar [desmexo'rar] vt (dañar) to impair, spoil; (MED) to weaken.

desmembrar [desmem'brar] vt (MED) to dismember; (fig) to separate.

desmentir [desmen'tir] vt (contradecir) to contradict; (refutar) to deny // vi: ~ **de** to refute; ~**se** vr to contradict o.s.

desmenuzar [desmenu'θar] vt (deshacer) to crumble; (examinar) to examine closely.

desmerecer [desmere'θer] vt to be unworthy of // vi (deteriorarse) to deteriorate.

desmesurado, a [desmesu'raðo, a] a disproportionate.

desmontar [desmon'tar] vt (deshacer) to dismantle; (tierra) to level // vi to dismount.

desmoralizar [desmorali'θar] vt to demoralize.

desmoronar [desmoro'nar] vt to wear away, erode; ~**se** vr (edificio, dique) to fall into disrepair; (sociedad) to decay; (economía) to decline.

desnivel [desni'βel] nm (de terreno) unevenness; **paso a** ~ (AUTO) flyover.

desnudar [desnu'ðar] vt (desvestir) to

undress; (*despojar*) to strip; ~**se** *vr* (*desvestirse*) to get undressed; **desnudo, a** *a* naked // *nm/f* nude; **desnudo de** devoid or bereft of.

desobedecer [desoβeðe'θer] *vt, vi* to disobey; **desobediencia** *nf* disobedience.

desocupación [desokupa'θjon] *nf* (*ocio*) leisure; (*desempleo*) unemployment; **desocupado, a** *a* at leisure; unemployed; (*deshabitado*) empty, vacant; **desocupar** *vt* to vacate.

desodorante [desoðo'rante] *nm* deodorant.

desolación [desola'θjon] *nf* (*lugar*) desolation; (*fig*) grief; **desolar** *vt* to ruin, lay waste; **desolarse** *vr* to grieve.

desorden [des'orðen] *nm* confusion; (*político*) disorder.

desorganizar [desorɣani'θar] *vt* (*desordenar*) to disorganize; (*deshacer*) to disrupt.

desorientar [desorjen'tar] *vt* (*extraviar*) to mislead; (*confundir, desconcertar*) to confuse; ~**se** *vr* (*perderse*) to lose one's way.

despabilado, a [despaβi'laðo, a] *a* (*despierto*) wide-awake; (*fig*) alert, sharp.

despabilar [despaβi'lar] *vt* (*vela*) to snuff; (*el ingenio*) to sharpen; (*fortuna, negocio*) to squander // *vi*, ~**se** *vr* to wake up.

despacio [des'paθjo] *ad* slowly.

despachar [despa'tʃar] *vt* (*negocio*) to do, complete; (*enviar*) to send, dispatch; (*vender*) to sell, deal in; (*billete*) to issue; (*mandar ir*) to send away.

despacho [des'patʃo] *nm* (*oficina*) office; (*de paquetes*) dispatch; (*venta*) sale; (*comunicación*) message; (*eficacia*) efficiency; (*rapidez*) promptness.

desparramar [desparra'mar] *vt* (*esparcir*) to scatter; (*noticia*) to spread; (*dinero, fortuna*) to squander; (*líquido*) to spill.

despavorido, a [despaβo'riðo, a] *a* terrified.

despectivo, a [despek'tiβo, a] *a* (*despreciativo*) derogatory; (*LING*) pejorative.

despecho [des'petʃo] *nm* spite; a ~ **de** in spite of.

despedazar [despeða'θar] *vt* to tear to pieces.

despedida [despe'ðiða] *nf* (*adios*) farewell; (*de obrero*) sacking.

despedir [despe'ðir] *vt* (*visita*) to see off, show out; (*licenciar: empleado*) to discharge; (*inquilino*) to evict; (*objeto*) to hurl; (*flecha*) to fire; (*olor etc*) to give out or off; ~**se** *vr*: ~**se de** to say goodbye to.

despegar [despe'ɣar] *vt* to unstick // *vi* to take off; ~**se** *vr* to come loose, come unstuck; **despego** *nm* detachment.

despegue [des'peɣe] *nm* takeoff.

despeinado, a [despei'naðo, a] *a* dishevelled, unkempt.

despejado, a [despe'xaðo, a] *a* (*lugar*) clear, free; (*cielo*) cloudless, clear; (*persona*) wide-awake.

despejar [despe'xar] *vt* (*gen*) to clear; (*misterio*) to clarify, clear up // *vi* (*el tiempo*) to clear; ~**se** *vr* (*tiempo, cielo*) to clear (up); (*misterio*) to become clearer; (*persona*) to relax.

despejo [des'pexo] *nm* (*de casa, calle etc*) brightness; (*desenvoltura*) self-confidence; (*talento, ingenio*) alertness.

despensa [des'pensa] *nf* larder.

despeñadero [despeɲa'ðero] *nm* (*GEO*) cliff, precipice.

desperdicio [desper'ðiθjo] *nm* (*despilfarro*) squandering; (*residuo*) waste.

desperezarse [despere'θarse] *vr* to stretch (o.s.).

desperfecto [desper'fekto] *nm* (*deterioro*) slight damage; (*defecto*) flaw, imperfection.

despertador [desperta'ðor] *nm* alarm clock.

despertar [desper'tar] *vt* (*persona*) to wake up; (*vocación*) to awaken; (*recuerdos*) to revive; (*apetito*) to arouse // *vi*, ~**se** *vr* to awaken, wake up // *nm* awakening.

despido [des'piðo] *nm* dismissal, sacking.

despierto *etc vb ver* **despertar**.

despierto, a [des'pjerto, a] *a* awake; (*fig*) sharp, alert.

despilfarro [despil'farro] *nm* (*derroche*) squandering; (*lujo desmedido*) extravagance.

despistar [despis'tar] *vt* to throw off the track or scent; (*fig*) to mislead, confuse; ~**se** *vr* to take the wrong road; (*fig*) to become confused.

desplazamiento [desplaθa'mjento] *nm* displacement; ~ **de tierras** landslip.

desplegar [desple'ɣar] *vt* (*tela, papel*) to unfold, open out; (*bandera*) to unfurl.

despoblar [despo'βlar] *vt* (*de gente*) to depopulate.

despojar [despo'xar] *vt* (*alguien: de sus bienes*) to divest of, deprive of; (*casa*) to strip, leave bare; (*alguien: de su cargo*) to strip of; **despojo** *nm* (*acto*) plundering; (*objetos*) plunder, loot; **despojos** *nmpl* waste *sg*; (*rocas, ladrillos*) debris *sg*.

desposado, a [despo'saðo, a] *a, nm/f* newly-wed.

desposeer [despose'er] *vt* (*despojar*) to dispossess.

déspota ['despota] *nm* despot.

despreciar [despre'θjar] *vt* (*desdeñar*) to despise, scorn; (*afrentar*) to slight; **desprecio** *nm* scorn, contempt; slight.

desprender [despren'der] *vt* (*separar*) to separate; (*desatar*) to unfasten; (*olor*) to give off; ~**se** *vr* (*botón: caerse*) to fall off; (: *abrirse*) to unfasten; (*olor, perfume*) to be given off; ~**se de** to follow from; **se desprende que** it transpires that.

desprendimiento [desprendi'mjento] *nm* (*gen*) loosening; (*de botón que se cae*) detachment; (*de botón que se abre*) unfastening; *(generosidad)* disinterestedness; *(indiferencia)* detachment; *(de gas)* release; *(de tierra, rocas)* landslide.

despreocupado, a [despreoku'paðo, a] *a (sin preocupación)* unworried, nonchalant; *(desprejuiciado)* impartial; *(negligente)* careless; **despreocuparse** *vr* to be carefree; **despreocuparse de** to have no interest in.

desprevenido, a [despreße'niðo, a] *a (no preparado)* unprepared, unready.

desproporción [despropor'θjon] *nf* disproportion, lack of proportion.

después [des'pwes] *ad* afterwards, later; *(próximo paso)* next; ~ **de comer** after lunch; **un año** ~ a year later; ~ **se debatió el tema** next the matter was discussed; ~ **de corregido el texto** after the text had been corrected; ~ **de todo** after all.

desquite [des'kite] *nm (satisfacción)* satisfaction; *(venganza)* revenge.

destacar [desta'kar] *vt* to emphasize, point up; *(MIL)* to detach, detail // *vi*, ~ **se** *vr (resaltarse)* to stand out; *(persona)* to be outstanding or exceptional.

destajo [des'taxo] *nm*: **trabajar a** ~ to do piecework.

destapar [desta'par] *vt (gen)* to open; *(cacerola)* to take the lid off, uncover; ~ **se** *vr (revelarse)* to reveal one's true character.

destartalado, a [destarta'laðo, a] *a (desordenado)* untidy; *(ruinoso)* tumbledown.

destello [des'teʎo] *nm (de estrella)* twinkle; *(de faro)* signal light.

destemplado, a [destem'plaðo, a] *a (MUS)* out of tune; *(voz)* harsh; *(MED)* out of sorts, indisposed.

desteñir [deste'ɲir] *vt* to fade // *vi*, ~ **se** *vr (color)* to fade; **esta tela no destiñe** this fabric will not run.

desterrar [deste'rrar] *vt (exilar)* to exile; *(fig)* to banish, dismiss.

destierro [des'tjerro] *nm* exile.

destilación [destila'θjon] *nf* distillation; **destilar** *vt* to distil; **destilería** *nf* distillery.

destinar [desti'nar] *vt* to destine; *(funcionario)* to appoint, assign; *(fondos)* to set aside (a for); ~ **se** *vr* to be destined.

destinatario, a [destina'tarjo, a] *nm/f* addressee.

destino [des'tino] *nm (suerte)* destiny; *(de viajero)* destination; *(función)* use.

destituir [destitu'ir] *vt* to dismiss.

destornillador [destorniʎa'ðor] *nm* screwdriver; **destornillar** *vt*, **destornillarse** *vr (tornillo)* to unscrew.

destreza [des'treθa] *nf (habilidad)* skill; *(maña)* dexterity; *(facilidad)* handiness.

destrozar [destro'θar] *vt (romper)* to smash, break (up); *(estropear)* to ruin; *(deshacer)* to shatter; *(el corazón)* to break.

destrozo [des'troθo] *nm (acción)*

destruction; *(desastre)* smashing; ~ **s** *nmpl (pedazos)* pieces; *(daños)* havoc *sg*.

destrucción [destruk'θjon] *nf* destruction.

destruir [destru'ir] *vt* to destroy.

desunir [desu'nir] *vt* to separate; *(TEC)* to disconnect; *(fig)* to cause a quarrel or rift between.

desusado, a [desu'saðo, a] *a (anticuado)* obsolete.

desvalido, a [desßa'liðo, a] *a (desprotegido)* destitute; *(POL)* underprivileged; *(sin fuerzas)* helpless.

desván [des'ßan] *nm* attic.

desvanecer [desßane'θer] *vt (disipar)* to dispel; *(borrar)* to blur; ~ **se** *vr (humo)* to vanish, disappear; *(color)* to fade; *(recuerdo)* to fade away.

desvanecimiento [desßaneθi'mjento] *nm (desaparición)* disappearance; *(de colores)* fading; *(evaporación)* evaporation; *(MED)* fainting fit.

desvariar [desßa'rjar] *vi (enfermo)* to be delirious; **desvarío** *nm* delirium.

desvelar [desße'lar] *vt* to keep awake; ~ **se** *vr* to stay awake; *(ser vigilante or watchful)* **desvelo** *nm* lack of sleep; *(insomnio)* sleeplessness; *(fig)* vigilance.

desventaja [desßen'taxa] *nf* disadvantage.

desventura [desßen'tura] *nf* misfortune.

desvergonzado, a [desßerxon'θaðo, a] *a* shameless.

desvergüenza [desßer'xwenθa] *nf (descaro)* shamelessness; *(insolencia)* impudence; *(mala conducta)* effrontery.

desviación [desßja'θjon] *nf* deviation.

desviar [des'ßjar] *vt* to turn aside; *(río)* to alter the course of; *(navío)* to divert, re-route; *(conversación)* to sidetrack; ~ **se** *vr (apartarse del camino)* to turn aside, deviate; (: *barco)* to go off course.

desvío [des'ßio] *nm (desviación)* detour, diversion; *(fig)* indifference.

desvirtuar [desßir'twar] *vt*, ~ **se** *vr* to spoil.

desvivirse [desßi'ßirse] *vr*: ~ **por** to long for, crave for.

detallar [deta'ʎar] *vt* to detail; *(COM)* to sell retail.

detalle [de'taʎe] *nm* detail; *(fig)* gesture, token; **al** ~ in detail.

detallista [deta'ʎista] *nm/f* retailer.

detener [dete'ner] *vt (tren, persona)* to stop; *(JUR)* to arrest; *(objeto)* to keep; ~ **se** *vr* to stop; *(demorarse)* ~ **se en** to delay over, linger over.

detenido, a [dete'niðo, a] *a (preso)* arrested, under arrest; *(minucioso)* detailed; *(tímido)* timid // *nm/f* person under arrest, prisoner.

detergente [deter'xente] *nm* detergent.

deteriorar [deterjo'rar] *vt* to spoil, damage; ~ **se** *vr* to deteriorate; *(relaciones)* to become damaged; **deterioro** *nm* deterioration.

determinación [determina'θjon] *nf (empeño)* determination; *(decisión)* decision; **determinar** *vt* (*plazo*) to fix; (*precio*) to settle; **determinarse** *vr* to decide.

detestar [detes'tar] *vt* to detest.

detonar [deto'nar] *vi* to detonate.

detrás [de'tras] *ad* behind; (*atrás*) at the back; ~ **de** behind.

detrimento [detri'mento] *nm* harm, damage; **en** ~ **de** to the detriment of.

deuda ['deuða] *nf* (*condición*) indebtedness, debt; (*cantidad*) debt.

deudor, a [deu'ðor, a] *a*: **saldo** ~ debit balance // *nm/f* debtor.

devaluación [deβalwa'θjon] *nf* devaluation.

devastar [deβas'tar] *vt* (*destruir*) to devastate.

devoción [deβo'θjon] *nf* devotion.

devolución [deβolu'θjon] *nf* devolution; (*reenvío*) return, sending back; (*reembolso*) repayment.

devolver [deβol'βer] *vt* (*gen*) to return; (*carta al correo*) to send back; (*com*) to repay, refund; (*visita, la palabra*) to return.

devorar [deβo'rar] *vt* to devour.

devoto, a [de'βoto, a] *a* devout // *nm/f* admirer.

di *vb ver* **dar; decir.**

día ['dia] *nm* day; ¿**qué** ~ **es?** what's the date?; **estar/poner al** ~ to be/keep up to date; **el** ~ **de hoy/de mañana** today/tomorrow; **al** ~ **siguiente** the following day; **vivir al** ~ to live from hand to mouth; **de** ~ by day, in daylight; **en pleno** ~ in full daylight.

diablo ['djaβlo] *nm* devil; **diablura** *nf* prank; **diabluras** *nfpl* mischief *sg.*

diabólico, a [dja'βoliko, a] *a* diabolical.

diafragma [dja'fraxma] *nm* diaphragm.

diagnosis [djax'nosis] *nf*, **diagnóstico** [djax'nostiko] *nm* diagnosis.

dialecto [dja'lekto] *nm* dialect.

diálogo ['djaloxo] *nm* dialogue.

diamante [dja'mante] *nm* diamond.

diapositiva [djaposi'tiβa] *nf* (*FOTO*) slide, transparency.

diario, a ['djarjo, a] *a* daily // *nm* newspaper.

diarrea [dja'rrea] *nf* diarrhoea.

dibujar [diβu'xar] *vt* to draw, sketch; **dibujo** *nm* drawing; **dibujos animados** cartoons.

diccionario [dikθjo'narjo] *nm* dictionary.

dice *etc vb ver* **decir.**

diciembre [di'θjembre] *nm* December.

dictado [dik'taðo] *nm* dictation.

dictador [dikta'ðor] *nm* dictator; **dictadura** *nf* dictatorship.

dictamen [dik'tamen] *nm* (*opinión*) opinion; (*juicio*) judgment.

dicho, a ['ditʃo, a] *pp de* **decir** // *a*: **en** ~**s países** in the aforementioned countries // *nm* saying // *nf* happiness.

diente ['djente] *nm* (*ANAT, TEC*) tooth; (*ZOOL*) fang; (: *de elefante*) tusk; (*de ajo*) clove; **da** ~ **con** ~ his teeth are chattering; **hablar entre** ~**s** to mutter, mumble.

dieron *vb ver* **dar.**

diesel ['disel] *a*: **motor** ~ diesel engine.

dieta ['djeta] *nf* diet.

diez [djeθ] *num* ten.

diferencia [dife'renθja] *nf* difference; **diferenciar** *vt* to differentiate between // *vi* to differ; **diferenciarse** *vr* to differ, be different; (*distinguirse*) to distinguish o.s.

diferente [dife'rente] *a* different.

difícil [di'fiθil] *a* difficult.

dificultad [difikul'taθ] *nf* difficulty; (*problema*) trouble.

dificultar [difikul'tar] *vt* (*complicar*) to complicate, make difficult; (*estorbar*) to obstruct.

difundir [difun'dir] *vt* (*esparcir*) to spread, diffuse; (*divulgar*) to divulge; ~**se** *vr* to spread (out).

difunto, a [di'funto, a] *a* dead, deceased // *nm/f* deceased (person).

digerir [dixe'rir] *vt* to digest; (*fig*) to absorb.

digital [dixi'tal] *a* digital.

dignarse [dix'narse] *vr* to deign to.

dignidad [dixni'ðað] *nf* dignity; (*honra*) honour.

digno, a ['dixno, a] *a* worthy.

digo *etc vb ver* **decir.**

dije *etc vb ver* **decir.**

dilatación [dilata'θjon] *nf* (*expansión*) dilation.

dilatado, a [dila'taðo, a] *a* dilated; (*ancho*) widened; (*largo*) long drawn-out; (*extenso*) extensive.

dilatar [dila'tar] *vt* (*cuerpo*) to dilate; (*prolongar*) to stretch; (*en el tiempo*) to prolong.

dilema [di'lema] *nm* dilemma.

diligencia [dili'xenθja] *nf* diligence; (*ocupación*) errand, job; ~**s** *nfpl* (*JUR*) formalities; **diligente** *a* diligent.

diluir [dilu'ir] *vt* to dilute.

diluvio [di'luβjo] *nm* deluge, flood.

dimensión [dimen'sjon] *nf* dimension.

diminuto, a [dimi'nuto, a] *a* tiny.

dimitir [dimi'tir] *vi* to resign.

dimos *vb ver* **dar.**

Dinamarca [dina'marka] *nf* Denmark; **dinamarqués, esa** *a* Danish // *nm/f* Dane.

dinámico, a [di'namiko, a] *a* dynamic.

dinamita [dina'mita] *nf* dynamite.

dínamo ['dinamo] *nf* dynamo.

dineral [dine'ral] *nm* large sum of money, fortune.

dinero [di'nero] *nm* money; ~ **efectivo** cash, ready cash.

dio *vb ver* **dar.**

dios [djos] *nm* god.

diosa ['djosa] *nf* goddess.

diplomacia [diplo'maθja] *nf* diplomacy; (*fig*) tact; **diplomático, a** *a* diplomatic // *nm/f* diplomat.

diputado, a [dipu'taðo, a] *nm/f* delegate; (*Cortes*) deputy.

diré *etc vb ver* **decir.**

dirección [direk'θjon] *nf* direction; (*señas*) address; (AUTO) steering; (*gerencia*) management; (POL) leadership; ~ **única** *o* **obligatoria** *o* **prohibida** one-way.

directo, a [di'rekto, a] *a* direct; **transmitir en** ~ to broadcast live.

director, a [direk'tor, a] *a* leading // *nm/f* director; ~ **de cine/de escena** producer/stage manager.

dirigir [diri'xir] *vt* to direct; (*carta*) to address; (*obra de teatro, film*) to produce, direct; (*coche, barco*) to steer; (*avión*) to fly; (MUS) to conduct; (*comercio*) to manage; ~**se a** *vr*: ~**se a** to go towards, make one's way towards; (*fig*) to speak to.

discernir [disθer'nir] *vt* (*distinguir, discriminar*) to discern.

disciplina [disθi'plina] *nf* discipline; **disciplinar** *vt* to discipline.

discípulo, a [dis'θipulo, a] *nm/f* disciple.

disco ['disko] *nm* disc; (DEPORTE) discus; (TELEC) dial; (AUTO) signal; (*fam*) boring affair; ~ **de larga duración/de duración extendida** long-playing record (L.P.)/extended play record (E.P.); ~ **de freno** brake disc.

discordia [dis'korðja] *nf* discord.

discoteca [disko'teka] *nf* discotheque.

discreción [diskre'θjon] *nf* discretion; (*reserva*) prudence; (*secreto*) secrecy; **comer a** ~ to eat as much as one wishes; **discrecional** *a* (*facultativo*) discretionary.

discrepancia [diskre'panθja] *nf* (*diferencia*) discrepancy; (*desacuerdo*) disagreement.

discreto, a [dis'kreto, a] *a* (*diplomático*) discreet; (*sensato*) sensible; (*listo*) shrewd; (*reservado*) quiet; (*sobrio*) sober; (*retraído*) unobtrusive; (*razonable*) reasonable.

discriminación [diskrimina'θjon] *nf* discrimination.

disculpa [dis'kulpa] *nf* excuse; (*pedir perdón*) apology; **disculpar** *vt* to excuse, pardon; **disculparse** *vr* to excuse o.s.; to apologize.

discurrir [disku'rrir] *vt* to invent // *vi* (*pensar, reflexionar*) to think, meditate; (*recorrer*) to roam, wander; (*el tiempo*) to pass, flow by.

discurso [dis'kurso] *nm* speech; (*razonamiento*) reasoning power.

discutir [disku'tir] *vt* (*debatir*) to discuss; (*pelear*) to argue about; (*contradecir*) to contradict.

diseminar [disemi'nar] *vt* to disseminate, spread.

diseño [di'seŋo] *nm* (*dibujo*) design.

disfraz [dis'fraθ] *nm* (*máscara*) disguise; (*excusa*) pretext; ~**ar** *vt* to disguise; ~**arse** *vr*: ~**arse de** to disguise o.s. as.

disfrutar [disfru'tar] *vt* to enjoy // *vi* to enjoy o.s.; ~ **de** to enjoy, possess.

disgustar [disxus'tar] *vt* (*no gustar*) to displease; (*contrariar, enojar*) to annoy,

upset; ~**se** *vr* to be annoyed; (*dos personas*) to fall out.

disgusto [dis'xusto] *nm* (*repugnancia*) disgust; (*contrariedad*) annoyance; (*tristeza*) grief; (*riña*) quarrel; (*avería*) misfortune.

disidente [disi'ðente] *nm* dissident.

disimular [disimu'lar] *vt* (*ocultar*) to hide, conceal; (*perdonar*) to excuse // *vi* to dissemble.

disipar [disi'par] *vt* to dispel; (*fortuna*) to squander; ~**se** *vr* (*nubes*) to vanish; (*indisciplinarse*) to dissipate.

disminución [disminu'θjon] *nf* diminution.

disminuir [disminu'ir] *vt* (*acortar*) to decrease; (*achicar*) to diminish; (*estrechar*) to lessen.

disoluto, a [diso'luto, a] *a* dissolute.

disolver [disol'βer] *vt* (*gen*) to dissolve; ~**se** *vr* to be dissolved.

disparar [dispa'rar] *vt, vi* to shoot, fire.

disparate [dispa'rate] *nm* (*tontería*) foolish remark; (*error*) blunder.

disparo [dis'paro] *nm* shot.

dispensar [dispen'sar] *vt* to dispense; (*disculpar*) to excuse.

dispersar [disper'sar] *vt* to disperse; ~**se** *vr* to scatter.

disponer [dispo'ner] *vt* (*arreglar*) to arrange; (*ordenar*) to put in order; (*preparar*) to prepare, get ready // *vi*: ~ **de** to have, own; ~**se** *vr*: ~**se para** to prepare to, prepare for.

disponible [dispo'niβle] *a* available.

disposición [disposi'θjon] *nf* arrangement, disposition; (*aptitud*) aptitude; **a la** ~ **de** at the disposal of.

dispuesto, a [dis'pwesto, a] *pp de* **disponer** // *a* (*arreglado*) arranged; (*preparado*) disposed.

disputar [dispu'tar] *vt* (*discutir*) to dispute, question; (*contender*) to contend for // *vi* to argue.

distanciar [distan'θjar] *vt* to space out; ~**se** *vr* to become estranged.

distante [dis'tante] *a* distant.

diste, disteis *vb ver* **dar.**

distinción [distin'θjon] *nf* (*gen*) distinction; (*claridad*) clarity; (*elegancia*) elegance; (*honor*) honour.

distinguir [distin'gir] *vt* to distinguish; (*escoger*) to single out; ~**se** *vr* to be distinguished.

distinto, a [dis'tinto, a] *a* different; (*claro*) clear.

distracción [distrak'θjon] *nf* (*pasatiempo*) hobby, pastime; (*olvido*) absent-mindedness, distraction.

distraer [distra'er] *vt* (*entretener*) to entertain; (*divertir*) to amuse; (*fondos*) to embezzle; ~**se** *vr* (*entretenerse*) to amuse o.s.; (*perder la concentración*) to allow one's attention to wander.

distraído, a [distra'iðo, a] *a* (*gen*) absent-minded; (*entretenido*) amusing.

distribuir [distriβu'ir] *vt* to distribute.

distrito [dis'trito] nm (sector, territorio) region; (barrio) district.

disturbio [dis'turβjo] nm disturbance.

disuadir [diswa'ðir] vt to dissuade.

disuelto [di'swelto] pp de **disolver.**

divagar [diβa'xar] vi (desviarse) to digress; (errar) to wander.

diván [di'βan] nm divan.

divergencia [diβer'xenθja] nf divergence.

diversidad [diβersi'ðað] nf diversity, variety.

diversificar [diβersifi'kar] vt to diversify.

diversión [diβer'sjon] nf (gen) entertainment; (actividad) hobby, pastime.

diverso, a [di'βerso, a] a diverse; ~s sundry.

divertir [diβer'tir] vt (entretener, recrear) to amuse, entertain; (apartar, distraer) to divert; ~se vr (pasarlo bien) to have a good time; (distraerse) to amuse o.s.

dividir [diβi'ðir] vt (gen) to divide; (separar) to separate; (distribuir) to distribute, share out.

divino, a [di'βino, a] a divine.

divisa [di'βisa] nf (emblema, moneda) emblem, badge; ~s nfpl currency sg.

división [diβi'sjon] nf (gen) division; (de partido) split; (de país) partition; (LING) hyphen; (divergencia) divergence.

divorciar [diβor'θjar] vt to divorce; ~se vr to get divorced; **divorcio** nm divorce.

divulgar [diβul'xar] vt (desparramar) to spread; (hacer circular) to divulge, circulate; ~se vr to leak out.

doblar [do'βlar] vt (gen) to double; (papel) to fold; (caño) to bend; (la esquina) to turn, go round; (film) to dub // vi to turn; (campana) to toll; ~se vr (plegarse) to fold (up), crease; (encorvarse) to bend; ~se de risa/dolor to be doubled up with laughter/pain.

doble ['doβle] a (gen) double; (de dos aspectos) dual; (fig) two-faced // nm double; (campana) toll(ing); ~s nmpl (DEPORTE) doubles sg // nm/f (TEATRO) double, stand-in; **con ~ sentido** with a double meaning.

doce ['doθe] num twelve.

docena [do'θena] nf dozen.

dócil ['doθil] a (pasivo) docile; (obediente) obedient.

doctor, a [dok'tor, a] nm/f doctor.

doctrina [dok'trina] nf doctrine, teaching.

documentación [dokumenta'θjon] nf documentation, papers pl.

documento [doku'mento] nm (certificado) document.

dólar ['dolar] nm dollar.

doler [do'ler] vt, vi to hurt; (fig) to grieve; ~se vr (de su situación) to grieve, feel sorry; (de las desgracias ajenas) to sympathize; **me duele el brazo** my arm hurts.

dolor [do'lor] nm pain; (fig) grief, sorrow.

domar [do'mar], **domesticar** [domesti'kar] vt to tame.

domicilio [domi'θiljo] nm home; ~ **particular** private residence; ~ **social** head office.

dominante [domi'nante] a dominant; (person) domineering.

dominar [domi'nar] vt (gen) to dominate; (idiomas etc) to have a command of // vi to dominate, prevail; ~se vr to control o.s.

domingo [do'mingo] nm Sunday.

dominio [do'minjo] nm (tierras) domain; (autoridad) power, authority; (de las pasiones) grip, hold; (de varios idiomas) command.

don [don] nm (talento) gift; ~ **Juan Gómez** Mr Juan Gomez or Juan Gomez Esq.

donaire [do'naire] nm charm.

doncella [don'θeʎa] nf (criada) maid; (muchacha) girl.

donde ['donde] ad where // prep: **el coche está allí ~ el farol** the car is over there by the lamppost or where the lamppost is; **por ~** through which; **en ~** where, in which.

dónde ['donde] ad interr where?; **¿a ~ vas?** where are you going (to)?; **¿de ~ vienes?** where have you come from?; **¿por ~?** where?, whereabouts?

dondequiera [donde'kjera] ad anywhere; **por ~** everywhere, all over the place // conj: ~ **que** wherever.

doña ['doɲa] nf título de mujer que no se traduce.

dorado, a [do'raðo, a] a (color) golden; (TEC) gilt.

dormir [dor'mir] vt: ~ **la siesta por la tarde** to have an afternoon nap // vi to sleep; ~se vr to go to sleep.

dormitar [dormi'tar] vi to doze.

dormitorio [dormi'torjo] nm bedroom; ~ **común** dormitory.

dos [dos] num two.

dosis ['dosis] nf inv dose, dosage.

dotado, a [do'taðo, a] a gifted; ~ **de** endowed with.

dotar [do'tar] vt to endow; **dote** nf dowry; **dotes** nfpl gifts.

doy vb ver **dar.**

drama ['drama] nm drama.

dramaturgo [drama'turxo] nm dramatist, playwright.

droga ['droxa] nf drug.

drogadicto, a [droxa'ðikto, a] nm/f drug addict.

ducha ['dutʃa] nf (baño) shower; (MED) douche; **ducharse** vr to take a shower.

duda ['duða] nf doubt.

dudoso, a [du'ðoso, a] a (incierto) hesitant; (sospechoso) doubtful.

duelo ['dwelo] nm (combate) duel; (luto) mourning.

duende ['dwende] nm imp, goblin.

dueño, a ['dweɲo, a] nm/f (propietario)

owner; (de casa) landlord/lady; (empresario) employer.
duermo etc vb ver **dormir.**
dulce ['dulθe] a sweet // ad gently, softly // nm sweet.
dulzura [dul'θura] nf sweetness; (ternura) gentleness.
duplicar [dupli'kar] vt (hacer el doble de) to duplicate; ~**se** vr to double.
duque ['duke] nm duke.
duquesa [du'kesa] nf duchess.
duración [dura'θjon] nf duration.
duradero, a [dura'ðero, a] a lasting.
durante [du'rante] ad during.
durar [du'rar] vi (permanecer) to last; (recuerdo) to remain.
dureza [du'reθa] nf (calidad) hardness.
durmí etc vb ver **dormir.**
durmiente [dur'mjente] nm/f sleeper.
duro, a ['duro, a] a (gen) hard; (carácter) tough // ad hard // nm (moneda) five peseta coin/note.

E

e [e] conj and.
E abr de **este.**
ebanista [eβa'nista] nm cabinetmaker.
ébano ['eβano] nm ebony.
ebrio, a ['eβrjo, a] a drunk.
ebullición [eβuʎi'θjon] nf boiling; (fig) ferment.
eclesiástico, a [ekle'sjastiko, a] a ecclesiastical.
eclipse [e'klipse] nm eclipse.
eco ['eko] nm echo; **tener** ~ to catch on.
ecología [ekolo'xia] nf ecology.
economato [ekono'mato] nm cooperative store.
economía [ekono'mia] nf (sistema) economy; (cualidad) thrift.
económico, a [eko'nomiko, a] a (barato) cheap, economical; (persona) thrifty; (COM. plan) financial; (: situación) economic.
economista [ekono'mista] nm/f economist.
ecuador [ekwa'ðor] nm equator; **el E**~ Ecuador.
ecuánime [e'kwanime] a (carácter) level-headed; (estado) calm.
ecuestre [e'kwestre] a equestrian.
echar [e'tʃar] vt to throw; (agua, vino) to pour (out); (empleado: despedir) to fire, sack; (bigotes) to grow; (hojas) to sprout; (cartas) to post; (humo) to emit, give out // vi: ~ **a correr/llorar** to break into a run/burst into tears; ~**se** vr to lie down; ~ **llave** a to lock (up); ~ **abajo** (gobierno) to overthrow; (edificio) to demolish; ~ **mano** a to lay hands on.
edad [e'ðað] nf age; ¿**qué** ~ **tienes?** how old are you?; **tiene ocho años de** ~ he is eight (years old); **de** ~ **media-na/avanzada** middle-aged/ advanced in years; **la E**~ **Media** the Middle Ages.

edición [eði'θjon] nf (acto) publication; (ejemplar) edition.
edicto [e'ðikto] nm edict, proclamation.
edificio [eði'fiθjo] nm building; (fig) edifice, structure.
editar [eði'tar] vt (publicar) to publish; (preparar textos) to edit.
editor, a [eði'tor, a] nm/f (que publica) publisher; (de periódico etc) editor // a: **casa** ~**a** a publishing house; ~**ial** a editorial // nm leading article, editorial; **casa** ~**ial** publishing house.
educación [eðuka'θjon] nf education; (crianza) upbringing; (modales) (good) manners pl.
educar [eðu'kar] vt to educate; (criar) to bring up; (voz) to train.
EE. UU. nmpl abr de **Estados Unidos** USA (United States of America).
efectivo, a [efek'tiβo, a] a effective; (real) actual, real // nm: **pagar en** ~ to pay (in) cash; **hacer** ~ **un cheque** to cash a cheque.
efecto [e'fekto] nm effect, result; ~**s** nmpl goods; (COM) assets; **en** ~ in fact; (respuesta) exactly, indeed.
efectuar [efek'twar] vt to carry out; (viaje) to make.
eficacia [efi'kaθja] nf (de persona) efficiency; (de medicamento) effectiveness.
eficaz [efi'kaθ] a (persona) efficient; (acción) effective.
egipcio, a [e'xipθjo, a] a, nm/f Egyptian.
Egipto [e'xipto] nm Egypt.
egoísmo [exo'ismo] nm egoism.
egoísta [exo'ista] a egoistical, selfish // nm/f egoist.
egregio, a [e'xrexjo, a] a eminent, distinguished.
Eire ['eire] nm Eire.
ej. abr de **ejemplo.**
eje ['exe] nm (GEO, MAT) axis; (de rueda) axle; (de máquina) shaft, spindle; **la idea** ~ the central idea.
ejecución [exeku'θjon] nf (gen) execution; (cumplimiento) fulfilment; (actuación) performance; (JUR: embargo de deudor) attachment, distraint.
ejecutar [exeku'tar] vt (gen) to execute, carry out; (matar) to execute; (cumplir) to fulfil; (MUS) to perform; (JUR: embargar) to attach, distrain (on).
ejecutivo, a [exeku'tiβo, a] a executive; **el poder** ~ the Executive (Power).
ejemplar [exem'plar] a exemplary // nm example; (ZOOL) specimen; (de libro) copy; (de periódico) number, issue.
ejemplo [e'xemplo] nm example; **por** ~ for example.
ejercer [exer'θer] vt to exercise; (influencia) to exert; (un oficio) to practise // vi (practicar) to practise (de as); (tener oficio) to hold office.
ejercicio [exer'θiθjo] nm exercise; (período) tenure; ~ **comercial** financial year.
ejército [e'xerθito] nm army; **entrar en**

el ~ to join the army, join up.

el [el] *det* the.

él [el] *pron* (*persona*) he; (*cosa*) it; (*después de prep: persona*) him; (: *cosa*) it.

elaborar [elaβo'rar] *vt* to elaborate; (*hacer*) to make; (*preparar*) to prepare; (*trabajar*) to work; (*calcular*) to work out.

elasticidad [elastiθi'ðað] *nf* elasticity; **elástico, a** *a* elastic; (*flexible*) flexible // *nm* elastic.

elección [elek'θjon] *nf* election; (*selección*) choice, selection.

electorado [elekto'raðo] *nm* electorate, voters *pl.*

electricidad [elektriθi'ðað] *nf* electricity.

electricista [elektri'θista] *nm/f* electrician.

eléctrico, a [e'lektriko, a] *a* electric // *nm* electric train.

electrizar [elektri'θar] *vt* to electrify.

electro... [elektro] *pref* electro...; ~**cardiógrafo** *nm* electrocardiograph; ~**cución** *nf* electrocution; ~**cutar** *vt* to electrocute; ~**chapado, a** *a* electroplated; **electrodo** *nm* electrode; ~**domésticos** *nmpl* (electrical) household appliances; ~**imán** *nm* electromagnet; ~**magnético, a** *a* electromagnetic; ~**motor** *nm* electric motor.

electrónico, a [elek'troniko, a] *a* electronic // *nf* electronics *sg.*

electrotecnia [elektro'teknja] *nf* electrical engineering; **electrotécnico, a** *nm/f* electrical engineer.

electrotermo [elektro'termo] *nm* immersion heater.

elefante [ele'fante] *nm* elephant; ~ **marino** elephant seal.

elegancia [ele'vanθja] *nf* (*gracia*) elegance, grace; (*estilo*) stylishness; **elegante** *a* elegant, graceful; stylish, fashionable.

elegía [ele'xia] *nf* elegy.

elegir [ele'xir] *vt* (*escoger*) to choose, select; (*optar*) to opt for; (*presidente*) to elect.

elemental [elemen'tal] *a* (*claro, obvio*) elementary; (*fundamental*) elemental, fundamental.

elemento [ele'mento] *nm* element; (*fig*) ingredient; ~**s** *nmpl* elements, rudiments.

elevación [eleβa'θjon] *nf* elevation; (*acto*) raising, lifting; (*de precios*) rise; (*GEO etc*) height, altitude; (*de persona*) loftiness; (*pey*) conceit, pride.

elevar [ele'βar] *vt* to raise, lift (up); (*precio*) to put up; ~**se** *vr* (*edificio*) to rise; (*precios*) to go up; (*transportarse, enajenarse*) to get carried away; (*engreírse*) to become conceited.

eliminar [elimi'nar] *vt* to eliminate, remove.

eliminatoria [elimina'torja] *nf* heat, preliminary (round).

elite [e'lite] *nf* elite.

elocuencia [elo'kwenθja] *nf* eloquence.

elogiar [elo'xjar] *vt* to praise, eulogize;

elogio *nm* praise; (*tributo*) tribute.

eludir [elu'ðir] *vt* (*evitar*) to avoid, evade; (*escapar*) to escape, elude.

ella ['eʎa] *pron* (*persona*) she; (*cosa*) it; (*después de prep: persona*) her; (: *cosa*) it.

ellas ['eʎas] *pron* (*personas y cosas*) they; (*después de prep*) them.

ello ['eʎo] *pron* it.

ellos ['eʎos] *pron* they; (*después de prep*) them.

emanar [ema'nar] *vi*: ~ **de** to emanate from, come from; (*derivar de*) to originate in.

emancipar [emanθi'par] *vt* to emancipate; ~**se** *vr* to become emancipated, free o.s.

embadurnar [embaður'nar] *vt* to smear.

embajada [emba'xaða] *nf* embassy; (*mensaje*) message, errand.

embajador, a [embaxa'ðor, a] *nm/f* ambassador/ambassadress.

embalar [emba'lar] *vt* (*envolver*) to parcel, wrap (up); (*envasar*) to package // *vi* to sprint.

embarazada, a [embara'θaða] *a* pregnant // *nf* pregnant woman.

embarazar [embara'θar] *vt* to obstruct, hamper; (*a una mujer*) to make pregnant; ~**se** *vr* (*aturdirse*) to become embarrassed; (*confundirse*) to get into a muddle; (*mujer*) to become pregnant.

embarazo [emba'raθo] *nm* (*de mujer*) pregnancy; (*impedimento*) obstacle, obstruction; (*timidez*) embarrassment.

embarcación [embarka'θjon] *nf* (*barco*) boat, craft; (*acto*) embarkation.

embarcadero [embarka'ðero] *nm* pier, landing stage.

embarcar [embar'kar] *vt* (*cargamento*) to ship, stow; (*persona*) to embark, put on board; ~**se** *vr* to embark, go on board.

embargar [embar'xar] *vt* (*impedir*) to impede, hinder; (*JUR*) to seize, impound.

embarque [em'barke] *nm* shipment, loading.

embaular [embau'lar] *vt* to pack (into a trunk); (*fig*) to stuff o.s. with.

embebecerse [embeβe'θerse] *vr* (*extasiarse*) to be lost in wonder, be amazed.

embeber [embe'βer] *vt* (*absorber*) to absorb, soak up; (*empapar*) to saturate // *vi* to shrink; ~**se** *vr*: ~**se en la lectura** to be engrossed *or* absorbed in a book.

embellecer [embeʎe'θer] *vt* to embellish, beautify.

embestida [embes'tiða] *nf* attack, onslaught; (*carga*) charge; **embestir** *vt* to attack assault; to charge, attack // *vi* to attack.

emblema [em'blema] *nm* emblem.

embobado, a [embo'βaðo, a] *a* (*atontado*) stunned, bewildered.

embocadura [emboka'ðura] *nf* narrow entrance; (*de río*) mouth; (*MUS*) mouthpiece.

émbolo ['embolo] *nm* (*AUTO*) piston.

embolsar [embol'sar] *vt* to pocket, put in one's pocket.

emborrachar [emborra'tʃar] *vt* to intoxicate, make drunk; ~**se** *vr* to get drunk.

emboscada [embos'kaða] *nf* (*celada*) ambush.

embotar [embo'tar] *vt* to blunt, dull; ~**se** *vr* (*adormecerse*) to go numb.

embotellar [embote'ʎar] *vt* to bottle; ~**se** *vr* (*circulación*) to get into a jam.

embozar [embo'θar] *vt* to muffle (up).

embragar [embra'xar] *vi* to let in the clutch.

embrague [em'braxe] *nm* (*también* **pedal de** ~) clutch.

embravecer [embraβe'θer] *vt* to enrage, infuriate; ~**se** *vr* to become furious; (*el mar*) to get rough; (*tormenta*) to rage.

embriagado, a [embrja'xaðo, a] *a* (*emborrachado*) intoxicated, drunk.

embriagar [embrja'xar] *vt* (*emborrachar*) to intoxicate, make drunk; (*alegrar*) to delight; ~**se** *vr* (*emborracharse*) to get drunk.

embriaguez [embrja'xeθ] *nf* (*borrachera*) drunkenness; (*fig*) rapture, delight.

embrollar [embro'ʎar] *vt* (*el asunto*) to confuse, complicate; (*persona*) to involve, embroil; ~**se** *vr* (*confundirse*) to get into a muddle *or* mess; ~**se con uno** to get into an argument with sb.

embrollo [em'broʎo] *nm* (*enredo*) muddle, confusion; (*aprieto*) fix, jam; (*pey: engaño*) fraud; (: *trampa*) trick.

embromar [embro'mar] *vt* (*burlarse de*) to tease, make fun of.

embrutecer [embrute'θer] *vt* (*brutalizar*) to brutalize; (: *depravar*) to deprave; (*atontar*) to stupefy; ~**se** *vr* to become brutal; to become depraved.

embudo [em'buðo] *nm* funnel; (*fig: engaño*) fraud; (: *trampa*) trick.

embuste [em'buste] *nm* trick; (*impostura*) imposture; (*mentira*) lie; (*hum*) fib; ~**ro, a** *a* lying, deceitful // *nm/f* (*tramposo*) cheat; (*impostor*) impostor; (*mentiroso*) liar; (*hum*) fibber.

embutido [embu'tiðo] *nm* (*CULIN*) sausage; (*TEC*) inlay.

embutir [embu'tir] *vt* (*TEC*) to inlay; (*llenar*) to pack tight, cram, stuff.

emergencia [emer'xenθja] *nf* emergency; (*surgimiento*) emergence.

emerger [emer'xer] *vi* to emerge, appear.

emigración [emixra'θjon] *nf* (*éxodo*) migration; (*destierro*) emigration.

emigrar [emi'xrar] *vi* (*pájaros*) to migrate; (*personas*) to emigrate.

eminencia [emi'nenθja] *nf* eminence; **eminente** *a* eminent, distinguished; (*GEO*) high.

emisario [emi'sarjo] *nm* emissary.

emisión [emi'sjon] *nf* (*acto*) emission; (*COM etc*) issue; (*RADIO, TV: acto*) broadcasting; (: *programa*) broadcast, programme.

emisora [emi'sora] *nf* (*de onda corta*) shortwave radio station; (*aparato*) broadcasting station.

emitir [emi'tir] *vt* (*olor etc*) to emit, give off; (*moneda etc*) to issue; (*opinión*) to express; (*RADIO*) to broadcast.

emoción [emo'θjon] *nf* emotion; (*excitación*) excitement; (*turbación*) worry, anxiety.

emocionante [emoθjo'nante] *a* (*excitante*) exciting, thrilling; (*conmovedor*) moving, touching; (*impresionante*) striking, impressive.

emocionar [emoθjo'nar] *vt* (*excitar*) to excite, thrill; (*conmover*) to move, touch; (*impresionar*) to impress.

empacho [em'patʃo] *nm* (*MED*) indigestion; (*fig*) embarrassment.

empalagoso, a [empala'xoso, a] *a* cloying; (*fig*) tiresome.

empalmar [empal'mar] *vt* to join, connect // *vi* (*dos caminos*) to meet, join; **empalme** *nm* joint, connection; junction; (*de trenes*) connection.

empanada [empa'naða] *nf* pie, patty.

empantanarse [empanta'narse] *vr* to get swamped; (*fig*) to get bogged down.

empañar [empa'ɲar] *vt* (*niño*) to swaddle, wrap up; ~**se** *vr* (*nublarse*) to get misty, steam up.

empapar [empa'par] *vt* (*mojar*) to soak, saturate; (*absorber*) to soak up, absorb; ~**se** *vr*: ~**se de** to soak up.

empapelar [empape'lar] *vt* (*paredes*) to paper; (*envolver con papel*) to wrap (up) in paper.

empaquetar [empake'tar] *vt* to pack, parcel up.

empastar [empas'tar] *vt* (*embadurnar*) to paste; (*diente*) to fill.

empatar [empa'tar] *vi* to draw, tie; **empate** *nm* draw, tie.

empedernido, a [empeðer'niðo, a] *a* hard, heartless; (*fijado*) hardened, inveterate.

empedernir [empeðer'nir] *vt* to harden.

empedrado, a [empe'ðraðo, a] *a* paved // *nm* paving; **empedrar** *vt* to pave.

empeñado, a [empe'ɲaðo, a] *a* (*objeto*) pawned; (*persona*) determined.

empeñar [empe'ɲar] *vt* (*objeto*) to pawn, pledge; (*persona*) to compel; ~**se** *vr* (*obligarse*) to bind o.s., pledge o.s.; (*endeudarse*) to get into debt; ~**se en** to be set on, be determined to.

empeño [em'peɲo] *nm* (*cosa prendada*) pledge; (*determinación, insistencia*) determination, insistence; **banco de** ~**s** pawnshop.

empeorar [empeo'rar] *vt* to make worse, worsen // *vi* to get worse, deteriorate.

empequeñecer [empekeɲe'θer] *vt* to dwarf; (*fig*) to belittle.

emperador [empera'ðor] *nm* emperor.

emperatriz [empera'triθ] *nf* empress.

empezar [empe'θar] *vt, vi* to begin, start.

empiezo *etc vb ver* **empezar.**

empinar [empi'nar] *vt* to raise (up) // *vi* (*fam*) to drink, booze (*fam*); ~**se** *vr* (*persona*) to stand on tiptoe; (*animal*) to rear up; (*camino*) to climb steeply; (*edificio*) to tower.

empírico, a [em'piriko, a] *a* empirical.

emplasto [em'plasto], **emplaste** [em-'plaste] *nm* (*MED*) plaster; (: *cataplasma*) poultice; (*componenda*) compromise.

emplazamiento [emplaθa'mjento] *nm* site, location; (*JUR*) summons *sg*.

emplazar [empla'θar] *vt* (*ubicar*) to site, place, locate; (*JUR*) to summons; (*convocar*) to summon.

empleado, a [emple'aðo, a] *nm/f* (*gen*) employee; (*de banco etc*) clerk.

emplear [emple'ar] *vt* (*usar*) to use, employ; (*dar trabajo a*) to employ; ~**se** *vr* (*conseguir trabajo*) to be employed; (*ocuparse*) to occupy o.s.

empleo [em'pleo] *nm* (*puesto*) job; (*puestos*: *colectivamente*) employment; (*uso*) use, employment.

empobrecer [empoβre'θer] *vt* to impoverish; ~**se** *vr* to become poor *or* impoverished; **empobrecimiento** *nm* impoverishment.

emporio [em'porjo] *nm* emporium, trading centre; (*gran almacén*) department store.

emprender [empren'der] *vt* (*empezar*) to begin, embark on; (*acometer*) to tackle, take on.

empreñar [empre'par] *vt* to make pregnant; ~**se** *vr* to become pregnant.

empresa [em'presa] *nf* enterprise.

empréstito [em'prestito] *nm* (public) loan.

empujar [empu'xar] *vt* to push, shove; **empuje** *nm* thrust; (*presión*) pressure; (*fig*) vigour, drive.

empujón [empu'xon] *nm* push, shove.

empuñar [empu'par] *vt* (*asir*) to grasp, take (firm) hold of.

emular [emu'lar] *vt* to emulate; (*rivalizar*) to rival.

émulo, a ['emulo, a] *nm/f* rival, competitor.

en [en] *prep* (*gen*): in; (*sobre*) on, upon; **meter** ~ **el bolsillo** to put in or into one's pocket; (*lugar*): **vivir** ~ **Toledo** to live in Toledo; ~ **casa** at home; (*tiempo*): **lo terminó** ~ **6 días** he finished it in 6 days; ~ **el mes de enero** in the month of January; ~ **aquel momento/aquella época** at that moment/that time; ~ **aquel día/aquella ocasión** on that day/that occasion; ~ **serio** seriously; ~ **fin** well, well then; **ir de puerta** ~ **puerta** to go from door to door; ~ **tren** by train.

enajenación [enaxena'θjon] *nf*, **enajenamiento** [enaxena'mjento] *nm* alienation; (*fig*: *distracción*) absent-mindedness; (: *embelesamiento*) rapture, trance; (*extrañamiento*) estrangement.

enajenar [enaxe'nar] *vt* to alienate; (*fig*)

to carry away; ~**se** *vr* (*de un bien*) to deprive o.s.; (*amigos*) to become estranged, fall out.

enamorado, a [enamo'raðo, a] *a* in love; **enamorar** *vt* to inspire love; **enamorarse** *vr* to fall in love.

enano, a [e'nano, a] *a* tiny // *nm/f* dwarf.

enardecer [enarðe'θer] *vt* (*pasiones*) to fire, inflame; (*persona*) to fill with enthusiasm; (: *llenar de ira*) to fill with anger; ~**se** *vr* to get excited; (*entusiasmarse*) to get enthusiastic (*por* about); (*de cólera*) to blaze.

encabezamiento [enkaβeθa'mjento] *nm* (*de carta*) heading; (*de periódico*) headline; (*preámbulo*) foreword, preface; (*registro*) roll, register.

encabezar [enkaβe'θar] *vt* (*manifestación*) to lead, head; (*lista*) to be at the top of; (*carta*) to put a heading to; (*libro*) to entitle; (*empadronar*) to register.

encadenar [enkaðe'nar] *vt* to chain (together); (*poner grilletes a*) to shackle.

encajar [enka'xar] *vt* (*ajustar*) to fit (into); (*golpe*) to give, deal; (*entrometer*) to insert // *vi* to fit (well); (*fig*: *corresponder a*) to match; ~**se** *vr* to intrude; ~**se en un sillón** to squeeze into a chair.

encaje [en'kaxe] *nm* (*labor*) lace; (*inserción*) insertion; (*ajuste*) fitting.

encajonar [enkaxo'nar] *vt* to box (up), put in a box.

encaminar [enkami'nar] *vt* to direct, send; ~**se** *vr*: ~**se a** to set out for.

encandilar [enkandi'lar] *vt* to dazzle; (*fuego*) to poke.

encantador, a [enkanta'ðor, a] *a* charming, lovely // *nm/f* magician, enchanter/tress.

encantar [enkan'tar] *vt* to charm, delight; (*hechizar*) to bewitch, cast a spell on; **encanto** *nm* (*magia*) spell, charm; (*fig*) charm, delight.

encarcelar [enkarθe'lar] *vt* to imprison, jail.

encarecer [enkare'θer] *vt* to put up the price of; (*pedir*) to recommend, urge // *vi*, ~**se** *vr* to get dearer.

encarecimiento [enkareθi'mjento] *nm* price increase; (*pedido insistente*) urging.

encargado, a [enkar'xaðo, a] *a* in charge // *nm/f* agent, representative; (*responsable*) person in charge; ~ **de negocios** chargé d'affaires.

encargar [enkar'xar] *vt* to entrust; (*recomendar*) to urge, recommend; ~**se** *vr*: ~**se de** to look after, take charge of.

encargo [en'karxo] *nm* (*pedido*) assignment, job; (*responsabilidad*) responsibility; (*recomendación*) recommendation; (*COM*) order.

encarnación [enkarna'θjon] *nf* incarnation, embodiment.

encarrilar [enkarri'lar] *vt* to correct, put on the right track; (*tren*) to put back on the rails.

encausar [enkau'sar] *vt* to prosecute, sue.

encauzar [enkau'θar] *vt* to channel.
enceguecer [enθexe'θer] *vt* to blind // *vi*, ~**se** *vr* to go blind.
encendedor [enθende'dor] *nm* lighter.
encender [enθen'der] *vt* (*con fuego*) to light; (*incendiar*) to set fire to; (*luz, radio*) to put on, switch on; (*inflarse*) to inflame; ~**se** *vr* to catch fire; (*excitarse*) to get excited; (*de cólera*) to flare up; (*el rostro*) to blush.
encendido [enθen'diðo] *nm* ignition.
encerrar [enθe'rrar] *vt* (*confinar*) to shut in, shut up; (*comprender, incluir*) to include, contain.
encía [en'θia] *nf* gum.
encierro [en'θierro] *nm* shutting in, shutting up; (*calabozo*) prison.
encima [en'θima] *ad* (*sobre*) above, over; (*además*) besides; ~ **de** (*en*) on, on top of; (*sobre*) above, over; (*además de*) besides, on top of; **por** ~ **de** over; **¿llevas dinero** ~**?** have you any money on you?; **se me vino** ~ it got on top of me.
encinta [en'θinta] *a* pregnant.
enclavar [enkla'βar] *vt* (*clavar*) to nail; (*atravesar*) to pierce; (*sitio*) to set; (*fig: fam*) to swindle.
encoger [enko'xer] *vt* (*gen*) to shrink, contract; (*fig: asustar*) to scare; (: *desanimar*) to discourage; ~**se** *vr* to shrink, contract; (*fig*) to cringe; ~**se de hombros** to shrug one's shoulders.
encojar [enko'xar] *vt* to lame; (*tullir*) to cripple; ~**se** *vr* to go lame; to become crippled.
encolar [enko'lar] *vt* (*engomar*) to glue, paste; (*pegar*) to stick down.
encolerizar [enkoleri'θar] *vt* to anger, provoke; ~**se** *vr* to get angry.
encomendar [enkomen'dar] *vt* to entrust, commend; ~**se** *vr:* ~**se a** to put one's trust in.
encomiar [enko'mjar] *vt* to praise, pay tribute to.
encomienda [enko'mjenda] *nf* (*encargo*) charge, commission; (*precio*) price; (*elogio*) tribute; ~ **postal** (*AM*) parcel post.
encomio [en'komjo] *nm* praise, tribute.
enconado, a [enko'naðo, a] *a* (*MED*) inflamed; (: *dolorido*) sore; (*fig*) angry.
enconar [enko'nar] *vt* (*MED*) to inflame; (*fig*) to anger, irritate; ~**se** *vr* (*MED*) to become inflamed; (*fig*) to get angry or irritated.
encono [en'kono] *nm* (*rencor*) rancour, spite; (*odio*) ill-feeling.
encontrado, a [enkon'traðo, a] *a* (*contrario*) contrary, conflicting; (*hostil*) hostile.
encontrar [enkon'trar] *vt* (*hallar*) to find; (*inesperadamente*) to meet, run into; ~**se** *vr* to meet (each other); (*situarse*) to be (situated); (*entrar en conflicto*) to crash, collide; ~**se con** to meet (with); ~**se bien de salud** to feel well.
encorvar [enkor'βar] *vt* to curve;

(*inclinar*) to bend (down); ~**se** *vr* to bend down, bend over, stoop.
encrespar [enkres'par] *vt* (*cabellos*) to curl; (*agua*) to ripple; (*fig*) to anger, irritate; ~**se** *vr* (*el mar*) to get rough; (*fig*) to get annoyed, irritated.
encrucijada [enkruθi'xaða] *nf* crossroads *sg*; (*empalme*) junction.
encuadernación [enkwaðerna'θjon] *nf* binding.
encuadernador, a [enkwaðerna'ðor, a] *nm/f* bookbinder.
encuadrar [enkwa'ðrar] *vt* (*retrato*) to frame; (*ajustar*) to fit, insert; (*encerrar*) to contain.
encubrir [enku'βrir] *vt* (*ocultar*) to hide, conceal; (*criminal*) to harbour, shelter.
encuentro *etc vb ver* **encontrar** // [en-'kwentro] *nm* (*de personas*) meeting; (*de trenes*) collision, crash; (*DEPORTE*) match, game; (*MIL*) encounter.
encuesta [en'kwesta] *nf* inquiry, investigation; ~ **judicial** post mortem.
encumbrado, a [enkum'braðo, a] *a* (*edificio*) lofty, towering; (*persona*) eminent, distinguished.
encumbrar [enkum'brar] *vt* (*edificio*) to raise; (*elevar*) to elevate; (*persona*) to exalt; ~**se** *vr* to rise, tower; (*fig*) to become conceited.
encharcado, a [entʃar'kaðo, a] *a* still; (*estancado*) stagnant.
enchufar [entʃu'far] *vt* (*ELEC*) to plug in; (*TEC*) to connect, fit together; **enchufe** *nm* (*ELEC: clavija*) plug; (: *toma*) plug, socket; (*de dos tubos*) joint, connection; (*fam: influencia*) contact, connection; (: *puesto*) cushy job.
endemoniado, a [endemo'njaðo, a] *a* possessed (of the devil); (*endiabolado*) devilish; (*furioso*) furious, wild.
endentar [enden'tar] *vt, vi* to engage, mesh.
enderezar [endere'θar] *vt* (*poner derecho*) to straighten (out); (: *verticalmente*) to set upright; (*carta*) to address; (*fig*) to straighten or sort out; (*dirigir*) to direct; ~**se** *vr* (*persona sentado*) to stand up; (*fig*) to correct one's ways.
endeudarse [endeu'ðarse] *vr* to get into debt.
endiablado, a [endja'βlaðo, a] *a* devilish, diabolical; (*hum*) mischievous; (*fig*) furious, angry.
endomingarse [endomin'garse] *vr* to dress up, put on one's best clothes.
endosar [endo'sar] *vt* (*cheque etc*) to endorse.
endulzar [endul'θar] *vt* to sweeten; (*fig*) to soften.
endurecer [endure'θer] *vt* to harden; (*fig*) to harden, toughen; ~**se** *vr* to harden, grow hard.
endurecido, a [endure'θiðo, a] *a* (*duro*) hard; (*fig*) hardy, tough; **estar** ~ **a algo** to be hardened or used to sth.
endurecimiento [endureθi'mjento] *nm*

(*acto*) hardening; (*tenacidad*) toughness; (*crueldad*) cruelty; (*insensibilidad*) callousness.

enemigo, a [ene'miɣo, a] *a* enemy, hostile // *nm/f* enemy // *nf* enmity, hostility.

enemistad [enemis'taθ] *nf* enmity.

enemistar [enemis'tar] *vt* to make enemies of, cause a rift between; ∼**se** *vr* to become enemies; (*amigos*) to fall out.

energía [ener'xia] *nf* (*vigor*) energy, drive; (*TEC, ELEC*) energy, power.

enérgico, a [e'nerxiko, a] *a* (*gen*) energetic; (*voz, modales*) forceful.

enero [e'nero] *nm* January.

enfadar [enfa'ðar] *vt* to anger, annoy; ∼**se** *vr* to get angry or annoyed.

enfado [en'faðo] *nm* (*enojo*) anger, annoyance; (*disgusto*) trouble, bother; ∼**so, a** *a* annoying; (*aburrido*) tedious.

énfasis ['enfasis] *nm* emphasis, stress.

enfático, a [en'fatiko, a] *a* emphatic; (*afectado*) pompous.

enfermar [enfer'mar] *vt* to make ill // *vi* to fall ill, be taken ill.

enfermedad [enferme'ðað] *nf* illness; ∼ **venérea** venereal disease.

enfermería [enferme'ria] *nf* infirmary; (*de colegio etc*) sick bay.

enfermero, a [enfer'mero, a] *nm/f* male nurse/nurse.

enfermizo, a [enfer'miθo, a] *a* (*persona*) sickly, unhealthy; (*lugar*) unhealthy.

enfermo, a [en'fermo, a] *a* ill, sick // *nm/f* invalid, sick person; (*en hospital*) patient.

enflaquecer [enflake'θer] *vt* (*adelgazar*) to make thin; (*debilitar*) to weaken; ∼**se** *vr* (*adelgazarse*) to become thin, lose weight; (*debilitarse*) to grow weak; (*fig*) to lose heart.

enfocar [enfo'kar] *vt* (*foto etc*) to focus; (*problema etc*) to approach, look at.

enfoque [en'foke] *nm* focus.

enfrentar [enfren'tar] *vt* (*peligro*) to face (up to), confront; (*oponer, carear*) to put face to face; ∼**se** *vr* (*dos personas*) to face or confront each other; (*dos equipos*) to meet; ∼**se a** *o* **con** to face up to, confront.

enfrente [en'frente] *ad* opposite; ∼ **de** *prep* opposite, facing; **la casa de** ∼ the house opposite, the house across the street.

enfriamiento [enfria'mjento] *nm* chilling, refrigeration; (*MED*) cold, chill.

enfriar [enfri'ar] *vt* (*alimentos*) to cool, chill; (*algo caliente*) to cool down; (*habitación*) to air, freshen; ∼**se** *vr* to cool down; (*MED*) to catch a chill; (*amistad*) to cool.

enfurecer [enfure'θer] *vt* to enrage, madden; ∼**se** *vr* to become furious, fly into a rage; (*mar*) to get rough.

engalanar [engala'nar] *vt* (*adornar*) to adorn; (*ciudad*) to decorate; ∼**se** *vr* to get dressed up.

enganchar [engan'tʃar] *vt* (*gen*) to hook; (*ropa*) to hang up; (*dos vagones*) to hitch up; (*TEC*) to couple, connect; (*MIL*) to

recruit; (*fig: fam: persona*) to rope into; ∼**se** *vr* (*MIL*) to enlist, join up.

enganche [en'gantʃe] *nm* hook; (*TEC*) coupling, connection; (*acto*) hooking (up); (: *ropa*) hanging up; (*MIL*) recruitment, enlistment.

engañar [enga'ɲar] *vt* to deceive; (*trampear*) to cheat, swindle; ∼**se** *vr* (*equivocarse*) to be wrong; (*disimular la verdad*) to deceive or kid o.s.

engaño [en'gaɲo] *nm* deceit; (*trampa*) trick, swindle; (*error*) mistake, misunderstanding; (*ilusión*) delusion; ∼**so, a** *a* (*tramposo*) crooked; (*mentiroso*) dishonest, deceitful; (*aspecto*) deceptive; (*consejo*) misleading, wrong.

engarzar [engar'θar] *vt* (*joya*) to set, mount; (*fig*) to link, connect.

engatusar [engatu'sar] *vt* (*fam*) to coax.

engendrar [enxen'drar] *vt* to breed; (*procrear*) to beget; (*fig*) to cause, produce; **engendro** *nm* (*BIO*) foetus; (*fig*) monstrosity; (*idea*) brainchild.

engolfarse [engol'farse] *vr*: ∼ **en** to bury o.s in, become deeply involved in.

engomar [engo'mar] *vt* to gum, glue, stick.

engordar [engor'ðar] *vt* to fatten // *vi* to get fat, put on weight.

engranaje [engra'naxe] *nm* gear.

engranar [engra'nar] *vt* to put into gear // *vi* to interlock.

engrandecer [engrande'θer] *vt* to enlarge, magnify; (*alabar*) to praise, speak highly of; (*exagerar*) to exaggerate.

engrasar [engra'sar] *vt* (*TEC: poner grasa*) to grease; (: *lubricar*) to lubricate, oil; (*manchar*) to make greasy; (*animal*) to fatten.

engreído, a [engre'iðo, a] *a* vain, conceited; **engreírse** *vr* to become conceited.

engrosar [engro'sar] *vt* (*ensanchar*) to enlarge; (*aumentar*) to increase; (*hinchar*) to swell // *vi* to get fat; ∼**se** *vr* to increase; to swell.

enhebrar [ene'βrar] *vt* to thread.

enhorabuena [enora'ðwena] *nf* congratulations *pl* // *ad* well and good.

enigma [e'niɣma] *nm* enigma; (*problema*) puzzle; (*misterio*) mystery.

enjabonar [enxaβo'nar] *vt* to soap; (*fam: adular*) to soft-soap; (: *regañar*) to scold.

enjambre [en'xamβre] *nm* swarm.

enjaular [enxau'lar] *vt* to put in a cage; (*fam*) to jail, lock up.

enjuagar [enxwa'ɣar] *vt* (*ropa*) to rinse (out).

enjugar [enxu'ɣar] *vt* to wipe (off); (*lágrimas*) to dry; (*déficit*) to wipe out.

enjuiciar [enxwi'θjar] *vt* (*JUR: procesar*) to prosecute, try; (*fig*) to judge.

enjuto, a [en'xuto, a] *a* dry, dried up; (*fig*) lean, skinny.

enlace [en'laθe] *nm* link, connection; (*relación*) relationship; (*casamiento*) marriage; (*de carretera, trenes*) connection; **agente**

de ~ broker; ~ **sindical** shop steward.

enlazar [enla'θar] *vt* (*atar*) to tie; (*conectar*) to link, connect; (AM) to lasso; ~**se** *vr* (*novios*) to get married; (*dos familias*) to become related by marriage; (*conectarse*) to link (up), be linked.

enlodar [enlo'ðar], **enlodazar** [enloða'θar] *vt* to muddy, cover in mud; (*fig: manchar*) to stain; (: *rebajar*) to debase.

enloquecer [enloke'θer] *vt* to drive mad // *vi*, ~**se** *vr* to go mad.

enlutar [enlu'tar] *vt* to dress in mourning; ~**se** *vr* to go into mourning.

enmarañar [enmara'ɲar] *vt* (*enredar*) to tangle (up), entangle; (*complicar*) to complicate; (*confundir*) to confuse; ~**se** *vr* (*enredarse*) to become entangled; (*confundirse*) to get confused; (*nublarse*) to cloud over.

enmascarar [enmaska'rar] *vt* to mask; ~**se** *vr* to put on a mask; ~**se de** to masquerade as.

enmendar [enmen'dar] *vt* to emend, correct; (*constitución etc*) to amend; (*compensar*) to make good; (*comportamiento*) to reform; ~**se** *vr* to reform, mend one's ways; **enmienda** *nf* correction; amendment; reform; (*compensación*) compensation, indemnity.

enmohecerse [enmoe'θerse] *vr* (*metal*) to rust, go rusty; (*muro, plantas*) to get mouldy.

enmudecer [enmuðe'θer] *vt* to silence // *vi*, ~**se** *vr* (*perder el habla*) to go silent; (*guardar silencio*) to keep quiet.

ennegrecer [enneɤre'θer] *vt* (*poner negro*) to blacken; (*oscurecer*) to darken; ~**se** *vr* to turn black; (*oscurecerse*) to get dark.

ennoblecer [ennoβle'θer] *vt* to ennoble; (*fig*) to embellish, adorn.

enojadizo, a [enoxa'ðiθo, a] *a* irritable, short-tempered.

enojar [eno'xar] *vt* (*encolerizar*) to anger; (*disgustar*) to annoy, upset; ~**se** *vr* to get angry; to get annoyed.

enojo [e'noxo] *nm* (*cólera*) anger; (*disgusto*) annoyance; ~**s** *nmpl* trials, problems; ~**so, a** *a* annoying.

enorgullecerse [enorɤuʎe'θerse] *vr* to be proud; ~ **de** to pride o.s. on, be proud of.

enorme [e'norme] *a* enormous, huge; (*fig*) monstrous; **enormidad** *nf* hugeness, immensity; (*despropósito*) absurdity, piece of nonsense; (*perversidad*) monstrosity.

enraizar [enrai'θar] *vi* to take root.

enredadera [enreða'ðera] *nf* (BOT) creeper, climbing plant.

enredar [enre'ðar] *vt* (*ovillo*) to tangle (up), entangle; (*peces*) to net; (*situación*) to complicate, confuse; (*meter cizaña*) to sow discord among or between; (*implicar*) to embroil, implicate; ~**se** *vr* to get entangled, get tangled (up); (*situación*) to get complicated; (*persona*) to get embroiled; (AM, *fam*) to meddle.

enredo [en'reðo] *nm* (*maraña*) tangle;

(*confusión*) mix-up, confusion; (*intriga*) intrigue.

enrevesado, a [enreße'saðo, a] *a* unruly, uncontrollable; (*enredado*) complicated, involved.

enriquecer [enrike'θer] *vt* to make rich, enrich; ~**se** *vr* to get rich.

enrojecer [enroxe'θer] *vt* to redden // *vi*, ~**se** *vr* (*metal*) to become red hot; (*persona*) to blush.

enrollar [enro'ʎar] *vt* to roll (up), wind (up).

enroscar [enros'kar] *vt* (*torcer, doblar*) to coil (round), wind; (*tornillo, rosca*) to screw in; ~**se** *vr* to coil, wind.

ensalada [ensa'laða] *nf* salad; **ensaladilla** *nf* Russian salad.

ensalzar [ensal'θar] *vt* (*alabar*) to praise, extol; (*exaltar*) to exalt.

ensambladura [ensambla'ðura] *nf*, **ensamblaje** [ensam'blaxe] *nm* assembly; (TEC) joint; **ensamblar** *vt* to assemble.

ensanchar [ensan'tʃar] *vt* (*hacer más ancho*) to widen; (*agrandar*) to enlarge, expand; ~**se** *vr* to get wider, expand; (*pey*) to give o.s. airs; **ensanche** *nm* (*de vestido, calle*) widening; (*de negocio*) expansion.

ensangrentar [ensangren'tar] *vt* to stain with blood; ~**se** *vr* (*fig*) to get angry.

ensañar [ensa'ɲar] *vt* to enrage; ~**se** *vr*: ~**se con** to delight in tormenting.

ensartar [ensar'tar] *vt* (*gen*) to string (together); (*aguja*) to thread.

ensayar [ensa'jar] *vt* to test, try (out); (TEATRO) to rehearse.

ensayista [ensa'jista] *nm/f* essayist.

ensayo [en'sajo] *nm* test, trial; (QUÍMICA) experiment; (TEATRO) rehearsal; (DEPORTE) try; (*obra literaria*) essay.

ensenada [ense'naða] *nf* inlet, cove.

enseñanza [ense'naɲθa] *nf* (*educación*) education; (*acción*) teaching; (*doctrina*) teaching, doctrine.

enseñar [ense'ɲar] *vt* (*educar*) to teach; (*instruir*) to teach, instruct; (*mostrar, señalar*) to show.

enseres [en'seres] *nmpl* goods and chattels, things.

ensimismarse [ensimis'marse] *vr* (*abstraerse*) to become lost in thought; (*estar absorto*) to be lost in thought; (AM) to become conceited.

ensoberbecerse [ensoßerße'θerse] *vr* to become proud; (*hacerse arrogante*) to become arrogant; (*mar*) to get rough.

ensordecer [ensorðe'θer] *vt* to deafen // *vi* to go deaf.

ensortijar [ensorti'xar] *vt*, ~**se** *vr* (*cabellos*) to curl.

ensuciar [ensu'θjar] *vt* (*manchar*) to dirty, soil; (*fig*) to defile; ~**se** *vr* (*mancharse*) to get dirty; (*fig*) to dirty/wet o.s.

ensueño [en'sweɲo] *nm* (*sueño*) dream, fantasy; (*ilusión*) illusion; (*soñando despierto*) reverie.

entablado [enta'ßlaðo] *nm* (*piso*)

floorboards pl; (armazón) boarding.

entablar [enta'ßlar] vt (recubrir) to board (up); (AJEDREZ, DAMAS) to set up; (conversación) to strike up; (JUR) to file // vi to draw.

entallar [enta'ʎar] vt (piedra) to sculpt; (madera) to carve; (grabar) to engrave; (traje) to tailor // vi: **el traje entalla bien** the suit fits well.

entender [enten'der] vt (comprender) to understand; (darse cuenta) to realize; (creer, pensar) to think, believe; (querer decir) to mean // vi: ~ **de** to know all about; ~ **en** to deal with, have to do with; ~**se** vr (comprenderse) to be understood; (ponerse de acuerdo) to understand one another, have an understanding; (aliarse) to agree, reach an agreement; (fam) to have an affair; **me entiendo con la mecánica** I'm (quite) good at mechanics.

entendido, a [enten'diðo, a] a (comprendido) understood; (hábil) skilled; (inteligente) knowledgeable // nm/f (experto) expert; (docto) knowledgeable person // excl agreed!; **entendimiento** nm (comprensión) understanding; (facultad intelectual) the mind, intellect; (juicio) judgement.

enterado, a [ente'raðo, a] a well-informed; **estar** ~ **de** to know about, be aware of.

enteramente [entera'mente] ad entirely, completely.

enterar [ente'rar] vt (informar) to inform, tell; ~**se** vr to find out, get to know.

entereza [ente'reθa] nf (totalidad) entirety; (fig: energía) strength of mind; (honradez) integrity; (severidad) strictness, severity.

enternecer [enterne'θer] vt (ablandar) to soften; (apiadar) to touch, move; ~**se** vr to be touched, be moved.

entero, a [en'tero, a] a (total) whole, entire; (fig: recto) honest; (: firme) firm, resolute // nm (COM: punto) point; (AM: pago) payment.

enterrador [enterra'ðor] nm gravedigger.

enterrar [ente'rrar] vt to bury.

entibiar [enti'ßjar] vt to cool; (fig) to cool (down).

entidad [enti'ðað] nf (empresa) firm, company; (organismo) body; (sociedad) society; (FILOSOFÍA) entity.

entiendo etc vb ver **entender**.

entierro [en'tjerro] nm (acción) burial; (funeral) funeral.

entomología [entomolo'xia] nf entomology.

entonación [entona'θjon] nf (LING) intonation; (fig) conceit.

entonado, a [ento'naðo, a] a (MUS) in tune; (fig) conceited.

entonar [ento'nar] vt (canción) to intone; (colores) to tone; (MED) to tone up // vi to be in tune; ~**se** vr (engreírse) to give o.s. airs.

entonces [en'tonθes] ad then, at that time;

desde ~ since then; **en aquel** ~ at that time; (pues) ~ and so.

entornar [entor'nar] vt (puerta, ventana) to half close, leave ajar; (los ojos) to screw up.

entorpecer [entorpe'θer] vt (adormecer los sentidos) to dull, benumb; (impedir) to obstruct, hinder; (: tránsito) to slow down, delay; **entorpecimiento** nm numbness; slowing-down, delay; (letargia) lethargy.

entrado, a [en'traðo, a] a: ~ **en años** elderly; **una vez** ~ **el verano** in the summer(time), when summer comes // nf (acción) entry, access; (sitio) entrance, way in; (COM) receipts pl, takings pl; (CULIN) entree; (DEPORTE) innings sg; (TEATRO) house, audience; (para el cine etc) ticket; (COM): ~**as y salidas** income and expenditure; (TEC): ~**a de aire** air intake or inlet.

entrante [en'trante] a next, coming // nm inlet; **ser** ~ **en una casa** to have the run of a house.

entraña [en'traɲa] nf (fig: centro) heart, core; (raíz) root; ~**s** nfpl (ANAT) entrails; **entrañable** a close, intimate.

entrar [en'trar] vt (introducir) to bring in // vi (meterse) to go/come in, enter; (comenzar): ~ **diciendo** to begin by saying; **no me entra** I can't get the hang of it; **el año que entra** next year.

entre ['entre] prep (dos) between; (más de dos) among(st); **pensaba** ~ **mí** I thought to myself.

entreabrir [entrea'ßrir] vt to half-open, open halfway.

entrecejo [entre'θexo] nm: **fruncir el** ~ to frown.

entredicho [entre'ðitʃo] nm prohibition, ban; (JUR) injunction.

entrega [en'trexa] nf (de mercancías) delivery; (rendición) surrender; **novela por** ~**s** serial, novel in instalments.

entregar [entre'var] vt (dar) to hand (over), deliver; (ceder) to give up; ~**se** vr (rendirse) to surrender, give in, submit; (dedicarse) to devote o.s.

entrelazar [entrela'θar] vt to entwine.

entremés [entre'mes] nm (CULIN) side-dish; **entremeses** nmpl hors d'œuvres.

entremeter [entreme'ter] vt to insert, put in; ~**se** vr to meddle, interfere; **entremetido, a** a meddling, interfering.

entremezclar [entremeθ'klar] vt, ~**se** vr to intermingle.

entrenador [entrena'ðor] nm trainer, coach; **entrenarse** vr to train.

entreoír [entreo'ir] vt to half hear.

entresacar [entresa'kar] vt to pick out, select.

entresuelo [entre'swelo] nm (sótano) basement.

entretanto [entre'tanto] ad meanwhile, meantime; **en el** ~ in the meantime.

entretejer [entrete'xer] vt to interweave.

entretener [entrete'ner] vt (divertir) to entertain, amuse; (detener) to hold up,

delay; (*cuidar*) to maintain; ~**se** *vr*
(*divertirse*) to amuse o.s.; (*retrasarse*) to
delay, linger; **entretenido, a** *a*
entertaining, amusing; **entretenimiento**
nm entertainment, amusement; (*cuidado*)
upkeep, maintenance.

entrever [entre'βer] *vt* to glimpse, catch
a glimpse of.

entreverar [entreβe'rar] *vt* to mix (up).

entrevista [entre'βista] *nf* interview;
entrevistar *vt* to interview;
entrevistarse *vr* to have an interview.

entristecer [entriste'θer] *vt* to sadden,
grieve; ~**se** *vr* to grow sad.

entrometer [entrome'ter] *etc* =
entremeter *etc*.

entroncar [entron'kar] *vi* to be connected
or related.

entronque [en'tronke] *nm* connection,
link.

entuerto [en'twerto] *nm* wrong, injustice.

entumecer [entume'θer] *vt* to numb,
benumb; ~**se** *vr* (*por el frío*) to go *or*
become numb; **entumecido, a** *a* numb,
stiff.

enturbiar [entur'βjar] *vt* (*el agua*) to
disturb, make cloudy; (*fig*) to fog, confuse;
~**se** *vr* (*oscurecerse*) to become cloudy;
(*fig*) to get confused, become obscure.

entusiasmar [entusjas'mar] *vt* to excite,
fill with enthusiasm; (*gustar mucho*) to
delight; ~**se** *vr*: ~**se con** *o* **por** to get
enthusiastic *or* excited about.

entusiasmo [entu'sjasmo] *nm*
enthusiasm; (*deleite*) delight; (*excitación*)
excitement.

entusiasta [entu'sjasta] *a* enthusiastic //
nm/f enthusiast.

enumerar [enume'rar] *vt* to enumerate.

enunciación [enunθja'θjon] *nf*,
enunciado [enun'θjaðo] *nm* enunciation;
(*declaración*) declaration, statement;
enunciar *vt* to enunciate; to declare,
state.

envainar [enβai'nar] *vt* to sheathe.

envalentonar [enβalento'nar] *vt* to give
courage to; ~**se** *vr* to take courage,
become bolder; (*pey: jactarse*) to boast,
brag.

envanecer [enβane'θer] *vt* to make
conceited; ~**se** *vr* to grow vain *or*
conceited.

envasar [enβa'sar] *vt* (*empaquetar*) to
pack, wrap; (*enfrascar*) to bottle; (*enlatar*)
to tin; (*embolsar*) to pocket // *vi* (*fig: fam:*
vino) to knock back; **envase** *nm* packing,
wrapping; bottling; tinning, canning;
pocketing; (*recipiente*) container;
(*paquete*) package; (*botella*) bottle; (*lata*)
tin, can.

envejecer [enβexe'θer] *vt* to make old,
age // *vi*, ~**se** *vr* (*volverse viejo*) to grow
old; (*fig*) to become old-fashioned.

envenenar [enβene'nar] *vt* to poison; (*fig*)
to embitter.

envergadura [enβerɣa'ðura] *nf* (*fig*)
scope, compass.

envés [en'βes] *nm* (*de tela*) back, wrong
side.

enviar [en'βjar] *vt* to send.

envidia [en'βiðja] *nf* (*deseo ferviente*)
envy; (*celos*) jealousy; **envidiar** *vt*
(*desear*) to envy; (*tener celos de*) to be
jealous of.

envilecer [enβile'θer] *vt* to debase,
degrade; ~**se** *vr* to lower o.s.

envío [en'βio] *nm* (*acción*) sending; (*de*
mercancías) consignment; (*COM*)
remittance.

enviudar [enβju'ðar] *vi* to be widowed.

envoltura [enβol'tura] *nf* (*cobertura*)
cover; (*embalaje*) wrapper, wrapping; (*fun-*
da) case.

envolver [enβol'βer] *vt* to wrap (up);
(*cubrir*) to cover; (*enemigo*) to surround;
(*implicar*) to involve, implicate; ~**se** *vr*
(*cubrirse*) to wrap o.s. up; (*implicarse*) to
become involved.

envuelto [en'βwelto] *pp de* **envolver.**

enzarzar [enθar'θar] *vt* (*fig*) to involve (in
a dispute).

épico, a ['epiko, a] *a* epic // *nf* epic.

epidemia [epi'ðemja] *nf* epidemic;
epidémico, a *a* epidemic.

epifanía [epifa'nia] *nf* Epiphany.

epilepsia [epi'lepsja] *nf* epilepsy.

epílogo [e'piloxo] *nm* epilogue.

episodio [epi'soðjo] *nm* episode.

epístola [e'pistola] *nf* epistle; (*fam*) letter.

epitafio [epi'tafjo] *nm* epitaph.

época ['epoka] *nf* period, time; (*HISTORIA*)
age, epoch; **hacer** ~ to be epoch-making.

equidad [eki'ðað] *nf* equity.

equilibrar [ekili'βrar] *vt* to balance;
equilibrio *nm* balance, equilibrium; **equi-**
librista *nm/f* (*funámbulo*) tightrope
walker; (*acróbata*) acrobat.

equipaje [eki'paxe] *nm* luggage; (*equipo*)
equipment, kit; (*NAUT: tripulación*) crew;
~ **de mano** hand luggage.

equipar [eki'par] *vt* (*proveer*) to equip.

equipararse [ekipa'rarse] *vr*: ~ **con** to
be on a level with.

equipo [e'kipo] *nm* (*materiales*)
equipment; (*grupo*) team; (: *de obreros*)
shift.

equis ['ekis] *nf* (the letter) X.

equitación [ekita'θjon] *nf* (*acto*) riding;
(*arte*) horsemanship.

equitativo, a [ekita'tiβo, a] *a* equitable,
fair.

equivalente [ekiβa'lente] *a, nm*
equivalent; **equivaler** *vi* to be equivalent
or equal.

equivocación [ekiβoka'θjon] *nf* mistake,
error; **equivocarse** *vr* to be wrong, make
a mistake; **equivocarse de camino** to
take the wrong road; **equívoco, a** *a* (*dudo-*
so) suspect; (*ambiguo*) ambiguous // *nm*
ambiguity; (*juego de palabras*) play on
words.

era *vb ver* **ser** // ['era] *nf* era, age.

erais *vb ver* **ser.**

éramos vb ver **ser.**
eran vb ver **ser.**
erario [e'rarjo] nm exchequer, treasury.
eras vb ver **ser.**
eres vb ver **ser.**
erguir [er'xir] vt to raise, lift; (poner derecho) to straighten; ~**se** vr to straighten
up; (fig) to swell with pride.
erigir [eri'xir] vt to erect, build; ~**se** vr:
~**se en** to set o.s. up as.
erizado, a [eri'θaðo, a] a bristly.
erizarse [eri'θarse] vr to stand on end.
erizo [e'riθo] nm hedgehog; (~ de mar)
sea-urchin.
ermitaño, a [ermi'taɲo, a] nm/f hermit.
erótico, a [e'rotiko, a] a erotic; **erotismo**
nm eroticism.
erradicar [erraði'kar] vt to eradicate.
errado, a [e'rraðo, a] a mistaken, wrong.
errante [e'rrante] a wandering, errant.
errar [e'rrar] vi (vagar) to wander, roam;
(equivocarse) to err, make a mistake // vt:
~ **el camino** to take the wrong road; ~
el tiro to miss.
erróneo, a [e'rroneo, a] a (equivocado)
wrong, mistaken; (falso) false, untrue.
error [e'rror] nm error, mistake; ~ **de
imprenta** misprint.
eructar [eruk'tar] vt to belch.
erudición [eruði'θjon] nf erudition,
learning.
erudito, a [eru'ðito, a] a erudite, learned.
erupción [erup'θjon] nf eruption; (MED)
rash.
es vb ver **ser.**
esa, esas det ver **ese.**
ésa, ésas pron ver **ése.**
esbelto, a [es'βelto, a] a slim, slender.
esbozo [es'βoθo] nm sketch, outline.
escabeche [eska'βetʃe] nm brine; (de
aceitunas etc) pickle; **pescado en** ~
pickled fish.
escabel [eska'βel] nm (low) stool.
escabroso, a [eska'βroso, a] a (accidentado) rough, uneven; (fig) tough, difficult; (:
atrevido) risqué.
escabullirse [eskaβuʎirse] vr to slip
away; (irse) to clear out.
escala [es'kala] nf (proporción, MUS) scale;
(de mano) ladder; (AVIAT) stopover; **hacer**
~ **en** to stop or call in at; ~ **de colores**
range of colours.
escalafón [eskala'fon] nm (escala de salarios) salary scale, wage scale; (lista etc)
list; (registro) register.
escalar [eska'lar] vt (montaña etc) to
climb, scale; (casa) to burgle, break into.
escalera [eska'lera] nf stairs pl, staircase;
(escala) ladder; (NAIPES) run; ~ **mecánica** escalator; ~ **de caracol** spiral
staircase.
escalinata [eskali'nata] nf outside
staircase.
escalofrío [eskalo'frio] nm chill; ~**s** nmpl
(fig) shivers; **escalofriante** a chilling.

escalón [eska'lon] nm step, stair; (de escalera) rung.
escama [es'kama] nf (de pez, serpiente)
scale; (de jabón) flake; (fig) resentment.
escamado, a [eska'maðo, a] a wary,
cautious.
escamotar [eskamo'tar], **escamotear**
[eskamote'ar] vt (quitar) to lift, swipe
(fam); (hacer desaparecer) to make
disappear.
escampar [eskam'par] vb impersonal to
stop raining; (del cielo) to clear (up).
escandalizar [eskandali'θar] vt to
scandalize, shock; ~**se** vr to be shocked;
(ofenderse) to be offended.
escándalo [es'kandalo] nm scandal;
(alboroto, tumulto) row, uproar;
escandaloso, a a scandalous, shocking.
escandinavo, a [eskandi'naβo, a] a, nm/f
Scandinavian.
escaño [es'kaɲo] nm bench; (POL) seat.
escapar [eska'par] vi (gen) to escape, run
away; (DEPORTE) to break away; ~**se** vr to
escape, get away; (gas) to leak (out).
escaparate [eskapa'rate] nm shop
window; (AM) wardrobe.
escape [es'kape] nm (de gas) leak; (de motor) exhaust; (de persona) escape.
escarabajo [eskara'βaxo] nm beetle; ~**s**
nmpl (fam) scribble sg.
escaramuza [eskara'muθa] nf skirmish;
(fig) brush.
escarbar [eskar'βar] vt (gallina) to
scratch; (dientes) to pick; (orejas) to clean;
(fig) to inquire into, investigate.
escarcha [es'kartʃa] nf frost.
escarlata [eskar'lata] a inv scarlet;
escarlatina nf scarlet fever.
escarmentar [eskarmen'tar] vt to punish
severely // vi to learn one's lesson;
escarmiento nm (ejemplo) lesson,
example; (castigo) punishment.
escarnecer [eskarne'θer] vt to mock,
ridicule; **escarnio, escarnecimiento** nm
mockery; (injuria) insult.
escarpado, a [eskar'paðo, a] a (abrupto)
sheer; (inclinado) steep; (accidentado)
craggy.
escasear [eskase'ar] vt to skimp (on) // vi
to be scarce.
escasez [eska'seθ] nf (falta) shortage,
scarcity; (pobreza) poverty; (mezquindad)
meanness.
escaso, a [es'kaso, a] a (poco) scarce;
(raro) rare; (ralo) thin, sparse; (limitado)
limited.
escatimar [eskati'mar] vt (limitar) to
skimp (on); (reducir) to curtail, cut down.
escena [es'θena] nf scene.
escenario [esθe'narjo] nm (TEATRO) stage;
(CINE) set; (fig) scene.
escepticismo [esθepti'θismo] nm
scepticism; **escéptico, a** a sceptical //
nm/f sceptic.
esclarecer [esklare'θer] vt (iluminar) to
light up, illuminate; (misterio, problema) to
shed light on; (ennoblecer) to ennoble.

esclavitud [eskla'ßi'tuð] *nf* slavery.
esclavizar [esklaßi'θar] *vt* to enslave.
esclavo, a [es'klaßo, a] *nm/f* slave.
escoba [es'koßa] *nf* broom.
escocer [esko'θer] *vt* to annoy // *vi* to burn, sting; **~se** *vr* to chafe, get chafed.
escocés, esa [esko'θes, esa] *a* Scottish // *nm/f* Scotsman/woman, Scot.
Escocia [es'koθja] *nf* Scotland.
escoger [esko'xer] *vt* to choose, pick, select; **escogido, a** *a* chosen, selected; *(calidad)* choice, select; **escogimiento** *nm* choice.
escolar [esko'lar] *a* school *cpd* // *nm/f* schoolboy/girl, pupil.
escolta [es'kolta] *nf* escort; **escoltar** *vt* to escort.
escombro [es'kombro] *nm* mackerel; **~s** *nmpl (basura)* rubbish *sg*; *(restos)* debris *sg*.
esconder [eskon'der] *vt* to hide, conceal; **~se** *vr* to hide; **escondite** *nm* hiding place; *(juego)* hide-and-seek.
escondrijo [eskon'drixo] *nm* hiding-place, hideout.
escopeta [esko'peta] *nf* shotgun.
escoplo [es'koplo] *nm* chisel.
Escorpio [es'korpjo] *nm* Scorpio.
escorpión [eskor'pjon] *nm* scorpion.
escote [es'kote] *nm (de vestido)* low neck; *(parte)* share; **pagar a ~** to share the expenses.
escotillón [eskoti'ʎon] *nm* trapdoor.
escozor [esko'θor] *nm (dolor)* sting(ing); *(fig)* grief, heartache.
escribano, a [eskri'ßano, a], **escribiente** [eskri'ßjente] *nm/f* clerk.
escribir [eskri'ßir] *vt, vi* to write; **~ a máquina** to type; **¿cómo se escribe?** how do you spell it?
escrito, a [es'krito, a] *pp de* **escribir** // *nm (documento)* document; *(manuscrito)* text, manuscript; **por ~** in writing.
escritor, a [eskri'tor, a] *nm/f* writer.
escritorio [eskri'torjo] *nm* desk; *(oficina)* office.
escritura [eskri'tura] *nf (acción)* writing; *(caligrafía)* (hand)writing; *(JUR: documento)* deed.
escrúpulo [es'krupulo] *nm* scruple; *(minuciosidad)* scrupulousness; **escrupuloso, a** *a* scrupulous.
escrutar [eskru'tar] *vt* to scrutinize, examine; *(votos)* to count.
escrutinio [eskru'tinjo] *nm (examen atento)* scrutiny; *(recuento de votos)* poll; *(resultado de elección)* voting, ballot.
escuadra [es'kwaðra] *nf (MIL etc)* squad; *(NAUT)* squadron; *(de coches etc)* fleet; **escuadrilla** *nf (de aviones)* squadron; *(AM: de obreros)* gang.
escuadrón [eska'ðron] *nm* squadron.
escuálido, a [es'kwaliðo, a] *a (flaco, macilento)* pale, wan; *(sucio)* squalid.
escuchar [esku'tʃar] *vt* to listen to // *vi* to listen.

escudilla [esku'ðiʎa] *nf* bowl, basin.
escudo [es'kuðo] *nm* shield.
escudriñar [eskuðri'ɲar] *vt (examinar)* to investigate, examine closely; *(mirar de lejos)* to scan.
escuela [es'kwela] *nf* school.
escueto, a [es'kweto, a] *a* plain, unadorned.
esculpir [eskul'pir] *vt* to sculpt; *(grabar)* to engrave; *(tallar)* to carve; **escultor, a** *nm/f* sculptor/tress; **escultura** *nf* sculpture.
escupidora [eskupi'ðora], **escupidera** [eskupi'ðera] *nf* spittoon; *(orinal)* bedpan.
escupir [esku'pir] *vt, vi* to spit (out).
escurridero [eskurri'ðero] *nm* draining-board.
escurridizo, a [eskurri'ðiθo, a] *a* slippery.
escurrir [esku'rrir] *vt (ropa)* to wring out; *(verduras)* to strain; *(platos)* to drain // *vi (los líquidos)* to drip; *(resbalarse)* to slip, slide; **~se** *vr (gotear)* to drip; *(secarse)* to drain; *(resbalarse)* to slip, slide; *(escaparse)* to slip away.
ese, esa, esos, esas ['ese, 'esa, 'esos, 'esas] *det (sg)* that; *(pl)* those.
ése, ésa, ésos, ésas ['ese, 'esa, 'esos, 'esas] *pron (sg)* that (one); *(pl)* those (ones); **~... éste...** the former... the latter...; **¡no me vengas con ~as** don't give me any more of that nonsense.
esencia [e'senθja] *nf* essence; **esencial** *a* essential.
esfera [es'fera] *nf* sphere; *(de reloj)* face; **esférico, a** *a* spherical.
esforzado, a [esfor'θaðo, a] *a (enérgico)* energetic, vigorous; *(valiente)* brave.
esforzar [esfor'θar] *vt (fortalecer)* to strengthen; *(alentar)* to encourage; **~se** *vr* to exert o.s., make an effort.
esfuerzo [es'fwerθo] *nm* effort; *(TEC)* stress; *(valor)* courage, spirit.
esfumarse [esfu'marse] *vr* to fade away.
esgrima [es'xrima] *nf* fencing.
esguince [es'xinθe] *nm (MED)* sprain; *(ademán)* swerve, dodge; *(ceño)* scowl, frown.
eslabón [esla'ßon] *nm* link; **eslabonar** *vt* to link, connect.
esmaltar [esmal'tar] *vt* to enamel; *(las uñas)* to paint, varnish; **esmalte** *nm* enamel; **esmalte de uñas** nail varnish, nail polish.
esmerado, a [esme'raðo, a] *a* careful, neat.
esmeralda [esme'ralda] *nf* emerald.
esmerarse [esme'rarse] *vr (aplicarse)* to take great pains, exercise great care; *(brillar)* to shine, do well.
esmero [es'mero] *nm* (great) care.
esnob [es'nob] *a inv (persona)* snobbish; *(coche etc)* posh // *nm/f* snob; **~ismo** *nm* snobbery.
eso ['eso] *pron* that, that thing *or* matter; **~ de su coche** all that about his car; **~ de ir al cine** all that about going to the cinema, the idea of going to the cinema; **a ~ de las cinco** at about five o'clock; **en**

~ thereupon, at that point; ~ **es** that's it; **¡~ sí que es vida!** now this is really living!; **por ~ te lo dije** that's why I told you.

esos ['esos] *det ver* **ese.**

ésos ['esos] *pron ver* **ése.**

espabilar [espaβi'lar] *vt* (*vela*) to snuff; ~**se** *vr* (*despertarse*) to wake up; (*animarse*) to liven up, look lively.

espacial [espa'θjal] *a inv* (*del espacio*) space *cpd*.

espaciar [espa'θjar] *vt* to space (out); (*divulgar*) to spread; ~**se** *vr*: ~**se en un tema** to enlarge on a subject.

espacio [es'paθjo] *nm* space; (*MUS*) interval; (*emisión*) (short) programme; spot; **el ~** space; ~**so, a** a spacious, roomy; (*lento*) slow.

espada [es'paða] *nf* sword; ~**s** *nfpl* (*NAIPES*) spades.

espaguetis [espa'xetis] *nmpl* spaghetti *sg*.

espalda [es'palda] *nf* (*gen*) back; ~**s** *nfpl* (*hombros*) shoulders; **a ~s de uno** behind sb's back; **cargado de ~s** round-shouldered; **tenderse de ~s** to lie (down) on one's back; **volver la ~ a alguien** to give sb the cold shoulder.

espaldar [espal'dar] *nm* (*de asiento*) back.

espaldilla [espal'ðiʎa] *nf* shoulder-blade.

espantadizo, a [espanta'ðiθo, a] *a* timid, easily frightened.

espantajo [espan'taxo] *nm*, **espanta-pájaros** [espanta'paxaros] *nmpl* scare-crow *sg*.

espantar [espan'tar] *vt* (*asustar*) to frighten, scare; (*ahuyentar*) to frighten off; (*asombrar*) to horrify, appal; ~**se** *vr* to get frightened *or* scared; to be appalled.

espanto [es'panto] *nm* (*susto*) fright; (*terror*) terror; (*fantasma*) ghost; (*asombro*) astonishment; ~**so, a** a frightening; terrifying; astonishing.

España [es'paɲa] *nf* Spain; **español, a** a Spanish // *nm/f* Spaniard // *nm* (*lengua*) Spanish.

esparadrapo [espara'ðrapo] *nm* sticking plaster.

esparcido, a [espar'θiðo, a] *a* scattered; (*fig*) jolly, cheerful.

esparcimiento [esparθi'mjento] *nm* (*de líquido*) spilling; (*dispersión*) spreading; (*derramamiento*) scattering; (*fig*) cheerfulness.

esparcir [espar'θir] *vt* to spread; (*derramar*) to scatter; (*líquido*) to spill; ~**se** *vr* to spread (out); to scatter; to spill; (*divertirse*) to enjoy o.s.

espárrago [es'parraxo] *nm* asparagus.

espasmo [es'pasmo] *nm* spasm.

especia [es'peθja] *nf* spice.

especial [espe'θjal] *a* special; ~**idad** *nf* speciality.

especie [es'peθje] *nf* (*BIO*) species; (*clase*) kind, sort; (*asunto*) matter; (*comentario*) remark, comment; **en ~** in kind.

especificar [espeθifi'kar] *vt* to specify; **específico, a** a specific.

espécimen [es'peθimen] (*pl* **especímenes**) *nm* specimen.

especioso, a [espe'θjoso, a] *a* (*perfecto*) perfect; (*fig*) deceitful.

espectáculo [espek'takulo] *nm* (*gen*) spectacle; (*TEATRO etc*) show.

espectador, a [espekta'ðor, a] *nm/f* spectator.

espectro [es'pektro] *nm* ghost; (*fig*) spectre.

especular [espeku'lar] *vt*, *vi* to speculate; **especulativo, a** a speculative.

espejismo [espe'xismo] *nm* mirage.

espejo [es'pexo] *nm* mirror; (*fig*) model; ~ **de retrovisión** rear-view mirror.

espeluznante [espeluθ'nante] *a inv* horrifying, hair-raising.

espera [es'pera] *nf* (*pausa, intervalo*) wait, period of waiting; (*JUR: plazo*) respite; **en ~ de** waiting for; (*con expectativa*) expecting.

esperanza [espe'ranθa] *nf* (*confianza*) hope; (*expectativa*) expectation; (*perspectiva*) prospect; **esperanzar** *vt* to give hope to.

esperar [espe'rar] *vt* (*aguardar*) to wait for; (*tener expectativa de*) to expect; (*desear*) to hope for // *vi* to wait; to expect; to hope.

esperma [es'perma] *nf* sperm.

espesar [espe'sar] *vt* to thicken; ~**se** *vr* to thicken, get thicker.

espeso, a [es'peso, a] *a* thick; **espesor** *nm* thickness.

espetar [espe'tar] *vt* (*pollo*) to put on a spit *or* skewer; (*pregunta*) to pop; (*dar: reto, sermón*) to give.

espetón [espe'ton] *nm* (*asador*) spit, skewer; (*aguja*) large pin; (*empujón*) jab, poke.

espía [es'pia] *nm/f* spy; **espiar** *vt* (*observar*) to spy on; (*acechar*) to watch out for.

espina [es'pina] *nf* thorn; (*de madera, astilla*) splinter; (*de pez*) bone; ~ **dorsal** spine.

espinaca [espi'naka] *nf* spinach.

espinar [espi'nar] *vt* (*herir*) to prick; (*fig*) to sting, hurt.

espinazo [espi'naθo] *nm* spine, backbone.

espino [es'pino] *nm* hawthorn.

espinoso, a [espi'noso, a] *a* (*planta*) thorny, prickly; (*fig*) bony.

espionaje [espjo'naxe] *nm* spying, espionage.

espiral [espi'ral] *a, nf* spiral.

espirar [espi'rar] *vt* to breathe out, exhale.

espiritista [espiri'tista] *a, nm/f* spiritualist.

espíritu [es'piritu] *nm* spirit; **espiritual** a spiritual.

espita [es'pita] *nf* tap; (*fig: fam*) drunkard.

esplendidez [esplendi'ðeθ] *nf* (*abundancia*) lavishness; (*magnificencia*) splendour.

esplendor [esplen'dor] *nm* splendour.

espolear [espole'ar] *vt* to spur on.
espolvorear [espolβore'ar] *vt* (*echar polvos*) to dust; (*esparcir*) to dust, sprinkle.
esponja [es'ponxa] *nf* sponge; (*fig*) sponger.
esponjarse [espon'xarse] *vr* (*fam: hincharse*) to swell with pride; (: *de salud*) to glow with health.
esponjoso, a [espon'xoso, a] *a* spongy, porous.
espontaneidad [espontanei'ðað] *nf* spontaneity; **espontáneo, a** *a* spontaneous.
esposa [es'posa] *nf* wife; **~s** *nfpl* handcuffs; **esposar** *vt* to handcuff.
esposo [es'poso] *nm* husband.
espuela [es'pwela] *nf* spur.
espuma [es'puma] *nf* foam; (*de cerveza*) froth, head; (*de jabón*) lather; **espumoso, a** *a* frothy, foamy; (*vino*) sparkling.
esqueleto [eske'leto] *nm* skeleton.
esquema [es'kema] *nm* (*diagrama*) diagram; (*dibujo*) plan; (*plan*) scheme; (*FILOSOFIA*) schema.
esquí [es'ki] (*pl* **esquís**) *nm* (*objeto*) ski; (*deporte*) skiing.
esquilar [eski'lar] *vt* to shear.
esquilmar [eskil'mar] *vt* (*cosechar*) to harvest; (*empobrecer: suelo*) to exhaust; (*fig*) to skin.
esquimal [eski'mal] *a, nm/f* Eskimo.
esquina [es'kina] *nf* corner.
esquirol [eski'rol] *nm* (*fam*) blackleg.
esquivar [eski'βar] *vt* to avoid; (*evadir*) to dodge, elude; **~se** *vr* to withdraw.
esquivez [eski'βeθ] *nf* (*altanería*) aloofness; (*desdeño*) scorn, disdain; **esquivo, a** *a* (*altanero*) aloof; (*desdeñoso*) scornful, disdainful.
esta ['esta] *det ver* **este**.
ésta ['esta] *pron ver* **éste**.
está *vb ver* **estar**.
estabilidad [estaβili'ðað] *nf* stability; **estable** *a* stable.
establecer [estaβle'θer] *vt* to establish; **~se** *vr* to establish o.s.; (*echar raíces*) to settle; **establecimiento** *nm* establishment.
estaca [es'taka] *nf* stake, post; (*para tiendas*) peg.
estacada [esta'kaða] *nf* (*cerca*) fence, fencing; (*palenque*) stockade.
estación [esta'θjon] *nf* station; (*del año*) season; **~ de autobuses** bus station.
estacionamiento [estaθjona'mjento] *nm* (*AUTO*) parking; (*MIL*) stationing; (*colocación*) placing.
estacionar [estaθjo'nar] *vt* (*AUTO*) to park; (*MIL*) to station; (*colocar*) to place; **~io, a** *a* stationary; (*COM: mercado*) slack.
estadio [es'taðjo] *nm* (*fase*) stage, phase; (*DEPORTE*) stadium.
estadista [esta'ðista] *nm* (*POL*) statesman; (*ESTADÍSTICA*) statistician.
estadística [esta'ðistika] *nf* (*una* **~**) figure, statistic; (*ciencia*) statistics *sg*.

estado [es'taðo] *nm* (*POL: condición*) state; (*social*) status; **~ de las cuentas** statement of accounts; **~ mayor** staff; **E~s Unidos (EE. UU.)** United States (USA).
estafa [es'tafa] *nf* swindle, trick; **estafar** *vt* to swindle, defraud.
estafeta [esta'feta] *nf* (*correo*) post; (*oficina de correos*) post office; **~ diplomática** diplomatic bag.
estallar [esta'ʎar] *vi* to burst; (*explotar*) to explode; (*epidemia, rebelión*) to break out; **~ en llanto** to burst into tears; **estallido** *nm* explosion; (*fig*) outbreak.
estampa [es'tampa] *nf* (*imagen*) image; (*impresión, imprenta*) print, engraving; (*imagen, figura: de persona*) appearance; (*fig: huella*) footprint.
estampado, a [estam'paðo, a] *a* printed // *nm* (*impresión: acción*) printing; (: *efecto*) print; (*marca*) stamping.
estampar [estam'par] *vt* (*imprimir*) to print; (*marcar*) to stamp; (*metal*) to engrave; (*poner sello en*) to stamp; (*fig*) to stamp, imprint.
estampida [estam'piða] *nf* stampede; (*estampido*) bang, report.
estampido [estam'piðo] *nm* bang, report.
estampilla [estam'piʎa] *nf* stamp.
están *vb ver* **estar**.
estancar [estan'kar] *vt* (*aguas*) to hold up, hold back; (*COM*) to monopolize; (*fig*) to block, hold up; **~se** *vr* to stagnate.
estancia [es'tanθja] *nf* (*permanencia*) stay; (*sala*) living-room; (*AM*) farm, ranch; **estanciero** *nm* farmer, rancher.
estanco, a [es'tanko, a] *a* watertight // *nm* (*monopolio*) state monopoly; (*tienda*) tobacconist's (shop).
estandarizar [estandari'θar] *vt* to standardize.
estandarte [estan'darte] *nm* banner, standard.
estanque [es'tanke] *nm* (*lago*) pool, pond; (*AGR*) reservoir.
estanquero, a [estan'kero, a], **estanquillero, a** [estanki'ʎero, a] *nm/f* tobacconist.
estante [es'tante] *nm* (*armario*) rack, stand; (*biblioteca*) bookcase; (*anaquel*) shelf; (*AM*) prop; **estantería** *nf* shelving, shelves *pl*.
estantigua [estan'tiɣwa] *nf* (*fantasma*) apparition.
estaño [es'taɲo] *nm* tin.
estar [es'tar] *vi* (*gen*) to be; (*en casa*) to be in; (*ubicarse*) to be found; (*presente*) to be present; **estamos a 2 de mayo** it is the 2nd May; **¿cómo está Ud?** how are you?; **~ enfermo** to be ill; **~ viejo/joven** (*parecerse*) to seem old/young; (*seguido de una preposición*): **¿a cuánto estamos de Madrid?** how far are we from Madrid?; **~ de fiesta** *o* **vacaciones** to be on holiday; **las uvas están a 5 pesetas** grapes are at 5 pesetas; **María no está** Maria isn't in; **~ por** (: *moción*) to be in

favour of; (: *persona*) to support, back; **está por hacer** it remains to be done; **¿estamos?** are we agreed?

estas ['estas] *det ver* **este.**

éstas ['estas] *pron ver* **éste.**

estás *vb ver* **estar.**

estatal [esta'tal] *a inv* state *cpd.*

estático, a [es'tatiko, a] *a* static.

estatificar [estatifi'kar] *vt* to nationalize.

estatua [es'tatwa] *nf* statue.

estatuir [estatu'ir] *vt* (*establecer*) to establish; (*determinar*) to prove.

estatura [esta'tura] *nf* stature, height.

estatuto [esta'tuto] *nm* (*JUR*) statute; (*de ciudad*) bye-law; (*de comité*) rule.

este ['este] *nm* east.

este, esta, estos, estas ['este, 'esta, 'estos, 'estas] *det* (*sg*) this; (*pl*) these.

éste, ésta, éstos, éstas ['este, 'esta, 'estos, 'estas] *pron* (*sg*) this (one); (*pl*) these (ones); **~... ése...** the latter... the former... .

esté *etc vb ver* **estar.**

estela [es'tela] *nf* wake, wash; (*fig*) trail.

estenografía [estenoxra'fia] *nf* shorthand, stenography.

estepa [es'tepa] *nf* (*GEO*) steppe.

estera [es'tera] *nf* mat(ting).

estereo... [estereo] *pref* stereo...; **~fónico, a** *a* stereophonic; **~tipar** *vt* to stereotype; **~tipo** *nm* stereotype.

estéril [es'teril] *a* sterile, barren; (*fig*) vain, futile.

esterlina [ester'lina] *a*: **libra ~** pound sterling.

estético, a [es'tetiko, a] *a* aesthetic // *nf* aesthetics *sg.*

estiércol [es'tjerkol] *nm* dung, manure.

estigma [es'tixma] *nm* stigma.

estilar [esti'lar] *vi,* **~se** *vr* to be in fashion, be used, be worn.

estilo [es'tilo] *nm* style; (*TEC*) stylus; (*DEPORTE*) stroke; **algo por el ~** something of the sort.

estima [es'tima] *nf* esteem, respect.

estimación [estima'θjon] *nf* (*evaluación*) estimation; (*aprecio, afecto*) esteem, regard.

estimar [esti'mar] *vt* (*evaluar*) to estimate; (*valorar*) to value; (*apreciar*) to esteem, respect; (*pensar, considerar*) to think, reckon; **¡se estima!** thanks very much!

estimulante [estimu'lante] *a* stimulating // *nm* stimulant; **estimular** *vt* to stimulate; (*excitar*) to excite; (*animar*) to encourage; **estímulo** *nm* stimulus; (*ánimo*) encouragement.

estío [es'tio] *nm* summer.

estipulación [estipula'θjon] *nf* stipulation, condition; **estipular** *vt* to stipulate.

estirado, a [esti'raðo, a] *a* (*tenso*) (stretched *or* drawn) tight; (*fig*) stiff, pompous.

estirar [esti'rar] *vt* to stretch; (*conversa-*

ción, presupuesto) to stretch out; **~se** *vr* to stretch.

estirón [esti'ron] *nm* pull, tug; (*crecimiento*) spurt, sudden growth; **dar un ~** to shoot up.

estirpe [es'tirpe] *nf* stock, lineage.

estival [esti'ßal] *a* summer *cpd.*

esto ['esto] *pron* this, this thing *or* matter; **~ de la boda** this business about the wedding.

estofa [es'tofa] *nf* (*tela*) quilting; (*calidad, clase*) quality, class.

estofado, a [esto'faðo, a] *a* (*CULIN*) stewed; (*bordado*) quilted // *nm* stew.

estofar [esto'far] *vt* (*bordar*) to quilt; (*CULIN*) to stew.

estoico, a [es'toiko, a] *a* (*FILOSOFÍA*) stoic(al); (*fig*) cold, indifferent.

estólido, a [es'toliðo, a] *a* stupid.

estómago [es'tomaxo] *nm* stomach; **tener ~** to be thick-skinned.

estorbar [estor'ßar] *vt* to hinder, obstruct; (*fig*) to bother, disturb // *vi* to be in the way; **estorbo** *nm* (*molestia*) bother, nuisance; (*obstáculo*) hindrance, obstacle.

estornudar [estornu'ðar] *vi* to sneeze.

estos ['estos] *det ver* **este.**

éstos ['estos] *pron ver* **éste.**

estoy *vb ver* **estar.**

estrafalario, a [estrafa'larjo, a] *a* odd, eccentric; (*desarreglado*) slovenly, sloppy.

estragar [estra'xar] *vt* to deprave, corrupt; (*deteriorar*) to ruin; **estrago** *nm* ruin, destruction; **hacer estragos en** to wreak havoc among.

estragón [estra'xon] *nm* (*CULIN*) tarragon.

estrangul [estran'gul] *nm* mouthpiece.

estrangulación [estrangula'θjon] *nf* strangulation.

estrangulador, a [estrangula'ðor, a] *nm/f* strangler // *nm* (*TEC*) throttle; (*AUTO*) choke.

estrangulamiento [estrangula'mjento] *nm* (*AUTO*) bottleneck.

estrangular [estrangu'lar] *vt* (*persona*) to strangle; (*MED*) to strangulate.

estraperlo [estra'perlo] *nm* black market.

estratagema [estrata'xema] *nf* (*MIL*) stratagem; (*astucia*) cunning.

estrategia [estra'texja] *nf* strategy; **estratégico, a** *a* strategic.

estratificar [estratifi'kar] *vt* to stratify.

estrato [es'trato] *nm* stratum, layer.

estrechar [estre'tʃar] *vt* (*reducir*) to narrow; (*vestido*) to take in; (*persona*) to hug, embrace; **~se** *vr* (*reducirse*) to narrow, grow narrow; (*apretarse*) to embrace; (*reducir los gastos*) to economize; **~ la mano** to shake hands; **~ amistad con alguien** to become very friendly with sb.

estrechez [estre'tʃeθ] *nf* narrowness; (*de ropa*) tightness; (*intimidad*) intimacy; (*COM*) want *or* shortage of money; **estrecheces** *nfpl* financial difficulties; **~ de conciencia** small-mindedness; **~ de miras** narrow-mindedness.

estrecho, a [es'tretʃo, a] a narrow; (apretado) tight; (íntimo) close, intimate; (miserable) mean // nm strait.

estregar [estre'xar] vt (sobar) to rub (hard); (rascar) to scrape.

estrella [es'treʎa] nf star; ~ **de mar** starfish.

estrellar [estre'ʎar] vt (hacer añicos) to smash (to pieces); (huevos) to fry; ~**se** vr to smash; (chocarse) to crash; (fracasar) to be smashed to pieces.

estremecer [estreme'θer] vt ~ to shake; ~**se** vr to shake, tremble; **estremecimiento** nm (conmoción) tremor; (sobresalto) shock; (temblor) trembling, shaking.

estrenar [estre'nar] vt (vestido) to wear for the first time; (casa) to move into; (película, obra de teatro) to present for the first time; ~**se** vr (persona) to make one's début; **estreno** nm (primer uso) first use; (en un empleo) début, first appearance; (CINE etc) première.

estreñir [estre'ɲir] vt to constipate; ~**se** vr to become constipated.

estrépito [es'trepito] nm noise, racket; (fig) fuss; **estrepitoso, a** a noisy; (fiesta) rowdy, boisterous.

estría [es'tria] nf groove.

estribar [estri'ßar] vi: ~ **en** to rest on, be supported by.

estribo [es'trißo] nm (de jinete) stirrup; (de coche, tren) step; (de puente) support; (fig) basis, foundation; (GEO) spur.

estribor [estri'ßor] nm starboard.

estricnina [estrik'nina] nf strychnine.

estricto, a [es'trikto, a] a (riguroso) strict; (severo) severe.

estro ['estro] nm inspiration.

estropajo [estro'paxo] nm scourer.

estropear [estrope'ar] vt (arruinar) to spoil; (dañar) to damage; (lisiar) to maim; (tullir) to cripple; ~**se** vr (objeto) to get damaged; (persona) to be crippled.

estructura [estruk'tura] nf structure.

estruendo [es'trwendo] nm (ruido) racket, din; (fig: alboroto) uproar, turmoil; (pompa) pomp.

estrujar [estru'xar] vt (apretar) to squeeze; (aplastar) to crush; (magullar) to bruise; (fig) to drain, bleed.

estuario [es'twarjo] nm estuary.

estuche [es'tutʃe] nm box, case.

estudiante [estu'ðjante] nm/f student; **estudiantil** a inv student cpd.

estudiantina [estuðjan'tina] nf student music group.

estudiar [estu'ðjar] vt to study.

estudio [es'tuðjo] nm study; (CINE, ARTE, RADIO) studio; ~**s** nmpl studies; (erudición) learning sg; ~**so, a** a studious.

estufa [es'tufa] nf heater, fire.

estulticia [estul'tiθja] nf foolishness.

estupefacto, a [estupe'fakto, a] a speechless, thunderstruck.

estupendo, a [estu'pendo, a] a wonderful,

terrific; (fam) great; ¡~! that's great!, fantastic!

estupidez [estupi'ðeθ] nf (torpeza) stupidity; (tontería) piece of nonsense.

estúpido, a [es'tupiðo, a] a stupid, silly.

estupor [estu'por] nm stupor; (fig) astonishment, amazement.

estupro [es'tupro] nm rape.

estuve etc vb ver **estar.**

etapa [e'tapa] nf stage; (DEPORTE) leg; (parada) stopping place; (fig) stage, phase.

eternidad [eterni'ðað] nf eternity; **eterno, a** a eternal, everlasting.

ético, a ['etiko, a] a ethical // nf ethics pl.

etíope [e'tiope] a, nm/f Ethiopian.

Etiopía [etjo'pia] nf Ethiopia.

etiqueta [eti'keta] nf (modales) etiquette; (papel) label, tag.

eucalipto [euka'lipto] nm eucalyptus.

Eucaristía [eukaris'tia] nf Eucharist.

eufemismo [eufe'mismo] nm euphemism.

euforia [eu'forja] nf euphoria.

eugenesia [euxe'nesja] nf, **eugenismo** [euxe'nismo] nm eugenics sg.

eunuco [eu'nuko] nm eunuch.

Europa [eu'ropa] nf Europe; **europeo, a** a, nm/f European.

éuscaro, a ['euskaro, a] a Basque // nm (lengua) Basque.

Euskadi [eus'kaði] nm the Basque Provinces pl.

eutanasia [euta'nasja] nf euthanasia.

evacuación [eßakwa'θjon] nf evacuation; **evacuar** vt to evacuate.

evadir [eßa'ðir] vt to evade, avoid; ~**se** vr to escape.

evaluar [eßa'lwar] vt to evaluate.

evangélico, a [eßan'xeliko, a] a evangelic(al).

evangelio [eßan'xeljo] nm gospel.

evaporación [eßapora'θjon] nf evaporation.

evaporar [eßapo'rar] vt to evaporate; ~**se** vr to vanish.

evasión [eßa'sjon] nf escape, flight; (fig) evasion.

evasivo, a [eßa'sißo, a] a evasive, noncommittal.

evento [e'ßento] nm unforeseen event; (eventualidad) eventuality; **a cualquier** ~ in any event.

eventual [eßen'twal] a possible, conditional (upon circumstances); (trabajador) casual, temporary.

evidencia [eßi'ðenθja] nf (certidumbre) evidence, proof; **evidenciar** vt (hacer patente) to make evident; (probar) to prove, show; **evidenciarse** vr to be evident.

evidente [eßi'ðente] a obvious, clear, evident.

evitar [eßi'tar] vt (evadir) to avoid; (impedir) to prevent.

evocar [eßo'kar] vt to evoke, call forth.

evolución [eßolu'θjon] nf (desarrollo) evolution, development; (cambio) change;

(*MIL*) manoeuvre; **evolucionar** *vi* to evolve; (*MIL, AVIAT*) to manoeuvre.

ex [eks] *a* ex-; **el ~ ministro** the former minister, the ex-minister.

exacerbar [eksaθer'βar] *vt* to irritate, annoy; (*agravar*) to aggravate.

exactitud [eksakti'tuð] *nf* exactness; (*precisión*) accuracy; (*puntualidad*) punctuality; **exacto, a** *a* exact; accurate; punctual; **¡exacto!** exactly!

exageración [eksaxera'θjon] *nf* exaggeration; **exagerar** *vt, vi* to exaggerate.

exaltado, a [eksal'taðo, a] *a* (*apasionado*) over-excited, worked-up; (*exagerado*) extreme; (*excitado*) elated.

exaltar [eksal'tar] *vt* to exalt, glorify; **~se** *vr* (*excitarse*) to get excited *or* worked-up; (*arrebatarse*) to get carried away.

examen [ek'samen] *nm* examination.

examinar [eksami'nar] *vt* to examine; **~se** *vr* to be examined, sit an examination.

exangüe [ek'sangwe] *a* (*desangrado*) bloodless; (*sin fuerzas*) weak.

exasperar [eksaspe'rar] *vt* to exasperate; **~se** *vr* to get exasperated, lose patience.

Exca. *abr de* **Excelencia.**

excedente [eksθe'ðente] *a, nm* excess, surplus.

exceder [eksθe'ðer] *vt* to exceed, surpass; **~se** *vr* (*extralimitarse*) to go too far; (*sobrepasarse*) to excel o.s.

excelencia [eksθe'lenθja] *nf* excellence; **E~** Excellency; **excelente** *a* excellent.

excelso, a [eks'θelso, a] *a* lofty, sublime.

excentricidad [eksθentriθi'ðað] *nf* eccentricity; **excéntrico, a** *a, nm/f* eccentric.

excepción [eksθep'θjon] *nf* exception; **excepcional** *a* exceptional.

excepto [eks'θepto] *ad* excepting, except (for).

exceptuar [eksθep'twar] *vt* to except, exclude.

excesivo, a [eksθe'siβo, a] *a* excessive.

exceso [eks'θeso] *nm* (*gen*) excess; (*COM*) surplus.

excitación [eksθita'θjon] *nf* (*sensación*) excitement; (*acción*) excitation.

excitado, a [eksθi'taðo, a] *a* excited; (*emociones*) aroused; **excitar** *vt* to excite; (*incitar*) to urge; **excitarse** *vr* to get excited.

exclamación [eksklama'θjon] *nf* exclamation; **exclamar** *vi* to exclaim.

excluir [eksklu'ir] *vt* to exclude; (*dejar fuera*) to shut out; (*descartar*) to reject; **exclusión** *nf* exclusion; (*descarte*) rejection; **con exclusión de** excluding.

exclusiva [eksklu'siβa], **exclusividad** [eksklusiβi'ðað] *nf* exclusiveness; (*PRENSA*) exclusive; (*COM*) sole right *or* agency.

exclusivo, a [eksklu'siβo, a] *a* exclusive; (*único*) sole.

Excmo. *abr de* **excelentísimo.**

excomulgar [ekskomul'ɣar] *vt* (*REL*) to excommunicate; (*excluir*) to ban, banish.

excomunión [ekskomu'njon] *nf* excommunication.

excoriar [eksko'rjar] *vt* to flay, skin.

excursión [ekskur'sjon] *nf* excursion, outing; **excursionismo** *nm* sightseeing.

excusa [eks'kusa] *nf* excuse; (*disculpa*) apology.

excusado, a [eksku'saðo, a] *a* unnecessary; (*disculpado*) excused, forgiven // *nm* lavatory, toilet.

excusar [eksku'sar] *vt* to excuse; (*evitar*) to avoid; (*impedir*) to prevent; **~se** *vr* (*rehusarse*) to decline a request; (*disculparse*) to apologize.

execrar [ekse'krar] *vt* to loathe.

exención [eksen'θjon] *nf* exemption.

exento, a [ek'sento, a] *pp de* **eximir** // *a* exempt; **~ de derechos** tax-free.

exequias [ek'sekjas] *nfpl* funeral rites, obsequies.

exhalación [eksala'θjon] *nf* (*del aire*) exhalation; (*vapor*) fumes *pl*, vapour; (*rayo*) shooting star.

exhalar [eksa'lar] *vt* to exhale, breathe out; (*olor etc*) to give off; (*suspiro*) to breathe, heave.

exhausto, a [ek'sausto, a] *a* exhausted.

exhibición [eksiβi'θjon] *nf* exhibition, display, show.

exhibir [eksi'βir] *vt* to exhibit, display, show.

exhortación [eksorta'θjon] *nf* exhortation; **exhortar** *vt*: **exhortar a** to exhort to.

exigencia [eksi'xenθja] *nf* demand, requirement; **exigente** *a* demanding.

exigir [eksi'xir] *vt* (*gen*) to demand, require; (*pago*) to exact.

exilio [ek'siljo] *nm* exile.

eximio, a [ek'simjo, a] *a* (*excelente*) choice, select; (*eminente*) distinguished, eminent.

eximir [eksi'mir] *vt* to exempt.

existencia [eksis'tenθja] *nf* existence; **~s** *nfpl* stock(s) (*pl*).

existir [eksis'tir] *vi* to exist, be.

éxito ['eksito] *nm* (*resultado*) result, outcome; (*triunfo*) success; **tener ~** to be successful.

exonerar [eksone'rar] *vt* to exonerate; **~ de una obligación** to free from an obligation.

exorcizar [eksorθi'θar] *vt* to exorcize.

exótico, a [ek'sotiko, a] *a* exotic.

expandir [ekspan'dir] *vt* to expand.

expansión [ekspan'sjon] *nf* expansion.

expatriarse [ekspa'trjarse] *vr* to emigrate; (*POL*) to go into exile.

expectativa [ekspekta'tiβa] *nf* (*espera*) expectation; (*perspectiva*) prospect.

expedición [ekspeði'θjon] *nf* (*excursión*) expedition; (*envío*) shipment; (*rapidez*) speed.

expediente [ekspe'ðjente] *nm* expedient; (*JUR: procedimento*) action, proceedings *pl*; (*: papeles*) dossier, file, record.

expedir [ekspe'ðir] *vt* (*despachar*) to send, forward; (*libreta cívica, pasaporte*) to issue; (*fig*) to deal with.

expedito, a [ekspe'ðito, a] *a* (*libre*) clear, free; (*pronto*) prompt, speedy.

expendedor, a [ekspende'ðor, a] *nm/f* (*vendedor*) dealer; (*aparato*) (vending) machine; ~ **de cigarrillos** cigarette machine.

expendeduría [ekspendedu'ria] *nf* shop; (*estanco*) tobacconist's (shop).

expensas [eks'pensas] *nfpl* expenses; **a** ~ **de** at the expense of.

experiencia [ekspe'rjenθja] *nf* experience; (*científica*) experiment.

experimentado, a [eksperimen'taðo, a] *a* experienced.

experimentar [eksperimen'tar] *vt* (*en laboratorio*) to experiment with; (*probar*) to test, try out; (*notar, observar*) to experience; (*sufrir*) to suffer; **experimento** *nm* experiment.

experto, a [eks'perto, a] *a* (*práctico*) expert; (*diestro*) skilled, experienced // *nm/f* expert.

expiar [ekspi'ar] *vt* to atone for.

expirar [ekspi'rar] *vi* to expire.

explayar [ekspla'jar] *vt* to extend, expand; ~**se** *vr* to extend, spread; ~**se con uno** to confide in sb.

explicación [eksplika'θjon] *nf* explanation; **explicar** *vt* to explain; **explicarse** *vr* to explain (o.s.).

explícito, a [eks'pliθito, a] *a* explicit.

explorador, a [eksplora'ðor, a] *nm/f* (*pionero*) explorer; (*MIL*) scout // *nm* (*MED*) probe; (*TEC*) (radar) scanner; **los E**~**es** the Scouts.

explorar [eksplo'rar] *vt* to explore; (*MED*) to probe; (*radar*) to scan.

explosión [eksplo'sjon] *nf* explosion; **explosivo, a** *a* explosive.

explotación [eksplota'θjon] *nf* exploitation; (*de planta etc*) running, operation; **explotar** *vt* to exploit; to run, operate // *vi* to explode.

exponer [ekspo'ner] *vt* to expose; (*cuadro*) to display; (*vida*) to risk; (*idea*) to explain; ~**se** *vr* to expose o.s., leave o.s. open.

exportación [eksporta'θjon] *nf* (*acción*) export; (*mercancías*) exports *pl*; **exportar** *vt* to export.

exposición [eksposi'θjon] *nf* (*gen*) exposure; (*de arte*) show, exhibition; (*petición*) petition; (*explicación*) explanation; (*narración*) account, statement.

exposímetro [ekspo'simetro] *nm* (*FOTO*) exposure meter.

exprés [eks'pres] *nm* (*AM*) express (train).

expresar [ekspre'sar] *vt* to express; **expresión** *nf* expression; **expresiones** *nfpl* regards.

expreso, a [eks'preso, a] *pp de* **expresar** // *a* (*claro*) specific, clear; (*rápido*) fast // *nm*: **mandar por** ~ to send by express (delivery).

exprimir [ekspri'mir] *vt* (*fruta*) to squeeze (out); (*ropa*) to wring out; (*fig*) to express emphatically.

expropiar [ekspro'pjar] *vt* to expropriate.

expuesto, a [eks'pwesto, a] *a* exposed; (*cuadro etc*) on show, on display.

expugnar [ekspux'nar] *vt* to take by storm.

expulsar [ekspul'sar] *vt* (*echar*) to eject; (*arrojar*) to throw out; (*expeler*) to expel; (*desalojar*) to drive out; (*despedir*) to sack, fire; (*a un futbolista*) to send off; **expulsión** *nf* expulsion; sending-off.

expurgar [ekspur'sar] *vt* to expurgate.

exquisito, a [ekski'sito, a] *a* exquisite; (*agradable*) delightful.

éxtasis ['ekstasis] *nm* ecstasy.

extender [eksten'der] *vt* (*gen*) to extend; (*los brazos*) to stretch out, hold out; (*mapa*) to spread (out), open (out); (*mantequilla*) to spread; (*certificado*) to issue; (*cheque, recibo*) to make out; (*documento*) to draw up; ~**se** *vr* (*gen*) to extend; (*en el suelo*) to stretch out; (*epidemia*) to spread; **extendido, a** *a* (*abierto*) spread out, open; (*brazos*) outstretched; (*prevaleciente*) widespread; **extensión** *nf* (*de país*) expanse, stretch; (*de libro*) extent; (*de tiempo*) length, duration; (*AM*) extension; **en toda la extensión de la palabra** in every sense of the word; **extenso, a** *a* extensive; (*prevaleciente*) widespread.

extenuar [ekste'nwar] *vi* (*agotar*) to exhaust; (*debilitar*) to weaken.

exterior [ekste'rjor] *a inv* (*de fuera*) external; (*afuera*) outside, exterior; (*apariencia*) outward; (*comercio*) foreign // *nm* (*gen*) exterior, outside; (*aspecto*) outward appearance; (*DEPORTE*) wing(er); **el** ~ foreign parts *pl*; **al** ~ outwardly, on the surface.

exterminar [ekstermi'nar] *vt* to exterminate; **exterminio** *nm* extermination.

externo, a [eks'terno, a] *a* (*exterior*) external, outside; (*superficial*) outward // *nm/f* day pupil.

extinguir [ekstin'gir] *vt* (*fuego*) to extinguish, put out; (*raza, población*) to wipe out; ~**se** *vr* (*fuego*) to go out; (*BIO*) to die out, become extinct.

extinto, a [eks'tinto, a] *a* extinct.

extintor [ekstin'tor] *nm* (fire) extinguisher.

extra ['ekstra] *a, nm/f* extra // *nm* extra; (*bono*) bonus.

extracción [ekstrak'θjon] *nf* extraction; (*en lotería*) draw.

extracto [eks'trakto] *nm* extract.

extraer [ekstra'er] *vt* to extract, take out.

extralimitarse [ekstralimi'tarse] *vr* to go too far.

extranjero, a [ekstran'xero, a] *a* foreign // *nm/f* foreigner // *nm* foreign lands *pl*; **en el** ~ abroad.

extrañar [ekstra'ɲar] *vt* (*desterrar*) to exile; (*sorprender*) to find strange *or* odd;

(AM) to miss; ~se vr (sorprenderse) to be amazed, be surprised; (distanciarse) to become estranged, grow apart.

extrañeza [ekstra'neθa] nf (rareza) strangeness, oddness; (asombro) amazement, surprise.

extraño, a [eks'traɲo, a] a (extranjero) foreign; (raro, sorprendente) strange, odd.

extraordinario, a [ekstraorði'narjo, a] a extraordinary; (edición, número) special // nm (plato) special dish; (de periódico) special edition; **horas ~as** overtime sg.

extravagancia [ekstraβa'xanθja] nf extravagance; **extravagante** a extravagant; (extraño) strange, odd; (excéntrico) eccentric; (estrafalario) outlandish.

extraviado, a [ekstra'βjaðo, a] a lost, missing.

extraviar [ekstra'βjar] vt (desviar) to mislead; (perder) to lose, misplace; ~se vr to lose one's way, get lost.

extravío [ekstra'βio] nm loss; (fig) deviation.

extremar [ekstre'mar] vt to carry to extremes; ~se vr to do one's utmost, make every effort.

extremaunción [ekstremaun'θjon] nf extreme unction.

extremeño, a [ekstre'meɲo, a] a, nm/f Extremaduran.

extremidad [ekstremi'ðað] nf (punta) extremity; (fila) edge; ~es nfpl (ANAT) extremities.

extremo, a [eks'tremo, a] a extreme; (último) last // nm end; (límite, grado sumo) extreme; **en último** ~ as a last resort; ~ **derecho/izquierdo** outside-right/outside-left.

extrínseco, a [eks'trinseko, a] a extrinsic.

extrovertido, a [ekstroβer'tiðo, a] a, nm/f extrovert.

exuberancia [eksuβe'ranθja] nf exuberance; **exuberante** a exuberant; (fig) luxuriant, lush.

exvoto [eks'βoto] nm votive offering.

eyacular [ejaku'lar] vt, vi to ejaculate.

F

f.a.b. abr de **franco a bordo** f.o.b. (free on board).

fábrica ['faβrika] nf factory; **marca de** ~ trademark; **precio de** ~ factory price.

fabricación [faβrika'θjon] nf (manufactura) manufacture; (producción) production; **de** ~ **casera** home-made; ~ **en serie** mass production.

fabricante [faβri'kante] nm/f manufacturer.

fabricar [faβri'kar] vt (hacer) to manufacture, make; (construir) to build; (elaborar) to fabricate, devise.

fabril [fa'βril] a: **industria** ~ manufacturing industry.

fábula ['faβula] nf (cuento) fable; (chisme) rumour.

facción [fak'θjon] nf (POL) faction; (del rostro) feature.

fácil ['faθil] a (simple) easy; (probable) likely.

facilidad [faθili'ðað] nf (capacidad) ease; (sencillez) simplicity; (de palabra) fluency; ~es nfpl facilities.

facilitar [faθili'tar] vt (hacer fácil) to make easy; (proporcionar) to provide; (hacer posible) to arrange; (hacer más fácil) to facilitate.

fácilmente ['faθilmente] ad easily.

factible [fak'tiβle] a feasible.

factor [fak'tor] nm factor.

factura [fak'tura] nf (cuenta) bill; (hechura) manufacture; **facturar** vt (COM) to invoice, charge for.

facultad [fakul'tað] nf (aptitud, ESCOL etc) faculty; (poder) power.

facha ['fatʃa] nf (fam: aspecto) look; (: desagradable) unpleasant sight.

fachada [fa'tʃaða] nf (ARQ) façade, front.

faena [fa'ena] nf (trabajo) work; (quehacer) task, job; ~s **de la casa** housework sg.

fagot [fa'got] nm (MUS) bassoon.

faisán [fai'san] nm pheasant.

faja ['faxa] nf (para la cintura) sash; (de mujer) corset; (de tierra) strip; (venda) bandage.

falange [fa'lanxe] nf (POL) Falange.

falda ['falda] nf (prenda de vestir) skirt.

falibilidad [faliβili'ðað] nf fallibility.

fálico, a ['faliko, a] a phallic.

falo ['falo] nm phallus.

falsedad [false'ðað] nf (hipocresía) falseness; (mentira) falsehood.

falsificar [falsifi'kar] vt (firma etc) to forge; (voto etc) to rig; (moneda) to counterfeit.

falso, a ['falso, a] a (gen) false; (erróneo) mistaken; (moneda etc) fake; **en** ~ falsely.

falta ['falta] nf (defecto) fault, flaw; (privación) lack, want; (ausencia) absence; (carencia) shortage; (equivocación) mistake; (DEPORTE) foul; **hacer** ~ to be missing or lacking.

faltar [fal'tar] vi (escasear) to be lacking, be wanting; (ausentarse) to be absent, be missing; (fallar: mecanismo) to go wrong, break down; **faltan 2 horas para llegar** there are 2 hours to go till arrival; ~ **el respeto a alguien** to be disrespectful to sb; **echar a** ~ **a alguien** to miss sb; **¡no faltaba más!** that's the last straw!

falto, a ['falto, a] a (desposeído) deficient, lacking; (necesitado) poor, wretched.

falla ['faʎa] nf (defecto) fault, flaw; (fracaso) failure.

fallar [fa'ʎar] vt (JUR) to pronounce sentence on // vi (memoria) to fail; (motor) to miss.

fallecer [faʎe'θer] vi to pass away, die; **fallecimiento** nm decease, demise.

fallo ['faʎo] nm (JUR) verdict, ruling; (fracaso) failure.

fama ['fama] *nf* (*renombre*) fame; (*reputación*) reputation.

familia [fa'milja] *nf* family.

familiar [fami'ljar] *a* (*relativo a la familia*) family *cpd*; (*conocido, informal*) familiar // *nm* relative; **~idad** *nf* (*gen*) familiarity; (*informalidad*) homeliness; **~izarse** *vr* to familiarize o.s. with.

famoso, a [fa'moso, a] *a* (*renombrado*) famous; (*fam: fabuloso*) great.

fanático, a [fa'natiko, a] *a* fanatical // *nm/f* (*gen*) fanatic; (*CINE etc*) fan; (*de deportes*) supporter; **fanatismo** *nm* fanaticism.

fanfarrón, ona [fanfa'rron, ona] *a* boastful; (*pey*) showy.

fango ['fango] *nm* mud; **~so, a** *a* muddy.

fantasía [fanta'sia] *nf* fantasy, imagination; (*fam*) conceit, vanity; **joyas de ~** imitation jewellery *sg*.

fantasma [fan'tasma] *nm* (*espectro*) ghost, apparition.

fantástico, a [fan'tastiko, a] *a* fantastic.

farmacéutico, a [farma'θeutiko, a] *a* pharmaceutical // *nm/f* chemist, pharmacist.

farmacia [far'maθja] *nf* chemist's (shop), pharmacy; **~ de turno** all-night chemist.

faro ['faro] *nm* (*NAUT. torre*) lighthouse; (*AUTO*) headlamp; **~s laterales** sidelights; **~s traseros** rear lights.

farol [fa'rol] *nm* (*luz*) lantern, lamp; (*de calle*) streetlamp.

farsa ['farsa] *nf* (*gen*) farce.

farsante [far'sante] *nm/f* fraud, fake.

fascinar [fasθi'nar] *vt* (*deslumbrar*) to fascinate.

fascismo [fas'θismo] *nm* fascism; **fascista** *a, nm/f* fascist.

fase ['fase] *nf* phase.

fastidiar [fasti'ðjar] *vt* (*disgustar*) to annoy, bother; (*estropear*) to spoil; (*aburrir*) to bore; **~se** *vr* (*dañarse*) to harm o.s.; (*disgustarse*) to get annoyed *or* cross.

fastidio [fas'tiðjo] *nm* (*disgusto*) annoyance; (*tedio*) boredom; **~so, a** *a* (*molesto*) annoying; (*aburrido*) tedious.

fatal [fa'tal] *a* (*gen*) fatal; (*inevitable*) unavoidable; (*desgraciado*) ill-fated; (*fam: malo, pésimo*) awful; **~idad** *nf* (*destino*) fate; (*mala suerte*) misfortune.

fatiga [fa'tixa] *nf* (*cansancio*) fatigue, weariness; **fatigar** *vt* to tire, weary; **fatigarse** *vr* to get tired; **fatigoso, a** *a* (*cansador*) tiring; (*aburrido*) tiresome.

fatuo, a [fa'twatuo, a] *a* (*vano*) fatuous; (*presuntuoso*) conceited.

fauces ['fauθes] *nfpl* jaws, mouth *sg*.

favor [fa'ßor] *nm* favour; **entrada de ~** complimentary ticket; **haga el ~ de...** would you be so good as to..., kindly...; **por ~** please; **~able** *a* favourable.

favorecer [faßore'θer] *vt* (*gen*) to favour; (*vestido etc*) to become, flatter; **este peinado le favorece** this hairstyle suits her.

favorito, a [faßo'rito, a] *a, nm/f* favourite.

faz [faθ] *nf*: **la ~ de la tierra** the face of the earth.

fe [fe] *nf* (*REL*) faith; (*confianza*) belief; (*documento*) certificate; (*lealtad*) fidelity, loyalty; **prestar ~ a** to believe, credit; **actuar con buena/mala ~** to act in good/bad faith; **dar ~ de** to bear witness to.

fealdad [feal'daθ] *nf* ugliness.

febrero [fe'ßrero] *nm* February.

febril [fe'ßril] *a* feverish.

fecundar [fekun'dar] *vt* (*generar*) to fertilize, make fertile; **fecundo, a** *a* (*fértil*) fertile; (*prolífico*) prolific; (*fructífero*) fruitful; (*abundante*) abundant; (*productivo*) productive.

fecha ['fetʃa] *nf* date; **en ~ próxima** soon; **hasta la ~** to date, so far; **poner ~** to date; **con ~ adelantada** post-dated.

federación [federa'θjon] *nf* federation.

federal [feðe'ral] *a* federal; **~ismo** *nm* federalism.

felicidad [feliθi'ðaθ] *nf* (*satisfacción, contento*) happiness; (*suerte feliz*) (good) luck; **~es** *nfpl* best wishes, congratulations.

felicitación [feliθita'θjon] *nf* congratulation; **felicitar** *vt* to congratulate.

feligrés, esa [feli'xres, esa] *nm/f* parishioner.

feliz [fe'liθ] *a* (*contento*) happy; (*afortunado*) lucky.

felonía [felo'nia] *nf* felony, crime.

felpudo [fel'puðo] *nm* doormat.

femenino, a [feme'nino, a] *a, nm* feminine.

feminista [femi'nista] *nf* feminist.

fénix ['feniks] *nm* (*ave*) phoenix.

fenómeno [fe'nomeno] *nm* phenomenon; (*fig*) freak, accident // *a inv* great // *excl* smashing!, marvellous!

feo, a [feo, a] *a* (*gen*) ugly; (*desagradable*) bad, nasty.

féretro ['feretro] *nm* (*ataúd*) coffin; (*sarcófago*) bier.

feria ['ferja] *nf* (*gen*) fair; (*AM*) village market; (*día de asueto*) holiday, rest day.

fermentar [fermen'tar] *vi* to ferment.

ferocidad [feroθi'ðaθ] *nf* fierceness, ferocity.

feroz [fe'roθ] *a* (*cruel*) cruel; (*salvaje*) fierce.

férreo, a ['ferreo, a] *a* iron.

ferretería [ferrete'ria], **ferrería** [ferre'ria] *nf* (*trastes*) ironmongery; (*tienda*) ironmonger's (shop), hardware store.

ferrocarril [ferroka'rril] *nm* railway; **~ de cremallera** rack railway.

fértil ['fertil] *a* (*productivo*) fertile; (*rico*) rich; **fertilidad** *nf* (*gen*) fertility; (*productividad*) fruitfulness; **fertilizar** *vt* to fertilize.

fervor [fer'ßor] *nm* fervour; **~oso, a** *a* fervent.

festejar [feste'xar] *vt* (*agasajar*) to

entertain lavishly; (*galantear*) to court; (*su cumpleaños*) to celebrate; **festejo** nm (*diversión*) entertainment; (*galanteo*) courtship; (*fiesta*) celebration.
festividad [festiβi'ðað] nf festivity.
festivo, a [fes'tiβo, a] a (*de fiesta*) festive; (*fig*) witty; (*CINE, LITERATURA*) humorous.
fétido, a ['fetiðo, a] a (*hediondo*) foul-smelling; (*podrido*) rotten.
fiado [fi'aðo] nm: **comprar al** ~ to buy on credit.
fiador, a [fia'ðor, a] nm/f (*JUR*) surety, guarantor; (*COM*) backer // nm (*de arma*) safety catch; (*cerrojo*) tumbler; **salir** ~ **por alguien** to go bail for sb.
fiambre ['fjambre] nm cold meat.
fianza ['fjanθa] nf surety; (*JUR*): **libertad bajo** ~ release on bail.
fiar [fi'ar] vt (*salir garante de*) to guarantee; (*vender a crédito*) to sell on credit // vi to trust; ~**se de uno** to rely on sb.
fiasco ['fjasko] nm fiasco.
fibra ['fiβra] nf fibre.
ficción [fik'θjon] nf fiction.
ficticio, a [fik'tiθjo, a] a (*imaginario*) fictitious; (*falso*) fabricated.
ficha ['fitʃa] nf (*en juegos*) token, counter; (*tarjeta*) (index) card; (*ELEC*) plug; **fichar** vt (*archivar*) to file, index; **estar fichado** to have a record; **fichero** nm card index.
fidelidad [fiðeli'ðað] nf (*lealtad*) fidelity, loyalty; **alta** ~ high fidelity, hi-fi.
fideos [fi'ðeos] nmpl noodles.
fiebre ['fjeβre] nf (*MED*) fever; (*fig*) feverish excitement; ~ **amarilla/del heno** yellow/hay fever; ~ **palúdica** malaria; **tener** ~ to have a temperature.
fiel [fjel] a (*leal*) faithful, loyal; (*fiable*) reliable; (*exacto*) accurate, exact // nm inspector; (*aguja*) needle, pointer; **los** ~**es** the faithful.
fieltro ['fjeltro] nm felt.
fiereza [fje'reθa] nf (*bravura*) fierceness; (*fealdad*) ugliness.
fiero, a ['fjero, a] a (*cruel*) cruel; (*feroz*) fierce; (*duro*) harsh // nf (*animal feroz*) wild animal or beast.
fiesta ['fjesta] nf party; (*de pueblo*) festival; ~**s** nfpl (*caricias*) endearments; (*vacaciones*) holiday sg; (*broma*) jokes; (*juerga*) fun and games; (*REL*): ~ **de guardar** day of obligation.
figura [fi'ɣura] nf (*gen*) figure; (*forma, imagen*) shape, form; (*cara*) face; (*TEATRO*) marionette; (*NAIPES*) face card.
figurar [fiɣu'rar] vt (*representar*) to represent; (*fingir*) to figure // vi to figure; ~**se** vr (*imaginarse*) to imagine; (*suponer*) to suppose.
fijar [fi'xar] vt (*gen*) to fix; (*estampilla*) to affix, stick (on); (*fig*) to settle (on), decide; ~ **con hilos** to sew on; ~**se** vr: ~**se en** to notice.
fijo, a ['fixo, a] a (*gen*) fixed; (*firme*) firm; (*permanente*) permanent // ad: **mirar** ~ to stare.

fila ['fila] nf row; (*cola, columna*) queue; (*cadena*) line; **ponerse en** ~ to line up, get into line.
filántropo [fi'lantropo] nm philanthropist.
filatelia [fila'telja] nf philately.
filete [fi'lete] nm (*carne*) steak; (*pescado*) fillet.
filial [fi'ljal] a filial // nf subsidiary.
Filipinas [fili'pinas] nfpl: **las** ~ the Philippines.
filmar [fil'mar] vt to film, shoot.
filo ['filo] nm (*gen*) edge; **sacar** ~ **a** to sharpen; **al** ~ **del mediodía** at about midday; **de doble** ~ double-edged.
filosofía [filoso'fia] nf philosophy; **filósofo** nm philosopher.
filtrar [fil'trar] vt, vi to filter, strain; ~**se** vr to filter; (*fig*) to dwindle; **filtro** nm (*TEC, utensilio*) filter; (*CULIN*) strainer.
fin [fin] nm (*gen*) end; (*objetivo*) aim, purpose; **al** ~ **y al cabo** when all's said and done; **a** ~ **de** in order to; **por** ~ finally; **en** ~ in short; ~ **de semana** weekend; ~ **al** ~ **final** // nm end, conclusion // nf final; ~**alista** nm/f finalist; ~**alizar** vt to end, finish // vi, ~**alizarse** vr to end, come to an end.
financiar [finan'θjar] vt to finance; **financiero, a** a financial.
finca ['finka] nf country estate; (*casa*) country house.
fingir [fin'xir] vt (*simular*) to simulate; (*pretextar*) to sham, fake // vi (*aparentar*) to pretend, feign; ~**se** vr to pretend to be.
finlandés, esa [finlan'des, esa] a Finnish // nm/f Finn // nm (*lengua*) Finnish.
Finlandia [fin'landja] nf Finland.
fino, a ['fino, a] a (*gen*) fine; (*delgado*) slender; (*puro*) pure; (*de buenas maneras*) polite, refined; (*inteligente*) shrewd.
firma ['firma] nf signature; (*COM*) firm, company; **firmar** vt to sign.
firme ['firme] a (*gen*) firm; (*estable*) stable; (*sólido*) solid; (*compacto*) compact; (*constante*) steady; (*decidido*) resolute // nm road (surface); ~**mente** ad firmly; ~**za** nf firmness; (*constancia*) steadiness; (*solidez*) solidity.
fiscal [fis'kal] a fiscal // nm Public Prosecutor.
fisgar [fis'ɣar] vt to pry into; (*pescar*) to spear, harpoon.
físico, a ['fisiko, a] a physical // nm physique // nm/f physicist // nf physics sg.
flaco, a ['flako, a] a (*muy delgado*) skinny, lean; (*débil*) weak, feeble.
flagrante [fla'ɣrante] a flagrant.
flamante [fla'mante] a (*brilliant*); (*nuevo*) brand-new.
flamenco, a [fla'menko, a] a (*de Flandes*) Flemish; (*agitanado*) gipsy // nm (*canto y baile*) flamenco.
flan [flan] nm creme caramel.
flaqueza [fla'keθa] nf (*delgadez*) leanness; (*fig*) weakness.
flash [flaʃ] nm (*FOTO*) flash.
flauta ['flauta] nf flute.

fleco ['fleko] nm fringe.

flecha ['fletʃa] nf arrow.

flema ['flema] nm phlegm.

flequillo [fle'kiʎo] nm (pelo) fringe.

flete ['flete] nm (carga) freight; (alquiler) charter; (precio) freightage.

flexible [flek'siβle] a flexible.

flojo, a ['floxo, a] a (gen) loose; (sin fuerzas) limp; (débil) weak.

flor [flor] nf flower; (piropo) compliment; **a ~ de** on the surface of; **~ecer** vi (BOT) to flower; (fig) to flourish; **~eciente a** (BOT) in flower, flowering; (fig) thriving.

flota ['flota] nf fleet.

flotar [flo'tar] vi (gen) to float; (colgar) to hang; **flote** nm: **a flote** afloat; **sacar a flote** (fig) to get back on one's feet.

fluctuar [fluk'twar] vi (oscilar) to fluctuate; (vacilar) to waver.

fluidez [flui'ðeθ] nf fluidity; (fig) fluency.

flúido, a ['fluiðo, a] a, nm fluid.

fluir [flu'ir] vi to flow.

flujo ['fluxo] nm flow; **~ y reflujo** ebb and flow; **~ de sangre** (MED) loss of blood.

foca ['foka] nf seal.

foco ['foko] nm focus; (ELEC) floodlight.

fogón [fo'xon] nm (de cocina) stove.

fogoso, a [fo'xoso, a] a spirited.

follaje [fo'ʎaxe] nm foliage.

folleto [fo'ʎeto] nm pamphlet.

fomentar [fomen'tar] vt (MED) to foment; **fomento** nm (MED) fomentation; (promoción) promotion; **Ministerio de Fomento** Ministry of Public Works.

fonda ['fonda] nf inn; (restaurante) buffet.

fondo ['fondo] nm (de mar) bottom; (cuarto) back; (ARTE etc) background; (reserva) fund; **~s** nmpl (COM) funds, resources; **una investigación a ~** a thorough investigation; **en el ~** at bottom, deep down.

fontanería [fontane'ria] nf plumbing; **fontanero** nm plumber.

forastero, a [foras'tero, a] a (extraño) alien, strange // nm/f stranger.

forcejear [forθexe'ar] vi (luchar) to struggle; (esforzarse) to make violent efforts.

forjar [for'xar] vt to forge.

forma ['forma] nf (figura) form, shape; (molde) mould, pattern; (MED) fitness; (método) way, means; **las ~s** the conventions.

formación [forma'θjon] nf (gen) formation; (educación) education.

formal [for'mal] a (gen) formal; (fig: persona) serious; **~idad** nf formality; seriousness.

formar [for'mar] vt (componer) to form, shape; (constituir) to make up, constitute; (ESCOL) to train, educate; **~se** vr (cobrar forma) to form, take form; (hacer línea) to form up; (desarrollarse) to develop.

formidable [formi'ðaβle] a (temible) formidable; (asombroso) tremendous.

formulario [formu'larjo] nm form.

fornido, a [for'niðo, a] a strapping, well-built.

foro ['foro] nm (gen) forum; (JUR) court.

forrar [fo'rrar] vt (abrigo) to line; (libro) to cover; **forro** nm (de cuaderno) cover; (costura) lining; (de sillón) upholstery; **forro de freno** brake lining.

fortalecer [fortale'θer] vt to strengthen.

fortaleza [forta'leθa] nf (gen) strength; (determinación) resolution.

fortuito, a [for'twito, a] a accidental.

fortuna [for'tuna] nf (suerte) fortune, (good) luck; (riqueza, caudal) fortune, wealth.

forzar [for'θar] vt (puerta) to force (open); (casa) to break into; (compeler) to compel.

forzoso, a [for'θoso, a] a necessary.

fosa ['fosa] nf (sepultura) grave; (en tierra) pit; (MED) cavity.

fósforo ['fosforo] nm (metaloide) phosphorus; (AM) match.

foso ['foso] nm ditch; (TEATRO) pit; (AUTO): **~ de reconocimiento** inspection pit.

foto ['foto] nf photo, snap(shot); **~copia** nf photocopy; **~copiador** nm photocopier; **~copiar** vt to photocopy.

fotografía [fotoxra'fia] nf (gen) photography; (una ~) photograph; **fotografiar** vt to photograph.

fotógrafo, a [fo'toxrafo, a] nm/f photographer.

fracaso [fra'kaso] nm (desgracia, revés) failure; **fracasar** vi (gen) to fail.

fracción [frak'θjon] nf fraction; (POL) faction; **fraccionar** vt to divide, break up.

fractura [frak'tura] nf fracture, break.

fragancia [fra'xanθja] nf (olor) fragrance; (perfume) perfume.

frágil ['fraxil] a (débil) fragile; (quebradizo) breakable; **fragilidad** nf fragility; (de persona) frailty.

fragmento [fraxmento] nm (pedazo) fragment.

fragor [fra'xor] nm (ruido intenso) din; (de gente) uproar.

fragua ['fraxwa] nf forge; **fraguar** vt to forge; (fig) to concoct // vi to harden.

fraile ['fraile] nm (REL) friar; (: monje) monk.

frambuesa [fram'bwesa] nf raspberry.

francés, esa [fran'θes, esa] a French // nm/f Frenchman/woman // nm (lengua) French.

Francia ['franθja] nf France.

franco, a ['franko, a] a (leal, abierto) frank, open; (generoso, liberal) generous, liberal; (COM: exento) free // nm franc.

francotirador, a [frankotira'ðor, a] nm/f sniper.

franela [fra'nela] nf flannel.

franja ['franxa] nf fringe.

franquear [franke'ar] vt (camino) to clear; (carta, paquete postal) to frank, stamp; (obstáculo) to overcome; **~se** vr (ceder) to give way; (confiarse a alguien) to unburden o.s.

franqueo [fran'keo] *nm* postage.

franqueza [fran'keθa] *nf* (*candor*) frankness; (*generosidad*) generosity.

frasco ['frasko] *nm* bottle; (*al vacío*) (vacuum) flask.

frase ['frase] *nf* sentence; ~ **hecha** set phrase.

fraude ['frauðe] *nm* (*cualidad*) dishonesty; (*acto*) fraud; **fraudulento, a** *a* fraudulent.

frecuencia [fre'kwenθja] *nf* frequency; **con** ~ frequently, often.

fregador [freɣa'ðor] *nm* sink.

fregar [fre'ɣar] *vt* (*frotar*) to scrub; (*platos*) to wash (up); (*AM*) to annoy.

freír [fre'ir] *vt* to fry.

frenar [fre'nar] *vt* to brake; (*fig*) to check.

frenesí [frene'si] *nm* frenzy; **frenético, a** *a* frantic.

freno ['freno] *nm* (*TEC, AUTO*) brake; (*de cabalgadura*) bit; (*fig*) check.

frente ['frente] *nm* (*ARQ, POL*) front; (*de objeto*) front part // *nf* forehead, brow; **en** ~ **de** in front of; (*en situación opuesta de*) opposite; **chocar de** ~ to crash head-on; **hacer** ~ **a** to face up to.

fresa ['fresa] *nf* strawberry.

fresco, a ['fresko, a] *a* (*nuevo*) fresh; (*frío*) cool // *nm* (*aire*) fresh air; (*ARTE*) fresco; (*fam*) shameless person; (*persona insolente*) impudent person // *nf* cool part of the day; **tomar el** ~ to get some fresh air; **frescura** *nf* freshness; (*descaro*) cheek, nerve; (*calma*) calmness.

frialdad [frial'dað] *nf* (*gen*) coldness; (*indiferencia*) indifference.

fricción [frik'θjon] *nf* (*gen*) friction; (*acto*) rub(bing); (*MED*) massage.

frigidez [frixi'ðeθ] *nf* frigidity.

frigorífico [friɣo'rifiko] *nm* refrigerator.

frijol [fri'xol] *nm* kidney bean.

frío, a ['frio, a] *a* cold // *nm* cold(ness).

frito, a ['frito, a] *a* fried; **me trae** ~ **ese hombre** I'm sick and tired of that man.

frívolo, a ['friβolo, a] *a* frivolous.

frontera [fron'tera] *nf* frontier; **fronterizo, a** *a* frontier *cpd*; (*contiguo*) bordering.

frontón [fron'ton] *nm* (*DEPORTE*) pelota court.

frotar [fro'tar] *vt* to rub; ~**se** *vr*: ~**se las manos** to rub one's hands.

fructífero, a [fruk'tifero, a] *a* fruitful.

frugal [fru'xal] *a* frugal.

fruncir [frun'θir] *vt* to pucker; (*costura*) to pleat; ~ **el ceño** to knit one's brow.

frustrar [frus'trar] *vt* to frustrate.

fruta ['fruta] *nf* fruit; **frutería** *nf* fruit shop.

fue *vb ver* **ser, ir.**

fuego ['fweɣo] *nm* (*gen*) fire; (*MED*) rash; **a** ~ **lento** on a low flame *or* gas; **¿tienes** ~? have you a light?

fuente ['fwente] *nf* (*de una plaza*) fountain; (*manantial, fig*) spring; (*origen*) source; (*plato*) large dish.

fuera *etc vb ver* **ser, ir** // ['fwera] *ad*

out(side); (*en otra parte*) away; (*excepto, salvo*) except, save // *prep*: ~ **de** outside; (*fig*) besides; ~ **de sí** beside o.s.

fuerte ['fwerte] *a* (*gen*) strong; (*golpe*) hard; (*ruido*) loud; (*comida*) rich; (*lluvia*) heavy; (*dolor*) intense // *ad* strongly; hard; loud(ly).

fuerza ['fwerθa] *nf* (*fortaleza*) strength; (*TEC, ELEC*) power; (*coacción*) force; (*MIL*) forces *pl*; **a** ~ **de** by dint of; **cobrar** ~**s** to recover one's strength; **tener** ~**s para** to have the strength to; **a la** ~, **por** ~ forcibly, by force.

fuga ['fuɣa] *nf* (*huida*) flight, escape; (*de gas*) leak; **fugarse** *vr* to flee, escape; **fugaz** *a* fleeting; **fugitivo, a** *a, nm/f* fugitive.

fui *vb ver* **ser, ir.**

fulano, a [fu'lano, a] *nm/f* so-and-so, what's-his-name.

fulgor [ful'xor] *nm* brilliance.

fumar [fu'mar] *vt, vi* to smoke; ~**se** *vr* (*disipar*) to squander; ~ **en pipa** to smoke a pipe.

funámbulo, a [fu'nambulo, a] *nm/f* tightrope-walker.

función [fun'θjon] *nf* function; (*de puesto*) duties *pl*; (*espectáculo*) show; **entrar en funciones** to take up one's duties; **funcionar** *vi* (*gen*) to function; (*máquina*) to work.

funcionario, a [funθjo'narjo, a] *nm/f* official; (*público*) civil servant.

funda ['funda] (*gen*) cover; (*de almohada*) pillowcase.

fundación [funda'θjon] *nf* foundation.

fundamental [fundamen'tal] *a* fundamental, basic.

fundamentar [fundamen'tar] *vt* (*poner base*) to lay the foundations of; (*establecer*) to found; (*fig*) to base; **fundamento** *nm* (*base*) foundation.

fundar [fun'dar] *vt* to found; (*dotar de fondos*) to endow; ~**se** *vr*: ~**se en** to be founded on.

fundición [fundi'θjon] *nf* fusing; (*fábrica*) foundry.

fundir [fun'dir] *vt* (*gen*) to fuse; (*metal*) to smelt, melt down; (*COM*) to merge; (*estatua*) to cast; ~**se** *vr* (*sólido*) to merge, blend; (*unirse*) to fuse together.

fúnebre ['funeβre] *a* funeral *cpd*, funereal.

funeral [fune'ral] *nm* funeral.

furgón [fur'xon] *nm* wagon.

furia ['furja] *nf* (*ira*) fury; (*violencia*) violence; **furibundo, a** *a* furious; **furioso, a** *a* (*iracundo*) furious; (*violento*) violent; **furor** *nm* (*cólera*) rage.

furtivo, a [fur'tiβo, a] *a* furtive.

furúnculo [fu'runkulo] *nm* (*MED*) boil.

fusible [fu'siβle] *nm* fuse.

fusil [fu'sil] *nm* rifle; ~**ar** *vt* to shoot.

fusión [fu'sjon] *nf* (*gen*) melting; (*unión*) fusion; (*COM*) merger.

fútbol ['futβol] *nm* football; **futbolín** *nm* table football; **futbolista** *nm* footballer.

fútil ['futil] *a* trifling; **futilidad, futileza** *nf* triviality.
futuro, a [fu'turo, a] *a, nm* future.

G

gabacho, a [ga'βatʃo, a] *a* Pyrenean; (*fam*) frenchified // *nm/f* Pyrenean villager.
gabán [ga'βan] *nm* overcoat.
gabardina [gaβar'ðina] *nf* raincoat, gabardine.
gabinete [gaβi'nete] *nm* (*POL*) cabinet; (*estudio*) study; (*de abogados etc*) office.
gaceta [ga'θeta] *nf* gazette; **gacetilla** *nf* (*en periódico*) news in brief; (*de personalidades*) gossip column.
gacha ['gatʃa] *nf* mush; ~**s** *nfpl* porridge *sg.*
gafas ['gafas] *nfpl* glasses; ~ **oscuras** dark glasses.
gaita ['gaita] *nf* flute; (~ *gallega*) bagpipes *pl.*
gajes ['gaxes] *nmpl* (*salario*) pay; **los** ~ **del oficio** occupational hazards.
gajo ['gaxo] *nm* (*árbol*) bough; (*de naranja*) segment.
gala ['gala] *nf* full dress; (*fig: lo mejor*) cream, flower; ~**s** *nfpl* finery *sg;* **estar de** ~ to be in one's best clothes; **hacer** ~ **de** to display, show off.
galán [ga'lan] *nm* lover, gallant; (*hombre atractivo*) ladies' man; (*TEATRO*): **primer** ~ leading man.
galano, a [ga'lano, a] *a* (*elegante*) elegant; (*bien vestido*) smart.
galante [ga'lante] *a* gallant; **galantear** *vt* (*hacer la corte a*) to court, woo; **galanteo** *nm* (*coqueteo*) flirting; (*de pretendiente*) wooing; **galantería** *nf* (*caballerosidad*) gallantry; (*cumplido*) politeness; (*comentario*) compliment.
galaxia [ga'laksja] *nf* galaxy.
galera [ga'lera] *nf* (*nave*) galley; (*carro*) wagon; (*MED*) hospital ward; (*IMPRENTA*) galley.
galería [gale'ria] *nf* (*gen*) gallery; (*balcón*) veranda(h); (*de casa*) corridor.
Gales ['gales] *nm* Wales; **galés, esa** *a* Welsh // *nm/f* Welshman/woman // (*lengua*) Welsh.
galgo [ga'l] *a* ['galʝo, a] *nm/f* greyhound.
galimatías [galima'tias] *nmpl* (*lenguaje*) gibberish *sg,* nonsense *sg.*
galón [ga'lon] *nm* (*MIL*) stripe; (*medida*) gallon.
galopar [galo'par] *vi* to gallop; **galope** *nm* gallop.
galvanizar [galβani'θar] *vt* to galvanize.
gallardía [gaʎar'ðia] *nf* (*galantería*) dash; (*valor*) bravery; (*elegancia*) elegance.
gallego, a [ga'ʎeɣo, a] *a, nm/f* Galician.
galleta [ga'ʎeta] *nf* biscuit.
gallina [ga'ʎina] *nf* hen // *nm* (*fam*) coward; ~ **ciega** blind man's buff.
gallo ['gaʎo] *nm* cock, rooster.

gama ['gama] *nf* (*MUS*) scale; (*fig*) range.
gamba ['gamba] *nf* prawn.
gamberro, a [gam'berro, a] *nm/f* hooligan, lout.
gamuza [ga'muθa] *nf* chamois.
gana ['gana] *nf* (*deseo*) desire, wish; (*apetito*) appetite; (*voluntad*) will; (*añoranza*) longing; **de buena** ~ willingly; **de mala** ~ reluctantly; **me da la** ~ **de** I feel like, I want to; **tener** ~**s de** to feel like.
ganadería [ganaðe'ria] *nf* (*ganado*) livestock; (*ganado vacuno*) cattle *pl;* (*cría, comercio*) cattle raising.
ganado [ga'naðo] *nm* livestock; ~ **lanar** sheep *pl;* ~ **vacuno** cattle *pl;* ~ **porcino** pigs *pl.*
ganador, a [gana'ðor, a] *a* winning // *nm/f* winner.
ganancia [ga'nanθja] *nf* (*lo ganado*) gain; (*aumento*) increase; (*beneficio*) profit; ~**s** *nfpl* (*ingresos*) earnings; (*beneficios*) profit *sg,* winnings.
ganapán [gana'pan] *nm* (*obrero casual*) odd-job man; (*individuo tosco*) lout.
ganar [ga'nar] *vt* (*obtener*) to get, obtain; (*sacar ventaja*) to gain; (*COM*) to earn; (*DEPORTE, premio*) to win; (*derrotar a*) to beat; (*alcanzar*) to reach // *vi* (*DEPORTE*) to win; ~**se** *vr:* ~**se la vida** to earn one's living.
gancho ['gantʃo] *nm* (*gen*) hook; (*colgador*) hanger.
gandul, a [gan'dul, a] *a, nm/f* good-for-nothing.
ganga ['ganga] *nf* (*cosa buena y barata*) bargain; (*buena situación*) cushy job.
gangrena [gan'grena] *nf* gangrene.
gansada [gan'saða] *nf* (*fam*) stupid thing to do.
ganso, a ['ganso, a] *nm/f* (*ZOOL*) gander/goose; (*fam*) idiot.
ganzúa [gan'θua] *nf* skeleton key // *nm/f* burglar.
gañán [ga'ɲan] *nm* farmhand, farm labourer.
garabato [gara'βato] *nm* (*gancho*) hook; (*garfio*) grappling iron; (*escritura*) scrawl, scribble; (*fam*) sex appeal.
garaje [ga'raxe] *nm* garage.
garante [ga'rante] *a* responsible // *nm/f* guarantor.
garantía [garan'tia] *nf* guarantee.
garantizar [garanti'θar], **garantir** [garan'tir] *vt* (*hacerse responsable de*) to vouch for; (*asegurar*) to guarantee.
garbanzo [gar'βanθo] *nm* chickpea.
garbo ['garβo] *nm* grace, elegance; ~**so, a** *a* graceful, elegant.
garfa ['garfa] *nf* claw.
garfio ['garfjo] *nm* grappling iron.
garganta [gar'ɣanta] *nf* (*interna*) throat; (*externa, de botella*) neck; **gargantilla** *nf* necklace.
gárgara ['garɣara] *nf* gargle, gargling.
gárgola ['garɣola] *nf* gargoyle.

garita [ga'rita] nf cabin, hut; (MIL) sentry box; (de camión) cab.

garra ['garra] nf (de gato, TEC) claw; (de ave) talon; (fam) hand, paw (fam).

garrafa [ga'rrafa] nf carafe, decanter.

garrido, a [ga'rriðo, a] a handsome.

garrote [ga'rrote] nm (palo) stick; (porra) cudgel; (suplicio) garrotte; (MED) tourniquet.

garrulería [garrule'ria] nf chatter.

gárrulo, a ['garrulo, a] a (charlatán) talkative; (ave) twittering; (arroyo) murmuring.

garzo, a ['garθo, a] a blue // nf heron.

gas [gas] nm gas.

gasa ['gasa] nf gauze.

gaseoso, a [gase'oso, a] a gassy, fizzy // nf lemonade, fizzy drink; (fam) pop.

gasolina [gaso'lina] nf petrol, gas(oline) (US); **gasolinera** nf petrol station.

gasómetro [ga'sometro] nm gasometer.

gastado, a [gas'taðo, a] a (rendido) spent; (raído) worn, threadbare; (usado: frase etc) trite.

gastar [gas'tar] vt (dinero, tiempo) to spend; (fuerzas) to use up; (desperdiciar) to waste; (llevar) to wear; ~se vr to wear out; (estropearse) to waste; ~ bromas to crack jokes.

gasto ['gasto] nm (desembolso) expenditure, spending; (consumo, uso) use; ~s nmpl (desembolsos) expenses; (cargos) charges, costs.

gatear [gate'ar] vi (andar a gatas) to go on all fours; (trepar) to climb // vt to scratch.

gatillo [ga'tiʎo] nm (de arma de fuego) trigger; (de dentista) forceps.

gato, a ['gato, a] nm/f cat // nm (TEC) jack; **andar a ~** as to go on all fours.

gatuno, a [ga'tuno, a] a feline.

gaucho ['gautʃo] nm gaucho.

gaveta [ga'βeta] nf drawer.

gavilla [ga'βiʎa] nf sheaf.

gaviota [ga'βjota] nf seagull.

gay [ge] a gay, homosexual.

gayo, a ['gajo, a] a gay, merry.

gazapera [gaθa'pera] nf (conejera) rabbit warren; (de gente) den of thieves; **gazapo** nm young rabbit; (fam) sly fellow.

gazmoño, a [gaθ'moɲo, a], **gazmoñero, a** [gaθmo'ɲero, a] a nm/f prude; (pretencioso) prig; (hipócrita) hypocrite.

gazpacho [gaθ'patʃo] nm gazpacho, cold vegetable soup.

gelatina [xela'tina] nf (plato) jelly; (polvos etc) gelatine.

gema ['xema] nf gem.

gemelo, a [xe'melo, a] a, nm/f twin; ~s nmpl (de camisa) cufflinks; **G~s** (ASTRO) Gemini sg; ~s de campo field glasses.

gemido [xe'miðo] nm (quejido) moan, groan; (aullido) howl.

gemir [xe'mir] vi (quejarse) to moan, groan; (aullar) to howl.

genealogía [xenealo'xia] nf genealogy.

generación [xenera'θjon] nf generation.

generador [xenera'ðor] nm generator.

general [xene'ral] a general // nm general; **por lo o en ~** in general; ~**idad** nf generality; **G~idat** nf Catalan parliament; ~**ización** nf generalization; ~**izar** vt to generalize; ~**izarse** vr to become generalised, spread; ~**mente** ad generally.

generar [xene'rar] vt to generate.

genérico, a [xe'neriko, a] a generic.

género ['xenero] nm (clase) kind, sort; (tipo) type; (BIO) genus; (LING) gender; (COM) material; ~ **humano** human race.

generosidad [xenerosi'ðað] nf generosity; **generoso, a** a generous.

genial [xe'njal] a inspired; (idea) brilliant; (afable) genial.

genio ['xenjo] nm (carácter) nature, disposition; (humor) temper; (facultad creadora) genius; **de mal ~** bad-tempered.

gente ['xente] nf (personas) people pl; (raza) race; (nación) nation; (parientes) relatives pl.

gentil [xen'til] a (elegante) graceful; (encantador) charming; ~**eza** nf grace; charm; (cortesía) courtesy.

gentío [xen'tio] nm crowd, throng.

genuflexión [xenuflek'sjon] nf genuflexion.

genuino, a [xe'nwino, a] a genuine.

geografía [xeoɣra'fia] nf geography.

geología [xeolo'xia] nf geology.

geometría [xeome'tria] nf geometry.

gerencia [xe'renθja] nf management; **gerente** nm (supervisor) manager; (jefe) director.

germen ['xermen] nm germ.

germinar [xermi'nar] vi to germinate.

gesticulación [xestikula'θjon] nf (ademán) gesticulation; (mueca) grimace.

gestión [xes'tjon] nf management; (diligencia, acción) negotiation; (esfuerzo) effort; **gestionar** vt (lograr) to try to arrange; (llevar) to manage; (discutir) to negotiate.

gesto ['xesto] nm (mueca) grimace; (ademán) gesture.

gestoría [xesto'ria] nf estate agent's.

Gibraltar [xiβral'tar] nm Gibraltar.

gigante [xi'ɣante] a, nm/f giant.

gilipollas [xili'poʎas] excl (fam) bastard! (fam).

gimnasia [xim'nasja] nf gymnastics pl; **gimnasio** nm gymnasium; **gimnásta** nm/f gymnast.

gimotear [ximote'ar] vi to whine, whimper.

ginebra [xi'neβra] nf gin.

ginecólogo, a [xine'koloɣo, a] nm/f gynecologist.

gira ['xira] nf tour, trip.

girar [xi'rar] vt (dar la vuelta) to turn (around); (: rápidamente) to spin; (COM: cheque) to draw; (comerciar: letra de cambio) to issue // vi to turn (round); (rápido) to spin; (COM) to draw.

girasol [xira'sol] *nm* sunflower.

giratorio, a [xira'torjo, a] *a* (*gen*) revolving; (*puente*) swing.

giro ['xiro] *nm* (*movimiento*) turn, revolution; (*LING*) expression; (*COM*) draft; ~ **bancario/postal** money/ postal order.

gitano, a [xi'tano, a] *a, nm/f* gypsy.

glacial [gla'θjal] *a* icy, freezing.

glándula ['glandula] *nf* gland.

globo ['gloβo] *nm* (*esfera*) globe, sphere; (*aeróstato, juguete*) balloon.

gloria ['glorja] *nf* glory; **gloriarse** *vr* to boast.

glorieta [glo'rjeta] *nf* (*de jardín*) bower, arbour; (*plazoleta*) roundabout.

glorificar [glorifi'kar] *vt* (*enaltecer*) to glorify, praise; ~**se** *vr:* ~**se de** to boast of.

glorioso, a [glo'rjoso, a] *a* glorious.

glosa ['glosa] *nf* comment; **glosar** *vt* (*comentar*) to comment on; (*fig*) to criticize.

glosario [glo'sarjo] *nm* glossary.

glotón, ona [glo'ton, ona] *a* gluttonous, greedy; **glotonería** *nf* gluttony, greed.

gobernación [goβerna'θjon] *nf* government, governing; **gobernador, a** *a* governing // *nm* governor; **gobernante** *a* governing.

gobernar [goβer'nar] *vt* (*dirigir*) to guide, direct; (*regir*) to rule, govern // *vi* to govern; (*NAUT*) to steer.

gobierno [go'βjerno] *nm* (*POL*) government; (*dirección*) guidance, direction; (*NAUT*) steering.

goce ['goθe] *nm* enjoyment.

gol [gol] *nm* goal.

gola ['gola] *nf* gullet; (*garganta*) throat.

golf [golf] *nm* golf.

golfa ['golfa] *nf* (*fam*) tart, whore.

golfo ['golfo] *nm* (*GEO*) gulf; (*fam: niño*) urchin; (*gamberro*) lout.

golondrina [golon'drina] *nf* swallow.

golosina [golo'sina] *nf* (*gen*) titbit; (*dulce*) sweet; **goloso, a** *a* sweet-toothed.

golpe ['golpe] *nm* (*gen*) blow; (*de puño*) punch; (*de mano*) smack; (*de corazón*) beat; (*de remo*) stroke; (*fig: choque*) clash; **no dar** ~ to be bone idle; **de un** ~ with one blow; **de** ~ suddenly; ~ **de estado** coup d'état; **golpear** *vt, vi* to strike, knock; (*asestar*) to beat; (*de puño*) to punch; (*golpetear*) to tap.

goma ['goma] *nf* (*caucho*) rubber; (*elástico*) elastic; ~ **espuma** foam rubber; ~ **de pegar** gum, glue.

gomita [go'mita] *nf* elastic band.

góndola ['gondola] *nf* (*barco*) gondola; (*de tren*) goods wagon.

gordo, a [gorðo, a] *a* (*gen*) fat; (*persona*) plump; (*tela*) coarse; (*fam*) enormous; **el premio** ~ (*en lotería*) first prize; **gordura** *nf* fat; (*corpulencia*) fatness, stoutness.

gorgojo [gor'xoxo] *nm* (*insecto*) grub; (*fam*) runt.

gorila [go'rila] *nm* gorilla.

gorjear [gorxe'ar] *vi* to twitter, chirp; **gorjeo** *nm* twittering, chirping.

gorra ['gorra] *nf* (*gen*) cap; (*de niño*) bonnet; (*militar*) bearskin // *nm* scrounger.

gorrión [go'rrjon] *nm* sparrow.

gorro ['gorro] *nm* (*gen*) cap; (*de niño, mujer*) bonnet.

gorrón [go'rron] *nm* pebble.

gota ['gota] *nf* (*gen*) drop; (*de sudor*) bead; (*MED*) gout; **gotear** *vi* to drip; (*lloviznar*) to drizzle; **gotera** *nf* leak.

gótico, a ['gotiko, a] *a* Gothic.

gozar [go'θar] *vi* to enjoy o.s.; ~ **de** (*disfrutar*) to enjoy; (*poseer*) to possess.

gozne ['goθne] *nm* hinge.

gozo ['goθo] *nm* (*alegría*) joy; (*placer*) pleasure; ~**so, a** *a* joyous, joyful.

grabación [graβa'θjon] *nf* recording.

grabado [gra'βaðo] *nm* print, engraving; **grabador** *nm* engraver.

grabadora [graβa'ðora] *nf* tape-recorder.

grabar [gra'βar] *vt* to engrave; (*discos, cintas*) to record.

gracejo [gra'θexo] *nm* (*humor*) wit, humour; (*elegancia*) grace.

gracia ['graθja] *nf* (*encanto*) grace, gracefulness; (*chiste*) joke; (*humor*) humour, wit; ¡~**s!** thanks!; **¡muchas** ~**s!** thanks very much!; ~**s a** thanks to; **tener** ~ to be funny; (*ser divertido*) to be enjoyable; **no me hace** ~ I am not keen; **gracioso, a** *a* (*divertido*) funny, amusing; (*cómico*) comical // *nm* (*TEATRO*) comic character.

grada ['graða] *nf* (*de escalera*) step; (*de anfiteatro*) tier, row.

gradación [graða'θjon] *nf* gradation.

gradería [graðe'ria] *nf* (*gradas*) (flight of) steps *pl*; (*de anfiteatro*) tiers *pl*, rows *pl*; ~ **cubierta** covered stand.

grado ['graðo] *nm* degree; (*de aceite, vino*) grade; (*grada*) step; (*MIL*) rank; **de buen** ~ willingly.

graduación [graðwa'θjon] *nf* (*del alcohol*) proof, strength; (*ESCOL*) graduation.

gradual [gra'ðwal] *a* gradual.

graduar [gra'ðwar] *vt* (*gen*) to graduate; (*clasificar*) to grade; (*MIL*) to commission; ~**se** *vr* to graduate.

gráfico, a ['grafiko, a] *a* graphic // *nm* diagram // *nf* graph.

grajo ['graxo] *nm* rook.

Gral *abr de* **General**.

gramática [gra'matika] *nf* grammar.

gramo ['gramo] *nm* gramme.

gran [gran] *a ver* **grande**.

grana ['grana] *nf* (*BOT*) seedling; (*ZOOL*) cochineal; (*color, tela*) scarlet.

Granada [gra'naða] *n* Granada.

granada [gra'naða] *nf* pomegranate; (*MIL*) grenade; **granadina** *nf* grenadine.

granadino, a [grana'ðino, a] *a* of Granada // *nm/f* native *or* inhabitant of Granada.

granado, a [gra'naðo, a] *a* choice, select // *nm* pomegranate tree.

granar [gra'nar] *vi* to seed.

granate [gra'nate] *nm* garnet.

Gran Bretaña [granbre'taɲa] *nf* Great Britain.

grande ['grande], **gran** [gran] *a* (*de tamaño*) big, large; (*alto*) tall; (*distinguido*) great; (*impresionante*) grand // *nm* grandee; **grandeza** *nf* greatness.

grandioso, a [gran'djoso, a] *a* magnificent, grand.

grandor [gran'dor] *nm* size.

granel [gra'nel]: **a ~** *ad* in abundance; (*COM*) in bulk.

granero [gra'nero] *nm* granary, barn.

granito [gra'nito] *nm* (*AGR*) small grain; (*roca*) granite; (*MED*) pimple.

granizado [grani'θaðo] *nm* iced drink; **granizar** *vi* to hail; **granizo** *nm* hail.

granja ['granxa] *nf* (*gen*) farm; (*lechería*) dairy; (*café*) milk bar.

granjear [granxe'ar] *vt* (*cobrar*) to earn; (*ganar*) to win; (*avanzar*) to gain; **granjería** *nf* (*COM*) profit; (*AGR*) farming.

grano ['grano] *nm* grain; (*semilla*) seed; (*baya*) berry; (*MED*) pimple; **~s** *nmpl* cereals.

granoso, a [gra'noso, a] *a* granulated.

granuja [gra'nuxa] *nf* grape seed // *nm* rogue; (*golfillo*) urchin.

grapa ['grapa] *nf* staple; (*TEC*) clamp.

grasa ['grasa] *nf* (*gen*) grease; (*de cocina*) fat, lard; (*sebo*) suet; (*mugre*) filth; (*escoria*) dross; **grasiento, a** *a* greasy; (*de aceite*) oily.

gratificación [gratifika'θjon] *nf* (*propina*) tip; (*bono*) bonus; (*recompensa*) reward; **gratificar** *vt* to tip; to reward.

gratis ['gratis] *ad* free.

gratitud [grati'tuð] *nf* gratitude.

grato, a ['grato, a] *a* (*agradable*) pleasant, agreeable; (*bienvenido*) welcome.

gratuito, a [gra'twito, a] *a* (*gratis*) free; (*sin razón*) gratuitous.

gravamen [gra'βamen] *nm* (*carga*) burden; (*impuesto*) tax.

gravar [gra'βar] *vt* to burden.

grave ['graβe] *a* heavy; (*serio*) grave, serious; **~dad** *nf* gravity.

grávido, a ['graβiðo, a] *a* (*preñada*) pregnant; (*lleno, cargado*) full.

gravitación [graβita'θjon] *nf* gravitation; **gravitar** *vi* to gravitate; **gravitar sobre** to rest on.

gravoso, a [gra'βoso, a] *a* (*pesado*) burdensome; (*costoso*) costly.

graznar [graθ'nar] *vi* (*cuervo*) to squawk; (*pato*) to quack; (*hablar ronco*) to croak; **graznido** *nm* squawk; croak.

Grecia ['greθja] *nf* Greece.

greguería [greɣe'ria] *nf* hubbub.

gremio ['gremjo] *nm* (*sindicato*) trade union; (*asociación*) professional association.

greña ['greɲa] *nf* (*cabellos*) shock of hair;

(*maraña*) tangle; **greñudo, a** *a* (*persona*) dishevelled; (*hair*) tangled.

gresca ['greska] *nf* uproar.

grey [grei] *nf* flock.

griego, a ['grjeɣo, a] *a, nm/f* Greek.

grieta ['grjeta] *nf* crack; **grietarse** *vr* = **agrietarse**.

grifo, a ['grifo, a] *a* curly, kinky // *nm* tap.

grillo ['griʎo] *nm* (*ZOOL*) cricket; (*BOT*) shoot; **~s** *nmpl* shackles, irons.

gripe ['gripe] *nf* flu, influenza.

gris [gris] *a* (*color*) grey.

grita ['grita] *nf* uproar; **gritar** *vt, vi* to shout, yell; **grito** *nm* shout, yell; (*de horror*) scream; **a grito pelado** at the top of one's voice.

grosella [gro'seʎa] *nf* (red)currant; **~ negra** blackcurrant.

grosería [grose'ria] *nf* (*actitud*) rudeness; (*comentario*) vulgar comment; **grosero, a** *a* (*poco cortés*) rude; (*ordinario*) vulgar, crude.

grosor [gro'sor] *nm* thickness.

grotesco, a [gro'tesko, a] *a* grotesque.

grúa ['grua] *nf* (*TEC*) crane; (*de petróleo*) derrick.

grueso, a ['grweso, a] *a* thick; (*voluminoso*) stout // *nm* bulk // *nf* gross; **el ~ de** the bulk of.

grulla ['gruʎa] *nf* crane.

gruñido [gru'niðo] *nm* grunt; (*fig*) grumble; **gruñir** *vi* (*animal*) to growl; (*fam*) to grumble.

grupa ['grupa] *nf* (*ZOOL*) rump.

grupo ['grupo] *nm* group; (*TEC*) unit, set.

gruta ['gruta] *nf* grotto.

guadamecí [gwaðame'θi], **guadamecil** [gwaðame'θil] *nm* embossed leather.

guadaña [gwa'ðaɲa] *nf* scythe; **guadañar** *vt* to scythe, mow.

guano ['gwano] *nm* (*AM*) guano.

guante ['gwante] *nm* glove.

guapo, a ['gwapo, a] *a* good-looking, attractive; (*hombre*) handsome; (*elegante*) smart // *nm* lover, gallant.

guarda ['gwarða] *nm* guard, keeper // *nf* guarding; (*custodia*) custody; **~bosque** *nm* gamekeeper; **~costas** *nm inv* coastguard vessel; **~dor, a** *a* protective // *nm/f* guardian, protector; **~espaldas** *nm/f inv* bodyguard; **~polvo** *nm* dust cover; (*de niño*) smock; (*para el trabajo*) overalls *pl*; **guardar** *vt* (*gen*) to keep; (*vigilar*) to guard, watch over; (*dinero: ahorrar*) to save, put by; **guardarse** *vr* (*preservarse*) to protect o.s.; (*evitar*) to avoid; **guardarropa** *nm* (*armario*) wardrobe; (*en establecimiento público*) cloakroom.

guardería [gwarðe'ria] *nf* (children's) nursery.

guardia ['gwarðja] *nf* (*MIL*) guard; (*cuidado*) care, custody // *nm* guard; (*policía*) policeman; **estar de ~** to be on guard; **montar ~** to mount guard; **G~ Civil** Civil Guard; **G~ Nacional** police; **~ urbano** traffic policeman.

uardián, ana [gwar'ðjan, ana] *nm/f* (*gen*) guardian, keeper; (*sereno*) watchman.

uardilla [gwar'ðiʎa] *nf* attic.

uarecer [gware'θer] *vt* (*proteger*) to protect; (*abrigar*) to shelter; ~**se** *vr* to take refuge.

uarida [gwa'riða] *nf* (*de animal*) den, lair; (*refugio*) refuge.

uarismo [gwa'rismo] *nm* figure, number.

uarnecer [gwarne'θer] *vt* (*equipar*) to provide; (*adornar*) to adorn; (*TEC*) to reinforce; **guarnición** *nf* (*de vestimenta*) trimming; (*de piedra*) mount; (*CULIN*) garnish; (*arneses*) harness; (*MIL*) garrison.

uarro, a [ˈgwarro, a] *nm/f* pig.

uasa [ˈgwasa] *nf* joke; **guasón, ona** *a* witty; (*bromista*) joking // *nm/f* wit; joker.

uatemala [gwate'mala] *nf* Guatemala.

ubernativo, a [gußerna'tiβo, a] *a* governmental.

uedeja [ge'ðexa] *nf* long hair; (*de león*) mane.

uerra [ˈgerra] *nf* war; (*pelea*) struggle; ~ **fría** cold war; **dar** ~ to annoy; **guerrear** *vi* to wage war; **guerrero, a** *a* fighting; (*carácter*) warlike // *nm/f* warrior.

uerrilla [ge'rriʎa] *nf* guerrilla warfare; (*tropas*) guerrilla band *or* group.

uía [ˈgia] *nm/f* guide // *nf* (*libro*) guidebook; ~ **de ferrocarriles** railway timetable; ~ **de teléfonos** telephone directory; **guiar** *vt* to guide, direct; (*AUT*) to steer; **guiarse** *vr*: **guiarse por** to be guided by.

uija [ˈgixa] *nf*, **guijarro** [gi'xarro] *nm* pebble; (*camino*) cobblestone.

uijo [ˈgixo] *nm* gravel; (*de playa*) shingle.

uillotina [giʎo'tina] *nf* guillotine.

uinda [ˈginda] *nf* morello cherry.

uindar [gin'dar] *vt* to hoist.

uindilla [gin'diʎa] *nf* Guinea pepper.

uiñapo [gi'napo] *nm* (*harapo*) rag; (*persona*) reprobate, rogue.

uiñar [gi'nar] *vi* to wink; (*parpadear*) to blink.

uión [gi'on] *nm* (*conductor*) leader; (*LING*) hyphen, dash; (*CINE*) script; **guionista** *nm/f* scriptwriter.

uirnalda [gir'nalda] *nf* garland.

uisa [ˈgisa] *nf*: **a** ~ **de** as, like, in the way of.

uisado [gi'saðo] *nm* stew.

uisante [gi'sante] *nm* pea; ~ **de olor** sweet pea.

uisar [gi'sar] *vt, vi* to cook; **guiso** *nm* cooked dish.

uita [ˈgita] *nf* twine.

uitarra [gi'tarra] *nf* guitar.

ula [ˈgula] *nf* gluttony, greed.

usano [gu'sano] *nm* maggot; (*lombriz*) earthworm; ~ **de luz** glow-worm; ~ **de seda** silk-worm.

ustar [gus'tar] *vt* to taste, sample // *vi* to please, be pleasing; ~ **de algo** to like *or*

enjoy sth; **me gustan las uvas** I like grapes.

gusto [ˈgusto] *nm* (*sentido, sabor*) taste; (*placer*) pleasure; **tiene** ~ **a menta** it tastes of mint; **tener buen** ~ to have good taste; **sentirse a** ~ to feel at ease; **mucho** ~ **en conocerle** pleased to meet you; **el** ~ **es mío** the pleasure is mine; **con** ~ willingly, gladly; ~**so, a** *a* (*sabroso*) tasty; (*agradable*) pleasant.

gutural [gutu'ral] *a* guttural.

H

ha *vb ver* **haber.**

haba [ˈaβa] *nf* bean.

Habana [a'βana] *nf*: **la** ~ Havana.

habano [a'βano] *nm* Havana cigar.

haber [a'ßer] *vb auxiliar* to have; **de** ~**lo sabido** if I had known (it); ~ **de** to have to // *vb impersonal*: **hay** there is/are; **hay que** it is necessary to, one must; **¿qué hay?** how's it going?; **no hay de qué** don't mention it // *nm* (*ingreso*) income; (*COM: crédito*) credit; ~**es** *nmpl* assets.

habichuela [aβi'tʃwela] *nf* kidney bean.

hábil [ˈaβil] *a* (*listo*) clever, smart; (*capaz*) fit, capable; (*experto*) expert; **día** ~ working day; **habilidad** *nf* (*gen*) skill, ability; (*inteligencia*) cleverness.

habilitación [aβilita'θjon] *nf* qualification; (*colocación de muebles*) fitting out; (*financiamiento*) financing.

habilitar [aβili'tar] *vt* (*capacitar*) to enable; (*dar instrumentos*) to equip; (*financiar*) to finance.

hábilmente [aβil'mente] *ad* skilfully, expertly.

habitación [aβita'θjon] *nf* (*cuarto*) room; (*casa*) dwelling, abode; (*BIO: morada*) habitat; ~ **sencilla** *o* **particular** single room; ~ **doble** *o* **matrimonial** double room.

habitante [aβi'tante] *nm/f* inhabitant.

habitar [aβi'tar] *vt* (*residir en*) to inhabit; (*ocupar*) to occupy // *vi* to live.

hábito [ˈaβito] *nm* habit; **habitual** *a* habitual.

habituar [aβi'twar] *vt* to accustom; ~**se** *vr*: ~**se a** to get used to.

habla [ˈaβla] *nf* (*capacidad de hablar*) speech; (*idioma*) language; (*dialecto*) dialect; **perder el** ~ to become speechless; **de** ~ **francesa** French-speaking; **estar al** ~ to be in contact; **¡González al** ~! Gonzalez speaking!

hablador, a [aβla'ðor, a] *a* talkative // *nm/f* chatterbox.

habladuría [aβlaðu'ria] *nf* rumour; (*sarcasmo*) sarcastic comment; ~**s** *nfpl* gossip *sg*.

hablar [a'βlar] *vt* to speak, talk // *vi* to speak; ~**se** *vr* to speak to each other; ~ **con** to speak to; ~ **de** to speak of *or* about; **'se habla inglés'** 'English spoken here'.

hablilla [a'βliʎa] *nf* story, rumour.

habré etc vb ver **haber.**

hacedero, a [aθe'ðero, a] a feasible.

hacedor, a [aθe'ðor, a] nm/f maker.

hacendoso, a [aθen'doso, a] a industrious.

hacer [a'θer] vt (gen) to make; (crear) to create; (TEC) to manufacture; (preparar) to prepare; (ejecutar) to do, execute; (obligar) to force, compel // vi (comportarse) to act, behave; (disimular) to pretend; (importar) to be important, matter; (convenir, ser apto) to be suitable; ~se vr (fabricarse) to be made, be done; (volverse) to become; (acostumbrarse a) to get used to; ~ la maleta to pack; ~ una pregunta to ask a question; ~ una visita to visit; ~ bien/mal to act rightly/wrongly; hace frío/calor it's cold/hot; hace dos años two years ago; hace poco a little while ago; ~ el malo (TEATRO) to play (the part of) the villain; ¿qué ~? what is to be done?; ~ como que o como si to act as though or as if; ~ de to act as; me hice un traje I had a suit made; ~se el sordo to turn a deaf ear; ~se viejo to grow old; ~se con algo to get hold of sth; ~se a un lado to stand aside.

hacia ['aθja] prep (en dirección de) towards; (cerca de) near; ~ arriba/abajo up(wards)/down(wards); ~ mediodía about noon.

hacienda [a'θjenda] nf (propiedad) property; (estancia) farm, ranch; (AM) plantation; ~ pública public finance; (Ministerio de) H~ Treasury, Exchequer.

hacina [a'θina] nf pile, stack.

hacha ['atʃa] nf axe; (antorcha) torch.

hache ['atʃe] nf (the letter) H.

hada ['aða] nf fairy.

hago etc vb ver **hacer.**

Haití [ai'ti] nm Haiti.

halagar [ala'xar] vt (mostrar afecto) to show affection for; (lisonjear) to flatter.

halago [a'laxo] nm pleasure, delight; (atractivo) attraction; (adulación) flattery; **halagüeño, a** a pleasing; attractive; flattering.

halcón [al'kon] nm falcon, hawk.

hálito ['alito] nm breath.

hallar [a'ʎar] vt (gen) to find; (descubrir) to discover; (toparse con) to run up against; ~se vr vr to be (situated); **hallazgo** nm discovery; (cosa) find.

hamaca [a'maka] nf hammock; ~ plegable deckchair.

hambre ['ambre] nf hunger; (carencia) famine; (fig) longing; **tener** ~ to be hungry; ~ar vi, vt to starve; **hambriento, a** a hungry, starving.

hamburguesa [ambur'xesa] nf hamburger.

hampa ['ampa] nf underworld; **hampón** nm tough.

han vb ver **haber.**

haragán, ana [ara'xan, ana] a, nm/f good-for-nothing; **haraganear** vi to idle, loaf about.

harapiento, a [ara'pjento, a] a tattered, in rags; **harapo** nm rag.

haré etc vb ver **hacer.**

harina [a'rina] nf flour; (polvo) powder; **harinero, a** nm/f flour merchant; **harinoso, a** a floury.

hartar [ar'tar] vt to satiate, glut; (fig) to tire, sicken; ~se vr (de comida) to fill o.s., gorge o.s.; (cansarse) to get fed up (de with); **hartazgo** nm surfeit, glut; **harto, a** a (lleno) full; (cansado) fed up // a (bastante) enough; (muy) very; **estar harto de** to be fed up with; **hartura** nf (exceso) surfeit; (abundancia) abundance; (satisfacción) satisfaction.

has vb ver **haber.**

hasta ['asta] ad even // prep (alcanzando a) as far as, up/down to; (de tiempo: a tal hora) till, until; (antes de) before // conj: ~ que until; ~ luego/la vista see you soon.

hastiar [as'tjar] vt (gen) to weary; (aburrir) to bore; (asquear) to disgust; ~se vr: ~se de to get fed up with; **hastío** nm weariness; boredom; disgust.

hato ['ato], **hatillo** [a'tiʎo] nm belonging, pl, kit; (víveres) provisions pl; (banda) gang, group; (montón) bundle, heap.

hay vb ver **haber.**

Haya ['aja] nf: **la** ~ The Hague.

haya etc vb ver **haber** // ['aja] nf beech tree; **hayal, hayedo** nm beech grove.

haz [aθ] vb ver **hacer** // nm bundle, bunch; (rayo: de luz) beam.

hazaña [a'θaɲa] nf feat, exploit.

hazmerreír [aθmerre'ir] nm laughing stock.

he vb ver **haber.**

hebilla [e'βiʎa] nf buckle, clasp.

hebra ['eβra] nf thread; (BOT: fibra) fibre, grain; **tabaco de** ~ loose tobacco.

hebreo, a [e'βreo, a] a, nm/f Hebrew // nm (lengua) Hebrew.

hectárea [ek'tarea] nf hectare.

hechizar [etʃi'θar] vt to cast a spell on, bewitch.

hechizo, a [e'tʃiθo, a] a (gen) false, artificial; (removible) detachable // nm witchcraft, magic; (acto de magía) spell, charm.

hecho, a ['etʃo, a] pp de **hacer** // a complete; (maduro) mature; (costura) ready-to-wear // nm deed, act; (dato) fact; (cuestión) matter; (suceso) event // excl agreed!, done!; ¡**bien** ~! well done!; **de** ~ in fact, as a matter of fact.

hechura [e'tʃura] nf making, creation; (producto) product; (forma) form, shape; (de persona) build; (TEC) craftsmanship; ~s nfpl (COSTURA) cost of making up sg.

heder [e'ðer] vt to stink, smell; (fig) to be unbearable.

hediondez [eðjon'deθ] nf stench, stink; (cosa) stinking thing; **hediondo, a** a stinking; (*insoportable*) repulsive, unbearable.

ledor [e'ðor] *nm* stench.

lelado, a [e'laðo, a] *a* frozen; (*glacial*) icy; (*fig*) chilly, cold // *nm* ice-cream // *nf* frost.

lelar [e'lar] *vt* to freeze, ice (up); (*dejar atónito*) to amaze; (*desalentar*) to discourage // *vi*, ~**se** *vr* to freeze.

lélice [e'liθe] *nf* spiral; (*TEC*) propeller.

lelicóptero [eli'koptero] *nm* helicopter.

lembra ['embra] *nf* (*BOT, ZOOL*) female; (*mujer*) woman; (*TEC*) nut.

lemorragia [emo'rraxja] *nf* haemorrhage.

lemorroides [emo'rroiðes] *nfpl* haemorrhoids.

lemos *vb ver* **haber.**

lenchir [en'tʃir] *vt* to fill, stuff; ~**se** *vr* (*llenarse de comida*) to stuff o.s. (with food); (*inflarse*) to swell (up).

lender [en'der] *vt* to cleave, split; **hendidura** *nf* crack, split; (*GEO*) fissure.

leno ['eno] *nm* hay.

lerbicida [erβi'θiða] *nm* weed-killer.

leredad [ere'ðaθ] *nf* landed property; (*granja*) farm.

eredar [ere'ðar] *vt* to inherit; **heredero, a** *nm/f* heir/heiress.

lereje [e'rexe] *nm/f* heretic; **herejía** *nf* heresy.

lerencia [e'renθja] *nf* inheritance.

lerido, a [e'riðo, a] *a* injured, wounded // *nm/f* casualty // *nf* wound, injury; (*insulto*) insult.

lerir [e'rir] *vt* to wound, injure; (*fig*) to offend.

lermanar [erma'nar] *vt* to match; (*unir*) to join.

lermandad [erman'daθ] *nf* brotherhood.

lermano, a [er'mano, a] *nm/f* brother/sister; ~ **gemelo** twin brother; ~ **politico** brother-in-law; ~**a politica** sister-in-law.

lermético, a [er'metiko, a] *a* hermetic; (*fig*) watertight.

lermoso, a [er'moso, a] *a* beautiful, lovely; (*estupendo*) splendid; (*guapo*) handsome; **hermosura** *nf* beauty.

léroe ['eroe] *nm* hero; **heroico, a** *a* heroic.

leroína [ero'ina] *nf* (*mujer*) heroine; (*droga*) heroin.

leroismo [ero'ismo] *nm* heroism.

lerrador [erra'ðor] *nm* blacksmith; **herradura** *nf*: **curva en herradura** hairpin bend.

lerramienta [erra'mjenta] *nf* tool; (*conjunto*) set of tools.

lerrería [erre'ria] *nf* smithy; (*TEC*) forge; **herrero** *nm* blacksmith.

lerrumbre [e'rrumbre] *nf* rust.

lervidero [erβi'ðero] *nm* (*burbujeo*) boiling, seething; (*fuente*) hot spring.

lervir [er'βir] *vi* (*gen*) to boil; (*burbujear*) to bubble; (*fig*): ~ **de** to teem with; ~ **a**

fuego lento to simmer; **hervor** *nm* boiling; (*fig*) ardour, fervour.

heterogéneo, a [etero'xeneo, a] *a* heterogeneous.

heterosexual [eterosek'swal] *a* heterosexual.

hice *etc vb ver* **hacer.**

hidráulico, a [i'ðrauliko, a] *a* hydraulic // *nf* hydraulics *sg*.

hidro... [iðro] *pref* hydro..., water-...; ~**ala** *nf* hovercraft; ~**avión** *nm* seaplane; ~**eléctrico, a** *a* hydroelectric; ~**fobia** *nf* hydrophobia, rabies; **hidrófugo, a** *a* damp-proof; **hidrógeno** *nm* hydrogen.

hiedra ['jeðra] *nf* ivy.

hiel [jel] *nf* gall, bile; (*fig*) bitterness.

hiela *etc vb ver* **helar.**

hielo ['jelo] *nm* (*gen*) ice; (*escarza*) frost; (*fig*) coldness, reserve.

hiena ['jena] *nf* hyena.

hierba ['jerβa] *nf* (*BOT*) grass; (*MED*) herb; **mala** ~ weed; (*fig*) evil influence; ~**buena** *nf* mint.

hierro ['jerro] *nm* (*metal*) iron; (*objeto*) iron object; (*herramienta*) tool; ~ **acanalado** corrugated iron; ~ **colado** *o* **fundido** cast iron.

hígado ['ixaðo] *nm* liver.

higiene [i'xjene] *nf* hygiene; **higiénico, a** *a* hygienic.

higo ['ixo] *nm* fig; ~ **paso** *o* **seco** dried fig; **higuera** *nf* fig tree.

hijastro, a [i'xastro, a] *nm/f* stepson/daughter.

hijo, a ['ixo, a] *nm/f* son/daughter, child; ~**s** *nmpl* children, sons and daughters; ~ **de papá/mamá** daddy's/mummy's boy; ~ **de puta** bastard, son of a bitch.

hilado, a [i'laðo, a] *a* spun // *nm* yarn.

hilandero, a [ilan'dero, a] *nm/f* spinner.

hilar [i'lar] *vt* to spin; ~ **delgado** to split hairs.

hilera [i'lera] *nf* row, file.

hilo ['ilo] *nm* (*gen*) thread; (*BOT*) fibre; (*metal*) wire; (*de agua*) trickle, thin stream; (*de luz*) beam, ray.

hilvanar [ilβa'nar] *vt* to tack; (*fig*) to do hurriedly.

Himalayas [ima'lajas] *nfpl*: **las** ~ the Himalayas.

himno ['imno] *nm* hymn; ~ **nacional** national anthem.

hincapié [inka'pje] *nm*: **hacer** ~ **en** to emphasize.

hincar [in'kar] *vt* to drive (in), thrust (in); ~**se** *vr*: ~**se de rodillas** to kneel down.

hinchado, a [in'tʃaðo, a] *a* (*gen*) swollen; (*persona*) pompous.

hinchar [in'tʃar] *vt* (*gen*) to swell; (*inflar*) to blow up, inflate; (*fig*) to exaggerate; ~**se** *vr* (*inflarse*) to swell up; (*fam*: *llenarse*) to stuff o.s.; **hinchazón** *nf* (*MED*) swelling; (*altivez*) arrogance.

hinojo [i'noxo] *nm* fennel.

hipar [i'par] *vi* to hiccup; (*perro*) to pant.

hipnotismo [ipno'tismo] *nm* hypnotism; **hipnotizar** *vt* to hypnotize.

hipo ['ipo] *nm* hiccups *pl*.

hipocresía [ipokre'sia] *nf* hypocrisy; **hipócrita** *a* hypocritical // *nm/f* hypocrite.

hipódromo [i'poðromo] *nm* racetrack.

hipopótamo [ipo'potamo] *nm* hippopotamus.

hipoteca [ipo'teka] *nf* mortgage.

hipótesis [i'potesis] *nf* hypothesis.

hiriente [i'rjente] *a* offensive, cutting.

hirsuto, a [ir'suto, a] *a* hairy; (*fig*) rough.

hispánico, a [is'paniko, a] *a* Hispanic.

hispano, a [is'pano, a] *a* Hispanic, Spanish, Hispano-; **H~américa** *nf* Spanish *or* Latin America; **~americano, a** *a, nm/f* Spanish *or* Latin American.

histeria [is'terja] *nf* hysteria.

historia [is'torja] *nf* (*gen*) history; (*cuento*) story, tale; **~s** *nfpl* (*chismes*) gossip *sg*; **dejarse de ~s** to come to the point; **pasar a la ~** to go down in history; **~dor, a** *nm/f* historian; **historiar** *vt* to chronicle, write the history of; **histórico, a** *a* historical; (*fig*) historic.

historieta [isto'rjeta] *nf* tale, anecdote; (*dibujos*) strip cartoon.

hito ['ito] *nm* (*gen*) landmark; (*objetivo*) goal, target.

hizo *vb ver* **hacer.**

hocico [o'θiko] *nm* snout; (*fig*) grimace; **caer** *o* **dar de ~s** to fall on one's face.

hockey ['xoki] *nm* hockey; **~ sobre patines** *o* **hielo** ice hockey.

hogar [o'xar] *nm* fireplace, hearth; (*casa*) home; (*vida familiar*) home life; **~eño, a** *a* home; (*persona*) home-loving.

hoguera [o'xera] *nf* (*gen*) bonfire; (*llamas*) blaze.

hoja ['oxa] *nf* (*gen*) leaf; (*de flor*) petal; (*de papel*) sheet; (*página*) page; **~ de afeitar** razor blade; **~ de estaño** tinfoil.

hojalata [oxa'lata] *nf* tin(plate).

hojear [oxe'ar] *vt* to leaf through, turn the pages of.

hola ['ola] *excl* hello!

Holanda [o'landa] *nf* Holland; **holandés, esa** *a* Dutch // *nm/f* Dutchman/woman // *nm* (*lengua*) Dutch.

holgado, a [ol'xaðo, a] *a* loose, baggy; (*libre*) free; (*desempleado*) idle; (*rico*) well-to-do.

holganza [ol'xanθa] *nf* (*ocio*) leisure; (*pereza*) idleness; (*diversión*) amusement.

holgar [ol'xar] *vi* (*descansar*) to rest; (*sobrar*) to be superfluous; **~se** *vr* to enjoy o.s.; **huelga decir que** it goes without saying that.

holgazán, ana [olxa'θan, ana] *a* idle, lazy // *nm/f* loafer.

holgura [ol'xura] *nf* looseness, bagginess; (*TEC*) play, free movement; (*vida*) comfortable living, luxury.

hollar [o'Aar] *vt* to tread (on), trample.

hollín [o'Ain] *nm* soot.

hombradía [ombra'ðia] *nf* manliness.

hombre ['ombre] *nm* (*gen*) man(kind); (*uno*) man // *excl* (*claro*) of course!; (*pa... énfasis*) man, old boy; (*sorpresa*) you don... say!; **~ de negocios** businessma... **~-rana** frogman; **~ de pro** *o* **d... provecho** honest man.

hombrera [om'brera] *nf* shoulder strap.

hombro ['ombro] *nm* shoulder.

hombruno, a [om'bruno, a] *a* mannish.

homenaje [ome'naxe] *nm* (*gen*) homag... (*lealtad*) allegiance; (*tributo*) tribute.

homicida [omi'θiða] *a* homicidal // *nm...* murderer; **homicidio** *nm* murde... homicide.

homosexual [omosek'swal] *a, nm...* homosexual.

hondo, a ['ondo, a] *a* deep; (*profundo*) lov... // *nm* depth(s) (*pl*), bottom; **~nada** ... hollow, depression; (*cañón*) ravine; (*GEO...* lowland; **hondura** *nf* depth, profundity.

Honduras [on'duras] *nf* Honduras.

hondureño, a [ondu'reɲo, a] *a, nm...* Honduran.

honestidad [onesti'ðað] *nf* purity, chastit... (*decencia*) decency; **honesto, a** *a* chaste... decent, honest; (*justo*) just.

hongo ['ongo] *nm* (*BOT. gen*) fungus; ... comestible) mushroom; (: *venenoso...* toadstool.

honor [o'nor] *nm* (*gen*) honour; (*gloria...* glory; **en ~ a la verdad** to be fai... **~able** *a* honourable.

honorario, a [ono'rarjo, a] *a* honorary ... **~s** *nmpl* fees.

honra ['onra] *nf* (*gen*) honour; (*nombre...* reputation; (*~dez*) *nf* honesty; (*de persona...* integrity; **~do, a** *a* honest, upright.

honrar [on'rar] *vt* to honour; **~se** v... **~se con algo/de hacer algo** to b... honoured by/to do sth.

honroso, a [on'roso, a] *a* (*honrado...* honourable; (*respetado*) respectable.

hora ['ora] *nf* (*gen*) time; (*específica*) hour... **¿qué ~ es?** what time is it?; **¿a qué ~...** at what time?; **media ~** half an hour; ... **la ~ de recreo** at playtime; **a primera...** **~** first thing (in the morning); **a última...** **~** at the last moment; **en las altas ~s** i... the small hours; **¡a buena ~!** it's hig... time!; **dar la ~** to strike the hour; **~s de...** **oficina/de trabajo** office/working hours... **~s de visita** visiting times; **~s extras...** extraordinarias overtime *sg*; **~s punta...** rush hours.

horadar [ora'ðar] *vt* to drill, bore.

horario, a [o'rarjo, a] *a* hourly, hour *cp...* // *nm* timetable.

horca ['orka] *nf* gallows *sg*.

horcajadas [orka'xaðas]: **a ~** *ad* astride.

horda ['orða] *nf* horde.

horizontal [oriθon'tal] *a* horizontal... **horizonte** *nm* horizon.

horma ['orma] *nf* mould.

hormiga [or'mixa] *nf* ant; **~s** *nfpl* (*MED...* pins and needles.

hormigón [ormi'xon] *nm* concrete; **~...**

armado/pretensado reinforced/prestressed concrete.

hormigueo [ormi'xeo] *nm* (*comezón*) itch; (*fig*) uneasiness; (*amontonamiento*) swarming.

hormona [or'mona] *nf* hormone.

hornillo [or'niʎo] *nm* small furnace; (*cocina*) portable stove.

horno ['orno] *nm* (*CULIN*) oven; (*TEC*) furnace; **alto** ~ blast furnace.

horóscopo [o'roskopo] *nm* horoscope.

horquilla [or'kiʎa] *nf* hairpin; (*AGR*) pitchfork.

horrendo, a [o'rrendo, a] *a* horrendous, frightful.

horrible [o'rriβle] *a* horrible, dreadful.

horripilante [orripi'lante] *a* hair-raising; (*espeluznante*) creepy.

horripilar [orripi'lar] *vt*: ~ **a uno** to horrify sb; ~**se** *vr* to be horrified.

horror [o'rror] *nm* horror, dread; (*atrocidad*) atrocity; **¡qué** ~! (*fam*) oh, my God!; ~**izar** *vt* to horrify, frighten; ~**izarse** *vr* to be horrified; ~**oso, a** *a* horrifying, ghastly.

hortaliza [orta'liθa] *nf* vegetable.

hortelano, a [orte'lano, a] *nm/f* (market) gardener.

hosco, a ['osko, a] *a* dark; (*triste, ceñudo*) sullen, gloomy.

hospedar [ospe'ðar] *vt* to put up, lodge; ~**se** *vr* to stay, lodge.

hospital [ospi'tal] *nm* hospital.

hospitalario, a [ospita'larjo, a] *a* hospitable; **hospitalidad** *nf* hospitality.

hosquedad [oske'ðað] *nf* sullenness.

hostal [os'tal] *nm* small hotel.

hostelero, a [oste'lero, a] *nm/f* innkeeper, landlord/lady.

hostería [oste'ria] *nf* hostelry.

hostia ['ostja] *nf* host, consecrated wafer; (*fam: golpe*) whack, punch // *excl*: ¡~**s!** damn it!

hostigar [osti'xar] *vt* to whip; (*fig*) to harass, pester.

hostil [os'til] *a* hostile; ~**idad** *nf* hostility.

hotel [o'tel] *nm* hotel; ~**ero, a** *a* hotel *cpd* // *nm/f* hotelier.

hoy [oi] *ad* (*este día*) today; (*el ahora*) now(adays) // *nm* present time; ~ **(en) día** now(adays).

hoya ['oja] *nf* pit; (*sepulcro*) grave; (*GEO*) valley.

hoyo ['ojo] *nm* hole, pit; **hoyuelo** *nm* dimple.

hoz [oθ] *nf* sickle.

hube *etc vb ver* **haber**.

hucha ['utʃa] *nf* money box; (*fig*) nest egg.

hueco, a ['weko, a] *a* (*vacío*) hollow, empty; (*blanco: papel*) blank; (*resonante*) booming // *nm* hollow, cavity.

huelga *etc vb ver* **holgar** // ['welxa] *nf* strike; **declararse en** ~ to go on strike, come out on strike; ~ **de brazos caídos/de hambre** sit-down/hunger strike; ~ **patronal** lockout.

huelgo *etc vb ver* **holgar** // ['welxo] *nm* breath; (*espacio*) room, space.

huelguista [wel'xista] *nm/f* striker.

huelo *etc vb ver* **oler**.

huella ['weʎa] *nf* (*acto de pisar, pisada*) tread(ing); (*marca del paso*) footprint, footstep; (: *de animal, máquina*) track; ~ **digital** fingerprint; ~ **del sonido** sound track.

huérfano, a ['werfano, a] *a* orphan(ed) // *nm/f* orphan.

huerta ['werta] *nf* market garden; (*área de regadío*) irrigated region.

huerto ['werto] *nm* orchard.

hueso ['weso] *nm* (*ANAT*) bone; (*de fruta*) stone.

huésped, a ['wespeð, a] *nm/f* (*invitado*) guest; (*habitante*) resident; (*anfitrión*) host.

huesudo, a [we'suðo, a] *a* bony, big-boned.

huevo ['weβo] *nm* egg; ~ **en cáscara/escalfado/estrellado** *o* **frito/pasado por agua** boiled/poached/fried/soft-boiled egg; ~**s revueltos** scrambled eggs.

huida [u'iða] *nf* escape, flight.

huidizo, a [ui'ðiθo, a] *a* (*tímido*) shy; (*pasajero*) fleeting.

huir [u'ir] *vt* (*escapar*) to flee, escape (from); (*evadir*) to avoid; ~**se** *vr* (*escaparse*) to escape; (*el tiempo*) to fly.

hule ['ule] *nm* (*goma*) rubber; (*encerado*) oilskin.

humanidad [umani'ðað] *nf* (*los hombres*) man(kind); (*cualidad*) humanity.

humanizar [umani'θar] *vt* to humanize.

humano, a [u'mano, a] *a* (*gen*) human; (*humanitario*) humane // *nm* human; **ser** ~ human being.

humareda [uma'reða] *nf* cloud of smoke.

humear [ume'ar] *vi* to smoke.

humedad [ume'ðað] *nf* (*del clima*) humidity; (*de pared etc*) dampness; **a prueba de** ~ damp-proof; **humedecer** *vt* to moisten, wet; **humedecerse** *vr* to get wet.

húmedo, a ['umeðo, a] *a* (*mojado*) damp, wet; (*tiempo etc*) humid.

humildad [umil'dað] *nf* humility, humbleness; **humilde** *a* humble, modest; (*pequeño: voz*) small.

humillación [umiʎa'θjon] *nf* humiliation; **humillante** *a* humiliating; **humillar** *vt* to humiliate; **humillarse** *vr* to humble o.s., grovel.

humo ['umo] *nm* (*de fuego*) smoke; (*gas nocivo*) fumes *pl*; ~**s** *nmpl* (*fig*) conceit *sg*.

humor [u'mor] *nm* (*disposición*) mood, temper; (*lo que divierte*) humour; **de buen/mal** ~ in a good/bad mood; ~**ada** *nf* witticism; ~**ismo** *nm* humour; ~**ista** *nm/f* humorist; ~**ístico, a** *a* funny, humorous.

hundido, a [un'diðo, a] *a* (*de mejillas*) sunken; (*de ojos*) deep-set.

hundimiento [undi'mjento] *nm* (*gen*) sinking; (*colapso*) collapse.

hundir [un'dir] *vt* to sink; (*edificio, plan*) to

ruin, destroy; ~**se** vr to sink, collapse.
húngaro, a ['ungaro, a] a, nm/f
Hungarian.
Hungría [un'gria] nf Hungary.
huracán [ura'kan] nm hurricane.
huraño, a [u'raɲo, a] a shy; (antisocial)
unsociable.
hurgar [ur'xar] vt to poke, jab; (remover)
to stir (up).
hurgonear [urxone'ar] vt to poke.
hurón, ona [u'ron, ona] a unsociable //
nm (ZOOL) ferret; (persona tímida) shy
person; (persona arisca) unsociable person.
hurtadillas [urta'ðiʎas]: **a ~** ad
stealthily, on the sly.
hurtar [ur'tar] vt to steal; ~**se** vr to hide,
withdraw; **hurto** nm theft, stealing.
husmear [usme'ar] vt (oler) to sniff out,
scent; (fam) to pry into // vi to smell bad;
husmo nm strong smell.
huyo etc vb ver **huir.**

I

iba etc vb ver **ir.**
ibérico, a [i'ßeriko, a] a Iberian.
iberoamericano, a [ißeroameri'kano, a]
a, nm/f Spanish American.
íbice ['ißiθe] nm ibex.
ibicenco, a [ißi'θenko, a] a Ibizan.
Ibiza [i'ßiθa] nf Ibiza.
ibón [i'ßon] nm lake, tarn.
iceberg ['aisßerʃ] nm iceberg.
ícono ['ikono] nm ikon, icon.
iconoclasta [ikono'klasta] a iconoclastic
// nm/f iconoclast.
ictericia [ikte'riθja] nf jaundice.
ida ['iða] nf going, departure; ~ **y vuelta**
round trip, return.
idea [i'ðea] nf idea; **darse/hacerse una**
~ de... to get an idea of....
ideal [iðe'al] a, nm ideal; ~**ista** nm/f
idealist; ~**izar** vt to idealize.
idear [iðe'ar] vt to think up; (aparato) to
invent; (viaje) to plan.
ídem ['iðem] pron ditto.
idéntico, a [i'ðentiko, a] a identical.
identidad [iðenti'ðað] nf identity; **carné**
de ~ identity card.
identificación [iðentifika'θjon] nf
identification; **identificar** vt to identify;
identificarse vr: **identificarse con** to
identify o.s. with.
ideología [iðeolo'xia] nf ideology;
ideológico, a a ideological.
idioma [i'ðjoma] nm (gen) language; (giro)
idiom.
idiota [i'ðjota] a idiotic // nm/f idiot;
idiotez nf idiocy.
idólatra [i'ðolatra] nm/f idolater/tress;
idolatría nf idolatry.
ídolo ['iðolo] nm idol.
idóneo, a [i'ðoneo, a] a (apto) fit; (conveniente) suitable.
iglesia [i'ɣlesja] nf church.
ignición [iɣni'θjon] nf ignition.

ignominia [iɣno'minja] nf ignominy;
ignominioso, a a ignominious.
ignorado, a [iɣno'raðo, a] a unknown;
(dato) obscure.
ignorancia [iɣno'ranθja] nf ignorance;
ignorante a ignorant, uninformed // nm/f
ignoramus.
ignorar [iɣno'rar] vt not to know, be
ignorant of.
ignoto, a [iɣ'noto, a] a unknown.
igual [i'ɣwal] a (gen) equal; (similar) like,
similar; (mismo) (the) same; (constante)
constant; (temperatura) even // nm/f
equal; **al ~ que** prep, conj like, just like.
igualada [iɣwa'laða] nf equaliser.
igualar [iɣwa'lar] vt (gen) to equalize,
make equal; (allanar, nivelar) to level (off),
even (out); ~**se** vr (platos de balanza) to
balance out; (equivaler) to be equal.
igualdad [iɣwal'dað] nf equality;
(similaridad) sameness; (uniformidad)
evenness, uniformity.
igualmente [iɣwal'mente] ad equally;
(también) also, likewise // excl the same
to you.
ikurriña [iku'rriɲa] nf Basque flag.
ilegal [ile'xal] a illegal.
ilegítimo, a [ile'xitimo, a] a illegitimate.
ileso, a [i'leso, a] a unhurt.
ilícito, a [i'liθito] a illicit.
ilimitado, a [ilimi'taðo, a] a unlimited.
ilógico, a [i'loxiko, a] a illogical.
iluminación [ilumina'θjon] nf (gen)
illumination; (alumbrado) lighting.
iluminar [ilumi'nar] vt to illuminate, light
(up); (fig) to enlighten.
ilusión [ilu'sjon] nf illusion; (quimera)
delusion; (esperanza) hope; **ilusionado, a**
a excited.
ilusionista [ilusjo'nista] nm/f conjurer.
iluso, a [i'luso, a] a easily deceived.
ilusorio, a [ilu'sorjo, a] a (de ilusión)
illusory, deceptive; (esperanza) vain.
ilustración [ilustra'θjon] nf illustration;
(saber) learning, erudition; **la I~** the En-
lightenment; **ilustrado, a** a illustrated;
learned.
ilustrar [ilus'trar] vt (gen) to illustrate;
(instruir) to instruct; (explicar) to explain,
make clear; ~**se** vr to acquire
knowledge.
ilustre [i'lustre] a famous, illustrious.
imagen [i'maxen] nf (gen) image; (dibujo)
picture; (semejanza) likeness.
imaginación [imaxina'θjon] nf
imagination.
imaginar [imaxi'nar] vt (gen) to imagine;
(idear) to think up; (suponer) to suppose;
~**se** vr to imagine; ~**io, a** a imaginary;
imaginativo, a a imaginative.
imán [i'man] nm magnet.
imbécil [im'beθil] nm/f imbecile, idiot;
imbecilidad nf imbecility.
imbuir [imbu'ir] vi to imbue.
imitación [imita'θjon] nf imitation; **imitar**

vt to imitate; (*parodiar, remedar*) to mimic, ape.

impaciencia [impa'θjenθja] *nf* impatience; **impaciente** *a* impatient; (*nervioso*) anxious.

impacto [im'pakto] *nm* impact.

impar [im'par] *a* odd.

imparcial [impar'θjal] *a* impartial, fair; ~ **idad** *nf* impartiality, fairness.

impartir [impar'tir] *vt* to impart, give.

impasible [impa'siβle] *a* impassive.

impavidez [impaβi'ðeθ] *nf* fearlessness, intrepidness; **impávido, a** *a* fearless, intrepid.

impecable [impe'kaβle] *a* impeccable.

impedimento [impeði'mento] *nm* impediment, obstacle.

impedir [impe'ðir] *vt* (*obstruir*) to impede, obstruct; (*estorbar*) to prevent.

impeler [impe'ler] *vt* to drive, propel; (*fig*) to impel.

impenetrabilidad [impenetraβili'ðað] *nf* impenetrability; **impenetrable** *a* impenetrable; (*fig*) incomprehensible.

impenitente [impeni'tente] *a* unrepentant.

impensado, a [impen'saðo, a] *a* unexpected.

imperar [impe'rar] *vi* (*reinar*) to rule, reign; (*fig*) to prevail, reign; (*precio*) to be current.

imperativo, a [impera'tiβo, a] *a* (*persona*) imperious; (*urgente*, LING) imperative.

imperceptible [imperθep'tiβle] *a* imperceptible.

imperdible [imper'ðiβle] *nm* safety pin.

imperdonable [imperðo'naβle] *a* unforgivable, inexcusable.

imperfección [imperfek'θjon] *nf* imperfection.

imperfecto, a [imper'fekto, a] *a* imperfect.

imperial [impe'rjal] *a* imperial; ~ **ismo** *nm* imperialism.

impericia [impe'riθja] *nf* (*torpeza*) unskilfulness; (*inexperiencia*) inexperience.

imperio [im'perjo] *nm* empire; (*reino, dominación*) rule, authority; (*fig*) pride, haughtiness; ~ **so, a** *a* imperious; (*urgente*) urgent; (*imperativo*) imperative.

impermeable [imperme'aβle] *a* impermeable; (*a prueba de agua*) waterproof // *nm* raincoat.

impersonal [imperso'nal] *a* impersonal.

impertérrito, a [imper'territo, a] *a* undaunted.

impertinencia [imperti'nenθja] *nf* (*inoportunidad*) irrelevant; (*insolencia*) impertinence; **impertinente** *a* irrelevant; impertinent.

imperturbable [impertur'βaβle] *a* imperturbable.

ímpetu ['impetu] *nm* (*impulso*) impetus, impulse; (*impetuosidad*) impetuosity; (*violencia*) violence.

impetuosidad [impetwosi'ðað] *nf* impetuousness; (*violencia*) violence; **impetuoso, a** *a* impetuous; (*persona*) headstrong; (*río*) rushing, violent; (*acto*) hasty.

impío, a [im'pio, a] *a* impious, ungodly.

implacable [impla'kaβle] *a* implacable.

implicar [impli'kar] *vt* (*gen*) to implicate, involve; (*entrañar*) to imply.

implícito, a [im'pliθito, a] *a* (*tácito*) implicit; (*sobreentendido*) implied.

implorar [implo'rar] *vt* to beg, implore.

imponente [impo'nente] *a* (*impresionante*) impressive, imposing; (*solemne*) grand // *nm/f* investor.

imponer [impo'ner] *vt* (*gen*) to impose; (*informar*) to inform, instruct; (*exigir*) to exact, command; (*COM*) to invest; ~ **se** *vr* to assert o.s.; (*prevalecer*) to prevail.

impopular [impopu'lar] *a* unpopular.

importación [importa'θjon] *nf* (*acto*) importing; (*objetos*) imports *pl*.

importancia [impor'tanθja] *nf* importance; (*valor*) value, significance; (*extensión*) size, magnitude; **importante** *a* important; valuable, significant.

importar [impor'tar] *vt* (*del extranjero*) to import; (*valer*) to amount to, be worth // *vi* to be important, matter; **me importa el rábano** I don't give a damn; **no importa** it doesn't matter.

importe [im'porte] *nm* (*total*) amount; (*valor*) value.

importunar [importu'nar] *vt* to bother, pester.

importuno, a [impor'tuno, a] *a* (*inoportuno, molesto*) inopportune; (*indiscreto*) troublesome.

imposibilidad [imposiβili'ðað] *nf* impossibility; **imposibilitar** *vt* to make impossible, prevent; (*incapacitar*) to disable, cripple.

imposible [impo'siβle] *a* (*gen*) impossible; (*insoportable*) unbearable, intolerable.

imposición [imposi'θjon] *nf* imposition; (*COM*) tax; (*enganche*) deposit.

impostor, a [impos'tor, a] *nm/f* impostor; **impostura** *nf* fraud, imposture.

impotencia [impo'tenθja] *nf* impotence; **impotente** *a* impotent, powerless.

impracticable [imprakti'kaβle] *a* (*irrealizable*) impracticable; (*intransitable*) impassable.

imprecar [impre'kar] *vi* to curse.

impregnar [impreɣ'nar] *vt* to impregnate; ~ **se** *vr* to become impregnated.

imprenta [im'prenta] *nf* (*gen*) printing; (*aparato*) press; (*casa*) printer's; (*letra*) print.

imprescindible [impresθin'diβle] *a* essential, indispensable.

impresión [impre'sjon] *nf* (*gen*) impression; (*IMPRENTA*) printing; (*edición*) edition; (*FOTO*) print; (*marca*) imprint; ~ **digital** fingerprint.

impresionable [impresjo'naβle] *a*

(*sensible*) impressionable; (*excitable*) emotional.

impresionante [impresjo'nante] *a* impressive; (*tremendo*) tremendous; (*maravilloso*) great, marvellous.

impresionar [impresjo'nar] *vt* (*conmover*) to move; (*afectar*) to impress, strike; (*película fotográfica*) to expose; ~**se** *vr* to be impressed; (*conmoverse*) to be moved.

impreso, a [im'preso, a] *pp de* **imprimir** // *a* printed // *nm* printed paper/book etc.

impresor [impre'sor] *nm* printer.

imprevisto, a [impre'ßisto, a] *a* (*gen*) unforeseen; (*inesperado*) unexpected.

imprimir [impri'mir] *vt* to imprint, impress, stamp; (*textos*) to print.

improbabilidad [improßaßili'ðað] *nf* (*sin seguridad*) improbability; (*inverosimilitud*) unlikelihood; **improbable** *a* improbable; unlikely.

improcedente [improθe'ðente] *a* (*inconveniente*) unsuitable; (*inadecuado*) inappropriate.

improductivo, a [improðuk'tißo, a] *a* unproductive.

improperio [impro'perjo] *nm* insult, taunt.

impropiedad [impropje'ðað] *nf* impropriety (of language).

impropio, a [im'propjo, a] *a* improper.

impróvido, a [im'proßiðo, a] *a* improvident.

improvisación [improßisa'θjon] *nf* improvisation; **improvisado, a** *a* improvised; **improvisar** *vt* to improvise.

improviso, a [impro'ßiso, a], **improvisto, a** [impro'ßisto, a] *a* unexpected, unforeseen; **de** ~ unexpectedly, suddenly.

imprudencia [impru'ðenθja] *nf* imprudence; (*indiscreción*) indiscretion; (*descuido*) carelessness; **imprudente** *a* imprudent; indiscreet; (*irreflexivo*) unwise.

impúdico, a [im'puðiko, a] *a* shameless, immodest; (*lujurioso*) lecherous, lewd.

impudor [impu'ðor] *nm* shamelessness, immodesty; (*lujuria*) lechery, lewdness.

impuesto, a [im'pwesto, a] *a* imposed; (*informado*) informed // *nm* tax.

impugnar [impux'nar] *vt* to oppose, contest; (*refutar*) to refute, impugn.

impulsar [impul'sar] *vt* = **impeler.**

impulsión [impul'sjon] *nf* (*TEC*) propulsion; (*fig*) impulse.

impulso [im'pulso] *nm* impulse; (*fuerza, empuje*) thrust, drive; (*rapto*) urge, impulse.

impune [im'pune] *a* unpunished; **impunidad** *nf* impunity.

impureza [impu'reθa] *nf* impurity; (*fig*) lewdness; **impuro, a** *a* impure; lewd.

imputación [imputa'θjon] *nf* imputation.

imputar [impu'tar] *vt* (*atribuir*) to attribute to; (*cargar*) to impute to.

inacabable [inaka'ßaßle] *a* (*infinito*) endless; (*interminable*) interminable.

inaccesible [inakθe'sißle] *a* inaccessible.

inacción [inak'θjon] *nf* (*gen*) inaction; (*desocupación*) inactivity; (*ocio*) idleness.

inaceptable [inaθep'taßle] *a* inacceptable.

inactividad [inaktißi'ðað] *nf* inactivity; (*pereza*) laziness, idleness; (*com*) dullness; **inactivo, a** *a* inactive.

inadaptación [inaðapta'θjon] *nf* maladjustment.

inadecuado, a [inaðe'kwaðo, a] *a* (*insuficiente*) inadequate; (*inapto*) unsuitable.

inadmisible [inaðmi'sißle] *a* inadmissible.

inadvertencia [inaðßer'tenθja] *nf* oversight.

inadvertido, a [inaðßer'tiðo, a] *a* (*distraído*) inattentive; (*no visto*) unnoticed; (*descuidado*) careless.

inagotable [inaɣo'taßle] *a* inexhaustible.

inaguantable [inaɣwan'taßle] *a* unbearable.

inalterable [inalte'raßle] *a* immutable, unchangeable; (*permanente*) permanent.

inanición [inani'θjon] *nf* starvation.

inanimado, a [inani'maðo, a] *a* inanimate.

inapto, a [in'apto] *a* unsuited.

inaudito, a [inau'ðito, a] *a* unheard-of.

inauguración [inauɣura'θjon] *nf* inauguration; (*de exposición*) opening; **inaugurar** *vt* to inaugurate; to open.

I.N.B. *abr de* **Instituto Nacional de Bachillerato** ≈ secondary school.

inca ['inka] *nm/f* Inca; ~**ico, a** *a* Inca.

incalculable [inkalku'laßle] *a* incalculable.

incandescente [inkandes'θente] *a* incandescent.

incansable [inkan'saßle] *a* tireless, untiring.

incapacidad [inkapaθi'ðað] *nf* incapacity; (*incompetencia*) incompetence; ~ **física/mental** physical/mental incapacity or disability.

incapacitar [inkapaθi'tar] *vt* (*inhabilitar*) to incapacitate, render unfit; (*descalificar*) to disqualify.

incapaz [inka'paθ] *a* incapable.

incautación [inkauta'θjon] *nf* confiscation; **incautarse** *vr*: **incautarse de** to seize, confiscate.

incauto, a [in'kauto, a] *a* (*imprudente*) incautious, unwary.

incendiar [inθen'djar] *vt* to set on fire; (*fig*) to inflame; ~**se** *vr* to catch fire; ~**io, a** *a* incendiary; (*fig*) inflammatory.

incendio [in'θendjo] *nm* fire.

incentivo [inθen'tißo] *nm* incentive.

incertidumbre [inθerti'ðumßre] *nf* (*inseguridad*) uncertainty; (*duda*) doubt.

incesante [inθe'sante], **incesable** [inθe'saßle] *a* incessant.

incesto [in'θesto] *nm* incest.

incidencia [inθi'ðenθja] nf (accidente) incident; (MAT) incidence.
incidente [inθi'ðente] a incidental // nm incident.
incidir [inθi'ðir] vi (influir) to influence; (afectar) to affect; ~ **en un error** to fall into error.
incienso [in'θjenso] nm incense.
incierto, a [in'θjerto, a] a uncertain.
incineración [inθinera'θjon] nf incineration; (de cadáveres) cremation; **incinerar** vt to burn; to cremate.
incipiente [inθi'pjente] a incipient.
incisión [inθi'sjon] nf incision.
incisivo, a [inθi'siβo, a] a sharp, cutting; (fig) incisive.
incitación [inθita'θjon] nf incitement.
incitante [inθi'tante] a (estimulante) exciting; (provocativo) provocative; **incitar** vt to incite, rouse.
incivil [inθi'βil] a rude, uncivil.
inclemencia [inkle'menθja] nf (severidad) harshness, severity; (del tiempo) inclemency; **inclemente** a harsh, severe; inclement.
inclinación [inklina'θjon] nf (gen) inclination; (de tierras) slope, incline; (de cabeza) nod, bow; (fig) leaning, bent.
inclinar [inkli'nar] vt to incline; (cabeza) to nod, bow; (tierras) to slope; (persuadir) to persuade; ~**se** vr to bow; (encorvarse) to stoop; ~**se a** to take after, resemble; ~**se ante** to bow down to; **me inclino a pensar que** I'm inclined to think that.
ínclito, a ['inklito, a] a illustrious, renowned.
incluir [inklu'ir] vt to include; (incorporar) to incorporate; (meter) to enclose.
inclusive [inklu'siβe] ad inclusive // prep including.
incluso, a [in'kluso, a] a included // ad inclusively; (hasta) even.
incógnito, a [in'koɣnito, a] a unknown // nm: **de** ~ incognito // nf unknown factor.
incoherente [inkoe'rente] a incoherent.
incoloro, a [inko'loro, a] a colourless.
incólume [in'kolume] a (gen) safe; (indemne) unhurt, unharmed.
incomodar [inkomo'ðar] vt to inconvenience; (molestar) to bother, trouble; (fastidiar) to annoy; ~**se** vr to put o.s. out; (fastidiarse) to get annoyed.
incomodidad [inkomoði'ðað] nf inconvenience; (fastidio, enojo) annoyance; (de vivienda) discomfort.
incómodo, a [in'komoðo, a] a (inconfortable) uncomfortable; (molesto) annoying; (inconveniente) inconvenient.
incomparable [inkompa'raβle] a incomparable.
incompatible [inkompa'tiβle] a incompatible.
incompetencia [inkompe'tenθja] nf incompetence; **incompetente** a incompetent.
incompleto, a [inkom'pleto, a] a incomplete, unfinished.

incomprensible [inkompren'siβle] a incomprehensible.
incomunicado, a [inkomuni'kaðo, a] a (aislado) cut off, isolated; (confinado) in solitary confinement.
inconcebible [inkonθe'βiβle] a inconceivable.
inconcluso, a [inkon'kluso, a] a (inacabado) unfinished; (incompleto) incomplete.
incondicional [inkondiθjo'nal] a unconditional; (apoyo) wholehearted; (partidario) staunch.
inconexo, a [inko'nekso, a] a (gen) unconnected; (desunido) disconnected.
inconfundible [inkonfun'diβle] a unmistakable.
incongruente [inkon'grwente] a incongruous.
inconmensurable [inkonmensu'raβle] a immeasurable, vast.
inconsciencia [inkons'θjenθja] nf unconsciousness; (fig) thoughtlessness; **inconsciente** a unconscious; thoughtless.
inconsecuencia [inkonse'kwenθja] nf inconsistency; **inconsecuente** a inconsistent.
inconsiderado, a [inkonsiðe'raðo, a] a inconsiderate.
inconsistente [inkonsis'tente] a weak; (tela) flimsy.
inconstancia [inkon'stanθja] nf (inconsecuencia, veleidad) inconstancy; (inestabilidad) unsteadiness; **inconstante** a inconstant.
incontestable [inkontes'taβle] a unanswerable; (innegable) undeniable.
incontinencia [inkonti'nenθja] nf incontinence; **incontinente** a incontinent.
inconveniencia [inkonβe'njenθja] nf unsuitability, inappropriateness; (incorrección) impoliteness; **inconveniente** a unsuitable; impolite // nm obstacle; (desventaja) disadvantage.
incorporación [inkorpora'θjon] nf incorporation; (del cuerpo) sitting/standing up; **incorporar** vt to incorporate; **incorporarse** vr to sit/stand up.
incorrección [inkorrek'θjon] nf (gen) incorrectness, inaccuracy; (descortesía) bad-mannered behaviour; **incorrecto, a** a (gen) incorrect, wrong; (facciones) irregular, odd; (comportamiento) bad-mannered.
incorregible [inkorre'xiβle] a incorrigible.
incorruptible [inkorrup'tiβle] a incorruptible; ~ **a la intemperie** rustproof.
incredulidad [inkreðuli'ðað] nf incredulity; (escepticismo) scepticism; **incrédulo, a** a incredulous, unbelieving; sceptical.
increíble [inkre'iβle] a incredible.
incremento [inkre'mento] nm increment; (aumento) rise, increase.
increpar [inkre'par] vt to reprimand.

incruento, a [in'krwento, a] a bloodless.
incrustar [inkrus'tar] vt to incrust;
(piedras: en joya) to inlay.
incubar [inku'ßar] vt to incubate; (fig) to
hatch.
inculcar [inkul'kar] vt to inculcate.
inculpar [inkul'par] vt (acusar) to accuse;
(achacar, atribuir) to charge, blame.
inculto, a [in'kulto, a] a (persona)
uneducated, uncultured; (terreno)
uncultivated // nm/f ignoramus.
incumplimiento [inkumpli'mjento] nm
non-fulfilment; ~ de contrato breach of
contract.
incurrir [inku'rrir] vi: ~ en to incur;
(crimen) to commit; ~ en un error to
fall into error.
indagación [indaɣa'θjon] nf investigation;
(búsqueda) search; (JUR) inquest; indagar
vt to investigate; to search; (averiguar) to
ascertain.
indecente [inde'θente] a indecent,
improper; (lascivo) obscene.
indecible [inde'θißle] a unspeakable;
(indescriptible) indescribable.
indeciso, a [inde'θiso, a] a (por decidir)
undecided; (vacilante) hesitant; (resultado)
indecisive.
indefectible [indefek'tißle] a unfailing.
indefenso, a [inde'fenso, a] a defenceless.
indefinido, a [indefi'niðo, a] a indefinite;
(vago) vague, undefined.
indeleble [inde'leßle] a indelible.
indemnizar [indemni'θar] vt to
indemnify; (compensar) to compensate.
independencia [indepen'denθja] nf
independence.
independiente [indepen'djente] a (libre)
independent; (autónomo) self-sufficient.
indeterminado, a [indetermi'naðo, a] a
indefinite; (desconocido) indeterminate.
India ['indja] nf: la ~ India.
indicación [indika'θjon] nf indication;
(señal) sign; (sugerencia) suggestion, hint;
(de termómetro) reading.
indicador [indika'ðor] nm indicator; (TEC)
gauge, meter.
indicar [indi'kar] vt (mostrar) to indicate,
show; (termómetro etc) to read, register;
(señalar) to point to.
índice ['indiθe] nm index; (catálogo)
catalogue; (ANAT) index finger, forefinger;
(de cuadrante) pointer, needle; (de reloj)
hand.
indicio [in'diθjo] nm indication, sign;
(huella) trace; (pesquisa) clue.
indiferencia [indife'renθja] nf
indifference; (apatía) apathy; indiferente
a indifferent.
indígena [in'dixena] a indigenous, native;
(aborigen) aboriginal // nm/f native;
aborigine.
indigencia [indi'xenθja] nf poverty, need.
indigestión [indixes'tjon] nf indigestion.
indigesto, a [indi'xesto, a] a undigested;
(indigestible) indigestible; (fig) turgid.

indignación [indixna'θjon] nf indignation;
indignado, a indignant.
indignar [indix'nar] vt to anger, make
indignant; ~se vr: ~se de o por to get
indignant about.
indignidad [indixni'ðað] nf (insulto)
indignity, insult; (ruindad) vile act;
indigno, a a (despreciable) low,
contemptible; (inmerecido) unworthy.
indio, a ['indjo, a] a, nm/f Indian.
indirecta [indi'rekta] nf insinuation,
innuendo; (sugerencia) hint.
indirecto, a [indi'rekto, a] a indirect.
indiscreción [indiskre'θjon] nf
(imprudencia) indiscretion; (irreflexión)
tactlessness; (acto) gaffe, tactless act.
indiscreto, a [indis'kreto, a] a indiscreet.
indiscutible [indisku'tißle] a indisputable,
unquestionable.
indispensable [indispen'saßle] a
indispensable.
indisponer [indispo'ner] vt to spoil, upset;
(salud) to make ill; ~se vr to fall ill; ~se
con uno to fall out with sb.
indisposición [indisposi'θjon] nf
indisposition.
indistinto, a [indis'tinto, a] a indistinct;
(vago) vague.
individual [indiβi'ðwal] a individual;
(habitación) single // nm (DEPORTE) singles
sg.
individuo, a [indi'βiðwo, a] a individual //
nm individual; (miembro, socio) member,
fellow.
indiviso, a [indi'βiso, a] a undivided.
índole ['indole] nf (naturaleza) nature;
(clase) sort, kind.
indolencia [indo'lenθja] nf indolence,
laziness.
indomable [indo'maßle] a indomitable;
(animal) untameable; (fig) unmanageable.
indómito, a [in'domito, a] a indomitable.
inducir [indu'θir] vt to induce; (inferir) to
infer; (persuadir) to persuade.
indudable [indu'ðaßle] a undoubted;
(incuestionable) unquestionable.
indulgencia [indul'xenθja] nf indulgence.
indultar [indul'tar] vt (perdonar) to
pardon, reprieve; (librar de pago) to
exempt; indulto nm pardon; exemption.
industria [in'dustrja] nf industry;
(habilidad) skill; industrial a industrial //
nm industrialist.
industrioso, a [indus'trjoso, a] a
industrious.
inédito, a [in'eðito, a] a (libro)
unpublished; (nuevo) unheard-of.
inefable [ine'faßle] a ineffable,
indescribable.
ineficaz [inefi'kaθ] a (inútil) ineffective;
(ineficiente) inefficient.
ineludible [inelu'ðißle] a inescapable,
unavoidable.
ineptitud [inepti'tuð] nf ineptitude,
incompetence; **inepto, a** a inept,
incompetent.

inequívoco, a [ine'kiθoko, a] *a* unequivocal; (*inconfundible*) unmistakable.

inercia [in'erθja] *nf* inertia; (*fig*) passivity.

inerme [in'erme] *a* (*sin armas*) unarmed; (*indefenso*) defenceless.

inerte [in'erte] *a* inert; (*fig*) passive.

inesperado, a [inespe'raðo, a] *a* unexpected, unforeseen.

inestable [ines'taβle] *a* unstable.

inevitable [ineβi'taβle] *a* inevitable.

inexactitud [ineksakti'tuð] *nf* inaccuracy; **inexacto, a** *a* inaccurate; (*falso*) untrue.

infamar [infa'mar] *vt* to dishonour; (*calumniar*) to defame, slander.

infame [in'fame] *a* infamous // *nm/f* vile person; **infamia** *nf* infamy; (*deshonra*) disgrace.

infancia [in'fanθja] *nf* infancy, childhood.

infante [in'fante] *nm* (*niño*) infant, child; (*hijo del rey*) prince.

infantería [infante'ria] *nf* infantry.

infantil [infan'til] *a* (*pueril, aniñado*) infantile; (*cándido*) childlike; (*literatura*) children's.

infarto [in'farto] *nm* heart attack.

infatigable [infati'xaβle] *a* tireless, untiring.

infausto, a [in'fausto, a] *a* unlucky.

infección [infek'θjon] *nf* infection; **infeccioso, a** *a* infectious.

infectar [infek'tar] *vt* to infect; ~**se** *vr* to become infected.

infelicidad [infeliθi'ðað] *nf* unhappiness.

infeliz [infe'liθ] *a* unhappy, wretched // *nm/f* wretch.

inferior [infe'rjor] *a* inferior; (*situación*) lower // *nm/f* inferior, subordinate.

inferir [infe'rir] *vt* (*deducir*) to infer, deduce; (*causar*) to cause.

infestar [infes'tar] *vt* (*infectar*) to infect; (*apestar*) to infest; (*fig*) to harass.

inficionar [infiθjo'nar] *vt* to infect; (*fig*) to corrupt.

infidelidad [infiðeli'ðað] *nf* (*gen*) infidelity, unfaithfulness; (*REL*) lack of faith.

infiel [in'fjel] *a* unfaithful, disloyal; (*falso*) inaccurate // *nm/f* infidel, unbeliever.

infierno [in'fjerno] *nm* hell.

ínfimo, a ['infimo, a] *a* vile, mean.

infinidad [infini'ðað] *nf* infinity; (*abundancia*) great quantity.

infinito, a [infi'nito, a] *a, nm* infinite.

inflación [infla'θjon] *nf* (*hinchazón*) swelling; (*monetaria*) inflation; (*fig*) conceit; **inflacionario, a** *a* inflationary.

inflamar [infla'mar] *vt* to set on fire; (*MED*) to inflame; ~**se** *vr* to catch fire; (*fig*) to become inflamed.

inflar [in'flar] *vt* (*hinchar*) to inflate, blow up; (*fig*) to exaggerate; ~**se** *vr* to swell (up); (*fig*) to get conceited.

inflexible [inflek'siβle] *a* inflexible; (*irrompible*) unbending; (*fig*) strict.

infligir [infli'xir] *vt* to inflict.

influencia [influ'enθja] *nf* influence; **influenciar** *vt* to influence.

influir [influ'ir] *vt* to influence.

influjo [in'fluxo] *nm* influence.

influyente [influ'jente] *a* influential.

información [informa'θjon] *nf* information; (*noticias*) news *sg*; (*JUR*) inquiry.

informal [infor'mal] *a* (*gen*) irregular, incorrect; (*persona*) unreliable; (*poco serio*) frivolous; (*trabajo*) disorganized; (*comportamiento*) unconventional.

informalidad [informali'ðað] *nf* (*impuntualidad*) unpunctuality; (*incorrección*) bad manners *pl*; (*ligereza*) frivolity.

informante [infor'mante] *nm/f* informant.

informar [infor'mar] *vt* (*gen*) to inform; (*revelar*) to reveal, make known // *vi* (*JUR*) to plead; (*denunciar*) to inform; (*dar cuenta de*) to report on; ~**se** *vr* to find out; ~**se de** to inquire into.

informe [in'forme] *a* shapeless // *nm* report.

infortunio [infor'tunjo] *nm* misfortune.

infracción [infrak'θjon] *nf* infraction, infringement; (*transgresión*) transgression.

infranqueable [infranke'aβle] *a* impassable; (*impracticable*) insurmountable.

infringir [infrin'xir] *vt* to infringe, contravene.

infructuoso, a [infruk'twoso, a] *a* fruitless, unsuccessful.

infundado, a [infun'daðo, a] *a* groundless, unfounded.

infundir [infun'dir] *vt* to infuse, instil.

ingeniar [inxe'njar] *vt* to think up, devise; ~**se** *vr*: ~**se para** to manage to.

ingeniería [inxenje'ria] *nf* engineering; **ingeniero, a** *nm/f* engineer; **ingeniero agrónomo/de sonido** agronomist/sound engineer.

ingenio [in'xenjo] *nm* (*talento*) talent; (*agudeza*) wit; (*habilidad*) ingenuity, inventiveness; (*TEC*): ~ **azucarero** sugar refinery.

ingenioso, a [inxe'njoso, a] *a* ingenious, clever; (*divertido*) witty.

ingénito, a [in'xenito, a] *a* innate.

ingenuidad [inxenwi'ðað] *nf* ingenuousness; (*candor*) candour; **ingenuo, a** *a* ingenuous.

ingerencia [inxe'renθja] *nf* = **injerencia.**

ingerir [inxe'rir] *vt* to ingest; (*tragar*) to swallow; (*consumir*) to consume.

Inglaterra [ingla'terra] *nf* England.

ingle ['ingle] *nf* groin.

inglés, esa [in'gles, esa] *a* English // *nm/f* Englishman/woman // *nm* (*lengua*) English.

ingratitud [ingrati'tuð] *nf* ingratitude; **ingrato, a** *a* (*gen*) ungrateful; (*desagradable*) unpleasant.

ingrediente [ingre'ðjente] *nm* ingredient.

ingresar [ingre'sar] vt (dinero) to deposit // vi to come in; ~ **en un club** to join a club; ~ **en el hospital** to go into hospital.

ingreso [in'greso] nm (entrada) entry; (: en hospital etc) admission; (de dinero) income, takings; **takings** pl.

inhábil [in'aβil] a unskilful, clumsy; **día** ~ non-working day.

inhabitable [inaβi'taβle] a uninhabitable.

inherente [ine'rente] a inherent.

inhibir [ini'βir] vt to inhibit; (REL) to restrain.

inhospitalario, a [inospita'larjo, a] a inhospitable.

inhumano, a [inu'mano, a] a inhuman.

I. N. I. ['ini] nm abr de **Instituto Nacional de Industria** = National Enterprise Board.

inicial [ini'θjal] a, nf initial.

iniciar [ini'θjar] vt (persona) to initiate; (estudios) to begin, commence; (conversación) to start up.

iniciativa [iniθja'tiβa] nf initiative; **la** ~ **privada** private enterprise.

inicuo, a [in'ikwo, a] a iniquitous.

ininterrumpido, a [ininterrum'piðo, a] a uninterrupted.

injerencia [inxe'renθja] nf interference.

injertar [inxer'tar] vt to graft; (inyectar) to inject; **injerto** nm graft.

injuria [in'xurja] nf (agravio, ofensa) offence; (insulto) insult; (daño) harm; **injuriar** vt to insult; to harm; **injurioso, a** a offensive; insulting; harmful.

injusticia [inxus'tiθja] nf injustice.

injusto, a [in'xusto, a] a unjust, unfair.

inmadurez [inmaðu'reθ] nf immaturity.

inmarcesible [inmarθe'siβle], **inmarchitable** [inmartʃi'taβle] a imperishable.

inmediaciones [inmeðja'θjones] nfpl neighbourhood sg, environs.

inmediato, a [inme'ðjato, a] a immediate; (contiguo) adjoining; (rápido) prompt; (próximo) close, next; **de** ~ immediately.

inmejorable [inmexo'raβle] a unsurpassable; (precio) unbeatable.

inmenso, a [in'menso, a] a immense, huge.

inmerecido, a [inmere'θiðo, a] a undeserved.

inmigración [inmixra'θjon] nf immigration.

inmiscuirse [inmisku'irse] vr to interfere, meddle.

inmobiliaria [inmoβi'ljarjo, a] a real-estate cpd // nf estate agency.

inmoderado, a [inmoðe'raðo, a] a immoderate, excessive.

inmolar [inmo'lar] vt to immolate, sacrifice.

inmoral [inmo'ral] a immoral.

inmortal [inmor'tal] a immortal; ~**izar** vt to immortalize.

inmotivado, a [inmoti'βaðo, a] a motiveless.

inmóvil [in'moβil] a immobile;

(inamovible) immovable; (invariable) unchanging; (parado) still, stationary.

inmueble [in'mweβle] nm property.

inmundicia [inmun'diθja] nf filth; **inmundo, a** a filthy.

inmunidad [inmuni'ðað] nf immunity.

inmutar [inmu'tar] vt to alter; ~**se** vr to turn pale.

innato, a [in'nato, a] a innate.

innecesario, a [inneθe'sarjo, a] a unnecessary.

innoble [in'noβle] a ignoble.

innocuo, a [in'nokwo, a] a innocuous.

innovación [innoβa'θjon] nf innovation; **innovar** vt to introduce.

inocencia [ino'θenθja] nf innocence.

inocentada [inoθen'taða] nf practical joke.

inocente [ino'θente] a (ingenuo) naive, simple; (inculpable) innocent // nm/f simpleton.

inodoro [ino'ðoro] nm toilet, lavatory.

inofensivo, a [inofen'siβo, a] a inoffensive.

inolvidable [inolβi'ðaβle] a unforgettable.

inoperante [inope'rante] a unworkable.

inopinado, a [inopi'naðo, a] a unexpected.

inoportuno, a [inopor'tuno, a] a untimely; (molesto) inconvenient.

inoxidable [inoksi'ðaβle] a: **acero** ~ stainless steel.

inquebrantable [inkeβran'taβle] a unbreakable.

inquietar [inkje'tar] vt to worry, trouble, disturb; ~**se** vr to worry, get upset; **inquieto, a** a anxious, worried; **inquietud** nf anxiety, worry.

inquilino, a [inki'lino, a] nm/f tenant.

inquirir [inki'rir] vt to enquire into, investigate.

insaciable [insa'θjaβle] a insatiable.

insalubre [insa'luβre] a unhealthy.

inscribir [inskri'βir] vt to inscribe; (lista) to list; (censo) to register; ~**se** vr to register; (ESCOL etc) to enrol.

inscripción [inskrip'θjon] nf inscription; (ESCOL etc) enrolment; (censo) registration.

insecto [in'sekto] nm insect.

inseguridad [insexuri'ðað] nf insecurity.

inseguro, a [inse'xuro, a] a insecure; (inconstante) unsteady; (incierto) uncertain.

insensato, a [insen'sato, a] a foolish, stupid.

insensibilidad [insensiβili'ðað] nf (gen) insensitivity; (dureza de corazón) callousness.

insensible [insen'siβle] a (gen) insensitive; (duro) callous; (movimiento) imperceptible; (sin sentido) numb.

insertar [inser'tar] vt to insert.

inservible [inser'βiβle] a useless.

insidioso, a [insi'ðjoso, a] a insidious.

insignia [in'sixnja] nf (señal distintivo)

badge; (*estandarte*) flag; (*condecoración*) decoration.

insignificante [insiɣnifi'kante] *a* insignificant.

insinuar [insi'nwar] *vt* to insinuate, imply; ~**se** *vr:* ~**se con uno** to ingratiate o.s. with sb.

insípido, a [in'sipiðo, a] *a* insipid.

insistencia [insis'tenθja] *nf* (*obstinación*) insistence; (*porfía*) persistence.

insistir [insis'tir] *vi* to insist; ~ **en algo** to stress sth.

insolación [insola'θjon] *nf* (MED) sunstroke.

insolencia [inso'lenθja] *nf* insolence; **insolente** *a* insolent.

insólito, a [in'solito, a] *a* unusual.

insoluble [inso'lußle] *a* insoluble.

insolvencia [insol'ßenθja] *nf* insolvency.

insomnio [in'somnjo] *nm* insomnia.

insondable [inson'daßle] *a* bottomless.

insoportable [insopor'taßle] *a* unbearable.

inspección [inspek'θjon] *nf* inspection, check; **inspeccionar** *vt* (*examinar*) to inspect, examine; (*controlar*) to check.

inspector, a [inspek'tor, a] *nm/f* inspector.

inspiración [inspira'θjon] *nf* inspiration; **inspirar** *vt* to inspire; (MED) to inhale; **inspirarse** *vr:* **inspirarse en** to be inspired by.

instalar [insta'lar] *vt* (*establecer*) to instal; (*erguir*) to set up, erect; ~**se** *vr* to establish o.s.

instancia [ins'tanθja] *nf* (JUR) petition; (*ruego*) request; **en última** ~ in the last resort.

instantáneo, a [instan'taneo, a] *a* instant, instantaneous // *nf* snap(shot).

instante [ins'tante] *nm* instant, moment.

instar [ins'tar] *vt* to press, urge // *vi* to be pressing *or* urgent.

instigar [insti'ɣar] *vt* to instigate.

instinto [ins'tinto] *nm* instinct; **por** ~ instinctively.

institución [institu'θjon] *nf* institution, establishment.

instituir [institu'ir] *vt* to establish; (*fundar*) to found; **instituto** *nm* (*gen*) institute; (*escuela*) high school.

instrucción [instruk'θjon] *nf* instruction.

instructivo, a [instruk'tißo, a] *a* instructive.

instruir [instru'ir] *vt* (*gen*) to instruct; (*enseñar*) to teach, educate; (MIL, DEPORTE) to train.

instrumento [instru'mento] *nm* (*gen*) instrument; (*herramienta*) tool, implement.

insubordinarse [insußorði'narse] *vr* to rebel.

insuficiencia [insufi'θjenθja] *nf* (*carencia*) lack; (*inadecuación*) inadequacy; **insuficiente** *a* (*gen*) insufficient; (*incompetente*) incompetent; (*nota*) inadequate.

insufrible [insu'frißle] *a* insufferable.

insular [insu'lar] *a* insular.

insulsez [insul'seθ] *nf* (*insipidez*) insipidity; (*fig*) dullness.

insultar [insul'tar] *vt* to insult; **insulto** *nm* insult.

insuperable [insupe'raßle] *a* (*excelente*) unsurpassable; (*arduo*) insurmountable.

insurgente [insur'xente] *a, nm/f* insurgent.

insurrección [insurrek'θjon] *nf* insurrection, rebellion.

intacto, a [in'takto, a] *a* intact.

intachable [inta'tʃaßle] *a* irreproachable.

integral [inte'ɣral] *a:* **pan** ~ wholemeal bread.

integrar [inte'ɣrar] *vt* to make up, compose; (COM) to repay; (MAT) to integrate.

integridad [inteɣri'ðað] *nf* wholeness; (*carácter*) integrity; **íntegro, a** *a* whole, entire; (*honrado*) honest.

intelectual [intelek'twal] *a, nm/f* intellectual.

inteligencia [inteli'xenθja] *nf* intelligence; (*ingenio*) ability; **inteligente** *a* intelligent.

intemperancia [intempe'ranθja] *nf* excess, intemperance.

intemperie [intem'perje] *nf* bad weather; **a la** ~ outdoors, in the open air.

intempestivo, a [intempes'tißo, a] *a* untimely.

intención [inten'θjon] *nf* (*gen*) intention; (*propósito*) purpose; **con segundas intenciones** maliciously; **de primera** ~ provisionally; **con** ~ deliberately.

intencionado, a [intenθjo'naðo, a] *a* deliberate; **bien/mal** ~ well-meaning/ill-disposed.

intendencia [inten'denθja] *nf* management, administration.

intenso, a [in'tenso, a] *a* intense; (*impresión*) vivid; (*sentimiento*) profound, deep.

intentar [inten'tar] *vt* (*tratar*) to try, attempt; **intento** *nm* (*intención*) intention, purpose; (*tentativa*) attempt.

intercalar [interka'lar] *vt* to insert.

intercambio [inter'kambjo] *nm* exchange, swap.

interceder [interθe'ðer] *vi* to intercede.

intercesión [interθe'sjon] *nf* intercession.

interés [inte'res] *nm* (*gen*) interest; (*parte*) share, part; (*pey*) self-interest; **intereses creados** vested interests.

interesado, a [intere'saðo, a] *a* interested; (*prejuiciado*) prejudiced; (*pey*) mercenary, self-seeking.

interesar [intere'sar] *vt, vi* to interest, be of interest to; ~**se** *vr:* ~**se en** *o* **por** to take an interest in.

interferir [interfe'rir] *vt* to interfere with; (TELEC) to jam // *vi* to interfere.

interior [inte'rjor] *a* inner, inside; (COM) domestic, internal // *nm* interior, inside; (*fig*) soul, mind; **Ministerio del I**~ Home Office.

interjección [interxek'θjon] *nf* interjection.

interlocutor, a [interloku'tor] *nm/f* speaker.

intermediario, a [interme'ðjarjo, a] *nm/f* intermediary // *nm* middleman.

intermedio, a [inter'meðjo, a] *a* intermediate // *nm* interval.

interminable [intermi'naβle] *a* endless.

intermitente [intermi'tente] *a* intermittent // *nm* indicator.

internacional [internaθjo'nal] *a* international.

internar [inter'nar] *vt* to intern; *(loco)* to commit; ~**se** *vr (en un hospital)* to go into hospital; *(penetrar)* to penetrate.

interno, a [in'terno, a] *a* internal, interior; *(POL etc)* domestic // *nm/f (alumno)* boarder.

interpelar [interpe'lar] *vt (rogar)* to implore; *(hablar)* to speak to.

interponer [interpo'ner] *vt* to interpose, put in; ~**se** *vr* to intervene.

interposición [interposi'θjon] *nf* insertion.

interpretación [interpreta'θjon] *nf* interpretation; **interpretar** *vt* to interpret; **intérprete** *nm/f* interpreter; *(traductor)* translator; *(músico, TEATRO)* performer, artist(e).

interrogación [interroxa'θjon] *nf* interrogation; *(LING)* question mark; **interrogar** *vt* to interrogate, question.

interrumpir [interrum'pir] *vt* to interrupt; *(ELEC)* to switch off, cut off.

interrupción [interrup'θjon] *nf* interruption.

interruptor [interrup'tor] *nm (ELEC)* switch.

intersección [intersek'θjon] *nf* intersection.

interurbano, a [interur'βano, a] *a*: **llamada** ~**a** trunk call.

intervalo [inter'βalo] *nm* interval; *(descanso)* break; **a** ~**s** at intervals, every now and then.

intervenir [interβe'nir] *vt (controlar)* to control, supervise; *(MED)* to operate on // *vi (participar)* to take part, participate; *(mediar)* to intervene.

interventor, a [interβen'tor, a] *nm/f* inspector; *(COM)* auditor.

interviú [inter'βju] *nf* interview.

intestino, a [intes'tino, a] *a* internal; *(doméstico)* domestic // *nm* intestine.

intimar [inti'mar] *vt* to intimate, announce // *vi* to become friendly.

intimidad [intimi'ðað] *nf* intimacy; *(confianza)* confidence; *(familiaridad)* familiarity; *(vida privada)* private life; *(soledad)* privacy.

íntimo, a ['intimo, a] *a* intimate.

intolerable [intole'raβle] *a* intolerable, unbearable.

intransitable [intransi'taβle] *a* impassable.

intrepidez [intrepi'ðeθ] *nf* courage, bravery; **intrépido, a** *a* intrepid.

intriga [in'trixa] *nf* intrigue; *(plan)* plot; **intrigar** *vt, vi* to intrigue.

intrincado, a [intrin'kaðo, a] *a* intricate.

intrínseco, a [in'trinseko, a] *a* intrinsic.

introducción [introðuk'θjon] *nf* introduction.

introducir [introðu'θir] *vt (gen)* to introduce; *(hacer penetrar)* to insert.

intruso, a [in'truso, a] *a* intrusive // *nm/f* intruder.

intuición [intwi'θjon] *nf* intuition.

inundación [inunda'θjon] *nf* flood(ing); **inundar** *vt* to flood; *(fig)* to swamp, inundate.

inusitado, a [inusi'taðo, a] *a* unusual.

inútil [in'util] *a* useless; *(esfuerzo)* vain, fruitless; **inutilidad** *nf* uselessness.

inutilizar [inutili'θar] *vt* to make useless, render useless; ~**se** *vr* to become useless.

invadir [inβa'ðir] *vt* to invade.

inválido, a [in'βaliðo, a] *a* invalid // *nm/f* invalid.

invariable [inβa'rjaβle] *a* invariable.

invasión [inβa'sjon] *nf* invasion.

invasor, a [inβa'sor, a] *a* invading // *nm/f* invader.

invención [inβen'θjon] *nf* invention.

inventar [inβen'tar] *vt* to invent.

inventario [inβen'tarjo] *nm* inventory.

inventiva [inβen'tiβa] *nf* inventiveness.

inventor, a [inβen'tor, a] *nm/f* inventor.

inverosímil [inβero'simil] *a* implausible; *(improbable)* unlikely, improbable.

inversión [inβer'sjon] *nf (COM)* investment; *(AUTO)* reversing; **inversionista** *nm/f* investor.

inverso, a [in'βerso, a] *a* inverse, opposite; **en el orden** ~ in reverse order; **a la** ~**a** inversely, the other way round.

invertir [inβer'tir] *vt (COM)* to invest; *(volcar)* to turn upside down; *(tiempo etc)* to spend; *(AUTO)* to reverse.

investigación [inβestiʝa'θjon] *nf* investigation; *(estudio)* research; **investigar** *vt* to investigate; *(estudiar)* to do research into.

inveterado, a [inβete'raðo, a] *a* inveterate, confirmed.

invicto, a [in'βikto, a] *a* unconquered.

invierno [in'βjerno] *nm* winter.

invitar [inβi'tar] *vt* to invite; *(incitar)* to entice; *(pagar)* to buy, pay for.

invocar [inβo'kar] *vt* to invoke, call on.

inyección [injek'θjon] *nf* injection.

inyectar [injek'tar] *vt* to inject.

ir [ir] *vi (gen)* to go; *(viajar)* to travel; *(ropa)* to suit; ~ **caminando** to walk; ~ **en coche/bicicleta/caballo/a pie** to drive/cycle/ride/walk; **¡voy!** I'm coming!; ~ **de viaje** to travel, go away; **voy para viejo** I'm getting on (in years); ~ **por/a por algo** to go for/go and get sth; **¡qué va!** *(no diga)* you don't say!; (: *¡no!*) no way!, rubbish!; **¡vamos!** come on!; **vaya susto que me has dado** what a fright

you gave me; ~**se** *vr* to go away, leave; (*mano etc*) to slip; **¡vete!** go away!
ira ['ira] *nf* anger, rage.
iracundo, a [ira'kundo, a] *a* irascible; (*colérico*) irate.
Irán [i'ran] *nm* Iran; **iranés, esa, iraní** *a, nm/f* Iranian.
iris ['iris] *nm* (*arco* ~) rainbow; (ANAT) iris.
Irlanda [ir'landa] *nf* Ireland; **irlandés, esa** *a* Irish // *nm/f* Irishman/woman.
ironía [iro'nia] *nf* irony; **irónico, a** *a* ironic(al).
irreal [irre'al] *a* unreal.
irreflexión [irreflek'sjon] *nf* thoughtlessness.
irremediable [irreme'ðjaβle] *a* incurable, hopeless.
irresoluto, a [irreso'luto, a] *a* irresolute, hesitant.
irrespetuoso, a [irrespe'twoso, a] *a* disrespectful.
irresponsable [irrespon'saβle] *a* irresponsible.
irrigar [irri'xar] *vt* to irrigate.
irrisorio, a [irri'sorjo, a] *a* derisory, ridiculous.
irritar [irri'tar] *vt* to irritate, annoy.
irrupción [irrup'θjon] *nf* irruption; (*invasión*) invasion.
isla ['isla] *nf* island.
islandés, esa [islan'des, esa] *a* Icelandic // *nm/f* Icelander.
Islandia [is'landja] *nf* Iceland.
isleño, a [is'leɲo, a] *a* island *cpd* // *nm/f* islander.
Israel [isra'el] *nm* Israel; **israelí** *a, nm/f* Israeli.
istmo ['istmo] *nm* isthmus.
Italia [i'talja] *nf* Italy; **italiano, a** *a, nm/f* Italian.
itinerario [itine'rarjo] *nm* itinerary, route.
izar [i'θar] *vt* to hoist.
izquierdista [iθkjer'ðista] *nm/f* left-winger, leftist.
izquierdo, a [iθ'kjerðo, a] *a* left // *nf* left; **a la** ~**a** on the left.

J

jabalí [xaβa'li] *nm* wild boar.
jabalina [xaβa'lina] *nf* javelin.
jabón [xa'βon] *nm* soap; **jabonar** *vt* to soap.
jaca ['xaka] *nf* pony.
jacinto [xa'θinto] *nm* hyacinth.
jactancia [xak'tanθja] *nf* boasting, boastfulness.
jactarse [xak'tarse] *vr* to boast, brag.
jadeante [xaðe'ante] *a* panting, gasping; **jadear** *vi* to pant, gasp for breath; **jadeo** *nm* panting, gasping.
jaez [xa'eθ] *nm* (*de caballerías*) harness; (*clase*) kind, sort.
jaguar [xa'ɣwar] *nm* jaguar.

jalar [xa'lar] *vt* to pull, haul.
jalbegue [xal'βeɣe] *nm* (*pintura*) white-wash; (*fig*) make-up.
jalea [xa'lea] *nf* jelly.
jaleo [xa'leo] *nm* racket, uproar; (*baile*) Andalusian popular dance; **estar de** ~ to be having a good time; **armar un** ~ to kick up a din.
Jamaica [xa'maika] *nf* Jamaica.
jamás [xa'mas] *ad* never; (*sin negación*) ever.
jamón [xa'mon] *nm* ham.
Japón [xa'pon] *nm*: **el** ~ Japan; **japonés, esa** *a, nm/f* Japanese.
jaque ['xake] *nm* cheque; (*fam*) bully; ~ **mate** checkmate.
jaqueca [xa'keka] *nf* (*severe*) headache, migraine.
jarabe [xa'raβe] *nm* syrup.
jarcia ['xarθja] *nf* (NAUT) ropes *pl*, rigging; (*para pescar*) (fishing) tackle; (*confusión, revoltijo*) jumble, mess.
jardín [xar'ðin] *nm* garden; **jardinería** *nf* gardening; **jardinero, a** *nm/f* gardener.
jarra ['xarra] *nf* jar.
jarro ['xarro] *nm* jug.
jaula ['xaula] *nf* cage.
jauría [xau'ria] *nf* pack of hounds.
J. C. *abr de* **Jesucristo.**
jefatura [xefa'tura] *nf*: ~ **de policía** police headquarters *sg*.
jefe ['xefe] *nm* (*gen*) chief, head; (*patrón*) boss; ~ **de camareros** head waiter; ~ **de cocina** chef; ~ **de estación** station-master; ~ **de estado** head of state; ~ **supremo** commander-in-chief; **ser el** ~ (*fig*) to be the boss.
jengibre [xen'xiβre] *nm* ginger.
jeque ['xeke] *nm* sheik.
jerarquía [xerar'kia] *nf* (*orden*) hierarchy; (*rango*) rank; **jerárquico, a** *a* hierarchic(al).
jerez [xe'reθ] *nm* sherry.
jerga ['xerɣa] *nf* (*tela*) coarse cloth; (*lenguaje*) jargon, slang.
jerigonza [xeri'ɣonθa] *nf* (*jerga*) jargon, slang; (*galimatías*) nonsense, gibberish.
jeringa [xe'ringa] *nf* syringe; (AM) annoyance, bother; ~ **de engrase** grease gun; **jeringar** *vt* to syringe; (*inyectar*) to inject; (AM) to annoy, bother.
jeroglífico [xero'xlifiko] *nm* hieroglyphic.
jersé, jersey (*pl* **jerseys**) [xer'sei] *nm* jersey, pullover, jumper.
Jerusalén [xerusa'len] *n* Jerusalem.
Jesucristo [xesu'kristo] *n* Jesus Christ.
jesuita [xe'swita] *a, nm* Jesuit.
Jesús [xe'sus] *nm* Jesus; **¡~!** good heavens!; (*al estornudar*) bless you!
jícara ['xikara] *nf* small cup.
jifero, a [xi'fero, a] *a* (*fam*) filthy // *nm* butcher's knife; (*matarife*) butcher, slaughterer.
jinete [xi'nete] *nm* (horse)rider.
jipijapa [xipi'xapa] *nm* (AM) straw hat.

jira ['xira] *nf* (*de tela*) strip; (*excursión*) picnic.

jirafa [xi'rafa] *nf* giraffe.

jirón [xi'ron] *nm* rag, shred.

jocosidad [xokosi'ðað] *nf* humour; (*chiste*) joke.

jocoso, a [xo'koso, a] *a* humorous, jocular.

jofaina [xo'faina] *nf* washbasin.

jornada [xor'naða] *nf* day's journey; (*camino o viaje entero*) journey; (*día de trabajo*) working day; (*fig*) lifetime.

jornal [xor'nal] *nm* (day's) wage; **~ero** *nm* (day) labourer.

joroba [xo'roßa] *nf* hump, hunched back; (*fam*) nuisance; **~do, a** *a* hunchbacked // *nm/f* hunchback.

jota ['xota] *nf* letter J; (*danza*) Aragonese dance; (*fam*) iota; **no saber ~** to have no idea.

joven ['xoßen] *a* young // *nm* young man, youth // *nf* young woman, girl.

jovial [xo'ßjal] *a* cheerful, jovial; **~idad** *nf* cheerfulness, joviality.

joya ['xoja] *nf* jewel, gem; (*fig: persona*) gem; **joyería** *nf* (*joyas*) jewellery; (*tienda*) jeweller's (shop); **joyero** *nm* (*persona*) jeweller; (*caja*) jewel case.

juanete [xwa'nete] *nm* bunion.

jubilación [xußila'θjon] *nf* (*retiro*) retirement; (*alegría*) jubilation.

jubilar [xußi'lar] *vt* to pension off, retire; (*fam*) to discard // *vi* to rejoice; **~se** *vr* to retire.

jubileo [xußi'leo] *nm* (*indulgencia*) jubilee; (*fam*) comings and goings *pl.*

júbilo ['xußilo] *nm* joy, jubilation, rejoicing; **~so, a** *a* jubilant.

judaísmo [xuða'ismo] *nm* Judaism.

judía [xu'ðia] *nf* Jewess; (*CULIN*) bean.

judicatura [xuðika'tura] *nf* (*cargo de juez*) office of judge; (*magistratura*) judicature.

judicial [xuði'θjal] *a* judicial.

judío, a [xu'ðio, a] *a* Jewish // *nm/f* Jew/ess.

juego *etc vb ver* **jugar** // ['xweɣo] *nm* (*gen*) play; (*pasatiempo, partido*) game; (*en casino*) gambling; (*conjunto*) set; **fuera de ~** (*persona*) offside; (*pelota*) out of play.

juerga ['xwerɣa] *nf* good time; (*fiesta*) party; **ir de ~** to go out on a spree.

jueves ['xweßes] *nm inv* Thursday.

juez [xweθ] *nm* judge; **~ de línea** linesman; **~ de salida** starter.

jugada [xu'ɣaða] *nf* play; **buena ~** good move/shot/stroke *etc.*

jugador, a [xuɣa'ðor, a] *nm/f* player; (*en casino*) gambler.

jugar [xu'ɣar] *vt, vi* to play; (*en casino*) to gamble; **~se** *vr* to gamble (away).

juglar [xu'ɣlar] *nm* minstrel.

jugo ['xuɣo] *nm* (*BOT*) juice; (*fig*) essence, substance; **~so, a** *a* juicy; (*fig*) substantial, important.

juguete [xu'ɣete] *nm* toy; (*TEATRO*) sketch; **~ar** *vi* to play; **~ría** *nf* toyshop.

juguetón, ona [xuɣe'ton, ona] *a* playful.

juicio ['xwiθjo] *nm* judgement; (*sana razón*) sanity, reason; (*opinión*) opinion; **estar fuera de ~** to be out of one's mind; **~so, a** *a* wise, sensible.

julio ['xuljo] *nm* July.

jumento, a [xu'mento, a] *nm/f* donkey.

junco ['xunko] *nm* rush, reed.

jungla ['xungla] *nf* jungle.

junio ['xunjo] *nm* June.

junta ['xunta] *nf ver* **junto.**

juntamente [xunta'mente] *ad* (*conjuntamente*) together; (*al mismo tiempo*) together, at the same time.

juntar [xun'tar] *vt* to join, unite; (*maquinaria*) to assemble, put together; (*dinero*) to collect; (*puerta*) to half-close, leave ajar; **~se** *vr* to join, meet; (*reunirse: personas*) to meet, assemble; (*arrimarse*) to approach, draw closer; (*vivir juntos*) to live together; **~se con uno** to join sb.

junto, a ['xunto, a] *a* (*unido*) joined, united; (*anexo*) near, close; (*continuo, próximo*) next, adjacent // *ad*: **todo ~** all at once // *nf* (*asamblea*) meeting, assembly; (*comité, consejo*) board, council, committee; (*articulación*) joint; **~ a** near (to), next to; **~s** together.

juntura [xun'tura] *nf* (*punto de unión*) join, junction; (*articulación*) joint.

jurado [xu'raðo] *nm* (*JUR*) juror; (*: conjunto de ~s*) jury; (*de concurso*) panel (of judges); (*: individuo*) member of a panel.

juramentar [xuramen'tar] *vt* to swear in, administer the oath to; **~se** *vr* to be sworn in, take the oath.

juramento [xura'mento] *nm* oath; (*maldición*) oath, curse; **prestar ~** to take the oath; **tomar ~ a** to swear in, administer the oath to.

jurar [xu'rar] *vt, vi* to swear; **~ en falso** to commit perjury; **jurárselas a uno** to have it in for sb.

jurídico, a [xu'riðiko, a] *a* legal.

jurisdicción [xurisðik'θjon] *nf* (*poder, autoridad*) jurisdiction; (*territorio*) district.

jurisprudencia [xurispru'ðenθja] *nf* jurisprudence.

jurista [xu'rista] *nm/f* jurist.

justamente [xusta'mente] *ad* justly, fairly; (*precisamente*) just, precisely, exactly.

justicia [xus'tiθja] *nf* justice; (*equidad*) fairness, justice; **justiciero, a** *a* just, righteous.

justificación [xustifika'θjon] *nf* justification; **justificar** *vt* to justify.

justo, a ['xusto, a] *a* (*equitativo*) just, fair, right; (*preciso*) exact, correct; (*ajustado*) tight // *ad* (*precisamente*) exactly, precisely.

juvenil [xuße'nil] *a* youthful.

juventud [xußen'tuð] *nf* (*adolescencia*) youth; (*jóvenes*) young people *pl.*

juzgado [xuθ'gaðo] *nm* tribunal; (*JUR*) court.

juzgar [xuθ'xar] *vt* to judge; **a ~ por...** to judge by..., judging by... .

K

kg *abr de* **kilogramo.**

kilo ['kilo] *nm* kilo // *pref:* ~**gramo** *nm* kilogramme; ~**litro** *nm* kilolitre; ~**metraje** *nm* distance in kilometres; **kilómetro** *nm* kilometre; ~**vatio** *nm* kilowatt.

kiosco ['kjosko] *nm* = **quiosco.**

km *abr de* **kilómetro.**

kv *abr de* **kilovatio.**

L

l *abr de* **litro.**

la [la] *det* the // *pron* her; (*Ud.*) you; (*cosa*) it // *nm* (*MUS*) la; ~ **del sombrero rojo** the girl in the red hat.

laberinto [laβe'rinto] *nm* labyrinth.

labia ['laβja] *nf* fluency; (*pey*) glibness.

labial [la'βja!] *a* labial; **lectura** ~ lip-reading.

labio ['laβjo] *nm* lip.

labor [la'βor] *nf* labour; (*AGR*) farm work; (*tarea*) job, task; (*costura*) needlework; ~**able** *a* workable; **día** ~**able** working day; ~ **ar** *vi* to work; ~**eo** *nm* (*AGR*) cultivation; (*de minas*) working; ~**ioso, a** *a* (*persona*) hard-working; (*trabajo*) tough; ~**ista** *a:* **Partido L~ista** Labour Party.

labrado, a [la'βraðo, a] *a* worked; (*cincelado*) carved; (*metal*) wrought // *nm* (*AGR*) cultivated field.

labrador, a [laβra'ðor, a] *a* farming // *nm/f* farmer.

labrantío, a [laβran'tio, a] *a* arable.

labranza [la'βranθa] *nf* (*AGR*) cultivation.

labrar [la'βrar] *vt* (*gen*) to work; (*madera etc*) to carve; (*fig*) to cause.

labriego, a [la'βrjeɣo, a] *nm/f* peasant.

laca ['laka] *nf* lacquer.

lacayo [la'kajo] *nm* lackey.

lacerar [laθe'rar] *vt* to lacerate.

lacio, a ['laθjo, a] *a* (*pelo*) lank; (*movimiento*) limp; (*BOT*) withered.

lacónico, a [la'koniko, a] *a* laconic.

lacrar [la'krar] *vt* (*MED*) to injure the health of; (*dañar*) to harm; (*cerrar*) to seal (with sealing wax); ~**se** *vr* to harm o.s.; **lacre** *nm* sealing wax.

lacrimoso, a [lakri'moso, a] *a* tearful.

lactar [lak'tar] *vt, vi* to suckle.

ladear [laðe'ar] *vt* to tip, tilt; (*ciudad, colina*) to skirt // *vi* to tilt; ~**se** *vr* to lean.

ladera [la'ðera] *nf* slope.

ladino, a [la'ðino, a] *a* cunning.

lado ['laðo] *nm* (*gen*) side; (*fig*) protection; (*MIL*) flank; **al** ~ **de** beside; **poner de** ~ to put on its side; **poner a un** ~ to put aside; **por todos** ~**s** on all sides, all round.

ladrar [la'ðrar] *vi* to bark; **ladrido** *nm* bark, barking.

ladrillo [la'ðriʎo] *nm* (*gen*) brick; (*azulejo*) tile; (*color*) brick red.

ladrón, ona [la'ðron, ona] *nm/f* thief.

lagar [la'ɣar] *nm* (wine/oil) press.

lagarto [la'ɣarto] *nm* (*ZOOL*) lizard; (*fig: fam*) sharp customer; ~ **de Indias** alligator.

lago ['laɣo] *nm* lake.

lágrima ['laɣrima] *nf* tear; **lagrimar** *vi* to weep.

laguna [la'ɣuna] *nf* (*lago*) lagoon; (*hueco*) gap.

laico, a ['laiko, a] *a* lay.

lamentable [lamen'taβle] *a* lamentable, regrettable; (*miserable*) pitiful.

lamentar [lamen'tar] *vt* (*sentir*) to regret; (*deplorar*) to lament; ~**se** *vr* to lament; **lamento** *nm* lament.

lamer [la'mer] *vt* to lick.

lámina ['lamina] *nf* (*plancha delgada*) sheet; (*para estampar, estampa*) plate; **laminar** *vt* (*en libro*) to laminate.

lámpara ['lampara] *nf* lamp; ~ **de alcohol/gas** spirit/gas lamp; ~ **de bolsillo** torch; ~ **de pie** standard lamp.

lampiño [lam'piɲo] *a* clean-shaven.

lana ['lana] *nf* wool.

lance ['lanθe] *nm* (*golpe*) stroke; (*suceso*) event, incident; (*riña*) quarrel; (*tirada*) throw; **libros de** ~ second-hand books.

lancha ['lantʃa] *nf* launch; ~ **automóvil** motorboat; ~ **de pesca** fishing boat; ~ **salvavidas/torpedera** lifeboat/torpedo boat; **lanchero** *nm* boatman.

lanero, a [la'nero, a] *a* woollen.

langosta [lan'gosta] *nf* (*insecto*) locust; (*crustáceo*) lobster; (*fig*) plague;· **langostín, langostino** *nm* prawn.

languidecer [langiðe'θer] *vi* to languish; **languidez** *nf* languor; **lánguido, a** *a* (*gen*) languid; (*sin energía*) listless.

lanilla [la'niʎa] *nf* nap.

lanudo, a [la'nuðo, a] *a* woolly.

lanza ['lanθa] *nf* (*arma*) lance, spear; (*de vagón*) pole.

lanzadera [lanθa'ðera] *nf* shuttle.

lanzamiento [lanθa'mjento] *nm* (*gen*) throwing; (*NAUT, COM*) launch, launching; ~ **de pesos** putting the shot.

lanzar [lan'θar] *vt* (*gen*) to throw; (*DEPORTE*) to bowl; (*NAUT, COM*) to launch; (*JUR*) to evict; (*MED*) to vomit; ~**se** *vr* to throw o.s.

laña ['laɲa] *nf* clamp.

lapa ['lapa] *nf* limpet.

lapicero [lapi'θero] *nm* propelling pencil.

lápida ['lapiða] *nf* stone; ~ **mortuoria** headstone; ~ **conmemorativa** memorial stone; **lapidar** *vt* to stone; **lapidario, a** *a, nm* lapidary.

lápiz ['lapiθ] *nm* pencil; ~ **de color** coloured pencil; ~ **de labios** lipstick.

lapón, ona [la'pon, ona] *nm/f* Laplander, Lapp.

lapso ['lapso] *nm* (*de tiempo*) interval; (*error*) error.

largar [lar'xar] *vt* (*soltar*) to release; (*aflojar*) to loosen; (*lanzar*) to launch;

(*fam*) to let fly; (*pelota*) to throw; (*velas*) to unfurl; (*AM*) to throw; ~**se** *vr* (*fam*) to beat it; (*NAUT*) to set sail; ~**se a** (*AM*) to start to.

largo, a ['larɣo, a] *a* (*longitud*) long; (*tiempo*) lengthy; (*persona: alta*) tall; (*fig*) generous // *nm* length; (*MUS*) largo // *ad* widely; **dos años** ~**s** two long years; **tiene 9 metros de** ~ it is 9 metres long; **a lo** ~ **de** along.

largueza [lar'ɣeθa] *nf* generosity.

lárice ['lariθe] *nm* larch.

laringe [la'rinxe] *nf* larynx; **laringitis** *nf* laryngitis.

larva ['larβa] *nf* larva.

las [las] *det* the // *pron* them; ~ **que cantan** the ones/women/girls who sing.

lascivo, a [las'θiβo, a] *a* lewd.

láser ['laser] *nm* laser.

lasitud [lasi'tuð] *nf* lassitude, weariness.

lástima ['lastima] *nf* (*pena*) pity; (*queja*) complaint; **dar** ~ to be pitiful; **es** ~ **que** it's a pity that; **¡qué** ~**!** what a pity!; **ella está hecha una** ~ she looks pitiful.

lastimar [lasti'mar] *vt* (*herir*) to wound; (*ofender*) to offend; (*compadecer*) to pity; ~**se** *vr* to hurt o.s.; ~**se de** to feel sorry for; **lastimero, a, lastimoso, a** *a* pitiful, pathetic.

lastre ['lastre] *nm* (*TEC, NAUT*) ballast; (*fig*) dead weight.

lata ['lata] *nf* (*metal*) tin; (*caja*) tin, can; (*fam*) nuisance; **hoja de** ~ tin(plate); **en** ~ tinned; **dar (la)** ~ to be a nuisance.

latente [la'tente] *a* latent.

lateral [late'ral] *a* side, lateral // (*TEATRO*) wings.

latido [la'tiðo] *nm* (*del corazón*) beat; (*de perro*) yelp.

latifundio [lati'fundjo] *nm* large estate; **latifundista** *nm* f owner of a large estate.

latigazo [lati'ɣaθo] *nm* (*golpe*) lash; (*sonido*) crack; (*fig: regaño*) sharp reproof; (*fam: bebida*) swig.

látigo ['latiɣo] *nm* whip.

latín [la'tin] *nm* Latin.

latino, a [la'tino, a] *a* Latin; ~**americano, a** *a, nm/f* Latin-American.

latir [la'tir] *vi* (*corazón, pulso*) to beat; (*perro*) to yelp.

latitud [lati'tuð] *nf* (*GEO*) latitude; (*fig*) breadth.

lato, a ['lato, a] *a* broad.

latón [la'ton] *nm* brass.

latoso, a [la'toso, a] *a* (*cansado*) annoying; (*aburrido*) boring.

latrocinio [latro'θinjo] *nm* robbery.

laúd [la'uð] *nm* lute.

laudo ['lauðo] *nm* (*JUR*) decision.

laureado, a [laure'aðo, a] *a* honoured // *nm* laureate.

laurel [lau'rel] *nm* (*BOT*) laurel; (*CULIN*) bay.

lava ['laβa] *nf* lava.

lavabo [la'βaβo] *nm* washbasin.

lavadero [laβa'ðero] *nm* laundry.

lavado [la'βaðo] *nm* washing; (*de ropa*) laundry; (*ARTE*) wash; ~ **de cerebro** brainwashing; ~ **en seco** dry cleaning.

lavadora [laβa'ðora] *nf* washing machine.

lavamanos [laβa'manos] *nm inv* washbasin.

lavandería [laβande'ria] *nf* laundry; ~ **automática** launderette.

lavaplatos [laβa'platos] *nm o f inv* dishwasher.

lavar [la'βar] *vt* to wash; (*borrar*) to wipe away; ~**se** *vr* to wash o.s.; ~**se las manos** to wash one's hands; ~ **y marcar** (*pelo*) to shampoo and set; ~ **en seco** to dry clean.

lavavajillas [laβaβa'xiʎas] *nm inv* dishwasher.

laxante [lak'sante] *nm* laxative.

laya ['laja] *nf* spade; **de la misma** ~ (*fig*) of the same sort.

lazada [la'θaða] *nf* bow.

lazo ['laθo] *nm* knot; (*lazada*) bow; (*de animales*) lasso; (*trampa*) snare; (*de camino*) hairpin bend; (*vínculo*) tie.

lb(s) *abr de* **libra(s)**.

le [le] *pron* (*directo*) him; (: *usted*) you; (*indirecto*) to him; (: *usted*) to you.

leal [le'al] *a* loyal; ~**tad** *nf* loyalty.

lebrel [le'βrel] *nm* greyhound.

lección [lek'θjon] *nf* lesson.

lector, a [lek'tor, a] *nm/f* reader.

lectura [lek'tura] *nf* reading.

leche ['letʃe] *nf* milk; **tener mala** ~ to be nasty; ~ **condensada/en polvo** condensed/powdered milk; ~ **desnatada** skimmed milk; ~ **de magnesia** milk of magnesia; ~**ra** *nf* (*vendedora*) milkmaid; (*para hervir*) milk pan; (*para servir*) milkjug; (*AM*) cow; ~**ría** *nf* dairy.

lecho ['letʃo] *nm* (*cama*) bed; (*de río*) bottom; (*GEO*) layer.

lechón [le'tʃon] *nm* sucking pig.

lechoso, a [le'tʃoso, a] *a* milky.

lechuga [le'tʃuɣa] *nf* lettuce.

lechuza [le'tʃuθa] *nf* owl.

leer [le'er] *vt* to read.

legación [leɣa'θjon] *nf* legation.

legado [le'xaðo] *nm* (*don*) bequest; (*herencia*) legacy; (*enviado*) legate.

legajo [le'xaxo] *nm* file.

legal [le'xal] *a* (*gen*) legal; (*persona*) trustworthy; ~**idad** *nf* legality; ~**izar** *vt* to legalize; (*documento*) to authenticate.

légamo ['leɣamo] *nm* (*cieno*) mud, ooze.

legar [le'xar] *vt* to bequeath, leave; **legatario, a** *nm/f* legatee.

legión [le'xjon] *nf* legion; **legionario, a** *a* legionary // *nm* legionnaire.

legislación [lexisla'θjon] *nf* legislation; **legislar** *vt* to legislate.

legitimar [lexiti'mar] *vt* to legitimize; **legítimo, a** *a* (*genuino*) authentic; (*legal*) legitimate.

lego, a ['leɣo, a] *a* (*REL*) secular; (*ignorante*) ignorant // *nm* layman.

legua ['leɣwa] *nf* league.

leguleyo [lexu'lejo] *nm* (*pey*) petty lawyer.

legumbre [le'xumbre] *nf* vegetable.

leído, a [le'iðo, a] a well-read.

lejanía [lexa'nia] *nf* distance; **lejano, a** *a* far-off; (*en el tiempo*) distant; (*fig*) remote.

lejía [le'xia] *nf* bleach.

lejos ['lexos] *ad* far, far away; **a lo ~** in the distance; **de o desde ~** from afar; **~ de** *prep* far from.

lelo, a ['lelo, a] a silly; (*fig*) open-mouthed // *nm/f* idiot.

lema ['lema] *nm* motto; (*POL*) slogan.

lencería [lenθe'ria] *nf* drapery.

lengua ['lengwa] *nf* tongue; **~ moderna** modern language; **morderse la ~** to hold one's tongue.

lenguado [len'gwaðo] *nm* sole.

lenguaje [len'gwaxe] *nm* language.

lenguaraz [lengwa'raθ] a talkative; (*pey*) foul-mouthed.

lengüeta [len'gweta] *nf* (*ANAT*) epiglottis; (*de balanza, zapatos, MUS*) tongue; (*herramienta*) needle.

lenidad [leni'ðað] *nf* lenience.

lente ['lente] *nm o f* lens; (*lupa*) magnifying glass; **~s** *npl* glasses; **~s de contacto** contact lenses.

lenteja [len'texa] *nf* lentil; **lentejuela** *nf* sequin.

lentitud [lenti'tuð] *nf* slowness; **con ~** slowly.

lento, a ['lento, a] a slow.

leña ['leɲa] *nf* firewood; **~dor, a, ~tero, a** *nm/f* woodcutter.

leño ['leɲo] *nm* (*trozo de árbol*) log; (*madera*) timber; (*fig*) blockhead.

Leo ['leo] *nm* Leo.

león [le'on] *nm* lion; (*AM*) puma; **~ marino** sea lion; **leonino, a** a leonine.

leontina [leon'tina] *nf* watch chain.

leopardo [leo'parðo] *nm* leopard.

lepra ['lepra] *nf* leprosy; **leproso, a** *nm/f* leper.

lerdo, a ['lerðo, a] a (*lento*) slow; (*patoso*) clumsy.

les [les] *pron* (*directo*) them; (: *ustedes*) you; (*indirecto*) to them; (: *ustedes*) to you.

lesbiana [les'βjana] a, *nf* lesbian.

lesión [le'sjon] *nf* (*daño*) lesion; (*fig*) injury; **lesionado, a** a injured // *nm/f* injured person.

letal [le'tal] a lethal.

letanía [leta'nia] *nf* litany.

letargo [le'tarɣo] *nm* (*MED*) lethargy.

letra ['letra] *nf* letter; (*escritura*) handwriting; (*MUS*) lyrics *pl*; **~ de cambio** bill of exchange; **~ de imprenta** print; **~do, a** learned; (*fam*) pedantic // *nm* lawyer; **letrero** *nm* (*cartel*) sign; (*etiqueta*) label.

leva ['leβa] *nf* (*NAUT*) weighing anchor; (*MIL*) levy; (*TEC*) lever.

levadizo [leβa'ðiθo] a: **puente ~** drawbridge.

levadura [leβa'ðura] *nf* (*para el pan*) yeast; (*de la cerveza*) brewer's yeast.

levantamiento [leβanta'mjento] *nm* raising, lifting; (*rebelión*) revolt, rising; **~ de pesos** weight-lifting.

levantar [leβan'tar] *vt* (*gen*) to raise; (*del suelo*) to pick up; (*hacia arriba*) to lift (up); (*plan*) to make, draw up; (*mesa*) to clear away; (*campamento*) to strike; (*fig*) to cheer up, hearten; **~se** *vr* to get up; (*enderezarse*) to straighten up; (*rebelarse*) to rebel; **~ el ánimo** to cheer up.

levante [le'βante] *nm* east coast; **el L~** the Near East, the Levant.

levar [le'βar] *vt* to weigh anchor; **~se** *vr* to set sail.

leve ['leβe] a light; (*fig*) trivial; **~dad** *nf* lightness.

levita [le'βita] *nf* frock coat.

léxico ['leksiko] *nm* lexicon, dictionary.

ley [lei] *nf* (*gen*) law; (*fig*) loyalty; (*metal*) standard.

leyenda [le'jenda] *nf* legend.

leyó *etc vb ver* **leer.**

liar [li'ar] *vt* to tie (up); (*unir*) to bind; (*envolver*) to wrap (up); (*enredar*) to confuse; (*cigarrillo*) to roll; **~se** *vr* (*fam*) to get involved; **~se a palos** to get involved in a fight.

Líbano ['liβano] *nm*: **el ~** the Lebanon.

libar [li'βar] *vt* to suck.

libelo [li'βelo] *nm* satire, lampoon; (*JUR*) petition.

libélula [li'βelula] *nf* dragonfly.

liberación [liβera'θjon] *nf* liberation; (*de la cárcel*) release.

liberal [liβe'ral] a, *nm/f* liberal; **~idad** *nf* liberality; (*lujo*) lavishness.

liberar [liβe'rar] *vt* to liberate.

libertad [liβer'tað] *nf* liberty; (*soltura*) freedom; **~ de culto/de prensa/de comercio** freedom of worship/the press/of trade; **~ condicional** probation; **~ bajo palabra** parole; **~ bajo fianza** bail.

libertar [liβer'tar] *vt* (*preso*) to set free; (*de una obligación*) to release; (*eximir*) to exempt.

libertino, a [liβer'tino, a] a loose-living // *nm/f* libertine.

libra ['liβra] *nf* pound; **L~** (*ASTRO*) Libra; **~ esterlina** pound sterling.

librador, a [liβra'ðor, a] *nm/f* drawer.

libramiento [liβra'mjento] *nm* rescue; (*COM*) delivery.

libranza [li'βranθa] *nf* (*COM*) draft; (*de letra de cambio*) bill of exchange.

librar [li'βrar] *vt* (*de peligro*) to save; (*batalla*) to wage, fight; (*de impuestos*) to exempt; (*secreto*) to reveal; (*mercancías*) to draw; (*cheque*) to make out; (*JUR*) to exempt // *vi* to give birth; **~se** *vr*: **~se de** to escape from, free o.s. from.

libre ['liβre] a (*gen*) free; (*lugar*) unoccupied; (*asiento*) vacant; (*de impuestos*) tax-free; (*de deudas*) free of debts; (*pey*) outspoken; **tiro ~** free kick; **los 100 metros ~** the 100 metres free-style (race); **al aire ~** in the open air.

librería [liβre'ria] *nf* (*biblioteca*) library; (*comercio*) bookshop; **librero, a** *nm/f* bookseller.

libreta [li'βreta] *nf* notebook; ~ **de ahorros** savings book; ~ **de banco** bank book.

libro ['liβro] *nm* book; ~ **en rústica/en pasta** *o* **encuadernado** paperback/hardback; ~ **de bolsillo** paperback; ~ **de caja** cashbook; ~ **de cheques** cheque book; ~ **de inventario** stock-list; ~ **de pedidos** order book; ~ **de texto** text-book.

Lic. *abr de* **licenciado, a.**

licencia [li'θenθja] *nf* (*gen*) licence; (*permiso*) permission; ~ **por enfermedad/con goce de sueldo** sick leave/paid leave; ~ **de caza/de conductor** game/driving licence; ~ **de derecho/de letras** law/arts degree; ~**do, a** *a* licensed // *nm/f* graduate; **licenciar** *vt* (*empleado*) to dismiss; (*permitir*) to permit, allow; (*soldado*) to discharge; (*estudiante*) to confer a degree upon; **licenciarse** *vr*: **licenciarse en letras** to graduate in arts.

licencioso, a [liθen'θjoso, a] *a* licentious.

liceo [li'θeo] *nm* (high) school.

licitador [liθita'ðor] *nm* bidder; (*AM*) auctioneer; **licitar** *vt* to bid for; (*AM*) to sell by auction.

lícito, a ['liθito, a] *a* (*legal*) lawful; (*justo*) fair, just; (*permisible*) permissible.

licor [li'kor] *nm* spirits *pl*; (*preparado*) liqueur.

licuadora [likwa'ðora] *nf* food-mixer, liquidizer; **licuar** *vt* to liquidize.

lid [lið] *nf* combat; (*fig*) controversy.

líder ['liðer] *nm/f* leader; **liderato** *nm* leadership.

lidia ['liðja] *nf* bullfight; **toros de** ~ fighting bulls; **lidiar** *vt, vi* to fight.

liebre ['ljeβre] *nf* hare.

lienzo ['ljenθo] *nm* linen; (*ARTE*) canvas; (*pañuelo*) handkerchief; (*ARQ*) wall.

liga ['liɣa] *nf* (*de medias*) garter, suspender; (*confederación*) league; (*venda*) band; (*aleación*) alloy; (*BOT*) mistletoe.

ligadura [liɣa'ðura] *nf* bond, tie; (*MED, MUS*) ligature.

ligamento [liɣa'mento] *nm* (*ANAT*) ligament; (*atadura*) tie; (*unión*) bond.

ligar [li'ɣar] *vt* (*atar*) to tie; (*unir*) to join; (*MED*) to bind up; (*MUS*) to slur; (*metales*) to alloy // *vi* to mix, blend; (*fam*) to pick up; (*entenderse*) to get on (well); ~**se** *vr* to commit o.s.

ligereza [lixe'reθa] *nf* lightness; (*rapidez*) swiftness; (*agilidad*) agility; (*superficialidad*) flippancy.

ligero, a [li'xero, a] *a* (*de peso*) light; (*tela*) thin; (*rápido*) swift, quick; (*ágil*) agile, nimble; (*de importancia*) slight; (*de carácter*) flippant, superficial // *ad*: **a la** ~**a** superficially.

lija ['lixa] *nf* (*ZOOL*) dogfish; (**papel de**) ~ sandpaper.

lila ['lila] *nf* lilac // *nm* (*fam*) twit.

lima ['lima] *nf* file; (*BOT*) lime; ~ **de carpintero** file; ~ **de uñas** nail-file; **limar** *vt* to file.

limitación [limita'θjon] *nf* limitation, limit.

limitar [limi'tar] *vt* to limit; (*reducir*) to reduce, cut down // *vi*: ~ **con** to border on; ~**se** *vr*: ~**se a** to limit o.s. to.

límite ['limite] *nm* (*gen*) limit; (*fin*) end; (*frontera*) border; ~ **de velocidad** speed limit.

limítrofe [li'mitrofe] *a* bordering, neighbouring.

limón [li'mon] *nm* lemon // *a*: **amarillo** ~ lemon-yellow; **limonada** *nf* lemonade; **limonero** *nm* lemon tree.

limosna [li'mosna] *nf* alms *pl*; **vivir de** ~ to live on charity.

limpiabotas [limpja'βotas] *nm inv* bootblack, shoeshine boy/girl.

limpiaparabrisas [limpjapara'βrisas] *nm inv* windscreen wiper.

limpiar [lim'pjar] *vt* (*gen*) to clean; (*con trapo*) to wipe; (*quitar*) to wipe away; (*zapatos*) to shine, polish; (*fig*) to clean up.

limpieza [lim'pjeθa] *nf* (*estado*) cleanliness; (*acto*) cleaning; (: *de las calles*) cleansing; (: *de zapatos*) polishing; (*habilidad*) skill; (*fig*) clean-up; (*pureza*) purity; (*MIL*): **operación de** ~ mopping-up operation; ~ **en seco** dry cleaning.

limpio, a ['limpjo, a] *a* clean; (*moralmente*) pure; (*COM*) clear, net; (*fam*) honest // *ad*: **jugar** ~ to play fair // *nm*: **pasar en** ~ to make a fair copy.

linaje [li'naxe] *nm* lineage, family; **linajudo, a** *a* highborn.

linaza [li'naθa] *nf* linseed; **aceite de** ~ linseed oil.

lince ['linθe] *nm* lynx.

linchar [lin'tʃar] *vt* to lynch.

lindante [lin'dante] *a* adjoining; ~ **con** bordering on.

lindar [lin'dar] *vi* to adjoin; ~ **con** to border on; **linde** *nm o f* boundary; **lindero, a** *a* adjoining // *nm* boundary.

lindo, a ['lindo, a] *a* pretty, lovely // *ad* (*AM*): **nos divertimos de lo** ~ we had a marvellous time; **canta muy** ~ he/she sings beautifully.

línea ['linea] *nf* (*gen*) line; ~ **aérea** airline; ~ **delantera** (*DEPORTE*) forward line; ~ **de meta** goal line; (*de carrera*) finishing line; ~ **de saque** service line, base line; ~ **recta** straight line.

lingüista [lin'gwista] *nm/f* linguist.

linimento [lini'mento] *nm* liniment.

lino ['lino] *nm* linen; (*BOT*) flax.

linóleo [li'noleo] *nm* lino, linoleum.

linterna [lin'terna] *nf* lantern, lamp; ~ **eléctrica** *o* **a pilas** torch.

lío ['lio] *nm* bundle; (*fam*) fuss; (*desorden*) muddle, mess; **armar un** ~ to make a fuss.

liquidación [likiða'θjon] *nf* liquidation; **venta de** ~ clearance sale.

liquidar [liki'ðar] vt (licuar) to liquidize; (eliminar) to liquidate; (mercaderías) to sell off; (pagar) to pay off; (terminar) to wind up; (AM) to ruin; ~**se** vr to liquefy.

líquido, a [li'kiðo, a] a liquid; (ganancia) net; (AM) accurate // nm liquid; ~ **imponible** net taxable income.

lira ['lira] nf (MUS) lyre; (moneda) lira.

lirio ['lirjo] nm (BOT) iris.

Lisboa [lis'βoa] n Lisbon.

lisiado, a [li'sjaðo, a] a injured // nm/f cripple.

lisiar [li'sjar] vt to maim; ~**se** vr to injure o.s.

liso, a ['liso, a] a (terreno) flat; (cabello) straight; (superficie) even; (tela) smooth.

lisonja [li'sonxa] nf flattery; **lisonjear** vt to flatter; (fig) to please; **lisonjero, a** a (gen) flattering; (agradable) gratifying, pleasing // nm/f flatterer.

lista ['lista] nf (gen) list; (de alumnos) school register; (de libros) catalogue; (de correos) poste restante; (de platos) menu; (de precios) price list; **pasar** ~ to call the roll; ~ **de espera** waiting list; **tela a** ~**s** striped material.

listado, a [lis'taðo, a] a striped.

listo, a ['listo, a] a (perspicaz) smart, clever; (preparado) ready.

listón [lis'ton] nm (tela) ribbon; (de madera, metal) strip.

litera [li'tera] nf (en barco, tren) berth; (en dormitorio) bunk, bunk bed.

literato, a [lite'rato, a] a literary // nm/f writer.

literatura [litera'tura] nf literature.

litigar [liti'var] vt to fight // vi (JUR) to go to law; (fig) to dispute, argue.

litigio [li'tixjo] nm (JUR) lawsuit; (fig): **en** ~ **con** in dispute with.

litografía [litovra'fia] nf lithography; (una ~) lithograph.

litoral [lito'ral] a coastal // nm coast, seaboard.

litro ['litro] nm litre.

liviano, a [li'βjano, a] a (persona) fickle; (cosa, objeto) trivial.

lívido, a [li'βiðo, a] a livid; (AM) pale.

ll... ver bajo la letra LL, después de L.

lo [lo] det neuter def art; ~ **bueno** the good // pron (persona) him; (cosa) it.

loa ['loa] nf praise; **loable** a praiseworthy; **loar** vt to praise.

lobato [lo'βato] nm wolf cub.

lobo ['loβo] nm wolf; ~ **de mar** sea dog; ~ **marino** seal.

lóbrego, a ['loβrevo, a] a dark; (fig) gloomy.

lóbulo ['loβulo] nm lobe.

locación [loka'θjon] nf lease.

local [lo'kal] a local // nm place, site; (oficinas) premises pl; ~**idad** nf (barrio) locality; (lugar) location; (TEATRO) seat, ticket; ~**izar** vt (ubicar) to locate, find; (restringir) to localize; (situar) to place.

loco, a ['loko, a] a mad // nm/f lunatic, mad person.

locomoción [lokomo'θjon] nf locomotion.

locomotora [lokomo'tora] nf engine.

locuaz [lo'kwaθ] a loquacious.

locución [loku'θjon] nf expression.

locura [lo'kura] nf madness; (acto) crazy act.

lodo ['loðo] nm mud; ~**s** nmpl (MED) mudbath sg.

lógico, a ['loxiko, a] a logical // nf logic.

logística [lo'xistika] nf logistics pl.

lograr [lo'srar] vt to achieve; (obtener) to get, obtain; ~ **hacer** to manage to do; ~ **que uno venga** to manage to get sb to come.

logro ['losro] nm achievement, success; **prestar a** ~ to lend at a high rate of interest.

loma ['loma] nf hillock.

lombriz [lom'briθ] nf worm; ~ **solitaria** tapeworm.

lomo ['lomo] nm (de animal) back; (de cerdo) pork loin; (de vaca) rib steak; (de libro) spine.

lona ['lona] nf canvas.

Londres ['londres] n London.

longaniza [longa'niθa] nf pork sausage.

longitud [lonxi'tuð] nf length; (GEO) longitude; **tener 3 metros de** ~ to be 3 metres long; ~ **de onda** wavelength.

lonja ['lonxa] nf slice; (de jamón) rasher; ~ **de pescado** fish market.

lontananza [lonta'nanθa] nf background.

loor [lo'or] nm praise.

loro ['loro] nm parrot.

los [los] det the // pron them; (ustedes) you; **mis libros y** ~ **de Ud** my books and yours.

losa ['losa] nf stone; ~ **sepulcral** gravestone.

lote ['lote] nm portion; (COM) lot.

lotería [lote'ria] nf lottery; (juego) lotto.

loza ['loθa] nf crockery.

lozanía [loθa'nia] nf (lujo) luxuriance; (orgullo) pride; **lozano, a** a luxuriant; (animado) lively; (altanero) haughty.

lubricante [luβri'kante] nm lubricant; **lubricar** vt to lubricate.

lucero [lu'θero] nm (ASTRO) bright star; (fig) brilliance.

lucidez [luθi'ðeθ] nf lucidity; **lúcido, a** a lucid.

luciente [lu'θjente] a shining.

luciérnaga [lu'θjernaxa] nf glow-worm.

lucimiento [luθi'mjento] nm (brillo) brilliance; (éxito) success.

lucir [lu'θir] vt to illuminate, light (up); (fig) to show off // vi (brillar) to shine; (tener éxito) to be successful; ~**se** vr to dress up.

lucrarse [lu'krarse] vr to enrich o.s.

lucro ['lukro] nm profit, gain.

luctuoso, a [luk'twoso, a] a mournful.

lucha ['lutʃa] nf fight, struggle; ~ **de**

clases class struggle; ~ **libre** wrestling; **luchar** vi to fight.

ludibrio [luˈðiβrjo] nm mockery.

luego [ˈlweɣo] ad (después) next; (más tarde) later, afterwards; (pronto) soon; **desde** ~ of course; **tan** ~ **como** as soon as.

lugar [luˈɣar] nm place; (sitio) spot; **en** ~ **de** instead of; **hacer** ~ to make room; **fuera de** ~ out of place; **tener** ~ to take place; ~ **común** commonplace.

lugareño, a [luɣaˈreɲo, a] a village cpd // nm/f villager.

lúgubre [ˈluɣuβre] a mournful.

lujo [ˈluxo] nm luxury; (fig) profusion, abundance; ~ **so, a** a luxurious.

lujuria [luˈxurja] nf lust; (fig) lewdness.

lumbre [ˈlumbre] nf (gen) light.

lumbrera [lumˈbrera] nf luminary; (en techo) skylight; (de barco) vent, port.

luminoso, a [lumiˈnoso, a] a luminous, shining.

luna [ˈluna] nf moon; (de un espejo) glass; (de gafas) lens; (fig) crescent; ~ **llena/nueva** full/new moon; **estar con** ~ to have one's head in the clouds.

lunar [luˈnar] a lunar // nm (ANAT) mole; **tela a** ~ **es** spotted material.

lunes [ˈlunes] nm inv Monday.

luneta [luˈneta] nf lens.

lupa [ˈlupa] nf magnifying glass.

lustrar [lusˈtrar] vt (mueble) to polish; (zapatos) to shine; **lustre** nm polish; (fig) lustre; **dar lustre a** to polish; **lustroso, a** a shining.

luterano, a [luteˈrano, a] a Lutheran.

luto [ˈluto] nm mourning; (congoja) grief, sorrow; ~ **s** nmpl mourning clothes; **llevar el** o **vestirse de** ~ to be in mourning.

Luxemburgo [luksemˈburxo] nm Luxembourg.

luz [luθ] (pl **luces**) nf light; **dar a** ~ **un niño** to give birth to a child; **sacar a** ~ to bring to light; (ELEC): **dar** ~ to switch on the light; **prender/apagar la** ~ to put the light on/off; **a todas luces** by any reckoning; **hacer la** ~ **sobre** to understand; **tener pocas luces** to be dim or stupid; ~ **roja/verde** red/green light; (AUTO): ~ **de costado** sidelight; ~ **de freno** brake light; ~ **del relámpago** flashlight; **luces de tráfico** traffic lights; **traje de luces** bullfighter's costume.

LL

llaga [ˈʎaɣa] nf wound.

llama [ˈʎama] nf flame; (ZOOL) llama.

llamada [ʎaˈmaða] nf call; ~ **al orden** call to order; **toque de** ~ (MIL) call-up; ~ **a pie de página** reference note.

llamamiento [ʎamaˈmjento] nm call.

llamar [ʎaˈmar] vt to call; (atención) to attract // vi (por teléfono) to telephone; (a la puerta) to knock/ring; (por señas) to beckon; (MIL) to call up; ~ **se** vr to be

called, be named; **¿cómo se llama Usted?** what's your name?

llamarada [ʎamaˈraða] nf (llamas) blaze; (rubor) flush; (fig) flare-up.

llamativo, a [ʎamaˈtiβo, a] a showy; (color) loud.

llamear [ʎameˈar] vi to blaze.

llaneza [ʎaˈneθa] nf (gen) simplicity; (honestidad) straightforwardness, frankness.

llano, a [ˈʎano, a] a (superficie) flat; (persona) straightforward; (estilo) clear // nm plain, flat ground.

llanta [ˈʎanta] nf (wheel) rim; (AM): ~ **de goma** tyre.

llanto [ˈʎanto] nm weeping.

llanura [ʎaˈnura] nf plain.

llave [ˈʎaβe] nf key; (del agua) tap; (MECÁNICA) spanner; (de la luz) switch; (MUS) key; ~ **inglesa** monkey wrench; ~ **de contacto** (AUTO) ignition key; **echar** ~ **a** to lock up; ~ **ro** nm keyring; **llavín** nm latchkey.

llegada [ʎeˈɣaða] nf arrival.

llegar [ʎeˈɣar] vi to arrive; (alcanzar) to reach; (bastar) to be enough; ~ **se** vr: ~ **se a** to approach; ~ **a** to manage to, succeed in; ~ **a ser** to become; ~ **a las manos de** to come into the hands of.

llenar [ʎeˈnar] vt (gen) to fill; (espacio) to cover; (formulario) to fill in or up; (deber) to fulfil; (fig) to heap.

lleno, a [ˈʎeno, a] a full, filled; (repleto) full up // nm (abundancia) abundance; (ASTRO) full moon; (TEATRO) full house; **dar de** ~ **contra un muro** to hit a wall head-on.

llevadero, a [ʎeβaˈðero, a] a bearable, tolerable.

llevar [ʎeˈβar] vt (gen) to take; (ropa) to wear; (cargar) to carry; (quitar) to take away; (conducir a alguien) to drive; (cargar hacia) to transport; (traer: dinero) to carry; (conducir) to lead; (MAT) to carry; ~ **se** vr to carry off, take away; **llevamos dos días aquí** we have been here for two days; **él me lleva 2 años** he's 2 years older than me; (COM): ~ **los libros** to keep the books; ~ **se bien** to get on well (together).

llorar [ʎoˈrar] vt, vi to weep; ~ **de risa** to cry with laughter.

lloriquear [ʎorikeˈar] vi to snivel, whimper.

lloro [ˈʎoro] nm weeping; **llorón, ona** a tearful // nm/f cry-baby; ~ **so, a** a (gen) weeping, tearful; (triste) sad, sorrowful.

llover [ʎoˈβer] vi to rain; ~ **se** vr (techo) to leak.

llovizna [ʎoˈβiθna] nf drizzle; **lloviznar** vi to drizzle.

llueve etc vb ver **llover.**

lluvia [ˈʎuβja] nf rain; ~ **radioactiva** radioactive fallout; **lluvioso, a** a rainy.

M

m abr de **metro; minuto.**

macarrones [maka'rrones] nmpl macaroni sg.

macerar [maθe'rar] vt to macerate; (fig) to mortify; ~**se** vr to mortify o.s.

maceta [ma'θeta] nf (de flores) pot of flowers; (para plantas) flowerpot; (mazo pequeño) mallet.

macilento, a [maθi'lento, a] a wan; (ojeroso) haggard.

macis ['maθis] nf mace.

macizo, a [ma'θiθo, a] a massive; (puerta) solid // nm mass, chunk; (de edificios) block; (AUTO) solid tyre.

mácula ['makula] nf stain, blemish; (ANAT) blind spot.

machacar [matʃa'kar] vt to crush, pound // vi to go on, keep on.

machamartillo [matʃamar'tiʎo]: **a ~** ad: cumplir **a ~** to carry out a task to the letter; eran cristianos **a ~** they were totally convinced Christians.

machete [ma'tʃete] nm (AM) machete, (large) knife.

macho ['matʃo] a male; (fig) virile // nm male; (fig) he-man.

machucar [matʃu'kar] vt to pound.

madeja [ma'ðexa] nf (de lana) skein, hank; (de pelo) mop.

madera [ma'ðera] nf wood; (fig) nature, character; **una ~** a piece of wood.

madero [ma'ðero] nm beam; (fig) ship.

madrastra [ma'ðrastra] nf stepmother.

madre ['maðre] a mother cpd; (AM) tremendous // nf mother; (causa) (AGR) main channel; (de vino etc) dregs pl; (de río) bed; ~ **política/soltera** mother-in-law/unmarried mother.

madreperla [maðre'perla] nf mother-of-pearl.

madreselva [maðre'selβa] nf honeysuckle.

madriguera [maðri'xera] nf burrow.

madrileño, a [maðri'leɲo, a] a of or from Madrid // nm/f native of Madrid.

madrina [ma'ðrina] nf (protectora) godmother; (ARQ) prop, shore; (TEC) brace; ~ **de boda** bridesmaid.

madrugada [maðru'xaða] nf early morning; (alba) dawn, daybreak; **madrugador, a** a early-rising; **madrugar** vi to get up early; (fig) to get ahead.

madurar [maðu'rar] vt, vi (fruta) to ripen; (fig) to mature; **madurez** nf ripeness; maturity; **maduro, a** a ripe; mature.

maestra [ma'estra] nf ver **maestro.**

maestría [maes'tria] nf mastery; (habilidad) skill, expertise.

maestro, a [ma'estro, a] a masterly; (perito) skilled, expert; (principal) main; (educado) trained // nm/f master/mistress; (que enseña) teacher // nm (autoridad) authority; (MUS) maestro;

(AM) skilled workman; **obra ~a** masterpiece; ~ **albañil** master mason.

magia ['maxja] nf magic; **mágico, a** a magic(al) // nm/f magician.

magisterio [maxis'terjo] nm (enseñanza) teaching; (profesión) teaching profession; (maestros) teachers pl.

magistrado [maxis'traðo] nm magistrate.

magistral [maxis'tral] a magisterial; (fig) masterly.

magnánimo, a [max'nanimo, a] a magnanimous.

magnate [max'nate] nm magnate, tycoon.

magnético, a [max'netiko, a] a magnetic; **magnetizar** vt to magnetize.

magnetofón [maxneto'fon], **magnetófono** [maxne'tofono] nm tape recorder; **magnetofónico, a** a: **cinta magnetofónica** recording tape.

magnífico, a [max'nifiko, a] a splendid, magnificent, wonderful.

magnitud [maxni'tuð] nf magnitude.

mago, a ['maxo, a] nm/f magician; los **Reyes M~s** the Magi, the Three Wise Men.

magro, a ['maxro, a] a (persona) thin, lean; (carne) lean.

magullar [maxu'ʎar] vt (amoratar) to bruise; (dañar) to damage; (fam: golpear) to bash, beat.

mahometano, a [maome'tano, a] a Mohammedan.

maíz [ma'iθ] nm maize, sweet corn.

majada [ma'xaða] nf (abrigo) sheepfold; (abono) dung.

majadero, a [maxa'ðero, a] a silly, stupid // nm (TEC) pestle; (canilla) bobbin.

majar [ma'xar] vt to crush, grind; (fig) to bother, pester.

majestad [maxes'tað] nf majesty; **majestuoso, a** a majestic.

majo, a ['maxo, a] a nice; (guapo) attractive, good-looking; (lujoso) smart.

mal [mal] ad badly; (equivocadamente) wrongly; (con dificultad) with difficulty // a = **malo** // nm evil; (desgracia) misfortune; (daño) harm, hurt; (MED) illness; ¡**menos ~!** just as well!; ~ **que bien** rightly or wrongly.

malabarismo [malaβa'rismo] nm juggling; **malabarista** nm/f juggler.

malaconsejado, a [malakonse'xaðo, a] a ill-advised.

malagueño, a [mala'xeɲo, a] a of or from Málaga.

malaria [ma'larja] nf malaria.

malbaratar [malβara'tar] vt (malgastar) to squander; (malvender) to sell off cheap.

malcontento, a [malkon'tento, a] a discontented.

malcriado, a [mal'krjaðo, a] a (grosero) rude, bad-mannered; (consentido) spoiled.

maldad [mal'dað] nf evil, wickedness.

maldecir [malde'θir] vt to curse // vi: ~ **de** to speak ill of.

maldición [maldi'θjon] nf curse.

maldito, a [mal'dito, a] *pp de* **maldecir** // *a* (*condenado*) damned; (*perverso*) wicked // *nf*: **soltar la** ~**a** to talk too much.

maleante [male'ante] *a* wicked // *nm/f* malefactor; **malear** *vt* to spoil; (*fig*) to corrupt.

malecón [male'kon] *nm* pier, jetty.

maledicencia [maleδi'θenθja] *nf* slander, scandal.

maleficiar [malefi'θjar] *vt* to harm, damage; (*hechizar*) to bewitch; **maleficio** *nm* curse, spell.

malestar [males'tar] *nm* (*gen*) discomfort; (*fig*) uneasiness; (*POL*) unrest.

maleta [ma'leta] *nf* case, suitcase; (*AUTO*) boot; **maletín** *nm* small case, bag.

malevolencia [maleßo'lenθja] *nf* malice, spite; **malévolo, a** *a* malicious, spiteful.

maleza [ma'leθa] *nf* (*hierbas malas*) weeds *pl*; (*arbustos*) thicket.

malgastar [malɣas'tar] *vt* (*tiempo, dinero*) to waste; (*salud*) to ruin.

malhechor, a [male'tʃor, a] *nm/f* malefactor; (*criminal*) criminal.

malicia [ma'liθja] *nf* (*maldad*) wickedness; (*astucia*) slyness, guile; (*mala intención*) malice, spite; (*carácter travieso*) mischievousness; ~**s** *nfpl* suspicions; **malicioso, a** *a* wicked, evil; sly, crafty; malicious, spiteful; mischievous.

malignidad [maliɣni'ðað] *nf* (*MED*) malignancy; (*malicia*) malice.

maligno, a [ma'liɣno, a] *a* evil; (*malévolo*) malicious; (*MED*) malignant.

malo, a ['malo, a] *a* bad; (*falso*) false // *nm/f* villain // *nf* spell of bad luck; **estar** ~ to be ill; **estar de** ~**as** to be in a bad mood.

malograr [malo'ɣrar] *vt* to spoil; (*plan*) to upset; (*tiempo, ocasión*) to waste; ~**se** *vr* (*plan etc*) to fail, come to grief; (*persona*) to die before one's time; **malogro** *nm* (*fracaso*) failure; (*pérdida*) waste; (*muerte*) early death.

malparado, a [malpa'raðo, a] *a*: **salir** ~ to come off badly.

malparir [malpa'rir] *vi* to have a miscarriage.

malquistar [malkis'tar] *vt* to estrange, cause a rift with/between.

malsano, a [mal'sano, a] *a* unhealthy.

Malta ['malta] *nf* Malta.

maltratar [maltra'tar] *vt* to ill-treat; **maltrato** *nm* ill-treatment; (*ofensa*) abuse, insults *pl*.

maltrecho, a [mal'tretʃo, a] *a* battered, damaged.

malvado, a [mal'ßaðo, a] *a* evil, villainous.

malvavisco [malßa'ßisko] *nm* marshmallow.

malversar [malßer'sar] *vt* to embezzle, misappropriate.

Malvinas [mal'ßinas]: **Islas** ~ *nfpl* Falkland Islands.

malla ['maʎa] *nf* mesh; (*de baño*) bathing costume; ~**s** *nfpl* tights; ~ **de alambre**

wire mesh; **hacer** ~ to knit.

Mallorca [ma'ʎorka] *nf* Majorca.

mama ['mama] *nf* (*de animal*) teat; (*de persona*) breast.

mamá [ma'ma] (*pl* ~**s**) *nf* (*fam*) mum, mummy.

mamar [ma'mar] *vt* (*pecho*) to suck; (*fig*) to absorb, assimilate // *vi* to suck.

mamarracho [mama'rratʃo] *nm* sight, mess.

mampara [mam'para] *nf* (*entre habitaciones*) partition; (*biombo*) screen.

mampostería [mamposte'ria] *nf* masonry.

mampuesto [mam'pwesto] *nm* (*piedra*) rough stone; (*muro*) wall, parapet; **de** ~ spare, emergency.

mamut [ma'mut] *nm* mammoth.

manada [ma'naða] *nf* (*rebaño*) herd; (*de ovejas*) flock; (*de lobos*) pack.

manantial [manan'tjal] *nm* spring; (*fuente*) fountain; (*fig*) source.

manar [ma'nar] *vt* to run with, flow with // *vi* to run, flow; (*abundar*) to abound.

mancebo [man'θeßo] *nm* (*joven*) young man; (*soltero*) bachelor; (*dependiente*) assistant.

mancilla [man'θiʎa] *nf* stain, blemish.

manco, a ['manko, a] *a* one-armed, one-handed; (*fig*) defective, faulty.

mancomún [manko'mun]: **de** ~ *ad* jointly, together; **mancomunar** *vt* to unite, bring together; (*recursos*) to pool; (*JUR*) to make jointly responsible; **mancomunarse** *vr* to unite, merge; **mancomunidad** *nf* union, association; (*POL*) commonwealth; (*JUR*) joint responsibility.

mancha ['mantʃa] *nf* stain, mark; (*boceto*) sketch, outline; **manchar** *vt* (*gen*) to stain, mark; (*ensuciar*) to soil, dirty.

manchego, a [man'tʃevo, a] *a* of *or* from La Mancha.

mandadero [manda'ðero] *nm* messenger; (*niño*) errand boy.

mandado [man'daðo] *nm* (*orden*) order; (*comisión*) commission, errand.

mandamiento [manda'mjento] *nm* (*orden*) order, command; (*REL*) commandment; ~ **judicial** warrant.

mandar [man'dar] *vt* (*ordenar*) to order; (*dirigir*) to lead, command; (*enviar*) to send; (*pedir*) to order, ask for // *vi* to be in charge; (*pey*) to be bossy; ~**se** *vr* (*MED*) to get about by o.s.; ¿**mande?** pardon?; ~ **hacer un traje** to have a suit made; ~**se cambiar** to go away, leave.

mandarín [manda'rin] *nm* mandarin // *nf* tangerine, mandarin.

mandatario, a [manda'tarjo, a] *nm/f* (*representante*) agent; (*AM*) leader.

mandato [man'dato] *nm* (*orden*) order; (*POL*) term of office; (: *territorio*) mandate; ~ **judicial** (*search*) warrant.

mandíbula [man'dißula] *nf* jaw.

mandil [man'dil] *nm* (*delantal*) apron; (*vestido*) pinafore dress.

mando ['mando] *nm* (MIL) command; (*de país*) rule; (*el primer lugar*) lead; (POL) term of office; (TEC) control; ~ **a la izquierda** left-hand drive; ~ **remoto** remote control.

mandolina [mando'lina] *nf* mandolin(e).

mandón, ona [man'don, ona] *a* bossy, domineering.

manea [ma'nea] *nf* hobble.

manejable [mane'xaβle] *a* manageable.

manejar [mane'xar] *vt* (*gen*) to manage; (*máquina*) to work, operate; (*idioma, caballo etc*) to handle; (*casa*) to run, manage; (AM) to drive; ~**se** *vr* (*comportarse*) to act, behave; (*arreglárselas*) to manage; (MED) to get about unaided; **manejo** *nm* management; handling; running; driving; (*facilidad de trato*) ease, confidence; **manejos** *nmpl* intrigues.

manera [ma'nera] *nf* way, manner, fashion; ~**s** *nfpl* manners; ~ **de ser** way of life; (*aire*) manner; **de ninguna** ~ no way, by no means; **de otra** ~ otherwise; **de todas** ~**s** at any rate; **no hay** ~ **de persuadirle** there's no way of convincing him.

manga ['manga] *nf* (*de camisa*) sleeve; (*de riego*) hose; (*tromba*) downpour; (*filtro*) filter; (NAUT) beam.

mangana [man'gana] *nf* lasso.

mango ['mango] *nm* handle; (BOT) mango.

mangonear [mangone'ar] *vt* to manage, boss about // *vi* (*meterse*) to meddle, interfere; (*ser mandón*) to boss people about.

manguera [man'gera] *nf* (*de riego*) hose; (*tubo*) pipe.

maní [ma'ni] *nm* (AM) peanut.

manía [ma'nia] *nf* (MED) mania; (*capricho*) rage, craze; (*disgusto*) dislike; (*malicia*) spite; **maníaco, a** *a* maniac(al) // *nm/f* maniac.

maniatar [manja'tar] *vt* to tie the hands of.

maniático, a [ma'njatiko, a] *a* maniac(al) // *nm/f* maniac.

manicomio [mani'komjo] *nm* asylum, mental hospital.

manifestación [manifesta'θjon] *nf* (*declaración*) statement, declaration; (*demostración*) show, manifestation; (POL) demonstration.

manifestar [manifes'tar] *vt* to show, manifest; (*declarar*) to state, declare; **manifiesto, a** *a* clear, manifest // *nm* manifesto.

manija [ma'nixa] *nf* handle.

manilla [ma'niʎa] *nf*: ~**s de hierro** handcuffs.

maniobra [ma'njoβra] *nf* manœuvring; (*maneja*) handling; (*fig*) manœuvre; (*estratagema*) stratagem; ~**s** *nfpl* manœuvres; **maniobrar** *vt* to manœuvre; (*manejar*) to handle.

manipulación [manipula'θjon] *nf* manipulation; **manipular** *vt* to

manipulate; (*manejar*) to handle.

maniquí [mani'ki] *nm* dummy // *nf* model.

manirroto, a [mani'rroto, a] *a* lavish, extravagant // *nm/f* spendthrift.

manivela [mani'βela] *nf* crank.

manjar [man'xar] *nm* (tasty) dish; ~ **blanco** blancmange.

mano ['mano] *nf* hand; (ZOOL) foot, paw; (*de pintura*) coat; (*serie*) lot, series; **a** ~ by hand; **a la** ~ on hand, within reach; **a** ~ **derecha/izquierda** on the right(-hand side)/left(-hand side); **de primera** ~ (at) first hand; **de segunda** ~ (at) second hand; **robo a** ~ **armada** armed robbery; ~ **de obra** labour, manpower; **estrechar la** ~ **a uno** to shake sb's hand.

manojo [ma'noxo] *nm* handful, bunch; ~ **de llaves** bunch of keys.

manoseado, a [manose'aðo, a] *a* well-worn; **manosear** *vt* (*tocar*) to handle, touch; (*desordenar*) to mess up, rumple; (*insistir en*) to overwork; (AM) to caress, fondle.

manotazo [mano'taθo] *nm* slap, smack.

mansalva [man'salβa]: **a** ~ *ad* without risk, without any danger.

mansedumbre [manse'ðumbre] *nf* gentleness, meekness.

mansión [man'sjon] *nf* mansion.

manso, a ['manso, a] *a* gentle, mild, meek; (*animal*) tame.

manta ['manta] *nf* blanket; (*abrigo*) shawl.

manteca [man'teka] *nf* fat; ~ **de cacahuete/cacao** peanut/cocoa butter; ~ **de cerdo** lard.

mantecado [mante'kaðo] *nm* ice-cream.

mantel [man'tel] *nm* tablecloth.

mantener [mante'ner] *vt* (*gen*) to support, maintain; (*alimentar*) to sustain; (*conservar*) to keep; (TEC) to maintain, service; ~**se** *vr* (*seguir de pie*) to be standing; (*no ceder*) to hold one's ground; (*subsistir*) to sustain o.s., keep going; **mantenimiento** *nm* maintenance; sustenance; (*sustento*) support.

mantequera [mante'kera] *nf* (*para hacer*) churn; (*para servir*) butter dish.

mantequilla [mante'kiʎa] *nf* butter.

mantilla [man'tiʎa] *nf* mantilla; ~**s** *nfpl* baby clothes.

manto ['manto] *nm* (*capa*) cloak; (*chal*) shawl; (*de ceremonia*) robe, gown.

mantón [man'ton] *nm* shawl.

manual [ma'nwal] *a* manual // *nm* manual, handbook.

manufactura [manufak'tura] *nf* manufacture; (*fábrica*) factory.

manuscrito, a [manus'krito, a] *a* hand-written // *nm* manuscript.

manutención [manuten'θjon] *nf* maintenance; (*sustento*) support.

manzana [man'θana] *nf* apple; (ARQ) block.

manzanilla [manθa'niʎa] *nf* (*planta*) camomile; (*infusión*) camomile tea; (*vino*) manzanilla.

manzano [man'θano] *nm* apple tree.

maña ['maɲa] nf (gen) skill, dexterity; (pey) guile; (costumbre) habit; (una ~) trick, knack.

mañana [ma'ɲana] ad tomorrow // nm future // nf morning; **de** o **por la** ~ in the morning; ¡**hasta** ~! see you tomorrow!; ~ **por la** ~ tomorrow morning; **mañanero, a** a early-rising.

mañoso, a [ma'ɲoso, a] a (hábil) skilful; (astuto) smart, clever.

mapa ['mapa] nm map.

maque ['make] nm lacquer.

maqueta [ma'keta] nf (scale) model.

maquillaje [maki'ʎaxe] nm make-up; (acto) making up; **maquillar** vt to make up; **maquillarse** vr to put on (some) make-up.

máquina ['makina] nf machine; (de tren) locomotive, engine; (cámara) camera; (fig) machinery; (: proyecto) plan, project; **escrito a** ~ typewritten; ~ **de afeitar** (safety) razor; ~ **de escribir** typewriter; ~ **de coser/lavar** sewing/washing machine.

maquinación [makina'θjon] nf machination, scheme, plot.

maquinal [maki'nal] a (fig) mechanical, automatic.

maquinaria [maki'narja] nf (máquinas) machinery; (mecanismo) mechanism, works pl.

maquinista [maki'nista] nm (de tren) engine driver; (TEC) operator; (NAUT) engineer.

mar [mar] nm o f sea; (marea) tide; ~ **adentro** o **afuera** out at sea; **en alta** ~ on the high seas; **la** ~ **de** (fam) lots of; **el M~ Negro/Báltico** the Black/Baltic Sea.

maraña [ma'raɲa] nf (maleza) thicket; (confusión) tangle.

maravilla [mara'βiʎa] nf marvel, wonder; (BOT) marigold; **maravillar** vt to astonish, amaze; **maravillarse** vr to be astonished, be amazed; **maravilloso, a** a wonderful, marvellous.

marca ['marka] nf (gen) mark; (sello) stamp; (COM) make, brand; **de** ~ excellent, outstanding; ~ **de fábrica** trademark.

marcado, a [mar'kaðo, a] a marked, strong.

marcar [mar'kar] vt (gen) to mark; (número de teléfono) to dial; (gol) to score; (números) to record, keep a tally of; (el pelo) to set; (fig) to indicate, point to // vi (DEPORTE) to score; (TELEC) to dial; ~**se** vr (NAUT) to take one's bearings; (fig) to make one's mark, stand out.

marcial [mar'θjal] a martial, military.

marciano, a [mar'θjano, a] a Martian.

marco ['marko] nm frame; (DEPORTE) goal-posts pl; (moneda) mark; (fig) framework; ~ **de chimenea** mantelpiece.

marcha ['martʃa] nf march; (TEC) running, working; (AUTO) gear; (velocidad) speed;

(fig) progress; (dirección) course; **poner en** ~ to put into gear; **dar** ~ **atrás** to reverse, put into reverse; **estar en** ~ to be under way, be in motion.

marchante, a [mar'tʃante, a] nm/f dealer, merchant; (AM: cliente) client, customer; (: buhonero) pedlar.

marchar [mar'tʃar] vi to go; (funcionar) to work, go; ~**se** vr to go away, leave.

marchitar [martʃi'tar] vt to wither, dry up; ~**se** vr to wither; (fig) to go into a decline; **marchito, a** a withered, faded; (fig) in decline.

marea [ma'rea] nf tide; (llovizna) drizzle.

marear [mare'ar] vt (NAUT) to sail, navigate; (fig) to annoy, upset; (MED): ~ **a uno** to make sb feel sick; ~**se** vr (tener náuseas) to feel/be sick; (desvanecerse) to feel faint; (aturdirse) to feel dizzy; (fam: emborracharse) to get a bit drunk.

maremoto [mare'moto] nm tidal wave.

mareo [ma'reo] nm (náusea) sick feeling; (aturdimiento) dizziness; (fam: lata) nuisance.

marfil [mar'fil] nm ivory.

margarina [marɣa'rina] nf margarine.

margarita [marɣa'rita] nf (BOT) daisy; (perla) pearl.

margen ['marxen] nm (borde) edge, border; (fig) margin, space // nf bank; **dar** ~ **para** to give an opportunity for; **mantenerse al** ~ to keep out (of things).

marica [ma'rika] nm magpie; (fam) sissy.

maricón [mari'kon] nm (fam) queer (fam).

marido [ma'riðo] nm husband.

marijuana [mari'xwana] nf marijuana, cannabis.

marina [ma'rina] nf navy; ~ **mercante** merchant navy.

marinero, a [mari'nero, a] a sea cpd; (barco) seaworthy // nm sailor, seaman.

marino, a [ma'rino, a] a sea cpd, marine // nm sailor.

marioneta [marjo'neta] nf puppet.

mariposa [mari'posa] nf butterfly.

mariscos [ma'riskos] nmpl shellfish, seafood sg.

marisma [ma'risma] nf marsh, swamp.

marítimo, a [ma'ritimo, a] a sea cpd, maritime.

marmita [mar'mita] nf pot.

mármol ['marmol] nm marble; **marmóreo, a** a marble.

marqués, esa [mar'kes, esa] nm/f marquis/marchioness.

marrar [ma'rrar] vi to miss.

marrón [ma'rron] a brown.

marroquí [marro'ki] a Moroccan // nm Morocco (leather).

Marruecos [ma'rrwekos] nm Morocco.

Marsellas [mar'seʎas] n Marseille.

martes ['martes] nm inv Tuesday.

martillar [marti'ʎar] vt to hammer.

martillo [mar'tiʎo] nm hammer; ~

neumático pneumatic drill; ~ **de orejas** claw-hammer.

mártir ['martir] nm/f martyr; **martirio** nm martyrdom; (fig) torture, torment.

marxismo [mark'sismo] nm Marxism; **marxista** nm/f Marxist.

marzo ['marθo] nm March.

mas [mas] conj but.

más [mas] a, ad more; (superlativo) most // conj and, plus; **es** ~ **de medianoche** it's after midnight; **el libro** ~ **leído del año** the most-read book of the year; **¡qué perro** ~ **feo!** what an ugly dog!; ~ **de,** ~ **de lo que,** ~ **que** more than; ~ **bien** rather; ~ **o menos** more or less.

masa ['masa] nf (mezcla) dough; (volumen) volume, mass; (FÍSICA) mass; (ELEC) earth; **en** ~ en masse; **las** ~**s** the masses.

masacre [ma'sakre] nm massacre.

masaje [ma'saxe] nm massage.

mascar [mas'kar] vt to chew; (fig) to mumble, mutter.

máscara ['maskara] nf (gen) mask // nm/f masked person; **mascarada** nf masquerade.

masculino, a [masku'lino, a] a masculine; (BIO) male.

mascullar [masku'ʎar] vt to mumble, mutter.

masilla [ma'siʎa] nf putty.

masivo, a [ma'siβo, a] a (enorme) massive; (en masa) mass, en masse.

masón [ma'son] nm (free)mason.

masoquista [maso'kista] nm/f masochist.

masticar [masti'kar] vt to chew; (fig) to ponder.

mástil ['mastil] nm (de navío) mast; (de guitarra) neck; (sostén) post, support.

mastín [mas'tin] nm mastiff; ~ **danés** Great Dane.

masturbación [masturβa'θjon] nf masturbation; **masturbarse** vr to masturbate.

mata ['mata] nf bush, shrub; (de hierbas) tuft; (campo) field; (AM) clump (of trees).

matadero [mata'ðero] nm slaughterhouse, abattoir.

matador, a [mata'ðor, a] a killing // nm/f killer // nm (TAUR) matador, bullfighter.

matanza [ma'tanθa] nf (de personas) killing; (de animales) slaughter(ing).

matar [ma'tar] vt, vi to kill; ~**se** vr (suicidarse) to kill o.s., commit suicide; (por otro) to be killed; ~ **el hambre** to stave off hunger.

mate ['mate] a (sin brillo: color) dull // nm (en ajedrez) (check)mate; (AM: hierba) maté; (: vasija) gourd.

matemáticas [mate'matikas] nfpl mathematics; **matemático, a** a mathematical // nm/f mathematician.

materia [ma'terja] nf (gen) matter; (TEC) material; **en** ~ **de** on the subject of; ~ **prima** raw material; **material** a material; (dolor) physical // nm material; (TEC) equipment; **materialismo** nm

materialism; **materialista** a materialist(ic); **materialmente** ad materially; (fig) absolutely.

maternal [mater'nal] a motherly, maternal.

maternidad [materni'ðað] nf motherhood, maternity; **materno, a** a motherly, maternal; (lengua) mother cpd.

matinal [mati'nal] a morning cpd.

matiz [ma'tiθ] nm shade; ~**ar** vt (dar tonos de) to tinge, tint; (variar) to vary; (ARTE) to blend.

matón [ma'ton] nm bully.

matorral [mato'rral] nm thicket.

matraca [ma'traka] nf rattle.

matrícula [ma'trikula] nf (registro) register; (AUTO) registration number; (: placa) licence plate; **matricular** vt to register, enrol.

matrimonial [matrimo'njal] a matrimonial.

matrimonio [matri'monjo] nm (boda) wedding; (pareja) (married) couple; (unión) marriage.

matriz [ma'triθ] nf womb; (TEC) mould; **casa** ~ (COM) head office.

matrona [ma'trona] nf (persona de edad) matron; (partera) midwife.

matute [ma'tute] nm contraband.

maullar [mau'ʎar] vi to mew, miaow.

mausoleo [mauso'leo] nm mausoleum.

maxilar [maksi'lar] nm jaw(bone).

máxima ['maksima] ver **máximo**.

máxime ['maksime] ad especially.

máximo, a ['maksimo, a] a maximum; (más alto) highest; (más grande) greatest // nm maximum // nf maxim.

mayo ['majo] nm May.

mayonesa [majo'nesa] nf mayonnaise.

mayor [ma'jor] a (gen) main, chief; (adulto) adult; (de edad avanzada) elderly; (MUS) major; (comparativo: de tamaño) bigger; (: de edad) older; (superlativo: de tamaño) biggest; (: de edad) oldest // nm chief, boss; **al por** ~ wholesale; ~ **de edad** adult; ~**es** nmpl ancestors.

mayoral [majo'ral] nm foreman.

mayordomo [major'ðomo] nm (criado) butler; (de hotel) steward.

mayoría [majo'ria] nf majority, greater part.

mayorista [majo'rista] nm/f wholesaler.

mayúsculo, a [ma'juskulo, a] a (fig) big, tremendous // nf capital (letter).

mazapán [maθa'pan] nm marzipan.

mazo ['maθo] nm (martillo) mallet; (de flores) bunch; (fig) bore; (DEPORTE) bat; (palo) club.

me [me] pron (directo) me; (indirecto) (to) me; (reflexivo) (to) myself; **¡démelo!** give it to me!

mecánico, a [me'kaniko, a] a mechanical // nm/f mechanic // a (estudio) mechanics sg; (mecanismo) mechanism.

mecanismo [meka'nismo] nm mechanism; (marcha) gear.

mecanografía [mekanoˑraˈfia] *nf* typewriting; **mecanógrafo, a** *nm/f* typist.

mecedor, a [meθeˈðor, a] *a* rocking // *nm* (*columpio*) swing // *nf* rocking chair.

mecer [meˈθer] *vt* (*cuna*) to rock; (*líquido*) to stir; ∼**se** *vr* to rock; (*ramo*) to sway.

mechero [meˈtʃero] *nm* (cigarette) lighter.

mechón [meˈtʃon] *nm* (*gen*) tuft; (*manojo*) bundle; (*de pelo*) lock.

medalla [meˈðaʎa] *nf* medal.

media [ˈmeðja] *nf ver* **medio.**

mediado, a [meˈðjaðo, a] *a* half-full; (*trabajo*) half-complete; **a** ∼**s de** in the middle of, halfway through.

mediano, a [meˈðjano, a] *a* (*regular*) medium, average; (*mediocre*) mediocre; (*indiferente*) indifferent.

medianoche [meðja'notʃe] *nf* midnight.

mediante [meˈðjante] *ad* by (means of), through.

mediar [meˈðjar] *vi* (*llegar a la mitad*) to get to the middle, get halfway; (*estar en medio*) to be in the middle; (*interceder*) to mediate, intervene.

medicación [meðikaˈθjon] *nf* medication, treatment.

medicamento [meðikaˈmento] *nm* medicine, drug.

medicina [meðiˈθina] *nf* medicine.

medición [meðiˈθjon] *nf* measurement.

médico, a [ˈmeðiko, a] *a* medical // *nm/f* doctor.

medida [meˈðiða] *nf* (*gen*) measure; (*medición*) measurement; (*prudencia*) moderation, prudence; **en cierta/gran** ∼ up to a point/to a great extent; **un traje a la** ∼ made-to-measure suit; ∼ **de cuello** collar size; **a** ∼ **de** in proportion to; (*de acuerdo con*) in keeping with.

medio, a [ˈmeðjo, a] *a* half (a); (*punto*) mid, middle; (*promedio*) average // *ad* half // *nm* (*centro*) middle, centre; (*promedio*) average; (*DEPORTE*) half-back; (*método*) means, way; (*ambiente*) environment // *nf* (*prenda de vestir*) stocking; (*promedio*) average; ∼**s** *nmpl* means, resources; ∼ **litro** half a litre; **las tres y** ∼ **a** half past three; **M**∼ **Oriente** Middle East; **a** ∼ **terminar** half finished; **pagar a** ∼**as** to share the cost; **hacer** ∼ **a** to knit.

mediocre [meˈðjokre] *a* middling, average; (*pey*) mediocre.

mediodía [meðjo'ðia] *nm* midday, noon.

medir [meˈðir] *vt* (*gen*) to measure; (*pesar*) to weigh up // *vi* to measure.

meditar [meðiˈtar] *vt* to ponder, think over, meditate (on); (*planear*) to think out.

mediterráneo, a [meðiteˈrraneo, a] *a* Mediterranean // *nm*: **el M**∼ the Mediterranean.

medroso, a [meˈðroso, a] *a* fearful, timid.

medusa [meˈðusa] *nf* jellyfish.

megáfono [meˈɣafono] *nm* megaphone.

megalómano, a [meɣaˈlomano, a] *nm/f* megalomaniac.

mejicano, a [mexiˈkano, a] *a, nm/f* Mexican.

Méjico [ˈmexiko] *nm* Mexico.

mejilla [meˈxiʎa] *nf* cheek.

mejor [meˈxor] *a, ad* (*comparativo*) better; (*superlativo*) best; **a lo** ∼ probably; (*quizá*) maybe; ∼ **dicho** rather; **tanto** ∼ so much the better.

mejora [meˈxora] *nf* improvement; **mejorar** *vt* to improve, make better // *vi*, **mejorarse** *vr* to improve, get better.

melancólico, a [melanˈkoliko, a] *a* (*triste*) sad, melancholy; (*soñador*) dreamy.

melena [meˈlena] *nf* (*de persona*) long hair; (*del león*) mane.

melocotón [meloko'ton] *nm* peach.

melodía [meloˈðia] *nf* melody; (*aire*) tune.

melodrama [meloˈðrama] *nm* melodrama; **melodramático, a** *a* melodramatic.

melón [meˈlon] *nm* melon.

meloso, a [meˈloso, a] *a* honeyed, sweet.

mellizo, a [meˈʎiθo, a] *a, nm/f* twin.

membrete [memˈbrete] *nm* letterhead.

memorable [memoˈraßle] *a* memorable.

memorándum [memoˈrandum] *nm* (*libro*) notebook; (*comunicación*) memorandum.

memoria [meˈmorja] *nf* (*gen*) memory; (*informe*) report; ∼**s** *nfpl* (*de autor*) memoirs.

mencionar [menθjo'nar] *vt* to mention.

mendigar [mendiˈɣar] *vt* to beg (for).

mendigo, a [menˈdixo, a] *nm/f* beggar.

mendrugo [menˈdruxo] *nm* crust.

menear [meneˈar] *vt* to move; (*fig*) to handle; ∼**se** *vr* to shake; (*balancearse*) to sway; (*moverse*) to move; (*fig*) to get a move on.

menester [menesˈter] *nm* (*necesidad*) necessity; (*ocupación*) job; ∼**es** *nmpl* (*deberes*) duties; (*instrumentos*) tackle *sg*, tools; **es** ∼ it is necessary.

mengua [ˈmengwa] *nf* (*disminución*) decrease; (*falta*) lack; (*pobreza*) poverty; (*fig*) discredit; ∼**do, a** *a* cowardly, timid; (*cicatero*) mean.

menguante [menˈgwante] *a* decreasing, diminishing; **menguar** *vt* to lessen, diminish; (*fig*) to discredit // *vi* to diminish, decrease; (*fig*) to decline.

menopausia [meno'pausja] *nf* menopause.

menor [meˈnor] *a* (*más pequeño*: *comparativo*) smaller; (: *superlativo*) smallest; (*más joven*: *comparativo*) younger; (: *superlativo*) youngest; (*MUS*) minor // *nm/f* (*joven*) young person, juvenile; **no tengo la** ∼ **idea** I haven't the slightest idea; **al por** ∼ retail; ∼ **de edad** person under age.

menos [ˈmenos] *a* (*comparativo*: *sg*) less; (: *pl*) fewer; (*superlativo*: *sg*) least; (: *pl*) fewest // *ad* (*comparativo*) less; (*superlativo*) least // *conj* except // *prep* (*MAT*) minus; **es lo** ∼ **que puedo hacer**

it's the least I can do; **lo ~ posible** as little as possible; **a ~ que** unless; **te echo de ~** I miss you; **al o por lo ~** at least.

menoscabar [menoska'ßar] vt (estropear) to damage, harm; (acortar) to lessen, reduce; (fig) to discredit.

menospreciar [menospre'θjar] vt to underrate, undervalue; (despreciar) to scorn, despise; **menosprecio** nm underrating, undervaluation; scorn, contempt.

mensaje [men'saxe] nm message; **~ro, a** nm/f messenger.

menstruar [mens'trwar] vi to menstruate; **menstruo** nm menstruation, period.

mensual [men'swal] a monthly; **100 ptas ~es** 100 ptas. a month.

menta ['menta] nf mint.

mental [men'tal] a mental.

mentar [men'tar] vt to mention, name.

mente ['mente] nf mind.

mentecato, a [mente'kato, a] a silly, stupid // nm/f fool, idiot.

mentir [men'tir] vi to lie; **~a** nf (una ~a) lie; (acto) lying; (invención) fiction; **parece ~a que...** it seems incredible that..., I can't believe that...; **~oso, a** a lying; (texto) full of errors // nm/f liar.

mentís [men'tis] nm: **dar el ~ a** to deny.

menú [me'nu] nm menu.

menudeo [menu'ðeo] nm: **vender al ~** to sell retail.

menudo, a [me'nuðo, a] a (pequeño) small, tiny; (sin importancia) petty, insignificant; (exacto) exact, meticulous; **¡~ negocio!** (fam) some deal!; **a ~** often, frequently; **por ~** in detail.

meñique [me'ɲike] nm little finger.

meollo [me'oʎo] nm (gen) marrow; (fig) core.

mercadería [merkaðe'ria] nf commodity; **~s** nfpl goods, merchandise sg.

mercado [mer'kaðo] nm market; **M~ Común** Common Market.

mercadotecnia [merkaðo'teknja] nf marketing.

mercancía [merkan'θia] nf commodity; **~s** nfpl goods, merchandise sg.

mercantil [merkan'til] a mercantile, commercial.

mercenario, a [merθe'narjo, a] a, nm mercenary.

mercurio [mer'kurjo] nm mercury.

merecer [mere'θer] vt to deserve, merit // vi to be deserving, be worthy; **merece la pena** it's worthwhile; **merecido, a** a (well) deserved; **llevar su merecido** to get one's deserts.

merendar [meren'dar] vt to have for tea // vi to have tea; (en el campo) to have a picnic.

merengue [me'renge] nm meringue.

merienda [me'rjenda] nf (light) tea, afternoon snack; (de campo) picnic.

mérito ['merito] nm merit; (valor) worth, value.

merluza [mer'luθa] nf hake.

merma ['merma] nf decrease; (pérdida) wastage; **mermar** vt to reduce, lessen // vi, **mermarse** vr to decrease, dwindle; (fig) to waste away.

mermelada [merme'laða] nf jam.

mero, a ['mero, a] a mere.

mes [mes] nm month; (salario) month's pay.

mesa ['mesa] nf table; (de trabajo) desk; (GEO) plateau; (ARQ) landing; **~ directiva** board; **poner/quitar la ~** to lay/clear the table.

meseta [me'seta] nf (GEO) meseta, tableland; (ARQ) landing.

mesón [me'son] nm olde-worlde bar.

mestizo, a [mes'tiθo, a] a half-caste, of mixed race; (ZOOL) crossbred // nm/f half-caste, half-breed.

mesura [me'sura] nf (moderación) moderation, restraint; (dignidad) dignity, calm; (cortesía) courtesy.

meta ['meta] nf goal; (de carrera) finish.

metáfora [me'tafora] nf metaphor.

metal [me'tal] nm (materia) metal; (MUS) brass; (fig) quality; **metálico, a** a metallic; (de metal) metal // nm cash.

metalurgia [meta'lurxja] nf metallurgy.

meteoro [mete'oro] nm meteor.

meter [me'ter] vt (colocar) to put, place; (introducir) to put in, insert; (añadir) to add; (involucrar) to involve; (causar) to make, cause; **~se** vr: **~se en** to go into, enter; (fig) to interfere in, meddle in; **~se a** to start; **~se a escritor** to become a writer; **~se con alguien** to provoke sb, pick a quarrel with sb.

meticuloso, a [metiku'loso, a] a meticulous, thorough.

metódico, a [me'toðiko, a] a methodical.

metodismo [meto'ðismo] nm Methodism.

método ['metoðo] nm method.

metralleta [metra'ʎeta] nf submachine gun.

métrico, a ['metriko, a] a metric.

metro ['metro] nm metre; (tren) underground, subway.

México ['meksiko] nm Mexico.

mezcla ['meθkla] nf mixture; (ARQ) mortar; **mezclar** vt to mix (up); (naipes) to shuffle; **mezclarse** vr to mix, mingle; **mezclarse en** to get mixed up in, get involved in.

mezquino, a [meθ'kino, a] a (cicatero) mean; (pobre) miserable.

mezquita [meθ'kita] nf mosque.

mi [mi] det my.

mí [mi] pron me; myself.

miaja ['mjaxa] nf crumb.

microbús [mikro'ßus] nm minibus.

micrófono [mi'krofono] nm microphone.

microlentillas [mikrolen'tiʎas] nfpl contact lenses.

microscopio [mikro'skopjo] nm microscope.

miedo [mjeðo] nm fear; (nerviosismo) apprehension, nervousness; **tener ~** to be afraid; **de** ~ wonderful, marvellous; **hace un frío de** ~ (*fam*) it's terribly cold; ~**so, a** *a* fearful, timid.

miel [mjel] *nf* honey.

miembro ['mjembro] *nm* limb; (*socio*) member; ~ **viril** penis.

mientes ['mjentes] *nfpl*: **no parar** ~ **en** to pay no attention to; **traer a las** ~ to recall.

mientras ['mjentras] *conj* while; (*duración*) as long as // *ad* meanwhile; ~ **tanto** meanwhile; ~ **más tiene, más quiere** the more he has, the more he wants.

miércoles ['mjerkoles] *nm inv* Wednesday.

mierda ['mjerða] *nf* (*fam*) shit.

miga ['miɣa] *nf* crumb; (*fig*) essence; **hacer buenas** ~**s** (*fam*) to get on well.

migración [miɣra'θjon] *nf* migration.

mil [mil] *num* thousand; **dos** ~ **libras** two thousand pounds.

milagro [mi'laɣro] *nm* miracle; ~**so, a** *a* miraculous.

mili ['mili] *nf*: **hacer la** ~ (*fam*) to do one's military service.

milicia [mi'liθja] *nf* (*MIL*) militia; (: *arte*) art of war; (*servicio militar*) military service.

milímetro [mi'limetro] *nm* millimetre.

militante [mili'tante] *a* militant.

militar [mili'tar] *a* (*del ejército*) military; (*guerrero*) warlike // *nm/f* soldier // *vi* to serve in the army; (*fig*) to be a member of a party.

milla ['miʎa] *nf* mile.

millar [mi'ʎar] *nm* thousand.

millón [mi'ʎon] *num* million; **millonario, a** *nm/f* millionaire.

mimar [mi'mar] *vt* (*gen*) to spoil, pamper; (*al poderoso*) to flatter.

mimbre ['mimbre] *nm* wicker.

mímica [mi'mika] *nf* (*para comunicarse*) sign language; (*imitación*) mimicry.

mimo ['mimo] *nm* (*caricia*) affectionate caress; (*de niño*) spoiling; (*TEATRO*) mime.

mina ['mina] *nf* mine; **minar** *vt* to mine; (*fig*) to undermine.

mineral [mine'ral] *a* mineral // *nm* (*GEO*) mineral; (*mena*) ore.

minero, a [mi'nero, a] *a* mining // *nm/f* miner.

miniatura [minja'tura] *a inv, nf* miniature.

minifalda [mini'falda] *nf* miniskirt.

mínimo, a [ˈminimo, a] *a, nm* minimum.

ministerio [minis'terjo] *nm* Ministry; **M~ de Hacienda/del Exterior** Treasury/Foreign Office.

ministro [mi'nistro] *nm* minister.

minorar [mino'rar] *vt* to reduce.

minoría [mino'ria] *nf* minority.

minucioso, a [minu'θjoso, a] *a* thorough, meticulous; (*prolijo*) very detailed.

minúsculo, a [mi'nuskulo, a] *a* tiny, minute // *nf* small letter.

minuta [mi'nuta] *nf* (*de comida*) menu;

(*borrador*) rough draft; (*apunte*) note.

minutero [minu'tero] *nm* minute hand.

minuto [mi'nuto] *nm* minute.

mío, a ['mio, a] *pron*: **el** ~ mine; **un amigo** ~ a friend of mine; **lo** ~ what is mine.

miope [mi'ope] *a* short-sighted.

mira ['mira] *nf* (*de arma*) sight(s) (*pl*) (*fig*) aim, intention; **estar a la** ~ to be on the look-out, keep watch; ~**da** *nf* look, glance; (*expresión*) look, expression; **echar una** ~**da a** to glance at; ~**do, a** *a* (*sensato*) sensible; (*considerado*) considerate; **bien/mal** ~**do** well/not well thought of.

mirador [mira'ðor] *nm* viewpoint, vantage point.

mirar [mi'rar] *vt* to look at; (*observar*) to watch; (*considerar*) to consider, think over; (*vigilar, cuidar*) to watch, look after // *vi* to look; (*ARQ*) to face; ~**se** *vr* (*dos personas*) to look at each other; ~ **bien/mal** to think highly of/have a poor opinion of; ~**se al espejo** to look at o.s. in the mirror.

mirlo ['mirlo] *nm* blackbird.

misa ['misa] *nf* mass.

miserable [mise'raβle] *a* (*avaro*) mean, stingy; (*nimio*) miserable, paltry; (*lugar*) squalid; (*fam*) vile, despicable // *nm/f* (*indigente*) wretch, poor person; (*perverso*) rotter.

miseria [mi'serja] *nf* misery; (*pobreza*) poverty; (*tacañería*) meanness, stinginess; (*condiciones*) squalor; **una** ~ a pittance.

misericordia [miseri'korðja] *nf* (*compasión*) compassion, pity; (*piedad*) mercy.

misil [mi'sil] *nm* missile.

misión [mi'sjon] *nf* mission; **misionero, a** *nm/f* missionary.

mismo, a [ˈmismo, a] *a* (*semejante*) same; (*después de pronombre*) -self; (*para énfasis*) very; **el** ~ **traje** the same suit; **en ese** ~ **momento** at that very moment; **vino el** ~ **Ministro** the minister himself came; **yo** ~ **lo vi** I saw it myself; **lo** ~ the same (thing); **da lo** ~ it's all the same; **quedamos en las** ~**as** we're no further forward // *ad*: **aquí/hoy** ~ right here/this very day; **ahora** ~ right now // *conj*: **lo** ~ **que** just like, just as; **por lo** ~ for the same reason.

misterio [mis'terjo] *nm* (*gen*) mystery; (*lo secreto*) secrecy.

mitad [mi'tað] *nf* (*medio*) half; (*centro*) middle; **a** ~ **de precio** (at) half-price; **en** **o a** ~ **del camino** halfway along the road; **cortar por la** ~ to cut through the middle.

mitin ['mitin] *nm* meeting.

mito ['mito] *nm* myth.

mixto, a ['miksto, a] *a* mixed.

mobiliario [moβi'ljarjo] *nm* furniture.

mocedad [moθe'ðað] *nf* youth.

moción [mo'θjon] *nf* motion.

mochila [mo'tʃila] *nf* rucksack.

moda ['moða] *nf* (*gen*) fashion; (*estilo*) style; **de** *o* **a la** ~ in fashion, fashionable; **pasado** *o* **fuera de** ~ out of fashion.

modales [mo'ðales] *nmpl* manners.

modalidad [moðali'ðað] *nf* kind, variety.

modelar [moðe'lar] *vt* to model.

modelo [mo'ðelo] *a inv, nm/f* model.

moderado, a [moðe'raðo, a] *a* moderate.

moderar [moðe'rar] *vt* to moderate; (*violencia*) to restrain, control; (*velocidad*) to reduce; ~**se** *vr* to restrain o.s., control o.s.

modernizar [moðerni'θar] *vt* to modernize.

moderno, a [mo'ðerno, a] *a* modern; (*actual*) present-day.

modestia [mo'ðestja] *nf* modesty; **modesto, a** *a* modest.

módico, a ['moðiko, a] *a* moderate, reasonable.

modificar [moðifi'kar] *vt* to modify.

modista [mo'ðista] *nm/f* dressmaker.

modo ['moðo] *nm* (*manera, forma*) way, manner; (*MUS*) mode; ~**s** *nmpl* manners; **de ningún** ~ in no way; **de todos** ~**s** at any rate; ~ **de empleo** directions *pl* (for use).

modorra [mo'ðorra] *nf* drowsiness.

modular [moðu'lar] *vt* to modulate.

mofa ['mofa] *nf* mockery, ridicule; **hacer** ~ **de** to mock; **mofar** *vi* to mock, scoff; **mofarse** *vr*: **mofarse de** to mock, scoff at.

mohíno, a [mo'ino, a] *a* (*triste*) gloomy, depressed; (*enojado*) sulky.

moho ['moo] *nm* (*BOT*) mould; (*oxidación*) rust; ~**so, a** *a* mouldy; rusty.

mojar [mo'xar] *vt* to wet; (*humedecer*) to damp(en), moisten; (*calar*) to soak // *vi*: ~ **en** to get involved in; ~**se** *vr* to get wet.

mojón [mo'xon] *nm* (*en un camino*) signpost; (*montón*) heap, pile.

molde ['molde] *nm* mould; (*de costura*) pattern; (*fig*) model; **el vestido le está de** ~ the dress is just right for her; ~**ar** *vt* to mould.

mole ['mole] *nf* mass, bulk.

moledora [mole'ðora] *nf* grinder, mill.

moler [mo'ler] *vt* to grind, crush; (*cansar*) to tire out, exhaust; (*irritar*) to annoy.

molestar [moles'tar] *vt* (*gen*) to bother; (*fastidiar*) to annoy; (*incomodar*) to inconvenience, put out // *vi* to be a nuisance; ~**se** *vr* to bother; (*incomodarse*) to go to trouble; (*ofenderse*) to take offence.

molestia [mo'lestja] *nf* (*gen*) bother, trouble; (*incomodidad*) inconvenience; (*MED*) discomfort; **es una** ~ it's a nuisance; **molesto, a** *a* (*que causa molestia*) annoying; (*incómodo*) inconvenient; (*inquieto*) uncomfortable, ill at ease; (*enfadado*) annoyed.

molinillo [moli'niʎo] *nm*: ~ **de café/carne** coffee grinder/mincer.

molino [mo'lino] *nm* (*edificio*) mill; (*máquina*) grinder.

momentáneo, a [momen'taneo, a] *a* momentary.

momento [mo'mento] *nm* (*gen*) moment; (*TEC*) momentum; **de** ~ at the moment, for the moment.

momia ['momja] *nf* mummy.

monarca [mo'narka] *nm/f* monarch, ruler; **monarquía** *nf* monarchy; **monarquista** *nm/f* royalist, monarchist.

monasterio [monas'terjo] *nm* monastery.

mondar [mon'dar] *vt* (*limpiar*) to clean; (*podar*) to prune, trim; (*pelar*) to peel; ~**se** *vr*: ~**se los dientes** to pick one's teeth.

moneda [mo'neða] *nf* (*tipo de dinero*) currency, money; (*pieza*) coin; **una** ~ **de 5p** a 5p piece; **monedero** *nm* purse; **monetario, a** *a* monetary, financial.

monja ['monxa] *nf* nun.

monje ['monxe] *nm* monk.

mono, a ['mono, a] *a* (*bonito*) lovely, pretty; (*gracioso*) nice, charming // *nm/f* monkey, ape // *nm* (*overoles*) overalls *pl*.

monopolio [mono'poljo] *nm* monopoly; **monopolizar** *vt* to monopolize.

monoriel [mono'riel] *nm* monorail.

monotonía [monoto'nia] *nf* (*sonido*) monotone; (*fig*) monotony.

monótono, a [mo'notono, a] *a* monotonous.

monstruo ['monstrwo] *nm* monster // *a* fantastic; ~**so, a** *a* monstrous.

monta ['monta] *nf* total, sum; **de poca** ~ unimportant, of little account.

montaje [mon'taxe] *nm* assembly; (*ARQ*) erection; (*TEATRO*) décor; (*CINE*) montage.

montaña [mon'taɲa] *nf* (*monte*) mountain; (*sierra*) mountains *pl*, mountainous area; (*AM*) forest; ~ **rusa** roller coaster; **montañés, esa** *a* mountain *cpd* // *nm/f* highlander; (*de Santander*) native of the Santander region.

montar [mon'tar] *vt* (*subir a*) to mount, get on; (*caballo etc*) to ride; (*TEC*) to assemble, put together; (*ARQ*) to erect; (*negocio*) to set up; (*arma*) to cock; (*colocar*) to lift on to // *vi* to mount, get on; (*sobresalir*) to overlap; ~ **a** to amount to, come to; ~ **en cólera** to get angry.

montaraz [monta'raθ] *a* mountain *cpd*, highland *cpd*; (*salvaje*) wild, untamed; (*pey*) uncivilized.

monte ['monte] *nm* (*montaña*) mountain; (*bosque*) woodland; (*área sin cultivar*) wild area, wild country; ~ **de Piedad** pawnshop; ~ **alto** forest; ~ **bajo** scrub(land).

monto ['monto] *nm* total, amount.

montón [mon'ton] *nm* heap, pile; (*fig*): **un** ~ **de** heaps of, lots of.

monumento [monu'mento] *nm* monument.

monzón [mon'θon] *nm* monsoon.

moña ['moɲa] *nf* hair ribbon.

moño ['moɲo] *nm* bun.

morado, a [mo'raðo, a] a purple; (*violado*) violet // *nm* bruise // *nf* (*casa*) dwelling, abode; (*período*) stay.

moral [mo'ral] a moral // *nf* (*ética*) ethics; (*moralidad*) morals *pl*, morality; (*ánimo*) morale.

moraleja [mora'lexa] *nf* moral.

moralizar [morali'θar] *vt* to moralize.

morboso, a [mor'βoso, a] a morbid.

morcilla [mor'θiʎa] *nf* blood sausage, black pudding.

mordaz [mor'ðaθ] a biting, scathing.

mordaza [mor'ðaθa] *nf* (*para la boca*) gag; (*TEC*) clamp.

morder [mor'ðer] *vt* to bite; (*mordisquear*) to nibble; (*consumir*) to eat away, eat into; **mordisco** *nm* bite.

moreno, a [mo'reno, a] a (*color*) (dark) brown; (*de tez*) dark; (*de pelo* ~) dark-haired; (*negro*) Negro.

moretón [more'ton] *nm* (*fam*) bruise.

morfina [mor'fina] *nf* morphine.

moribundo, a [mori'βundo, a] a dying.

morir [mo'rir] *vi* (*gen*) to die; (*fuego*) to die down; (*luz*) to go out; ~**se** *vr* (*gen*) to die; (*pierna etc*) to go to sleep, go numb; (*fig*) to be dying; **fue muerto en un accidente** he was killed in an accident; ~**se por algo** to be dying for sth.

morisco, a [mo'risko, a], **moro, a** ['moro, a] a Moorish // *nm/f* Moor.

morral [mo'rral] *nm* haversack.

morsa ['morsa] *nf* walrus.

mortaja [mor'taxa] *nf* shroud; (*TEC*) mortise; (*AM*) cigarette paper.

mortal [mor'tal] a mortal; (*golpe*) deadly; ~**idad, mortandad** *nf* mortality.

mortero [mor'tero] *nm* mortar.

mortífero, a [mor'tifero, a] a deadly, lethal.

mortificar [mortifi'kar] *vt* (*MED*) to damage, affect seriously; (*fig*) to mortify; ~**se** *vr* to be (very) embarrassed.

mosca ['moska] *nf* fly.

Moscú [mos'ku] *n* Moscow.

mosquitero [moski'tero] *nm* mosquito net.

mosquito [mos'kito] *nm* mosquito.

mostaza [mos'taθa] *nf* mustard.

mostrador [mostra'ðor] *nm* (*de tienda*) counter; (*de café*) bar; (*de reloj*) face, dial.

mostrar [mos'trar] *vt* (*gen*) to show; (*exhibir*) to display, exhibit; (*explicar*) to explain; ~**se** *vr*: ~**se amable** to be kind, to prove to be kind; **no se muestra muy inteligente** he doesn't seem (to be) very intelligent.

mostrenco, a [mos'trenko, a] a ownerless, unclaimed; (*perro*) stray; (*persona*) homeless; (*fam*) dense, slow.

mota ['mota] *nf* speck, tiny piece; (*en diseño*) dot.

mote ['mote] *nm* (*apodo*) nickname; (*sentencia*) motto.

motín [mo'tin] *nm* (*del pueblo*) revolt, rising; (*del ejército*) mutiny.

motivar [moti'βar] *vt* (*causar*) to cause, motivate; (*explicar*) to explain, justify; **motivo, a** a *motive* // *nm* motive, reason.

moto ['moto] *nf*, **motocicleta** [motoθi'kleta] *nf* motorbike.

motoniveladora [motoniβela'ðora] *nf* bulldozer.

motor [mo'tor] *nm* motor, engine; ~ **a chorro o de reacción/de explosión** jet engine/internal combustion engine.

motora [mo'tora] *nf*, **motorbote** [motor'βote] *nm* motorboat.

motosierra [moto'sjerra] *nf* mechanical saw.

movedizo, a [moβe'ðiθo, a] a easily moved, movable; (*inseguro*) unsteady; (*fig*) unsettled, changeable; (*persona*) fickle.

mover [mo'βer] *vt* (*gen*) to move; (*cabeza*) to shake; (*accionar*) to drive; (*fig*) to cause, provoke; ~**se** *vr* to move; (*fig*) to get a move on.

móvil ['moβil] a mobile; (*pieza de máquina*) moving; (*mueble*) movable // *nm* motive; **movilidad** *nf* mobility; **movilizar** *vt* to mobilize.

movimiento [moβi'mjento] *nm* (*gen*) movement; (*TEC*) motion; (*actividad*) activity; **el M**~ the Falangist Movement.

mozo, a ['moθo, a] a (*joven*) young; (*soltero*) single, unmarried // *nm/f* (*joven*) youth, lad/girl; (*criado*) servant // *nm* (*camarero*) waiter.

muchacho, a [mu'tʃatʃo, a] *nm/f* (*niño*) boy/girl; (*criado*) servant/servant o maid.

muchedumbre [mutʃe'ðumbre] *nf* crowd.

mucho, a ['mutʃo, a] a (*sg*) a lot of; (*gen en frase negativa o interrogativa*) much; (*pl*) many, a lot of, lots of // *ad* (*en cantidad*) a lot, a great deal, much; (*del tiempo*) long; (*muy*) very // *pron*: **tengo** ~ **que hacer** I have a lot to do; ~**s dicen que** a lot of people say that; **ni** ~ **menos** far from it.

mudanza [mu'ðanθa] *nf* (*cambio*) change; (*de casa*) move; ~**s** *nfpl* (*fig*) moodiness *sg*.

mudar [mu'ðar] *vt* to change; (*ZOOL*) to shed // *vi* to change; ~**se** *vr* (*la ropa*) to change; (*de casa*) to move (house).

mudo, a ['muðo, a] a dumb; (*callado, CINE*) silent.

mueble ['mweβle] *nm* piece of furniture; ~**s** *nmpl* furniture *sg*; ~**ría** *nf* furniture shop.

mueca ['mweka] *nf* face, grimace; **hacer** ~**s a** to make faces at.

muela ['mwela] *nf* (*diente*) tooth; (: *de atrás*) molar.

muelle ['mweʎe] a (*blando*) soft; (*elástico*) springy; (*fig*) soft, easy // *nm* spring; (*NAUT*) wharf; (*malecón*) jetty.

muero *etc vb ver* **morir**.

muerte ['mwerte] *nf* death; (*homicidio*) murder; **dar** ~ **a** to kill.

muerto, a ['mwerto, a] *pp de* **morir** // a dead; (*color*) dull // *nm/f* dead man/woman; (*difunto*) deceased;

(*cadáver*) corpse; **estar ~ de cansancio** to be dead tired.

muestra ['mwestra] *nf* (*señal*) indication, sign; (*demostración*) demonstration; (*prueba*) proof; (*estadística*) sample; (*modelo*) model, pattern; (*testimonio*) token; **muestreo** *nm* sample, sampling.

muestro etc *vb ver* **mostrar.**

muevo etc *vb ver* **mover.**

mugir [mu'xir] *vi* (*vaca*) to moo; (*persona*) to roar, howl.

mugre ['muxre] *nf* dirt, filth; **mugriento, a** *a* dirty, filthy.

mujer [mu'xer] *nf* (*de sexo femenino*) woman; (*esposa*) wife; **~iego** *nm* womaniser.

mula ['mula] *nf* mule.

muladar [mula'ðar] *nm* dungheap, dung-hill.

muleta [mu'leta] *nf* (*para andar*) crutch; (*TAUR*) stick with red cape attached; (*fig*) prop, support.

multa ['multa] *nf* fine; **multar** *vt* to fine.

multicopista [multiko'pista] *nm* duplicator.

múltiple ['multiple] *a* multiple; (*pl*) many, numerous.

multiplicar [multipli'kar] *vt* (*MAT*) to multiply; (*fig*) to increase; **~se** *vr* (*BIO*) to multiply; (*fig*) to attend to a lot of things at one time.

multitud [multi'tuð] *nf* (*gentío, muchedumbre*) crowd; **~ de** lots of.

mullido, a [mu'ʎiðo, a] *a* (*cama*) soft; (*hierba*) soft, springy // *nm* stuffing, filling.

mundano, a [mun'dano, a] *a* worldly; (*de moda*) fashionable.

mundial [mun'djal] *a* world-wide, universal; (*guerra, récord*) world *cpd.*

mundo ['mundo] *nm* world; **todo el ~** everybody; **tener ~** to be experienced, know one's way around.

munición [muni'θjon] *nf* (*MIL*) stores *pl*, supplies *pl*; (*de arma*) ammunition.

municipio [muni'θipjo] *nm* (*municipalidad*) town council, corporation; (*comuna*) town, municipality.

muñeca [mu'peka] *nf* (*ANAT*) wrist; (*juguete*) doll; (*maniquí*) dummy.

muñeco [mu'neko] *nm* (*figura*) figure; (*marioneta*) puppet; (*maniquí*) dummy; (*fig*) puppet, pawn.

muralla [mu'raʎa] *nf* (*city*) wall(s) (*pl*).

murciélago [mur'θjelaxo] *nm* bat.

murmullo [mur'muʎo] *nm* murmur(ing); (*cuchicheo*) whispering; (*de arroyo*) murmur, rippling.

murmuración [murmura'θjon] *nf* gossip; **murmurar** *vi* to murmur, whisper; (*criticar*) to criticize; (*cotillear*) to gossip.

muro ['muro] *nm* wall.

muscular [musku'lar] *a* muscular.

músculo ['muskulo] *nm* muscle.

museo [mu'seo] *nm* museum.

musgo ['musxo] *nm* moss.

músico, a ['musiko, a] *a* musical // *nm/f* musician // *nf* music.

musitar [musi'tar] *vt*, *vi* to mutter, mumble.

muslo ['muslo] *nm* thigh.

mustio, a ['mustjo, a] *a* (*persona*) depressed, gloomy; (*planta*) faded, withered.

musulmán, ana [musul'man, ana] *nm/f* Moslem.

mutación [muta'θjon] *nf* (*BIO*) mutation; (*cambio*) (sudden) change.

mutilar [muti'lar] *vt* to mutilate; (*a una persona*) to maim.

mutuamente [mutwa'mente] *ad* mutually; **mutuo, a** *a* mutual.

muy [mwi] *ad* very; (*demasiado*) too; **M~ Señor mío** Dear Sir; **~ de noche** very late at night; **eso es ~ de él** that's just like him.

N

N *abr de* **norte.**

n/ *abr de* **nuestro, a.**

nabo ['naβo] *nm* turnip; (*raíz*) root.

nácar ['nakar] *nm* mother-of-pearl.

nacer [na'θer] *vi* to be born; (*de huevo*) to hatch; (*vegetal*) to sprout; (*río*) to rise; **~ al amor** to awaken to love; **nació una sospecha en su mente** a suspicion formed in her mind; **nacido, a** *a* born; **recién nacido** newborn; **naciente** *a* new, emerging; (*sol*) rising; **nacimiento** *nm* birth; (*fig*) birth, origin; (*de Navidad*) Nativity; (*linaje*) descent, family; (*de río*) source.

nación [na'θjon] *nf* nation; **nacional** *a* national; **nacionalismo** *nm* nationalism; **nacionalista** *nm/f* nationalist; **nacionalizar** *vt* to nationalize; **nacionalizarse** *vr* to become naturalized.

nada ['naða] *pron* nothing // *ad* not at all, in no way; **no decir ~** to say nothing, not to say anything; **de ~** don't mention it.

nadaderas [naða'ðeras] *nfpl* waterwings.

nadador, a [naða'ðor, a] *nm/f* swimmer.

nadar [na'ðar] *vi* to swim.

nadie ['naðje] *pron* nobody, no-one; **~ habló** nobody spoke; **no había ~** there was nobody there, there wasn't anybody there.

nado ['naðo] : **a ~** *ad*: **pasar a ~** to swim across.

naipe ['naipe] *nm* playing card; **~s** *nmpl* cards.

nalgas ['nalxas] *nfpl* buttocks.

nana ['nana] *nf* (*fam: abuela*) grandma (*fam*), granny (*fam*); (: *canción*) lullaby.

naranja [na'ranxa] *a*, *nf* orange; **media ~** (*fam*) better half (*fam*); **~do, a** *a* orange // *nf* orangeade; **naranjo** *nm* orange tree.

narciso [nar'θiso] *nm* narcissus.

narcótico, a [nar'kotiko, a] *a*, *nm* narcotic; **narcotizar** *vt* to drug.

nardo ['narðo] *nm* lily.

narigón, ona [nari'ɣon, ona], **narigudo, a** [nari'ɣuðo, a] *a* big-nosed.

nariz [na'riθ] *nf* nose; **narices** *nfpl* nostrils; **en las narices de uno** under one's (very) nose.

narración [narra'θjon] *nf* narration; **narrador, a** *nm/f* narrator.

narrar [na'rrar] *vt* to narrate, recount; **narrativa** *nf* narrative, story.

nata ['nata] *nf* cream.

natación [nata'θjon] *nf* swimming.

natal [na'tal] *a:* **ciudad** ~ home town; ~**icio** *nm* birthday; ~**idad** *nf* birth rate.

natillas [na'tiʎas] *nfpl* custard *sg.*

natividad [natiβi'ðað] *nf* nativity.

nativo, a [na'tiβo, a] *a* native; (*innato*) innate, natural // *nm/f* native.

nato, a ['nato, a] *a* born; **un músico** ~ *a* born musician.

natural [natu'ral] *a* natural; (*fruta etc*) fresh // *nm/f* native // *nm* nature; ~**eza** *nf* nature; (*género*) nature, kind; ~**eza muerta** still life; ~**idad** *nf* naturalness; ~**ización** *nf* naturalization; ~**izarse** *vr* to become naturalized; (*aclimatarse*) to become acclimatized; ~**mente** *ad* naturally.

naufragar [naufra'ɣar] *vi* to sink; **naufragio** *nm* shipwreck; **náufrago, a** *nm/f* castaway, shipwrecked person.

náusea ['nausea] *nf* nausea; **me da** ~ it makes me feel sick; **nauseabundo, a** *a* nauseating, sickening.

náutico, a [na'utiko, a] *a* nautical.

nava ['naβa] *nf* (*GEO*) level plain.

navaja [na'βaxa] *nf* (*cortaplumas*) clasp knife, penknife; (*de barbero, peluquero*) razor.

navarro, a [na'βarro, a] *a* Navarrese.

nave ['naβe] *nf* (*barco*) ship, vessel; (*ARQ*) nave; ~ **espacial** spaceship.

navegación [naβeɣa'θjon] *nf* navigation; (*viaje*) sea journey; ~ **aérea** air traffic; ~ **costera** coastal shipping; **navegante** *nm/f* navigator; **navegar** *vi* (*barco*) to sail; (*avión*) to fly // *vt* to sail; to fly; (*dirigir el rumbo*) to navigate.

navidad [naβi'ðað] *nf* Christmas; **navideño, a** *a* Christmas *cpd.*

navío [na'βio] *nm* ship.

nazi ['naθi] *a, nm/f* Nazi.

neblina [ne'βlina] *nf* mist.

nebuloso, a [neβu'loso, a] *a* foggy; (*calinoso*) misty; (*cielo*) cloudy; (*indefinido*) nebulous, vague // *nf* nebula.

necedad [neθe'ðað] *nf* foolishness; (*una* ~) foolish act.

necesario, a [neθe'sarjo, a] *a* necessary.

neceser [neθe'ser] *nm* vanity case; (*bolsa*) holdall; ~ **de viaje** travelling case.

necesidad [neθesi'ðað] *nf* need; (*lo inevitable*) necessity; (*miseria*) poverty, need; **en caso de** ~ in case of need or emergency; **hacer sus** ~**es** to relieve o.s.

necesitado, a [neθesi'taðo, a] *a* needy, poor; ~ **de** in need of.

necesitar [neθesi'tar] *vt* to need, require // *vi:* ~ **de** to have need of.

necio, a ['neθjo, a] *a* foolish.

necrología [nekrolo'xia] *nf* obituary.

necrópolis [ne'kropolis] *nf* cemetery.

nectarina [nekta'rina] *nf* nectarine.

nefando, a [ne'fando, a] *a* unspeakable.

nefasto, a [ne'fasto, a] *a* ill-fated, unlucky.

negación [neɣa'θjon] *nf* negation; (*rechazo*) refusal, denial.

negar [ne'ɣar] *vt* (*renegar, rechazar*) to refuse; (*prohibir*) to refuse, deny; (*desmentir*) to deny; ~**se** *vr:* ~**se a** to refuse to.

negativo, a [neɣa'tiβo, a] *a, nm* negative // *nf* (*gen*) negative; (*rechazo*) refusal, denial.

negligencia [neɣli'xenθja] *nf* negligence; **negligente** *a* negligent.

negociable [neɣo'θjaβle] *a* (*COM*) negotiable.

negociado [neɣo'θjaðo] *nm* department, section.

negociante [neɣo'θjante] *nm/f* businessman/woman; (*comerciante*) merchant.

negociar [neɣo'θjar] *vt, vi* to negotiate; ~ **en** to deal in, trade in.

negocio [ne'ɣoθjo] *nm* (*COM*) business; (*asunto*) affair, business; (*operación comercial*) deal, transaction; (*AM*) firm; (*lugar*) place of business; **los** ~**s** business *sg*; **hacer** ~ to do business.

negro, a ['neɣro, a] *a* black; (*suerte*) awful // *nm* black // *nm/f* Negro/Negress, black // *nf* (*MUS*) crotchet; **negrura** *nf* blackness.

nene, a ['nene, a] *nm/f* baby, small child; (*fam*) dear.

nenúfar [ne'nufar] *nm* water lily.

neologismo [neolo'xismo] *nm* neologism.

neoyorquino, a [neojor'kino, a] *a* (of) New York.

nepotismo [nepo'tismo] *nm* nepotism.

nervio ['nerβjo] *nm* (*ANAT*) nerve; (*tendón*) tendon; (*fig*) vigour; ~**sidad** *nf* nervousness, nerves *pl*; ~**so, a, nervudo, a** *a* nervous.

neto, a ['neto, a] *a* clear; (*verdad etc*) pure; (*limpio*) clean; (*COM*) net.

neumático, a [neu'matiko, a] *a* pneumatic // *nm* tyre; ~ **de recambio** spare tyre.

neuralgia [neu'ralxja] *nf* neuralgia.

neurastenia [neuras'tenja] *nf* nervous exhaustion.

neuritis [neu'ritis] *nf* neuritis.

neurólogo, a [neu'roloxo, a] *nm/f* neurologist.

neurosis [neu'rosis] *nf inv* neurosis.

neutral [neu'tral] *a* neutral; ~**izar** *vt* to neutralize; (*contrarrestar*) to counteract.

neutro, a ['neutro, a] *a* (*BIO*) neuter, sexless; (*LING*) neuter.

neutrón [neu'tron] *nm* neutron; **bomba de neutrones** neutron bomb.

nevada [ne'ßaða] *nf* snowstorm; (*caída de nieve*) snowfall.

nevar [ne'ßar] *vi* to snow; **nevasca** *nf* snowstorm.

nevera [ne'ßera] *nf* refrigerator, icebox.

nevisca [ne'ßiska] *nf* flurry of snow; (*aguanieve*) sleet; **neviscar** *vi* to snow lightly; to sleet.

ni [ni] *conj* nor, neither; (~ *siquiera*) not ... even; ~ **que** not even if; ~ **blanco** ~ **negro** neither white nor black.

Nicaragua [nika'raɣwa] *nf* Nicaragua; **nicaragüense** *a, nm/f* Nicaraguan.

nicotina [niko'tina] *nf* nicotine.

nicho ['nitʃo] *nm* niche.

nido ['niðo] *nm* nest; (*fig*) hiding place; (*lugar predilecto*) haunt.

niebla ['njeßla] *nf* fog; (*neblina*) mist.

niego *etc vb ver* **negar**.

nieto, a ['njeto, a] *nm/f* grandson/daughter; ~**s** *nmpl* grandchildren.

nieva *etc vb ver* **nevar**.

nieve ['njeße] *nf* snow.

nigromancia [niɣro'manθja] *nf* necromancy, black magic.

nihilismo [nii'lismo] *nm* nihilism.

Nilo ['nilo] *nm*: **el** ~ the Nile.

nimbo ['nimbo] *nm* (*aureola*) halo; (*nube*) nimbus.

nimiedad [nimje'ðað] *nf* small-mindedness; (*prolijidad*) long-windedness; (*trivialidad*) triviality.

nimio, a ['nimjo, a] *a* (*insignificante*) trivial, insignificant; (*escrupuloso*) fussy, overparticular.

ninfa ['ninfa] *nf* nymph.

ninfómana [nin'fomana] *nf* nymphomaniac.

ninguno, a [nin'guno, a], **ningún** [nin-'gun] *a* no // *pron* (*nadie*) nobody; (*ni uno*) none, not one; (*ni uno ni otro*) neither; **de** ~**a manera** by no means, not at all.

niña ['niɲa] *nf ver* **niño**.

niñera [ni'ɲera] *nf* nursemaid, nanny; **niñería** *nf* childish act.

niñez [ni'ɲeθ] *nf* childhood; (*infancia*) infancy.

niño, a ['niɲo, a] *a* (*joven*) young; (*inmaduro*) immature // *nm* (*chico*) boy, child // *nf* (*chica*) girl, child; (*ANAT*) pupil.

nipón, ona [ni'pon, ona] *a, nm/f* Japanese.

níquel ['nikel] *nm* nickel; **niquelar** *vt* (*TEC*) to nickel-plate.

nitidez [niti'ðeθ] *nf* (*claridad*) clarity; (: *de atmósfera*) brightness; (: *de imagen*) sharpness; **nítido, a** *a* clear; sharp.

nitrato [ni'trato] *nm* nitrate.

nitrógeno [ni'troxeno] *nm* nitrogen.

nitroglicerina [nitroxliθe'rina] *nf* nitroglycerine.

nivel [ni'ßel] *nm* (*GEO*) level; (*norma*) level, standard; (*altura*) height; ~ **de aceite** oil level; ~ **de aire** spirit level; ~ **de vida** standard of living; ~**ar** *vt*

(*terreno*) to level out; (*equilibrar: mueble*) to even up; (*COM*) to balance.

NN. UU. *nfpl abr de* **Naciones Unidas** U.N. *sg* (United Nations).

no [no] *ad* no; not; (*con verbo*) not // *excl* no!; ~ **tengo nada** I don't have anything, I have nothing; ~ **es el mío** it's not mine; **ahora** ~ not now; ¿~ **lo sabes?** don't you know?; ~ **mucho** not much; ~ **bien termine, lo entregaré** as soon as I finish I'll hand it over; ¡**a que** ~ **lo sabes!** I bet you don't know!; ¡**cuándo** *o* **cómo** ~**!** of course!; **los países** ~ **alineados** the non-aligned countries; **el** ~ **conformismo** non-conformism; **la** ~ **intervención** non-intervention.

NO *abr de* **noroeste.**

no. *abr de* **número.**

noble ['noßle] *a, nm/f* noble; ~**za** *nf* nobility.

noción [no'θjon] *nf* notion.

nocivo, a [no'θißo, a] *a* harmful.

noctambulismo [noktamßu'lismo] *nm* sleepwalking; **noctámbulo, a** *nm/f* sleepwalker.

nocturno, a [nok'turno, a] *a* (*de la noche*) nocturnal, night *cpd*; (*de la tarde*) evening *cpd* // *nm* nocturne.

noche ['notʃe] *nf* night, night-time; (*la tarde*) evening; (*fig*) darkness; **de** ~, **por la** ~ at night.

nochebuena [notʃe'ßwena] *nf* Christmas Eve.

nochevieja [notʃe'ßjexa] *nf* New Year's Eve.

nodriza [no'ðriθa] *nf* wet nurse.

nogal [no'ɣal] *nm* walnut tree.

nómada ['nomaða] *a* nomadic // *nm/f* nomad.

nombradía [nombra'ðia] *nf* fame.

nombramiento [nombra'mjento] *nm* naming; (*a un empleo*) appointment.

nombrar [nom'brar] *vt* (*designar*) to name; (*mencionar*) to mention; (*dar puesto a*) to appoint.

nombre ['nombre] *nm* name; (*sustantivo*) noun; (*fama*) renown; ~ **y apellidos** name in full; ~ **común/propio** common/proper noun; ~ **de pila/de soltera** Christian/maiden name.

nomenclatura [nomenkla'tura] *nf* nomenclature.

nomeolvides [nomeol'ßiðes] *nm inv* forget-me-not.

nómina ['nomina] *nf* (*lista*) list; (*COM*) payroll.

nominal [nomi'nal] *a* nominal.

nominativo, a [nomina'tißo, a] *a* (*COM*): **cheque** ~ **a X** cheque made out to X.

non [non] *a* odd, uneven // *nm* odd number.

nonada [no'naða] *nf* trifle.

nono, a ['nono, a] *a* ninth.

nordeste [nor'ðeste] *a* north-east, north-eastern, north-easterly // *nm* north-east.

nórdico, a ['norðiko, a] *a* (*del norte*) northern, northerly; (*escandinavo*) Nordic.

noria ['norja] nf (AGR) waterwheel; (de carnaval) big wheel.

normal [nor'mal] a (corriente) normal; (habitual) usual, natural; **(gasolina)** ~ two-star petrol; ~**idad** nf normality; **restablecer la** ~**idad** to restore order; ~**izar** vt (reglamentar) to normalize; (TEC) to standardize; ~**izarse** vr to return to normal.

normando, a [nor'mando, a] a, nm/f Norman.

noroeste [noro'este] a north-west, north-western, north-westerly // nm north-west.

norte ['norte] a north, northern, northerly // nm north; (fig) guide.

norteamericano, a [norteameri'kano, a] a, nm/f (North) American.

noruego, a [nor'rweɣo, a] a, nm/f Norwegian; N~a nf Norway.

nos [nos] pron (directo) us; (indirecto) us; to us; for us; from us; (reflexivo) (to) ourselves; (recíproco) (to) each other; ~ **levantamos a las 7** we get up at 7.

nosotros [no'sotros] pron (sujeto) we; (después de prep) us.

nostalgia [nos'talxja] nf nostalgia.

nota ['nota] nf note; (ESCOL) mark.

notabilidad [notaβili'ðað] nf (persona) notable.

notable [no'taβle] a, nm/f notable.

notación [nota'θjon] nf (nota) note; (MAT, MUS) notation.

notar [no'tar] vt (advertir) to notice, note; (anotar, asentar) to note (down); (censurar) to criticize; ~**se** vr to be obvious.

notarial [nota'rjal] a: **acta** ~ affidavit.

notario [no'tarjo] nm notary.

noticia [no'tiθja] nf (información) piece of news; **las** ~**s** the news sg; **tener** ~**s de alguien** to hear from sb.

noticiar [noti'θjar] vt to notify; ~**io** nm (CINE) newsreel; (TV) news bulletin; **noticioso, a** a well-informed.

notificación [notifika'θjon] nf notification; **notificar** vt to notify, inform.

notoriedad [notorje'ðað] nf fame, renown; **notorio, a** a (público) well-known; (evidente) obvious.

novato, a [no'βato, a] a inexperienced // nm/f beginner.

novecientos [noθe'θjentos] num nine hundred.

novedad [noβe'ðað] nf (calidad de nuevo) newness; (noticia) piece of news; (cambio) change, (new) development.

novedoso, a [noβe'ðoso, a] a novel.

novel [no'βel] a new; (inexperto) inexperienced // nm/f beginner.

novela [no'βela] nf novel.

novelero, a [noβe'lero, a] a highly imaginative; (voluble) fickle; (chismoso) gossipy.

novelesco, a [noβe'lesko, a] a fictional; (romántico) romantic; (fantástico) fantastic.

noveno, a [no'βeno, a] a ninth.

noventa [no'βenta] num ninety.

novia ['noβja] nf ver **novio.**

noviazgo [no'βjaɣo] nm engagement.

novicio, a [no'βiθjo, a] nm/f novice.

noviembre [no'βjembre] nm November.

novilla [no'βiʎa] nf heifer; ~**da** nf (TAUR) bullfight with young bulls; **novillero** nm novice bullfighter; **novillo** nm young bull; **hacer novillos** (fam) to play truant.

novio, a ['noβjo, a] nm/f boyfriend/girlfriend; (prometido) fiancé/fiancée; (recién casado) bridegroom/bride; **los** ~**s** the newly-weds.

N. S. abr de **Nuestro Señor.**

nubarrón [nuβa'rron] nm storm cloud.

nube ['nuβe] nf cloud.

nublado, a [nu'βlaðo, a] a cloudy // nm storm cloud; **nublar** vt (oscurecer) to darken; (confundir) to cloud; **nublarse** vr to grow dark.

nuca ['nuka] nf nape of the neck.

nuclear [nukle'ar] a nuclear.

núcleo ['nukleo] nm (centro) core; (FÍSICA) nucleus.

nudillo [nu'ðiʎo] nm knuckle.

nudo ['nuðo] nm (gen) knot; (unión) bond; (de problema) crux; (de comunicaciones) centre; ~**so, a** a knotty.

nuera ['nwera] nf daughter-in-law.

nuestro, a ['nwestro, a] det our // pron ours; ~ **padre** our father; **un amigo** ~ a friend of ours; **es el** ~ it's ours.

nueva ['nweβa] nf ver **nuevo.**

nuevamente [nweβa'mente] ad (otra vez) again; (de nuevo) anew.

nueve ['nweβe] num nine.

nuevo, a ['nweβo, a] a (gen) new // nf piece of news; **de** ~ again; **N~a York** n New York; **N~a Zelandia** nf New Zealand.

nuez [nweθ] (pl **nueces**) nf (fruto) nut; (del nogal) walnut; ~ **de Adán** Adam's apple; ~ **moscada** nutmeg.

nulidad [nuli'ðað] nf (incapacidad) incompetence; (abolición) nullity.

nulo, a ['nulo, a] a (inepto, torpe) useless; (inválido) (null and) void; (DEPORTE) drawn, tied.

núm. abr de **número.**

numen ['numen] nm inspiration.

numeración [numera'θjon] nf (cifras) numbers pl; (arábiga, romana etc) numerals pl.

numeral [nume'ral] nm numeral.

numerar [nume'rar] vt to number.

numerario [nume'rarjo] nm hard cash.

numérico, a [nu'meriko, a] a numerical.

número ['numero] nm (gen) number; (tamaño: de zapato) size; (ejemplar: de diario) number, issue; **sin** ~ numberless, unnumbered; ~ **de matrícula/telefónico** registration/telephone number; **atrasado** back number.

numeroso, a [nume'roso, a] a numerous.

nunca ['nunka] ad (jamás) never; ~ **lo pensé** I never thought it; **no vino** ~ he

never came; ~ **más** never again.
nuncio ['nunθjo] nm (REL) nuncio.
nupcias ['nupθjas] nfpl wedding sg, nuptials.
nutria ['nutrja] nf otter.
nutrición [nutri'θjon] nf nutrition.
nutrido, a [nu'triðo, a] a (alimentado) nourished; (fig: grande) large; (abundante) abundant.
nutrir [nu'trir] vt (alimentar) to nourish; (dar de comer) to feed; (alentar) to encourage; (esperanzas) to cherish; **nutritivo, a** a nourishing, nutritious.
nylon [ni'lon] nm nylon.

Ñ

ñame ['ɲame] nm yam.
ñaque ['ɲake] nm junk.
ñato, a ['ɲato, a] a (AM) snub-nosed.
ñoñería [ɲoɲe'ria], **ñoñez** [ɲo'ɲeθ] nf insipidness.
ñoño, a ['ɲoɲo, a] a (AM: tonto) silly, stupid; (soso) insipid; (persona) spineless.

O

o [o] conj or.
O abr de **oeste.**
o/ abr de **orden.**
oasis [o'asis] nm oasis.
obcecar [oβθe'kar] vt to blind.
obedecer [oβeðe'θer] vt to obey; **obediencia** nf obedience; **obediente** a obedient.
obertura [oβer'tura] nf overture.
obesidad [oβesi'ðað] nf obesity; **obeso, a** a obese.
obispo [o'βispo] nm bishop.
objeción [oβxe'θjon] nf objection; **objetar** vt, vi to object.
objetivo, a [oβxe'tiβo, a] a, nm objective.
objeto [oβ'xeto] nm (cosa) object; (fin) aim.
oblicuo, a [o'βlikwo, a] a oblique; (mirada) sidelong.
obligación [oβlixa'θjon] nf obligation; (COM) bond.
obligar [oβli'xar] vt to force; ~**se** vr to bind o.s.; **obligatorio, a** a compulsory, obligatory.
oboe [o'βoe] nm oboe.
obra ['oβra] nf (gen) work; (hechura) piece of work; (ARQ) construction, building; (TEATRO) play; ~ **maestra** masterpiece; **(Ministerio de) O~s Públicas** Ministry of Public Works; **en** ~ **de** in about; **por** ~ **de** thanks to (the efforts of); **obrar** vt to work; (tener efecto) to have an effect on // vi to act, behave; (tener efecto) to have an effect; **la carta obra en su poder** the letter is in his/her possession; **obrero, a** a working, labour cpd; **clase obrera** working class // nm/f (gen) worker; (sin oficio) labourer.

obscenidad [oβsθeni'ðað] nf obscenity; **obsceno, a** a obscene.
obscu... = oscu... .
obsequiar [oβse'kjar] vt (ofrecer) to present with; (agasajar) to make a fuss of, lavish attention on; **obsequio** nm (regalo) gift; (cortesía) courtesy, attention; **obsequioso, a** a attentive.
observación [oβserβa'θjon] nf observation; (reflexión) remark.
observancia [oβser'βanθja] nf observance.
observar [oβser'βar] vt to observe; (anotar) to notice; ~**se** vr to keep to, observe.
obsesión [oβse'sjon] nf obsession; **obsesionar** vt to obsess.
obstaculizar [oβstakuli'θar] vt (dificultar) to hinder; (impedir) to stand in the way of.
obstáculo [oβs'takulo] nm (gen) obstacle; (impedimento) hindrance, drawback.
obstante [oβ'stante]: **no** ~ ad nevertheless // prep in spite of.
obstar [oβs'tar] vi: ~ **a** to hinder.
obstetricia [oβste'triθja] nf obstetrics sg; **obstétrico, a** a obstetric // nm/f obstetrician.
obstinado, a [oβsti'naðo, a] a (gen) obstinate; (terco) stubborn.
obstinarse [oβsti'narse] vr to be obstinate; ~ **en** to persist in.
obstrucción [oβstruk'θjon] nf obstruction; **obstruir** vt to obstruct.
obtener [oβte'ner] vt (conseguir) to obtain; (ganar) to gain.
obtuso, a [oβ'tuso, a] a (filo) blunt; (MAT, fig) obtuse.
obviar [oβ'βjar] vt to clear away // vi to stand in the way.
obvio, a ['oββjo, a] a obvious.
ocasión [oka'sjon] nf (oportunidad) opportunity, chance; (momento) occasion, time; (causa) cause; **de** ~ secondhand; **ocasionar** vt to cause.
ocaso [o'kaso] nm (oeste) west; (fig) decline.
occidente [okθi'ðente] nm west.
océano [o'θeano] nm ocean; **el** ~ **Índico** the Indian Ocean.
O.C.E.D. nf abr de **Organización de Cooperación Económica y Desarrollo** OECD (Organization for Economic Cooperation and Development).
ocio ['oθjo] nm (tiempo) leisure; (pey) idleness; ~**s** nmpl pastime sg; ~**sidad** nf idleness; ~**so, a** a (inactivo) idle; (inútil) useless.
octanaje [okta'naxe] nm: **de alto** ~ high octane; **octano** nm octane.
octavín [okta'βin] nm piccolo.
octavo, a [ok'taβo, a] a eighth.
octogenario, a [oktoxe'narjo, a] a octogenarian.
octubre [ok'tuβre] nm October.
ocular [oku'lar] a ocular, eye cpd; **testigo** ~ eyewitness.

oculista [oku'lista] nm/f oculist.

ocultar [okul'tar] vt (esconder) to hide; (callar) to withhold; **oculto, a** a hidden; (fig) secret.

ocupación [okupa'θjon] nf occupation.

ocupado, a [oku'paðo, a] a (persona) busy; (sitio) occupied; (teléfono) engaged; **ocupar** vt (gen) to occupy; **ocuparse** vr: **ocuparse con** o **de** o **en** (gen) to concern o.s. with; (cuidar) to look after.

ocurrencia [oku'rrenθja] nf (ocasión) occurrence; (agudeza) witticism.

ocurrir [oku'rrir] vi to happen; ~**se** vr: **se me ocurre que...** it occurs to me that... .

ochenta [o'tʃenta] num eighty.

ocho [o'tʃo] num eight.

odiar [o'ðjar] vt to hate; **odio** nm (gen) hate, hatred; (disgusto) dislike; **odioso, a** a (gen) hateful; (malo) nasty.

O.E.A. nf abr de **Organización de Estados Americanos** O.A.S. (Organization of American States).

oeste [o'este] nm west; **una película del** ~ a western.

ofender [ofen'der] vt (agraviar) to offend; (ser ofensivo a) to be offensive to; ~**se** vr to take offence; **ofensa** nf offence; **ofensivo, a** a (insultante) insulting; (MIL) offensive // nf offensive.

oferta [o'ferta] nf offer; (propuesta) proposal; **la** ~ **y la demanda** supply and demand; **artículos en** ~ goods on offer.

oficial [ofi'θjal] a official // nm official; (MIL) officer.

oficina [ofi'θina] nf office; **oficinista** nm/f clerk.

oficio [o'fiθjo] nm (profesión) profession; (puesto) post; (REL) service; **ser del** ~ to be an old hand; **tener mucho** ~ to have a lot of experience; ~ **de difuntos** funeral service; **de** ~ officially.

oficiosidad [ofiθjosi'ðað] nf helpfulness; (pey) officiousness.

oficioso, a [ofi'θjoso, a] a (diligente) attentive; (pey) officious; (no oficial) unofficial, informal.

ofrecer [ofre'θer] vt (dar) to offer; (proponer) to propose; ~**se** vr (persona) to offer o.s., volunteer; (situación) to present itself; **¿qué se le ofrece?, ¿se le ofrece algo?** what can I do for you?, can I get you anything?

ofrecimiento [ofreθi'mjento] nm offer, offering.

ofrendar [ofren'dar] vt to offer, contribute.

oftálmico, a [of'talmiko, a] a ophthalmic.

ofuscación [ofuska'θjon] nf, **ofuscamiento** [ofuska'mjento] nm (fig) bewilderment; **ofuscar** vt (confundir) to bewilder; (enceguecer) to dazzle, blind.

oída [o'iða] nf hearing; **de** ~**s** by hearsay.

oído [o'iðo] nm ear; (sentido) hearing.

oigo etc vb ver **oír**.

oír [o'ir] vt (gen) to hear; (atender a) to listen to; **¡oiga!** listen!; ~ **misa** to attend mass.

O.I.T. nf abr de **Organización Internacional del Trabajo** I.L.O. (International Labour Organization).

ojal [o'xal] nm buttonhole.

ojalá [oxa'la] excl if only it were so!, some hope(s)! // conj if only...!, would that...!; ~ **que venga hoy** I hope he comes today.

ojeada [oxe'aða] nf glance; **ojear** vt (mirar fijo) to stare at; (examinar) to eye; (mirar de reojo) to glance at.

ojera [o'xera] nf: **tener** ~**s** to have rings or circles under the eyes.

ojeriza [oxe'riθa] nf ill-will.

ojeroso, a [oxe'roso, a] a haggard.

ojete [o'xete] nm eye(let).

ojo ['oxo] nm eye; (de puente) span; (de cerradura) keyhole // excl careful!; **tener** ~ **para** to have an eye for; ~ **de buey** porthole.

ola ['ola] nf wave.

olé [o'le] excl bravo!, olé!

oleada [ole'aða] nf big wave, swell; (fig) surge.

oleaje [ole'axe] nm swell.

óleo ['oleo] nm oil; **oleoducto** nm (oil) pipeline.

oler [o'ler] vt (gen) to smell; (husmear) to pry into; (fig) to sniff out // vi: ~ **a** to smell of.

olfatear [olfate'ar] vt to smell; (fig) to sniff out; (husmear) to pry into; **olfato** nm sense of smell.

oliente [o'ljente] a smelling; **bien/mal** ~ sweet-/foul-smelling.

oligarquía [olixar'kia] nf oligarchy.

olimpiada [olim'piaða] nf: **las O**~**s** the Olympics.

oliva [o'liβa] nf (aceituna) olive; (árbol) olive tree; **aceite de** ~ olive oil; **olivo** nm olive tree.

olmo ['olmo] nm elm (tree).

olor [o'lor] nm smell; ~**oso, a** a scented.

olvidadizo, a [olβiða'ðiθo, a] a (desmemoriado) forgetful; (distraído) absent-minded.

olvidar [olβi'ðar] vt to forget; (omitir) to omit; ~**se** vr to forget o.s.; **se me olvidó** I forgot.

olvido [ol'βiðo] nm oblivion.

olla ['oʎa] nf pan; (comida) stew; ~ **a presión** o **autopresión** pressure cooker; ~ **podrida** Spanish stew.

ombligo [om'bliɣo] nm navel.

ominoso, a [omi'noso, a] a ominous.

omisión [omi'sjon] nf (abstención) omission; (descuido) neglect.

omiso, a [o'miso, a] a: **hacer caso** ~ **de** to ignore, pass over.

omitir [omi'tir] vt to omit.

omnipotente [omnipo'tente] a omnipotent.

omnívoro, a [om'niβoro, a] a omnivorous.

omóplato [o'moplato] nm shoulder blade.

O.M.S. nf abr de **Organización Mundial**

de la Salud W.H.O. (World Health Organization).

once [ˈonθe] *num* eleven; **las ~** (*fam*) elevenses.

onda [ˈonda] *nf* wave; **~ corta/larga/media** short/long/ medium wave; **~s acústicas/ hertzianas** acoustic/Hertzian waves; **ondear** *vt* to wave // *vi* to wave; (*tener ondas*) to be wavy; (*pelo*) to flow; (*agua*) to ripple; **ondearse** *vr* to swing, sway.

ondulación [ondulaˈθjon] *nf* undulation; **ondulado, a** *a* wavy // *nm* wave; **ondulante** *a* undulating; (*cartón, chapa*) corrugated.

ondular [onduˈlar] *vt* (*el pelo*) to wave // *vi*, **~se** *vr* to undulate.

oneroso, a [oneˈroso, a] *a* onerous.

ONU *nf abr de* **Organización de las Naciones Unidas** UNO (United Nations Organization).

O.P. *nfpl abr de* **Obras Públicas** Public Works.

opaco, a [oˈpako, a] *a* opaque; (*fig*) dull.

opalescente [opalesˈθente] *a* opalescent.

ópalo [ˈopalo] *nm* opal.

opción [opˈθjon] *nf* (*gen*) option; (*derecho*) right, option.

ópera [ˈopera] *nf* opera; **~ bufa** *o* **cómica** comic opera.

operación [operaˈθjon] *nf* (*gen*) operation; (*COM*) transaction, deal.

operador, a [operaˈðor, a] *nm/f* operator; (*en cine*) projectionist; (*de cine*) camera operator.

operante [opeˈrante] *a* operating.

operar [opeˈrar] *vt* (*producir*) to produce, bring about; (*MED*) to operate on // *vi* (*COM*) to operate, deal; **~se** *vr* to occur; (*MED*) to have an operation.

opereta [opeˈreta] *nf* operetta.

opinar [opiˈnar] *vt* (*estimar*) to think // *vi* (*enjuiciar*) to give one's opinion; **opinión** *nf* (*creencia*) belief; (*criterio*) opinion.

opio [ˈopjo] *nm* opium.

oponente [opoˈnente] *nm/f* opponent.

oponer [opoˈner] *vt* (*resistencia*) to put up, offer; (*negativa*) to raise; **~se** *vr* (*objetar*) to object; (*estar frente a frente*) to be opposed; (*dos personas*) to oppose each other; **~ A a B** to set A against B; **me opongo a pensar que...** I refuse to believe or think that... .

oportunidad [oportuniˈðað] *nf* (*ocasión*) opportunity; (*posibilidad*) chance.

oportunismo [oportuˈnismo] *nm* opportunism; **oportunista** *nm/f* opportunist.

oportuno, a [oporˈtuno, a] *a* (*apto*) appropriate, suitable; (*en su tiempo*) opportune; (*conveniente*) convenient; **en el momento ~** at the right moment.

oposición [oposiˈθjon] *nf* opposition; **oposiciones** *nfpl* public examinations.

opositor, a [oposiˈtor, a] *nm/f* (*adversario*) opponent; (*concurrente*) competitor.

opresión [opreˈsjon] *nf* oppression;

opresivo, a *a* oppressive; **opresor, a** *nm/f* oppressor.

oprimir [opriˈmir] *vt* to squeeze; (*fig*) to oppress.

oprobio [oˈproβjo] *nm* (*infamia*) ignominy; (*descrédito*) shame.

optar [opˈtar] *vi* (*elegir*) to choose; **~ a** *o* **por** to opt for.

óptico, a [ˈoptiko, a] *a* optic(al) // *nm/f* optician.

optimismo [optiˈmismo] *nm* optimism; **optimista** *nm/f* optimist.

óptimo, a [ˈoptimo, a] *a* (*bueno*) very good; (*el mejor*) very best.

opuesto, a [oˈpwesto, a] *a* (*contrario*) opposite; (*antagónico*) opposing.

opugnar [opuɣˈnar] *vt* to attack.

opulencia [opuˈlenθja] *nf* opulence; **opulento, a** *a* opulent.

oquedad [okeˈðað] *nf* (*fig*) void.

ora [ˈora] *ad*: **~ tú ~ yo** now you, now me.

oración [oraˈθjon] *nf* (*discurso*) speech; (*REL*) prayer; (*LING*) sentence.

oráculo [oˈrakulo] *nm* oracle.

orador, a [oraˈðor, a] *nm/f* (*predicador*) preacher; (*conferenciante*) speaker.

oral [oˈral] *a* oral.

orangután [oranguˈtan] *nm* orang-utan.

orar [oˈrar] *vi* (*REL*) to pray; (*hablar*) to make a speech.

oratoria [oraˈtorja] *nf* oratory.

órbita [ˈorβita] *nf* orbit.

orden [ˈorðen] *nm* (*gen*) order // *nf* (*gen*) order; **~ del día** agenda; **de primer ~** first-rate; **en ~ de prioridad** in order of priority.

ordenado, a [orðeˈnaðo, a] *a* (*metódico*) methodical; (*arreglado*) orderly.

ordenador [orðenaˈðor] *nm* computer.

ordenanza [orðeˈnanθa] *nf* ordinance.

ordenar [orðeˈnar] *vt* (*mandar*) to order; (*poner orden*) to put in order, arrange; **~se** *vr* (*REL*) to be ordained.

ordeñadora [orðeɲaˈðora] *nf* milking machine.

ordeñar [orðeˈnar] *vt* to milk.

ordinario, a [orðiˈnarjo, a] *a* (*común*) ordinary, usual; (*bajo*) vulgar, common.

orégano [oˈreɣano] *nm* oregano.

oreja [oˈrexa] *nf* ear; (*de zapatos*) tongue; (*MECÁNICA*) lug, flange.

orfandad [orfanˈdað] *nf* orphanhood.

orfebrería [orfeβreˈria] *nf* gold/silver work.

organillo [orɣaˈniʎo] *nm* barrel organ.

organismo [orɣaˈnismo] *nm* (*BIO*) organism; (*POL*) organization.

organista [orɣaˈnista] *nm/f* organist.

organización [orɣaniθaˈθjon] *nf* organization; **organizar** *vt* to organize.

órgano [ˈorɣano] *nm* organ.

orgasmo [orˈɣasmo] *nm* orgasm.

orgía [orˈxia] *nf* orgy.

orgullo [orˈɣuʎo] *nm* (*altanería*) pride; (*autorespeto*) self-respect; **orgulloso, a** *a* (gen) proud; (altanero) haughty.

orientación [orjenta'θjon] nf (posición) position; (dirección) direction; (entrenamiento) training.

orientar [orjen'tar] vt (situar) to orientate; (señalar) to point; (dirigir) to direct; (informar) to guide; ~**se** vr to get one's bearings; (decidirse) to decide on a course of action.

oriente [o'rjente] nm east; **Cercano/Medio/Lejano O~** Near/ Middle/Far East.

origen [o'rixen] nm (germen) origin; (nacimiento) lineage, birth.

original [orixi'nal] a (nuevo) original; (extraño) odd, strange; ~**idad** nf originality.

originar [orixi'nar] vt to originate; ~**se** vr to originate; ~**io, a** a (nativo) native; (primordial) original.

orilla [o'riʎa] nf (borde) border; (de río) bank; (de bosque, tela) edge; (de taza etc) rim, lip; (de calle) pavement; **orillar** vt (bordear) to skirt, go round; (resolver) to wind up; (tocar: asunto) to touch briefly on.

orín [o'rin] nm rust.

orina [o'rina] nf urine; **orinal** nm (chamber) pot; **orinar** vi to urinate; **orinarse** vr to wet o.s.; **orines** nmpl urine sg.

oriundo, a [o'rjundo, a] a: ~ **de** native of.

orlar [or'lar] vt (adornar) to adorn, decorate; (encuadrar) to frame.

ornamentar [ornamen'tar] vt (adornar, ataviar) to adorn; (revestir) to bedeck.

ornamento [orna'mento] nm ornament.

ornar [or'nar] vt to adorn.

oro ['oro] nm gold; ~**s** nmpl (NAIPES) hearts.

oropel [oro'pel] nm tinsel.

orozuz [oro'θuθ] nm liquorice.

orquesta [or'kesta] nf orchestra; ~ **de cámara/sinfónica** chamber/symphony orchestra.

orquídea [or'kiðea] nf orchid.

ortiga [or'tixa] nf nettle.

ortodoxo, a [orto'ðokso, a] a orthodox.

ortografía [ortoɤra'fia] nf spelling.

ortopedia [orto'peðja] nf orthopaedics sg.

oruga [o'ruxa] nf caterpillar; (BOT) rocket.

orzuelo [or'θwelo] nm (MED) stye.

os [os] pron (gen) you; (a vosotros) to you.

osa ['osa] nf (she-)bear; **O~ Mayor/Menor** Great/Little Bear.

osadía [osa'ðia] nf daring.

osar [o'sar] vi to dare.

oscilación [osθila'θjon] nf (movimiento) oscillation; (fluctuación) fluctuation; (vacilación) hesitation; (columpio) swinging, movement to and fro; **oscilar** vi to oscillate; to fluctuate; to hesitate.

ósculo ['oskulo] nm kiss.

oscurecer [oskure'θer] vt to darken // vi to grow dark; ~**se** vr to grow or get dark.

oscuridad [oskuri'ðað] nf obscurity; (tinieblas) darkness.

oscuro, a [os'kuro, a] a dark; (fig) obscure; **a** ~**as** in the dark.

óseo, a ['oseo, a] a bony.

oso ['oso] nm bear; ~ **de peluche** teddy bear; ~ **hormiguero** anteater.

ostensible [osten'sißle] a obvious.

ostentación [ostenta'θjon] nf (gen) ostentation; (acto) display; **ostentar** vt (gen) to show; (pey) to flaunt, show off; (poseer) to have, possess; **ostentoso, a** a ostentatious, showy.

osteópata [oste'opata] nm/f osteopath.

ostra ['ostra] nf oyster.

ostracismo [ostra'θismo] nm ostracism.

osuno, a [o'suno, a] a bear-like.

OTAN ['otan] nf abr de **Organización del Tratado del Atlántico Norte** NATO (North Atlantic Treaty Organization).

otear [ote'ar] vt to observe; (fig) to look into.

otitis [o'titis] nf earache.

otoñal [oto'nal] a autumnal.

otoño [o'toɲo] nm autumn.

otorgamiento [otorɤa'mjento] nm conferring, granting; (JUR) execution.

otorgar [otor'ɤar] vt (conceder) to concede; (dar) to grant.

otro, a ['otro, a] a (sg) another; (pl) other // pron another one; ~**s** others; ~**a cosa** something else; **de** ~**a manera** otherwise; **en** ~ **tiempo** formerly, once; **ni uno ni** ~ neither one nor the other; ~ **tanto** the same again.

ovación [oßa'θjon] nf ovation.

oval [o'ßal], **ovalado, a** [oßa'laðo, a] a oval; **óvalo** nm oval.

oveja [o'ßexa] nf sheep; **ovejuno, a** a sheep cpd.

overol [oße'rol] nm overalls pl.

ovillar [oßi'ʎar] vt to wind (into a ball); ~**se** vr to curl up into a ball.

OVNI ['oßni] nm abr de **objeto volante no identificado** UFO (unidentified flying object).

ovulación [oßula'θjon] nf ovulation; **óvulo** nm ovum.

oxidación [oksiða'θjon] nf rusting; **oxidar** vt to rust; **oxidarse** vr to become rusty.

óxido ['oksiðo] nm oxide.

oxigenado, a [oksixe'naðo, a] a (QUÍMICA) oxygenated; (pelo) bleached // nm peroxide.

oxígeno [ok'sixeno] nm oxygen.

oyente [o'jente] nm/f listener, hearer.

oyes, oyó etc vb ver **oír**.

P

P abr de **padre**.

pabellón [paße'ʎon] nm bell tent; (ARQ) pavilion; (de hospital etc) block, section; (bandera) flag.

pábilo ['paßilo] nm wick.

pacer [pa'θer] vi to graze // vt to graze on.

paciencia [pa'θjenθja] nf patience.

paciente [pa'θjente] a, nm/f patient.

pacificación [paθifika'θjon] *nf* pacification; **pacificar** *vt* to pacify; (*tranquilizar*) to calm.

pacífico, a [pa'θifiko, a] *a* (*persona*) peace-loving; (*existencia*) pacific; **el** (*océano*) **P~** the Pacific (Ocean).

pacifismo [paθi'fismo] *nm* pacifism; **pacifista** *nm/f* pacifist.

pactar [pak'tar] *vt* to agree to, agree on // *vi* to come to an agreement.

pacto ['pakto] *nm* (*tratado*) pact; (*acuerdo*) agreement.

padecer [paðe'θer] *vt* (*sufrir*) to suffer; (*soportar*) to endure, put up with; (*ser víctima de*) to be a victim of; **padecimiento** *nm* suffering.

padrastro [pa'ðrastro] *nm* stepfather.

padre ['paðre] *nm* father // *a* (*fam*): **un éxito ~** a tremendous success; **~s** *nmpl* parents.

padrino [pa'ðrino] *nm* (*REL*) godfather; (*fig*) sponsor, patron; **~s** *nmpl* godparents; **~ de boda** best man.

padrón [pa'ðron] *nm* (*censo*) census, roll; (*de socios*) register; (*TEC*) pattern.

paella [pa'eʎa] *nf* paella, *dish of rice with meat, shellfish etc*.

paga ['paɣa] *nf* (*dinero pagado*) payment; (*sueldo*) pay, wages *pl*.

pagadero, a [paɣa'ðero, a] *a* payable; **~ a la entrega/a plazos** payable on delivery/in instalments.

pagador, a [paɣa'ðor, a] *nm/f* (*quien paga*) payer; (*cajero*) cashier.

pagano, a [pa'ɣano, a] *a*, *nm/f* pagan, heathen.

pagar [pa'ɣar] *vt* (*gen*) to pay; (*las compras, crimen*) to pay for; (*fig: favor*) to repay // *vi* to pay; **~ al contado/a plazos** to pay (in) cash/in instalments; **~se** *vr*: **~se con algo** to be content with sth; **~se de sí mismo** to be conceited.

pagaré [paɣa're] *nm* I.O.U.

página ['paxina] *nf* page.

pago ['paɣo] *nm* (*dinero*) payment; (*fig*) return; (*barrio*) district; (*AM*) home region, home area; **estar ~** to be even or quits; **~ anticipado/a cuenta/a la entrega/en especie** advance payment/payment on account/cash on delivery/payment in kind.

país [pa'is] *nm* (*gen*) country; (*región*) land; (*paisaje*) landscape; **los P~es Bajos** the Low Countries; **el P~ Vasco** the Basque Country; **paisaje** *nm* countryside, scenery.

paisano, a [pai'sano, a] *a* of the same country // *nm/f* (*compatriota*) fellow countryman/woman; (*campesino*) peasant; **vestir de ~** (*soldado*) to be in civvies (*fam*); (*guardia*) to be in plain clothes.

paja ['paxa] *nf* straw; (*fig*) trash, rubbish.

pájara ['paxara] *nf* hen bird; (*cometa*) kite; (*mujer*) thief.

pájaro ['paxaro] *nm* bird.

pajita [pa'xita] *nf* (drinking) straw.

pala ['pala] *nf* (*de mango largo*) spade; (*de mango corto*) shovel; (*raqueta etc*) bat; (: *de tenis*) racquet; (*CULIN*) slice; **~ matamoscas** fly swat.

palabra [pa'laβra] *nf* (*gen*) word; (*facultad*) (power of) speech; (*derecho de hablar*) right to speak; **palabrota** *nf* swearword.

palacio [pa'laθjo] *nm* palace; (*mansión*) mansion, large house; **~ de justicia** courthouse; **~ municipal** town/city hall.

paladar [pala'ðar] *nm* (*gen*) palate; **paladear** *vt* to taste.

palanca [pa'lanka] *nf* lever; (*fig*) pull, influence.

palangana [palan'gana] *nf* washbasin.

palco ['palko] *nm* box.

palenque [pa'lenke] *nm* (*cerca*) stockade, fence; (*área*) arena, enclosure; (*de gallos*) pit.

Palestina [pales'tina] *nf* Palestine.

paliar [pa'ljar] *vt* (*mitigar*) to mitigate; (*disfrazar*) to conceal; **paliativo** *nm* palliative.

palidecer [paliðe'θer] *vi* to turn pale; **palidez** *nf* paleness; **pálido, a** *a* pale.

palillo [pa'liʎo] *nm* small stick; (*para dientes*) toothpick.

paliza [pa'liθa] *nf* beating, thrashing.

palizada [pali'θaða] *nf* fence; (*lugar cercado*) enclosure.

palma ['palma] *nf* (*ANAT*) palm; (*árbol*) palm tree; **batir o dar ~s** to clap, applaud; **~da** *nf* slap; **~s** *nfpl* clapping *sg*, applause *sg*.

palmear [palme'ar] *vi* to clap.

palmo ['palmo] *nm* (*medida*) span; (*fig*) small amount; **~ a ~** inch by inch.

palmotear [palmote'ar] *vi* to clap, applaud; **palmoteo** *nm* clapping, applause; (*palmada*) slap.

palo ['palo] *nm* stick; (*poste*) post, pole; (*mango*) handle, shaft; (*golpe*) blow, hit; (*de golf*) club; (*de béisbol*) bat; (*NAUT*) mast; (*NAIPES*) suit; **~ de tienda** tent pole.

paloma [pa'loma] *nf* dove, pigeon.

palomilla [palo'miʎa] *nf* moth; (*TEC: tuerca*) wing nut; (: *hierro*) angle iron.

palomitas [palo'mitas] *nfpl* popcorn *sg*.

palpar [pal'par] *vt* to touch, feel; (*acariciar*) to caress, fondle; (*caminar a tientas*) to grope one's way along; (*fig*) to appreciate, understand; **~ a uno** to frisk sb.

palpitación [palpita'θjon] *nf* palpitation; **palpitante** *a* palpitating; (*fig*) burning; **palpitar** *vi* to palpitate; (*latir*) to beat.

palúdico, a [pa'luðiko, a] *a* marshy.

paludismo [palu'ðismo] *nm* malaria.

pampa ['pampa] *nf* (*AM*) pampa(s), prairie.

pan [pan] *nm* (*en general*) bread; (*una barra*) loaf; (*trigo*) wheat; **de ~ llevar** arable; **~ integral** wholemeal bread; **~ molido** breadcrumbs *pl*.

pana ['pana] *nf* corduroy.

panadería [panaðe'ria] *nf* baker's (shop); **panadero, a** *nm/f* baker.

Panamá [pana'ma] *nm* Panama; **panameño, a** *a* a Panamanian.
pancarta [pan'karta] *nf* placard, banner.
panda ['panda] *nf* panda.
pandereta [pande'reta] *nf* tambourine.
pandilla [pan'diʎa] *nf* set, group; (*de criminales*) gang; (*pey*) clique.
pando, a ['pando, a] *a* sagging.
panel [pa'nel] *nm* panel.
pánico [pa'niko] *nm* panic.
panorama [pano'rama] *nm* panorama; (*vista*) view.
pantalones [panta'lones] *nmpl* trousers.
pantalla [pan'taʎa] *nf* (*de cine*) screen; (*cubre-luz*) lampshade.
pantano [pan'tano] *nm* (*ciénaga*) marsh, swamp; (*depósito: de agua*) reservoir; (*fig*) jam, fix, difficulty.
pantera [pan'tera] *nf* panther.
pantimedias [panti'meðjas] *nfpl* tights.
pantomima [panto'mima] *nf* pantomime.
pantorrilla [panto'rriʎa] *nf* calf (of the leg).
pantufla [pan'tufla] *nf* slipper.
panza ['panθa] *nf* belly, paunch; **panzudo, a, panzón, ona** *a* fat, potbellied.
pañal [pa'ɲal] *nm* nappy; **~es** *nmpl* (*fig*) early stages, infancy *sg*.
pañería [paɲe'ria] *nf* drapery; **pañero, a** *nm/f* draper.
paño ['paɲo] *nm* (*tela*) cloth; (*pedazo de tela*) (piece of) cloth; (*trapo*) duster, rag; **~ higiénico** sanitary towel; **~s menores** underclothes.
pañuelo [pa'ɲwelo] *nm* handkerchief, hanky (*fam*); (*para la cabeza*) (head)scarf.
papa ['papa] *nf* (*AM*) potato // *nm*: **el P~** the Pope.
papá [pa'pa] (*pl* **~s**) *nm* (*fam*) dad, daddy.
papagayo [papa'vajo] *nm* parrot.
papamoscas [papa'moskas] *nm inv* fly-catcher.
papanatas [papa'natas] *nm inv* (*fam*) sucker, simpleton.
papar [pa'par] *vt* to swallow, gulp (down).
paparrucha [papa'rrutʃa] *nf* (*tontería*) piece of nonsense; (*engaño*) hoax.
papaya [pa'paja] *nf* papaya.
papel [pa'pel] *nm* (*en general*) paper; (*hoja de papel*) sheet of paper; (*TEATRO*) part, role; **~ de calcar/carbón/de cartas** tracing paper/carbon paper/stationery; **~ de envolver/de empapelar** brown paper, wrapping paper/wallpaper; **~ de estaño/higiénico** tinfoil/toilet paper; **~ de lija** sandpaper; **~ moneda** paper money; **~ secante** blotting paper.
papeleo [pape'leo] *nm* red tape.
papelera [pape'lera] *nf* (*cesto*) wastepaper basket; (*escritorio*) desk.
papelería [papele'ria] *nf* (*papeles*) mass of papers; (*tienda*) stationer's (shop).
papeleta [pape'leta] *nf* (*pedazo de papel*) slip *or* bit of paper; (*tarjeta de archivo*) index card; (*POL*) ballot paper; (*ESCOL*) report.

paperas [pa'peras] *nfpl* mumps.
paquete [pa'kete] *nm* (*caja*) packet; (*bulto*) parcel; (*AM: fam*) nuisance, bore.
par [par] *a* (*igual*) like, equal; (*MAT*) even // *nm* equal; (*de guantes*) pair; (*de veces*) couple; (*dignidad*) peer; (*GOLF, COM*) par; **abrir de ~ en ~** to open wide.
para ['para] *prep* (*gen*) for; **no es ~ comer** it's not for eating; **decir ~ sí** to say to o.s.; **¿~ qué lo quieres?** what do you want it for?; **se casaron ~ separarse otra vez** they married only to separate again; **lo tendré ~ mañana** I'll have it for tomorrow; **ir ~ casa** to go home, head for home; **~ profesor es muy estúpido** he's very stupid for a teacher; **¿quién es usted ~ gritar así?** who are you to shout like that?; **tengo bastante ~ vivir** I have enough to live on; **estoy ~ cantar** I'm about to sing.
parabién [para'βjen] *nm* congratulations *pl*.
parábola [pa'raβola] *nf* parable; (*MAT*) parabola.
parabrisas [para'βrisas] *nm inv* windscreen.
paracaídas [paraka'iðas] *nm inv* parachute; **paracaidista** *nm/f* parachutist; (*MIL*) paratrooper.
parachoques [para'tʃokes] *nm inv* bumper; (*en auto*) shock absorber.
parada [pa'raða] *nf ver* **parado**.
paradero [para'ðero] *nm* stopping-place; (*situación*) whereabouts; (*fin*) end.
parado, a [pa'raðo, a] *a* (*persona*) motionless, standing still; (*fábrica*) closed, at a standstill; (*coche*) stopped; (*AM*) standing (up); (*sin empleo*) unemployed, idle; (*confuso*) confused // *nm* (*gen*) stop; (*acto*) stopping; (*de industria*) shutdown, stoppage; (*de pagos*) suspension; (*lugar*) stopping-place; (*apuesta*) bet; **~a de autobús** bus stop.
paradoja [para'ðoxa] *nf* paradox.
parador [para'ðor] *nm* (*luxury*) hotel.
paráfrasis [pa'rafrasis] *nm inv* paraphrase.
paragolpes [para'volpes] *nm inv* bumper.
paraguas [pa'raxwas] *nm inv* umbrella.
Paraguay [para'xwai] *nm*: **el ~** Paraguay.
paraíso [para'iso] *nm* paradise, heaven.
paraje [pa'raxe] *nm* place, spot.
paralelo, a [para'lelo, a] *a* parallel.
parálisis [pa'ralisis] *nf* paralysis; **paralítico, a** *a, nm/f* paralytic; **paralizar** *vt* to paralyse; **paralizarse** *vr* to become paralysed; (*fig*) to come to a standstill.
paramilitar [paramili'tar] *a* para-military.
páramo ['paramo] *nm* bleak plateau.
parangón [paran'gon] *nm*: **sin ~** incomparable.
paranoico, a [para'noiko, a] *nm/f* paranoiac.
parapléjico, a [para'plexiko, a] *a, nm/f* paraplegic.

parar [pa'rar] *vt* to stop; (*golpe*) to ward off // *vi* to stop; ~**se** *vr* to stop; (*AM*) to stand up; **ha parado de llover** it has stopped raining; **van a ~ en la comisaria** they're going to end up in the police station; ~**se en** to pay attention to.

parásito, a [pa'rasito, a] *nm/f* parasite.

parasol [para'sol] *nm* parasol, sunshade.

parcela [par'θela] *nf* plot, piece of ground.

parcial [par'θjal] *a* (*pago*) part-; (*eclipse*) partial; (*juez*) prejudiced, biased; ~**idad** *nf* (*prejuicio*) prejudice, bias; (*partido, facción*) party, faction.

parco, a ['parko, a] *a* (*frugal*) frugal; (*mezquino*) mean; (*moderado*) moderate.

parche ['partʃe] *nm* (*MED*) sticking plaster; (*gen*) patch.

parear [pare'θer] *vt* (*juntar, hacer par*) to match, put together; (*calcetines*) to put into pairs; (*BIO*) to mate, pair.

parecer [pare'θer] *nm* (*opinión*) opinion, view; (*aspecto*) looks *pl* // *vi* (*tener apariencia*) to seem, look; (*asemejarse*) to look like, seem like; (*aparecer, llegar*) to appear; ~**se** *vr* to look alike, resemble each other; ~**se a** to look like, resemble; **según** *o* **a lo que parece** evidently, apparently; **me parece que** I think (that), it seems to me that; **parecido, a** *a* similar // *nm* similarity, likeness, resemblance; **bien parecido** good-looking, nice-looking.

pared [pa'reð] *nf* wall.

parejo, a [pa'rexo, a] *a* (*igual*) equal; (*liso*) smooth, even // *nf* (*dos*) pair; (: *de personas*) couple; (*el otro: de un par*) other one (of a pair); (: *persona*) partner.

parentela [paren'tela] *nf* relations *pl*.

parentesco [paren'tesko] *nm* relationship.

paréntesis [pa'rentesis] *nm inv* parenthesis; (*digresión*) digression; (*en escrito*) bracket.

parezco *etc vb ver* **parecer.**

pariente, a [pa'rjente, a] *nm/f* relative, relation.

parihuela [pari'wela] *nf* stretcher.

parir [pa'rir] *vt* to give birth to // *vi* (*mujer*) to give birth, have a baby.

París [pa'ris] *n* Paris.

parlamentar [parlamen'tar] *vi* (*hablar*) to talk, converse; (*negociar*) to parley.

parlamentario, a [parlamen'tarjo, a] *a* parliamentary // *nm/f* member of parliament.

parlamento [parla'mento] *nm* (*POL*) parliament; (*conversación*) parley.

parlanchín, ina [parlan'tʃin, ina] *a* loose-tongued, indiscreet // *nm/f* chatterbox.

parlar [par'lar] *vi* to chatter (away), talk (a lot); (*chismear*) to gossip; **parlero, a** *a* talkative; gossipy; (*pájaro*) singing.

paro ['paro] *nm* (*huelga*) stoppage (of work), strike; (*desempleo*) unemployment; **subsidio de ~** unemployment benefit; **hay ~ en la industria** work in the industry is at a standstill.

parodia [pa'roðja] *nf* parody; **parodiar** *vt* to parody.

parpadear [parpaðe'ar] *vi* (*los ojos*) to blink; (*luz*) to flicker.

párpado ['parpaðo] *nm* eyelid.

parque ['parke] *nm* (*lugar verde*) park; (*depósito*) depot; ~ **de atracciones/de estacionamiento/zoológico** fairground/car park/zoo.

parquímetro [par'kimetro] *nm* parking meter.

párrafo ['parrafo] *nm* paragraph; **echar un ~** (*fam*) to have a chat.

parranda [pa'rranda] *nf* (*fam*) spree, binge.

parrilla [pa'rriʎa] *nf* (*CULIN*) grill; (*de coche*) grille; **(carne de) ~** barbecue; ~**da** *nf* barbecue.

párroco ['parroko] *nm* parish priest.

parroquia [pa'rrokja] *nf* parish; (*iglesia*) parish church; (*COM*) clientele, customers *pl*; ~**no, a** *nm/f* parishioner; client, customer.

parte ['parte] *nm* message; (*informe*) report // *nf* (*gen*) part; (*lado, cara*) side; (*de reparto*) share; (*JUR*) party; **en alguna ~ de Europa** somewhere in Europe; **en cualquier ~** anywhere; **en gran ~** to a large extent; **la mayor ~ de los españoles** most Spaniards; **de algún tiempo a esta ~** for some time past; **de ~ de alguien** on sb's behalf; **por ~ de** on the part of; **yo por mi ~** I for my part; **por otra ~** on the other hand; **dar ~** to inform; **tomar ~** to take part.

partera [par'tera] *nf* midwife.

partición [parti'θjon] *nf* division, sharing-out; (*POL*) partition.

participación [partiθipa'θjon] *nf* (*acto*) participation, taking part; (*parte, COM*) share; (*de lotería*) small prize; (*aviso*) notice, notification.

participante [partiθi'pante] *nm/f* participant; **participar** *vt* to notify, inform // *vi* to take part, participate; (*compartir*) to share.

partícipe [par'tiθipe] *nm/f* participant.

particular [partiku'lar] *a* (*especial*) particular, special; (*individual, personal*) private, personal // *nm* (*punto, asunto*) particular, point; (*individuo*) individual; **tiene coche ~** he has a car of his own; ~**izar** *vt* to distinguish; (*especificar*) to specify; (*detallar*) to give details about.

partida [par'tiða] *nf* (*salida*) departure; (*COM*) entry, item; (*juego*) game; (*apuesta*) bet; (*grupo, bando*) band, group; **mala ~** dirty trick; ~ **de nacimiento/matrimonio/defunción** birth/marriage/death certificate.

partidario, a [parti'ðarjo, a] *a* partisan // *nm/f* (*DEPORTE*) supporter; (*POL*) partisan.

partido [par'tiðo] *nm* (*POL*) party; (*encuentro*) game, match; (*apoyo*) support; (*equipo*) team; **sacar ~ de** to profit from, benefit from; **tomar ~** to take sides.

partir [par'tir] *vt* (*dividir*) to split, divide;

(*compartir, distribuir*) to share (out), distribute; (*romper*) to break open, split open; (*rebanada*) to cut (off) // *vi* (*tomar camino*) to set off, set out; (*comenzar*) to start (off or out); ~**se** *vr* to crack or split or break (in two *etc*); **a** ~ **de** (starting) from.

parto ['parto] *nm* birth; (*fig*) product, creation; **estar de** ~ to be in labour.

parvulario [parβu'larjo] *nm* nursery school, kindergarten.

pasa ['pasa] *nf* raisin; ~ **de Corinto/de Esmirna** currant/sultana.

pasada [pa'saða] *nf ver* **pasado.**

pasadizo [pasa'ðiθo] *nm* (*pasillo*) passage, corridor; (*callejuela*) alley.

pasado, a [pa'saðo, a] *a* past; (*malo: comida, fruta*) bad; (*muy cocido*) overdone; (*anticuado*) out of date // *nm* past // *nf* passing, passage; (*acción de pulir*) rub, polish; ~**s** *nmpl* ancestors; ~ **mañana** the day after tomorrow; **el mes** ~ last month; **de** ~**a** in passing, incidentally; **una mala** ~**a** a dirty trick.

pasador [pasa'ðor] *nm* (*gen*) bolt; (*de pelo*) pin, grip; ~**es** *nmpl* cufflinks.

pasaje [pa'saxe] *nm* (*gen*) passage; (*pago de viaje*) fare; (*los pasajeros*) passengers *pl*; (*pasillo*) passageway.

pasajero, a [pasa'xero, a] *a* passing; (*calle*) busy // *nm/f* passenger; (*viajero*) traveller.

pasamanos [pasa'manos] *nm* rail, handrail; (*de escalera*) banister.

pasaporte [pasa'porte] *nm* passport.

pasar [pa'sar] *vt* (*gen*) to pass; (*tiempo*) to spend; (*durezas*) to suffer, endure; (*noticia*) to give, pass on; (*río*) to cross; (*barrera*) to pass through; (*falta*) to overlook, tolerate; (*contrincante*) to surpass, do better than; (*coche*) to overtake; (*enfermedad*) to give, infect with // *vi* (*gen*) to pass; (*terminarse*) to be over; (*ocurrir*) to happen; ~**se** *vr* (*flores*) to fade; (*comida*) to go bad, go off; (*fig*) to overdo it, go too far; ~ **de** to go beyond, exceed; **¡pase!** come in!; ~**se al enemigo** to go over to the enemy; **se me pasó** I forgot; **no se le pasa nada** nothing escapes him, he misses nothing; **pase lo que pase** come what may.

pasarela [pasa'rela] *nf* footbridge; (*en barco*) gangway.

pasatiempo [pasa'tjempo] *nm* pastime; (*distracción*) amusement.

Pascua ['paskwa] *nf*: ~ (**de Resurrección**) Easter; ~ **de Navidad** Christmas; ~**s** *nfpl* Christmas time; **¡felices** ~**s!** Merry Christmas.

pase ['pase] *nm* pass.

pasear [pase'ar] *vt* to take for a walk; (*exhibir*) to parade, show off // *vi*, ~**se** *vr* to walk, go for a walk; (*holgazanear*) to idle, loaf about; ~ **en coche** to go for a drive; **paseo** *nm* (*avenida*) avenue; (*distancia corta*) short walk; **dar un paseo** to go for a walk.

pasillo [pa'siʎo] *nm* passage, corridor.

pasión [pa'sjon] *nf* passion.

pasivo, a [pa'siβo, a] *a* passive; (*inactivo*) inactive // *nm* (*COM*) liabilities *pl*, debts *pl*.

pasmar [pas'mar] *vt* (*asombrar*) to amaze, astonish; (*enfriar*) to chill (to the bone); **pasmo** *nm* amazement, astonishment; chill; (*fig*) wonder, marvel; **pasmoso, a** *a* amazing, astonishing.

paso, a ['paso, a] *a* dried // *nm* (*gen*) step; (*modo de andar*) walk; (*huella*) footprint; (*rapidez*) speed, pace, rate; (*camino accesible*) way through, passage; (*cruce*) crossing; (*pasaje*) passing, passage; (*GEO*) pass; (*estrecho*) strait; **a ese** ~ (*fig*) at that rate; **salir al** ~ **de** *o* **a** to waylay; **estar de** ~ to be passing through; ~ **elevado** flyover; **prohibido el** ~ no entry; **ceda el** ~ give way.

pasta ['pasta] *nf* (*gen*) paste; (*CULIN: masa*) dough; (: *de bizcochos etc*) pastry; (*cartón*) cardboard; (*fam*) money, dough (*fam*); ~**s** *nfpl* (*bizcochos*) pastries, small cakes; (*fideos, espaguetis etc*) noodles, spaghetti *sg etc*; ~ **de dientes** *o* **dentífrica** toothpaste; ~ **de madera** wood pulp.

pastar [pas'tar], **pastear** [paste'ar] *vt, vi* to graze.

pastel [pas'tel] *nm* (*dulce*) cake; (*de carne*) pie; (*pintura*) pastel; ~**ería** *nf* cake shop, pastry shop.

pasteurizado, a [pasteuri'θaðo, a] *a* pasteurized.

pastilla [pas'tiʎa] *nf* (*de jabón, chocolate*) cake, bar; (*píldora*) tablet, pill.

pasto ['pasto] *nm* (*hierba*) grass; (*lugar*) pasture, field.

pastor, a [pas'tor, a] *nm/f* shepherd/ess // *nm* clergyman, pastor.

pata ['pata] *nf* (*pierna*) leg; (*pie*) foot; (*de muebles*) leg; ~**s arriba** upside down; **meter la** ~ to put one's foot in it; (*TEC*): ~ **de cabra** crowbar; **tener buena/mala** ~ to be lucky/unlucky; ~**da** *nf* stamp; (*puntapié*) kick.

patalear [patale'ar] *vi* to stamp one's feet.

patata [pa'tata] *nf* potato; ~**s fritas** *o* **a la española** chips, French fries; ~**s inglesas** crisps.

patear [pate'ar] *vt* (*pisar*) to stamp on, trample (on); (*pegar con el pie*) to kick // *vi* to stamp (with rage), stamp one's foot.

patente [pa'tente] *a* obvious, evident; (*COM*) patent // *nf* patent; **patentizar** *vt* to show, reveal, make evident.

paternal [pater'nal] *a* fatherly, paternal; **paterno, a** *a* paternal.

patético, a [pa'tetiko, a] *a* pathetic, moving.

patillas [pa'tiʎas] *nfpl* sideburns.

patín [pa'tin] *nm* skate; (*de tobogán*) runner; **patinaje** *nm* skating; **patinar** *vi* to skate; (*resbalarse*) to skid, slip; (*fam*) to slip up, blunder.

patio ['patjo] *nm* (*de casa*) patio, courtyard; ~ **de recreo** playground.

pato ['pato] *nm* duck; **pagar el** ~ (*fam*) to take the blame, carry the can.

patológico, a [pato'loxiko, a] *a* pathological.

patraña [pa'traɲa] *nf* story, fib.

patria ['patrja] *nf* native land, mother country.

patrimonio [patri'monjo] *nm* inheritance; (*fig*) heritage.

patriota [pa'trjota] *nm/f* patriot; **patriotismo** *nm* patriotism.

patrocinar [patroθi'nar] *vt* to sponsor; (*apoyar*) to back, support; **patrocinio** *nm* sponsorship; backing, support.

patrón, ona [pa'tron, ona] *nm/f* (*jefe*) boss, chief, master/mistress; (*propietario*) landlord/lady; (*REL*) patron saint // *nm* (*TEC, costura*) pattern; **patronal** *a*: **la clase patronal** management; **patronato** *nm* sponsorship; (*acto*) patronage; (*COM*) employers' association.

patrulla [pa'truʎa] *nf* patrol.

pausa ['pausa] *nf* pause; (*intervalo*) break; (*interrupción*) interruption.

pausado, a [pau'saðo, a] *a* slow, deliberate.

pauta ['pauta] *nf* line, guide line.

pavo ['paβo] *nm* turkey; ~ **real** peacock.

pavor [pa'βor] *nm* dread, terror.

payaso, a [pa'jaso, a] *nm/f* clown.

paz [paθ] *nf* peace; (*tranquilidad*) peacefulness, tranquillity; **hacer las paces** to make peace; (*fig*) to make up.

P.C.E. *abr de* **Partido Comunista Español**.

peaje [pe'axe] *nm* toll.

peatón [pea'ton] *nm* pedestrian.

peca ['peka] *nf* freckle.

pecado [pe'kaðo] *nm* sin; **pecador, a** *a* sinful // *nm/f* sinner.

pecaminoso, a [pekami'noso, a] *a* sinful.

pecar [pe'kar] *vi* (*REL*) to sin; (*fig*): **peca de generoso** he is too generous.

peculiar [peku'ljar] *a* special, peculiar; (*característico*) typical, characteristic; ~**idad** *nf* peculiarity; special feature, characteristic.

pecho ['petʃo] *nm* (*ANAT*) chest; (*de mujer*) breast(s) (*pl*), bosom; (*corazón*) heart, breast; (*valor*) courage, spirit; **dar el** ~ **a** to breast-feed; **tomar algo a** ~ to take sth to heart.

pechuga [pe'tʃuɣa] *nf* breast (of chicken *etc*).

pedal [pe'ðal] *nm* pedal; ~**ear** *vi* to pedal.

pedante [pe'ðante] *a* pedantic // *nm/f* pedant; ~**ría** *nf* pedantry.

pedazo [pe'ðaθo] *nm* piece, bit; **hacerse** ~**s** to fall to pieces; (*romperse*) to smash, shatter.

pedernal [peðer'nal] *nm* flint.

pediatra [pe'ðjatra] *nm/f* pediatrician.

pedicuro, a [peðiˈkuro, a] *nm/f* chiropodist.

pedido [pe'ðiðo] *nm* (*COM: mandado*) order; (*petición*) request.

pedir [pe'ðir] *vt* to ask for, request; (*comida, COM: mandar*) to order; (*exigir:*

precio) to ask; (*necesitar*) to need, demand, require // *vi* to ask; **me pidió que cerrara la puerta** he asked me to shut the door; **¿cuánto piden por el coche?** how much are they asking for the car?

pegadizo, a [peɣaˈðiθo, a] *a* sticky; (*MED*) infectious // *nm/f* sponger, hanger-on (*fam*).

pegajoso, a [peɣaˈxoso, a] *a* sticky, adhesive; (*MED*) infectious.

pegamento [peɣaˈmento] *nm* gum, sticky stuff.

pegar [pe'ɣar] *vt* (*papel, sellos*) to stick (on); (*cartel*) to post, stick up; (*coser*) to sew (on); (*unir: partes*) to join, fix together; (*MED*) to give, infect with; (*dar: golpe*) to give, deal // *vi* (*adherirse*) to stick, adhere; (*prender: fuego*) to catch; (*ir juntos: colores*) to match, go together; (*golpear*) to hit; (*quemar: el sol*) to strike hot, burn (*fig*); ~**se** *vr* (*gen*) to stick; (*dos personas*) to hit each other, fight; (*fam*): ~ **un grito** to let out a yell; ~ **un salto** to jump (with fright); ~ **en** to touch; ~**se un tiro** to shoot o.s.

peinado [pei'naðo] *nm* (*en peluquería*) hairdo; (*estilo*) hair style.

peinador, a [peina'ðor, a] *nm/f* hairdresser.

peinar [pei'nar] *vt* to comb; (*hacer estilo*) to style; ~**se** *vr* to comb one's hair.

peine ['peine] *nm* comb; ~**ta** *nf* ornamental comb.

Pekín [pe'kin] *n* Pekin(g).

pelado, a [pe'laðo, a] *a* (*cabeza*) shorn; (*fruta*) peeled; (*campo, fig*) bare // *nm* bare patch; (*fig*) wretch, poor devil.

pelaje [pe'laxe] *nm* (*ZOOL*) fur, coat; (*fig*) appearance.

pelambre [pe'lambre] *nm* (*pelo largo*) long hair, mop; (*piel de animal cortado*) fur; (: *de oveja*) fleece; (*parte sin piel*) bare patch.

pelar [pe'lar] *vt* (*cortar el pelo a*) to cut the hair of; (*quitar la piel: animal*) to skin; ~**se** *vr* (*la piel*) to peel off; (*persona*) to lose one's hair; **voy a** ~**me** I'm going to get my hair cut.

peldaño [pel'daɲo] *nm* step.

pelea [pe'lea] *nf* (*lucha*) fight; (*discusión*) quarrel, row; **pelear** *vi* to fight; **pelearse** *vr* to fight; (*reñirse*) to fall out, quarrel.

peletería [pelete'ria] *nf* furrier's, fur shop.

pelicano [peli'kano], **pelícano** [pe'likano] *nm* pelican.

pelicorto, a [peli'korto, a] *a* short-haired.

película [pe'likula] *nf* film; (*cobertura ligera*) thin covering; (*FOTO: rollo*) roll or reel of film.

peligro [pe'liɣro] *nm* danger; (*riesgo*) risk; **correr** ~ **de** to be in danger of; ~**so, a** *a* dangerous; risky.

pelirrojo, a [peli'rroxo, a] *a* red-haired, red-headed.

pelo ['pelo] *nm* (*cabellos*) hair; (*de barba, bigote*) whisker; (*de animal: pellejo*) fur, coat; (de perro etc) hair, coat; **al ~** just right; **venir al ~** to be exactly what one needs; **un hombre de ~ en pecho** a brave man; **por los ~s** by the skin of one's teeth; **no tener ~s en la lengua** to be outspoken, not mince words; **tomar el ~ a uno** to pull sb's leg.

pelón, ona [pe'lon, ona] a a hairless, bald; (fig) broke, skint (fam).

pelota [pe'lota] nf ball; (fam: cabeza) nut (fam); **en ~** stark naked; **~ vasca** pelota.

pelotón [pelo'ton] nm (pelota) big ball; (muchedumbre) crowd; (MIL) squad, detachment.

peluca [pe'luka] nf wig.

peluche [pe'lutʃe] nm felt.

peludo, a [pe'luðo, a] a hairy, shaggy.

peluquería [peluke'ria] nf hairdresser's; (para hombres) barber's (shop); **peluquero, a** nm/f hairdresser; barber.

pelleja [pe'ʎexa] nf skin, hide; (fam) whore.

pellejo [pe'ʎexo] nm (de animal) skin, hide; (de fruta) skin, peel.

pellizcar [peʎiθ'kar] vt to pinch, nip.

pena ['pena] nf (congoja) grief, sadness; (ansia) anxiety; (remordimiento) regret; (dificultad) trouble; (dolor) pain; **merecer o valer la ~** to be worthwhile; **a duras ~s** with great difficulty; **~ de muerte** death penalty; **~ pecuniaria** fine; **¡qué ~!** what a shame!

penal [pe'nal] a penal // nm (cárcel) prison; (FÚTBOL) penalty.

penalidad [penali'ðað] nf (problema, dificultad) trouble, hardship; (JUR) penalty, punishment.

penar [pe'nar] vt to penalize; (castigar) to punish // vi to suffer; **~se** vr to grieve, mourn.

pender [pen'der] vi (colgar) to hang; (JUR) to be pending.

pendiente [pen'djente] a (colgante) hanging; (por resolver) pending, unsettled // nm earring // nf hill, slope.

pene ['pene] nm penis.

penetración [penetra'θjon] nf (acto) penetration; (agudeza) sharpness, insight.

penetrante [pene'trante] a (herida) deep; (persona, arma) sharp; (sonido) penetrating, piercing; (mirada) searching; (viento, ironía) biting.

penetrar [pene'trar] vt to penetrate, pierce; (entender) to grasp // vi to penetrate, go in; (líquido) to soak in; (emoción) to pierce.

penicilina [peniθi'lina] nf penicillin.

península [pe'ninsula] nf peninsula; **peninsular** a peninsular.

penitencia [peni'tenθja] nf (remordimiento) penitence; (castigo) penance; **penitencial** a penitential; **~ría** nf prison, penitentiary.

penoso, a [pe'noso, a] a (afligido) painful, distressing; (trabajoso) laborious, difficult.

pensador, a [pensa'ðor, a] nm/f thinker.

pensamiento [pensa'mjento] nm (gen) thought; (mente) mind; (idea) idea; (intento) intention.

pensar [pen'sar] vt to think; (considerar) to think over, think out; (proponerse) to intend, plan, propose; (imaginarse) to think up, invent // vi to think; **~ en** to aim at, aspire to; **pensativo, a** a thoughtful, pensive.

pensión [pen'sjon] nf (casa) boarding house, guest house; (dinero) pension; (cama y comida) board and lodging; (beca) scholarship; **pensionista** nm/f (jubilado) (old-age) pensioner; (quien vive en pensión) lodger.

penúltimo, a [pe'nultimo, a] a penultimate, second last.

penumbra [pe'numbra] nf half-light, semi-darkness.

penuria [pe'nurja] nf shortage, want.

peña ['peɲa] nf (roca) rock; (cuesta) cliff, crag; (grupo) group, circle.

peñascal [peɲas'kal] nm rocky place; **peñasco** nm large rock, boulder.

peñón [pe'ɲon] nm mass of rock; **el P~** the Rock (of Gibraltar).

peón [pe'on] nm labourer; (AM) farm labourer, farmhand; (eje) spindle, shaft, axle; (AJEDREZ) pawn.

peor [pe'or] a (comparativo) worse; (superlativo) worst // ad worse; worst; **de mal en ~** from bad to worse.

pepino [pe'pino] nm cucumber; **(no) me importa un ~** I don't care two hoots.

pepita [pe'pita] nf (BOT) pip; (MINERÍA) nugget.

pequeñez [peke'neθ] nf smallness, littleness; (infancia) infancy; (trivialidad) trifle, triviality.

pequeño, a [pe'keɲo, a] a small, little.

pera ['pera] nf pear; **peral** nm pear tree.

percance [per'kanθe] nm setback, misfortune.

percatarse [perka'tarse] vr: **~ de** to notice, take note of.

percepción [perθep'θjon] nf (vista) perception; (idea) notion, idea; (colecta de fondos) collection.

perceptible [perθep'tiβle] a perceptible, noticeable; (COM) payable, receivable.

percibir [perθi'βir] vt to perceive, notice; (COM) to earn, receive, get.

percusión [perku'sjon] nf percussion.

percha ['pertʃa] nf (poste) pole, support; (ganchos) coat stand; (colgador) coat hanger; (de ave) perch.

perdedor, a [perðe'ðor, a] a (que pierde) losing; (olvidadizo) forgetful // nm/f loser.

perder [per'ðer] vt (gen) to lose; (tiempo, palabras) to waste; (oportunidad) to lose, miss; (tren) to miss // vi to lose; **~se** vr (extraviarse) to get lost; (desaparecer) to disappear, be lost to view; (arruinarse) to be ruined; (hundirse) to sink; **echar a ~** (comida) to spoil, ruin; (oportunidad) to waste.

perdición [perði'θjon] nf perdition, ruin.

pérdida ['perðiða] *nf* (*gen*) loss; (*de tiempo*) waste; ~**s** *nfpl* (*COM*) losses.

perdido, a [per'ðiðo, a] *a* lost; (*incorregible*) incorrigible; ~**so, a** *a* (*que pierde*) losing; (*fácilmente* ~) easily lost.

perdiz [per'ðiθ] *nf* partridge.

perdón [per'ðon] *nm* (*disculpa*) pardon, forgiveness; (*clemencia*) mercy; ¡~! sorry!, I beg your pardon!; **perdonar** *vt* to pardon, forgive; (*la vida*) to spare; (*excusar*) to exempt, excuse.

perdurable [perðu'raβle] *a* lasting; (*eterno*) everlasting; **perdurar** *vi* (*resistir*) to last, endure; (*seguir existiendo*) to stand, still exist.

perecer [pere'θer] *vi* (*morir*) to perish, die; (*objeto*) to shatter.

peregrinación [pereɣrina'θjon] *nf* long tour, travels *pl*; (*REL*) pilgrimage; **peregrino, a** *a* travelling; (*nuevo*) newly-introduced // *nm/f* pilgrim.

perejil [pere'xil] *nm* parsley.

perenne [pe'renne] *a* everlasting, perennial.

perentorio, a [peren'torjo, a] *a* (*urgente*) urgent, peremptory; (*fijo*) set, fixed.

pereza [pe'reθa] *nf* (*flojera*) laziness; (*lentitud*) sloth, slowness; **perezoso, a** *a* lazy; slow, sluggish.

perfección [perfek'θjon] *nf* perfection; (*acto*) completion; **perfeccionar** *vt* to perfect; (*acabar*) to complete, finish.

perfecto, a [per'fekto, a] *a* perfect; (*terminado*) complete, finished.

perfidia [per'fiðja] *nf* perfidy, treachery.

perfil [per'fil] *nm* (*parte lateral*) profile; (*silueta*) silhouette, outline; (*ARQ*) (cross) section; ~**es** *nmpl* features; (*fig*) social graces; ~**ado, a** *a* (*bien formado*) well-shaped; (*largo: cara*) long; ~**ar** *vt* (*trazar*) to outline; (*dar carácter a*) to shape, give character to.

perforación [perfora'θjon] *nf* perforation; (*con taladro*) drilling; **perforadora** *nf* drill.

perforar [perfo'rar] *vt* to perforate; (*agujero*) to drill, bore; (*papel*) to punch a hole in // *vi* to drill, bore.

perfumado, a [perfu'maðo, a] *a* scented, perfumed.

perfume [per'fume] *nm* perfume, scent.

pericia [pe'riðja] *nf* skill, expertise.

periferia [peri'ferja] *nf* periphery; (*de ciudad*) outskirts *pl*.

perímetro [pe'rimetro] *nm* perimeter.

periódico, a [pe'rjoðiko, a] *a* periodic(al) // *nm* newspaper; **periodismo** *nm* journalism; **periodista** *nm/f* journalist.

periodo [pe'rjoðo], **período** [pe'rioðo] *nm* period.

perito, a [pe'rito, a] *a* (*experto*) expert; (*diestro*) skilled, skilful // *nm/f* expert; skilled worker; (*técnico*) technician.

perjudicar [perxuði'kar] *vt* (*gen*) to damage, harm; *ese vestido le perjudica* that dress doesn't suit her; **perjudicial** *a* damaging, harmful; (*en detrimento*) detri-

mental; **perjuicio** *nm* damage, harm; (*pérdidas*) financial loss.

perjurar [perxu'rar] *vi* to commit perjury.

perla ['perla] *nf* pearl; **me viene de** ~ it suits me fine.

permanecer [permane'θer] *vi* (*quedarse*) to stay, remain; (*seguir*) to continue to be.

permanencia [perma'nenθja] *nf* (*duración*) permanence; (*estancia*) stay.

permanente [perma'nente] *a* (*que queda*) permanent; (*constante*) constant // *nf* perm.

permisible [permi'siβle] *a* permissible, allowable.

permiso [per'miso] *nm* permission; (*licencia*) permit, licence; **con** ~ excuse me; **estar de** ~ (*MIL*) to be on leave; ~ **de conducir** *o* **conductor** driving licence.

permitir [permi'tir] *vt* to permit, allow.

pernicioso, a [perni'θjoso, a] *a* (*maligno, MED*) pernicious; (*persona*) wicked.

pernio ['pernjo] *nm* hinge.

perno ['perno] *nm* bolt.

pero ['pero] *conj* but; (*aún*) yet // *nm* (*defecto*) flaw, defect; (*reparo*) objection.

perorar [pero'rar] *vi* to make a speech.

perpendicular [perpendiku'lar] *a* perpendicular; **el camino es** ~ **al río** the road is at right angles to the river.

perpetrar [perpe'trar] *vt* to perpetrate.

perpetuamente [perpetwa'mente] *ad* perpetually; **perpetuar** *vt* to perpetuate; **perpetuo, a** *a* perpetual.

perplejo, a [per'plexo, a] *a* perplexed, bewildered.

perra ['perra] *nf* bitch; (*fam*) mania, crazy idea.

perrera [pe'rrera] *nf* kennel.

perrillo [pe'rriʎo] *nm* puppy.

perro ['perro] *nm* dog; ~ **caliente** hot dog.

persa ['persa] *a, nm/f* Persian.

persecución [perseku'θjon] *nf* pursuit, hunt, chase; (*REL, POL*) persecution.

perseguir [perse'xir] *vt* to pursue, hunt; (*cortejar*) to chase after; (*molestar*) to pester, annoy; (*REL, POL*) to persecute.

perseverante [perseβe'rante] *a* persevering, persistent; **perseverar** *vi* to persevere, persist; **perseverar en** *o* **sobre** to persevere in, persist with.

persiana [per'sjana] *nf* (Venetian) blind.

persignarse [persix'narse] *vr* to cross o.s.

persistente [persis'tente] *a* persistant; **persistir** *vi* to persist.

persona [per'sona] *nf* person; **10** ~**s** 10 people.

personaje [perso'naxe] *nm* important person, celebrity; (*TEATRO*) character.

personal [perso'nal] *a* (*particular*) personal; (*para una persona*) single, for one person // *nm* personnel, staff; ~**idad** *nf* personality.

personarse [perso'narse] *vr* to appear in person.

personificar [personifi'kar] *vt* to personify.

perspectiva [perspek'tiβa] *nf* perspective; (*vista, panorama*) view, panorama; (*posibilidad futura*) outlook, prospect.

perspicacia [perspi'kaθja] *nf* keensightedness; (*fig*) discernment, perspicacity.

perspicaz [perspi'kaθ] *a* (*agudo: de la vista*) keen; (*fig*) shrewd.

persuadir [perswa'ðir] *vt* (*gen*) to persuade; (*convencer*) to convince; ~**se** *vr* to become convinced; **persuasión** *nf* (*acto*) persuasion; (*estado de mente*) conviction; **persuasivo, a** *a* persuasive; convincing.

pertenecer [pertene'θer] *vi* to belong; (*fig*) to concern; **pertenencia** *nf* ownership; **pertenencias** *nfpl* possessions, property *sg*; **perteneciente** *a*: **perteneciente a** belonging to.

pertinaz [perti'naθ] *a* (*persistente*) persistent; (*terco*) obstinate.

pertinente [perti'nente] *a* relevant, pertinent; (*apropiado*) appropriate; ~ **a** concerning, relevant to.

perturbación [perturβa'θjon] *nf* (*POL*) disturbance; (*MED*) upset, disturbance.

perturbado, a [pertur'βaðo, a] *a* mentally unbalanced.

perturbador, a [perturβa'ðor, a] *a* (*que perturba*) perturbing, disturbing; (*subversivo*) subversive.

perturbar [pertur'βar] *vt* (*el orden*) to disturb; (*MED*) to upset, disturb; (*mentalmente*) to perturb.

Perú [pe'ru] *nm*: **el** ~ Peru; **peruano, a** *a*, *nm/f* Peruvian.

perversión [perβer'sjon] *nf* perversion; **perverso, a** *a* perverse; (*depravado*) depraved; **pervertido, a** *a* perverted // *nm/f* pervert; **pervertir** *vt* to pervert, corrupt; (*distorsionar*) to distort.

pesa ['pesa] *nf* weight; (*DEPORTE*) shot.

pesadez [pesa'ðeθ] *nf* (*calidad de pesado*) heaviness; (*lentitud*) slowness; (*aburrimiento*) tediousness.

pesadilla [pesa'ðiʎa] *nf* nightmare, bad dream.

pesado, a [pe'saðo, a] *a* (*gen*) heavy; (*lento*) slow; (*difícil, duro*) tough, hard; (*aburrido*) tedious, boring; (*bochornoso*) sultry.

pesadumbre [pesa'ðumbre] *nf* grief, sorrow.

pésame ['pesame] *nm* expression of condolence, message of sympathy.

pesar [pe'sar] *vt* to weigh // *vi* to weigh; (*ser pesado*) to weigh a lot, be heavy; (*fig: opinión*) to carry weight // *nm* (*sentimiento*) regret; (*pena*) grief, sorrow; **a** ~ **de** *o* **pese a (que)** in spite of, despite.

pesario [pe'sarjo] *nm* pessary.

pesca ['peska] *nf* (*acto*) fishing; (*cantidad de pescado*) catch; **ir de** ~ to go fishing.

pescadería [peskaðe'ria] *nf* fish shop.

pescado [pes'kaðo] *nm* fish.

pescador, a [peska'ðor, a] *nm/f* fisherman/woman.

pescar [pes'kar] *vt* (*coger*) to catch; (*tratar de coger*) to fish for; (*conseguir: trabajo*) to manage to get // *vi* to fish, go fishing; **viene a** ~ **un marido** she's come to get a husband.

pescuezo [pes'kweθo] *nm* neck.

pesebre [pe'seβre] *nm* manger.

peseta [pe'seta] *nf* peseta.

pesimista [pesi'mista] *a* pessimistic // *nm/f* pessimist.

pésimo, a ['pesimo, a] *a* abominable, vile.

peso ['peso] *nm* weight; (*balanza*) scales *pl*; (*moneda*) peso; ~ **bruto/neto** gross/net weight; **vender a** ~ to sell by weight.

pesquero, a [pes'kero, a] *a* fishing *cpd*.

pesquisa [pes'kisa] *nf* inquiry, investigation.

pestaña [pes'taɲa] *nf* (*ANAT*) eyelash; (*borde*) rim; **pestañear, pestañar** *vi* to blink.

peste ['peste] *nf* (*gen*) plague; (*mal olor*) stink, stench.

pesticida [pesti'θiða] *nm* pesticide.

pestilencia [pesti'lenθja] *nf* (*plaga*) pestilence, plague; (*mal olor*) stink, stench.

pétalo ['petalo] *nm* petal.

petardista [petar'ðista] *nm/f* (*tramposo*) cheat; (*rompehuelgas*) blackleg.

petición [peti'θjon] *nf* (*pedido*) request, plea; (*memorial*) petition; (*JUR*) plea.

petrificar [petrifi'kar] *vt* to petrify.

petróleo [pe'troleo] *nm* oil, petroleum; **petrolero, a** *a* petroleum *cpd* // *nm* (*COM*) oil man; (*extremista*) extremist, revolutionary; (*buque*) (oil) tanker.

peyorativo, a [pejora'tiβo, a] *a* pejorative.

pez [peθ] *nm* fish.

pezón [pe'θon] *nm* teat, nipple; (*MECÁNICA*) nipple, lubrication point.

piadoso, a [pja'ðoso, a] *a* (*devoto*) pious, devout; (*misericordioso*) kind, merciful.

pianista [pja'nista] *nm/f* pianist.

piano ['pjano] *nm* piano.

piar [pi'ar] *vi* to cheep.

picadillo [pika'ðiʎo] *nm* mince, minced meat.

picado, a [pi'kaðo, a] *a* pricked, punctured; (*mar*) choppy; (*diente*) bad; (*tabaco*) cut; (*enfadado*) cross // *nf* prick; (*de abeja*) sting; (*de mosquito*) bite.

picador [pika'ðor] *nm* (*TAUR*) picador; (*entrenador de caballos*) horse trainer; (*minero*) faceworker.

picadura [pika'ðura] *nf* (*diente*) bad tooth; (*pinchazo*) puncture; (*de abeja*) sting; (*de mosquito*) bite; (*tabaco picado*) cut tobacco.

picante [pi'kante] *a* hot; (*comentario*) racy, spicy.

picar [pi'kar] *vt* (*agujerear, perforar*) to prick, puncture; (*abeja*) to sting; (*mosquito, serpiente*) to bite; (*incitar*) to incite, goad; (*dañar, irritar*) to annoy, bother; (*quemar*:

lengua) to burn, sting // *vi* (*pez*) to bite, take the bait; (*el sol*) to burn, scorch; (*abeja*, MED) to sting; (*mosquito*) to bite; ~**se** *vr* (*decaer*) to decay; (*agriarse*) to turn sour, go off; (*ofenderse*) to take offence; ~ **en** (*fig*) to dabble in.

picardía [pikar'ðia] *nf* villainy; (*astucia*) slyness, craftiness; (*una* ~) dirty trick; (*palabra*) rude/bad word *or* expression.

pícaro, a ['pikaro, a] *a* (*malicioso*) villainous; (*travieso*) mischievous // *nm* (*ladrón*) crook; (*astuto*) sly sort; (*sinvergüenza*) rascal, scoundrel.

pico ['piko] *nm* (*de ave*) beak; (*punto agudo*) peak, sharp point; (TEC) pick, pickaxe; (GEO) peak, summit; **y** ~ **and a bit.**

picotear [pikote'ar] *vt* to peck // *vi* to nibble, pick; (*fam*) to chatter; ~**se** *vr* to squabble.

picudo, a [pi'kuðo, a] *a* pointed, with a point.

pichón [pi'tʃon] *nm* young pigeon.

pido, pidió *etc vb ver* **pedir.**

pie [pje] (*pl* ~**s**) *nm* (*gen*) foot; (*fig: motivo*) motive, basis; (: *fundamento*) foothold; **ir a** ~ to go on foot, walk; **estar de** ~ to be standing (up); **ponerse de** ~ to stand up; **al** ~ **de la letra** (*citar*) literally, verbatim; (*copiar*) exactly, word for word; **en** ~ **de guerra** on a war footing; **dar** ~ **a** to give cause for.

piedad [pje'ðað] *nf* (*lástima*) pity, compassion; (*clemencia*) mercy; (*devoción*) piety, devotion.

piedra ['pjeðra] *nf* stone; (*roca*) rock; (*de mechero*) flint; (METEOROLOGÍA) hailstone.

piel [pjel] *nf* (ANAT) skin; (ZOOL) skin, hide; (*de oso*) fur; (*cuero*) leather; (BOT) skin, peel; ~ **de ante** *o* **de Suecia** suede.

pienso *etc vb ver* **pensar.**

pierdo *etc vb ver* **perder.**

pierna ['pjerna] *nf* leg.

pieza ['pjeθa] *nf* piece; (*habitación*) room; ~ **de recambio** *o* **repuesto** spare (part).

pigmeo, a [piɣ'meo, a] *a, nm/f* pigmy.

pijama [pi'xama] *nm* pyjamas *pl.*

pila ['pila] *nf* (ELEC) battery; (*montón*) heap, pile; (*fuente*) sink.

píldora ['pildora] *nf* pill; **la** ~ **(anticonceptiva)** the pill.

pileta [pi'leta] *nf* basin, bowl; (AM) swimming pool.

pilón [pi'lon] *nm* pillar, post; (ELEC) pylon.

piloto [pi'loto] *nm* pilot; (*de aparato*) rear light, tail light; (AUTO) driver.

pillaje [pi'ʎaxe] *nm* pillage, plunder.

pillar [pi'ʎar] *vt* (*saquear*) to pillage, plunder; (*fam: coger*) to catch; (: *agarrar*) to grasp, seize; (: *entender*) to grasp, catch on to.

pillo, a ['piʎo, a] *a* villainous; (*astuto*) sly, crafty // *nm/f* rascal, rogue, scoundrel.

pimentón [pimen'ton] *nm* (*polvo*) paprika; (*pimiento*) red pepper.

pimienta [pi'mjenta] *nf* pepper.

pimiento [pi'mjento] *nm* pepper, pimiento.

pinacoteca [pinako'teka] *nf* art gallery.

pinar [pi'nar] *nm* pinewood.

pincel [pin'θel] *nm* paintbrush.

pinchar [pin'tʃar] *vt* (*perforar*) to prick, pierce; (*neumático*) to puncture; (*incitar*) to prod; (*herir*) to wound.

pinchazo [pin'tʃaθo] *nm* (*perforación*) prick; (*de llanta*) puncture; (*fig*) prod.

pinchitos [pin'tʃitos] *nmpl* bar snacks.

pingüino [pin'gwino] *nm* penguin.

pino ['pino] *nm* pine (tree); **en** ~ upright, vertical.

pinta ['pinta] *nf* spot; (*medida*) spot, drop; (*aspecto*) appearance, look(s) (*pl*); ~**do, a** spotted; (*de muchos colores*) colourful.

pintar [pin'tar] *vt* to paint // *vi* to paint; (*fam*) to count, be important; ~**se** *vr* to put on make-up.

pintor, a [pin'tor, a] *nm/f* painter.

pintoresco, a [pinto'resko, a] *a* picturesque.

pintura [pin'tura] *nf* painting; ~ **a la acuarela** watercolour; ~ **al óleo** oil painting; ~ **rupestre** cave painting.

pinza ['pinθa] *nf* (ZOOL) claw; (*para colgar ropa*) clothes peg; (TEC) pincers *pl*; ~**s** *nfpl* (*para depilar*) tweezers *pl.*

piña ['piɲa] *nf* (*fruto del pino*) pine cone; (*fruta*) pineapple; (*fig*) group.

pío, a ['pio, a] *a* (*devoto*) pious, devout; (*misericordioso*) merciful // *nm* cheep, chirp.

piojo [pi'joxo] *nm* louse.

pionero, a [pjo'nero, a] *a* pioneering // *nm/f* pioneer.

pipa ['pipa] *nf* pipe; (BOT) edible sunflower seed.

pipí [pi'pi] *nm* (*fam*): **hacer** ~ to have a wee(wee).

pique ['pike] *nm* (*resentimiento*) pique, resentment; (*rivalidad*) rivalry, competition; **irse a** ~ to sink; (*familia*) to be ruined.

piquera [pi'kera] *nf* hole, vent.

piqueta [pi'keta] *nf* pick(axe).

piquete [pi'kete] *nm* (*herida*) prick, jab; (*agujerito*) small hole; (MIL) squad, party; (*de obreros*) picket.

piragua [pi'raɣwa] *nf* canoe; **piragüismo** *nm* (DEPORTE) canoeing.

pirámide [pi'ramiðe] *nf* pyramid.

pirata [pi'rata] *a, nm* pirate.

Pirineo(s) [piri'neo(s)] *nm*(*pl*) Pyrenees *pl.*

piropo [pi'ropo] *nm* compliment, (*piece of*) flattery.

pisada [pi'saða] *nf* (*paso*) footstep; (*huella*) footprint.

pisar [pi'sar] *vt* (*caminar sobre*) to walk on, tread on; (*apretar con el pie*) to press; (*fig*) to trample on, walk all over // *vi* to tread, step, walk.

piscina [pis'θina] *nf* swimming pool; (*para peces*) fishpond.

Piscis ['pisθis] *nm* Pisces.
piso ['piso] *nm* (*suelo, de edificio*) floor; (*apartamento*) flat, apartment.
pisotear [pisote'ar] *vt* to trample (on *or* underfoot).
pista ['pista] *nf* track, trail; (*indicio*) clue; ~ **de aterrizaje** runway; ~ **de baile** dance floor; ~ **de tenis** tennis court; ~ **de hielo** ice rink.
pistola [pis'tola] *nf* pistol; (*TEC*) spray-gun; **pistolero, a** *nm/f* gunman, gangster // *nf* holster.
pistón [pis'ton] *nm* (*TEC*) piston; (*MUS*) key.
pitar [pi'tar] *vt* (*hacer sonar*) to blow; (*rechiflar*) to whistle at, boo // *vi* to whistle; (*AUTO*) to sound *or* toot one's horn; (*AM*) to smoke.
pitillo [pi'tiʎo] *nm* cigarette.
pito ['pito] *nm* whistle; (*de coche*) horn.
pitón [pi'ton] *nm* (*ZOOL*) python; (*protuberancia*) bump, lump; (*de jarro*) spout.
pitonisa [pito'nisa] *nf* fortune-teller.
pizarra [pi'θarra] *nf* (*piedra*) slate; (*encerado*) blackboard.
pizca ['piθka] *nf* pinch, spot; (*fig*) spot, speck, trace; **ni** ~ not a bit.
placa ['plaka] *nf* plate; ~ **de matrícula** number plate.
placentero, a [plaθen'tero, a] *a* pleasant, agreeable.
placer [pla'θer] *nm* pleasure // *vt* to please.
plácido, a ['plaθiðo, a] *a* placid.
plaga ['plaxa] *nf* pest; (*MED*) plague; (*abundancia*) abundance; **plagar** *vt* to infest, plague; (*llenar*) to fill.
plagio ['plaxjo] *nm* plagiarism.
plan [plan] *nm* (*esquema, proyecto*) plan; (*idea, intento*) idea, intention; **tener** ~ (*fam*) to have a date; **tener un** ~ (*fam*) to have an affair; **en** ~ **económico** (*fam*) on the cheap; **vamos en** ~ **de turismo** we're going as tourists; **si te pones en ese** ~... if that's your attitude... .
plana ['plana] *nf ver* **plano.**
plancha ['plantʃa] *nf* (*para planchar*) iron; (*rótulo*) plate, sheet; (*NAUT*) gangway; ~ **do** *nm* ironing; **planchar** *vt* to iron // *vi* to do the ironing.
planeador [planea'ðor] *nm* glider; ~**a** *nf* bulldozer.
planear [plane'ar] *vt* to plan // *vi* to glide.
planeta [pla'neta] *nm* planet.
planicie [pla'niθje] *nf* plain.
planificación [planifika'θjon] *nf* planning; ~ **familiar** family planning.
plano, a ['plano, a] *a* flat, level, even // *nm* (*MAT, TEC, AVIAT*) plane; (*FOTO*) shot; (*ARQ*) plan; (*GEO*) map; (*de ciudad*) map, street plan // *nf* sheet (of paper), page; (*TEC*) trowel; **primer** ~ close-up; **caer de** ~ to fall flat; **en primera** ~**a** on the front page; ~**a mayor** staff.
planta ['planta] *nf* (*BOT, TEC*) plant; (*ANAT*) sole of the foot, foot; ~ **baja** ground floor.

plantación [planta'θjon] *nf* (*AGR*) plantation; (*acto*) planting.
plantar [plan'tar] *vt* (*BOT*) to plant; (*levantar*) to erect, set up; ~**se** *vr* to stand firm; ~ **a uno en la calle** to chuck sb out; **dejar plantado a uno** (*fam*) to stand sb up.
plantear [plante'ar] *vt* (*problema*) to pose; (*dificultad*) to raise; (*planificar*) to plan; (*institución*) to set up, establish; (*reforma*) to implant.
plantilla [plan'tiʎa] *nf* (*de zapato*) insole; (*de media*) sole; (*personal*) personnel; **ser de** ~ to be on the staff.
plantío [plan'tio] *nm* (*acto*) planting; (*lugar*) plot, bed, patch.
plantón [plan'ton] *nm* (*MIL*) guard, sentry; (*fam*) long wait; **dar (un)** ~ **a uno** to stand sb up.
plañidero, a [plaɲi'ðero, a] *a* mournful, plaintive.
plañir [pla'ɲir] *vi* to mourn.
plasmar [plas'mar] *vt* (*dar forma*) to mould, shape; (*representar*) to represent // *vi:* ~ **en** to take the form of.
plasticina [plasti'θina] *nf* plasticine.
plástico, a [a ['plastiko, a] *a* plastic // *nf* (art of) sculpture, modelling // *nm* plastic.
plata ['plata] *nf* (*metal*) silver; (*cosas hechas de plata*) silverware; (*AM*) money; **hablar en** ~ to speak bluntly *or* frankly.
plataforma [plata'forma] *nf* platform; ~ **de lanzamiento/perforación** launch(ing) pad/drilling rig.
plátano ['platano] *nm* (*fruta*) banana; (*árbol*) banana tree.
platea [pla'tea] *nf* (*TEATRO*) pit.
plateado, a [plate'aðo, a] *a* silver; (*TEC*) silver-plated.
platería [plate'ria] *nf* silversmith's.
plática ['platika] *nf* talk, chat; **platicar** *vi* to talk, chat.
platillo [pla'tiʎo] *nm* saucer; ~**s** *nmpl* cymbals; ~ **volador** *o* **volante** flying saucer.
platino [pla'tino] *nm* platinum; ~**s** *nmpl* (*AUTO*) contact points.
plato ['plato] *nm* plate, dish; (*parte de comida*) course; (*guiso*) dish.
playa ['plaja] *nf* beach; (*lugar veraniego*) seaside resort; (*costa*) seaside; ~ **de estacionamiento** (*AM*) car park.
playera [pla'jera] *nf* T-shirt.
plaza ['plaθa] *nf* square; (*mercado*) market(place); (*sitio*) room, space; (*en vehículo*) seat, place; (*colocación*) post, job.
plazco *etc vb ver* **placer.**
plazo ['plaθo] *nm* (*lapso de tiempo*) time, period, term; (*fecha de vencimiento*) expiry date; (*pago parcial*) instalment; **a corto/largo** ~ short-/long-term; **comprar a** ~**s** to buy on hire purchase, pay for in instalments.
plazoleta [plaθo'leta], **plazuela** [pla-'θwela] *nf* small square.
pleamar [plea'mar] *nf* high tide.
plebe ['pleβe] *nf:* **la** ~ the common

people *pl*, the masses *pl*; (*pey*) the plebs *pl*; ~**yo, a** *a* plebeian; (*pey*) coarse, common.
plebiscito [pleβis'θito] *nm* plebiscite.
plegable [ple'xaβle], **plegadizo, a** [plexa'ðiθo, a] *a* pliable; (*silla*) folding.
plegar [ple'xar] *vt* (*doblar*) to fold, bend; (*COSTURA*) to pleat; ~**se** *vr* to yield, submit.
pleito ['pleito] *nm* (*JUR*) lawsuit, case; (*fig*) dispute, feud.
plenilunio [pleni'lunjo] *nm* full moon.
plenitud [pleni'tuð] *nf* plenitude, fullness; (*abundancia*) abundance.
pleno, a ['pleno, a] *a* (*gen*) full; (*completo*) complete // *nm* plenum; **en ~ día** in broad daylight; **en ~ verano** at the height of summer; **en ~a cara** full in the face.
pleuresía [pleure'sia] *nf* pleurisy.
plexiglás [pleksi'xlas] *nm* perspex.
pliego ['pljexo] *nm* (*hoja*) sheet (of paper); (*carta*) sealed letter/document; ~ **de condiciones** details *pl*, specifications *pl*.
pliegue ['pljexe] *nm* fold, crease; (*de vestido*) pleat.
plisado [pli'saðo] *nm* pleating; ~ **de acordeón** accordion pleats *pl*.
plomero [plo'mero] *nm* plumber.
plomo ['plomo] *nm* (*metal*) lead; (*ELEC*) fuse.
pluma ['pluma] *nf* (*gen*) feather; (*para escribir*) pen.
plural [plu'ral] *a* plural; ~**idad** *nf* plurality; **una ~idad de votos** a majority of votes.
plus [plus] *nm* bonus.
plutocracia [pluto'kraθja] *nf* plutocracy.
población [poβla'θjon] *nf* population; (*pueblo, ciudad*) town, city; **poblado, a** *a* inhabited // *nm* (*aldea*) village; (*pueblo*) (small) town; **densamente poblado** densely populated.
poblador, a [poβla'ðor, a] *nm/f* settler, colonist; (*fundador*) founder.
poblar [po'βlar] *vt* (*colonizar*) to colonize; (*fundar*) to found; (*habitar*) to inhabit.
pobre ['poβre] *a* poor // *nm/f* poor person; **¡~!** poor thing!; ~**za** *nf* poverty.
pocilga [po'θilxa] *nf* pigsty.
poción [po'θjon], **pócima** ['poθima] *nf* potion.
poco, a ['poko, a] *a* little; ~**s** few // *ad* (*no mucho*) little, not much // *nm*: **un ~ a** little, a bit; **tener a uno en ~** to think little *or* not think much of sb; **por ~** almost, nearly; ~ **a ~** little by little, gradually; **dentro de ~** (+ *presente o futuro*) shortly; (+ *pasado*) soon after; **hace ~** a short time ago, not long ago.
podar [po'ðar] *vt* to prune.
podenco [po'ðenko] *nm* hound.
poder [po'ðer] *vi* can; (*sujeto: persona*) to be able to, can; (*permiso*) can, may; (*posibilidad, hipótesis*) may // *nm* (*gen*) power; (*autoridad*) authority; **puede que sea así** it may be, maybe; **¿se puede?** may I come in?; **¿puedes con eso?** can

you manage that?; **a más no ~** to the utmost; **no ~ menos de hacer algo** not to be able to help doing sth; **no ~ más** to have had enough; ~**ío** *nm* power; (*autoridad*) authority; ~**oso, a** *a* powerful.
podrido, a [po'ðriðo, a] *a* rotten, bad; (*fig*) rotten, corrupt.
podrir [po'ðrir] = **pudrir.**
poema [po'ema] *nm* poem.
poesía [poe'sia] *nf* poetry.
poeta [po'eta] *nm* poet; **poético, a** *a* poetic(al).
póker ['poker] *nm* poker.
polaco, a [po'lako, a] *a* Polish // *nm/f* Pole.
polar [po'lar] *a* polar; ~**idad** *nf* polarity; ~**izarse** *vr* to polarize.
polea [po'lea] *nf* pulley.
polémica [po'lemika] *nf* (*gen*) polemics *sg*; (*una ~*) controversy.
policía [poli'θia] *nm/f* policeman/woman // *nf* police; ~**co, a** *a* police *cpd*; **novela ~ca** detective story.
poligamia [poli'xamja] *nf* polygamy.
polilla [po'liʎa] *nf* moth.
polio ['poljo] *nm* polio.
politécnico [poli'tekniko] *nm* polytechnic.
politene [poli'tene], **politeno** [poli'teno] *nm* polythene.
político, a [po'litiko, a] *a* political; (*discreto*) tactful; (*de familia*) in-law // *nm/f* politician // *nf* politics *sg*; (*económica, agraria*) policy; **padre ~** father-in-law; **politicastro** *nm* (*pey*) politician, politico.
póliza ['poliθa] *nf* insurance policy.
polo ['polo] *nm* (*GEO, ELEC*) pole; (*helado*) iced lolly; (*DEPORTE*) polo; (*suéter*) polo-neck; ~ **Norte/Sur** North/South Pole.
Polonia [po'lonja] *nf* Poland.
poltrona [pol'trona] *nf* reclining chair, easy chair.
polución [polu'θjon] *nf* pollution.
polvera [pol'βera] *nf* powder compact, vanity case.
polvo ['polβo] *nm* dust; (*QUÍMICA, CULIN, MED*) powder; ~**s** *nmpl* powder *sg*; ~ **de talco** talcum powder; **estar hecho ~** to be worn out *or* exhausted.
pólvora ['polβora] *nf* gunpowder; (*fuegos artificiales*) fireworks *pl*.
polvoriento, a [polβo'rjento, a] *a* (*superficie*) dusty; (*sustancia*) powdery.
pollería [poʎe'ria] *nf* poulterer's (shop).
pollo ['poʎo] *nm* chicken.
pomada [po'maða] *nf* pomade.
pomelo [po'melo] *nm* grapefruit.
pómez ['pomeθ] *nf*: **piedra ~** pumice stone.
pompa ['pompa] *nf* (*burbuja*) bubble; (*bomba*) pump; (*esplendor*) pomp, splendour; **pomposo, a** *a* splendid, magnificent; (*pey*) pompous.
pómulo ['pomulo] *nm* cheekbone.
pon [pon] *vb ver* **poner.**
ponche ['pontʃe] *nm* punch.

poncho ['pontʃo] *nm* (*AM*) poncho, cape.
ponderado, a [ponde'raðo, a] *a* calm, steady, balanced.
ponderar [ponde'rar] *vt* (*considerar*) to weigh up, consider; (*elogiar*) to praise highly, speak in praise of.
pondré *etc vb ver* **poner.**
poner [po'ner] *vt* (*gen*) to put; (*colocar*) to place, set; (*ropa*) to put on; (*problema, la mesa*) to set; (*telegrama*) to send; (*TELEC*) to connect; (*radio, TV*) to switch on, turn on; (*tienda*) to open, set up; (*nombre*) to give; (*añadir*) to add; (*TEATRO, CINE*) to put on; (+ *adjetivo*) to make, turn; (*suponer*) to suppose // *vi* (*ave*) to lay (eggs); ~se *vr* to put *or* place o.s.; (*ropa*) to put on; (+ *adjetivo*) to turn, get, become; (*el sol*) to set; **póngame con el Señor X** get me Mr X, put me through to Mr X; ~se de zapatero to take a job as a shoemaker; ~se a bien con uno to get on good terms with sb; ~se con uno to quarrel with sb; ~se rojo to blush; ~se a to begin to.
pongo *etc vb ver* **poner.**
pontificado [pontifi'kaðo] *nm* papacy, pontificate; **pontífice** *nm* pope, pontiff.
pontón [pon'ton] *nm* pontoon.
ponzoña [pon'θoɲa] *nf* poison, venom; **ponzoñoso, a** *a* poisonous, venomous.
popa ['popa] *nf* stern.
popular [popu'lar] *a* popular; (*del pueblo*) of the people; ~idad *nf* popularity; ~izarse *vr* to become popular.
poquedad [poke'ðað] *nf* (*escasez*) scantiness; (*una* ~) small thing, trifle; (*fig*) timidity.
por [por] *prep* (*con el fin de*) in order to; (*a favor de, hacia*) for; (*a causa de*) out of, because of, from; (*según*) according to; (*por agencia de*) by; (*a cambio de*) for, in exchange for; (*en lugar de*) instead of, in place of; (*durante*) for; **10 ~ 10 son 100** 10 times 10 are 100; **será ~ poco tiempo** it won't be for long; ~ **correo/avión** by post/plane; ~ **centenares** by the hundred; (**el**) **10 ~ ciento** 10 per cent; ~ **orden** in order; **ir a Bilbao ~ Santander** to go to Bilbao via Santander; **pasar ~ Madrid** to pass through Madrid; **camina ~ la izquierda** walk on the left; ~ **todo el país** throughout the country; **entra ~ delante/detrás** come/go in by the front/back (door); ~ **la calle** along the street; ~ **la mañana** in the morning; ~ **la noche** at night; **£2 ~ hora** £2 an hour; ~ **allí** over there; **está ~ el norte** it's somewhere in the north; ~ **mucho que quisiera, no puedo** much as I would like to, I can't; ~**que** because; ¿~ **qué?** why?; ~ (**lo**) **tanto** so, therefore; ~ **cierto** (*seguro*) certainly; (*a propósito*) by the way; ~ **ejemplo** for example; ~ **favor** please; ~ **fuera/dentro** outside/inside; ~ **si (acaso)** just in case; ~ **sí mismo** *o* **sólo** by o.s.

porcelana [porθe'lana] *nf* porcelain; (*china*) china.
porcentaje [porθen'taxe] *nm* percentage.
porción [por'θjon] *nf* (*parte*) portion, share; (*cantidad*) quantity, amount.
pordiosear [porðjose'ar] *vi* to beg; **pordiosero, a** *nm/f* beggar.
porfía [por'fia] *nf* persistence; (*terquedad*) obstinacy; **porfiado, a** *a* persistent, obstinate; **porfiar** *vi* to persist, insist; (*disputar*) to argue stubbornly.
pormenor [porme'nor] *nm* detail, particular.
pornografía [pornoxra'fia] *nf* pornography.
poro ['poro] *nm* pore; ~**so, a** *a* porous.
porque ['porke] *conj* (*a causa de*) because; (*ya que*) since; (*con el fin de*) so that, in order that.
porqué [por'ke] *nm* reason, cause.
porquería [porke'ria] *nf* (*suciedad*) filth, muck, dirt; (*acción*) dirty trick; (*objeto*) small thing, trifle; (*fig*) rubbish.
porro, a ['porro, a] *a* (*fam*) stupid // *nm* (*arma*) stick, club; (*TEC*) large hammer; (*fam*) bore.
porrón, ona [po'rron, ona] *a* slow, stupid // *nm* glass wine jar with a long spout.
portada [por'taða] *nf* (*entrada*) porch, doorway; (*de revista*) cover.
portador, a [porta'ðor, a] *nm/f* carrier, bearer.
portaequipajes [portaeki'paxes] *nm inv* boot; (*arriba del coche*) luggage rack.
portal [por'tal] *nm* (*entrada*) vestibule, hall; (*portada*) porch, doorway; (*puerta de entrada*) main door; (*de ciudad*) gate; (*DEPORTE*) goal.
portaligas [porta'lixas] *nm inv* suspender belt.
portamaletas [portama'letas] *nm inv* boot.
portamonedas [portamo'neðas] *nm inv* purse.
portarse [por'tarse] *vr* to behave, conduct o.s.
portátil [por'tatil] *a* portable.
portaviones [porta'βjones] *nm inv* aircraft carrier.
portavoz [porta'βoθ] *nm* (*megáfono*) megaphone, loudhailer; (*vocero*) spokesman/woman.
portazo [por'taθo] *nm*: **dar un ~** to slam the door.
porte ['porte] *nm* (*com*) transport; (*precio*) transport charges *pl*; (*comportamiento*) conduct, behaviour.
portento [por'tento] *nm* marvel, wonder; ~**so, a** *a* marvellous, extraordinary.
porteño, a [por'teɲo, a] *a* of *or* from Buenos Aires.
portería [porte'ria] *nf* (*oficina*) porter's office; (*gol*) goal.
portero, a [por'tero, a] *nm/f* porter; (*conserje*) caretaker; (*ujier*) doorman // *nm* goalkeeper.

pórtico ['portiko] *nm* (*patio*) portico, porch; (*fig*) gateway; (*arcada*) arcade.

portilla [por'tiʎa] *nf* porthole.

portillo [por'tiʎo] *nm* (*abertura*) gap, opening; (*GEO*) narrow pass.

portorriqueño, a [portorri'keɲo, a] *a* Puerto Rican.

Portugal [portu'ɣal] *nm* Portugal; **portugués, esa** *a*, *nm/f* Portuguese.

porvenir [porβe'nir] *nm* future.

pos [pos] *prep*: **en ~ de** after, in pursuit of.

posada [po'saða] *nf* (*refugio*) shelter, lodging; (*mesón*) guest house; **dar ~ a** to give shelter to, take in.

posaderas [posa'ðeras] *nfpl* backside *sg*, buttocks.

posar [po'sar] *vt* (*en el suelo*) to lay down, put down; (*la mano*) to place, put gently // *vi* to sit, pose; **~ se** *vr* to settle; (*pájaro*) to perch ; (*avión*) to land, come down.

posdata [pos'ðata] *nf* postscript.

pose ['pose] *nf* pose.

poseedor, a [posee'ðor, a] *nm/f* owner, possessor; (*de récord, puesto*) holder.

poseer [pose'er] *vt* to have, possess, own; (*ventaja*) to enjoy; (*récord, puesto*) to hold; **poseído, a** *a* possessed; **posesión** *nf* possession; **posesionarse** *vr*: **posesionarse de** to take possession of, take over; **posesivo, a** *a* possessive.

posibilidad [posiβili'ðað] *nf* possibility; (*oportunidad*) chance; **posibilitar** *vt* to make possible, permit; (*hacer factible*) to make feasible.

posible [po'siβle] *a* possible; (*factible*) feasible; **de ser ~** if possible; **en lo ~** as far as possible.

posición [posi'θjon] *nf* (*gen*) position; (*rango social*) status.

positivo, a [posi'tiβo, a] *a* positive // *nf* (*FOTO*) print.

poso ['poso] *nm* sediment.

posponer [pospo'ner] *vt* to put behind/below; (*AM*) to postpone.

posta ['posta] *nf* (*de caballos*) relay, team; (*pedazo*) slice // *nm* courier.

postal [pos'tal] *a* postal // *nf* postcard.

poste ['poste] *nm* (*de telégrafos*) post, pole; (*columna*) pillar; **dar ~ a uno** (*fam*) to keep sb hanging about.

postergar [poster'ɣar] *vt* (*AM: posponer*) to postpone, delay.

posteridad [posteri'ðað] *nf* posterity.

posterior [poste'rjor] *a* back, rear; (*siguiente*) following, subsequent; (*más tarde*) later; **~idad** *nf*: **con ~idad** later, subsequently.

postizo, a [pos'tiθo, a] *a* false, artificial // *nm* hairpiece.

postor, a [pos'tor, a] *nm/f* bidder.

postrado, a [pos'traðo, a] *a* prostrate; **postrar** *vt* (*derribar*) to cast down, overthrow; (*humillar*) to humble; (*MED*) to weaken, exhaust.

postre ['postre] *nm* sweet, dessert.

postremo, a [pos'tremo, a] **postrer,**

ero, a [pos'trer, ero, a] *a* (*último*) last; (*que viene detrás*) rear.

postulado [postu'laðo] *nm* postulate; **postular** *vt* (*empleo*) to apply for; (*pedir*) to seek, demand; (*proponer*) to postulate.

póstumo, a ['postumo, a] *a* posthumous.

postura [pos'tura] *nf* (*del cuerpo*) posture, position; (*fig*) attitude, position.

potable [po'taβle] *a* drinkable.

potaje [po'taxe] *nm* stew; **~s** *nmpl* mixed vegetables.

pote ['pote] *nm* pot, jar.

potencia [po'tenθja] *nf* power.

potencial [poten'θjal] *a, nm* potential.

potente [po'tente] *a* powerful.

pozo ['poθo] *nm* well; (*de río*) deep pool; (*de mina*) shaft.

práctica ['praktika] *nf ver* **práctico.**

practicable [prakti'kaβle] *a* practicable; (*camino*) passable, usable.

practicante [prakti'kante] *nm/f* (*MED: ayudante de doctor*) medical assistant; (: *enfermero*) male nurse; (*quien practica algo*) practitioner // *a* practising.

practicar [prakti'kar] *vt* to practise; (*deporte*) to go in for, play; (*realizar*) to carry out, perform.

práctico, a ['praktiko, a] *a* (*gen*) practical; (*conveniente*) handy; (*instruído: persona*) skilled, expert // *nf* practice; (*método*) method; (*arte, capacidad*) skill; **en la ~a** in practice.

pradera [pra'ðera] *nf* meadow; (*de Canadá*) prairie.

prado ['praðo] *nm* (*campo*) meadow, field; (*pastizal*) pasture.

Praga ['praɣa] *n* Prague.

pragmático, a [praɣ'matiko, a] *a* pragmatic.

preámbulo [pre'ambulo] *nm* preamble, introduction.

precario, a [pre'karjo, a] *a* precarious.

precaución [prekau'θjon] *nf* (*medida preventiva*) preventive measure, precaution; (*prudencia*) caution, wariness.

precaver [preka'βer] *vt* to guard against; (*impedir*) to forestall; **~se** *vr*: **~se de o contra algo** to (be on one's) guard against sth; **precavido, a** *a* cautious, wary.

precedencia [preθe'ðenθja] *nf* precedence; (*prioridad*) priority; (*superioridad*) greater importance, superiority; **precedente** *a* preceding; (*anterior*) former // *nm* precedent; **preceder** *vt*, *vi* to precede, go/come before.

precepto [pre'θepto] *nm* precept.

preciado, a [pre'θjaðo, a] *a* (*estimado*) esteemed, valuable; (*vanidoso*) presumptuous; **preciar** *vt* to esteem, value; **preciarse** *vr* to boast; **preciarse de** to pride o.s. on, boast of being.

precio ['preθjo] *nm* (*de mercado*) price; (*costo*) cost; (*valor*) value, worth; (*de viaje*) fare; **~ al contado/de coste/de**

oportunidad cash/cost/bargain price; ~ **tope** top price.

preciosidad [preθjosi'ðað] *nf* (*valor*) (high) value, (great) worth; (*encanto*) charm; (*cosa bonita*) beautiful thing; **es una** ~ it's lovely, it's really beautiful; **precioso, a** *a* precious; (*de mucho valor*) valuable; (*fam*) lovely, beautiful.

precipicio [preθi'piθjo] *nm* cliff, precipice; (*fig*) abyss.

precipitación [preθipita'θjon] *nf* haste; (*lluvia*) rainfall.

precipitado, a [preθipi'taðo, a] *a* hasty, rash; (*salida*) hasty, sudden.

precipitar [preθipi'tar] *vt* (*arrojar*) to hurl down, throw; (*acelerar*) to hasten; (*acelerar*) to speed up, accelerate; ~**se** *vr* to throw o.s.; (*apresurarse*) to rush; (*actuar sin pensar*) to act rashly.

precipitoso, a [preθipi'toso, a] *a* (*escarpado*) steep, sheer; (*a la carrera, imprudente*) hasty, rash.

precisamente [preθisa'mente] *ad* precisely; (*justo*) precisely, exactly, just.

precisar [preθi'sar] *vt* (*necesitar*) to need, require; (*fijar*) to determine exactly, fix; (*especificar*) to specify // *vi* to be necessary.

precisión [preθi'sjon] *nf* (*exactitud*) precision; (*necesidad*) need, necessity.

preciso, a [pre'θiso, a] *a* (*exacto*) precise; (*necesario*) necessary, essential.

preconcebido, a [prekonθe'ßiðo, a] *a* preconceived.

preconizar [prekoni'θar] *vt* (*aconsejar*) to advise; (*prever*) to foresee.

precoz [pre'koθ] *a* (*persona*) precocious; (*calvicie*) premature.

precursor, a [prekur'sor, a] *nm/f* precursor.

predecir [preðe'θir] *vt* to predict, foretell, forecast.

predestinado, a [preðesti'naðo, a] *a* predestined.

predeterminar [preðetermi'nar] *vt* to predetermine.

prédica ['preðika] *nf* sermon; **predicador, a** *nm/f* preacher; **predicar** *vt, vi* to preach.

predicción [preðik'θjon] *nf* prediction.

predilecto, a [preði'lekto, a] *a* favourite.

predio ['preðjo] *nm* property, estate.

predisponer [preðispo'ner] *vt* to predispose; (*pey*) to prejudice; **predisposición** *nf* predisposition, inclination; prejudice, bias.

predominante [preðomi'nante] *a* predominant.

predominar [preðomi'nar] *vt* to dominate // *vi* to predominate; (*prevalecer*) to prevail; **predominio** *nm* predominance, prevalence.

prefabricado, a [prefaßri'kaðo, a] *a* prefabricated.

prefacio [pre'faθjo] *nm* preface.

preferencia [prefe'renθja] *nf* preference; **de** ~ preferably, for preference;

preferible *a* preferable; **preferir** *vt* to prefer.

prefigurar [prefixu'rar] *vt* to foreshadow, prefigure.

pregonar [prexo'nar] *vt* to proclaim, announce.

pregunta [pre'xunta] *nf* question; **hacer una** ~ to ask *or* put a question.

preguntar [prexun'tar] *vt* to ask; (*cuestionar*) to question // *vi* to ask; ~**se** *vr* to wonder; ~ **por alguien** to ask for sb; **preguntón, ona** *a* inquisitive.

prehistórico, a [preis'toriko, a] *a* prehistoric.

prejuicio [pre'xwiθjo] *nm* prejudgement; (*preconcepción*) preconception; (*pey*) prejudice, bias.

prelación [prela'θjon] *nf* priority.

preliminar [prelimi'nar] *a* preliminary.

preludio [pre'luðjo] *nm* prelude.

prematuro, a [prema'turo, a] *a* premature.

premeditación [premeðita'θjon] *nf* premeditation; **premeditar** *vt* to premeditate.

premiar [pre'mjar] *vt* to reward; (*en un concurso*) to give a prize to; **premio** *nm* reward; prize; (*COM*) premium.

premonición [premoni'θjon] *nf* premonition.

premura [pre'mura] *nf* (*aprieto*) pressure; (*prisa*) haste, urgency.

prenatal [prena'tal] *a* antenatal, prenatal.

prenda ['prenda] *nf* (*ropa*) garment, article of clothing; (*garantía*) pledge; ~**s** *nfpl* talents, gifts.

prendar [pren'dar] *vt* to captivate, enchant; ~**se de uno** to fall in love with sb.

prendedor [prende'ðor] *nm* brooch.

prender [pren'der] *vt* (*captar*) to catch, capture; (*detener*) to arrest; (*coser*) to pin, attach; (*sujetar*) to fasten // *vi* to catch; (*arraigar*) to take root; ~**se** *vr* (*encenderse*) to catch fire; (*engalanarse*) to dress up.

prensa ['prensa] *nf* press; **la P** ~ the press; **prensar** *vt* to press.

preñada, a [pre'naðo, a] *a* (*mujer*) pregnant; ~ **de** pregnant with, full of; **preñez** *nf* pregnancy.

preocupación [preokupa'θjon] *nf* worry, concern; (*ansiedad*) anxiety; **preocupado, a** *a* worried, concerned; anxious.

preocupar [preoku'par] *vt* to worry; ~**se** *vr* to worry; ~**se de algo** (*hacerse cargo*) to worry about sth, take care of sth.

preparación [prepara'θjon] *nf* (*acto*) preparation; (*estado*) preparedness, readiness; (*entrenamiento*) training; **preparado, a** *a* (*dispuesto*) prepared; (*CULIN*) ready (to serve) // *nm* preparation.

preparador, a [prepara'ðor, a] *nm/f* trainer.

preparar [prepa'rar] *vt* (*disponer*) to prepare, get ready; (*TEC: tratar*) to

prepare, process, treat; (*entrenar*) to teach, train; ~se *vr*: **~se a** *o* **para** to prepare to *or* for, get ready to *or* for; **preparativo, a** *a* preparatory, preliminary; **preparativos** *nmpl* preparations; **preparatorio, a** *a* preparatory.

prerrogativa [prerroxa'tiβa] *nf* prerogative, privilege.

presa ['presa] *nf* (*captura*) capture, seizure; (*cosa apresada*) catch; (*víctima*) victim; (*de animal*) prey; (*de agua*) dam.

presbítero [pres'βitero] *nm* priest.

prescindible [presθin'diβle] *a* dispensable.

prescindir [presθin'dir] *vi*: ~ **de** (*privarse de*) to do without, go without; (*descartar*) to dispense with.

prescribir [preskri'βir] *vt* to prescribe; **prescripción** *nf* prescription.

presencia [pre'senθja] *nf* presence; **presencial** *a*: **testigo presencial** eye-witness; (*asistir a*) to attend; (*ver*) to see, witness.

presentación [presenta'θjon] *nf* presentation; (*introducción*) introduction.

presentador, a [presenta'ðor, a] *nm/f* compère.

presentar [presen'tar] *vt* to present; (*ofrecer*) to offer; (*mostrar*) to show, display; (*a una persona*) to introduce; **~se** *vr* (*llegar inesperadamente*) to appear, turn up; (*ofrecerse: como candidato*) to run, stand; (*aparecer*) to show, appear; (*solicitar empleo*) to apply.

presente [pre'sente] *a* present // *nm* present; **hacer** ~ to state, declare; **tener** ~ to remember, bear in mind.

presentimiento [presenti'mjento] *nm* premonition, presentiment; **presentir** *vt* to have a premonition of.

preservación [preserβa'θjon] *nf* protection, preservation; **preservar** *vt* to protect, preserve; **preservativo** *nm* sheath, condom.

presidencia [presi'ðenθja] *nf* presidency; (*de comité*) chairmanship; **presidente** *nm/f* president; chairman/woman.

presidiario [presi'ðjarjo] *nm* convict; **presidio** *nm* (*penitenciaría*) prison, penitentiary; (*trabajo forzoso*) hard labour; (*MIL*) garrison.

presidir [presi'ðir] *vt* (*dirigir*) to preside at, preside over; (: *comité*) to take the chair at; (*dominar*) to dominate, rule // *vi* to preside; to take the chair.

presión [pre'sjon] *nf.* pressure; **presionar** *vt* to press; (*fig*) to press, put pressure on // *vi*: **presionar para** *o* **por** to press for.

preso, a ['preso, a] *nm/f* prisoner; **tomar** *o* **llevar** ~ **a uno** to arrest sb, take sb prisoner.

prestado, a [pres'taðo, a] *a* on loan; **pedir** ~ to borrow.

prestamista [presta'mista] *nm/f* moneylender.

préstamo ['prestamo] *nm* loan.

prestar [pres'tar] *vt* to lend, loan; (*atención*) to pay; (*ayuda*) to give // *vi* to give, stretch.

prestatario, a [presta'tarjo, a] *nm/f* borrower.

presteza [pres'teθa] *nf* speed, promptness.

prestigio [pres'tixjo] *nm* prestige; **~so, a** *a* (*honorable*) prestigious; (*famoso, renombrado*) renowned, famous.

presto, a ['presto, a] *a* (*rápido*) quick, prompt; (*dispuesto*) ready // *ad* at once, right away.

presumir [presu'mir] *vt* to presume // *vi* (*tener aires*) to be conceited; **según cabe** ~ as may be presumed, presumably; **presunción** *nf* presumption; **presunto, a** *a* (*supuesto*) supposed, presumed; (*así llamado*) so-called; **presuntuoso, a** *a* conceited, presumptuous.

presuponer [presupo'ner] *vt* to presuppose.

presupuesto [presu'pwesto] *nm* (*FINANZAS*) budget; (*estimación: de costo*) estimate.

presuroso, a [presu'roso, a] *a* (*rápido*) quick, speedy; (*que tiene prisa*) hasty.

pretencioso, a [preten'θjoso, a] *a* pretentious.

pretender [preten'der] *vt* (*intentar*) to try to, seek to; (*reivindicar*) to claim; (*buscar*) to seek, try for; (*cortejar*) to woo, court; ~ **que** to expect that; **pretendiente** *nm/f* (*candidato*) candidate, applicant; (*amante*) suitor; **pretensión** *nf* (*aspiración*) aspiration; (*reivindicación*) claim; (*orgullo*) pretension.

pretexto [pre'teksto] *nm* pretext; (*excusa*) excuse.

prevalecer [preβale'θer] *vi* to prevail; **prevaleciente** *a* prevailing, prevalent.

prevalerse [preβa'lerse] *vr*: ~ **de** to avail o.s. of.

prevención [preβen'θjon] *nf* (*preparación*) preparation; (*estado*) preparedness, readiness; (*el evitar*) prevention; (*previsión*) foresight, forethought; (*prejuicio*) bias, prejudice; (*precaución*) precaution.

prevenido, a [preβe'niðo, a] *a* prepared, ready; (*cauteloso*) cautious.

prevenir [preβe'nir] *vt* (*impedir*) to prevent; (*prever*) to foresee, anticipate; (*predisponer*) to prejudice, bias; (*avisar*) to warn; (*preparar*) to prepare, get ready; **~se** *vr* to get ready, prepare; **~se contra** to take precautions against; **preventivo, a** *a* preventive, precautionary.

prever [pre'βer] *vt* to foresee.

previo, a ['preβjo, a] *a* (*anterior*) previous; (*preliminar*) preliminary // *prep*: ~ **acuerdo de los otros** subject to the agreement of the others.

previsión [preβi'sjon] *nf* (*perspicacia*) foresight; (*predicción*) forecast; ~ **social** social security.

prieto, a ['prjeto, a] *a* (*oscuro*) dark; (*fig*) mean; (*comprimido*) tight, compressed.

prima ['prima] *nf ver* **primo.**
primacía [prima'θia] *nf* primacy.
primario, a [pri'marjo, a] *a* primary.
primavera [prima'ßera] *nf* (*temporada*) spring; (*período*) springtime.
primer, primero, a [pri'mer, pri'mero, a] *a* first; (*fig*) prime // *ad* first; (*más bien*) sooner, rather // *nf* (*AUTO*) first gear; (*FERRO*) first class; **de ~a** (*fam*) first-class, first-rate; **~a plana** front page.
primitivo, a [primi'tißo, a] *a* primitive; (*original*) original.
primo, a ['primo, a] *nm/f* cousin; (*fam*) fool, dupe // *nf* (*COM*) bonus; **~ hermano** first cousin; **materias ~as** raw materials.
primogénito, a [primo'xenito, a] *a* first-born.
primordial [primor'ðjal] *a* basic, fundamental.
primoroso, a [primo'roso, a] *a* exquisite, delicate.
princesa [prin'θesa] *nf* princess.
principal [prinθi'pal] *a* principal, main // *nm* (*jefe*) chief, principal.
príncipe ['prinθipe] *nm* prince.
principiante [prinθi'pjante] *nm/f* beginner; **principiar** *vt* to begin.
principio [prin'θipjo] *nm* (*comienzo*) beginning, start; (*origen*) origin; (*primera etapa*) rudiment, basic idea; (*moral*) principle; **a ~s de** at the beginning of; **tener** *o* **tomar en ~** to start from, be based on.
pringue ['pringe] *nm* (*grasa*) grease, fat, dripping; (*mancha*) grease stain.
prioridad [priori'ðað] *nf* priority.
prisa ['prisa] *nf* (*apresuramiento*) hurry, haste; (*rapidez*) speed; (*urgencia*) (sense of) urgency; **a** *o* **de ~** quickly; **correr ~** to be urgent; **darse ~** to hurry up; **estar de** *o* **tener ~** to be in a hurry.
prisión [pri'sjon] *nf* (*cárcel*) prison; (*período de cárcel*) imprisonment; **prisionero, a** *nm/f* prisoner.
prismáticos [pris'matikos] *nmpl* binoculars.
privación [priβa'θjon] *nf* deprivation; (*falta*) want, privation.
privado, a [pri'ßaðo, a] *a* private.
privar [pri'ßar] *vt* to deprive; (*prohibir*) to forbid // *vi* (*gozar de favor*) to be in favour; (*prevalecer*) to prevail; **privativo, a** *a* exclusive.
privilegiado, a [prißile'xjaðo, a] *a* privileged; (*memoria*) very good; **privilegiar** *vt* to grant a privilege to; (*favorecer*) to favour.
privilegio [prißi'lexjo] *nm* privilege; (*concesión*) concession; **~ de invención** patent.
pro [pro] *nm o f* profit, advantage // *prep*: **asociación ~ ciegos** association for the blind // *pref*: **~ soviético/americano** pro-Soviet/American; **en ~ de** on behalf of, for; **los ~s y los contras** the pros and cons.

probabilidad [proßaßili'ðað] *nf* probability, likelihood; (*oportunidad*, *posibilidad*) chance, prospect; **probable** *a* probable, likely.
probanza [pro'ßanθa] *nf* proof, evidence.
probar [pro'ßar] *vt* (*demostrar*) to prove; (*someter a prueba*) to test, try out; (*ropa*) to try on; (*comida*) to taste // *vi* to try; **~se un traje** to try on a suit.
probeta [pro'ßeta] *nf* test tube.
problema [pro'ßlema] *nm* problem.
procaz [pro'kaθ] *a* insolent, impudent.
procedente [proθe'ðente] *a* (*razonable*) reasonable; (*conforme a derecho*) proper, fitting; **~ de** coming from, originating in.
proceder [proθe'ðer] *vi* (*avanzar*) to proceed; (*actuar*) to act; (*ser correcto*) to be right (and proper), be fitting // *nm* (*acción*) course of action; (*comportamiento*) behaviour, conduct; **procedimiento** *nm* procedure; (*proceso*) process; (*método*) means, method.
procesado, a [proθe'saðo, a] *nm/f* accused (person); **procesar** *vt* to try, put on trial.
procesión [proθe'sjon] *nf* procession.
proceso [pro'θeso] *nm* process; (*JUR*) trial; (*lapso*) course (of time).
proclama [pro'klama] *nf* (*acto*) proclamation; (*cartel*) poster; **proclamar** *vt* to proclaim.
procreación [prokrea'θjon] *nf* procreation; **procrear** *vt*, *vi* to procreate.
procurador, a [prokura'ðor, a] *nm/f* attorney.
procurar [proku'rar] *vt* (*intentar*) to try, endeavour; (*conseguir*) to get, obtain; (*asegurar*) to secure; (*producir*) to produce.
prodigio [pro'ðixjo] *nm* prodigy; (*milagro*) wonder, marvel; **~so, a** *a* prodigious, marvellous.
pródigo, a ['proðixo, a] *a*: **hijo ~** prodigal son.
producción [proðuk'θjon] *nf* production; (*suma de productos*) output; (*producto*) product; **~ en serie** mass production.
producir [proðu'θir] *vt* to produce; (*generar*) to cause, bring about; **~se** *vr* (*gen*) to come about, happen; (*hacerse*) to be produced, be made; (*estallar*) to break out.
productividad [proðuktißi'ðað] *nf* productivity; **productivo, a** *a* productive; (*provechoso*) profitable.
producto [pro'ðukto] *nm* product; (*producción*) production.
productor, a [proðuk'tor, a] *a* productive, producing // *nm/f* producer.
proeza [pro'eθa] *nf* exploit, feat.
profanar [profa'nar] *vt* to desecrate, profane; **profano, a** *a* profane // *nm/f* layman/woman.
profecía [profe'θia] *nf* prophecy.
proferir [profe'rir] *vt* (*palabra, sonido*) to utter; (*injuria*) to hurl, let fly.
profesar [profe'sar] *vt* (*declarar*) to profess; (*practicar*) to practise.

profesión [profe'sjon] *nf* profession; **profesional** *a* professional.

profesor, a [profe'sor, a] *nm/f* teacher; ~**ado** *nm* teaching profession.

profeta [pro'feta] *nm/f* prophet; **profetizar** *vt, vi* to prophesy.

prófugo, a [pro'fuɣo, a] *nm/f* fugitive; (*desertor*) deserter.

profundidad [profundi'ðað] *nf* depth; **profundizar** *vt* (*fig*) to go deeply into; **profundo, a** *a* deep; (*misterio, pensador*) profound.

progenie [pro'xenje] *nf* offspring.

progenitor [proxeni'tor] *nm* ancestor; ~**es** *nmpl* (*fam*) parents.

programa [pro'ɣrama] *nm* programme; ~**ción** *nf* programming; ~**dor, a** *nm/f* programmer; **programar** *vt* to programme.

progresar [proɣre'sar] *vi* to progress, make progress; **progresista** *a, nm/f* progressive; **progresivo, a** *a* progressive; (*gradual*) gradual; (*continuo*) continuous; **progreso** *nm* progress.

prohibición [proißi'θjon] *nf* prohibition, ban; **prohibir** *vt* to prohibit, ban, forbid; **se prohibe fumar** no smoking.

prohijar [proi'xar] *vt* to adopt.

prójimo, a ['proximo, a] *nm/f* fellow man, neighbour.

proletariado [proleta'rjaðo] *nm* proletariat; **proletario, a** *a, nm/f* proletarian.

proliferación [prolifera'θjon] *nf* proliferation; **proliferar** *vi* to proliferate; **prolífico, a** *a* prolific.

prolijo, a [pro'lixo, a] *a* long-winded, tedious.

prólogo ['proloxo] *nm* prologue.

prolongación [prolonga'θjon] *nf* extension; **prolongado, a** *a* (*largo*) long; (*alargado*) lengthy; **prolongar** *vt* (*gen*) to extend; (*en el tiempo*) to prolong; (*calle, tubo*) to make longer, extend.

promedio [pro'meðjo] *nm* average; (*de distancia*) middle, mid-point.

promesa [pro'mesa] *nf* promise.

prometer [prome'ter] *vt* to promise // *vi* to show promise; ~**se** *vr* (*dos personas*) to get engaged; **prometido, a** *a* promised; engaged // *nm/f* fiancé/fiancée.

prominente [promi'nente] *a* prominent.

promiscuo, a [pro'miskwo, a] *a* (*mezclado*) mixed(-up), in disorder; (*ambiguo*) ambiguous.

promoción [promo'θjon] *nf* promotion.

promotor [promo'tor] *nm* promoter; (*instigador*) instigator.

promover [promo'ßer] *vt* to promote; (*causar*) to cause; (*instigar*) to instigate, stir up.

promulgar [promul'xar] *vt* to promulgate; (*fig*) to proclaim.

pronosticar [pronosti'kar] *vt* to predict, foretell, forecast; **pronóstico** *nm* prediction, forecast.

prontitud [pronti'tuð] *nf* speed, quickness;

(*de ingenio*) quickness, sharpness.

pronto, a ['pronto, a] *a* (*rápido*) prompt, quick; (*preparado*) ready; (*astuto*) quick, sharp // *ad* quickly, promptly; (*en seguida*) at once, right away; (*dentro de poco*) soon; (*temprano*) early // *nm*: **tener** ~**s de enojo** to be quick-tempered; **al** ~ at first; **de** ~ suddenly; **por lo** ~ meanwhile, for the present.

pronunciación [pronunθja'θjon] *nf* pronunciation; **pronunciar** *vt* to pronounce; (*discurso*) to make, deliver; **pronunciarse** *vr* to revolt, rise, rebel; (*declararse*) to declare o.s.

propagación [propaɣa'θjon] *nf* propagation.

propaganda [propa'ɣanda] *nf* (*política*) propaganda; (*comercial*) advertising.

propagar [propa'xar] *vt* to propagate.

propensión [propen'sjon] *nf* inclination, propensity; **propenso, a** *a* inclined to; **ser propenso a** to be inclined to, have a tendency to.

propiamente [propja'mente] *ad* properly; (*realmente*) really, exactly.

propicio, a [pro'piθjo, a] *a* favourable, propitious.

propiedad [propje'ðað] *nf* (*gen*) property; (*posesión*) possession, ownership; ~ **industrial** patent rights *pl*; ~ **literaria** copyright; ~ **particular** private property.

propietario, a [propje'tarjo, a] *nm/f* owner, proprietor.

propina [pro'pina] *nf* tip.

propio, a ['propjo, a] *a* own, of one's own; (*característico*) characteristic, typical; (*conveniente*) proper; (*mismo*) selfsame, very; **el** ~ **ministro** the minister himself; **¿tienes casa** ~**a?** have you a house of your own?

proponer [propo'ner] *vt* to propose, put forward; (*problema*) to pose; ~**se** *vr* to propose, plan, intend.

proporción [propor'θjon] *nf* proportion; (*MAT*) ratio; (*oportunidad*) chance, opportunity; **proporciones** *nfpl* dimensions; (*fig*) size *sg*; **proporcionado, a** *a* proportionate; (*regular*) medium, middling; (*justo*) just right; **proporcionar** *vt* (*dar*) to give, supply, provide; (*adaptar*) to adjust, adapt.

proposición [proposi'θjon] *nf* proposition; (*propuesta*) proposal.

propósito [pro'posito] *nm* purpose; (*intento*) aim, intention // *a*: **a** ~ appropriate, suitable // *ad*: **a** ~ **by the** way, incidentally; **a** ~ **de** about, with regard to; **de** ~ on purpose, deliberately.

propuesta [pro'pwesta] *nf* proposal.

propulsar [propul'sar] *vt* to drive, propel; (*fig*) to promote, encourage; **propulsión** *nf* propulsion; **propulsión a chorro** *o* **por reacción** jet propulsion.

prórroga ['prorroxa] *nf* (*gen*) extension; (*JUR*) stay; (*COM*) deferment; **prorrogar** *vt* (*período*) to extend; (*decisión*) to defer, postpone.

prorrumpir [prorrum'pir] *vi* to burst forth, break out.

prosa ['prosa] *nf* prose.

proscribir [proskri'βir] *vt* to prohibit, ban; (*desterrar*) to exile, banish; (*partido*) to proscribe; **proscripción** *nf* prohibition, ban; banishment; proscription.

prosecución [proseku'θjon] *nf* continuation; (*persecución*) pursuit.

proseguir [prose'xir] *vt* to continue, carry on, proceed with // *vi* to continue, go on.

prospección [prospek'θjon] *nf* exploration; (*del petróleo, del oro*) prospecting.

prospecto [pros'pekto] *nm* prospectus.

prosperar [prospe'rar] *vi* to prosper, thrive, flourish; **prosperidad** *nf* prosperity; (*éxito*) success; **próspero, a** *a* prosperous, thriving, flourishing; (*que tiene éxito*) successful.

prostíbulo [pros'tiβulo] *nm* brothel.

prostitución [prostitu'θjon] *nf* prostitution; **prostituir** *vt* to prostitute; **prostituirse** *vr* to prostitute o.s., become a prostitute; **prostituta** *nf* prostitute.

protagonista [protaxo'nista] *nm/f* protagonist.

protección [protek'θjon] *nf* protection.

protector, a [protek'tor, a] *a* protective, protecting // *nm/f* protector.

proteger [prote'xer] *vt* to protect; **protegido, a** *nm/f* protégé/ protégée.

proteína [prote'ina] *nf* protein.

protesta [pro'testa] *nf* protest; (*declaración*) protestation.

protestante [protes'tante] *a* Protestant.

protestar [protes'tar] *vt* to protest, declare; (*fé*) to protest // *vi* to protest.

protocolo [proto'kolo] *nm* protocol.

prototipo [proto'tipo] *nm* prototype.

provecho [pro'βetʃo] *nm* advantage, benefit; (*FINANZAS*) profit; ¡**buen** ~! bon appétit!; **en** ~ **de** to the benefit of; **sacar** ~ **de** to benefit from, profit by.

proveer [proβe'er] *vt* to provide, supply; (*preparar*) to provide, get ready; (*vacante*) to fill; (*negocio*) to transact, dispatch // *vi*: ~ **a** to provide for.

provenir [proβe'nir] *vi*: ~ **de** to come from, stem from.

proverbio [pro'βerβjo] *nm* proverb.

providencia [proβi'ðenθja] *nf* providence; (*previsión*) foresight; ~**s** *nfpl* measures, steps.

provincia [pro'βinθja] *nf* province; ~**no, a** *a* provincial; (*del campo*) country *cpd*.

provisión [proβi'sjon] *nf* provision; (*abastecimiento*) provision, supply; (*medida*) measure, step.

provisional [proβisjo'nal] *a* provisional.

provocación [proβoka'θjon] *nf* provocation; **provocar** *vt* to provoke; (*alentar*) to tempt, invite; (*causar*) to bring about, lead to; (*promover*) to promote;

(*estimular*) to rouse, stir, stimulate; **provocativo, a** *a* provocative.

próximamente [proksima'mente] *ad* shortly, soon.

proximidad [proksimi'ðað] *nf* closeness, proximity; **próximo, a** *a* near, close; (*vecino*) neighbouring; (*el que viene*) next.

proyectar [projek'tar] *vt* (*objeto*) to hurl, throw; (*luz*) to cast, shed; (*CINE*) to screen, show; (*planear*) to plan.

proyectil [projek'til] *nm* projectile, missile; (*MIL*) missile.

proyecto [pro'jekto] *nm* plan; (*estimación de costo*) detailed estimate.

proyector [projek'tor] *nm* (*CINE*) projector; (*MIL*) searchlight; (*de teatro*) spotlight.

prudencia [pru'ðenθja] *nf* (*sabiduría*) wisdom, prudence; (*cautela*) care; **prudente** *a* sensible, wise, prudent; (*conductor*) careful.

prueba ['prweβa] *nf* proof; (*ensayo*) test, trial; (*saboreo*) testing, sampling; (*de ropa*) fitting; ~**s** *nfpl* trials; **a** ~ on trial; **a** ~ **de** proof against; **a** ~ **de agua/fuego** waterproof/fireproof; **sala de** ~**s** fitting room; **someter a** ~ to put to the test.

prurito [pru'rito] *nm* itch; (*de bebé*) nappy rash.

psico... [siko] *pref* psycho...; ~**análisis** *nm* psychoanalysis; ~**logía** *nf* psychology; ~**lógico, a** *a* psychological; **psicólogo, a** *nm/f* psychologist; **psicópata** *nm/f* psychopath; ~**sis** *nf inv* psychosis.

psiquiatra [si'kjatra] *nm/f* psychiatrist; **psiquiátrico, a** *a* psychiatric.

psíquico, a ['sikiko, a] *a* psychic(al).

PSOE *abr de* **Partido Socialista Obrero Español.**

púa ['pua] *nf* sharp point; (*para guitarra*) plectrum; **alambre de** ~ barbed wire.

pubertad [puβer'tað] *nf* puberty.

publicación [puβlika'θjon] *nf* publication; **publicar** *vt* (*editar*) to publish; (*hacer público*) to publicize; (*vulgarizar*) to make public, divulge.

publicidad [puβliθi'ðað] *nf* publicity; (*COM*) advertising; **publicitario, a** *a* publicity *cpd*; advertising *cpd*.

público, a ['puβliko, a] *a* public // *nm* public; (*TEATRO etc*) audience.

puchero [pu'tʃero] *nm* stew; **hacer** ~**s** to pout.

pude *etc vb ver* **poder.**

púdico, a ['puðiko, a] *a* modest.

pudiera *etc vb ver* **poder.**

pudor [pu'ðor] *nm* modesty.

pudrir [pu'ðrir] *vt* to rot; (*fam*) to upset, annoy; ~**se** *vr* to rot, decay.

pueblo ['pweβlo] *nm* people; (*nación*) nation; (*aldea*) village.

puedo *etc vb ver* **poder.**

puente ['pwente] *nm* (*gen*) bridge; ~ **aéreo** airlift; ~ **colgante** suspension bridge; **hacer el** ~ (*fam*) to take an extra day off work between 2 public holidays.

puerco, a ['pwerko, a] *nm/f* pig/sow //

(*sucio*) dirty, filthy; (*obsceno*) disgusting; ~ **de mar** porpoise; ~ **marino** dolphin.

pueril [pwe'ril] *a* childish.

puerro ['pwerro] *nm* leek.

puerta ['pwerta] *nf* door; (*de jardín*) gate; (*portal*) doorway; (*fig*) gateway; (*gol*) goal; **a ~ cerrada** behind closed doors; ~ **giratoria** swing door, revolving door.

puertaventana [pwertaßen'tana] *nf* shutter.

puerto ['pwerto] *nm* port; (*paso*) pass; (*fig*) haven, refuge.

Puerto Rico [pwerto'riko] *nm* Puerto Rico; **puertorriqueño, a** *a* Puerto Rican.

pues [pwes] *ad* (*entonces*) then; (¡*entonces!*) well, well then; (*así que*) so // *conj* (*ya que*) since; ; ~! (*sí*) yes!, certainly!

puesto, a ['pwesto, a] *pp de* **poner** // *a* dressed // *nm* (*lugar, posición*) place; (*trabajo*) post, job; (*COM*) stall // *conj*: ~ **que** since, as // *a* (*apuesta*) bet, stake; ~**a en marcha** starting; ~**a del sol** sunset.

púgil ['puxil] *nm* boxer.

pugna ['puxna] *nf* battle, conflict; ~**cidad** *nf* pugnacity, aggressiveness; **pugnar** *vi* (*luchar*) to struggle, fight; (*pelear*) to fight.

pulcro, a ['pulkro, a] *a* neat, tidy; (*bello*) exquisite.

pulga ['pulxa] *nf* flea.

pulgada [pul'xaða] *nf* inch.

pulgar [pul'xar] *nm* thumb.

pulir [pu'lir], **pulimentar** [pulimen'tar] *vt* to polish; (*alisar*) to smooth; (*fig*) to polish up, touch up.

pulmón [pul'mon] *nm* lung; **pulmonía** *nf* pneumonia.

pulpa ['pulpa] *nf* pulp; (*de fruta*) flesh, soft part.

púlpito ['pulpito] *nm* pulpit.

pulpo ['pulpo] *nm* octopus.

pulsación [pulsa'θjon] *nf* beat, pulsation; (*ANAT*) throb(bing).

pulsador [pulsa'ðor] *nm* button, push button.

pulsar [pul'sar] *vt* (*tecla*) to touch, tap; (*MUS*) to play; (*botón*) to press, push // *vi* to pulsate; (*latir*) to beat, throb; (*MED*): ~ **a uno** to take sb's pulse.

pulsera [pul'sera] *nf* bracelet.

pulso ['pulso] *nm* (*ANAT*) pulse; (: *muñeca*) wrist; (*fuerza*) strength; (*firmeza*) steadiness, steady hand; (*tacto*) tact, good sense.

pulverizador [pulßeriða'ðor] *nm* spray, spray gun; **pulverizar** *vt* to pulverize; (*líquido*) to spray.

pulla ['puʎa] *nf* cutting remark; (*expresión grosera*) obscene remark.

pungir [pun'xir] *vt* to puncture, prick, pierce; (*fig*) to cause suffering to.

punición [puni'θjon] *nf* punishment; **punitivo, a** *a* punitive.

punta ['punta] *nf* point, tip; (*extremidad*) end; (*fig*) touch, trace; **horas** ~**s** peak hours, rush hours; **sacar** ~ **a** to sharpen; **estar de** ~ to be edgy.

puntada [pun'taða] *nf* (*COSTURA*) stitch; (*fam*) hint; **no ha dado** ~ he hasn't done a stroke.

puntal [pun'tal] *nm* prop, support.

puntapié [punta'pje] *nm* kick.

puntear [punte'ar] *vt* (*marcar*) to tick, mark; (*coser*) to stitch (up).

puntería [punte'ria] *nf* (*de arma*) aim, aiming; (*destreza*) marksmanship.

puntiagudo, a [puntja'xuðo, a] *a* sharp, pointed.

puntilla [pun'tiʎa] *nf* (*de pluma*) point, nib; (**andar**) **de** ~**s** (to walk) on tiptoe.

punto ['punto] *nm* (*gen*) point; (*señal diminuta*) spot, dot; (*lugar*) spot, place; (*momento*) point, moment; **a** ~ ready; **estar a** ~ **de** to be on the point of *or* about to; **en** ~ on the dot; ~ **de arranque** starting point; ~ **muerto** dead centre; (*AUTO*) neutral (gear); ~ **y coma** semicolon; ~ **de interrogación** question mark.

puntuación [puntwa'θjon] *nf* punctuation; (*puntos: en examen*) mark(s) (*pl*); (*DEPORTE*) score.

puntual [pun'twal] *a* (*a tiempo*) punctual; (*exacto*) exact, accurate; (*seguro*) reliable; ~**idad** *nf* punctuality; exactness, accuracy; reliability; ~**izar** *vt* to fix, specify; (*en la memoria*) to fix in one's mind/memory.

punzante [pun'θante] *a* (*dolor*) shooting, sharp; (*herramienta*) sharp; **punzar** *vt* to prick, pierce // *vi* to shoot, stab.

puñado [pu'ɲaðo] *nm* handful.

puñal [pu'ɲal] *nm* dagger; ~**ada** *nf* stab; ~**ada de misericordia** coup de grâce.

puñetazo [puɲe'taθo] *nm* punch.

puño ['puɲo] *nm* (*ANAT*) fist; (*cantidad*) fistful, handful; (*COSTURA*) cuff; (*de herramienta*) handle.

pupila [pu'pila] *nf* pupil.

pupitre [pu'pitre] *nm* desk.

puré [pu're] *nm* puree; (*sopa*) (thick) soup; ~ **de patatas** mashed potatoes.

pureza [pu'reθa] *nf* purity.

purga ['purxa] *nf* purge; **purgante** *a, nm* purgative; **purgar** *vt* to purge.

purgatorio [purxa'torjo] *nm* purgatory.

purificar [purifi'kar] *vt* to purify; (*refinar*) to refine.

puritano, a [puri'tano, a] *a* (*actitud*) puritanical; (*iglesia, tradición*) puritan // *nm/f* puritan.

puro, a ['puro, a] *a* pure; (*cielo*) clear; (*verdad*) simple, plain // *ad*: **de** ~ **cansado** out of sheer tiredness // *nm* cigar.

púrpura ['purpura] *nf* purple; **purpúreo, a** *a* purple.

puse, pusiera etc *vb ver* **poner**.

pústula ['pustula] *nf* pimple, sore.

puta ['puta] *nf* whore, prostitute.

putrefacción [putrefak'θjon] *nf* rotting, putrefaction.

pútrido, a ['putriðo, a] *a* rotten.

Q

q.e.p.d. abr de **que en paz descanse.**

q.e.s.m. abr de **que estrecha su mano.**

que [ke] pron (sujeto) who, that; (: cosa) which, that; (complemento) whom, that; (: cosa) which, that // conj that; **el momento en ~ llegó** the moment he arrived; **lo ~ digo** what I say; **dar ~ hablar** to give cause to talk, cause talk; **le ruego ~ se calle** I'm asking you to keep quiet; **te digo ~ sí** I'm telling you, I assure you; **yo ~ tú** if I were you.

qué [ke] a what?, which? // pron what?; ¡~ divertido! how funny!; ¿~ edad tiene Ud? how old are you?; ¿de ~ me hablas? what are you saying to me?; ¿~ tal? how are you?, how are things?; ¿~ hay (de nuevo)? what's new?

quebrada [ke'ßraða] nf ver **quebrado.**

quebradizo, a [keßra'ðiθo, a] a fragile; (persona) frail.

quebrado, a [ke'ßraðo, a] a (roto) broken; (pálido) pale; (COM) bankrupt // nm/f bankrupt // nf ravine.

quebradura [keßra'ðura] nf (fisura) fissure; (GEO) gorge; (MED) rupture.

quebrantadura [keßranta'ðura] nf, **quebrantamiento** [keßranta'mjento] nm (acto) breaking; (estado) exhaustion.

quebrantar [keßran'tar] vt (romper) to break; (infringir) to violate, transgress; **~se** vr (persona) to fail in health; (deshacerse) to break.

quebranto [ke'ßranto] nm damage, harm; (decaimiento) exhaustion; (debilidad) weakness; (dolor) grief, pain.

quebrar [ke'ßrar] vt to break, smash; (interrumpir) to interrupt // vi to go bankrupt; **~se** vr to break, get broken; (MED) to be ruptured.

quedar [ke'ðar] vi (permanecer) to stay; (seguir siendo) to remain; (encontrarse) to be; (restar) to remain, be left; **~se** vr to remain, stay (behind); **~se con** to keep; **~ en** (acordar) to agree on/to; (acabar siendo) to end up as; **~ por hacer** to be still to be done; **~ ciego/mudo** to be left blind/dumb; **no te queda bien ese vestido** that dress doesn't suit you; **quedamos a las seis** we agreed to meet at six.

quedo, a ['keðo, a] a still // ad softly, gently.

quehacer [kea'θer] nm task, job; (doméstico) chore.

queja ['kexa] nf complaint; **quejarse** vr (enfermo) to moan, groan; (protestar) to complain; **quejido** nm moan; **quejoso, a** a complaining.

quemado, a [ke'maðo, a] a burnt.

quemadura [kema'ðura] nf burn, scald.

quemar [ke'mar] vt to burn; (fig) to burn up, squander // vi to be burning hot; **~se** vr to burn (up); (del sol) to get sunburnt.

quemarropa [kema'rropa]: **a ~** ad point-blank.

quemazón [kema'θon] nf burn; (calor) intense heat; (sensación) itch.

quepo etc vb ver **caber.**

querella [ke're/a] nf (JUR) charge; (disputa) dispute.

querer [ke'rer] vt (desear) to want, wish; (amar a) to love; **~ hacer algo** to want to do sth; **querido, a** dear // nm/f darling // nf mistress.

quesería [kese'ria] nf dairy, cheese factory.

queso ['keso] nm cheese; **~ crema** cream cheese; **~ helado** ice-cream brick.

quicio ['kiθjo] nm hinge; **sacar a uno de ~** to get on sb's nerves.

quiebra ['kjeßra] nf break, split; (COM) bankruptcy; (ECON) slump.

quiebro ['kjeßro] nm (del cuerpo) swerve.

quien [kjen] pron who; **hay ~ piensa que** there are those who think that; **no hay ~ lo haga** no-one will do it.

quién [kjen] pron who, whom; ¿~ es? who's there?

quienquiera [kjen'kjera] (pl **quienesquiera**) pron whoever.

quiero etc vb ver **querer.**

quieto, a ['kjeto, a] a still; (carácter) placid; **quietud** nf stillness.

quijada [ki'xaða] nf jaw, jawbone.

quilate [ki'late] nm carat.

quimera [ki'mera] nf chimera; **quimérico, a** a fantastic.

químico, a ['kimiko, a] a chemical // nm/f chemist // nf chemistry.

quincalla [kin'ka/a] nf hardware, ironmongery.

quince ['kinθe] num fifteen; **~na** nf fortnight; (pago) fortnightly pay; **~nal** a fortnightly.

quiniela [ki'njela] nf pools coupon; **~s** nfpl football pools.

quinientos [ki'njentos] num five hundred.

quinina [ki'nina] nf quinine.

quinqui ['kinki] nm gangster.

quinto, a ['kinto, a] a fifth // nf country house; (MIL) call-up, draft.

quiosco ['kjosko] nm (de música) bandstand; (de periódicos) news stand.

quirúrgico, a [ki'rurxiko, a] a surgical.

quise, quisiera etc vb ver **querer.**

quisquilloso, a [kiski'/oso, a] a touchy; (fam) pernickety.

quiste ['kiste] nm cyst.

quita ['kita] nf remission of debt; **de ~ y pon** detachable.

quitaesmalte [kitaes'malte] nm nail-polish remover.

quitamanchas [kita'mantʃas] nm inv stain remover.

quitar [ki'tar] vt to remove, take away; (ropa) to take off; (dolor) to kill, stop; **¡quita de ahí!** get away!; **~se** vr to withdraw; **se quitó el sombrero** he took off his hat.

quitsol [kita'sol] nm sunshade.

quite ['kite] nm (esgrima) parry; (evasión) dodge.

quizá(s) [ki'θa(s)] ad perhaps, maybe.

R

rábano ['raβano] nm radish; **me importa un ~** I don't give a damn.

rabia ['raβja] nf (MED) rabies; (fig) fury, rage; **rabiar** vi to have rabies; to rage, be furious; **rabiar por algo** to be dying for or long for sth.

rabieta [ra'βjeta] nf tantrum, fit of temper.

rabino [ra'βino] nm rabbi.

rabioso, a [ra'βjoso, a] a rabid; (fig) furious.

rabo ['raβo] nm tail.

racial [ra'θjal] a racial, race cpd.

racimo [ra'θimo] nm bunch.

raciocinio [raθjo'θinjo] nm reason.

ración [ra'θjon] nf portion; **raciones** nfpl rations.

racional [raθjo'nal] a (razonable) reasonable; (lógico) rational; **~izar** vt to rationalize.

racionar [raθjo'nar] vt to ration (out).

racismo [ra'θismo] nm racialism, racism; **racista** a, nm/f racist.

racha ['ratʃa] nf gust of wind.

radar [ra'ðar] nm radar.

radiador [raðja'ðor] nm radiator.

radiante [ra'ðjante] a radiant.

radical [raði'kal] a, nm/f radical.

radicar [raði'kar] vi to take root; **~ en** to lie or consist in; **~se** vr to establish o.s., put down (one's) roots.

radio ['raðjo] nf radio; (aparato) radio (set) // nm (MAT) radius; (QUÍMICA) radium; **~activo, a** a radioactive; **~difusión** nf broadcasting; **~emisora** nf transmitter, radio station; **~escucha** nm/f listener; **~grafía** nf X-ray; **~grafiar** vt to X-ray; **~terapia** nf radiotherapy; **radioyente** nm/f listener.

raer [ra'er] vt to scrape (off).

ráfaga ['rafaxa] nf gust; (de luz) flash; (de tiros) burst.

raído, a [ra'iðo, a] a (ropa) threadbare; (persona) shameless.

raigambre [rai'xambre] nf (BOT) roots pl; (fig) tradition.

raíz [ra'iθ] (pl **raíces**) nf root; **~ cuadrada** square root; **a ~ de** as a result of.

raja ['raxa] nf (de melón etc) slice; (grieta) crack; **rajar** vt to split; (fam) to slash; (fruta etc) to slice; **rajarse** vr to split, crack; (AM) to quit.

rajatabla [raxa'taβla]: **a ~** ad (estrictamente) strictly, to the letter; (cueste lo que cueste) at all costs.

ralo, a ['ralo, a] a thin, sparse.

rallado, a [ra'ʎaðo, a] a grated; **rallador** nm grater; **rallar** vt to grate.

rama ['rama] nf branch; **~da** nf, **~je** nm branches pl, foliage; **ramal** nm (de cuerda) strand; (FERRO) branch line; (AUTO) branch (road).

rambla ['rambla] nf (de agua) stream; (avenida) avenue.

ramera [ra'mera] nf whore.

ramificación [ramifika'θjon] nf ramification; **ramificarse** vr to branch out.

ramillete [rami'ʎete] nm bouquet; (fig) select group.

ramo ['ramo] nm branch; (COM) department, section.

rampa ['rampa] nf (MED) cramp; (plano) ramp.

ramplón, ona [ram'plon, ona] a uncouth, coarse.

rana ['rana] nf frog; **~ toro** bullfrog; **salto de ~** leapfrog.

rancio, a [ra'ranθjo, a] a rancid; (vino) aged, mellow; (fig) ancient.

rancho ['rantʃo] nm grub (fam); (AM) farm.

rango ['rango] nm rank, standing.

ranura [ra'nura] nf groove; (de teléfono) slot.

rapacidad [rapaθi'ðað] nf rapacity.

rapar [ra'par] vt to shave; (los cabellos) to crop; (fam) to pinch, nick (fam).

rapaz [ra'paθ] a (ladrón) thieving; (ZOOL) predatory.

rapaz, a [ra'paθ, a] nm/f young boy/girl.

rape ['rape] nm quick shave; **al ~** cropped.

rapé [ra'pe] nm snuff.

rapidez [rapi'ðeθ] nf speed, rapidity; **rápido, a** a rapid, fast, quick // ad quickly // nm (tren) express; **rápidos** nmpl rapids.

rapiña [ra'piɲa] nm robbery; **ave de ~** bird of prey.

raptar [rap'tar] vt to kidnap; **rapto** nm kidnapping; (impulso) sudden impulse; (éxtasis) ecstasy, rapture.

raqueta [ra'keta] nf racquet.

raquítico, a [ra'kitiko, a] a stunted; (fig) poor, inadequate; **raquitismo** nm rickets sg.

rareza [ra'reθa] nf rarity; (fig) eccentricity.

raro, a ['raro, a] a (poco común) rare; (extraño) odd, strange; (excepcional) remarkable.

ras [ras] nm: **a ~ de** level with; **a ~ de tierra** at ground level.

rasar [ra'sar] vt (igualar) to level; (frotar) to graze.

rascacielos [raska'θjelos] nm inv skyscraper.

rascar [ras'kar] vt (con las uñas) to scratch; (raspar) to scrape; **~se** vr to scratch (o.s.).

rasgadura [rasxa'ðura] nf tear, rip; **rasgar** vt to tear, rip (up).

rasgo ['rasxo] nm stroke; **~s** nmpl

features, characteristics; **a grandes ~s** in outline, broadly.

rasguñar [rasɣu'ɲar] *vt* to scratch; **rasguño** *nm* scratch.

raso, a ['raso, a] *a* (*liso*) flat, level; (*a baja altura*) very low // *nm* satin; **cielo ~** clear sky; **soldado ~** private.

raspador [raspa'ðor] *nm* scraper.

raspadura [raspa'ðura] *nf* scrape; (*marca*) scratch; **~s** *nfpl* scrapings; **raspar** *vt* to scrape; (*arañar*) to scratch; (*limar*) to file.

rastra ['rastra] *nf* (*huella*) track; (*AGR*) rake; **a ~s** by dragging; (*fig*) unwillingly; **pescar a la ~** to trawl.

rastreador [rastrea'ðor] *nm* tracker; (*NAUT*) trawler; **~ de minas** minesweeper; **rastrear** *vt* to track; (*laguna, río*) to dredge, drag.

rastrero, a [ras'trero, a] *a* creeping; (*vestido*) trailing; (*fig*) despicable, mean.

rastrillar [rastri'ʎar] *vt* to rake; **rastrillo** *nm* rake.

rastro ['rastro] *nm* (*AGR*) rake; (*pista*) track, trail; (*curso*) course; (*vestigio*) trace; (*matadero*) slaughterhouse; **el R~** the Madrid fleamarket.

rastrojo [ras'troxo] *nm* stubble.

rasurador [rasura'ðor] *nm*, **rasuradora** [rasura'ðora] *nf* electric shaver; **rasurarse** *vr* to shave.

rata ['rata] *nf* rat.

ratear [rate'ar] *vt* (*robar*) to steal; (*distribuir*) to share out.

ratería [rate'ria] *nf* petty theft.

ratero, a [ra'tero, a] *a* light-fingered // *nm/f* pickpocket.

ratificar [ratifi'kar] *vt* to ratify.

rato ['rato] *nm* while, short time; **a ~s** at times; **hay para ~** there's still a long way to go; **pasar el ~** to kill time; **pasar un buen/mal ~** to have a good/rough time.

ratón [ra'ton] *nm* mouse; **ratonera** *nf* mousetrap.

raudal [rau'ðal] *nm* torrent; **a ~es** in abundance.

raya ['raja] *nf* line; (*marca*) scratch; (*en tela*) stripe; (*de pelo*) parting; (*límite*) boundary; **tener a ~** to keep in check; **rayar** *vt* to line; to scratch; (*subrayar*) to underline // *vi*: **rayar en o con** to border on.

rayo ['rajo] *nm* (*del sol*) ray, beam; (*de luz*) shaft; (*en una tormenta*) lightning, flash of lightning; **~s X** X-rays.

rayón [ra'jon] *nm* rayon.

raza ['raθa] *nf* race; **~ humana** human race.

razón [ra'θon] *nf* (*gen*) reason; (*justicia*) right, justice; (*razonamiento*) reasoning; (*motivo*) course; (*MAT*) ratio; **a ~ de 10 cada día** at the rate of 10 a day; '**~: ...**' "inquiries to ...''; **en ~ de** with regard to; **dar ~ a uno** to agree that sb is right; **tener ~** to be right; **~ directa/inversa** direct/inverse proportion; **~ de ser**

raison d'être; **razonable** *a* reasonable; (*justo, moderado*) fair; **razonamiento** *nm* (*juicio*) judgement; (*argumento*) reasoning; **razonar** *vt* to reason, argue; (*cuenta*) to itemize // *vi* to reason, argue.

reabastecer [reaβaste'θer] *vt* to refuel.

reabrir [rea'βrir] *vt* to reopen.

reacción [reak'θjon] *nf* reaction; **avión a ~** jet plane; **~ en cadena** chain reaction; **reaccionar** *vi* to react; **reaccionario, a** *a* reactionary.

reacio, a [re'aθjo, a] *a* stubborn.

reactor [reak'tor] *nm* reactor.

readaptación [reaðapta'θjon] *nf*: **~ profesional** industrial retraining.

reafirmar [reafir'mar] *vt* to reaffirm.

reagrupar [reaɣru'par] *vt* to regroup.

reajuste [rea'xuste] *nm* readjustment.

real [re'al] *a* real; (*del rey, fig*) royal.

realce [re'alθe] *nm* (*TEC*) embossing; (*lustre, fig*) splendour; (*ARTE*) highlight; **poner de ~** to emphasize.

realidad [reali'ðað] *nf* reality, fact; (*verdad*) truth.

realista [rea'lista] *nm/f* realist.

realización [realiθa'θjon] *nf* fulfilment; (*COM*) sale, selling-up.

realizador, a [realiθa'ðor, a] *nm/f* (*TV etc*) producer.

realizar [reali'θar] *vt* (*objetivo*) to achieve; (*plan*) to carry out; (*viaje*) to make, undertake; (*COM*) to sell up; **~se** *vr* to come about, come true.

realmente [real'mente] *ad* really, actually.

realzar [real'θar] *vt* (*TEC*) to raise; (*embellecer*) to enhance; (*acentuar*) to highlight.

reanimar [reani'mar] *vt* to revive; (*alentar*) to encourage; **~se** *vr* to revive.

reanudar [reanu'ðar] *vt* (*renovar*) to renew; (*retomar*) to resume.

reaparición [reapari'θjon] *nf* reappearance.

rearme [re'arme] *nm* rearmament.

reata [re'ata] *nf* rope, rein; **de ~** in single file.

rebaja [re'βaxa] *nf* (*COM*) reduction; (*menoscabo*) lessening; **rebajar** *vt* (*bajar*) to lower; (*reducir*) to reduce; (*disminuir*) to lessen; (*humillar*) to humble.

rebanada [reβa'naða] *nf* slice.

rebaño [re'βaɲo] *nm* herd; (*de ovejas*) flock.

rebasar [reβa'sar] *vt* (*también* **~ de**) to exceed; (*AUTO*) to overtake.

rebatir [reβa'tir] *vt* to refute; (*descontar*) to deduct.

rebato [re'βato] *nm* alarm; (*ataque*) surprise attack.

rebelarse [reβe'larse] *vr* to rebel, revolt.

rebelde [re'βelde] *a* rebellious; (*indócil*) unruly // *nm/f* rebel; **rebeldía** *nf* rebelliousness; (*desobediencia*) disobedience; **rebelión** *nf* rebellion.

reblandecer [reβlande'θer] *vt* to soften.

rebosante [reβo'sante] *a* overflowing; **rebosar** *vi* to overflow; (*abundar*) to abound, be plentiful.

rebotar [reβo'tar] *vt* to bounce; (*rechazar*) to repel; ~**se** *vr* (*pelota*) to rebound; (*bala*) to ricochet; **rebote** *nm* rebound; **de rebote** on the rebound.

rebozar [reβo'θar] *vt* to wrap up; (*CULIN*) to fry in batter; **rebozo** *nm* muffler; (*AM*) shawl; **decir algo sin rebozo** to call a spade a spade.

rebuscado, a [reβus'kaðo, a] *a* affected.

rebuscar [reβus'kar] *vt* to search carefully; (*objeto*) to search for carefully.

rebuznar [reβuθ'nar] *vi* to bray.

recabar [reka'βar] *vt* to manage to get.

recado [re'kaðo] *nm* errand; (*mensaje*) message; **tomar un** ~ (*TELEC*) to take a message.

recaer [reka'er] *vi* to relapse; ~ **en** to fall to *or* on; **recaída** *nf* relapse.

recalcar [rekal'kar] *vt* (*fig*) to stress, emphasize.

recalcitrante [rekalθi'trante] *a* recalcitrant.

recalcitrar [rekalθi'trar] *vi* (*echarse atrás*) to step back; (*resistir*) to resist, be stubborn.

recalentar [rekalen'tar] *vt* (*volver a calentar*) to reheat; (*demasiado*) to overheat.

recambio [re'kambjo] *nm* spare; (*de pluma*) refill.

recapacitar [rekapaθi'tar] *vt* to think over // *vi* to reflect.

recargado, a [rekar'xaðo, a] *a* overloaded; **recargar** *vt* to overload; (*batería*) to recharge; **recargar los precios** to increase prices; **recargo** *nm* surcharge; (*aumento*) increase.

recatado, a [reka'taðo, a] *a* modest, demure; (*prudente*) cautious.

recatar [reka'tar] *vt* to hide; ~**se** *vr* to hide o.s.

recato [re'kato] *nm* modesty, demureness; (*cautela*) caution.

recaudación [rekauða'θjon] *nf* collection; (*suma*) takings *pl*; (*en deporte*) gate; **recaudador** *nm* tax collector.

recelar [reθe'lar] *vt*: ~ **que** (*sospechar*) to suspect that; (*temer*) to fear that // *vi*, ~**se** *vr*: ~(**se**) **de** to distrust; **recelo** *nm* distrust, suspicion; **receloso, a** *a* distrustful, suspicious.

recepción [reθep'θjon] *nf* reception; **recepcionista** *nm/f* receptionist.

receptáculo [reθep'takulo] *nm* receptacle.

receptivo, a [reθep'tiβo, a] *a* receptive.

receptor, a [reθep'tor, a] *nm/f* recipient // *nm* receiver.

recesión [reθe'sjon] *nf* recession.

receta [re'θeta] *nf* (*CULIN*) recipe; (*MED*) prescription.

recibidor, a [reθiβi'ðor, a] *nm/f* receiver, recipient.

recibimiento [reθiβi'mjento] *nm*

(*recepción*) reception; (*acogida*) welcome.

recibir [reθi'βir] *vt* (*gen*) to receive; (*dar la bienvenida*) to welcome // *vi* to entertain; ~**se** *vr*: ~**se de** to qualify as; **recibo** *nm* receipt.

reciedumbre [reθje'ðumbre] *nf* strength; (*vigor*) vigour.

recién [re'θjen] *ad* recently, newly; **el** ~ **llegado** the newcomer; **el** ~ **nacido** the newborn child.

reciente [re'θjente] *a* recent; (*fresco*) fresh.

recinto [re'θinto] *nm* (*gen*) enclosure; (*área*) area, place.

recio, a ['reθjo, a] *a* strong, tough; (*voz*) loud; (*tiempo*) harsh // *ad* hard; loud(ly).

recipiente [reθi'pjente] *nm* receptacle.

reciprocidad [reθiproθi'ðað] *nf* reciprocity; **recíproco, a** *a* reciprocal.

recital [reθi'tal] *nm* (*MUS*) recital; (*LITERATURA*) reading; **recitar** *vt* to recite.

reclamación [reklama'θjon] *nf* claim, demand; (*queja*) complaint.

reclamar [rekla'mar] *vt* to claim, demand // *vi*: ~ **contra** to complain about; ~ **en justicia** to take to court; **reclamo** *nm* (*anuncio*) advertisement; (*tentación*) attraction.

reclinar [rekli'nar] *vt* to recline, lean; ~**se** *vr* to lean back.

recluir [reklu'ir] *vt* to intern, confine.

reclusión [reklu'sjon] *nf* (*prisión*) prison; (*refugio*) seclusion; ~ **perpetua** life imprisonment.

recluta [re'kluta] *nm/f* recruit // *nf* recruitment.

reclutamiento [rekluta'mjento] *nm* recruitment.

recobrar [reko'βrar] *vt* (*recuperar*) to recover; (*rescatar*) to get back; ~**se** *vr* to recover.

recodo [re'koðo] *nm* (*de río, camino*) bend.

recogedor, a [rekoxe'ðor, a] *nm/f* picker, harvester.

recoger [reko'xer] *vt* (*gen*) to collect; (*AGR*) to harvest; (*levantar*) to pick up; (*juntar*) to gather; (*pasar a buscar*) to come for, fetch; (*dar asilo*) to give shelter to; (*faldas*) to gather up; (*pelo*) to put up; ~**se** *vr* (*retirarse*) to retire; **recogido, a** *a* (*lugar*) quiet, secluded; (*persona*) modest, retiring; (*pequeño*) small // *nf* (*del correo*) collection; (*AGR*) harvest.

recolección [rekolek'θjon] *nf* (*de las mieses*) harvesting; (*colecta*) collection.

recomendación [rekomenda'θjon] *nf* (*sugerencia*) suggestion, recommendation; (*elogio*) praise; **recomendar** *vt* to suggest, recommend; to praise; (*confiar*) to entrust.

recompensa [rekom'pensa] *nf* reward, recompense; **recompensar** *vt* to reward, recompense; (*por pérdidas*) to compensate.

recomponer [rekompo'ner] *vt* to mend; ~**se** *vr* (*fam*) to doll up.

reconciliación [rekonθilja'θjon] *nf* reconciliation; **reconciliar** *vt* to reconcile; **reconciliarse** vr to become reconciled.

reconfortar [rekonfor'tar] vt to comfort; ~**se** vr: ~**se con** to fortify o.s. with.

reconocer [rekono'θer] vt to recognize; (registrar) to search; (MED) to examine; **reconocido, a** a recognized; (agradecido) grateful; **reconocimiento** nm recognition; search; examination; gratitude; (confesión) admission.

reconquista [rekon'kista] nf reconquest.

reconstituyente [rekonstitu'jente] nm tonic.

reconstruir [rekonstru'ir] vt to reconstruct.

recopilación [rekopila'θjon] nf (sumario) summary; (compendio) compilation; **recopilar** vt to compile.

récord ['rekorð] a inv, nm record.

recordar [rekor'ðar] vt (acordarse de) to remember; (acordar a otro) to remind // vi to remember.

recorrer [reko'rrer] vt (país) to cross, travel through; (distancia) to cover; (repasar) to go over, look over; **recorrido** nm run, journey; **tren de largo recorrido** main-line train.

recortado, a [rekor'taðo, a] a uneven, irregular.

recortar [rekor'tar] vt to cut out; **recorte** nm (acción) cutting; (de prensa) cutting, clipping; (de telas, chapas) trimming.

recostado, a [rekos'taðo, a] a leaning; **estar** ~ to be lying down.

recostar [rekos'tar] vt to lean; ~**se** vr to lie down.

recoveco [reko'ßeko] nm bend; (en casa) cubby hole.

recreación [rekrea'θjon] nf recreation; (TEATRO, CINE) interval, intermission.

recrear [rekre'ar] vt (entretener) to entertain; (volver a crear) to recreate; **recreativo, a** a recreational; **recreo** nm recreation; (ESCOL) break, playtime.

recriminar [rekrimi'nar] vt to reproach // vi to recriminate; ~**se** vr to reproach each other.

recrudecer [rekruðe'θer] vt, vi, ~**se** vr to worsen.

recrudecimiento [rekruðeθi'mjento] nm, **recrudescencia** [rekruðes'θenθja] nf upsurge.

recta ['rekta] nf ver **recto.**

rectángulo, a [rek'tangulo, a] a rectangular // nm rectangle.

rectificar [rektifi'kar] vt to rectify; (volverse recto) to straighten // vi to correct o.s.

rectitud [rekti'tuð] nf (exactitud) correctness; (fig) rectitude.

recto, a ['rekto, a] a straight; (persona) honest, upright // nm rectum // nf straight line.

rector, a [rek'tor, a] a governing.

recua ['rekwa] nf mule train.

recuento [re'kwento] nm inventory; **hacer el** ~ **de** to count or reckon up.

recuerdo [re'kwerðo] nm souvenir; ~**s** nmpl memories; ¡~**s a tu madre!** give my regards to your mother.

recular [reku'lar] vi to fall back; (fig) to back down.

recuperable [rekupe'raßle] a recoverable; **recuperación** nf recovery.

recuperar [rekupe'rar] vt to recover; (tiempo) to make up; ~**se** vr to recuperate.

recurrir [reku'rrir] vi (JUR) to appeal; ~ **a** to resort to; (persona) to turn to; **recurso** nm resort; (medios) means pl, resources pl; (JUR) appeal.

recusar [reku'sar] vt to reject, refuse.

rechazar [retʃa'θar] vt to repel, drive back; (idea) to reject; (oferta) to turn down.

rechazo [re'tʃaθo] nm (retroceso) recoil; (rebote) rebound; (negación) rebuff.

rechifla [re'tʃifla] nf hissing, booing; (fig) derision; **rechiflar** vt to hiss, boo; **rechiflarse** vr to take things as a joke.

rechinar [retʃi'nar] vi to creak; (gruñir) to grumble; (dientes) to grind.

rechoncho, a [re'tʃontʃo, a] a (fam) chubby, thickset.

red [reð] nf net, mesh; (de ferrocarriles etc) network; (trampa) trap.

redacción [reðak'θjon] nf editing; (oficina) newspaper office; (personal) editorial staff.

redactar [reðak'tar] vt to draw up, draft; (periódico) to edit.

redada [re'ðaða] nf: ~ **policíaca** police raid, round-up.

rededor [reðe'ðor] nm: **al** o **en** ~ around, round about.

redención [reðen'θjon] nf redemption; **redentor, a** a redeeming.

redescubrir [reðesku'ßrir] vt to rediscover.

redicho, a [re'ðitʃo, a] a affected, stilted.

redil [re'ðil] nm sheepfold.

redimir [reði'mir] vt to redeem.

rédito ['reðito] nm interest, yield.

redoblar [reðo'ßlar] vt to redouble; (plegar) to fold back // vi (tambor) to play a roll on the drums.

redomado, a [reðo'maðo, a] a sly, crafty.

redonda [re'ðonda] nf ver **redondo.**

redondear [reðonde'ar] vt to round, round off; ~**se** vr to become wealthy.

redondel [reðon'del] nm (círculo) circle; (TAUR) bullring, arena.

redondo, a [re'ðondo, a] a (circular) round; (directo) straight; (completo) complete // nf: **a la** ~**a** around, round about.

reducción [reðuk'θjon] nf reduction; (MED) setting.

reducido, a [reðu'θiðo, a] a reduced; (limitado) limited; (pequeño) small; **reducir** vt to reduce; to limit; (MED) to set a bone; **reducirse** vr to diminish.

redundancia [reðun'danθja] *nf* redundancy.

reembolsar [reembol'sar] *vt* to reimburse; (*depósito*) to refund; **reembolso** *nm* reimbursement; refund.

reemplazar [reempla'θar] *vt* to replace; **reemplazo** *nm* replacement; **de reemplazo** (MIL) reserve.

refacción [refak'θjon] *nf* (AM) repair(s) (*pl*).

refajo [re'faxo] *nm* (*enagua*) flannel underskirt; (*falda*) short skirt.

referencia [refe'renθja] *nf* reference; (*informe*) report; **con ~ a** with reference to.

referente [refe'rente] *a*: **~ a** concerning, relating to.

referir [refe'rir] *vt* (*contar*) to tell, recount; (*relacionar*) to refer, relate; **~se** *vr*: **~se a** to refer to.

refilón [refi'lon]: **de ~** *ad* obliquely, aslant.

refinado, a [refi'naðo, a] *a* refined; **refinamiento** *nm* refinement; **refinar** *vt* to refine; (*fig*) to perfect, polish.

reflejar [refle'xar] *vt* (*gen*) to reflect; **reflejo, a** *a* reflected; (*movimiento*) reflex // *nm* reflection; (ANAT) reflex.

reflexión [reflek'sjon] *nf* reflection; **reflexionar** *vt* to reflect on // *vi* to reflect; (*detenerse*) to pause (to think).

reflexivo, a [reflek'siβo, a] *a* thoughtful; (LING, fig) reflexive.

reflujo [re'fluxo] *nm* ebb.

refocilar [refoθi'lar] *vt* to cheer up.

reforma [re'forma] *nf* reform; (ARQ etc) repair; **~ agraria** agrarian reform.

reformar [refor'mar] *vt* (*modificar*) to change, alter; (*formar de nuevo*) to reform; (ARQ) to repair; **~se** *vr* to mend one's ways.

reformatorio [reforma'torjo] *nm* reformatory.

reforzar [refor'θar] *vt* (*gen*) to strengthen; (ARQ) to reinforce; (*fig*) to encourage.

refractario, a [refrak'tarjo, a] *a* stubborn; (TEC) heat-resistant.

refrán [re'fran] *nm* proverb, saying.

refregar [refre'xar] *vt* to scrub.

refrenar [refre'nar] *vt* to check, restrain.

refrendar [refren'dar] *vt* (*firma*) to endorse, countersign; (*pasaporte*) to stamp; (*ley*) to approve.

refrescar [refres'kar] *vt* (*gen*) to refresh // *vi* to cool down; **~se** *vr* to get cooler; (*tomar aire fresco*) to go out for a breath of fresh air.

refresco [re'fresko] *nm* soft drink, cool drink; "**~s**" "refreshments".

refriega [re'frjexa] *nf* scuffle, brawl.

refrigeración [refrixera'θjon] *nf* refrigeration; (*de casa*) air-conditioning; **refrigerador** *nm* refrigerator; **refrigerar** *vt* to refrigerate; to air-condition.

refuerzo [re'fwerθo] *nm* reinforcement; (TEC) support.

refugiado, a [refu'xjaðo, a] *nm/f* refugee; **refugiarse** *vr* to take refuge, shelter; **refugio** *nm* refuge; (*protección*) shelter.

refulgencia [reful'xenθja] *nf* brilliance; **refulgir** *vi* to shine, be dazzling.

refundición [refundi'θjon] *nf* recasting, revision; **refundir** *vt* to recast.

refunfuñar [refunfu'ɲar] *vi* to grunt, growl; (*quejarse*) to grumble.

refutación [refuta'θjon] *nf* refutation; **refutar** *vt* to refute.

regadera [rexa'ðera] *nf* watering can.

regadío [rexa'ðio] *nm* irrigated land.

regalado, a [rexa'laðo, a] *a* comfortable, luxurious; (*gratis*) free, for nothing; (*pey*) soft.

regalar [rexa'lar] *vt* (*dar*) to give, present; (*entregar*) to give away; (*mimar*) to pamper, make a fuss of.

regalía [rexa'lia] *nf* privilege, prerogative; (COM) bonus; (*de autor*) royalty.

regaliz [rexa'liθ] *nm*, **regaliza** [rexa'liθa] *nf* liquorice.

regalo [re'xalo] *nm* (*obsequio*) gift, present; (*gusto*) pleasure; (*comodidad*) comfort.

regalón, ona [rexa'lon, ona] *a* spoiled, pampered.

regañadientes [rexaɲa'ðjentes]: **a ~** *ad* reluctantly.

regañar [rexa'ɲar] *vt* to scold // *vi* to grumble; **regaño** *nm* scolding, telling-off; (*queja*) grumble; **regañón, ona** *a* grumbling; (*mujer*) nagging.

regar [re'xar] *vt* to water, irrigate; (*fig*) to scatter, sprinkle.

regatear [rexate'ar] *vt* to bargain over; (*guardar*) to be mean with // *vi* to bargain, haggle; (DEPORTE) to dribble; **regateo** *nm* bargaining; dribbling; (*del cuerpo*) swerve, dodge.

regazo [re'xaθo] *nm* lap.

regeneración [rexenera'θjon] *nf* regeneration; **regenerar** *vt* to regenerate.

regentar [rexen'tar] *vt* to direct, manage; **regente** *nm* manager; (POL) regent.

régimen ['reximen] (*pl* **regímenes**) *nm* regime; (MED) diet.

regimiento [rexi'mjento] *nm* regiment; (*organización*) administration.

regio, a ['rexjo, a] *a* royal, regal; (*fig: suntuoso*) splendid.

región [re'xjon] *nf* region; **regionalista** *nm/f* regionalist.

regir [re'xir] *vt* to govern, rule; (*dirigir*) to manage, run // *vi* to apply, be in force.

registrador [rexistra'ðor] *nm* registrar, recorder.

registrar [rexis'trar] *vt* (*buscar en cajón*) to look through, search; (*inspeccionar*) to inspect; (*anotar*) to register, record; **~se** *vr* to register; (*ocurrir*) to happen.

registro [re'xistro] *nm* registration; (MUS, *libro*) register; (*inspección*) inspection,

search; ~ **civil** registry office.
regla ['reɣla] nf (ley) rule, regulation; (de medir) ruler, rule; **la** ~ (MED) periods pl; **salir de** ~ to step out of line.
reglamentación [reɣlamenta'θjon] nf (acto) regulation; (lista) rules pl; **reglamentar** vt to regulate; **reglamentario, a** a statutory; **reglamento** nm rules pl, regulations pl.
reglar [re'ɣlar] vt (papel) to rule; (actos) to regulate.
regocijado, a [reɣoθi'xaðo, a] a merry; **regocijar** vt to cheer up, gladden; **regocijarse** vr to have a good time, make merry; (alegrarse) to rejoice; **regocijo** nm joy, happiness.
regodearse [reɣoðe'arse] vr to be glad, be delighted; **regodeo** nm delight.
regresar [reɣre'sar] vi to come/go back, return; **regresivo, a** a backward; (fig) regressive; **regreso** nm return.
reguero [re'ɣero] nm irrigation ditch.
regulador [reɣula'ðor] nm (gen) regulator; (de radio etc) knob, control.
regular [reɣu'lar] a (gen) regular; (normal) normal, usual; (común) ordinary; (organizado) regular, orderly; (mediano) average; (fam) not bad, so-so // ad so-so, alright // vt (controlar) to control, regulate; (TEC) to adjust; **por lo** ~ as a rule; ~**idad** nf regularity; ~**izar** vt to regularize.
regusto [re'ɣusto] nm aftertaste.
rehabilitación [reaβilita'θjon] nf rehabilitation; (ARQ) restoration; **rehabilitar** vt to rehabilitate; to restore; (reintegrar) to reinstate.
rehacer [rea'θer] vt (reparar) to mend, repair; (volver a hacer) to redo, repeat; ~**se** vr (MED) to recover; (dominarse) to pull o.s. together.
rehén [re'en] nm hostage.
rehilete [rei'lete] nm (dardo) dart; (DEPORTE) badminton, shuttlecock.
rehuir [reu'ir] vt to avoid, shun.
rehusar [reu'sar] vt, vi to refuse.
reina ['reina] nf queen; ~**do** nm reign; **reinante** a (fig) prevailing; **reinar** vi to reign.
reincidir [reinθi'ðir] vi to relapse.
reincorporarse [reinkorpo'rarse] vr: ~ **a** to rejoin.
reino ['reino] nm kingdom; **el R** ~ **Unido** the United Kingdom.
reintegrar [reinte'ɣrar] vt (reconstituir) to reconstruct; (persona) to reinstate; (dinero) to return, pay back; ~**se** vr: ~**se a** to return to.
reír [re'ir] vi, ~**se** vr to laugh; ~**se de** to laugh at.
reiterar [reite'rar] vt to reiterate.
reivindicación [reiβindika'θjon] nf (demanda) claim, demand; (justificación) vindication; **reivindicar** vt to claim; (restaurar) to restore.
reja ['rexa] nf (de ventana) grille, bars pl;

(en la calle) grating; (del arado) ploughshare.
rejilla [re'xiʎa] nf (de ventana) grille; (de silla) wickerwork; (de ventilación) vent; (de coche) luggage rack.
rejoneador [rexonea'ðor] nm mounted bullfighter.
rejuvenecer [rexuβene'θer] vt, vi to rejuvenate; ~**se** vr to be rejuvenated.
relación [rela'θjon] nf relation, relationship; (MAT) ratio; (informe) report; **relaciones públicas** public relations; **con** ~ **a** o **en** ~ **con** in relation to; **relacionar** vt to relate, connect; **relacionarse** vr to be connected, be linked.
relajación [relaxa'θjon] nf relaxation; **relajado, a** a (disoluto) loose; (cómodo) relaxed; (MED) ruptured; **relajar** vt, **relajarse** vr to relax.
relamer [rela'mer] vt to lick (repeatedly); ~**se** vr to lick one's lips.
relamido, a [rela'miðo, a] a (pulcro) overdressed; (afectado) affected.
relámpago [re'lampaɣo] nm flash of lightning; **visita/huelga** ~ lightning visit/strike; **relampaguear** vi to flash.
relatar [rela'tar] vt to tell, relate.
relativo, a [rela'tiβo, a] a relative; **en lo** ~ **a** concerning.
relato [re'lato] nm (narración) story, tale; (informe) report.
relegar [rele'ɣar] vt to relegate.
relevante [rele'βante] a eminent, outstanding.
relevar [rele'βar] vt (sustituir) to relieve; ~**se** vr to relay; ~ **a uno de un cargo** to relieve sb of his post.
relevo [re'leβo] nm relief; **carrera de** ~**s** relay race.
relieve [re'ljeβe] nm (ARTE, TEC) relief; (fig) prominence, importance; ~**s** nmpl left-overs; **bajo** ~ bas-relief.
religión [reli'xjon] nf religion; **religiosidad** nf religiosity; **religioso, a** a religious // nm/f monk/nun // nm cleric.
relinchar [relin'tʃar] vi to neigh; **relincho** nm neigh; (acto) neighing.
reliquia [re'likja] nf relic; ~ **de familia** family heirloom.
reloj [re'lo(x)] nm watch; (de iglesia etc) clock; ~ **de pulsera** wristwatch; ~ **despertador** alarm clock; ~**ero, a** nm/f watchmaker; clockmaker.
reluciente [relu'θjente] a brilliant, shining; **relucir** vi to shine; (fig) to excel.
relumbrante [relum'brante] a dazzling; **relumbrar** vi to dazzle, shine brilliantly.
rellano [re'ʎano] nm (ARQ) landing.
rellenar [reʎe'nar] vt (llenar) to fill up; (CULIN) to stuff; (COSTURA) to pad; **relleno, a** a full up; stuffed // nm stuffing; (de tapicería) padding.
remachar [rema'tʃar] vt to rivet; (fig) to hammer home, drive home; **remache** nm rivet.
remanente [rema'nente] nm remainder;

(*COM*) balance; (*de producto*) surplus.
remanso [re'manso] *nm* pool; (*fig*) quiet place.
remar [re'mar] *vi* to row.
rematado, a [rema'taðo, a] *a* complete, utter.
rematar [rema'tar] *vt* to finish off; (*COM*) to sell off cheap // *vi* to end, finish off.
remate [re'mate] *nm* end, finish; (*punta*) tip; (*DEPORTE*) shot; (*ARQ*) top; (*COM*) auction sale; **de** *o* **para** ~ to crown it all.
remedar [reme'ðar] *vt* to imitate.
remediar [reme'ðjar] *vt* (*gen*) to remedy; (*subsanar*) to make good, repair; (*ayudar*) to help; (*evitar*) to avoid.
remedio [re'meðjo] *nm* remedy; (*alivio*) relief, help; (*JUR*) recourse, remedy; **poner** ~ **a** to correct, stop; **no tener más** ~ to have no alternative; **¡qué** ~! there's no choice; **sin** ~ hopeless, incurable.
remedo [re'meðo] *nm* imitation; (*pey*) parody.
remendar [remen'dar] *vt* to repair; (*con parche*) to patch.
remesa [re'mesa] *nf* remittance; (*COM*) shipment; **remesar** *vt* to remit, send.
remiendo [re'mjendo] *nm* (*gen*) mend; (*con parche*) patch; (*cosido*) darn.
remilgado, a [remil'xaðo, a] *a* prim; (*afectado*) affected; **remilgo** *nm* primness; affectation.
reminiscencia [reminis'θenθja] *nf* reminiscence.
remisión [remi'sjon] *nf* (*acto*) sending, shipment.
remiso, a [re'miso, a] *a* remiss.
remitir [remi'tir] *vt* to remit, send; (*perdonar*) to pardon; (*posponer*) to postpone // *vi* to slacken; (*en carta*): **remite: X** sender: X; **remitente** *nm/f* sender.
remo ['remo] *nm* (*de barco*) oar; (*deporte*) rowing.
remoción [remo'θjon] *nf* removal.
remojar [remo'xar] *vt* to steep, soak; (*galleta etc*) to dip.
remojo [re'moxo] *nm*: **dejar la ropa a** ~ to leave clothes to soak.
remolacha [remo'latʃa] *nf* beet, beetroot.
remolcador [remolka'ðor] *nm* (*NAUT*) tug; (*AUTO*) breakdown lorry.
remolinar [remoli'nar] *vi* to whirl, eddy; **remolino** *nm* (*gen*) eddy; (*de agua*) whirlpool; (*de viento*) whirlwind; (*de gente*) throng.
remolque [re'molke] *nm* tow, towing; (*cuerda*) towrope; **llevar a** ~ to tow.
remontar [remon'tar] *vt* to mend; ~**se** *vr* to soar; ~**se a** (*COM*) to amount to; ~ **el vuelo** to soar.
rémora ['remora] *nf* hindrance.
remorder [remor'ðer] *vt* to distress, disturb; ~**se** *vr* to suffer remorse; ~**se la conciencia** to have a troubled conscience; **remordimiento** *nm* remorse.
remoto, a [re'moto, a] *a* remote.

remover [remo'ßer] *vt* to stir; (*tierra*) to turn over; (*objetos*) to move around; (*quitar*) to remove.
remozar [remo'θar] *vt* to rejuvenate; ~**se** *vr* to be rejuvenated, look younger.
remuneración [remunera'θjon] *nf* remuneration; **remunerar** *vt* to remunerate; (*premiar*) to reward.
renacer [rena'θer] *vi* to be reborn; (*fig*) to revive; **renacimiento** *nm* rebirth; **el Renacimiento** the Renaissance.
renal [re'nal] *a* renal, kidney *cpd*.
rencilla [ren'θiʎa] *nf* quarrel.
rencor [ren'kor] *nm* rancour, bitterness; ~**oso, a** *a* spiteful.
rendición [rendi'θjon] *nf* surrender.
rendido, a [ren'diðo, a] *a* (*sumiso*) submissive; (*cansado*) worn-out.
rendimiento [rendi'mjento] *nm* (*MIL*) surrender; (*producción*) output; (*agotamiento*) exhaustion; (*TEC, COM*) efficiency.
rendir [ren'dir] *vt* (*vencer*) to defeat; (*producir*) to produce; (*dar beneficio*) to yield; (*agotar*) to exhaust; (*dominar*) to dominate // *vi* to pay; ~**se** *vr* (*someterse*) to surrender; (*cansarse*) to wear o.s. out; ~ **homenaje** *o* **culto a** to pay homage to.
renegado, a [rene'xaðo, a] *a, nm/f* renegade.
renegar [rene'xar] *vi* (*renunciar*) to renounce; (*blasfemar*) to blaspheme; (*fam*) to curse; (*quejarse*) to complain.
RENFE *nf abr de* **Red Nacional de los Ferrocarriles Españoles.**
renglón [ren'glon] *nm* (*línea*) line; (*COM*) item, article; **a** ~ **seguido** immediately after.
reniego [re'njexo] *nm* curse, oath; (*queja*) grumble, complaint.
renombrado, a [renom'braðo, a] *a* renowned; **renombre** *nm* renown.
renovación [renoßa'θjon] *nf* (*de contrato*) renewal; (*ARQ*) renovation; **renovar** *vt* to renew; to renovate.
renta ['renta] *nf* (*ingresos*) income; (*beneficio*) profit; (*alquiler*) rent; ~ **vitalicia** annuity; **rentable** *a* profitable; **rentar** *vt* to produce, yield.
rentero, a [ren'tero, a] *nm/f* tenant farmer.
rentista [ren'tista] *nm/f* stockholder.
renuencia [re'nwenθja] *nf* reluctance; **renuente** *a inv* reluctant.
renuncia [re'nunθja] *nf* (*gen*) resignation.
renunciar [renun'θjar] *vt* to renounce // *vi* to resign; ~ **a hacer algo** to give up doing sth.
reñido, a [re'ɲiðo, a] *a* (*batalla*) bitter, hard-fought; **estar** ~ **con uno** to be on bad terms with sb.
reñir [re'ɲir] *vt* (*regañar*) to scold // *vi* (*estar peleado*) to quarrel, fall out; (*combatir*) to fight.
reo [re'o] *nm/f* culprit, offender; ~ **de muerte** prisoner condemned to death.
reojo [re'oxo]: **de** ~ *ad* out of the corner of one's eye; (*fig*) askance.

reorganizar [reorɣani'θar] vt to reorganize.

reorientar [reorjen'tar] vt to reorientate; (reajustar) to readjust.

reparación [repara'θjon] nf (acto) mending, repairing; (TEC) repair; (fig) amends, reparation; **reparar** vt to repair; to make amends for; (suerte) to retrieve; (observar) to observe // vi: **reparar en** (darse cuenta de) to notice; (poner atención en) to pay attention to.

reparo [re'paro] nm (reparación) repair; (advertencia) observation; (duda) doubt; (dificultad) difficulty; (resguardo) defence.

reparón, ona [repa'ron, ona] a carping.

repartición [reparti'θjon] nf distribution; (división) division; **repartidor, a** nm/f distributor.

repartir [repar'tir] vt to distribute, share out; (correo) to deliver; **reparto** nm distribution; delivery; (TEATRO, CINE) cast.

repasar [repa'sar] vt (sitio) to pass by again; (lección) to revise; (MECANICA) to check; **repaso** nm revision; overhaul, checkup; (de ropa) mending.

repatriar [repa'trjar] vt to repatriate.

repecho [re'petʃo] nm steep incline; **a ~** uphill.

repelente [repe'lente] a repellent, repulsive; **repeler** vt to repel.

repensar [repen'sar] vt to reconsider.

repente [re'pente] nm: **de ~** suddenly; **un ~ de ira** a fit of anger.

repentino, a [repen'tino, a] a sudden.

repercusión [reperku'sjon] nf repercussion.

repercutir [reperku'tir] vi to rebound; (sonido) to echo; **~se** vr to reverberate; **~ en** to have repercussions on.

repertorio [reper'torjo] nm list; (TEATRO) repertoire.

repetición [repeti'θjon] nf repetition; **repetir** vt to repeat; (plato) to have a second helping // vi to repeat; **repetirse** vr (volver sobre tema) to repeat o.s.; (sabor) to come back.

repicar [repi'kar] vt (desmenuzar) to chop up finely; (campanas) to ring; **~se** vr to boast.

repique [re'pike] nm pealing, ringing; **~teo** nm pealing; (de tambor) drumming.

repisa [re'pisa] nf ledge, shelf; **~ de chimenea** mantelpiece.

repito etc vb ver **repetir**.

replegar [reple'xar] vt to fold over; **~se** vr to fall back, retreat.

repleto, a [re'pleto, a] a replete, full up.

réplica ['replika] nf answer; (ARTE) replica.

replicar [repli'kar] vi to answer; (objetar) to argue, answer back.

repliegue [re'pljexe] nm (MIL) withdrawal.

repoblación [repoβla'θjon] nf repopulation; (de río) restocking; **~ forestal** reafforestation; **repoblar** vt to repopulate; to reafforest.

repollo [re'poʎo] nm cabbage.

reponer [repo'ner] vt to replace, put back; (TEATRO) to revive; **~se** vr to recover; **~ que** to reply that.

reportaje [repor'taxe] nm report, article.

reposacabezas [reposaka'βeθas] nm inv headrest.

reposado, a [repo'saðo, a] a (descansado) restful; (tranquilo) calm; **reposar** vi to rest, repose.

reposición [reposi'θjon] nf replacement; (CINE) remake.

repositorio [reposi'torjo] nm repository.

reposo [re'poso] nm rest.

repostar [repos'tar] vt to replenish; (AUTO) to fill up (with petrol).

repostería [reposte'ria] nf confectioner's (shop); (depósito) pantry, larder; **repostero, a** nm/f confectioner.

reprender [repren'der] vt to reprimand; **reprensión** nf rebuke, reprimand.

represa [re'presa] nf dam; (lago artificial) lake, pool.

represalia [repre'salja] nf reprisal.

representación [representa'θjon] nf representation; (TEATRO) performance; **representante** nm/f representative; performer.

representar [represen'tar] vt to represent; (TEATRO) to play; (edad) to look; **~se** vr to imagine; **representativo, a** a representative.

represión [repre'sjon] nf repression.

reprimir [repri'mir] vt to repress.

reprobar [repro'βar] vt to censure, reprove.

réprobo, a ['reproβo, a] nm/f reprobate.

reprochar [repro'tʃar] vt to reproach; **reproche** nm reproach.

reproducción [reproðuk'θjon] nf reproduction.

reproducir [reproðu'θir] vt to reproduce; **~se** vr to breed; (situación) to recur.

reptil [rep'til] nm reptile.

república [re'puβlika] nf republic; **republicano, a** a, nm/f republican.

repudiar [repu'ðjar] vt to repudiate; (fe) to renounce; **repudio** nm repudiation.

repuesto [re'pwesto] nm (pieza de recambio) spare (part); (abastecimiento) supply; **rueda de ~** spare wheel.

repugnancia [repux'nanθja] nf repugnance; **repugnante** a repugnant, repulsive.

repugnar [repux'nar] vt to disgust // vi, **~se** vr (contradecirse) to conflict; (dar asco) to be disgusting.

repujar [repu'xar] vt to emboss.

repulgar [repul'xar] vt to hem.

repulido, a [repu'liðo, a] a (gen) polished; (persona) dressed up, dolled up.

repulsa [re'pulsa] nf rebuff; (fig) reprimand.

repulsión [repul'sjon] nf repulsion, aversion; **repulsivo, a** a repulsive.

reputación [reputa'θjon] nf reputation.

reputar [repu'tar] vt to consider, deem.
requemado, a [reke'maðo, a] a (quemado) scorched; (bronceado) tanned.
requerimiento [rekeri'mjento] nm request; (JUR) summons.
requerir [reke'rir] vt (rogar) to ask, request; (exigir) to require; (llamar) to send for, summon.
requesón [reke'son] nm cottage cheese.
requete... [re'kete] pref extremely.
réquiem ['rekjem] nm requiem.
requisa [re'kisa] nf (inspección) survey, inspection; (MIL) requisition.
requisito [reki'sito] nm requirement, requisite.
res [res] nf beast, head of cattle.
resabio [re'saßjo] nm (maña) vice, bad habit; (dejo) aftertaste.
resaca [re'saka] nf (en el mar) undertow, undercurrent; (fig) backlash; (fam) hangover.
resalado, a [resa'laðo, a] a (fam) lively.
resaltar [resal'tar] vi to project, stick out; (persona) to stand out, be conspicuous.
resarcimiento [resarθi'mjento] nm compensation; **resarcir** vt to compensate; **resarcirse** vr to make up for.
resbaladero [resßala'ðero] nm (gen) slippery place; (en parque infantil) slide.
resbaladizo, a [resßala'ðiθo, a] a slippery.
resbalar [resßa'lar] vi, **~se** vr to slip, slide; (fig) to slip (up).
rescatar [reska'tar] vt (heridos) to save, rescue; (objeto) to get back, recover; (cautivos) to ransom.
rescate [res'kate] nm rescue, recovery; **pagar un ~** to pay a ransom.
rescindir [resθin'dir] vt to rescind.
rescisión [resθi'sjon] nf cancellation.
rescoldo [res'koldo] nm embers pl; (fig) scruple.
resecar [rese'kar] vt to dry thoroughly; (MED) to remove; **~se** vr to dry up.
reseco, a [re'seko, a] a very dry; (fig) skinny.
resentido, a [resen'tiðo, a] a resentful; **resentimiento** nm resentment, bitterness.
resentirse [resen'tirse] vr (debilitarse: persona) to suffer; **~ con** to resent; **~ de** (consecuencias) to feel the effects of.
reseña [re'seɲa] nf (cuenta) account; (informe) report; (LITERATURA) review; **reseñar** vt to describe; to review.
reserva [re'serßa] nf (gen) reserve; (reservación) reservation; **a ~ de** except for; **con toda ~** in strictest confidence.
reservado, a [reser'ßaðo, a] a reserved; (retraído) cold, distant // nm private room.
reservar [reser'ßar] vt (guardar) to keep; (habitación, entrada) to reserve; (callar) to keep to o.s.; **~se** vr to save o.s.
resfriado [resfri'aðo] nm cold; **resfriarse** vr to cool; (MED) to catch (a) cold.
resguardar [resɣwar'ðar] vt to protect,

shield; **~se** vr: **~se de** to guard against; **resguardo** nm defence; (custodia) protection; (garantía) guarantee; (vale) voucher.
residencia [resi'ðenθja] nf residence.
residente [resi'ðente] a, nm/f resident.
residir [resi'ðir] vi to reside, live; **~ en** to reside in, lie in.
residuo [re'siðwo] nm residue.
resignación [resiɣna'θjon] nf resignation; **resignar** vt to resign; **resignarse** vr: **resignarse a** o **con** to resign o.s. to, be resigned to.
resistencia [resis'tenθja] nf (dureza) endurance, strength; (oposición, eléctrica) resistance; **resistente** a strong, hardy; resistant.
resistir [resis'tir] vt (soportar) to bear; (oponerse a) to resist, oppose; (aguantar) to put up with // vi to resist; (aguantar) to last, endure; **~se** vr: **~se a** to refuse to, resist.
resma ['resma] nf ream.
resol [re'sol] nm glare of the sun.
resolución [resolu'θjon] nf (gen) resolution; (decisión) decision; **resoluto, a** a resolute.
resolver [resol'ßer] vt to resolve; (solucionar) to solve, resolve; (decidir) to decide, settle; **~se** vr to make up one's mind.
resollar [reso'ʎar] vi to breathe noisily, wheeze.
resonancia [reso'nanθja] nf (del sonido) resonance; (repercusión) repercussion; **resonante** a resonant, resounding; (fig) tremendous; **resonar** vi to ring, echo.
resoplar [reso'plar] vi to snort; **resoplido** nm heavy breathing.
resorte [re'sorte] nm (pieza) spring; (elasticidad) elasticity; (fig) lever.
respaldar [respal'dar] vt to endorse; (fig) to back (up), support; **~se** vr to lean back; **~se con** o **en** to take one's stand on; **respaldo** nm (de cama) headboard; (de sillón) back; (fig) support, backing.
respectivo, a [respek'tiβo, a] a respective; **en lo ~ a** with regard to.
respecto [res'pekto] nm: **al ~** on this matter; **con ~ a**, **~ de** with regard to, in relation to.
respetable [respe'taßle] a respectable; **respetar** vt to respect; **respeto** nm respect; (acatamiento) deference; **respetos** nmpl respects; **respetuoso, a** a respectful.
respingar [respin'gar] vi to shy; **respingo** nm start, jump; (fig) gesture of disgust.
respiración [respira'θjon] nf breathing; (MED) respiration; (ventilación) ventilation; **respirar** vi to breathe; (inhalar) to inhale; **respiratorio, a** a respiratory; **respiro** nm breathing; (fig) respite.
resplandecer [resplande'θer] vi to shine; **resplandeciente** a resplendent, shining;

resplandor nm brilliance, brightness; (del fuego) blaze.

responder [respon'der] vt to answer // vi to answer; (fig) to respond; (pey) to answer back; ~ **de** o **por** to answer for.

responsabilidad [responsaβili'ðað] nf responsibility; **responsable** a responsible.

respuesta [res'pwesta] nf answer, reply.

resquebrajar [reskeβra'xar] vt, ~**se** vr to crack, split.

resquemor [reske'mor] nm resentment.

resquicio [res'kiθjo] nm chink; (hendedura) crack.

restablecer [restaβle'θer] vt to re-establish, restore; ~**se** vr to recover.

restallar [resta'ʎar] vi to crack.

restante [res'tante] a remaining; **lo** ~ the remainder.

restar [res'tar] vt (MAT) to subtract; (fig) to take away // vi to remain, be left.

restauración [restaura'θjon] nf restoration.

restaurán [restau'ran], **restaurante** [restau'rante] nm restaurant.

restaurar [restau'rar] vt to restore.

restitución [restitu'θjon] nf return, restitution.

restituir [restitu'ir] vt (devolver) to return, give back; (rehabilitar) to restore; ~**se** vr: ~**se a** to rejoin.

resto ['resto] nm (residuo) rest, remainder; (apuesta) stake; ~**s** nmpl remains.

restregar [restre'xar] vt to scrub, rub.

restricción [restrik'θjon] nf restriction.

restrictivo, a [restrik'tiβo, a] a restrictive.

restringir [restrin'xir] vt to restrict, limit.

resucitar [resuθi'tar] vt, vi to resuscitate, revive.

resuelto, a [re'swelto, a] pp de **resolver** // a resolute, determined.

resuello [re'sweʎo] nm breath.

resultado [resul'taðo] nm (conclusión) outcome; (consecuencia) result, consequence; **resultante** a resulting, resultant.

resultar [resul'tar] vi (llegar a ser) to turn out to be; (salir bien) to turn out well; (COM) to amount to; ~ **de** to stem from; **me resulta difícil hacerlo** it's difficult for me to do it.

resumen [re'sumen] nm summary, résumé; **en** ~ in short.

resumir [resu'mir] vt to sum up; (cortar) to abridge, cut down.

retablo [re'taβlo] nm altarpiece.

retaguardia [reta'xwarðja] nf rearguard.

retahíla [reta'ila] nf series, string.

retal [re'tal] nm remnant.

retama [re'tama] nf (AM) broom.

retar [re'tar] vt (gen) to challenge; (desafiar) to defy, dare.

retardar [retar'ðar] vt (demorar) to delay; (hacer más lento) to slow down; (retener) to hold back; **retardo** nm delay.

retazo [re'taθo] nm snippet.

rete... ['rete] pref very, extremely.

retén [re'ten] nm (TEC) catch; (reserva) store, reserve.

retener [rete'ner] vt (guardar) to retain, keep; (intereses) to withhold.

retina [re'tina] nf retina.

retintín [retin'tin] nm jangle.

retirada [reti'raða] nf (MIL, refugio) retreat; (de dinero) withdrawal; (de embajador) recall; **retirado, a** (distante) remote; (tranquilo) quiet; (jubilado) retired.

retirar [reti'rar] vt to withdraw; (quitar) to remove; (jubilar) to retire, pension off; ~**se** vr to retreat, withdraw; to retire; (acostarse) to retire, go to bed; **retiro** nm retreat; retirement; (pago) pension.

reto ['reto] nm dare, challenge.

retocar [reto'kar] vt (fotografía) to touch up, retouch.

retoño [re'toɲo] nm sprout, shoot; (fig) offspring, child.

retoque [re'toke] nm retouching; (MED) symptom.

retorcer [retor'θer] vt (gen) to twist; (manos, lavado) to wring; ~**se** vr to become twisted; (mover el cuerpo) to writhe.

retorcimiento [retorθi'mjento] nm twist, twisting; (fig) deviousness.

retórica [re'torika] nf rhetoric; (fig) affectedness.

retornar [retor'nar] vt to return, give back // vi to return, go/come back; **retorno** nm return.

retortijón [retorti'xon] nm twist, twisting.

retozar [reto'θar] vi (juguetear) to frolic, romp; (saltar) to gambol; **retozón, ona** a playful.

retracción [retrak'θjon] nf, **retractación** [retrakta'θjon] nf retraction.

retractar [retrak'tar] vt to retract; ~**se** vr to retract; **me retracto** I take that back.

retraer [retra'er] vt to dissuade; ~**se** vr to retreat, withdraw; **retraído, a** a shy, retiring; **retraimiento** nm (gen) retirement; (timidez) shyness; (lugar) retreat.

retransmisión [retransmi'sjon] nf repeat (broadcast); **retransmitir** vt (mensaje) to relay; (TV etc) to retransmit; (: en vivo) to broadcast live.

retrasado, a [retra'saðo, a] a late; (MED) mentally retarded; (país etc) backward, underdeveloped; **retrasar** vt (demorar) to postpone, put off; (retardar) to slow down // vi, **retrasarse** vr (atrasarse) to be late; (reloj) to be slow; (producción) to fall (away); (quedarse atrás) to lag behind.

retraso [re'traso] nm (demora) delay; (lentitud) slowness; (tardanza) lateness; (atraso) backwardness; **llegar con** ~ to arrive late; ~ **mental** mental deficiency.

retratar [retra'tar] vt (ARTE) to paint the portrait of; (fotografiar) to photograph; (fig) to depict; ~**se** vr to have one's

portrait painted; to have one's photograph taken; **retrato** nm portrait; (fig) likeness; **retrato-robot** nm identikit picture.
retreta [re'treta] nf retreat.
retrete [re'trete] nm toilet, lavatory.
retribución [retriβu'θjon] nf (recompensa) reward; (pago) pay, payment; **retribuir** vt to reward; to pay.
retro... [retro] pref retro... .
retroactivo, a [retroak'tiβo, a] a retroactive, retrospective.
retroceder [retroθe'ðer] vi (echarse atrás) to move back(wards); (tropas) to fall back, retreat; (arma de fuego) to recoil; (fig) to back down.
retroceso [retro'θeso] nm backward movement; (MIL) withdrawal, retreat; (MED) relapse; (fig) backing down.
retrógrado, a [re'troxraðo, a] a (atrasado) retrograde; (POL) reactionary.
retropropulsión [retropropul'sjon] nf jet propulsion.
retrospectivo, a [retrospek'tiβo, a] a retrospective.
retrovisor [retroβi'sor] nm driving or rear-view mirror.
retumbante [retum'bante] a resounding; **retumbar** vi to echo, resound.
reuma ['reuma] nm rheumatism; **reumático, a** a rheumatic; **reumatismo** nm rheumatism.
reunificar [reunifi'kar] vt to reunify.
reunión [reu'njon] nf (asamblea) meeting; (fiesta) party; (reencuentro) reunion.
reunir [reu'nir] vt (juntar) to reunite, join; (recoger) to gather; (personas) to assemble; (cualidades) to combine; ~se vr to meet, gather.
revalidar [reβali'ðar] vt to confirm, ratify.
revalorar [reβalo'rar] vt to revalue, reassess.
revancha [re'βantʃa] nf revenge.
revelación [reβela'θjon] nf revelation.
revelado [reβe'laðo] nm developing.
revelar [reβe'lar] vt to reveal; (FOTO) to develop.
revendedor, a [reβende'ðor, a] nm/f retailer; (pey) ticket tout.
reventar [reβen'tar] vt to burst, explode; (fam: plan) to ruin // vi, ~se vr (estallar) to burst, explode; (fam: morirse) to kick the bucket (fam); ~ **por** to be bursting to.
reventón [reβen'ton] nm burst, explosion; (AUTO) blow-out, puncture.
reverberación [reβerβera'θjon] nf reverberation; **reverberar** vi to reverberate; **reverbero** nm reverberation.
reverdecer [reβerðe'θer] vi (fig) to revive, come to life again.
reverencia [reβe'renθja] nf reverence; **reverenciar** vt to revere.
reverendo, a [reβe'renðo, a] a reverend; **reverente** a reverent.
reversión [reβer'sjon] nf reversion.

reverso [re'βerso] nm back, wrong side; (de moneda) reverse.
revertir [reβer'tir] vi to revert.
revés [re'βes] nm back, wrong side; (fig) reverse, setback; (DEPORTE) backhand; **hacer al** ~ to do sth the wrong way round; **volver algo al** ~ to turn sth round; (ropa) to turn sth inside out.
revestir [reβes'tir] vt to put on; (cubrir) to cover, coat; ~ **con** o **de** to invest with.
revisar [reβi'sar] vt (examinar) to check; (rever) to revise; **revisión** nf revision.
revisor, a [reβi'sor, a] nm/f inspector; (FERRO) ticket collector.
revista [re'βista] nf magazine, review; (TEATRO) revue; (inspección) inspection; **pasar** ~ a to review, inspect.
revivir [reβi'βir] vi to revive.
revocación [reβoka'θjon] nf repeal; **revocar** vt to revoke.
revolcar [reβol'kar] vt to knock down, send flying; ~se vr to roll about.
revolotear [reβolote'ar] vi to flutter; **revoloteo** nm fluttering.
revoltijo [reβol'tixo] nm mess, jumble.
revoltoso, a [reβol'toso, a] a (travieso) naughty, unruly; (rebelde) rebellious.
revolución [reβolu'θjon] nf revolution; **revolucionar** vt to revolutionize; **revolucionario, a** a, nm/f revolutionary.
revólver [re'βolβer] nm revolver.
revolver [reβol'βer] vt (desordenar) to disturb, mess up; (mover) to move about; (poner al revés) to turn over; (investigar) to look through; (adentrarse en) to go into; (POL) to stir up; (hacer paquete) to wrap up // vi: ~ **en** to go through, rummage (about) in; ~se vr to turn round; (por dolor) to writhe; (volver contra) to turn on or against.
revuelco [re'βwelko] nm fall, tumble.
revuelo [re'βwelo] nm fluttering; (fig) commotion.
revuelto, a [re'βwelto, a] pp de **revolver** // a (mezclado) mixed-up; (huevos) scrambled; (descontento) discontented; (travieso) mischievous // nf (motín) revolt; (conmoción) commotion.
revulsivo [reβul'siβo] nm enema.
rey [rei] nm king.
reyerta [re'jerta] nf quarrel, brawl.
rezagado, a [reθa'xaðo, a] nm/f straggler.
rezagar [reθa'xar] vt (dejar atrás) to leave behind; (retrasar) to delay, postpone.
rezar [re'θar] vi to pray; ~ **con** (fam) to concern, have to do with; **rezo** nm prayer.
rezongar [reθon'gar] vi to grumble.
rezumar [reθu'mar] vt to ooze // vi to leak; ~se vr to leak out.
ría ['ria] nf estuary.
riada [ri'aða] nf flood.
ribera [ri'βera] nf (de río) bank; (: área) riverside; (del mar) shore.
ribete [ri'βete] nm (de vestido) border; (fig) addition; ~ar vt to edge, border.
rico, a ['riko, a] a (gen) rich; (adinerado)

wealthy; (*lujoso*) luxurious; (*comida*) tasty, delicious // *nm/f* rich person.

rictus ['riktus] *nm* (*mueca*) sneer, grin.

ridiculez [riðiku'leθ] *nf* absurdity; **ridiculizar** *vt* to ridicule.

ridículo, a [ri'ðikulo, a] *a* ridiculous; **hacer el ~** to make o.s. ridiculous; **poner a uno en ~** to ridicule sb.

riego ['rjeɣo] *nm* (*aspersión*) watering; (*irrigación*) irrigation.

riel [rjel] *nm* rail.

rienda ['rjenda] *nf* rein; **dar ~ suelta a** to give free rein to.

riente ['rjente] *a* laughing.

riesgo ['rjesɣo] *nm* risk; **correr el ~ de** to run the risk of.

rifa ['rifa] *nf* (*lotería*) raffle; (*disputa*) quarrel; **rifar** *vt* to raffle // *vi* to quarrel; **rifarse** *vr*: **rifarse algo** to fight over sth.

rifle ['rifle] *nm* rifle.

rigidez [rixi'ðeθ] *nf* rigidity, stiffness; (*fig*) strictness; **rígido, a** *a* rigid, stiff; strict, inflexible.

rigor [ri'ɣor] *nm* strictness, rigour; (*inclemencia*) harshness; **de ~** de rigueur, essential; **riguroso, a** *a* rigorous; harsh; (*severo*) severe.

rimar [ri'mar] *vi* to rhyme.

rimbombante [rimbom'bante] *a* resounding; (*fig*) pompous.

rincón [rin'kon] *nm* (inside) corner.

rinoceronte [rinoθe'ronte] *nm* rhinoceros.

riña ['riɲa] *nf* (*disputa*) argument; (*pelea*) brawl.

riñón [ri'ɲon] *nm* (*gen*) kidney; **tener riñones** to have guts.

río *etc vb ver* **reír** // ['rio] *nm* river; (*fig*) torrent, stream; **~ abajo/arriba** downstream/upstream.

rioplatense [riopla'tense] *a* of the River Plate region.

ripio ['ripjo] *nm* (*residuo*) refuse, waste; (*cascotes*) rubble, debris.

riqueza [ri'keθa] *nf* wealth, riches *pl*; (*cualidad*) richness.

risa ['risa] *nf* (*una ~*) laugh; (*gen*) laughter.

risco ['risko] *nm* crag, cliff; **~so, a** *a* steep.

risible [ri'sißle] *a* (*ridículo*) ludicrous; (*jocoso*) laughable.

risotada [riso'taða] *nf* guffaw.

ristra ['ristra] *nf* string.

risueño, a [ri'sweɲo, a] *a* (*sonriente*) smiling; (*contento*) cheerful.

ritmo ['ritmo] *nm* rhythm; **a ~ lento** slowly; **trabajar a ~ lento** to go slow.

rito ['rito] *nm* rite.

ritual [ri'twal] *a, nm* ritual.

rival [ri'ßal] *a, nm/f* rival; **~idad** *nf* rivalry; **~izar** *vi*: **~izar con** to rival, vie with.

rizado, a [ri'θaðo, a] *a* curly // *nm* curls *pl*; **rizar** *vt* to curl; **rizarse** *vr* (*el pelo*) to

curl; (*el mar*) to ripple; **rizo** *nm* curl; ripple.

RNE *nf abr de* **Radio Nacional de España**.

robar [ro'ßar] *vt* to rob; (*objeto*) to steal; (*casa etc*) to break into; (*NAIPES*) to draw.

roble ['roßle] *nm* oak; **~do, ~dal** *nm* oakwood.

roblón [ro'ßlon] *nm* rivet.

robo [ro'ßo] *nm* robbery, theft; **~ relámpago** smash-and-grab raid.

robot [ro'ßo(t)] *nm* robot.

robustecer [roßuste'θer] *vt* to strengthen.

robusto, a [ro'ßusto, a] *a* robust, strong.

roca ['roka] *nf* rock.

rocalla [ro'kaʎa] *nf* pebbles *pl*.

roce ['roθe] *nm* (*caricia*) brush; (*TEC*) friction; (*en la piel*) graze; **tener ~ con** to be in close contact with.

rociada [ro'θjaða] *nf* (*aspersión*) sprinkling; (*fig*) hail, shower; **rociar** *vt* to spray.

rocín [ro'θin] *nm* nag, hack.

rocío [ro'θio] *nm* dew.

rocoso, a [ro'koso, a] *a* rocky.

rodado, a [ro'ðaðo, a] *a* (*con ruedas*) wheeled; (*redondo*) round // *nf* rut.

rodaja [ro'ðaxa] *nf* (*raja*) slice; (*rueda*) small wheel.

rodaje [ro'ðaxe] *nm* (*TEC*) wheels *pl*, set of wheels; (*CINE*) shooting, filming; (*AUTO*): **en ~** running in.

rodar [ro'ðar] *vt* (*vehículo*) to wheel; (*escalera*) to roll down; (*viajar por*) to travel (over) // *vi* to roll; (*coche*) to go, run; (*CINE*) to shoot, film.

rodear [roðe'ar] *vt* to surround // *vi* to go round; **~se** *vr*: **~se de amigos** to surround o.s. with friends.

rodeo [ro'ðeo] *nm* (*ruta indirecta*) detour; (*evasión*) evasion; (*AM*) rodeo; **hablar sin ~s** to come to the point, speak plainly.

rodilla [ro'ðiʎa] *nf* knee; **de ~s** kneeling.

rodillo [ro'ðiʎo] *nm* roller; (*CULIN*) rolling-pin; **~ apisonador** *o* **de vapor** steamroller.

rododendro [roðo'ðendro] *nm* rhododendron.

roedor, a [roe'ðor, a] *a* gnawing // *nm* rodent.

roer [ro'er] *vt* (*masticar*) to gnaw; (*corroer*, *fig*) to corrode.

rogar [ro'ɣar] *vt, vi* (*pedir*) to ask for; (*suplicar*) to beg, plead; **se ruega no fumar** please do not smoke.

rojete [ro'xete] *nm* rouge.

rojizo, a [ro'xiθo, a] *a* reddish.

rojo, a ['roxo, a] *a, nm* red; **al ~ vivo** red-hot; **~ de labios** lipstick.

rol [rol] *nm* list, roll; (*AM*: *papel*) role.

rollizo, a [ro'ʎiθo, a] *a* (*objeto*) cylindrical; (*persona*) plump.

rollo ['roʎo] *nm* (*gen*) roll; (*de cuerda*) coil; (*madera*) log; (*fam*) bore; **¡qué ~!** what a carry-on!

Roma ['roma] *n* Rome.

romance [ro'manθe] *nm* Romance language; (*LITERATURA*) ballad; **hablar en** ~ to speak plainly.

romántico, a [ro'mantiko, a] *a* romantic.

romería [rome'ria] *nf* (*REL*) pilgrimage; (*excursión*) trip, outing.

romero, a [ro'mero, a] *nm/f* pilgrim // *nm* rosemary.

romo, a ['romo, a] *a* blunt; (*fig*) dull.

rompecabezas [rompeka'βeθas] *nm inv* riddle, puzzle; (*juego*) jigsaw.

rompehuelgas [rompe'welɣas] *nm inv* strikebreaker, blackleg.

rompeolas [rompe'olas] *nm inv* breakwater.

romper [rom'per] *vt* (*gen*) to break; (*hacer pedazos*) to smash; (*papel etc*) to tear, rip // *vi* (*olas*) to break; (*sol, diente*) to break through; ~ **un contrato** to break a contract; ~ **a** to start (suddenly) to; ~ **en llanto** to burst into tears; ~ **con uno** to fall out with sb.

rompimiento [rompi'mjento] *nm* breaking; (*fig*) break; (*quiebra*) crack; ~ **de hostilidades** outbreak of hostilities.

ron [ron] *nm* rum.

roncar [ron'kar] *vi* to snore.

ronco, a ['ronko, a] *a* (*sin voz*) hoarse; (*áspero*) raucous.

roncha ['rontʃa] *nf* weal; (*contusión*) bruise.

ronda ['ronda] *nf* (*gen*) round; (*patrulla*) patrol; **rondar** *vt* to patrol // *vi* to patrol; (*fig*) to prowl round.

rondón [ron'don]: **de** ~ *ad* unexpectedly.

ronquear [ronke'ar] *vi* to be hoarse; **ronquedad** *nf* hoarseness.

ronquido [ron'kiðo] *nm* snore, snoring.

ronronear [ronrone'ar] *vi* to purr; **ronroneo** *nm* purr.

ronzal [ron'θal] *nm* halter.

roña ['roɲa] *nf* scab; (*mugre*) crust (of dirt).

roñoso, a [ro'ɲoso, a] *a* (*mugriento*) filthy; (*inútil*) useless; (*tacaño*) mean.

ropa ['ropa] *nf* clothes *pl*, clothing; ~ **blanca** linen; ~ **de cama** bed linen; ~ **interior** underwear; ~**je** *nm* gown, robes *pl*; ~**vejero, a** *nm/f* second-hand clothes dealer.

ropero [ro'pero] *nm* linen cupboard; (*guardarropa*) wardrobe.

roque ['roke] *nm* rook, castle.

roquedal [roke'ðal] *nm* rocky place.

rosa ['rosa] *a inv* pink // *nf* rose; (*ANAT*) red birthmark; ~ **de los vientos** the compass; ~**s** *nfpl* popcorn *sg*.

rosado, a [ro'saðo, a], **rosáceo, a** [ro-'saθeo, a] *a* pink // *nm* rosé.

rosal [ro'sal] *nm* rosebush.

rosario [ro'sarjo] *nm* (*REL*) rosary; **rezar el** ~ to say the rosary.

rosca ['roska] *nf* (*de tornillo*) thread; (*de humo*) coil, spiral; (*pan, postre*) ring-shaped roll/pastry.

rosetón [rose'ton] *nm* rosette; (*ARQ*) rose

window; (*AUTO*) cloverleaf (junction).

rostro ['rostro] *nm* (*cara*) face.

rotación [rota'θjon] *nf* rotation; ~ **de cultivos** crop rotation.

rotativo, a [rota'tiβo, a] *a* rotary.

roto, a ['roto, a] *pp de* **romper** // *a* broken; (*disipado*) debauched.

rótula ['rotula] *nf* kneecap; (*TEC*) ball-and-socket joint.

rotular [rotu'lar] *vt* (*titular, encabezar*) to head, entitle; (*etiquetar*) to label; **rótulo** *nm* heading, title; label.

rotundo, a [ro'tundo, a] *a* round; (*enfático*) emphatic.

rotura [ro'tura] *nf* (*rompimiento*) breaking; (*quiebra*) crack; (*MED*) fracture.

roturar [rotu'rar] *vt* to plough.

rozado, a [ro'θaðo, a] *a* worn.

rozadura [roθa'ðura] *nf* abrasion, graze.

rozar [ro'θar] *vt* (*frotar*) to rub; (*arañar*) to scratch; (*arrugar*) to crumple; (*AGR*) to graze; (*tocar ligeramente*) to shave, touch lightly; ~**se** *vr* to rub (together); (*trabarse*) to trip over one's own feet; ~ **con** (*fam*) to rub shoulders with.

roznar [roθ'nar] *vi* to bray.

rte *abr de* **remite, remitente** sender.

rubí [ru'βi] *nm* ruby.

rubicundo, a [ruβi'kundo, a] *a* ruddy; (*de salud*) rosy with health.

rubio, a ['ruβjo, a] *a* fair-haired // *nm/f* blond/blonde; **tabaco** ~ Virginia tobacco.

rubor [ru'βor] *nm* (*timidez*) bashfulness; (*sonrojo*) blush; ~**izarse** *vr* to blush; ~**oso, a** *a* blushing.

rúbrica ['ruβrika] *nf* title, heading; (*de la firma*) flourish; **rubricar** *vt* (*firmar*) to sign with a flourish; (*concluir*) to sign and seal.

rucio, a ['ruθjo, a] *a* grey.

rudeza [ru'ðeθa] *nf* (*tosquedad*) coarseness; (*sencillez*) simplicity.

rudimento [ruði'mento] *nm* rudiment.

rudo, a ['ruðo, a] *a* (*sin pulir*) unpolished; (*tosco*) coarse; (*violento*) violent; (*vulgar*) common; (*estúpido*) stupid.

rueda ['rweða] *nf* (*gen*) wheel; (*círculo*) ring, circle; (*rodaja*) slice, round; ~ **delantera/trasera/de repuesto** front/back/spare wheel; ~ **de prensa** press conference.

ruedo ['rweðo] *nm* (*contorno*) edge, border; (*de vestido*) hem; (*círculo*) circle; (*TAUR*) arena, bullring.

ruego *etc vb ver* **rogar** // ['rweɣo] *nm* request.

rufián [ru'fjan] *nm* scoundrel.

rugby ['ruxβi] *nm* rugby.

rugido [ru'xiðo] *nm* roar; **rugir** *vi* to roar.

rugoso, a [ru'xoso, a] *a* (*arrugado*) wrinkled; (*áspero*) rough; (*desigual*) ridged.

ruibarbo [rui'βarβo] *nm* rhubarb.

ruido ['rwiðo] *nm* (*gen*) noise; (*sonido*) sound; (*alboroto*) racket, row; (*escándalo*) commotion, rumpus; **~so, a** *a* noisy, loud; (*fig*) sensational.

ruin [ru'in] *a* contemptible, mean.

ruina ['rwina] *nf* (*gen*) ruin; (*colapso*) collapse; (*de persona*) ruin, downfall; (*de imperio*) decline.

ruindad [rwin'dað] *nf* lowness, meanness; (*acto*) low or mean act.

ruinoso, a [rui'noso, a] *a* ruinous; (*destartalado*) dilapidated, tumbledown; (*COM*) disastrous.

ruiseñor [rwise'ɲor] *nm* nightingale.

rula ['rula], **ruleta** [ru'leta] *nf* roulette.

Rumania [ru'manja] *nf* Rumania.

rumba ['rumba] *nf* rumba.

rumbo ['rumbo] *nm* (*ruta*) route, direction; (*ángulo de dirección*) course, bearing; (*fig*) course of events.

rumboso, a [rum'boso, a] *a* generous.

rumiante [ru'mjante] *nm* ruminant.

ruminar [rumi'nar] *vt* to chew; (*fig*) to chew over // *vi* to chew the cud.

rumor [ru'mor] *nm* (*ruido sordo*) low sound; (*murmuración*) murmur, buzz; **~earse** *vr*: **se ~ea que** it is rumoured that; **~eo** *nm* murmur.

rupestre [ru'pestre] *a* rock *cpd.*

ruptura [rup'tura] *nf* (*MED*) fracture; (*fig*) rupture.

rural [ru'ral] *a* rural.

Rusia ['rusja] *nf* Russia; **ruso, a** *a, nm/f* Russian.

rústico, a ['rustiko, a] *a* rustic; (*ordinario*) coarse, uncouth // *nm/f* yokel // *nf*: **libro en ~a** paperback.

ruta ['ruta] *nf* route.

rutina [ru'tina] *nf* routine; **~rio, a** *a* a routine.

S *abr de* **santo, a; sur.**

s. *abr de* **siglo; siguiente.**

sábado ['saβaðo] *nm* Saturday.

sábana ['saβana] *nf* sheet.

sabandija [saβan'dixa] *nf* bug, insect.

sabañón [saβa'ɲon] *nm* chilblain.

sabelotodo [saβelo'toðo] *nm/f inv* know-all.

saber [sa'βer] *vt* to know; (*llegar a conocer*) to find out, learn; (*tener capacidad de*) to know how to // *vi*: **~ a** to taste of, taste like // *nm* knowledge, learning; **a ~** namely; **¿sabes nadar?** can you swim?; **¿sabes ir?** do you know the way?

sabiduría [saβiðu'ria] *nf* (*conocimientos*) wisdom; (*instrucción*) knowledge, learning.

sabiendas [sa'βjendas]: **a ~** *ad* knowingly.

sabio, a ['saβjo,a] *a* (*docto*) learned; (*prudente*) wise, sensible.

sabor [sa'βor] *nm* taste, flavour; **~ear** *vt* to savour, relish; (*dar ~ a*) to flavour.

sabotaje [saβo'taxe] *nm* sabotage; **sabotear** *vt* to sabotage.

sabré *etc vb ver* **saber.**

sabroso, a [sa'βroso, a] *a* tasty; (*fig: fam*) racy, salty.

sacacorchos [saka'kortʃos] *nm inv* corkscrew.

sacapuntas [saka'puntas] *nm inv* pencil sharpener.

sacar [sa'kar] *vt* (*gen*) to take out; (*fig*) to get (out); (*quitar*) to remove, get out; (*hacer salir*) to bring out; (*conclusión*) to draw; (*novela etc*) to publish, bring out; (*ropa*) to take off; (*obra*) to make; (*FOTO*) to take; (*premio*) to receive; (*entradas*) to get; **~ adelante** to bring up; **~ a alguien a bailar** to get sb up to dance; **~ apuntes** to take notes; **~ la cara por alguien** to stick up for sb; **~ la lengua** to stick out one's tongue.

sacarina [saka'rina] *nf* saccharin(e).

sacerdote [saθer'ðote] *nm* priest.

saco ['sako] *nm* (*gen*) bag; (*grande*) sack; (*su contenido*) bagful; (*AM*) jacket; **~ de dormir** sleeping bag.

sacramento [sakra'mento] *nm* sacrament.

sacrificar [sakrifi'kar] *vt* to sacrifice; **sacrificio** *nm* sacrifice.

sacrilegio [sakri'lexjo] *nm* sacrilege; **sacrílego, a** *a* sacrilegious.

sacristía [sakris'tia] *nf* sacristy.

sacro, a ['sakro, a] *a* sacred.

sacudida [saku'ðiða] *nf* (*zarandeada*) shake, shaking; (*sacudimiento*) jolt, bump; **~ eléctrica** electric shock; **sacudir** *vt* to shake; (*golpear*) to hit.

sádico, a ['saðiko, a] *a* sadistic; **sadismo** *nm* sadism.

saeta [sa'eta] *nf* (*flecha*) arrow; (*de reloj*) hand; (*brújula*) magnetic needle.

sagacidad [saɣaθi'ðað] *nf* shrewdness, cleverness; **sagaz** *a* shrewd, clever; (*astuto*) astute.

sagrado, a [sa'ɣraðo, a] *a* sacred, holy // *nm* sanctuary, asylum.

Sáhara ['saara] *nm*: **el ~** the Sahara (desert).

sahumar [sau'mar] *vt* to fumigate.

sal [sal] *vb ver* **salir** // *nf* salt; **~ de la Higuera** Epsom salts.

sala ['sala] *nf* (*cuarto grande*) large room; (**~ de estar**) living room; (*TEATRO*) house, auditorium; (*de hospital*) ward; **~ de apelación** court; **~ de espera** waiting room.

salado, a [sa'laðo, a] *a* salty; (*fig*) witty, amusing; **agua ~a** salt water; **salar** *vt* to salt, add salt to.

salario [sa'larjo] *nm* wage, pay.

salchicha [sal'tʃitʃa] *nf* pork sausage; **salchichón** *nm* (salami-type) sausage.

saldar [sal'dar] *vt* to pay; (*vender*) to sell off; (*fig*) to settle, resolve; **saldo** *nm* (*pago*) settlement; (*de una cuenta*) balance; (*lo restante*) remnant(s) (*pl*), remainder.

saldré *etc vb ver* **salir.**

salero [sa'lero] *nm* salt cellar.

salgo *etc vb ver* **salir.**

salida [sa'liða] nf exit, way out, (acto) leaving, going out; (de tren, AVIAT) departure; (TEC) output, production; (fig) way out; (COM) opening; (GEO, válvula) outlet; (de gas, aire) escape, leak; **calle sin ~** cul-de-sac; **~ de emergencia** emergency exit.

saliente [sa'ljente] a (ARQ) projecting; (que se retira) outgoing, retiring; (el sol) rising; (fig) outstanding.

salir [sa'lir] vi (gen) to come/go out; (resultar) to turn out; (partir) to leave, depart; (aparecer) to appear; (sobresalir) to project, jut out; **~se** vr (vasija) to leak; (animal) to escape, get out; **~ con** to go out with; **~ a la superficie** to come to the surface; **~ caro/barato** to work out expensive/cheap.

saliva [sa'lißa] nf saliva.

salmantino, a [salman'tino, a] a of Salamanca.

salmo ['salmo] nm psalm.

salmón [sal'mon] nm salmon.

salmuera [sal'mwera] nf pickle, brine.

salón [sa'lon] nm (de casa) living-room, lounge; (muebles) lounge suite; **~ de belleza** beauty parlour; **~ de pintura** art gallery; **~ de baile** dance hall.

salpicadero [salpika'ðero] nm dashboard.

salpicar [salpi'kar] vt (rociar) to sprinkle, spatter; (esparcir) to scatter.

salsa ['salsa] nf sauce; (con carne asada) gravy; (fig) spice.

saltamontes [salta'montes] nm inv grasshopper.

saltar [sal'tar] vt to jump (over), leap (over); (dejar de lado) to skip, miss out // vi to jump, leap; (pelota) to bounce; (al aire) to fly up; (quebrarse) to break; (al agua) to dive; (fig) to explode, blow up.

saltear [salte'ar] vt (robar) to rob (in a holdup); (asaltar) to assault, attack; (CULIN) to sauté.

saltimbanqui [saltim'banki] nm/f acrobat.

salto ['salto] nm jump, leap; (al agua) dive; (DEPORTE) jump; **~ de agua** waterfall.

saltón, ona [sal'ton, ona] a (ojos) bulging, popping; (dientes) protruding.

salubre [sa'lußre] a healthy, salubrious.

salud [sa'luð] nf health; **¡(a su) ~!** good health!; **~able** a (de buena ~) healthy; (provechoso) good, beneficial.

saludar [salu'ðar] vt to greet; (MIL) to salute; **saludo** nm greeting; **saludos** (en carta) best wishes, regards, greetings.

salvación [salßa'θjon] nf (gen) salvation; (rescate) rescue.

salvaguardar [salßaɣwar'ðar] vt to safeguard.

salvaje [sal'ßaxe] a wild; (tribú) savage; **salvajismo** nm, **salvajez** nf savagery.

salvar [sal'ßar] vt (rescatar) to save, rescue; (resolver) to overcome, resolve; (cubrir distancias) to cover, travel; (hacer excepción) to except, exclude; (un barco) to salvage.

salvavidas [salßa'ßiðas] nm inv lifebelt // a: **bote/chaleco/cinturón ~** lifeboat/jacket/belt.

salvia ['salßja] nf sage.

salvo, a ['salßo, a] a safe // ad except (for), save; **a ~ out** of danger; **~ que** unless; **~ conducto** nm safe-conduct.

san [san] a saint; **~ Juan** St. John.

sanar [sa'nar] vt (herida) to heal; (persona) to cure // vi (persona) to get well, recover; (herida) to heal.

sanatorio [sana'torjo] nm sanatorium.

sanción [san'θjon] nf sanction; **sancionar** vt to sanction.

sandalia [san'dalja] nf sandal.

sandía [san'dia] nf watermelon.

sandwich ['sandwitʃ] nm sandwich.

saneamiento [sanea'mjento] nm sanitation; (de la tierra) drainage; (indemnización) compensation; (fig) remedy; **sanear** vt to drain; to compensate; to remedy, repair; (garantizar) to guarantee; (asegurar) to insure.

sangrar [san'grar] vt, vi to bleed; **sangre** nf blood.

sangría [san'gria] nf sangria, sweetened drink of red wine with fruit.

sangriento, a [san'grjento, a] a (herido) bleeding; (batalla) bloody.

sanguinario, a [sangi'narjo, a] a bloodthirsty.

sanguíneo, a [san'gineo, a] a blood cpd.

sanidad [sani'ðað] nf sanitation; (calidad de sano) health, healthiness; **~ pública** public health.

sanitario, a [sani'tarjo, a] a sanitary; (de la salud) health cpd.

sano, a ['sano, a] a healthy; (sin daños) sound; (comida) good, (entero) whole, intact; **~ y salvo** safe and sound.

santidad [santi'ðað] nf holiness, sanctity; **santificar** vt to sanctify, make holy.

santiguar [santi'war] vt (fig) to slap, hit; **~se** vr to make the sign of the cross.

santo, a ['santo, a] a holy; (fig) wonderful, miraculous // nm/f saint // nm saint's day; **~ y seña** password.

santuario [san'twarjo] nm sanctuary, shrine.

saña ['sana] nf rage, fury.

sapo ['sapo] nm toad.

saque ['sake] nm (TENIS) service, serve; (FÚTBOL) throw-in; **~ de esquina** corner (kick).

saquear [sake'ar] vt (MIL) to sack; (robar) to loot, plunder; (fig) to ransack; **saqueo** nm sacking; looting, plundering; ransacking.

sarampión [saram'pjon] nm measles sg.

sarcasmo [sar'kasmo] nm sarcasm; **sarcástico, a** a sarcastic.

sardina [sar'ðina] nf sardine.

sardónico, a [sar'ðoniko, a] a sardonic; (irónico) ironical, sarcastic.

sargento [sar'xento] nm sergeant.

sarna ['sarna] *nf* itch; (*MED*) scabies.
sartén [sar'ten] *nf* frying pan.
sastre ['sastre] *nm* tailor; ~**ría** *nf* (*arte*) tailoring; (*tienda*) tailor's (shop).
satélite [sa'telite] *nm* satellite.
sátira ['satira] *nf* satire.
satisfacción [satisfak'θjon] *nf* satisfaction; **satisfacer** *vt* to satisfy; (*gastos*) to meet; (*pérdida*) to make good; **satisfacerse** *vr* to satisfy o.s., be satisfied; (*vengarse*) to take revenge; **satisfecho, a** *a* satisfied; (*contento*) content(ed), happy; (*vanidoso*) self-satisfied, smug.
saturar [satu'rar] *vt* to saturate.
sauce ['sauθe] *nm* willow; ~ **llorón** weeping willow.
sauna ['sauna] *nf* sauna.
savia ['saβja] *nf* sap.
saxofón [sakso'fon], **saxófono** [sak-'sofono] *nm* saxophone.
sayo ['sajo] *nm* smock.
sazonado, a [saθo'naðo, a] *a* (*fruta*) ripe; (*CULIN*) flavoured, seasoned; **sazonar** *vt* to ripen; to flavour, season.
se [se] *pron reflexivo* oneself; (*sg: m*) himself; (: *f*) herself; (: *de una cosa*) itself; (: *de Ud*) yourself; (*pl*) themselves; (: *de Uds*) yourselves; (*de uno*) oneself; ~ **mira en el espejo** he looks at himself in the mirror; (*recíproco*) each other, one another; ~ **ayudan** they help each other; ~ **miraron (el uno al otro)** they looked at one another; (*uso impersonal*): ~ **compró hace 3 años** it was bought 3 years ago; **en esa parte** ~ **habla francés** in that area French is spoken *or* people speak French; (*dativo*): ~ **lo daré** I'll give it to him/her/you; **él** ~ **ha comprado un sombrero** he has bought himself a hat.
SE *abr de* **sudeste.**
sé *vb ver* **saber, ser.**
sea *etc vb ver* **ser.**
sebo ['seβo] *nm* fat, grease.
seca ['seka] *nf ver* **seco.**
secador [seka'ðor] *nm*: ~ **de cabello** *o* **para el pelo** hair-dryer.
secadora [seka'ðora] *nf* wringer; ~ **centrífuga** spin-dryer.
secar [se'kar] *vt* to dry; ~**se** *vr* to dry (off); (*río, planta*) to dry up.
sección [sek'θjon] *nf* section.
seco, a ['seko, a] *a* dry; (*carácter*) cold; (*respuesta*) sharp, curt; (*coñac*) straight // *nf* drought; **vivir a pan** ~ to live by bread alone; **habrá pan a** ~**as** there will be just bread; **decir algo a** ~**as** to say sth curtly; **parar en** ~ to stop dead.
secretaría [sekreta'ria] *nf* secretariat; **secretario, a** *nm/f* secretary.
secreto, a [se'kreto, a] *a* secret; (*persona*) secretive // *nm* secret; (*calidad*) secrecy.
secta ['sekta] *nf* sect; ~**rio, a** *a* sectarian.
sector [sek'tor] *nm* sector.
secuela [se'kwela] *nf* consequence.
secuestrar [sekwes'trar] *vt* to kidnap; (*bienes*) to seize, confiscate; **secuestro**

nm kidnapping; seizure, confiscation.
secular [seku'lar] *a* secular.
secundar [sekun'dar] *vt* to second, support.
secundario, a [sekun'darjo, a] *a* secondary.
sed [seð] *nf* thirst; **tener** ~ to be thirsty.
seda ['seða] *nf* silk.
sedal [se'ðal] *nm* fishing line.
sedante [se'ðante], **sedativo** [seða'tiβo] *nm* sedative.
sede ['seðe] *nf* (*de gobierno*) seat; (*de compañía*) headquarters *pl*; **Santa S**~ Holy See.
sediento, a [se'ðjento, a] *a* thirsty.
sedimentar [seðimen'tar] *vt* to deposit; ~**se** *vr* to settle; **sedimento** *nm* sediment.
seducción [seðuk'θjon] *nf* seduction; **seducir** *vt* to seduce; (*sobornar*) to bribe; (*cautivar*) to charm, fascinate; **seductor, a** *a* seductive; charming, fascinating; (*engañoso*) deceptive, misleading // *nm/f* seducer.
segadora-trilladora [seɣa'ðora triʎa-'ðora] *nf* combine harvester.
seglar [se'ɣlar] *a* secular, lay.
segregación [seɣreɣa'θjon] *nf* segregation; ~ **racial** racial segregation; **segregar** *vt* to segregate, separate.
seguido, a [se'ɣiðo, a] *a* (*continuo*) continuous, unbroken; (*recto*) straight; ~**s** consecutive, successive // *ad* (*directo*) straight (on); (*después*) after // *nf*: **en** ~**a** at once, right away; **5 días** ~**s** 5 days running, 5 days in a row.
seguimiento [seɣi'mjento] *nm* chase, pursuit; (*continuación*) continuation.
seguir [se'ɣir] *vt* (*gen*) to follow; (*venir después*) to follow on, come after; (*proseguir*) to continue; (*perseguir*) to chase, pursue // *vi* (*gen*) to follow; (*continuar*) to continue, carry or go on; ~**se** *vr* to follow; **sigo sin comprender** I still don't understand; **sigue lloviendo** it's still raining.
según [se'ɣun] *prep* according to // *ad* according to circumstances; ~ **y conforme** it all depends; ~ **esté el tiempo** depending on the weather.
segundo, a [se'ɣundo, a] *a* second // *nm* second // *nf* second meaning; **de** ~**a mano** second hand.
segur [se'ɣur] *nf* (*hacha*) axe; (*hoz*) sickle.
seguramente [seɣura'mente] *ad* surely; (*con certeza*) for sure, with certainty.
seguridad [seɣuri'ðað] *nf* (*gen*) safety; (*del estado, de casa etc*) security; (*certidumbre*) certainty; (*confianza*) confidence; (*estabilidad*) stability; ~ **social** social security.
seguro, a [se'ɣuro, a] *a* (*cierto*) sure, certain; (*fiel*) trustworthy; (*libre de peligro*) safe; (*bien defendido, firme*) secure // *ad* for sure, certainly // *nm* (*COM*) insurance; ~ **contra terceros/a todo riesgo** third party/comprehensive insurance; ~**s sociales** social security *sg*.

seis [seis] *num* six.
seismo ['seismo] *nm* tremor, earthquake.
selección [selek'θjon] *nf* selection; **seleccionar** *vt* to pick, choose, select; **selecto, a** *a* select, choice; (*escogido*) selected.
selva ['selβa] *nf* (*bosque*) forest, woods *pl*; (*jungla*) jungle.
sello ['seʎo] *nm* stamp; (*medicinal*) capsule, pill.
semáforo [se'maforo] *nm* (*AUTO*) traffic lights *pl*; (*FERRO*) signal.
semana [se'mana] *nf* week; **entre ~** during the week; **semanal, semanario, a** *a* weekly.
semblante [sem'blante] *nm* face; (*fig*) face, appearance.
sembrar [sem'brar] *vt* to sow; (*objetos*) to sprinkle, scatter about; (*noticias*) to spread.
semejante [seme'xante] *a* (*parecido*) similar; **~s** alike, similar // *nm* fellow man, fellow creature; **no he dicho cosa ~** I have not said any such thing; **semejanza** *nf* similarity, resemblance.
semejar [seme'xar] *vi* to seem like, resemble; **~se** *vr* to look alike, be similar.
semen ['semen] *nm* semen; **~tal** *nm* stud.
semestral [semes'tral] *a* half-yearly, bi-annual.
semicírculo [semi'θirkulo] *nm* semicircle.
semiconsciente [semikons'θjente] *a* semiconscious.
semilla [se'miʎa] *nf* seed.
seminario [semi'narjo] *nm* (*REL*) seminary; (*en universidad*) seminar.
sémola ['semola] *nf* semolina.
sempiterno, a [sempi'terno, a] *a* everlasting // *nf* evergreen.
Sena ['sena] *nm*: **el ~** the (river) Seine.
senado [se'naðo] *nm* senate; **senador, a** *nm/f* senator.
sencillez [senθi'ʎeθ] *nf* (*gen*) simplicity; (*naturalidad*) naturalness; **sencillo, a** *a* simple; natural, unaffected.
senda ['senda] *nf*, **sendero** [sen'dero] *nm* path, track.
sendos, as ['sendos, as] *apl*: **les dio ~ golpes** he hit both of them.
senil [se'nil] *a* senile.
seno ['seno] *nm* (*ANAT*) bosom, bust; (*fig*) bosom; (*vacío*) hollow; **~s** breasts.
sensación [sensa'θjon] *nf* (*gen*) sensation; (*sentido*) sense; (*sentimiento*) feeling.
sensato, a [sen'sato, a] *a* sensible.
sensible [sen'sible] *a* sensitive; (*apreciable*) perceptible, appreciable; (*pérdida*) considerable.
sensitivo, a [sensi'tiβo, a], **sensorio, a** [sen'sorjo, a], **sensorial** [senso'rjal] *a* sensory.
sensual [sen'swal] *a* sensual.
sentado, a [sen'taðo, a] *a* (*establecido*) settled; (*carácter*) sensible; **estar ~** to sit, be sitting (down) // *nf* sitting; **dar por ~** to take for granted, assume.

sentar [sen'tar] *vt* to sit, seat; (*fig*) to establish // *vi* (*vestido*) to suit; (*alimento*): **~ bien/mal a** to agree/disagree with; **~se** *vr* (*persona*) to sit, sit down; (*el tiempo*) to settle (down); (*los depósitos*) to settle.
sentencia [sen'tenθja] *nf* (*máxima*) maxim, saying; (*JUR*) sentence; **sentenciar** *vt* to sentence // *vi* to give one's opinion.
sentido, a [sen'tiðo, a] *a* (*pérdida*) regrettable; (*carácter*) sensitive // *nm* (*gen*) sense; (*sentimiento*) feeling; (*significado*) sense, meaning; (*dirección*) direction; **mi más ~ pésame** my deepest sympathy; **~ del humor** sense of humour; **~ único** one-way (street).
sentimental [sentimen'tal] *a* sentimental; **vida ~** love life.
sentimiento [senti'mjento] *nm* (*emoción*) feeling, emotion; (*sentido*) sense; (*pesar*) regret, sorrow.
sentir [sen'tir] *vt* (*gen*) to feel; (*percibir*) to perceive, sense; (*lamentar*) to regret, be sorry for // *vi* (*tener la sensación*) to feel; (*lamentarse*) to feel sorry // *nm* opinion, judgement; **~se bien/mal** to feel well/ill; **lo siento** I'm sorry.
seña ['seɲa] *nf* sign; (*MIL*) password; **~s** *nfpl* address *sg*; **~s personales** personal details.
señal [se'ɲal] *nf* (*gen*) sign; (*síntoma*) symptom; (*FERRO, TELEC*) signal; (*marca*) mark; (*COM*) deposit; **en ~ de** as a token of, as a sign of; **~ar** *vt* to mark; (*indicar*) to point out, indicate; (*fijar*) to fix, settle; **~arse** *vr* to make one's mark.
señor [se'ɲor] *nm* (*hombre*) man; (*caballero*) gentleman; (*dueño*) owner, master; (*trato: antes de nombre propio*) Mr; (*: directo*) sir; **muy ~ mío** Dear Sir; **el ~ alcalde/presidente** the mayor/president.
señora [se'ɲora] *nf* (*dama*) lady; (*trato*) Mrs; (*tratamiento de cortesía*) madam; (*fam*) wife; **Nuestra S~** Our Lady.
señorita [seɲo'rita] *nf* (*gen*) Miss; (*mujer joven*) young lady.
señuelo [se'ɲwelo] *nm* decoy.
sepa *etc vb ver* **saber.**
separación [separa'θjon] *nf* separation; (*división*) division; (*distancia*) gap, distance.
separar [sepa'rar] *vt* to separate; (*dividir*) to divide; **~se** *vr* (*parte*) to come away; (*partes*) to come apart; (*persona*) to leave, go away; (*matrimonio*) to separate; **separatismo** *nm* separatism.
sepia ['sepja] *nf* cuttlefish.
séptico, a ['septiko, a] *a* septic.
septiembre [sep'tjembre] *nm* September.
séptimo, a ['septimo, a] *a, nm* seventh.
sepultar [sepul'tar] *vt* to bury; **sepultura** *nf* (*acto*) burial; (*tumba*) grave, tomb; **sepulturero, a** *nm/f* gravedigger.
sequedad [seke'ðað] *nf* dryness; (*fig*) brusqueness, curtness.

sequía [se'kia] *nf* drought.
séquito ['sekito] *nm* followers *pl*, retinue.
ser [ser] *vi* (*gen*) to be; (*devenir*) to become // *nm* being; ~ **de** (*origen*) to be from, come from; (*hecho de*) to be (made) of; (*pertenecer a*) to belong to; **es la una** it is one o'clock; **es de esperar que** it is to be hoped that; **era de ver** it was worth seeing, you should have seen it; **a no** ~ **que** unless; **de no** ~ **así** if it were not so, were it not so; **o sea** that is to say; **sea como sea** be that as it may.
serenarse [sere'narse] *vr* to calm down.
sereno, a [se'reno, a] *a* (*persona*) calm, unruffled; (*el tiempo*) fine, settled; (*ambiente*) calm, peaceful // *nm* night watchman.
serie ['serje] *nf* series; (*cadena*) sequence, succession; **fuera de** ~ out of order; **fabricación en** ~ mass production.
seriedad [serje'ðað] *nf* seriousness; (*formalidad*) reliability; (*de crisis*) gravity, seriousness; **serio, a** *a* serious; reliable, dependable; grave, serious; **en serio** *ad* seriously.
sermón [ser'mon] *nm* (*REL*) sermon.
serpentear [serpente'ar] *vi* to wriggle; (*fig*) to wind, snake.
serpentina [serpen'tina] *nf* streamer.
serpiente [ser'pjente] *nf* snake; ~ **boa** boa constrictor; ~ **pitón** python; ~ **de cascabel** rattlesnake.
serranía [serra'nia] *nf* mountainous area; **serrano, a** *a* highland *cpd*, hill *cpd* // *nm/f* highlander.
serrar [se'rrar] *vt* = **aserrar**.
serrín [se'rrin] *nm* = **aserrín**.
serrucho [se'rrutʃo] *nm* saw.
servicio [ser'ßiθjo] *nm* service; ~**s** toilet(s).
servidor, a [serßi'ðor, a] *nm/f* servant; **su seguro** ~ (**s.s.s.**) yours faithfully; **servidumbre** *nf* (*sujeción*) servitude; (*criados*) servants *pl*, staff.
servil [ser'ßil] *a* servile.
servilleta [serßi'ʎeta] *nf* serviette, napkin.
servir [ser'ßir] *vt* to serve // *vi* to serve; (*tener utilidad*) to be of use, be useful; ~**se** *vr* to serve or help o.s.; ~**se de algo** to make use of sth, use sth; **sírvase pasar** please come in.
sesenta [se'senta] *num* sixty.
sesgado, a [ses'xaðo, a] *a* slanted, slanting; **sesgo** *nm* slant; (*fig*) slant, twist.
sesión [se'sjon] *nf* (*POL*) session, sitting; (*CINE*) showing.
seso ['seso] *nm* brain; **sesudo, a** *a* sensible, wise.
seta ['seta] *nf* mushroom.
setenta [se'tenta] *num* seventy.
seudo... ['seuðo] *pref* pseudo... .
seudónimo [seu'ðonimo] *nm* pseudonym.
severidad [seßeri'ðað] *nf* severity; **severo, a** *a* severe.
Sevilla [se'ßiʎa] *n* Seville.

sexo ['sekso] *nm* sex.
sexto, a ['seksto, a] *a*, *nm* sixth.
sexual [sek'swal] *a* sexual; **vida** ~ **sex** life.
si [si] *conj* if; **me pregunto** ~ ... I wonder if or whether... .
sí [si] *ad* yes // *nm* consent // *pron* (*gen*) oneself; (*sg: m*) himself; (: *f*) herself; (: *de cosa*) itself; (*de usted*) yourself; (*pl*) themselves; (*de ustedes*) yourselves; (*recíproco*) each other; **él no quiere pero yo** ~ he doesn't want to but I do; **ella** ~ **vendrá** she will certainly come, she is sure to come; **claro que** ~ of course; **creo que** ~ I think so.
siderúrgico, a [siðe'rurxiko, a] *a* iron and steel *cpd* // *nf*: **la** ~**a** the iron and steel industry.
sidra ['siðra] *nf* cider.
siembra ['sjembra] *nf* sowing.
siempre ['sjempre] *ad* (*gen*) always; (*todo el tiempo*) all the time; ~ **que** *conj* (*cada vez*) whenever; (*dado que*) provided that; **para** ~ for ever.
sien [sjen] *nf* temple.
siento *etc vb ver* **sentar, sentir.**
sierra ['sjerra] *nf* (*TEC*) saw; (*cadena de montañas*) mountain range.
siervo, a ['sjerßo, a] *nm/f* slave.
siesta ['sjesta] *nf* siesta, nap.
siete ['sjete] *num* seven.
sífilis ['sifilis] *nf* syphilis.
sifón [si'fon] *nm* syphon; **whisky con** ~ whisky and soda.
sigla ['sixla] *nf* symbol.
siglo ['sixlo] *nm* century; (*fig*) age.
significación [sixnifika'θjon] *nf* significance.
significado [sixnifi'kaðo] *nm* significance; (*de palabra*) meaning.
significar [sixnifi'kar] *vt* to mean, signify; (*notificar*) to make known, express; ~**se** *vr* to become known, make a name for o.s.; **significativo, a** *a* significant.
signo ['sixno] *nm* sign; ~ **de admiración** *o* **exclamación** exclamation mark; ~ **de interrogación** question mark.
sigo *etc vb ver* **seguir.**
siguiente [si'xjente] *a* next, following.
siguió *etc vb ver* **seguir.**
sílaba ['silaßa] *nf* syllable.
silbar [sil'ßar] *vt*, *vi* to whistle; **silbato** *nm* whistle; **silbido** *nm* whistle, whistling.
silenciador [silenθja'ðor] *nm* silencer.
silenciar [silen'θjar] *vt* (*persona*) to silence; (*escándalo*) to hush up; **silencio** *nm* silence, quiet; **silencioso, a** *a* silent, quiet.
silicio [si'liθjo] *nm* silicon.
silueta [si'lweta] *nf* silhouette; (*de edificio*) outline; (*figura*) figure.
silvestre [sil'ßestre] *a* rustic, rural; (*salvaje*) wild.
silla ['siʎa] *nf* (*asiento*) chair; (*de jinete*) saddle.

sillón [si'ʎon] *nm* armchair, easy chair; ~ **de ruedas** wheelchair.

simbólico, a [sim'boliko, a] *a* symbolic(al); **símbolo** *nm* symbol.

simetría [sime'tria] *nf* symmetry.

simiente [si'mjente] *nf* seed.

similar [simi'lar] *a* similar.

simio ['simjo] *nm* ape.

simpatía [simpa'tia] *nf* liking; (*afecto*) affection; (*amabilidad*) kindness; (*solidaridad*) mutual support, solidarity; **simpático, a** *a* nice, pleasant; kind; **simpatizante** *nm/f* sympathiser; **simpatizar** *vi*: **simpatizar con** to get on well with.

simple ['simple] *a* (*gen*) simple; (*elemental*) simple, easy; (*mero*) mere; (*puro*) pure, sheer // *nm/f* simpleton; ~**za** *nf* simpleness; (*necedad*) silly thing; **simplicidad** *nf* simplicity; **simplificar** *vt* to simplify.

simular [simu'lar] *vt* to simulate.

simultáneo, a [simul'taneo, a] *a* simultaneous.

sin [sin] *prep* without; **la ropa está ~ lavar** the clothes are unwashed; ~ **que** *conj* without; ~ **embargo** however, still.

sinagoga [sina'ɣoɣa] *nf* synagogue.

sinceridad [sinθeri'ðað] *nf* sincerity; **sincero, a** *a* sincere.

sincronizar [sinkroni'θar] *vt* to synchronize.

sindical [sindi'kal] *a* union *cpd*, trade-union *cpd*; ~**ista** *nm/f* trade-unionist; **sindicato** *nm* (*de trabajadores*) trade(s) union; (*de negociantes*) syndicate.

sinfín [sin'fin] *nm*: **un ~ de** a great many, no end of.

sinfonía [sinfo'nia] *nf* symphony.

singular [singu'lar] *a* singular; (*fig*) outstanding, exceptional; (*pey*) peculiar, odd; ~**idad** *nf* singularity, peculiarity; ~**izar** *vt* to single out; ~**izarse** *vr* to distinguish o.s., stand out.

siniestro, a [si'njestro, a] *a* left; (*fig*) sinister.

sinnúmero [sin'numero] *nm* = **sinfín**.

sino ['sino] *nm* fate, destiny // *conj* (*pero*) but; (*salvo*) except, save.

sinónimo [si'nonimo] *nm* synonym.

sinrazón [sinra'θon] *nf* wrong, injustice.

síntesis ['sintesis] *nf* synthesis; **sintético, a** *a* synthetic; **sintetizar** *vt* to synthesize.

sintió *vb ver* **sentir**.

síntoma ['sintoma] *nm* symptom.

sinvergüenza [sinβer'ɣwenθa] *nm/f* shameless person.

sionismo [sjo'nismo] *nm* Zionism.

siquiera [si'kjera] *conj* even if, even though // *ad* at least; **ni ~** not even.

sirena [si'rena] *nf* siren.

sirviente, a [sir'βjente, a] *nm/f* servant.

sirvo *etc vb ver* **servir**.

sisear [sise'ar] *vt, vi* to hiss.

sismógrafo [sis'moɣrafo] *nm* seismograph.

sistema [sis'tema] *nm* system; (*método*) method; **sistemático, a** *a* systematic.

sitiar [si'tjar] *vt* to besiege, lay seige to.

sitio ['sitjo] *nm* (*lugar*) place; (*espacio*) room, space; (MIL) siege.

situación [sitwa'θjon] *nf* situation, position; (*estatus*) position, standing.

situar [si'twar] *vt* to place, put; (*edificio*) to locate, situate.

slip [slip] *nm* pants *pl*, briefs *pl*.

smoking ['smokin] (*pl* ~**s**) *nm* dinner jacket.

so [so] *prep* under.

SO *abr de* **sudoeste**.

sobaco [so'βako] *nm* armpit.

soberanía [soβera'nia] *nf* sovereignty; **soberano, a** *a* sovereign; (*fig*) supreme // *nm/f* sovereign.

soberbio, a [so'βerβjo, a] *a* (*orgulloso*) proud; (*altivo*) haughty, arrogant; (*fig*) magnificent, superb // *nf* pride; haughtiness, arrogance; magnificence; (*cólera*) anger.

sobornar [soβor'nar] *vt* to bribe; **soborno** *nm* bribe.

sobra ['soβra] *nf* excess, surplus; ~**s** *nfpl* left-overs, scraps; **de ~** extra, surplus; **tengo de ~** I've more than enough; ~**do, a** (*de ~*) more than enough; (*excesivo*) excessive // *ad* too, exceedingly; **sobrante** *a* remaining, extra // *nm* surplus, remainder; **sobrar** *vt* to exceed, surpass // *vi* (*tener de más*) to be more than enough; (*quedar*) to remain, be left (over).

sobre ['soβre] *prep* (*gen*) on; (*encima*) on (top of); (*por, encima de, arriba de*) over, above; (*más que*) more than; (*además*) in addition to, besides; (*alrededor de, tratando de*) about // *nm* envelope.

sobrecama [soβre'kama] *nf* bedspread.

sobrecargar [soβrekar'xar] *vt* (*camión*) to overload; (COM) to surcharge.

sobrehumano, a [soβreu'mano, a] *a* superhuman.

sobrellevar [soβreʎe'βar] *vt* (*fig*) to bear, endure.

sobremarcha [soβre'martʃa] *nf* (AUTO) overdrive.

sobrenatural [soβrenatu'ral] *a* supernatural.

sobrepasar [soβrepa'sar] *vt* to exceed, surpass.

sobreponer [soβrepo'ner] *vt* (*poner encima*) to put on top; (*añadir*) to add; ~**se** *vr*: ~**se a** to win through, pull through.

sobreprecio [soβre'preθjo] *nm* surcharge.

sobresaliente [soβresa'ljente] *a* projecting; (*fig*) outstanding, excellent; **sobresalir** *vi* to project, jut out; to stand out, excel.

sobresaltar [soβresal'tar] *vt* (*asustar*) to scare, frighten; (*sobrecoger*) to startle; **sobresalto** *nm* (*movimiento*) start; (*susto*) scare; (*turbación*) sudden shock; **de sobresalto** suddenly.

sobrescrito [soβres'krito] nm address.

sobretodo [soβre'toðo] nm overcoat.

sobreviviente [soβreβi'βjente] a surviving // nm/f survivor; **sobrevivir** vi to survive.

sobriedad [soβrje'ðað] nf sobriety, soberness; (moderación) moderation, restraint.

sobrino, a [so'βrino, a] nm/f nephew/niece.

sobrio, a ['soβrjo, a] a sober; (moderado) moderate, restrained.

socarrón, ona [soka'rron, ona] a (sarcástico) sarcastic, ironic(al); (astuto) crafty, cunning.

sociable [so'θjaβle] a (persona) sociable, friendly; (animal) social.

social [so'θjal] a social; (COM) company cpd.

socialdemócrata [soθjalde'mokrata] nm/f social democrat.

socialista [soθja'lista] a, nm/f socialist.

socializar [soθjali'θar] vt to socialize.

sociedad [soθje'ðað] nf (gen) society; (COM) company; ~ **anónima (SA)** limited company.

socio, a ['soθjo, a] nm/f (miembro) member; (COM) partner; ~ **comandatario** sleeping partner.

sociología [soθjolo'xia] nf sociology.

socorrer [soko'rrer] vt to help; **socorro** nm (ayuda) help, aid; (MIL) relief; **¡socorro!** help!

soda ['soða] nf (sosa) soda; (bebida) soda water.

sofá [so'fa] (pl ~s) nm sofa, settee; ~-**cama** studio couch.

sofisticación [sofistika'θjon] nf sophistication.

sofocar [sofo'kar] vt to suffocate; (apagar) to smother, put out; ~**se** vr to suffocate; (fig) to blush, feel embarrassed; **sofoco** nm suffocation; embarrassment.

soga ['soxa] nf rope.

sois vb ver **ser**.

sojuzgar [soxuθ'xar] vt to subdue, rule despotically.

sol [sol] nm sun; (luz) sunshine, sunlight; **hace** ~ it is sunny.

solamente [sola'mente] ad only, just.

solapa [so'lapa] nf (de ropa) lapel; (de libro) jacket.

solar [so'lar] a solar, sun cpd.

solaz [so'laθ] nm recreation, relaxation; (alivio) solace; ~**ar** vt (divertir) to amuse; (aliviar) to console.

soldada [sol'daða] nf pay.

soldado [sol'daðo] nm soldier.

soldador [solda'ðor] nm soldering iron; (persona) welder; **soldar** vt to solder, weld; (unir) to join, unite.

soledad [sole'ðað] nf solitude; (estado infeliz) loneliness; (nostalgia) grieving, mourning.

solemne [so'lemne] a solemn; **solemnidad** nf solemnity.

soler [so'ler] vi to be in the habit of, be accustomed to.

solfa ['solfa] nf, **solfeo** [sol'feo] nm solfa; (conjunto de signos) musical notation.

solicitación [soliθita'θjon] nf request; (de votos) canvassing; **solicitar** vt (permiso) to ask for, seek; (puesto) to apply for; (votos) to canvass; (atención) to attract; (persona) to pursue, chase after.

solícito, a [so'liθito, a] a (diligente) diligent; (cuidadoso) careful; **solicitud** nf (calidad) great care; (petición) request; (memorial) petition; (a un puesto) application.

solidaridad [soliðari'ðað] nf solidarity; **solidario, a** a (participación) joint, common; (compromiso) mutually binding.

solidez [soli'ðeθ] nf solidity; **sólido, a** a solid.

soliloquio [soli'lokjo] nm soliloquy, monologue.

solista [so'lista] nm/f soloist.

solitario, a [soli'tarjo, a] a a lonely, solitary // nm/f recluse; (en la sociedad) loner // nm solitaire.

soliviar [soli'βjar] vt to lift.

solo, a ['solo, a] a (único) single, sole; (sin compañía) alone; (solitario) lonely; **hay una** ~**a dificultad** there is just one difficulty; **a** ~**as** alone, by o.s.

sólo ['solo] ad only, just.

solomillo [solo'miʎo] nm sirloin.

soltar [sol'tar] vt (dejar ir) to let go of; (desprender) to unfasten, loosen; (librar) to release, set free; (estornudo, risa) to let out.

soltero, a [sol'tero, a] a single, unmarried // nm bachelor // nf single woman, spinster.

soltura [sol'tura] nf looseness, slackness; (de los miembros) agility, ease of movement; (en el hablar) fluency, ease; (MED) diarrhoea.

soluble [so'luβle] a (QUÍMICA) soluble; (problema) solvable.

solución [solu'θjon] nf solution; **solucionar** vt (problema) to solve; (asunto) to settle.

solventar [solβen'tar] vt (pagar) to settle, pay; (resolver) to resolve.

sollozar [soʎo'θar] vi to sob; **sollozo** nm sob.

sombra ['sombra] nf shadow; (como protección) shade; ~**s** nfpl darkness sg; **tener buena/mala** ~ to be lucky/unlucky.

sombreador [sombrea'ðor] nm: ~ **de ojos** eyeshadow.

sombrero [som'brero] nm hat.

sombrilla [som'briʎa] nf parasol, sunshade.

sombrío, a [som'brio, a] a (oscuro) dark; (sombreado) shaded; (fig) sombre, sad; (persona) gloomy.

somero, a [so'mero, a] a superficial.

someter [some'ter] vt (país) to conquer; (persona) to subject to one's will; (informe) to present, submit; ~**se** vr to give in, yield, submit; ~ **a** to subject to.

somnambulismo [somnambu'lismo] *nm* sleepwalking; **somnámbulo, a** *a nm/f* sleepwalker.

somnífero [som'nifero] *nm* sleeping pill.

somos *vb ver* **ser.**

son [son] *vb ver* **ser** // *nm* sound; **en ~ de broma** as a joke.

sonar [so'nar] *vt* to ring // *vi* to sound; *(hacer ruido)* to make a noise; *(pronunciarse)* to be sounded, be pronounced; *(ser conocido)* to sound familiar; *(campana)* to ring; *(reloj)* to strike, chime; ~**se** *vr*: ~**se (las narices)** to blow one's nose; **me suena ese nombre** that name rings a bell.

sonda ['sonda] *nf (NAUT)* sounding; *(TEC)* bore, drill; *(MED)* probe; **sondear** *vt* to sound; to bore (into), drill; to probe, sound; *(fig)* to sound out; **sondeo** *nm* sounding; boring, drilling; *(fig)* sound, enquiry.

sónico, a ['soniko, a] *a* sonic, sound *cpd.*

sonido [so'niðo] *nm* sound.

sonoro, a [so'noro, a] *a* sonorous; *(resonante)* loud, resonant.

sonreír [sonre'ir] *vi*, ~**se** *vr* to smile; **sonriente** a smiling; **sonrisa** *nf* smile.

sonrojo [son'roxo] *nm* blush.

soñador, a [sopa'ðor, a] *nm/f* dreamer; **soñar** *vt, vi* to dream; **soñar con** to dream about, dream of.

soñoliento, a [sopo'ljento, a] *a* sleepy, drowsy.

sopa ['sopa] *nf* soup.

soplador [sopla'ðor] *nm* fan, ventilator.

soplar [so'plar] *vt (polvo)* to blow away, blow off; *(inflar)* to blow up; *(vela)* to blow out // *vi* to blow; ~**se** *vr (fam: ufanarse)* to get conceited; **soplo** *nm* blow, puff; *(de viento)* puff, gust.

soporífero [sopo'rifero] *nm* sleeping pill.

soportable [sopor'taßle] *a* bearable; **soportar** *vt* to bear, carry; *(fig)* to bear, put up with; **soporte** *nm* support; *(fig)* pillar, support.

soprano [so'prano] *nf* soprano.

sorber [sor'ßer] *vt (chupar)* to sip; *(inhalar)* to inhale; *(tragar)* to swallow (up); *(absorber)* to soak up, absorb.

sorbete [sor'ßete] *nm* iced fruit drink.

sorbo ['sorßo] *nm (trago)* gulp, swallow; *(chupada)* sip.

sordera [sor'ðera] *nf* deafness.

sórdido, a ['sorðiðo, a] *a* dirty, squalid; *(palabra)* nasty, dirty; *(fig)* mean.

sordo, a ['sorðo, a] *a (persona)* deaf; *(máquina)* quiet // *nm/f* deaf person; a ~**as** on the quiet; ~**mudo, a** a deaf and dumb.

sorprendente [sorpren'dente] *a* surprising; **sorprender** *vt* to surprise; **sorpresa** *nf* surprise.

sortear [sorte'ar] *vt* to draw lots for; *(objeto)* to raffle; *(dificultad)* to avoid; **sorteo** *nm* drawing lots; raffle.

sosegado, a [sose'xaðo, a] *a* quiet, calm; **sosegar** *vt* to quieten, calm; *(el ánimo)* to

reassure // *vi* to rest; **sosiego** *nm* quiet(ness), calm(ness).

soslayo [sos'lajo]: **al** *o* **de ~** *ad* obliquely, sideways.

soso, a ['soso, a] *a (CULIN)* tasteless; *(fig)* dull, uninteresting.

sospecha [sos'petʃa] *nf* suspicion; **sospechar** *vt* to suspect; **sospechoso, a** *a* suspicious; *(testimonio, opinión)* suspect // *nm/f* suspect.

sostén [sos'ten] *nm (apoyo)* support; *(prenda femenina)* bra, brassière; *(alimentación)* sustenance, food.

sostener [soste'ner] *vt* to support; *(mantener)* to keep up, maintain; *(alimentar)* to sustain, keep going; ~**se** *vr* to support o.s.; *(seguir)* to continue, remain; **sostenido, a** *a* continuous, sustained; *(prolongado)* prolonged.

sótano ['sotano] *nm* basement.

soterrar [sote'rrar] *vt* to bury.

soviético, a [so'ßjetiko, a] *a* Soviet.

soy *vb ver* **ser.**

sport [sport] *nm* sport.

Sr *abr de* **Señor.**

Sra *abr de* **Señora.**

S.R.C. *abr de* **se ruega contestación** R.S.V.P.

Sta *abr de* **Santa; Señorita.**

status ['status] *nm inv* status.

Sto *abr de* **Santo.**

su [su] *pron (de él)* his; *(de ella)* her; *(de una cosa)* its; *(de ellos, ellas)* their; *(de usted, ustedes)* your.

suave ['swaße] *a* gentle; *(superficie)* smooth; *(trabajo)* easy; *(música, voz)* soft, sweet; **suavidad** *nf* gentleness; smoothness; softness, sweetness; **suavizar** *vt* to soften; *(quitar la aspereza)* to smooth (out).

subalimentado, a [sußalimen'taðo, a] *a* undernourished.

subasta [su'ßasta] *nf* auction; **subastar** *vt* to auction (off).

subconsciencia [sußkons'θjenθja] *nf* subconscious; **subconsciente** *a* subconscious.

subdesarrollado, a [sußðesarro'ʎaðo, a] *a* underdeveloped; **subdesarrollo** *nm* underdevelopment.

súbdito, a ['sußðito, a] *nm/f* subject.

subdividir [sußðißi'ðir] *vt* to subdivide.

subestimar [sußesti'mar] *vt* to underestimate, underrate; *(propiedad)* to undervalue.

subexpuesto, a [sußeks'pwesto, a] *a* underexposed.

subido, a [su'ßiðo, a] *a (color)* bright, strong; *(precio)* high // *nf (gen)* ascent, climb; *(de precio)* rise, increase; *(camino)* way up; *(pendiente)* slope, hill.

subir [su'ßir] *vt (objeto)* to raise, lift up; *(cuesta, calle)* to go up; *(montaña)* to climb; *(precio)* to raise, put up // *vi* to go/come up; *(a un coche)* to get in; *(a un autobús)* to get on; *(precio)* to rise, go up; *(río)* to rise; ~**se** *vr* to get up, climb.

súbito, a ['suβito, a] *a* (*repentino*) sudden; (*imprevisto*) unexpected; (*precipitado*) hasty, rash // *ad*: **(de)** ~ suddenly.

sublevación [suβleβa'θjon] *nf* revolt, rising.

sublime [su'βlime] *a* sublime.

submarino, a [suβma'rino, a] *a* underwater // *nm* submarine.

subordinado, a [suβorði'naðo, a] *a, nm/f* subordinate.

subrayar [suβra'jar] *vt* to underline.

subrepticio, a [suβrep'tiθjo, a] *a* surreptitious.

subsanar [suβsa'nar] *vt* (*reparar*) to make good; (*perdonar*) to excuse; (*sobreponerse a*) to overcome.

subscribir [suβskri'βir] *vt* = **suscribir**.

subsidiario, a [suβsi'ðjarjo, a] *a* subsidiary.

subsidio [suβ'siðjo] *nm* (*ayuda*) aid, financial help; (*subvención*) subsidy, grant; (*de enfermedad, paro etc*) benefit.

subsistencia [suβsis'tenθja] *nf* subsistence; **subsistir** *vi* (*gen*) to subsist; (*vivir*) to live; (*sobrevivir*) to survive, endure.

subterráneo, a [suβte'rraneo, a] *a* underground, subterranean // *nm* underpass, underground passage.

suburbano, a [suβur'βano, a] *a* suburban.

suburbio [su'βurβjo] *nm* (*barrio*) slum quarter; (*afueras*) suburbs *pl*.

subvencionar [suββenθjo'nar] *vt* to subsidize.

subversión [suββer'sjon] *nf* subversion; **subversivo, a** *a* subversive.

subyugar [suβju'ɣar] *vt* (*país*) to subjugate, subdue; (*enemigo*) to overpower; (*voluntad*) to dominate.

suceder [suθe'ðer] *vt, vi* to happen; (*seguir*) to succeed, follow; **lo que sucede es que...** the fact is that...; **sucesión** *nf* succession; (*serie*) sequence, series.

sucesivamente [suθesiβa'mente] *ad*: **y así** ~ and so on.

sucesivo, a [suθe'siβo, a] *a* successive, following; **en lo** ~ in future, from now on.

suceso [su'θeso] *nm* (*hecho*) event, happening; (*incidente*) incident; (*resultado*) outcome.

suciedad [suθje'ðað] *nf* (*estado*) dirtiness; (*mugre*) dirt, filth.

sucinto, a [su'θinto, a] *a* succinct, concise.

sucio, a ['suθjo, a] *a* dirty.

suculento, a [suku'lento, a] *a* succulent.

sucumbir [sukum'bir] *vi* to succumb.

sucursal [sukur'sal] *nf* branch (office).

sudamericano, a [suðameri'kano, a] *a* South American.

sudar [su'ðar] *vt, vi* to sweat.

sudeste [su'ðeste] *nm* south-east; **sudoeste** *nm* south-west.

sudor [su'ðor] *nm* sweat; ~**oso, a**, **sudoso, a**, ~**iento, a** *a* sweaty, sweating.

Suecia ['sweθja] *nf* Sweden; **sueco, a** *a* Swedish // *nm/f* Swede.

suegro, a ['sweɣro, a] *nm/f* father-/mother-in-law.

suela ['swela] *nf* sole.

sueldo ['sweldo] *nm* pay, wage(s) (*pl*); **el** ~ **mínimo** the minimum wage.

suele *etc vb ver* **soler.**

suelo ['swelo] *nm* (*tierra*) ground; (*de casa*) floor.

suelto, a ['swelto, a] *a* loose; (*libre*) free; (*separado*) detached, individual; (*ágil*) quick, agile; (*corriente*) fluent, flowing // *nm* (loose) change, small change.

sueño *etc vb ver* **soñar** // ['sweɲo] *nm* sleep; (*somnolencia*) sleepiness, drowsiness; (*lo soñado, fig*) dream; **tener** ~ to be sleepy.

suero ['swero] *nm* serum.

suerte ['swerte] *nf* (*fortuna*) luck; (*azar*) chance; (*destino*) fate, destiny; (*condición*) lot; (*género*) sort, kind; **tener** ~ to be lucky; **de otra** ~ otherwise, if not; **de** ~ **que** so that, in such a way that.

suéter ['sweter] *nm* sweater.

suficiente [sufi'θjente] *a* enough, sufficient; (*capaz*) capable.

sufragio [su'fraxjo] *nm* (*voto*) vote; (*derecho de voto*) suffrage; (*ayuda*) help, aid.

sufrimiento [sufri'mjento] *nm* (*dolor*) suffering; (*paciencia*) patience; (*tolerancia*) tolerance.

sufrir [su'frir] *vt* (*padecer*) to suffer; (*soportar*) to bear, stand, put up with; (*apoyar*) to hold up, support // *vi* to suffer.

sugerencia [suxe'renθja] *nf* suggestion; **sugerir** *vt* to suggest; (*sutilmente*) to hint.

sugestión [suxes'tjon] *nf* suggestion; (*sutil*) hint; **sugestionar** *vt* to influence.

sugestivo, a [suxes'tiβo, a] *a* stimulating; (*fascinante*) fascinating.

suicida [sui'θiða] *a* suicidal // *nm/f* suicidal person; (*muerto*) suicide, person who has committed suicide; **suicidio** *nm* suicide.

Suiza ['swiθa] *nf* Switzerland; **suizo, a** *a, nm/f* Swiss.

sujeción [suxe'θjon] *nf* subjection.

sujetador [suxeta'ðor] *nm* fastener, clip; (*de papeles*) paper clip.

sujetar [suxe'tar] *vt* (*fijar*) to fasten; (*detener*) to hold down; (*fig*) to subject, subjugate; ~**se** *vr* to subject o.s.; **sujeto, a** *a* fastened, secure // *nm* subject; (*individuo*) individual; **sujeto a** subject to.

suma ['suma] *nf* (*cantidad*) total, sum; (*de dinero*) sum; (*acto*) adding (up), addition; (*resumen*) summary; (*esencia*) essence; **en** ~ in short; ~**dora** *nf* adding machine.

sumamente [suma'mente] *ad* extremely, exceedingly.

sumar [su'mar] *vt* to add (up); (*reunir*) to collect, gather; (*abreviar*) to summarize, sum up // *vi* to add up.

sumario, a [su'marjo, a] *a* brief, concise // *nm* summary.

sumergir [sumer'xir] *vt* to submerge; (*hundir*) to sink; (*bañar*) to immerse, dip;

sumersión *nf* submersion; *(fig)* absorption.

sumidero [sumi'ðero] *nm* drain; *(TEC)* sump.

suministrador, a [suministra'ðor, a] *nm/f* supplier; **suministrar** *vt* to supply, provide; **suministro** *nm* supply; *(acto)* supplying, providing.

sumir [su'mir] *vt* to sink, submerge; *(fig)* to plunge.

sumisión [sumi'sjon] *nf (acto)* submission; *(calidad)* submissiveness, docility; **sumiso, a** *a* submissive, docile.

sumo, a ['sumo, a] *a* great, extreme; *(mayor)* highest, supreme.

supe *etc vb ver* **saber**.

super... [super] *pref* super..., over... // **de** high-grade fuel.

superar [supe'rar] *vt (sobreponerse a)* to overcome; *(rebasar)* to surpass, do better than; *(pasar)* to go beyond; **~se** *vr* to excel o.s.

superávit [supe'raßit] *nm* surplus.

supercarburante [superkarßu'rante] *nm* high-grade fuel.

superestructura [superestruk'tura] *nf* superstructure.

superficial [superfi'θjal] *a* superficial; *(medida)* surface *cpd*, of the surface.

superficie [super'fiθje] *nf* surface; *(área)* area.

superfluo, a [su'perflwo, a] *a* superfluous.

superintendente [superinten'dente] *nm/f* supervisor, superintendent.

superior [supe'rjor] *a (piso, clase)* upper; *(temperatura, número, nivel)* higher; *(mejor: calidad, producto)* superior, better // *nm/f* superior; **~idad** *nf* superiority.

supermercado [supermer'kaðo] *nm* supermarket.

supersónico, a [super'soniko, a] *a* supersonic.

superstición [supersti'θjon] *nf* superstition; **supersticioso, a** *a* superstitious.

supervisor, a [superßi'sor, a] *nm/f* supervisor.

supervivencia [superßi'ßenθja] *nf* survival.

supiera *etc vb ver* **saber**.

suplementario, a [suplemen'tarjo, a] *a* supplementary; **suplemento** *nm* supplement.

suplente [su'plente] *a, nm/f* substitute.

súplica ['suplika] *nf* request; *(REL)* supplication.

suplicante [supli'kante] *nm/f* applicant.

suplicar [supli'kar] *vt (cosa)* to beg (for), plead for; *(persona)* to beg, plead with.

suplicio [su'pliθjo] *nm* torture.

suplir [su'plir] *vt (compensar)* to make good, make up for; *(reemplazar)* to replace, substitute // *vi:* **~ a** *o* **por** to take the place of, substitute for.

suponer [supo'ner] *vt* to suppose // *vi* to have authority; **suposición** *nf* supposition; *(autoridad)* authority.

supremacía [suprema'θia] *nf* supremacy.

supremo, a [su'premo, a] *a* supreme.

supresión [supre'sjon] *nf* suppression; *(de derecho)* abolition; *(de dificultad)* removal; *(de palabra)* deletion; *(de restricción)* cancellation, lifting.

suprimir [supri'mir] *vt* to suppress; *(derecho, costumbre)* to abolish; *(dificultad)* to remove; *(palabra)* to delete; *(restricción)* to cancel, lift.

supuesto, a [su'pwesto, a] *a (hipotético)* supposed; *(falso)* false // *nm* assumption, hypothesis; **~ que** *conj* since; **por ~** of course.

sur [sur] *nm* south.

surcar [sur'kar] *vt* to plough, furrow; *(superficie)* to cut, score; **surco** *nm* groove; *(AGR)* furrow.

surgir [sur'xir] *vi* to arise, emerge; *(dificultad)* to come up, crop up.

surtido, a [sur'tiðo, a] *a* mixed, assorted // *nm (gen)* selection, assortment; *(abastecimiento)* supply, stock.

surtir [sur'tir] *vt* to supply, provide // *vi* to spout, spurt.

susceptible [susθep'tißle] *a* susceptible; *(sensible)* sensitive; **~ de** capable of.

suscitar [susθi'tar] *vt* to cause, provoke; *(interés)* to arouse.

suscribir [suskri'ßir] *vt (firmar)* to sign; *(respaldar)* to subscribe to; endorse; **~se** *vr* to subscribe; **suscripción** *nf* subscription.

suspender [suspen'der] *vt (objeto)* to hang (up), suspend; *(trabajo)* to stop, suspend; *(a estudiante)* to fail; **suspensión** *nf* suspension; *(fig)* stoppage, suspension.

suspenso, a [sus'penso, a] *a* hanging, suspended; *(estudiante)* failed; *(admirado)* astonished, amazed // *nm:* **quedar** *o* **estar en ~** to be pending.

suspicacia [suspi'kaθja] *nf* suspicion, mistrust; **suspicaz** *a* suspicious, distrustful.

suspirar [suspi'rar] *vi* to sigh; **suspiro** *nm* sigh.

sustancia [sus'tanθja] *nf* substance.

sustentar [susten'tar] *vt (alimentar)* to sustain, nourish; *(objeto)* to hold up, support; *(idea, teoría)* to maintain, uphold; *(fig)* to sustain, keep going; **sustento** *nm* support; *(alimento)* sustenance, food.

sustituir [substitu'ir] *vt* to substitute, replace; **sustituto, a** *nm/f* substitute, replacement.

susto ['susto] *nm* fright, scare.

sustraer [sustra'er] *vt* to remove, take away; *(MAT)* to subtract; **~se** *vr (evitar)* to avoid; *(retirarse)* to withdraw.

susurrar [susu'rrar] *vi* to whisper; **susurro** *nm* whisper.

sutil [su'til] *a* subtle; *(tenue)* thin; **~eza** *nf* subtlety; thinness.

suyo, a ['sujo, a] *a (con artículo o después del verbo ser: de él)* his; *(: de ella)* hers; *(: de ellos, ellas)* theirs; *(: de Ud, Uds)* yours; *(después de un nombre: de él)* of his; *(: de* *ella*) of hers; (: *de ellos, ellas*) of theirs; (: *de Ud, Uds*) of yours.

T

t *abr de* **tonelada.**

taba ['taβa] *nf* (ANAT) ankle bone; (*juego*) jacks *sg.*

tabaco [ta'βako] *nm* tobacco; (*fam*) cigarettes *pl.*

taberna [ta'βerna] *nf* bar; **tabernero, a** *nm/f* (*encargado*) publican; (*camarero*) barman.

tabique [ta'βike] *nm* (*pared*) thin wall; (*para dividir*) partition.

tabla ['taβla] *nf* (*de madera*) plank; (*estante*) shelf; (*de anuncios*) board; (*lista, catálogo*) list; (*mostrador*) counter; (*de vestido*) pleat; (ARTE) panel; ~s (TAUR, TEATRO) boards; **hacer** ~s to draw; ~**do** *nm* (*plataforma*) platform; (*suelo*) plank floor; (TEATRO) stage.

tablero [ta'βlero] *nm* (*de madera*) plank, board; (*de ajedrez, damas*) board; (AUTO) dashboard.

tablilla [ta'βliʎa] *nf* small board; (MED) splint.

tablón [ta'βlon] *nm* (*de suelo*) plank; (*de techo*) beam; (*de anuncios*) notice board.

tabú [ta'βu] *nm* taboo.

tabular [taβu'lar] *vt* to tabulate.

taburete [taβu'rete] *nm* stool.

tacaño, a [ta'kaɲo, a] *a* (*avaro*) mean; (*astuto*) crafty.

tácito, a ['taθito, a] *a* tacit.

taciturno, a [taθi'turno, a] *a* (*callado*) silent; (*malhumorado*) sullen.

taco ['tako] *nm* (BILLAR) cue; (*libro de billetes*) book; (*manojo de billetes*) wad; (AM) heel; (*tarugo*) peg; (*fam: bocado*) snack; (: *palabrota*) swear word; (: *trago de vino*) swig.

tacón [ta'kon] *nm* heel; **de** ~ **alto** high heeled; **taconeo** *nm* (heel) stamping.

táctico, a ['taktiko, a] *a* tactical // *nf* tactics *pl.*

tacto ['takto] *nm* touch; (*acción*) touching.

tacha ['tatʃa] *nf* flaw; (TEC) stud; **poner** ~ **a** to find fault with; **tachar** *vt* (*borrar*) to cross out; (*corregir*) to correct; (*criticar*) to criticize; **tachar de** to accuse of.

tafetán [tafe'tan] *nm* taffeta; **tafetanes** *nmpl* (*fam*) frills; ~ **adhesivo** *o* **inglés** sticking plaster.

tafilete [tafi'lete] *nm* morocco leather.

tahona [ta'ona] *nf* (*panadería*) bakery; (*molino*) flourmill.

tahur [ta'ur] *nm* gambler; (*pey*) cheat.

taimado, a [tai'maðo, a] *a* (*astuto*) sly; (*resentido*) sullen.

taja ['taxa] *nf* (*corte*) cut; (*repartición*) division; ~**da** *nf* slice; ~**dera** *nf* (*instrumento*) chopper; (*madera*) chopping block; **tajante** *a* sharp.

tajar [ta'xar] *vt* to cut; **tajo** *nm* (*corte*) cut; (*filo*) cutting edge; (GEO) cleft.

tal [tal] *a* such; ~ **vez** perhaps // *pron* (*persona*) someone, such a one; (*cosa*) something, such a thing; ~ **como** such as; ~ **para cual** tit for tat; (*dos iguales*) two of a kind // *ad*: ~ **como** (*igual*) just as; ~ **cual** (*como es*) just as it is; ~ **el padre, cual el hijo** like father, like son; **¿qué** ~? how are things?; **¿qué** ~ **te gusta?** how do you like it? // *conj*: **con** ~ **de que** provided that.

talabartero [talaβar'tero] *nm* saddler.

taladrar [tala'ðrar] *vt* to drill; **taladro** *nm* (*gen*) drill; (*hoyo*) drill hole; **taladro neumático** pneumatic drill.

talante [ta'lante] *nm* (*humor*) mood; (*voluntad*) will, willingness.

talar [ta'lar] *vt* to fell, cut down; (*fig*) to devastate.

talco ['talko] *nm* (*polvos*) talcum powder; (MINEROLOGÍA) talc.

talego [ta'lexo] *nm*, **talega** [ta'lexa] *nf* sack.

talento [ta'lento] *nm* talent; (*capacidad*) ability; (*don*) gift.

talidomida [taliðo'miða] *nm* thalidomide.

talismán [talis'man] *nm* talisman.

talmente [tal'mente] *ad* (*de esta forma*) in such a way; (*hasta tal punto*) to such an extent; (*exactamente*) exactly.

talón [ta'lon] *nm* (*gen*) heel; (COM) counterfoil.

talonario [talo'narjo] *nm* (*de cheques*) chequebook; (*de billetes*) book of tickets; (*de recibos*) receipt book.

talud [ta'luð] *nm* slope.

talla ['taʎa] *nf* (*estatura, fig,* MED) height, stature; (*palo*) measuring rod; (ARTE) carving.

tallado, a [ta'ʎaðo, a] *a* carved // *nm* carving; **tallar** *vt* (*trabajar*) to work, carve; (*grabar*) to engrave; (*medir*) to measure; (*repartir*) to deal // *vi* to deal.

tallarín [taʎa'rin] *nm* noodle.

talle ['taʎe] *nm* (ANAT) waist; (*medida*) size; (*física*) build; (: *de mujer*) figure; (*fig*) appearance.

taller [ta'ʎer] *nm* (TEC) workshop; (*de artista*) studio.

tallo ['taʎo] *nm* (*de planta*) stem; (*de hierba*) blade; (*brote*) shoot; (*col*) cabbage; (CULIN) candied peel.

tamaño, a [ta'maɲo] *a* such a (*big/small*) // *nm* size; **de** ~ **natural** full-size.

tamarindo [tama'rindo] *nm* tamarind.

tambalearse [tambale'arse] *vr* (*persona*) to stagger; (*vehículo*) to sway.

también [tam'bjen] *ad* (*igualmente*) also, too, as well; (*además*) besides.

tambor [tam'bor] *nm* drum; (ANAT) eardrum; ~ **del freno** brake drum.

tamiz [ta'miθ] *nm* sieve; ~**ar** *vt* to sieve.

tamo ['tamo] *nm* fluff.

tampoco [tam'poko] *ad* nor, neither; **yo** ~ **lo compré** I didn't buy it either.

tampón [tam'pon] *nm* plug; (MED) tampon.

tan [tan] *ad* so; ~ **es así que** so much so that.

tanda ['tanda] *nf* (*gen*) series; (*juego*) set; (*turno*) shift; (*grupo*) gang.

tangente [tan'xente] *nf* tangent.

Tánger ['tanxer] *n* Tangier(s).

tangible [tan'xiβle] *a* tangible.

tanque ['tanke] *nm* (*gen*) tank; (*AUTO, NAUT*) tanker.

tantear [tante'ar] *vt* (*calcular*) to reckon (up); (*medir*) to take the measure of; (*probar*) to test, try out; (*tomar la medida: persona*) to take the measurements of; (*considerar*) to weigh up // *vi* (*DEPORTE*) to score; **tanteo** *nm* (*cálculo*) (rough) calculation; (*prueba*) test, trial; (*DEPORTE*) scoring; (*adivinanzas*) guesswork; **al tanteo** by trial and error.

tanto, a ['tanto, a] *a* (*cantidad*) so much, as much; ~**s** so many, as many; **20 y** ~**s** 20-odd // *ad* (*cantidad*) so much, as much; (*tiempo*) so long, as long; ~ **tú como yo** both you and I; ~ **como eso** it's not as bad as that; ~ **más ... cuanto que** it's all the more ... because; ~ **mejor/peor** so much the better/the worse; ~ **si viene como si va** whether he comes or whether he goes; ~ **es así que** so much so that; **por** *o* **por lo** ~ therefore; **me he vuelto ronco de** *o* **con** ~ **hablar** I have become hoarse with so much talking // *conj:* **con** ~ **que** provided (that); **en** ~ **que** while; **hasta** ~ **(que)** until such time as; **un** ~ (*suma*) certain amount; (*proporción*) so much; (*punto*) point; (*gol*) goal; **al** ~ **up to date; un** ~ **perezoso** somewhat lazy; **al** ~ **de que** because of the fact that // *pron:* **cada uno paga** ~ each one pays so much; **a** ~**s de agosto** on such and such a day in August.

tapar [ta'par] *vt* (*cubrir*) to cover; (*envolver*) to wrap *or* cover up; (*la vista*) to obstruct; (*persona, falta*) to conceal; (*AM*) to fill; ~**se** *vr* to wrap o.s. up.

taparrabo [tapa'rraβo] *nm* (*bañador*) (bathing *or* swimming) trunks *pl.*

tapete [ta'pete] *nm* table cover.

tapia ['tapja] *nf* (garden) wall; **tapiar** *vt* to wall in.

tapicería [tapiθe'ria] *nf* tapestry; (*para muebles*) upholstery; (*tienda*) upholsterer's (shop); **tapiz** *nm* (*alfombra*) carpet; (*tela tejida*) tapestry; **tapizar** *vt* (*pared*) to wallpaper; (*suelo*) to carpet; (*muebles*) to upholster.

tapón [ta'pon] *nm* (*corcho*) stopper; (*TEC*) plug; (*MED*) tampon; ~ **de rosca** *o* **de tuerca** screw-top.

taquigrafía [takiχra'fia] *nf* shorthand; **taquígrafo, a** *nm/f* shorthand writer.

taquilla [ta'kiʎa] *nf* (*donde se compra*) booking office; (*suma recogida*) takings *pl;* **taquillero, a** *a:* **función taquillera** box office success // *nm/f* ticket clerk.

taquímetro [ta'kimetro] *nm* speedometer; (*de control*) tachymeter.

tara ['tara] *nf* (*defecto*) defect; (*COM*) tare.

tarántula [ta'rantula] *nf* tarantula.

tararear [tarare'ar] *vi* to hum.

tardanza [tar'ðanθa] *nf* (*demora*) delay; (*lentitud*) slowness.

tardar [tar'ðar] *vi* (*tomar tiempo*) to take a long time; (*llegar tarde*) to be late; (*demorar*) to delay; **¿tarda mucho el tren?** does the train take long?; **a más** ~ at the latest; **no tardes en venir** come soon, come before long.

tarde ['tarðe] *ad* (*hora*) late; (*después de tiempo*) too late // *nf* (*de día*) afternoon; (*al anochecer*) evening; **de** ~ **en** ~ from time to time; **¡buenas** ~**s!** (*de día*) good afternoon!; (*de noche*) good evening!; **a** *o* **por la** ~ in the afternoon; in the evening.

tardío [tar'ðio] *a* (*retrasado*) late; (*lento*) slow (to arrive).

tardo, a ['tarðo, a] *a* (*lento*) slow; (*torpe*) dull.

tarea [ta'rea] *nf* task; (*ESCOL*) homework; ~ **de ocasión** chore.

tarifa [ta'rifa] *nf* (*lista de precios*) price list; (*COM*) tariff; ~ **completa** all-in cost.

tarima [ta'rima] *nf* (*plataforma*) platform; (*taburete*) stool; (*litera*) bunk.

tarjeta [tar'xeta] *nf* card; ~ **postal/de crédito/de Navidad** postcard/credit card/Christmas card.

tarro ['tarro] *nm* jar, pot.

tarta ['tarta] *nf* (*pastel*) cake; (*torta*) tart.

tartamudear [tartamuðe'ar] *vi* to stammer; **tartamudo, a** *a* stammering // *nm/f* stammerer.

tartana [tar'tana] *nf* (*barco*) dinghy.

tartárico [tar'tariko, a] *a:* **ácido** ~ tartaric acid.

tártaro ['tartaro] *a, nm* Tartar.

tasa ['tasa] *nf* (*precio*) (fixed) price, rate; (*valoración*) valuation; (*medida, norma*) measure, standard; ~ **de interés** rate of interest; ~**ción** *nf* (*gen*) valuation; (*de oro etc*) appraisal; ~**dor** *nm* valuer.

tasajo [ta'saxo] *nm* dried beef.

tasar [ta'sar] *vt* (*arreglar el precio*) to fix a price for; (*valorar*) to value, assess; (*limitar*) to limit.

tasca ['taska] *nf* (*fam*) pub.

tatarabuelo [tatara'βwelo] *nm* great-great-grandfather.

tatuaje [ta'twaxe] *nm* (*dibujo*) tattoo; (*acto*) tattooing; **tatuar** *vt* to tattoo.

taumaturgo [tauma'turxo] *nm* miracle-worker.

taurino, a [tau'rino, a] *a* bullfighting *cpd.*

Tauro ['tauro] *nm* Taurus.

tauromaquia [tauro'makja] *nf* tauromachy.

tautología [tautolo'xia] *nf* tautology.

taxi ['taksi] *nm* taxi.

taxidermia [taksi'ðermja] *nf* taxidermy.

taxista [tak'sista] *nm/f* taxi driver.

taza ['taθa] *nf* cup; (*de retrete*) bowl; ~ **para café** coffee cup; **tazón** *nm* (~ *grande*) large cup; (*escudilla*) basin.

te [te] *pron* (*complemento de objeto*) you; (*complemento indirecto*) (to) you; (*reflexivo*) (to) yourself; **¿** ~ **duele**

mucho el brazo? does your arm hurt a lot?; ~ **equivocas** you're wrong; ¡**cálma**~! calm yourself!

té [te] *nm* tea.

tea ['tea] *nf* torch.

teatral [tea'tral] *a* theatre *cpd*; (*fig*) theatrical; **teatro** *nm* (*gen*) theatre; (*LITERATURA*) plays *pl*, drama.

tebeo [te'βeo] *nm* children's comic.

tecla ['tekla] *nf* key; ~**do** *nm* keyboard; **teclear** *vi* to strum; (*fam*) to drum; **tecleo** *nm* (*MUS; sonido*) strumming; (*forma de tocar*) fingering; (*fam*) drumming.

técnico, a ['tekniko, a] *a* technical // *nm* technician; (*experto*) expert // *nf* (*procedimientos*) technique; (*arte, oficio*) craft.

tecnócrata [tek'nokrata] *nm/f* technocrat.

tecnología [teknolo'xia] *nf* technology; **tecnológico, a** *a* technological; **tecnólogo** *nm* technologist.

techo ['tetʃo] *nm* (*externo*) roof; (*interno*) ceiling; **techumbre** *nf* roof.

tedio ['teðjo] *nm* (*aburrimiento*) boredom; (*apatía*) apathy; (*fastidio*) depression; ~**so, a** *a* boring; (*cansado*) wearisome, tedious.

teja ['texa] *nf* (*azulejo*) tile; (*BOT*) lime (tree); ~**do** *nm* (tiled) roof.

tejanos [te'xanos] *nmpl* jeans.

tejemaneje [texema'nexe] *nm* (*bullicio*) bustle; (*lío*) fuss; (*aspaviento*) to-do; (*intriga*) intrigue.

tejer [te'xer] *vt* to weave; (*AM*) to knit; (*fig*) to fabricate; **tejido** *nm* fabric; (*telaraña*) web; (*estofa, tela*) (knitted) material; (*ANAT*) tissue; (*textura*) texture.

tel, teléf *abr de* **teléfono.**

tela ['tela] *nf* (*material*) material; (*telaraña*) web; (*de fruta, en líquido*) skin; (*del ojo*) film; **telar** *nm* (*máquina*) loom; (*de teatro*) gridiron; **telares** *nmpl* textile mill *sg.*

telaraña [tela'raɲa] *nf* cobweb.

tele ['tele] *nf* (*fam*) TV.

tele... [tele] *pref* tele...; ~**comunicación** *nf* telecommunication; ~**control** *nm* remote control; ~**diario** *nm* television news; ~**difusión** *nf* (television) broadcast; ~**dirigido, a** *a* remote-controlled; ~**férico** *nm* (*tren*) cable-railway; (*de esquí*) ski-lift; ~**fonear** *vi* to telephone; ~**fónico, a** *a* telephone *cpd*; ~**fonista** *nm/f* telephonist; **teléfono** *nm* telephone; ~**foto** *nf* telephoto; ~**grafía** *nf* telegraphy; **telégrafo** *nm* telegraph; (*fam: persona*) telegraph boy; ~**grama** *nm* telegram; ~**impresor** *nm* teleprinter; **telémetro** *nm* rangefinder; ~**objetivo** *nm* telephoto lens; ~**pático, a** *a* telepathic; ~**scópico, a** *a* telescopic; ~**scopio** *nm* telescope; ~**silla** *nf* chairlift; ~**spectador, a** *nm/f* viewer; ~**squí** *nm* ski-lift; ~**tipista** *nm/f* teletypist; ~**tipo** *nm* teletype; ~**vidente** *nm/f* viewer; ~**visar** *vt* to televise;

~**visión** *nf* television; ~**visión en colores** colour television; ~**visor** *nm* television set.

telex [te'leks] *nm* telex.

telón [te'lon] *nm* curtain; ~ **de boca/seguridad** front/safety curtain; ~ **de acero** (*POL*) iron curtain; ~ **de fondo** backcloth, background.

tema ['tema] *nm* (*asunto*) subject, topic; (*MUS*) theme // *nf* (*obsesión*) obsession; (*manía*) ill-will; **tener** ~ **a uno** to have a grudge against sb; **temático, a** *a* thematic.

tembladera [tembla'ðera] *nf* shaking; (*AM*) quagmire.

temblar [tem'blar] *vi* to shake, tremble; (*de frío*) to shiver; **tembleque** *a* shaking // *nm* = **tembladera; temblón, ona** *a* shaking; **temblor** *nm* trembling; (*AM: de tierra*) earthquake; **tembloroso, a** *a* trembling.

temer [te'mer] *vt* to fear // *vi* to be afraid; **temo que llegue tarde** I am afraid he may be late.

temerario, a [teme'rarjo, a] *a* (*descuidado*) reckless; (*arbitrario*) hasty; **temeridad** *nf* (*imprudencia*) rashness; (*audacia*) boldness.

temeroso, a [teme'roso, a] *a* (*miedoso*) fearful; (*que inspira temor*) frightful.

temible [te'miβle] *a* fearsome.

temor [te'mor] *nm* (*miedo*) fear; (*duda*) suspicion.

témpano ['tempano] *nm* (*MUS*) kettledrum; ~ **de hielo** ice-flow; ~ **de tocino** flitch of bacon.

temperamento [tempera'mento] *nm* temperament.

temperatura [tempera'tura] *nf* temperature.

temperie [tem'perje] *nf* state of the weather.

tempestad [tempes'tað] *nf* storm; **tempestuoso, a** *a* stormy.

templado, a [tem'plaðo, a] *a* (*moderado*) moderate; (: *en el comer*) frugal; (: *en el beber*) abstemious; (*agua*) lukewarm; (*clima*) mild; (*MUS*) well-tuned; **templanza** *nf* moderation; abstemiousness; mildness.

templar [tem'plar] *vt* (*moderar*) to moderate; (*furia*) to restrain; (*calor*) to reduce; (*solución*) to dilute; (*afinar*) to tune (up); (*acero*) to temper; (*tuerca*) to tighten up // *vi* to moderate; ~**se** *vr* to be restrained; **temple** *nm* (*humor*) mood; (*ajuste*) tempering; (*afinación*) tuning; (*clima*) temperature; (*pintura*) tempera.

templete [tem'plete] *nm* bandstand.

templo ['templo] *nm* (*iglesia*) church; (*pagano etc*) temple.

temporada [tempo'raða] *nf* time, period; (*estación*) season.

temporal [tempo'ral] *a* (*no permanente*) temporary; (*REL*) temporal // *nm* storm.

tempranero, a [tempra'nero, a] *a* (*BOT*) early; (*persona*) early-rising.

temprano, a [tem'prano, a] *a* early;

(*demasiado pronto*) too soon, too early.
ten *vb ver* **tener.**
tenacidad [tenaθi'ðað] *nf* (*gen*) tenacity; (*dureza*) toughness; (*terquedad*) stubbornness.
tenacillas [tena'θiʎas] *nfpl* (*gen*) tongs; (*para el pelo*) curling tongs; (*MED*) forceps.
tenaz [te'naθ] *a* (*material*) tough; (*persona*) tenacious; (*pegajoso*) sticky; (*terco*) stubborn.
tenaza(s) [te'naθa(s)] *nf(pl)* (*MED*) forceps; (*TEC*) pliers; (*ZOOL*) pincers.
tendal [ten'dal] *nm* awning.
tendedero [tende'ðero] *nm* (*para ropa*) drying-place; (*cuerda*) clothes line.
tendencia [ten'denθja] *nf* tendency; (*proceso*) trend; **tener ~ a** to tend or have a tendency to; **tendencioso, a** *a* tendentious.
tender [ten'der] *vt* (*extender*) to spread out; (*colgar*) to hang out; (*vía férrea, cable*) to lay; (*cuerda*) to stretch // *vi* to tend; **~se** *vr* to lie down; (*fig: dejarse llevar*) to let o.s. go; (: *dejar ir*) to let things go; **~ la cama/la mesa** (*AM*) to make the bed/lay the table.
ténder ['tender] *nm* tender.
tenderete [tende'rete] *nm* (*puesto*) stall; (*carretilla*) barrow; (*exposición*) display of goods; (*jaleo*) mess.
tendero, a [ten'dero, a] *nm/f* shopkeeper.
tendido, a [ten'diðo, a] *a* (*acostado*) lying down, flat; (*colgado*) hanging // *nm* (*ropa*) washing; (*TAUR*) front rows of seats; (*colocación*) laying; (*ARQ: enyesado*) coat of plaster; **a galope ~** flat out.
tendón [ten'don] *nm* tendon.
tendré *etc vb ver* **tener.**
tenducho [ten'dutʃo] *nm* small dirty shop.
tenebroso, a [tene'βroso, a] *a* (*oscuro*) dark; (*fig*) gloomy; (*siniestro*) sinister.
tenedor [tene'ðor] *nm* (*CULIN*) fork; (*poseedor*) holder; **~ de libros** book-keeper.
teneduría [teneðu'ria] *nf* keeping; **~ de libros** book-keeping.
tenencia [te'nenθja] *nf* (*de casa*) tenancy; (*de oficio*) tenure; (*de propiedad*) possession.
tener [te'ner] *vt* (*poseer*) to have; (*en la mano*) to hold; (*caja*) to hold, contain; (*considerar*) to consider; **~ suerte** to be lucky; **~ permiso** to have permission; **tiene 10 años** he is 10 years old; **¿cuántos años tienes?** how old are you?; **~ sed/hambre/frío/calor** to be thirsty/hungry/cold/hot; **~ ganas (de)** to want (to); **~ celos** to be jealous; **~ cuidado** to be careful; **~ razón** to be right; **~ un metro de ancho/de largo** to be one metre wide/long; **~ a bien** to see fit to; **~ en cuenta** to bear in mind, take into account; **~ a menos** to consider it beneath o.s.; **~ a uno en más** (*estima*) to think with the more of sb; **~ a uno por...** to think sb...; **~ por seguro** to be sure; **~ presente** to remember, bear in mind; **~**

que (*obligación*) to have to; **tiene que ser así** it has to be this way; **nos tiene preparada una sorpresa** he has prepared a surprise for us; **¿qué tiene?** what's the matter with him?; **¿ésas tenemos?** what's all this?; **tiene un mes de muerto** he has been dead for a month; **~se** *vr* (*erguirse*) to stand; (*apoyarse*) to lean (on); (*fig*) to control o.s.; (*considerarse*) to consider o.s.
tenería [tene'ria] *nf* tannery.
tengo *etc vb ver* **tener.**
tenia ['tenja] *nf* tapeworm.
teniente [te'njente] *nm* (*rango*) lieutenant; (*ayudante*) deputy.
tenis ['tenis] *nm* tennis; **~ta** *nm/f* tennis player.
tenor [te'nor] *nm* (*tono*) tone; (*sentido*) meaning; (*MUS*) tenor; **a ~ de** on the lines of.
tensar [ten'sar] *vt* to tauten; (*arco*) to draw.
tensión [ten'sjon] *nf* (*gen*) tension; (*TEC*) stress; (*MED*): **~ arterial** blood pressure; **tener la ~ alta** to have high blood pressure; **tenso, a** *a* tense.
tentación [tenta'θjon] *nf* temptation.
tentáculo [ten'takulo] *nm* tentacle.
tentador, a [tenta'ðor, a] *a* tempting // *nm/f* tempter/temptress.
tentar [ten'tar] *vt* (*tocar*) to touch, feel; (*seducir*) to tempt; (*atraer*) to attract; (*probar*) to try (out); (*lanzarse a*) to venture; (*MED*) to probe; **tentativa** *nf* attempt; **tentativa de asesinato** attempted murder.
tentempié [tentem'pje] *nm* (*fam*) snack.
tenue ['tenwe] *a* (*delgado*) thin, slender; (*alambre*) fine; (*insustancial*) tenuous; (*sonido*) faint; (*neblina*) light; (*lazo, vínculo*) slight; **tenuidad** *nf* thinness, fineness; (*ligereza*) lightness; (*sencillez*) simplicity.
teñir [te'ɲir] *vt* to dye; (*fig*) to tinge; **~se** *vr* to dye; **~se el pelo** to dye one's hair.
teología [teolo'xia] *nf* theology.
teorema [teo'rema] *nm* theorem.
teoría [teo'ria] *nf* theory; **en ~** in theory; **teóricamente** *ad* theoretically; **teórico, a** *a* theoretic(al) // *nm/f* theoretician, theorist; **teorizar** *vi* to theorize.
terapéutico, a [tera'peutiko, a] *a* therapeutic.
terapia [te'rapja] *nf* therapy; **~ laboral** occupational therapy.
tercer [ter'θer] *a ver* **tercero.**
tercería [terθe'ria] *nf* (*mediación*) mediation; (*arbitraje*) arbitration.
tercero, tercer, a [ter'θero, ter'θer, a] *a* third // *nm* (*árbitro*) mediator; (*JUR*) third party.
terceto [ter'θeto] *nm* trio.
terciado, a [ter'θjaðo, a] *a* slanting; **azúcar ~** brown sugar.
terciar [ter'θjar] *vt* (*MAT*) to divide into three; (*inclinarse*) to slope; (*llevar*) to wear (across the shoulder) // *vi* (*participar*) to take part; (*hacer de árbitro*) to mediate;

~se vr to come up; ~io, a a tertiary.
tercio [ter'θjo] nm third.
terciopelo [terθjo'pelo] nm velvet.
terco, a ['terko, a] a obstinate; (material) tough.
tergiversación [terxiβersa'θjon] nf (deformación) distortion; (evasivas) prevarication; **tergiversar** vt to distort // vi to prevaricate.
termas ['termas] nfpl hot springs.
terminación [termina'θjon] nf (final) end; (conclusión) conclusion, ending; **terminal** a, nm, nf terminal; **terminante** a (final) final, definitive; (tajante) categorical; **terminar** vt (completar) to complete, finish; (concluir) to end // vi (llegar a su fin) to end; (parar) to stop; (acabar) to finish; **terminarse** vr to come to an end; **terminar por hacer algo** to end up (by) doing sth; **término** nm end, conclusion; (parada) terminus; (límite) boundary; **término medio** average; (fig) middle way; **en último término** (a fin de cuentas) in the last analysis; (como último recurso) as a last resort; **en términos de** in terms of.
terminología [terminolo'xia] nf terminology.
termodinámico, a [termoði'namiko, a] a thermodynamic.
termómetro [ter'mometro] nm thermometer.
termonuclear [termonukle'ar] a thermonuclear.
termo(s) ['termo(s)] nm thermos.
termostato [termo'stato] nm thermostat.
ternero, a [ter'nero, a] nm/f (animal) calf // nf (carne) veal.
terneza [ter'neθa] nf tenderness.
terno ['terno] nm (traje) three-piece suit; (conjunto) set of three.
ternura [ter'nura] nf (trato) tenderness; (palabra) endearment; (cariño) fondness.
terquedad [terke'ðað] nf obstinacy; (dureza) harshness.
terrado [te'rraðo] nm terrace.
terraplén [terra'plen] nm (AGR) terrace; (FERRO) embankment; (MIL) rampart; (cuesta) slope.
terrateniente [terrate'njente] nm landowner.
terraza [te'rraθa] nf (balcón) balcony; (techo) flat roof; (AGR) terrace.
terremoto [terre'moto] nm earthquake.
terrenal [terre'nal] a earthly.
terreno [te'rreno] nm (tierra) land; (parcela) plot; (suelo) soil; (fig) field; **un ~** a piece of land.
terrero, a [te'rrero, a] a (de la tierra) earthy; (vuelo) low; (fig) humble.
terrestre [te'rrestre] a terrestrial; (ruta) land cpd.
terrible [te'rriβle] a (espantoso) terrible; (aterrador) dreadful; (tremendo) awful.
territorio [terri'torjo] nm territory.
terrón [te'rron] nm (de azúcar) lump; (de tierra) clod, lump; **terrones** nmpl land sg.

terror [te'rror] nm terror; **~ífico, a** a terrifying; **~ista** a, nm/f terrorist.
terroso, a [te'rroso, a] a earthy.
terruño [te'rruɲo] nm (pedazo) clod; (parcela) plot; (fig) native soil.
terso, a ['terso, a] a (liso) smooth; (pulido) polished; (fig: estilo) flowing; **tersura** nf smoothness; (brillo) shine.
tertulia [ter'tulja] nf (reunión informal) social gathering; (grupo) group, circle; (sala) clubroom.
tesar [te'sar] vt to tighten up.
tesis ['tesis] nf inv thesis.
tesón [te'son] nm (firmeza) firmness; (tenacidad) tenacity.
tesorero, a [teso'rero, a] nm/f treasurer; **tesoro** nm (gen) treasure; (FIN, POL) treasury.
testaferro [testa'ferro] nm figurehead.
testamentaría [testamenta'ria] nf execution of a will.
testamentario, a [testamen'tarjo, a] a testamentary // nm/f executor/executrix; **testamento** nm will; **testar** vi to make a will.
testarudo, a [testa'ruðo, a] a stubborn.
testero, a [tes'tero, a] nm/f (gen) front // nm (ARQ) front wall.
testes ['testes] nmpl testes.
testículo [tes'tikulo] nm testicle.
testificar [testifi'kar] vt to testify; (fig) to attest // vi to give evidence.
testigo [tes'tixo] nm/f witness; **~ de cargo/descargo** witness for the prosecution/defence; **~ ocular** eye witness.
testimoniar [testimo'njar] vt to testify to; (fig) to show; **testimonio** nm testimony.
teta ['teta] nf (de biberón) teat; (ANAT) nipple; (fam) breast.
tétanos ['tetanos] nm tetanus.
tetera [te'tera] nf teapot.
tetilla [te'tiʎa] nf (ANAT) nipple; (de biberón) teat.
tétrico, a ['tetriko, a] a gloomy, dismal.
textil [teks'til] a textile; **~es** nmpl textiles.
texto ['teksto] nm text; **textual** a textual.
textura [teks'tura] nf (de tejido) texture; (de mineral) structure.
tez [teθ] nf (cutis) complexion; (color) colouring.
ti [ti] pron you; (reflexivo) yourself.
tía ['tia] nf (pariente) aunt; (mujer cualquiera) girl, bird (col); (fam: pej: vieja) old bag; (: prostituta) whore.
tibia ['tiβja] nf tibia.
tibieza [ti'βjeθa] nf (temperatura) tepidness; (fig) coolness; **tibio, a** a lukewarm.
tiburón [tiβu'ron] nm shark.
tic [tik] nm (ruido) click; (de reloj) tick; (MED): **~ nervioso** nervous tic.
tictac [tik'tak] nm (de reloj) tick tock.
tiempo ['tjempo] nm (gen) time; (época, período) age, period; (METEOROLOGÍA) weather; (LING) tense; (edad) age; (de

juego) half; **a** ~ in time; **a un** *o* **al mismo** ~ at the same time; **al poco** ~ very soon (after); **de** ~ **en** ~ from time to time; **hace buen/mal** ~ the weather is fine/bad; **estar a** ~ to be in time; **hace** ~ some time ago; **hacer** ~ to while away the time; **motor de 2** ~**s** two-stroke engine.

tienda ['tjenda] *nf* (*gen*) shop; (*más grande*) store; (*NAUT*) awning; ~ **de campaña** tent.

tienes *etc vb ver* **tener.**

tienta ['tjenta] *nf* (*MED*) probe; (*fig*) tact; **andar a** ~**s** to grope one's way along.

tiento ['tjento] *nm* (*tacto*) touch; (*precaución*) wariness; (*pulso*) steady hand; (*ZOOL*) feeler; (*de ciego*) blind man's stick.

tierno, a ['tjerno, a] *a* (*blando, dulce*) tender; (*fresco*) fresh.

tierra ['tjerra] *nf* earth; (*suelo*) soil; (*mundo*) world; (*país*) country, land; ~ **adentro** inland.

tieso, a ['tjeso, a] *a* (*rígido*) rigid; (*duro*) stiff; (*fig: testarudo*) stubborn; (*fam: orgulloso*) conceited // *ad* strongly.

tiesto ['tjesto] *nm* flowerpot; (*pedazo*) piece of pottery.

tiesura [tje'sura] *nf* rigidity; (*fig*) stubbornness; (*fam*) conceit.

tifo ['tifo] *nm* typhus.

tifoidea [tifoi'ðea] *nf* typhoid.

tifón [ti'fon] *nm* (*huracán*) typhoon; (*de mar*) tidal wave.

tifus ['tifus] *nm* typhus.

tigre ['tixre] *nm* tiger.

tijera [ti'xera] *nf* (*AM*) scissors *pl*; (*ZOOL*) claw; (*persona*) gossip; **de** ~ folding; ~**s** *nfpl* scissors; (*para plantas*) shears; **tijeretear** *vt* to snip // *vi* (*fig*) to meddle.

tildar [til'dar] *vt*: ~ **de** to brand as.

tilde ['tilde] *nf* (*defecto*) defect; (*trivialidad*) triviality; (*TIPOGRAFÍA*) tilde.

tilín [ti'lin] *nm* tinkle.

tilo ['tilo] *nm* lime tree.

timar [ti'mar] *vt* (*robar*) to steal; (*estafar*) to swindle; ~**se** *vr* (*fam*) to make eyes (*con uno* at sb).

timbal [tim'bal] *nm* small drum.

timbrar [tim'brar] *vt* to stamp.

timbre ['timbre] *nm* (*sello*) stamp; (*campanilla*) bell; (*tono*) timbre; (*COM*) stamp duty.

timidez [timi'ðeθ] *nf* shyness; **tímido, a** *a* shy.

timo ['timo] *nm* swindle.

timón [ti'mon] *nm* helm, rudder; **timonel** *nm* helmsman.

tímpano ['timpano] *nm* (*ANAT*) eardrum; (*MUS*) small drum.

tina ['tina] *nf* tub; (*baño*) bathtub; **tinaja** *nf* large jar.

tinglado [tin'glaðo] *nm* (*cobertizo*) shed; (*fig: truco*) trick; (*intriga*) intrigue.

tinieblas [ti'njeßlas] *nfpl* (*gen*) darkness *sg*; (*sombras*) shadows.

tino ['tino] *nm* (*habilidad*) skill; (*MIL*) marksmanship; (*juicio*) insight; (*moderación*) moderation.

tinta ['tinta] *nf* ink; (*TEC*) dye; (*ARTE*) colour.

tinte ['tinte] *nm* (*acto*) dyeing; (*carácter*) tinge; (*barniz*) veneer.

tinterillo [tinte'riʎo] *nm* penpusher.

tintero [tin'tero] *nm* inkwell.

tintinear [tintine'ar] *vt* to tinkle.

tinto, a ['tinto, a] *a* (*teñido*) dyed; (*manchado*) stained // *nm* red wine.

tintorera [tinto'rera] *nf* shark.

tintorería [tintore'ria] *nf* dry cleaner's.

tintura [tin'tura] *nf* (*acto*) dyeing; (*QUÍMICA*) dye; (*farmacéutico*) tincture.

tío ['tio] *nm* (*pariente*) uncle; (*fam: viejo*) old fellow; (: *individuo*) bloke, chap.

tiovivo [tio'ßißo] *nm* roundabout.

típico, a ['tipiko, a] *a* typical.

tiple ['tiple] *nm* soprano (voice) // *nf* soprano.

tipo ['tipo] *nm* (*clase*) type, kind; (*norma*) norm; (*patrón*) pattern; (*hombre*) fellow; (*ANAT*) build; (: *de mujer*) figure; (*IMPRENTA*) type; ~ **bancario/de descuento/de interés/de cambio** bank/discount/interest/exchange rate.

tipografía [tipoxra'fia] *nf* (*tipo*) printing; (*lugar*) printing press; **tipográfico, a** *a* printing; **tipógrafo, a** *nm/f* printer.

tiquismiquis [tikis'mikis] *nm* fussy person // *nmpl* (*querellas*) squabbling *sg*; (*escrúpulos*) silly scruples.

tira ['tira] *nf* strip; (*fig*) abundance; ~ **y afloja** give and take.

tirabuzón [tiraßu'θon] *nm* corkscrew.

tirado, a [ti'raðo, a] *a* (*barato*) dirt-cheap; (*fam: fácil*) very easy // *nf* (*acto*) cast, throw; (*distancia*) distance; (*serie*) series; (*TIPOGRAFÍA*) printing, edition; **de una** ~**a** at one go.

tirador [tira'ðor] *nm* (*mango*) handle; (*ELEC*) flex.

tiranía [tira'nia] *nf* tyranny; **tirano, a** *a* tyrannical // *nm/f* tyrant.

tirante [ti'rante] *a* (*cuerda*) tight, taut; (*relaciones*) strained // *nm* (*ARQ*) brace; (*TEC*) stay; (*correa*) shoulder strap; ~**s** *nmpl* braces; **tirantez** *nf* tightness; (*fig*) tension.

tirar [ti'rar] *vt* (*aventar*) to throw; (*dejar caer*) to drop; (*volcar*) to upset; (*derribar*) to knock down *or* over; (*jalar*) to pull; (*desechar*) to throw out *or* away; (*disipar*) to squander; (*imprimir*) to print; (*dar: golpe*) to deal // *vi* (*disparar*) to shoot; (*jalar*) to pull; (*fig*) to draw; (*fam: andar*) to go; (*tender a, buscar realizar*) to tend to; (*DEPORTE*) to shoot; ~**se** *vr* to throw o.s.; (*fig*) to cheapen o.s.; ~ **abajo** to bring down, destroy; **tira más a su padre** he takes more after his father; **ir tirando** to manage; **a todo** ~ at the most.

tirita [ti'rita] *nf* (sticking) plaster.

tiritar [tiri'tar] *vi* to shiver.

tiro ['tiro] *nm* (*lanzamiento*) throw;

(*disparo*) shot; (*disparar*) shooting; (*DEPORTE*) drive; (*alcance*) range; (*de escalera*) flight (of stairs); (*golpe*) blow; (*engaño*) hoax; ~ **al blanco** target practice; **caballo de** ~ cart-horse; **andar de** ~**s largos** to be all dressed up; **al** ~ (*AM*) at once.

tirón [ti'ron] *nm* (*sacudida*) pull, tug; **de un** ~ in one go.

tirotear [tirote'ar] *vt* to shoot at; ~**se** *vr* to exchange shots; **tiroteo** *nm* exchange of shots, shooting.

tísico, a ['tisiko, a] *a* consumptive.

títere ['titere] *nm* puppet.

titilar [titi'lar] *vi* (*luz, estrella*) to twinkle; (*parpado*) to flutter.

titiritero, a [titiri'tero, a] *nm/f* puppeteer.

titubeante [tituβe'ante] *a* (*inestable*) shaky, tottering; (*farfullante*) stammering; (*dudoso*) hesitant; **titubear** *vi* to stagger; (*fig*) to hesitate; **titubeo** *nm* staggering; stammering; hesitation.

titulado, a [titu'laðo, a] *a* (*libro*) entitled; (*persona*) titled; **titular** *a* titular // *nm/f* occupant // *nm* headline // *vt* to title; **titularse** *vr* to be entitled; **título** *nm* (*gen*) title; (*de diario*) headline; (*certificado*) professional qualification; (*universitario*) university degree; (*fig*) right; **a título de** in the capacity of.

tiza ['tiθa] *nf* chalk.

tizna ['tiθna] *nf* grime; **tiznar** *vt* to blacken; (*fig*) to tarnish.

tizón [ti'θon], **tizo** ['tiθo] *nm* brand; (*fig*) stain.

toalla [to'aʎa] *nf* towel.

tobillo [to'βiʎo] *nm* ankle.

tobogán [toβo'xan] *nm* toboggan; (*montaña rusa*) switchback; (*resbaladilla*) chute, slide.

toca ['toka] *nf* headdress.

tocadiscos [toka'ðiskos] *nm inv* record player.

tocado, a [to'kaðo, a] *a* rotten; (*fam*) touched // *nm* headdress.

tocador [toka'ðor] *nm* (*mueble*) dressing table; (*cuarto*) boudoir; (*neceser*) toilet case; (*fam*) ladies' toilet.

tocante [to'kante]: ~ **a** *prep* with regard to.

tocar [to'kar] *vt* to touch; (*MUS*) to play; (*topar con*) to run into, strike; (*referirse a*) to allude to; (*padecer*) to suffer; (*el pelo*) to do // *vi* (*a la puerta*) to knock (on *or* at the door); (*ser de turno*) to fall to, be the turn of; (*ser hora*) to be due; (*barco, avión*) to call at; (*atañer*) to concern; ~**se** *vr* (*cubrirse la cabeza*) to cover one's head; (*tener contacto*) to touch (each other); **por lo que a mí me toca** as far as I am concerned; **esto toca en la locura** this verges on madness.

tocayo, a [to'kajo, a] *nm/f* namesake.

tocino [to'θino] *nm* bacon.

todavía [toða'βia] *ad* (*aun*) still; (*aún*) yet; ~ **más** yet more; ~ **no** not yet.

todo, a ['toðo, a] *a* all; (*cada*) every;

(*entero*) whole; (*sentido negativo*): **en** ~ **el día lo he visto** I haven't seen him all day; ~**as las semanas**/~**s los martes** every week/Tuesday // *ad* all, completely // *nm* everything // *pron*: ~**s**/~**as** everyone; **a** ~**a velocidad** at full speed; **estaba** ~ **ojos** he was all eyes; **puede ser** ~ **lo honesto que quiera** he can be as honest as he likes; **ante** ~ above all; **en un** ~ as a whole; **corriendo y** ~, **no llegaron a tiempo** even though they ran, they still didn't arrive in time; **con** ~ still, even so; **del** ~ completely.

todopoderoso, a [toðopoðe'roso, a] *a* all powerful; (*REL*) almighty.

toga ['toxa] *nf* toga; (*ESCOL*) gown.

Tokio ['tokjo] *n* Tokyo.

toldo ['toldo] *nm* (*para el sol*) sunshade; (*tienda*) marquee; (*fig*) pride.

tole ['tole] *nm* (*fam*) commotion.

tolerable [tole'raβle] *a* tolerable; **tolerancia** *nf* tolerance; **tolerar** *vt* to tolerate; (*resistir*) to endure.

toma ['toma] *nf* (*gen*) taking; (*MED*) dose.

tomar [to'mar] *vt* (*gen*) to take; (*aspecto*) to take on; (*beber*) to drink // *vi* to take; (*AM*) to drink; ~**se** *vr* to take; ~**se por** to consider o.s. to be; ~ **a bien/a mal** to take well/badly; ~ **en serio** to take seriously; ~ **el pelo a alguien** to pull sb's leg; ~**la con uno** to pick a quarrel with sb.

tomate [to'mate] *nm* tomato; ~**ra** *nf* tomato plant.

tomillo [to'miʎo] *nm* thyme.

tomo ['tomo] *nm* (*libro*) volume; (*tamaño*) size; (*fig*) importance.

ton [ton] *abr de* **tonelada** // *nm*: **sin** ~ **ni son** without rhyme or reason.

tonada [to'naða] *nf* tune.

tonalidad [tonali'ðað] *nf* tone.

tonel [to'nel] *nm* barrel.

tonelada [tone'laða] *nf* ton; **tonelaje** *nm* tonnage.

tonelero [tone'lero] *nm* cooper.

tónico, a ['toniko, a] *a* tonic // *nm* (*MED*) tonic // *nf* (*MUS*) tonic; (*fig*) keynote.

tonificar [tonifi'kar] *vt* to tone up.

tonillo [to'niʎo] *nm* monotonous voice.

tono ['tono] *nm* tone; **fuera de** ~ inappropriate; **darse** ~ to put on airs.

tontería [tonte'ria] *nf* (*estupidez*) foolishness; (*una* ~) stupid remark; ~**s** *nfpl* rubbish *sg*, nonsense *sg*.

tonto, a ['tonto, a] *a* stupid; (*sentimental*) silly // *nm/f* fool; (*payaso*) clown.

topacio [to'paθjo] *nm* topaz.

topar [to'par] *vt* (*tropezar*) to bump into; (*encontrar*) to find, come across; (*ZOOL*) to butt // *vi*: ~ **contra** *o* **en** to run into; ~ **con** to run up against; **el problema topa en eso** that's where the problem lies.

tope ['tope] *a* maximum // *nm* (*fin*) end; (*limite*) limit; (*riña*) quarrel; (*FERRO*) buffer; (*AUTO*) bumper; **al** ~ end to end.

tópico, a ['topiko, a] *a* topical // *nm* platitude.

topo ['topo] *nm* (*ZOOL*) mole; (*fig*) blunderer.

topografía [topoɤra'fia] *nf* topography; **topógrafo, a** *nm/f* topographer.

toque ['toke] *nm* touch; (*MUS*) beat; (*de campana*) peal; (*fig*) crux; **dar un ~ a** to test; **~ de queda** curfew; **~tear** *vt* to handle.

toquilla [to'kiʎa] *nf* (*bufanda*) headscarf; (*chal*) shawl.

torbellino [torbe'ʎino] *nm* whirlwind; (*fig*) whirl.

torcedura [torθe'ðura] *nf* twist; (*MED*) sprain.

torcer [tor'θer] *vt* to twist; (*la esquina*) to turn; (*MED*) to sprain; (*cuerda*) to plait; (*ropa, manos*) to wring; (*persona*) to corrupt // *vi* (*desviar*) to turn off; (*pelota*) to spin; **~se** *vr* (*ladearse*) to bend; (*desviarse*) to go astray; (*fracasar*) to go wrong; **torcido, a** *a* twisted; (*fig*) crooked // *nm* curl.

tordo, a ['torðo, a] *a* dappled // *nm* thrush.

torear [tore'ar] *vt* (*fig: evadir*) to avoid; (*jugar con*) to tease // *vi* to fight bulls; **toreo** *nm* bullfighting; **torero, a** *nm/f* bullfighter.

tormenta [tor'menta] *nf* storm; (*fig: confusión*) turmoil; (*desgracia*) misfortune.

tormento [tor'mento] *nm* torture; (*fig*) anguish.

tornar [tor'nar] *vt* (*devolver*) to return, give back; (*transformar*) to transform // *vi* to go back; **~se** *vr* (*ponerse*) to become; (*volver*) to return.

tornasol [torna'sol] *nm* (*BOT*) sunflower; **papel de ~** litmus paper; **~ado, a** *a* (*brillante*) iridescent; (*reluciente*) shimmering.

torneo [tor'neo] *nm* tournament.

tornero, a [tor'nero, a] *nm/f* machinist.

tornillo [tor'niʎo] *nm* screw.

torniquete [torni'kete] *nm* (*puerta*) turnstile; (*MED*) tourniquet.

torno ['torno] *nm* (*TEC*) winch; (*tambor*) drum; **en ~ (a)** round, about.

toro ['toro] *nm* bull; (*fam*) he-man; **los ~s** bullfighting.

toronja [to'ronxa] *nf* grapefruit.

torpe ['torpe] *a* (*poco hábil*) clumsy, awkward; (*necio*) dim; (*lento*) slow; (*indecente*) crude; (*no honrado*) dishonest.

torpedo [tor'peðo] *nm* torpedo.

torpeza [tor'peθa] *nf* (*falta de agilidad*) clumsiness; (*lentitud*) slowness; (*rigidez*) stiffness; (*error*) mistake; (*crudeza*) obscenity.

torre ['torre] *nf* tower; (*de petróleo*) derrick.

torrente [to'rrente] *nm* torrent.

tórrido, a ['torriðo, a] *a* torrid.

torrija [to'rrixa] *nf* fried bread; **~s** French toast *sg*.

torsión [tor'sjon] *nf* twisting.

torso ['torso] *nm* torso.

torta ['torta] *nf* cake; (*fam*) slap.

tortícolis [tor'tikolis] *nm* stiff neck.

tortilla [tor'tiʎa] *nf* omelette; (*AM*) maize pancake; **~ francesa/española** plain/potato omelette.

tórtola ['tortola] *nf* turtledove.

tortuga [tor'tuxa] *nf* tortoise.

tortuoso, a [tor'twoso, a] *a* winding.

tortura [tor'tura] *nf* torture; **torturar** *vt* to torture.

tos [tos] *nf* cough; **~ ferina** whooping cough.

tosco, a ['tosko, a] *a* coarse.

toser [to'ser] *vi* to cough.

tostado, a [tos'taðo, a] *a* toasted; (*por el sol*) dark brown; (*piel*) tanned // *nf* tan; **tostador** *nm* toaster; **tostar** *vt* to toast; (*café*) to roast; (*al sol*) to tan; **tostarse** *vr* to get brown.

total [to'tal] *a* total // *ad* in short; (*al fin y al cabo*) when all is said and done // *nm* total; **~ que** to cut a long story short.

totalidad [totali'ðað] *nf* whole.

totalitario, a [totali'tarjo, a] *a* totalitarian.

tóxico, a ['toksiko, a] *a* toxic // *nm* poison.

tozudo, a [to'θuðo, a] *a* obstinate.

traba ['traβa] *nf* bond, tie; (*cadena*) fetter.

trabajador, a [traβaxa'ðor, a] *nm/f* worker // *a* hard-working.

trabajar [traβa'xar] *vt* to work; (*arar*) to till; (*empeñarse en*) to work at; (*empujar: persona*) to push; (*convencer*) to persuade // *vi* to work; (*esforzarse*) to strive; **trabajo** *nm* work; (*tarea*) task; (*POL*) labour; (*fig*) effort; **tomarse el trabajo de** to take the trouble to; **trabajo por turno/a destajo** shift work/ piecework; **trabajoso, a** *a* hard; (*MED*) pale.

trabalenguas [traβa'lengwas] *nm inv* tongue twister.

trabar [tra'βar] *vt* (*juntar*) to join, unite; (*atar*) to tie down, fetter; (*agarrar*) to seize; (*amistad*) to strike up; **~se** *vr* to become entangled; (*reñir*) to squabble; **trabazón** *nf* (*TEC*) joining, assembly; (*fig*) bond, link.

trabucar [traβu'kar] *vt* (*confundir*) to confuse, mix up; (*palabras*) to misplace.

tracción [trak'θjon] *nf* traction; **~ delantera/trasera** front-wheel/rear-wheel drive.

tractor [trak'tor] *nm* tractor.

tradición [traði'θjon] *nf* tradition; **tradicional** *a* traditional.

traducción [traðuk'θjon] *nf* translation; **traducir** *vt* to translate; **traductor, a** *nm/f* translator.

traer [tra'er] *vt* (*gen*) to bring; (*llevar*) to carry; (*ropa*) to wear; (*imán*) to draw; (*incluir*) to carry; (*fig*) to cause; **~se** *vr*: **~se algo** to be up to sth; **~se bien/mal** to dress well/badly.

traficar [trafi'kar] *vi* to trade.

tráfico ['trafiko] *nm* (*COM*) trade; (*AUTO*) traffic.

tragaluz [traxa'luθ] *nm* skylight.

tragamonedas [traxamo'neðas] *nm inv,*

tragaperras [traˣa'perras] *nm inv* slot machine.

tragar [tra'ˣar] *vt* to swallow; (*devorar*) to devour, bolt down; ~**se** *vr* to swallow.

tragedia [tra'ˣeðja] *nf* tragedy; **trágico, a** *a* tragic.

trago ['traˣo] *nm* (*líquido*) drink; (*comido de golpe*) gulp; (*fam: de bebida*) swig; (*desgracia*) blow.

traición [trai'ɵjon] *nf* treachery; (*JUR*) treason; (*una* ~) act of treachery; **traicionar** *vt* to betray; **traidor, a, traicionero, a** *a* treacherous // *nm/f* traitor.

traigo *etc vb ver* **traer.**

traje ['traxe] *vb ver* **traer** // *nm* (*gen*) dress; (*de hombre*) suit; (*vestimenta típica*) costume; (*fig*) garb; ~ **de baño** swimsuit; ~ **de luces** bullfighter's costume.

trajera *etc vb ver* **traer.**

trajín [tra'xin] *nm* haulage; (*fam: movimiento*) bustle; **trajines** *nmpl* goings-on; **trajinar** *vt* (*llevar*) to carry, transport // *vi* (*moverse*) to bustle about; (*viajar*) to travel around.

trama ['trama] *nf* (*fig*) link; (: *intriga*) plot; (*de tejido*) weft; **tramar** *vt* to plot; (*TEC*) to weave.

tramitar [trami'tar] *vt* (*asunto*) to transact; (*negociar*) to negotiate; (*manejar*) to handle; **trámite** *nm* (*paso*) step; (*JUR*) transaction; **trámites** *nmpl* (*burocracia*) paperwork *sg*, procedures; (*JUR*) proceedings.

tramo ['tramo] *nm* (*de tierra*) plot; (*de escalera*) flight; (*de vía*) section.

tramoya [tra'moja] *nf* (*TEATRO*) piece of stage machinery; (*fig*) trick; **tramoyista** *nm/f* scene shifter; (*fig*) trickster.

trampa ['trampa] *nf* (*gen*) trap; (*en el suelo*) trapdoor; (*prestidigitación*) conjuring trick; (*engaño*) trick; (*fam*) fiddle; (*de pantalón*) fly; **trampear** *vt, vi* to cheat; **trampista** *nm/f* = **tramposo.**

trampolín [trampo'lin] *nm* trampoline; (*de piscina etc*) diving board.

tramposo, a [tram'poso, a] *a* crooked, cheating // *nm/f* crook, cheat.

tranca ['tranka] *nf* (*palo*) stick; (*viga*) beam; (*de puerta, ventana*) bar; **trancar** *vt* to bar // *vi* to stride along.

trance ['tranɵe] *nm* (*momento difícil*) difficult moment; (*situación crítica*) critical situation; (*estado hipnotizado*) trance.

tranco ['tranko] *nm* stride.

tranquilidad [trankili'ðað] *nf* (*calma*) calmness, stillness; (*paz*) peacefulness; **tranquilizar** *vt* (*calmar*) to calm (down); (*asegurar*) to reassure; **tranquilo, a** *a* (*calmado*) calm; (*apacible*) peaceful; (*mar*) calm; (*mente*) untroubled.

transacción [transak'ɵjon] *nf* transaction.

transar [tran'sar] *vt* = **transigir.**

transbordador [transβorða'ðor] *nm* ferry.

transbordar [transβor'ðar] *vt* to transfer; ~**se** *vr* to change; **transbordo** *nm*

transfer; **hacer transbordo** to change (trains).

transcurrir [transku'rrir] *vi* (*tiempo*) to pass; (*hecho*) to turn out.

transcurso [trans'kurso] *nm*: ~ **del tiempo** lapse (of time).

transeúnte [transe'unte] *a* transient // *nm/f* passer-by.

transferencia [transfe'renɵja] *nf* transference; (*COM*) transfer; **transferir** *vt* to transfer; (*de tiempo*) to postpone.

transfigurar [transfiˣu'rar] *vt* to transfigure.

transformador [transforma'ðor] *nm* transformer.

transformar [transfor'mar] *vt* to transform; (*convertirse*) to convert.

tránsfuga ['transfuˣa] *nm/f* (*MIL*) deserter; (*POL*) turncoat.

transgresión [transˣre'sjon] *nf* transgression.

transición [transi'ɵjon] *nf* transition.

transido, a [tran'siðo, a] *a* overcome.

transigir [transi'xir] *vi* to compromise, make concessions.

transistor [transis'tor] *nm* transistor.

transitar [transi'tar] *vi* to go (from place to place); **tránsito** *nm* transit; (*AUTO*) traffic; (*parada*) stop; **transitorio, a** *a* transitory.

transmisión [transmi'sjon] *nf* (*TEC*) transmission; (*transferencia*) transfer; ~ **en directo/exterior** live/outside broadcast; **transmitir** *vt* (*gen*) to transmit; (*RADIO, TV*) to broadcast.

transparencia [transpa'renɵja] *nf* transparency; (*claridad*) clearness, clarity; (*foto*) slide; **transparentar** *vt* to reveal // *vi* to be transparent; **transparente** *a* transparent; clear; (*ligero*) diaphanous // *nm* curtain.

transpirar [transpi'rar] *vi* to perspire; (*fig*) to transpire.

transponer [transpo'ner] *vt* to transpose; (*cambiar de sitio*) to change the place of // *vi* (*desaparecer*) to disappear; (*ir más allá*) to go beyond; ~**se** *vr* to change places; (*ocultarse*) to hide; (*sol*) to go down.

transportación [transporta'ɵjon] *nf* transportation; **transportar** *vt* to transport; (*llevar*) to carry; **transporte** *nm* transport; (*COM*) haulage.

tranvía [tran'βia] *nm* tram.

trapecio [tra'peɵjo] *nm* trapeze; **trapecista** *nm/f* trapeze artist.

trapero, a [tra'pero, a] *nm/f* ragman.

trapicheos [trapi'tʃeos] *nmpl* (*fam*) schemes, fiddles.

trapisonda [trapi'sonda] *nf* (*jaleo*) row; (*estafa*) swindle.

trapo ['trapo] *nm* (*tela*) rag; (*de cocina*) cloth.

traqueteo [trake'teo] *nm* (*crujido*) crack; (*golpeteo*) rattling.

tras [tras] *prep* (*detrás*) behind; (*después*) after; ~ **de** besides.

trascendencia [trasɵen'denɵja] *nf*

(*importancia*) importance; (*filosofía*) transcendence; **trascendental** a important; transcendental; **trascender** vi (*oler*) to smell; (*evocar*) to evoke, suggest; (*noticias*) to come out; (*suceso*) to have a wide effect; **trascender a** to smack of.

trasegar [trase'xar] vt (*moverse*) to move about; (*vino*) to decant.

trasero, a [tra'sero, a] a back // nm (*ANAT*) bottom; ~s nmpl ancestors.

trasfondo [tras'fondo] nm background.

trasgredir [trasɣre'ðir] vt to contravene.

trashumante [trasu'mante] a migrating.

trasladar [trasla'ðar] vt (*gen*) to move; (*persona*) to transfer; (*postergar*) to postpone; (*copiar*) to copy; (*interpretar*) to interpret; **traslado** nm (*gen*) move; (*mudanza*) move, removal; (*copia*) copy.

traslucir [traslu'θir] vt to show; ~se vr to be translucent; (*fig*) to be revealed.

trasluz [tras'luθ] nm reflected light; **al** ~ against or up to the light.

trasnochar [trasno'tʃar] vi (*acostarse tarde*) to stay up late; (*no dormir*) to have a sleepless night; (*pasar la noche*) to stay the night.

traspasar [traspa'sar] vt (*bala*) to pierce, go through; (*propiedad*) to sell, transfer; (*calle*) to cross over; (*límites*) to go beyond; (*ley*) to break; **traspaso** nm transfer; (*fig*) anguish.

traspié [tras'pje] nm (*caída*) stumble; (*tropezón*) trip; (*fig*) blunder.

trasplantar [trasplan'tar] vt to transplant.

traste ['traste] nm (*MUS*) fret; **dar al** ~ **con algo** to ruin sth.

trastienda [tras'tjenda] nf backshop; **obtener algo por la** ~ to get sth by underhand means.

trasto ['trasto] nm (*mueble*) piece of furniture; (*tarro viejo*) old pot; (*pey: cosa*) piece of junk; (: *persona*) dead loss; ~s nmpl (*TEATRO*) scenery sg.

trastornado, a [trastor'naðo, a] a (*loco*) mad; (*agitado*) crazy; **trastornar** vt to overturn, upset; (*fig: ideas*) to confuse; (: *nervios*) to shatter; (: *persona*) to drive crazy; **trastornarse** vr (*plan*) to fall through; **trastorno** nm (*acto*) overturning; (*confusión*) confusion.

trasunto [tra'sunto] nm copy.

tratable [tra'taβle] a friendly.

tratado [tra'taðo] nm (*POL*) treaty; (*COM*) agreement.

tratamiento [trata'mjento] nm treatment.

tratar [tra'tar] vt (*ocuparse de*) to treat; (*manejar, TEC*) to handle; (*MED*) to treat; (*dirigirse a: persona*) to address // vi: ~ **de** (*hablar sobre*) to deal with, be about; (*intentar*) to try to; ~ **con** (*COM*) to trade in; (*negociar*) to negotiate with; (*tener contactos*) to have dealings with; ~se vr to treat each other; **trato** nm dealings pl; (*relaciones*) relationship; (*comportamiento*) manner; (*COM*) agreement; (*título*) (form of) address.

trauma ['trauma] nm trauma.

través [tra'βes] nm (*fig*) reverse; **al** ~ ad across, crossways; **a** ~ **de** prep across; (*sobre*) over; (*por*) through.

travesaño [traβe'saɲo] nm (*ARQ*) crossbeam; (*DEPORTE*) crossbar.

travesía [traβe'sia] nf (*calle*) cross-street; (*NAUT*) crossing.

travesura [traβe'sura] nf (*broma*) prank; (*ingenio*) wit; **travieso, a** a (*niño*) naughty; (*adulto*) restless; (*ingenioso*) witty // nf crossing; (*ARQ*) crossbeam.

trayecto [tra'jekto] nm (*ruta*) road, way; (*viaje*) journey; (*tramo*) stretch; (*curso*) course; ~**ria** nf trajectory; (*fig*) path.

traza ['traθa] nf (*ARQ*) plan, design; (*aspecto*) looks pl; (*señal*) sign; (*engaño*) trick; (*habilidad*) skill; ~**do, a** a: **bien** ~**do** shapely, well-formed // nm (*ARQ*) plan, design; (*fig*) outline; **trazar** vt (*ARQ*) to plan; (*ARTE*) to sketch; (*fig*) to trace; (*plan*) to follow; **trazo** nm (*línea*) line; (*bosquejo*) sketch.

trébol ['treβol] nm (*BOT*) clover.

trece ['treθe] num thirteen.

trecho ['tretʃo] nm (*distancia*) distance; (*de tiempo*) while; (*fam*) piece; **de** ~ **en** ~ at intervals.

tregua ['treɣwa] nf (*MIL*) truce; (*fig*) lull.

treinta ['treinta] num thirty.

tremendo, a [tre'mendo, a] a (*terrible*) terrible; (*imponente: cosa*) imposing; (*fam: fabuloso*) tremendous; (*divertido*) entertaining.

trémulo, a ['tremulo, a] a quivering.

tren [tren] nm train; ~ **de aterrizaje** undercarriage.

trenza ['trenθa] nf (*de pelo*) plait; **trenzar** vt (*el pelo*) to plait // vi (*en baile*) to weave in and out; **trenzarse** vr (*AM*) to become involved with.

trepadora [trepa'ðora] nf (*BOT*) climber; **trepar** vt, vi to climb; (*TEC*) to drill.

trepidación [trepiða'θjon] nf shaking, vibration; **trepidar** vi to shake, vibrate.

tres [tres] num three.

tresillo [tre'siʎo] nm three-piece suite; (*MUS*) triplet.

treta ['treta] nf (*COM etc*) gimmick; (*fig*) trick.

triángulo ['trjangulo] nm triangle.

tribu ['triβu] nf tribe.

tribuna [tri'βuna] nf (*plataforma*) platform; (*DEPORTE*) stand; (*fig*) public speaking.

tribunal [triβu'nal] nm (*juicio*) court; (*comisión, fig*) tribunal.

tributar [triβu'tar] vt to pay; (*las gracias*) to give; (*cariño*) to show; **tributo** nm (*COM*) tax.

trigal [tri'xal] nm wheat field; **trigo** nm wheat; **trigos** nmpl wheat field(s) (pl).

trigueño, a [tri'xeɲo, a] a (*pelo*) corn-coloured; (*piel*) olive-skinned.

trillado, a [tri'ʎaðo, a] a threshed; (*fig*)

trite, hackneyed; **trilladora** *nf* threshing machine; **trillar** *vt* (*fig*) to frequent; (*AGR*) to thresh.

trimestral [trimes'tral] *a* quarterly; (*ESCOL*) termly; **trimestre** *nm* (*ESCOL*) term.

trincar [trin'kar] *vt* (*atar*) to tie up; (*NAUT*) to lash; (*agarrar*) to pinion.

trinchar [trin'tʃar] *vt* to carve.

trinchera [trin'tʃera] *nf* (*fosa*) trench; (*para vía*) cutting; (*impermeable*) trench-coat.

trineo [tri'neo] *nm* sledge.

trinidad [trini'ðað] *nf* trio; (*REL*): **la T~** the Trinity.

trino ['trino] *nm* trill.

trinquete [trin'kete] *nm* (*TEC*) pawl; (*NAUT*) foremast.

tripa ['tripa] *nf* (*ANAT*) intestine; (*fam*) insides *pl*.

triple ['triple] *a* triple.

triplicado [tripli'kaðo] *a*: **por ~** in triplicate.

tripulación [tripula'θjon] *nf* crew; **tripulante** *nm/f* crewman/woman; **tripular** *vt* (*barco*) to man; (*AUTO*) to drive.

triquiñuela [triki'ɲwela] *nf* trick.

tris [tris] *nm* crack; **en un ~** in an instant.

triste ['triste] *a* (*afligido*) sad; (*sombrío*) melancholy, gloomy; (*desolado*) desolate; (*lamentable*) sorry, miserable; (*viejo*) old; **~za** *nf* (*aflicción*) sadness; (*melancolía*) melancholy.

triturar [tritu'rar] *vt* (*moler*) to grind; (*mascar*) to chew.

triunfar [trjun'far] *vi* (*tener éxito*) to triumph; (*ganar*) to win; **triunfo** *nm* triumph.

trivial [tri'βjal] *a* trivial; **~izar** *vt* to minimize, play down.

triza ['triθa] *nf* bit, piece; **hacer ~s** to smash to bits; **trizar** *vt* to smash to bits.

trocar [tro'kar] *vt* (*COM*) to exchange; (*dinero, de lugar*) to change; (*palabras*) to exchange; (*confundir*) to confuse; (*vomitar*) to vomit.

trocha ['trotʃa] *nf* (*sendero*) by-path; (*atajo*) short cut.

troche ['trotʃe]: **a ~ y moche** *ad* helter-skelter, pell-mell.

trofeo [tro'feo] *nm* (*premio*) trophy; (*éxito*) success.

troj(e) ['trox(e)] *nf* granary.

tromba ['tromba] *nf* whirlwind.

trombón [trom'bon] *nm* trombone.

trombosis [trom'bosis] *nf* thrombosis.

trompa ['trompa] *nf* horn; (*trompo*) humming top; (*hocico*) snout; (*fam*): **cogerse una ~** to get tight.

trompeta [trom'peta] *nf* trumpet; (*clarín*) bugle.

trompo ['trompo] *nm* spinning top.

trompón [trom'pon] *nm* bump.

tronado, a [tro'naðo, a] *a* broken-down.

tronar [tro'nar] *vt* (*AM*) to shoot // *vi* to

thunder; (*fig*) to rage; (*fam*) to go broke.

tronco ['tronko] *nm* (*de árbol, ANAT*) trunk; (*de planta*) stem.

tronchar [tron'tʃar] *vt* (*árbol*) to chop down; (*fig: vida*) to cut short; (*esperanza*) to shatter; (*persona*) to tire out; **~se** *vr* to fall down.

tronera [tro'nera] *nf* (*MIL*) loophole; (*ARQ*) small window.

trono ['trono] *nm* throne.

tropa ['tropa] *nf* (*MIL*) troop; (*soldados*) soldiers *pl*; (*gentío*) mob.

tropel [tro'pel] *nm* (*muchedumbre*) crowd; (*prisa*) rush; (*montón*) throng.

tropelía [trope'lia] *nm* outrage.

tropezar [trope'θar] *vi* to trip, stumble; (*fig*) to slip up; **~ con** (*encontrar*) to run into; (*topar con*) to bump into; (*reñir*) to fall out with; **tropezón** *nm* tripe; (*fig*) blunder.

tropical [tropi'kal] *a* tropical; **trópico** *nm* tropic.

tropiezo [tro'pjeθo] *nm* (*error*) slip, blunder; (*desgracia*) misfortune; (*obstáculo*) snag; (*discusión*) quarrel.

trotamundos [trota'mundos] *nm inv* globetrotter.

trotar [tro'tar] *vi* to trot; **trote** *nm* trot; (*fam*) travelling; **de mucho trote** hard-wearing.

trozo [tro'θo] *nm* bit, piece.

truco ['truko] *nm* (*habilidad*) knack; (*engaño*) trick; **~s** *nmpl* billiards *sg*.

trucha ['trutʃa] *nf* (*pez*) trout; (*TEC*) crane.

trueno ['trweno] *nm* (*gen*) thunder; (*estampido*) boom; (*de arma*) bang.

trueque ['trweke] *nm* exchange; (*COM*) barter.

trufa ['trufa] *nf* (*BOT*) truffle; (*fig: fam*) fib.

truhán, ana [tru'an, ana] *nm/f* rogue.

truncado, a [trun'kaðo, a] *a* truncated; **truncar** *vt* (*cortar*) to truncate; (*la vida etc*) to cut short; (*el desarrollo*) to stunt.

tu [tu] *a* your.

tú [tu] *pron* you.

tubérculo [tu'βerkulo] *nm* (*BOT*) tuber.

tuberculosis [tuβerku'losis] *nf* tuberculosis.

tubería [tuβe'ria] *nf* pipes *pl*; (*conducto*) pipeline; **tubo** *nm* tube, pipe; **tubo de ensayo** test-tube; **tubo de escape** exhaust (pipe).

tuerca ['twerka] *nf* nut.

tuerto, a ['twerto, a] *a* (*torcido*) twisted; (*ciego*) blind in one eye // *nm* one-eyed person; (*ofensa*) wrong; **a ~as** upside-down.

tuétano ['twetano] *nm* (*gen*) marrow; (*BOT*) pith.

tufo ['tufo] *nm* vapour; (*fig: pey*) stench.

tul [tul] *nm* tulle.

tulipán [tuli'pan] *nm* tulip.

tullido, a [tu'ʎiðo, a] *a* crippled; (*cansado*) exhausted.

tumba ['tumba] *nf* (*sepultura*) tomb; (*sacudida*) shake; (*voltereta*) somersault.

tumbar [tum'bar] *vt* to knock down; (*doblar*) to knock over; (*fam: suj: olor*) to overpower // *vi* to fall down; ~**se** (*echarse*) to lie down; (*extenderse*) to stretch out.

tumbo ['tumbo] *nm* (*caída*) fall; (*de vehículo*) jolt; (*momento crítico*) critical moment.

tumido, a [tu'miðo, a] *a* swollen.

tumor [tu'mor] *nm* tumour.

tumulto [tu'multo] *nm* turmoil.

tuna ['tuna] *nf ver* **tuno.**

tunante [tu'nante] *a* rascally.

tunda ['tunda] *nf* (*de tela*) shearing; (*golpeo*) beating; **tundir** *vt* (*tela*) to shear; (*hierba*) to mow; (*fig*) to exhaust; (*fam: golpear*) to beat.

túnel ['tunel] *nm* tunnel.

Túnez ['tuneθ] *nm* Tunisia; (*ciudad*) Tunis.

tuno, a ['tuno, a] *nm/f* (*fam*) rogue // *nf* (*BOT*) prickly pear; (*MUS*) student music group.

tuntún [tun'tun]: **al** ~ *ad* thoughtlessly.

tupido, a [tu'piðo, a] *a* (*denso*) dense; (*fig*) dim; (*tela*) close-woven.

turba ['turßa] *nf* crowd.

turbación [turßa'θjon] *nf* (*molestia*) disturbance; (*preocupación*) worry; **turbado, a** *a* (*molesto*) disturbed; (*preocupado*) worried; **turbar** *vt* (*molestar*) to disturb; (*incomodar*) to upset; **turbarse** *vt* to be disturbed.

turbina [tur'ßina] *nf* turbine.

turbio, a ['turßjo, a] *a* cloudy; (*lenguaje*) confused //-*ad* indistinctly.

turbión [tur'ßjon] *nf* (*fig*) shower.

turbohélice [turßo'eliθe] *nm* turboprop.

turbulencia [turßu'lenθja] *nf* turbulence; (*fig*) restlessness; **turbulento, a** *a* turbulent; (*fig: intranquilo*) restless; (: *ruidoso*) noisy.

turco, a ['turko, a] *a* Turkish.

turismo [tu'rismo] *nm* tourism; (*coche*) saloon car; **turista** *nm/f* tourist; **turístico, a** *a* tourist *cpd.*

turnar [tur'nar] *vi*, ~**se** *vr* to take (it in) turns; **turno** *nm* (*INDUSTRIA*) shift; (*oportunidad, orden de prioridad*) opportunity; (*DEPORTE etc*) turn.

turquesa [tur'kesa] *nf* turquoise.

Turquía [tur'kia] *nf* Turkey.

turrón [tu'rron] *nm* (*dulce*) nougat; (*fam*) sinecure.

tutear [tute'ar] *vt* to address as familiar 'tú'; ~**se** *vr* to be on familiar terms.

tutela [tu'tela] *nf* (*legal*) guardianship; (*instrucción*) guidance; **tutelar** *a* tutelary // *vt* to protect.

tutor, a [tu'tor, a] *nm/f* (*legal*) guardian; (*ESCOL*) tutor.

tuve, tuviera *etc vb ver* **tener.**

tuyo, a ['tujo, a] *a* yours, of yours // *pron* yours; **los** ~**s** (*fam*) your relations, your family.

TVE *nf abr de* **Televisión Española.**

U

u [u] *conj* or.

ubérrimo, a [u'ßerrimo, a] *a* very rich, fertile.

ubicar [ußi'kar] *vt* (*AM*) to place, situate; (: *fig*) to install in a post; ~**se** *vr* to lie, be located.

ubicuo, a [u'ßikwo, a] *a* ubiquitous.

ubre ['ußre] *nf* udder.

U.C.D. *abr de* **Unión del Centro Democrático.**

Ud(s) *abr de* **usted(es).**

ufanarse [ufa'narse] *vr* to boast; ~ **de** to pride o.s. on; **ufano, a** *a* (*arrogante*) arrogant; (*presumido*) conceited.

U.G.T. *abr de* **Unión General de Trabajadores.**

ujier [u'xjer] *nm* usher; (*portero*) doorkeeper.

úlcera ['ulθera] *nf* ulcer; **ulcerar** *vt* to make sore; **ulcerarse** *vr* to ulcerate.

ulterior [ulte'rjor] *a* (*más allá*) farther, further; (*subsecuente, siguiente*) subsequent; ~**mente** *ad* later, subsequently.

últimamente [ultima'mente] *ad* (*recientemente*) lately, recently; (*finalmente*) finally; (*como último recurso*) as a last resort.

ultimar [ulti'mar] *vt* to finish; (*finalizar*) to finalize; (*AM: rematar*) to finish off.

último, a ['ultimo, a] *a* last; (*más reciente*) latest, most recent; (*más bajo*) bottom; (*más alto*) top; (*fig*) final, extreme; **en las** ~**as** on one's last legs; **por** ~ finally.

ultra ['ultra] *a* ultra // *nm/f* extreme right-winger.

ultrajar [ultra'xar] *vt* (*escandalizar*) to outrage; (*insultar*) to insult, abuse; **ultraje** *nm* outrage; insult.

ultramar [ultra'mar] *nm*: **de** *o* **en** ~ abroad, overseas; ~**ino, a** *a* overseas, foreign; ~**inos** *nmpl* groceries; **tienda de** ~**inos** grocer's (shop).

ultranza [ul'tranθa]: **a** ~ *ad* to the death; (*a todo trance*) at all costs; (*completo*) outright.

ultrasónico, a [ultra'soniko, a] *a* ultrasonic.

ulular [ulu'lar] *vi* to howl; (*búho*) to hoot.

umbral [um'bral] *nm* (*gen*) threshold.

umbroso, a [um'broso, a], **umbrío, a** [um'brio, a] *a* shady.

un, una [un, 'una] *det a* // *num* one; *ver* **uno.**

unánime [u'nanime] *a* unanimous; **unanimidad** *nf* unanimity.

unción [un'θjon] *nf* anointing; **extrema** ~ Extreme Unction.

undécimo, a [un'deθimo, a] *a* eleventh.

undular [undu'lar] *vi ver* **ondular.**

ungir [un'xir] *vt* to rub with ointment; (*REL*) to anoint.

ungüento [un'gwento] nm ointment; (fig) salve, balm.

únicamente ['unikamente] ad solely; (solamente) only; **único, a** a only; (solo) sole, single; (sin par) unique.

unidad [uni'ðað] nf unity; (TEC) unit.

unido, a [u'niðo, a] a joined, linked; (fig) united.

unificar [unifi'kar] vt to unite, unify.

uniformar [unifor'mar] vt to make uniform, level up; (persona) to put into uniform; **uniforme** a uniform, equal; (superficie) even // nm uniform; **uniformidad** nf uniformity; (llaneza) levelness, evenness.

unilateral [unilate'ral] a unilateral.

unión [u'njon] nf (gen) union; (acto) uniting, joining; (calidad) unity; (TEC) joint; (fig) closeness, togetherness; **la U~ Soviética** the Soviet Union.

unir [u'nir] vt (juntar) to join, unite; (atar) to tie, fasten; (combinar) to combine // vi to mix well; **~se** vr to join together, unite; (empresas) to merge.

unísono [u'nisono] nm: **al ~** in unison.

universal [uniβer'sal] a universal; (mundial) world cpd.

universidad [uniβersi'ðað] nf university.

universo [uni'βerso] nm universe.

uno ['uno] num, det one // pron one; (alguien) someone, somebody; **~s** some, a few; **~ a ~, ~ por ~** one by one; **cada ~** each or every one; **estar en ~** to be at one; **~ que otro** some, a few; **~s y otros** all of them; **~ y otro** both.

untar [un'tar] vt (gen) to rub; (engrasar) to grease, oil; (MED) to rub with ointment; (fig) to bribe; **~se** vr to be crooked; **unto** nm animal fat; (MED) ointment; (fam) slush fund.

uña ['uɲa] nf (ANAT) nail; (garra) claw; (casco) hoof; (arrancaclavos) claw.

uranio [u'ranjo] nm uranium.

urbanidad [urβani'ðað] nf courtesy, politeness.

urbanismo [urβa'nismo] nm town planning.

urbanización [urβaniθa'θjon] nf housing scheme.

urbano, a [ur'βano, a] a (de ciudad) urban; (cortés) courteous, polite.

urbe [ur'βe] nf large city.

urdimbre [ur'ðimbre] nf (de tejido) warp; (intriga) intrigue; **urdir** vt to warp; (fig) to plot, contrive.

urgencia [ur'xenθja] nf urgency; (prisa) haste, rush; **servicios de ~** emergency services; **urgente** a urgent; (insistente) insistent; **urgir** vi to be urgent.

urinario, a [uri'narjo, a] a urinary // nm urinal.

urna ['urna] nf urn; (POL) ballot box.

urraca [u'rraka] nf magpie.

URSS nf: **la ~** the USSR.

Uruguay [uru'xwai] nm: **el ~** Uruguay; **uruguayo, a** a, nm/f Uruguayan.

usado, a [u'saðo, a] a (gen) used; (ropa etc) worn.

usanza [u'sanθa] nf custom, usage.

usar [u'sar] vt to use; (ropa) to wear; (tener costumbre) to be in the habit of; **~se** vr to be used; **uso** nm use; wear; (costumbre) usage, custom; (moda) fashion; **al uso** in keeping with custom; **al uso de** in the style of.

usted [us'teð] pron you.

usual [u'swal] a usual.

usuario, a [usu'arjo, a] nm/f user.

usura [u'sura] nf usury; **usurero, a** nm/f usurer.

usurpar [usur'par] vt to usurp.

utensilio [uten'siljo] nm tool; (CULIN) utensil.

útero ['utero] nm uterus, womb.

útil ['util] a useful // nm tool; **utilidad** nf usefulness; (COM) profit; **utilizar** vt to use, utilize.

utopía [uto'pia] nf Utopia; **utópico, a** a Utopian.

uva ['uβa] nf grape.

V

v abr de **voltio.**

va vb ver **ir.**

vaca ['baka] nf (animal) cow; (carne) beef; (cuero) cowhide.

vacaciones [baka'θjones] nfpl holidays.

vacante [ba'kante] a vacant, empty // nf vacancy.

vacar [ba'kar] vi to fall vacant; **~ a o en** to devote o.s. to.

vaciado, a [ba'θjaðo, a] a (hecho en molde) cast in a mould; (hueco) hollow // nm cast.

vaciar [ba'θjar] vt to empty out; (ahuecar) to hollow out; (moldear) to cast // vi (río) to flow (en into); **~se** vr to empty; (fig) to blab, spill the beans.

vaciedad [baθje'ðað] nf emptiness.

vacilación [baθila'θjon] nf hesitation; **vacilante** a unsteady; (habla) faltering; (fig) hesitant; **vacilar** vi to be unsteady; to falter; to hesitate, waver; (persona) to stagger, stumble; (memoria) to fail.

vacío, a [ba'θio, a] a empty; (puesto) vacant; (desocupado) idle; (vano) vain // nm emptiness; (FÍSICA) vacuum; (un ~) (empty) space.

vacuna [ba'kuna] nf vaccine; **vacunar** vt to vaccinate.

vacuno, a [ba'kuno, a] a bovine.

vacuo, a ['bakwo, a] a empty.

vadear [baðe'ar] vt (río) to ford; (problema) to overcome; (persona) to sound out; **vado** nm ford; (solución) solution; (descanso) respite.

vagabundo, a [baxa'βundo, a] a wandering; (pey) vagrant // nm tramp.

vagamente [baxa'mente] ad vaguely.

vagancia [ba'xanθja] nf vagrancy; **vagar** vi (gen) to wander; (no hacer nada) to idle // nm leisure.

vagido [ba'xiðo] *nm* wail.

vagina [ba'xina] *nf* vagina.

vago, a ['baɣo, a] *a* vague; (*perezoso*) lazy; (*ambulante*) wandering // *nm/f* (*vagabundo*) tramp; (*flojo*) lazybones *sg*, idler.

vagón [ba'xon] *nm* (*de pasajeros*) carriage; (*de mercancías*) wagon.

vaguedad [baɣe'ðað] *nf* vagueness.

vaho ['bao] *nm* (*vapor*) vapour, steam; (*olor*) smell; (*respiración*) breath.

vaina ['baina] *nf* sheath.

vainilla [bai'niʎa] *nf* vanilla.

vais *vb ver* **ir**.

vaivén [bai'ßen] *nm* to-and-fro movement; (*de tránsito*) coming and going; **vaivenes** *nmpl* (*fig*) ups and downs.

vajilla [ba'xiʎa] *nf* crockery, dishes *pl*.

val, valdré *etc vb ver* **valer**.

vale ['bale] *nm* (*vapor*) voucher; (*recibo*) receipt; (*pagaré*) I.O.U.

valedero, a [bale'ðero, a] *a* valid.

valenciano, a [balen'θjano, a] *a* Valencian.

valentía [balen'tia] *nf* courage, bravery; (*pey*) boastfulness; (*acción*) heroic deed; **valentón, ona** *a* blustering.

valer [ba'ler] *vt* to aid, protect; (*MAT*) to equal // *vi* to be worth; (*costar*) to cost; (*ser útil*) to be useful; (*ser válido*) to be valid; **~se** *vr* to defend o.s.; **~se de** to make use of, take advantage of // *nm* worth, value; **~ la pena** to be worthwhile; **¿vale?** O. K.?

valgo *etc vb ver* **valer**.

validar [bali'ðar] *vt* to validate; **validez** *nf* validity; **válido, a** *a* valid.

valiente [ba'ljente] *a* brave, valiant; (*pey*) boastful // *nm* hero.

valija [ba'lixa] *nf* case; (*mochila*) satchel.

valioso, a [ba'ljoso, a] *a* valuable; (*rico*) wealthy.

valor [ba'lor] *nm* value, worth; (*precio*) price; (*valentía*) valour, courage; (*importancia*) importance; **~es** *nmpl* (*COM*) securities; **~ación** *nf* valuation; **~ar** *vt* to value.

vals [bals] *nm* waltz.

válvula ['balßula] *nf* valve.

valla ['baʎa] *nf* fence; (*DEPORTE*) hurdle; (*fig*) barrier; **vallar** *vt* to fence in.

valle ['baʎe] *nm* valley, vale.

vamos *vb ver* **ir**.

vampiro, resa [bam'piro, i'resa] *nm/f* vampire.

van *vb ver* **ir**.

vanagloriarse [banaɣlo'rjarse] *vr* to boast.

vándalo, a ['bandalo, a] *nm/f* vandal; **vandalismo** *nm* vandalism.

vanguardia [ban'gwarðja] *nf* vanguard; (*ARTE*) avant-garde.

vanidad [bani'ðað] *nf* vanity; (*irrealidad*) unreality; **vanidoso, a** *a* vain, conceited.

vano, a ['bano, a] *a* (*irreal*) unreal; (*irracional*) unreasonable; (*inútil*) useless;

(*persona*) vain, conceited; (*frívolo*) frivolous.

vapor [ba'por] *nm* vapour; (*vaho*) steam; (*neblina*) mist; **~es** *nmpl* (*MED*) hysterics; **al ~** (*CULIN*) steamed; **~izar** *vt* to vaporize; **~oso, a** *a* vaporous; (*vahoso*) steamy.

vaquero, a [ba'kero, a] *a* cattle *cpd* // *nm* cowboy; **~s** *nmpl* jeans.

vara ['bara] *nf* stick, wand; (*TEC*) rod.

varear [bare'ar] *vt* to hit, beat.

variable [ba'rjaßle] *a, nf* variable; **variación** *nf* variation; **variar** *vt* to vary; (*modificar*) to modify; (*cambiar de posición*) to switch around // *vi* to vary; **variedad** *nf* variety.

varilla [ba'riʎa] *nf* stick; (*BOT*) twig; (*TEC*) rod; (*de rueda*) spoke.

vario, a ['barjo, a] *a* (*variado*) varied; (*multicolor*) motley; (*cambiable*) changeable; **~s** various, several.

varón [ba'ron] *nm* male, man; **varonil** *a* manly.

Varsovia [bar'soßja] *n* Warsaw.

vas *vb ver* **ir**.

vascongado, a [baskon'xaðo, a], **vascuence** [bas'kwenθe], **vasco, a** ['basko, a] *a* Basque; **las Vascongadas** the Basque Country.

vaselina [base'lina] *nf* vaseline.

vasija [ba'sixa] *nf* container, vessel.

vaso ['baso] *nm* glass, tumbler; (*ANAT*) vessel.

vástago ['bastaxo] *nm* (*BOT*) shoot; (*TEC*) rod; (*fig*) offspring.

vasto, a ['basto, a] *a* vast, huge.

Vaticano [bati'kano] *nm*: **el ~** the Vatican.

vaticinio [bati'θinjo] *nm* prophecy.

vatio ['batjo] *nm* (*ELEC*) watt.

vaya *etc vb ver* **ir**.

Vd(s) *abr de* **usted(es)**.

ve *vb ver* **ir, ver**.

vecindad [beθin'dað] *nf*, **vecindario** [beθin'darjo] *nm* neighbourhood; (*habitantes*) residents *pl*; **vecino, a** *a* neighbouring // *nm/f* neighbour; (*residente*) resident.

veda ['beða] *nf* prohibition.

vedado [be'ðaðo] *nm* preserve.

vedar [be'ðar] *vt* (*prohibir*) to ban, prohibit; (*impedir*) to stop, prevent.

vegetación [bexeta'θjon] *nf* vegetation.

vegetal [bexe'tal] *a, nm* vegetable.

vehemencia [bee'menθja] *nf* (*insistencia*) vehemence; (*pasión*) passion; (*fervor*) fervour; (*violencia*) violence; **vehemente** *a* vehement; passionate; fervent.

vehículo [be'ikulo] *nm* vehicle; (*MED*) carrier.

veía *etc vb ver* **ver**.

veinte ['beinte] *num* twenty.

vejación [bexa'θjon] *nf* vexation; (*humillación*) humiliation.

vejamen [be'xamen] *nm* satire.

vejar [be'xar] vt (irritar) to annoy, vex; (humillar) to humiliate.

vejez [be'xeθ] nf old age.

vejiga [be'xixa] nf (ANAT) bladder.

vela ['bela] nf (de cera) candle; (NAUT) sail; (insomnio) sleeplessness; (vigilia) vigil; (MIL) sentry duty; (fam) snot; **estar a dos ~s** (fam) to be skint (fam).

velado, a [be'laðo, a] a veiled; (sonido) muffled; (FOTO) blurred // nf soirée.

velador [bela'ðor] nm watchman; (candelero) candlestick.

velar [be'lar] vt (hacer guardia) to keep watch over; (cubrir) to veil // vi to stay awake; **~ por** to watch over, look after.

veleidad [belei'ðað] nf (ligereza) fickleness; (capricho) whim.

velero [be'lero] nm (NAUT) sailing ship; (AVIAT) glider.

veleta [be'leta] nf weather vane.

velo ['belo] nm veil.

velocidad [beloθi'ðað] nf speed; (TEC, AUTO) gear.

velocímetro [belo'θimetro] nm speedometer.

velódromo [be'loðromo] nm cycle track.

veloz [be'loθ] a fast.

vello ['beλo] nm down, fuzz; **vellón** nm fleece; **~so, a** a fuzzy; **velludo, a** a shaggy // nm plush, velvet.

ven vb ver **venir**.

vena ['bena] nf vein.

venablo [be'naβlo] nm javelin.

venado [be'naðo] nm deer.

venal [be'nal] a (ANAT) venous; (pey) venal; **~idad** nf venality.

vencedor, a [benθe'ðor, a] a victorious // nm/f victor, winner.

vencer [ben'θer] vt (dominar) to defeat, beat; (derrotar) to vanquish; (superar, controlar) to overcome, master // vi (triunfar) to win (through), triumph; (plazo) to expire; **vencido, a** a (derrotado) defeated, beaten; (COM) due // ad: **pagar vencido** to pay in arrears; **vencimiento** nm collapse; (COM) maturity.

venda ['benda] nf bandage; **~je** nm bandage, dressing; **vendar** vt to bandage; **vendar los ojos** to blindfold.

vendaval [benda'βal] nm (viento) gale; (huracán) hurricane.

vendedor, a [bende'ðor, a] nm/f seller.

vender [ben'der] vt to sell; **~ al contado/al por mayor/al por menor** to sell for cash/wholesale/retail.

vendimia [ben'dimja] nf grape harvest.

vendré etc vb ver **venir**.

veneno [be'neno] nm poison, venom; **~so, a** a poisonous.

venerable [bene'raβle] a venerable; **veneración** nf veneration; **venerar** vt (reconocer) to venerate; (adorar) to worship.

venéreo, a [be'nereo, a] a venereal.

venero [be'nero] nm (veta) seam, lode; (fuente) spring.

venezolano, a [beneθo'lano, a] a Venezuelan.

Venezuela [bene'θwela] nf Venezuela.

venganza [ben'ganθa] nf vengeance, revenge; **vengar** vt to avenge; **vengarse** vr to take revenge; **vengativo, a** a (persona) vindictive.

vengo etc vb ver **venir**.

venia ['benja] nf (perdón) pardon; (permiso) consent.

venial [be'njal] a venial.

venida [be'niða] nf (llegada) arrival; (regreso) return; (fig) rashness.

venidero, a [beni'ðero, a] a coming, future.

venir [be'nir] vi to come; (llegar) to arrive; (fig) to stem from; (ocurrir) to happen; **~ bien/mal** to be suitable/unsuitable; **el año que viene** next year; **~se abajo** to collapse.

venta ['benta] nf (COM) sale; **~ a plazos** hire purchase; **~ al contado/al por mayor/al por menor** o **al detalle** cash sale/ wholesale/retail; **~ de liquidación** clearance sale.

ventaja [ben'taxa] nf advantage; **ventajoso, a** a advantageous.

ventana [ben'tana] nf window; **~ de guillotina/saladiza** sash/bay window; **ventanilla** nf (de taquilla) window (of booking office etc).

ventear [bente'ar] vt (ropa) to hang out to dry; (oler) to sniff // vi (investigar) to investigate; (soplar) to blow; **~se** vr (romperse) to crack; (ANAT) to break wind.

ventilación [bentila'θjon] nf ventilation; (corriente) draught; **ventilar** vt to ventilate; (a secar) to put out to dry; (fig) to air, discuss.

ventisca [ben'tiska] nf, **ventisquero** [bentis'kero] nm blizzard; (nieve amontonada) snowdrift.

ventosear [bentose'ar] vi to break wind.

ventoso, a [ben'toso, a] a windy.

ventrílocuo, a [ben'trilokwo, a] nm/f ventriloquist; **ventriloquia** nf ventriloquism.

ventura [ben'tura] nf (felicidad) happiness; (buena suerte) luck; (destino) fortune; **a la (buena) ~** at random; **venturoso, a** a happy; (afortunado) lucky, fortunate.

veo etc vb ver **ver**.

ver [ber] vt, vi to see; (mirar) to look at, watch; (investigar) to look into; **~se** vr (encontrarse) to meet; (dejarse ~) to be seen; (hallarse: en un apuro) to find o.s., be // nm looks pl, appearance; **a ~** let's see; **dejarse ~** to become apparent; **no tener nada que ~ con** to have nothing to do with; **a mi modo de ~** as I see it.

vera ['bera] nf edge, verge; (de río) bank.

veracidad [beraθi'ðað] nf truthfulness.

veranear [berane'ar] vi to spend the summer; **veraneo** nm summer holiday; **veraniego, a** a summer cpd; **verano** nm summer.

veras ['beras] *nfpl* truth *sg*; **de** ~ really, truly.

veraz [be'raθ] *a* truthful.

verbal [ber'βal] *a* verbal.

verbena [ber'βena] *nf* street party.

verbigracia [berβi'ɣraθja] *ad* for example.

verbo [ber'βo] *nm* verb; ~**so, a** *a* verbose.

verdad [ber'ðað] *nf* (*lo verídico*) truth; (*fiabilidad*) reliability // *ad* really; **de** ~ *a* real, proper; **a decir** ~ to tell the truth; ~**ero, a** *a* (*veraz*) true, truthful; (*fiable*) reliable; (*fig*) real.

verde ['berðe] *a* green; (*sucio*) blue, dirty // *nm* green; **viejo** ~ dirty old man; ~**ar,** ~**cer** *vi* to turn green; **verdor** *nm* (*lo* ~) greenness; (*BOT*) verdure; (*fig*) youthful vigour.

verdugo [ber'ðuɣo] *nm* executioner; (*BOT*) shoot; (*cardenal*) weal.

verdulero, a [berðu'lero, a] *nm/f* greengrocer.

verdura [ber'ðura] *nf* greenness; ~**s** *nfpl* (*CULIN*) greens.

vereda [be'reða] *nf* path.

veredicto [bere'ðikto] *nm* verdict.

vergonzoso, a [berɣon'θoso, a] *a* shameful; (*tímido*) timid, bashful.

vergüenza [ber'ɣwenθa] *nf* shame, sense of shame; (*timidez*) bashfulness; (*pudor*) modesty.

verídico, a [be'riðiko, a] *a* true, truthful.

verificar [berifi'kar] *vt* to check; (*corroborar*) to verify; (*llevar a cabo*) to carry out; ~**se** *vr* to occur, happen.

verja ['berxa] *nf* grating.

vermut [ber'mut] *nm* vermouth.

verosímil [bero'simil] *a* likely, probable; (*relato*) credible.

verruga [be'rruɣa] *nf* wart.

versado, a [ber'saðo, a] *a*: ~ **en** versed in.

versar [ber'sar] *vi* to go round, turn.

versátil [ber'satil] *a* versatile.

versión [ber'sjon] *nf* version; (*traducción*) translation.

verso ['berso] *nm* (*gen*) verse; **un** ~ a line of poetry.

vértebra ['berteβra] *nf* vertebra.

verter [ber'ter] *vt* (*vaciar*) to empty, pour (out); (*tirar*) to dump // *vi* to flow.

vertical [berti'kal] *a* vertical.

vértice ['bertiθe] *nm* vertex, apex.

vertiente [ber'tjente] *nf* slope.

vertiginoso, a [bertixi'noso, a] *a* giddy, dizzy; **vértigo** *nm* vertigo; (*mareo*) dizziness.

vesícula [be'sikula] *nf* blister.

vespertino, a [besper'tino, a] *a* evening *cpd*.

vestíbulo [bes'tiβulo] *nm* hall; (*de teatro*) foyer.

vestido [bes'tiðo] *nm* (*ropa*) clothes *pl*, clothing; (*de mujer*) dress, frock.

vestigio [bes'tixjo] *nm* (*trazo*) trace; (*señal*) sign; ~**s** *nmpl* remains.

vestimenta [besti'menta] *nf* clothing.

vestir [bes'tir] *vt* (*poner: ropa*) to put on; (*llevar: ropa*) to wear; (*cubrir*) to clothe, cover; (*pagar: la ropa*) to pay for the clothing of; (*sastre*) to make clothes for // *vi* (*ponerse: ropa*) to dress; (*verse bien*) to look good; ~**se** *vr* to get dressed, dress o.s.

vestuario [bes'twarjo] *nm* clothes *pl*, wardrobe; (*TEATRO*) dressing room; (*DEPORTE*) changing room.

veta ['beta] *nf* (*vena*) vein, seam; (*raya*) streak; (*de madera*) grain.

vetar [be'tar] *vt* to veto.

veterano, a [bete'rano, a] *a, nm* veteran.

veterinario, a [beteri'narjo, a] *nm/f* vet(erinary surgeon) // *nf* veterinary science.

veto ['beto] *nm* veto.

vetusto, a [be'tusto, a] *a* ancient.

vez [beθ] *nf* time; (*turno*) turn; **a la** ~ **que** at the same time as; **a su** ~ in its turn; **cada** ~ **más/menos** more and more/less and less; **una** ~ once; **de una** ~ in one go; **de una** ~ **para siempre** once and for all; **en** ~ **de** instead of; **a veces** sometimes; **una** ~ **y otra** ~ repeatedly; **de** ~ **en cuando** from time to time; **7 veces 9** 7 times 9; **hacer las veces de** to stand in for; **tal** ~ perhaps.

v. g., v. gr. *abr de* **verbigracia.**

vía ['bia] *nf* track, route; (*FERRO*) line; (*fig*) way; (*ANAT*) passage, tube // *prep* via, by way of; **por** ~ **judicial** by legal means; **por** ~ **oficial** through official channels; **por** ~ **de** by way of; **en** ~**s de** in the process of; ~ **aérea** airway.

viaducto [bja'ðukto] *nm* viaduct.

viajante [bja'xante] *nm* commercial traveller.

viajar [bja'xar] *vi* to travel; **viaje** *nm* journey; (*gira*) tour; (*NAUT*) voyage; **estar de viaje** to be on a journey; **viaje de ida y vuelta** round trip; **viaje de novios** honeymoon; **viajero, a** *a* travelling; (*ZOOL*) migratory // *nm/f* (*quien viaja*) traveller; (*pasajero*) passenger.

vial [bjal] *a* road *cpd*, traffic *cpd*.

víbora ['biβora] *nf* viper.

vibración [biβra'θjon] *nf* vibration; **vibrador** *nm* vibrator; **vibrante** *a* vibrant; **vibrar** *vt*, *vi* to vibrate.

vicario [bi'karjo] *nm* curate.

vicepresidente [biθepresi'ðente] *nm/f* vice president.

viciado, a [bi'θjaðo, a] *a* (*corrompido*) corrupt; (*contaminado*) foul, contaminated; **viciar** *vt* (*pervertir*) to pervert; (*adulterar*) to adulterate; (*falsificar*) to falsify; (*JUR*) to nullify; (*estropear*) to spoil; (*sentido*) to twist; **viciarse** *vr* to become corrupted.

vicio ['biθjo] *nm* (*libertinaje*) vice; (*mala costumbre*) bad habit; (*mimo*) spoiling; (*alabeo*) warp, warping; ~**so, a** *a* (*muy malo*) vicious; (*corrompido*) depraved; (*mimado*) spoiled // *nm/f* depraved person.

vicisitud [biθisi'tuð] *nf* vicissitude.

víctima ['biktima] nf victim.

victoria [bik'torja] nf victory; **victorioso, a** a victorious.

vicuña [bi'kuɲa] nf vicuna.

vid [bið] nf vine.

vida ['biða] nf (gen) life; (duración) lifetime; **de por ~** for life; **en la/mi ~** never; **estar con ~** to be still alive; **ganarse la ~** to earn one's living.

vidriero, a [bi'ðrjero, a] nm/f glazier // nf (ventana) stained-glass window; (puerta) glass door.

vidrio ['biðrjo] nm glass; **~so, a** a glassy; (frágil) fragile, brittle; (resbaladizo) slippery.

viejo, a ['bjexo, a] a old // nm/f old man/woman.

vienes etc vb ver **venir**.

vienés, esa [bje'nes, esa] a Viennese.

viento ['bjento] nm wind; (olfato) scent.

vientre ['bjentre] nm belly; (matriz) womb; **~s** nmpl bowels.

viernes ['bjernes] nm inv Friday.

Vietnam [bjet'nam] nm: **el ~** Vietnam; **vietnamita** a Vietnamese.

viga ['biɣa] nf beam, rafter.

vigencia [bi'xenθja] nf validity; **estar en ~** to be in force; **vigente** a valid, in force; (imperante) prevailing.

vigésimo, a [bi'xesimo, a] a twentieth.

vigía [bi'xia] nm look-out // nf (atalaya) watchtower; (acción) watching.

vigilancia [bixi'lanθja] nf vigilance; **vigilar** vt to watch over // vi (gen) to be vigilant; (hacer guardia) to keep watch.

vigilia [vi'xilja] nf wakefulness, being awake; (REL) fast; **comer de ~** to fast.

vigor [bi'ɣor] nm vigour, vitality; **en ~** in force; **entrar/poner en ~** to take/put into effect; **~oso, a** a vigorous.

vil [bil] a vile, low; **~eza** nf vileness; (acto) base deed.

vilipendiar [bilipen'djar] vt to vilify, revile.

vilo ['bilo]: **en ~** ad in the air, suspended.

villa ['biʎa] nf (pueblo) small town; (municipalidad) municipality.

villorrio [bi'ʎorrjo] nm one-horse town, dump (fam).

vinagre [bi'naɣre] nm vinegar.

vinculación [binkula'θjon] nf (lazo) link, bond; (acción) linking; **vincular** vt to link, bind; **vínculo** nm link, bond.

vindicar [bindi'kar] vt to vindicate; (vengar) to avenge; (JUR) to claim.

vine etc vb ver **venir**.

vinicultura [binikul'tura] nf wine growing.

viniera etc vb ver **venir**.

vino ['bino] nm wine.

viña ['biɲa] nf, **viñedo** [bi'ɲeðo] nm vineyard.

violación [bjola'θjon] nf violation; **~ (sexual)** rape; **violar** vt to violate; to rape.

violencia [bjo'lenθja] nf (fuerza) violence, force; (embarazo) embarrassment; (acto injusto) unjust act; **violentar** vt to force; (casa) to break into; (agredir) to assault; (violar) to violate; **violento, a** a violent; (furioso) furious; (situación) embarrassing; (acto) forced, unnatural; (difícil) awkward.

violeta [bjo'leta] nf violet.

violín [bjo'lin] nm violin.

violón [bjo'lon] nm double bass.

viraje [bi'raxe] nm turn; (de vehículo) swerve; (de carretera) bend; (fig) change of direction; **virar** vt, vi to change direction.

virgen ['birxen] a, nf virgin.

Virgo ['birxo] nm Virgo.

viril [bi'ril] a virile; **~idad** nf virility.

virtualmente [birtwal'mente] ad virtually.

virtud [bir'tuð] nf virtue; **virtuoso, a** a virtuous // nm/f virtuoso.

viruela [bi'rwela] nf smallpox; **~s** nfpl pockmarks; **~s locas** chickenpox.

virulento, a [biru'lento, a] a virulent.

virus ['birus] nm virus.

visado [bi'saðo] nm visa.

viscoso, a [bis'koso, a] a viscous.

visera [bi'sera] nf visor.

visibilidad [bisiβili'ðað] nf visibility; **visible** a visible; (fig) obvious.

visión [bi'sjon] nf (ANAT) vision, (eye)sight; (fantasía) vision, fantasy; (panorama) view; **visionario, a** a (que preve) visionary; (alucinado) deluded // nm/f visionary; (chalado) lunatic.

visita [bi'sita] nf call, visit; (persona) visitor; **visitar** vt to visit, call on; (inspeccionar) to inspect.

vislumbrar [bislum'brar] vt to glimpse, catch a glimpse of; **vislumbre** nf glimpse; (centelleo) gleam; (idea vaga) glimmer.

viso ['biso] nm (del metal) glint, gleam; (de tela) sheen; (aspecto) appearance.

visón [bi'son] nm mink.

visor [bi'sor] nm (FOTO) viewfinder.

víspera ['bispera] nf eve, day before.

vista ['bista] nf sight, vision; (capacidad de ver) (eye)sight; (mirada) look(s) (pl) // nm customs officer; **a primera ~** at first glance; **hacer la ~ gorda** to turn a blind eye; **volver la ~** to look back; **está a la ~ que** it's obvious that; **en ~ de** in view of; **en ~ de que** in view of the fact that; **¡hasta la ~!** so long!, see you!; **con ~s a** with a view to; **~zo** nm glance; **dar o echar un ~zo a** to glance at.

visto etc vb ver **vestir**.

visto, a ['bisto, a] pp de ver // a seen; (considerado) considered // nm: **~ bueno** approval; **'~ bueno'** approved; **por lo ~** evidently; **está ~ que** it's clear that; **está bien/mal ~** it's acceptable/unacceptable; **~ que** conj since, considering that.

vistoso, a [bis'toso, a] a colourful; (alegre) gay; (pey) gaudy.

vital [bi'tal] a life cpd, living cpd; (fig) vital; (persona) lively, vivacious; **~icio, a** a for life.

vitamina [bita'mina] *nf* vitamin.
viticultor, a [bitikul'tor, a] *nm/f* vine grower; **viticultura** *nf* vine growing.
vitorear [bitore'ar] *vt* to cheer, acclaim.
vítreo, a ['bitreo, a] *a* vitreous.
vitrina [bi'trina] *nf* glass case.
vituperar [bitupe'rar] *vt* to condemn; **vituperio** *nm* (*condena*) condemnation; (*censura*) censure; (*insulto*) insult.
viudo, a ['bjuðo, a] *nm/f* widower/widow; **viudez** *nf* widowhood.
vivacidad [biβaθi'ðað] *nf* (*vigor*) vigour; (*vida*) vivacity.
vivaracho, a [biβa'ratʃo, a] *a* jaunty, lively; (*ojos*) bright, twinkling.
vivaz [bi'βaθ] *a* (*que dura*) enduring; (*vigoroso*) vigorous; (*vivo*) lively.
víveres ['biβeres] *nmpl* provisions.
viveza [bi'βeθa] *nf* liveliness; (*agudeza*) sharpness.
vivienda [bi'βjenda] *nf* (*alojamiento*) housing; (*morada*) dwelling.
0**Aviviente** [bi'βjente] *a* living.
vivificar [biβifi'kar] *vt* to give life to.
vivir [bi'βir] *vt, vi* to live // *nm* life, living.
vivo, a ['biβo, a] *a* living, live, alive; (*fig*) /vivid; (*astuto*) smart, clever; **llegar a lo** ~ to cut to the quick.
vocablo [bo'kaβlo] *nm* (*palabra*) word; (*término*) term.
vocabulario [bokaβu'larjo] *nm* vocabulary.
vocación [boka'θjon] *nf* vocation.
vocal [bo'kal] *a* vocal // *nf* vowel; ~**izar** *vt* to vocalize.
vocear [boθe'ar] *vt* (*para vender*) to cry; (*aclamar*) to acclaim; (*fig*) to proclaim // *vi* to yell; **vocerío** *nm*, **vocería** *nf* shouting.
vocero [bo'θero] *nm/f* spokesman/woman.
vociferar [boθife'rar] *vt* to shout; (*jactarse*) to proclaim boastfully // *vi* to yell.
vocinglero, a [boθin'glero, a] *a* vociferous; (*gárrulo*) garrulous; (*fig*) blatant.
vodka ['boðka] *nf* vodka.
vol *abr de* **volumen.**
volador, a [bola'ðor, a] *a* flying.
volante [bo'lante] *a* flying // *nm* (*de máquina, coche*) steering wheel; (*de reloj*) balance.
volar [bo'lar] *vt* (*demoler*) to blow up, demolish // *vi* to fly.
volátil [bo'latil] *a* volatile; (*fig*) changeable.
volcán [bol'kan] *nm* volcano; ~**ico, a** *a* volcanic.
volcar [bol'kar] *vt* to upset, overturn; (*tumbar, derribar*) to knock over; (*vaciar*) to empty out // *vi* to overturn; ~**se** *vr* to tip over.
volibol [boli'βol] *nm* volleyball.
volición [boli'θjon] *nf* volition.
voltaje [bol'taxe] *nm* voltage.
volteador, a [boltea'ðor, a] *nm/f* acrobat.

voltear [bolte'ar] *vt* to turn over; (*volcar*) to turn upside down; (*doblar*) to peal // *vi* to roll over.
voltio ['boltjo] *nm* volt.
voluble [bo'luβle] *a* fickle.
volumen [bo'lumen] *nm* volume; **voluminoso, a** *a* voluminous; (*enorme*) massive.
voluntad [bolun'tað] *nf* will, willpower; (*deseo*) desire, wish; (*afecto*) fondness.
voluntario, a [bolun'tarjo, a] *a* voluntary // *nm/f* volunteer.
voluntarioso, a [bolunta'rjoso, a] *a* headstrong.
voluptuoso, a [bolup'twoso, a] *a* voluptuous.
volver [bol'βer] *vt* (*gen*) to turn; (*dar vuelta*) to turn (over); (*voltear*) to turn round, turn upside down; (*poner al revés*) to turn inside out; (*devolver*) to return; (*transformar*) to change, transform // *vi* to return, go/come back; ~**se** *vr* to turn round; (*llegar a ser*) to become; ~ **la espalda** to turn one's back; ~ **bien por mal** to return good for evil; ~ **a hacer** to do again; ~ **en sí** to come to; ~**se loco** to go mad.
vomitar [bomi'tar] *vt, vi* to vomit; **vómito** *nm* (*acto*) vomiting; (*resultado*) vomit.
voraz [bo'raθ] *a* voracious; (*fig*) fierce.
vórtice ['bortiθe] *nm* whirlpool; (*de aire*) whirlwind.
vosotros [bo'sotros] *pron* you.
votación [bota'θjon] *nf* (*acto*) voting; (*voto*) vote; **votar** *vi* to vote; **voto** *nm* vote; (*promesa*) vow; (*maldición*) oath, curse; **votos** (*good*) wishes.
voy *vb ver* **ir.**
voz [boθ] *nf* voice; (*grito*) shout; (*chisme*) rumour; (*LING*) word; **dar voces** to shout, yell; **a media** ~ in a low voice; **a** ~ **en cuello** *o* **en grito** at the top of one's voice; **de viva** ~ verbally; **en** ~ **alta** aloud; ~ **de mando** command.
vuelco ['bwelko] *nm* spill, overturning; (*fig*) collapse.
vuelo ['bwelo] *vb ver* **volar** // *nm* flight; (*encaje*) lace, frill; (*fig*) importance; **coger al** ~ to catch in flight.
vuelta ['bwelta] *nf* (*gen*) turn; (*curva*) bend, curve; (*regreso*) return; (*revolución*) revolution; (*paseo*) stroll; (*circuito*) lap; (*de papel, tela*) reverse; (*cambio*) change; **V~ de Francia** Tour de France; ~ **cerrada** hairpin bend; **a la** ~ on one's return; **a** ~ **de correo** by return of post; **dar** ~**s** to turn, revolve; **dar** ~**s a una idea** to turn over an idea (in one's head); **estar de** ~ (*fam*) to be back; **dar una** ~ to go for a walk.
vuelto *pp de* **volver.**
vuelvo *etc vb ver* **volver.**
vuestro, a ['bwestro, a] *a* your; **un amigo** ~ a friend of yours // *pron*: **el** ~/**la** ~/**a**/**los** ~**s**/**las** ~**as** yours.
vulgar [bul'γar] *a* (*ordinario*) vulgar; (*común*) common; ~**idad** *nf* commonness; (*acto*) vulgarity; (*expresión*) coarse

expression; ~**idades** *nfpl* banalities; ~**izar** *vt* to popularize.
vulgo ['bulxo] *nm* common people.
vulnerable [bulne'raβle] *a* vulnerable.
vulnerar [bulne'rar] *vt* to harm, damage.
vulpino, a [bul'pino, a] *a* vulpine; *(fig)* foxy.

W

wáter ['bater] *nm* lavatory.
wátman ['watman] *a inv (fam)* cool.
whisky ['wiski] *nm* whisky.

X

xenofobia [kseno'foβja] *nf* xenophobia.
xilófono [ksi'lofono] *nm* xylophone.

Y

y [i] *conj* and.
ya [ja] *ad (gen)* already; *(ahora)* now; *(en seguida)* at once; *(pronto)* soon // *excl* all right! // *conj (ahora que)* now that; ~ **lo sé** I know; ~ **dice que sí,** ~ **dice que no** first he says yes, then he says no; ~ **que** since.
yacer [ja'θer] *vi* to lie.
yacimiento [jaθi'mjento] *nm* bed, deposit.
yanqui ['janki] *a* Yankee.
yate ['jate] *nm* yacht.
yazco *etc vb ver* **yacer.**
yedra ['jeðra] *nf* ivy.
yegua ['jeɣwa] *nf* mare.
yema ['jema] *nf (del huevo)* yoke; *(BOT)* leaf bud; *(fig)* best part; ~ **del dedo** fingertip.
yergo *etc vb ver* **erguir.**
yermo, a ['jermo, a] *a* uninhabited // *nm* waste land.
yerno ['jerno] *nm* son-in-law.
yerro *etc vb ver* **errar.**
yerto, a ['jerto, a] *a* stiff.
yesca ['jeska] *nf* tinder.
yeso ['jeso] *nm (GEO)* gypsum; *(ARQ)* plaster.
yodo ['joðo] *nm* iodine.
yugo ['juxo] *nm* yoke.
Yugoslavia [juxos'laβja] *nf* Yugoslavia.
yugular [juxu'lar] *a* jugular.
yunque ['junke] *nm* anvil.
yunta ['junta] *nf* yoke; **yuntero** *nm* ploughman.
yute ['jute] *nm* jute.
yuxtaponer [jukstapo'ner] *vt* to juxtapose; **yuxtaposición** *nf* juxtaposition.

Z

zafar [θa'far] *vt (soltar)* to untie; *(superficie)* to clear; ~**se** *vr (escaparse)* to escape; *(ocultarse)* to hide o.s. away; *(TEC)* to slip off.
zafio, a ['θafjo, a] *a* coarse.

zafiro [θa'firo] *nm* sapphire.
zaga ['θaxa] *nf* rear; **a la** ~ behind, in the rear.
zagal, a [θa'xal, a] *nm/f* boy/girl, lad/lass.
zaguán [θa'xwan] *nm* hallway.
zahareño, a [θaa'reɲo, a] *a (salvaje)* wild; *(arisco)* unsociable.
zaherir [θae'rir] *vt (criticar)* to criticize; *(fig: herir)* to wound.
zahorí [θao'ri] *nm* clairvoyant.
zaino, a ['θaino, a] *a (color de caballo)* chestnut; *(pérfido)* treacherous; *(animal)* vicious.
zalamería [θala'merja] *nf* flattery; **zalamero, a** *a* flattering; *(relamido)* suave.
zamarra [θa'marra] *nf (piel)* sheepskin; *(saco)* sheepskin jacket.
zambra ['θambra] *nf* gypsy dance.
zambullirse [θambu'ʎirse] *vr* to dive; *(ocultarse)* to hide o.s.
zampar [θam'par] *vt (esconder)* to hide or put away (hurriedly); *(comer)* to gobble; *(arrojar)* to hurl // *vi* to eat voraciously; ~**se** *vr (chocar)* to bump; *(fig)* to gatecrash.
zanahoria [θana'orja] *nf* carrot.
zancada [θan'kaða] *nf* stride.
zancadilla [θanka'ðiʎa] *nf* trip; *(fig)* stratagem.
zancajo [θan'kaxo] *nm (ANAT)* heel; *(fig)* dwarf.
zanco ['θanko] *nm* stilt.
zancudo, a [θan'kuðo, a] *a* long-legged // *nm (AM)* mosquito.
zángano ['θangano] *nm* drone.
zanja ['θanxa] *nf (fosa)* ditch; *(tumba)* grave; **zanjar** *vt (fosa)* to ditch, trench; *(problema)* to surmount; *(conflicto)* to resolve.
zapapico [θapa'piko] *nm* pick, pickaxe.
zapata [θa'pata] *nf* half-boot; *(MECÁNICA)* shoe.
zapatear [θapate'ar] *vt (tocar)* to tap with one's foot; *(patear)* to kick; *(fam)* to ill-treat // *vi* to tap with one's feet.
zapatería [θapate'ria] *nf (oficio)* shoemaking; *(tienda)* shoe-shop; *(fábrica)* shoe factory; **zapatero, a** *nm/f* shoemaker.
zapatilla [θapa'tiʎa] *nf* slipper.
zapato [θa'pato] *nm* shoe.
zarabanda [θara'βanda] *nf* saraband; *(fig)* whirl.
zaranda [θa'randa] *nf* sieve; **zarandear** *vt* to sieve; *(fam)* to shake vigorously.
zarcillo [θar'θiʎo] *nm* earring.
zarpa ['θarpa] *nf (garra)* claw.
zarpar [θar'par] *vi* to weigh anchor.
zarza ['θarθa] *nf (BOT)* bramble; **zarzal** *nm (matorral)* bramble patch.
zarzamora [θarθa'mora] *nf* blackberry.
zarzuela [θar'θwela] *nf* Spanish light opera.
zigzag [θix'θax] *a* zigzag; **zigzaguear** *vi* to zigzag.

zinc [θink] *nm* zinc.

zócalo ['θokalo] *nm* (*ARQ*) plinth, base.

zona ['θona] *nf* zone; ~ **fronteriza** border area.

zoología [θoolo'xia] *nf* zoology; **zoológico, a** *a* zoological // *nm* zoo; **zoólogo, a** *nm/f* zoologist.

zopilote [θopi'lote] *nm* (*AM*) buzzard.

zoquete [θo'kete] *nm* (*madera*) block; (*pan*) crust; (*fam*) blockhead.

zorro, a ['θorro, a] *a* crafty // *nm/f* fox/vixen.

zozobra [θo'θoβra] *nf* (*fig*) anxiety; **zozobrar** *vi* (*hundirse*) to capsize; (*fig*) to fail.

zueco ['θweko] *nm* clog.

zumbar [θum'bar] *vt* (*burlar*) to tease; (*golpear*) to hit // *vi* to buzz; (*fam*) to be very close; ~**se** *vr*: ~**se de** to tease; **zumbido** *nm* buzzing; (*fam*) punch.

zumo ['θumo] *nm* juice; (*ganancia*) profit.

zurcir [θur'θir] *vt* (*coser*) to darn; (*fig*) to put together.

zurdo, a ['θurðo, a] *a* (*mano*) left; (*persona*) left-handed.

zurrar [θu'rrar] *vt* (*TEC*) to dress; (*fam: pegar duro*) to wallop; (: *aplastar*) to flatten; (: *criticar*) to criticize harshly.

zurriago [θu'rrjaxo] *nm* whip, lash.

zurrón [θu'rron] *nm* pouch.

zutano, a [θu'tano, a] *nm/f* so-and-so.

ENGLISH - SPANISH
INGLÉS - ESPAÑOL

A

a, an [eɪ, ə, æn, ən, n] *det* un(a); **3 a day/week** 3 por día/semana; **10 km an hour** 10 km por hora.

A.A. *n abbr of* **Automobile Association; Alcoholics Anonymous.**

aback [ə'bæk] *ad:* **to be taken ~** quedar desconcertado.

abandon [ə'bændən] *vt* abandonar; (*renounce*) renunciar a // *n* abandono; (*wild behaviour*) desenfreno.

abashed [ə'bæʃt] *a* avergonzado, confuso.

abate [ə'beɪt] *vi* moderarse; (*lessen*) disminuir; (*calm down*) calmarse.

abattoir ['æbətwɑ:*] *n* matadero.

abbey ['æbɪ] *n* monasterio.

abbot ['æbət] *n* abad *m*.

abbreviate [ə'bri:vɪeɪt] *vt* abreviar; **abbreviation** [-'eɪʃən] *n* (*short form*) abreviatura; (*act*) abreviación *f*.

abdicate ['æbdɪkeɪt] *vt, vi* abdicar; **abdication** [-'keɪʃən] *n* abdicación *f*.

abdomen ['æbdəmən] *n* abdomen *m*.

abduct [æb'dʌkt] *vt* raptar, secuestrar; **~ion** [-'dʌkʃən] *n* rapto, secuestro.

aberration [æbə'reɪʃən] *n* aberración *f*.

abet [ə'bɛt] *vt* (*incite*) incitar; (*aid*) ser cómplice de.

abeyance [ə'beɪəns] *n:* **in ~** (*law*) en desuso; (*matter*) en suspenso.

abhor [əb'hɔ:*] *vt* aborrecer, abominar (de); **~rent** [ə'brenɪv] *a* detestable.

abide [ə'baɪd] *pt, pp* **abode** *or* **abided** *vt* aguantar, soportar; **to ~ by** *vt fus* atenerse a.

ability [ə'bɪlɪtɪ] *n* habilidad *f*, capacidad *f*; (*talent*) talento.

ablaze [ə'bleɪz] *a* en llamas, ardiendo.

able ['eɪbl] *a* capaz; (*skilled*) hábil; **to be ~ to do sth** poder hacer algo; **~-bodied** *a* sano; **ably** *ad* hábilmente.

abnormal [æb'nɔ:məl] *a* anormal; **~ity** [-'mælɪtɪ] *n* anormalidad *f*.

aboard [ə'bɔ:d] *ad* a bordo // *prep* a bordo de.

abode [ə'bəud] *pt, pp of* **abide** // *n* domicilio.

abolish [ə'bɔlɪʃ] *vt* suprimir, abolir; **abolition** [æbəu'lɪʃən] *n* supresión *f*, abolición *f*.

abominable [ə'bɔmɪnəbl] *a* abominable.

aborigine [æbə'rɪdʒɪnɪ] *n* aborigen *m*.

abort [ə'bɔ:t] *vt* abortar; **~ion** [ə'bɔ:ʃən] *n* aborto (provocado); **to have an ~ion** abortarse, hacerse abortar; **~ive** *a* fracasado.

abound [ə'baund] *vi* abundar.

about [ə'baut] *prep* (*subject*) acerca de, sobre; (*place*) alrededor de, por // *ad* casi, más o menos, a eso de; **to walk ~ the town** andar por la ciudad; **it takes ~ 10 hours** es cosa de 10 horas más o menos; **at ~ 2 o'clock** a eso de las 2; **to be ~ to** estar a punto de; **what** *or* **how ~ doing this?** ¿qué tal si hacemos esto?; **~ turn** *n* media vuelta.

above [ə'bʌv] *ad* encima, por encima, arriba // *prep* encima de; **mentioned ~** susodicho; **~ all** sobre todo; **~ board** *a* legítimo.

abrasion [ə'breɪʒən] *n* (*on skin*) abrasión *f*; **abrasive** [ə'breɪzɪv] *a* abrasivo.

abreast [ə'brest] *ad* de frente; **to keep ~ of** mantenerse al corriente de.

abridge [ə'brɪdʒ] *vt* abreviar.

abroad [ə'brɔ:d] *ad* (*to be*) en el extranjero; (*to go*) al extranjero.

abrupt [ə'brʌpt] *a* (*sudden*) brusco; (*gruff*) áspero.

abscess ['æbsɪs] *n* absceso.

abscond [əb'skɔnd] *vi* fugarse.

absence ['æbsəns] *n* ausencia.

absent ['æbsənt] *a* ausente; **~ee** [-'ti:] *n* ausente *m/f*; **~eeism** [-'ti:ɪzəm] *n* absentismo; **~-minded** *a* distraído.

absolute ['æbsəlu:t] *a* absoluto; **~ly** [-'lu:tlɪ] *ad* absolutamente.

absolve [əb'zɔlv] *vt:* **to ~ sb (from)** absolver a alguien (de).

absorb [əb'zɔ:b] *vt* absorber; **to be ~ed in a book** estar absorto en un libro; **~ent** *a* absorbente; **~ing** *a* absorbente.

abstain [əb'steɪn] *vi:* **to ~ (from)** abstenerse (de).

abstention [əb'stɛnʃən] *n* abstención *f*.

abstinence ['æbstɪnəns] *n* abstinencia.

abstract ['æbstrækt] *a* abstracto.

absurd [əb'sɔ:d] *a* absurdo; **~ity** *n* absurdo.

abundance [ə'bʌndəns] *n* abundancia; **abundant** [-dənt] *a* abundante.

abuse [ə'bju:s] *n* (*insults*) improperios *mpl*, injurias *fpl*; (*misuse*) abuso // *vt* [ə'bju:z] (*ill-treat*) maltratar; (*take advantage of*) abusar de; **abusive** *a* ofensivo.

abysmal [ə'bɪzməl] *a* abismal; (*ignorance etc*) profundo.

abyss [ə'bɪs] *n* abismo.

academic [ækə'demɪk] *a* académico, universitario; (*pej: issue*) puramente teórico.

academy [ə'kædəmɪ] *n* (*learned body*) academia; (*school*) instituto, colegio.

accede [æk'si:d] *vi:* **to ~ to** (*request*) consentir en; (*throne*) subir a.

accelerate [æk'seləreit] vt acelerar // vi acelerarse; **acceleration** [-'reiʃən] n aceleración f; **accelerator** n acelerador m.

accent ['æksent] n acento.

accept [ək'sept] vt aceptar; (approve) aprobar; (permit) admitir; **~able** a aceptable; admisible; **~ance** n aceptación f; aprobación f.

access ['ækses] n acceso; **to have ~ to** tener libre acceso a; **~ible** [-'sesəbl] a accesible.

accessory [æk'sesəri] n accesorio; **toilet accessories** npl artículos mpl de tocador.

accident ['æksidənt] n accidente m; (chance) casualidad f; **by ~** (unintentionally) sin querer; (by coincidence) por casualidad; **~al** [-'dentl] a accidental, fortuito; **~ally** [-'dentəli] ad sin querer; por casualidad; **~-prone** a con tendencia a sufrir/causar accidentes.

acclaim [ə'kleim] vt aclamar, aplaudir // n aclamación f, aplausos mpl.

acclimatize [ə'klaimətaiz] vt: **to become ~d** aclimatarse.

accommodate [ə'kɔmədeit] vt alojar, hospedar; (reconcile) componer; (oblige, help) complacer; (adapt): **to ~ one's plans to** acomodar sus proyectos a; **accommodating** a servicial, complaciente.

accommodation [əkɔmə'deiʃən] n alojamiento; (space) sitio.

accompaniment [ə'kʌmpənimənt] n acompañamiento; **accompany** [-ni] vt acompañar.

accomplice [ə'kʌmplis] n cómplice m/f.

accomplish [ə'kʌmpliʃ] vt (finish) acabar, alcanzar; (achieve) realizar, llevar a cabo; **~ed** a experto, hábil; **~ment** n (ending) conclusión f; (bringing about) realización f; (skill) talento.

accord [ə'kɔːd] n acuerdo // vt concordar; **of his own ~** espontáneamente; **~ance** n: **in ~ance with** de acuerdo con; **~ing to** prep según; (in accordance with) conforme a; **~ingly** ad (thus) por consiguiente.

accordion [ə'kɔːdiən] n acordeón m.

accost [ə'kɔst] vt abordar, dirigirse a.

account [ə'kaunt] n (COMM) cuenta, factura; (report) informe m; **of little ~** de poca importancia; **on ~** a cuenta; **on no ~** de ninguna manera, bajo ningún concepto; **on ~ of** a causa de, por motivo de; **to take into ~, take ~ of** tomar en cuenta; **to ~ for** vt (answer for) responder de; (explain) dar cuenta o razón de; **~able** a responsable.

accountancy [ə'kauntənsi] n contabilidad f; **accountant** [-tənt] n contador/a m/f.

accumulate [ə'kjuːmjuleit] vt acumular // vi acumularse; **accumulation** [-'leiʃən] n acumulación f.

accuracy ['ækjurəsi] n exactitud f, precisión f; **accurate** [-rit] a (number) exacto; (answer) acertado; (shot) certero.

accusation [ækjuːˈzeiʃən] n acusación f; **accuse** [ə'kjuːz] vt acusar; (blame) echar la culpa a; **accused** [ə'kjuːzd] n acusado/a.

accustom [ə'kʌstəm] vt acostumbrar; **~ed** a: **~ed to** acostumbrado a.

ace [eis] n as m.

ache [eik] n dolor m // vi doler; **my head ~s** me duele la cabeza.

achieve [ə'tʃiːv] vt (reach) alcanzar; (realize) llevar a cabo; (victory, success) lograr, conseguir; **~ment** n (completion) realización f; (success) éxito.

acid ['æsid] a ácido; (bitter) agrio // n ácido; **~ity** [ə'siditi] n acidez f; (MED) acedía.

acknowledge [ək'nɔlidʒ] vt (letter) acusar recibo de; (fact) reconocer; **~ment** n acuse m de recibo; reconocimiento.

acne ['ækni] n acné m.

acorn ['eikɔːn] n bellota.

acoustic [ə'kuːstik] a acústico; **~s** n, npl acústica sg.

acquaint [ə'kweint] vt: **to ~ sb with sth** (warn) avisar a uno de algo; (inform) poner a uno al corriente de algo; **to be ~ed with** (person) conocer; (fact) estar al corriente de; **~ance** n conocimiento; (person) conocido/a.

acquiesce [ækwi'es] vt: **to ~ in** consentir en, conformarse con.

acquire [ə'kwaiə*] vt adquirir; (achieve) conseguir; **acquisition** [ækwi'ziʃən] n adquisición f; **acquisitive** [ə'kwizitiv] a codicioso.

acquit [ə'kwit] vt absolver, exculpar; **to ~ o.s. well** defenderse, salir con éxito; **~tal** n absolución f, exculpación f.

acre ['eikə*] n acre m.

acrimonious [ækri'məuniəs] a (remark) mordaz; (argument) reñido.

acrobat ['ækrəbæt] n acróbata m/f; **~ics** [ækrəu'bætiks] n, npl acrobacia sg.

across [ə'krɔs] prep (on the other side of) al otro lado de, del otro lado de; (crosswise) a través de // ad de un lado a otro, de una parte a otra; a través, al través; **to run/swim ~** atravesar corriendo/nadando; **~ from** enfrente de.

act [ækt] n acto, acción f; (THEATRE) acto; (in music-hall etc) número; (LAW) decreto, ley f // vi (machine) funcionar, marchar; (person) actuar, comportarse; (THEATRE) actuar, trabajar; (pretend) fingir; (take action) obrar // vt (part) hacer el papel de, representar; **to ~ as** actuar o hacer de; **~ing** a suplente // n: **to do some ~ing** ser actor/actriz.

action ['ækʃən] n acción f, acto; (MIL) acción f, batalla; (LAW) proceso, demanda; **to take ~** tomar medidas.

activate ['æktiveit] vt (mechanism) activar.

active ['æktiv] a activo, enérgico; (volcano) en actividad; **activity** [-'tiviti] n actividad f.

actor ['æktə*] n actor m; **actress** [-trɪs] n actriz f.
actual ['æktjuəl] a verdadero, real; **~ly** ad realmente, en realidad.
acupuncture ['ækjupʌŋktʃə*] n acupuntura.
acute [ə'kju:t] a (gen) agudo.
ad [æd] n abbr of **advertisement**.
A.D. ad abbr of **Anno Domini** A.C. (año de Cristo).
Adam ['ædəm] n Adán; **~'s apple** n nuez f de la garganta.
adamant ['ædəmənt] a firme, inflexible.
adapt [ə'dæpt] vt adaptar; (reconcile) acomodar // vi: to ~ (to) adaptarse (a), ajustarse (a); **~able** a (device) adaptable; (person) que se adapta; **~ation** [ædæp-'teɪʃən] n adaptación f; **~er** n (ELEC) adaptador m.
add [æd] vt añadir, agregar; (figures: also: ~ up) sumar // vi: to ~ to (increase) aumentar, acrecentar; **it doesn't ~ up** no tiene sentido.
adder ['ædə*] n víbora.
addict ['ædɪkt] n (enthusiast) entusiasta m/f; (to drugs etc) adicto/a; **~ed** [ə'dɪktɪd] a: **to be ~ed to** ser aficionado de; ser adicto a; **addiction** [ə'dɪkʃən] n (enthusiasm) afición f; (dependence) hábito morboso.
adding machine ['ædɪŋməʃi:n] n calculadora.
addition [ə'dɪʃən] n (adding up) adición f; (thing added) añadidura, añadido; **in ~** además, por añadidura; **in ~ to** además de; **~al** a adicional.
additive ['ædɪtɪv] n aditivo.
address [ə'drɛs] n dirección f, señas fpl; (speech) discurso // vt (letter) dirigir; (speak to) dirigirse a, dirigir la palabra a; **~ee** [ædrɛ'siː] n destinatario/a.
adenoids ['ædɪnɔɪdz] npl vegetaciones fpl adenoideas.
adept ['ædɛpt] a: ~ **at** experto o hábil en.
adequate ['ædɪkwɪt] a (apt) adecuado; (enough) suficiente.
adhere [əd'hɪə*] vi: to ~ **to** pegarse a; (fig: abide by) observar; (: hold to) adherirse a; **adherent** n partidario/a.
adhesive [əd'hi:zɪv] a, n adhesivo.
adjacent [ə'dʒeɪsənt] a: ~ **to** contiguo a, inmediato a.
adjective ['ædʒɛktɪv] n adjetivo.
adjoining [ə'dʒɔɪnɪŋ] a contiguo, vecino.
adjourn [ə'dʒɜːn] vt aplazar; (session) suspender, levantar // vi suspenderse.
adjudicate [ə'dʒuːdɪkeɪt] vi sentenciar; **adjudicator** n juez m, árbitro.
adjust [ə'dʒʌst] vt (change) modificar; (arrange) arreglar; (machine) ajustar // vi: to ~ (to) adaptarse (a); **~able** a ajustable; **~ment** n modificación f; arreglo; (of prices, wages) ajuste m.
adjutant ['ædʒətənt] n ayudante m.
ad-lib [æd'lɪb] vt, vi improvisar; **ad lib** ad a voluntad, a discreción.
administer [əd'mɪnɪstə*] vt proporcionar;

(justice) administrar; **administration** [-'treɪʃən] n administración f; (government) gobierno; **administrative** [-trətɪv] a administrativo; **administrator** [-treɪtə*] n administrador/a m/f.
admirable ['ædmərəbl] a admirable.
admiral ['ædmərəl] n almirante m; **A~ty** n Ministerio de Marina, Almirantazgo.
admiration [ædmə'reɪʃən] n admiración f.
admire [əd'maɪə*] vt admirar; **admirer** n admirador/a m/f; (suitor) pretendiente m.
admission [əd'mɪʃən] n (entry) entrada; (enrolment) ingreso; (confession) confesión f.
admit [əd'mɪt] vt dejar entrar, dar entrada a; (permit) admitir; (acknowledge) reconocer; (accept) aceptar; **to ~ to** confesarse culpable de; **~tance** n entrada; **~tedly** ad de acuerdo que.
admonish [əd'mɒnɪʃ] vt amonestar; (advise) aconsejar.
ado [ə'du:] n: **without (any) more ~** sin más (ni más).
adolescence [ædəu'lɛsns] n adolescencia; **adolescent** [-'lɛsnt] a, n adolescente m/f.
adopt [ə'dɒpt] vt adoptar; **~ion** [ə'dɒpʃən] n adopción f; **~ed** a adoptivo.
adore [ə'dɔ:*] vt adorar.
adorn [ə'dɔ:n] vt adornar.
adrenalin [ə'drɛnəlɪn] n adrenalina.
Adriatic [eɪdrɪ'ætɪk] n: **the ~ (Sea)** el (Mar) Adriático.
adrift [ə'drɪft] ad a la deriva; **to come ~** desprenderse.
adult ['ædʌlt] n (gen) adulto.
adulterate [ə'dʌltəreɪt] vt adulterar.
adultery [ə'dʌltərɪ] n adulterio.
advance [əd'vɑ:ns] n (gen) adelanto, progreso; (money) anticipo, préstamo; (MIL) avance m // vt avanzar, adelantar; anticipar, prestar // vi avanzar, adelantarse; **in ~** por adelantado; **~d** a avanzado; (SCOL: studies) adelantado; **~d in years** entrado en años; **~ment** n progreso; (in rank) ascenso.
advantage [əd'vɑ:ntɪdʒ] n (also TENNIS) ventaja; **to take ~ of** (use) aprovecharse de; (gain by) sacar partido de; **~ous** [ædvən'teɪdʒəs] a ventajoso, provechoso.
advent ['ædvənt] n advenimiento; **A~** Adviento.
adventure [əd'vɛntʃə*] n aventura; **adventurous** [-tʃərəs] a aventurero.
adverb ['ædvɜːb] n adverbio.
adversary ['ædvəsərɪ] n adversario, contrario.
adverse ['ædvɜːs] a adverso, contrario; ~ **to** adverso a.
adversity [əd'vɜːsɪtɪ] n infortunio.
advert ['ædvɜːt] n abbr of **advertisement**.
advertise ['ædvətaɪz] vi hacer propaganda; (in newspaper etc) poner un anuncio // vt anunciar; **~ment** [əd-'vɜːtɪsmənt] n (COMM) anuncio; **advertising** n publicidad f, propaganda; anuncios mpl.

advice [əd'vaɪs] n consejo, consejos mpl; (notification) aviso; **to take legal** ~ consultar a un abogado.

advisable [əd'vaɪzəbl] a aconsejable, conveniente.

advise [əd'vaɪz] vt aconsejar; (inform) avisar; **adviser** n consejero; (business adviser) asesor m; **advisory** a consultivo.

advocate ['ædvəkeɪt] vt (argue for) abogar por; (give support to) ser partidario de // n [-kɪt] abogado.

aerial ['ɛərɪəl] n antena // a aéreo.

aeroplane ['ɛərəpleɪn] n avión m.

aerosol ['ɛərəsɔl] n aerosol m.

aesthetic [iːs'θetɪk] a estético.

afar [ə'fɑː*] ad: **from** ~ desde lejos.

affable ['æfəbl] a afable.

affair [ə'fɛə*] n asunto; (also: love ~) aventura o relación f (amorosa).

affect [ə'fekt] vt afectar, influir en; (move) conmover; ~ation [æfek'teɪʃən] n afectación f; ~ed a afectado.

affection [ə'fekʃən] n afecto, cariño; ~ate a afectuoso, cariñoso.

affiliated [ə'fɪlɪeɪtɪd] a afiliado.

affinity [ə'fɪnɪtɪ] n afinidad f.

affirmation [æfə'meɪʃən] n afirmación f.

affirmative [ə'fɜːmətɪv] a afirmativo.

affix [ə'fɪks] (signature) poner, añadir; (stamp) p~

afflict [ə'flɪkt] vt afligir; ~ion [ə'flɪkʃən] n enfermedad f, aflicción f.

affluence ['æfluəns] n opulencia, riqueza; **affluent** [-ənt] a opulento, acaudalado.

afford [ə'fɔːd] vt (provide) dar, proporcionar; **can we** ~ **it?** ¿tenemos bastante dinero para comprarlo?

affront [ə'frʌnt] n afrenta, ofensa.

afield [ə'fiːld] ad: **far** ~ muy lejos.

afloat [ə'fləut] ad (floating) a flote; (at sea) en el mar.

afoot [ə'fut] ad: **there is something** ~ algo se está tramando.

aforesaid [ə'fɔːsed] a susodicho.

afraid [ə'freɪd] a: **to be** ~ **of** (person) tener miedo a; (thing) tener miedo de; **to be** ~ **to** tener miedo de, temer; **I am** ~ **that** me temo que.

afresh [ə'freʃ] ad de nuevo, otra vez.

Africa ['æfrɪkə] n África; ~n a, n africano/a.

aft [ɑːft] ad (to be) en popa; (to go) a popa.

after ['ɑːftə*] prep (time) después de; (place, order) detrás de, tras // ad después // conj después (de) que; **what/who are you** ~? ¿qué/a quién busca Usted?; **to ask** ~ **sb** preguntar por alguien; ~ **all** después de todo, al fin y al cabo; ~ **you!** ¡pase Usted!; ~**birth** n secundinas fpl; ~**effects** npl consecuencias fpl, efectos mpl; ~**life** n vida futura; ~**math** n consecuencias fpl, resultados mpl; ~**noon** n tarde f; ~**shave** (lotion) n loción f para después del afeitado; ~**thought** n ocurrencia (tardía), más tarde; ~**wards** ad después, más tarde.

again [ə'gen] ad otra vez, de nuevo; **to do sth** ~ volver a hacer algo; ~ **and** ~ una y otra vez; **now and** ~ de vez en cuando.

against [ə'genst] prep (opposed) contra, en contra de; (close to) contra, junto a.

age [eɪdʒ] n (gen) edad f; (old ~) vejez f; (period) época // vi envejecer(se) // vt envejecer; **to come of** ~ llegar a la mayoría de edad; **it's been** ~**s since** hace muchísimo tiempo que; ~**d a** ['eɪdʒɪd] viejo, anciano // a [eɪdʒd]: ~**d 10** de 10 años de edad; ~ **group** n: **to be in the same** ~ **group** tener la misma edad; ~**less** a (eternal) eterno; (ever young) siempre joven; ~ **limit** n edad mínima/máxima.

agency ['eɪdʒənsɪ] n agencia; **through** or **by the** ~ **of** por medio de.

agenda [ə'dʒendə] n orden m del día.

agent ['eɪdʒənt] n (gen) agente m/f; (representative) representante m/f, delegado/a.

aggravate ['ægrəveɪt] vt agravar; (annoy) irritar, exasperar; **aggravation** [-'veɪʃən] n agravación f.

aggregate ['ægrɪgeɪt] n (whole) conjunto; (collection) agregado.

aggression [ə'greʃən] n agresión f; **aggressive** [ə'gresɪv] a agresivo; (zealous) enérgico.

aggrieved [ə'griːvd] a ofendido, agraviado.

aghast [ə'gɑːst] a horrorizado; **to be** ~ pasmarse.

agile ['ædʒaɪl] a ágil.

agitate ['ædʒɪteɪt] vt (shake) agitar; (trouble) inquietar; **to** ~ **for** hacer campaña pro o en favor de; **agitator** n agitador/a m/f.

ago [ə'gəu] ad: **2 days** ~ hace 2 días; **not long** ~ hace poco; **how long** ~? ¿hace cuánto tiempo?

agog [ə'gɔg] a (anxious) ansiado; (excited) emocionado.

agonizing ['ægənaɪzɪŋ] a (pain) atroz, agudo; (suspense) angustioso.

agony ['ægənɪ] n (pain) dolor m agudo; (distress) angustia; **to be in** ~ sufrir atrozmente.

agree [ə'griː] vt (price) acordar, quedar en // vi (statements etc) coincidir, concordar; **to** ~ (**with**) (person) estar de acuerdo (con), ponerse de acuerdo (con); **to** ~ **to do** aceptar hacer; **to** ~ **to sth** consentir en algo; **to** ~ **that** (admit) estar de acuerdo en que; **garlic doesn't** ~ **with me** el ajo no me sienta bien; ~**able** a agradable; (person) simpático; (willing) de acuerdo, conforme; ~**d a** (time, place) convenido; ~**ment** n acuerdo; (COMM) contrato; **in** ~**ment** de acuerdo, conforme.

agricultural [ægrɪ'kʌltʃərəl] a agrícola; **agriculture** ['ægrɪkʌltʃə*] n agricultura.

aground [ə'graund] ad: **to run** ~ encallar, embarrancar.

ahead [ə'hed] ad delante; ~ **of** delante de;

(*fig: schedule etc*) antes de; ~ **of time** antes de la hora; **to be ~ of sb** (*fig*) llevar la ventaja a alguien; **go right** *or* **straight ~** ¡siga adelante!

aid [eid] *n* ayuda, auxilio // *vt* ayudar, auxiliar; **in ~ of** a beneficio de; **to ~ and abet** (*LAW*) ser cómplice de.

aide [eid] *n* (*person*) edecán *m*.

ailment ['eilmənt] *n* enfermedad *f*, achaque *m*.

aim [eim] *vt* (*gun, camera*) apuntar; (*missile, remark*) dirigir; (*blow*) asestar // *vi* (*also:* **take ~**) apuntar // *n* puntería; (*objective*) propósito, meta; **to ~ at** (*objective*) aspirar a, pretender; **to ~ to do** tener la intención de hacer; **~less** a sin propósito, sin objeto; **~lessly** *ad* a la ventura, a la deriva.

air [ɛəʳ] *n* aire *m*; (*appearance*) aspecto // *vt* ventilar; (*grievances, ideas*) airear // *cpd* (*currents, attack etc*) aéreo, aeronáutico; **~borne** a (*in the air*) en el aire; (*MIL.*) aerotransportado; **~conditioned** a con aire acondicionado; **~ conditioning** *n* aire acondicionado; **~craft** *n, pl inv* avión *m*; **~craft carrier** *n* porta(a)viones *m inv*; **A~ Force** *n* Fuerzas Aéreas *fpl*, aviación *f*; **~gun** *n* escopeta de aire comprimido; **~ hostess** *n* azafata; **~ letter** *n* carta aérea; **~lift** *n* puente *m* aéreo; **~line** *n* línea aérea; **~liner** *n* avión *m* de pasajeros; **~lock** *n* esclusa de aire; **~mail** *n*: **by ~mail** por avión; **~port** *n* aeropuerto; **~ raid** *n* ataque *m* aéreo; **~sick** a: **to be ~sick** marearse (en un avión); **~strip** *n* pista de aterrizaje; **~tight** a hermético; **~y** a (*room*) bien ventilado; (*manners*) ligero.

aisle [ail] *n* (*of church*) nave *f*; (*of theatre*) pasillo.

ajar [ə'dʒɑ:ʳ] a entreabierto.

akin [ə'kin] a: **~ to** relacionado con.

alarm [ə'lɑ:m] *n* alarma; (*anxiety*) inquietud *f* // *vt* asustar, inquietar; **~ clock** *n* despertador *m*.

Albania [æl'beiniə] *n* Albania.

album ['ælbəm] *n* álbum *m*; (*L.P.*) elepé *m*.

alcohol ['ælkəhɔl] *n* alcohol *m*; **~ic** [-'hɔlik] a, *n* alcohólico/a; **~ism** *n* alcoholismo.

alcove ['ælkəuv] *n* nicho, hueco.

alderman ['ɔ:ldəmən] *n, pl* **-men** concejal *m*.

ale [eil] *n* cerveza.

alert [ə'lɔ:t] a alerta; (*sharp*) despierto, despabilado // *n* alerta *m*, alarma // *vt* poner sobre aviso; **to be on the ~** estar alerta o sobre aviso.

algebra ['ældʒibrə] *n* álgebra.

Algeria [æl'dʒiəriə] *n* Argelia; **~n** a, *n* argelino/a.

alias ['eiliəs] *ad* alias, por otro nombre // *n* alias *m*.

alibi ['ælibai] *n* coartada.

alien ['eiliən] *n* extranjero/a // a: **~ to** distinto de, ajeno a; **~ate** *vt* enajenar, alejar; **~ation** [-'neiʃən] *n* enajenación *f*.

alight [ə'lait] a ardiendo, quemando // *vi* apearse, bajar.

align [ə'lain] *vt* alinear; **~ment** *n* alineación *f*.

alike [ə'laik] a semejantes, iguales // *ad* igualmente, del mismo modo; **to look ~** parecerse.

alimony ['æliməni] *n* (*payment*) alimentos *mpl*.

alive [ə'laiv] a (*gen*) vivo; (*lively*) activo, enérgico.

alkali ['ælkəlai] *n* álcali *m*.

all [ɔ:l] a todo; (*pl*) todos(as) // *pron* todo; (*pl*) todos(as) // *ad* completamente, del todo; **~ alone** completamente solo; **at ~** en absoluto, del todo; **~ the time/his life** todo el tiempo/toda su vida; **~ five** todos los cinco; **~ of them** todos (ellos); **~ of us went** fuimos todos; **not as hard as ~ that** no tan difícil; **~ in ~** con todo, así y todo.

allay [ə'lei] *vt* (*fears*) aquietar; (*pain*) aliviar.

allegation [æli'geiʃən] *n* aseveración *f*, alegación *f*.

allege [ə'ledʒ] *vt* afirmar, pretender.

allegiance [ə'li:dʒəns] *n* lealtad *f*.

allegory ['æligəri] *n* alegoría.

allergic [ə'lɔ:dʒik] a: **~ to** alérgico a; **allergy** ['ælədʒi] *n* alergia.

alleviate [ə'li:vieit] *vt* aliviar, mitigar.

alley ['æli] *n* (*street*) callejuela; (*in garden*) paseo.

alliance [ə'laiəns] *n* alianza *f*; **allied** ['ælaid] a aliado; (*related*) relacionado.

alligator ['æligeitəʳ] *n* caimán *m*.

all-in ['ɔ:lin] a (*also ad: charge*) todo incluido; **~ wrestling** *n* lucha libre.

alliteration [əlitə'reiʃən] *n* aliteración *f*.

all-night ['ɔ:l'nait] a (*café, behaviour*) abierto toda la noche; (*party*) que dura toda la noche.

allocate ['æləkeit] *vt* (*share out*) repartir, distribuir; (*devote*) asignar; **allocation** [-'keiʃən] *n* (*of money*) ración *f*, cuota; (*distribution*) reparto.

allot [ə'lɔt] *vt* asignar; **~ment** *n* ración *f*, porción *f*; (*garden*) parcela.

all-out ['ɔ:laut] a (*effort etc*) máximo; **all out** *ad* con todas sus fuerzas; (*speed*) a máxima velocidad.

allow [ə'lau] *vt* (*practice, behaviour*) permitir, dejar; (*sum to spend etc*) pagar, dar; (*a claim*) admitir; (*sum, time estimated*) dar, conceder; (*concede*): **to ~ that** reconocer que; **to ~ sb to do** permitir a alguien hacer; **to ~ for** *vt fus* tener en cuenta, tomar en consideración; **~ance** *n* (*gen*) concesión *f*; (*payment*) subvención *f*, pensión *f*; (*discount*) descuento, rebaja; **family ~ance** subsidio familiar; **to make ~ances for** ser indulgente con; tener en cuenta.

alloy ['ælɔi] *n* (*mix*) mezcla.

all: **~ right** *ad* (*well*) bien; (*correct*) correcto; (*as answer*) ¡conforme!, ¡está bien!; **~round** a (*gen*) completo; (*view*) amplio; (*person*) que hace de todo;

~-**time** a (record) de todos los tiempos.

allude [ɔ'lu:d] vi: **to** ~ **to** aludir a.

alluring [ɔ'ljuɔrɪŋ] a seductor(a), atractivo.

allusion [ɔ'lu:ʒɔn] n referencia, alusión f.

ally ['ælaɪ] n aliado/a // vr [ɔ'laɪ]: **to** ~ **o.s. with** aliarse con.

almighty [ɔːl'maɪtɪ] a todopoderoso, omnipotente.

almond ['ɑːmɔnd] n (fruit) almendra; (tree) almendro.

almost ['ɔːlmɔust] ad casi, por poco.

alms [ɑːmz] npl limosna sg.

aloft ['ɔ'lɔft] ad arriba, en alto.

alone [ɔ'lɔun] a solo // ad sólo, solamente; **to leave sb** ~ dejar a uno solo o en paz; **to leave sth** ~ no tocar algo, dejar algo sin tocar; **let** ~ sin hablar de.

along [ɔ'lɔŋ] prep a lo largo de, por // ad: **is he coming** ~ **with us?** ¿nos acompaña?; **he was limping** ~ iba cojeando; ~ **with** junto con, además de; ~**side** prep junto a, al lado de // ad (NAUT) al costado.

aloof [ɔ'lu:f] a reservado // ad: **to stand** ~ mantenerse a distancia.

aloud [ɔ'laud] ad en voz alta.

alphabet ['ælfɔbet] n alfabeto; ~**ical** [-'bɛtɪkɔl] a alfabético.

alpine ['ælpaɪn] a alpino, alpestre.

Alps [ælps] npl: **the** ~ los Alpes.

already [ɔːl'redɪ] ad ya.

alright ['ɔːl'raɪt] ad = **all right.**

also ['ɔːlsəu] ad también, además.

altar ['ɔːltə*] n aitar m.

alter ['ɔːltə*] vt cambiar, modificar // vi cambiarse, mudarse; (worsen) alterarse; ~**ation** [ɔːltə'reɪʃən] n cambio, modificación f, alteración f.

alternate [ɔl'tɔːnɪt] a alterno, alternativo // vi ['ɔːltɔːneɪt] alternarse; **on** ~ **days** un día sí y otro no; ~**ly** ad alternativamente, por turno; **alternating** [-'neɪtɪŋ] a (current) alterno.

alternative [ɔl'tɔːnɪtɪv] a alternativo // n alternativa; ~**ly** ad: ~**ly one could...** por otra parte se podría... .

alternator ['ɔːltɔːneɪtə*] n (AUT) alternador m.

although [ɔːl'ðəu] conj aunque; (given that) si bien.

altitude ['æltɪtjuːd] n altitud f, altura.

alto ['æltəu] n (female) contralto f; (male) alto.

altogether [ɔːltɔ'gɛðə*] ad enteramente, del todo; (on the whole, in all) en total, en conjunto.

aluminium [ælju'mɪnɪəm], **aluminum** [ɔ'luːmɪnəm] (US) n aluminio.

always ['ɔːlweɪz] ad siempre.

am [æm] vb see **be.**

a.m. ad abbr of **ante meridiem** de la mañana, antes de mediodía.

amalgamate [ɔ'mælgəmeɪt] vi amalgamarse, unirse // vt amalgamar,

unir; **amalgamation** [-'meɪʃən] n (COMM) amalgamación f, unión f.

amass [ɔ'mæs] vt amontonar, acumular.

amateur ['æmɔtə*] n aficionado/a, amateur m/f.

amaze [ɔ'meɪz] vt asombrar, pasmar; ~**ment** n asombro, sorpresa.

Amazon ['æmɔzɔn] n (GEO) Amazonas m.

ambassador [æm'bæsɔdɔ*] n embajador m.

amber ['æmbɔ*] n ámbar m; **at** ~ (AUT) en el amarillo.

ambidextrous [æmbɪ'dɛkstrɔs] a ambidextro.

ambiguity [æmbɪ'gjuɪtɪ] n ambigüedad f; (of meaning) doble sentido; **ambiguous** [-'bɪgjuɔs] a ambiguo.

ambition [æm'bɪʃɔn] n ambición f; **ambitious** [-ʃɔs] a ambicioso; (plan) grandioso.

ambivalent [æm'bɪvɔlɔnt] a ambivalente; (pej) equívoco.

amble ['æmbl] vi (gen: ~ **along**) deambular, andar sin prisa.

ambulance ['æmbjulɔns] n ambulancia.

ambush ['æmbuʃ] n emboscada // vt tender una emboscada a; (fig) coger por sorpresa.

amenable [ɔ'miːnɔbl] a: ~ **to** (advice etc) sensible a.

amend [ɔ'mɛnd] vt (law, text) enmendar; (habits) corregir, mejorar; **to make** ~**s** compensar, dar satisfacción por; ~**ment** n enmienda.

amenities [ɔ'miːnɪtɪz] npl conveniencias fpl, comodidades fpl.

America [ɔ'mɛrɪkɔ] n Estados Unidos mpl; ~**n** a, n norteamericano/a.

amiable ['eɪmɪɔbl] a (kind) amable, simpático; (hearty) bonachón(ona).

amicable ['æmɪkɔbl] a amistoso, amigable.

amid(st) [ɔ'mɪd(st)] prep entre, en medio de.

amiss [ɔ'mɪs] ad: **to take sth** ~ tomar algo a mal.

ammonia [ɔ'mɔunɪɔ] n amoníaco.

ammunition [æmju'nɪʃɔn] n municiones fpl.

amnesia [æm'niːzɪɔ] n amnesia.

amnesty ['æmnɪstɪ] n amnistía.

amok [ɔ'mɔk] ad: **to run** ~ enloquecerse, desbocarse.

among(st) [ɔ'mʌŋ(st)] prep entre, en medio de.

amoral [æ'mɔrɔl] a amoral.

amorous ['æmɔrɔs] a amoroso; (in love) enamorado.

amount [ɔ'maunt] n (gen) cantidad f; (of bill etc) suma, importe m // vi: **to** ~ **to** (reach) alcanzar; (total) sumar; (be same as) equivaler a, significar.

amp(ère) ['æmp(ɛɔ*)] n amperio.

amphibian [æm'fɪbɪɔn] n anfibio; **amphibious** [-bɪɔs] a anfibio.

amphitheatre ['æmfɪθɪɔtɔ*] n anfiteatro.

ample ['æmpl] *a* (*spacious*) amplió, ancho; (*abundant*) abundante; (*enough*) bastante, suficiente.

amplifier ['æmplɪfaɪə*] *n* amplificador *m*.

amplify ['æmplɪfaɪ] *vt* amplificar, aumentar; (*explain*) explicar.

amputate ['æmpjuteɪt] *vt* amputar.

amuck [ə'mʌk] *ad* = **amok.**

amuse [ə'mju:z] *vt* divertir; (*distract*) distraer, entretener; ~**ment** *n* diversión *f*; (*pastime*) pasatiempo; (*laughter*) risa.

an [æn, ən, n] *det see* **a.**

anaemia [ə'ni:mɪə] *n* anemia; **anaemic** [-mɪk] *a* anémico; (*fig*) soso, insípido.

anaesthetic [ænɪs'θetɪk] *n* anestesia; **anaesthetist** [æ'ni:sθɪtɪst] *n* anestesista *m/f*.

analgesic [ænæl'dʒi:sɪk] *a*, *n* analgésico.

analogy [ə'nælədʒɪ] *n* análogo.

analyse ['ænəlaɪz] *vt* analizar; **analysis** [ə'næləsɪs], *pl* **-ses** [-si:z] *n* análisis *m inv*; **analyst** [-lɪst] *n* (*US*) analista *m/f*; **analytic(al)** ['lɪtɪk(ol)] *a* analítico.

anarchist ['ænəkɪst] *a*, *n* anarquista *m/f*; **anarchy** [-kɪ] *n* anarquía, desorden *m*.

anatomy [ə'nætəmɪ] *n* anatomía.

ancestor ['ænsɪstə*] *n* antepasado; **ancestry** [-trɪ] *n* ascendencia, abolengo.

anchor ['æŋkə*] *n* ancla, áncora // *vi* anclar // *vt* (*fig*) sujetar, asegurar; **to weigh** ~ levar anclas; ~**age** *n* ancladero.

anchovy ['æntʃəvɪ] *n* anchoa.

ancient ['eɪnʃənt] *a* antiguo.

and [ænd] *conj* y; (*before i, hi*) e; ~ **so on** etcétera, y así sucesivamente; **try** ~ **come** procure *o* intente venir; **better** ~ **better** cada vez mejor.

Andes ['ændiːz] *npl*: **the** ~ los Andes.

anecdote ['ænɪkdəut] *n* anécdota.

anew [ə'nju:] *ad* de nuevo, otra vez.

angel ['eɪndʒəl] *n* ángel *m*.

anger ['æŋgə*] *n* cólera, ira // *vt* enojar, provocar.

angina [æn'dʒaɪnə] *n* angina (de pecho).

angle ['æŋgl] *n* ángulo; **from their** ~ desde su punto de vista.

angler ['æŋglə*] *n* pescador/a *m/f* (de caña).

Anglican ['æŋglɪkən] *a*, *n* anglicano/a.

angling ['æŋglɪŋ] *n* pesca con caña.

Anglo- ['æŋgləu] *pref* anglo....

angrily ['æŋgrɪlɪ] *ad* con enojo, airadamente.

angry ['æŋgrɪ] *a* enfadado, enojado; **to be** ~ **with sb/at sth** estar enfadado con alguien/por algo; **to get** ~ enfadarse, enojarse.

anguish ['æŋgwɪʃ] *n* (*physical*) dolor *m* agudo; (*mental*) angustia.

angular ['æŋgjulə*] *a* (*shape*) angular; (*features*) anguloso.

animal ['ænɪməl] *n* animal *m*, bestia; (*insect*) bicho // *a* animal.

animate ['ænɪmeɪt] *vt* (*enliven*) animar;

(*encourage*) estimular, alentar; ~**d** *a* vivo, animado.

animosity [ænɪ'mɔsɪtɪ] *n* animosidad *f*, rencor *m*.

aniseed ['ænisiːd] *n* anís *m*.

ankle ['æŋkl] *n* tobillo *m*.

annex ['æneks] *n* (*also*: **annexe**) (*edificio*) anexo, dependencia // *vt* [æ'neks] (*territory*) anexar; (*document*) adjuntar.

annihilate [ə'naɪəleɪt] *vt* aniquilar.

anniversary [ænɪ'vɜːsərɪ] *n* aniversario.

annotate ['ænəuteɪt] *vt* anotar, comentar.

announce [ə'nauns] *vt* comunicar, anunciar; ~**ment** *n* anuncio, aviso, declaración *f*; **announcer** *n* (*RADIO, TV*) locutor/a *m/f*.

annoy [ə'nɔɪ] *vt* molestar, fastidiar, irritar; **don't get** ~**ed!** ¡no se enfade!; ~**ance** *n* enojo; (*thing*) molestia; ~**ing** *a* molesto, fastidioso; (*person*) pesado.

annual ['ænjuəl] *a* anual // *n* (*BOT*) anual *m*; (*book*) anuario; ~**ly** *ad* anualmente, cada año.

annuity [ə'nju:ɪtɪ] *n* renta *o* pensión *f* vitalicia.

annul [ə'nʌl] *vt* anular, cancelar; (*law*) revocar; ~**ment** *n* anulación *f*, cancelación *f*.

annum ['ænəm] *n see* **per.**

anoint [ə'nɔɪnt] *vt* untar.

anomaly [ə'nɔmɔlɪ] *n* anomalía.

anonymity [ænə'nɪmɪtɪ] *n* anonimato; **anonymous** [ə'nɔnɪməs] *a* anónimo.

anorak ['ænəræk] *n* anorak *m*.

anorexia [ænə'reksɪə] *n* (*MED*) anorexia.

another [ə'nʌðə*] *a*: ~ **book** (*one more*) otro libro; (*a different one*) un libro distinto // *pron* otro; *see also* **one.**

answer ['ɑːnsə*] *n* contestación *f*, respuesta; (*to problem*) solución *f* // *vi* contestar, responder // *vt* (*reply to*) contestar a, responder a; (*problem*) resolver; **to** ~ **the phone** contestar el teléfono; **in** ~ **to your letter** contestando *o* en contestación a su carta; **to** ~ **the bell** *or* **the door** acudir a la puerta; **to** ~ **back** *vi* replicar, ser respondón(ona); **to** ~ **for** *vt fus* responder de *o* por; **to** ~ **to** *vt fus* (*description*) corresponder a; (*needs*) satisfacer; ~**able** *a*: ~**able to sb for sth** responsable ante uno de algo.

ant [ænt] *n* hormiga.

antacid [ænt'æsɪd] *a* antiácido.

antagonist [æn'tægənɪst] *n* antagonista *m/f*, adversario/a; ~**ic** [-'nɪstɪk] *a* antagónico; (*opposed*) contrario, opuesto; **antagonize** [-naɪz] *vt* enemistarse con.

Antarctic [ænt'ɑːktɪk] *n*: **the** ~ el Antártico; ~**a** *n* Antártida.

antelope ['æntɪləup] *n* antílope *m*.

antenatal ['æntɪ'neɪtl] *a* antenatal, prenatal; ~ **clinic** *n* clínica prenatal.

antenna [æn'tenə], *pl* ~**e** [-niː] *n* antena.

anthem ['ænθəm] *n*: **national** ~ himno nacional.

anthology [æn'θɔlədʒɪ] *n* antología.

anthropologist [ænθrə'pɔlədʒɪst] n
antropólogo; **anthropology** [-dʒi] n
antropología.
anti... [æntɪ] pref anti...; **∼-aircraft** a
antiaéreo.
antibiotic [æntɪbaɪ'ɔtɪk] a, n antibiótico.
anticipate [æn'tɪsɪpeɪt] vt (foresee)
prever; (expect) esperar, contar con;
(forestall) anticiparse a, adelantarse a;
(look forward to) prometerse;
anticipation [-'peɪʃən] n previsión f;
esperanza; anticipación f, prevención f.
anticlimax [æntɪ'klaɪmæks] n decepción f.
anticlockwise [æntɪ'klɔkwaɪz] ad en
dirección contraria a la de las agujas del
reloj.
antics ['æntɪks] npl payasadas fpl; (of
child) travesuras fpl.
anticyclone [æntɪ'saɪkləun] n anticiclón
m.
antidote ['æntɪdəut] n antídoto.
antifreeze ['æntɪfriːz] n anticongelante m,
solución f anticongelante.
antihistamine [æntɪ'hɪstəmiːn] n
antihistamínico.
antiquated ['æntɪkweɪtɪd] a anticuado.
antique [æn'tiːk] n antigüedad f, antigualla
// a antiguo, anticuado; **∼ dealer** n
anticuario; **∼ shop** n tienda de
antigüedades.
antiquity [æn'tɪkwɪtɪ] n antigüedad f.
antiseptic [æntɪ'septɪk] a, n antiséptico.
antisocial [æntɪ'səuʃəl] a antisocial.
antlers ['æntləz] npl cuernas fpl.
anus ['eɪnəs] n ano.
anvil ['ænvɪl] n yunque m.
anxiety [æŋ'zaɪətɪ] n (worry) inquietud f;
(eagerness) ansia, anhelo; (MED) ansiedad
f.
anxious ['æŋkʃəs] a (worried) inquieto;
(keen) deseoso; **∼ly** ad con inquietud, de
manera angustiada.
any ['enɪ] a (in negative and interrogative
sentences = some) algún, alguna, alguna;
(negative sense) ningún, ninguno, ninguna;
(no matter which) cualquier(a); (each and
every) todo; **I haven't ∼ money/books**
no tengo dinero/libros; **have you ∼ but-
ter/children?** ¿tiene mantequilla/hijos?;
at ∼ moment en cualquier momento; **in
∼ case** de todas formas, de todas
maneras; **at ∼ rate** de todas formas, sea
como sea // pron alguno; ninguno; (anybody) cualquiera; (in negative and
interrogative sentences): **I haven't ∼** no
tengo ninguno; **have you got ∼?** ¿tiene
algunos?; **can ∼ of you sing?** ¿alguno de
Ustedes sabe cantar?; (in negative
sentences) nada; (in interrogative and conditional constructions) algo; **I can't hear
him ∼** more no le oigo más; **do you
want ∼ more soup?** ¿quiere más sopa?;
∼body pron cualquiera, cualquier
persona; (in interrogative sentences)
alguien; (in negative sentences): **I don't
see ∼body** no veo a nadie; **∼how** ad de
todos modos, de todas maneras;

(carelessly) de cualquier manera; **∼one
= ∼body;** **∼thing** pron (see **∼body**)
algo, cualquier cosa; algo; (in negative
sentences) nada; (everything) todo; **∼time**
ad (at any moment) en cualquier momento,
de un momento a otro; (whenever) no
importa cuándo, cuando quiera; **∼way** ad
de todas maneras; de cualquier modo;
∼where ad (see **∼body**) dondequiera;
en algún sitio; (negative sense) en ningún
sitio; (everywhere) en or por todas partes;
I don't see him ∼where no le veo en
ningún sitio.
apart [ə'pɑːt] ad aparte, separadamente;
10 miles ∼ separados por 10 millas; **∼
from** prep aparte de.
apartheid [ə'pɑːteɪt] n apartheid m.
apartment [ə'pɑːtmənt] n (US) piso,
apartamento; (room) cuarto.
apathetic [æpə'θetɪk] a apático,
indiferente; **apathy** ['æpəθɪ] n apatía,
indiferencia.
ape [eɪp] n mono // vt imitar, remedar.
aperitif [ə'perɪtɪv] n aperitivo.
aperture ['æpətʃuə*] n rendija, resquicio;
(PHOT) abertura.
apex ['eɪpeks] n ápice m; (fig) cumbre f.
aphrodisiac [æfrəu'dɪzɪæk] a, n
afrodisíaco.
apiece [ə'piːs] ad cada uno.
apologetic [əpɔlə'dʒetɪk] a (tone, letter)
lleno de disculpas.
apologize [ə'pɔlədʒaɪz] vi: **to ∼ (for sth
to sb)** disculparse (con alguien de algo);
apology [-dʒɪ] n disculpa, excusa.
apostle [ə'pɔsl] n apóstol m/f.
apostrophe [ə'pɔstrəfɪ] n apóstrofe m.
appal [ə'pɔːl] vt horrorizar, espantar;
∼ling a espantoso; (awful) pésimo.
apparatus [æpə'reɪtəs] n aparato.
apparent [ə'pærənt] a aparente; (obvious)
manifiesto, claro; **∼ly** ad por lo visto, al
parecer.
apparition [æpə'rɪʃən] n aparición f;
(ghost) fantasma m.
appeal [ə'piːl] vi (LAW) apelar // n (LAW)
apelación f; (request) llamamiento; (plea)
súplica, ruego; (charm) atractivo, encanto;
to ∼ for suplicar, reclamar; **to ∼ to**
(subj: person) rogar a, suplicar a; (subj:
thing) atraer, interesar; **to ∼ to sb for
mercy** rogarle misericordia a alguien; **it
doesn't ∼ to me** no me atrae, no me
llama la atención; **∼ing** a (nice)
atrayente, atractivo; (touching) conmove-
dor(a), emocionante.
appear [ə'pɪə*] vi aparecer, presentarse;
(LAW) comparecer; (publication) salir (a
luz), publicarse; (seem) parecer; **it would
∼ that** parecería que; **∼ance** n aparición f; (look, aspect) apariencia, aspecto.
appease [ə'piːz] vt (pacify) apaciguar;
(satisfy) satisfacer, saciar.
appendicitis [əpendɪ'saɪtɪs] n apendicitis
f.
appendix [ə'pendɪks], pl **-dices** [-dɪsiːz] n
apéndice m.

appetite ['æpɪtaɪt] n apetito; (fig) deseo, anhelo.

appetizing ['æpɪtaɪzɪŋ] a apetitoso.

applaud [ə'plɔːd] vt, vi aplaudir; **applause** [-ɔːz] n aplausos mpl.

apple ['æpl] n manzana; ~ **tree** n manzano.

appliance [ə'plaɪəns] n aparato.

applicable [ə'plɪkəbl] a aplicable, pertinente.

applicant ['æplɪkənt] n candidato/a, solicitante m/f.

application [æplɪ'keɪʃən] n aplicación f; (for a job, a grant etc) solicitud f, petición f; ~ **form** n formulario.

apply [ə'plaɪ] vt: to ~ (to) aplicar (a); (fig) emplear (para) // vi: to ~ to (ask) presentarse a, ser candidato a; (be suitable for) ser aplicable a; (be relevant to) tener que ver con; to ~ for (permit, grant, job) solicitar; to ~ the brakes aplicar los frenos; to ~ o.s. to aplicarse a, dedicarse a.

appoint [ə'pɔɪnt] vt (to post) nombrar; (date, place) fijar, señalar; ~ment n (engagement) cita; (date) compromiso; (act) nombramiento; (post) puesto.

apportion [ə'pɔːʃən] vt repartir, distribuir; (blame) dar.

appraisal [ə'preɪzl] n tasación f, valoración f.

appreciable [ə'priːʃəbl] a sensible.

appreciate [ə'priːʃɪeɪt] vt (like) apreciar, tener en mucho; (be grateful for) agradecer; (assess) valorar, apreciar; (be aware of) comprender, percibir // vi (COMM) aumentar(se) en valor, subir; **appreciation** [-'eɪʃən] n aprecio; reconocimiento, agradecimiento; aumento en valor.

appreciative [ə'priːʃɪətɪv] a (person) agradecido; (comment) elogioso.

apprehend [æprɪ'hɛnd] vt percibir, comprender; (arrest) detener.

apprehension [æprɪ'hɛnʃən] n (fear) recelo, aprensión f; **apprehensive** [-'hɛnsɪv] a aprensivo.

apprentice [ə'prɛntɪs] n aprendiz/a m/f; ~ship n aprendizaje m.

approach [ə'prəutʃ] vi acercarse // vt acercarse a; (be approximate) aproximarse a; (ask, apply to) dirigirse a // n acercamiento; aproximación f; (access) acceso; (proposal) proposición f; ~able a (person) abordable; (place) accesible.

appropriate [ə'prəuprɪeɪt] vt (take) apropiarse; (allot): to ~ sth for destinar algo a // a [-rɪɪt] (apt) apropiado, conveniente; (relevant) competente.

approval [ə'pruːvəl] n aprobación f, visto bueno; on ~ (COMM) a prueba.

approve [ə'pruːv] vt aprobar; ~d **school** n correccional m.

approximate [ə'prɔksɪmɪt] a aproximado // vt [-meɪt] aproximarse a, acercarse a;

approximation [-'meɪʃən] n aproximación f.

apricot ['eɪprɪkɔt] n albaricoque m.

April ['eɪprəl] n abril m; ~ **Fool's Day** n Día m de los Inocentes.

apron ['eɪprən] n delantal m.

apt [æpt] a (suitable) acertado, oportuno; (appropriate) conveniente; (likely): ~ **to do** con tendencia a hacer.

aptitude ['æptɪtjuːd] n aptitud f, capacidad f.

aqualung ['ækwəlʌŋ] n aparato de buceo autónomo.

aquarium [ə'kwɛərɪəm] n acuario.

Aquarius [ə'kwɛərɪəs] n Acuario.

aquatic [ə'kwætɪk] a acuático.

aqueduct ['ækwɪdʌkt] n acueducto.

Arab ['ærəb] n árabe m/f.

Arabia [ə'reɪbɪə] n Arabia; ~**n** a árabe.

Arabic ['ærəbɪk] n árabe m.

arable ['ærəbl] a cultivable.

arbitrary ['ɑːbɪtrərɪ] a arbitrario.

arbitrate ['ɑːbɪtreɪt] vi arbitrar; **arbitration** [-'treɪʃən] n arbitraje m; **arbitrator** n juez m árbitro.

arc [ɑːk] n arco.

arcade [ɑː'keɪd] n arcada; (round a square) soportales mpl; (passage with shops) galería, pasaje m.

arch [ɑːtʃ] n arco; (vault) bóveda; (of foot) empeine m // vt arquear.

archaeologist [ɑːkɪ'ɔlədʒɪst] n arqueólogo; **archaeology** [-dʒɪ] n arqueología.

archaic [ɑː'keɪɪk] a arcaico.

archbishop [ɑːtʃ'bɪʃəp] n arzobispo.

arch-enemy ['ɑːtʃ'ɛnɪmɪ] n enemigo jurado.

archer ['ɑːtʃə*] n arquero; ~y n tiro con arco.

archetype ['ɑːkɪtaɪp] n arquetipo.

archipelago [ɑːkɪ'pɛlɪgəu] n archipiélago.

architect ['ɑːkɪtɛkt] n arquitecto; ~**ural** [-'tɛktʃərəl] a arquitectónico; ~**ure** n arquitectura.

archives ['ɑːkaɪvz] npl archivo sg.

archway ['ɑːtʃweɪ] n arco, arcada.

Arctic ['ɑːktɪk] a ártico // n: the ~ el Ártico.

ardent ['ɑːdənt] a (passionate) ardiente, apasionado; (fervent) fervoroso; **ardour** ['ɑːdə*] n ardor m; fervor m.

arduous ['ɑːdjuəs] a (gen) arduo; (journey) penoso.

are [ɑː*] vb see **be**.

area ['ɛərɪə] n (gen) área; (MATH etc) superficie f, extensión f; (zone) región f, zona.

arena [ə'riːnə] n arena; (of circus) pista; (for bullfight) plaza, ruedo.

aren't [ɑːnt] = **are not**.

Argentina [ɑːdʒən'tiːnə] n Argentina; **Argentinian** [-'tɪnɪən] a, n argentino/a.

argue ['ɑːgjuː] vi (quarrel) discutir; (reason) argüir, discurrir; to ~ **that** sostener que; **argument** n (reasons) argumento; (*quarrel*) discusión f; (*debate*) debate *m*, disputa; **argumentative** [-mentətiv] a discutidor(a).

aria ['ɑ:rɪə] *n* (MUS) aria.

arid ['ærɪd] *a* árido.

Aries ['ɛərɪz] *n* Aries *m*.

arise [ə'raɪz], *pt* **arose**, *pp* **arisen** [ə'rɪzn] *vi* (*rise up*) levantarse, alzarse; (*emerge*) surgir, presentarse; **to ~ from** resultar de.

aristocracy [ærɪs'tɔkrəsɪ] *n* aristocracia; **aristocrat** ['ærɪstəkræt] *n* aristócrata *m/f*.

arithmetic [ə'rɪθmətɪk] *n* aritmética.

ark [ɑ:k] *n*: **Noah's A~** Arca de Noé.

arm [ɑ:m] *n* (ANAT) brazo; (*weapon*, MIL: *branch*) arma // *vt* armar; **~s** *npl* (*weapons*) armas *fpl*; (HERALDRY) escudo *sg*; **~s race** carrera de armamentos; **in ~** cogidos del brazo; **~band** *n* brazalete *m*; **~chair** *n* sillón *m*; **~ed** *a* armado; **~ed robbery** *n* robo a mano armada; **~ful** *n* brazado, brazada.

armistice ['ɑ:mɪstɪs] *n* armisticio.

armour ['ɑ:mə*] *n* armadura; **~ed car** *n* coche *m* blindado; **~y** *n* armería, arsenal *m*.

armpit ['ɑ:mpɪt] *n* sobaco, axila.

army ['ɑ:mɪ] *n* ejército.

aroma [ə'rəumə] *n* aroma *m*, fragancia; **~tic** [ærə'mætɪk] *a* aromático, fragante.

arose [ə'rəuz] *pt of* **arise.**

around [ə'raund] *ad* alrededor; (*in the area*) a la redonda // *prep* alrededor de, en torno a; (*fig*: *about*) alrededor de.

arouse [ə'rauz] *vt* despertar.

arrange [ə'reɪndʒ] *vt* arreglar, ordenar; (*programme*) organizar; **~ment** *n* arreglo; (*agreement*) acuerdo; **~ments** *npl* (*plans*) planes *mpl*, medidas *fpl*; (*preparations*) preparativos *mpl*.

arrears [ə'rɪəz] *npl* atrasos *mpl*; **to be in ~ with one's rent** atrasarse en el arriendo.

arrest [ə'rɛst] *vt* detener; (*sb's attention*) llamar // *n* detención *f*; **under ~** detenido.

arrival [ə'raɪvəl] *n* llegada; **new ~** recién llegado.

arrive [ə'raɪv] *vi* llegar.

arrogance ['ærəgəns] *n* arrogancia; **arrogant** [-gənt] *a* arrogante.

arrow ['ærəu] *n* flecha.

arsenal ['ɑ:sɪnl] *n* arsenal *m*.

arsenic ['ɑ:snɪk] *n* arsénico.

arson ['ɑ:sn] *n* delito de incendiar.

art [ɑ:t] *n* arte *m*; (*craft*) artes *fpl* y oficios *mpl*; (*skill*) destreza; (*technique*) técnica; **A~s** *npl* (SCOL) Letras *fpl*; **~ gallery** *n* museo de bellas artes; (*small and private*) galería de arte.

artery ['ɑ:tərɪ] *n* (MED) arteria; (*fig*) vía principal.

arthritis [ɑ:'θraɪtɪs] *n* artritis f.

artichoke ['ɑ:tɪtʃəuk] *n* alcachofa; **Jerusalem ~** aguaturma.

article ['ɑ:tɪkl] *n* artículo, objeto, cosa; (*in*

newspaper) artículo; (LAW: *training*): **~s** *npl* contrato *sg* de aprendizaje.

articulate [ɑ:'tɪkjulɪt] *a* claro o distinto en el hablar // *vt* [-leɪt] articular; **~d lorry** *n* camión *m* articulado.

artificial [ɑ:tɪ'fɪʃəl] *a* artificial; (*teeth etc*) postizo; **~ respiration** *n* respiración f artificial.

artillery [ɑ:'tɪlərɪ] *n* artillería.

artisan ['ɑ:tɪzæn] *n* artesano.

artist ['ɑ:tɪst] *n* artista *m/f*; (MUS) intérprete *m/f*; **~ic** [ɑ:'tɪstɪk] *a* artístico; **~ry** *n* arte *m*, habilidad f artística.

artless ['ɑ:tlɪs] *a* (*innocent*) natural, sencillo; (*clumsy*) desmañado.

as [æz, əz] *conj* (*cause*) como, ya que; (*time*: *moment*) como, cuando; (: *duration*) mientras; (*manner*) como, lo mismo que, tal como; (*in the capacity of*) como; **~ big ~** tan grande como; **twice ~ big ~** dos veces más grande que; **~ she said** como ella dijo; **~ if** *or* **though** como si; **~ for** *or* **to that** en cuanto a eso, en lo que a eso se refiere; **~ or so long ~** *conj* mientras (que); **~ much/many ~** tanto(s)... como; **~ soon ~** *conj* tan pronto como; **~ such** *ad* como tal; **~ well** *ad* también, además; **~ well ~** *conj* así como; *see also* **such.**

asbestos [æz'bɛstəs] *n* asbesto, amianto.

ascend [ə'sɛnd] *vt* subir; **~ancy** *n* ascendiente *m*, dominio.

ascent [ə'sɛnt] *n* subida; (*slope*) cuesta, pendiente *m*; (*promotion*) ascenso.

ascertain [æsə'teɪn] *vt* averiguar, determinar.

ascetic [ə'sɛtɪk] *a* ascético.

ascribe [ə'skraɪb] *vt*: **to ~ sth to** atribuir algo a.

ash [æʃ] *n* ceniza; (*tree*) fresno.

ashamed [ə'feɪmd] *a* avergonzado; **to be ~ of** avergonzarse de.

ashen ['æʃn] *a* ceniciento, pálido.

ashore [ə'fɔ:*] *ad* en tierra.

ashtray ['æʃtreɪ] *n* cenicero.

Asia ['eɪʃə] *n* Asia; **~n, ~tic** [eɪsɪ'ætɪk] *a*, *n* asiático/a.

aside [ə'saɪd] *ad* aparte, a un lado.

ask [ɑ:sk] *vt* (*question*) preguntar; (*demand*) pedir; (*invite*) invitar; **to ~ sb sth/to do sth** preguntar algo a alguien/pedir a alguien que haga algo; **to ~ sb about sth** preguntar algo a alguien; **to ~ (sb) a question** hacer una pregunta (a alguien); **to ~ sb out to dinner** invitar a comer a uno; **to ~ for** *vt fus* pedir.

askance [ə'skɑ:ns] *ad*: **to look ~ at sb** mirar con recelo a uno.

askew [ə'skju:] *ad* sesgado, ladeado, oblicuamente.

asleep [ə'sli:p] *a* dormido; **to fall ~** dormirse, quedarse dormido.

asparagus [əs'pærəgəs] *n* espárragos *mpl*.

aspect ['æspɛkt] *n* aspecto, apariencia; (*direction in which a building etc faces*) orientación f.

aspersions [əs'pəːʃənz] npl: **to cast ~ on** difamar a, calumniar a.

asphalt ['æsfælt] n asfalto; (place) pista asfaltada.

asphyxiate [æs'fıksıeıt] vt asfixiar // vi asfixiarse; **asphyxiation** [-'eıʃən] n asfixia.

aspiration [æspə'reıʃən] n (fig) anhelo, deseo, ambición f.

aspire [əs'paıə*] vi: **to ~ to** aspirar a, ambicionar.

aspirin ['æsprın] n aspirina.

ass [æs] n asno, burro; (col) imbécil m.

assailant [ə'seılənt] n asaltador/a m/f, agresor/a m/f.

assassin [ə'sæsın] n asesino; **~ate** vt asesinar; **~ation** [-'neıʃən] n asesinato.

assault [ə'sɔːlt] n (gen: attack) asalto, ataque m // vt asaltar, atacar; (sexually) violar.

assemble [ə'sɛmbl] vt reunir, juntar; (TECH) montar // vi reunirse, juntarse.

assembly [ə'sɛmblı] n (meeting) reunión f, asamblea; (people) concurrencia; (construction) montaje m; **~ line** n línea de producción.

assent [ə'sɛnt] n asentimiento, aprobación f // vi consentir, asentir.

assert [ə'səːt] vt afirmar; (claim etc) hacer valer; **~ion** [ə'səːʃən] n afirmación f.

assess [ə'sɛs] vt valorar, calcular; (tax, damages) fijar; (property etc: for tax) gravar; **~ment** n valoración f; gravamen m; **~or** n asesor/a m/f; (of tax) tasador/a m/f.

asset ['æsɛt] n posesión f; (quality) ventaja sg; **~s** npl (funds) activo sg, fondos mpl.

assiduous [ə'sıdjuəs] a asiduo.

assign [ə'saın] vt (date) fijar; (task) asignar; (resources) destinar; (property) traspasar; **~ment** n asignación f; (task) tarea.

assimilate [ə'sımıleıt] vt asimilar.

assist [ə'sıst] vt ayudar; (progress etc) fomentar; **~ance** n ayuda, auxilio; (welfare) subsidio; **~ant** n ayudante m/f, auxiliar m/f; (also: **shop ~ant**) dependiente/a m/f.

assizes [ə'saızız] npl sesión f de un tribunal.

associate [ə'səuʃıt] a asociado // n asociado, colega m/f; (in crime) cómplice m/f; (member) miembro / (vb: [-ʃıeıt]) vt asociar, relacionar // vi: **to ~ with sb** tratar con alguien.

association [əsəusı'eıʃən] n asociación f; (COMM) sociedad f.

assorted [ə'sɔːtıd] a surtido, variado.

assortment [ə'sɔːtmənt] n surtido.

assume [ə'sjuːm] vt (suppose) suponer, dar por sentado; (responsibilities etc) asumir; (attitude, name) adoptar, tomar.

assumption [ə'sʌmpʃən] n (supposition) suposición f, presunción f; (act) asunción f.

assurance [ə'ʃuərəns] n garantía, promesa; (confidence) confianza, aplomo; (certainty) certeza; (insurance) seguro.

assure [ə'ʃuə*] vt asegurar.

asterisk ['æstərısk] n asterisco.

astern [ə'stəːn] ad a popa, por la popa.

asteroid ['æstərɔıd] n asteroide m.

asthma ['æsmə] n asma; **~tic** [æs'mætık] a, n asmático/a.

astonish [ə'stɔnıʃ] vt asombrar, pasmar; **~ment** n asombro, sorpresa.

astound [ə'staund] vt asombrar, pasmar.

astray [ə'streı] ad: **to go ~** extraviarse; **to lead ~** llevar por mal camino.

astride [ə'straıd] ad a horcajadas // prep a caballo o horcajadas sobre.

astrologer [əs'trɔlədʒə*] n astrólogo; **astrology** [-dʒı] n astrología.

astronaut ['æstrənɔːt] n astronauta m/f.

astronomer [əs'trɔnəmə*] n astrónomo; **astronomical** [æstrə'nɔmıkəl] a astronómico; (fig) tremendo, enorme; **astronomy** [-mı] n astronomía.

astute [əs'tjuːt] a astuto.

asunder [ə'sʌndə*] ad: **to tear ~** romper en dos, hacer pedazos.

asylum [ə'saıləm] n (refuge) asilo; (hospital) manicomio.

at [æt] prep en, a; **~ the top** en la cumbre; **~ 4 o'clock** a las cuatro; **~ £1 a kilo** a libra el kilo; **~ night** de noche, por la noche; **~ a stroke** de un golpe; **two ~ a time** de dos en dos; **~ times** a veces.

ate [eıt] pt of **eat**.

atheist ['eıθııst] n ateo/a.

Athens ['æθınz] n Atenas f.

athlete ['æθliːt] n atleta m/f.

athletic [æθ'lɛtık] a atlético; **~s** n atletismo.

Atlantic [ət'læntık] n: **the ~ (Ocean)** el (Océano) Atlántico.

atlas ['ætləs] n atlas m.

atmosphere ['ætməsfıə*] n atmósfera; (fig) ambiente m.

atom ['ætəm] n átomo; **~ic** [ə'tɔmık] a atómico; **~(ic) bomb** n bomba atómica; **~izer** ['ætəmaızə*] n atomizador m.

atone [ə'təun] vi: **to ~ for** expiar.

atrocious [ə'trəuʃəs] a (very bad) atroz; (fig) horrible, infame.

atrocity [ə'trɔsıtı] n atrocidad f.

attach [ə'tætʃ] vt (gen) sujetar, pegar; (document, letter) adjuntar; **to be ~ed to sb/sth** (to like) tener cariño a alguien/algo.

attaché [ə'tæʃeı] n agregado; **~ case** n maletín m.

attachment [ə'tætʃmənt] n (tool) accesorio; (love): **~ (to)** cariño (a).

attack [ə'tæk] vt (MIL) atacar; (criminal) agredir, asaltar; (task etc) emprender // n ataque m, asalto; (on sb's life) atentado; **heart ~** ataque al corazón o cardíaco; **~er** n agresor/a m/f, asaltante m/f.

attain [ə'teın] vt (also: **~ to**) alcanzar; (achieve) lograr, conseguir; **~ments** npl dotes fpl, talento sg.

attempt [ə'tɛmpt] n tentativa, intento; (attack) atentado // vt intentar, tratar de.

attend [ə'tɛnd] *vt* asistir a; (*patient*) atender; **to ~ to** *vt fus* (*needs, affairs etc*) ocuparse de; (*speech etc*) prestar atención a; (*customer*) atender a; **~ance** *n* asistencia, presencia; (*people present*) concurrencia; **~ant** *n* sirviente/a *m/f*, mozo/a; (*THEATRE*) acomodador/a *m/f* // *a* concomitante.

attention [ə'tɛnʃən] *n* atención *f* // *excl* (*MIL*) ¡firme(s)!; **for the ~ of...** (*ADMIN*) atención... .

attentive [ə'tɛntɪv] *a* atento; (*polite*) cortés.

attest [ə'tɛst] *vi*: **to ~ to** dar fe de.

attic ['ætɪk] *n* desván *m*, ático.

attitude ['ætɪtjuːd] *n* (*gen*) actitud *f*; (*disposition*) disposición *f*.

attorney [ə'tɔːnɪ] *n* (*lawyer*) abogado; (*having proxy*) apoderado; **A~ General** *n* (*Brit*) fiscal *m* de la corona; (*US*) procurador *m* general.

attract [ə'trækt] *vt* atraer; (*attention*) llamar; **attraction** [ə'trækʃən] *n* (*gen pl*) encantos *mpl*; (*amusements*) diversiones *fpl*; (*PHYSICS*) atracción *f*; (*fig: towards sth*) atractivo; **~ive** *a* atractivo; (*interesting*) atrayente; (*pretty*) guapo, mono.

attribute ['ætrɪbjuːt] *n* atributo // *vt* [ə'trɪbjuːt]: **to ~ sth to** atribuir o achacar algo a.

aubergine ['əʊbəʒiːn] *n* berenjena.

auburn ['ɔːbən] *a* castaño rojizo.

auction ['ɔːkʃən] *n* (*also: sale by ~*) subasta // *vt* subastar; **~eer** [-'nɪə*] *n* subastador/a *m/f*.

audacious [ɔː'deɪʃəs] *a* audaz, atrevido; (*pej*) descarado; **audacity** [ɔː'dæsɪtɪ] *n* audacia, atrevimiento; (*pej*) descaro.

audible ['ɔːdɪbl] *a* audible, que se puede oír.

audience ['ɔːdɪəns] *n* auditorio, público; (*interview*) audiencia.

audio-visual [ɔːdɪəʊ'vɪzjʊəl] *a* audiovisual.

audit ['ɔːdɪt] *vt* revisar, intervenir.

audition [ɔː'dɪʃən] *n* audición *f*.

auditor ['ɔːdɪtə*] *n* interventor/a *m/f*, censor/a *m/f* de cuentas.

auditorium [ɔːdɪ'tɔːrɪəm] *n* auditorio.

augment [ɔːg'mɛnt] *vt* aumentar // *vi* aumentarse.

augur ['ɔːgə*] *vi*: **it ~s well** es de buen agüero.

August ['ɔːgəst] *n* agosto.

aunt [ɑːnt] *n* tía; **~ie, ~y** *n* diminutive of **aunt**.

au pair ['əʊ'pɛə*] *n* (*also: ~ girl*) au pair *f*.

aura ['ɔːrə] *n* emanación *f*; (*atmosphere*) ambiente *m*.

auspices ['ɔːspɪsɪz] *npl*: **under the ~ of** bajo los auspicios de.

auspicious [ɔːs'pɪʃəs] *a* propicio, de buen augurio.

austere [ɔs'tɪə*] *a* austero; (*manner*) adusto; **austerity** [ɔs'stɛrətɪ] *n* austeridad *f*.

Australia [ɔs'treɪlɪə] *n* Australia; **~n** *a, n* australiano/a.

Austria ['ɔstrɪə] *n* Austria; **~n** *a, n* austríaco/a.

authentic [ɔː'θɛntɪk] *a* auténtico.

author ['ɔːθə*] *n* autor/a *m/f*.

authoritarian [ɔːθɔrɪ'tɛərɪən] *a* autoritario.

authoritative [ɔː'θɔrɪtətɪv] *a* autorizado; (*manner*) autoritario.

authority [ɔː'θɔrɪtɪ] *n* autoridad *f*; **the authorities** *npl* las autoridades.

authorize ['ɔːθəraɪz] *vt* autorizar.

auto ['ɔːtəʊ] *n* (*US*) coche *m*, automóvil *m*.

autobiography [ɔːtəbaɪ'ɔgrəfɪ] *n* autobiografía.

autocratic [ɔːtə'krætɪk] *a* autocrático.

autograph ['ɔːtəgrɑːf] *n* autógrafo // *vt* firmar; (*photo etc*) dedicar.

automatic [ɔːtə'mætɪk] *a* automático // *n* (*gun*) pistola automática.

automation [ɔːtə'meɪʃən] *n* automatización *f*.

automaton [ɔː'tɔmətən], *pl* **-mata** [-tə] *n* autómata *m/f*.

automobile ['ɔːtəməbiːl] *n* (*US*) coche *m*, automóvil *m*.

autonomous [ɔː'tɔnəməs] *a* autónomo.

autopsy ['ɔːtɔpsɪ] *n* autopsia.

autumn ['ɔːtəm] *n* otoño.

auxiliary [ɔːg'zɪlɪərɪ] *a* auxiliar.

Av. *abbr of* **avenue.**

avail [ə'veɪl] *vt*: **to ~ o.s. of** aprovechar(se) de, valerse de // *n*: **to no ~** en vano, sin resultado.

availability [əveɪlə'bɪlɪtɪ] *n* disponibilidad *f*.

available [ə'veɪləbl] *a* disponible; (*usable*) asequible.

avalanche ['ævəlɑːnʃ] *n* alud *m*, avalancha.

avant-garde ['ævã'gɑːd] *a* de vanguardia.

avaricious [ævə'rɪʃəs] *a* avaro, avariento.

Ave. *abbr of* **avenue.**

avenge [ə'vɛndʒ] *vt* vengar.

avenue ['ævənjuː] *n* avenida; (*path*) camino.

average ['ævərɪdʒ] *n* promedio, término medio // *a* (*mean*) medio, de término medio; (*ordinary*) regular, corriente // *vt* calcular el promedio de, prorratear; **on ~** por regla general; **to ~ out** *vi*: **to ~ out at** resultar por promedio, ser por regla general.

averse [ə'vɜːs] *a*: **to be ~ to sth/doing** sentir aversión o antipatía por algo/por hacer; **aversion** [ə'vɜːʃən] *n* aversión *f*, repugnancia.

avert [ə'vɜːt] *vt* prevenir; (*blow*) desviar; (*one's eyes*) apartar.

aviary ['eɪvɪərɪ] *n* pajarera, avería.

aviation [eɪvɪ'eɪʃən] *n* aviación *f*.

avid ['ævɪd] *a* ávido, ansioso.

avocado [ævə'kɑːdəʊ] *n* (*also: ~ pear*) aguacate *m*.

avoid [ə'vɔɪd] *vt* evitar, eludir; **~able** *a*

evitable, eludible; ~**ance** n el evitar, evitación f.

await [ə'weɪt] vt esperar, aguardar.

awake [ə'weɪk] a despierto // (vb: pt **awoke**, pp **awoken** or **awaked**) vt despertar // vi despertarse; ~**ning** n el despertar.

award [ə'wɔːd] n (prize) premio, condecoración f; (LAW) fallo, sentencia; (act) concesión f // vt (prize) otorgar; conceder; (LAW: damages) adjudicar, decretar.

aware [ə'wɛə*] a consciente; (awake) despierto; (informed) enterado; **to become** ~ **of** darse cuenta de, enterarse de; ~**ness** n conciencia, conocimiento.

awash [ə'wɔʃ] a inundado.

away [ə'weɪ] ad (gen) fuera; (far ~) lejos; **two kilometres** ~ a dos kilómetros de distancia; **two hours** ~ **by car** a dos horas en coche; **the holiday was two weeks** ~ faltaba dos semanas para las vacaciones; ~ **from** lejos de, fuera de; **he's** ~ **for a week** estará ausente una semana; **to take** ~ vt llevar(se); **to work/pedal** ~ seguir trabajando/pedaleando; **to fade** ~ desvanecerse; (sound) apagarse; ~ **match** n (SPORT) partido de fuera.

awe [ɔː] n pavor m, respeto, temor m reverencial; ~-**inspiring**, ~**some** a imponente, pasmoso; ~**struck** a pasmado.

awful ['ɔːfəl] a tremendo, terrible, pasmoso; ~**ly** ad (very) terriblemente.

awhile [ə'waɪl] ad durante un rato, un rato, algún tiempo.

awkward ['ɔːkwəd] a (clumsy) desmañado, torpe; (shape) incómodo; (problem) difícil; (embarrassing) delicado, desagradable.

awning ['ɔːnɪŋ] n (of shop) toldo; (of window etc) marquesina.

awoke [ə'wəuk], **awoken** [-kən] pt, pp of **awake**.

awry [ə'raɪ] ad: **to be** ~ estar de través o al sesgo; **to go** ~ salir mal, fracasar.

axe, ax (US) [æks] n hacha // vt (employee) despedir; (project etc) parar, cortar; (jobs) reducir.

axiom ['æksɪəm] n axioma m.

axis ['æksɪs], pl **axes** [-siːz] n eje m.

axle ['æksl] n eje m, árbol m.

ay(e) [aɪ] excl (yes) sí; **the ayes** npl los que votan a favor.

Aztec ['æztɛk] n azteca m/f.

B

B.A. abbr of **Bachelor of Arts** licenciado en letras.

babble ['bæbl] vi barbullar.

baboon [bə'buːn] n mandril m.

baby ['beɪbɪ] n nene/a m/f; ~ **carriage** n (US) cochecito; ~-**ish** a infantil; ~-**sit** vi hacer de canguro; ~-**sitter** n canguro m/f.

bachelor ['bætʃələ*] n soltero.

back [bæk] n (of person) espalda; (of animal) lomo; (of hand) dorso; (of house, car, train) parte f de atrás; (of chair) respaldo; (of page) reverso; (FOOTBALL) defensa m // vt (candidate: also: ~ **up**) respaldar, apoyar; (horse: at races) apostar a; (car) dar marcha atrás a o con // vi (car etc) dar marcha atrás // a (in compounds) tras; ~ **seats/wheels** (AUT) asientos mpl/ruedas fpl de atrás; ~ **payments** pagos mpl con efecto retroactivo; ~ **rent** renta atrasada // ad (not forward) (hacia) atrás; (returned): **he's** ~ **está** de vuelta, ha vuelto; **he ran** ~ retrocedió corriendo; (restitution): **throw the ball** ~ devuelve la pelota; **can I have it** ~? ¿me lo devuelve?; (again): **he called** ~ llamó de nuevo; **to** ~ **down** vi echarse atrás; **to** ~ **out** vi (of promise) volverse atrás.

back: ~**ache** n dolor m de espalda; ~**bencher** n miembro del parlamento sin portafolio; ~**biting** n murmuración f; ~**bone** n columna vertebral; ~**cloth** n telón m de foro; ~**date** vt (letter) poner fecha atrasada a; ~**dated pay rise** alza de sueldo con efecto retroactivo; ~**er** n partidario; (COMM) promotor m; ~**fire** vi (AUT) petardear; (plans) fallar, salir al revés; ~**gammon** n backgammon m; ~**ground** n fondo; (of events) antecedentes mpl; (basic knowledge) bases fpl; (experience) conocimientos mpl, educación f; **family** ~**ground** origen m, antecedentes mpl; ~**hand** n (TENNIS: also: ~**hand stroke**) revés m; ~**handed** a (fig) ambiguo, equívoco; ~**hander** n (bribe) soborno; ~**ing** n (fig) apoyo, respaldo; ~**lash** n reacción f, resaca; ~**log** n: ~**log of work** atrasos mpl; ~**number** n (of magazine etc) número atrasado; ~**pay** n pago atrasado; ~**side** n (col) trasero, culo; ~**stage** ad entre bastidores; ~**stroke** n braza de espaldas; ~**ward** a (movement) hacia atrás; (person, country) atrasado; (shy) tímido; ~**wards** ad (move, go) hacia atrás; (read a list) al revés; (fall) de espaldas; ~**water** n (fig) lugar m atrasado o apartado; ~**yard** n traspatio.

bacon ['beɪkən] n tocino.

bacteria [bæk'tɪərɪə] npl bacteria sg.

bad [bæd] a malo; (serious) grave; (meat, food) podrido, pasado; **to go** ~ echarse a perder.

badge [bædʒ] n insignia; (of policeman) chapa, placa.

badger ['bædʒə*] n tejón m.

badly ['bædlɪ] ad (work, dress etc) mal; ~ **wounded** gravemente herido; **he needs it** ~ le hace gran falta; **to be** ~ **off (for money)** andar mal de dinero.

badminton ['bædmɪntən] n badminton m.

bad-tempered ['bæd'tɛmpəd] a de mal genio o carácter; (temporary) de mal humor.

baffle ['bæfl] vt (puzzle) desconcertar, confundir.

bag [bæg] n bolsa, saco; (handbag) bolso; (satchel) mochila; (case) maleta; (of hunter) caza // vt (col: take) coger, pescar; ~**ful** n saco (lleno); ~**gage** n equipaje m; ~**gy** a que hace bolsas; ~**pipes** npl gaita sg.

bail [beɪl] n fianza, caución f // vt (prisoner: gen: give ~ to) poner en libertad bajo fianza; (boat: also: ~ out) achicar; **to ~ sb out** obtener la libertad de uno bajo fianza; see also **bale**.

bailiff ['beɪlɪf] n alguacil m.

bait [beɪt] n cebo // vt cebar, poner el cebo en.

bake [beɪk] vt cocer (al horno) // vi (cook) cocerse; (be hot) hacer un calor terrible; ~**d beans** npl judías fpl en salsa de tomate; **baker** n panadero; ~**ry** n (for bread) panadería; (for cakes) pastelería; **baking** n (act) cocción f; (batch) hornada; **baking powder** n polvos mpl de levadura.

balaclava [bælə'klɑːvə] n (also: ~ **helmet**) pasamontañas m inv.

balance ['bæləns] n equilibrio; (COMM: sum) balance m; (remainder) resto; (scales) balanza // vt equilibrar; (budget) nivelar; (account) saldar; (compensate) contrapesar; ~ **of trade/payments** balanza de comercio/pagos; ~**d** a (personality, diet) equilibrado; ~ **sheet** n balance m.

balcony ['bælkənɪ] n (open) balcón m; (closed) galería.

bald [bɔːld] a calvo; ~**ness** n calvicie f.

bale [beɪl] n (AGR) paca, fardo; **to ~ out** (of a plane) lanzarse en paracaídas; **to ~ sb out of a difficulty** sacar a uno de un problema.

baleful ['beɪlful] a (look) triste; (sinister) funesto, siniestro.

ball [bɔːl] n bola; (football) balón m; (for tennis, golf) pelota; (dance) baile m.

ballad ['bæləd] n balada, romance m.

ballast ['bæləst] n lastre m.

ballerina [bælə'riːnə] n bailarina.

ballet ['bæleɪ] n ballet m, baile m; ~ **dancer** n bailarín/ina m/f.

balloon [bə'luːn] n globo; ~**ist** n ascensionista m/f.

ballot ['bælət] n votación f; ~ **box** n urna (electoral); ~ **paper** n papeleta.

ball-point pen ['bɔːlpɔɪnt'-] n bolígrafo.

ballroom ['bɔːlrum] n salón m de baile.

balmy ['bɑːmɪ] a (breeze, air) suave, fragante; (col) = **barmy**.

Baltic ['bɔːltɪk] n: **the ~ (Sea)** el (Mar) Báltico.

balustrade ['bæləstreɪd] n barandilla.

bamboo [bæm'buː] n bambú m.

ban [bæn] n prohibición f, proscripción f // vt prohibir, proscribir; (exclude) excluir.

banal [bə'nɑːl] a banal, vulgar.

banana [bə'nɑːnə] n plátano.

band [bænd] n (group) banda; (gang) pandilla; (strip) faja, tira; (at a dance)

orquesta; (MIL) banda; **to ~ together** vi juntarse, asociarse.

bandage ['bændɪdʒ] n venda, vendaje m // vt vendar.

bandit ['bændɪt] n bandido; **one-armed ~** máquina tragaperras.

bandstand ['bændstænd] n quiosco.

bandwagon ['bændwægən] n: **to jump on the ~** (fig) seguir la corriente o la moda.

bandy ['bændɪ] vt (jokes, insults) cambiar.

bandy-legged ['bændɪ'lɛgd] a estevado.

bang [bæŋ] n estallido; (of door) portazo; (blow) golpe m // vt hacer estallar; (door) cerrar de golpe // vi estallar.

banger ['bæŋə*] n (car: gen: old ~) chatarra.

bangle ['bæŋgl] n ajorca.

banish ['bænɪʃ] vt desterrar.

banister(s) ['bænɪstə(z)] n(pl) pasamanos m inv.

banjo ['bændʒəu], pl ~**es** or ~**s** n banjo.

bank [bæŋk] n (COMM) banco; (of river, lake) ribera, orilla; (of earth) terraplén m // vi (AVIAT) ladearse; **to ~ on** vt fus contar con; **to ~ with** tener la cuenta con; ~ **account** n cuenta de banco; ~**er** n banquero; **B~ holiday** n día m festivo; ~**ing** n banca; ~**note** n billete m de banco; ~ **rate** n tipo de interés bancario.

bankrupt ['bæŋkrʌpt] n quebrado/a // a quebrado, insolvente; **to go ~** quebrar; **to be ~** estar en quiebra; ~**cy** n quiebra; (fraudulent) bancarrota.

banner ['bænə*] n bandera; (in demonstration) pancarta.

banns [bænz] npl amonestaciones fpl.

banquet ['bæŋkwɪt] n banquete m.

baptism ['bæptɪzəm] n bautismo.

baptize [bæp'taɪz] vt bautizar.

bar [bɑː*] n barra; (of window etc) tranca; (of soap) pastilla; (fig: hindrance) obstáculo; (prohibition) proscripción f; (pub) bar m; (counter: in pub) mostrador m; (MUS) barra // vt (road) obstruir; (window) atrancar; (person) excluir; (activity) prohibir; **behind ~s** en la cárcel; **the B~** (profession) la abogacía; (people) el cuerpo de abogados; ~ **none** sin excepción.

barbaric [bɑː'bærɪk] a bárbaro.

barbarous ['bɑːbərəs] a bárbaro.

barbecue ['bɑːbɪkjuː] n barbacoa.

barbed wire ['bɑːbd-] n alambre m de púas.

barber ['bɑːbə*] n peluquero, barbero.

barbiturate [bɑː'bɪtjurɪt] n barbitúrico.

bare [bɛə*] a desnudo; (head) descubierto // vt desnudar; **to ~ one's teeth** enseñar los dientes; ~**back** ad sin montura; ~**faced** a descarado; ~**foot** a, ad descalzo; ~**ly** ad apenas.

bargain ['bɑːgɪn] n pacto, negocio; (good buy) ganga // vi negociar; (haggle) regatear; **into the ~** además, por añadidura.

barge [bɑːdʒ] n barcaza; **to ~ in** vi

irrumpir, entrar sin permiso; **to ~ into** vt fus dar contra.

baritone ['bærɪtəʊn] n barítono.

bark [bɑːk] n (of tree) corteza; (of dog) ladrido // vi ladrar.

barley ['bɑːlɪ] n cebada.

barmaid ['bɑːmeɪd] n camarera.

barman ['bɑːmən] n camarero, barman m.

barmy ['bɑːmɪ] a (col) chiflado, lelo.

barn [bɑːn] n granero.

barnacle ['bɑːnəkl] n percebe m.

barometer [bə'rɒmɪtə*] n barómetro.

baron ['bærən] n barón m; **~ess** n baronesa.

barracks ['bærəks] npl cuartel m.

barrage ['bærɑːʒ] n (MIL) descarga, bombardeo; (dam) presa.

barrel ['bærəl] n tonel m, barril m; (of gun) cañón m.

barren ['bærən] a estéril, árido.

barricade ['bærɪ'keɪd] n barricada // vt levantar barricadas.

barrier ['bærɪə*] n barrera.

barring ['bɑːrɪŋ] prep excepto, salvo.

barrister ['bærɪstə*] n abogado m/f.

barrow ['bærəʊ] n (cart) carretilla (de mano).

bartender ['bɑːtendə*] n (US) camarero, barman m.

barter ['bɑːtə*] vt: **to ~ sth for sth** trocar algo por algo.

base [beɪs] n base f // vt: **to ~ sth on** basar o fundar algo en // a bajo, infame; **~ball** n béisbol m; **~ment** n sótano.

bash [bæʃ] vt (col) golpear.

bashful ['bæʃful] a tímido, vergonzoso.

bashing ['bæʃɪŋ] n (col) tunda.

basic ['beɪsɪk] a básico; **~ally** ad fundamentalmente, en el fondo.

basil ['bæzl] n albahaca.

basin ['beɪsn] n (vessel) cuenco, tazón m; (GEO) cuenca; (also: **wash~**) palangana, jofaina.

basis ['beɪsɪs] pl **-ses** [-siːz] n base f.

bask [bɑːsk] vi: **to ~ in the sun** tomar el sol.

basket ['bɑːskɪt] n cesta, cesto; (with handle) canasta; **~ball** n baloncesto; **~work** n cestería.

Basque [bæsk] a, n vasco/a; **~ Country** Euskadi m, País m Vasco.

bass [beɪs] n (MUS) contrabajo.

bassoon [bə'suːn] n bajón m.

bastard ['bɑːstəd] n bastardo.

baste [beɪst] vt (CULIN) pringar.

bastion ['bæstɪən] n baluarte m.

bat [bæt] n (ZOOL) murciélago; (for ball games) palo; (for cricket, baseball) bate m; (for table tennis) raqueta; **he didn't ~ an eyelid** ni pestañeó.

batch [bætʃ] n (of bread) hornada; (of papers) colección f, lote m.

bated ['beɪtɪd] a: **with ~ breath** sin respiración.

bath [bɑːθ, pl bɑːðz] n (~ tub) baño, bañera; (also: **~s** pl) baño, piscina // vt bañar; **to**

have a ~ bañarse, tomar un baño; **~chair** n silla de ruedas.

bathe [beɪð] vi bañarse // vt bañar; **bather** n bañista m/f.

bathing ['beɪðɪŋ] n el bañarse; **~ cap** n gorro de baño; **~ costume** n traje m de baño; **~ trunks** npl bañador m.

bath: **~mat** n estera de baño; **~room** n (cuarto de) baño; **~s** npl piscina sg; **~ towel** n toalla de baño.

baton ['bætən] n (MUS) batuta.

battalion [bə'tælɪən] n batallón m.

batter ['bætə*] vt apalear, azotar // n batido; **~ed** a (hat, pan) estropeado.

battery ['bætərɪ] n batería; (of torch) pila.

battle ['bætl] n batalla; (fig) lucha // vi luchar; **~field** n campo m de batalla; **~ments** npl almenas fpl; **~ship** n acorazado.

bawdy ['bɔːdɪ] a indecente; (joke) verde.

bawl [bɔːl] vi chillar, gritar.

bay [beɪ] n (GEO) bahía; (BOT) laurel m // vi aullar; **to hold sb at ~** mantener a alguien a raya.

bayonet ['beɪənɪt] n bayoneta.

bay window ['beɪ-] n ventana sa/ediza.

bazaar [bə'zɑː*] n bazar m.

bazooka [bə'zuːkə] n bazuca.

b. & b., B. & B. abbr of **bed and breakfast** cama y desayuno.

BBC n abbr of **British Broadcasting Corporation.**

B.C. ad abbr of **before Christ** a. de J.C. (antes de Jesucristo).

be [biː] pt **was, were,** pp **been** vi (of state) ser; (of place, temporary condition) estar; **I am English** soy inglés; **I am tired** estoy cansado; **how are you?** ¿cómo está Usted?; **who is it?** ¿quién es?; **it is raining** está lloviendo; **I am warm** tengo calor; **it is cold** hace frío; **how much is it?** ¿cuánto es o cuesta?; **he is four (years old)** tiene cuatro años; **2 and 2 are 4** dos más dos son cuatro; **where have you been?** ¿dónde has estado?, ¿de dónde vienes?

beach [biːtʃ] n playa // vt varar.

beacon ['biːkən] n (lighthouse) faro; (marker) guía.

bead [biːd] n cuenta, abalorio; (of sweat) gota.

beak [biːk] n pico.

beaker ['biːkə*] n jarra.

beam [biːm] n (ARCH) viga, travesaño; (of light) rayo, haz m de luz // vi brillar; (smile) sonreír; **~ing** a (sun, smile) radiante.

bean [biːn] n judía; **runner/broad ~** habichuela/haba; **coffee ~** grano de café.

bear [bɛə*] n oso // (vb: pt **bore,** pp **borne**) vt (weight etc) llevar; (cost) pagar; (responsibility) tener; (endure) soportar, aguantar; (stand up to) resistir a; (children) parir // vi: **to ~ right/left** torcer a la derecha/izquierda; **~able** a soportable.

beard [bɪəd] n barba; **~ed** a barbado.

bearing ['bɛərɪŋ] *n* porte *m*, comportamiento; (*connection*) relación *f*; (**ball**) ~s *npl* cojinetes *mpl* a bolas; **to take a** ~ marcarse; **to find one's** ~**s** orientarse.

beast [bi:st] *n* bestia; (*col*) bruto, salvaje *m*; ~**ly** a bestial; (*awful*) horrible.

beat [bi:t] *n* (*of heart*) latido; (*MUS*) ritmo, compás *m*; (*of policeman*) ronda // *pt* **beat**, *pp* **beaten**) *vt* (*hit*) golpear; (*eggs*) batir; (*defeat*) vencer, derrotar; (*better*) sobrepasar; (*drum*) tocar; (*rhythm*) marcar // *vi* (*heart*) latir; **to ~ about the bush** ir por rodeos; **to** ~ **it** largarse; **to** ~ **off** *vt* rechazar; **to** ~ **up** *vt* (*col: person*) dar una paliza a; ~**er** *n* (*for eggs, cream*) batidora; ~**ing** *n* golpeo.

beautiful ['bju:tiful] a hermoso, bello; ~**ly** *ad* maravillosamente; **beautify** [-faɪ] *vt* embellecer.

beauty ['bju:tɪ] *n* belleza, hermosura; (*person*) belleza; ~ **salon** *n* salón *m* de belleza; ~ **spot** *n* lunar *m* postizo; (*TOURISM*) lugar *m* de excepcional belleza.

beaver ['bi:və*] *n* castor *m*.

becalmed [bɪ'ka:md] a encalmado.

became [bɪ'keɪm] *pt of* **become**.

because [bɪ'kɔz] *conj* porque; ~ **of** *prep* debido a, a causa de.

beck [bɛk] *n*: **to be at the** ~ **and call of** estar a disposición de.

beckon ['bɛkən] *vt* (*also:* ~ **to**) llamar con señas.

become [bɪ'kʌm] (*irg: like* **come**) *vt* (*suit*) favorecer, sentar a // *vi* (+ *noun*) hacerse, llegar a ser; (+ *adj*) ponerse, volverse; **to** ~ **fat** engordarse.

becoming [bɪ'kʌmɪŋ] a (*behaviour*) decoroso; (*clothes*) favorecedor(a).

bed [bɛd] *n* cama; (*of flowers*) macizo; (*of coal, clay*) capa; **to go to** ~ acostarse; **single/double** ~ cama individual/matrimonial; ~**clothes** *npl* ropa *sg* de cama; ~**ding** *n* ropa de cama.

bedlam ['bɛdləm] *n* confusión *f*.

bedraggled [bɪ'dræɡld] a mojado, ensuciado.

bed: ~**ridden** a postrado (en cama); ~**room** *n* dormitorio, alcoba; ~**side** *n*: **at sb's** ~**side** a la cabecera de alguien; ~**sit(ter)** *n* apartamento; ~**spread** *n* sobrecama *m*, colcha.

bee [bi:] *n* abeja.

beech [bi:tʃ] *n* haya.

beef [bi:f] *n* carne *f* de vaca; **roast** ~ rosbif *m*.

bee: ~**hive** *n* colmena; ~**line** *n*: **to make a** ~**line for** ir derecho a.

been [bi:n] *pp of* **be**.

beer [bɪə*] *n* cerveza.

beetle ['bi:tl] *n* escarabajo.

beetroot ['bi:tru:t] *n* remolacha.

before [bɪ'fɔ:*] *prep* (*of time*) antes de; (*of space*) delante de // *conj* antes (de) que // *ad* (*time*) antes, anteriormente; (*space*) delante, adelante; **the week** ~ la semana

anterior; **I've never seen it** ~ no lo he visto nunca.

befriend [bɪ'frɛnd] *vt* ofrecer amistad a, ayudar.

beg [bɛɡ] *vi* pedir, rogar; (*as beggar*) pedir limosna // *vt* pedir, rogar; (*entreat*) suplicar.

began [bɪ'ɡæn] *pt of* **begin**.

beggar ['bɛɡə*] *n* mendigo.

begin [bɪ'ɡɪn], *pt* **began**, *pp* **begun** *vt*, *vi* empezar, comenzar; ~**ner** *n* principiante *m/f*; ~**ning** *n* principio, comienzo.

begrudge [bɪ'ɡrʌdʒ] *vt*: **to** ~ **sb sth** tenerle envidia a alguien por algo.

begun [bɪ'ɡʌn] *pp of* **begin**.

behalf [bɪ'hɑ:f] *n*: **on** ~ **of** en nombre de, por.

behave [bɪ'heɪv] *vi* (*person*) portarse, comportarse; (*thing*) funcionar; (*well: also:* ~ **o.s.**) portarse bien; **behaviour, behavior** (*US*) *n* comportamiento, conducta.

behind [bɪ'haɪnd] *prep* detrás de // detrás, por detrás, atrás // *n* trasero; ~ **time** atrasado.

behold [bɪ'həuld] (*irg: like* **hold**) *vt* contemplar.

beige [beɪʒ] a beige.

being ['bi:ɪŋ] *n* ser *m*; **to come into** ~ nacer, aparecer.

belated [bɪ'leɪtɪd] a atrasado, tardío.

belch [bɛltʃ] *vi* eructar // *vt* (*gen:* ~ **out:** *smoke etc*) arrojar.

belfry ['bɛlfrɪ] *n* campanario.

Belgian ['bɛldʒən] a, *n* belga *m/f*.

Belgium ['bɛldʒəm] *n* Bélgica.

belie [bɪ'laɪ] *vt* desmentir, contradecir.

belief [bɪ'li:f] *n* (*opinion*) opinión *f*; (*trust, faith*) fe *f*; (*acceptance as true*) creencia.

believable [bɪ'li:vəbl] a creíble.

believe [bɪ'li:v] *vt, vi* creer; **believer** *n* creyente *m/f*, fiel *m/f*; (*POL*) partidario/a.

belittle [bɪ'lɪtl] *vt* minimizar, despreciar.

bell [bɛl] *n* campana; (*small*) campanilla; (*on door*) timbre *m*; (*animal's*) cencerro; (*on toy etc*) cascabel *m*.

belligerent [bɪ'lɪdʒərənt] a (*at war*) beligerante; (*fig*) agresivo.

bellow ['bɛləu] *vi* bramar; (*person*) rugir // *vt* (*orders*) gritar, vociferar.

bellows ['bɛləuz] *npl* fuelle *m*.

belly ['bɛlɪ] *n* barriga, panza.

belong [bɪ'lɔŋ] *vi*: **to** ~ **to** pertenecer a; (*club etc*) ser socio de; ~**ings** *npl* pertenencias *fpl*.

beloved [bɪ'lʌvɪd] a, *n* querido/a, amado/a.

below [bɪ'ləu] *prep* bajo, debajo de // *ad* abajo, (por) debajo; **see** ~ véase más abajo.

belt [bɛlt] *n* cinturón *m*; (*MED*) faja; (*TECH*) correa, cinta // *vt* (*thrash*) golpear con correa.

bench [bɛntʃ] *n* banco; **the B**~ (*LAW*) tribunal *m*; (*people*) judicatura.

bend [bɛnd], *pt, pp* **bent** *vt* doblar, inclinar;

(*leg, arm*) torcer // *vi* doblarse, inclinarse // *n* (*in road*) recodo, vuelta; (*in pipe, river*) ángulo, curva; **to ~ down** *vi* inclinar, doblar; **to ~ over** *vi* inclinarse.

beneath [bɪˈniːθ] *prep* bajo, debajo de; (*unworthy of*) indigno de // *ad* abajo, (por) debajo.

benefactor [ˈbɛnɪfæktə*] *n* bienhechor *m*.

beneficial [bɛnɪˈfɪʃəl] *a* provechoso, beneficioso.

benefit [ˈbɛnɪfɪt] *n* beneficio, provecho; (*profit*) utilidad *f*; (*money*) subsidio // *vt* beneficiar, aprovechar // *vi*: **he'll ~ from it** le sacará provecho.

Benelux [ˈbɛnɪlʌks] *n* Benelux *m*.

benevolent [bɪˈnevələnt] *a* benévolo.

bent [bɛnt] *pt, pp of* **bend** // *n* inclinación *f* // *a*: **to be ~ on** estar empeñado en.

bequeath [bɪˈkwiːð] *vt* legar.

bequest [bɪˈkwɛst] *n* legado.

bereaved [bɪˈriːvd] *n*: **the ~** los afligidos *mpl*; **bereavement** [-ˈriːvmənt] *n* aflicción *f*.

beret [ˈbɛreɪ] *n* boina.

berry [ˈbɛrɪ] *n* baya.

berserk [bəˈsɔːk] *a*: **to go ~** perder los estribos.

berth [bəːθ] *n* (*bed*) litera; (*cabin*) camarote *m*; (*for ship*) amarradero // *vi* atracar, amarrar.

beseech [bɪˈsiːtʃ], *pt, pp* **besought** [-ˈsɔːt] *vt* suplicar.

beset [bɪˈsɛt], *pt, pp* **beset** *vt* rodear; (*person*) acosar.

beside [bɪˈsaɪd] *prep* junto a, al lado de; **to be ~ o.s. (with anger)** estar fuera de sí.

besides [bɪˈsaɪdz] *ad* además // *prep* (*as well as*) además de; (*except*) fuera de, excepto.

besiege [bɪˈsiːdʒ] *vt* (*town*) sitiar; (*fig*) asediar.

best [bɛst] *a* (el/la) mejor // *ad* (lo) mejor; **the ~ part of** (*quantity*) la mayor parte de; **at ~** en el mejor de los casos; **to make the ~ of sth** sacar el mejor partido de algo; **to the ~ of my knowledge** como yo sepa; **to the ~ of my ability** como mejor puedo; **~ man** *n* padrino de boda.

bestow [bɪˈstəu] *vt* otorgar; (*affection*) ofrecer.

bestseller [ˈbɛstˈsɛlə*] *n* éxito de librería, bestseller *m*.

bet [bɛt] *n* apuesta // *vt, vi, pt, pp* **bet** *or* **betted** apostar, jugar.

betray [bɪˈtreɪ] *vt* traicionar; (*denounce*) delatar; **~al** *n* traición *f*.

better [ˈbɛtə*] *a* mejor // *ad* mejor // *vt* mejorar; (*go above*) superar // *n*: **to get the ~ of** quedar por encima de alguien; **you had ~ do it** más vale que lo haga; **he thought ~ of it** cambió de parecer; **to get ~** mejorar(se); (*MED*) reponerse; **~ off** a más acomodado.

betting [ˈbɛtɪŋ] *n* juego, el apostar; **~ shop** *n* agencia de apuestas.

between [bɪˈtwiːn] *prep* entre // *ad* en medio.

beverage [ˈbɛvərɪdʒ] *n* bebida.

bevy [ˈbɛvɪ] *n*: **a ~ of** una bandada de.

beware [bɪˈwɛə*] *vi*: **to ~ (of)** precaverse de, tener cuidado con // *excl* ¡cuidado!

bewildered [bɪˈwɪldəd] *a* aturdido, perplejo.

bewitching [bɪˈwɪtʃɪŋ] *a* hechicero, encantador(a).

beyond [bɪˈjɔnd] *prep* (*in space*) más allá de; (*exceeding*) además de, fuera de; (*above*) superior a // *ad* más allá, más lejos; **~ doubt** fuera de toda duda; **~ repair** irreparable.

bias [ˈbaɪəs] *n* (*prejudice*) prejuicio, pasión *f*; (*preference*) predisposición *f*; **~(s)ed** *a* (*against*) con prejuicios; (*towards*) partidario.

bib [bɪb] *n* babero.

Bible [ˈbaɪbl] *n* Biblia.

bibliography [bɪblɪˈɔgrəfɪ] *n* bibliografía.

bicker [ˈbɪkə*] *vi* reñir.

bicycle [ˈbaɪsɪkl] *n* bicicleta.

bid [bɪd] *n* (*at auction*) oferta, postura; (*attempt*) tentativa, conato // (*vb: pt* **bade** [bæd] *or* **bid**, *pp* **bidden** [ˈbɪdn] *or* **bid**) *vi* hacer una oferta // *vt* mandar, ordenar; **to ~ sb good day** dar a uno los buenos días; **~der** *n*: **the highest ~der** el mejor postor; **~ding** *n* (*at auction*) ofertas *fpl*; (*order*) orden *f*, mandato.

bide [baɪd] *vt*: **to ~ one's time** esperar el momento adecuado.

bidet [ˈbiːdeɪ] *n* bidet *m*.

bier [bɪə*] *n* féretro.

big [bɪg] *a* grande.

bigamy [ˈbɪgəmɪ] *n* bigamia.

bigheaded [ˈbɪgˈhɛdɪd] *a* engreído.

bigot [ˈbɪgət] *n* fanático, intolerante *m/f*; **~ed** *a* fanático, intolerante; **~ry** *n* fanatismo, intolerancia.

bike [baɪk] *n* bici *f*.

bikini [bɪˈkiːnɪ] *n* bikini *m*.

bile [baɪl] *n* bilis *f*.

bilingual [baɪˈlɪŋgwəl] *a* bilingüe.

bill [bɪl] *n* (*account*) cuenta; (*invoice*) factura; (*POL*) proyecto de ley; (*US: banknote*) billete *m*; (*of bird*) pico; **stick no ~s** prohibido fijar carteles.

billet [ˈbɪlɪt] *n* alojamiento.

billfold [ˈbɪlfəuld] *n* (*US*) cartera.

billiards [ˈbɪlɪədz] *n* billar *m*.

billion [ˈbɪlɪən] *n* (*Brit*) billón *m*; (*US*) mil millones.

billy goat [ˈbɪlɪ-] *n* macho cabrío.

bin [bɪn] *n* (*gen*) cubo; **bread/litter ~** nasa/papelera.

bind [baɪnd], *pt, pp* **bound** *vt* atar, liar; (*wound*) vendar; (*book*) encuadernar; (*oblige*) obligar; **~ing** *a* (*contract*) obligatorio.

binge [bɪndʒ] *n* borrachera, juerga.

bingo [ˈbɪŋgəu] *n* bingo *m*.

binoculars [bɪˈnɔkjuləz] *npl* gemelos *mpl*, prismáticos *mpl*.

bio... [baɪə] *pref*: **~chemistry** *n* bioquímica; **~graphy** [baɪˈɔgrəfɪ] *n* biografía; **~logical** *a* biológico; **~logy** [baɪˈɔlədʒɪ] *n* biología.

birch [bɔːtʃ] *n* abedul *m*; (*cane*) vara.

bird [bɔːd] *n* ave *f*, pájaro; (*col: girl*) chica; **~cage** *n* jaula; **~'s eye view** *n* vista de pájaro; **~ watcher** *n* ornitólogo.

birth [bɔːθ] *n* nacimiento; (*MED*) parto; **to give ~ to** parir, dar a luz; **~ certificate** *n* partida de nacimiento; **~ control** *n* control *m* de natalidad; (*methods*) métodos *mpl* anticonceptivos; **~day** *n* cumpleaños *m*; **~place** *n* lugar *m* de nacimiento; **~rate** *n* (tasa de) natalidad *f*.

biscuit [ˈbɪskɪt] *n* galleta.

bisect [baɪˈsɛkt] *vt* bisecar.

bishop [ˈbɪʃəp] *n* obispo.

bit [bɪt] *pt of* **bite** // *n* trozo, pedazo, pedacito; (*of horse*) freno, bocado; **a ~ of** un poco de; **a ~ mad** algo loco; **~ by ~** poco a poco.

bitch [bɪtʃ] *n* (*dog*) perra.

bite [baɪt], *pt* **bit**, *pp* **bitten** *vt, vi* morder; (*insect etc*) picar // *n* mordedura; (*insect ~*) picadura; (*mouthful*) bocado; **let's have a ~ (to eat)** comamos algo.

biting [ˈbaɪtɪŋ] *a* penetrante, cortante; (*sharp*) mordaz.

bitten [ˈbɪtn] *pp of* **bite**.

bitter [ˈbɪtə*] *a* amargo; (*wind, criticism*) cortante, penetrante; (*battle*) encarnizado // *n* (*beer*) cerveza clara; **~ness** *n* amargura; (*anger*) rencor *m*.

bizarre [bɪˈzɑː*] *a* raro, estrafalario.

blab [blæb] *vi* chismear, soplar // *vt* (*also: ~ out*) revelar, contar.

black [blæk] *a* (*colour*) negro; (*dark*) oscuro // *n* negro; (*colour*) color *m* negro // *vt* (*shoes*) lustrar; (*INDUSTRY*) boicotear; **to give sb a ~ eye** darle a uno una bofetada (en el ojo); **~ and blue** *a* amoratado; **~berry** *n* zarzamora; **~bird** *n* mirlo; **~board** *n* pizarra; **~currant** *n* grosella negra; **~en** *vt* ennegrecer; (*fig*) denigrar; **~leg** *n* esquirol *m*, rompehuelgas *m inv*; **~list** *n* lista negra; **~mail** *n* chantaje *m* // *vt* chantajear; **~mailer** *n* chantajista *m/f*; **~ market** *n* mercado negro; **~out** *n* apagón *m*; (*fainting*) desmayo, pérdida de conocimiento; **~smith** *n* herrero.

bladder [ˈblædə*] *n* vejiga.

blade [bleɪd] *n* hoja; (*cutting edge*) filo; **a ~ of grass** una brizna de hierba.

blame [bleɪm] *n* culpa // *vt*: **to ~ sb for sth** echar a uno la culpa de algo; **to be to ~** tener la culpa de; **~less** *a* (*person*) inocente.

bland [blænd] *a* suave; (*taste*) soso.

blank [blæŋk] *a* en blanco; (*shot*) sin bala; (*look*) sin expresión // *n* blanco, espacio en blanco; cartucho sin bala o de fogueo.

blanket [ˈblæŋkɪt] *n* manta // *vt* envolver.

blare [blɛə*] *vi* (*brass band, horns, radio*) resonar.

blasé [ˈblɑːzeɪ] *a* hastiado.

blasphemy [ˈblæsfɪmɪ] *n* blasfemia.

blast [blɑːst] *n* (*of wind*) ráfaga, soplo; (*of whistle*) toque *m*; (*of explosive*) carga explosiva; (*force*) choque *m* // *vt* (*blow up*) volar; (*blow open*) abrir con carga explosiva; **~-off** *n* (*SPACE*) lanzamiento.

blatant [ˈbleɪtənt] *a* descarado.

blaze [bleɪz] *n* (*fire*) fuego; (*flames*) llamarada; (*fig*) arranque *m* // *vi* (*fire*) arder en llamas; (*fig*) brillar // *vt*: **to ~ a trail** (*fig*) abrir (un) camino.

blazer [ˈbleɪzə*] *n* chaqueta ligera.

bleach [bliːtʃ] *n* (*also: household ~*) lejía // *vt* (*linen*) blanquear; **~ed** *a* (*hair*) decolorado.

bleak [bliːk] *a* (*countryside*) desierto; (*prospect*) poco prometedor(a).

bleary-eyed [ˈblɪərɪˈaɪd] *a* de ojos legañosos.

bleat [bliːt] *vi* balar.

bleed [bliːd], *pt, pp* **bled** [blɛd] *vt, vi* sangrar.

blemish [ˈblɛmɪʃ] *n* mancha, tacha.

blend [blɛnd] *n* mezcla // *vt* mezclar // *vi* (*colours etc*) combinarse, mezclarse.

bless [blɛs], *pt, pp* **blessed** *or* **blest** [blɛst] *vt* bendecir; **~ing** *n* bendición *f*; (*advantage*) beneficio, ventaja.

blew [bluː] *pt of* **blow**.

blight [blaɪt] *vt* (*hopes etc*) frustrar, arruinar.

blimey [ˈblaɪmɪ] *excl* (*col*) ¡caray!

blind [blaɪnd] *a* ciego // *n* (*for window*) persiana // *vt* cegar; (*dazzle*) deslumbrar; **~ alley** *n* callejón *m* sin salida; **~ corner** *n* esquina escondida; **~fold** *n* venda // *a, ad* con los ojos vendados // *vt* vendar los ojos a; **~ly** *ad* a ciegas, ciegamente; **~ness** *n* ceguera; **~ spot** *n* mácula.

blink [blɪŋk] *vi* parpadear, pestañear; (*light*) oscilar; **~ers** *npl* anteojeras *fpl*.

blinking [ˈblɪŋkɪŋ] *a* (*col*): **this ~...** este condenado...

bliss [blɪs] *n* felicidad *f*; (*fig*) éxtasis *m*.

blister [ˈblɪstə*] *n* (*on skin*) ampolla // *vi* (*paint*) ampollarse; **~ing** *a* (*heat*) abrasador(a).

blithe [blaɪð] *a* alegre.

blithering [ˈblɪðərɪŋ] *a* (*col*): **this ~ idiot** este tonto perdido.

blitz [blɪts] *n* bombardeo aéreo.

blizzard [ˈblɪzəd] *n* ventisca.

bloated [ˈbləʊtɪd] *a* hinchado.

blob [blɔb] *n* (*drop*) gota; (*stain, spot*) mancha.

block [blɔk] *n* bloque *m*; (*in pipes*) obstáculo; (*of buildings*) manzana // *vt* (*gen*) obstruir, cerrar; (*progress*) estorbar; **~ade** [-ˈkeɪd] *n* bloqueo // *vt* bloquear; **~age** *n* estorbo, obstrucción *f*; **~ of flats** *n* bloque *m* de pisos; **~ letters** *npl* letras *fpl* de molde.

bloke [bləʊk] *n* (*col*) tipo, tío.

blond(e) [blɔnd] *a, n* rubio/a.

blood [blʌd] *n* sangre *f*; **~ donor** *n*

donador/a m/f de sangre; ~ **group** n grupo sanguíneo; ~ **hound** n sabueso; ~ **pressure** n presión f sanguínea; ~**shed** n matanza; ~**shot** a inyectado en sangre; ~**stained** a manchado de sangre; ~**stream** n corriente f sanguínea; ~**thirsty** a sanguinario; ~ **transfusion** n transfusión f de sangre; ~**y** a sangriento; (coll): **this** ~**y...** este condenado/puñetero...; ~**y strong/ good** (col!) terriblemente fuerte/ bueno; ~**y-minded** a (col) malintencionado.

bloom [blu:m] n floración f; (fig) perfección f, plenitud f // vi florecer; ~**ing** a (col): **this** ~**ing...** este condenado... .

blossom ['blɔsəm] n flor f // vi florecer; (fig) desarrollarse.

blot [blɔt] n borrón m // vt secar; (ink) manchar; **to** ~ **out** vt (view) oscurecer, hacer desaparecer.

blotchy ['blɔtʃɪ] a (complexion) enrojecido, lleno de manchas.

blotting paper ['blɔtɪŋ-] n papel m secante.

blouse [blauz] n blusa.

blow [bləu] n golpe m // (vb: pt **blew**, pp **blown** [bləun]) vi soplar // vt (glass) soplar; (fuse) quemar; (instrument) tocar; **to** ~ **one's nose** sonarse; **to** ~ **away** vt llevarse, arrancar; **to** ~ **down** vt derribar; **to** ~ **off** vt arrebatar; **to** ~ **out** vi apagarse; **to** ~ **over** vi pasar, quedar olvidado; **to** ~ **up** vi estallar // vt volar; (tyre) inflar; (PHOT) ampliar; ~**lamp** n soplete m, lámpara de soldar; ~**-out** n (of tyre) pinchazo.

biubber ['blʌbə•] n grasa de ballena // vi (pej) lloriquear.

blue [blu:] a azul; ~ **film/joke** film/chiste verde; **to have the** ~**s** estar melancólico; ~**bell** n campanilla, campánula azul; ~**bottle** n moscarda, mosca azul; ~**jeans** npl bluejean m inv, vaqueros mpl; ~**print** n (fig) anteproyecto.

bluff [blʌf] vi hacer un bluff, farolear // n bluff m, farol m.

blunder ['blʌndə•] n error m garrafal, metedura de pata // vi cometer un error, meter la pata.

blunt [blʌnt] a embotado, desafilado; (person) franco, directo // vt embotar, desafilar; ~**ness** n (of person) franqueza, brusquedad f.

blur [blə:•] n aspecto borroso // vt hacer borroso, desdibujar.

blurt [blə:t]: ~ **out** vt (say) descolgarse con, dejar escapar.

blush [blʌʃ] vi ruborizarse, ponerse colorado // n rubor m.

blustering ['blʌstərɪŋ] a (person) fanfarrón(ona).

blustery ['blʌstərɪ] a (weather) tempestuoso, tormentoso.

board [bɔ:d] n tabla, tablero; (on wall) tablón m; (for chess etc) tablero; (committee) junta, consejo; (in firm) mesa o junta

directiva // vt (ship) embarcarse en; (train) subir a; **full** ~ pensión f completa; **to go by the** ~ (fig) ser abandonado/olvidado; **to** ~ **up** vt (door) entablar, enmaderar; ~ **and lodging** n pensión f; ~**er** n huésped/a m/f; (SCOL) interno; ~**ing house** n casa de huéspedes; ~**ing school** n internado; ~**room** n sala de juntas.

boast [bəust] vi jactarse, presumir // vt ostentar // n alarde m, baladronada; ~**ful** a presumido, jactancioso.

boat [bəut] n barco, buque m; (small) barca, bote m; ~**er** n (hat) sombrero de paja; ~**ing** n canotaje m; ~**man** n barquero; ~**swain** ['bəusn] n contramaestre m.

bob [bɔb] vi (boat, cork on water: also: ~ **up and down**) menearse, balancearse; **to** ~ **up** vi aparecer, levantarse // n (col) = **shilling.**

bobbin ['bɔbɪn] n (of sewing machine) carrete m, bobina.

bobby ['bɔbɪ] n (col) poli m/f.

bobsleigh ['bɔbsleɪ] n bob m.

bodice ['bɔdɪs] n corpiño.

bodily ['bɔdɪlɪ] a corpóreo, corporal // ad (in person) en persona; (lift) en peso.

body ['bɔdɪ] n cuerpo; (corpse) cadáver m; (of car) caja, carrocería; (fig: society) conjunto; (fig: quantity) parte f principal; **in a** ~ en bloque, en conjunto; ~**guard** n guardaespaldas m inv; ~**work** n carrocería.

bog [bɔg] n pantano, ciénaga // vt: **to get** ~**ged down** (fig) empantanarse, atascarse.

boggle ['bɔgl] vi: **the mind** ~**s** le deja boquiabierto a uno.

bogus ['bəugəs] a falso, fraudulento; (person) fingido.

boil [bɔɪl] vt cocer; (eggs) pasar por agua // vi hervir // n (MED) furúnculo, divieso; **to come to the** ~ comenzar a hervir; **to** ~ **down to** (fig) reducirse a; ~**er** n caldera; ~**er suit** n mono; ~**ing point** n punto de ebullición f.

boisterous ['bɔɪstərəs] a (noisy) bullicioso; (excitable) exuberante; (crowd) tumultuoso.

bold [bəuld] a (brave) valiente, audaz; (excessively) atrevido; (pej) descarado; (outline, colour) fuerte; ~**ness** n valor m, audacia; (cheek) descaro.

Bolivia [bə'lɪvɪə] n Bolivia.

bollard ['bɔləd] n (AUT) poste m.

bolster ['bəulstə•] n (noisy) travesero, cabezal m; **to** ~ **up** vt reforzar; (fig) alentar.

bolt [bəult] n (lock) cerrojo; (with nut) perno, tornillo // vt (door) echar el cerrojo a; (food) engullir // vi fugarse; (horse) desbocarse.

bomb [bɔm] n bomba // vt bombardear; ~**ard** [-'bɑ:d] vt bombardear; (fig) asediar; ~**ardment** [-'bɑ:dmənt] n bombardeo.

bombastic [bɔm'bæstɪk] a rimbombante; (*person*) farolero.

bomb: ~ **disposal** n desmontaje m de explosivos; ~**er** n (AVIAT) bombardero; ~**shell** n obús m, granada; (*fig*) bomba.

bona fide ['bəunə'faɪdɪ] a genuino, auténtico.

bond [bɔnd] n (*binding promise*) fianza; (FINANCE) bono; (*link*) vínculo, lazo.

bondage [bɔndɪdʒ] n esclavitud f.

bone [bəun] n hueso; (*of fish*) espina // vt deshuesar; quitar las espinas a; ~-**dry** a completamente seco; ~ **idle** a gandul.

bonfire ['bɔnfaɪə*] n hoguera, fogata.

bonnet ['bɔnɪt] n gorra; (*Brit: of car*) capó m.

bonus ['bəunəs] n sobrepaga, prima.

bony ['bəunɪ] a (*arm, face*, MED. *tissue*) huesudo; (*meat*) lleno de huesos; (*fish*) lleno de espinas.

boo [bu:] vt abuchear, rechiflar.

booby trap ['bu:bɪ-] n trampa explosiva.

book [buk] n libro; (*notebook*) libreta; (*of stamps etc*) librito; (COMM) ~**s** las cuentas, el balance // vt (*ticket*) sacar; (*seat, room*) reservar; (*driver*) fichar; ~**case** n librería, estante m para libros; ~**ing office** n (RAIL) despacho de billetes; (THEATRE) taquilla; ~-**keeping** n teneduría de libros; ~**let** n folleto; ~**maker** n corredor m de apuestas; ~**seller** n librero; ~**shop** n librería; ~**stall** n quiosco de libros.

boom [bu:m] n (*noise*) trueno, estampido; (*in prices etc*) alza rápida; (ECON) boom m, prosperidad f repentina.

boomerang ['bu:məræŋ] n bumerang m.

boon [bu:n] n favor m, beneficio.

boost [bu:st] n estímulo, empuje m // vt estimular, empujar; ~**er** n (MED) reinyección f.

boot [bu:t] n bota; (*Brit: of car*) maleta, maletero // vt dar un puntapié a; **to** ~ (*in addition*) además, por añadidura.

booth [bu:ð] n (*at fair*) barraca; (*telephone* ~, *voting* ~) cabina.

booty ['bu:tɪ] n botín m.

booze [bu:z] (*col*) n bebida, trago // vi emborracharse.

border ['bɔ:də*] n borde m, margen m, orilla; (*of a country*) frontera // a fronterizo; **the B**~**s** región fronteriza entre Escocia e Inglaterra; **to** ~ **on** vt fus lindar con; (*fig*) rayar en; ~**line** n (*fig*) frontera.

bore [bɔ:*] pt of **bear** // vt (*hole*) taladrar, agujerear; (*person*) aburrir // n (*person*) pelmazo, pesado; (*of gun*) calibre m; ~**dom** n aburrimiento.

boring ['bɔ:rɪŋ] a aburrido.

born [bɔ:n] a: **to be** ~ nacer; **I was** ~ **in 1960** nací en 1960.

borne [bɔ:n] pp of **bear**.

borough ['bʌrə] n municipio.

borrow ['bɔrəu] vt: **to** ~ **sth (from sb)** pedir algo prestado a alguien.

borstal ['bɔ:stl] n reformatorio (de menores).

bosom ['buzəm] n pecho; (*fig*) seno; ~ **friend** n amigo del alma o íntimo.

boss [bɔs] n jefe m; (*employer*) patrón/ona m/f; (*political etc*) cacique m // vt regentar, dar órdenes a; ~**y** a mandón(ona).

bosun ['bəusn] n contramaestre m.

botanist ['bɔtənɪst] n botanista m/f; **botany** [-nɪ] n botánica.

botch [bɔtʃ] vt (*also:* ~ **up**) arruinar, estropear.

both [bəuθ] a, pron ambos(as), los dos; ~ **of us went, we** ~ **went** fuimos los dos, ambos fuimos // ad: ~ **A and B** tanto A como B.

bother ['bɔðə*] vt (*worry*) preocupar; (*disturb*) molestar, fastidiar // vi (*gen:* ~ **o.s.**) molestarse; **to** ~ **doing** tomarse la molestia de hacer o; **what a** ~! ¡qué lata!

bottle ['bɔtl] n botella; (*small*) frasco; (*baby's*) biberón m // vt embotellar; **to** ~ **up** vt embotellar, contener; ~**neck** n embotellamiento; ~-**opener** n destapador m, abrebotellas m inv.

bottom ['bɔtəm] n (*of box, sea*) fondo; (*buttocks*) trasero, culo; (*of page, list*) pie m // a (*low*) inferior, más bajo; (*last*) último; ~**less** a sin fondo, insondable.

bough [bau] n rama.

bought [bɔ:t] pt, pp of **buy**.

boulder ['bəuldə*] n canto rodado.

bounce [bauns] vi (*ball*) (re)botar; (*cheque*) ser rechazado o incobrable // vt hacer (re)botar // n (*rebound*) (re)bote m.

bound [baund] pt, pp of **bind** // n (*leap*) salto; (*gen pl: limit*) límite m // vi (*leap*) saltar // a: ~ **by** (*limited by*) rodeado de, confinado con; **to be** ~ **to do sth** (*obliged*) tener el deber de hacer algo; (*likely*) estar seguro de hacer algo; **out of** ~**s** prohibido el paso; ~ **for** con destino a.

boundary ['baundrɪ] n límite m, lindero.

boundless ['baundlɪs] a ilimitado.

bouquet ['bukeɪ] n (*of flowers*) ramo; (*of wine*) aroma m.

bout [baut] n (*of malaria etc*) ataque m; (BOXING *etc*) combate m, encuentro.

bow [bəu] n (*knot*) lazo; (*weapon*, MUS) arco // n [bau] (*of the head*) reverencia; (NAUT) proa // vi [bau] inclinarse, hacer una reverencia; (*yield*): **to** ~ **to** or **before** ceder ante, someterse a.

bowels [bauəlz] npl intestinos mpl, vientre m.

bowl [bəul] n tazón m, cuenco; (*for washing*) palangana, jofaina; (*ball*) bola // vi (CRICKET) arrojar la pelota; ~**s** n juego de las bochas, bolos mpl.

bow-legged ['bəulegd] a estevado.

bowler ['bəulə*] n (CRICKET) lanzador m (de la pelota); (*also:* ~ **hat**) hongo, bombín m.

bowling ['bəulɪŋ] n (*game*) bochas fpl, bolos mpl; ~ **alley** n bolera; ~ **green** n pista para bochas.

bow tie ['bəu-] *n* corbata de lazo.
box [bɒks] *n* (*also:* **cardboard** ~) caja, cajón *m*; (*for jewels*) estuche *m*; (*for money*) cofre *m*; (THEATRE) palco // *vt* encajonar // *vi* (SPORT) boxear; ~**er** *n* (*person*) boxeador *m*; (*dog*) boxer *m*; ~**ing** *n* (SPORT) boxeo; **B**~**ing Day** *n* Día de San Esteban, 26 de diciembre; ~**ing gloves** *npl* guantes *mpl* de boxeo; ~**ing ring** *n* ring *m*, cuadrilátero; ~ **office** *n* taquilla; ~**room** *n* trastero.
boy [bɔɪ] *n* (*young*) niño; (*older*) muchacho; (*servant*) criado.
boycott ['bɔɪkɔt] *n* boicot *m* // *vt* boicotear.
boyfriend ['bɔɪfrɛnd] *n* novio.
boyish ['bɔɪʃ] *a* muchachil.
B.R. *abbr of* **British Rail.**
bra [brɑ:] *n* sostén *m*.
brace [breɪs] *n* refuerzo, abrazadera; (*on teeth*) aparato; (*tool*) berbiquí *m* // *vt* asegurar, reforzar; ~**s** *npl* tirantes *mpl*; **to** ~ **o.s.** (*fig*) fortalecer el ánimo.
bracelet ['breɪslɪt] *n* pulsera, brazalete *m*.
bracing ['breɪsɪŋ] *a* vigorizante, tónico.
bracken ['brækən] *n* helecho.
bracket ['brækɪt] *n* (TECH) soporte *m*, puntal *m*; (*group*) clase *f*, categoría; (*also:* **brace** ~) soporte *m*, abrazadera; (*also:* **round** ~) paréntesis *m inv*; (*gen:* **square** ~) corchete *m* // *vt* (*group*) agrupar.
brag [bræg] *vi* jactarse.
braid [breɪd] *n* (*trimming*) galón *m*; (*of hair*) trenza.
Braille [breɪl] *n* Braille *m*.
brain [breɪn] *n* cerebro; ~**s** *npl* sesos *mpl*; ~**child** *n* parto del ingenio; ~**wash** *vt* lavar el cerebro a; ~**wave** *n* idea luminosa; ~**y** *a* muy listo *o* inteligente.
braise [breɪz] *vt* cocer a fuego lento.
brake [breɪk] *n* (*on vehicle*) freno // *vt, vi* frenar; ~ **drum** *n* tambor *m* de freno; ~ **fluid** *n* líquido para freno.
bramble ['bræmbl] *n* zarza.
branch [brɑ:ntʃ] *n* rama; (*fig*) ramo; (*road*) ramal *m*; (COMM) sucursal *f* // *vi* (*also:* ~ **out**) ramificarse; (: *fig*) extenderse.
brand [brænd] *n* marca; (*iron*) hierro de marcar // *vt* (*cattle*) marcar con hierro candente.
brandish ['brændɪʃ] *vt* blandir.
brand-new ['brænd'nju:] *a* flamante, completamente nuevo.
brandy ['brændɪ] *n* coñac *m*, brandy *m*.
brash [bræʃ] *a* (*rough*) tosco; (*cheeky*) descarado.
brass [brɑ:s] *n* latón *m*; ~ **band** *n* banda de metal.
brassière ['bræsɪə*] *n* sostén *m*.
brat [bræt] *n* (*pej*) mocoso.
bravado [brə'vɑ:dəu] *n* baladronada.
brave [breɪv] *a* valiente, valeroso // *n* valiente *m* // *vt* (*challenge*) desafiar; (*resist*) aguantar; ~**ry** *n* valor *m*, valentía.
brawl [brɔ:l] *n* pendencia, reyerta // *vi* pelearse.

brawn [brɔ:n] *n* fuerza; (*meat*) carne *f* en gelatina; ~**y** *a* fornido, musculoso.
bray [breɪ] *n* rebuzno // *vi* rebuznar.
brazen ['breɪzn] *a* descarado, cínico // *vt*: **to** ~ **it out** defenderse con descaro.
brazier ['breɪzɪə*] *n* brasero.
Brazil [brə'zɪl] *n* (el) Brasil; ~**ian** *a, n* brasileño/a.
breach [bri:tʃ] *vt* abrir brecha en // *n* (*gap*) brecha; (*breaking*): ~ **of contract** infracción *f* de contrato; ~ **of the peace** perturbación *f* del órden público.
bread [brɛd] *n* pan *m*; ~ **and butter** *n* pan *m* con mantequilla; (*fig*) pan (de cada día) // *a* común y corriente; ~**crumbs** *npl* migajas *fpl*; (CULIN) pan molido.
breadth [brɛtθ] *n* anchura; (*fig*) amplitud *f*.
breadwinner ['brɛdwɪnə*] *n* sostén *m* de la familia.
break [breɪk], *pt* **broke,** *pp* **broken** *vt* (*gen*) romper; (*promise*) faltar a; (*fall*) amortiguar; (*journey*) interrumpir; (*law*) violar, infringir; (*record*) batir; (*news*) comunicar // *vi* romperse, quebrarse; (*storm*) estallar // *n* (*gap*) abertura; (*crack*) grieta; (*fracture*) fractura; (*breakdown*) ruptura, rompimiento; (*rest*) descanso; (*time*) intérvalo; (: *at school*) (período de) recreo; (*chance*) oportunidad *f*; (*escape*) evasión *f*, fuga; **to** ~ **down** *vt* (*figures, data*) analizar, descomponer; (*undermine*) acabar con // *vi* estropearse; (MED) sufrir un colapso; (AUT) averiarse; (*person*) romper a llorar; **to** ~ **even** *vi* salir sin ganar ni perder; **to** ~ **free** *or* **loose** *vi* abrirse paso; **to** ~ **in** *vt* (*horse etc*) domar // *vi* (*burglar*) forzar una entrada; **to** ~ **into** *vt fus* (*house*) forzar; **to** ~ **off** *vi* (*speaker*) pararse, detenerse; (*branch*) partir; **to** ~ **open** *vt* (*door etc*) abrir por la fuerza, forzar; **to** ~ **out** *vi* estallar; **to** ~ **out in spots** salir a uno granos; **to** ~ **up** *vi* romperse // *vt* romper, intervenir en; ~**able** *a* quebradizo; ~**age** *n* rotura; ~**down** *n* (AUT) avería; (*in communications*) interrupción *f*; (MED: *also:* **nervous** ~**down**) colapso, crisis *f* nerviosa; ~**down lorry** *n* grúa, camión *m* grúa; ~**er** *n* rompiente *m*, ola grande.
breakfast ['brɛkfəst] *n* desayuno.
break: ~**through** *n* ruptura; (*fig*) avance *m*, adelanto; ~**water** *n* rompeolas *m inv*.
breast [brɛst] *n* (*of woman*) pecho, seno; (*chest*) pecho; (*of bird*) pechuga; ~-**stroke** *n* braza de pecho.
breath [brɛθ] *n* aliento, respiración *f*; **out of** ~ sin aliento, sofocado; ~**alyser** *n* prueba de alcohol por el aliento.
breathe [bri:ð] *vt, vi* respirar; (*noisily*) resollar; ~**r** *n* respiro.
breath: ~**less** *a* sin aliento, jadeante; ~**taking** *a* imponente, pasmoso.
breed [bri:d], *pt, pp* **bred** [brɛd] *vt* criar, engendrar // *vi* reproducirse, procrear // *n* raza, casta; ~**er** *n* (*person*) criador/a *m/f*; ~**ing** *n* (*of person*) educación *f*.

breeze [briːz] n brisa.
breezy ['briːzi] a de mucho viento, ventoso; (person) despreocupado.
brevity ['brɛvɪti] n brevedad f.
brew [bruː] vt (tea) hacer; (beer) elaborar // vi hacerse, prepararse; (fig) amenazar; ~**er** n cervecero; ~**ery** n fábrica de cerveza.
bribe [braɪb] n soborno // vt sobornar, cohechar; ~**ry** n soborno, cohecho.
brick [brɪk] n ladrillo; ~**layer** n albañil m; ~**works** n ladrillar m.
bridal ['braɪdl] a nupcial.
bride [braɪd] n novia; ~**groom** n novio; **bridesmaid** n dama de honor.
bridge [brɪdʒ] n puente m; (NAUT) puente m de mando; (of nose) caballete m; (CARDS) bridge m // vt (river) tender un puente sobre; ~**head** n cabeza de puente.
bridle ['braɪdl] n brida, freno // vt poner la brida a; (fig) reprimir, refrenar; ~ **path** n camino de herradura.
brief [briːf] a breve, corto // n (LAW) escrito // vt (inform) informar; (instruct) dar órdenes a; ~**s** npl (for men) calzoncillos mpl; (for women) bragas fpl; ~**case** n cartera; ~**ing** n (PRESS) informe m.
brigade [brɪˈgeɪd] n (MIL) brigada.
brigadier [brɪgəˈdɪə*] n general m de brigada.
bright [braɪt] a claro, luminoso; (weather) de sol; (person: clever) listo, inteligente; (: lively) alegre, animado; (colour) vivo; ~**en** vt (room) hacer más alegre // vi (weather) despejarse; (person: gen: ~**en up**) animarse, alegrarse.
brilliance ['brɪljəns] n brillo, brillantez f; **brilliant** [-ənt] a brillante; (clever) genial.
brim [brɪm] n borde m; (of hat) ala; ~**ful** a lleno hasta el borde; (fig) rebosante (de).
brine [braɪn] n (CULIN) salmuera.
bring [brɪŋ], pt, pp **brought** vt (thing) traer; (person) conducir; **to ~ about** vt ocasionar, producir; **to ~ back** vt volver a traer; (return) devolver; **to ~ down** vt bajar; (price) rebajar; **to ~ forward** vt adelantar; **to ~ in** vt (harvest) recoger; **to ~ off** vt (task, plan) lograr, conseguir; **to ~ out** vt (object) sacar; **to ~ round** vt (unconscious person) hacer volver en sí; (convince) convencer, ganar; **to ~ up** vt (person) educar, criar; (carry up) subir; (question) sacar a colación.
brink [brɪŋk] n borde m.
brisk [brɪsk] a enérgico, vigoroso; (speedy) rápido; (trade) activo.
brisket ['brɪskɪt] n carne f de vaca para asar.
bristle ['brɪsl] n cerda // vi erizarse.
Britain ['brɪtən] n Gran Bretaña.
British ['brɪtɪʃ] a británico; **the ~** npl los británicos; **the ~ Isles** npl las Islas Británicas.
Briton ['brɪtən] n británico/a.
brittle ['brɪtl] a quebradizo, frágil.
broach [brəʊtʃ] vt (subject) abordar.

broad [brɔːd] a ancho, amplio; (accent) cerrado; **in ~ daylight** en pleno día; ~**cast** n emisión f // (vb: pt, pp ~**cast**) vt (RADIO) emitir; (TV) transmitir // vi hablar o tocar por la radio; ~**casting** n radiodifusión f, difusión f; ~**en** vt ensanchar // vi ensancharse; ~**ly** ad en general; ~**-minded** a tolerante, liberal.
brochure ['brəʊʃjuə*] n folleto.
broke [brəʊk] pt of **break** // a (col) pelado, sin blanca.
broken ['brəʊkən] pp of **break** // a: ~ **leg** pierna rota; **in ~ English** en un inglés imperfecto; ~**-hearted** con el corazón partido.
broker ['brəʊkə*] n agente m/f, bolsista m/f.
bronchitis [brɔŋˈkaɪtɪs] n bronquitis f.
bronze [brɔnz] n bronce m.
brooch [brəʊtʃ] n prendedor m.
brood [bruːd] n camada, cría; (children) progenie f; (: pej) prole f // vi (hen) empollar; (obsessively) darle vueltas (a).
brook [bruk] n arroyo.
broom [brum] n escoba; (BOT) retama; ~**stick** n palo de escoba.
Bros. abbr of **Brothers.**
broth [brɔθ] n caldo.
brothel ['brɔθl] n burdel m.
brother ['brʌðə*] n hermano; ~**-in-law** n cuñado.
brought [brɔːt] pt, pp of **bring.**
brow [brau] n ceja; (forehead) frente m; (of hill) cumbre f.
brown [braun] a moreno; (hair) castaño; (tanned) bronceado // n (colour) color m moreno o pardo // vt poner moreno; (tan) broncear; (CULIN) dorar; ~**ie** n niña Girl Guide.
browse [brauz] vi (among books) hojear libros.
bruise [bruːz] n cardenal m, contusión f // vt magullar.
brunette [bruːˈnɛt] n morena.
brunt [brʌnt] n: **the ~ of** lo más fuerte de, lo peor de.
brush [brʌʃ] n cepillo; (large) escoba; (for painting, shaving etc) brocha; (artist's) pincel m; (BOT) maleza; (quarrel) escaramuza, encuentro // vt cepillar; (gen: ~ **past**, ~ **against**) rozar al pasar; **to ~ aside** vt rechazar, no hacer caso a; **to ~ up** vt (knowledge) repasar, refrescar; ~**wood** n (bushes) maleza; (sticks) leña.
brusque [bruːsk] a brusco, áspero.
Brussels ['brʌslz] n Bruselas; ~ **sprout** n colecilla de Bruselas.
brutal ['bruːtl] a brutal; ~**ity** [-ˈtælɪti] n brutalidad f.
brute [bruːt] n bruto; (person) bestia.
B.Sc. abbr of **Bachelor of Science** licenciado en ciencias.
bubble ['bʌbl] n burbuja, ampolla // vi burbujear, borbotar; ~ **gum** n chicle m de globo.
buck [bʌk] n macho; (US: col) dólar m // vi

corcovear; **to pass the** ~ **(to sb)** echar
(a uno) el muerto; **to** ~ **up** vi (cheer up)
animarse, cobrar ánimo.

bucket ['bʌkɪt] n cubo, balde m.

buckle ['bʌkl] n hebilla // vt abrochar con
hebilla // vi torcerse, combarse.

bud [bʌd] n brote m, yema; (of flower)
capullo // vi brotar, echar brotes; (fig)
florecer.

Buddhism ['budɪzm] n Budismo.

budding ['bʌdɪŋ] a en ciernes, en embrión.

buddy ['bʌdɪ] n (US) compañero,
compinche m.

budge [bʌdʒ] vt mover; (fig) hacer ceder
// vi moverse.

budgerigar ['bʌdʒərɪgaː*] n periquito.

budget ['bʌdʒɪt] n presupuesto.

budgie ['bʌdʒɪ] n = budgerigar.

buff [bʌf] a (colour) color m de ante // n
(enthusiast) entusiasta m/f.

buffalo ['bʌfələu], pl ~ or ~es n búfalo.

buffer ['bʌfə*] n amortiguador m.

buffet ['bufeɪ] n (bar) bar m, cafetería;
(food) buffet m // vt ['bʌfɪt] (strike)
abofetear; (wind etc) golpear; ~ **car** n
coche-comedor m.

buffoon [bə'fuːn] n bufón m.

bug [bʌg] n (insect) chinche m; (: gen)
bicho, sabandija; (: fig: germ) microbio,
bacilo; (spy device) micrófono oculto; (tap)
intervención f; (machine for tapping)
aparato de intervención // vt (fam)
fastidiar; (spy on) poner micrófono oculto
en.

bugle ['bjuːgl] n corneta, clarín m.

build [bɪld] n (of person) talle m, tipo // vt,
pt, pp **built** construir, edificar; ~**er** n
constructor m; (contractor) contratista
m/f; ~**ing** n (act of) construcción f;
(habitation, offices) edificio; ~**ing society**
n sociedad f inmobiliaria, cooperativa de
construcciones; **to** ~ **up** vt (MED)
fortalecer; (stocks) acumular.

built [bɪlt] pt, pp of build // a: ~**-in**
(cupboard) empotrado; (device) interior,
incorporado; ~**-up** (area) urbanizado.

bulb [bʌlb] n (BOT) bulbo; (ELEC) bombilla.

Bulgaria [bʌl'gɛərɪə] n Bulgaria; ~**n** a, n
búlgaro/a.

bulge [bʌldʒ] n bombeo, pandeo // vi
bombearse, pandearse; (pocket etc) hacer
bulto.

bulk [bʌlk] n (mass) bulto, volumen m;
(major part) grueso; **in** ~ (COMM) a
granel; **the** ~ **of** la mayor parte de;
~**head** n mamparo; ~**y** a voluminoso,
abultado.

bull [bul] n toro; ~**dog** n dogo.

bulldozer ['buldəuzə*] n aplanadora,
motoniveladora.

bullet ['bulɪt] n bala; ~**proof** a a prueba
de balas; ~ **wound** n balazo.

bulletin ['bulɪtɪn] n anuncio, parte m.

bullfight ['bulfaɪt] n corrida de toros;
~**er** n torero; ~**ing** n los toros mpl, el
toreo; (art of ~**ing**) tauromaquia.

bullion ['buljən] n oro o plata en barras.

bullock ['bulək] n novillo.

bull's-eye ['bulzaɪ] n centro del blanco.

bully ['bulɪ] n valentón m, matón m // vt
intimidar, tiranizar.

bum [bʌm] n (col: backside) culo, trasero;
(tramp) vagabundo.

bumblebee ['bʌmblbiː] n (ZOOL) abejorro.

bump [bʌmp] n (blow) tope m, choque m;
(jolt) sacudida; (on road etc, on head) bollo,
abolladura // vt (strike) chocar contra,
topetar // vi dar sacudidas; **to** ~ **into** vt
fus chocar contra, tropezar con; (person)
topar; ~**er** n (Brit) parachoques m inv //
a: ~**er crop/harvest** cosecha
abundante.

bumpy ['bʌmpɪ] a (road) lleno de baches;
(journey) zarandeado.

bun [bʌn] n bollo; (of hair) moño.

bunch [bʌntʃ] n (of flowers) ramo; (of keys)
manojo; (of bananas) piña; (of people)
grupo; (pej) pandilla.

bundle ['bʌndl] n (gen) bulto, fardo; (of
sticks) haz f; (of papers) legajo // vt (also:
~ **up**) atar, envolver; (put): **to** ~ **sth/sb
into** meter algo/a alguien
precipitadamente en.

bung [bʌŋ] n tapón m, bitoque m // vt
(throw: gen: ~ **into**) arrojar.

bungalow ['bʌŋgələu] n bungalow m,
chalé m.

bungle ['bʌŋgl] vt chapucear.

bunion ['bʌnjən] n juanete m.

bunk [bʌŋk] n tonterías fpl; ~ **beds** npl
literas fpl.

bunker ['bʌŋkə*] n (coal store) carbonera;
(MIL) refugio; (GOLF) bunker m.

bunny ['bʌnɪ] n (also: ~ **rabbit**) conejito.

bunting ['bʌntɪŋ] n empavesada, banderas
fpl.

buoy [bɔɪ] n boya; **to** ~ **up** vt mantener a
flote; (fig) animar; ~**ant** a boyante.

burden ['bəːdn] n carga // vt cargar.

bureau [bjuə'rəu], pl ~**x** [-z] n (furniture)
escritorio, buró m; (office) oficina,
agencia.

bureaucracy [bjuə'rɔkrəsɪ] n burocracia;
bureaucrat ['bjuərəkræt] n burócrata m/f.

burglar ['bəːglə*] n ladrón/ona m/f; ~
alarm n alarma f de ladrones; ~**y** n robo
con allanamiento, robo de una casa;
burgle ['bəːgl] vt robar (con
allanamiento).

burial ['berɪəl] n entierro; ~ **ground** n
cementerio.

burlesque [bəː'lesk] n parodia.

burly ['bəːlɪ] a fornido, membrudo.

Burma ['bəːmə] n Birmania.

burn [bəːn], pt, pp **burned** or **burnt** vt
quemar; (house) incendiar // vi quemarse,
arder; incendiarse; (sting) escocer // n
quemadura; **to** ~ **down** vt incendiar;
~**er** n (gas) quemador m, fuego; ~**ing** a
ardiente.

burp [bəːp] (col) n eructo // vi eructar.

burrow ['bʌrəu] n madriguera // vt hacer
una madriguera.

bursar ['bɔːsə*] n tesorero; (student)
becario; ~y n beca.

burst [bɔːst], pt, pp **burst** vt (balloon, pipe)
reventar; (banks etc) romper // vi
reventarse; romperse; (tyre) pincharse;
(bomb) estallar // n (gen) reventón m;
(explosion) estallido; (shots) ráfaga de
tiros; a ~ of energy una explosión f de
energía; to ~ into flames estallar en
llamas; to ~ into laughter soltar la
carcajada; to ~ into tears deshacerse
en lágrimas; to be ~ing with reventar
por o de; to ~ into vt fus (room etc)
irrumpir en; to ~ open vi abrirse de
golpe.

bury ['bɛrɪ] vt enterrar; (body) enterrar,
sepultar.

bus [bʌs] n autobús m.

bush [buʃ] n arbusto; (scrub land) monte m;
to beat about the ~ ir por rodeos; ~y a
(thick) espeso, poblado.

busily ['bɪzɪlɪ] ad atareadamente,
afanosamente.

business ['bɪznɪs] n (matter) negocio;
(trading) comercio, negocios mpl; (firm)
empresa, casa; (occupation) oficio; (affair)
asunto; it's my ~ to... me toca o
corresponde...; it's none of my ~ yo no
tengo nada que ver; he means ~ habla
en serio; ~like a formal, metódico;
~man n hombre m de negocios.

bus-stop ['bʌsstɔp] n parada de autobús.

bust [bʌst] n (ANAT) pecho // a (broken)
roto, estropeado; to go ~ quebrarse.

bustle ['bʌsl] n bullicio, movimiento // vi
menearse, apresurarse; **bustling** a (town)
animado, bullicioso.

busy ['bɪzɪ] a ocupado, atareado; (shop,
street) concurrido, animado // vr: to ~
o.s. with ocuparse en; ~body n
entrometido.

but [bʌt] conj pero // prep excepto, menos;
nothing ~ nada más que; ~ for a no ser
por, si no fuera por; all ~ finished casi
terminado.

butane ['bjuːteɪn] n butano.

butcher ['butʃə*] n carnicero // vt hacer
una carnicería con; (cattle etc for meat)
matar; ~'s (shop) n carnicería.

butler ['bʌtlə*] n mayordomo.

butt [bʌt] n (cask) tonel m; (for rain) tina;
(thick end) cabo, extremo; (of gun) culata;
(of cigarette) colilla; (fig: target) blanco //
vt dar cabezadas contra, topetar.

butter ['bʌtə*] n mantequilla // vt untar
con mantequilla; ~ bean n judía blanca;
~cup n ranúnculo.

butterfly ['bʌtəflaɪ] n mariposa.

buttocks ['bʌtəks] npl nalgas fpl.

button ['bʌtn] n botón m // vt abotonar,
abrochar; // vi abrocharse; ~hole n ojal
m; (flower) flor f que se lleva en el ojal //
vt obligar a escuchar.

buttress ['bʌtrɪs] n contrafuerte m; (fig)
apoyo, sostén m.

buxom ['bʌksəm] a (baby) rollizo; (woman)
frescachona.

buy [baɪ], pt, pp **bought** vt comprar // n
compra; to ~ sb sth/sth from sb
comprar algo para alguien/comprarle
algo a alguien; ~er n comprador/a m/f.

buzz [bʌz] n zumbido; (col: phone call)
llamada (por teléfono) // vi zumbar.

buzzard ['bʌzəd] n águila ratonera.

buzzer ['bʌzə*] n zumbador m, vibrador m.

by [baɪ] prep por; (beside) junto a, cerca de;
(according to) según, de acuerdo con;
(before): ~ 4 o'clock para las cuatro //
ad see pass, go etc; ~ bus/car en
autobús/coche; paid ~ the hour pagado
por horas; ~ night/day de noche/día;
(all) ~ oneself (completamente) solo;
~ the way a propósito, por cierto; ~
and large en general; ~ and ~ luego,
más tarde.

bye(-bye) ['baɪ('baɪ)] excl adiós, hasta
luego.

by(e)-law ['baɪlɔː] n ordenanza municipal.

by-election ['baɪɪlɛkʃən] n elección f
parcial.

bygone ['baɪgɔn] a pasado, del pasado //
n: let ~s be ~s lo pasado, pasado está.

bypass ['baɪpɑːs] n carretera de
circunvalación // vt evitar.

by-product ['baɪprɔdʌkt] n subproducto,
derivado.

bystander ['baɪstændə*] n espectador/a
m/f.

byword ['baɪwɔːd] n: to be a ~ for ser
conocidísimo por.

C

C. abbr of **centigrade.**

C.A. abbr of **chartered accountant.**

cab [kæb] n taxi m; (of truck) cabina.

cabaret ['kæbəreɪ] n cabaret m.

cabbage ['kæbɪdʒ] n col m, berza.

cabin ['kæbɪn] n cabaña; (on ship)
camarote m; ~ cruiser n yate m de
motor.

cabinet ['kæbɪnɪt] n (POL) consejo de
ministros; (furniture) armario; (also:
display ~) vitrina; ~-maker n ebanista
m.

cable ['keɪbl] n cable m // vt cablegrafiar;
~-car n coche m de teleférico, tren m
aéreo.

cackle ['kækl] vi cacarear.

cactus ['kæktəs], pl -ti [-taɪ] n cacto.

caddie ['kædɪ] n cadi m.

cadet [kə'dɛt] n (MIL) cadete m.

cadge [kædʒ] vt gorronear; **cadger** n
gorrón/ona m/f.

Caesarean (section) [siː'zɛərɪən] n
cesárea.

café ['kæfeɪ], **cafeteria** [kæfɪ'tɪərɪə] n
café m.

caffein(e) ['kæfiːn] n cafeína.

cage [keɪdʒ] n jaula // vt enjaular.

cagey ['keɪdʒɪ] a (col) cauteloso,
reservado.

Cairo ['kaɪərəu] n el Cairo.

cajole [kə'dʒəul] vt engatusar.

cake [keik] n (large) pastel m; (small) pasta, bizcocho; (of soap) pastilla; **~d with** cubierto de.

calamitous [kə'læmitəs] a calamitoso; **calamity** [-iti] n calamidad f.

calcium ['kælsiəm] n calcio.

calculate ['kælkjuleit] vt calcular; **calculating** a (clever) astuto; (devious) calculador(a); **calculation** [-'leiʃən] n cálculo, cómputo; **calculator** n calculadora.

calculus ['kælkjuləs] n cálculo.

calendar ['kæləndəˀ] n calendario; **~ month/year** mes m/año civil.

calf [kɑːf], pl **calves** n (of cow) ternero, becerro; (of other animals) cría; (also: **~skin**) piel m de becerro; (ANAT) pantorrilla.

calibre, caliber (US) ['kælibəˀ] n calibre m.

call [kɔːl] vt (gen, also TEL) llamar // vi (shout) llamar; (telephone) llamar por teléfono; (visit: also: **~ in**, **~ round**) hacer una visita // n (shout, TEL) llamada; (of bird) canto; (appeal) llamamiento; **to ~ for** vt fus (demand) pedir, exigir; (fetch) venir por; **to ~ off** vt suspender; (cancel) cancelar; **to ~ on** vt fus (visit) visitar; (turn to) acudir. a; **to ~ out** vi gritar, dar voces; **to ~ up** vt (MIL) llamar al servicio militar; **~box** n cabina telefónica; **~er** n visita m/f; (TEL) usuario; **~ girl** n prostituta; **~ing** n vocación f, profesión f.

callous ['kæləs] a insensible, cruel.

calm [kɑːm] n calma, tranquilidad f // vt calmar, tranquilizar // a (gen) tranquilo; (sea) liso, en calma; **~ly** ad tranquilamente, con calma; **~ness** n calma; **to ~ down** vi calmarse, tranquilizarse // vt calmar, tranquilizar.

calorie ['kæləri] n caloría.

calve [kɑːv] vi parir.

calves [kɑːvz] pl of **calf**.

camber ['kæmbəˀ] n (of road) combadura, comba.

Cambodia [kæm'bəudjə] n Camboya.

came [keim] pt of **come**.

camel ['kæməl] n camello.

cameo ['kæmiəu] n camafeo.

camera ['kæmərə] n máquina fotográfica; (CINEMA, TV) cámara; **in ~** en secreto; **~man** n cámaraman m, cámara m/f.

camouflage ['kæməflɑːʒ] n camuflaje m // vt camuflar.

camp [kæmp] n campo, campamento // vi acampar // a afectado, afeminado.

campaign [kæm'pein] n (MIL, POL etc) campaña // vi hacer campaña.

camp: ~bed n cama de campaña; **~er** n campista m/f; (vehicle) caravana; **~ing** n camping m; **to go ~ing** hacer camping; **~site** n camping m.

campus ['kæmpəs] n ciudad f universitaria.

can [kæn] auxiliary vb (gen) poder; (know

how to) saber; **I ~ swim** sé nadar // n (of oil, water) lata, bote m // vt enlatar; (preserve) conservar en lata.

Canada ['kænədə] n el Canadá; **Canadian** [kə'neidiən] a, n canadiense m/f.

canal [kə'næl] n canal m.

canary [kə'nɛəri] n canario; **C~ Islands** npl las (Islas) Canarias fpl.

cancel ['kænsəl] vt cancelar; (train) suprimir; (appointment) anular; (cross out) tachar, borrar; **~lation** [-'leiʃən] n cancelación f; supresión f.

cancer ['kænsəˀ] n cáncer m; **C~** (ASTRO) Cáncer m.

candid ['kændid] a franco, abierto.

candidate ['kændideit] n candidato.

candle ['kændl] n vela; (in church) cirio; **~stick** n (also: **~ holder**) (single) candelero; (low) palmatoria; (bigger, ornate) candelabro.

candour ['kændəˀ] n franqueza.

candy ['kændi] n azúcar m cande; (US) dulce m, caramelo.

cane [kein] n (BOT) caña; (stick) vara, palmeta // vt (SCOL) castigar (con palmeta).

canine ['kænain] a canino.

canister ['kænistəˀ] n bote m, lata.

cannabis ['kænəbis] n cáñamo, marijuana.

canned [kænd] a en lata, de lata.

cannibal ['kænibəl] n caníbal m/f; **~ism** n canibalismo.

cannon ['kænən], pl **~ or ~s** n cañón m; **~ball** n bala (de cañón).

cannot ['kænɔt] = **can not.**

canny ['kæni] a astuto.

canoe [kə'nuː] n canoa; (SPORT) piragua; **~ing** n (SPORT) piragüismo; **~ist** n piragüista m/f.

canon ['kænən] n (clergyman) canónigo; (standard) canon m.

canonize ['kænənaiz] vt canonizar.

can opener ['kænəupnəˀ] n abrelatas m inv.

canopy ['kænəpi] n dosel m, toldo; (ARCH) baldaquín m.

can't [kænt] = **can not.**

cantankerous [kæn'tæŋkərəs] a arisco, malhumorado.

canteen [kæn'tiːn] n cantina; (bottle) cantimplora; (of cutlery) juego (de cubiertos).

canter ['kæntəˀ] n medio galope // vi ir a medio galope.

canvas ['kænvəs] n (gen) lona; (painting) lienzo; (NAUT) velas fpl; **under ~** (camping) bajo lona.

canvass ['kænvəs] vt (POL) solicitar votos de.

canyon ['kænjən] n cañón m.

cap [kæp] n gorra; (of pen) capuchón m; (of bottle) tapa, cápsula; (MED) diafragma m // vt coronar, poner remate a; (outdo) superar; (FOOTBALL) seleccionar (para el equipo nacional).

capability [keɪpə'bɪlɪtɪ] n capacidad f; **capable** ['keɪpəbl] a capaz.
capacity [kə'pæsɪtɪ] n capacidad f; (position) calidad f.
cape [keɪp] n capa; (GEO) cabo.
caper ['keɪpə*] n (CULIN: gen: ~s) alcaparra; (prank) travesura.
capital ['kæpɪtl] n (also: ~ city) capital f; (money) capital m; (also: ~ letter) mayúscula; ~**ism** n capitalismo; ~**ist** a, n capitalista m/f; ~ **punishment** n pena de muerte.
capitulate [kə'pɪtjuleɪt] vi capitular, rendirse; **capitulation** [-'leɪʃən] n capitulación f, rendición f.
capricious [kə'prɪʃəs] a caprichoso.
Capricorn ['kæprɪkɔ:n] n Capricornio.
capsize [kæp'saɪz] vt volcar, hacer zozobrar // vi volcarse, zozobrar.
capstan ['kæpstən] n cabrestante m.
capsule ['kæpsju:l] n cápsula.
captain ['kæptɪn] n capitán m // vt capitanear, ser el capitán de.
caption ['kæpʃən] n (heading) título; (to picture) leyenda.
captivate ['kæptɪveɪt] vt cautivar, encantar.
captive ['kæptɪv] a, n cautivo/a; **captivity** [-'tɪvɪtɪ] n cautiverio.
capture ['kæptʃə*] vt prender, apresar; (place) tomar; (attention) captar, llamar // n apresamiento; toma; (thing taken) presa.
car [kɑ:*] n coche m, automóvil m; (RAIL) vagón m.
carafe [kə'ræf] n garrafa.
caramel ['kærəməl] n caramelo.
carat ['kærət] n quilate m.
caravan ['kærəvæn] n caravana, rulota; (of camels) caravana.
caraway ['kærəweɪ] n: ~ **seed** carvi m.
carbohydrate [kɑ:bəu'haɪdreɪt] n hidrato de carbono; (food) fécula.
carbon ['kɑ:bən] n carbono; ~ **copy** n copia al carbón; ~ **paper** n papel m carbón.
carburettor [kɑ:bju'rɛtə*] n carburador m.
carcass ['kɑ:kəs] n cadáver m de animal.
card [kɑ:d] n carta, naipe m; (visiting ~, post~ etc) tarjeta; ~**board** n cartón m, cartulina; ~ **game** n juego de naipes.
cardiac ['kɑ:dɪæk] a cardíaco.
cardigan ['kɑ:dɪgən] n rebeca.
cardinal ['kɑ:dɪnl] a cardinal // n cardenal m.
card index n fichero.
care [kɛə*] n (gen) cuidado; (worry) inquietud f, solicitud f; (charge) cargo, custodia // vi: to ~ **about** preocuparse de, tener interés en; **in sb's** ~ a cargo de alguien; **to take** ~ **to** cuidarse o tener cuidado de; **to take** ~ **of** vt cuidar; **to** ~ **for** vt fus cuidar a; (like) querer; **I don't** ~ no me importa.
career [kə'rɪə*] n carrera // vi (also: ~

along) correr a toda velocidad.
carefree ['kɛəfri:] a despreocupado.
careful ['kɛəful] a cuidadoso; (cautious) cauteloso; **(be)** ~! ¡tenga cuidado!; ~**ly** ad con cuidado, cuidadosamente.
careless ['kɛəlɪs] a descuidado; (heedless) poco atento; ~**ly** ad sin cuidado, a la ligera; ~**ness** n descuido, falta de atención.
caress [kə'rɛs] n caricia // vt acariciar.
caretaker ['kɛəteɪkə*] n portero, conserje m/f.
car-ferry ['kɑ:fɛrɪ] n transbordador m para coches.
cargo ['kɑ:gəu], pl ~**es** n cargamento, carga.
Caribbean [kærɪ'bi:ən] n: **the** ~ **(Sea)** el Caribe.
caricature ['kærɪkətjuə*] n caricatura.
carnal ['kɑ:nl] a carnal.
carnation [kɑ:'neɪʃən] n clavel m.
carnival ['kɑ:nɪvəl] n fiesta, feria, carnaval m.
carnivore ['kɑ:nɪvɔ:*] n carnívoro.
carol ['kærəl] n: **(Christmas)** ~ villancico.
carp [kɑ:p] n (fish) carpa; **to** ~ **at** vt fus quejarse de.
car park n aparcamiento, parking m.
carpenter ['kɑ:pɪntə*] n carpintero; **carpentry** [-trɪ] n carpintería.
carpet ['kɑ:pɪt] n alfombra // vt alfombrar; ~ **slippers** npl zapatillas fpl.
carriage ['kærɪdʒ] n coche m; (RAIL) vagón m; (for goods) transporte m; (bearing) porte m; ~**way** n (part of road) carretera; **dual** ~**way** carretera de doble calzada.
carrier ['kærɪə*] n trajinista m/f; (company) empresa de transportes; ~ **bag** n bolsa (de papel).
carrot ['kærət] n zanahoria.
carry ['kærɪ] vt (gen) llevar; (transport) transportar; (a motion, bill) aprobar; (involve: responsibilities etc) entrañar, implicar // vi (sound) oírse; **to** ~ **on** vi (continue) seguir (adelante), continuar; (fam: complain) quejarse, protestar // vt proseguir, continuar; **to** ~ **out** vt (orders) cumplir; (investigation) llevar a cabo, realizar.
cart [kɑ:t] n carro, carreta // vt acarrear, llevar (en carro).
cartilage ['kɑ:tɪlɪdʒ] n cartílago.
cartographer [kɑ:'tɔgrəfə*] n cartógrafo.
carton ['kɑ:tən] n (box) caja (de cartón); (of yogurt) pote m.
cartoon [kɑ:'tu:n] n (PRESS) caricatura; (comic strip) tira cómica; (film) dibujos mpl animados; ~**ist** n caricaturista m/f; dibujante m/f.
cartridge ['kɑ:trɪdʒ] n cartucho.
carve [kɑ:v] vt (meat) trinchar; (wood, stone) cincelar, esculpir; (on tree) grabar; **to** ~ **up** dividir, repartir; **carving** n (in wood etc) escultura, (obra de) talla; **carving knife** n trinchante m.

car wash *n* lavado de coches.

cascade [kæs'keɪd] *n* salto de agua, cascada; (*fig*) chorro // *vi* caer a chorros *o* en forma de cascada.

case [keɪs] *n* (*container*) caja; (*MED*) caso; (*for jewels etc*) estuche *m*; (*LAW*) causa, proceso; (*also*: **suit**~) maleta; **in ~ (of)** en caso de (que), por si; **in any ~** en todo caso; **just in ~** por si acaso; **to make a good ~** tener buenos argumentos.

cash [kæʃ] *n* (dinero en) efectivo, dinero contante // *vt* cobrar, hacer efectivo; **to pay (in) ~** pagar al contado; **~ on delivery** cóbrese al entregar; **~book** *n* libro de caja; **~desk** *n* caja.

cashew [kæ'ʃuː] *n* (*also*: **~ nut**) anacardo.

cashier [kæ'ʃɪə*] *n* cajero.

cashmere [kæʃ'mɪə*] *n* casimir *m*, cachemira.

cash register *n* caja.

casing ['keɪsɪŋ] *n* envoltura; (*of boiler etc*) revestimiento.

casino [kə'siːnəu] *n* casino.

cask [kɑːsk] *n* tonel *m*, barril *m*.

casket ['kɑːskɪt] *n* cofre *m*, estuche *m*; (*US*: *coffin*) ataúd *m*.

casserole ['kæsərəul] *n* cacerola; (*food*) cazuela.

cassette [kæ'sɛt] *n* cassette *m*; **~ player** *n* tocacassettes *m inv*.

cassock ['kæsək] *n* sotana.

cast [kɑːst], *pt*, *pp* **cast** *vt* (*throw*) echar, arrojar, lanzar; (*skin*) mudar, perder; (*metal*) fundir; (*THEATRE*) hacer el reparto de // *vi* (*FISHING*) lanzar // *n* (*THEATRE*) reparto; (*mould*) forma, molde *m*; (*also*: **plaster ~**) vaciado; **to ~ away** *vt* desechar; **to ~ down** *vt* derribar; **to ~ loose** soltar; **to ~ one's vote** dar el voto; **to ~ off** *vi* (*NAUT*) desamarrar.

castanets [kæstə'nɛts] *npl* castañuelas *fpl*.

castaway ['kɑːstəwɔɪ] *n* náufrago.

caste [kɑːst] *n* casta.

casting vote ['kɑːstɪŋ] *n* voto decisivo.

cast iron *n* hierro fundido.

castle ['kɑːsl] *n* castillo; (*CHESS*) torre *f*.

castor ['kɑːstə*] *n* (*wheel*) ruedecilla; **~ oil** *n* aceite *m* de ricino; **~ sugar** *n* azúcar *m* extrafino.

castrate [kæs'treɪt] *vt* castrar.

casual ['kæʒjul] *a* (*by chance*) fortuito; (*irregular*: *work etc*) eventual, temporero; (*unconcerned*) despreocupado; (*informal*: *clothes*) de sport; **~ly** *ad* por casualidad; de manera despreocupada.

casualty ['kæʒjultɪ] *n* víctima *m/f*, herido; (*dead*) muerto; (*MIL*) baja; **casualties** *npl* pérdidas *fpl*.

cat [kæt] *n* gato.

Catalan ['kætəlæn] *a*, *n* Catalán/ana *m/f*.

catalogue, catalog (*US*) ['kætələg] *n* catálogo // *vt* catalogar.

Catalonia [kætə'ləunɪə] *n* Cataluña.

catalyst ['kætəlɪst] *n* catalizador *m*.

catapult ['kætəpʌlt] *n* tirador *m*.

cataract ['kætərækt] *n* (*also* MED) catarata.

catarrh [kə'tɑː*] *n* catarro.

catastrophe [kə'tæstrəfɪ] *n* catástrofe *m*; **catastrophic** [kætə'strɔfɪk] *a* catastrófico.

catch [kætʃ], *pt*, *pp* **caught** *vt* (*gen*) coger; (*arrest*) detener; (*grasp*) asir; (*breath*) suspender; (*person*: *by surprise*) sorprender; (*attract*: *attention*) ganar; (*MED*) contagiarse de, coger; (*also*: **~ up**) alcanzar // *vi* (*fire*) encenderse; (*in branches etc*) enredarse // *n* (*fish etc*) pesca; (*act of catching*) cogida; (*trick*) trampa; (*of lock*) pestillo, cerradura; **to ~ on** *vi* (*understand*) caer en la cuenta; (*grow popular*) hacerse popular; **to ~ sight of** divisar; **to ~ up** *vi* (*fig*) ponerse al día.

catch: **~ing** *a* (*MED*) contagioso; **~ment area** *n* zona de captación; **~ phrase** *n* lema *m*, slogan *m*; **~y** *a* (*tune*) pegadizo.

catechism ['kætɪkɪzəm] *n* (*REL*) catequismo.

categoric(al) [kætɪ'gɔrɪk(əl)] *a* categórico, terminante.

categorize ['kætɪgəraɪz] *vt* clasificar; **category** [-rɪ] *n* categoría, clase *f*.

cater ['keɪtə*] *vi*: **to ~ for** abastecer a; (*needs*) atender a; (*consumers*) proveer a; **~er** *n* abastecedor *m*, proveedor *m*; **~ing** *n* servicio de comidas; (*trade*) abastecimiento.

caterpillar ['kætəpɪlə*] *n* oruga, gusano; **~ track** *n* rodado de oruga.

cathedral [kə'θiːdrəl] *n* catedral *f*.

catholic ['kæθəlɪk] *a* católico; **C~** *a*, *n* (*REL*) católico/a.

cattle ['kætl] *npl* ganado *sg*.

catty ['kætɪ] *a* malicioso, rencoroso.

Caucasus ['kɔːkəsəs] *n* Cáucaso.

caught [kɔːt] *pt*, *pp of* **catch**.

cauliflower ['kɔlɪflauə*] *n* coliflor *f*.

cause [kɔːz] *n* causa, motivo, razón *f* // *vt* causar; (*provoke*) provocar.

causeway ['kɔːzweɪ] *n* (*road*) carretera elevada; (*embankment*) terraplén *m*.

caustic ['kɔːstɪk] *a* cáustico; (*fig*) mordaz.

caution ['kɔːʃən] *n* cautela, prudencia; (*warning*) advertencia, amonestación *f* // *vt* amonestar.

cautious ['kɔːʃəs] *a* cauteloso, prudente, precavido; **~ly** *ad* con cautela; **~ness** *n* cautela.

cavalier [kævə'lɪə*] *a* arrogante, desdeñoso.

cavalry ['kævəlrɪ] *n* caballería.

cave [keɪv] *n* cueva, caverna; **to ~ in** *vi* (*roof etc*) derrumbarse, hundirse; **~man** *n* cavernícola *m/f*, troglodita *m/f*.

cavern ['kævən] *n* caverna.

caviar(e) ['kævɪɑː*] *n* caviar *m*.

cavity ['kævɪtɪ] *n* hueco, cavidad *f*.

cavort [kə'vɔːt] *vi* dar cabrioladas.

caw [kɔː] *vi* graznar.

CBI *n abbr of* **Confederation of British Industries**.

cc *abbr of* **cubic centimetres; carbon copy.**

cease [si:s] *vt, vi* cesar; ~**fire** *n* cese *m* de hostilidades *o* fuego; ~**less** *a* incesante; ~**lessly** *ad* sin cesar.

cedar ['si:də*] *n* cedro.

cede [si:d] *vt* ceder.

ceiling ['si:lɪŋ] *n* techo; (*fig*) límite *m*.

celebrate ['sɛlɪbreɪt] *vt* celebrar; (*marriage*) solemnizar // *vi* divertirse; ~**d** *a* célebre; **celebration** [-'breɪʃən] *n* fiesta, celebración *f*.

celebrity [sɪ'lɛbrɪtɪ] *n* celebridad *f*.

celery ['sɛlərɪ] *n* apio.

celestial [sɪ'lɛstɪəl] *a* (*of sky*) celeste; (*divine*) celestial.

celibacy ['sɛlɪbəsɪ] *n* celibato.

cell [sɛl] *n* celda; (*BIOL*) célula; (*ELEC*) elemento.

cellar ['sɛlə*] *n* sótano; (*for wine*) bodega.

'cello ['tʃɛləu] *n* violoncelo.

cellophane ['sɛləfeɪn] *n* celofán *m*.

cellular ['sɛljulə*] *a* celular.

cellulose ['sɛljuləus] *n* celulosa.

Celt [kɛlt, sɛlt] *a, n* celta *m/f*; ~**ic** *a* celta.

cement [sə'mɛnt] *n* cemento // *vt* cementar; (*fig*) cimentar, fortalecer.

cemetery ['sɛmɪtrɪ] *n* cementerio.

cenotaph ['sɛnətɑ:f] *n* cenotafio.

censor ['sɛnsə*] *n* censor // *vt* (*cut*) tachar, suprimir; ~**ship** *n* censura.

censure ['sɛnʃə*] *vt* censurar.

census ['sɛnsəs] *n* censo.

cent [sɛnt] *n* (*US: coin*) centavo, céntimo; *see also* **per.**

centenary [sɛn'ti:nərɪ] *n* centenario.

centi... [sɛntɪ] *pref:* ~**grade** *a* centígrado; ~**litre** *n* centilitro; ~**metre** *n* centímetro; ~**pede** *n* ciempiés *m*.

central ['sɛntrəl] *a* central; (*of town*) céntrico; **C**~ **American** *a* centroamericano; ~ **heating** *n* calefacción *f* central; ~**ize** *vt* centralizar.

centre ['sɛntə*] *n* centro // *vt* centrar; ~-**forward** *n* (*SPORT*) delantero centro; ~-**half** *n* (*SPORT*) medio centro.

century ['sɛntjurɪ] *n* siglo; **20th** ~ siglo veinte.

ceramic [sɪ'ræmɪk] *a* cerámico; ~**s** *n* cerámica.

cereal ['si:rɪəl] *n* cereal *m*.

ceremony ['sɛrɪmənɪ] *n* ceremonia.

certain ['sə:tən] *a* (*gen*) seguro; (*correct*) cierto; (*person*) seguro; (*a particular*) cierto; **for** ~ a ciencia cierta; ~**ly** *ad* desde luego, por cierto; ~**ty** *n* certeza, certidumbre *f*, seguridad *f*.

certificate [sə'tɪfɪkɪt] *n* certificado.

certify ['sə:tɪfaɪ] *vt* certificar.

cervix ['sə:vɪks] *n* cerviz *f*.

cessation [sə'seɪʃən] *n* cesación *f*, suspensión *f*.

cf. *abbr* = **compare** cfr.

chafe [tʃeɪf] *vt* (*rub*) rozar; (*wear*) desgastar; (*irritate*) irritar.

chaffinch ['tʃæfɪntʃ] *n* pinzón *m* vulgar.

chagrin ['ʃægrɪn] *n* disgusto, desazón *f*.

chain [tʃeɪn] *n* (*gen*) cadena // *vt* (*also:* ~ **up**) encadenar; ~ **reaction** *n* reacción *f* en cadena; ~ **store** *n* tienda de una cadena.

chair [tʃɛə*] *n* silla; (*armchair*) sillón *m*; (*of university*) cátedra // *vt* (*meeting*) presidir; ~**lift** *n* telesilla; ~**man** *n* presidente *m*.

chalet ['ʃæleɪ] *n* chalet *m*.

chalice ['tʃælɪs] *n* cáliz *m*.

chalk [tʃɔ:k] *n* (*GEO*) creta; (*for writing*) tiza.

challenge ['tʃælɪndʒ] *n* desafío, reto // *vt* desafiar, retar; (*statement, right*) poner en duda, cuestionar; **to** ~ **sb to do sth** retar a uno a que haga algo; **challenger** *n* (*SPORT*) contrincante *m/f*; **challenging** *a* desafiante; (*tone*) de desafío.

chamber ['tʃeɪmbə*] *n* cámara, sala; ~ **of commerce** cámara de comercio; ~**maid** *n* camarera; ~ **music** *n* música de cámara.

chamois ['ʃæmwɑ:] *n* gamuza.

champagne [ʃæm'peɪn] *n* champaña, champán *m*.

champion ['tʃæmpɪən] *n* campeón/ona *m/f*; ~**ship** *n* campeonato.

chance [tʃɑ:ns] *n* (*luck*) casualidad *f*, suerte *f*; (*fate*) azar *m*; (*opportunity*) ocasión *f*, oportunidad *f*; (*likelihood*) posibilidad *f*; (*risk*) riesgo // *vt* arriesgar, probar // *a* fortuito, casual; **to** ~ **it** aventurarse, arriesgarse; **to take a** ~ arriesgarse; **by** ~ por casualidad.

chancel ['tʃɑ:nsəl] *n* coro y presbiterio.

chancellor ['tʃɑ:nsələ*] *n* canciller *m*; **C**~ **of the Exchequer** *n* Ministro de Hacienda.

chandelier [ʃændə'lɪə*] *n* araña (de luces).

change [tʃeɪndʒ] *vt* (*gen*) cambiar; (*replace*) reemplazar; (*gear, clothes, house*) cambiar de, mudar de; (*exchange*) trocar; (*transform*) transformar // *vi* (*gen*) cambiar(se), mudar; (*trains*) hacer transbordo; **to** ~ **into** transformarse en // *n* cambio, modificación *f*, transformación *f*; (*coins*) moneda suelta, suelto; (*money returned*) vuelta; **for a** ~ para variar; ~**able** *a* (*weather*) cambiable, mudable; ~**less** *a* inmutable; ~**over** *n* (*to new system*) cambio.

changing ['tʃeɪndʒɪŋ] *a* cambiante; ~ **room** *n* vestuario.

channel ['tʃænl] *n* (*TV*) canal *m*; (*of river*) cauce *m*; (*of sea*) estrecho; (*groove, fig: medium*) conducto, medio // *vt* canalizar, encauzar; **the (English) C**~ el Canal (de la Mancha); **the C**~ **Islands** las Islas Normandas *fpl*.

chant [tʃɑ:nt] *n* canto // *vt* cantar; (*fig*) recitar en tono monótono.

chaos ['keɪɔs] *n* caos *m*; **chaotic** [keɪ'ɔtɪk] *a* caótico, desordenado.

chap [tʃæp] *n* (*col: man*) tío, tipo // *vi* (*skin*) agrietarse.

chapel ['tʃæpəl] n capilla.
chaperon ['ʃæpərəʊn] n carabina.
chaplain ['tʃæplɪn] n capellán m.
chapter ['tʃæptə*] n capítulo.
char [tʃɑ:*] vt (burn) carbonizar, chamuscar // n = **charlady.**
character ['kærɪktə*] n carácter m, naturaleza, índole f, calidad f; (in novel, film) personaje m; (role) papel m; ~**istic** [-'rɪstɪk] a característico // n característica; ~**ize** vt caracterizar.
charade [ʃə'rɑ:d] n charada.
charcoal ['tʃɑ:kəʊl] n carbón m vegetal; (ART) carboncillo.
charge [tʃɑ:dʒ] n carga; (LAW) cargo, acusación f; (cost) precio, coste m; (responsibility) cargo; (task) encargo // vt (LAW) acusar (with de); (gun, battery, MIL: enemy) cargar; (price) pedir; (customer) cobrar; (sb with task) encargar // vi cargar, precipitarse; (make pay) cobrar; ~**s** npl: **bank ~s** suplemento cobrado por el banco; **free of ~** gratis; **to reverse the ~s** (TEL) poner una conferencia por cobrar; **to take ~ of** hacerse cargo de, encargarse de; **to be in ~ of** estar a cargo de o encargado de; **how much do you ~?** ¿cuánto cobra Usted?; **to ~ an expense (up) to sb's account** cargar algo a cuenta de alguien.
charitable ['tʃærɪtəbl] a caritativo.
charity ['tʃærɪtɪ] n (gen) caridad f; (sympathy) compasión f; (organization) sociedad f benéfica.
charlady ['tʃɑ:leɪdɪ] n mujer f de la limpieza.
charm [tʃɑ:m] n encanto, atractivo; (spell) hechizo; (object) amuleto // vt encantar; hechizar; ~**ing** a encantador(a), simpático.
chart [tʃɑ:t] n cuadro; (graph) gráfica; (map) carta de navegación // vt (course) trazar.
charter ['tʃɑ:tə*] vt (plane) alquilar; (ship) fletar // n (document) carta; ~**ed accountant** n perito contable; ~ **flight** n vuelo charter.
charwoman ['tʃɑ:wʊmən] n = **charlady.**
chase [tʃeɪs] vt (follow) perseguir; (hunt) cazar // n persecución f; caza; **to ~ after** correr tras.
chasm ['kæzəm] n abismo.
chassis ['ʃæsɪ] n chasis m.
chaste [tʃeɪst] a casto; **chastity** ['tʃæstɪtɪ] n castidad f.
chat [tʃæt] vi (also: **have a ~**) charlar // n charla.
chatter ['tʃætə*] vi (person) charlar; (teeth) castañetear // n (of birds) parloteo; (of people) charla, cháchara; ~**box** n parlanchín/ina m/f.
chatty ['tʃætɪ] a (style) familiar; (person) hablador(a), locuaz.
chauffeur ['ʃəʊfə*] n chófer m.
cheap [tʃi:p] a barato; (trick) malo; (poor quality) barato, de poca calidad // ad barato; ~**en** vt rebajar el precio,

abaratar; **to ~en o.s.** rebajarse; ~**ly** ad barato, a bajo precio.
cheat [tʃi:t] vi hacer trampa // vt defraudar, timar // n trampa, fraude m; (person) tramposo; ~**ing** n trampa, fraude m.
check [tʃɛk] vt (examine) controlar; (facts) comprobar; (count) contar; (halt) parar, detener; (restrain) refrenar, restringir // n (inspection) control m, inspección f; (curb) freno; (bill) nota, cuenta; (obstacle) impedimento, estorbo; (token) ficha; (pattern: gen pl) cuadro; **to ~ in** vi (in hotel, airport) registrarse // vt (luggage) facturar; **to ~ out** vi (of hotel) pagar la cuenta y marcharse; **to ~ up** vi: **to ~ up on sth** comprobar algo; **to ~ up on sb** investigar a una persona; ~**mate** n jaque m mate; ~**out** n caja; ~**point** n (punto de) control m; ~**up** n (MED) reconocimiento general; (of machine) repaso.
cheek [tʃi:k] n mejilla; (impudence) descaro; ~**bone** n pómulo; ~**y** a fresco, descarado.
cheer [tʃɪə*] vt vitorear, aplaudir; (gladden) alegrar, animar // vi aplaudir, gritar con entusiasmo // n grito (de entusiasmo); ~**s** npl aplausos mpl; ~**s!** ¡salud!; **to ~ up** vi animarse, cobrar ánimos // vt alegrar, animar; ~**ful** a alegre; ~**fulness** n alegría; **cheerio** excl ¡hasta luego!; ~**less** a triste, sombrío.
cheese [tʃi:z] n queso.
chef [ʃef] n jefe/a m/f de cocina.
chemical ['kemɪkəl] a químico // n elemento químico.
chemist ['kemɪst] n farmacéutico; (scientist) químico; ~**ry** n química; ~**'s (shop)** n farmacia.
cheque [tʃek] n cheque m; ~**book** n libro de cheques, chequera.
chequered ['tʃekəd] a (fig) variado, accidentado.
cherish ['tʃerɪʃ] vt (love) querer, apreciar; (protect) cuidar; (hope etc) abrigar.
cherry ['tʃerɪ] n cereza.
chess [tʃes] n ajedrez m; ~**board** n tablero (de ajedrez); ~**man** n pieza, trebejo.
chest [tʃest] n (ANAT) pecho; (box) cofre m, cajón m; ~ **of drawers** n cómoda.
chestnut ['tʃesnʌt] n castaña; ~ **(tree)** n castaño.
chew [tʃu:] vt mascar, masticar; ~**ing gum** n chicle m.
chic [ʃi:k] a elegante.
chick [tʃɪk] n pollito, polluelo; (fam) chica.
chicken ['tʃɪkɪn] n gallina, pollo; (food) pollo; ~**pox** n varicela.
chickpea ['tʃɪkpi:] n garbanzo.
chicory ['tʃɪkərɪ] n (for coffee) achicoria; (salad) escarola.
chief [tʃi:f] n jefe/a m/f // a principal; ~**ly** ad principalmente.
chiffon ['ʃɪfɔn] n gasa.
chilblain ['tʃɪlbleɪn] n sabañón m.

child [tʃaɪld], pl ~**ren** ['tʃɪldrən] n niño/a; (offspring) hijo/a; ~**birth** n parto; ~**hood** n niñez f, infancia; ~**ish** a pueril, aniñado; ~**like** a como (de) niño; ~ **minder** n cuidadora de niños.

Chile ['tʃɪlɪ] n Chile m; ~**an** a, n chileno/a.

chill [tʃɪl] n frío; (MED) escalofrío, resfriado // vt enfriar; (CULIN) congelar; ~**y** a frío.

chime [tʃaɪm] n (peal) repique m, campanada // vi repicar, sonar.

chimney ['tʃɪmnɪ] n chimenea; ~ **sweep** n deshollinador m.

chimpanzee [tʃɪmpæn'ziː] n chimpancé m.

chin [tʃɪn] n barba, barbilla.

china ['tʃaɪnə] n porcelana; (gen) loza.

China ['tʃaɪnə] n China; **Chinese** [tʃaɪ'niːz] a chino // n chino/a; (LING) el chino.

chink [tʃɪŋk] n (opening) grieta, hendedura; (noise) tintineo.

chip [tʃɪp] n (gen pl: CULIN) patata frita; (of wood) astilla; (of glass, stone) lasca; (at poker) ficha // vt (cup, plate) astillar; to ~ **in** vi interrumpir; (contribute) compartir los gastos.

chiropodist [kɪ'rɔpədɪst] n pedicuro.

chirp [tʃəːp] vi gorjear, piar; (cricket) chirriar.

chisel ['tʃɪzl] n (for wood) formón m; (for stone) cincel m.

chit [tʃɪt] n nota.

chitchat ['tʃɪttʃæt] n chismes mpl, habladurías fpl.

chivalrous ['ʃɪvəlrəs] a caballeroso; **chivalry** [-rɪ] n caballerosidad f.

chives [tʃaɪvz] npl cebollino sg.

chlorine ['klɔːriːn] n cloro.

chock [tʃɔk]: ~**-a-block**, ~**-full** a de bote en bote, atestado.

chocolate ['tʃɔklɪt] n chocolate m.

choice [tʃɔɪs] n elección f, selección f; (preference) preferencia // a selecto, elegido.

choir ['kwaɪə*] n coro; ~**boy** n corista m.

choke [tʃəuk] vi sofocarse; (on food) atragantarse // vt ahogar, sofocar; (block) obstruir // n (AUT) estrangulador m; **choker** n (necklace) gargantilla.

cholera ['kɔlərə] n cólera m.

choose [tʃuːz], pt **chose**, pp **chosen** vt escoger, elegir; (team) seleccionar.

chop [tʃɔp] vt (wood) cortar, tajar; (CULIN: also: ~ **up**) desmenuzar; (meat) picar // n golpe m cortante; (CULIN) chuleta; ~**s** npl (jaws) boca sg, labios mpl; ~**py** a (sea) picado, agitado; ~**sticks** npl palillos mpl.

choral ['kɔːrəl] a coral.

chord [kɔːd] n (MUS) acorde m.

chore [tʃɔː*] n faena, tarea; (routine task) trabajo rutinario.

choreographer [kɔrɪ'ɔgrəfə*] n coreógrafo.

chorister ['kɔrɪstə*] n corista m/f.

chortle ['tʃɔːtl] vi reír entre dientes.

chorus ['kɔːrəs] n coro; (repeated part of song) estribillo.

chose [tʃəuz], **chosen** ['tʃəuzn] pt, pp of **choose**.

Christ [kraɪst] n Cristo.

christen ['krɪsn] vt bautizar; ~**ing** n bautizo.

Christian ['krɪstɪən] a, n cristiano/a; ~**ity** [-'ænɪtɪ] n cristianismo; ~ **name** n nombre m de pila.

Christmas ['krɪsməs] n Navidad f; **Merry** ~! ¡Felices Pascuas!; ~ **Eve** n Nochebuena.

chrome [krəum], **chromium** ['krəumɪəm] n cromo.

chromosome ['krəuməsəum] n cromosoma m.

chronic ['krɔnɪk] a crónico.

chronicle ['krɔnɪkl] n crónica.

chronological [krɔnə'lɔdʒɪkəl] a cronológico.

chrysanthemum [krɪ'sænθəməm] n crisantemo.

chubby ['tʃʌbɪ] a rechoncho.

chuck [tʃʌk] vt lanzar, arrojar; to ~ **out** vt echar (fuera), tirar; to ~ (**up**) vt abandonar.

chuckle ['tʃʌkl] vi reírse entre dientes.

chug [tʃʌg] vi resoplar; to ~ **along** vi (fig) ir tirando.

chum [tʃʌm] n compinche m, compañero.

chunk [tʃʌŋk] n pedazo, trozo.

church [tʃəːtʃ] n iglesia; ~**yard** n campo santo.

churlish ['tʃəːlɪʃ] a grosero, hosco.

churn [tʃəːn] n (for butter) mantequera; (for milk) lechera // vt revolver, agitar.

chute [ʃuːt] n (also: **rubbish** ~) vertedero; (children's slide) tobogán m.

chutney ['tʃʌtnɪ] n salsa picante.

CID n abbr of **Criminal Investigation Department** B.I.C. (Brigada de Investigación Criminal).

cider ['saɪdə*] n sidra.

cigar [sɪ'gɑː*] n puro.

cigarette [sɪgə'rɛt] n cigarrillo; (fam) pitillo; ~ **case** n pitillera; ~ **end** n colilla; ~ **holder** n boquilla.

Cinderella [sɪndə'rɛlə] n la Cenicienta.

cinders ['sɪndəz] npl cenizas fpl.

cine [sɪnɪ]: ~**camera** n cámara cinematográfica; ~**film** n película cinematográfica.

cinema ['sɪnəmə] n cine m.

cinnamon ['sɪnəmən] n canela.

cipher ['saɪfə*] n cifra.

circle ['səːkl] n círculo; (in cinema) anfiteatro // vi dar vueltas // vt (surround) rodear, cercar; (move round) dar la vuelta a.

circuit ['səːkɪt] n circuito; (tour) gira; (track) pista; (lap) vuelta; ~**ous** [səː'kjuɪtəs] a tortuoso, indirecto.

circular ['səːkjulə*] a circular // n circular f.

circulate ['səːkjuleɪt] vi circular // vt poner en circulación, hacer circular;

circulation [-'leɪʃən] n circulación f; (of newspaper) tirada.
circumcise ['sɜːkəmsaɪz] vt circuncidar.
circumference [sə'kʌmfərəns] n circunferencia.
circumspect ['sɜːkəmspekt] a circunspecto, prudente.
circumstances ['sɜːkəmstənsɪz] npl circunstancias fpl; (financial condition) situación f económica.
circus ['sɜːkəs] n circo; (roundabout) glorieta.
cistern ['sɪstən] n tanque m, depósito; (in toilet) cisterna.
cite [saɪt] vt citar.
citizen ['sɪtɪzn] n (POL) ciudadano/a; (resident) vecino/a, habitante m/f; ~ship n ciudadanía.
citrus fruit ['sɪtrəs-] n agrios mpl.
city ['sɪtɪ] n ciudad f; the C~ centro financiero de Londres.
civic ['sɪvɪk] a cívico, municipal.
civil ['sɪvɪl] a civil; (polite) atento, cortés; (defence) pasivo; (well-bred) educado; ~ engineer n ingeniero civil; C~ Service administración f pública; ~ian [sɪ'vɪlɪən] a civil, de paisano // n civil m/f, paisano.
civilization [sɪvɪlaɪ'zeɪʃən] n civilización f.
civilized ['sɪvɪlaɪzd] a civilizado.
claim [kleɪm] vt exigir, reclamar; (rights etc) reivindicar; (assert) pretender // vi (for insurance) reclamar // n reclamación f; (LAW) demanda; (pretension) pretensión f; ~ant n (ADMIN, LAW) demandante m/f.
clairvoyant [kleə'vɔɪənt] n clarividente m/f.
clam [klæm] n almeja.
clamber ['klæmbə*] vi subir gateando, trepar.
clammy ['klæmɪ] a (cold) frío y húmedo; (sticky) pegajoso.
clamp [klæmp] n abrazadera, grapa // vt afianzar (con abrazadera); to ~ down on vt fus suprimir, restringir.
clan [klæn] n clan m.
clang [klæŋ] n sonido metálico // vi sonar, hacer estruendo.
clap [klæp] vi aplaudir // vt (hands) batir; (put) poner // n (of hands) palmada; (of thunder) estampido (de trueno); ~ping n aplausos mpl.
claret ['klærət] n clarete m.
clarification [klærɪfɪ'keɪʃən] n aclaración f; **clarify** ['klærɪfaɪ] vt aclarar.
clarinet [klærɪ'net] n clarinete m.
clarity ['klærɪtɪ] n claridad f.
clash [klæʃ] n estruendo; (fig) choque m // vi (meet) encontrarse; (battle) chocar; (disagree) estar en desacuerdo.
clasp [klɑːsp] n broche m; (on jewels) cierre m // vt abrochar; (hand) apretar, estrechar; (embrace) abrazar.
class [klɑːs] n (gen) clase f // a clasista, de clase // vt clasificar.
classic ['klæsɪk] a clásico // n (work) obra clásica; ~al a clásico.

classification [klæsɪfɪ'keɪʃən] n clasificación f; **classify** ['klæsɪfaɪ] vt clasificar.
class: ~**mate** n compañero de clase; ~**room** n aula.
clatter ['klætə*] n ruido, estruendo; (of hooves) trápala // vi hacer ruido o estruendo.
clause [klɔːz] n cláusula; (LING) oración f.
claustrophobia [klɔːstrə'fəubɪə] n claustrofobia.
claw [klɔː] n (of cat) uña; (of bird of prey) garra; (of lobster) pinza; (TECH) garfio // vt: to ~ at arañar; (tear) desgarrar.
clay [kleɪ] n arcilla.
clean [kliːn] a limpio; (clear) neto, bien definido // vt limpiar; to ~ out vt limpiar; to ~ up vt limpiar, asear; ~-cut a (person) de buen parecer; (clear) nítido; ~er n (person) asistenta; ~ing n (gen) limpieza, (clothes) limpieza en seco; ~liness ['klenlɪnɪs] n limpieza; ~-shaven a sin barba, lampiño.
cleanse [klenz] vt limpiar; **cleanser** n agente m de limpieza; (for face) desmaquillador m; **cleansing department** n departamento de limpieza.
clear [klɪə*] a claro; (road, way) limpio, libre; (complete) completo // vt (space) despejar, limpiar; (LAW: suspect) absolver; (obstacle) salvar, saltar por encima de; (debt) liquidar // vi (gen) aclararse; (fog etc) despejarse // ad: ~ of a distancia de; to ~ up vt limpiar; (mystery) aclarar, resolver; ~ance n (removal) despeje m; (permission) acreditación f; ~-cut a bien definido, nítido; ~ing n (in wood) claro; ~ing bank n cámara de compensación; ~ly ad claramente; ~way n (Brit) carretera donde no se puede aparcar.
cleaver ['kliːvə] n cuchilla (de carnicero).
clef [klef] n (MUS) clave f.
clemency ['klemənsɪ] n clemencia.
clench [klentʃ] vt apretar, cerrar.
clergy ['klɜːdʒɪ] n clero; ~man n clérigo.
clerical ['klerɪkəl] a oficinista; (REL) clerical.
clerk [klɑːk, (US) klɜːrk] n empleado, oficinista m/f.
clever ['klevə*] a (mentally) inteligente, listo; (deft, crafty) hábil; (device, arrangement) ingenioso.
cliché ['kliːʃeɪ] n cliché m, frase f hecha.
click [klɪk] vt (tongue) chasquear; (heels) taconear.
client ['klaɪənt] n cliente m/f; ~ele [kliːɑːn'tel] n clientela.
cliff [klɪf] n acantilado.
climate ['klaɪmɪt] n clima m; (fig) ambiente m.
climax ['klaɪmæks] n colmo, punto culminante; (sexual) clímax m.
climb [klaɪm] vi subir, trepar // vt (stairs) subir; (tree) trepar a; (hill) escalar // n subida; ~er n alpinista m/f, montañista m/f; ~ing n alpinismo.

clinch [klɪntʃ] vt (deal) cerrar; (argument) remachar.

cling [klɪŋ], pt, pp **clung** [klʌŋ] vi: **to ~ to** pegarse a, quedar pegado a; (of clothes) ajustarse a.

clinic ['klɪnɪk] n clínica; ~**al** a clínico.

clink [klɪŋk] vi tintinar.

clip [klɪp] n (for hair) prendido; (also: **paper** ~) sujetapapeles m inv; (clamp) grapa // vt (cut) cortar; (shorten) acortar; (clamp) sujetar; ~**pers** npl (for gardening) tijeras fpl; (for hair) maquinilla sg; (for nails) cortauñas m inv; ~**ping** n recorte m.

clique [kli:k] n camarilla, pandilla.

cloak [kləuk] n capa, manto // vt (fig) encubrir, disimular; ~**room** n guardarropa; (in station) consigna; (WC) lavabo, aseos mpl.

clock [klɔk] n reloj m; (in taxi) taxímetro; (fam) cara; ~**wise** ad en el sentido de las agujas del reloj; ~**work** n aparato de relojería // a de cuerda.

clog [klɔg] n zueco, chanclo // vt atascar // vi atascarse.

cloister ['klɔɪstə*] n claustro.

close a, ad and derivatives [kləus] a cercano, próximo; (print, weave) tupido, compacto; (friend) íntimo; (connection) estrecho; (examination) detallado, minucioso; (weather) bochornoso; (atmosphere) sofocante; (room) mal ventilado // ad cerca // vb and derivatives [kləuz] vt (shut) cerrar; (end) concluir, terminar // vi (shop etc) cerrarse; (end) concluirse, terminarse // n (end) fin m, final m, conclusión f; **to ~ down** vi cerrarse definitivamente; **to ~ up** vi (crowd) arrimarse; ~**d** a (shop etc) cerrado; ~**d shop** n acuerdo de emplear sólo trabajadores sindicados; ~**ly** ad (exactly) fielmente; (carefully) atentamente.

closet ['klɔzɪt] n (cupboard) armario; (wc) lavabo.

close-up ['kləusʌp] n primer plano.

closure ['kləuʒə*] n (close-down) cierre m, clausura; (end) fin m.

clot [klɔt] n (gen: blood ~) embolia; (fam: idiot) imbécil m/f // vi (blood) cuajarse, coagularse.

cloth [klɔθ] n (material) tela, paño; (rag) trapo.

clothe [kləuð] vt vestir; (fig) revestir; ~**s** npl ropa sg; ~**s brush** n cepillo (para la ropa); ~**s line** n cuerda (para tender la ropa); ~**s peg** n pinza; **clothing** n = **clothes**.

cloud [klaud] n nube f; (storm~) nubarrón m; ~**burst** n chaparrón m; ~**y** a nublado, nubloso; (liquid) turbio.

clout [klaut] vt dar un tortazo a.

clove [kləuv] n clavo; ~ **of garlic** diente m de ajo.

clover ['kləuvə*] n trébol m.

clown [klaun] n payaso // vi (also: ~ **about**, ~ **around**) hacer el payaso.

club [klʌb] n (society) club m; (weapon)

porra, cachiporra; (also: **golf** ~) palo // vt aporrear // vi: **to ~ together** hacer una colecta; ~**s** npl (CARDS) tréboles mpl; ~**house** n sala de reunión.

cluck [klʌk] vi cloquear.

clue [klu:] n pista; (in crosswords) indicación f; **I haven't a** ~ no tengo idea.

clump [klʌmp] n (of trees) grupo.

clumsy ['klʌmzi] a (person) torpe, desmañado; (movement) pesado.

cluster ['klʌstə*] n grupo; (BOT) racimo // vi agruparse, apiñarse.

clutch [klʌtʃ] n (grip, grasp) apretón m, agarro; (AUT) embrague m; (pedal) pedal m de embrague // vt sujetar, empuñar.

clutter ['klʌtə*] vt atestar, llenar desordenadamente.

Co. abbr of county; company.

c/o abbr of care of c/a (en casa de), a/c (a cuidado de).

coach [kəutʃ] n (bus) autocar m; (horse-drawn) coche m; (of train) vagón m, coche m; (SPORT) entrenador m, instructor m // vt (SPORT) entrenar; (student) preparar, enseñar.

coagulate [kəu'ægjuleɪt] vi coagularse.

coal [kəul] n carbón m; ~ **face** n frente m de carbón; ~**field** n yacimiento de carbón.

coalition [kəuə'lɪʃən] n coalición f.

coal: ~man, ~ merchant n carbonero; ~**mine** n mina de carbón.

coarse [kɔːs] a basto, burdo; (vulgar) grosero, ordinario.

coast [kəust] n costa, litoral m // vi (AUT) ir en punto muerto; ~**al** a costero, costanero; ~**er** n buque m costero, barco de cabotaje; ~**guard** n guardacostas m inv; ~**line** n litoral m.

coat [kəut] n (jacket) chaqueta; (overcoat) abrigo; (of animal) pelo, lana; (of paint) mano f, capa // vt cubrir, revestir; ~ **of arms** n escudo de armas; ~ **hanger** n percha; ~**ing** n capa, baño.

coax [kəuks] vt engatusar.

cob [kɔb] n see **corn.**

cobbler ['kɔblə] n zapatero remendón.

cobbles ['kɔblz], **cobblestones** ['kɔblstəunz] npl guijarros mpl.

cobra ['kəubrə] n cobra.

cobweb ['kɔbwɛb] n telaraña.

cocaine [kə'keɪn] n cocaína.

cock [kɔk] n (rooster) gallo; (male bird) macho // vt (gun) amartillar; ~**atoo** n cacatúa; ~**erel** n gallito.

cockle ['kɔkl] n berberecho.

cockney ['kɔkni] n habitante m/f de ciertos barrios bajos de Londres.

cockpit ['kɔkpɪt] n (in aircraft) carlinga, cabina.

cockroach ['kɔkrəutʃ] n cucaracha.

cocktail ['kɔkteɪl] n combinado, coctel m; ~ **cabinet** n mueble-bar m; ~ **party** n coctel m, cóctel m.

cocoa ['kəukəu] n cacao; (drink) chocolate m.

coconut ['kəukənʌt] *n* coco.

cocoon [kə'ku:n] *n* capullo.

cod [kɒd] *n* bacalao.

code [kəud] *n* código; (*cipher*) clave *f*; **codify** *vt* codificar.

coerce [kəu'ə:s] *vt* forzar, obligar; **coercion** [-'ə:ʃən] *n* coacción *f*.

coexistence ['kəuig'zistəns] *n* coexistencia.

coffee ['kɒfi] *n* café *m*; ~ **bean** *n* grano de café; ~ **grounds** *npl* heces *fpl* de café; ~ **pot** *n* cafetera.

coffin ['kɒfin] *n* ataúd *m*.

cog [kɒg] *n* diente *m*; ~ **wheel** *n* rueda dentada.

cognac ['kɒnjæk] *n* coñac *m*.

coherent [kəu'hiərənt] *a* coherente.

coil [kɔil] *n* rollo; (*rope*) adujada; (*ELEC*) bobina, carrete *m*; (*contraceptive*) espiral *f* // *vi* enrollarse, arrollarse.

coin [kɔin] *n* moneda // *vt* (*word*) inventar, idear; ~ **age** *n* moneda; ~ **box** *n* caja de monedas.

coincide [kəuin'said] *vi* coincidir; (*agree*) estar de acuerdo; **coincidence** [kəu'insidəns] *n* casualidad *f*.

coke [kəuk] *n* (*coal*) coque *m*; (*drink*) Coca Cola *f*.

colander ['kɒləndə*] *n* colador *m*, escurridor *m*.

cold [kəuld] *a* frío // *n* frío; (*MED*) resfriado; **it's** ~ hace frío; **to be** ~ tener frío; **to catch** ~ resfriarse, acatarrarse; **to** ~ **shoulder** tratar con frialdad; ~ **ly** *a* fríamente; ~ **sore** *n* herpes *m* labial.

coleslaw ['kəulslɔ:] *n* ensalada de col.

colic ['kɒlik] *n* cólico.

collaborate [kə'læbəreit] *vi* colaborar; **collaboration** [-'reiʃən] *n* colaboración *f*.

collage [kɒ'lɑ:ʒ] *n* collage *m*.

collapse [kə'læps] *vi* (*gen*) hundirse, derrumbarse; (*MED*) sufrir colapso // *n* (*gen*) hundimiento; (*MED*) colapso; **collapsible** *a* plegable.

collar ['kɒlə*] *n* (*of coat, shirt*) cuello; ~ **bone** *n* clavícula.

collate [kɒ'leit] *vt* cotejar.

colleague ['kɒli:g] *n* colega *m/f*.

collect [kə'lekt] *vt* reunir; (*as a hobby*) coleccionar; (*call and pick up*) recoger; (*wages*) cobrar; (*debts*) recaudar; (*donations, subscriptions*) colectar // *vi* reunirse; coleccionar; ~ **ion** [kə'lekʃən] *n* colección *f*; cobro; (*of people*) grupo; (*of donations*) recaudación *f*; (*of post*) recogida.

collective [kə'lektiv] *a* colectivo.

collector [kə'lektə*] *n* coleccionista *m/f*; (*of taxes etc*) recaudador *m*.

college ['kɒlidʒ] *n* colegio.

collide [kə'laid] *vi* chocar.

collie ['kɒli] *n* perro pastor.

collision [kə'liʒən] *n* choque *m*.

colloquial [kə'ləukwiəl] *a* familiar, coloquial.

colon ['kəulən] *n* (*sign*) dos puntos; (*MED*) colón *m*.

colonel ['kə:nl] *n* coronel *m*.

colonial [kə'ləuniəl] *a* colonial.

colonize ['kɒlənaiz] *vt* colonizar.

colony ['kɒləni] *n* colonia.

colossal [kə'lɒsl] *a* colosal.

colour, color (*US*) ['kʌlə*] *n* color *m* // *vt* color(e)ar; (*with crayons*) pintar; (*dye*) teñir // *vi* (*blush*) sonrojarse; ~ **s** *npl* (*of party, club*) colores *mpl*; ~ **blind** *a* daltoniano; ~ **ed** *a* de color; (*photo*) a colores; ~ **eds** *npl* gente *f* de color; ~ **film** *n* película en colores; ~ **ful** *a* lleno de color; (*personality*) animado; ~ **ing** *n* colorido; ~ **less** *a* incoloro, sin color; ~ **scheme** *n* combinación *f* de colores; ~ **television** *n* televisión *f* en color(es).

colt [kəult] *n* potro.

column ['kɒləm] *n* columna; ~ **ist** ['kɒləmnist] *n* columnista *m/f*.

coma ['kəumə] *n* coma *m*.

comb [kəum] *n* peine *m*; (*ornamental*) peineta // *vt* (*hair*) peinar; (*area*) registrar.

combat ['kɒmbæt] *n* combate *m* // *vt* combatir.

combination [kɒmbi'neiʃən] *n* (*gen*) combinación *f*.

combine [kəm'bain] *vt* combinar; (*qualities*) reunir // *vi* combinarse // *n* ['kɒmbain] (*ECON*) asociación *f*; (*pej*) monopolio; ~ (**harvester**) *n* cosechadora.

combustion [kəm'bʌstʃən] *n* combustión *f*.

come [kʌm], *pt* **came**, *pp* **come** *vi* venir; **to** ~ **about** *vi* suceder, ocurrir; **to** ~ **across** *vt fus* (*person*) topar; (*thing*) dar con; **to** ~ **away** *vi* marcharse; **to** ~ **back** *vi* volver; **to** ~ **by** *vt fus* (*acquire*) conseguir; **to** ~ **down** *vi* bajar; (*plane*) aterrizarse; (*crash*) estrellarse; (*buildings*) desplomarse; **to** ~ **forward** *vi* presentarse; **to** ~ **in** *vi* entrar; (*train*) llegar; (*fashion*) ponerse de moda; **to** ~ **in for** *vt fus* (*criticism etc*) merecer; **to** ~ **into** *vt fus* (*money*) heredar; **to** ~ **off** *vi* (*button*) soltarse, desprenderse; (*attempt*) tener lugar; **to** ~ **on** *vi* (*pupil, undertaking*) crecer, desarrollarse // *vt* (*find*) encontrar; ~ **on!** ¡vamos!; **to** ~ **out** *vi* salir, aparecer; (*be revealed*) salir a luz; **to** ~ **out for/against** declararse por/contra; **to** ~ **to** *vi* volver en sí; (*total*) sumar; **to** ~ **up** *vi* subir; (*sun*) salir; (*problem*) surgir; **to** ~ **up against** *vt fus* (*resistance, difficulties*) tropezar con; **to** ~ **up with** *vt fus* (*idea*) sugerir, proponer; **to** ~ **upon** *vt fus* dar o topar con; ~ **back** *n* (*THEATRE*) reaparición *f*.

comedian [kə'mi:diən] *n* cómico; **comedienne** [-'en] *n* cómica.

comedown ['kʌmdaun] *n* (*fam*) revés *m*, bajón *m*.

comedy ['kɒmidi] *n* comedia.

comet ['kɒmit] *n* cometa *m*.

comfort ['kʌmfət] *n* comodidad *f*, confort

m; (well-being) bienestar m; (solace) consuelo; (relief) alivio // vt consolar; aliviar; ~able a cómodo.

comic ['kɔmɪk] a (also: ~al) cómico // n (magazine) tebeo; ~ **strip** n tira cómica.

coming ['kʌmɪŋ] n venida, llegada // a que viene; ~(s) **and going(s)** n(pl) ir y venir m, ajetreo.

comma ['kɔmə] n coma.

command [kə'mɑ:nd] n orden f, mandato; (MIL: authority) mando; (mastery) dominio // vt (troops) mandar; (give orders to) mandar, ordenar; (dispose of) disponer de; (deserve) merecer; ~**eer** [kɔmən'dɪə*] vt requisar; ~**er** n (MIL) comandante m/f, jefe/a m/f.

commando [kə'mɑ:ndəu] n comando.

commemorate [kə'meməreɪt] vt conmemorar; **commemoration** [-'reɪʃən] n conmemoración f; **commemorative** [-rətɪv] a conmemorativo.

commence [kə'mens] vt, vi comenzar, empezar.

commend [kə'mend] vt (praise) elogiar, alabar; (recommend) recomendar; (entrust) encomendar; ~**ation** [kɔmen'deɪʃən] n elogio, encomio; recomendación f.

commensurate [kə'menʃərɪt] a equivalente (with a).

comment ['kɔment] n comentario // vi hacer comentarios; ~**ary** ['kɔmentərɪ] n comentario; ~**ator** ['kɔmenteɪtə*] n comentador m.

commerce ['kɔmə:s] n comercio.

commercial [kə'mə:ʃəl] a comercial // n (TV) anuncio (comercial); ~ **break** n emisión f publicitaria; ~**ize** vt comercializar.

commiserate [kə'mɪzəreɪt] vi: to ~ with compadecerse de, condolerse de.

commission [kə'mɪʃən] n (fee) comisión f; (act) perpetración f // vt (MIL) nombrar; (work of art) encargar; **out of** ~ inutilizado; ~**aire** [kəmɪʃə'nɛə*] n portero; ~**er** n comisario; (POLICE) jefe/a m/f de policía.

commit [kə'mɪt] vt (act) cometer; (to sb's care) entregar; to ~ **o.s. (to do)** comprometerse (a hacer); to ~ **suicide** suicidarse; ~**ment** n compromiso.

committee [kə'mɪtɪ] n comité m.

commodity [kə'mɔdɪtɪ] n mercancía.

common ['kɔmən] a (gen) común; (pej) ordinario // n campo común; **the C~s** npl (la Cámara de) los Comunes; **in** ~ en común; ~**er** n plebeyo; ~ **law** n ley f consuetudinaria; ~**ly** ad comúnmente; **C~ Market** n Mercado Común; ~**place** a vulgar, trivial; ~**room** n salón m común; ~ **sense** n sentido común; **the C~wealth** n la Mancomunidad.

commotion [kə'məuʃən] n tumulto, confusión f.

communal ['kɔmju:nl] a comunal.

commune ['kɔmju:n] n (group) comuna //

vi [kə'mju:n]: to ~ **with** comulgar o conversar con.

communicate [kə'mju:nɪkeɪt] vt comunicar // vi: to ~ **(with)** comunicarse (con).

communication [kəmju:nɪ'keɪʃən] n comunicación f; ~ **cord** n timbre m de alarma.

communion [kə'mju:nɪən] n (also: **Holy C~**) comunión f.

communiqué [kə'mju:nɪkeɪ] n comunicado, parte m.

communism ['kɔmjunɪzəm] n comunismo; **communist** a, n comunista m/f.

community [kə'mju:nɪtɪ] n comunidad f; (large group) colectividad f; (locals) vecindario; ~ **centre** n centro social.

commute [kə'mju:t] vi viajar a diario // vt conmutar; **commuter** n persona que viaja a menudo.

compact [kəm'pækt] a compacto; (style) conciso; (packed) apretado // n ['kɔmpækt] (pact) pacto; (for powder) polvera.

companion [kəm'pænɪən] n compañero; ~**ship** n compañerismo.

company ['kʌmpənɪ] n. (gen) compañía; (COMM) sociedad f, compañía; **to keep sb** ~ acompañar a uno; **limited** ~ sociedad f anónima.

comparable ['kɔmpərəbl] a comparable.

comparative [kəm'pærətɪv] a relativo.

compare [kəm'pɛə*] vt comparar; (set side by side) cotejar // vi: to ~ **(with)** compararse (con); **comparison** [-'pærɪsn] n comparación f; cotejo; **in comparison (with)** en comparación (con).

compartment [kəm'pɑ:tmənt] n (also RAIL) departamento.

compass ['kʌmpəs] n brújula; ~**es** npl compás m.

compassion [kəm'pæʃən] n compasión f; ~**ate** a compasivo.

compatible [kəm'pætɪbl] a compatible.

compel [kəm'pel] vt obligar; ~**ling** a (fig: argument) convincente.

compendium [kəm'pendɪəm] n compendio.

compensate ['kɔmpənseɪt] vt compensar // vi: to ~ **for** compensar; **compensation** [-'seɪʃən] n (for loss) indemnización f.

compère ['kɔmpɛə*] n presentador m.

compete [kəm'pi:t] vi (take part) tomar parte, concurrir; (vie with) competir, hacer competencia.

competence ['kɔmpɪtəns] n capacidad f, aptitud f; **competent** [-ənt] a competente, capaz.

competition [kɔmpɪ'tɪʃən] n (contest) concurso; (ECON) competencia; (rivalry) competencia.

competitive [kəm'petɪtɪv] a (ECON) competitivo; (spirit) competidor(a), de competencia.

competitor [kəm'petɪtə*] n (rival)

(*participant*) competidor/a *m/f*; (*participant*) concursante *m/f.*
compile [kəm'paɪl] *vt* recopilar, compilar.
complacency [kəm'pleɪsnsɪ] *n* satisfacción *f* de sí mismo; **complacent** [-sənt] *a* complacido.
complain [kəm'pleɪn] *vi* (*gen*) quejarse; ~**t** *n* (*gen*) queja; (*JUR*) demanda, querella; (*MED*) enfermedad *f.*
complement ['kɒmplɪmənt] *n* complemento; (*esp ship's crew*) dotación *f*; ~**ary** [kɒmplɪ'mɛntərɪ] *a* complementario.
complete [kəm'pliːt] *a* (*full*) completo; (*finished*) acabado // *vt* (*fulfil*) completar; (*finish*) acabar; (*a form*) llenar; ~**ly** *ad* completamente; **completion** *n* (*gen*) conclusión *f*, terminación *f*; (*of contract etc*) realización *f.*
complex ['kɒmplɛks] *a* complejo // *n* (*gen*) complejo.
complexion [kəm'plɛkʃən] *n* (*of face*) tez *f*, cutis *m*; (*fig*) aspecto.
complexity [kəm'plɛksɪtɪ] *n* complejidad *f.*
compliance [kəm'plaɪəns] *n* (*submission*) sumisión *f*; (*agreement*) conformidad *f*; **in** ~ **with** de acuerdo con; **compliant** [-ənt] *a* sumiso; conforme.
complicate ['kɒmplɪkeɪt] *vt* complicar; ~**d** *a* complicado; **complication** [-'keɪʃən] *n* complicación *f.*
compliment *n* ['kɒmplɪmənt] (*formal*) cumplido; (*lovers'*) piropo; ~**s** *npl* saludos *mpl*; **to pay sb a** ~ (*amorously*) piropear, echar piropos a alguien; ~**ary** [-'mɛntərɪ] *a* lisonjero; (*free*) de favor.
comply [kəm'plaɪ] *vi*: **to** ~ **with** cumplir con.
component [kəm'pəunənt] *a* componente // *n* (*TECH*) pieza.
compose [kəm'pəuz] *vt* componer; **to be** ~**d of** componerse de, constar de; **to** ~ **o.s.** tranquilizarse; ~**d** *a* sosegado; **composer** *n* (*MUS*) compositor *m.*
composite ['kɒmpəzɪt] *a* compuesto.
composition [kɒmpə'zɪʃən] *n* composición *f.*
compost ['kɒmpɒst] *n* abono compuesto.
composure [kəm'pəuʒə*] *n* serenidad *f*, calma.
compound ['kɒmpaund] *n* (*CHEM, LING*) compuesto; (*enclosure*) recinto // *a* (*gen*) compuesto; (*fracture*) complicado.
comprehend [kɒmprɪ'hɛnd] *vt* comprender; **comprehension** [-'hɛnʃən] *n* comprensión *f.*
comprehensive [kɒmprɪ'hɛnsɪv] *a* (*broad*) extenso; (*general*) de conjunto; (*INSURANCE*) contra todo riesgo; ~ **(school)** *n* integrado.
compress [kəm'prɛs] *vt* comprimir // *n* ['kɒmprɛs] (*MED*) compresa; ~**ion** [-'prɛʃən] *n* compresión *f.*
comprise [kəm'praɪz] *vt* (*also*: **be** ~**d of**) comprender, constar de.
compromise ['kɒmprəmaɪz] *n*

(*agreement*) componenda, arreglo; (*midpoint*) término medio // *vt* comprometer // *vi* transigir.
compulsion [kəm'pʌlʃən] *n* obligación *f.*
compulsive [kəm'pʌlsɪv] *a* compulsivo; (*PSYCH*) empedernido.
compulsory [kəm'pʌlsərɪ] *a* obligatorio.
computer [kəm'pjuːtə*] *n* ordenador *m*, computador *m*, computadora; ~**ize** *vt* computerizar; ~ **programmer** *n* programador/a *m/f*; ~ **programming** *n* programación *f*; ~ **science** *n* ciencia de computadoras.
comrade ['kɒmrɪd] *n* camarada *m/f*; ~**ship** *n* camaradería, compañerismo.
con [kɒn] *vt* estafar // *n* estafa.
concave ['kɒn'keɪv] *a* cóncavo.
conceal [kən'siːl] *vt* ocultar.
concede [kən'siːd] *vt* conceder // *vi* ceder, darse por vencido.
conceit [kən'siːt] *n* presunción *f*; ~**ed** *a* presumido.
conceivable [kən'siːvəbl] *a* concebible.
conceive [kən'siːv] *vt*, *vi* concebir.
concentrate ['kɒnsəntreɪt] *vi* concentrarse // *vt* concentrar.
concentration [kɒnsən'treɪʃən] *n* concentración *f*; ~ **camp** *n* campo de concentración.
concept ['kɒnsɛpt] *n* concepto.
conception [kən'sɛpʃən] *n* (*idea*) concepto, idea; (*BIOL*) concepción *f.*
concern [kən'səːn] *n* (*matter*) asunto; (*COMM*) empresa; (*anxiety*) preocupación *f* // *vt* tener que ver con; **to be** ~**ed** (*about*) interesarse (por), preocuparse (por); ~**ing** *prep* sobre, acerca de.
concert ['kɒnsət] *n* concierto; ~ **hall** *n* sala de conciertos.
concertina [kɒnsə'tiːnə] *n* concertina.
concerto [kən'tʃəːtəu] *n* concierto.
concession [kən'sɛʃən] *n* concesión *f*; **tax** ~ privilegio fiscal.
conciliation [kənsɪlɪ'eɪʃən] *n* conciliación *f*; **conciliatory** [-'sɪlɪətrɪ] *a* conciliador(a).
concise [kən'saɪs] *a* conciso.
conclude [kən'kluːd] *vt* (*finish*) concluir; (*treaty etc*) firmar; (*agreement*) llegar a; (*decide*) llegar a la conclusión de; **conclusion** [-'kluːʒən] *n* conclusión *f*; **conclusive** [-'kluːsɪv] *a* decisivo, concluyente.
concoct [kən'kɒkt] *vt* (*gen*) confeccionar; (*plot*) tramar.
concrete ['kɒnkriːt] *n* hormigón *m* // *a* concreto.
concur [kən'kəː*] *vi* estar de acuerdo, asentir.
concurrently [kən'kʌrntlɪ] *ad* al mismo tiempo.
concussion [kən'kʌʃən] *n* conmoción *f* cerebral.
condemn [kən'dɛm] *vt* condenar; ~**ation** [kɒndɛm'neɪʃən] *n* (*gen*) condenación *f*; (*blame*) censura.

condensation [kɔndɛn'seiʃɔn] *n* condensación *f*.

condense [kɔn'dɛns] *vi* condensarse // *vt* condensar, abreviar; ~**d milk** *n* leche *f* condensada.

condescend [kɔndi'sɛnd] *vi* condescender, dignarse; ~**ing** *a* condescendiente.

condition [kɔn'diʃɔn] *n* condición *f* // *vt* condicionar; **on** ~ **that** a condición (de) que.

condolences [kɔn'dɔulɔnsiz] *npl* pésame *m*.

condone [kɔn'dɔun] *vt* condonar.

conducive [kɔn'djuːsiv] *a*: ~ **to** conducente a.

conduct ['kɔndʌkt] *n* conducta, comportamiento // *vt* [kɔn'dʌkt] (*lead*) conducir; (*manage*) llevar, dirigir; (*MUS*) dirigir // *vi* (*MUS*) llevar la batuta; **to** ~ **o.s.** comportarse; ~**or** *n* (*of orchestra*) director *m*; (*on bus*) cobrador *m*; (*ELEC*) conductor *m*; ~**ress** *n* (*on bus*) cobradora.

cone [kɔun] *n* cono; (*for ice-cream*) barquillo.

confectioner [kɔn'fɛkʃɔnɔ*] *n* pastelero; ~**'s (shop)** *n* pastelería; (*sweet shop*) confitería; ~**y** *n* (*cakes*) pasteles *mpl*; (*sweets*) dulces *mpl*.

confederation [kɔnfɛdɔ'reiʃɔn] *n* confederación *f*.

confer [kɔn'fɔː*] *vt* otorgar (*on* a) // *vi* conferenciar.

conference ['kɔnfɔrns] *n* (*meeting*) congreso.

confess [kɔn'fɛs] *vt* confesar // *vi* confesarse; ~**ion** [-'fɛʃɔn] *n* confesión *f*; ~**ional** [-'fɛʃɔnl] *n* confesionario; ~**or** *n* confesor *m*.

confetti [kɔn'fɛti] *n* confeti *m*.

confide [kɔn'faid] *vi*: **to** ~ **in** confiar en, fiarse de.

confidence ['kɔnfidns] *n* (*gen*) confianza; (*secret*) confidencia; ~ **trick** *n* timo; **confident** *a* seguro de sí mismo; **confidential** [kɔnfi'dɛnʃɔl] *a* confidencial; (*secretary*) de confianza.

confine [kɔn'fain] *vt* (*limit*) limitar; (*shut up*) encerrar; ~**d** *a* (*space*) reducido; ~**ment** *n* (*prison*) prisión *f*; (*enclosure*) encierro; (*MED*) parto, sobreparto; ~**s** ['kɔnfainz] *npl* confines *mpl*.

confirm [kɔn'fɔːm] *vt* confirmar; ~**ation** [kɔnfɔ'meiʃɔn] *n* confirmación *f*; ~**ed** *a* empedernido.

confiscate ['kɔnfiskeit] *vt* confiscar; **confiscation** [-'keiʃɔn] *n* incautación *f*.

conflict ['kɔnflikt] *n* conflicto // *vi* [kɔn'flikt] (*opinions*) chocar; ~**ing** *a* contrario.

conform [kɔn'fɔːm] *vi* conformarse; **to** ~ **to** ajustarse a, cuadrar con; ~**ist** *n* conformista *m/f*.

confound [kɔn'faund] *vt* confundir; ~**ed** *a* condenado.

confront [kɔn'frʌnt] *vt* (*problems*) encararse con; (*enemy*, *danger*)

enfrentarse con; ~**ation** [kɔnfrɔn'teiʃɔn] *n* enfrentamiento.

confuse [kɔn'fjuːz] *vt* (*perplex*) aturdir, desconcertar; (*mix up*) confundir; ~**d** *a* confuso; (*person*) perplejo, despistado; **confusing** *a* confuso; **confusion** [-'fjuːʒɔn] *n* confusión *f*.

congeal [kɔn'dʒiːl] *vi* (*freeze*) congelarse; (*coagulate*) coagularse.

congenial [kɔn'dʒiːniɔl] *a* simpático, agradable.

congenital [kɔn'dʒɛnitl] *a* congénito.

congested [kɔn'dʒɛstid] *a* (*gen*) lleno; (*area*) superpoblado; **congestion** [-'dʒɛstʃɔn] *n* congestión *f*.

conglomeration [kɔnglɔmɔ'reiʃɔn] *n* conglomeración *f*.

congratulate [kɔn'grætjuleit] *vt* felicitar; **congratulations** [-'leiʃɔnz] *npl* felicidades *fpl*.

congregate ['kɔngrigeit] *vi* congregarse; **congregation** [-'geiʃɔn] *n* (*in church*) fieles *mpl*; (*assembly*) reunión *f*.

congress ['kɔngrɛs] *n* congreso; ~**man** *n* (*US*) diputado.

conical ['kɔnikl] *a* cónico.

conifer ['kɔnifɔ*] *n* conífera; ~**ous** [kɔ'nifɔrɔs] *a* (*forest*) conífero.

conjecture [kɔn'dʒɛktʃɔ*] *n* conjetura.

conjugal ['kɔndʒugl] *a* conyugal.

conjugate ['kɔndʒugeit] *vt* conjugar.

conjunction [kɔn'dʒʌŋkʃɔn] *n* conjunción *f*.

conjure ['kʌndʒɔ*] *vi* hacer juegos de manos; **to** ~ **up** *vt* (*ghost, spirit*) hacer aparecer; (*memories*) evocar; **conjurer** *n* ilusionista *m/f*; **conjuring trick** *n* ilusionismo, juego de manos.

conk [kɔŋk]: ~ **out** *vi* (*col*) estropearse.

con man ['kɔn-] *n* timador *m*.

connect [kɔ'nɛkt] *vt* juntar, unir; (*ELEC*) conectar; (*fig*) relacionar, asociar // *vi*: **to** ~ **with** (*train*) enlazar con; ~**ion** *n* juntura, unión *f*; (*ELEC*) conexión *f*; (*RAIL*) correspondencia; (*TEL*) comunicación *f*; (*fig*) relación *f*.

connive [kɔ'naiv] *vi*: **to** ~ **at** hacer la vista gorda a.

connoisseur [kɔni'sɔ*] *n* experto, entendido.

connotation [kɔnɔ'teiʃɔn] *n* connotación *f*.

conquer ['kɔŋkɔ*] *vt* (*gen*) conquistar; (*enemy*) vencer; (*feelings*) dominar; ~**or** *n* conquistador *m*.

conquest ['kɔŋkwɛst] *n* conquista.

cons [kɔnz] *npl see* **pro**.

conscience ['kɔnʃɔns] *n* conciencia.

conscientious [kɔnʃi'ɛnʃɔs] *a* concienzudo; (*objection*) de conciencia.

conscious ['kɔnʃɔs] *a* consciente; ~**ness** *n* conciencia; (*MED*) conocimiento.

conscript ['kɔnskript] *n* recluto *m/f*; ~**ion** [kɔn'skripʃɔn] *n* servicio militar (obligatorio).

consecrate ['kɔnsikreit] *vt* consagrar.

consecutive [kən'sɛkjutɪv] *a* sucesivo, seguido.

consensus [kən'sɛnsəs] *n* consenso.

consent [kən'sɛnt] *n* consentimiento // *vi*: to ~ to consentir en.

consequence ['kɔnsɪkwəns] *n* consecuencia.

consequently ['kɔnsɪkwəntlɪ] *ad* por consiguiente.

conservation [kɔnsə'veɪʃən] *n* conservación *f.*

conservative [kən'sɔːvətɪv] *a* conservador(a); (*cautious*) cauteloso; **C**~ *a, n* conservador/a *m/f.*

conservatory [kən'sɔːvətrɪ] *n* (*greenhouse*) invernadero.

conserve [kən'sɔːv] *vt* conservar // *n* conserva.

consider [kən'sɪdə*] *vt* (*gen*) considerar; (*take into account*) tomar en cuenta; (*study*) estudiar, examinar; ~**able** *a* considerable; (*sum*) importante.

considerate [kən'sɪdərɪt] *a* considerado; **consideration** [-'reɪʃən] *n* consideración *f*; (*reward*) retribución *f.*

considering [kən'sɪdərɪŋ] *prep* en consideración a.

consign [kən'saɪn] *vt* consignar; ~**ment** *n* envío.

consist [kən'sɪst] *vi*: to ~ of consistir en.

consistency [kən'sɪstənsɪ] *n* (*of person etc*) consecuencia; (*thickness*) consistencia.

consistent [kən'sɪstənt] *a* (*person*) consecuente; (*even*) constante.

consolation [kɔnsə'leɪʃən] *n* consuelo.

console [kən'səul] *vt* consolar // *n* ['kɔnsəul] consola.

consolidate [kən'sɔlɪdeɪt] *vt* consolidar.

consommé [kən'sɔmeɪ] *n* consomé *m*, caldo.

consonant ['kɔnsənənt] *n* consonante *f.*

consortium [kən'sɔːtɪəm] *n* consorcio.

conspicuous [kən'spɪkjuəs] *a* (*visible*) visible; (*garish etc*) llamativo; (*outstanding*) notable.

conspiracy [kən'spɪrəsɪ] *n* conjura, complot *m.*

conspire [kən'spaɪə*] *vi* conspirar.

constable ['kʌnstəbl] *n* policía *m/f*; **chief** ~ jefe *m* de policía.

constabulary [kən'stæbjulərɪ] *n* policía.

constant ['kɔnstənt] *a* (*gen*) constante; (*loyal*) leal, fiel.

constellation [kɔnstə'leɪʃən] *n* constelación *f.*

consternation [kɔnstə'neɪʃən] *n* consternación *f.*

constipated ['kɔnstɪpeɪtəd] *a* estreñido.

constituency [kən'stɪtjuənsɪ] *n* (*POL*) distrito electoral; **constituent** [-ənt] *n* (*POL*) elector/a *m/f*; (*part*) componente *m.*

constitute ['kɔnstɪtjuːt] *vt* constituir.

constitution [kɔnstɪ'tjuːʃən] *n* constitución *f*; ~**al** *a* constitucional.

constrain [kən'streɪn] *vt* obligar; ~**ed** *a*:

to feel ~ed to... sentirse en la necesidad de...; ~**t** *n* (*force*) fuerza; (*confinement*) encierro; (*shyness*) reserva.

constrict [kən'strɪkt] *vt* apretar, estrechar.

construct [kən'strʌkt] *vt* construir; ~**ion** [-ʃən] *n* construcción *f*; ~**ive** *a* constructivo.

construe [kən'struː] *vt* interpretar.

consul ['kɔnsl] *n* cónsul *m/f*; ~**ate** ['kɔnsjulɪt] *n* consulado.

consult [kən'sʌlt] *vt, vi* consultar; ~**ant** *n* (*MED*) especialista *m/f*; (*other specialist*) asesor *m*; ~**ation** [kɔnsəl'teɪʃən] *n* consulta; ~**ing room** *n* consultorio.

consume [kən'sjuːm] *vt* (*eat*) comerse; (*drink*) beberse; (*fire etc, COMM*) consumir; **consumer** *n* consumidor/a *m/f*; **consumer goods** *npl* bienes *mpl* de consumo; **consumer society** *n* sociedad *f* de consumo.

consummate ['kɔnsʌmeɪt] *vt* consumar.

consumption [kən'sʌmpʃən] *n* consumo.

cont. *abbr of* **continued.**

contact ['kɔntækt] *n* contacto; (*pej*) enchufe *m* // *vt* ponerse en contacto con; **he has good** ~**s** tiene buenas relaciones; ~ **lenses** *npl* lentes *fpl* de contacto, microlentillas *fpl.*

contagious [kən'teɪdʒəs] *a* contagioso.

contain [kən'teɪn] *vt* contener; **to** ~ **o.s.** contenerse; ~**er** *n* recipiente *m*; (*for shipping etc*) contenedor *m.*

contaminate [kən'tæmɪneɪt] *vt* contaminar; **contamination** [-'neɪʃən] *n* contaminación *f.*

cont'd *abbr of* **continued.**

contemplate ['kɔntəmpleɪt] *vt* (*gen*) contemplar; (*expect*) contar con; (*intend*) pensar; **contemplation** [-'pleɪʃən] *n* contemplación *f.*

contemporary [kən'tɛmpərərɪ] *a, n* contemporáneo/a.

contempt [kən'tɛmpt] *n* desprecio; ~**ible** *a* despreciable; ~**uous** *a* despectivo, desdeñoso.

contend [kən'tɛnd] *vt* (*argue*) afirmar // *vi* (*struggle*) luchar; ~**er** *n* contendiente *m/f.*

content [kən'tɛnt] *a* (*happy*) contento; (*satisfied*) satisfecho // *vt* contentar; satisfacer // *n* ['kɔntɛnt] contenido; satisfacción *f*; ~**s** *npl* contenido *sg*; ~**ed** *a* contento; satisfecho.

contention [kən'tɛnʃən] *n* contienda; (*argument*) argumento.

contentment [kən'tɛntmənt] *n* contento.

contest ['kɔntɛst] *n* contienda; (*competition*) concurso // *vt* [kən'tɛst] (*dispute*) impugnar; (*legal case*) defender; (*POL*) ser candidato en; ~**ant** [kən'tɛstənt] *n* concursante *m/f*; (*in fight*) contendiente *m/f.*

context ['kɔntɛkst] *n* contexto.

continent ['kɔntɪnənt] *n* continente *m*; **the C**~ el continente europeo; ~**al** [-'nɛntl] *a* continental.

contingency [kən'tɪndʒənsɪ] n contingencia; **contingent** [-ənt] n contingente m.

continual [kən'tɪnjuəl] a continuo; ~**ly** ad constantemente.

continuation [kəntɪnju'eɪʃən] n prolongación f; (after interruption) continuación f.

continue [kən'tɪnju:] vi seguir, continuar // vt seguir, continuar; (start again) proseguir.

continuity [kɒntɪ'njuɪtɪ] n continuidad f.

continuous [kən'tɪnjuəs] a continuo.

contort [kən'tɔ:t] vt retorcer; ~**ion** [-'tɔ:ʃən] n contorsión f; ~**ionist** [-'tɔ:ʃənɪst] n contorsionista m/f.

contour ['kɒntuə*] n contorno; (also: ~ line) curva de nivel.

contraband ['kɒntrəbænd] n contrabando.

contraception [kɒntrə'sɛpʃən] n contracepción f; **contraceptive** [-'sɛptɪv] a, n anticonceptivo.

contract ['kɒntrækt] n contrato // (vb: [kən'trækt]) vi (COMM): to ~ to do sth comprometerse por contrato a hacer algo; (become smaller) contraerse, encogerse // vt contraer; ~**ion** [-ʃən] n contracción f; ~**or** n contratista m/f.

contradict [kɒntrə'dɪkt] vt (deny) desmentir; (be contrary to) contradecir; ~**ion** [-ʃən] n contradicción f.

contralto [kən'træltəu] n contralto.

contraption [kən'træpʃən] n (pej) armatoste m.

contrary ['kɒntrərɪ] a, n contrario.

contrast ['kɒntrɑ:st] n contraste m // vt [kən'trɑ:st] comparar; ~**ing** a opuesto.

contravene [kɒntrə'vi:n] vt oponerse a; (law) contravenir.

contribute [kən'trɪbju:t] vi contribuir // vt: to ~ to (gen) contribuir a; (newspaper) escribir para; **contribution** [kɒntrɪ'bju:ʃən] n (money) aportación f; (to debate) intervención f; (to journal) colaboración f; **contributor** n (to newspaper) colaborador m.

contrive [kən'traɪv] vt (invent) idear; (carry out) efectuar; (plot) tramar // vi: to ~ to do lograr hacer.

control [kən'trəul] vt (gen) controlar; (traffic etc) dirigir; (machinery) regular; (temper) dominar // n (command) control m; (of car) conducción f; (check) freno; ~**s** npl mando sg; ~ **panel** n tablero de instrumentos; ~ **room** n sala de mando; ~ **tower** n (AVIAT) torre f de control.

controversial [kɒntrə'vɜ:ʃl] a discutible; **controversy** ['kɒntrəvɜ:sɪ] n controversia.

convalesce [kɒnvə'lɛs] vi convalecer; **convalescence** n convalecencia; **convalescent** a, n convaleciente m/f.

convector [kən'vɛktə*] n (heater) calentador m de convección.

convene [kən'vi:n] vt convocar // vi reunirse.

convenience [kən'vi:nɪəns] n (comfort) comodidad f; (advantage) ventaja; at your ~ cuando le sea conveniente; **public** ~ aseos públicos mpl; **convenient** [-ənt] a cómodo; (useful) útil; (place) accesible; (time) oportuno, conveniente.

convent ['kɒnvənt] n convento; ~ **school** n colegio de monjas.

convention [kən'vɛnʃən] n convención f; (meeting) asamblea; ~**al** a convencional.

converge [kən'vɜ:dʒ] vi converger.

conversant [kən'vɜ:snt] a: to be ~ with ser enterado de.

conversation [kɒnvə'seɪʃən] n conversación f; ~**al** a (familiar) familiar; (talkative) locuaz.

converse ['kɒnvɜ:s] n inversa // vi [kən-'vɜ:s] conversar; ~**ly** [-'vɜ:slɪ] ad a la inversa.

conversion [kən'vɜ:ʃən] n conversión f; ~ **table** n tabla de conversión.

convert [kən'vɜ:t] vt (REL, COMM) convertir; (alter) transformar // n ['kɒnvɜ:t] converso/a; ~**ible** a convertible // n descapotable m.

convex ['kɒn'vɛks] a convexo.

convey [kən'veɪ] vt (gen) llevar; (thanks) comunicar; (idea) expresar; ~**or belt** n cinta transportadora.

convict [kən'vɪkt] vt (gen) condenar; (sentence) declarar culpable // n ['kɒnvɪkt] presidiario; ~**ion** [-ʃən] n condena; (belief) creencia, convicción f.

convince [kən'vɪns] vt convencer; **convincing** a convincente.

convoy ['kɒnvɔɪ] n convoy m.

convulse [kən'vʌls] vt convulsionar; (laughter) hacer morir de la risa; **convulsion** [-'vʌlʃən] n convulsión f; (laughter) paroxismo.

coo [ku:] vi arrullar.

cook [kuk] vt (gen) cocinar; (stew etc) guisar; (meal) preparar // vi cocer; (person) cocinar // n cocinero; ~**er** n cocina; ~**ery** n (dishes) cocina; (art) arte m de cocinar; ~**ery book** n libro de cocina; ~**ie** n (US) bizcocho; ~**ing** n cocina.

cool [ku:l] a fresco; (not hot) tibio; (not afraid) tranquilo; (unfriendly) frío // vt enfriar // vi enfriarse; ~**ness** n frescura; tranquilidad f; (hostility) frialdad f; (indifference) falta de entusiasmo.

coop [ku:p] n gallinero // vt: to ~ up (fig) encerrar.

co-op ['kəuɒp] n abbr of **Cooperative (Society)**.

cooperate [kəu'ɒpəreɪt] vi cooperar, colaborar; **cooperation** [-'reɪʃən] n cooperación f, colaboración f; **cooperative** [-rətɪv] a cooperativo // n cooperativa.

coordinate [kəu'ɔ:dɪneɪt] vt coordinar; **coordination** [-'neɪʃən] n coordinación f.

cop [kɒp] n (col) poli m.

cope [kəup] vi: to ~ with poder con; (problem) hacer frente a.

co-pilot ['kəu'paɪlət] n copiloto.

copious ['kəupɪəs] a copioso, abundante.

copper ['kɔpə*] n (metal) cobre m; (col: policeman) poli m; ~s npl monedas fpl de poco valor.

coppice ['kɔpɪs], **copse** [kɔps] n bosquecillo.

copulate ['kɔpjuleɪt] vi copularse; **copulation** [-'leɪʃən] n cópula.

copy ['kɔpɪ] n copia; (of book etc) ejemplar m; (of writing) original m // vt copiar; ~**right** n derechos mpl de autor.

coral ['kɔrəl] n coral m; ~ **reef** n arrecife m (de coral).

cord [kɔːd] n cuerda; (ELEC) cordón m; (fabric) pana.

cordial ['kɔːdɪəl] a afectuoso // n cordial m.

cordon ['kɔːdn] n cordón m; **to** ~ **off** vt acordonar.

corduroy ['kɔːdərɔɪ] n pana.

core [kɔː*] n (gen) centro, núcleo; (of fruit) corazón m // vt quitar el corazón de.

coriander [kɔrɪ'ændə*] n culantro.

cork [kɔːk] n corcho; (tree) alcornoque m; ~**screw** n sacacorchos m inv.

cormorant ['kɔːmərnt] n cormorán m grande.

corn [kɔːn] n (wheat) trigo; (US: maize) maíz m; (cereals) granos mpl; (on foot) callo; ~ **on the cob** (CULIN) maíz en la mazorca.

corned beef ['kɔːnd-] n carne f de vaca acecinada.

corner ['kɔːnə*] n (gen) ángulo; (outside) esquina; (inside) rincón m; (in road) curva; (FOOTBALL) córner m // vt (trap) arrinconar; (COMM) acaparar // vi (in car) tomar una curva; ~**stone** n piedra angular.

cornet ['kɔːnɪt] n (MUS) corneta; (of ice-cream) barquillo.

cornflour ['kɔːnflauə*] n harina de maíz.

Cornwall ['kɔːnwəl] n Cornualles m.

corny ['kɔːnɪ] a (col) viejo, gastado.

corollary [kə'rɔlərɪ] n corolario.

coronary ['kɔrənərɪ] n: ~ (**thrombosis**) trombosis f coronaria.

coronation [kɔrə'neɪʃən] n coronación f.

coroner ['kɔrənə*] n juez m de primera instancia.

coronet ['kɔrənɪt] n corona.

corporal ['kɔːpərl] n cabo // a corporal.

corporate ['kɔːpərɪt] a corporativo.

corporation [kɔːpə'reɪʃən] n (of town) ayuntamiento; (COMM) corporación f.

corps [kɔː*], pl **corps** [kɔːz] n cuerpo.

corpse [kɔːps] n cadáver m.

corpuscle ['kɔːpʌsl] n corpúsculo.

corral [kə'rɑːl] n corral m.

correct [kə'rɛkt] a (accurate) justo, exacto; (proper) correcto // vt corregir; (exam) calificar; ~**ion** [-ʃən] n rectificación f; (erasure) tachadura.

correlate ['kɔrɪleɪt] vt correlacionar.

correspond [kɔrɪs'pɔnd] vi (write) escribirse; (be equal to) corresponder; ~**ence** n correspondencia; ~**ence**

course n curso por correspondencia; ~**ent** n corresponsal m/f; ~**ing** a correspondiente.

corridor ['kɔrɪdɔː*] n pasillo.

corroborate [kə'rɔbəreɪt] vt corroborar.

corrode [kə'rəud] vt corroer // vi corroerse; **corrosion** [-'rəuʒən] n corrosión f.

corrugated ['kɔrəgeɪtɪd] a ondulado; ~ **iron** n chapa ondulada.

corrupt [kə'rʌpt] a corrompido; (person) venal // vt corromper; (bribe) sobornar; ~**ion** [-ʃən] n corrupción f.

corset ['kɔːsɪt] n faja.

Corsica ['kɔːsɪkə] n Córcega.

cortège [kɔː'teɪʒ] n cortejo, desfile m.

cortisone ['kɔːtɪzəun] n cortisona.

cosh [kɔʃ] n cachiporra.

cosiness ['kəuzɪnɪs] n comodidad f; (atmosphere) lo holgado.

cos lettuce [kɔs-] n lechuga cos.

cosmetic [kɔz'mɛtɪk] n cosmético.

cosmic ['kɔzmɪk] a cósmico.

cosmonaut ['kɔzmənɔːt] n cosmonauta m/f.

cosmopolitan [kɔzmə'pɔlɪtn] a cosmopolita.

cosmos ['kɔzmɔs] n cosmos m.

cost [kɔst] n (gen) coste m, costo; (price) precio; ~**s** npl costes mpl // vi, pt, pp **cost** costar, valer // vt preparar el presupuesto de; **at the** ~ **of** a costa de; **how much does it** ~? ¿cuánto cuesta?

co-star ['kəustɑː*] n colega m/f de reparto.

Costa Rican ['kɔstə'riːkən] a costarriqueño.

costly ['kɔstlɪ] a (expensive) costoso; (valuable) suntuoso.

cost price n precio de coste.

costume ['kɔstjuːm] n traje m; (also: **swimming** ~) traje de baño.

cosy ['kəuzɪ] a cómodo; (atmosphere) acogedor(a); (life) holgado.

cot [kɔt] n (child's) cuna.

cottage ['kɔtɪdʒ] n casita de campo; (rustic) barraca; ~ **cheese** n requesón m.

cotton ['kɔtn] n algodón m; (thread) hilo; **to** ~ **on to** vt (col) caer en la cuenta de; ~ **wool** n algodón m (hidrófilo).

couch [kautʃ] n sofá m.

cough [kɔf] vi toser // n tos f; **to** ~ **up** vt escupir; ~ **drop** n pastilla para la tos.

could [kud] pt of **can**; ~**n't** = **could not**.

council ['kaunsl] n consejo; **city** or **town** ~ consejo municipal; ~ **estate** n polígono de renta limitada; ~ **house** n vivienda de renta limitada; ~**lor** n concejal m/f.

counsel ['kaunsl] n (advice) consejo; (lawyer) abogado // vt aconsejar; ~**lor** n consejero.

count [kaunt] vt (gen) contar; (include) incluir // vi contar // n (gen) cuenta; (of votes) escrutinio; (nobleman) conde m; (sum) total m, suma; **to** ~ **on** vt fus contar con; **that doesn't** ~! ¡eso no vale!;

~**down** n cuenta hacia atrás.
counter ['kauntə*] n (in shop) mostrador m; (in games) ficha // vt contrarrestar; (blow) parar; (attack) contestar a // ad: ~ to contrario a; ~**act** vt contrarrestar; ~**attack** n contrataque m // vi contratacar; ~**balance** n contrapeso; ~**espionage** n contraespionaje m.
counterfeit ['kauntəfɪt] n moneda falsa // vt falsificar // a falso, falsificado.
counterfoil ['kauntəfɔɪl] n talón m.
counterpart ['kauntəpɑːt] n (of person) colega m/f.
counter-revolution [kauntərɛvə'luːʃən] n contrarrevolución f.
countersign ['kauntəsaɪn] vt refrendar.
countess ['kauntɪs] n condesa.
countless ['kauntlɪs] a incontable.
country ['kʌntrɪ] n país m; (native land) patria; (as opposed to town) campo; (region) región f, tierra; ~ **dancing** n baile m regional; ~ **house** n quinta, finca; ~**side** n campo.
county ['kauntɪ] n condado; ~ **town** n cabeza de partido.
coup [kuː], pl ~**s** [-z] n golpe m; ~ **d'état/de grâce** golpe de estado/de gracia.
coupé [kuː'peɪ] n cupé m.
couple ['kʌpl] n (of things) par m; (of people) pareja; (married ~) matrimonio // vt (ideas, names) unir, juntar; (machinery) acoplar; a ~ of un par de.
coupling ['kʌplɪŋ] n (RAIL) enganche m.
coupon ['kuːpɔn] n cupón m; (pools ~) boleto.
courage ['kʌrɪdʒ] n valor m, valentía; ~**ous** [kə'reɪdʒəs] a valiente.
courier ['kurɪə*] n estafeta; (diplomatic) correo; (for tourists) agente m/f de turismo.
course [kɔːs] n (direction) dirección f; (of river, ESCOL) curso; (of ship) rumbo, derrota; (of bullet) trayectoria; (fig) proceder m; (GOLF) campo; (part of meal) plato; **of** ~ ad desde luego, naturalmente; **of** ~! ¡claro!; **in due** ~ en el momento oportuno.
court [kɔːt] n (royal) corte m; (LAW) tribunal m, juzgado; (TENNIS) pista, cancha // vt (woman) cortejar, hacer la corte a; (danger etc) buscar; **to take to** ~ demandar.
courteous ['kɔːtɪəs] a cortés.
courtesan [kɔːtɪ'zæn] n cortesana.
courtesy ['kɔːtəsɪ] n cortesía; **by** ~ **of** con permiso de.
court-house ['kɔːthaus] n (US) palacio de justicia.
courtier ['kɔːtɪə*] n cortesano.
court: ~**-martial,** pl ~**s-martial** n consejo de guerra // vt someter a consejo de guerra; ~**room** n sala de justicia; ~**yard** n patio.
cousin ['kʌzn] n primo/a; **first** ~ primo carnal.
cove [kəuv] n cala, ensenada.

covenant ['kʌvənənt] n convenio.
cover ['kʌvə*] vt (gen) cubrir; (with lid) tapar; (chairs etc) revestir; (distance) recorrer; (include) abarcar; (protect) abrigar; (journalist) investigar; (issues) tratar // n (gen) cubierta; (lid) tapa; (for chair etc) funda; (for bed) cobertor m; (envelope) sobre m; (for book) forro; (of magazine) portada; (shelter) abrigo; (insurance) cobertura; **under** ~ (indoors) bajo techo; **under** ~ **of** al abrigo de; (fig) so capa de; **to** ~ **up for sb** encubrir a uno; ~**age** n alcance m; ~ **charge** n precio del cubierto; ~**ing** n cubierta, envoltura; ~**ing letter** n carta explicatoria.
covet ['kʌvɪt] vt codiciar.
cow [kau] n vaca // vt intimidar.
coward ['kauəd] n cobarde m/f; ~**ice** [-ɪs] n cobardía; ~**ly** a cobarde.
cowboy ['kaubɔɪ] n vaquero.
cower ['kauə*] vi encogerse (de miedo).
cowshed ['kauʃed] n establo.
coxswain ['kɔksn] n (abbr: cox) timonel m/f.
coy [kɔɪ] a tímido.
coyote [kɔɪ'əutɪ] n coyote m.
crab [kræb] n cangrejo; ~ **apple** n manzana silvestre.
crack [kræk] n grieta; (noise) crujido; (: of whip) chasquido; (fam) chiste m // vt agrietar, romper; (nut) cascar; (safe) forzar; (whip etc) chasquear; (knuckles) crujir; (joke) contar // a (expert) experto; **to** ~ **up** vi (MED) sufrir un colapso nervioso; ~**er** n (biscuit) cräcker m; (Christmas cracker) sorpresa.
crackle ['krækl] vi crepitar; **crackling** n (of fire) crepitación f; (of leaves etc) crujido; (of pork) chicharrón m.
cradle ['kreɪdl] n cuna.
craft [krɑːft] n (skill) arte m; (trade) oficio; (cunning) astucia; (boat) barco.
craftsman ['krɑːftsmən] n artesano; ~**ship** n artesanía.
crafty ['krɑːftɪ] a astuto.
crag [kræg] n peñasco; ~**gy** a escarpado.
cram [kræm] vt (fill) llenar, henchir; ~**med** a atestado.
cramp [kræmp] n (MED) calambre m; (TECH) grapa // vt (limit) restringir; (annoy) estorbar; ~**ed** a apretado, estrecho.
crampon ['kræmpən] n crampón m.
cranberry ['krænbərɪ] n arándano agrio.
crane [kreɪn] n (TECH) grúa; (bird) grulla.
crank [kræŋk] n manivela; (person) chiflado; ~**shaft** n eje m del cigüeñal.
cranky ['kræŋkɪ] a (eccentric) maniático; (bad-tempered) irritable.
cranny ['krænɪ] n see **nook.**
crash [kræʃ] n (noise) estruendo; (of cars etc) choque m; (of plane) accidente m de avión; (COMM) quiebra // vt (plane) estrellar // vi (plane) estrellarse; (two cars) chocar; (fall noisily) caer con estrépito; ~ **course** n curso acelerado; ~

helmet n casco (protector); ~ **landing** n aterrizaje m forzoso.

crate [kreɪt] n cajón m de embalaje; (fam) armatoste m.

crater ['kreɪtə*] n cráter m.

cravat(e) [krə'væt] n pañuelo.

crave [kreɪv] vt: **to** ~ **for** ansiar, anhelar; **craving** n (of pregnant woman) antojo.

crawl [krɔːl] vi (gen) arrastrarse; (child) andar a gatas, gatear; (vehicle) avanzar a paso de tortuga // n (SWIMMING) crol m.

crayfish ['kreɪfɪʃ] n, pl inv langostino.

crayon ['kreɪɔn] n pastel m, lápiz m de color.

craze [kreɪz] n manía; (fashion) moda.

crazy ['kreɪzɪ] a (person) loco; (idea) disparatado.

creak [kriːk] vi chirriar, rechinar; (door etc) crujir.

cream [kriːm] n (of milk) nata; (gen) crema; (fig) flor y nata // a (colour) color m (de) crema; ~ **cake** n pastel m de nata; ~ **cheese** n queso de nata; ~**y** a cremoso.

crease [kriːs] n (fold) pliegue m; (in trousers) raya; (wrinkle) arruga // vt (fold) doblar, plegar; (wrinkle) arrugar // vi (wrinkle up) arrugarse.

create [kriː'eɪt] vt crear; **creation** [-ʃən] n creación f; **creative** a creador(a); **creator** n creador m.

creature ['kriːtʃə*] n (animal) animal m, bicho; (living thing) criatura.

crèche, creche [krɛʃ] n guardería infantil.

credentials [krɪ'dɛnʃlz] npl credenciales fpl.

credibility [krɛdɪ'bɪlɪtɪ] n credibilidad f.

credible ['krɛdɪbl] a creíble.

credit ['krɛdɪt] n (gen) crédito; (merit) honor m, mérito // vt (COMM) abonar; (believe) creer, prestar fe a // a crediticio; ~**s** npl (CINEMA) fichas técnicas; ~**able** a estimable, digno de elogio; ~ **card** n tarjeta de crédito; ~**or** n acreedor m.

credulity [krɪ'djuːlɪtɪ] n credulidad f.

creed [kriːd] n credo.

creek [kriːk] n cala, ensenada; (US) riachuelo.

creep [kriːp], pt, pp **crept** vi (animal) deslizarse; (gen) arrastrarse; (plant) trepar; ~**er** n enredadera; ~**y** a (frightening) horripilante.

cremate [krɪ'meɪt] vt incinerar; **cremation** [-ʃən] n incineración f.

crematorium [krɛmə'tɔːrɪəm], pl **-ria** [-rɪə] n (horno) crematorio.

creosote ['krɪəsəut] n creosota.

crêpe [kreɪp] n (fabric) crespón m; (rubber) crepé m; ~ **bandage** n venda de crepé.

crept [krɛpt] pt, pp of **creep.**

crescent ['krɛsnt] n media luna; (street) calle f en semicírculo.

cress [krɛs] n mastuerzo.

crest [krɛst] n (of bird) cresta; (of hill)

cima, cumbre f; (of helmet) cimera; (of coat of arms) blasón m; ~**fallen** a alicaído.

Crete [kriːt] n Creta.

crevasse [krɪ'væs] n grieta.

crevice [krɪ'vɪs] n grieta, hendedura.

crew [kruː] n (of ship etc) tripulación f; (gang) banda; (MIL) dotación f; ~**-cut** n corte m al rape; ~**-neck** n cuello plano.

crib [krɪb] n pesebre m // vt (col) plagiar.

crick [krɪk] n (in neck) tortícolis m.

cricket ['krɪkɪt] n (insect) grillo; (game) críquet m.

crime [kraɪm] n crimen m; (less serious) delito; **criminal** ['krɪmɪnl] n criminal m, delincuente m // a criminal, delictivo; (law) penal; **the Criminal Investigation Department (CID)** Brigada de Investigación Criminal (B.I.C.).

crimson ['krɪmzn] a carmesí.

cringe [krɪndʒ] vi agacharse, encogerse.

crinkle ['krɪŋkl] vt arrugar.

cripple ['krɪpl] n lisiado, mutilado // vt lisiar, tullir.

crisis ['kraɪsɪs], pl **-ses** [-siːz] n crisis f.

crisp [krɪsp] a fresco; (cooked) tostado; (hair) crespo; (manner) seco; ~**s** npl papas fritas fpl.

criss-cross ['krɪskrɔs] a entrelazado.

criterion [kraɪ'tɪərɪən], pl **-ria** [-rɪə] n criterio.

critic ['krɪtɪk] n (gen) criticón/ona m/f; (paper) crítico; ~**al** a (gen) crítico; (illness) grave; ~**ally** ad (ill) gravemente; ~**ism** ['krɪtɪsɪzm] n crítica; ~**ize** ['krɪtɪsaɪz] vt criticar.

croak [krəuk] vi (frog) croar; (raven) graznar // n graznido.

crochet ['krəuʃeɪ] n ganchillo.

crockery ['krɔkərɪ] n loza, vajilla.

crocodile ['krɔkədaɪl] n cocodrilo.

crocus ['krəukəs] n azafrán m.

croft [krɔft] n granja pequeña; ~**er** n pequeño granjero.

croissant ['krwæsã] n croissant m, medialuna.

crone [krəun] n bruja.

crony ['krəunɪ] n compinche m/f.

crook [kruk] n (fam) maleante m/f; (of shepherd) cayado; (of arm) pliegue m; ~**ed** ['krukɪd] a torcido; (path) tortuoso; (action) poco limpio.

crop [krɔp] n (species) cultivo; (quantity) cosecha // vt cortar, recortar; **to** ~ **up** vi surgir, presentarse.

croquet ['krəukeɪ] n croquet m.

croquette [krə'kɛt] n croqueta.

cross [krɔs] n cruz f // vt (street etc) cruzar, atravesar // a de mal humor, malhumorado; **to** ~ **o.s.** santiguarse; **to** ~ **out** vt tachar; **to** ~ **over** vi cruzar; ~**bar** n travesaño; (SPORT) larguero; ~**country (race)** n carrera a campo traviesa, cross m; ~**-examination** n repregunta, interrogatorio; ~**-examine** vt repreguntar; ~**-eyed** a bizco; ~**ing** n (*road*) cruce *m*; (*rail*) paso a nivel; (*sea-passage*) travesía; (*also:* **pedestrian** ~**ing**) paso para peatones; ~ **purposes** *npl*: **to be at** ~ **purposes** malentenderse uno a otro; ~**-reference** *n* contra-rreferencia; ~**roads** *n* cruce *m*, encrucijada; ~ **section** *n* corte *m* transversal; (*of population*) sección *f* representativa; ~**wind** *n* viento de costado; ~**word** *n* crucigrama *m*.

crotch [krɔtʃ] *n* (*of garment*) entrepierna.

crotchet ['krɔtʃit] *n* (*MUS*) negra.

crotchety ['krɔtʃiti] *a* (*person*) arisco.

crouch [krautʃ] *vi* agacharse, acurrucarse.

croupier ['kru:piə] *n* crupier *m/f.*

crow [krəu] *n* (*bird*) cuervo; (*of cock*) canto, cacareo // *vi* (*cock*) cantar, cacarear.

crowbar ['krəubɑ:*] *n* palanca.

crowd [kraud] *n* muchedumbre *f*; (*SPORT*) público; (*unruly*) tropel *m*; (*common herd*) vulgo // *vt* (*gather*) amontonar; (*fill*) llenar // *vi* (*gather*) reunirse; (*pile up*) amontonarse; ~**ed** *a* (*full*) atestado; (*well-attended*) concurrido.

crown [kraun] *n* corona; (*of head*) coronilla; (*of hat*) copa; (*of hill*) cumbre *f* // *vt* coronar; ~ **jewels** *npl* joyas *fpl* reales; ~ **prince** *n* príncipe *m* heredero.

crucial ['kru:ʃl] *a* decisivo.

crucifix ['kru:sifiks] *n* crucifijo; ~**ion** [-'fikʃən] *n* crucifixión *f*; **crucify** [-fai] *vt* crucificar.

crude [kru:d] *a* (*materials*) bruto; (*fig:* *basic*) tosco; (*: vulgar*) ordinario; ~ (**oil**) *n* aceite *m* crudo.

cruel [kruəl] *a* cruel; ~**ty** *n* crueldad *f.*

cruet ['kru:it] angarillas *fpl.*

cruise [kru:z] *n* crucero, viaje *m* por mar // *vi* (*ship*) hacer un crucero; (*car*) circular lentamente; **cruiser** *n* crucero.

crumb [krʌm] *n* miga, migaja.

crumble ['krʌmbl] *vt* desmenuzar // *vi* (*gen*) desmenuzarse; (*building*) desmoro-narse; **crumbly** *a* desmenuzable.

crumpet ['krʌmpit] *n* bollo blando.

crumple ['krʌmpl] *vt* (*paper*) estrujar; (*material*) arrugar.

crunch [krʌntʃ] *vt* (*food etc*) mascar; (*underfoot*) hacer crujir // *n* (*fig*) crisis *f*; ~**y** *a* crujiente.

crusade [kru:'seid] *n* cruzada.

crush [krʌʃ] *n* (*people*) agolpamiento; (*crowd*) aglomeración *f*; (*drink*): **lemon** ~ limonada // *vt* (*gen*) aplastar; (*paper*) estrujar; (*cloth*) arrugar; (*fruit*) exprimir; ~**ing** *a* aplastante; (*burden*) agobiador(a).

crust [krʌst] *n* corteza; (*MED*) costra.

crutch [krʌtʃ] *n* muleta.

crux [krʌks] *n* lo esencial.

cry [krai] *vi* llorar; (*shout*) gritar // *n* grito.

crypt [kript] *n* cripta.

cryptic ['kriptik] *a* enigmático, secreto.

crystal ['kristl] *n* cristal *m*; ~**-clear** *a* transparente, claro como el agua; **crystallize** *vt* cristalizar // *vi* cristalizarse.

cub [kʌb] *n* cachorro.

Cuba ['kju:bə] *n* Cuba; ~**n** *a*, *n* cubano/a.

cubbyhole ['kʌbihəul] *n* chiribitil *m.*

cube [kju:b] *n* cubo; (*of sugar*) terrón *m* // *vt* (*MATH*) cubicar; ~ **root** *n* raíz *f* cúbica; **cubic** *a* cúbico.

cubicle ['kju:bikl] *n* (*at pool*) caseta; (*for bed*) camarilla.

cuckoo ['kuku:] *n* cuco; ~ **clock** *n* reloj *m* de cuclillo.

cucumber ['kju:kʌmbə*] *n* pepino.

cuddle ['kʌdl] *vt* abrazar amorosamente // *vi* abrazarse; **cuddly** *a* mimoso.

cue [kju:] *n* (*snooker*) taco; (*THEATRE etc*) entrada, apunte *m.*

cuff [kʌf] *n* (*of shirt, coat etc*) puño; (*blow*) bofetada; **off the** ~ *ad* de improviso; ~**links** *npl* gemelos *mpl.*

cuisine [kwi'zi:n] *n* cocina.

cul-de-sac ['kʌldəsæk] *n* callejón *m* sin salida.

culinary ['kʌlinəri] *a* culinario.

cull [kʌl] *vt* (*flowers*) coger; (*select*) entresacar.

culminate ['kʌlmineit] *vi*: **to** ~ **in** terminar en; **culmination** [-'neiʃən] *n* culminación *f*, colmo.

culpable ['kʌlpəbl] *a* culpable.

culprit ['kʌlprit] *n* (*persona*) culpable, delincuente *m/f.*

cult [kʌlt] *n* culto.

cultivate ['kʌltiveit] *vt* (*also fig*) cultivar; **cultivation** [-'veiʃən] *n* cultivo; (*fig*) cultura.

cultural ['kʌltʃərəl] *a* cultural.

culture ['kʌltʃə*] *n* (*also fig*) cultura; ~**d** *a* culto.

cumbersome ['kʌmbəsəm] *a* molesto, incómodo.

cumulative ['kju:mjulətiv] *a* cumulativo.

cunning ['kʌniŋ] *n* astucia // *a* astuto.

cup [kʌp] *n* taza; (*prize, event*) copa.

cupboard ['kʌbəd] *n* armario; (*on wall*) alacena.

Cupid ['kju:pid] *n* Cupido.

cupola ['kju:pələ] *n* cúpula.

cup-tie ['kʌptai] *n* partido de copa.

cur [kə:] *n* perro de mala raza; (*person*) canalla *m/f.*

curable ['kjuərəbl] *a* curable.

curate ['kjuərit] *n* cura *m.*

curator [kjuə'reitə*] *n* director *m.*

curb [kə:b] *vt* refrenar // *n* freno.

curdle ['kə:dl] *vi* cuajarse.

curds [kə:dz] *npl* requesón *m.*

cure [kjuə*] *vt* curar // *n* cura, curación *f.*

curfew ['kə:fju:] *n* toque *m* de queda.

curio ['kjuəriəu] *n* curiosidad *f.*

curiosity [kjuəri'ɔsiti] *n* curiosidad *f*; **curious** ['kjuəriəs] *a* curioso.

curl [kə:l] *n* rizo, bucle *m* // *vt* (*hair*) rizar; (*paper*) arrollar; (*lip*) fruncir // *vi* rizarse; arrollarse; **to** ~ **up** *vi* arrollarse; (*person*) hacer un ovillo; (*fam*) morirse de risa; ~**er** *n* bigudí *m*, chincho; ~**y** *a* rizado.

currant ['kʌrnt] n pasa; (black, red) grosella.

currency ['kʌrnsɪ] n moneda.

current ['kʌrnt] n corriente f // a corriente, actual; ~ **account** n cuenta corriente; ~ **affairs** npl actualidades fpl; ~**ly** ad actualmente.

curriculum [kə'rɪkjuləm], pl ~**s** or **-la** [-lə] n plan m de estudios; ~ **vitae** n currículum m.

curry ['kʌrɪ] n curry m // vt: **to** ~ **favour with** buscar favores con; ~ **powder** n polvos mpl de curry.

curse [kə:s] vi echar pestes // vt maldecir, echar pestes de // n maldición f; (swearword) palabrota.

cursory ['kə:sərɪ] a rápido, superficial.

curt [kə:t] a corto, seco.

curtail [kə:'teɪl] vt (visit etc) acortar; (expenses etc) restringir.

curtain ['kə:tn] n cortina; (THEATRE) telón m; ~ **ring** n anilla.

curts(e)y ['kə:tsɪ] n reverencia // vi hacer una reverencia.

curve [kə:v] n curva // vt encorvar, torcer // vi encorvarse, torcerse; (road) hacer (una) curva.

cushion ['kuʃən] n cojín m; (SNOOKER) banda // vt (seat) acolchar; (shock) amortiguar.

custard ['kʌstəd] n (for pouring) natilla.

custodian [kʌs'təudɪən] n custodio.

custody ['kʌstədɪ] n custodia; **to take into** ~ detener.

custom ['kʌstəm] n costumbre f; (COMM) clientela; ~**ary** a acostumbrado.

customer ['kʌstəmə*] n cliente m/f.

custom-made ['kʌstəm'meɪd] a hecho a la medida.

customs ['kʌstəmz] npl aduana sg; ~ **duty** n derechos mpl de aduana; ~ **officer** n aduanero.

cut [kʌt], pt, pp **cut** vt cortar; (price) rebajar; (record) grabar; (reduce) reducir // vi cortar; (intersect) cruzarse // n (gen) eorte m; (of clothes) corte m; (with sword) tajo; (of knife) cuchillada; (in salary etc) rebaja; (of meat) tajada; **power** ~ apagón m; **to** ~ **a tooth** salirle a uno un diente; **to** ~ **down** vt (tree) derribar; (reduce) reducir; **to** ~ **off** vt (gen) cortar; (retreat) impedir; (troops) cercar; **to** ~ **out** vt (shape) recortar; (delete) suprimir; **to** ~ **through** vi abrirse camino; ~**back** n reducción f.

cute [kju:t] a lindo; (shrewd) listo.

cuticle ['kju:tɪkl] n cutícula.

cutlery ['kʌtlərɪ] n cubiertos mpl.

cutlet ['kʌtlɪt] n chuleta.

cut: ~**out** n recortable m; ~-**price** a a precio reducido; ~**throat** n asesino // a intenso.

cutting ['kʌtɪŋ] a (gen) cortante; (remark) mordaz // n (PRESS) recorte m; (RAIL) desmonte m.

cwt abbr of **hundredweight(s).**

cyanide ['saɪənaɪd] n cianuro.

cyclamen ['sɪkləmən] n ciclamen m.

cycle ['saɪkl] n ciclo; (bicycle) bicicleta // vi ir en bicicleta; **cycling** n ciclismo; **cyclist** n ciclista m/f.

cyclone ['saɪkləun] n ciclón m.

cygnet ['sɪgnɪt] n pollo de cisne.

cylinder ['sɪlɪndə*] n cilindro; ~ **block** n bloque m de cilindros; ~ **capacity** n cilindrada; ~ **head** n culata de cilindro; ~-**head gasket** n junta de culata.

cymbals ['sɪmblz] npl platillos mpl.

cynic ['sɪnɪk] n cínico; ~**al** a cínico; ~**ism** ['sɪnɪsɪzəɪn] n cinismo.

cypress ['saɪprɪs] n ciprés m.

Cypriot ['sɪprɪət] a, n chipriota m/f.

Cyprus ['saɪprəs] n Chipre f.

cyst [sɪst] n quiste m; ~**itis** n cistitis f.

czar [zɑ:*] n zar m.

Czech [tʃɛk] a, n checo/a.

Czechoslovakia [tʃɛkəslə'vækɪə] n Checoslovaquia.

D

dab [dæb] vt (eyes, wound) tocar (ligeramente); (paint, cream) mojar ligeramente // n (of paint) brochazo; (of liquid) gota; (amount) pequeña cantidad f.

dabble ['dæbl] vi: **to** ~ **in** interesarse por.

dad [dæd], **daddy** ['dædɪ] n papá m; **daddy-long-legs** n típula.

daffodil ['dæfədɪl] n narciso trompón.

daft [dɑ:ft] a estúpido, tonto.

dagger ['dægə*] n puñal m, daga; **to look** ~**s at sb** apuñalar a alguien con la mirada.

daily ['deɪlɪ] a diario, cotidiano // n (paper) diario; (domestic help) asistenta // ad a diario, cada día.

dainty ['deɪntɪ] a delicado; (tasteful) elegante, primoroso.

dairy ['dɛərɪ] n (shop) lechería; (on farm) vaquería // a lechero; ~ **farm** n granja; ~ **produce** n productos mpl lácteos.

daisy ['deɪzɪ] n margarita.

dale [deɪl] n valle m.

dam [dæm] n presa // vt represar.

damage ['dæmɪdʒ] n daño, perjuicio; (to machine) avería // vt dañar, perjudicar; averiar; ~**s** npl (LAW) daños y perjuicios.

damn [dæm] vt condenar; (curse) maldecir // n (col): **I don't give a** ~ me trae sin cuidado // a (col) maldito; ~ **(it)!** ¡mecachis!; ~**ing** a (evidence) irrecusable.

damp [dæmp] a húmedo, mojado // n humedad f // vt (also: ~**en**) (cloth, rag) mojar; (enthusiasm etc) desalentar; ~**ness** n humedad f.

damson ['dæmzən] n ciruela damascena.

dance [dɑ:ns] n baile m // vi bailar; ~ **hall** n salón m de baile; **dancer** n bailador/a m/f; (professional) bailarín/ina m/f; **dancing** n baile m.

dandelion ['dændɪlaɪən] n diente m de león.

dandruff ['dændrəf] n caspa.
Dane [deɪn] n danés/esa m/f.
danger ['deɪndʒɔ*] n peligro; (risk) riesgo;
~! (on sign) ¡peligro de muerte!; **to be in
~ of** correr riesgo de; **~ous** a peligroso;
~**ously** ad peligrosamente.
dangle ['dæŋgl] vt colgar // vi pender,
estar colgado.
Danish ['deɪnɪʃ] a, n danés/esa m/f.
dare [dɛə*] vt: **to ~ sb to do** desafiar a
uno a hacer algo // vi: **to ~ (to) do sth**
atreverse a hacer algo; ~**devil** n
temerario, atrevido; **daring** a atrevido,
osado // n atrevimiento, osadía.
dark [dɑːk] a (gen) oscuro; (hair,
complexion) moreno; (cheerless) triste,
sombrío; (fig) secreto, escondido // n
(gen) oscuridad f; (night) tinieblas fpl; **to
be left in the ~ about** (fig) quedar sin
saber nada de; **after ~** después del
anochecer; ~**en** vt oscurecer; (colour)
hacer más oscuro // vi oscurecerse; (sky)
anublarse; ~ **glasses** npl gafas fpl
oscuras; ~**ness** n oscuridad f, tinieblas
fpl; ~ **room** n cuarto oscuro.
darling ['dɑːlɪŋ] a, n querido/a.
darn [dɑːn] vt zurcir.
dart [dɑːt] n dardo; (in game) rehilete m;
(in sewing) sisa // vi precipitarse; **to ~
away/along** irse/seguir precipitado;
~**board** n blanco; ~**s** n juego de
rehiletes.
dash [dæʃ] n (sign) guión m; (: long) raya;
(rush) carrera // vt (break) romper,
estrellar; (hopes) defraudar // vi
precipitarse, ir de prisa; **to ~ away** or **off**
vi marcharse apresuradamente; ~**board**
n tablero de instrumentos; ~**ing** a
gallardo.
data ['deɪtə] npl datos mpl; ~ **processing**
n procesamiento de datos.
date [deɪt] n (day) fecha; (with friend) cita;
(fruit) dátil m; (tree) palmera // vt fichar;
citar; **to ~ ad** hasta la fecha; **out of ~**
fuera de moda; **up to ~** moderno, al día;
~**d** a anticuado.
daub [dɔːb] vt manchar.
daughter ['dɔːtə*] n hija; ~-**in-law** n
nuera, hija política.
daunting ['dɔːntɪŋ] a desalentador(a).
dawdle ['dɔːdl] vi (waste time) perder el
tiempo; (go slow) andar muy despacio.
dawn [dɔːn] n alba, amanecer m // vi
(day) amanecer; (fig): **it ~ed on him
that...** cayó en la cuenta de que... .
day [deɪ] n día m; (working ~) jornada; **the
~ before** el día anterior; **the following
~** el día siguiente; **by ~** de día; ~**break**
n amanecer m; ~**dream** n ensueño // vi
soñar despierto; ~**light** n luz f (del día);
~**time** n día m // a de día.
daze [deɪz] vt (stun) aturdir // n: **in a ~**
aturdido.
dazzle ['dæzl] vt deslumbrar; **dazzling** a
deslumbrante.
dead [dɛd] a (gen) muerto; (deceased)
difunto; (telephone) cortado; (ELEC) sin

corriente // ad (gen) totalmente; (exactly)
justo; ~ **tired** muerto de cansancio; **to
stop ~** parar en seco; **the ~** los
muertos; ~**en** vt (blow, sound)
amortiguar; (make numb) calmar, aliviar;
~ **end** n callejón m sin salida; ~ **heat** n
(SPORT) empate m; ~**line** n fecha o hora
tope; ~**lock** n punto muerto; ~**ly** a
mortal, fatal; ~**pan** a sin expresión.
deaf [dɛf] a sordo; ~-**aid** n audífono; ~**en**
vt ensordecer; ~**ening** a
ensordecedor(a); ~**ness** n sordera;
~-**mute** n sordomudo/a.
deal [diːl] n (agreement) pacto, convenio;
(business) negocio, trato; (CARDS) reparto
// vt, pt, pp **dealt** [dɛlt] (gen) dar; **a great
~ (of)** bastante, mucho; **to ~ in** tratar
en, comerciar en; **to ~ with** vt fus
(people) tratar con; (problem) ocuparse
de; (subject) tratar de; (punish) castigar;
~**er** n comerciante m, tratante m; (CARDS)
mano f; ~**ings** npl transacciones fpl;
(relations) relaciones fpl.
dear [dɪə*] a querido; (expensive) caro //
n: **my ~** mi querido/a // excl: ~ **me!**
¡Dios mío!; **D~ Sir/Madam** (in letter)
Muy Señor Mío, estimado Señor/estimada
Señora; ~**ly** ad (love) tiernamente; (pay)
caro.
death [dɛθ] n muerte f; ~**bed** n lecho de
muerte; ~ **certificate** n partida de
defunción; ~ **duties** npl (Brit) derechos
mpl de herencia; ~**ly** a mortal; (silence)
profundo; ~ **penalty** n pena de muerte;
~ **rate** n mortalidad f.
debar [dɪ'bɑː*] vt (exclude) excluir.
debase [dɪ'beɪs] vt degradar.
debate [dɪ'beɪt] n debate m // vt discutir.
debauchery [dɪ'bɔːtʃərɪ] n libertinaje m.
debit ['dɛbɪt] n debe m // vt: **to ~ a sum
to sb** or **to sb's account** cargar una suma
en cuenta a alguien.
debris ['dɛbriː] n escombros mpl.
debt [dɛt] n deuda; **to be in ~** tener
deudas; ~**or** n deudor/a m/f.
début ['deɪbjuː] n presentación f.
decade ['dɛkeɪd] n decenio.
decadence ['dɛkədəns] n decadencia.
decay [dɪ'keɪ] n decadencia; (of building)
desmoronamiento; (fig) deterioro;
(rotting) pudrición f; (of tooth) caries f //
vi (rot) pudrirse; (fig) decaer.
deceased [dɪ'siːst] a difunto.
deceit [dɪ'siːt] n engaño; ~**ful** a engañoso.
deceive [dɪ'siːv] vt engañar.
decelerate [diː'sɛləreɪt] vt moderar la
marcha de // vi decelerar.
December [dɪ'sɛmbə*] n diciembre m.
decency ['diːsənsɪ] n decencia.
decent ['diːsənt] a (proper) decente;
(person) amable, bueno.
decentralize [diː'sɛntrəlaɪz] vt
descentralizar.
deception [dɪ'sɛpʃən] n engaño;
deceptive [-tɪv] a engañoso.
decibel ['dɛsɪbɛl] n decibel(io) m.
decide [dɪ'saɪd] vt (person) decidir;

(*question, argument*) resolver // vi decidir;
to ~ on sth decidir por algo; **~d** a
(*resolute*) decidido; (*clear, definite*)
indudable; **~dly** [-dɪdlɪ] ad decididamente.
deciduous [dɪˈsɪdjuəs] a de hoja caduca.
decimal [ˈdesɪməl] a decimal // n decimal
f; **~ point** n coma de decimales.
decimate [ˈdesɪmeɪt] vt diezmar.
decipher [dɪˈsaɪfə*] vt descifrar.
decision [dɪˈsɪʒən] n decisión f.
decisive [dɪˈsaɪsɪv] a decisivo; (*conclusive*)
terminante; (*manner*) tajante.
deck [dek] n (*NAUT*) cubierta f; (*of bus*) piso;
(*of cards*) baraja; **~chair** n tumbona,
hamaca.
declaration [dekləˈreɪʃən] n declaración f;
declare [dɪˈkleə*] vt (*gen*) declarar.
decline [dɪˈklaɪn] n decaimiento,
decadencia; (*lessening*) disminución f // vt
rehusar // vi decaer; disminuir; (*fall*)
bajar.
declutch [ˈdiːˈklʌtʃ] vi desembragar.
decode [diːˈkəud] vt descifrar.
decompose [diːkəmˈpəuz] vi
descomponerse; **decomposition**
[diːkɔmpəˈzɪʃən] n descomposición f.
decontaminate [diːkənˈtæmɪneɪt] vt
descontaminar.
décor [ˈdeɪkɔ:*] n decoración f; (*THEATRE*)
decorado.
decorate [ˈdekəreɪt] vt adornar, decorar;
(*paint*) pintar; (*paper*) empapelar;
decoration [-ˈreɪʃən] n adorno; (*act*)
decoración f; (*medal*) condecoración f;
decorator n (*painter*) pintor m.
decoy [ˈdiːkɔɪ] n señuelo.
decrease [diːˈkriːs] n disminución f // (vb:
[diːˈkriːs]) vt disminuir, reducir // vi
reducirse.
decree [dɪˈkriː] n decreto; **~ nisi** n orden
f disolución de divorcio.
decrepit [dɪˈkrepɪt] a decrépito.
dedicate [ˈdedɪkeɪt] vt dedicar;
dedication [-ˈkeɪʃən] n (*devotion*)
dedicación f; (*in book*) dedicatoria f.
deduce [dɪˈdjuːs] vt deducir.
deduct [dɪˈdʌkt] vt restar; (*from wage etc*)
descontar; **~ion** [dɪˈdʌkʃən] n descuento;
(*conclusion*) deducción f, conclusión f.
deed [diːd] n hecho, acto; (*feat*) hazaña;
(*LAW*) escritura.
deem [diːm] vt juzgar.
deep [diːp] a (*gen*) profundo; (*voice*) bajo;
(*breath*) profundo, a pleno pulmón;
(*person*) insondable // ad: **the spectators
stood 20 ~** los espectadores se formaron
de 20 en fondo; **to be 4 metres ~** tener 4
metros de profundo; **~en** vt ahondar,
profundizar // vi (*darkness*) intensificarse;
~-freeze n congeladora; **~-fry** vt freír
en aceite abundante; **~-sea diving** n
buceo de altura; **~-seated** a (*beliefs*)
(profundamente) arraigado; **~-set** a
(*eyes*) hundido.
deer [dɪə*] n, pl inv ciervo; **~skin** n
gamuza, piel f de ciervo.
deface [dɪˈfeɪs] vt desfigurar, mutilar.

defamation [defəˈmeɪʃən] n difamación f.
default [dɪˈfɔːlt] vi no pagar; (*SPORT*) dejar
de presentarse // n: **by ~** (*LAW*) en
rebeldía; (*SPORT*) por no presentarse al
adversario; **~er** n (*in debt*) moroso/a.
defeat [dɪˈfiːt] n derrota // vt derrotar,
vencer; (*fig: efforts*) frustrar; **~ist** a, n
derrotista m/f.
defect [ˈdiːfekt] n defecto // vi [dɪˈfekt]
desertar; **~ive** [dɪˈfektɪv] a (*gen*)
defectuoso; (*person*) anormal.
defence [dɪˈfens] n defensa; **~less** a
indefenso.
defend [dɪˈfend] vt defender; **~ant** n
acusado/a; (*in civil case*) demandado/a;
~er n defensor m.
defensive [dɪˈfensɪv] a defensivo; **on the
~** a la defensiva.
defer [dɪˈfɜ:*] vt (*postpone*) aplazar; **to ~
to** diferir a; **~ence** [ˈdefərəns] n
deferencia, respeto.
defiance [dɪˈfaɪəns] n desafío; **in ~ of** en
contra de; **defiant** [-ənt] a (*insolent*)
insolente; (*challenging*) retador(a).
deficiency [dɪˈfɪʃənsɪ] n (*lack*) falta;
(*defect*) defecto; **deficient** [-ənt] a
(*lacking*) insuficiente; (*incomplete*)
incompleto; (*defective*) defectuoso;
(*mentally*) anormal; **deficient in** falto de.
deficit [ˈdefɪsɪt] n déficit m.
defile [dɪˈfaɪl] vt manchar, deshonrar.
define [dɪˈfaɪn] vt definir.
definite [ˈdefɪnɪt] a (*fixed*) determinado;
(*clear, obvious*) claro, categórico; **he was
~ about it** no dejó lugar a dudas (sobre
ello); **~ly** ad claramente.
definition [defɪˈnɪʃən] n definición f.
definitive [dɪˈfɪnɪtɪv] a definitivo.
deflate [diːˈfleɪt] vt (*gen*) desinflar;
(*person*) quitar los humos a.
deflect [dɪˈflekt] vt desviar.
deform [dɪˈfɔːm] vt deformar; **~ed** a
deformado; **~ity** n deformación f.
defraud [dɪˈfrɔːd] vt estafar; **to ~ sb of
sth** estafar algo a uno.
defrost [diːˈfrɔst] vt (*fridge*) deshelar,
descongelar.
deft [deft] a diestro, hábil.
defunct [dɪˈfʌŋkt] a difunto.
defuse [diːˈfjuːz] vt quitar el fusible a.
defy [dɪˈfaɪ] vt (*resist*) oponerse
resueltamente a; (*challenge*) desafiar;
(*order*) contravenir.
degenerate [dɪˈdʒenəreɪt] vi degenerar //
a [dɪˈdʒenərɪt] degenerado.
degradation [degrəˈdeɪʃən] n degradación
f; **degrading** [dɪˈɡreɪdɪŋ] a degradante.
degree [dɪˈɡriː] n grado; (*SCOL*) título; **~ in
maths** licencia en matemáticas.
dehydrated [diːhaɪˈdreɪtɪd] a
deshidratado; (*milk*) en polvo.
de-ice [diːˈaɪs] vt (*windscreen*) deshelar.
deign [deɪn] vi: **to ~ to do** dignarse
hacer.
deity [ˈdiːɪtɪ] n deidad f, divinidad f.
dejected [dɪˈdʒektɪd] a abatido,

desanimado; (face) cariacontecido; **dejection** [-'ʃən] n abatimiento.

delay [dɪ'leɪ] vt demorar, aplazar; (person) entretener; (trains) retrasar // vi tardar // n (gen) dilación f; (a ~) demora, retraso; **without ~** en seguida, sin tardar.

delegate ['dɛlɪgɪt] n delegado/a // vt ['dɛlɪgeɪt] delegar; **delegation** [-'geɪʃən] n delegación f.

delete [dɪ'liːt] vt suprimir, tachar.

deliberate [dɪ'lɪbərɪt] a (intentional) intencionado; (slow) pausado, lento // vi [dɪ'lɪbəreɪt] deliberar; **~ly** ad (on purpose) a propósito; (slowly) pausadamente.

delicacy ['dɛlɪkəsɪ] n delicadeza; (choice food) golosina.

delicate ['dɛlɪkɪt] a (gen) delicado; (fragile) frágil; (skilled) fino.

delicatessen [dɛlɪkə'tɛsn] n tienda especializada en comida exótica.

delicious [dɪ'lɪʃəs] a delicioso, rico.

delight [dɪ'laɪt] n (feeling) placer m, deleite m; (object) encanto, delicia // vt encantar, deleitar; **to take ~ in** deleitarse con; **~ful** a encantador(a), delicioso.

delinquency [dɪ'lɪŋkwənsɪ] n delincuencia; **delinquent** [-ənt] a, n delincuente m/f.

delirious [dɪ'lɪrɪəs] a delirante; **delirium** [-ɪəm] n delirio.

deliver [dɪ'lɪvə*] vt (distribute) repartir; (hand over) entregar; (message) comunicar; (speech) pronunciar; (blow) lanzar, dar; (MED) **to be ~ed** dar a luz; **~y** n reparto; entrega; (distribution) distribución f; (of speaker) modo de expresarse; (MED) parto, alumbramiento; (saving) liberación f; **to take ~y of** recibir.

delta ['dɛltə] n delta m.

delude [dɪ'luːd] vt engañar.

deluge ['dɛljuːdʒ] n diluvio // vt inundar.

delusion [dɪ'luːʒən] n ilusión f, engaño.

de luxe [də'lʌks] a de lujo.

delve [dɛlv] vi: **to ~ into** ahondar en.

demand [dɪ'mɑːnd] vt (gen) exigir; (rights) reclamar // n (gen) exigencia; (claim) reclamación f; (ECON) demanda; **to be in ~** ser muy solicitado; **on ~** a solicitud; **~ing** a (boss) exigente; (work) absorbente.

demarcation [diːmɑː'keɪʃən] n demarcación f.

demean [dɪ'miːn] vt: **to ~ o.s.** rebajarse.

demeanour [dɪ'miːnə*] n porte m, conducta.

demented [dɪ'mɛntɪd] a demente.

demister [diː'mɪstə*] n (AUT) de(s)fuminador m de vapores.

democracy [dɪ'mɒkrəsɪ] n democracia; **democrat** ['dɛməkræt] n demócrata m/f; **democratic** [dɛmə'krætɪk] a democrático.

demolish [dɪ'mɒlɪʃ] vt derribar, demoler; **demolition** [dɛmə'lɪʃən] n derribo, demolición f.

demonstrate ['dɛmənstreɪt] vt demostrar

// vi manifestarse; **demonstration** [-'streɪʃən] n (POL) manifestación f; (proof) prueba, demostración f; **demonstrator** n (POL) manifestante m/f.

demoralize [dɪ'mɒrəlaɪz] vt desmoralizar.

demote [dɪ'məut] vt degradar.

demure [dɪ'mjuə*] a recatado.

den [dɛn] n (of animal) guarida; (study) estudio.

denial [dɪ'naɪəl] n (refusal) negativa; (of report etc) desmentimiento; **self-~** abnegación f.

denim ['dɛnɪm] n dril m; **~s** npl vaqueros mpl.

Denmark ['dɛnmɑːk] n Dinamarca.

denomination [dɪnɒmɪ'neɪʃən] n valor m; (REL) confesión f.

denominator [dɪ'nɒmɪneɪtə*] n denominador m.

denote [dɪ'nəut] vt indicar, significar.

denounce [dɪ'nauns] vt denunciar.

dense [dɛns] a (thick) espeso; (: foliage etc) tupido; (stupid) torpe, duro de mollera; **~ly** ad: **~ly populated** con gran densidad de población.

density ['dɛnsɪtɪ] n densidad f.

dent [dɛnt] n abolladura // vt (also: **make a ~ in**) abollar.

dental ['dɛntl] a dental; **~ surgeon** n odontólogo.

dentist ['dɛntɪst] n dentista m/f; **~ry** n odontología.

dentures ['dɛntʃəz] npl dentadura sg (postiza).

deny [dɪ'naɪ] vt (gen) negar; (charge) rechazar; (report) desmentir; **to ~ o.s.** privarse (de).

deodorant [diː'əudərənt] n desodorante m.

depart [dɪ'pɑːt] vi irse, marcharse; (train) salir; **to ~ from** (fig: differ from) apartarse de.

department [dɪ'pɑːtmənt] n (COMM) sección f; (SCOL) ramo; (POL) ministerio; **~ store** n gran almacén m.

departure [dɪ'pɑːtʃə*] n partida, ida; (of train) salida; **a new ~** un nuevo rumbo.

depend [dɪ'pɛnd] vi: **to ~ on** depender de; (rely on) contar con; **it ~s** ¡depende!, ¡según!; **~able** a (person) formal, serio; **~ence** n dependencia; **~ant, ~ent** n dependiente m/f.

depict [dɪ'pɪkt] vt (in picture) pintar; (describe) representar.

depleted [dɪ'pliːtɪd] a reducido.

deplorable [dɪ'plɔːrəbl] a lamentable, deplorable; **deplore** [dɪ'plɔː*] vt lamentar, deplorar.

deploy [dɪ'plɔɪ] vt desplegar.

depopulation ['diːpɒpju'leɪʃən] n despoblación f.

deport [dɪ'pɔːt] vt deportar; **~ation** [-'teɪʃən] n deportación f; **~ment** n comportamiento.

depose [dɪ'pəuz] vt deponer.

deposit [dɪ'pɒzɪt] n (gen) depósito; (CHEM) sedimento; (of ore, oil) yacimiento // vt (*gen*) depositar; ~ **account** *n* cuenta de ahorros; ~**or** *n* cuentacorrentista *m/f*.

depot ['dɛpəu] *n* (*storehouse*) depósito; (*for vehicles*) parque *m*.

depraved [dɪ'preɪvd] *a* depravado, vicioso; **depravity** [-'prævɪtɪ] *n* depravación *f*, vicio.

depreciate [dɪ'priːʃɪeɪt] *vi* depreciarse, perder valor; **depreciation** [-'eɪʃən] *n* depreciación *f*.

depress [dɪ'prɛs] *vt* deprimir; (*press down*) presionar; ~**ed** *a* deprimido; ~**ing** *a* deprimente; ~**ion** [dɪ'prɛʃən] *n* depresión *f*.

deprivation [dɛprɪ'veɪʃən] *n* privación *f*; (*loss*) pérdida.

deprive [dɪ'praɪv] *vt*: **to** ~ **sb of** privar a alguien de; ~**d** *a* pobre.

depth [dɛpθ] *n* (*gen*) profundidad *f*; (*of room etc*) fondo; **in the** ~**s of** en lo más hondo de.

deputation [dɛpju'teɪʃən] *n* delegación *f*.

deputize ['dɛpjutaɪz] *vi*: **to** ~ **for sb** sustituir por uno.

deputy ['dɛpjutɪ] *a*: ~ **head** subdirector/a *m/f* // *n* sustituto/a, suplente *m*; (*POL*) diputado; (*agent*) representante *m*.

derail [dɪ'reɪl] *vt*: **to be** ~**ed** descarrilarse; ~**ment** *n* descarrilamiento.

deranged [dɪ'reɪndʒd] *a* (*person*) vuelto loco, trastornado (mentalmente).

derelict ['dɛrɪlɪkt] *a* abandonado.

deride [dɪ'raɪd] *vt* ridiculizar, mofarse de; **derision** [-'rɪʒən] *n* irrisión *f*, mofas *fpl*.

derivative [dɪ'rɪvətɪv] *n* derivado // *a* derivado; (*work*) poco original.

derive [dɪ'raɪv] *vt* derivar // *vi*: **to** ~ **from** derivarse de.

dermatitis [dəːmə'taɪtɪs] *n* dermatitis *f*; **dermatology** [-'tɒlədʒɪ] *n* dermatología.

derogatory [dɪ'rɒgətərɪ] *a* despectivo.

derrick ['dɛrɪk] *n* torre *f* de perforación.

descend [dɪ'sɛnd] *vt*, *vi* descender, bajar; **to** ~ **from** descender de; ~**ant** *n* descendiente *m/f*.

descent [dɪ'sɛnt] *n* descenso; (*GEO*) pendiente *m*, declive *m*; (*origin*) descendencia.

describe [dɪs'kraɪb] *vt* describir; **description** [-'krɪpʃən] *n* descripción *f*; (*sort*) clase *f*, género; **descriptive** [-'krɪptɪv] *a* descriptivo.

desecrate ['dɛsɪkreɪt] *vt* profanar.

desert ['dɛzət] *n* desierto // (*vb*: [dɪ'zəːt]) *vt* abandonar, desamparar // *vi* (*MIL*) desertar; ~**er** *n* desertor *m*; ~**ion** [dɪ'zəːʃən] *n* deserción *f*.

deserve [dɪ'zəːv] *vt* merecer, ser digno de; **deserving** *a* (*person*) digno; (*action, cause*) meritorio.

design [dɪ'zaɪn] *n* (*sketch*) bosquejo; (*layout, shape*) diseño; (*pattern*) dibujo; (*intention*) propósito, intención *f* // *vt* (*gen*) diseñar; (*plan*) proyectar.

designate ['dɛzɪgneɪt] *vt* (*point to*) señalar; (*appoint*) nombrar; (*destine*)

designar // *a* ['dɛzɪgnɪt] designado; **designation** [-'neɪʃən] *n* (*appointment*) nombramiento; (*name*) denominación *f*.

designer [dɪ'zaɪnə*] *n* (*ART*) dibujante *m*; (*TECH*) diseñador *m*; (*fashion* ~) modista *m/f*.

desirable [dɪ'zaɪərəbl] *a* (*proper*) deseable; (*attractive*) atractivo.

desire [dɪ'zaɪə*] *n* deseo // *vt* desear.

desk [dɛsk] *n* (*in office*) escritorio; (*for pupil*) pupitre *m*; (*in hotel, at airport*) recepción *f*.

desolate ['dɛsəlɪt] *a* (*place*) desierto; (*person*) afligido; **desolation** [-'leɪʃən] *n* (*of place*) desolación *f*; (*of person*) aflicción *f*.

despair [dɪs'pɛə*] *n* desesperación *f* // *vi*: **to** ~ **of** desesperarse de.

despatch [dɪs'pætʃ] *n*, *vt* = **dispatch**.

desperate ['dɛspərɪt] *a* desesperado; (*fugitive*) peligroso; ~**ly** *ad* desesperadamente; (*very*) terriblemente, gravemente.

desperation [dɛspə'reɪʃən] *n* desesperación *f*; **in** ~ desesperado.

despicable [dɪs'pɪkəbl] *a* vil, despreciable.

despise [dɪs'paɪz] *vt* despreciar.

despite [dɪs'paɪt] *prep* a pesar de, pese a.

despondent [dɪs'pɒndənt] *a* deprimido, abatido.

dessert [dɪ'zəːt] *n* postre *m*; ~**spoon** *n* cuchara (de postre).

destination [dɛstɪ'neɪʃən] *n* destino.

destiny ['dɛstɪnɪ] *n* destino.

destitute ['dɛstɪtjuːt] *a* desamparado, indigente.

destroy [dɪs'trɔɪ] *vt* (*gen*) destruir; (*finish*) acabar con; ~**er** *n* (*NAUT*) destructor *m*.

destruction [dɪs'trʌkʃən] *n* destrucción *f*; (*fig*) ruina; **destructive** [-tɪv] *a* destructivo, destructor(a).

detach [dɪ'tætʃ] *vt* separar; (*unstick*) despegar; ~**able** *a* separable; (*TECH*) desmontable; ~**ed** *a* (*attitude*) objetivo, imparcial; (*house*) independiente, solo; ~**ment** *n* (*gen*) separación *f*; (*MIL*) destacamento; (*fig*) objetividad *f*, imparcialidad *f*.

detail ['diːteɪl] *n* detalle *m* // *vt* (*gen*) detallar; (*MIL*) destacar; **in** ~ en detalle; ~**ed** *a* detallado.

detain [dɪ'teɪn] *vt* retener; (*in captivity*) detener.

detect [dɪ'tɛkt] *vt* (*gen*) descubrir; (*MED, POLICE*) identificar; (*MIL, RADAR, TECH*) detectar; ~**ion** [dɪ'tɛkʃən] *n* descubrimiento; identificación *f*; ~**ive** *n* detective *m*; ~**ive story** *n* novela policíaca; ~**or** *n* detector *m*.

détente [deɪ'tɑːnt] *n* detente *f*.

detention [dɪ'tɛnʃən] *n* detención *f*, arresto.

deter [dɪ'təː*] *vt* (*discourage*) desalentar; (*dissuade*) disuadir; (*prevent*) impedir.

detergent [dɪ'təːdʒənt] *n* detergente *m*.

deteriorate [dɪ'tɪərɪəreɪt] *vi* deteriorarse; **deterioration** [-'reɪʃən] *n* deterioro.

determination [dɪtəːmɪ'neɪʃən] *n* (*gen*)

determinación f; (resolve) resolución f.
determine [dɪ'tɜːmɪn] vt (gen) determinar; (limits etc) definir; (dispute) resolver; ~**d** a (person) resuelto.
deterrent [dɪ'tɛrənt] n fuerza de disuasión.
detest [dɪ'tɛst] vt aborrecer; ~**able** a aborrecible.
detonate ['dɛtəneɪt] vi estallar // vt hacer detonar; **detonator** n detonador m, fulminante m.
detour ['diːtuə*] n rodeo.
detract [dɪ'trækt] vt: **to ~ from** quitar mérito a, desvirtuar.
detriment ['dɛtrɪmənt] n: **to the ~ of** en perjuicio de; ~**al** [dɛtrɪ'mɛntl] a perjudicial (to a).
devaluation [diːvæljuː'eɪʃən] n devaluación f; **devalue** ['-'væljuː] vt devaluar.
devastate ['dɛvəsteɪt] vt devastar; **he was ~d by the news** las noticias le dejaron desolado; **devastating** a devastador(a); (fig) arrollador(a).
develop [dɪ'vɛləp] vt (gen) desarrollar; (PHOT) revelar; (disease) coger; (engine trouble) empezar a tener // vi desarrollarse; (advance) progresar; (appear) aparecer; ~**ing country** país m en desarrollo; ~**ment** n desarrollo; (advance) progreso; (of affair, case) desenvolvimiento; (of land) urbanización f.
deviate ['diːvieɪt] vi desviarse; **deviation** ['-'eɪʃən] n desviación f.
device [dɪ'vaɪs] n (scheme) estratagema f, recurso; (apparatus) aparato, mecanismo.
devil ['dɛvl] n diablo, demonio; ~**ish** a diabólico.
devious ['diːvɪəs] a intricado, enrevesado; (person) taimado.
devise [dɪ'vaɪz] vt idear, inventar.
devoid [dɪ'vɔɪd] a: ~ **of** desprovisto de.
devote [dɪ'vəut] vt: **to ~ sth to** dedicar algo a; ~**d** a (loyal) leal, fiel; **the book is ~d to politics** el libro trata de la política; **devotee** [dɛvəu'tiː] n devoto/a.
devotion [dɪ'vəuʃən] n dedicación f; (REL) devoción f.
devour [dɪ'vauə*] vt devorar.
devout [dɪ'vaut] a devoto.
dew [djuː] n rocío.
dexterity [dɛks'tɛrɪtɪ] n destreza.
diabetes [daɪə'biːtiːz] n diabetes f; **diabetic** ['-'bɛtɪk] a, n diabético/a.
diagnose [daɪəg'nəuz] vt diagnosticar; **diagnosis** ['-'nəusɪs], pl **-ses** ['-'nəusiːz] n diagnóstico.
diagonal [daɪ'ægənl] a diagonal // n diagonal f.
diagram ['daɪəgræm] n diagrama m, esquema m.
dial ['daɪəl] n esfera, cuadrante m // vt (number) marcar; ~**ling tone** n tono de marcar.
dialect ['daɪəlɛkt] n dialecto.
dialogue ['daɪəlɔg] n diálogo.
diameter [daɪ'æmɪtə*] n diámetro.

diamond ['daɪəmənd] n diamante m; ~**s** npl (CARDS) oros mpl.
diaper ['daɪəpə*] n (US) pañal m.
diaphragm ['daɪəfræm] n diafragma m.
diarrhoea, diarrhea (US) [daɪə'riːə] n diarrea.
diary ['daɪərɪ] n (daily account) diario; (book) agenda m.
dice [daɪs] n, pl inv dados mpl // vt (CULIN) cortar en cuadritos.
dictate [dɪk'teɪt] vt dictar; ~**s** ['dɪkteɪts] npl dictados mpl; **dictation** ['-'teɪʃən] n dictado.
dictator [dɪk'teɪtə*] n dictador m; ~**ship** n dictadura.
diction ['dɪkʃən] n dicción f.
dictionary ['dɪkʃənrɪ] n diccionario.
did [dɪd] pt of **do.**
die [daɪ] vi morir; **to ~ away** vi (sound, light) extinguirse lentamente; **to ~ down** vi (gen) apagarse; (wind) amainar; **to ~ out** vi desaparecer, extinguirse.
diesel ['diːzəl]: ~ **engine** n motor m Diesel; ~ **(oil)** n gas-oil m.
diet ['daɪət] n dieta; (restricted food) régimen m // vi (also: **be on a ~**) estar a dieta, hacer régimen.
differ ['dɪfə*] vi (be different) ser distinto de, diferenciarse de; (disagree) discrepar; ~**ence** n diferencia; (quarrel) desacuerdo; ~**ent** a diferente, distinto; ~**entiate** ['-'rɛnʃɪeɪt] vt distinguir // vi diferenciarse; **to ~entiate between** distinguir entre; ~**ently** ad de otro modo, en forma distinta.
difficult ['dɪfɪkəlt] a difícil; ~**y** n dificultad f.
diffidence ['dɪfɪdəns] n timidez f; **diffident** ['-ənt] a tímido.
diffuse [dɪ'fjuːs] a difuso // vt [dɪ'fjuːz] difundir.
dig [dɪg], pt, pp **dug** vt (hole) cavar; (garden) cultivar; (coal) extraer; (nails etc) hincar // n (prod) empujón m; (archaeological) excavación f; (remark) indirecta; **to ~ in** vi atrincherarse; **to ~ into** vt (savings) consumir; **to ~ out** vt (hole) excavar; (fig) sacar; **to ~ up** vt desenterrar; (plant) desarraigar.
digest [daɪ'dʒɛst] vt (food) digerir; (facts) asimilar // n ['daɪdʒɛst] resumen m; ~**ion** [dɪ'dʒɛstʃən] n digestión f.
digital ['dɪdʒɪtəl] a digital.
dignified ['dɪgnɪfaɪd] a grave, solemne; (action) decoroso.
dignity ['dɪgnɪtɪ] n dignidad f.
digress [daɪ'grɛs] vi: **to ~ from** apartarse de; ~**ion** [daɪ'grɛʃən] n digresión f.
digs [dɪgz] npl (Brit: col) pensión f, alojamiento.
dilapidated [dɪ'læpɪdeɪtɪd] a desmoronado, ruinoso.
dilate [daɪ'leɪt] vt dilatar // vi dilatarse.
dilemma [daɪ'lɛmə] n dilema m.
diligent ['dɪlɪdʒənt] a diligente.
dilute [daɪ'luːt] vt diluir // a diluido.

dim [dɪm] a (*light*) débil; (*sight*) turbio; (*outline*) indistinto; (*stupid*) lerdo; (*room*) oscuro // vt (*light*) bajar; (AUT) poner a media luz.

dime [daɪm] n (US) moneda de diez centavos.

dimension [dɪ'mɛnʃən] n dimensión f.

diminish [dɪ'mɪnɪʃ] vi disminuirse.

diminutive [dɪ'mɪnjutɪv] a diminuto // n (LING) diminutivo.

dimly ['dɪmlɪ] ad débilmente; (*not clearly*) indistintamente.

dimple ['dɪmpl] n hoyuelo.

din [dɪn] n estruendo, estrépito.

dine [daɪn] vi cenar; **diner** n (*person*) comensal m/f; (RAIL) = **dining car.**

dinghy ['dɪŋgɪ] n bote m; **rubber ~** lancha (neumática).

dingy ['dɪndʒɪ] a (*room*) sombrío; (*dirty*) sucio; (*dull*) deslucido.

dining ['daɪnɪŋ]: **~ car** n coche-comedor m; **~ room** n comedor m.

dinner ['dɪnə*] n (*evening meal*) cena; (*lunch*) comida; (*public*) cena, banquete m; **~ jacket** n smoking m; **~ party** n cena; **~ time** n hora de cenar o comer.

diocese ['daɪəsɪs] n diócesis f.

dip [dɪp] n (*slope*) pendiente m; (*in sea*) baño // vt (*in water*) mojar; (*ladle etc*) meter; (AUT: *lights*) poner a media luz // vi inclinarse hacia abajo.

diphtheria [dɪf'θɪərɪə] n difteria.

diploma [dɪ'pləʊmə] n diploma m.

diplomacy [dɪ'pləʊməsɪ] n diplomacia; **diplomat** ['dɪpləmæt] n diplomático; **diplomatic** [dɪplə'mætɪk] a diplomático.

dipstick ['dɪpstɪk] n (AUT) varilla graduada, indicador m de nivel (del aceite).

dire [daɪə*] a calamitoso.

direct [daɪ'rɛkt] a (*gen*) directo // vt dirigir; **can you ~ me to...?** ¿puede indicarme dónde está...?

direction [dɪ'rɛkʃən] n dirección f; **~s** npl (*advice*) órdenes fpl, instrucciones fpl; **~s for use** modo de empleo.

directly [dɪ'rɛktlɪ] ad (*in straight line*) directamente; (*at once*) en seguida.

director [dɪ'rɛktə*] n director m; **managing ~** director gerente.

directory [dɪ'rɛktərɪ] n (TEL) guía (telefónica).

dirt [dɜːt] n suciedad f; **~-cheap** a tirado, muy barato; **~y** a sucio; (*joke*) verde // vt ensuciar; (*stain*) manchar; **~y trick** n juego sucio.

disability [dɪsə'bɪlɪtɪ] n incapacidad f; **disabled** [dɪs'eɪbld] a disminuido, minusválido.

disadvantage [dɪsəd'vɑːntɪdʒ] n desventaja, inconveniente m.

disagree [dɪsə'griː] vi (*differ*) discrepar; (*be against, think otherwise*): **to ~ (with)** no estar de acuerdo (con); **~able** a desagradable; **~ment** n (*gen*) desacuerdo; (*quarrel*) riña.

disallow ['dɪsə'laʊ] vt (*goal*) anular.

disappear [dɪsə'pɪə*] vi desaparecer; **~ance** n desaparición f.

disappoint [dɪsə'pɔɪnt] vt decepcionar; (*hopes*) defraudar; **~ing** a decepcionante; **~ment** n decepción f.

disapproval [dɪsə'pruːvəl] n desaprobación f.

disapprove [dɪsə'pruːv] vi: **to ~ of** desaprobar.

disarm [dɪs'ɑːm] vt desarmar; **~ament** n desarme m; **~ing** a encantador(a).

disaster [dɪ'zɑːstə*] n desastre m; **disastrous** a desastroso.

disband [dɪs'bænd] vt disolver // vi desbandarse.

disbelief [dɪsbə'liːf] n incredulidad f.

disc [dɪsk] n disco.

discard [dɪs'kɑːd] vt (*old things*) tirar; (*fig*) descartar.

discern [dɪ'sɜːn] vt percibir, discernir; **~ing** a perspicaz.

discharge [dɪs'tʃɑːdʒ] vt (*duties*) cumplir, desempeñar; (*ship etc*) descargar; (*patient*) dar de alta; (*employee*) despedir; (*soldier*) licenciar; (*defendant*) poner en libertad // n ['dɪstʃɑːdʒ] (ELEC) descarga; (*dismissal*) despedida; (*of duty*) desempeño; (*of debt*) pago, descargo.

disciple [dɪ'saɪpl] n discípulo.

discipline ['dɪsɪplɪn] n disciplina // vt disciplinar.

disclaim [dɪs'kleɪm] vt negar.

disclose [dɪs'kləʊz] vt revelar; **disclosure** [-'kləʊʒə*] n revelación f.

disco ['dɪskəʊ] n abbr of **discothèque.**

discoloured [dɪs'kʌləd] a descolorado.

discomfort [dɪs'kʌmfət] n incomodidad f; (*unease*) inquietud f; (*physical*) malestar m.

disconcert [dɪskən'sɜːt] vt desconcertar.

disconnect [dɪskə'nɛkt] vt (*gen*) separar; (ELEC etc) desconectar.

discontent [dɪskən'tɛnt] n descontento; **~ed** a descontento.

discontinue [dɪskən'tɪnjuː] vt interrumpir; (*payments*) suspender.

discord ['dɪskɔːd] n discordia; (MUS) disonancia; **~ant** [dɪs'kɔːdənt] a disonante.

discothèque ['dɪskəʊtɛk] n discoteca.

discount ['dɪskaʊnt] n descuento // vt [dɪs-'kaʊnt] descontar.

discourage [dɪs'kʌrɪdʒ] vt desalentar; (*oppose*) oponerse a; **discouraging** a desalentador(a).

discourteous [dɪs'kɔːtɪəs] a descortés.

discover [dɪs'kʌvə*] vt descubrir; **~y** n descubrimiento.

discredit [dɪs'krɛdɪt] vt desacreditar.

discreet [dɪ'skriːt] a (*tactful*) discreto; (*careful*) circunspecto, prudente; **~ly** ad discretamente.

discrepancy [dɪ'skrɛpənsɪ] n (*difference*) diferencia; (*disagreement*) discrepancia.

discretion [dɪ'skrɛʃən] n (*tact*) discreción f; (*care*) prudencia, circunspección f.

discriminate [dɪ'skrɪmɪneɪt] *vi*: to ~ between distinguir entre; to ~ against discriminar contra; **discriminating** *a* perspicaz; **discrimination** [-'neɪʃən] *n* (*discernment*) perspicacia; (*bias*) discriminación *f*.

discuss [dɪ'skʌs] *vt* (*gen*) discutir; (*a theme*) tratar; ~**ion** [dɪ'skʌʃən] *n* discusión *f*.

disdain [dɪs'deɪn] *n* desdén *m* // *vt* desdeñar.

disease [dɪ'ziːz] *n* enfermedad *f*.

disembark [dɪsɪm'baːk] *vt*, *vi* desembarcar.

disengage [dɪsɪn'geɪdʒ] *vt* soltar; (*clutch*) desembragar.

disentangle [dɪsɪn'tæŋgl] *vt* desenredar.

disfigure [dɪs'fɪgə*] *vt* desfigurar.

disgrace [dɪs'greɪs] *n* ignominia; (*downfall*) caída; (*shame*) vergüenza, escándalo // *vt* deshonrar; ~**ful** *a* vergonzoso; (*behaviour*) escandaloso.

disgruntled [dɪs'grʌntld] *a* disgustado, malhumorado.

disguise [dɪs'gaɪz] *n* disfraz *m* // *vt* disfrazar; **in** ~ disfrazado.

disgust [dɪs'gʌst] *n* repugnancia // *vt* repugnar, dar asco a; ~**ing** *a* repugnante, asqueroso.

dish [dɪʃ] *n* (*gen*) plato; **to do** *or* **wash the** ~**es** fregar los platos; **to** ~ **up** *vt* servir; **to** ~ **out** *vt* repartir; ~**cloth** *n* paño de cocina, bayeta.

dishearten [dɪs'haːtn] *vt* desalentar.

dishevelled [dɪ'ʃevəld] *a* despeinado, desmelenado.

dishonest [dɪs'ɒnɪst] *a* (*person*) poco honrado, tramposo; (*means*) fraudulento; ~**y** *n* falta de honradez.

dishonour [dɪs'ɒnə*] *n* deshonra; ~**able** *a* deshonroso.

dishwasher ['dɪʃwɒʃə*] *n* lavaplatos *m inv*; (*person*) friegaplatos *m/f inv*.

disillusion [dɪsɪ'luːʒən] *vt* desilusionar.

disinfect [dɪsɪn'fɛkt] *vt* desinfectar; ~**ant** *n* desinfectante *m*.

disintegrate [dɪs'ɪntɪgreɪt] *vi* disgregarse, desintegrarse.

disinterested [dɪs'ɪntrəstɪd] *a* desinteresado.

disjointed [dɪs'dʒɔɪntɪd] *a* inconexo.

disk [dɪsk] *n* = **disc.**

dislike [dɪs'laɪk] *n* antipatía, aversión *f* // *vt* tener antipatía a.

dislocate ['dɪsləkeɪt] *vt* dislocar.

dislodge [dɪs'lɒdʒ] *vt* sacar; (*enemy*) desalojar.

disloyal [dɪs'lɔɪəl] *a* desleal.

dismal ['dɪzml] *a* (*dark*) sombrío; (*depressing*) triste; (*depressed*) abatido; (*very bad*) fatal.

dismantle [dɪs'mæntl] *vt* desmontar, desarmar.

dismay [dɪs'meɪ] *n* consternación *f* // *vt* consternar.

dismiss [dɪs'mɪs] *vt* (*worker*) despedir;

(*official*) destituir; (*idea*, *LAW*) rechazar; (*possibility*) descartar // *vi* (*MIL*) romper filas; ~**al** *n* despedida; destitución *f*.

dismount [dɪs'maunt] *vi* apearse.

disobedience [dɪsə'biːdɪəns] *n* desobediencia; **disobedient** [-ənt] *a* desobediente.

disobey [dɪsə'beɪ] *vt* desobedecer.

disorder [dɪs'ɔːdə*] *n* desorden *m*; (*rioting*) disturbio; (*MED*) trastorno; (*disease*) enfermedad *f*; ~**ly** *a* (*untidy*) desordenado; (*meeting*) alborotado; (*conduct*) escandaloso.

disorganized [dɪs'ɔːgənaɪzd] *a* desorganizado.

disorientated [dɪs'ɔːrɪenteɪtəd] *a* desorientado.

disown [dɪs'əun] *vt* desconocer.

disparaging [dɪs'pærɪdʒɪŋ] *a* despreciativo.

disparity [dɪs'pærɪtɪ] *n* disparidad *f*.

dispatch [dɪs'pætʃ] *vt* enviar; (*kill*) despachar // *n* (*sending*) envío; (*speed*) prontitud *f*; (*PRESS*) informe *m*; (*MIL*) parte *m*.

dispel [dɪs'pɛl] *vt* disipar, dispersar.

dispensary [dɪs'pɛnsərɪ] *n* dispensario, farmacia.

dispense [dɪs'pɛns] *vt* dispensar, repartir; **to** ~ **with** *vt fus* prescindir de; **dispenser** *n* (*container*) distribuidor *m* automático; **dispensing chemist** *n* farmacéutico.

dispersal [dɪs'pəːsl] *n* dispersión *f*; **disperse** [-'pəːs] *vt* dispersar // *vi* dispersarse.

displace [dɪs'pleɪs] *vt* (*shift*) sacar de su sitio; ~**d person** *n* (*POL*) desplazado/a; ~**ment** *n* cambio de sitio.

display [dɪs'pleɪ] *n* (*exhibition*) exposición *f*; (*MIL*) alarde *m*; (*of feeling*) manifestación *f*; (*pej*) aparato, pompa // *vt* exponer; manifestar; (*ostentatiously*) lucir.

displease [dɪs'pliːz] *vt* (*offend*) ofender; (*annoy*) enojar, enfadar; (*be unpleasant to*) desagradar; ~**d with** disgustado con; **displeasure** [-'plɛʒə*] *n* disgusto.

disposable [dɪs'pəuzəbl] *a* para (usar y) tirar.

disposal [dɪs'pəuzl] *n* (*sale*) venta; (*of house*) traspaso; (*arrangement*) colocación *f*; (*of rubbish*) destrucción *f*; **at one's** ~ a disposición de uno.

dispose [dɪs'pəuz] *vt*: **to** ~ **of** (*time, money*) disponer de; (*unwanted goods*) deshacerse de; (*throw away*) tirar; ~**d** *a*: ~**d to do** dispuesto a hacer; **disposition** [-'zɪʃən] *n* disposición *f*.

disproportionate [dɪsprə'pɔːʃənət] *a* desproporcionado.

disprove [dɪs'pruːv] *vt* refutar.

dispute [dɪs'pjuːt] *n* disputa; (*verbal*) discusión *f*; (*also*: **industrial** ~) conflicto (laboral) // *vt* (*argue*) disputar; (*question*) cuestionar.

disqualification [dɪskwɒlɪfɪ'keɪʃən] *n*

inhabilitación f; (SPORT, from driving) descalificación f.

disqualify [dɪs'kwɔlɪfaɪ] vt (SPORT) descalificar; **to ~ sb for sth/from doing sth** inhabilitar a alguien para algo/hacer algo.

disregard [dɪsrɪ'gɑːd] vt desatender; (ignore) no hacer caso de.

disrepair [dɪsrɪ'pɛə*] n: **to fall into ~** desmoronarse.

disreputable [dɪs'rɛpjutəbl] a (person) de mala fama; (behaviour) vergonzoso.

disrespectful [dɪsrɪ'spɛktful] a irrespetuoso.

disrupt [dɪs'rʌpt] vt (plans) desbaratar; (conversation) interrumpir; **~ion** [-'rʌpʃən] n trastorno; desbaratamiento; interrupción f.

dissatisfaction [dɪssætɪs'fækʃən] n disgusto, descontento; **dissatisfied** [-'sætɪsfaɪd] a insatisfecho.

dissect [dɪ'sɛkt] vt disecar.

dissent [dɪ'sɛnt] n disensión f.

disservice [dɪs'sɔːvɪs] n: **to do sb a ~** perjudicar a alguien.

dissident ['dɪsɪdnt] a, n disidente m/f.

dissipate ['dɪsɪpeɪt] vt disipar; (waste) desperdiciar.

dissociate [dɪ'səuʃɪeɪt] vt disociar.

dissolute ['dɪsəluːt] a disoluto.

dissolve [dɪ'zɔlv] vt disolver // vi disolverse.

dissuade [dɪ'sweɪd] vt: **to ~ sb (from)** disuadir a alguien (de).

distance ['dɪstns] n distancia; **in the ~** a lo lejos.

distant ['dɪstnt] a (manner) reservado, frío.

distaste [dɪs'teɪst] n repugnancia; **~ful** a repugnante, desagradable.

distil [dɪs'tɪl] vt destilar; **~lery** n destilería.

distinct [dɪs'tɪŋkt] a (different) distinto; (clear) claro; (unmistakeable) inequívoco; **as ~ from** a diferencia de; **~ion** [dɪs'tɪŋkʃən] n distinción f; (in exam) sobresaliente m; **~ive** a distintivo; **~ly** ad claramente.

distinguish [dɪs'tɪŋgwɪʃ] vt distinguir; **~ed** a (eminent) distinguido; **~ing** a (feature) distintivo.

distort [dɪs'tɔːt] vt torcer, retorcer; **~ion** [dɪs'tɔːʃən] n deformación f; (of sound) distorsión f.

distract [dɪs'trækt] vt distraer; (attention) apartar; (bewilder) aturdir; **~ed** a distraído; **~ion** [dɪs'trækʃən] n distracción f; (confusion) aturdimiento; (amusement) diversión f.

distraught [dɪs'trɔːt] a turbado, enloquecido.

distress [dɪs'trɛs] n (anguish) angustia; (misfortune) desgracia; (want) miseria; (pain) dolor m; (danger) peligro // vt (cause anguish) apenar, afligir; (pain) doler; **~ing** a doloroso; **~ signal** n señal f de socorro.

distribute [dɪs'trɪbjuːt] vt (gen) distribuir; (share out) repartir; **distribution** [-'bjuːʃən] n distribución f; **distributor** n (AUT) distribuidor m; (COMM) distribuidora.

district ['dɪstrɪkt] n (of country) zona, región f; (of town) barrio; (ADMIN) distrito; **~ attorney** n (US) fiscal m/f; **~ nurse** n (Brit) enfermera que asiste a domicilio.

distrust [dɪs'trʌst] n desconfianza // vt desconfiar de.

disturb [dɪs'tɔːb] vt (gen) perturbar; (bother) molestar; (interrupt) interrumpir; (upset) trastornar; (disorganize) desordenar; **~ance** n (gen) perturbación f; (political etc) disturbio; (violence) alboroto; (of mind) trastorno; **~ing** a inquietante, perturbador(a).

disuse [dɪs'juːs] n: **to fall into ~** caer en desuso.

disused [dɪs'juːzd] a abandonado.

ditch [dɪtʃ] n zanja; (irrigation ~) acequia // vt (col) deshacerse de.

dither ['dɪðə*] vi vacilar.

ditto ['dɪtəu] ad ídem, lo mismo.

divan [dɪ'væn] n diván m.

dive [daɪv] n (from board) salto; (underwater) buceo; (of submarine) sumersión f; (AVIAT) picada // vi saltar; bucear; sumergirse; picar; **diver** n (SPORT) saltador/a m/f; (underwater) buzo.

diverge [daɪ'vɔːdʒ] vi divergir.

diverse [daɪ'vɔːs] a diversos(as), varios(as).

diversify [daɪ'vɔːsɪfaɪ] vt diversificar.

diversion [daɪ'vɔːʃən] n (AUT) desviación f; (distraction, MIL) diversión f.

diversity [daɪ'vɔːsɪtɪ] n diversidad f.

divert [daɪ'vɔːt] vt (turn aside) desviar; (amuse) divertir.

divest [daɪ'vɛst] vt: **to ~ sb of sth** despojar a alguien de algo.

divide [dɪ'vaɪd] vt dividir; (separate) separar // vi dividirse; (road) bifurcarse.

dividend ['dɪvɪdɛnd] n dividendo; (fig) beneficio.

divine [dɪ'vaɪn] a divino.

diving ['daɪvɪŋ] n (SPORT) salto; (underwater) buceo; **~ board** n trampolín m; **~ suit** n escafandra.

divinity [dɪ'vɪnɪtɪ] n divinidad f; (SCOL) teología.

division [dɪ'vɪʒən] n división f; (sharing out) repartimiento; (disagreement) discordia; (POL) votación f.

divorce [dɪ'vɔːs] n divorcio // vt divorciarse de; **~d** a divorciado; **divorcee** [-'siː] n divorciado/a.

divulge [daɪ'vʌldʒ] vt divulgar, revelar.

D.I.Y. a, n abbr of **do-it-yourself.**

dizziness ['dɪzɪnɪs] n vértigo.

dizzy ['dɪzɪ] a (person) mareado; (height) vertiginoso; **to feel ~** marearse, estar mareado.

DJ n abbr of **disc jockey.**

do [duː] pt **did**, pp **done** vt, vi (gen) hacer; (speed) ir a; (THEATRE) representar // n (col) fiesta; **he didn't laugh** no se rió; **she swims better than I** ~ nada mejor que yo; **he laughed, didn't he?** se rió ¿no?; **that will** ~! ¡basta!; **to make** ~ **with** contentarse con; ~ **you agree?** ¿está Usted de acuerdo?; ' **to** ~ **one's hair** (comb) peinarse; (style) arreglarse el pelo; **will it** ~? ¿sirve?, ¿conviene?; **to** ~ **well** prosperar, tener éxito; **to** ~ **without sth** prescindir de algo; **to** ~ **away with** vt fus (kill) exterminar; (suppress) suprimir; **to** ~ **up** vt (laces) liar, atar; (room) renovar.

docile ['dəusaıl] a dócil.

dock [dɔk] n (NAUT) muelle m; (LAW) banquillo (de los acusados); ~**s** npl muelles mpl, puerto // vi (arrive) llegar; (enter ~) atracar al muelle; (pay etc) rebajar; ~**er** n trabajador m portuario, estibador m; ~ **yard** n astillero.

doctor ['dɔktə*] n médico; (Ph.D. etc) doctor/a m/f // vt (fig) arreglar, falsificar; (drink etc) adulterar.

doctrine ['dɔktrın] n doctrina.

document ['dɔkjumənt] n documento; ~**ary** [-'mɛntəri] a documental // n documental m; ~**ation** [-'teıʃən] n documentación f.

dodge [dɔdʒ] n (of body) regate m; (fig) truco // vt (gen) evadir; (blow) esquivar.

dodgems ['dɔdʒəmz] npl coches mpl de choque.

dog [dɔg] n perro // vt seguir los pasos de; ~ **biscuits** npl galletas fpl de perro; ~**collar** n collar m de perro; (fig) cuello de cura.

dogged ['dɔgıd] a tenaz, obstinado.

dogma ['dɔgmə] n dogma m; ~**tic** [-'mætık] a dogmático.

doings ['duıŋz] npl (events) sucesos mpl; (acts) hechos mpl.

do-it-yourself [du:ıtjɔ:'sɛlf] n bricolaje m.

doldrums ['dɔldrəmz] npl: **to be in the** ~ (person) estar abatido; (business) estar encalmado.

dole [dəul] n (Brit) (payment) subsidio de paro; **on the** ~ parado; **to** ~ **out** vt repartir.

doleful ['dəulful] a triste, lúgubre.

doll [dɔl] n muñeca; **to** ~ **o.s. up** ataviarse.

dollar ['dɔlə*] n dólar m.

dolphin ['dɔlfın] n delfín m.

domain [də'meın] n campo, competencia; (empire) dominio.

dome [dəum] n (ARCH) cúpula; (shape) bóveda.

domestic [də'mɛstık] a (gen) doméstico; (national) nacional; (home-loving) hogareño; (internal: trade) interior; (: strife) interno; ~**ated** a domesticado; (home-loving) casero, hogareño.

dominant ['dɔmınənt] a dominante.

dominate ['dɔmıneıt] vt dominar; **domination** [-'neıʃən] n dominación f.

domineering [dɔmı'nıərıŋ] a dominante.

dominion [də'mınıən] n dominio.

domino ['dɔmınəu], pl ~**es** n ficha de dominó; ~**es** n (game) dominó.

donate [də'neıt] vt donar; **donation** [də'neıʃən] n donativo.

done [dʌn] pp of **do**.

donkey ['dɔŋkı] n burro.

donor ['dəunə*] n donante m/f.

don't [dəunt] = **do not**.

doom [du:m] n (fate) suerte f; (death) muerte f // vt: **to be** ~**ed to failure** ser condenado al fracaso.

door [dɔ:*] n puerta; (entry) entrada; **next** ~ en la casa de al lado; ~**bell** n timbre m; ~ **handle** n tirador m; (of car) manija; ~ **knocker** n aldaba; ~**man** n (in hotel) portero; ~**mat** n felpudo, estera; ~**step** n peldaño.

dope [dəup] n (col: person) imbécil m/f // vt (horse etc) drogar.

dopey ['dəupı] a (dizzy) mareado.

dormant ['dɔ:mənt] a inactivo; (latent) latente.

dormitory ['dɔ:mıtrı] n dormitorio.

dormouse ['dɔ:maus], pl -**mice** [-maıs] n lirón m.

dosage ['dəusıdʒ] n dósis f inv.

dose [dəus] n dósis f inv // vt: **to** ~ **o.s.** medicinarse.

doss house ['dɔss-] n pensión f de mala muerte.

dot [dɔt] n punto; ~**ted with** salpicado de; **on the** ~ en punto.

dote [dəut]: **to** ~ **on** vt fus adorar, idolatrar.

double ['dʌbl] a doble // ad (twice): **to cost** ~ costar el doble // n (gen) doble m // vt doblar; (efforts) redoblar // vi doblarse; **at the** ~ corriendo; ~**s** n (TENNIS) juego de dobles; ~ **bass** n contrabajo; ~ **bed** n cama matrimonial; ~**bend** n doble curva; ~**breasted** a cruzado; ~**cross** vt (trick) engañar; (betray) traicionar; ~**decker** n autobús m de dos pisos; ~ **room** n cuarto para dos; **doubly** ad doblemente.

doubt [daut] n duda // vt dudar; (suspect) dudar de; **to** ~ **that** dudar que; **there is no** ~ **that** no cabe duda de que; ~**ful** a dudoso; (person) sospechoso; ~**less** ad sin duda.

dough [dəu] n masa, pasta; ~**nut** n buñuelo.

dove [dʌv] n paloma; ~**tail** vi (fig) encajar.

dowdy ['daudı] a desaliñado; (inelegant) poco elegante.

down [daun] n (fluff) pelusa; (feathers) plumón m, flojel m // ad (~ wards) abajo, hacia abajo; (on the ground) por/en tierra // prep abajo // vt (col: drink) beberse; (: food) devorar; **the D**~**s** zona de colinas del sur de Inglaterra; ~ **with X!** ¡abajo X!; ~**-at-heel** a venido a menos; (appearance) desaliñado; ~**cast** a abatido; ~**fall** n caída, ruina; ~**hearted** a desanimado; ~**hill** ad: **to go** ~**hill** ir cuesta abajo; ~ **payment** n enganche m, pago al contado; ~**pour** n aguacero; ~**right** a (clear) manifiesto; (out-and-out) terminante, definitivo; ~**stairs** ad (below) (en la casa) de abajo; (~wards) escaleras abajo; ~**stream** ad aguas o río abajo; ~**to-earth** a práctico; ~**town** ad en el centro de la ciudad; ~**ward** a, ad, ~**wards** ad hacia abajo.

dowry ['dauri] n dote f.

doz. abbr of **dozen.**

doze [dəuz] vi dormitar; **to** ~ **off** vi quedarse medio dormido.

dozen ['dʌzn] n docena.

Dr. abbr of **doctor; drive.**

drab [dræb] a gris, monótono.

draft [drɑ:ft] n (first copy) borrador m; (COMM) giro; (US: call-up) quinta f // vt (plan) redactar; (send) mandar; (conscript) quintar; (write roughly) hacer un borrador de; see also **draught.**

drag [dræg] vt arrastrar; (river) dragar, rastrear // vi arrastrarse por el suelo // n (col) lata; **to** ~ **on** vi ser interminable.

dragonfly ['drægənflai] n libélula.

drain [drein] n desaguadero; (in street) sumidero; (source of loss) desagüe m; (loss) pérdida; (on resources) sumidero // vt (land, marshes) desaguar; (MED) drenar; (reservoir) desecar; (fig) agotar // vi escurrirse; ~**age** n (act) desagüe m; (MED, AGR) drenaje m; (sewage) alcantarillado; ~**ing board**, ~**board** (US) n escurridera, escurridor m; ~**pipe** n tubo de desagüe.

dram [dræm] n (drink) trago.

drama ['drɑ:mə] n (art) teatro; (play) drama m; ~**tic** [drə'mætik] a dramático; ~**tist** ['dræmətist] n dramaturgo.

drank [dræŋk] pt of **drink.**

drape [dreip] vt cubrir; ~**s** npl (US) cortinas fpl; **draper** n pañero.

drastic ['dræstik] a (measure) severo; (change) radical; (forceful) enérgico.

draught [drɑ:ft] n (of air) corriente f; (drink) trago; (NAUT) calado; ~**s** n juego de damas; **on** ~ (beer) de barril; ~**board** n tablero de damas.

draughtsman ['drɑ:ftsmən] n proyectista m, delineante m.

draw [drɔ:], pt **drew**, pp **drawn** vt (pull) tirar; (take out) sacar; (attract) atraer; (picture) dibujar; (money) retirar // vi (SPORT) empatar // n (SPORT) empate m; (lottery) sorteo; (attraction) atracción f; **to** ~ **near** vi acercarse; **to** ~ **out** vi (lengthen) alargar; **to** ~ **up** vi (stop) pararse // vt (document) redactar; ~**back** n inconveniente m, desventaja; ~**bridge** n puente m levadizo.

drawer [drɔ:*] n cajón m.

drawing ['drɔ:iŋ] n dibujo; ~ **board** n tablero de (dibujante); ~ **pin** n chinche m; ~ **room** n salón m.

drawl [drɔ:l] n habla lenta y cansina.

drawn [drɔ:n] pp of **draw.**

dread [drɛd] n pavor m, terror m // vt

temer, tener miedo o pavor a; ~**ful** a espantoso.

dream [dri:m] n sueño // vt, vi, pt, pp **dreamed** or **dreamt** [drɛmt] soñar; ~**er** n soñador/a m/f; ~**y** a (distracted) soñador(a), distraído; (music) de sueño.

dreary ['driəri] a monótono, aburrido.

dredge [drɛdʒ] vt dragar; **dredger** n (ship) draga; (also: **sugar dredger**) espolvoreador m.

dregs [drɛgz] npl heces fpl.

drench [drɛntʃ] vt empapar; **to get** ~**ed** mojarse hasta los huesos.

dress [drɛs] n vestido; (clothing) ropa // vt vestir; (wound) vendar; (CULIN) aliñar // vi vestirse; **to** ~ **up** vi vestirse de etiqueta; (in fancy dress) disfrazarse; ~ **circle** n principal m; ~**er** n (furniture) aparador m; (: US) cómoda con espejo; ~**ing** n (MED) vendaje m; (CULIN) aliño; ~**ing gown** n bata; ~**ing room** n (THEATRE) camarín m; (SPORT) vestidor m; ~**ing table** n tocador m; ~**maker** n modista, costurera; ~**making** n costura; ~ **rehearsal** n ensayo general; ~ **shirt** n camisa de frac.

drew [dru:] pt of **draw.**

dribble ['dribl] vi gotear, caer gota a gota; (baby) babear // vt (ball) regatear.

dried [draid] a (gen) seco; (fruit) paso; (milk) en polvo.

drift [drift] n (of current etc) velocidad f; (of sand etc) montón m; (distance off course) deriva; (meaning) significado // vi (boat) ir a la deriva; (sand, snow) amontonarse; ~**wood** n madera de deriva.

drill [dril] n taladro; (bit) broca; (of dentist) fresa; (for mining etc) perforadora, barrena; (MIL) instrucción f // vt perforar, taladrar // vi (for oil) perforar.

drink [driŋk] n bebida // vt, vi, pt **drank**, pp **drunk** beber; **to have a** ~ tomar; ~**er** n bebedor/a m/f; ~**ing water** n agua potable.

drip [drip] n (act) goteo; (one ~) gota; (MED) gota a gota m // vi gotear, caer gota a gota; ~-**dry** a (shirt) de lava y pon; ~**ping** n pringue m; ~**ping wet** a calado.

drive [draiv] n paseo (en coche); (journey) viaje m; (also: ~**way**) entrada; (energy) energía, vigor m; (PSYCH) impulso; (SPORT) ataque m // (vb: pt **drove**, pp **driven** ['drivn]) vt (car) conducir; (urge) hacer trabajar; (by power) mover; (nail) clavar; (push) empujar; (TECH: motor) impulsar // vi (AUT. at controls) conducir; (: travel) pasearse en coche, viajar // ~ conducción f a la izquierda/derecha.

driver ['draivə*] n conductor m; (of taxi, bus) chofer m; ~**'s license** n (US) permiso de conducir.

driving ['draiviŋ] n el conducir, automovilismo; ~ **instructor** n instructor m de conducción; ~ **lesson** n clase f de conducción; ~ **licence** n (Brit) permiso de conducir; ~ **mirror** n retrovisor m; ~ **school** n autoescuela; ~ .**test** n examen m de conducción.

drizzle ['drɪzl] n llovizna // vi lloviznar.

drone [drəun] n zumbido; (*male bee*) zángano.

drool [dru:l] vi babear; **to** ~ **over sth** extasiarse ante algo.

droop [dru:p] vi colgar; (*fig*) decaer, desanimarse.

drop [drɔp] n (*of water*) gota; (*lessening*) baja; (*fall*) caída; (*of cliff*) pendiente m, declive m // vt (*allow to fall*) dejar caer; (*voice, eyes, price*) bajar; (*set down from car*) dejar; (*omit*) omitir // vi caer; (*price, temperature*) bajar; (*wind*) amainar; **to** ~ **off** vi (*sleep*) dormirse // vt (*passenger*) bajar; **to** ~ **out** vi (*withdraw*) retirarse; ~**out** n marginado; ~ **per** n cuentagotas m inv; ~**pings** npl excremento sg (de animal).

drought [draut] n sequía.

drove [drəuv] pt of **drive**.

drown [draun] vt ahogar // vi ahogarse.

drowsy ['drauzɪ] a soñoliento; **to be** ~ tener sueño.

drudgery ['drʌdʒərɪ] n trabajo monótono.

drug [drʌg] n medicamento; (*narcotic*) droga // vt drogar; ~ **addict** n drogadicto/a; ~**gist** n (*US*) farmacéutico; ~ **store** n (*US*) farmacia.

drum [drʌm] n tambor m; (*large*) bombo; (*for oil, petrol*) bidón m; ~**s** npl batería sg // vi tocar el tambor; (*with fingers*) tamborilear; ~**mer** n tambor m; ~**stick** n (*MUS*) palillo; (*of chicken*) muslo.

drunk [drʌŋk] pp of **drink** // a borracho // n (*also*: ~**ard**) borracho/a; ~**en** a borracho; ~**enness** n embriaguez f.

dry [draɪ] a seco; (*day*) sin lluvia; (*climate*) árido, seco // vt secar; (*tears*) enjugarse // vi secarse; **to** ~ **up** vi agotarse; (*in speech*) atascarse; ~**cleaner's** n tintorería; ~-**cleaning** n lavado en seco; ~**er** n lavadora; ~**ness** n sequedad f; ~ **rot** n putrefacción f fungoide.

dual ['djuəl] a doble; ~-**control** a de doble mando; ~ **nationality** n doble nacionalidad f; ~-**purpose** a de doble uso.

dubbed [dʌbd] a (*CINEMA*) doblado.

dubious ['dju:bɪəs] a dudoso; (*reputation, company*) sospechoso.

duchess ['dʌtʃɪs] n duquesa.

duck [dʌk] n pato // vi agacharse; ~**ling** n patito.

duct [dʌkt] n conducto, canal m.

dud [dʌd] n (*shell*) obús m que no estalla; (*object, tool*): **it's a** ~ es una filfa // a: ~ **cheque** cheque m sin fondos.

due [dju:] a (*proper*) debido; (*expected*) esperado; (*fitting*) conveniente, oportuno // n (*debt*) deuda; (*desert*) lo que merece uno // ad: ~ **north** derecho al norte; ~**s** npl (*for club, union*) cuota sg; (*in harbour*) derechos mpl; **in** ~ **course** a su debido tiempo; ~ **to** debido a.

duel ['djuəl] n duelo.

duet [dju:'et] n dúo.

dug [dʌg] pt, pp of **dig**.

duke [dju:k] n duque m.

dull [dʌl] a (*light*) apagado; (*slow*) torpe; (*boring*) pesado; (*sound, pain*) sordo; (*weather, day*) gris // vt (*pain, grief*) aliviar; (*mind, senses*) entorpecer.

duly ['dju:lɪ] ad debidamente; (*on time*) a su debido tiempo.

dumb [dʌm] a mudo; (*stupid*) estúpido; ~**founded** [dʌm'faundɪd] a pasmado.

dummy ['dʌmɪ] n (*tailor's model*) maniquí m; (*for baby*) chupete m // a falso, postizo.

dump [dʌmp] n (*heap*) montón m; (*place*) basurero, vaciadero; (*col*) casucha; (*MIL*) depósito // vt (*put down*) verter, vaciar; (*get rid of*) deshacerse de; (*goods*) inundar el mercado con; ~**ing** n (*ECON*) dumping m; (*of rubbish*): '**no** ~**ing**' 'prohibido verter basura'.

dumpling ['dʌmplɪŋ] n bola de masa hervida.

dunce [dʌns] n zopenco.

dune [dju:n] n duna.

dung [dʌŋ] n estiércol m.

dungarees [dʌŋgə'ri:z] npl mono sg.

dungeon ['dʌndʒən] n calabozo.

dupe [dju:p] n (*victim*) víctima // vt engañar.

duplicate ['dju:plɪkət] n duplicado // vt ['dju:plɪkeɪt] duplicar; (*on machine*) multicopiar; **in** ~ por duplicado; **duplicator** n multicopista m.

durable ['djuərəbl] a duradero.

duration [djuə'reɪʃən] n duración f.

duress [djuə'rɛs] n: **under** ~ por compulsión.

during ['djuərɪŋ] prep durante.

dusk [dʌsk] n crepúsculo, anochecer m.

dust [dʌst] n polvo // vt (*furniture*) desempolvorar; (*cake etc*): **to** ~ **with** espolvorear de; ~**bin** n (*Brit*) cubo de la basura; ~**er** n paño, trapo, bayeta; (*feather* ~) plumero; ~ **jacket** n sobrecubierta; ~**man** n (*Brit*) basurero; ~**y** a polvoriento.

Dutch [dʌtʃ] a holandés(esa) // n (*LING*) holandés m; ~**man/woman** n holandés/esa m/f.

duty ['dju:tɪ] n deber m; (*tax*) derechos mpl de aduana; **on** ~ de servicio; (*at night etc*) de guardia; **off** ~ libre (de servicio); ~-**free** a libre de derechos de aduana.

dwarf [dwɔ:f], pl **dwarves** [dwɔ:vz] n enano // vt empequeñecer.

dwell [dwel], pt, pp **dwelt** [dwelt] vi morar; **to** ~ **on** vt fus explayarse en; ~**ing** n vivienda.

dwindle ['dwɪndl] vi menguar, disminuir.

dye [daɪ] n tinte m // vt teñir.

dying ['daɪɪŋ] a moribundo, agonizante; (*moments*) final; (*words*) último.

dynamic [daɪ'næmɪk] a dinámico; ~**s** n, npl dinámica sg.

dynamite ['daɪnəmaɪt] n dinamita.

dynamo ['daɪnəməu] n dinamo f.
dynasty ['dɪnəstɪ] n dinastía.

E

each [i:tʃ] det cada inv // pron cada uno; ~ **other** el uno al otro; **they hate ~ other** se odian (entre ellos o mutuamente); **they have 2 books** ~ tiene 2 libros por persona.
eager ['i:gə*] a (gen) impaciente; (hopeful) ilusionado; (ambitious) ambicioso; **to be ~ to do sth** ansiar hacer algo, impacientarse por hacer algo; **to be ~ for** ansiar, anhelar.
eagle ['i:gl] n águila.
ear [ɪə*] n oreja; (MUS) oído; (of corn) espiga; ~**ache** n dolor m de oídos; ~**drum** n tímpano.
earl [ɔ:l] n conde m.
early ['ɔ:lɪ] ad (gen) temprano; (before time) con tiempo, con anticipación // a (gen) temprano; (reply) pronto; (first) primero; (work) juvenil; **have an ~ night** acuéstate temprano; **in the ~ or ~ in the spring/19th century** a principios de primavera/del siglo diez y nueve; **as ~ as possible** cuánto antes, lo más pronto posible.
earmark ['ɪəmɑ:k] vt reservar (for para), destinar (for a).
earn [ɔ:n] vt (gen) ganar; (salary) percibir; (interest) devengar; (praise) merecerse.
earnest ['ɔ:nɪst] a serio, formal; **in ~** ad en serio.
earnings ['ɔ:nɪŋz] npl (personal) sueldo, ingresos mpl; (company) ganancias fpl.
ear: ~**phones** npl auriculares mpl; ~**ring** n pendiente m, arete m; ~**shot** n: **within ~shot** al alcance del oído.
earth [ɔ:θ] n (gen) tierra; (ELEC) cable m de toma de tierra // vt (ELEC) conectar a tierra; ~**enware** n loza de barro; ~**quake** n terremoto; ~**y** a (fig: vulgar) grosero; (: sensual) sensual.
earwig ['ɪəwɪg] n tijereta.
ease [i:z] n (gen) facilidad f; (relief) alivio; (calm) tranquilidad f; (relaxed state) comodidad f // vt facilitar; aliviar; (loosen) soltar; (relieve: pressure) aflojar; (weight) aligerar; (help pass): **to ~ sth in/out** meter/sacar con cuidado; **at ~!** (MIL) ¡descanso!; **to ~ off** or **up** vi (gen) suavizarse; (at work) dejar de trabajar tanto; (wind) amainar; (rain) moderarse.
easel ['i:zl] n caballete m.
east [i:st] n este m, oriente m // a del este, oriental // ad al este, hacia el este; **the E~** el Oriente.
Easter ['i:stə*] n Pascua (de Resurrección).
easterly ['i:stəlɪ] a (to the east) al este; (from the east) del este.
eastern ['i:stən] a del este, oriental.
East Germany n Alemania Oriental.
eastward(s) ['i:stwədz)] ad hacia el este.

easy ['i:zɪ] a (gen) fácil; (simple) sencillo; (slow) lento, pausado; (comfortable) holgado, cómodo; (relaxed) natural, llano // ad: **to take it** or **things ~** (not worry) tomarlo con calma; (go slowly) ir despacio; (rest) descansar; ~ **chair** n sillón m; ~ **going** a acomodadizo.
eat [i:t] pt **ate**, pp **eaten** ['i:tn] vt (gen) comer; (supper) cenar; **to ~ into, to ~ away at** vt fus corroer; ~**able** a comestible.
eau de Cologne [əudəkə'ləun] n (agua de) Colonia.
eaves [i:vz] npl alero sg.
eavesdrop ['i:vzdrɔp] vi escuchar a escondidas (on sb a uno).
ebb [ɛb] n reflujo // vi bajar; (fig: also: ~ away) decaer; ~ **tide** n marea menguante.
ebony ['ɛbənɪ] n ébano.
eccentric [ɪk'sɛntrɪk] a, n excéntrico/a.
ecclesiastical [ɪkli:zɪ'æstɪkəl] a eclesiástico.
echo ['ɛkəu], pl ~**es** n eco m // vt (sound) repetir // vi resonar, hacer eco.
eclipse [ɪ'klɪps] n eclipse m // vt eclipsar.
ecology [ɪ'kɔlədʒɪ] n ecología.
economic [i:kə'nɔmɪk] a económico; (business etc) rentable; ~**al** a económico; ~**s** n (la) economía; **economist** [ɪ'kɔnəmɪst] n economista m/f.
economize [ɪ'kɔnəmaɪz] vi economizar, ahorrar.
economy [ɪ'kɔnəmɪ] n economía.
ecstasy ['ɛkstəsɪ] n éxtasis m; **ecstatic** [-'tætɪk] a extático.
ecumenical [i:kju'mɛnɪkl] a ecuménico.
eczema ['ɛksɪmə] n eczema m.
edge [ɛdʒ] n (of knife etc) filo; (of object) borde m; (of lake etc) orilla // vt (SEWING) ribetear; **on ~** (fig) = **edgy; to ~ away from** alejarse poco a poco; ~**ways** ad: **he couldn't get a word in** ~**ways** no pudo meter baza; **edging** n (SEWING) ribete m; (of path) borde m.
edgy ['ɛdʒɪ] a nervioso, inquieto.
edible ['ɛdɪbl] a comestible.
edict ['i:dɪkt] n edicto.
edifice ['ɛdɪfɪs] n edificio.
edit ['ɛdɪt] vt (be editor of) dirigir; (cut) cortar; ~**ion** [ɪ'dɪʃən] n (gen) edición f; (number printed) tirada; ~**or** n (of newspaper) director m; (of book) autor m de la edición; ~**orial** [-'tɔ:rɪəl] a editorial, de la dirección // n editorial m.
educate ['ɛdjukeɪt] vt (gen) educar; (instruct) instruir.
education [ɛdju'keɪʃən] n educación f; (schooling) enseñanza; (ESCOL) pedagogía; ~**al** a (policy etc) educacional; (teaching) docente; (instructive) educativo.
EEC n abbr of **European Economic Community** CEE (Comunidad Económica Europea).
eel [i:l] n anguila.
eerie ['ɪərɪ] a (strange) extraño; (mysterious) misterioso.

effect [ı'fɛkt] n efecto // vt efectuar, llevar a cabo; ~s npl efectos mpl; **to take ~** (drug) surtir efecto; **in ~** en realidad; ~**ive** a (gen) eficaz; (striking) impresionante; (real) efectivo; **to become ~ive** entrar en vigor; ~**iveness** n eficacia.

effeminate [ı'fɛmɪnɪt] a afeminado.

effervescent [ɛfə'vɛsnt] a efervescente.

efficiency [ı'fɪʃənsı] n (gen) eficiencia; (of machine) rendimiento.

efficient [ı'fɪʃənt] a eficiente.

effigy ['ɛfɪdʒı] n efigie f.

effort ['ɛfət] n esfuerzo; **to make an ~ to** esforzarse por; ~**less** a sin esfuerzo (alguno).

effrontery [ı'frʌntərı] n descaro.

effusive [ı'fjuːsɪv] a efusivo.

e.g. ad abbr of **exempli gratia** p. ej. (por ejemplo).

egg [ɛg] n huevo; **hard-boiled/poached/soft-boiled ~** huevo duro/escalfado/pasado por agua; **scrambled ~s** huevos revueltos; **to ~ on** vt incitar; ~**cup** n huevera; ~**shell** n cáscara de huevo.

ego ['iːgəʊ] n ego; ~**ism** n egoísmo; ~**ist** n egoísta m/f.

Egypt ['iːdʒɪpt] n Egipto; ~**ian** [ı'dʒɪpʃən] a, n egipcio/a.

eiderdown ['aɪdədaʊn] n edredón m.

eight [eɪt] num ocho; ~**een** num diez y ocho, dieciocho; ~**th** a, n octavo; ~**y** num ochenta.

Eire ['ɛərə] n Eire m.

either ['aɪðə*] det cualquier ... de los dos; (both, each) uno u otro; **on ~ side** en ambos lados // pron: ~ **(of them)** cualquiera (de los dos); **I don't like ~** no me gusta ni uno ni otro // ad tampoco; **no, I don't ~** no, yo tampoco // conj: ~ **yes or no** o sí o no.

eject [ı'dʒɛkt] vt echar; (tenant) desahuciar; ~**or seat** n asiento proyectable.

eke [iːk]: **to ~ out** vt (make last) escatimar; (add to) suplir las deficiencias de.

elaborate [ı'læbərıt] a complicado; (decorated) rebuscado // (vb: [ı'læbəreɪt]) vt elaborar // vi explicarse con muchos detalles.

elapse [ı'læps] vi transcurrir.

elastic [ı'læstık] a, n elástico; ~ **band** n gomita.

elated [ı'leɪtıd] a: **to be ~** regocijarse; **elation** [ı'leɪʃən] n regocijo.

elbow ['ɛlbəʊ] n codo.

elder ['ɛldə*] a mayor // n (tree) saúco; (person) mayor; (of tribe) anciano; ~**ly** a de edad, mayor // n: **the ~ly** la gente mayor.

eldest ['ɛldıst] a, n el/la mayor.

elect [ı'lɛkt] vt elegir; **to ~ to do** optar por hacer // a: **the president ~** el presidente electo; ~**ion** [ı'lɛkʃən] n elección f; ~**ioneering** [ılɛkʃə'nɪərıŋ] n campaña electoral; ~**or** n elector/a m/f;

~**oral** a electoral; ~**orate** n electorado.

electric [ı'lɛktrık] a eléctrico; ~**al** a eléctrico; ~ **blanket** n manta eléctrica; ~ **chair** n silla eléctrica; ~ **cooker** n cocina eléctrica; ~ **fire** n estufa eléctrica.

electrician [ılɛk'trıʃən] n electricista m/f.

electricity [ılɛk'trısıtı] n electricidad f.

electrify [ı'lɛktrıfaı] vt (RAIL) electrificar; (audience) electrizar.

electro... [ılɛktrəʊ] pref: ~**cute** [-kjuːt] vt electrocutar; **electrode** [ı'lɛktrəʊd] n electrodo; ~**magnetic** a electromagnético.

electron [ı'lɛktrɔn] n electrón m.

electronic [ılɛk'trɔnık] a electrónico; ~**s** n electrónica.

elegance ['ɛlıgəns] n elegancia; **elegant** [-gənt] a elegante.

element ['ɛlımənt] n (gen) elemento; **to brave the ~s** salir a la intemperie; ~**ary** [-'mɛntərı] a (gen) elemental; (primitive) rudimentario; (school, education) de primera enseñanza.

elephant ['ɛlıfənt] n elefante m.

elevate ['ɛlıveıt] vt (gen) elevar; (in rank) ascender.

elevation [ɛlı'veıʃən] n elevación f; (rank) ascenso; (height) altura.

elevator ['ɛlıveıtə*] n (US) ascensor m.

eleven [ı'lɛvn] num once; ~**ses** npl las once; ~**th** a undécimo.

elf [ɛlf], pl **elves** [ɛlvz] n duende m.

elicit [ı'lısıt] vt: **to ~ (from)** sacar (de).

eligible ['ɛlıdʒəbl] a elegible; **to be ~ for sth** llenar los requisitos para algo.

eliminate [ı'lımıneıt] vt eliminar; (strike out) suprimir; (suspect) descartar; **elimination** [-'neıʃən] n eliminación f; supresión f.

élite [eı'liːt] n élite f.

elm [ɛlm] n olmo.

elocution [ɛlə'kjuːʃən] n elocución f.

elongated ['iːlɔŋgeıtıd] a alargado, estirado.

elope [ı'ləʊp] vi fugarse con su amante; ~**ment** n fuga.

eloquence ['ɛləkwəns] n elocuencia; **eloquent** [-wənt] a elocuente.

else [ɛls] ad lo(s) demás; **something ~** otra cosa; **somewhere ~** en otra parte; **everywhere ~** en todas partes (menos aquí); **where ~?** ¿dónde más?, ¿en qué otra parte?; **there was little ~ to do** apenas quedaba otra cosa que hacer; **nobody ~** spoke no habló nadie más; ~**where** ad (be) en otra parte; (go) a otra parte.

elucidate [ı'luːsıdeıt] vt aclarar, elucidar.

elude [ı'luːd] vt (gen) eludir; (blow) esquivar; (pursuer) escaparse de, zafarse de.

elusive [ı'luːsıv] a esquivo; (answer) difícil de encontrar.

emaciated [ı'meısıeıtıd] a demacrado.

emanate ['ɛməneıt] vi emanar, proceder.

emancipate [ɪ'mænsɪpeɪt] vt emancipar; ~d a liberado; **emancipation** [-'peɪʃən] n emancipación f, liberación f.

embalm [ɪm'bɑːm] vt embalsamar.

embankment [ɪm'bæŋkmənt] n terraplén m; (riverside) dique m.

embargo [ɪm'bɑːgəʊ], pl ~es n prohibición f.

embark [ɪm'bɑːk] vi embarcarse // vt embarcar; **to** ~ **on** (fig) emprender, lanzarse a; ~ation [ɛmbɑː'keɪʃən] n (people) embarco; (goods) embarque m.

embarrass [ɪm'bærəs] vt desconcertar, azorar; (financially etc) poner en un aprieto; ~ing a desconcierto, azoramiento; (financial) apuros mpl.

embassy ['ɛmbəsɪ] n embajada.

embed [ɪm'bɛd] vt (gen) empotrar; (teeth etc) clavar.

embellish [ɪm'bɛlɪʃ] vt embellecer; (fig) adornar.

embers ['ɛmbəz] npl rescoldo sg, ascua sg.

embezzle [ɪm'bɛzl] vt desfalcar, malversar; ~ment n desfalco, malversación f.

embitter [ɪm'bɪtə*] vt amargar; (fig) envenenar; ~ed a resentido, amargado.

emblem ['ɛmbləm] n emblema m.

embody [ɪm'bɔdɪ] vt (features) encarnar; (ideas) expresar.

embossed [ɪm'bɔst] a realzado; ~ **with** con grabado en relieve.

embrace [ɪm'breɪs] vt abrazar, dar un abrazo a; (include) abarcar; (adopt: idea) adherirse a // vi abrazarse // n abrazo.

embroider [ɪm'brɔɪdə*] vt bordar; (fig: story) adornar, embellecer; ~y n bordado.

embryo ['ɛmbrɪəʊ] n (also fig) embrión m.

emerald ['ɛmərəld] n esmeralda.

emerge [ɪ'mɜːdʒ] vi (gen) salir, aparecer; (arise) surgir; **emergence** n salida, aparición f; surgimiento.

emergency [ɪ'mɜːdʒənsɪ] n (event) emergencia; (crisis) crisis f; (need) necesidad f urgente; **in an** ~ en caso de urgencia; **state of** ~ estado de emergencia; ~ **exit** n salida de emergencia; ~ **landing** n aterrizaje m forzoso; ~ **meeting** n reunión f extraordinaria.

emery ['ɛmərɪ] ~ **board** n lima de uñas; ~ **paper** n papel m de esmeril.

emetic [ɪ'mɛtɪk] n emético.

emigrant ['ɛmɪgrənt] n emigrante m/f.

emigrate ['ɛmɪgreɪt] vi emigrarse; **emigration** [-'greɪʃən] n emigración f.

eminence ['ɛmɪnəns] n eminencia; **eminent** [-ənt] a eminente.

emission [ɪ'mɪʃən] n emisión f.

emit [ɪ'mɪt] vt (gen) emitir; (smoke) arrojar; (smell) despedir; (sound) producir.

emotion [ɪ'məʊʃən] n emoción f; ~al a (person) sentimental; (scene) conmovedor(a), emocionante; ~ally ad con emoción.

emotive [ɪ'məʊtɪv] a emotivo.

emperor ['ɛmpərə*] n emperador m.

emphasis ['ɛmfəsɪs], pl ~ses [-siːz] n énfasis m inv.

emphasize ['ɛmfəsaɪz] vt (word, point) subrayar, recalcar; (feature) hacer resaltar.

emphatic [ɛm'fætɪk] a (strong) enérgico; (unambiguous, clear) enfático; ~ally ad con énfasis.

empire ['ɛmpaɪə*] n imperio.

empirical [ɛm'pɪrɪkl] a empírico.

employ [ɪm'plɔɪ] vt emplear; ~ee [-'iː] n empleado/a; ~er n patrón/ona m/f, empresario; ~ment n (gen) empleo; (work) trabajo; **full** ~ment pleno empleo; ~ment **agency** n agencia de colocaciones; ~ment **exchange** n bolsa de trabajo.

empower [ɪm'paʊə*] vt: **to** ~ **sb to do sth** autorizar a uno a hacer algo.

empress ['ɛmprɪs] n emperatriz f.

emptiness ['ɛmptɪnɪs] n (gen) vacío; (of life etc) vaciedad f.

empty ['ɛmptɪ] a vacío; (place) desierto; (house) desocupado; (threat) vano // n (bottle) envase m // vt vaciar; (place) dejar vacío // vi vaciarse; (house) quedar desocupado; (place) quedar desocupado; ~-handed a con las manos vacías.

emulate ['ɛmjʊleɪt] vt emular.

emulsion [ɪ'mʌlʃən] n emulsión f.

enable [ɪ'neɪbl] vt: **to** ~ **sb to do sth** (allow) permitir a uno hacer algo; (prepare) capacitar a uno para hacer algo.

enact [ɪn'ækt] vt (law) promulgar; (play) representar; (role) hacer.

enamel [ɪ'næməl] n esmalte m.

enamoured [ɪ'næməd] a: **to be** ~ **of** (person) estar enamorado de; (activity etc) tener gran afición a; (idea) aferrarse a.

encased [ɪn'keɪst] a: ~ **in** (enclosed) encerrado en; (covered) revestido de.

enchant [ɪn'tʃɑːnt] vt encantar; ~ing a encantador(a).

encircle [ɪn'sɜːkl] vt (gen) rodear; (waist) ceñir.

encl. abbr of **enclosed** adj. (adjunto).

enclose [ɪn'kləʊz] vt (land) cercar; (with letter etc) adjuntar; (in receptacle) encerrar; **please find** ~d le adjunto.

enclosure [ɪn'kləʊʒə*] n cercado, recinto; (comm) carta adjunta.

encore [ɔŋ'kɔː*] excl ¡otra!, ¡bis! // n bis m.

encounter [ɪn'kaʊntə*] n encuentro // vt encontrar, encontrarse con; (difficulty) tropezar con.

encourage [ɪn'kʌrɪdʒ] vt alentar, animar; (growth) estimular; ~ment n estímulo; (of industry) fomento.

encroach [ɪn'krəʊtʃ] vi: **to** ~ (up)on (gen) invadir; (time) ocupar.

encrusted [ɪn'krʌstəd] a: ~ **with** incrustado de.

encumber [ɪn'kʌmbə*] vt: **to be** ~ed **with** (carry) tener que cargar con; (debts) estar gravado de.

encyclop(a)edia [ɛnsaɪkləu'piːdɪə] *n* enciclopedia.

end [ɛnd] *n* (*gen, also aim*) fin *m*; (*of table*) extremo; (*of street*) final *m*; (*SPORT*) lado // *vt* terminar, acabar; (*also*: **bring to an ~, put an ~ to**) acabar con // *vi* terminar, acabar; **in the ~** al fin, por fin, finalmente; **on ~** (*object*) de punta, de cabeza; **to stand on ~** (*hair*) erizarse; **for hours on ~** horas seguidas; **to ~ up** *vi*: **to ~ up in** terminar en; (*place*) ir a parar en.

endanger [ɪn'deɪndʒə*] *vt* poner en peligro.

endear [ɪn'dɪə*] *vr*: **to ~ o.s. to** hacerse querer de; **~ing** *a* simpático, atractivo; **~ment** *n* cariño, palabra cariñosa.

endeavour [ɪn'dɛvə*] *n* esfuerzo; (*attempt*) tentativa; (*striving*) empeño // *vi*: **to ~ to do** esforzarse por hacer; (*try*) procurar hacer.

ending ['ɛndɪŋ] *n* fin *m*, conclusión *f*; (*of book*) desenlace *m*; (*LING*) terminación *f*.

endless ['ɛndlɪs] *a* interminable, inacabable.

endorse [ɪn'dɔːs] *vt* (*cheque*) endosar; (*approve*) aprobar; **~ment** *n* (*on driving licence*) nota de inhabilitación.

endow [ɪn'dau] *vt* (*provide with money*) dotar; (*: institution*) fundar; **to be ~ed with** estar dotado de.

endurance [ɪn'djuərəns] *n* resistencia; **endure** *vt* (*bear*) aguantar, soportar; (*resist*) resistir // *vi* (*last*) durar; (*resist*) resistir.

enemy ['ɛnəmɪ] *a, n* enemigo/a.

energetic [ɛnə'dʒɛtɪk] *a* enérgico.

energy ['ɛnədʒɪ] *n* energía.

enforce [ɪn'fɔːs] *vt* (*LAW*) hacer cumplir; **~d** *a* forzoso, forzado.

engage [ɪn'geɪdʒ] *vt* (*attention*) llamar; (*in conversation*) abordar; (*worker*) contratar; (*taxi*) alquilar; (*clutch*) embragar // *vi* (*TECH*) engranar con; **to ~ in** dedicarse a, ocuparse en; **~d** *a* (*busy, in use*) ocupado; (*betrothed*) prometido; **to get ~d** prometerse; **he is ~d in research** se dedica a la investigación; **~d tone** *n* señal *f* de comunicando; **~ment** *n* (*appointment*) compromiso, cita; (*battle*) combate *m*; (*to marry*) compromiso; (*period*) noviazgo; **~ment ring** *n* alianza, anillo de prometida.

engaging [ɪn'geɪdʒɪŋ] *a* atractivo, simpático.

engender [ɪn'dʒɛndə*] *vt* engendrar.

engine ['ɛndʒɪn] *n* (*AUT*) motor *m*; (*RAIL*) locomotora; **~ driver** *n* maquinista *m*.

engineer [ɛndʒɪ'nɪə*] *n* ingeniero; (*US: RAIL*) maquinista *m*; **~ing** *n* ingeniería.

England ['ɪŋglənd] *n* Inglaterra.

English ['ɪŋglɪʃ] *a* inglés(esa) // *n* (*LING*) el inglés; **the ~** los ingleses; **~man/woman** *n* inglés/esa *m/f*.

engrave [ɪn'greɪv] *vt* grabar; **engraving** *n* grabado.

engrossed [ɪn'grəust] *a*: **~ in** absorto en.

engulf [ɪn'gʌlf] *vt* sumergir, hundir.

enhance [ɪn'hɑːns] *vt* (*gen*) intensificar, aumentar; (*beauty*) realzar.

enigma [ɪ'nɪgmə] *n* enigma *m*; **~tic** [ɛnɪg-'mætɪk] *a* enigmático.

enjoy [ɪn'dʒɔɪ] *vt* (*possess*) poseer; (*have: health, fortune*) disfrutar de, gozar de; (*food*) comer con gusto; **to ~ o.s.** divertirse, pasarlo bien; **~able** *a* (*pleasant*) agradable; (*amusing*) divertido; **~ment** *n* (*use*) disfrute *m*; (*joy*) placer *m*.

enlarge [ɪn'lɑːdʒ] *vt* aumentar; (*broaden*) extender; (*PHOT*) ampliar // *vi*: **to ~ on** (*subject*) tratar con más detalles; **~ment** *n* (*PHOT*) ampliación *f*.

enlighten [ɪn'laɪtn] *vt* (*inform*) informar, instruir; **~ed** *a* (*cultured*) culto; (*knowledgeable*) bien informado; (*tolerant*) comprensivo; **~ment** *n* (*HISTORY*): **the E~ment** la Ilustración, el Siglo de las Luces.

enlist [ɪn'lɪst] *vt* alistar; (*support*) conseguir // *vi* alistarse.

enmity ['ɛnmɪtɪ] *n* enemistad *f*.

enormity [ɪ'nɔːmɪtɪ] *n* enormidad *f*; **enormous** [-məs] *a* enorme.

enough [ɪ'nʌf] *a*: **~ time/books** bastante tiempo/bastantes libros // *n*: **have you got ~?** ¿tiene Usted bastante? // *ad*: **big ~** bastante grande; **he has not worked ~** no ha trabajado bastante; **~!** ¡basta ya!; **that's ~, thanks** con eso basta, gracias; **I've had ~ of him** estoy harto de él; **... which, funnily ~ ...** lo que, por extraño que parezca... .

enquire [ɪn'kwaɪə*] *vt, vi* = **inquire.**

enrage [ɪn'reɪdʒ] *vt* enfurecer, hacer rabiar.

enrich [ɪn'rɪtʃ] *vt* enriquecer.

enrol [ɪn'rəul] *vt* inscribir; (*SCOL*) matricular // *vi* inscribirse; matricularse; **~ment** *n* inscripción *f*; matriculación *f*.

en route [ɔn'ruːt] *ad* (*on the way to*) camino de; (*on the way*) en camino.

ensign ['ɛnsaɪn] *n* (*flag*) bandera; (*MIL*) alférez *m*.

enslave [ɪn'sleɪv] *vt* esclavizar.

ensue [ɪn'sjuː] *vi* seguirse; (*result*) resultar; (*happen*) sobrevenir.

ensure [ɪn'ʃuə*] *vt* asegurar.

entail [ɪn'teɪl] *vt* (*imply*) suponer; (*result in*) acarrear.

entangle [ɪn'tæŋgl] *vt* enredar, enmarañar; **~ment** *n* enredo.

enter ['ɛntə*] *vt* (*room*) entrar en; (*club*) hacerse socio de; (*army*) alistarse en; (*sb for a competition*) inscribir; (*write down*) anotar, apuntar // *vi* entrar; **to ~ for** *vt fus* presentarse para; **to ~ into** *vt fus* (*relations*) establecer; (*plans*) formar parte de; (*debate*) tomar parte en; (*agreement*) llegar a, firmar; **to ~ (up)on** *vt fus* (*career*) emprender.

enteritis [ɛntə'raɪtɪs] *n* enteritis *f*.

enterprise ['ɛntəpraɪz] *n* empresa; (*spirit*) iniciativa; **free ~** la libre empresa; **private ~** la iniciativa privada;

enterprising a emprendedor(a).
entertain [ɛntə'teɪn] vt (amuse) divertir; (receive: guest) recibir (en casa); (idea) abrigar; (plan) estudiar; ~ er n artista m/f; ~ing a divertido, entretenido; ~ment n (amusement) diversión f; (show) espectáculo; (party) fiesta.
enthralled [ɪn'θrɔːld] a encantado, cautivado.
enthusiasm [ɪn'θuːzɪæzəm] n entusiasmo.
enthusiast [ɪn'θuːzɪæst] n entusiasta m/f; ~ic [-'æstɪk] a entusiasta inv; to be ~ic about entusiasmarse por.
entice [ɪn'taɪs] vt tentar; (seduce) seducir; **enticing** a atractivo, tentador(a).
entire [ɪn'taɪə*] a entero, completo; (in total) total, todo; ~ly ad totalmente; ~ty [ɪn'taɪərətɪ] n: **in its ~ty** en su totalidad.
entitle [ɪn'taɪtl] vt: to ~ sb to sth dar a uno derecho a algo; ~d a (book) que se titula; to be ~d to do tener derecho a hacer.
entourage [ɒntu'rɑːʒ] n séquito.
entrails ['ɛntreɪlz] npl entrañas fpl.
entrance ['ɛntrəns] n entrada // vt [ɪn-'trɑːns] encantar, hechizar; to gain ~ to (university etc) ingresar en; ~ examination n examen m de ingreso; ~ fee n cuota.
entrant ['ɛntrənt] n participante m/f.
entreat [ɛn'triːt] vt rogar, suplicar; ~y n ruego, súplica.
entrée ['ɒntreɪ] n (CULIN) entrada.
entrenched [ɛn'trɛntʃd] a atrincherado.
entrepreneur [ɒntrəprə'nəː] n empresario; (of works) contratista m/f.
entrust [ɪn'trʌst] vt: to ~ sth to sb confiar algo a uno.
entry ['ɛntrɪ] n entrada; (permission to enter) acceso; (in register) apunte m; (in account) partida; ~ form n boleto de inscripción; **no ~** prohibido el paso; (AUT) dirección prohibida.
enumerate [ɪ'njuːməreɪt] vt enumerar.
enunciate [ɪ'nʌnsɪeɪt] vt pronunciar; (principle etc) enunciar.
envelop [ɪn'vɛləp] vt envolver.
envelope ['ɛnvələup] n sobre m.
envious ['ɛnvɪəs] a envidioso; (look) de envidia.
environment [ɪn'vaɪərnmənt] n medio ambiente; ~al [-'mɛntl] a ambiental.
envisage [ɪn'vɪzɪdʒ] vt (foresee) prever; (imagine) concebir, representarse.
envoy ['ɛnvɔɪ] n enviado.
envy ['ɛnvɪ] n envidia // vt tener envidia a; to ~ sb sth envidiar algo a uno.
enzyme ['ɛnzaɪm] n enzima.
ephemeral [ɪ'fɛmərl] a efímero.
epic ['ɛpɪk] n épica // a épico.
epidemic [ɛpɪ'dɛmɪk] n epidemia.
epilepsy ['ɛpɪlɛpsɪ] n epilepsia; **epileptic** [-'lɛptɪk] a, n epiléptico/a.
episode ['ɛpɪsəud] n episodio.
epistle [ɪ'pɪsl] n epístola.
epitaph ['ɛpɪtɑːf] n epitafio.

epitome [ɪ'pɪtəmɪ] n epítome m; **epitomize** vt epitomar, resumir.
epoch ['iːpɔk] n época.
equable ['ɛkwəbl] a uniforme, igual; (character) tranquilo, afable.
equal ['iːkwl] a (gen) igual; (treatment) equitativo // n igual m/f // vt ser igual a; to be ~ to (task) estar a la altura de; ~ity [iːˈkwɔlɪtɪ] n igualdad f; ~ize vt, vi igualar; (SPORT) lograr el empate; ~ly ad igualmente; (share etc) por igual.
equanimity [ɛkwə'nɪmɪtɪ] n ecuanimidad f.
equate [ɪ'kweɪt] vt: to ~ sth with considerar algo equivalente a; **equation** [ɪ'kweɪʃən] n (MATH) ecuación f.
equator [ɪ'kweɪtə*] n ecuador m; ~ial [ɛkwə'tɔːrɪəl] a ecuatorial.
equilibrium [iːkwɪ'lɪbrɪəm] n equilibrio.
equinox ['iːkwɪnɔks] n equinoccio.
equip [ɪ'kwɪp] vt (gen) equipar; (person) proveer; to be well ~ped estar bien dotado; ~ment n equipo; (tools) avíos mpl.
equitable ['ɛkwɪtəbl] a equitativo.
equivalent [ɪ'kwɪvəlnt] a equivalente; to be ~ to equivaler a // n equivalente m.
equivocal [ɪ'kwɪvəkl] a equivoco; (open to suspicion) ambiguo.
era ['ɪərə] n era, época.
eradicate [ɪ'rædɪkeɪt] vt erradicar, extirpar.
erase [ɪ'reɪz] vt borrar; **eraser** n goma de borrar.
erect [ɪ'rɛkt] a erguido // vt erigir, levantar; (assemble) montar.
erection [ɪ'rɛkʃən] n construcción f; (assembly) montaje m; (structure) edificio; (MED) erección f.
ermine ['əːmɪn] n armiño.
erode [ɪ'rəud] vt (GEO) erosionar; (metal) corroer, desgastar; **erosion** [ɪ'rəuʒən] n erosión f; desgaste m.
erotic [ɪ'rɔtɪk] a erótico; ~ism [ɪ'rɔtɪsɪzm] n erotismo.
err [əː*] vi errar, equivocarse; (REL) pecar.
errand ['ɛrnd] n recado, mandado; ~ boy n recadero.
erratic [ɪ'rætɪk] a irregular; (uneven) desigual, poco uniforme.
erroneous [ɪ'rəunɪəs] a erróneo.
error ['ɛrə*] n error m, equivocación f.
erupt [ɪ'rʌpt] vi estar en erupción; (MED) hacer erupción; (fig) estallar; ~ion [ɪ'rʌpʃən] n erupción f; (fig) explosión f.
escalate ['ɛskəleɪt] vi extenderse, intensificarse; **escalation** [-'leɪʃən] n escalamiento, intensificación f.
escalator ['ɛskəleɪtə*] n escalera móvil.
escapade [ɛskə'peɪd] n travesura.
escape [ɪ'skeɪp] n (gen) fuga; (from duties) escapatoria; (from chase) fuga, evasión f // vi (gen) escaparse; (flee) huir, evadirse; (leak) fugarse // vt evitar, eludir; (consequences) escapar a; to ~ from

(*place*) escaparse de; (*person*) escaparse a; (*clutches*) librarse de; **escapism** *n* escapismo.

escort ['ɛskɔːt] *n* acompañante *m/f*; (*MIL*) escolta; (*NAUT*) convoy *m* // *vt* [ɪ'skɔːt] acompañar; (*MIL, NAUT*) escoltar.

Eskimo ['ɛskɪməu] *n* esquimal *m/f*.

especially [ɪ'spɛʃlɪ] *ad* (*gen*) especialmente; (*above all*) sobre todo; (*particularly*) en particular.

espionage ['ɛspɪənɑːʒ] *n* espionaje *m*.

esplanade [ɛspləˈneɪd] *n* (*by sea*) paseo marítimo.

espouse [ɪ'spauz] *vt* adherirse a.

Esquire [ɪ'skwaɪə] *n* (*abbr* **Esq.**): **J. Brown,** ~ Sr. Don J. Brown.

essay ['ɛseɪ] *n* (*SCOL*) ensayo.

essence ['ɛsns] *n* esencia.

essential [ɪ'sɛnʃl] *a* (*necessary*) imprescindible; (*basic*) esencial; ~**ly** *ad* esencialmente.

establish [ɪ'stæblɪʃ] *vt* establecer; (*facts*) verificar; (*proof*) demostrar; (*relations*) entablar; ~**ed** *a* (*business*) de buena reputación; (*staff*) de plantilla; ~**ment** *n* establecimiento; **the E**~**ment** la clase dirigente.

estate [ɪ'steɪt] *n* (*land*) finca, hacienda; (*property*) propiedad *f*; (*inheritance*) herencia; (*POL*) estado; ~ **housing** *n* urbanización *f*; **industrial** ~ polígono industrial; ~ **agent** *n* agente *m/f* inmobiliario; ~ **car** *n* (*Brit*) furgoneta.

esteem [ɪ'stiːm] *n*: **to hold sb in high** ~ estimar en mucho a uno // *vt* estimar.

estimate ['ɛstɪmət] *n* estimación *f*, apreciación *f*; (*assessment*) tasa, cálculo; (*COMM*) presupuesto // *vt* [-meɪt] estimar; tasar, calcular; **estimation** [-'meɪʃən] *n* opinión *f*, juicio; (*esteem*) aprecio.

estrange [ɪ'streɪndʒ] *vt* enajenar.

estuary ['ɛstjuərɪ] *n* estuario, ría.

etching ['ɛtʃɪŋ] *n* aguafuerte *f*.

eternal [ɪ'tɜːnl] *a* eterno.

eternity [ɪ'tɜːnɪtɪ] *n* eternidad *f*.

ether ['iːθə] *n* éter *m*.

ethical ['ɛθɪkl] *a* ético; (*honest*) honrado; **ethics** ['ɛθɪks] *n* ética // *npl* moralidad *f*.

ethnic ['ɛθnɪk] *a* étnico.

etiquette ['ɛtɪkɛt] *n* etiqueta.

eucalyptus [juːkə'lɪptəs] *n* eucalipto.

euphemism ['juːfəmɪzm] *n* eufemismo.

euphoria [juː'fɔːrɪə] *n* euforia.

Europe ['juərəp] *n* Europa; **European** [-'piːən] *a*, *n* europeo/a.

euthanasia [juːθə'neɪzɪə] *n* eutanasia.

evacuate [ɪ'vækjueɪt] *vt* desocupar; **evacuation** [-'eɪʃən] *n* evacuación *f*.

evade [ɪ'veɪd] *vt* evadir, eludir.

evaluate [ɪ'væljueɪt] *vt* evaluar; (*value*) tasar; (*evidence*) interpretar.

evangelist [ɪ'vændʒəlɪst] *n* evangelizador *m*, evangelista *m/f*.

evaporate [ɪ'væpəreɪt] *vi* evaporarse, desvanecerse // *vt* evaporar; ~**d milk** *n*

leche *f* evaporada; **evaporation** [-'reɪʃən] *n* evaporación *f*.

evasion [ɪ'veɪʒən] *n* evasiva, evasión *f*; **evasive** [-sɪv] *a* evasivo.

eve [iːv] *n*: **on the** ~ **of** en vísperas de.

even ['iːvn] *a* (*level*) llano; (*smooth*) liso; (*speed, temperature*) uniforme; (*number*) par; (*nature*) ecuánime; (*SPORT*) igual(es) // *ad* hasta, aun, siquiera; ~ **more** aun más; ~ **so** aun así; **not** ~ ni siquiera; ~ **he was there** hasta él estuvo allí; ~ **on Sundays** incluso los domingos; **to** ~ **out** *vi* nivelarse; **to get** ~ **with sb** ajustar cuentas con uno.

evening ['iːvnɪŋ] *n* tarde *f*; (*dusk*) atardecer *m*; (*night*) noche *f*; (*event*) velada; **in the** ~ por la tarde; ~ **class** *n* clase *f* nocturna; ~ **dress** *n* (*man's*) traje *m* de etiqueta; (*woman's*) traje *m* de noche.

event [ɪ'vɛnt] *n* suceso, acontecimiento; (*SPORT*) prueba; **in the** ~ **of** en caso de (que); ~**ful** *a* accidentado; (*game etc*) lleno de emoción.

eventual [ɪ'vɛntʃuəl] *a* (*last*) final; (*resulting*) consiguiente; ~**ity** [-'ælɪtɪ] *n* eventualidad *f*; ~**ly** *ad* (*finally*) finalmente, al fin y al cabo; (*in time*) a la larga.

ever ['ɛvə*] *ad* nunca, jamás; (*at all times*) alguna vez; **the best** ~ el/la mejor que se ha visto jamás; **have you** ~ **seen it?** ¿lo ha visto Usted jamás?; **better than** ~ mejor que nunca; ~ **since** *ad* desde entonces // *conj* después de que; ~**green** *n* árbol *m* de hoja perenne; ~**lasting** *a* eterno, perpetuo.

every ['ɛvrɪ] *det* (*each*) cada; (*all*) todo; ~ **day** cada día; ~ **other car** cada dos coches; ~ **now and then** en vez en cuando; ~**body** *pron* todos *pl*, todo el mundo; ~**day** *a* (*daily*) diario, cotidiano; (*usual*) corriente; (*common*) vulgar; (*routine*) rutinario; ~**one** = ~**body**; ~**thing** *pron* todo; ~**where** *ad* (*be*) en todas partes; (*go*) a *o* por todas partes.

evict [ɪ'vɪkt] *vt* desahuciar; ~**ion** [ɪ'vɪkʃən] *n* desahucio.

evidence ['ɛvɪdəns] *n* (*proof*) prueba; (*of witness*) testimonio; (*facts*) datos *mpl*, hechos *mpl*; **to give** ~ prestar declaración, dar testimonio.

evident ['ɛvɪdənt] *a* evidente, manifiesto; ~**ly** *ad* naturalmente.

evil ['iːvl] *a* malo; (*influence*) funesto; (*smell*) horrible // *n* mal *m*, maldad *f*; ~**doer** *n* malhechor/a *m/f*.

evocative [ɪ'vɔkətɪv] *a* sugestivo, evocador(a).

evoke [ɪ'vəuk] *vt* evocar.

evolution [iːvə'luːʃən] *n* evolución *f*, desarrollo.

evolve [ɪ'vɔlv] *vt* desarrollar // *vi* evolucionar, desarrollarse.

ewe [juː] *n* oveja.

ex-... [ɛks] *pref* ex.

exact [ɪg'zækt] *a* exacto // *vt*: **to** ~ **sth**

(from) exigir algo (de); ~**ing** a exigente; *(conditions)* arduo; ~**itude** n exactitud f; ~**ly** ad exactamente; *(time)* en punto.

exaggerate [ɪgˈzædʒəreɪt] vt, vi exagerar; **exaggeration** [-ˈreɪʃən] n exageración f.

exalted [ɪgˈzɔːltɪd] a exaltado, elevado.

exam [ɪgˈzæm] n abbr of **examination**.

examination [ɪgzæmɪˈneɪʃən] n *(gen)* examen m; *(LAW)* interrogación f; *(inquiry)* investigación f.

examine [ɪgˈzæmɪn] vt *(gen)* examinar; *(inspect)* inspeccionar, escudriñar; *(SCOL, LAW: person)* interrogar; *(at customs: luggage)* registrar; **examiner** n inspector m.

example [ɪgˈzɑːmpl] n ejemplo; *(copy)* ejemplar m; **for ~** por ejemplo.

exasperate [ɪgˈzɑːspəreɪt] vt exasperar, irritar; **exasperating** a irritante.

excavate [ˈɛkskəveɪt] vt excavar; **excavation** [-ˈveɪʃən] n excavación f.

exceed [ɪkˈsiːd] vt exceder; *(number)* pasar de; *(speed limit)* sobrepasar; *(limits)* rebasar; *(powers)* excederse en; *(hopes)* superar; ~**ingly** ad sumamente, sobremanera.

excel [ɪkˈsɛl] vi sobresalir.

excellence [ˈɛksələns] n excelencia.

Excellency [ˈɛksələnsɪ] n: **His ~** Su Excelencia.

excellent [ˈɛksələnt] a excelente.

except [ɪkˈsɛpt] prep *(also: ~ **for**, ~**ing**)* excepto, salvo, con excepción de // vt exceptuar, excluir; ~ **if/when** excepto si/cuando; ~ **that** salvo que; ~**ion** [ɪkˈsɛpʃən] n excepción f; **to take ~ ion to** ofenderse por; ~**ional** [ɪkˈsɛpʃənl] a excepcional.

excerpt [ˈɛksɜːpt] n extracto.

excess [ɪkˈsɛs] n exceso; *(COMM)* excedente m; ~ **baggage** n exceso de equipaje; ~ **fare** n suplemento; ~**ive** a excesivo.

exchange [ɪksˈtʃeɪndʒ] n cambio; *(of goods)* canje m; *(of ideas)* intercambio; *(also: **telephone ~**)* central f (telefónica) // vt cambiar; canjear.

exchequer [ɪksˈtʃɛkə*] n hacienda.

excise [ˈɛksaɪz] n impuestos mpl sobre el comercio exterior // vt [ɛkˈsaɪz] suprimir.

excite [ɪkˈsaɪt] vt *(stimulate)* excitar; *(awaken)* despertar; *(move)* entusiasmar; **to get ~d** emocionarse; ~**ment** n emoción f; *(anticipation)* ilusión f; *(agitation)* agitación f; **exciting** a emocionante.

exclaim [ɪkˈskleɪm] vi exclamar; **exclamation** [ɛksklɚˈmeɪʃən] n exclamación f; **exclamation mark** n punto de admiración.

exclude [ɪkˈskluːd] vt excluir; *(except)* exceptuar; **exclusion** [ɪkˈskluːʒən] n exclusión f.

exclusive [ɪkˈskluːsɪv] a exclusivo; *(club, district)* selecto; ~ **of tax** excluyendo impuestos; ~**ly** ad únicamente.

excommunicate [ɛkskəˈmjuːnɪkeɪt] vt excomulgar.

excrement [ˈɛkskrəmənt] n excremento.

excrete [ɪkˈskriːt] vi excretar.

excruciating [ɪkˈskruːʃɪeɪtɪŋ] a agudísimo, atroz.

excursion [ɪkˈskɔːʃən] n excursión f.

excusable [ɪkˈskjuːzəbl] a perdonable.

excuse [ɪkˈskjuːs] n disculpa, excusa; *(evasion)* pretexto // [ɪkˈskjuːz] disculpar, perdonar; **to ~ sb from doing sth** dispensar a uno de hacer algo; ~ **me!** ¡perdón!; **if you will ~ me** con su permiso.

execute [ˈɛksɪkjuːt] vt *(plan)* realizar; *(order)* cumplir; *(person)* ajusticiar, ejecutar; **execution** n realización f; cumplimiento; ejecución f; **executioner** n verdugo.

executive [ɪgˈzɛkjutɪv] n *(COMM, POL)* ejecutivo // a ejecutivo.

executor [ɪgˈzɛkjutə*] n albacea m, testamentario.

exemplary [ɪgˈzɛmplərɪ] a ejemplar.

exemplify [ɪgˈzɛmplɪfaɪ] vt ejemplificar.

exempt [ɪgˈzɛmpt] a: ~ **from** exento de // vt: **to ~ sb from** eximir a uno de; ~**ion** [ɪgˈzɛmpʃən] n exención f; *(immunity)* inmunidad f.

exercise [ˈɛksəsaɪz] n ejercicio // vt ejercer; *(right)* valerse de; *(dog)* llevar de paseo // vi hacer ejercicio(s); ~ **book** n cuaderno.

exert [ɪgˈzɜːt] vt ejercer; **to ~ o.s.** esforzarse, afanarse; *(overdo things)* trabajar demasiado; ~**ion** n esfuerzo.

exhaust [ɪgˈzɔːst] n *(pipe)* escape m; *(fumes)* gases mpl de escape // vt agotar; ~**ion** [ɪgˈzɔːstʃən] n agotamiento; **nervous ~ion** postración f nerviosa; ~**ive** a exhaustivo.

exhibit [ɪgˈzɪbɪt] n *(ART)* obra expuesta; *(LAW)* objeto expuesto // vt *(show)* manifestar; *(emotion)* acusar; *(film)* presentar; *(paintings)* exponer; ~**ion** [ɛksɪˈbɪʃən] n exposición f; ~**ionist** [ɛksɪˈbɪʃənɪst] n exhibicionista m/f.

exhilarating [ɪgˈzɪləreɪtɪŋ] a estimulante, tónico.

exhort [ɪgˈzɔːt] vt exhortar.

exile [ˈɛksaɪl] n exilio; *(person)* exiliado/a // vt desterrar, exiliar.

exist [ɪgˈzɪst] vi existir; *(live)* vivir; ~**ence** n existencia; *(life)* vida; ~**ing** a existente, actual.

exit [ˈɛksɪt] n salida.

exonerate [ɪgˈzɒnəreɪt] vt: **to ~ from** exculpar de.

exorcize [ˈɛksɔːsaɪz] vt exorcizar.

exotic [ɪgˈzɒtɪk] a exótico.

expand [ɪkˈspænd] vt *(widen)* ensanchar; *(number)* aumentar // vi *(trade etc)* expandirse; *(gas, metal)* dilatarse.

expanse [ɪkˈspæns] n extensión f; *(of wings)* envergadura.

expansion [ɪkˈspænʃən] n *(of town)* ensanche m; *(of trade)* expansión f.

expatriate [ɛksˈpætrɪət] n expatriado/a.

expect [ɪkˈspɛkt] vt *(gen)* esperar; *(count*

on) contar con; (*suppose*) suponer // *vi*: **to be ~ing** estar encinta; **~ant mother** *n* mujer *f* encinta; **~ation** [ɛkspɛk'teɪʃən] *n* esperanza, expectativa.

expedience [ɛk'spiːdɪəns]. **expediency** [ɛk'spiːdɪənsɪ] *n* conveniencia; **expedient** *a* conveniente, oportuno // *n* recurso, expediente *m*.

expedition [ɛkspə'dɪʃən] *n* expedición *f*.

expel [ɪk'spɛl] *vt* arrojar; (*SCOL*) expulsar.

expend [ɪk'spɛnd] *vt* gastar; (*use up*) consumir; **~able** *a* prescindible; **~iture** *n* gastos *mpl*, desembolso.

expense [ɪk'spɛns] *n* gasto, gastos *mpl*; (*high cost*) costa; **~s** *npl* (*COMM*) gastos *mpl*; **at the ~ of** a costa o expensas de; **~ account** *n* cuenta de gastos.

expensive [ɪk'spɛnsɪv] *a* caro, costoso.

experience [ɪk'spɪərɪəns] *n* experiencia // *vt* experimentar; (*suffer*) sufrir; **~d** *a* experimentado.

experiment [ɪk'spɛrɪmənt] *n* experimento // *vi* hacer experimentos; **~al** [-'mɛntl] *a* experimental.

expert ['ɛkspət] *a* experto, perito // *n* experto, perito; (*specialist*) especialista *m/f*; **~ise** [-'tiːz] *n* pericia.

expire [ɪk'spaɪə*] *vi* (*gen*) expirar; (*end*) terminar; (*run out*) caducar, vencerse; **expiry** *n* expiración *f*; terminación *f*; vencimiento.

explain [ɪk'spleɪn] *vt* explicar; (*clarify*) aclarar; (*demonstrate*) exponer; **explanation** [ɛksplə'neɪʃən] *n* explicación *f*, aclaración *f*; **explanatory** [ɪk'splænətrɪ] *a* explicativo; aclaratorio.

explicit [ɪk'splɪsɪt] *a* explícito.

explode [ɪk'spləud] *vi* estallar, explotar; (*with anger*) reventar // *vt* volar, explotar.

exploit ['ɛksplɔɪt] *n* hazaña // *vt* [ɪk'splɔɪt] explotar; **~ation** [-'teɪʃən] *n* explotación *f*.

exploration [ɛksplə'reɪʃən] *n* exploración *f*; **exploratory** [ɪk'splɔrətrɪ] *a* (*fig*: *talks*) exploratorio, de sondaje.

explore [ɪk'splɔ:*] *vt* explorar; (*fig*) examinar, sondar; **explorer** *n* explorador *m*.

explosion [ɪk'spləuʒən] *n* explosión *f*; **explosive** [-sɪv] *a*, *n* explosivo.

exponent [ɪk'spəunənt] *n* exponente *m/f*, intérprete *m/f*.

export [ɛk'spɔːt] *vt* exportar // *n* ['ɛkspɔːt] exportación *f* // *cpd* de exportación; **~ation** [-'teɪʃən] *n* exportación *f*; **~er** *n* exportador *m*.

expose [ɪk'spəuz] *vt* exponer; (*unmask*) desenmascarar; **~d** *a* expuesto; (*position*) desabrigado.

exposure [ɪk'spəuʒə*] *n* exposición *f*; (*PHOT*) revelación *f*; (: *shot*) fotografía; **to die from ~** (*MED*) morir de frío; **~ meter** *n* fotómetro.

expound [ɪk'spaund] *vt* exponer, explicar.

express [ɪk'sprɛs] *a* (*definite*) expreso, explícito; (*letter etc*) urgente // *n* (*train*) rápido // *ad* (*send*) por carta urgente // *vt* expresar; (*squeeze*) exprimir; **~ion** [ɪk-

'sprɛʃən] *n* expresión *f*; **~ive** *a* expresivo; **~ly** *ad* expresamente.

expulsion [ɪk'spʌlʃən] *n* expulsión *f*.

exquisite [ɛk'skwɪzɪt] *a* exquisito.

extend [ɪk'stɛnd] *vt* (*visit*, *street*) prolongar; (*building*) ensanchar; (*offer*) ofrecer // *vi* (*land*) extenderse.

extension [ɪk'stɛnʃən] *n* extensión *f*; (*building*) ampliación *f*; (*TEL*: *line*) línea derivada; (: *telephone*) extensión *f*; (*of deadline*) prórroga.

extensive [ɪk'stɛnsɪv] *a* (*gen*) extenso; (*broad*) vasto, ancho; (*frequent*) general, común; **he's travelled ~ly** ha viajado por muchos países.

extent [ɪk'stɛnt] *n* (*breadth*) extensión *f*; (*scope*) alcance *m*; **to some ~** hasta cierto punto; **to the ~ of...** hasta el punto de...; **to such an ~ that...** hasta tal punto que...; **to what ~?** ¿hasta qué punto?

exterior [ɛk'stɪərɪə*] *a* exterior, externo // *n* exterior *m*; (*appearance*) aspecto.

exterminate [ɪk'stɜːmɪneɪt] *vt* exterminar; **extermination** [-'neɪʃən] *n* exterminación *f*.

external [ɪk'stɜːnl] *a* externo, exterior; **~ly** *ad* por fuera.

extinct [ɪk'stɪŋkt] *a* extinto; **~ion** [ɪk-'stɪŋkʃən] *n* extinción *f*.

extinguish [ɪk'stɪŋgwɪʃ] *vt* extinguir, apagar; **~er** *n* extintor *m*.

extort [ɪk'stɔːt] *vt* sacar a la fuerza (*from sb* de uno); **~ion** [ɪk'stɔːʃən] *n* exacción *f*; **~ionate** [ɪk'stɔːʃnət] *a* excesivo, exorbitante.

extra ['ɛkstrə] *a* adicional; (*excessive*) de más, de sobra; (*bonus*: *payment*) extraordinario // *ad* (*in addition*) especialmente // *n* (*addition*) extra *m*, suplemento; (*THEATRE*) extra *m/f*, comparsa *m/f*; (*newspaper*) edición *f* extraordinaria.

extra... [ɛkstrə] *pref* extra... .

extract [ɪk'strækt] *vt* sacar, extraer; (*confession*) arrancar, obtener // *n* ['ɛkstrækt] extracto.

extradite ['ɛkstrədaɪt] *vt* (*from country*) conceder la extradición de; (*to country*) obtener la extradición de; **extradition** [-'dɪʃən] *n* extradición *f*.

extramarital [ɛkstrə'mærɪtl] *a* extra-matrimonial.

extramural [ɛkstrə'mjuərl] *a* de extramuros.

extraordinary [ɪk'strɔːdnrɪ] *a* extra-ordinario; (*odd*) raro.

extravagant [ɪk'strævəgənt] *a* (*lavish*) pródigo; (*wasteful*) derrochador(a); (*price*) exorbitante; (*praise*) excesivo; (*odd*) raro.

extreme [ɪk'striːm] *a* extremo; (*poverty etc*) extremado; (*case*) excepcional // *n* extremo, extremidad *f*; **~ly** *ad* sumamente, extremadamente; **extremist** *a*, *n* extremista *m/f*.

extremity [ɪk'strɛmətɪ] *n* extremidad *f*, punta; (*need*) apuro, necesidad *f*.

extricate ['ɛkstrɪkeɪt] *vt* librar.

extrovert ['ɛkstrəvɔːt] n extrovertido/a.
exuberant [ɪg'zjuːbərnt] a (person) eufórico; (style) exuberante.
exude [ɪg'zjuːd] vt rezumar, sudar.
exult [ɪg'zʌlt] vi regocijarse.
eye [aɪ] n ojo // vt mirar de soslayo, ojear; **to keep an ~ on** vigilar, estar pendiente de; **~ball** n globo del ojo; **~bath** n ojera; **~brow** n ceja; **~brow pencil** n lápiz m de cejas; **~-catching** a llamativo; **~drops** npl gotas fpl para los ojos; **~lash** n pestaña; **~lid** n párpado; **~-opener** n revelación f, gran sorpresa; **~shadow** n sombreador m de ojos; **~sight** n vista; **~sore** n monstruosidad f; **~wash** n (fig) disparates mpl, tonterías fpl; **~ witness** n testigo m // f presencial.
eyrie ['ɪərɪ] n aguilera.

F

F. abbr of **Fahrenheit.**
fable ['feɪbl] n fábula.
fabric ['fæbrɪk] n tejido, tela.
fabrication [fæbrɪ'keɪʃən] n invención f.
fabulous ['fæbjuləs] a fabuloso.
façade [fə'sɑːd] n fachada.
face [feɪs] n cara; (ANAT) cara, rostro; (of clock) esfera; (side, surface) superficie f // vt (person) encararse con; (building) dar a; **to lose ~** desprestigiarse; **in the ~ of** (difficulties etc) en vista de; **on the ~ of it** a primera vista; **~ to ~** cara a cara; **to ~ up to** vt fus hacer frente a, arrostrar; **~ cloth** n paño; **~ cream** n crema (de belleza); **~ lift** n cirujía estética; **~ powder** n polvos mpl; **~-saving** a para salvar las apariencias.
facet ['fæsɪt] n faceta.
facetious [fə'siːʃəs] a chistoso.
face value ['feɪs'væljuː] n (of stamp) valor m nominal; **to take sth at ~** (fig) tomar algo en sentido literal, aceptar las apariencias de algo.
facial ['feɪʃəl] a de la cara.
facile ['fæsaɪl] a superficial, ligero.
facilitate [fə'sɪlɪteɪt] vt facilitar.
facilities [fə'sɪlɪtɪz] npl facilidades fpl.
facing ['feɪsɪŋ] prep frente a // a de enfrente.
fact [fækt] n hecho; **in ~** en realidad.
faction ['fækʃən] n facción f.
factor ['fæktə*] n factor m.
factory ['fæktərɪ] n fábrica.
factual ['fæktjuəl] a objetivo.
faculty ['fækəltɪ] n facultad f; (US: teaching staff) profesorado.
fade [feɪd] vi desteñirse; (sound, hope) desvanecerse; (light) apagarse; (flower) marchitarse.
fag [fæg] n (col: cigarette) pitillo; **~ end** n colilla; **~ged out** a (col) agotado.
fail [feɪl] vt (candidate) suspender; (exam) no aprobar // vi acabarse; (engine) fallar; (voice) desfallecer; (patient) debilitarse; **to ~ to do sth** (neglect) dejar de hacer algo;

(be unable) no poder hacer algo; **without ~** sin falta; **~ing** n falta, defecto // prep a falta de; **~ure** ['feɪljə*] n fracaso; (person) fracasado/a; (mechanical etc) fallo.
faint [feɪnt] a débil; (recollection) vago; (mark) apenas visible // n desmayo // vi desmayarse; **to feel ~** estar mareado, marearse; **~-hearted** a pusilánime; **~ly** ad débilmente; vagamente; **~ness** n debilidad f.
fair [fɛə*] a justo; (colour) rubio; (weather) bueno; (good enough) suficiente; (sizeable) considerable // ad (play) limpio // n feria; (funfair) parque m de atracciones; **~ly** ad (justly) con justicia; (equally) equitativamente; (quite) bastante; **~ness** n justicia; (impartiality) imparcialidad f.
fairy ['fɛərɪ] n hada; **~ tale** n cuento de hadas.
faith [feɪθ] n fe f; (trust) confianza; (sect) religión f; **~ful** a fiel; **~fully** ad fielmente; **yours ~fully** le saluda atentamente.
fake [feɪk] n (painting etc) falsificación f; (person) impostor m // a falso // vt fingir; (painting etc) falsificar; **his illness is a ~** su enfermedad es una invención.
falcon ['fɔːlkən] n halcón m.
fall [fɔːl] n caída; (US: autumn) otoño // vi, pt **fell**, pp **fallen** ['fɔːlən] caer, caerse; (price) bajar; **~s** npl (waterfall) cascada, salto de agua; **to ~ flat** vi (on one's face) caerse (boca abajo); (plan) fracasar; **to ~ back** vi retroceder; **to ~ back on** vt fus (remedy etc) recurrir a; **to ~ backwards** vi caer de espaldas; **to ~ behind** vi quedarse atrás; **to ~ down** vi (person) caerse; (building, hopes) derrumbarse; **to ~ for** vt fus (trick) dejarse engañar por; (person) enamorarse de; **to ~ in** vi (roof) hundirse; (MIL) alinearse; **to ~ off** vi caerse; (diminish) disminuir; **to ~ out** vi (friends etc) reñir; (MIL) romper filas; **to ~ through** vi (plan, project) fracasar.
fallacy ['fæləsɪ] n (error) error m; (lie) mentira.
fallible ['fæləbl] a falible.
fallout ['fɔːlaut] n lluvia radioactiva; **~ shelter** n refugio contra ataques nucleares.
false [fɔːls] a (gen) falso; (hair, teeth etc) postizo; (disloyal) desleal, traidor(a); **under ~ pretences** con engaños; **~hood** n (lie) mentira; (falseness) falsedad f; **~ly** ad (accuse) falsamente; **~ teeth** npl dentadura postiza sg.
falter ['fɔːltə*] vi vacilar.
fame [feɪm] n fama.
familiar [fə'mɪlɪə*] a familiar; (well-known) conocido; (tone) de confianza; **to be ~ with** (subject) estar enterado de; **~ity** [fəmɪlɪ'ærɪtɪ] n familiaridad f; **~ize** [fə'mɪlɪəraɪz] vr: **to ~ize o.s. with** familiarizarse con.
family ['fæmɪlɪ] n familia; **~ business** n

negocio familiar; ~ **doctor** n médico de cabecera.

famine ['fæmɪn] n hambre f.

famished ['fæmɪʃt] a hambriento.

famous ['feɪməs] a famoso, célebre; ~**ly** ad (get on) estupendamente.

fan [fæn] n abanico; (ELEC) ventilador m; (person) aficionado/a // vt abanicar; (fire, quarrel) atizar; **to ~ out** vi desparramarse.

fanatic [fə'nætɪk] n fanático/a; ~**al** a fanático.

fan belt ['fænbɛlt] n correa de ventilador.

fanciful ['fænsɪful] a (gen) fantástico; (imaginary) imaginario.

fancy ['fænsɪ] n (whim) capricho, antojo; (taste) afición f, gusto; (imagination) imaginación f; (delusion) quimera // a (decorative) hermoso; (luxury) de lujo; (as decoration) de adorno // vt (feel like, want) tener ganas de; (imagine) imaginarse; (think) creer; **to take a ~ to** encapricharse por, tomar afición a; **it took** or **caught my ~** me cayó en gracia; **to ~ that...** imaginarse que...; **he fancies her** le gusta (ella); ~ **dress** n disfraz m; ~**-dress ball** n baile m de disfraces.

fang [fæŋ] n colmillo.

fantastic [fæn'tæstɪk] a fantástico.

fantasy ['fæntəzɪ] n fantasía.

far [fɑ:*] a (distant) lejano // ad lejos; ~ **away**, ~ **off** (a lo) lejos; ~ **better** mucho mejor; ~ **from** lejos de; **by** ~ con mucho; **go as** ~ **as the farm** vaya hasta la granja; **as** ~ **as I know** que yo sepa; **how** ~? ¿hasta dónde?; (fig) ¿hasta qué punto?; **the F ~ East** el Extremo Oriente; ~**away** a remoto.

farce [fɑ:s] n farsa; **farcical** a absurdo.

fare [fɛə*] n (on trains, buses) precio (del billete); (in taxi: fare) tarifa; (: passenger) pasajero; (food) comida.

farewell [fɛə'wɛl] excl, n adiós m.

farm [fɑ:m] n granja, finca, estancia (AM) // vt cultivar; ~**er** n granjero, estanciero (AM); ~**hand** n peón m; ~**house** n casa de labranza; ~**ing** n (gen) agricultura; (tilling) cultivo; ~**land** n tierra de cultivo; ~ **worker** n = ~**hand**; ~**yard** n corral m.

far-sighted ['fɑ:'saɪtɪd] a previsor(a).

fart [fɑ:t] (col!) n pedo // vi tirarse un pedo.

farther ['fɑ:ðə*] ad más lejos, más allá.

farthest ['fɑ:ðɪst] superlative of **far**.

fascinate ['fæsɪneɪt] vt fascinar; **fascination** ['neɪʃən] n fascinación f.

fascism ['fæʃɪzəm] n fascismo; **fascist** [-ɪst] a, n fascista m/f.

fashion ['fæʃən] n (gen) moda; (manner) manera // vt formar; **in** ~ a la moda; **out of** ~ pasado de moda; ~**able** a de moda; ~ **show** n desfile m de modelos.

fast [fɑ:st] a rápido; (dye, colour) sólido; (clock): **to be** ~ estar adelantado // ad rápidamente, de prisa; (stuck, held) firmemente // n ayuno // vi ayunar; ~

asleep profundamente dormido.

fasten ['fɑ:sn] vt asegurar, sujetar; (coat, belt) abrochar // vi cerrarse; ~**er**, ~**ing** n (gen) cierre m; (of door etc) cerrojo; **zip** ~**er** cremallera.

fastidious [fæs'tɪdɪəs] a (fussy) delicado; (demanding) exigente.

fat [fæt] a gordo; (meat) con mucha grasa; (greasy) grasiento // n grasa; (on person) carnes fpl; (lard) manteca.

fatal ['feɪtl] a (gen) fatal; (injury) mortal; (consequence) funesto; ~**ism** n fatalismo; ~**ity** [fə'tælɪtɪ] n (road death etc) víctima m/f; ~**ly** ad: ~**ly injured** herido a muerte.

fate [feɪt] n destino; (of person) suerte f; ~**ful** a fatídico.

father ['fɑ:ðə*] n padre m; ~**hood** n paternidad f; ~**-in-law** n suegro; ~**ly** a paternal.

fathom ['fæðəm] n braza // vt (NAUT) sondear; (unravel) desentrañar; (understand) lograr comprender.

fatigue [fə'ti:g] n fatiga, cansancio.

fatten ['fætn] vt, vi engordar.

fatty ['fætɪ] a (food) graso // n (fam) gordito/a, gordinflón/ona m/f.

faucet ['fɔ:sɪt] n (US) grifo.

fault [fɔ:lt] n (error) falta; (blame) culpa; (defect: in character) defecto; (in manufacture) desperfecto; (GEO) falla // vt tachar; **it's my** ~ es culpa mía; **to find** ~ **with** criticar, poner peros a; **at** ~ culpable; ~**less** a (action) intachable; (person) sin defectos; ~**y** a defectuoso.

fauna ['fɔ:nə] n fauna.

faux pas ['fəu'pɑ:] n paso en falso; (gaffe) plancha.

favour, favor (US) ['feɪvə*] n favor m; (support) apoyo; (approval) aprobación f // vt (proposition) estar a favor de, aprobar; (person etc) favorecer; (assist) ser propicio a; **to ask a** ~ de pedir un favor a; **to do sb a** ~ hacer un favor a uno; **to find** ~ **with** caer en gracia de; **in** ~ **of** a favor de; ~**able** a favorable; ~**ite** [-rɪt] a, n favorito, preferido; ~**itism** n favoritismo.

fawn [fɔ:n] n cervato // a (also: ~**-coloured**) color de cervato, leonado.

fear [fɪə*] n miedo, temor m // vt tener miedo a o de, temer; **for** ~ **of** por temor a; ~**ful** a temeroso, miedoso; (cowardly) tímido; (awful) terrible; ~**less** a (gen) sin miedo o temor; (bold) audaz.

feasible ['fi:zəbl] a factible.

feast [fi:st] n banquete m; (REL: also: ~ **day**) fiesta // vt, vi banquetear.

feat [fi:t] n hazaña.

feather ['fɛðə*] n pluma; ~**-weight** n (BOXING) peso pluma.

feature ['fi:tʃə*] n (gen) característica; (ANAT) rasgo; (article) crónica // vt (subj: film) presentar // vi figurar; ~**s** npl (of face) facciones fpl; ~ **film** n película (de largo metraje).

February ['fɛbruərɪ] n febrero.

fed [fɛd] pt, pp of **feed.**

federal ['fɛdərəl] a federal; **federation** [-'reiʃən] n federación f.

fed-up [fɛd'ʌp] a: **to be ~** estar harto.

fee [fi:] n derechos mpl, honorarios mpl; (of school) matrícula; (of club) cuota.

feeble ['fi:bl] a débil; **~-minded** a imbécil.

feed [fi:d] n (gen) comida; (of baby) alimento infantil; (of animal) pienso // vt, pt, pp **fed** (gen) alimentar; (baby: breastfeed) dar el pecho a; (animal) dar de comer a; (data, information): **to ~ into** suministrar a; **to ~ on** vt fus alimentarse de; **~ing bottle** n biberón m.

feel [fi:l] n (sensation) sensación f; (sense of touch) tacto // vt, pt, pp **felt** tocar, palpar; (cold, pain etc) sentir; (think, believe) creer; **to ~ hungry/cold** tener hambre/frío; **to ~ lonely/better** sentirse solo/ mejor; **it ~s soft** es suave al tacto; **to ~ like** (want) tener ganas de; **to ~ about** or **around** tantear; **~er** n (of insect) antena; **to put out ~ers** (fig) sondear; **~ing** n (gen) sensación f; (foreboding) presentimiento; (opinion) opinión f; (emotion) sentimiento.

feet [fi:t] pl of **foot.**

feign [fein] vt fingir.

feline ['fi:lain] a felino.

fell [fɛl] pt of **fall** // vt (tree) talar.

fellow ['fɛləu] n (gen) tipo; (fam) tío; (of learned society) socio; **~ students** compañeros mpl de curso, condiscípulos mpl; **~ citizen** n conciudadano; **~ countryman** n compatriota m/f; **~ men** npl semejantes mpl; **~ship** n compañerismo; (grant) beca.

felony ['fɛləni] n crimen m.

felt [fɛlt] pt, pp of **feel** // n fieltro; **~-tip pen** n rotulador m.

female ['fi:meil] n (woman) mujer f; (ZOOL) hembra // a femenino.

feminine ['fɛminin] a femenino.

feminist ['fɛminist] n feminista.

fence [fɛns] n valla, cerca // vt (also: ~ in) cercar // vi hacer esgrima; **fencing** n esgrima.

fend [fɛnd] vi: **to ~ for o.s.** arreglárselas por su cuenta.

fender ['fɛndə*] n guardafuego; (US: AUT) parachoques m inv; (: RAIL) trompa.

ferment [fə'mɛnt] vi fermentar // n ['fɜ:mɛnt] (fig) agitación f; **~ation** [-'teiʃən] n fermentación f.

fern [fɜ:n] n helecho.

ferocious [fə'rəuʃəs] a feroz; **ferocity** [-'rɔsiti] n ferocidad f.

ferret ['fɛrit] n hurón m // vt: **to ~ out** descubrir.

ferry ['fɛri] n (small) barca (de pasaje), balsa; (large: also: **~boat**) transbordador m // vt transportar.

fertile ['fɜ:tail] a fértil; (BIOL) fecundo; **fertility** [fə'tiliti] n fertilidad f; fecundidad f; **fertilize** ['fɜ:tilaiz] vt fertilizar; fecundar; (AGR) abonar; **fertilizer** n fertilizante m.

fervent ['fɜ:vənt] a ardiente, apasionado.

fester ['fɛstə*] vi ulcerarse.

festival ['fɛstivəl] n (REL) fiesta; (ART, MUS) festival m.

festive ['fɛstiv] a festivo; **the ~ season** (Christmas) las Navidades.

festivities [fɛs'tivitiz] npl fiestas fpl.

fetch [fɛtʃ] vt ir a buscar; (sell for) venderse por.

fetching ['fɛtʃiŋ] a atractivo.

fête [feit] n fiesta.

fetish ['fɛtiʃ] n fetiche m.

fetters ['fɛtəz] npl grillos mpl.

feud [fju:d] n (hostility) enemistad f; (quarrel) disputa.

feudal ['fju:dl] a feudal; **~ism** n feudalismo.

fever ['fi:və*] n fiebre f; **~ish** a febril.

few [fju:] a (not many) pocos; (some) algunos, unos; **a ~** a unos pocos // pron algunos; **~er** a menos; **~est** a los/las menos.

fiancé [fi'ã:ŋsei] n novio, prometido; **~e** n novia, prometida.

fiasco [fi'æskəu] n fiasco.

fibre, fiber (US) ['faibə*] n fibra; **~-glass** n fibra de vidrio.

fickle ['fikl] a inconstante.

fiction ['fikʃən] n (gen) ficción f; **~al** a novelesco; **fictitious** [fik'tiʃəs] a ficticio.

fiddle ['fidl] n (MUS) violín m; (cheating) trampa; (swindle) estafa // vt (accounts) falsificar; **to ~ with** vt fus jugar con; **fiddler** n violinista m/f.

fidelity [fi'dɛliti] n fidelidad f.

fidget ['fidʒit] vi moverse nerviosamente; **~y** a nervioso.

field [fi:ld] n campo; (ELEC) prado; (fig) esfera, especialidad f; (competitors) competidores mpl; (entrants) concurrentes mpl; **~ glasses** npl gemelos mpl; **~ marshal** n mariscal m; **~work** n trabajo de campo.

fiend [fi:nd] n demonio; **~ish** a diabólico.

fierce [fiəs] a feroz; (wind, attack) violento; (heat) intenso; (fighting, enemy) encarnizado.

fiery ['faiəri] a (burning) ardiente; (temperament) apasionado.

fifteen [fif'ti:n] num quince.

fifth [fifθ] a, n quinto.

fiftieth ['fiftiiθ] a quincuagésimo.

fifty ['fifti] num cincuenta.

fig [fig] n higo.

fight [fait] n (gen) pelea; (MIL) combate m; (struggle) lucha // vt, pt, pp **fought** vt luchar contra; (cancer, alcoholism) combatir // vi pelear, luchar; **~er** n combatiente m/f; (fig) luchador/a m/f; (plane) caza; **~ing** n (gen) el luchar; (battle) combate m.

figment ['figmənt] n: **a ~ of the imagination** una quimera.

figurative ['figjurətiv] a figurado.

figure 260 **fit**

figure ['fɪgə*] n (DRAWING, GEOM) figura, dibujo; (number, cipher) cifra; (body, outline) talle m, tipo // vt (esp US) imaginar // vi (appear) figurar; **to ~ out** vt (understand) comprender; **~head** n mascarón m de proa; **~ skating** n patinaje m de figuras.

file [faɪl] n (tool) lima; (dossier) expediente m; (folder) carpeta; (row) fila // vt limar; (papers) clasificar; (LAW: claim) presentar; (store) archivar; **to ~ in/out** vi entrar/salir en fila; **to ~ past** vt fus desfilar ante; **filing** n el archivar; **filing cabinet** n fichero, archivo.

fill [fɪl] vt llenar // n: **to eat one's ~** llenarse; **to ~ in** vt rellenar; **to ~ up** vt llenar (hasta el borde) // vi (AUT) poner gasolina.

fillet ['fɪlɪt] n filete m.

filling ['fɪlɪŋ] n (CULIN) relleno; (for tooth) empaste m; **~ station** n estación f de servicio.

film [fɪlm] n película // vt (scene) filmar // vi rodar (una película); **~ star** n astro, estrella de cine; **~strip** n tira de película.

filter ['fɪltə*] n filtro // vt filtrar; **~ tip** n boquilla.

filth [fɪlθ] n suciedad f; **~y** a sucio; (language) obsceno.

fin [fɪn] n (gen) aleta.

final ['faɪnl] a (last) final, último; (definitive) definitivo, terminante // n (SPORT) final f; **~s** npl (SCOL) exámenes mpl finales.

finale [fɪ'nɑːlɪ] n final m.

final: ~ist n (SPORT) finalista m/f; **~ize** vt concluir, completar; **~ly** ad (lastly) por último, finalmente; (eventually) por fin; (irrevocably) de modo definitivo.

finance [faɪ'næns] n (money) fondos mpl; **~s** npl finanzas fpl // vt financiar; **financial** [-'nænʃəl] a financiero; (economic) económico; **financier** n (gen) financiero; (investor) inversionista m/f.

find [faɪnd] pt, pp **found** vt (gen) encontrar, hallar; (come upon) descubrir // n hallazgo; descubrimiento; **to ~ sb guilty** (LAW) declarar culpable a uno; **to ~ out** vt averiguar; (truth, secret) descubrir; **to ~ out about** (by chance) enterarse de; **~ings** npl (LAW) veredicto sg, fallo sg; (of report) recomendaciones fpl.

fine [faɪn] a (delicate) fino; (good) bueno; (beautiful) bonito // ad (well) bien; (small) delgado // n (LAW) multa // vt (LAW) multar; **to be ~** (weather) hacer buen tiempo; **~ arts** npl bellas artes fpl.

finery ['faɪnərɪ] n adornos mpl.

finesse [fɪ'nɛs] n sutileza.

finger ['fɪŋgə*] n dedo // vt (touch) manosear; (MUS) tocar (distraídamente); **little/index ~** dedo meñique/índice; **~nail** n uña; **~print** n huella dactilar; **~tip** n yema del dedo.

finicky ['fɪnɪkɪ] a (fussy) delicado.

finish ['fɪnɪʃ] n (end) fin m; (goal) meta;

(polish etc) acabado // vt, vi terminar; **to ~ off** vt acabar, terminar; (kill) acabar con; **to ~ third** llegar el tercero; **~ing line** n línea de llegada o meta.

finite ['faɪnaɪt] a finito.

Finland ['fɪnlənd] n Finlandia.

Finn [fɪn] n finlandés/esa m/f; **~ish** a finlandés(esa) // n (LING) finlandés m.

fiord [fjɔːd] n fiordo.

fir [fə*] n abeto.

fire ['faɪə*] n (gen) fuego; (accidental) incendio // vt (gun) disparar; (set fire to) incendiar; (excite) exaltar; (interest) despertar; (dismiss) despedir // vi encenderse; **on ~** ardiendo, en llamas; **~ alarm** n alarma de incendios; **~arm** n arma de fuego; **~ brigade** n (cuerpo de) bomberos mpl; **~ engine** n coche m de bomberos; **~ escape** n escalera de incendios; **~ extinguisher** n extintor m (de fuego); **~man** n bombero; **~place** n chimenea; **~proof** a a prueba de fuego; **~side** n hogar m; **~ station** n parque m de bomberos; **~wood** n leña; **~works** npl fuegos mpl artificiales.

firing ['faɪərɪŋ] n (MIL) disparos mpl, tiroteo; **~ squad** n pelotón m de ejecución.

firm [fəːm] a firme // n firma; **~ly** ad firmemente; **~ness** n firmeza.

first [fəːst] a primero // ad (before others) primero; (when listing reasons etc) en primer lugar, primeramente // n (person: in race) primero; (AUT) primera; **at ~** al principio; **~ of all** ante todo; **~-aid kit** n botiquín m; **~-class** a de primera clase; **~-hand** a de primera mano; **~ly** ad en primer lugar; **~ name** n nombre m de pila; **~-rate** a de primera clase.

fir tree n abeto.

fiscal ['fɪskəl] a fiscal.

fish [fɪʃ] n, pl inv pez m; (food) pescado // vt, vi pescar; **to go ~ing** ir de pesca; **~erman** n pescador m; **~ery** n pesquería; **~ fingers** npl dedos mpl de pescado; **~ing boat** n barca de pesca; **~ing line** n sedal m; **~ing rod** n caña (de pescar); **~ing tackle** n aparejo (de pescar); **~ market** n mercado de pescado; **~monger** n pescadero; **~monger's (shop)** n pescadería; **~y** a (fig) sospechoso.

fission ['fɪʃən] n fisión f.

fissure ['fɪʃə*] n fisura.

fist [fɪst] n puño.

fit [fɪt] a (MED, SPORT) en (buena) forma; (proper) adecuado, apropiado // vt (clothes) sentar bien a; (try on: clothes) probar; (facts) cuadrar o corresponder con; (accommodate) ajustar, adaptar; (correspond exactly) encajar en // vi (clothes) entallar; (in space, gap) caber; (correspond) corresponder // n (MED) ataque m; **~ to apto para**; **~ for** apropiado para; **this dress is a good ~** este vestido me sienta bien; **to ~ in** vi (gen) encajarse; (fig: person) llevarse bien

(con todos); **to ~ out** (*also:* ~ **up**) *vt*
equipar; **~ful** *a* espasmódico,
intermitente; **~ment** *n* mueble *m*;
~ness *n* (*MED*) salud *f*; (*of remark*)
conveniencia; **~ter** *n* ajustador *m*; **~ting**
a apropiado // *n* (*of dress*) prueba;
~tings *npl* instalaciones *fpl*.

five [faɪv] *num* cinco; **fiver** *n* (*Brit: col*)
billete *m* de cinco libras.

fix [fɪks] *vt* (*secure*) fijar, asegurar; (*mend*)
arreglar // *n*: **to be in a ~** estar en un
aprieto; **~ed** [fɪkst] *a* (*prices etc*) fijo;
~ture ['fɪkstʃəʳ] *n* cosa fija; (*furniture*)
mueble *m* fijo; (*SPORT*) partido.

fizz [fɪz] *vi* hacer efervescencia.

fizzle ['fɪzl] **~ out** *vi* apagarse.

fizzy ['fɪzɪ] *a* (*drink*) gaseoso; (*gen*)
efervescente.

fjord [fjɔːd] = **fiord**.

flabbergasted ['flæbəgɑːstɪd] *a* pasmado.

flabby ['flæbɪ] *a* flojo; (*fat*) gordo.

flag [flæg] *n* bandera; (*stone*) losa // *vi*
acabarse, decaer; **to ~ sb down** hacer
signos a uno para que se detenga; **~pole**
n asta de bandera.

flagrant ['fleɪgrənt] *a* flagrante.

flair [flɛəʳ] *n* aptitud *f* especial.

flake [fleɪk] *n* (*of rust, paint*) escama; (*of
snow, soap powder*) copo // *vi* (*also:* ~ **off**)
desprenderse en escamas.

flamboyant [flæm'bɔɪənt] *a* (*dress*)
vistoso; (*person*) extravagante.

flame [fleɪm] *n* llama.

flamingo [flə'mɪŋgəu] *n* flamenco.

flammable ['flæməbl] *a* inflamable.

flan [flæn] *n* tarta.

flank [flæŋk] *n* flanco; (*of person*) costado
// *vt* flanquear.

flannel ['flænl] *n* (*also:* **face ~**) paño;
(*fabric*) franela; (*col*) coba; **~s** *npl*
pantalones *mpl* de franela.

flap [flæp] *n* (*of pocket*) cartera; (*of
envelope*) solapa; (*of table*) hoja
(plegadiza); (*wing movement*) aletazo // *vt*
(*wings*) aletear // *vi* (*sail, flag*) ondear.

flare [flɛəʳ] *n* llamarada; (*MIL*) bengala; (*in
skirt etc*) vuelo; **to ~ up** *vi* encenderse;
(*fig: person*) encolerizarse; (*: revolt*)
estallar.

flash [flæʃ] *n* relámpago; (*also:* **news ~**)
noticias *fpl* de última hora; (*PHOT*) flash *m*
// *vt* (*light, headlights*) encender y apagar
(la luz); (*torch*) encender // *vi* brillar,
relampaguear; **in a ~** en un instante; **he
~ed by or past** pasó como un rayo;
~back *n* flashback *m*; **~bulb** *n* bombilla
fusible; **~er** *n* (*AUT*) intermitente *m*.

flashy ['flæʃɪ] *a* (*pej*) ostentoso.

flask [flɑːsk] *n* frasco; (*also:* **vacuum ~**)
termo.

flat [flæt] *a* llano; (*smooth*) liso; (*tyre*)
desinflado; (*beer*) muerto; (*MUS*)
desafinado // *n* (*apartment*) piso,
apartamento; (*AUT*) pinchazo; (*MUS*)
pinchazo; **~ly** *ad* terminantemente, de
plano; **~ness** *n* (*of land*) llanura, lo llano;
~ten *vt* (*also:* **~ten out**) allanar;

(*smooth out*) alisar; (*demolish*) aplastar.

flatter ['flætəʳ] *vt* adular, halagar; **~er** *n*
adulador/a *m/f*; **~ing** *a* halagüeño; **~y** *n*
adulación *f*.

flatulence ['flætjuləns] *n* flatulencia.

flaunt [flɔːnt] *vt* ostentar, lucir.

flavour, flavor (*US*) ['fleɪvəʳ] *n* sabor *m*,
gusto // *vt* sazonar, condimentar; **~ed
with** con sabor a; **~ing** *n* condimento.

flaw [flɔː] *n* defecto; **~less** *a* intachable.

flax [flæks] *n* lino; **~en** *a* rubio.

flea [fliː] *n* pulga; **~pit** *n* cine *m* de baja
categoría.

flee [fliː], *pt, pp* **fled** [flɛd] *vt* huir de,
abandonar // *vi* huir, fugarse.

fleece [fliːs] *n* vellón *m*; (*wool*) lana // *vt*
(*col*) pelar.

fleet [fliːt] *n* (*gen*) flota; (*of lorries etc*)
escuadra.

fleeting ['fliːtɪŋ] *a* fugaz.

Flemish ['flemɪʃ] *a* flamenco.

flesh [fleʃ] *n* carne *f*; (*of fruit*) pulpa; **of ~
and blood** de carne y hueso.

flew [fluː] *pt of* **fly**.

flex [fleks] *n* cordón *m* // *vt* (*muscles*)
tensar; **~ibility** [-ı'bılıtı] *n* flexibilidad *f*;
~ible *a* flexible.

flick [flık] *n* golpecito; (*with finger*)
capirotazo; (*with whip*) chasquido // *vt* dar
un golpecito a; **to ~ through** *vt fus*
hojear.

flicker ['flıkəʳ] *vi* (*light*) parpadear;
(*flame*) vacilar // *n* parpadeo.

flier ['flaɪəʳ] *n* aviador/a *m/f*.

flight [flaɪt] *n* vuelo; (*escape*) huida, fuga;
(*also:* ~ **of steps**) tramo (de escaleras);
to take ~ huir, darse a la fuga; **to put to
~** ahuyentar; **~ deck** *n* (*AVIAT*) cabina.

flimsy ['flımzı] *a* (*thin*) muy ligero; (*weak*)
débil.

flinch [flıntʃ] *vi* acobardarse.

fling [flıŋ], *pt, pp* **flung** *vt* arrojar.

flint [flınt] *n* pedernal *m*; (*in lighter*)
piedra.

flip [flıp] *vt* dar la vuelta a; (*coin*) echar a
cara o cruz.

flippant ['flıpənt] *a* poco serio.

flirt [flɜːt] *vi* coquetear, flirtear // *n*
coqueta *m/f*; **~ation** [-'teıʃən] *n* coqueteo,
flirteo.

flit [flıt] *vi* revolotear.

float [fləut] *n* flotador *m*; (*in procession*)
carroza // *vi* flotar; (*swimmer*) hacer la
plancha // *vt* (*gen*) hacer flotar;
(*company*) lanzar.

flock [flɔk] *n* (*of sheep*) rebaño; (*of birds*)
bandada; (*of people*) multitud *f*.

flog [flɔg] *vt* azotar; (*col*) vender.

flood [flʌd] *n* inundación *f*; (*of words, tears
etc*) torrente *m* // *vt* inundar; **~ing** *n*
inundación *f*; **~light** *n* foco.

floor [flɔːʳ] *n* suelo; (*storey*) piso; (*of sea*)
fondo; (*dance ~*) pista // *vt* (*fig*) dejar sin
respuesta; **ground ~** (*Brit*), **first ~** (*US*)
planta baja; **first ~** (*Brit*), **second ~**

(US) primer piso; ~**board** n tabla; ~**show** n cabaret m.

flop [flɔp] n fracaso // vi *(fail)* fracasar.

floppy ['flɔpɪ] a flojo.

flora ['flɔːrə] n flora; **floral** ['flɔːrl] a floral.

florid ['flɔrɪd] a *(style)* florido.

florist ['flɔrɪst] n florista m/f; ~**'s (shop)** n florería.

flounce [flauns] n volante m; **to** ~ **out** vi salir enfadado.

flounder ['flaundə*] vi tropezar.

flour ['flauə*] n harina.

flourish ['flʌrɪʃ] vi florecer; ~**ing** a floreciente.

flout [flaut] vt burlarse de.

flow [fləu] n *(movement)* flujo; *(direction)* curso; *(tide)* corriente f // vi correr, fluir; *(blood)* derramarse.

flower ['flauə*] n flor f // vi florecer; ~**bed** n macizo; ~**pot** n tiesto; ~**y** a florido.

flown [fləun] pp of **fly.**

flu [fluː] n gripe f.

fluctuate ['flʌktjueɪt] vi fluctuar; **fluctuation** [-'eɪʃən] n fluctuación f.

fluent ['fluːənt] a *(speech)* elocuente; **he speaks** ~ **French, he's** ~ **in French** domina el francés; ~**ly** ad con fluidez.

fluff [flʌf] n pelusa; ~**y** a velloso.

fluid ['fluːɪd] a, n fluido, líquido.

fluke [fluːk] n *(col)* chiripa.

flung [flʌŋ] pt, pp of **fling.**

fluorescent [fluə'rɛsnt] a fluorescente.

fluoride ['fluəraɪd] n fluoruro.

flurry ['flʌrɪ] n *(of snow)* ráfago; *(haste)* agitación f; ~ **of activity** frenesí m de actividad.

flush [flʌʃ] n *(on face)* rubor m; *(plenty)* plenitud f, abundancia // vt limpiar con agua // vi ruborizarse // a: ~ **with** a ras de; **to** ~ **the toilet** hacer funcionar el WC; ~**ed** a ruborizado.

flustered ['flʌstəd] a aturdido.

flute [fluːt] n flauta.

flutter ['flʌtə*] n emoción f; *(of wings)* revoloteo, aleteo; *(fam: bet)* apuesta // vi revolotear.

flux [flʌks] n flujo; **in a state of** ~ cambiando continuamente.

fly [flaɪ] n *(insect)* mosca; *(on trousers: also:* **flies)** bragueta // *(vb: pt* **flew,** *pp* **flown)** vt *(gen)* hacer volar; *(plane)* pilot(e)ar; *(cargo)* transportar (en avión); *(distances)* recorrer (en avión) // vi volar; *(passengers)* ir o subir en avión; *(escape)* evadirse; *(flag)* ondear; **to let** ~ desahogarse; ~**ing** n *(activity)* (el) volar // a: ~**ing visit** visita relámpago; **with** ~**ing colours** con lucimiento; ~**ing saucer** n platillo volante; ~**over** n *(Brit: bridge)* paso a desnivel o superior; ~**past** n desfile m aéreo; ~**sheet** n *(for tent)* doble techo.

foal [fəul] n potro.

foam [fəum] n espuma // vi echar espuma; ~ **rubber** n espuma de caucho.

fob [fɔb] vt: **to** ~ **sb off** deshacerse de alguien con excusas.

focal ['fəukəl] a focal.

focus ['fəukəs], pl ~**es** n foco // vt *(field glasses etc)* enfocar; **to** ~ **on** enfocar a; **in/out of** ~ enfocado/desenfocado.

fodder ['fɔdə*] n pienso.

foe [fəu] n enemigo.

foetus ['fiːtəs] n feto.

fog [fɔg] n niebla; ~**gy** a: **it's** ~**gy** hay niebla, está brumoso.

foil [fɔɪl] vt frustrar // n hoja; *(also:* **kitchen** ~**)** papel m (de) aluminio; *(FENCING)* florete m.

fold [fəuld] n *(bend, crease)* pliegue m; *(of skin)* arruga; *(AGR)* redil m // vt doblar; **to** ~ **up** vi *(map etc)* plegarse, doblarse; *(business)* quebrar // vt *(map etc)* plegar; ~**er** n *(for papers)* carpeta; *(brochure)* folleto; ~**ing** a *(chair, bed)* plegable.

foliage ['fəulɪdʒ] n follaje m.

folk [fəuk] npl gente f // a popular, folklórico; ~**s** npl familia, parientes mpl; ~**lore** ['fəuklɔː*] n folklore m; ~**song** n canción f popular o folklórica.

follow ['fɔləu] vt seguir // vi seguir; *(result)* resultar; **he** ~**ed suit** hizo lo mismo; **to** ~ **up** vt *(letter, offer)* responder a; *(case)* investigar; ~**er** n seguidor/a m/f; *(POL)* partidario/a; ~**ing** a siguiente // n afición f, partidarios mpl.

folly ['fɔlɪ] n locura.

fond [fɔnd] a *(loving)* cariñoso; **to be** ~ **of** tener cariño a.

fondle ['fɔndl] vt acariciar.

fondness ['fɔndnɪs] n *(for things)* gusto; *(for people)* cariño.

font [fɔnt] n pila bautismal.

food [fuːd] n comida; ~ **mixer** n batidora; ~ **poisoning** n botulismo; ~**stuffs** npl comestibles mpl.

fool [fuːl] n tonto/a; *(CULIN)* puré m de frutas con nata // vt engañar // vi *(gen:* ~ **around)** bromear; *(waste time)* perder el tiempo; ~**hardy** a temerario; ~**ish** a tonto; *(stupid)* estúpido; *(careless)* imprudente; ~**proof** a *(plan etc)* infalible.

foot [fut], pl **feet** n pie m; *(measure)* pie m *(= 304 mm)*; *(of animal)* pata // vt *(bill)* pagar; **on** ~ a pie; ~**ball** n balón m; *(game)* fútbol m; ~**baller** n futbolista m; ~**brake** n freno de pie; ~**bridge** n puente m para peatones; ~**hills** npl estribaciones fpl; ~**hold** n pie m firme; ~**ing** n *(fig)* posición f; **to lose one's** ~**ing** perder el pie; **on an equal** ~**ing** en pie de igualdad; ~**lights** npl candilejas fpl; ~**man** n lacayo; ~**note** n nota de pie; ~**path** n sendero; *(pavement)* acera; ~**sore** a con los pies adoloridos; ~**step** n paso; ~**wear** n calzado.

for [fɔː*] prep *(gen)* para; *(as, in exchange for, because of)* por; *(during)* durante; *(in spite of)* a pesar de // conj pues, ya que; **it was sold** ~ **100 pesetas** se vendió por 100 pesetas; **what** ~? ¿para qué?; **what's it** ~? ¿para qué sirve?; **he was away** ~

2 years estuvo fuera 2 años; **he went ~ the paper** fue a buscar el periódico; **~ sale** se vende.

forage ['fɔrɪdʒ] n forraje m.

foray ['fɔreɪ] n incursión f.

forbid [fə'bɪd], pt **forbad(e)** [fə'bæd], pp **forbidden** [fə'bɪdn] vt prohibir; **~ding** a (gloomy) lúgubre; (severe) severo.

force [fɔːs] n fuerza f // vt forzar; **to ~ o.s.** to hacer un esfuerzo por; **the F~s** npl las Fuerzas Armadas; **in ~** en vigor; **~d** [fɔːst] a forzado; **~ful** a enérgico.

forceps ['fɔːsɛps] npl fórceps m inv.

forcibly ['fɔːsəblɪ] ad a la fuerza.

ford [fɔːd] n vado // vt vadear.

forearm ['fɔːrɑːm] n antebrazo.

foreboding [fɔː'bəudɪŋ] n presagio.

forecast ['fɔːkɑːst] n pronóstico // vt (irg: like **cast**) pronosticar.

forefathers ['fɔːfɑːðəz] npl antepasados mpl.

forefinger ['fɔːfɪŋgə*] n (dedo) índice m.

forego ['fɔːgəu] = **forgo**.

foregone ['fɔːgɔn] a: **it's a ~ conclusion** es una conclusión inevitable.

foreground ['fɔːgraund] n primer plano.

forehead ['fɔrɪd] n frente f.

foreign ['fɔrɪn] a extranjero; (trade) exterior; **~er** n extranjero; **~ exchange** n divisas fpl; **F~ Minister** n Ministro de Asuntos Exteriores; **F~ Office** n Ministerio de Asuntos Exteriores.

foreleg ['fɔːlɛg] n pata delantera.

foreman ['fɔːmən] n capataz m; (in construction) maestro de obras.

foremost ['fɔːməust] a principal.

forensic [fə'rɛnsɪk] a forense.

forerunner ['fɔːrʌnə*] n precursor/a m/f.

foresee [fɔː'siː] (irg: like **see**) vt prever; **~able** a previsible.

foresight ['fɔːsaɪt] n previsión f.

forest ['fɔrɪst] n bosque m.

forestall [fɔː'stɔːl] vt prevenir.

forestry ['fɔrɪstrɪ] n silvicultura.

foretaste ['fɔːteɪst] n (gen) anticipo; (sample) muestra.

foretell [fɔː'tɛl] (irg: like **tell**) vt predecir, pronosticar.

forever [fə'rɛvə*] ad para siempre.

foreword ['fɔːwəːd] n prefacio.

forfeit ['fɔːfɪt] n pérdida; (fine) multa // vt perder (derecho a).

forgave [fə'geɪv] pt of **forgive**.

forge [fɔːdʒ] n fragua; (smithy) herrería // vt (signature, money) falsificar; (metal) forjar; **to ~ ahead** vi avanzar constantemente; **forger** n falsificador/a m/f; **~ry** n falsificación f.

forget [fə'gɛt], pt **forgot**, pp **forgotten** vt olvidar // vi olvidarse; **~ful** a olvidadizo; **~fulness** n (gen) olvido; (thoughtlessness) descuido; (oblivion) falta de memoria.

forgive [fə'gɪv], pt **forgave**, pp **forgiven** vt perdonar; **to ~ sb for sth** perdonar algo a uno; **~ness** n perdón m.

forgo [fɔː'gəu] (irg: like **go**) vt (give up)

renunciar a; (go without) privarse de.

forgot [fə'gɔt] pt of **forget**.

forgotten [fə'gɔtn] pp of **forget**.

fork [fɔːk] n (for eating) tenedor m; (for gardening) horca; (of roads) bifurcación f; (in tree) horcadura // vi (road) bifurcarse; **to ~ out** vt (col: pay) desembolsar; **~ed** [fɔːkt] a (lightning) en zigzag; **~-lift truck** n elevadora-transportadora de horquilla.

form [fɔːm] n forma; (scol) clase f; (questionnaire) formulario // vt formar; **in top ~** en plena forma.

formal ['fɔːməl] a (offer, receipt) oficial; (person etc) ceremonioso; (occasion, dinner) oficial, protocolario; (dress) de etiqueta; **~ity** [-'mælɪtɪ] n ceremonia; **~ities** npl formalidades fpl; **~ly** ad oficialmente.

format ['fɔːmæt] n formato.

formation [fɔː'meɪʃən] n formación f.

formative ['fɔːmətɪv] a (years) formativo.

former ['fɔːmə*] a anterior; (earlier) antiguo; (ex) ex; **the ~ ... the latter ...** aquél ... éste ...; **~ly** ad antiguamente.

formidable ['fɔːmɪdəbl] a formidable.

formula ['fɔːmjulə] n fórmula f.

formulate ['fɔːmjuleɪt] vt formular.

forsake [fə'seɪk], pt **forsook** [fə'suk], pp **forsaken** [fə'seɪkən] vt (gen) abandonar; (plan) renunciar a.

fort [fɔːt] n fuerte m.

forte ['fɔːtɪ] n fuerte m.

forth [fɔːθ] ad en adelante; **back and ~** de acá para allá; **and so ~** y así sucesivamente; **~coming** a próximo, venidero; (character) comunicativo; **~right** a franco.

fortieth ['fɔːtɪɪθ] a cuadragésimo.

fortification [fɔːtɪfɪ'keɪʃən] n fortificación f; **fortify** ['fɔːtɪfaɪ] vt fortalecer.

fortitude ['fɔːtɪtjuːd] n fortaleza.

fortnight ['fɔːtnaɪt] n quincena; **~ly** a quincenal // ad quincenalmente.

fortress ['fɔːtrɪs] n fortaleza.

fortuitous [fɔː'tjuːɪtəs] a fortuito.

fortunate ['fɔːtʃənɪt] a: **to be ~** tener suerte; **it is ~ that...** es afortunado que...; **~ly** ad afortunadamente.

fortune ['fɔːtʃən] n suerte f; (wealth) fortuna; **~-teller** n adivina.

forty ['fɔːtɪ] num cuarenta.

forum ['fɔːrəm] n foro.

forward ['fɔːwəd] a (movement, position) avanzado; (front) delantero; (not shy) atrevido // n (sport) delantero // vt (letter) remitir; (career) progresar; **to move ~** avanzar; **~(s)** ad (hacia) adelante.

fossil ['fɔsl] n fósil m.

foster ['fɔstə*] vt fomentar; **~ brother** n hermano de leche; **~ child** n hijo adoptivo; **~ mother** n madre f adoptiva.

fought [fɔːt] pt, pp of **fight**.

foul [faul] a (gen) sucio, puerco; (weather) horrible; (smell etc) asqueroso // n (FOOTBALL) falta (en contra) // vt (dirty) ensuciar; (block) atascar; (football player) cometer una falta contra; ~ **play** n (SPORT) mala jugada; (LAW) muerte f violenta.

found [faund] pt, pp of **find** // vt (establish) fundar; ~**ation** [-'deɪʃən] n (act) fundación f; (basis) base f; (also: ~**ation cream**) crema base; ~**ations** npl (of building) cimientos mpl.

founder ['faundə*] n fundador/a m/f // vi hundirse.

foundry ['faundrɪ] n fundición f.

fountain ['fauntɪn] n fuente f; ~ **pen** n pluma-fuente f.

four [fɔ:*] num cuatro; **on all** ~**s** a gatas; ~-**poster** n cama a columnas; ~**some** ['fɔ:səm] n grupo de cuatro personas; ~**teen** num catorce; ~**teenth** a décimocuarto; ~**th** a cuarto.

fowl [faul] n ave f (de corral).

fox [fɔks] n zorro // vt confundir; ~**trot** n fox m.

foyer ['fɔɪeɪ] n vestíbulo.

fracas ['frækɑ:] n gresca, riña.

fraction ['frækʃən] n fracción f.

fracture ['fræktʃə*] n fractura // vt fracturar.

fragile ['frædʒaɪl] a frágil.

fragment ['frægmənt] n fragmento; ~**ary** a fragmentario.

fragrance ['freɪgrəns] n fragancia; **fragrant** [-ənt] a fragante, oloroso.

frail [freɪl] a (fragile) frágil, quebradizo; (weak) delicado.

frame [freɪm] n (gen) estructura; (body) talle m; (TECH) armazón m; (of picture, door etc) marco; (of spectacles: also: ~**s**) montura // vt encuadrar; (reply) formular; (fam) incriminar; ~ **of mind** n estado de ánimo; ~**work** n marco.

France [frɑ:ns] n Francia.

franchise ['fræntʃaɪz] n (POL) derecho de votar, sufragio.

frank [fræŋk] a franco // vt (letter) franquear; ~**ly** ad francamente; ~**ness** n franqueza.

frantic ['fræntɪk] a frenético.

fraternal [frə'tə:nl] a fraterno; **fraternity** [-nɪtɪ] n (club) fraternidad f; (US) club m de estudiantes; (guild) cofradía; **fraternize** ['frætənaɪz] vi confraternizar.

fraud [frɔ:d] n fraude m; (person) impostor m; ~**ulent** a fraudulento.

fraught [frɔ:t] a: ~ **with** cargado de.

fray [freɪ] n combate m, lucha // vi deshilacharse; **tempers were** ~**ed** tenían los nervios a punto.

freak [fri:k] n (person) fenómeno; (event) suceso anormal; (thing) cosa insólita.

freckle ['frekl] n peca.

free [fri:] a (gen) libre; (not fixed) suelto; (gratis) gratuito; (unoccupied) desocupado; (liberal) generoso // vt (prisoner etc) poner en libertad; (jammed object) soltar; ~ **(of charge)** ad gratis; ~**dom** ['fri:dəm] n libertad f; ~-**for-all** n riña general; ~ **kick** n tiro libre; ~**lance** a

independiente; ~**ly** ad libremente; generosamente; ~**mason** n francmasón m; ~ **trade** n libre comercio; ~**way** n (US) autopista; ~**wheel** vi ir en punto muerto; ~ **will** n libre albedrío; **of one's own** ~ **will** por su propia voluntad.

freeze [fri:z], pt **froze**, pp **frozen** vi helarse, congelarse // vt helar; (prices, food, salaries) congelar // n helada; congelación f; **freezer** n congelador m.

freezing ['fri:zɪŋ] a helado; ~ **point** n punto de congelación; **3 degrees below** ~ tres grados bajo cero.

freight [freɪt] n (goods) carga; (money charged) flete m; ~ **car** n (US) vagón m de mercancías.

French [frentʃ] a francés(esa) // n (LING) francés m; **the** ~ los franceses; ~ **fried (potatoes)** npl patatas fpl fritas; ~**man/woman** n francés/esa m/f; ~ **window** n puertaventana.

frenzy ['frenzɪ] n frenesí m.

frequency ['fri:kwənsɪ] n frecuencia; **frequent** [-ənt] a frecuente // vt [frɪ'kwent] frecuentar; **frequently** [-əntlɪ] ad frecuentemente, a menudo.

fresco ['freskəu] n fresco.

fresh [freʃ] a (gen) fresco; (new) nuevo; (water) dulce; ~**en** vi (wind, air) soplar más recio; **to** ~**en up** vi (person) lavarse, arreglarse; ~**ly** ad (newly) nuevamente; (recently) recientemente; ~**ness** n frescura.

fret [fret] vi inquietarse.

friar ['fraɪə*] n fraile m; (before name) fray.

friction ['frɪkʃən] n fricción f.

Friday ['fraɪdɪ] n viernes m.

fridge [frɪdʒ] n nevera.

friend [frend] n amigo/a; ~**liness** n simpatía; ~**ly** a simpático; ~**ship** n amistad f.

frieze [fri:z] n friso.

frigate ['frɪgɪt] n fragata.

fright [fraɪt] n susto; **to take** ~ asustarse; ~**en** vt asustar; ~**ening** a espantoso; ~**ful** a espantoso, horrible; ~**fully** ad terriblemente.

frigid ['frɪdʒɪd] a (MED) frígido, frío; ~**ity** [frɪ'dʒɪdɪtɪ] n frialdad f; (MED) frigidez f.

frill [frɪl] n volante m.

fringe [frɪndʒ] n flequillo; (edge: of forest etc) borde m, margen m; ~ **benefits** npl ventajas fpl supletorias.

frisky ['frɪskɪ] a juguetón(ona), fogoso.

fritter ['frɪtə*] n buñuelo; **to** ~ **away** vt desperdiciar.

frivolous ['frɪvələs] a frívolo.

frizzy ['frɪzɪ] a rizado.

fro [frəu] see **to**.

frock [frɔk] n vestido.

frog [frɔg] n rana; ~**man** n hombre-rana m.

frolic ['frɔlɪk] vi juguetear.

from [frɔm] prep de; ~ **January (on)** a partir de enero; ~ **what he says** por lo que dice.

front [frʌnt] n (foremost part) parte f delantera; (of house) fachada; (promenade: also: sea ~) paseo marítimo; (MIL, POL, METEOROLOGY) frente m; (fig: appearances) apariencias fpl // a delantero, primero; **in ~ (of)** delante (de); **~al** a frontal; **~door** n puerta principal; **~ier** ['frʌntɪə*] n frontera; **~ page** n primera plana; **~room** n (Brit) salón m, sala; **~-wheel drive** n tracción f delantera.

frost [frɔst] n (gen) helada; (visible) escarcha; (visible) congelación f; **~ed** a (glass) deslustrado; **~y** a (window) cubierto de escarcha; (welcome) glacial.

froth [frɔθ] n espuma.

frown [fraun] n ceño // vi fruncir el ceño.

froze [frəuz] pt of **freeze**.

frozen ['frəuzn] pp of **freeze**.

frugal ['fru:gəl] a frugal.

fruit [fru:t] n, pl inv fruta; **~erer** n frutero; **~erer's (shop)** n frutería; **~ful** a provechoso; **~ion** [fru:'ɪʃən] n: **to come to ~ion** realizarse; **~ machine** n máquina tragaperras.

frustrate [frʌs'treɪt] vt frustrar; **~d** a frustrado; **frustration** [-'treɪʃən] n frustración f.

fry [fraɪ], pt, pp **fried** vt freír; **small ~** gente f menuda; **~ing pan** n sartén f.

ft. abbr of **foot, feet**.

fuchsia ['fju:ʃə] n fucsia.

fudge [fʌdʒ] n (CULIN) dulce m de azúcar, manjar m.

fuel [fjuəl] n (for heating) combustible m; (coal) carbón m; (wood) leña; (for propelling) carburante m; **~ oil** n aceite m combustible; **~ tank** n depósito de combustible.

fugitive ['fju:dʒɪtɪv] n fugitivo.

fulfil [ful'fɪl] vt (function) cumplir con; (condition) satisfacer; (wish, desire) realizar; **~ment** n satisfacción f; realización f.

full [ful] a lleno; (fig) pleno; (complete) completo; (information) detallado // ad: **~well** perfectamente; **I'm ~** estoy lleno; **~ employment** pleno empleo; **~ fare** pasaje m completo; **a ~ two hours** dos horas completas; **at ~ speed** a máxima velocidad; **in ~** (reproduce, quote) íntegramente; **~-length** a (portrait) de cuerpo entero; **~ moon** n luna llena; **~-sized** a (portrait etc) de tamaño natural; **~ stop** n punto; **~-time** a (work) de tiempo completo // n (SPORT) final m; **~y** ad completamente; **~y-fledged** a (teacher, barrister) diplomado.

fumble ['fʌmbl] **to ~ with** vt fus revolver, manosear.

fume [fju:m] vi humear, echar humo; **~s** npl humo sg, gases mpl.

fumigate ['fju:mɪgeɪt] vt fumigar.

fun [fʌn] n (amusement) diversión f; (joy) alegría; **to have ~** divertirse; **for ~** en broma; **to make ~ of** vt fus burlarse de.

function ['fʌŋkʃən] n función f // vi funcionar; **~al** a funcional.

fund [fʌnd] n fondo; (source, store) fuente f; **~s** npl fondos mpl.

fundamental [fʌndə'mentl] a fundamental.

funeral ['fju:nərəl] n (burial) entierro; (ceremony) funerales mpl; **~ service** n misa de difuntos.

funfair ['fʌnfɛə*] n parque m de atracciones.

fungus ['fʌŋgəs], pl **-gi** [-gaɪ] n hongo.

funnel ['fʌnl] n embudo; (of ship) chimenea.

funnily ['fʌnɪlɪ] ad de modo divertido.

funny ['fʌnɪ] a gracioso, divertido; (strange) curioso, raro.

fur [fə:*] n piel f; (in kettle etc) sarro; **~coat** n abrigo de pieles.

furious ['fjuərɪəs] a furioso; (effort) violento; **~ly** ad con furia.

furlong ['fə:lɔŋ] n octava parte de una milla.

furlough ['fə:ləu] n (US) licencia.

furnace ['fə:nɪs] n horno.

furnish ['fə:nɪʃ] vt amueblar; (supply) suministrar; **~ings** npl muebles mpl.

furniture ['fə:nɪtʃə*] n muebles mpl; **piece of ~** mueble m; **~ polish** n cera de lustrar.

furrier ['fʌrɪə*] n peletero.

furrow ['fʌrəu] n surco.

furry ['fə:rɪ] a peludo.

further ['fə:ðə*] a (new) nuevo, adicional; (place) más lejano // ad más lejos; (more) más; (moreover) además // vt promover, adelantar; **~ education** n educación f superior; **~more** [fə:ðə'mɔ:*] ad además.

furthest ['fə:ðɪst] superlative of **far**.

furtive ['fə:tɪv] a furtivo.

fury ['fjuərɪ] n furia.

fuse, fuze (US) [fju:z] n fusible m; (for bomb etc) mecha // vt (metal) fundir; (fig) fusionar // vi fundirse; fusionarse; (ELEC): **to ~ the lights** fundir los plomos; **~ box** n caja de fusibles.

fuselage ['fju:zəlɑ:ʒ] n fuselaje m.

fusion ['fju:ʒən] n fusión f.

fuss [fʌs] n (noise) bulla; (dispute) lío; (complaining) protesta; (ceremony) ceremonias fpl; **to make a ~** armar un lío o jaleo; **~y** a (person) exigente.

futile ['fju:taɪl] a vano; **futility** [-'tɪlɪtɪ] n inutilidad f.

future ['fju:tʃə*] a (gen) futuro; (coming) venidero // n futuro; **futuristic** [-'rɪstɪk] a futurístico.

fuzzy ['fʌzɪ] a (PHOT) borroso; (hair) muy rizado.

G

gabble ['gæbl] vi hablar atropelladamente; (gossip) cotorrear.

gable ['geɪbl] n aguilón m.

gadget ['gædʒɪt] n aparato.

Gaelic ['geɪlɪk] n (LING) gaélico.

gag [gæg] n (joke) chiste m // vt amordazar.

gaiety ['geɪtɪ] n alegría.

gaily ['geɪlɪ] ad alegremente.

gain [geɪn] n ganancia // vt ganar // vi (watch) adelantarse; **to ~ by sth** sacar provecho de algo; **to ~ on sb** ir ganando terreno a uno.

gait [geɪt] n modo de andar.

gala ['gɑːlə] n fiesta.

galaxy ['gæləksɪ] n galaxia.

gale [geɪl] n (wind) vendaval m.

gallant ['gælənt] a valiente; (towards ladies) atento; **~ry** n valentía; (courtesy) cortesía.

gall-bladder ['gɔːlblædə*] n vesícula biliar.

gallery ['gælərɪ] n galería; (also: **art ~**) museo.

galley ['gælɪ] n (ship's kitchen) cocina; (ship) galera.

gallon ['gæln] n galón m (4.543 litros).

gallop ['gæləp] n galope m // vi galopar.

gallows ['gæləʊz] n horca.

gallstone ['gɔːlstəʊn] n cálculo biliario.

gamble ['gæmbl] n (risk) riesgo; (bet) apuesta // vt: **to ~ on** apostar a; (fig) confiar en que // vi jugar; (COMM) especular; **gambler** n jugador/a m/f; **gambling** n el juego.

game [geɪm] n (gen) juego; (match) partido; (of cards) partida; (HUNTING) caza // a valiente; (ready): **to be ~ for anything** atreverse a todo; **~ bird** n ave f de caza; **~keeper** n guardabosques m inv.

gammon ['gæmən] n (bacon) tocino ahumado; (ham) jamón m ahumado.

gang [gæŋ] n pandilla; (of workmen) brigada // vi: **to ~ up on sb** conspirar contra uno.

gangrene ['gæŋgriːn] n gangrena.

gangster ['gæŋstə*] n gángster m.

gangway ['gæŋweɪ] n (in theatre etc) pasillo; (on ship) pasarela; (on dock) pasadera.

gaol [dʒeɪl] = **jail**.

gap [gæp] n vacío, hueco; (in trees, traffic) claro; (in time) intervalo.

gape [geɪp] vi estar o quedarse boquiabierto; **gaping** a (hole) muy abierto.

garage ['gærɑːʒ] n garaje m.

garbage ['gɑːbɪdʒ] n basura; **~ can** n (US) cubo de la basura.

garbled ['gɑːbld] a (distorted) falsificado, amañado.

garden ['gɑːdn] n jardín m; **~er** n jardinero; **~ing** n jardinería.

gargle ['gɑːgl] vi hacer gárgaras.

gargoyle ['gɑːgɔɪl] n gárgola.

garish ['gɛərɪʃ] a chillón(ona).

garland ['gɑːlənd] n guirnalda.

garlic ['gɑːlɪk] n ajo.

garment ['gɑːmənt] n prenda (de vestir).

garnish ['gɑːnɪʃ] vt adornar; (CULIN) aderezar.

garrison ['gærɪsn] n guarnición f // vt guarnecer.

garrulous ['gærjuləs] a gárrulo.

garter ['gɑːtə*] n liga; **~ belt** portaligas m inv.

gas [gæs] n gas m; (US: gasoline) gasolina // vt asfixiar con gas; **~ cooker** n cocina de gas; **~ cylinder** n bombona de gas; **~ fire** n estufa de gas.

gash [gæʃ] n raja; (on face) cuchillada // vt (gen) rajar; (with knife) acuchillar.

gasket ['gæskɪt] n (AUT) junta.

gas: ~mask n careta antigás; **~ meter** n contador m de gas.

gasoline ['gæsəliːn] n (US) gasolina.

gasp [gɑːsp] n grito sofocado // vi (pant) jadear; **to ~ out** vt (say) decir con voz entrecortada.

gas: ~ ring n hornillo de gas; **~ stove** n cocina de gas; **~sy** a gaseoso; **~ tap** n llave f del gas.

gastric ['gæstrɪk] a gástrico; **~ ulcer** n úlcera gástrica.

gate [geɪt] n puerta; (RAIL) barrera; **~crash** vt colarse de gorra en; **~way** n puerta.

gather ['gæðə*] vt (flowers, fruit) coger; (assemble) reunir; (pick up) recoger; (SEWING) fruncir; (understand) entender // vi (assemble) reunirse; **~ing** n reunión f, asamblea.

gauche [gəʊʃ] a torpe.

gaudy ['gɔːdɪ] a chillón(ona).

gauge [geɪdʒ] n medida; (RAIL) entrevía; (instrument) indicador m // vt medir.

gaunt [gɔːnt] a descarnado; (grim, desolate) desolado.

gauntlet ['gɔːntlɪt] n (fig): **to run the ~** correr baquetas; **to throw down the ~** arrojar el guante.

gauze [gɔːz] n gasa.

gave [geɪv] pt of **give**.

gay [geɪ] a (person) alegre; (colour) vistoso, vivo; (homosexual) gay.

gaze [geɪz] n mirada fija; **to ~ at sth** mirar algo con fijeza.

gazelle [gə'zɛl] n gacela.

gazetteer [gæzə'tɪə*] n diccionario geográfico.

G.B. abbr of **Great Britain.**

G.C.E. n abbr of **General Certificate of Education.**

gear [gɪə*] n equipo, herramientas fpl; (TECH) engranaje m; (AUT) velocidad f, marcha; **top/low ~** tercera (o cuarta)/primera velocidad; **in ~** en marcha; **~ box** n caja de cambios; **~ lever, ~ shift** (US) n palanca de velocidades; **~ wheel** n rueda dentada.

geese [giːs] pl of **goose.**

gelatin(e) ['dʒɛlətiːn] n gelatina.

gelignite ['dʒɛlɪgnaɪt] n gelignita.

gem [dʒɛm] n joya.

Gemini ['dʒɛmɪnaɪ] n Géminis m, Gemelos mpl.

gender ['dʒɛndə*] n género.

general ['dʒɛnərl] *n* general *m // a* general; **in ~** en general; **~ election** *n* elecciones *fpl* generales; **~ization** [-aɪ'zeɪʃən] *n* generalización *f*; **~ize** *vi* generalizar; **~ly** *ad* generalmente, en general; **~ practitioner (G.P.)** *n* médico general.

generate ['dʒɛnəreɪt] *vt* (ELEC) generar; (*fig*) producir.

generation [dʒɛnə'reɪʃən] *n* generación *f*.

generator ['dʒɛnəreɪtə*] *n* generador *m*.

generosity [dʒɛnə'rɔsɪtɪ] *n* generosidad *f*; **generous** ['dʒɛnərəs] *a* generoso; (*helping etc*) abundante.

genetics [dʒɪ'nɛtɪks] *n* genética.

Geneva [dʒɪ'niːvə] *n* Ginebra.

genial ['dʒiːnɪəl] *a* afable, simpático.

genitals ['dʒɛnɪtlz] *npl* órganos *mpl* genitales.

genius ['dʒiːnɪəs] *n* genio.

genocide ['dʒɛnəusaɪd] *n* genocidio.

gent [dʒɛnt] *n abbr of* **gentleman.**

genteel [dʒɛn'tiːl] *a* fino, elegante.

gentle ['dʒɛntl] *a* (*sweet*) amable, dulce; (*touch etc*) ligero, suave; (*animal*) manso.

gentleman ['dʒɛntlmən] *n* señor *m*; (*well-bred man*) caballero.

gentleness ['dʒɛntlnɪs] *n* dulzura; (*of touch*) suavidad *f*; (*of animal*) mansedumbre *f*.

gently ['dʒɛntlɪ] *ad* suavemente.

gentry ['dʒɛntrɪ] *n* alta burguesía.

gents [dʒɛnts] *n* (aseos de) caballeros *mpl*.

genuine ['dʒɛnjuɪn] *a* auténtico; (*person*) sincero.

geographic(al) [dʒɪə'græfɪk(l)] *a* geográfico; **geography** [dʒɪ'ɔgrəfɪ] *n* geografía.

geological [dʒɪə'lɔdʒɪkl] *a* geológico; **geologist** [dʒɪ'ɔlədʒɪst] *n* geólogo; **geology** [dʒɪ'ɔlədʒɪ] *n* geología.

geometric(al) [dʒɪə'mɛtrɪk(l)] *a* geométrico; **geometry** [dʒɪ'ɔmətrɪ] *n* geometría.

geranium [dʒɪ'reɪnjəm] *n* geranio.

germ [dʒəːm] *n* (*gen*) microbio, bacteria; (BIO, *fig*) germen *m*.

German ['dʒəːmən] *a* alemán(ana) *// n* alemán/ana *m/f*; (LING) alemán *m*; **~ measles** *n* rubéola.

Germany ['dʒəːmənɪ] *n* Alemania.

germination [dʒəːmɪ'neɪʃən] *n* germinación *f*.

gesticulate [dʒɛs'tɪkjuleɪt] *vi* gesticular.

gesture ['dʒɛstʃə*] *n* gesto.

get [gɛt], *pt*, *pp* **got**, *pp* **gotten** (US) *vt* (*obtain*) obtener; (*receive*) recibir; (*achieve*) conseguir; (*find*) encontrar; (*catch*) coger; (*fetch*) traer, ir a buscar; (*understand*) entender *// vi* (*become*) hacerse, volverse; **to ~ old** hacerse viejo, envejecer; **to ~ to** (*place*) llegar a; **he got under the fence** pasó por debajo de la barrera; **to ~ ready/washed** prepararse/lavarse; **to ~ sb to do sth** hacer que alguien haga algo; **to ~ sth**

out of sth sacar algo de algo; **to ~ about** *vi* salir mucho, viajar mucho; (*news*) divulgarse; **to ~ along** *vi* (*agree*) entenderse; (*depart*) marcharse; (*manage*) = **to get by**; **to ~ at** *vt fus* (*attack*) atacar; (*reach*) llegar a; (*the truth*) descubrir; **to ~ away** *vi* marcharse; (*on holiday*) irse de vacaciones; (*escape*) escaparse; **to ~ away with** *vt fus* hacer impunemente; **to ~ back** *vi* (*return*) volver *// vt* recobrar; **to ~ by** *vi* (*pass*) lograr pasar; (*manage*) arreglárselas; **to ~ down** *vi* bajarse *// vt* (*object*) bajar; (*depress*) deprimir; **to ~ down to** *vt fus* (*work*) ponerse a (hacer); **to ~ in** *vi* (*train*) llegar; (*arrive home*) volver a casa, regresar; **to ~ off** *vi* (*from train etc*) bajar; (*depart: person, car*) marcharse *// vt fus* (*train, bus*) bajar de; **to ~ on** *vi* (*at exam etc*) tener éxito; (*agree*) entenderse *// vt* (*horse*) subir; **to ~ out** *vi* salir; (*of vehicle*) bajar; (*news*) saberse *// vt* (*take out*) sacar; **to ~ out of** *vt fus* (*duty etc*) escaparse de; **to ~ over** *vt* (*illness*) recobrarse de; (*put across*) hacer comprender; **to ~ round** *vt fus* rodear; (*fig: person*) engatusar a; **to ~ through to** *vt* (TEL) comunicar con; **to ~ together** *vi* reunirse; **to ~ up** *vi* (*rise*) levantarse *// vt fus* levantar; **to ~ up to** *vt fus* (*reach*) llegar a; (*prank etc*) hacer; **~away** *n* fuga, escape *m*.

geyser ['giːzə*] *n* calentador *m* de agua; (GEO) géiser *m*.

Ghana ['gɑːnə] *n* Ghana.

ghastly ['gɑːstlɪ] *a* horrible; (*pale*) pálido.

gherkin ['gəːkɪn] *n* pepinillo.

ghetto ['gɛtəu] *n* ghetto.

ghost [gəust] *n* fantasma *m*; **~ly** *a* fantasmal.

giant ['dʒaɪənt] *n* gigante *m // a* gigantesco, gigante.

gibberish ['dʒɪbərɪʃ] *n* galimatías *m*.

gibe [dʒaɪb] *n* pulla.

giblets ['dʒɪblɪts] *npl* menudillos *mpl*.

giddiness ['gɪdɪnɪs] *n* vértigo; **giddy** *a* (*dizzy*) mareado; (*speed*) vertiginoso; (*frivolous*) atolondrado; **it makes me giddy** me marea.

gift [gɪft] *n* (*gen*) regalo; (*offering*) obsequio; (*ability*) talento; **~ed** *a* dotado.

gigantic [dʒaɪ'gæntɪk] *a* gigantesco.

giggle ['gɪgl] *vi* reírse con risa tonta *// n* risilla tonta.

gill [dʒɪl] *n* (*measure*) = 0.14 l *// n* [gɪl] (*of fish*) agalla, branquia.

gilt [gɪlt] *a*, *n* dorado; **~-edged** *a* (COMM) del Estado.

gimmick ['gɪmɪk] *n* truco.

gin [dʒɪn] *n* (*liquor*) ginebra.

ginger ['dʒɪndʒə*] *n* jengibre *m*; **~ ale** *n* cerveza de jengibre; **~bread** *n* pan *m* de jengibre; **~-haired** *a* pelirrojo.

gingerly ['dʒɪndʒəlɪ] *ad* con pies de plomo.

gipsy ['dʒɪpsɪ] *n* gitano/a.

giraffe [dʒɪ'rɑːf] *n* jirafa.

girder ['gəːdə*] *n* viga.

girdle ['gɔːdl] n (corset) faja // vt ceñir.
girl [gɔːl] n (small) niña; (young woman) chica, joven f, muchacha; **an English ~** una (chica) inglesa; **~friend** n (of girl) amiga; (of boy) novia; **~ish** a de niña.
girth [gɔːθ] n circunferencia; (stoutness) gordura.
gist [dʒɪst] n lo esencial.
give [gɪv], pt **gave**, pp **given** vt (gen) dar; (deliver) entregar; (as gift) regalar // vi (break) romperse; (stretch: fabric) dar de sí; **to ~ sb sth,** **~ sth to sb** dar algo a uno; **to ~ away** vt (give free) regalar; (betray) traicionar; (disclose) revelar; **to ~ back** vt devolver; **to ~ in** vi ceder // vt entregar; **to ~ off** vt despedir; **to ~ out** vt distribuir; **to ~ up** vi renunciar, darse por vencido // vt renunciar a; **to ~ up smoking** dejar de fumar; **to ~ way** vi ceder, (AUT) ceder el paso.
glacier ['glæsɪə*] n glaciar m.
glad [glæd] a contento; **~den** vt alegrar.
gladioli [glædɪ'əulaɪ] npl gladíolos mpl.
gladly ['glædlɪ] ad con mucho gusto.
glamorous ['glæmərəs] a encantador(a), atractivo; **glamour** n encanto, atractivo.
glance [glɑːns] n ojeada, mirada // vi: **to ~ at** echar una ojeada a; **to ~ off** (bullet) rebotar; **glancing** a (blow) oblicuo.
gland [glænd] n glándula.
glare [glɛə*] n luz f deslumbradora, brillo // vi deslumbrar; **to ~ at** mirar ferozmente a; **glaring** a (mistake) notorio.
glass [glɑːs] n vidrio, cristal m; (for drinking) vaso; (: with stem) copa; (also: looking ~) espejo; **~es** npl gafas fpl; **~house** n invernadero; **~ware** n cristalería; **~y a** (eyes) vidrioso.
glaze [gleɪz] vt (door) poner cristal a; (pottery) barnizar // n barniz m; **~d** a (eye) vidrioso; (pottery) barnizado.
glazier ['gleɪzɪə*] n vidriero.
gleam [gliːm] n destello // vi brillar; **~ing** a reluciente.
glee [gliː] n alegría, regocijo.
glen [glɛn] n cañada, valle m estrecho.
glib [glɪb] a de mucha labia; **~ness** n labia.
glide [glaɪd] vi deslizarse; (AVIAT, birds) planear // n deslizamiento; (AVIAT) vuelo sin motor; **glider** n (AVIAT) planeador m; **gliding** n (AVIAT) vuelo sin motor.
glimmer ['glɪmə*] n luz f trémula.
glimpse [glɪmps] n vista momentánea, vislumbre m // vt vislumbrar, entrever.
glint [glɪnt] n destello; (in the eye) chispa // vi centellear.
glisten ['glɪsn] vi relucir, brillar.
glitter ['glɪtə*] vi relucir, brillar // n brillo.
gloat [gləut] vi: **to ~ (over)** recrearse en, saborear.
global ['gləubl] a mundial; (sum) global.
globe [gləub] n globo, esfera.
gloom [gluːm] n tinieblas fpl, oscuridad f; (sadness) tristeza, melancolía; **~y a**

(dark) oscuro; (sad) triste; (pessimistic) pesimista.
glorify ['glɔːrɪfaɪ] vt glorificar; (praise) alabar.
glorious ['glɔːrɪəs] a glorioso; **glory** n gloria.
gloss [glɔs] n (shine) brillo; (paint) pintura brillante o esmalte; **to ~ over** vt fus encubrir.
glossary ['glɔsərɪ] n glosario.
glossy ['glɔsɪ] a lustroso.
glove [glʌv] n guante m; **~ compartment** n (AUT) guantera.
glow [gləu] vi (shine) brillar; (fire) arder // n brillo.
glower ['glauə*] vi: **to ~ at** mirar con ceño.
glucose ['gluːkəus] n glucosa.
glue [gluː] n goma (de pegar) // vt pegar.
glum [glʌm] a (mood) abatido; (person, tone) melancólico.
glut [glʌt] n superabundancia.
glutton ['glʌtn] n glotón/ona m/f; **a ~ for work** un trabajador incansable; **~y** n gula, glotonería.
glycerin(e) ['glɪsəriːn] n glicerina.
gnarled [nɑːld] a nudoso.
gnat [næt] n mosquito.
gnaw [nɔː] vt roer.
gnome [nəum] n gnomo.
go [gəu], pt **went**, pp **gone** vi ir; (travel) viajar; (depart) irse, marcharse; (work) funcionar, marchar; (be sold) venderse; (time) pasar; (fit, suit): **to ~ with** hacer juego con; (become) ponerse; (break etc) estropearse, romperse // n, pl **~es: to be have a ~ (at)** probar suerte (con); **to be on the ~** moverse, estar trabajando; **whose ~ is it?** ¿a quién le toca?; **he's going to do it** va a hacerlo; **to ~ for a walk** ir de paseo; **to ~ dancing** ir a bailar; **how did it ~?** ¿qué tal salió o resultó?, ¿cómo ha ido?; **to ~ about** vi (rumour) propagarse // vt fus: **how do I ~ about this?** ¿cómo me las arreglo para hacer esto?; **to ~ ahead** vi (make progress) avanzar; (get going) seguir; **to ~ along** vi ir // vt fus bordear; **to ~ along with** estar de acuerdo con; **to ~ away** vi irse, marcharse; **to ~ back** vi volver; **to ~ back on** vt fus (promise) faltar a; **to ~ by** vi (years, time) pasar // vt fus guiarse por; **to ~ down** vi bajar; (ship) hundirse; (sun) ponerse // vt fus bajar por; **to ~ for** vt fus (fetch) ir por; (like) gustar; (attack) atacar; **to ~ in** vi entrar; **to ~ in for** vt fus (competition) presentarse a; **to ~ into** vt fus entrar en; (investigate) investigar; (embark on) embarcarse en; **to ~ off** vi irse, marcharse; (food) pasarse; (explode) estallar; (event) realizarse // vt fus dejar de gustar; **to ~ on** vi seguir, continuar; (happen) pasar, ocurrir; **to ~ on doing sth** seguir haciendo algo; **to ~ out** vi salir; (fire, light) apagarse; **to ~ over** vi (ship) zozobrar // vt fus (check) revisar; **to**

~ **through** vt fus (town etc) atravesar; **to** ~ **up** vi subir; **to** ~ **without** vt fus pasarse sin.

goad [gəud] vt aguijonear.

go-ahead ['gəuəhɛd] a emprendedor(a) // n luz f verde.

goal [gəul] n meta; (score) gol m; ~**keeper** n portero; ~**-post** n poste m de la portería.

goat [gəut] n cabrío, cabra m/f.

gobble ['gɔbl] vt (also: ~ **down**, ~ **up**) engullirse (ávidamente).

goblet ['gɔblit] n copa.

goblin ['gɔblin] n duende m.

go-cart ['gəukɑ:t] n go-cart m.

god [gɔd] n dios m; G~ n Dios m; ~**child** n ahijado/a; ~**dess** n diosa; ~**father** n padrino; ~**-forsaken** a dejado de la mano de Dios; ~**mother** n madrina; ~**send** n don m del cielo; ~**son** n ahijado.

goggles ['gɔglz] npl gafas fpl submarinas.

going ['gəuiŋ] n (conditions) estado del terreno / a: **the** ~ **rate** la tarifa corriente o en vigor.

gold [gəuld] n oro // a de oro; ~**en** a (made of ~) de oro; (~ in colour) dorado; ~**fish** n pez m de colores; ~**mine** n mina de oro.

golf [gɔlf] n golf m; ~ **club** n club m de golf; (stick) palo (de golf); ~ **course** n campo de golf; ~**er** n jugador/a m/f de golf.

gondola ['gɔndələ] n góndola.

gone [gɔn] pp of **go**.

gong [gɔŋ] n gong m.

gonorrhea [gɔnə'riə] n gonorrea.

good [gud] a (gen) bueno; (kind) bueno, amable; (well-behaved) educado; (useful) útil // n bien m, provecho; ~**s** npl bienes mpl; (COMM) mercancías fpl; **to be** ~ **at** tener, aptitud para; **to be** ~ **for** servir para; **it's** ~ **for you** te hace bien; **would you be** ~ **enough to...?** ¿podría hacerme el favor de...?, ¿sería tan amable de...?; **a** ~ **deal (of)** mucho; **a** ~ **many** muchos; **to make** ~ reparar; **for** ~ para siempre, definitivamente; ~ **morning/afternoon!** ¡buenos días/buenas tardes!; ~ **evening!** ¡buenas noches!; ~ **night!** ¡buenas noches!; ~**bye!** ¡adiós!; **to say** ~**bye** despedirse; G~ **Friday** n Viernes m Santo; ~**-looking** a guapo; ~**ness** n (of person) bondad f; **for** ~**ness sake!** ¡Por Dios!; ~**ness gracious!** ¡Dios mío!; ~**will** n buena voluntad f.

goose [gu:s], pl **geese** n ganso, oca.

gooseberry ['guzbəri] n grosella espinosa.

gooseflesh ['gu:sfleʃ] n, **goose pimples** npl carne f de gallina.

gore [gɔ:*] vt cornear // n sangre f.

gorge [gɔ:dʒ] n barranco // vr: **to** ~ **o.s. (on)** atracarse (de).

gorgeous ['gɔ:dʒəs] a magnífico, maravilloso.

gorilla [gə'rilə] n gorila m.

gorse [gɔ:s] n aulaga.

gory ['gɔ:ri] a sangriento.

go-slow ['gəu'sləu] n huelga de trabajo lento.

gospel ['gɔspl] n evangelio.

gossip ['gɔsip] n (scandal) chismorreo, chismes mpl; (chat) charla; (scandalmonger) chismoso/a; (talker) hablador/a m/f // vi cotillear.

got [gɔt] pt, pp of **get**; ~**ten** (US) pp of **get**.

gout [gaut] n gota.

govern ['gʌvən] vt (gen) gobernar; (dominate) dominar.

governess ['gʌvənis] n institutriz f.

government ['gʌvnmənt] n gobierno; ~**al** [-'mentl] a gubernamental.

governor ['gʌvənə*] n gobernador m; (of jail) director/a m/f.

gown [gaun] n traje m; (of teacher, judge) toga.

G.P. n abbr of **general practitioner**.

GPO n abbr of **General Post Office**.

grab [græb] vt coger, arrebatar.

grace [greis] n (REL) gracia; (gracefulness) elegancia, finura // vt (favour) honrar; (adorn) adornar; **5 days'** ~ un plazo de 5 días; **to say** ~ bendecir la mesa; ~**ful** a elegante, gracioso; **gracious** ['greiʃəs] a amable.

grade [greid] n (quality) clase f, calidad f; (degree) grado; (US: SCOL) clase f // vt clasificar.

gradient ['greidiənt] n pendiente f.

gradual ['grædjuəl] a paulatino; ~**ly** ad paulatinamente.

graduate ['grædjuit] n graduado, licenciado // vi ['grædjueit] graduarse, licenciarse; **graduation** [-'eiʃən] n graduación f.

graft [grɑ:ft] n (AGR, MED) injerto; (bribery) corrupción f // vt injertar.

grain [grein] n grano; (corn) granos mpl, cereales mpl; (in wood) fibra.

gram [græm] n gramo.

grammar ['græmə*] n gramática; **grammatical** [grə'mætikl] a gramatical.

gramme [græm] n = **gram**.

gramophone ['græməfəun] n tocadiscos m inv.

granary ['grænəri] n granero, troj f.

grand [grænd] a magnífico, imponente; ~**children** npl nietos mpl; ~**dad** n yayo, abuelito; ~**daughter** n nieta; ~**eur** ['grændjə*] n magnificencia, lo grandioso; ~**father** n abuelo; ~**iose** ['grændiəuz] a grandioso; (pej) pomposo; ~**ma** n yaya, abuelita; ~**mother** n abuela; ~**pa** n = ~**dad**; ~ **piano** n piano de cola; ~**son** n nieto; ~**stand** n (SPORT) tribuna.

granite ['grænit] n granito.

granny ['græni] n abuelita, yaya.

grant [grɑ:nt] vt (concede) conceder; (admit) asentir // n (SCOL) beca; **to take sth for** ~**ed** dar algo por sentado.

granulated sugar ['grænjuleitid-] n azúcar m granulado.

granule ['grænju:l] n gránulo.

grape [greɪp] n uva; **sour** ~s (fig) envidia.

grapefruit ['greɪpfruːt] n pomelo, toronja (AM).

graph [grɑːf] n gráfica; ~ic a gráfico.

grapple ['græpl] vi: **to** ~ **with** sth esforzarse por resolver algo.

grasp [grɑːsp] vt agarrar, asir; (understand) comprender // n (grip) asimiento; (reach) alcance m; (understanding) comprensión f; ~ing a avaro.

grass [grɑːs] n hierba; (lawn) césped m; ~**hopper** n saltamontes m inv; ~**land** n pradera; ~**-roots** a popular; ~ **snake** n culebra; ~**y** a cubierto de hierba.

grate [greɪt] n (fireplace) chimenea; (of iron) parrilla // vi rechinar // vt (CULIN) rallar.

grateful ['greɪtful] a agradecido.

grater ['greɪtə*] n rallador m.

gratify ['grætɪfaɪ] vt complacer; (whim) satisfacer; ~**ing** a grato.

grating ['greɪtɪŋ] n (iron bars) rejilla // a (noise) áspero.

gratitude ['grætɪtjuːd] n agradecimiento.

gratuity [grə'tjuːɪtɪ] n gratificación f.

grave [greɪv] n tumba // a serio, grave; ~**digger** n sepulturero.

gravel ['grævl] n grava.

grave: ~**stone** n lápida; ~**yard** n cementerio, camposanto.

gravity ['grævɪtɪ] n gravedad f; (seriousness) seriedad f.

gravy ['greɪvɪ] n salsa.

gray [greɪ] a = **grey**.

graze [greɪz] vi pacer // vt (touch lightly) rozar; (scrape) raspar // n (MED) rasguño.

grease [griːs] n (fat) grasa; (lubricant) lubricante m // vt engrasar; ~**proof** a a prueba de grasa; (paper) apergaminado; **greasy** a grasiento.

great [greɪt] a grande; (col) magnífico, estupendo; **G~ Britain** n Gran Bretaña; ~**-grandfather/mother** n bisabuelo/a; ~**ly** ad sumamente, mucho, muy; ~**ness** n grandeza.

Greece [griːs] n Grecia.

greed [griːd] n (also: ~**iness**) codicia, avaricia; (for food) gula; ~**ily** ad con avidez; ~**y** a avaro; (for food) glotón(ona).

Greek [griːk] a griego // n griego/a; (LING) griego.

green [griːn] a verde; (inexperienced) novato // n verde m; (stretch of grass) césped m; ~s npl verduras fpl; ~**gage** n claudia; ~**grocer** n verdulero; ~**house** n invernadero; ~**ish** a verdoso.

Greenland ['griːnlənd] n Groenlandia.

greet [griːt] vt saludar; (welcome) dar la bienvenida a; ~**ing** n (gen) saludo; (welcome) bienvenida.

gregarious [grə'gɛərɪəs] a gregario.

grenade [grə'neɪd] n granada.

grew [gruː] pt of **grow**.

grey [greɪ] a gris; ~**-haired** a canoso; ~**hound** n galgo.

grid [grɪd] n reja; (ELEC) red f.

grief [griːf] n dolor m, pena.

grievance ['griːvəns] n motivo de queja, agravio.

grieve [griːv] vi afligirse, acongojarse // vt dar pena a; **to** ~ **for** llorar por.

grievous ['griːvəs] a penoso.

grill [grɪl] n (on cooker) parrilla // vt asar a la parrilla; (question) interrogar duramente.

grille [grɪl] n reja; (AUT) rejilla.

grim [grɪm] a siniestro; (fam) horrible.

grimace [grɪ'meɪs] n mueca // vi hacer muecas.

grime [graɪm] n mugre f; **grimy** a mugriento.

grin [grɪn] n sonrisa abierta // vi sonreír abiertamente.

grind [graɪnd] pt, pp **ground** vt (coffee, pepper etc) moler; (make sharp) afilar // n (work) trabajo pesado y aburrido; **to** ~ **one's teeth** rechinar los dientes.

grip [grɪp] n (hold) asimiento; (of hands) apretón m; (handle) asidero; (of racquet etc) mango; (holdall) maletín m; (understanding) comprensión f // vt agarrar; **to come to** ~**s with** luchar a brazo partido con; ~**ping** a absorbente.

grisly ['grɪzlɪ] a horripilante, horrible.

gristle ['grɪsl] n cartílago.

grit [grɪt] n gravilla; (courage) valor m // vt (road) poner gravilla en; **to** ~ **one's teeth** apretar los dientes.

groan [grəʊn] n gemido, quejido // vi gemir, quejarse.

grocer ['grəʊsə*] n tendero de ultramarinos; ~**ies** npl comestibles mpl; ~'**s (shop)** n tienda de ultramarinos.

groggy ['grɔgɪ] a aturdido; (BOXING) grogui.

groin [grɔɪn] n ingle f.

groom [gruːm] n mozo de caballos; (also: **bride**~) novio // vt (horse) cuidar; **well-**~**ed** a acicalado.

groove [gruːv] n ramura, surco.

grope [grəʊp] vi ir a tientas; **to** ~ **for** vt fus buscar a tientas.

gross [grəʊs] a grueso; (COMM) bruto; ~**ly** ad (greatly) enormemente.

grotesque [grə'tɛsk] a grotesco.

grotto ['grɔtəʊ] n gruta.

ground [graʊnd] pt, pp of **grind** // n suelo, tierra; (SPORT) campo, terreno; (reason: gen pl) causa, razón f // vt (plane) mantener en tierra; (US. ELEC) conectar con tierra // vi (ship) varar, encallar; ~**s** npl (of coffee etc) poso sg; (gardens etc) jardines mpl, parque m; **on the** ~ en el suelo; **to the** ~ al suelo; ~**floor** n planta baja; ~**ing** n (in education) conocimientos mpl básicos; ~**less** a infundado; ~**sheet** n tela impermeable; ~ **staff** n personal m de tierra; ~**work** n preparación f.

group [gruːp] n grupo; (musical) conjunto

// (vb: also: ~ **together**) vt agrupar // vi agruparse.

grouse [graus] n, pl inv (bird) urogallo // vi (complain) quejarse.

grove [grəuv] n arboleda.

grovel ['grɔvl] vi (fig) humillarse.

grow [grəu], pt **grew**, pp **grown** vi (gen) crecer; (plants) cultivarse; (increase) aumentarse; (spread) extenderse, desarrollarse; (become) volverse; **to ~ rich/weak** enriquecerse/debilitarse // vt cultivar, dejar crecer; **to ~ up** vi crecer, hacerse hombre/mujer; **~er** n cultivador/a m/f, productor/a m/f; **~ing** a creciente.

growl [graul] vi gruñir.

grown [grəun] pp of **grow**; **~-up** n adulto, persona mayor.

growth [grəuθ] n crecimiento, desarrollo; (what has grown) brote m; (MED) acceso, tumor m.

grub [grʌb] n gusano; (col: food) comida.

grubby ['grʌbɪ] a sucio, mugriento.

grudge [grʌdʒ] n motivo de rencor // vt: **to ~ sb sth** dar algo a uno de mala gana, escatimar algo a uno; **to bear sb a ~** guardar rencor a uno; **he ~s (giving) the money** da el dinero de mala gana.

gruelling ['gruəlɪŋ] a penoso, duro.

gruesome ['gru:səm] a horrible.

gruff [grʌf] a (voice) bronco; (manner) brusco.

grumble ['grʌmbl] vi refunfuñar, quejarse.

grumpy ['grʌmpɪ] a gruñón(ona).

grunt [grʌnt] vi gruñir // n gruñido.

guarantee [gærən'ti:] n garantía // vt garantizar.

guarantor [gærən'tɔ:*] n garante m/f, fiador/a m/f.

guard [gɑ:d] n guardia; (RAIL) jefe m de tren // vt guardar; **~ed** a (fig) cauteloso; **~ian** n guardián/ana m/f; (of minor) tutor/a m/f; **~'s van** n (RAIL) furgón m.

guerrilla [gə'rɪlə] n guerrillero; **~ warfare** n guerra de guerrillas.

guess [gɛs] vi, vt (gen) adivinar; (suppose) suponer // n suposición f, conjetura; **to take** or **have a ~** tratar de adivinar; **~ work** n conjeturas fpl.

guest [gɛst] n invitado/a; (in hotel) huésped/a m/f; **~-house** n casa de huéspedes, pensión f; **~ room** n cuarto de huéspedes.

guffaw [gʌ'fɔ:] n carcajada // vi reírse a carcajadas.

guidance ['gaɪdəns] n (gen) dirección f; (advice) consejos mpl.

guide [gaɪd] n (person) guía m/f; (book, fig) guía // vt guiar; **(girl) ~** n exploradora; **~book** n guía; **~ dog** n perro guía; **~lines** npl (fig) principios mpl generales.

guild [gɪld] n gremio; **~hall** n (Brit) ayuntamiento.

guile [gaɪl] n astucia; **~less** a cándido.

guillotine ['gɪlətiːn] n guillotina.

guilt [gɪlt] n culpabilidad f; **~y** a culpable.

guinea pig ['gɪnɪpɪg] n conejillo de Indias.

guise [gaɪz] n: **in** or **under the ~ of** so capa de.

guitar [gɪ'tɑ:*] n guitarra; **~ist** n guitarrista m/f.

gulf [gʌlf] n golfo; (abyss) abismo.

gull [gʌl] n gaviota.

gullet ['gʌlɪt] n esófago; (fam) garganta.

gullible ['gʌlɪbl] a crédulo.

gully ['gʌlɪ] n barranco.

gulp [gʌlp] vi tragar saliva // vt (also: ~ **down**) tragarse // n: **at one ~** de un trago.

gum [gʌm] n (ANAT) encía; (glue) goma; (sweet) caramelo de goma; (also: **chewing-~**) chiclé m // vt engomar, pegar con goma; **~boots** npl botas fpl de goma.

gun [gʌn] n (gen) arma de fuego; (small) pistola; (shotgun) escopeta; (rifle) fusil m; (cannon) cañón m; **~boat** n cañonero; **~fire** n fuego, disparos mpl; **~man** n pistolero; **~ner** n artillero; **at ~point** bajo la amenaza de un arma; **~powder** n pólvora; **~shot** n escopetazo, cañonazo; **~smith** n armero.

gurgle ['gə:gl] vi gorgotear.

gush [gʌʃ] vi chorrear; (fig) deshacerse en efusiones.

gusset ['gʌsɪt] n escudete m.

gust [gʌst] n (of wind) ráfaga.

gusto ['gʌstəu] n entusiasmo.

gut [gʌt] n intestino, tripa; (MUS etc) cuerda de tripa; **~s** npl (courage) valor m.

gutter ['gʌtə*] n (of roof) canalón m; (in street) arroyo.

guttural ['gʌtərl] a gutural.

guy [gaɪ] n (also: **~rope**) cuerda; (col: man) tío, tipo.

guzzle ['gʌzl] vi tragar // vt engullir.

gym [dʒɪm] n (also: **gymnasium**) gimnasio; (also: **gymnastics**) gimnasia; **~nast** n gimnasta m/f; **~nastics** n gimnasia; **~ shoes** npl zapatillas fpl de gimnasia; **~ slip** n túnica de colegiala.

gynaecologist, gynecologist (US) [gaɪnɪ'kɔlədʒɪst] n ginecólogo; **gynaecology, gynecology** (US) [-nə'kɔlədʒɪ] n ginecología.

gypsy ['dʒɪpsɪ] n = **gipsy**.

gyrate [dʒaɪ'reɪt] vi girar.

H

haberdashery ['hæbə'dæʃərɪ] n mercería.

habit ['hæbɪt] n hábito, costumbre f; (costume) hábito.

habitable ['hæbɪtəbl] a habitable.

habitual [hə'bɪtjuəl] a acostumbrado, habitual; (drinker, liar) empedernido; **~ly** ad por costumbre.

hack [hæk] vt (cut) cortar; (slice) tajar // n corte m; (axe blow) hachazo.

hackneyed ['hæknɪd] a trillado, gastado.

had [hæd] pt, pp of **have**.

haddock ['hædək], pl ~ or ~s n especie de merluza.

hadn't ['hædnt] = had not.

haemorrhage, hemorrhage (US) ['hɛmərɪdʒ] n hemorragia.

haemorrhoids, hemorrhoids (US) ['hɛmərɔɪdz] npl hemorroides fpl.

haggard ['hægəd] a ojeroso.

haggle ['hægl] vi (argue) discutir; (bargain) regatear.

Hague [heɪg] n: The ~ La Haya.

hail [heɪl] n (weather) granizo // vt saludar; (call) llamar a // vi granizar; ~**stone** n (piedra de) granizo.

hair [heə*] n (gen) pelo, cabellos mpl; (one ~) pelo, cabello; (head of ~) cabellera; (on legs) vello; **grey** ~ canas fpl; ~**brush** n cepillo (del pelo); ~**cut** n corte m de pelo; ~**do** n peinado; ~**dresser** n peluquero; ~**dresser's** n peluquería; ~**drier** n secador m de pelo; ~**net** n redecilla; ~**piece** n trenza postiza; ~**pin** n horquilla; ~**pin bend** n curva de horquilla; ~**raising** a espeluznante; ~ **remover** n depilador m; (cream) crema depilatoria; ~ **spray** n laca; ~**style** n peinado; ~**y** a peludo; velludo.

half [hɑːf], pl **halves** n mitad f // a medio // ad medio, a medias; ~-**an-hour** media hora; **two and a** ~ dos y media; ~ **a pound** media libra; **to cut sth in** ~ cortar algo por la mitad; ~ **asleep** medio dormido; ~-**price** a mitad de precio; ~-**back** n (SPORT) medio; ~-**breed**, ~-**caste** n mestizo; ~-**hearted** a indiferente, poco entusiasta; ~-**hour** n media hora; ~-**penny** ['heɪpnɪ] n medio penique; ~-**time** n medio tiempo; ~**way** ad a medio camino.

halibut ['hælɪbət] n, pl inv halibut m.

hall [hɔːl] n (for concerts) sala; (entrance way) hall m, vestíbulo; **town** ~ palacio municipal; ~ **of residence** n residencia (universitaria).

hallmark ['hɔːlmɑːk] n (mark) marca; (seal) sello.

hallo [hə'ləu] excl = **hello**.

hallucination [həluːsɪ'neɪʃən] n alucinación f.

halo ['heɪləu] n (of saint) aureola.

halt [hɔːlt] n (stop) alto, parada; (RAIL) apeadero // vt parar // vi pararse; (process) interrumpirse.

halve [hɑːv] vt partir por la mitad.

halves [hɑːvz] pl of **half**.

ham [hæm] n jamón m (cocido); (actor) comicastro.

hamburger ['hæmbɔːgə*] n hamburguesa.

hamlet ['hæmlɪt] n aldea.

hammer ['hæmə*] n martillo // vt amartillar // vi (on door) golpear.

hammock ['hæmək] n hamaca.

hamper ['hæmpə*] vt estorbar // n cesto.

hand [hænd] n mano f; (of clock) manecilla; (writing) letra; (applause) aplausos mpl; (worker) obrero; (measure) palmo // vt

(give) dar, pasar; (deliver) entregar; **to give sb a** ~ dar una mano a uno, ayudar a uno; **at** ~ a la mano; **in** ~ entre manos; **on the one** ~ ..., **on the other** ~ ... por una parte ... por otra (parte) ...; **to** ~ **in** vt entregar; **to** ~ **out** vt distribuir; **to** ~ **over** vt (deliver) entregar; (surrender) ceder; ~**bag** n bolso; ~**basin** n lavabo; ~**book** n manual m; ~**brake** n freno de mano; ~**cuffs** npl esposas fpl; ~**ful** n puñado.

handicap ['hændɪkæp] n handicap m, desventaja // vt estorbar; **mentally/physically** ~**ped** incapacitado mentalmente/físicamente.

handicraft ['hændɪkrɑːft] n artesanía.

handkerchief ['hæŋkətʃɪf] n pañuelo.

handle ['hændl] n (of door etc) tirador m, manija; (of cup etc) asa; (of knife etc) mango; (for winding) manivela; (fam: name) título // vt (touch) tocar; (deal with) encargarse de; (treat: people) manejar; '~ **with care**' 'tratar con cuidado'; **to fly off the** ~ perder los estribos; ~**bar(s)** n(pl) manillar m.

hand-luggage ['hændlʌgɪdʒ] n equipaje m de mano.

handmade ['hændmeɪd] a hecho a mano.

handout ['hændaut] n (distribution) repartición f; (charity) limosna; (leaflet) folleto.

handshake ['hændʃeɪk] n apretón m de manos.

handsome ['hænsəm] a guapo.

handwriting ['hændraɪtɪŋ] n letra.

handy ['hændɪ] a (close at hand) a mano; (convenient) práctico; (skilful) hábil, diestro; ~**man** n (hombre) mañoso.

hang [hæŋ], pt, pp **hung** vt colgar; (criminal: pt, pp **hanged**) ahorcar; (head) bajar // vi colgar; **to** ~ **about** vi haraganear; **to** ~ **on** vi (wait) esperar; **to** ~ **up** vi (TEL) colgar.

hangar ['hæŋə*] n hangar m.

hanger ['hæŋə*] n percha; ~-**on** n parásito.

hangover ['hæŋəuvə*] n (after drinking) resaca.

hang-up ['hæŋʌp] n complejo.

hanker ['hæŋkə*] vi: **to** ~ **after** (miss) echar de menos; (long for) añorar.

hankie, hanky ['hæŋkɪ] n abbr of **handkerchief**.

haphazard [hæp'hæzəd] a fortuito.

happen ['hæpən] vi suceder, ocurrir; (take place) tener lugar, realizarse; **to** ~ **upon** tropezar con; ~**ing** n suceso, acontecimiento.

happily ['hæpɪlɪ] ad (luckily) afortunadamente; (cheerfully) alegremente.

happiness ['hæpɪnɪs] n (gen) felicidad f; (joy) alegría.

happy ['hæpɪ] a feliz, alegre; **to be** ~ (**with**) estar contento (con); **to be** ~ **ser** feliz.

harass ['hærəs] vt acosar, hostigar;

~**ment** n persecución f; (worry) preocupación f.

harbour, harbor (US) ['hɑːbə*] n puerto // vt (hope etc) abrigar; (hide) esconder.

hard [hɑːd] a (gen) duro; (difficult) difícil; (work) arduo; (person) severo // ad (work) mucho, duro, duramente; (think, try) seriamente; **to look** ~ mirar fijo o fijamente; **no** ~ **feelings!** sin rencor; **to be** ~ **of hearing** ser duro de oído; **to be** ~ **done by** ser tratado injustamente; ~**back** n libro encuadernado; ~**board** n chapa de madera; ~**en** vt endurecer; (fig) curtir // vi endurecerse; ~-**headed** a poco sentimental, práctico; ~ **labour** n trabajos mpl forzados.

hardly ['hɑːdlɪ] ad (scarcely) apenas; **that can** ~ **be true** difícilmente puede ser cierto; ~ **ever** casi nunca.

hardness ['hɑːdnɪs] n dureza.

hardship ['hɑːdʃɪp] n (troubles) penas fpl; (financial) apuro.

hard-up [hɑːd'ʌp] a (col) pelado.

hardware ['hɑːdwɛə*] n ferretería; (COMPUTERS) material m; ~ **shop** n ferretería.

hard-wearing [hɑːd'wɛərɪŋ] a resistente, duradero.

hard-working [hɑːd'wɜːkɪŋ] a trabajador(a).

hardy ['hɑːdɪ] a fuerte; (plant) resistente.

hare [hɛə*] n liebre f; ~-**brained** a casquivano.

harem [hɑːˈriːm] n harén m.

haricot (bean) ['hærɪkəʊ] n alubia.

harm [hɑːm] n daño, mal m // vt (person) hacer daño a, perjudicar; (thing) dañar; **out of** ~'s **way** a salvo; ~**ful** a perjudicial; (pest) dañino; ~**less** a inofensivo.

harmonica [hɑːˈmɒnɪkə] n armónica.

harmonious [hɑːˈməʊnɪəs] a armonioso; **harmonize** ['hɑːmənaɪz] vt, vi armonizar; **harmony** ['hɑːmənɪ] n armonía.

harness ['hɑːnɪs] n arreos mpl // vt (horse) enjaezar; (resources) aprovechar.

harp [hɑːp] n arpa f // vi: **to** ~ **on about** hablar constantemente de; ~**ist** n arpista m/f.

harpoon [hɑːˈpuːn] n arpón m.

harrowing ['hærəʊɪŋ] a horroroso.

harsh [hɑːʃ] a (hard) duro, cruel; (severe) severo; (unpleasant) desagradable; (: colour) chillón(ona); (contrast) violento; ~**ness** n dureza.

harvest ['hɑːvɪst] n cosecha; (of grapes) vendimia // vt, vi cosechar; ~**er** n (machine) cosechadora.

has [hæz] vb see **have**.

hash [hæʃ] n (CULIN) picadillo; (fig: mess) lío.

hashish ['hæʃɪʃ] n hachís m, hachich m.

hasn't ['hæznt] = **has not.**

hassle ['hæsl] n pelea // vt molestar a.

haste [heɪst] n prisa; **hasten** ['heɪsn] vt acelerar // vi darse prisa; **hastily** ad de prisa; **hasty** a apresurado.

hat [hæt] n sombrero.

hatch [hætʃ] n (NAUT: also: ~**way**) escotilla // vi salir del cascarón // vt incubar; (plot) tramar.

hatchback ['hætʃbæk] n (AUT) coche m con puerta trasera.

hatchet ['hætʃɪt] n hacha.

hate [heɪt] vt odiar, aborrecer // n odio; ~**ful** a odioso; **hatred** n odio.

hat trick ['hættrɪk] n (SPORT, also fig) tres triunfos seguidos.

haughty ['hɔːtɪ] a altanero, arrogante.

haul [hɔːl] vt tirar; (by lorry) transportar // n (of fish) redada; (of stolen goods etc) botín m; ~**age** n transporte m; (costs) gastos mpl de transporte; ~**ier** n contratista m de transportes.

haunch [hɔːntʃ] n anca; (of meat) pierna.

haunt [hɔːnt] vt (subj: ghost) aparecer en; (frequent) frecuentar; (obsess) obsesionar // n guarida; ~**ed house** casa de fantasmas.

have [hæv], pt, pp **had** vt (gen) tener; (possess) poseer; (meal, shower) tomar; **to** ~ **sth done** hacer hacer algo; **she has to do it** tiene que hacerlo; **I had better leave** más vale que me marche; **I won't** ~ **it** no lo tolero; **he has gone** se ha ido; **to** ~ **it out with sb** ajustar cuentas con alguien; **to** ~ **a baby** parir, dar a luz.

haven ['heɪvn] n puerto; (fig) refugio.

haven't ['hævnt] = **have not.**

haversack ['hævəsæk] n mochila.

havoc ['hævək] n estragos mpl.

hawk [hɔːk] n halcón m.

hay [heɪ] n heno; ~ **fever** n fiebre f del heno; ~**stack** n almiar m.

haywire ['heɪwaɪə*] a (col): **to go** ~ (person) volverse loco; (plan) embarullarse.

hazard ['hæzəd] n riesgo // vt aventurar; ~**ous** a (dangerous) peligroso; (risky) arriesgado.

haze [heɪz] n neblina.

hazelnut ['heɪzlnʌt] n avellana.

hazy ['heɪzɪ] a brumoso; (idea) vago.

he [hiː] pron él; ~ **who...** él que..., quien...; ~-**man** n macho.

head [hɛd] n cabeza; (leader) jefe/a m/f // vt (list) encabezar; (group) capitanear; ~**s (or tails)** cara (o cruz); ~ **first** de cabeza; ~ **over heels** patas arriba; **to** ~ **the ball** cabecear (la pelota); **to** ~ **for** vt fus dirigirse a; ~**ache** n dolor m de cabeza; ~**ing** n título; ~**lamp** n faro; ~**land** n promontorio; ~**light** = ~**lamp**; ~**line** n titular m; ~**long** ad (fall) de cabeza; (rush) precipitadamente; ~**master/** **mistress** n director/a m/f (de escuela); ~**office** n oficina central, central f; ~-**on** a (collision) de frente; ~**phones** npl auriculares mpl; ~**quarters (HQ)** npl sede f central; (MIL) cuartel m general; ~-**rest** n reposacabezas m inv; ~**room** n (in car) espacio para la cabeza; (under bridge) luz f; ~**scarf** n pañuelo (de cabeza); ~**stone** n lápida mortuoria; ~**strong** *a* voluntarioso; ~ **waiter** *n* jefe *m* de camareros; ~**way** *n* progreso; to **make** ~**way** avanzar; ~**wind** *n* viento contrario.

heal [hiːl] *vt* curar // *vi* cicatrizarse.

health [hɛlθ] *n* salud *f*; **good** ~! ¡salud y pesetas!; ~ **food** *n* comida natural; **H**~ **Service** *n* Seguro de Enfermedad; ~**y** *a* (*gen*) sano.

heap [hiːp] *n* montón *m* // *vt* amontonar; (*plate*) colmar.

hear [hɪə*], *pt, pp* **heard** [hɑːd] *vt* oír; (*perceive*) sentir; (*listen to*) escuchar; (*lecture*) asistir a // *vi* oír; **to** ~ **about** oír hablar de; **to** ~ **from sb** tener noticias de alguien; ~**ing** *n* (*sense*) oído; (*LAW*) vista; ~**ing aid** *n* audífono; ~**say** *n* rumores *mpl*, habillas *fpl*.

hearse [hɑːs] *n* coche *m* fúnebre.

heart [hɑːt] *n* corazón *m*; ~**s** *npl* (*CARDS*) corazones *mpl*; **at** ~ en el fondo; **by** ~ (*learn, know*) de memoria; ~ **attack** *n* ataque *m* cardíaco; ~**beat** *n* latido (del corazón); ~**breaking** *a* desgarrador(a); **to be** ~**broken** estar angustiado; ~ **failure** *n* fallo cardíaco; ~**felt** *a* (*cordial*) cordial; (*deeply felt*) más sentido.

hearth [hɑːθ] *n* (*gen*) hogar *m*; (*fireplace*) chimenea.

heartily ['hɑːtɪlɪ] *ad* sinceramente, cordialmente; (*laugh*) a carcajadas; (*eat*) con buen apetito.

heartless ['hɑːtlɪs] *a* cruel.

hearty ['hɑːtɪ] *a* cordial.

heat [hiːt] *n* (*gen*) calor *m*; (*ardour*) ardor *m*; (*SPORT: also:* **qualifying** ~) prueba eliminatoria // *vt* calentar; (*fig*) acalorar; **to** ~ **up** *vi* (*gen*) calentarse; ~**ed** *a* caliente; (*fig*) acalorado; ~**er** *n* calentador *m*.

heath [hiːθ] *n* (*Brit*) brezal *m*.

heathen ['hiːðn] *a, n* pagano/a.

heather ['hɛðə*] *n* brezo.

heating ['hiːtɪŋ] *n* calefacción *f*.

heatstroke ['hiːtstrəuk] *n* insolación *f*.

heatwave ['hiːtweɪv] *n* ola de calor.

heave [hiːv] *vt* (*pull*) tirar de; (*push*) empujar con esfuerzo; (*lift*) levantar (con esfuerzo) // *vi* (*water*) agitarse // *n* tirón *m*; empujón *m*; (*effort*) esfuerzo; (*throw*) echada.

heaven ['hɛvn] *n* cielo; (*REL*) paraíso; ~**ly** *a* celestial; (*REL*) divino.

heavily ['hɛvɪlɪ] *ad* pesadamente; (*drink, smoke*) con exceso; (*sleep, sigh*) profundamente.

heavy ['hɛvɪ] *a* pesado; (*work*) duro; (*sea, rain, meal*) fuerte; (*drinker, smoker*) gran; (*eater*) comilón(ona); ~**weight** *n* (*SPORT*) peso pesado.

Hebrew ['hiːbruː] *a* hebreo.

heckle ['hɛkl] *vt* interrumpir.

hectic ['hɛktɪk] *a* febril, agitado.

he'd [hiːd] = **he would; he had.**

hedge [hɛdʒ] *n* seto // *vt* cercar (con un seto) // *vi* contestar con evasivas; **to** ~ **one's bets** (*fig*) cubrirse.

hedgehog ['hɛdʒhɔg] *n* erizo.

heed [hiːd] *vt* (*also:* **take** ~ **of**) (*attend to*) hacer caso de; (*bear in mind*) tener en cuenta; ~**less** *a* desatento.

heel [hiːl] *n* talón *m* // *vt* (*shoe*) poner tacón a.

hefty ['hɛftɪ] *a* (*person*) fornido; (*piece*) grande; (*price*) gordo.

heifer ['hɛfə*] *n* novilla, ternera.

height [haɪt] *n* (*of person*) talle *m*; (*of building*) altura; (*high ground*) cerro; (*altitude*) altitud *f*; ~**en** *vt* elevar; (*fig*) aumentar.

heir [ɛə*] *n* heredero; ~**ess** *n* heredera; ~**loom** *n* reliquia de familia.

held [hɛld] *pt, pp of* **hold.**

helicopter ['hɛlɪkɔptə*] *n* helicóptero.

hell [hɛl] *n* infierno; ~! ¡demonios!

he'll [hiːl] = **he will, he shall.**

hellish ['hɛlɪʃ] *a* infernal; (*fam*) horrible.

hello [hə'ləu] *excl* ¡hola!; (*surprise*) ¡caramba!

helm [hɛlm] *n* (*NAUT*) timón *m*.

helmet ['hɛlmɪt] *n* casco.

help [hɛlp] *n* ayuda; (*charwoman*) criada, asistenta; (*assistant etc*) empleado // *vi* ayudar; ~! ¡socorro!; ~ **yourself** sírvete; **he can't** ~ **it** no es culpa suya; ~**er** *n* ayudante *m/f*; ~**ful** *a* útil, servicial; ~**ing** *n* ración *f*; ~**less** *a* (*incapable*) incapaz; (*defenceless*) indefenso.

hem [hɛm] *n* dobladillo; **to** ~ **in** *vt* cercar.

hemisphere ['hɛmɪsfɪə*] *n* hemisferio.

hen [hɛn] *n* gallina.

hence [hɛns] *ad* (*therefore*) por lo tanto; **2 years** ~ de aquí a 2 años; ~**forth** *ad* de hoy en adelante.

henchman ['hɛntʃmən] *n* (*pej*) secuaz *m*.

henpecked ['hɛnpɛkt] *a* dominado por su mujer.

her [həː*] *pron* (*direct*) la; (*indirect*) le; (*stressed, after prep*) ella // *a* su.

herald ['hɛrəld] *n* (*forerunner*) precursor/a *m/f* // *vt* anunciar.

heraldry ['hɛrəldrɪ] *n* heráldica.

herb [həːb] *n* hierba.

herd [həːd] *n* rebaño.

here [hɪə*] *ad* aquí; ~! (*present*) presente; ~ **she is** aquí está; ~**after** *ad* en el futuro // *n*: **the** ~**after** (la vida de) ultratumba; ~**by** *ad* (*in letter*) por la presente.

hereditary [hɪ'rɛdɪtrɪ] *a* hereditario; **heredity** [-tɪ] *n* herencia.

heresy ['hɛrəsɪ] *n* herejía.

heretic ['hɛrətɪk] *n* hereje *m/f*; ~**al** [hɪ'rɛtɪkl] *a* herético.

heritage ['hɛrɪtɪdʒ] *n* (*gen*) herencia; (*fig*) patrimonio.

hermit ['həːmɪt] *n* ermitaño.

hernia ['həːnɪə] *n* hernia.

hero ['hɪərəu], *pl* ~**es** *n* héroe *m*; (*in book, film*) protagonista *m*; ~**ic** [hɪ'rəuɪk] *a* heroico.

heroin ['herəʊɪn] n heroína.
heroine ['herəʊɪn] n heroína; (in book, film) protagonista.
heroism ['herəʊɪzm] n heroísmo.
heron ['herən] n garza.
herring ['herɪŋ] n arenque m.
hers [hɜːz] pron (el) suyo/(la) suya etc.
herself [hɜː'self] pron (reflexive) se; (emphatic) ella misma; (after prep) sí (misma).
he's [hiːz] = **he is; he has**.
hesitant ['hezɪtənt] a vacilante, dudoso.
hesitate ['hezɪteɪt] vi dudar, vacilar; **hesitation** ['-teɪʃən] n indecisión f.
hew [hjuː] vt cortar con hacha.
hexagon ['heksəgən] n hexágono; ~al [-'sægənl] a hexagonal.
hi [haɪ] excl ¡oye!, ¡hola!
hibernate ['haɪbəneɪt] vi invernar.
hiccough, hiccup ['hɪkʌp] vi hipar; ~s npl hipo sg.
hid [hɪd] pt of **hide**.
hidden ['hɪdn] pp of **hide**.
hide [haɪd] n (skin) piel f // (vb: pt **hid**, pp **hidden**) vt esconder, ocultar // vi: **to ~ (from sb)** esconderse o ocultarse (de alguien); ~-**and-seek** n escondite m; ~-**away** n escondite m.
hideous ['hɪdɪəs] a horrible.
hiding ['haɪdɪŋ] n (beating) paliza; **to be in ~** (concealed) estar escondido; ~ **place** n escondrijo.
hierarchy ['haɪərɑːkɪ] n jerarquía.
high [haɪ] a (gen) alto; (speed, number) grande; (price) elevado; (wind) fuerte; (voice) agudo // a alto, a gran altura; **it is 20 m ~** tiene 20 m de altura; ~ **in the air** en las alturas; ~**brow** a culto; ~**chair** n silla alta; ~**handed** a despótico; ~**heeled** a de tacón alto; ~**jack** = **hijack**; ~ **jump** n (SPORT) salto de altura; ~**light** n (fig: of event) punto culminante // vt subrayar; ~**ly** ad sumamente; ~**ly strung** a hipertenso; **H~ Mass** n misa mayor; ~**ness** n altura; **Her H~ness** Su Alteza; ~-**pitched** a agudo; ~-**rise block** n torre f de pisos; ~ **school** n colegio de segunda enseñanza, Instituto; ~ **street** n calle f mayor; ~**way** n carretera.
hijack ['haɪdʒæk] vt secuestrar; ~**er** n secuestrador/a m/f.
hike [haɪk] vi (go walking) ir de excursión; (tramp) caminar // n caminata; **hiker** n excursionista m/f.
hilarious [hɪ'leərɪəs] a (behaviour, event) regocijante.
hill [hɪl] n colina; (high) montaña; (slope) cuesta; ~**side** n ladera; ~**y** a montañoso; (uneven) accidentado.
hilt [hɪlt] n (of sword) empuñadura; **to the ~** completamente.
him [hɪm] pron (direct) le, lo; (indirect) le; (stressed, after prep) él; ~**self** pron (reflexive) se; (emphatic) él mismo; (after prep) sí (mismo).
hind [haɪnd] a posterior // n cierva.

hinder ['hɪndə*] vt estorbar, impedir; **hindrance** ['hɪndrəns] n estorbo, obstáculo.
Hindu ['hɪnduː] n hindú m/f.
hinge [hɪndʒ] n bisagra, gozne m // vi (fig): **to ~ on** depender de.
hint [hɪnt] n indirecta; (advice) consejo // vt: **to ~ that** insinuar que // vi soltar indirectas; **to ~ at** hacer una alusión a.
hip [hɪp] n cadera; ~ **pocket** n bolsillo de atrás.
hippopotamus [hɪpə'pɒtəməs], pl ~**es** or -**mi** [-maɪ] n hipopótamo.
hire ['haɪə*] vt (car, equipment) alquilar; (worker) contratar // n alquiler m; (of person) salario; **for ~** se alquila; (taxi) libre; ~ **purchase (H.P.)** n compra a plazos.
his [hɪz] pron (el) suyo/(la) suya etc // a su.
Hispanic [hɪs'pænɪk] a hispánico.
hiss [hɪs] vi silbar, sisear // n silbido, siseo.
historian [hɪ'stɔːrɪən] n historiador/a m/f.
historic(al) [hɪ'stɒrɪk(l)] a histórico.
history ['hɪstərɪ] n historia.
hit [hɪt], pt, pp **hit** vt (strike) golpear, pegar; (reach: target) alcanzar; (collide with: car) chocar contra // n golpe m; (success) éxito, sensación f; **to ~ it off with sb** hacer buenas migas con alguien.
hitch [hɪtʃ] vt (fasten) atar, amarrar; (also: ~ **up**) alzar // n (difficulty) dificultad f; **to ~ a lift** hacer autostop.
hitch-hike ['hɪtʃhaɪk] vi hacer autostop; **hitch-hiker** n autostopista m/f.
hive [haɪv] n colmena.
hoard [hɔːd] n acumulación f // vt acumular; ~**ing** n acumulación f; (for posters) cartelera.
hoarfrost ['hɔːfrɒst] n escarcha.
hoarse [hɔːs] a ronco.
hoax [həʊks] n trampa.
hobble ['hɒbl] vi cojear // vt (horse) manear.
hobby ['hɒbɪ] n pasatiempo, afición f; ~-**horse** n (fig) tema, manía.
hobo ['həʊbəʊ] n (US) vagabundo.
hockey ['hɒkɪ] n hockey m.
hoe [həʊ] n azadón m // vt azadonar.
hog [hɒg] n cerdo, puerco // vt (fig) acaparar; **to go the whole ~** liarse la manta a la cabeza.
hoist [hɔɪst] n (lift) montacargas m inv; (crane) grúa.
hold [həʊld], pt, pp **held** vt tener; (contain) contener; (keep back) retener; (believe) sostener; (take ~ of) coger; (take weight) soportar; (meeting) celebrar // vi (withstand pressure) resistir; (be valid) valer; (stick) pegarse // n (handle) asidero; (grasp) asimiento; (fig) dominio; (WRESTLING) presa; (NAUT) bodega; ~ **the line!** (TEL) no cuelgue; **to ~ one's own** (fig) defenderse; **to catch** or **get (a) ~ of** agarrarse, asirse de; **to ~ back** vt retenerse; (secret) guardarse; **to ~ down** vt (person) sujetar; (job) conservar; **to ~ off** vt (enemy) rechazar; **to ~ on** vi

agarrarse bien; (*wait*) esperar; ~ **on!** (*TEL*) no cuelgue; **to ~ on to** *vt fus* agarrarse a; (*keep*) guardar; **to ~ out** *vt* alargar // *vi* (*resist*) resistir; **to ~ up** *vt* (*raise*) levantar; (*support*) apoyar; (*delay*) atrasar; (*rob*) asaltar; **~all** *n* funda, neceser *m*; **~er** *n* (*of* ticket, record) poseedor/a *m/f*; (*of office, title etc*) titular *m/f*; **~ing** *n* (*share*) interés *m*; **~up** *n* (*robbery*) atraco; (*delay*) parada; (*in traffic*) embotellamiento.

hole [haul] *n* agujero // *vt* agujerear.

holiday ['holədɪ] *n* vacaciones *fpl*; (*day off*) (día de) fiesta, feriado; **~-maker** *n* veraneante *m/f*; **~ resort** *n* punto de veraneo.

holiness ['haulɪnɪs] *n* santidad *f*.

Holland ['holənd] *n* Holanda.

hollow ['holəu] *a* hueco, vacío; (*eyes*) hundido; (*sound*) sordo; (*doctrine*) falso // *n* (*gen*) hueco; (*in ground*) hoyo // *vt*: **to ~ out** ahuecar.

holly ['holɪ] *n* acebo; **~hock** *n* malva loca.

holster ['haulstə*] *n* pistolera.

holy ['hauli] *a* (*gen*) santo, sagrado; (*water*) bendito; **H~ Ghost** *or* **Spirit** *n* Espíritu *m* Santo.

homage ['homɪdʒ] *n* homenaje *m*; **to pay ~ to** rendir homenaje a.

home [haum] *n* casa; (*country*) patria; (*institution*) asilo // *a* (*domestic*) casero, de casa; (*ECON, POL*) nacional // *ad* (*direction*) a casa; **at ~** en casa; **to go/come ~** ir/volver a casa; **make yourself at ~** ¡estás en tu casa!; **~ address** *n* señas *fpl*; **~land** *n* tierra natal; **~less** *a* sin hogar, sin casa; **~ly** *a* (*domestic*) casero; (*simple*) sencillo; **~-made** *a* hecho en casa; **~ rule** *n* autonomía; **H~ Secretary** *n* (*Brit*) Ministro del Interior; **~sick** *a*: **to be ~sick** tener morriña, tener nostalgia; **~ town** *n* ciudad *f* natal; **~ward** ['haumwəd] *a* (*journey*) hacia casa; **~work** *n* tarea.

homicide ['homisaɪd] *n* (*US*) homicidio.

homosexual [homəu'sɛksjuəl] *a, n* homosexual *m*.

honest ['ɔnɪst] *a* honrado; (*sincere*) franco, sincero; **~ly** *ad* honradamente; francamente; **~y** *n* honradez *f*.

honey ['hʌnɪ] *n* miel *f*; **~comb** *n* panal *m*; (*pattern*) nido de abejas; **~moon** *n* luna de miel; (*trip*) viaje de novios.

honk [hɔŋk] *vi* (*AUT*) tocar la bocina.

honorary ['ɔnərərɪ] *a* no remunerado; (*duty, title*) honorario.

honour, honor (*US*) ['ɔnə*] *vt* honrar // *n* honor *m*, honra; **~able** *a* honorable; **~s degree** *n* (*SCOL*) título universitario.

hood [hud] *n* capucha; (*Brit: AUT*) capota; (*US: AUT*) capó *m*.

hoodlum ['hu:dləm] *n* matón *m*.

hoof [hu:f], *pl* **hooves** *n* pezuña.

hook [huk] *n* gancho; (*on dress*) corchete *m*, broche *m*; (*for fishing*) anzuelo // *vt* enganchar.

hooligan ['hu:lɪgən] *n* gamberro.

hoop [hu:p] *n* aro.

hoot [hu:t] *vi* (*AUT*) tocar la bocina; (*siren*) tocar la sirena // *n* bocinazo; toque *m* de sirena; **to ~ with laughter** morirse de risa; **~er** *n* (*AUT*) bocina; (*NAUT*) sirena.

hooves [hu:vz] *pl of* **hoof.**

hop [hop] *vi* saltar, brincar; (*on one foot*) saltar con un pie // *n* salto, brinco.

hope [haup] *vt, vi* esperar // *n* esperanza; **I ~ so/not** espero que sí/no; **~ful** *a* (*person*) optimista, lleno de esperanzas; (*situation*) prometedor(a); **~fully** *ad* con optimismo, con esperanza; **~less** *a* desesperado.

hops [hops] *npl* lúpulo *sg*.

horde [hɔ:d] *n* horda.

horizon [hə'raɪzn] *n* horizonte *m*; **~tal** [hɔrɪ'zɔntl] *a* horizontal.

hormone ['hɔ:məun] *n* hormona.

horn [hɔ:n] *n* cuerno; (*MUS*) trompa; (*AUT*) bocina; **~-rimmed** de concha; **~ed** *a* (*animal*) con cuernos.

hornet ['hɔ:nɪt] *n* avispón *m*.

horny ['hɔ:nɪ] *a* (*material*) córneo; (*hands*) calloso.

horoscope ['hɔrəskəup] *n* horóscopo.

horrible ['hɔrɪbl] *a* horrible.

horrid ['hɔrɪd] *a* horrible, horroroso.

horrify ['hɔrɪfaɪ] *vt* horrorizar.

horror ['hɔrə*] *n* horror *m*; **~ film** *n* película de horror.

hors d'œuvre [ɔ:'də:vrə] *n* entremeses *mpl*.

horse [hɔ:s] *n* caballo; **on ~back** a caballo; **~man/woman** *n* jinete *m*/amazona; **~-power (h.p.)** *n* caballo (de fuerza); **~-racing** *n* carreras *fpl* de caballos; **~radish** *n* rábano picante; **~shoe** *n* herradura.

horticulture ['hɔ:tɪkʌltʃə*] *n* horticultura.

hose [hauz] *n* (*also:* **~pipe**) manga.

hosiery ['hauzɪərɪ] *n* calcetería.

hospitable ['hɔspɪtəbl] *a* hospitalario.

hospital ['hɔspɪtl] *n* hospital *m*.

hospitality [hɔspɪ'tælɪtɪ] *n* hospitalidad *f*.

host [haust] *n* anfitrión *m*; (*in hotel etc*) huésped *m*; (*large number*): **a ~ of** multitud de; (*REL*) hostia.

hostage ['hɔstɪdʒ] *n* rehén *m*.

hostel ['hɔstl] *n* hostal *m*; **youth ~** *n* albergue *m* de juventud.

hostess ['haustɪs] *n* anfitriona; (*air ~*) azafata; (*in night-club*) cabaretera.

hostile ['hɔstaɪl] *a* hostil; **hostility** [-'stɪlɪtɪ] *n* hostilidad *f*.

hot [hɔt] *a* caliente; (*weather*) caluroso, de calor; (*as opposed to only warm*) muy caliente; (*spicy*) picante; (*fig*) ardiente, acalorado; **~ dog** *n* perro caliente.

hotel [hau'tɛl] *n* hotel *m*; **~ier** *n* hotelero.

hot: **~headed** *a* exaltado; **~house** *n* invernadero; **~ly** *ad* con pasión, apasionadamente; **~-water bottle** *n* bolsa de agua caliente.

hound [haund] *vt* acosar // *n* perro de caza.

hour ['auə*] n hora; ~ly ad cada hora.
house [haus, pl: 'hauzɪz] n (also: firm) casa; (POL) cámara; (THEATRE) sala // vt [hauz] (person) alojar; **on the** ~ (fig) la casa invita; ~ **arrest** n arresto domiciliario; ~**boat** n casa flotante; ~**breaking** n robo (en una casa); ~**coat** n bata; ~**hold** n familia; ~**keeper** n ama de claves; ~**keeping** n (work) trabajos domésticos mpl; ~**keeping (money)** dinero para gastos domésticos; ~-**warming party** n fiesta de estreno de casa; ~**wife** n ama de casa; ~**work** n faenas fpl (de la casa).
housing ['hauzɪŋ] n (act) alojamiento; (houses) viviendas fpl; ~ **estate** n bloque m de viviendas.
hovel ['hɔvl] n pocilga.
hover ['hɔvə*] vi flotar (en el aire); ~**craft** n hidroala m, aerodeslizador m.
how [hau] ad cómo; ~ **are you?** ¿cómo está Vd?, ¿cómo estás?; ~ **long have you been here?** ¿cuánto tiempo hace que estás aquí?; ~ **lovely!** ¡qué bonito!; ~ **many/much?** ¿cuántos/cuánto?; ~ **old are you?** ¿cuántos años tienes?; ~**ever** ad de cualquier manera; (+ adjective) por muy ... que; (in questions) cómo // conj sin embargo, no obstante.
howl [haul] n aullido // vi aullar.
h.p., H.P. abbr of hire purchase; horse power.
HQ abbr of **headquarters.**
hub [hʌb] n (of wheel) centro.
hubbub ['hʌbʌb] n barahúnda, barullo.
hubcap ['hʌbkæp] n tapacubo.
huddle ['hʌdl] vi: **to** ~ **together** amontonarse.
hue [hju:] n color m, matiz m; ~ **and cry** n alarma.
huff [hʌf] n: **in a** ~ con rabieta.
hug [hʌg] vt abrazar // n abrazo.
huge [hju:dʒ] a enorme.
hulk [hʌlk] n (wreck) barco viejo; (hull) casco.
hull [hʌl] n (of ship) casco.
hullo [hə'ləu] excl = **hello.**
hum [hʌm] vt tararear, canturrear // vi tararear, canturrear; (insect) zumbar // n zumbido.
human ['hju:mən] a, n humano.
humane [hju:'meɪn] a humano, humanitario.
humanity [hju:'mænɪtɪ] n humanidad f.
humble ['hʌmbl] a humilde // vt humillar; **humbly** ad humildemente.
humbug ['hʌmbʌg] n embustes mpl; (sweet) caramelo de menta.
humdrum ['hʌmdrʌm] a (boring) monótono, aburrido; (routine) rutinario.
humid ['hju:mɪd] a húmedo; ~**ity** [-'mɪdɪtɪ] n humedad f.
humiliate [hju:'mɪlɪeɪt] vt humillar; **humiliation** [-'eɪʃən] n humillación f.
humility [hju:'mɪlɪtɪ] n humildad f.
humorist ['hju:mərɪst] n humorista m/f.

humorous ['hju:mərəs] a gracioso, divertido.
humour, humor (US) ['hju:mə*] n humorismo, sentido del humor; (mood) humor m // vt (person) complacer.
hump [hʌmp] n (in ground) montículo; (camel's) giba.
hunch [hʌntʃ] n (premonition) presentimiento; ~**back** n joroba; ~**ed** a jorobado.
hundred ['hʌndrəd] num ciento; (before n) cien; ~**weight** n (Brit) = 50.8 kg; 112 lb; (US) = 45.3 kg; 100 lb.
hung [hʌŋ] pt, pp of hang.
Hungarian [hʌŋ'gɛərɪən] a, n húngaro/a.
Hungary ['hʌŋgərɪ] n Hungría.
hunger ['hʌŋgə*] n hambre f // vi: **to** ~ **for** (gen) tener hambre de; (desire) anhelar; ~ **strike** n huelga de hambre; **hungrily** [-grəlɪ] ad ávidamente, con ganas; **hungry** [-grɪ] a hambriento; **to be hungry** tener hambre.
hunt [hʌnt] vt (seek) buscar; (SPORT) cazar // vi cazar // n caza, cacería; ~**er** n cazador m; ~**ing** n caza.
hurdle ['hə:dl] n (SPORT) valla; (fig) obstáculo.
hurl [hə:l] vt lanzar, arrojar.
hurrah [hu'rɑ:], **hurray** [hu'reɪ] n ¡viva!, ¡vítor!
hurricane ['hʌrɪkən] n huracán m.
hurried ['hʌrɪd] a (fast) apresurado; (rushed) hecho de prisa; ~**ly** ad con prisa, apresuradamente.
hurry ['hʌrɪ] n prisa // vi apresurarse, darse prisa // vt (person) dar prisa a; (work) apresurar; **to be in a** ~ tener prisa.
hurt [hə:t], pt, pp **hurt** vt hacer daño a // vi doler // a lastimado; ~**ful** a (gen) dañoso; (remark) hiriente.
hurtle ['hə:tl] vi: **to** ~ **past** pasar como un rayo; **to** ~ **down** caer con violencia.
husband ['hʌzbənd] n marido.
hush [hʌʃ] n silencio // vt hacer callar; (cover up) encubrir; ~! ¡chitón!, ¡cállate!
husk [hʌsk] n (of wheat) cáscara.
husky ['hʌskɪ] a ronco; (burly) fornido // n perro esquimal.
hustle ['hʌsl] vt (push) empujar; (hurry) dar prisa a // n bullicio, actividad f febril; ~ **and bustle** n vaivén m.
hut [hʌt] n cabaña; (shed) cobertizo.
hutch [hʌtʃ] n conejera.
hyacinth ['haɪəsɪnθ] n jacinto.
hybrid ['haɪbrɪd] a, n híbrido.
hydrant ['haɪdrənt] n (also: fire ~) boca de incendios.
hydraulic [haɪ'drɔ:lɪk] a hidráulico.
hydroelectric [haɪdrəu'lektrɪk] a hidroeléctrico.
hydrogen ['haɪdrədʒən] n hidrógeno.
hyena [haɪ'i:nə] n hiena.
hygiene ['haɪdʒi:n] n higiene f; **hygienic** [-'dʒi:nɪk] a higiénico.
hymn [hɪm] n himno.

hyphen ['haɪfn] n guión m.
hypnosis [hɪp'nəusɪs] n hipnosis f;
hypnotic [-'nɒtɪk] a hipnótico; **hypnotism**
['hɪpnɒtɪzm] n hipnotismo; **hypnotist**
['hɪpnɒtɪst] n hipnotista m/f; **hypnotize**
['hɪpnɒtaɪz] vt hipnotizar.
hypocrisy [hɪ'pɒkrɪsɪ] n hipocresía;
hypocrite ['hɪpɒkrɪt] n hipócrita m/f;
hypocritical [hɪpɒ'krɪtɪkl] a hipócrita.
hypothesis [haɪ'pɒθɪsɪs], pl **-ses** [-siːz] n
hipótesis f; **hypothetic(al)** [-pəu'θɛtɪk(l)] a
hipotético.
hysteria [hɪ'stɪərɪə] n histeria; **hysterical**
[-'stɛrɪkl] a histérico; **hysterics** [-'stɛrɪks]
npl histeria sg, histerismo sg.

I

I [aɪ] pron yo.
ice [aɪs] n hielo // vt (cake) alcorzar;
(drink) helar // vi (also: ~ **over**, ~ **up**)
helarse; ~ **age** n período glacial; ~ **axe**
n piolei m; **~berg** n iceberg m; ~ **box** n
(US) nevera; **~-cold** a helado; ~ **cream**
n helado; ~ **cube** n cubito de hielo; ~
hockey n hockey m sobre hielo.
Iceland ['aɪslənd] n Islandia; **~er** n
islandés/esa m/f; **~ic** [-'lændɪk] a
islandés(esa).
ice: ~ **rink** n pista de hielo; ~ **skating** n
patinaje m sobre hielo.
icicle ['aɪsɪkl] n carámbano.
icing ['aɪsɪŋ] n (CULIN) alcorza, garapiña;
(AVIAT etc) formación f de hielo; ~ **sugar**
n azúcar m de alcorza.
icon ['aɪkɒn] n ícono.
icy ['aɪsɪ] a (road) helado; (fig) glacial.
I'd [aɪd] = **I would; I had.**
idea [aɪ'dɪə] n idea.
ideal [aɪ'dɪəl] n ideal m // a ideal; **~ist** n
idealista m/f.
identical [aɪ'dɛntɪkl] a idéntico.
identification [aɪdɛntɪfɪ'keɪʃən] n
identificación f; **means of** ~ documentos
mpl personales.
identify [aɪ'dɛntɪfaɪ] vt identificar.
identikit picture [aɪ'dɛntɪkɪt-] n retrato-
robot m.
identity [aɪ'dɛntɪtɪ] n identidad f.
ideological [aɪdɪə'lɒdʒɪkəl] a ideológico;
ideology [-dɪ'ɒlɒdʒɪ] n ideología.
idiocy ['ɪdɪəsɪ] n idiotez f; (stupid act)
estupidez f.
idiom ['ɪdɪəm] n modismo; (style of
speaking) lenguaje m.
idiosyncrasy [ɪdɪəu'sɪŋkrəsɪ] n
idiosincrasia.
idiot ['ɪdɪət] n (gen) idiota m/f; (fool)
tonto/a; **~ic** [-'ɒtɪk] a idiota; tonto.
idle ['aɪdl] a (gen) ocioso; (lazy)
holgazán(ana); (unemployed) desocupado;
(pointless) inútil // vi (machine) marchar
en vacío // vt: **to** ~ **away the time**
malgastar el tiempo; **~ness** n ociosidad f;
holgazanería; desocupación f.
idol ['aɪdl] n ídolo; **~ize** vt idolatrar.

if [ɪf] conj si.
igloo ['ɪgluː] n iglú m.
ignite [ɪg'naɪt] vt encender; (set fire to)
incendiar // vi encenderse.
ignition [ɪg'nɪʃən] n (AUT) encendido; **to
switch on/off the** ~ encender/apagar
el motor; ~ **key** n (AUT) llave f de
contacto.
ignorance ['ɪgnərəns] n ignorancia;
ignorant [-ənt] a ignorante; **to be
ignorant of** ignorar.
ignore [ɪg'nɔ:*] vt (person) no hacer caso
de; (fact) pasar por alto.
I'll [aɪl] = **I will, I shall.**
ill [ɪl] a enfermo, malo; (bad) malo // n mal
m; (fig) infortunio // ad mal; **to take** or **be
taken** ~ ponerse enfermo, enfermar;
~-advised a poco recomendable;
(misled) mal aconsejado; **~-at-ease** a
incómodo.
illegal [ɪ'liːgl] a ilegal.
illegible [ɪ'lɛdʒɪbl] a ilegible.
illegitimate [ɪlɪ'dʒɪtɪmət] a ilegítimo.
ill: **~-fated** a malogrado; ~ **feeling** n
rencor m.
illicit [ɪ'lɪsɪt] a ilícito.
illiterate [ɪ'lɪtərət] a analfabeto.
ill-mannered [ɪl'mænəd] a mal educado.
illness ['ɪlnɪs] n enfermedad f.
illogical [ɪ'lɒdʒɪkl] a ilógico.
ill-treat [ɪl'triːt] vt maltratar.
illuminate [ɪ'luːmɪneɪt] vt (room, street)
iluminar, alumbrar; (subject) aclarar;
illumination [-'neɪʃən] n alumbrado;
illuminations npl luminarias fpl.
illusion [ɪ'luːʒən] n ilusión f; **to be under
the** ~ **that...** estar bajo la ilusión de
que...; **illusory** [-sərɪ] a ilusorio.
illustrate ['ɪləstreɪt] vt (gen) ilustrar;
(subject) aclarar; (point) poner ejemplos a;
illustration [-'streɪʃən] n (example)
ejemplo; (explanation) aclaración f; (in
book) lámina.
illustrious [ɪ'lʌstrɪəs] a ilustre.
ill will [ɪl'wɪl] n rencor m.
I'm [aɪm] = **I am.**
image ['ɪmɪdʒ] n imagen f.
imaginary [ɪ'mædʒɪnərɪ] a imaginaiio;
imagination [-'neɪʃən] n imaginación f;
(inventiveness) inventiva; (illusion)
fantasía; **imaginative** [-nətɪv] a
imaginativo; **imagine** vt imaginarse;
(delude o.s.) hacerse la ilusión de (que).
imbalance [ɪm'bæləns] n (gen)
desequilibrio; (inequality) falta de
correspondencia.
imbecile ['ɪmbəsiːl] n imbécil m/f.
imbue [ɪm'bjuː] vt: **to** ~ **sth with** imbuir
algo de.
imitate ['ɪmɪteɪt] vt imitar; **imitation**
[-'teɪʃən] n imitación f; (copy) copia;
(mimicry) mímica.
immaculate [ɪ'mækjulət] a perfectamente limpio; (REL) inmaculado.
immaterial [ɪmə'tɪərɪəl] a incorpóreo; **it
is** ~ **whether...** no importa si... .

immature [ımə'tjuə*] a (person) poco maduro; (of one's youth) juvenil.
immediate [ı'mi:dıət] a inmediato; (pressing) urgente, apremiante; ~ly ad (at once) en seguida; ~ly next to muy junto a.
immense [ı'mɛns] a inmenso, enorme.
immerse [ı'mɔ:s] vt (submerge) sumergir; (sink) hundir; **to be ~d in** (fig) estar absorto en.
immersion heater [ı'mɔ:ʃn-] n calentador m de inmersión.
immigrant ['ımıgrənt] n inmigrante m/f; **immigrate** [-greıt] vi inmigrar; **immigration** [-'greıʃən] n inmigración f.
imminent ['ımınənt] a inminente.
immobile [ı'məubaıl] a inmóvil; **immobilize** [-bılaız] vt inmovilizar.
immoral [ı'mɔrl] a inmoral; ~ity [-'rælıtı] n inmoralidad f.
immortal [ı'mɔ:tl] a inmortal; ~ize vt inmortalizar.
immune [ı'mju:n] a: ~ **(to)** inmune (contra); **immunity** n (MED) inmunidad f; (COMM) exención f.
immunization [ımjunaı'zeıʃən] n inmunización f; **immunize** ['ımjunaız] vt inmunizar.
imp [ımp] n diablillo.
impact ['ımpækt] n (gen) impacto.
impair [ım'pɛə*] vt perjudicar.
impale [ım'peıl] vt atravesar.
impart [ım'pa:t] vt comunicar.
impartial [ım'pa:ʃl] a imparcial; ~ity [ımpa:ʃı'ælıtı] n imparcialidad f.
impassable [ım'pa:səbl] a (barrier) infranqueable; (river) invadeable; (road) intransitable.
impatience [ım'peıʃəns] n impaciencia; **impatient** [-ənt] a impaciente; **to get** or **grow impatient** impacientarse.
impeccable [ım'pɛkəbl] a impecable.
impede [ım'pi:d] vt estorbar, dificultar.
impediment [ım'pɛdımənt] n obstáculo, estorbo; (also: **speech** ~) defecto (del habla).
impending [ım'pɛndıŋ] a (near) próximo.
impenetrable [ım'pɛnıtrəbl] a (gen) impenetrable; (unfathomable) insondable.
imperative [ım'pɛrətıv] a (tone) imperioso; (necessary) indispensable; (pressing) urgente // n (LING) imperativo.
imperceptible [ımpə'sɛptıbl] a imperceptible, insensible.
imperfect [ım'pə:fıkt] a imperfecto; (goods etc) defectuoso; ~**ion** [-'fɛkʃən] n (blemish) desperfecto; (state) imperfección f.
imperial [ım'pıərıəl] a imperial; ~**ism** n imperialismo.
imperil [ım'pɛrıl] vt arriesgar, poner en peligro.
impersonal [ım'pə:sənl] a impersonal.
impersonate [ım'pə:səneıt] vt hacerse pasar por; (THEATRE) imitar.

impertinent [ım'pə:tınənt] a impertinente, insolente.
impervious [ım'pə:vıəs] a impermeable; (fig): ~ **to** insensible a.
impetuous [ım'pɛtjuəs] a impetuoso, irreflexivo.
impetus ['ımpətəs] n ímpetu m; (fig) impulso.
impinge [ım'pındʒ]: **to ~ on** vt fus invadir, abusar de; (affect) afectar a.
implausible [ım'plɔ:zıbl] a inverosímil.
implement ['ımplımənt] n instrumento, herramienta // vt ['ımplıment] hacer efectivo; (carry out) realizar.
implicate ['ımplıkeıt] vt (compromise) comprometer; (involve) enredar; **implication** [-'keıʃən] n consecuencia, implicancia (AM).
implicit [ım'plısıt] a (gen) implícito; (complete) absoluto.
implore [ım'plɔ:*] vt (person) suplicar.
imply [ım'plaı] vt (involve) implicar; (mean) significar; (hint) dar a entender que; **it is implied** se sobreentiende.
impolite [ımpə'laıt] a mal educado.
import [ım'pɔ:t] vt importar // n ['ımpɔ:t] (COMM) importación f; (: article) artículo importado; (meaning) significado, sentido.
importance [ım'pɔ:təns] n importancia; **important** [-ənt] a importante; **it's not important** no importa, no tiene importancia.
importer [ım'pɔ:tə*] n importador/a m/f.
impose [ım'pəuz] vt imponer // vi: **to ~ on sb** abusar de uno; **imposing** a imponente, impresionante.
impossible [ım'pɔsıbl] a imposible; (person) insoportable.
impostor [ım'pɔstə*] n impostor/a m/f.
impotence ['ımpətəns] n impotencia; **impotent** [-ənt] a impotente.
impound [ım'paund] vt embargar.
impoverished [ım'pɔvərıʃt] a necesitado; (land) agotado.
impracticable [ım'præktıkəbl] a no factible, irrealizable.
impractical [ım'præktıkl] a (person) poco práctico.
imprecise [ımprı'saıs] a impreciso.
impregnable [ım'prɛgnəbl] a invulnerable; (castle) inexpugnable.
impregnate ['ımprɛgneıt] vt (gen) impregnar; (soak) empapar; (fertilize) fecundar.
impresario [ımprı'sa:rıəu] n empresario.
impress [ım'prɛs] vt impresionar; (mark) estampar // vi hacer buena impresión; **to ~ sth on sb** convencer a uno de algo; **it ~ed itself on me** se me grabó (en la memoria).
impression [ım'prɛʃən] n impresión f; (footprint etc) huella; (print run) edición f; **to be under the ~ that** tener la impresión de que; ~**able** a influenciable; (sensitive) sensible; ~**ist** n impresionista m/f.
impressive [ım'prɛsıv] a impresionante.

imprint ['ımprınt] n impresión f, huella.
imprison [ım'prızn] vt encarcelar;
~**ment** n encarcelamiento, cárcel f.
improbable [ım'prɔbəbl] a improbable,
inverosímil.
impromptu [ım'prɔmptjuː] a improvisado
// ad de improviso.
improper [ım'prɔpə*] a (incorrect)
impropio; (unseemly) indecoroso;
(indecent) indecente.
impropriety [ımprə'praıətı] n falta de
decoro; (indecency) indecencia; (of
language) impropiedad f.
improve [ım'pruːv] vt mejorar // vi
mejorarse; (become perfect) per-
feccionarse; (pupils) hacer progresos;
~**ment** n mejoramiento; perfección f;
progreso.
improvise ['ımprəvaız] vt, vi improvisar.
imprudent [ım'pruːdnt] a imprudente.
impudent ['ımpjudnt] a descarado,
insolente.
impulse ['ımpʌls] n impulso; **to act on** ~
obrar sin reflexión; **impulsive** [-'pʌlsıv] a
irreflexivo.
impunity [ım'pjuːnıtı] n: **with** ~
impunemente.
impure [ım'pjuə*] a (adulterated)
adulterado; (not pure) impuro; **impurity** n
(gen) impureza.
in [ın] prep en; (within) dentro de; (with
time: during, within): ~ **2 days** en 2 días;
(: after): ~ **2 weeks** dentro de 2
semanas; (with town, country): **it's** ~
France está en Francia // ad dentro,
adentro; (fashionable) de moda; **is he** ~?
¿está en casa? ~ **the country** en el
campo; ~ **the distance** a lo lejos; ~
town en el centro (de la ciudad); ~ **the
sun** al sol, bajo el sol; ~ **the rain** bajo la
lluvia; ~ **French** en francés; **1** ~ **10** uno
sobre 10, uno de cada 10; ~ **hundreds**
por centenares; **the best pupil** ~ **the
class** el mejor alumno de la clase;
written ~ **pencil** escrito con lápiz; ~
saying this at their party is ~
su partido ha llegado al poder; **to ask
sb** ~ invitar a uno a entrar; **to run/limp**
~ entrar corriendo/cojeando; **the** ~**s
and outs** los recovecos.
in., ins abbr of **inch(es).**
inability [ınə'bılıtı] n incapacidad f.
inaccessible [ınæk'sɛsıbl] a inaccesible.
inaccuracy [ın'ækjurəsı] n inexactitud f;
inaccurate [-rət] a inexacto, incorrecto.
inactivity [ınæk'tıvıtı] n inactividad f.
inadequate [ın'ædıkwət] a (insufficient)
insuficiente; (unsuitable) inadecuado;
(person) incapaz.
inadvertently [ınəd'vɜːtntlı] ad por
equivocación o descuido.
inadvisable [ınəd'vaızəbl] a no
aconsejable.
inane [ı'neın] a necio, fatuo.
inanimate [ın'ænımət] a inanimado.
inapplicable [ın'æplıkəbl] a inaplicable.
inappropriate [ınə'prəuprıət] a

inoportuno, inconveniente; (word,
expression) impropio.
inapt [ın'æpt] a impropio; ~**itude** n
incapacidad f.
inarticulate [ınɑː'tıkjulət] a (person)
incapaz de expresarse; (speech)
inarticulado.
inasmuch as [ınəz'mʌtʃæz] ad (given that)
puesto que; (since) ya que.
inattentive [ınə'tɛntıv] a distraído.
inaudible [ın'ɔːdıbl] a inaudible.
inaugural [ı'nɔːgjurəl] a (speech) de
apertura; **inaugurate** [-reıt] vt inaugurar;
inauguration [-'reıʃən] n ceremonia de
apertura.
in-between [ınbı'twiːn] a intermedio, de
entre medio.
inborn [ın'bɔːn] a (feeling) innato.
inbred [ın'brɛd] a innato; (family)
engendrado por endogamia.
incalculable [ın'kælkjuləbl] a
incalculable.
incapable [ın'keıpəbl] a incapaz.
incapacitate [ınkə'pæsıteıt] vt: **to** ~ **sb**
incapacitar a uno.
incapacity [ınkə'pæsıtı] n (inability)
incapacidad f.
incarcerate [ın'kɑːsəreıt] vt encarcelar.
incarnate [ın'kɑːnıt] a en persona // vt
['ınkɑːneıt] encarnar; **incarnation**
[-'neıʃən] n encarnación f.
incendiary [ın'sɛndıərı] a incendiario.
incense ['ınsɛns] n incienso // vt [ın'sɛns]
(anger) indignar, encolerizar.
incentive [ın'sɛntıv] n incentivo, estímulo.
incessant [ın'sɛsnt] a incesante, contínuo;
~**ly** ad constantemente.
incest ['ınsɛst] n incesto.
inch [ıntʃ] n pulgada; **to be within an** ~
of estar a dos dedos de; **he didn't give an**
~ no dio concesión alguna; **to** ~
forward avanzar palmo a palmo.
incidence ['ınsıdns] n (of crime, disease)
frecuencia.
incident ['ınsıdnt] n incidente m, suceso;
(in book) episodio.
incidental [ınsı'dɛntl] a no esencial,
accesorio; (unplanned) fortuito; ~ **to** al
margen de; ~**ly** [-'dɛntəlı] ad (by the way)
a propósito.
incinerator [ın'sınəreıtə*] n incinerador
m.
incipient [ın'sıpıənt] a incipiente.
incision [ın'sıʒən] n corte m.
incisive [ın'saısıv] a (mind) penetrante;
(tone) mordaz; (remark etc) tajante.
incite [ın'saıt] vt provocar.
inclination [ınklı'neıʃən] n (tendency)
tendencia, inclinación f.
incline ['ınklaın] n pendiente m, cuesta //
(vb: [ın'klaın]) vt (slope) inclinar; (head)
poner de lado // vi inclinarse; **to be** ~**d
to** (tend) ser propenso a; (be willing) estar
dispuesto a.
include [ın'kluːd] vt incluir, comprender;

(*in letter*) adjuntar; **including** *prep* incluso, inclusive.

inclusion [ɪn'kluːʒən] *n* inclusión *f*; **inclusive** [-sɪv] *a* inclusivo // *ad* inclusive.

incognito [ɪnkɔg'niːtəu] *ad* de incógnito.

incoherent [ɪnkəu'hɪərənt] *a* incoherente.

income ['ɪŋkʌm] *n* (*personal*) ingresos *mpl*; (*from property etc*) renta; (*profit*) rédito; ~ **tax** *n* impuesto sobre la renta; ~ **tax inspector** *n* inspector/a *m/f* fiscal; ~ **tax return** *n* registro fiscal.

incoming ['ɪnkʌmɪŋ] *a*: ~ **flight** vuelo entrante.

incomparable [ɪn'kɔmpərəbl] *a* incomparable, sin par.

incompatible [ɪnkəm'pætɪbl] *a* incompatible.

incompetence [ɪn'kɔmpɪtəns] *n* incompetencia; **incompetent** [-ənt] *a* incompetente.

incomplete [ɪnkəm'pliːt] *a* incompleto; (*unfinished*) sin terminar.

incomprehensible [ɪnkɔmprɪ'hensɪbl] *a* incomprensible.

inconceivable [ɪnkən'siːvəbl] *a* inconcebible.

inconclusive [ɪnkən'kluːsɪv] *a* sin resultado (definitivo); (*argument*) poco convincente.

incongruous [ɪn'kɔŋgruəs] *a* (*foolish*) absurdo, estrafalario; (*remark, act*) disonante, nada lógico.

inconsiderate [ɪnkən'sɪdərət] *a* desconsiderado; **how ~ of him!** ¡qué falta de consideración (de su parte)!

inconsistent [ɪnkən'sɪstnt] *a* inconsecuente; ~ **with** (que) no concuerda con.

inconspicuous [ɪnkən'spɪkjuəs] *a* poco llamativo, modesto; **to make o.s. ~** no llamar la atención.

inconstant [ɪn'kɔnstnt] *a* inconstante.

incontinent [ɪn'kɔntɪnənt] *a* incontinente.

inconvenience [ɪnkən'viːnjəns] *n* (*gen*) inconvenientes *mpl*; (*trouble*) molestia, incomodidad *f* // *vt* incomodar; **inconvenient** [-ənt] *a* incómodo, poco práctico; (*time, place*) inoportuno.

incorporate [ɪn'kɔːpəreɪt] *vt* incorporar; (*contain*) comprender; (*add*) agregar; ~**d** *a*: ~**d company** (*US: abbr* **Inc.**) Sociedad Anónima (S.A.).

incorrect [ɪnkə'rɛkt] *a* incorrecto.

incorruptible [ɪnkə'rʌptɪbl] *a* (*gen*) incorruptible; (*not open to bribes*) insobornable.

increase ['ɪnkriːs] *n* aumento // *vi* [ɪn-'kriːs] aumentarse; (*grow*) crecer; (*price*) subir; **increasing** *a* (*number*) creciente, en aumento; **increasingly** *ad* de más en más, cada vez más.

incredible [ɪn'krɛdɪbl] *a* increíble.

incredulous [ɪn'krɛdjuləs] *a* incrédulo.

increment ['ɪnkrɪmənt] *n* aumento, incremento.

incriminate [ɪn'krɪmɪneɪt] *vt* incriminar.

incubation [ɪnkju'beɪʃən] *n* incubación *f*;

incubator ['ɪnkjubeɪtə*] *n* incubadora.

incumbent [ɪn'kʌmbənt] *n* ocupante *m/f* // *a*: **it is ~ on him to...** le incumbe... .

incur [ɪn'kə:*] *vt* (*expenses*) contraer; (*gen*) incurrir en.

incurable [ɪn'kjuərəbl] *a* incurable; (*fig*) irremediable.

incursion [ɪn'kəːʃən] *n* incursión *f*.

indebted [ɪn'dɛtɪd] *a*: **to be ~ to sb** estar en deuda con uno.

indecent [ɪn'diːsnt] *a* indecente; ~ **assault** *n* atentado contra el pudor; ~ **exposure** *n* exhibicionismo.

indecisive [ɪndɪ'saɪsɪv] *a* indeciso; (*discussion*) no resuelto, inconcluyente.

indeed [ɪn'diːd] *ad* de hecho, realmente; **yes ~!** claro que sí.

indefinite [ɪn'dɛfɪnɪt] *a* indefinido; (*uncertain*) incierto; ~**ly** *ad* (*wait*) indefinidamente.

indelible [ɪn'dɛlɪbl] *a* imborrable.

indemnify [ɪn'dɛmnɪfaɪ] *vt* indemnizar, resarcir.

indentation [ɪndɛn'teɪʃən] *n* mella; (*TYP*) sangría.

independence [ɪndɪ'pɛndns] *n* independencia; **independent** [-ənt] *a* independiente; **to become independent** independizarse.

index ['ɪndɛks] *n* (*pl*: ~**es**: *in book*) índice *m*; (: *in library etc*) catálogo; (*pl*: **indices** ['ɪndɪsiːz]: *ratio, sign*) exponente *m*; ~ **card** *n* ficha; ~ **finger** *n* índice *m*; ~**-linked** *a* vinculado al índice del coste de la vida.

India ['ɪndɪə] *n* la India; ~**n** *a, n* indio/a; **Red ~n** *n* piel roja *m/f*.

indicate ['ɪndɪkeɪt] *vt* indicar; **indication** [-'keɪʃən] *n* indicio, señal *f*; **indicator** *n* (*gen*) indicador *m*.

indices ['ɪndɪsiːz] *pl* de **index**.

indict [ɪn'daɪt] *vt* acusar; ~**ment** *n* acusación *f*.

indifference [ɪn'dɪfrəns] *n* indiferencia; **indifferent** [-ənt] *a* indiferente; (*poor*) regular.

indigenous [ɪn'dɪdʒɪnəs] *a* indígena *inv*.

indigestion [ɪndɪ'dʒɛstʃən] *n* indigestión *f*, empacho.

indignant [ɪn'dɪgnənt] *a*: **to be ~ about sth** indignarse por algo; **indignation** [-'neɪʃən] *n* indignación *f*.

indignity [ɪn'dɪgnɪtɪ] *n* indignidad *f*; (*insult*) ultraje *m*, afrenta.

indigo ['ɪndɪgəu] *a* color de añil // *n* añil *m*.

indirect [ɪndɪ'rɛkt] *a* indirecto; ~**ly** *ad* indirectamente.

indiscreet [ɪndɪ'skriːt] *a* indiscreto; (*rash*) imprudente; **indiscretion** [-'skrɛʃən] *n* indiscreción *f*; imprudencia.

indiscriminate [ɪndɪ'skrɪmɪnət] *a* indistinto.

indispensable [ɪndɪ'spɛnsəbl] *a* indispensable, imprescindible.

indisposed [ɪndɪ'spəuzd] *a* (*unwell*) indispuesto.

indisputable [ˌɪndɪˈspjuːtəbl] *a* incontestable.

indistinct [ˌɪndɪˈstɪŋkt] *a* indistinto; (*memory, noise*) confuso.

individual [ˌɪndɪˈvɪdjuəl] *n* individuo // *a* individual; (*personal*) personal; (*for/of one only*) particular; ~**ist** *n* individualista *m/f*; ~**ity** [-ˈælɪtɪ] *n* individualidad *f*; ~**ly** *ad* individualmente; particularmente.

indoctrinate [ɪnˈdɔktrɪneɪt] *vt* adoctrinar; **indoctrination** [-ˈneɪʃən] *n* adoctrinamiento.

indolent [ˈɪndələnt] *a* indolente, perezoso.

indoor [ˈɪndɔː*] *a* (*inner*) interior; (*household*) de casa; (*inside*) de puertas adentro; (*swimming-pool*) cubierto; (*games*) de salón; (*sport*) bajo cubierta; ~**s** [ɪnˈdɔːz] *ad* dentro; (*at home*) en casa.

induce [ɪnˈdjuːs] *vt* inducir; (*bring about*) producir; (*provoke*) provocar; ~**ment** *n* (*incentive*) incentivo, aliciente *m*.

induction [ɪnˈdʌkʃən] *n* (MED: *of birth*) inducción *f*; ~ **course** *n* curso de inducción.

indulge [ɪnˈdʌldʒ] *vt* (*desire*) dar rienda suelta a; (*whim*) condescender con; (*person*) complacer; (*child*) consentir // *vi*: **to** ~ **in** darse el lujo de; **indulgence** *n* (*of desire*) gratificación *f*; (*leniency*) complacencia; **indulgent** *a* indulgente.

industrial [ɪnˈdʌstrɪəl] *a* industrial; ~ **action** *n* huelga; ~ **estate** *n* zona industrial; ~**ist** *n* industrial *m/f*; ~**ize** *vt* industrializar.

industrious [ɪnˈdʌstrɪəs] *a* (*gen*) trabajador(a); (*student*) aplicado.

industry [ˈɪndəstrɪ] *n* industria; (*diligence*) aplicación *f*.

inebriated [ɪˈniːbrɪeɪtɪd] *a* borracho.

inedible [ɪnˈedɪbl] *a* incomible; (*plant etc*) no comestible.

ineffective [ˌɪnɪˈfɛktɪv] *a* ineficaz, inútil.

inefficiency [ˌɪnɪˈfɪʃənsɪ] *n* ineficacia; **inefficient** [-ənt] *a* ineficaz, ineficiente.

ineligible [ɪnˈɛlɪdʒɪbl] *a* (*candidate*) inelegible; **to be** ~ **for sth** no tener derecho a algo.

inept [ɪˈnɛpt] *a* incompetente, incapaz.

inequality [ˌɪnɪˈkwɔlɪtɪ] *n* desigualdad *f*.

inert [ɪˈnɜːt] *a* inerte, inactivo; (*immobile*) inmóvil; ~**ia** [ɪˈnɜːʃə] *n* inercia; (*laziness*) pereza.

inescapable [ˌɪnɪˈskeɪpəbl] *a* ineludible.

inestimable [ɪnˈɛstɪməbl] *a* inestimable.

inevitable [ɪnˈɛvɪtəbl] *a* inevitable; (*necessary*) forzoso.

inexcusable [ˌɪnɪksˈkjuːzəbl] *a* imperdonable.

inexhaustible [ˌɪnɪgˈzɔːstɪbl] *a* inagotable.

inexorable [ɪnˈɛksɔrəbl] *a* inexorable, implacable.

inexpensive [ˌɪnɪkˈspɛnsɪv] *a* económico.

inexperience [ˌɪnɪkˈspɪərɪəns] *n* falta de experiencia; ~**d** *a* inexperto.

inexplicable [ˌɪnɪkˈsplɪkəbl] *a* inexplicable.

inextricable [ɪnɪkˈstrɪkəbl] *a* inextricable.

infallible [ɪnˈfælɪbl] *a* infalible.

infamous [ˈɪnfəməs] *a* infame; **infamy** [-mɪ] *n* infamia.

infancy [ˈɪnfənsɪ] *n* infancia.

infant [ˈɪnfənt] *n* (*baby*) criatura; (*young child*) niño/a; ~**ile** *a* infantil; (*pej*) aniñado; ~ **school** *n* escuela de párvulos.

infantry [ˈɪnfəntrɪ] *n* infantería; ~**man** *n* soldado (de infantería).

infatuated [ɪnˈfætjueɪtɪd] *a*: ~ **with** (*gen*) encaprichado por; (*in love*) enamorado de; **infatuation** [-ˈeɪʃən] *n* encaprichamiento; enamoramiento.

infect [ɪnˈfɛkt] *vt* (*wound*) infectar; (*person*) contagiar; (*fig: pej*) corromper; ~**ed with** (*illness*) contagiado de; ~**ion** [ɪnˈfɛkʃən] *n* infección *f*; (*fig*) contagio; ~**ious** [ɪnˈfɛkʃəs] *a* contagioso; (*also: fig*) infeccioso.

infer [ɪnˈfɜː*] *vt* deducir, inferir; ~**ence** [ˈɪnfərəns] *n* deducción *f*, inferencia.

inferior [ɪnˈfɪərɪə*] *a, n* inferior *m/f*; ~**ity** [-rɪˈɔrətɪ] *n* inferioridad *f*; ~**ity complex** *n* complejo de inferioridad.

infernal [ɪnˈfɜːnl] *a* infernal.

inferno [ɪnˈfɜːnəu] *n* infierno; (*fig*) hoguera.

infertile [ɪnˈfɜːtaɪl] *a* estéril, infecundo; **infertility** [-ˈtɪlɪtɪ] *n* esterilidad *f*, infecundidad *f*.

infested [ɪnˈfɛstɪd] *a*: ~ (**with**) plagado (de).

infidelity [ˌɪnfɪˈdɛlɪtɪ] *n* infidelidad *f*.

in-fighting [ˈɪnfaɪtɪŋ] *n* (*fig*) luchas *fpl* internas.

infiltrate [ˈɪnfɪltreɪt] *vt* (*troops etc*) infiltrarse en // *vi* infiltrarse.

infinite [ˈɪnfɪnɪt] *a* infinito.

infinitive [ɪnˈfɪnɪtɪv] *n* infinitivo.

infinity [ɪnˈfɪnɪtɪ] *n* (*also* MATH) infinito; (*an* ~) infinidad *f*.

infirm [ɪnˈfɜːm] *a* enfermo, débil; ~**ary** *n* hospital *m*; ~**ity** *n* debilidad *f*; (*illness*) enfermedad *f*, achaque *m*.

inflame [ɪnˈfleɪm] *vt* inflamar.

inflammable [ɪnˈflæməbl] *a* inflamable; (*explosive*) explosivo.

inflammation [ˌɪnfləˈmeɪʃən] *n* inflamación *f*.

inflate [ɪnˈfleɪt] *vt* (*tyre, balloon*) inflar; (*fig*) hinchar; ~**d** *a* (*style*) exagerado; (*value*) excesivo; **inflation** [ɪnˈfleɪʃən] *n* (ECON) inflación *f*; **inflationary** [ɪnˈfleɪʃnərɪ] *a* inflacionario.

inflexible [ɪnˈflɛksɪbl] *a* inflexible.

inflict [ɪnˈflɪkt] *vt*: **to** ~ **on** infligir en; (*tax etc*) imponer a; ~**ion** [ɪnˈflɪkʃən] *n* imposición *f*.

inflow [ˈɪnfləu] *n* afluencia.

influence [ˈɪnfluəns] *n* influencia // *vt* influir en, influenciar; (*persuade*) sugestionar; **under the** ~ **of alcohol** en estado de embriaguez; **influential** [-ˈɛnʃl] *a* influyente.

influenza [ˌɪnfluˈɛnzə] *n* gripe *f*.

influx [ˈɪnflʌks] *n* afluencia.

inform [ɪnˈfɔːm] vt: **to ~ sb of sth** informar a uno sobre o de algo; (warn) avisar a uno de algo; (communicate) comunicar algo a uno // vi soplar; **to ~ on sb** delatar a uno.

informal [ɪnˈfɔːml] a (person, manner) desenvuelto; (tone) familiar; (visit, discussion) extraoficial; (intimate) de confianza; **~ity** [-ˈmælɪtɪ] n falta de ceremonia; (intimacy) intimidad f; (familiarity) familiaridad f; (ease) afabilidad f.

information [ɪnfəˈmeɪʃən] n información f, informes mpl; (news) noticias fpl; (knowledge) conocimientos mpl; (LAW) delatación f; **a piece of ~** un dato.

informative [ɪnˈfɔːmətɪv] a informativo.

informer [ɪnˈfɔːmə*] n delator/a m/f; (also: **police ~**) soplón/ona m/f.

infra-red [ɪnfrəˈred] a infrarrojo.

infrequent [ɪnˈfriːkwənt] a infrecuente.

infringe [ɪnˈfrɪndʒ] vt infringir, violar // vi: **to ~ on** invadir, abusar de; **~ment** n infracción f; (of rights) invasión f; (SPORT) falta.

infuriate [ɪnˈfjuərɪeɪt] vt enfurecer; **infuriating** a enloquecedor(a).

ingenious [ɪnˈdʒiːnjəs] a ingenioso; **ingenuity** [-dʒɪˈnjuːɪtɪ] n ingeniosidad f.

ingenuous [ɪnˈdʒenjuəs] a ingenuo.

ingot [ˈɪŋgət] n lingote m, barra.

ingrained [ɪnˈgreɪnd] a arraigado.

ingratiate [ɪnˈgreɪʃɪeɪt] vt: **to ~ o.s. with** congraciarse con.

ingratitude [ɪnˈgrætɪtjuːd] n ingratitud f.

ingredient [ɪnˈgriːdɪənt] n ingrediente m.

inhabit [ɪnˈhæbɪt] vt habitar, vivir en; (occupy) ocupar; **~ant** n habitante m/f.

inhale [ɪnˈheɪl] vt inhalar // vi (in smoking) aspirar.

inherent [ɪnˈhɪərənt] a: **~ in** or **to** inherente a.

inherit [ɪnˈherɪt] vt heredar; **~ance** n herencia; (fig) patrimonio.

inhibit [ɪnˈhɪbɪt] vt inhibir, impedir; **to ~ sb from doing sth** impedir a uno hacer algo; **~ion** [-ˈbɪʃən] n inhibición f.

inhospitable [ɪnhɔsˈpɪtəbl] a (person) inhospitalario; (place) inhóspito.

inhuman [ɪnˈhjuːmən] a inhumano.

inimitable [ɪˈnɪmɪtəbl] a inimitable.

iniquity [ɪˈnɪkwɪtɪ] n inicuidad f; (injustice) injusticia.

initial [ɪˈnɪʃl] a inicial; (first) primero // n inicial f // vt firmar con las iniciales; **~s** npl iniciales fpl; (abbreviation) siglas fpl; **~ly** ad al principio, en primer lugar.

initiate [ɪˈnɪʃɪeɪt] vt (start) iniciar, dar comienzo a; **to ~ sb into a secret** iniciar a uno en un secreto; **to ~ proceedings against sb** (LAW) entablar proceso contra uno; **initiation** [-ˈeɪʃən] n (into secret etc) iniciación f; (beginning) comienzo.

initiative [ɪˈnɪʃɪətɪv] n iniciativa.

inject [ɪnˈdʒekt] vt (liquid) inyectar; (fig) injertar; **~ion** [ɪnˈdʒekʃən] n inyección f.

injunction [ɪnˈdʒʌŋkʃən] n interdicto.

injure [ˈɪndʒə*] vt herir, lastimar; (fig) perjudicar; (offend) ofender; **injury** n herida, lesión f; (wrong) perjuicio, daño; **injury time** n (SPORT) descuento.

injustice [ɪnˈdʒʌstɪs] n injusticia.

ink [ɪŋk] n tinta.

inkling [ˈɪŋklɪŋ] n sospecha; (idea) idea, atisbo.

inlaid [ˈɪnleɪd] a taraceado, entarimado.

inland [ˈɪnlənd] a interior, del interior // ad [ɪnˈlænd] tierra adentro; **I~ Revenue** n (Brit) el fisco.

in-laws [ˈɪnlɔːz] npl parientes mpl políticos.

inlet [ˈɪnlet] n (GEO) ensenada, cala; (TECH) admisión f, entrada.

inmate [ˈɪnmeɪt] n (in prison) presidiario; (in asylum) internado/a.

inn [ɪn] n posada, mesón m.

innate [ɪˈneɪt] a innato.

inner [ˈɪnə*] a interior, interno; **~ city** n centro de la ciudad; **~ tube** n (of tyre) cámara.

innocence [ˈɪnəsns] n inocencia; **innocent** [-nt] a inocente.

innocuous [ɪˈnɔkjuəs] a innocuo.

innovation [ɪnəuˈveɪʃən] n novedad f.

innuendo [ɪnjuˈendəu] pl **~es** n indirecta.

innumerable [ɪˈnjuːmrəbl] a innumerable.

inoculation [ɪnɔkjuˈleɪʃən] n inoculación f.

inopportune [ɪnˈɔpətjuːn] a inoportuno.

inordinately [ɪˈnɔːdɪnɪtlɪ] ad desmesuradamente.

inorganic [ɪnɔːˈgænɪk] a inorgánico.

in-patient [ˈɪnpeɪʃənt] n paciente m/f interno/a.

input [ˈɪnput] n (ELEC) entrada; (COMM) inversión f.

inquest [ˈɪnkwest] n pesquisa judicial; (coroner's) encuesta judicial.

inquire [ɪnˈkwaɪə*] vi pedir informes // vt (ask) preguntar; (seek information about) pedir informes sobre; **to ~ about** vt fus (person) preguntar por; (fact) informarse de; **to ~ into** vt fus investigar, indagar; **inquiring** a (mind) penetrante; (look) interrogativo; **inquiry** n pregunta; (LAW) investigación f, pesquisa; (commission) comisión f investigadora; **inquiry office** n oficina de informaciones.

inquisitive [ɪnˈkwɪzɪtɪv] a (curious) activo, inquiridor(a); (prying) preguntón(ona), fisgón(ona).

inroad [ˈɪnrəud] n incursión f; (fig) invasión f.

insane [ɪnˈseɪn] a loco; (MED) demente.

insanitary [ɪnˈsænɪtərɪ] a insalubre.

insanity [ɪnˈsænɪtɪ] n demencia, locura.

insatiable [ɪnˈseɪʃəbl] a insaciable.

inscribe [ɪnˈskraɪb] vt inscribir; (book etc): **to ~ (to sb)** dedicar (a uno).

inscription [ɪnˈskrɪpʃən] n (gen) inscripción f; (in book) dedicatoria.

inscrutable [ɪnˈskruːtəbl] a inescrutable, insondable.

insect ['ɪnsɛkt] n insecto; ~**icide** [ɪn-'sɛktɪsaɪd] n insecticida m.

insecure [ɪnsɪ'kjuə*] a inseguro; **insecurity** n inseguridad f.

insensible [ɪn'sɛnsɪbl] a impasible, insensible; (unconscious) inconsciente.

insensitive [ɪn'sɛnsɪtɪv] a insensible.

inseparable [ɪn'sɛprəbl] a inseparable; **they were ~ friends** les unía una estrecha amistad.

insert [ɪn'sɜːt] vt (between things) intercalar; (into sth) introducir; (in paper) publicar; (: advert) poner // a ['ɪnsɜːt] hoja suelta (intercalada); ~**ion** [ɪn'sɔːʃən] n inserción f; (publication) publicación f; (of pages) materia añadida.

inshore [ɪn'ʃɔː*] a cercano a la orilla o costa // ad (be) cerca de la orilla; (move) hacia la orilla.

inside ['ɪn'saɪd] n interior m; (lining) forro // a interior, interno; (secret) secreto // ad (within) (por) dentro; (with movement) hacia dentro; (fam: in prison) en la cárcel // prep dentro de; (of time): ~ **10 minutes** en menos de 10 minutos; ~**s** npl (col) tripas fpl; ~ **forward** n (SPORT) delantero interior; ~ **lane** n (AUT. in Britain) el lado o carril izquierdo; ~ **out** ad (turn) al revés; (know) a fondo.

insidious [ɪn'sɪdɪəs] a insidioso; (underground) clandestino.

insight ['ɪnsaɪt] n perspicacia.

insignificant [ɪnsɪg'nɪfɪknt] a insignificante.

insincere [ɪnsɪn'sɪə*] a poco sincero; **insincerity** [-'sɛrɪtɪ] n falta de sinceridad, doblez f.

insinuate [ɪn'sɪnjueɪt] vt insinuar; **insinuation** [-'eɪʃən] n insinuación f; (hint) indirecta.

insipid [ɪn'sɪpɪd] a soso, insulso.

insist [ɪn'sɪst] vi insistir; **to ~ on doing** empeñarse en hacer; **to ~ that** insistir en que; (claim) exigir que; ~**ence** n insistencia; (stubbornness) empeño; ~**ent** a insistente; empeñado.

insole ['ɪnsəul] n plantilla.

insolence ['ɪnsələns] n insolencia, descaro; **insolent** [-ənt] a insolente, descarado.

insoluble [ɪn'sɔljubl] a insoluble.

insolvent [ɪn'sɔlvənt] a insolvente.

insomnia [ɪn'sɔmnɪə] n insomnio.

inspect [ɪn'spɛkt] vt inspeccionar, examinar; (troops) pasar revista a; ~**ion** [ɪn'spɛkʃən] n inspección f, examen m; ~**or** n inspector/a m/f; (RAIL) revisor m.

inspiration [ɪnspə'reɪʃən] n inspiración f; **inspire** [ɪn'spaɪə*] vt inspirar.

instability [ɪnstə'bɪlɪtɪ] n inestabilidad f.

install [ɪn'stɔːl] vt instalar; ~**ation** [ɪnstə'leɪʃən] n instalación f.

instalment, installment (US) [ɪn-'stɔːlmənt] n plazo; (of story) entrega; (of TV serial etc) episodio.

instance ['ɪnstəns] n ejemplo, caso; **for ~**

por ejemplo; **in the first ~** en primer lugar.

instant ['ɪnstənt] n instante m, momento // a instantáneo, inmediato; (coffee) en polvo; ~**ly** ad en seguida.

instead [ɪn'stɛd] ad en cambio; ~ **of** en lugar de, en vez de.

instep ['ɪnstɛp] n empeine m.

instigation [ɪnstɪ'geɪʃən] n instigación f.

instil [ɪn'stɪl] vt: **to ~ into** infundir a, inculcar en.

instinct ['ɪnstɪŋkt] n instinto; ~**ive** [-'stɪŋktɪv] a instintivo; ~**ively** [-'stɪŋktɪvlɪ] ad por instinto.

institute ['ɪnstɪtjuːt] n instituto; (professional body) colegio // vt (inquiry) iniciar, empezar; (proceedings) entablar.

institution [ɪnstɪ'tjuːʃən] n (gen) institución f; (beginning) iniciación f; (organization) instituto; (MED. home) asilo; (asylum) manicomio; (custom) costumbre f.

instruct [ɪn'strʌkt] vt: **to ~ sb in sth** instruir a uno en o sobre algo; **to ~ sb to do sth** dar instrucciones a uno de hacer algo; ~**ion** [ɪn'strʌkʃən] n (teaching) instrucción f; ~**ions** npl órdenes fpl; ~**ions (for use)** modo sg de empleo; ~**ive** a aleccionador(a); ~**or** n instructor/a m/f.

instrument ['ɪnstrumənt] n instrumento; ~**al** [-'mɛntl] a (MUS) instrumental; **to be ~al in** contribuir materialmente a; ~ **panel** n tablero (de instrumentos).

insubordinate [ɪnsə'bɔːdənɪt] a insubordinado; **insubordination** [-'neɪʃən] n insubordinación f; (disobedience) desobediencia.

insufferable [ɪn'sʌfrəbl] a insufrible.

insufficient [ɪnsə'fɪʃənt] a insuficiente.

insular ['ɪnsjulə*] a insular; (outlook) de miras estrechas.

insulate ['ɪnsjuleɪt] vt aislar; **insulating tape** n cinta aislante; **insulation** [-'leɪʃən] n aislamiento.

insulin ['ɪnsjulɪn] n insulina.

insult ['ɪnsʌlt] n insulto; (offence) ofensa // vt [ɪn'sʌlt] insultar, injuriar; ofender; ~**ing** a insultante; ofensivo.

insuperable [ɪn'sjuːprəbl] a insuperable.

insurance [ɪn'ʃuərəns] n seguro; **fire/life ~** seguro sobre la vida/contra incendios; ~ **agent** n agente m/f de seguros; ~ **policy** n póliza (de seguros).

insure [ɪn'ʃuə*] vt asegurar.

insurrection [ɪnsə'rɛkʃən] n insurrección f.

intact [ɪn'tækt] a íntegro; (unharmed) ileso, sano.

intake ['ɪnteɪk] n (TECH) entrada, toma; (: pipe) tubo de admisión; (of food) cantidad admitida; (SCOL): **an ~ of 200 a year** 200 matriculados al año.

intangible [ɪn'tændʒɪbl] a intangible.

integral ['ɪntɪgrəl] a (whole) íntegro; (part) integrante.

integrate ['ɪntɪgreɪt] vt integrar // vi integrarse.

integrity [ɪn'tɛgrɪtɪ] n honradez f, rectitud f.

intellect ['ɪntəlekt] n intelecto; ~ual [-'lektjuəl] a, n intelectual m/f.

intelligence [ɪn'tɛlidʒəns] n inteligencia; (MIL etc) informes mpl; **I~ Service** n Servicio de Inteligencia; **intelligent** [-ənt] a inteligente.

intelligible [ɪn'tɛlidʒɪbl] a inteligible, comprensible.

intend [ɪn'tɛnd] vt (gift etc): **to ~ sth for** destinar algo a; **to ~ to do sth** tener intención de o proponerse hacer algo; **~ed a** (effect) deseado // n prometido/a.

intense [ɪn'tɛns] a intenso; (person) nervioso; ~ly ad intensamente; (very) sumamente.

intensify [ɪn'tɛnsɪfaɪ] vt intensificar; (increase) aumentar.

intensity [ɪn'tɛnsɪtɪ] n intensidad f; (strength) fuerza.

intensive [ɪn'tɛnsɪv] a intensivo; ~ **care unit** n centro de cuidados intensivos.

intent [ɪn'tɛnt] n propósito // a (absorbed) absorto; (attentive) atento; **to all ~s and purposes** prácticamente; **to be ~ on doing sth** estar resuelto a hacer algo.

intention [ɪn'tɛnʃən] n intento, propósito; (plan) proyecto; ~al a intencional, deliberado; ~ally a propósito.

intently [ɪn'tɛntlɪ] ad atentamente, fijamente.

inter [ɪn'tə:*] vt enterrar.

interact [ɪntər'ækt] vi influirse mutuamente; ~ion [-'ækʃən] n influencia mútua, acción f recíproca.

intercede [ɪntə'si:d] vi: **to ~ (with)** interceder (con).

intercept [ɪntə'sɛpt] vt interceptar; (stop) detener; ~ion [-'sɛpʃən] n interceptación f; detención f.

interchange ['ɪntətʃeɪndʒ] n intercambio; (exchange) canje m; (on motorway) paso a desnivel // vt [ɪntə'tʃeɪndʒ] intercambiar; canjear; ~able a intercambiable.

intercom ['ɪntəkɔm] n sistema m de intercomunicación.

interconnect [ɪntəkə'nɛkt] vi (rooms) conectarse.

intercourse ['ɪntəkɔ:s] n (sexual) relaciones fpl; (social) trato.

interest ['ɪntrɪst] n (also COMM) interés m; (profit) ventaja, provecho // vt interesar; **to be ~ed in** interesarse por; ~ing a interesante.

interfere [ɪntə'fɪə*] vi: **to ~ in** (quarrel, other people's business) entrometerse o mezclarse en; **to ~ with** (hinder) estorbar; (damage) estropear; (radio) interferir con.

interference [ɪntə'fɪərəns] n (gen) intromisión f; (RADIO, TV) interferencia.

interim ['ɪntərɪm] n: **in the ~** entretanto, en el interino.

interior [ɪn'tɪərɪə*] n interior m // a interior.

interject [ɪntə'dʒɛkt] vt interponerse; ~ion [-'dʒɛkʃən] n interyección f.

interlock [ɪntə'lɔk] vi entrelazarse; (wheels etc) endentarse.

interloper ['ɪntələupə*] n intruso.

interlude ['ɪntəlu:d] n intérvalo; (rest) descanso; (THEATRE) intermedio.

intermarry [ɪntə'mærɪ] vi casarse (parientes).

intermediary [ɪntə'mi:dɪərɪ] n intermediario.

intermediate [ɪntə'mi:dɪət] a intermedio, medio.

intermission [ɪntə'mɪʃən] n (THEATRE) descanso.

intermittent [ɪntə'mɪtnt] a intermitente.

intern [ɪn'tə:n] vt internar; (enclose) encerrar // n ['ɪntə:n] (US) interno.

internal [ɪn'tə:nl] a interno, interior; ~ly ad interiormente; **'not to be taken ~ly'** 'uso externo'; ~ **revenue** n (US) rentas fpl públicas.

international [ɪntə'næʃənl] a internacional; ~ **game** partido internacional; ~ **player** jugador/a m/f internacional.

interplay ['ɪntəpleɪ] n interacción f.

interpret [ɪn'tə:prɪt] vt interpretar; (translate) traducir; (understand) entender // vi hacer de intérprete; ~ation [-'teɪʃən] n interpretación f; traducción f; entendimiento; ~er n intérprete m/f.

interrelated [ɪntərɪ'leɪtɪd] a interrelacionado.

interrogate [ɪn'tɛrougeɪt] vt interrogar; **interrogation** [-'geɪʃən] n interrogatorio; **interrogative** [ɪntə'rɔgətɪv] a interrogativo.

interrupt [ɪntə'rʌpt] vt, vi interrumpir; ~ion [-'rʌpʃən] n interrupción f.

intersect [ɪntə'sɛkt] vt cruzar // vi (roads) cruzarse; ~ion [-'sɛkʃən] n intersección f; (of roads) cruce m.

intersperse [ɪntə'spə:s] vt esparcir, entremezclar.

intertwine [ɪntə'twaɪn] vt entrelazar // vi entrelazarse.

interval ['ɪntəvl] n intérvalo; (SCOL) recreo; (THEATRE, SPORT) descanso; **at ~s** a ratos, de vez en cuando.

intervene [ɪntə'vi:n] vi (gen) intervenir; (take part) participar; (occur) sobrevenir; **intervention** [-'vɛnʃən] n intervención f.

interview ['ɪntəvju:] n (RADIO, TV etc) entrevista // vt entrevistarse con; ~ee [-'i:] n entrevistado/a; ~er n entrevistador/a m/f.

intestine [ɪn'tɛstɪn] n: **large/small ~** intestino grueso/delgado.

intimacy ['ɪntɪməsɪ] n intimidad f; (relations) amistades fpl íntimas.

intimate ['ɪntɪmət] a íntimo; (friendship) estrecho; (knowledge) profundo // vt ['ɪntɪmeɪt] (announce) dar a entender.

intimidate [ɪn'tɪmɪdeɪt] vt intimidar,

amedrentar; intimidation [-'deiʃən] *n* intimidación *f*.

into ['intu] *prep* (*gen*) en; (*towards*) a; (*inside*) hacia el interior de; ~ **3 pieces/French** en 3 pedazos/ francés.

intolerable [ɪn'tɔlərəbl] *a* intolerable, insufrible; **intolerance** [-rəns] *n* intolerancia; **intolerant** [-rənt] *a:* **intolerant of** intolerante con *o* para.

intonation [ɪntəʊ'neiʃən] *n* entonación *f*.

intoxicate [ɪn'tɔksɪkeit] *vt* embriagar; ~**d** *a* embriagado; **intoxication** [-'keiʃən] *n* embriaguez *f*.

intractable [ɪn'træktəbl] *a* (*child*) intratable; (*material*) difícil de trabajar; (*problem*) espinoso.

intransigent [ɪn'trænsidʒənt] *a* intransigente.

intransitive [ɪn'trænsitɪv] *a* intransitivo.

intravenous [ɪntrə'viːnəs] *a* intravenoso.

intrepid [ɪn'trepid] *a* intrépido.

intricate ['ɪntrɪkət] *a* intrincado; (*complex*) complejo.

intrigue [ɪn'triːg] *n* intriga // *vt* interesar, fascinar // *vi* andar en intrigas; **intriguing** *a* intrigante.

intrinsic [ɪn'trɪnsɪk] *a* intrínseco.

introduce [ɪntrə'djuːs] *vt* introducir, meter; **to** ~ **sb (to sb)** presentar uno (a otro); **to** ~ **sb to** (*pastime, technique*) introducir a uno a; **introduction** [-'dʌkʃən] *n* introducción *f*; (*of person*) presentación *f*; **introductory** [-'dʌktəri] *a* preliminar.

introspective [ɪntrəʊ'spektɪv] *a* introspectivo.

introvert ['ɪntrəʊvəːt] *a, n* introvertido/a.

intrude [ɪn'truːd] *vi* (*person*) entrometerse; **to** ~ **on** *or* **into** estorbar; **intruder** *n* intruso/a; **intrusion** [-ʒən] *n* invasión *f*; **intrusive** [-sɪv] *a* intruso.

intuition [ɪntjuː'ɪʃən] *n* intuición *f*; **intuitive** [-'tjuːɪtɪv] *a* intuitivo.

inundate ['ɪnʌndeit] *vt*: **to** ~ **with** inundar de.

invade [ɪn'veid] *vt* invadir; **invader** *n* invasor/a *m/f*.

invalid ['ɪnvəlɪd] *n* inválido/a // *a* [ɪn-'vælɪd] (*not valid*) inválido, nulo; ~**ate** [ɪn-'vælɪdeit] *vt* invalidar, anular.

invaluable [ɪn'væljuəbl] *a* inestimable.

invariable [ɪn'vɛərɪəbl] *a* invariable.

invasion [ɪn'veiʒən] *n* invasión *f*.

invent [ɪn'vent] *vt* inventar; ~**ion** [ɪn-'venʃən] *n* invento; (*inventiveness*) inventiva; (*lie*) ficción *f*, mentira; ~**ive** *a* ingenioso; ~**iveness** *n* ingenio, inventiva; ~**or** *n* inventor/a *m/f*.

inventory ['ɪnvəntri] *n* inventario.

inverse [ɪn'vəːs] *a, n* inverso; ~**ly** *ad* a la inversa.

invert [ɪn'vəːt] *vt* invertir, volver al revés; ~**ed commas** *npl* comillas *fpl*.

invertebrate [ɪn'vəːtibrət] *n* invertebrado.

invest [ɪn'vest] *vt, vi* invertir.

investigate [ɪn'vestigeit] *vt* investigar; (*study*) estudiar, examinar; **investigation**

[-'geiʃən] *n* investigación *f*, pesquisa; examen *m*; **investigator** *n* investigador/a *m/f*.

investiture [ɪn'vestɪtʃə*] *n* investidura.

investment [ɪn'vestmənt] *n* inversión *f*.

investor [ɪn'vestə*] *n* inversionista *m/f*.

inveterate [ɪn'vetərət] *a* empedernido.

invigorating [ɪn'vɪgəreitɪŋ] *a* vigorizante.

invincible [ɪn'vɪnsɪbl] *a* invencible.

inviolate [ɪn'vaɪələt] *a* inviolado.

invisible [ɪn'vɪzibl] *a* invisible; ~ **ink** *n* tinta simpática.

invitation [ɪnvɪ'teiʃən] *n* invitación *f*.

invite [ɪn'vait] *vt* (*gen*) invitar; (*to drink, food*) convidar; (*opinions etc*) solicitar, pedir; (*trouble*) buscarse; **inviting** *a* atractivo; (*look*) incitante; (*food*) apetitoso.

invoice ['ɪnvɔis] *n* factura // *vt* facturar.

invoke [ɪn'vəʊk] *vt* invocar; (*aid*) implorar; (*law*) recurrir a.

involuntary [ɪn'vɔləntri] *a* involuntario.

involve [ɪn'vɔlv] *vt* (*entail*) suponer, implicar; **to** ~ **sb (in)** comprometer a uno (con); ~**d** *a* complicado; ~**ment** *n* (*gen*) enredo; (*obligation*) compromiso; (*difficulty*) apuro.

invulnerable [ɪn'vʌlnərəbl] *a* invulnerable.

inward ['ɪnwəd] *a* (*movement*) interior, interno; (*thought, feeling*) íntimo; ~**ly** *ad* (*feel, think etc*) para sí, para dentro; ~**(s)** *ad* hacia dentro.

iodine ['aɪəʊdiːn] *n* yodo.

iota [aɪ'əʊtə] *n* (*fig*) jota, ápice *m*.

IOU *n abbr of* **I owe you** pagaré *m*.

IQ *n abbr of* **intelligence quotient** cociente *m* intelectual.

Iran [ɪ'raːn] *n* Irán *m*; ~**ian** [ɪ'reɪnɪən] *a, n* iraní *m/f*.

Iraq [ɪ'raːk] *n* El Irak; ~**i** *a, n* irakí *m/f*.

irascible [ɪ'ræsɪbl] *a* irascible.

irate [aɪ'reit] *a* enojado, indignado.

Ireland ['aɪələnd] *n* Irlanda.

iris ['aɪrɪs], *pl* ~**es** *n* (ANAT) iris *m*; (BOT) lirio.

Irish ['aɪrɪʃ] *a* irlandés(esa) // *npl*: **the** ~ los irlandeses; ~**man/ woman** *n* irlandés/esa *m/f*.

irk [əːk] *vt* fastidiar; ~**some** *a* fastidioso.

iron ['aɪən] *n* hierro; (*for clothes*) plancha // *a* de hierro // *vt* (*clothes*) planchar; ~**s** *npl* (*chains*) grillos *mpl*; **to** ~ **out** *vt* (*crease*) quitar; (*fig*) allanar.

ironic(al) [aɪ'rɔnɪk(l)] *a* irónico.

ironing ['aɪənɪŋ] *n* (*act*) planchado; (*ironed clothes*) ropa planchada; (*to be ironed*) ropa por planchar; ~ **board** *n* tabla de planchar.

ironmonger ['aɪənmʌŋgə*] *n* ferretero; ~**'s (shop)** *n* ferretería, quincallería.

iron ore ['aɪən'ɔː*] *n* mineral *m* de hierro.

irony ['aɪrəni] *n* ironía; **the** ~ **of it is that...** lo irónico es que...

irreconcilable [ɪrekən'saɪləbl] *a*

inconciliable, irreconciliable.
irrefutable [ɪrɪˈfjuːtəbl] a irrefutable.
irregular [ɪˈrɛgjulə*] a irregular; (surface) desigual; (illegal) ilegal; ~**ity** [-ˈlærɪtɪ] n irregularidad f; desigualdad f.
irrelevant [ɪˈrɛləvənt] a fuera de lugar, inoportuno.
irreparable [ɪˈrɛprəbl] a irreparable.
irreplaceable [ɪrɪˈpleɪsəbl] a irremplazable.
irrepressible [ɪrɪˈprɛsəbl] a irrefrenable.
irreproachable [ɪrɪˈprəʊtʃəbl] a irreprochable.
irresistible [ɪrɪˈzɪstɪbl] a irresistible.
irresolute [ɪˈrɛzəluːt] a indeciso.
irrespective [ɪrɪˈspɛktɪv]: ~ **of** prep sin tener en cuenta, no importa.
irresponsible [ɪrɪˈspɒnsɪbl] a (act) irresponsable; (person) poco serio.
irreverent [ɪˈrɛvərnt] a irreverente, irrespetuoso.
irrevocable [ɪˈrɛvəkəbl] a irrevocable.
irrigate [ˈɪrɪgeɪt] vt regar; **irrigation** [-ˈgeɪʃən] n riego.
irritable [ˈɪrɪtəbl] a irritable; (mood) de mal humor.
irritate [ˈɪrɪteɪt] vt irritar; (MED) picar; **irritation** [-ˈteɪʃən] n irritación f, enojo; picazón m, picor m.
is [ɪz] vb see **be**.
Islam [ˈɪzlɑːm] n Islam m.
island [ˈaɪlənd] n isla; (also: **traffic** ~) refugio; ~**er** n isleño/a.
isle [aɪl] n isla.
isn't [ˈɪznt] = **is not**.
isolate [ˈaɪsəleɪt] vt aislar; ~**d** a aislado; **isolation** [-ˈleɪʃən] n aislamiento.
isotope [ˈaɪsəutəup] n isótopo.
Israel [ˈɪzreɪl] n Israel m; ~**i** [ɪzˈreɪlɪ] a, n israelí m/f.
issue [ˈɪsjuː] n cuestión f, asunto; (outcome) resultado; (of banknotes etc) emisión f; (of newspaper etc) número; (offspring) sucesión f, descendencia // vt (rations, equipment) distribuir, repartir; (orders) dar; (certificate) expedir; (decree) promulgar; (book) publicar; (cheques) extender; (banknotes, stamps) emitir.
isthmus [ˈɪsməs] n istmo.
it [ɪt] pron (subject) él/ella; (direct object) lo/la; (indirect object) le; (impersonal) ello; (after prep) él/ella/ello; ~'**s raining** llueve, está lloviendo; **where is** ~? ¿dónde está?; **he's proud of** ~ le enorgullece; **he agreed to** ~ está de acuerdo (con ello).
Italian [ɪˈtæljən] a italiano // n italiano/a; (LING) el italiano.
italic [ɪˈtælɪk] a cursivo; ~**s** npl cursiva sg.
Italy [ˈɪtəlɪ] n Italia.
itch [ɪtʃ] n comezón m; (fig) prurito // vi (person) sentir o tener comezón; (part of body) picar; **I'm** ~**ing to do sth** rabio por hacer algo; ~**ing** n comezón m; ~**y** a: **to be** ~**y** picar.
it'd [ˈɪtd] = **it would**; **it had**.

item [ˈaɪtəm] n (gen) artículo; (detail) detalle m; (on agenda) asunto a tratar; (in programme) número; (also: **news** ~) noticia; ~**ize** vt detallar.
itinerant [ɪˈtɪnərənt] a ambulante.
itinerary [aɪˈtɪnərərɪ] n itinerario.
it'll [ˈɪtl] = **it will, it shall**.
its [ɪts] a su // pron (el) suyo/(la) suya.
it's [ɪts] = **it is**; **it has**.
itself [ɪtˈsɛlf] pron (reflexive) sí mismo/a; (emphatic) él mismo/ella misma.
ITV n abbr of **Independent Television**.
I.U.D. n abbr of **intra-uterine device** DIU.
I've [aɪv] = **I have**.
ivory [ˈaɪvərɪ] n marfil m; ~ **tower** n (fig) torre f de marfil.
ivy [ˈaɪvɪ] n hiedra.

J

jab [dʒæb] vt (elbow) dar un codazo a; (punch) dar un golpe rápido a; **to** ~ **sth into sth** clavar algo en algo // n codazo; golpe m (rápido); (MED: col) pinchazo.
jabber [ˈdʒæbə*] vt, vi farfullar.
jack [dʒæk] n (AUT) gato; (BOWLS) boliche m; (CARDS) sota; **to** ~ **up** vt (AUT) alzar con gato.
jackdaw [ˈdʒækdɔː] n grajilla.
jacket [ˈdʒækɪt] n chaqueta, americana; (of boiler etc) camisa; (of book) sobrecubierta; **potatoes in their** ~**s** patatas con su piel.
jack-knife [ˈdʒæknaɪf] n navaja.
jackpot [ˈdʒækpɒt] n premio gordo.
jade [dʒeɪd] n (stone) jade m.
jaded [ˈdʒeɪdɪd] a (tired) cansado; (fed-up) hastiado.
jagged [ˈdʒægɪd] a dentado.
jail [dʒeɪl] n cárcel f; ~**break** n fuga o evasión f (de la cárcel); ~**er** n carcelero.
jam [dʒæm] n mermelada; (also: **traffic** ~) embotellamiento; (difficulty) apuro // vt (passage etc) obstruir, cerrar; (mechanism, drawer etc) atascar; (RADIO) interferir // vi atascarse, trabarse; **to** ~ **sth into sth** meter algo por la fuerza en algo.
Jamaica [dʒəˈmeɪkə] n Jamaica.
jangle [ˈdʒæŋgl] vi sonar (de manera) discordante.
janitor [ˈdʒænɪtə*] n (caretaker) portero, conserje m.
January [ˈdʒænjuərɪ] n enero.
Japan [dʒəˈpæn] n (el) Japón; ~**ese** [dʒæpəˈniːz] a japonés(esa) // n, pl inv japonés/esa m/f; (LING) japonés m.
jar [dʒɑː*] n (glass: large) jarra; (: small) tarro // vi (sound) chirriar; (colours) desentonar.
jargon [ˈdʒɑːgən] n jerga.
jasmin(e) [ˈdʒæzmɪn] n jazmín m.
jaundice [ˈdʒɔːndɪs] n ictericia; ~**d** a (fig: embittered) amargado; (: disillusioned) desilusionado.

jaunt [dʒɔ:nt] n excursión f; ~y a alegre.
javelin ['dʒævlin] n jabalina.
jaw [dʒɔ:] n mandíbula.
jaywalker ['dʒeiwɔ:kə*] n peatón m imprudente.
jazz [dʒæz] n jazz m; **to** ~ **up** vt (liven up) animar, avivar; ~y a de colores llamativos.
jealous ['dʒɛləs] a (gen) celoso; (envious) envidioso; **to be** ~ tener celos; ~y n celos mpl; envidia.
jeans [dʒi:nz] npl (pantalones) vaqueros o tejanos mpl.
jeep [dʒi:p] n jeep m.
jeer [dʒiə*] vi: **to** ~ (**at**) (boo) abuchear; (mock) mofarse (de).
jelly ['dʒɛli] n jalea, gelatina; ~**fish** n medusa.
jeopardize ['dʒɛpədaiz] vt arriesgar, poner en peligro; **jeopardy** [-di] n: **to be in jeopardy** estar en peligro o a riesgo.
jerk [dʒɔ:k] n (jolt) sacudida; (wrench) tirón m // vt dar una sacudida a // vi (vehicle) traquetear.
jerkin ['dʒɔ:kin] n cazadora.
jerky ['dʒɔ:ki] a espasmódico.
jersey ['dʒɔ:zi] n jersey m.
jest [dʒɛst] n broma.
jet [dʒɛt] n (of gas, liquid) chorro; (AVIAT) avión m a reacción; ~-**black** a de azabache; ~ **engine** n motor m a reacción.
jettison ['dʒɛtisn] vt desechar.
jetty ['dʒɛti] n muelle m, embarcadero.
Jew [dʒu:] n judío; ~**ess** n judía.
jewel ['dʒu:əl] n joya; (in watch) rubí m; ~**ler**, n joyero; ~**ler's (shop)** n joyería; ~**lery** n joyas fpl, alhajas fpl.
Jewish ['dʒu:iʃ] a judío.
jibe [dʒaib] n pulla.
jiffy ['dʒifi] n (col): **in a** ~ en un instante.
jig [dʒig] n jiga.
jigsaw ['dʒigsɔ:] n (also: ~ **puzzle**) rompecabezas m inv.
jilt [dʒilt] vt dar calabazas a.
jingle ['dʒiŋgl] n (advert) estribillo // vi tintinear.
jinx [dʒiŋks] n (col) gafe m, maldición f.
jitters ['dʒitəz] npl (col): **to get the** ~ ponerse nervioso.
job [dʒɔb] n (gen) trabajo; (task) tarea; (duty) deber m; (post) empleo; (fam: difficulty) dificultad f; **it's a good** ~ **that...** menos mal que...; **just the** ~! ¡estupendo!; ~**less** a sin trabajo.
jockey ['dʒɔki] n jockey m // vi: **to** ~ **for position** maniobrar para conseguir una posición.
jocular ['dʒɔkjulə*] a (humorous) jocoso; (merry) alegre.
jog [dʒɔg] vt empujar (ligeramente) // vi (run) hacer footing; **to** ~ **along** ir tirando; **to** ~ **sb's memory** refrescar la memoria a uno; ~**ging** n footing m.
join [dʒɔin] vt (things) juntar, unir; (become member of) inscribirse en, afiliarse a;

(meet: people) reunirse o encontrarse con // vi (roads, rivers) confluir // n juntura; **to** ~ **up** vi unirse; (MIL) alistarse.
joiner ['dʒɔinə*] n carpintero; ~**y** n carpintería.
joint [dʒɔint] n (TECH) junta, unión f; (wood) ensambladura; (ANAT) articulación f; (CULIN) asado; (col: place) garito // a (common) común; (combined) combinado; (committee) mixto; **by** ~ **agreement** por común acuerdo; ~**ly** ad (gen) mutuamente, en común; (collectively) colectivamente; (together) conjuntamente.
joke [dʒəuk] n chiste m; (also: **practical** ~) broma // vi bromear; **to play a** ~ **on** gastar una broma a; **joker** n chistoso/a, bromista m/f; (CARDS) comodín m.
jolly ['dʒɔli] a (merry) alegre; (enjoyable) divertido // ad (col) muy, terriblemente.
jolt [dʒəult] n (shake) sacudida; (blow) golpe m; (shock) susto // vt sacudir; asustar.
Jordan ['dʒɔ:dən] n Jordania.
jostle ['dʒɔsl] vt dar empellones a, codear.
jot [dʒɔt] n: **not one** ~ ni jota, ni pizca; **to** ~ **down** vt apuntar; ~**ter** n bloc m; (SCOL) cuaderno.
journal ['dʒɔ:nl] n (paper) periódico; (magazine) revista; (diary) diario; ~**ese** [-'li:z] n (pej) lenguaje m periodístico; ~**ism** n periodismo; ~**ist** n periodista m/f.
journey ['dʒɔ:ni] n viaje m; (distance covered) trayecto // vi viajar; **return** ~ viaje de regreso.
joy [dʒɔi] n alegría; ~**ful**, ~**ous** a alegre; ~ **ride** n paseo en coche; (illegal) paseo en coche robado.
J.P. n abbr of **Justice of the Peace.**
Jr, Jun., Junr abbr of **junior.**
jubilant ['dʒu:bilnt] a jubiloso; **jubilation** [-'leiʃən] n júbilo.
jubilee ['dʒu:bili:] n aniversario.
judge [dʒʌdʒ] n juez m // vt (gen) juzgar; (estimate) considerar; **judg(e)ment** n juicio; (punishment) sentencia, fallo.
judicial [dʒu:'diʃl] a judicial.
judicious [dʒu:'diʃəs] a juicioso.
judo ['dʒu:dəu] n judo.
jug [dʒʌg] n jarro.
juggernaut ['dʒʌgənɔ:t] n (huge truck) mastodonte m.
juggle ['dʒʌgl] vi hacer juegos malabares; **juggler** n malabarista m/f.
Jugoslav ['ju:gəu'sla:v] a, n = **Yugoslav.**
juice [dʒu:s] n zumo, jugo; **juicy** a jugoso.
jukebox ['dʒu:kbɔks] n rocola.
July [dʒu:'lai] n julio.
jumble ['dʒʌmbl] n revoltijo // vt (also: ~ **up**: mix up) revolver; (: disarrange) mezclar; ~ **sale** n (Brit) venta de objetos usados.
jumbo (jet) ['dʒʌmbəu] n jumbo-jet m.
jump [dʒʌmp] vi saltar, dar saltos; (start) asustarse, sobresaltarse; (increase) aumentar // vi saltar // n salto; aumento; **to** ~ **the queue** colarse.

jumper ['dʒʌmpə*] n suéter m, jersey m.
jumpy ['dʒʌmpi] a nervioso.
junction ['dʒʌŋkʃən] n (of roads) cruce m; (RAIL) empalme m.
juncture ['dʒʌŋktʃə*] n: at this ~ en este momento, en esta coyuntura.
June [dʒuːn] n junio.
jungle ['dʒʌŋgl] n selva, jungla.
junior ['dʒuːniə*] a (in age) menor, más joven; (competition) juvenil; (position) subalterno // n menor m/f, joven m/f; ~ **school** n escuela primaria.
junk [dʒʌŋk] n (cheap goods) baratijas fpl, (lumber) trastos viejos mpl; (rubbish) basura; (ship) junco; ~**shop** n tienda de objetos usados.
jurisdiction [dʒuərɪs'dɪkʃən] n jurisdicción f.
jurisprudence [dʒuərɪs'pruːdəns] n jurisprudencia.
jury ['dʒuərɪ] n jurado.
just [dʒʌst] a justo // ad (exactly) exactamente; (only) sólo, solamente; he's ~ done it/left acaba de hacerlo/irse; ~ **right** perfecto, perfectamente; ~ **two o'clock** las dos en punto; ~ **as well that...** menos mal que...; ~ **as he was leaving** en el momento en que se marchaba; ~ **before/enough** justo antes/lo suficiente; ~ **here** aquí mismo; he ~ **missed** ha fallado por poco; ~ **listen** escucha (solamente).
justice ['dʒʌstɪs] n justicia; J~ **of the Peace (J.P.)** n juez m de paz.
justifiable [dʒʌstɪ'faɪəbl] a justificable; **justifiably** ad justificadamente.
justification [dʒʌstɪfɪ'keɪʃən] n justificación f; **justify** ['dʒʌstɪfaɪ] vt justificar.
justly ['dʒʌstlɪ] ad (gen) justamente; (with reason) con razón.
justness ['dʒʌstnɪs] n justicia.
jut [dʒʌt] vi (also: ~ out) sobresalir.
juvenile ['dʒuːvənaɪl] a juvenil; (court) de menores; (books) para jóvenes // n joven m/f, menor m/f de edad.
juxtapose ['dʒʌkstəpəuz] vt yuxtaponer.

K

kaleidoscope [kə'laɪdəskəup] n calidoscopio.
kangaroo [kæŋgə'ruː] n canguro.
keel [kiːl] n quilla; **on an even** ~ (fig) en equilibrio.
keen [kiːn] a (interest, desire) grande, vivo; (eye, intelligence) agudo; (competition) intenso; (edge) afilado; (eager) entusiasta inv; **to be** ~ **to do** or **on doing sth** tener muchas ganas de hacer algo; **to be** ~ **on sth/sb** interesarse por algo/alguien; ~**ness** n (eagerness) entusiasmo, interés m.
keep [kiːp], pt, pp **kept** vt (retain, preserve) guardar; (hold back) quedarse con; (shop, diary) llevar; (feed: family etc) mantener; (promise) cumplir; (chickens, bees etc) criar // vi (food) conservarse; (remain) seguir, continuar // n (of castle) torreón m; (food etc) comida, subsistencia; **to** ~ **doing sth** seguir haciendo algo; **to** ~ **sb from doing sth** impedir a alguien hacer algo; **to** ~ **sth from happening** impedir que algo ocurra; **to** ~ **sb happy** hacer a alguien feliz; **to** ~ **a place tidy** mantener un lugar limpio; **to** ~ **sth to o.s.** guardar algo para sí mismo; **to** ~ **sth (back) from sb** ocultar algo a alguien; **to** ~ **time** (clock) mantener la hora exacta; **to** ~ **on** vi seguir, continuar; **to** ~ **out** vi (stay out) permanecer fuera; **'**~ **out'** prohibida la entrada; **to** ~ **up** vt mantener, conservar // vi no retrasarse; **to** ~ **up with** (pace) ir al paso de; (level) mantenerse a la altura de; ~**er** n guardián m; ~**ing** n (care) cuidado; **in** ~**ing with** de acuerdo con; ~**sake** n recuerdo.
keg [keg] n barrilete m, barril m.
kennel ['kenl] n perrera; ~**s** npl criadero sg de perros.
Kenya ['kenjə] n Kenia.
kept [kept] pt, pp of **keep.**
kerb [kəːb] n bordillo.
kernel ['kəːnl] n almendra.
kerosene ['kerəsiːn] n keroseno.
ketchup ['ketʃəp] n salsa de tomate, catsup m.
kettle ['ketl] n hervidor m, olla.
key [kiː] n (gen) llave f; (MUS) tono; (of piano, typewriter) tecla; ~**board** n teclado; ~**hole** n ojo (de la cerradura); ~**note** n (MUS) tónica; ~**ring** n llavero; ~**stone** n piedra clave.
khaki ['kɑːki] n caqui.
kick [kɪk] vt (person) dar una patada a; (ball) dar un puntapié a // vi (horse) dar coces // n patada; puntapié m; (of rifle) culetazo; (thrill): he does it for ~s lo hace para divertirse; **to** ~ **off** vi (SPORT) hacer el saque inicial; ~-**off** n (SPORT) saque m inicial.
kid [kɪd] n (child) chiquillo m; (animal) cabrito; (leather) cabritilla // vi (col) bromear.
kidnap ['kɪdnæp] vt secuestrar; ~**per** n secuestrador/a m/f; ~**ping** n secuestro.
kidney ['kɪdnɪ] n riñón m.
kill [kɪl] vt (gen) matar; (murder) asesinar; (destroy) destruir; (finish off) acabar con // n acto de matar; ~**er** n asesino; ~**ing** n (one) asesinato; (several) matanza // a (funny) divertido.
kiln [kɪln] n horno.
kilo ['kiːləu] n kilo; ~**gram(me)** ['kɪləugræm] n kilo, kilogramo; ~**metre**, ~**meter** (US) ['kɪləmiːtə*] n kilómetro; ~**watt** ['kɪləuwɔt] n kilovatio.
kilt [kɪlt] n falda escocesa.
kimono [kɪ'məunəu] n quimono.
kin [kɪn] n parientes mpl.
kind [kaɪnd] a (generous) bondadoso; (good) bueno, amable // n clase f, especie f; (species) género; **in** ~ (COMM) en

especie; **a ~ of** una especie de; **two of a ~** dos de la misma especie.

kindergarten ['kɪndəgɑːtn] n jardín m de infancia.

kind-hearted [kaɪnd'hɑːtɪd] a bondadoso, de buen corazón.

kindle ['kɪndl] vt encender.

kindly ['kaɪndlɪ] a (gen) bondadoso; (good) bueno; (gentle) cariñoso // ad bondadosamente, amablemente; **will you ~...** sea Usted tan amable de.... .

kindness ['kaɪndnɪs] n bondad f, amabilidad f.

kindred ['kɪndrɪd] n familia, parientes mpl // a: **~ spirit** espíritu m afín.

king [kɪŋ] n rey m; **~dom** n reino; **~fisher** n martín m pescador; **~-size** a de tamaño extra.

kink [kɪŋk] n (of rope) enroscadura.

kinky ['kɪŋkɪ] a (odd) excéntrico; (pej) pervertido.

kiosk ['kiːɔsk] n quiosco; (TEL) cabina.

kipper ['kɪpə*] n arenque m ahumado.

kiss [kɪs] n beso // vt besar; **to ~ (each other)** besarse.

kit [kɪt] n (gen) avíos mpl; (equipment) equipo; (set of tools etc) (caja de) herramientas fpl; (for assembly) mecano.

kitchen ['kɪtʃɪn] n cocina; **~ garden** n huerto; **~ sink** n fregadero; **~ware** n batería de cocina.

kite [kaɪt] n (toy) cometa.

kitten ['kɪtn] n gatito.

kitty ['kɪtɪ] n (pool of money) fondo común; (CARDS) polla.

kleptomaniac [klɛptəʊ'meɪnɪæk] n cleptómano/a.

knack [næk] n: **to have the ~ of doing sth** tener el don de hacer algo.

knapsack ['næpsæk] n mochila.

knead [niːd] vt amasar.

knee [niː] n rodilla; **~cap** n rótula.

kneel [niːl], pt, pp **knelt** vi arrodillarse.

knell [nɛl] n toque m de difuntos.

knelt [nɛlt] pt, pp of **kneel.**

knew [njuː] pt of **know.**

knickers ['nɪkəz] npl bragas fpl.

knife [naɪf], pl **knives** n cuchillo // vt acuchillar.

knight [naɪt] n caballero; (CHESS) caballo; **~hood** n caballería; (title): **to get a ~hood** recibir el título de sir.

knit [nɪt] vt hacer a punto; (brows) fruncir // vi hacer punto; (bones) soldarse; **to ~ together** (fig) unir, juntar; **~ting** n labor f de punto; **~ting machine** n máquina de tricotar; **~ting needle** n aguja de hacer punto; **~wear** n géneros mpl de punto.

knives [naɪvz] pl of **knife.**

knob [nɔb] n (of door) tirador m; (of stick) puño; (lump) bulto; (fig): **a ~ of butter** una porción de mantequilla.

knock [nɔk] vt (strike) golpear; (bump into) chocar contra; (fig: col) denigrar // n golpe m; (on door) llamada; **to ~ at** or **on the door** llamar a la puerta; **to ~ down**

vt atropellar; **to ~ off** vi (col: finish) despachar // vt (col: steal) birlar; **to ~ out** vt dejar sin sentido; (BOXING) poner fuera de combate, dejar K.O.; **~er** n (on door) aldaba; **~-kneed** a patizambo; **~out** n (BOXING) K.O. m, knockout m.

knot [nɔt] n (gen) nudo // vt anudar; **~ty** a (fig) complicado.

know [nəʊ], pt **knew**, pp **known** vt (gen) saber; (person, author, place) conocer; **to ~ that...** saber que...; **to ~ how to swim** saber nadar; **~-all** n sabelotodo m/f; **~-how** n habilidad f; **~ing** a (look: of complicity) de complicidad; (: spiteful) malicioso; **~ingly** ad (purposely) adrede; (spitefully) maliciosamente.

knowledge ['nɔlɪdʒ] n (gen) conocimiento; (range of learning) saber m, conocimientos mpl; (learning) erudición f, ciencia; **~able** a entendido, erudito.

known [nəʊn] pp of **know.**

knuckle ['nʌkl] n nudillo.

K.O. n abbr of **knockout.**

Koran [kɔ'rɑːn] n Corán m.

L

l. abbr of **litre.**

lab [læb] n abbr of **laboratory.**

label ['leɪbl] n etiqueta; (brand: of record) marca // vt poner etiqueta a.

laboratory [lə'bɔrətərɪ] n laboratorio.

laborious [lə'bɔːrɪəs] a penoso.

labour, labor (US) ['leɪbə*] n (task) trabajo; (~ force) mano f de obra; (workers) trabajadores mpl; (MED) (dolores mpl del) parto // vi: **to ~ (at)** trabajar (en) // vi insistir en; **in ~** (MED) de parto; **L~, the L~ party** el partido laborista; **hard ~** trabajos mpl forzados; **~ed** a (movement) penoso; (style) pesado; **~er** n peón m; (on farm) peón m, bracero; (day ~er) jornalero.

labyrinth ['læbɪrɪnθ] n laberinto.

lace [leɪs] n encaje m; (of shoe etc) cordón m // vt (shoe) atar.

lack [læk] n (absence) falta; (scarcity) escasez f // vt no tener, carecer de; **through** or **for ~ of** por falta de; **to be ~ing** faltar, no haber.

lackadaisical [lækə'deɪzɪkl] a (careless) descuidado; (indifferent) indiferente.

laconic [lə'kɔnɪk] a lacónico.

lacquer ['lækə*] n laca.

lad [læd] n muchacho, chico; (in stable etc) mozo.

ladder ['lædə*] n escalera (de mano); (in tights) carrera // vt (tights) hacer una carrera en.

laden ['leɪdn] a: **~ (with)** cargado (de).

ladle ['leɪdl] n cucharón m.

lady ['leɪdɪ] n señora; (distinguished, noble) dama; **young ~** señorita; **'ladies' (toilets)** 'señoras'; **~bird, ~bug** (US) n mariquita; **~-in-waiting** n dama de honor; **~like** a fino.

lag [læg] vi (also: **~ behind**) retrasarse.

quedarse atrás // vt (*pipes*) calorifugar.
lager ['lɑːgə*] n cerveza (rubia).
lagging ['lægɪŋ] n revestimiento.
lagoon [lə'guːn] n laguna.
laid [leɪd] pt, pp of **lay.**
lain [leɪn] pp of **lie.**
lair [lɛə*] n guarida.
lake [leɪk] n lago.
lamb [læm] n cordero; (*meat*) carne f de cordero; ~ **chop** n chuleta de cordero; **lambswool** n lana de cordero.
lame [leɪm] a cojo; (*weak*) débil, poco convincente.
lament [lə'mɛnt] n lamento // vt lamentarse de; ~**able** ['læməntəbl] a lamentable.
laminated ['læmineɪtɪd] a laminado.
lamp [læmp] n lámpara.
lampoon [læm'puːn] vt satirizar.
lamp: ~**post** n farol m; ~**shade** n pantalla.
lance [lɑːns] n lanza // vt (MED) abrir con lanzeta; ~ **corporal** n soldado de primera clase.
lancet ['lɑːnsit] n lanceta.
land [lænd] n (*gen*) tierra; (*country*) país m; (*piece of* ~) terreno; (*estate*) tierras fpl, finca; (AGR) campo // vi (*from ship*) desembarcar; (AVIAT) aterrizar; (*fig: fall*) caer, terminar // vt (*obtain*) conseguir; (*passengers, goods*) desembarcar; **to ~ up in/at** ir a parar a/en; ~**ing** n desembarco; aterrizaje m; (*of staircase*) rellano; ~**ing craft** n barca de desembarco; ~**ing gear** n tren m de aterrizaje; ~**ing stage** n desembarcadero; ~**ing strip** n pista de aterrizaje; ~**lady** n (*of boarding house*) patrona; (*owner*) dueña; ~**locked** a cercado de tierra; ~**lord** n propietario; (*of pub etc*) patrón m; ~**lubber** n hombre m de tierra; ~**mark** n lugar m conocido; **to be a ~mark** (*fig*) hacer época; ~**owner** n terrateniente m/f.
landscape ['lændskeɪp] n paisaje m; ~**d** a reformado artísticamente.
landslide ['lændslaɪd] n (GEO) corrimiento de tierras; (*fig: pol*) victoria arrolladora.
lane [leɪn] n (*in country*) vereda; (*in town*) callejón m; (AUT) carril m; (*in race*) calle f; (*for air or sea traffic*) ruta.
language ['læŋgwɪdʒ] n lenguaje m; (*national tongue*) idioma m, lengua; **bad ~** lenguaje indecente.
languid ['læŋgwɪd] a lánguido.
languish ['læŋgwɪʃ] vi languidecer.
lank [læŋk] a (*hair*) lacio.
lanky ['læŋkɪ] a larguirucho.
lantern ['læntn] n linterna; (NAUT) farol m.
lap [læp] n (*of track*) vuelta; (*of body*): **to sit on sb's** ~ sentarse en las rodillas de uno // vt (*also*: ~ **up**) lamer // vi (*waves*) chapotear; ~**dog** n perro faldero.
lapel [lə'pɛl] n solapa.
Lapland ['læplænd] n Laponia; **Lapp** [læp] a, n lapón/ona m/f.
lapse [læps] n error m, equivocación f;

(*moral*) desliz m // vi (*expire*) caducar; (LAW) equivocarse; (*morally*) caer en un desliz; (*time*) pasar, transcurrir; **to ~ into bad habits** volver a las andadas; ~ **of time** lapso, período.
larceny ['lɑːsənɪ] n latrocinio; **petty ~** robo de menor cuantía.
lard [lɑːd] n manteca (de cerdo).
larder ['lɑːdə*] n despensa.
large [lɑːdʒ] a (*gen*) grande; (*fat*) gordo; **at ~** (*free*) en libertad; (*generally*) en general; ~**ly** ad en gran parte; ~-**scale** a (*map*) en gran escala; (*fig*) importante.
lark [lɑːk] n (*bird*) alondra; (*joke*) travesura, broma; **to ~ about** vi bromear, divertirse tontamente.
larva ['lɑːvə], pl -**vae** [-viː] n larva.
laryngitis [lærɪn'dʒaɪtɪs] n laringitis f.
larynx ['lærɪŋks] n laringe f.
lascivious [lə'sɪvɪəs] a lascivo.
laser ['leɪzə*] n laser m.
lash [læʃ] n latigazo; (*punishment*) azote m; (*gen*: **eyelash**) pestaña // vt azotar; (*tie*) atar; **to ~ out** vi: **to ~ out at** or **against sb** atacar violentamente a alguien; **to ~ out** (*col: spend*) gastar generosamente.
lass [læs] n chica.
lasso [læ'suː] n lazo // vt coger con lazo.
last [lɑːst] a (*gen*) último; (*final*) último, final // ad por último // vi (*endure*) durar; (*continue*) continuar, seguir; ~ **week** la semana pasada; ~ **night** anoche; **at ~** por fin; ~ **but one** penúltimo; ~**ing** a duradero; ~-**minute** a de última hora.
latch [lætʃ] n picaporte m, pestillo; ~**key** n llavín m.
late [leɪt] a (*not on time*) tarde, atrasado; (*far on in day etc*) tardío; (*hour*) avanzado; (*recent*) reciente; (*former*) antiguo, ex; (*dead*) fallecido // ad tarde; (*behind time, schedule*) con retraso; **of ~** últimamente; **in ~ May** hacia fines de mayo; **the ~ Mr X** el difunto Sr X; ~**comer** n recién llegado; ~**ly** ad últimamente; ~**ness** n (*of person*) retraso; (*of event*) lo tardío.
latent ['leɪtnt] a latente.
later ['leɪtə*] a (*date etc*) posterior; (*version etc*) más reciente // ad más tarde, después.
lateral ['lætərl] a lateral.
latest ['leɪtɪst] a último; **at the ~** a más tardar.
lathe [leɪð] n torno.
lather ['lɑːðə*] n espuma (de jabón) // vt enjabonar // vi hacer espuma.
Latin ['lætɪn] n latín m // a latino; ~ **America** n América latina; ~-**American** a latinoamericano.
latitude ['lætɪtjuːd] n latitud f.
latrine [lə'triːn] n letrina.
latter ['lætə*] a último; (*of two*) segundo // n: **the ~** el último, éste; ~**ly** ad últimamente.
lattice ['lætɪs] n enrejado; (*on window*) reja.
laudable ['lɔːdəbl] a loable.
laugh [lɑːf] n risa; (*loud*) carcajada // vi

reírse, reír; reírse a carcajadas; **to ~ at**
vt fus reírse de; **to ~ off** *vt* tomar algo a
risa; **~able** *a* risible, ridículo; **to be the
~ing stock of the town** ser el
hazmerreír de la ciudad; **~ter** *n* risa.

launch [lɔːntʃ] *n* (*boat*) lancha; *see also*
~ing // *vt* (*ship, rocket, plan*) lanzar;
~ing *n* (*of rocket etc*) lanzamiento;
(*inauguration*) estreno; **~(ing) pad** *n*
plataforma de lanzamiento.

launder [ˈlɔːndə*] *vt* lavar.

launderette [lɔːnˈdrɛt] *n* lavandería
(automática).

laundry [ˈlɔːndrɪ] *n* lavandería; (*clothes*)
ropa sucia; **to do the ~** hacer la colada.

laureate [ˈlɔːrɪət] *a see* **poet**.

laurel [ˈlɔrl] *n* laurel *m*.

lava [ˈlɑːvə] *n* lava.

lavatory [ˈlævətərɪ] *n* lavabo; **lavatories**
npl servicios *mpl*, aseos *mpl*.

lavender [ˈlævəndə*] *n* lavanda.

lavish [ˈlævɪʃ] *a* abundante; (*giving freely*):
~ with pródigo en // *vt*: **to ~ sth on sb**
colmar a uno de algo.

law [lɔː] *n* ley *f*; (*study*) derecho; (*of game*)
regla; **~-abiding** *a* que cumple la ley;
~ and order *n* órden *m* público; **~breaker**
n infractor *m* (de la ley); **~ court** *n*
tribunal *m* (de justicia); **~ful** *a* legítimo,
lícito; **~fully** *ad* legalmente; **~less** *a*
(*act*) ilegal; (*person*) rebelde; (*country*)
desordenado.

lawn [lɔːn] *n* césped *m*; **~mower** *n*
cortacésped *m*; **~ tennis** [-ˈtɛnɪs] *n* tenis
m.

law: ~ school *n* facultad *f* de derecho; **~
student** *n* estudiante *m/f* de derecho.

lawsuit [ˈlɔːsuːt] *n* pleito.

lawyer [ˈlɔːjə*] *n* abogado; (*for sales, wills
etc*) notario.

lax [læks] *a* flojo; (*negligent*) negligente.

laxative [ˈlæksətɪv] *n* laxante *m*.

laxity [ˈlæksɪtɪ] *n* flojedad *f*; (*moral*)
relajamiento; (*negligence*) negligencia.

lay [leɪ] *pt of* **lie** // *a* laico; (*not expert*)
profano // *vt, pt, pp* **laid** (*place*) colocar;
(*eggs, table*) poner; (*trap*) tender; **to ~
aside** *or* **by** *vt* dejar a un lado; **to ~ down**
vt (*pen etc*) dejar; (~ *flat*) acostar; (*arms*)
rendir; (*policy*) asentar; **to ~ down the
law** imponer la ley; **to ~ off** *vt* (*workers*)
despedir, poner en paro; **to ~ on** *vt*
(*water, gas*) instalar; (*provide*) proveer; **to
~ out** *vt* (*design*) diseñar; (*spend*)
gastar; **to ~ up** *vt*
(*store*) guardar; (*ship*) desarmar; (*subj:
illness*) obligar a guardar cama; **~about**
n vago/a; **~-by** *n* apartadero.

layer [ˈleɪə*] *n* capa.

layette [leɪˈɛt] *n* canastilla, ajuar *m* (de
niño).

layman [ˈleɪmən] *n* persona no experta;
(*REL*) lego.

layout [ˈleɪaʊt] *n* (*design*) plan *m*, trazado;
(*disposition*) disposición *f*; (*PRESS*)
composición *f*.

laze [leɪz] *vi* no hacer nada; (*pej*)

holgazanear; **laziness** *n* pereza; **lazy** *a*
perezoso, vago.

lb. *abbr of* **pound** (*weight*).

lead [liːd] *n* (*front position*) delantera;
(*SPORT*) liderato; (*distance, time ahead*)
ventaja; (*clue*) pista; (*ELEC*) cable *m*; (*for
dog*) correa; (*THEATRE*) papel *m* principal
// *n* [lɛd] plomo; (*in pencil*) mina // (*vb: pt,
pp* **led**) *vt* conducir; (*induce*) llevar; (*be
leader of*) dirigir; (*SPORT*) ir en cabeza de
// *vi* ir primero; **to ~ to** llevar a, salir a;
to ~ astray *vt* llevar por mal camino; **to
~ away** *vt* llevar; **to ~ back** *vt* hacer
volver; **to ~ on** *vt* (*tease*) coquetear con;
to ~ on to *vt* (*induce*) incitar a; **to ~ up
to** conducir a.

leader [ˈliːdə*] *n* (*gen*) jefe *m*, líder *m*; (*of
union etc*) dirigente *m/f*; (*of gang*)
cabecilla *m*; (*guide*) guía *m/f*; (*of
newspaper*) artículo de fondo; **~ship** *n*
dirección *f*; (*quality*) dotes *fpl* de mando.

leading [ˈliːdɪŋ] *a* (*main*) principal;
(*outstanding*) destacado; (*first*) primero;
(*front*) delantero; **~ lady** *n* (*THEATRE*)
primera actriz *f*; **~ light** *n* (*person*)
figura principal.

leaf [liːf], *pl* **leaves** *n* hoja // *vi*: **to ~
through** hojear; **to turn over a new ~**
reformarse.

leaflet [ˈliːflɪt] *n* folleto.

league [liːg] *n* sociedad *f*; (*FOOTBALL*) liga;
to be in ~ with estar de manga con.

leak [liːk] *n* (*of liquid, gas*) escape *m*, fuga;
(*hole*) agujero; (*in roof*) gotera; (*of money*)
filtración *f* // *vi* (*shoes, ship*) hacer agua;
(*pipe*) tener (un) escape; (*roof*) gotear;
(*container*) salirse; (*gas*) escaparse; (*fig:
news*) filtrarse // *vt* (*gen*) dejar escapar;
(*exude*) rezumar; **the information was
~ed to the enemy** las informaciones se
pasaron al enemigo; **the news ~ed out**
trascendió la noticia.

lean [liːn] *a* (*thin*) flaco; (*meat*) magro //
(*vb: pt, pp* **leaned** *or* **leant** [lɛnt]) *vt*: **to ~
sth on** apoyar algo en // *vi* (*slope*)
inclinarse; (*rest*): **to ~ against** apoyarse
contra; **to ~ on** apoyarse en; (*fig: rely on*)
contar con (el apoyo de); **to ~
back/forward** *vi* inclinarse hacia
atrás/hacia adelante; **to ~ over** *vi*
ladearse; **~ing** *a* inclinado // *n*: **~ing
(towards)** inclinación *f* (hacia); **~-to** *n*
colgadizo.

leap [liːp] *n* salto // *vi, pt, pp* **leaped** *or*
leapt [lɛpt] saltar; **~frog** *n* pídola; **~
year** *n* año bisiesto.

learn [lɜːn], *pt, pp* **learned** *or* **learnt** *vt*
(*gen*) aprender; (*come to know of*)
enterarse de // *vi* aprender; **to ~ how to
do sth** aprender a hacer algo; **~ed**
[ˈlɜːnɪd] *a* erudito; **~er** *n* principiante *m/f*;
~ing *n* el saber *m*, conocimientos *mpl*.

lease [liːs] *n* arriendo // *vt* arrendar.

leash [liːʃ] *n* cuerda.

least [liːst] *a* (*slightest*) menor; (*smallest*)
más pequeño; (*smallest amount of*) mínimo
// *ad* menos // *n*: **the ~** lo menos; **the ~**

possible effort el mínimo de esfuerzo posible; **at ~** por lo menos, al menos; **not in the ~** en absoluto.

leather ['lɛðə*] n cuero.

leave [liːv], pt, pp **left** vt dejar; (go away from) abandonar // vi irse; (train) salir // n permiso; **to be left** quedar, sobrar; **there's some milk left over** sobra o queda algo de leche; **on ~** de permiso; **to take one's ~ of** despedirse de; **to ~ out** vt omitir.

leaves [liːvz] pl of **leaf**.

Lebanon ['lɛbənən] n Líbano.

lecherous ['lɛtʃərəs] a lascivo.

lecture ['lɛktʃə*] n conferencia; (SCOL) clase f // vi dar una clase // vt (scold) sermonear; **to give a ~ on** dar una conferencia sobre; **lecturer** n conferenciante m/f; (at university) profesor adjunto/profesora adjunta m/f.

led [lɛd] pt, pp of **lead**.

ledge [lɛdʒ] n (of window, on wall) repisa, reborde m; (of mountain) plataforma.

ledger ['lɛdʒə*] n libro mayor.

lee [liː] n sotavento.

leek [liːk] n puerro.

leer [lɪə*] vi: **to ~ at sb** mirar impúdicamente a alguien.

leeway ['liːweɪ] n (fig): **to have some ~** tener cierta libertad de acción.

left [lɛft] pt, pp of **leave** // a izquierdo; (POL) de izquierda // n izquierda // ad a la izquierda; **the L~** (POL) la izquierda; **~-handed** a zurdo; **the ~-hand side** n la izquierda; **~-luggage (office)** n consigna; **~-overs** npl sobras fpl; **~-wing** a (POL) de izquierdas, izquierdista.

leg [lɛg] n pierna; (of animal) pata; (of chair) pie m; (CULIN: of meat) pierna; (of journey) etapa; **1st/2nd ~** (SPORT) partido de ida/de vuelta; **to pull sb's ~** bromear con uno.

legacy ['lɛgəsɪ] n legado.

legal ['liːgl] a (gen) lícito; (of law) legal; (enquiry etc) jurídico; **~ize** vt legalizar; **~ly** ad legalmente; **~ tender** n moneda corriente.

legend ['lɛdʒənd] n leyenda; **~ary** a legendario.

legible ['lɛdʒəbl] a legible.

legion ['liːdʒən] n legión f.

legislate ['lɛdʒɪsleɪt] vi legislar; **legislation** [-'leɪʃən] n legislación f; **legislative** [-lətɪv] a legislativo; **legislature** [-lətʃə*] n cuerpo legislativo.

legitimacy [lɪ'dʒɪtɪməsɪ] n legitimidad f; **legitimate** [-mət] a legítimo.

leg-room ['lɛgruːm] n espacio para las piernas.

leisure ['lɛʒə*] n ocio, tiempo libre; **at ~** con tranquilidad; **~ centre** n centro de diversiones; **~ly** a pausado, lento.

lemon ['lɛmən] n limón m; **~ade** [-'neɪd] n (fruit juice) limonada; (fizzy) gaseosa.

lend [lɛnd], pt, pp **lent** vt: **to ~ sth to sb** prestar algo a alguien; **~er** n prestador/a

m/f; **~ing library** n biblioteca circulante.

length [lɛŋθ] n largo, longitud f; (section: of road, pipe etc) tramo; **at ~** (at last) por fin, finalmente; (lengthily) largamente; **~en** vt alargar // vi alargarse; **~ways** ad de largo; **~y** a largo, extenso; (meeting) prolongado.

leniency ['liːnɪənsɪ] n indulgencia; **lenient** [-ənt] a indulgente.

lens [lɛnz] n (of spectacles) lente f; (of camera) objetivo.

lent [lɛnt] pt, pp of **lend**.

Lent [lɛnt] n Cuaresma.

lentil ['lɛntɪl] n lenteja.

Leo ['liːəu] n Leo.

leopard ['lɛpəd] n leopardo.

leotard ['liːətɑːd] n leotardo.

leper ['lɛpə*] n leproso/a; **leprosy** [-prəsɪ] n lepra.

lesbian ['lɛzbɪən] n lesbiana.

less [lɛs] det a (in size, degree etc) menor; (in quantity) menos // pron, ad menos; **~ than half** menos de la mitad; **~ and ~** cada vez menos; **the ~ he works...** cuanto menos trabaja... .

lessen ['lɛsn] vi disminuir, menguar // vt disminuir, reducir.

lesson ['lɛsn] n lección f; **a maths ~** una clase o una lección de matemáticas.

lest [lɛst] conj: **~ it happen** para que no pase.

let [lɛt], pt, pp **let** vt (allow) dejar, permitir; (lease) alquilar; **~'s go** ¡vamos!; **~ him come** que venga; **'to ~'** 'se alquila'; **to ~ down** vt (lower) bajar; (dress) alargar; (tyre) desinflar; (hair) soltar; (disappoint) defraudar; **to ~ go** vi soltar; (fig) dejarse ir // vt abandonar; **to ~ in** vt dejar entrar; (visitor etc) hacer pasar; **to ~ off** vt dejar libre; (firework etc) disparar; (smell etc) despedir; **to ~ on** vi (col) divulgar (that que); **to ~ out** vt dejar salir; (dress) ensanchar; **to ~ up** vi amainar, disminuir.

lethal ['liːθl] a mortífero; (wound) mortal.

lethargic [lɛ'θɑːdʒɪk] a letárgico; **lethargy** ['lɛθədʒɪ] n letargo.

letter ['lɛtə*] n (of alphabet) letra; (correspondence) carta; **~ bomb** n carta con bomba explosiva; **~box** n buzón m; **~ing** n letras fpl.

lettuce ['lɛtɪs] n lechuga.

let-up ['lɛtʌp] n descanso, tregua.

leukaemia, leukemia (US) [luː'kiːmɪə] n leucemia.

level ['lɛvl] a (flat) llano; (flattened) nivelado; (uniform) igual // ad a nivel // n nivel m; (flat place) llano // vt nivelar, allanar; **to be ~ with** estar a nivel de; **~s** npl Bachillerato Superior, B.U.P.; **'O' ~s** npl bachillerato elemental, octavo de básica; **on the ~** (fig: honest) en serio; **to ~ off** or **out** vi (prices etc) estabilizarse; **~ crossing** n paso a nivel; **~-headed** a sensato.

lever ['liːvə*] n palanca // vt: **to ~ up**

alzar con palanca; ~**age** n (fig: influence) influencia.

levity ['lɛvɪtɪ] n frivolidad f, informalidad f.

levy ['lɛvɪ] n impuesto // vt exigir, recaudar.

lewd [lu:d] a impúdico, obsceno.

liability [laɪə'bɪlətɪ] n responsabilidad f; (handicap) desventaja; (risk) riesgo; **liabilities** npl obligaciones fpl; (COMM) deudas fpl, pasivo sg.

liable ['laɪəbl] a (subject): ~ to sujeto a; **to be** ~ **for** ser responsable de; **to be** ~ **to** (likely) tener tendencia a.

liaison [li:'eɪzɔn] n (coordination) enlace m; (affair) relaciones fpl amorosas.

liar ['laɪə*] n mentiroso/a.

libel ['laɪbl] n calumnia // vt calumniar.

liberal ['lɪbərl] a (gen) liberal; (generous): ~ **with** generoso con.

liberate ['lɪbəreɪt] vt liberar; **liberation** [-'reɪʃən] n liberación f.

liberty ['lɪbətɪ] n libertad f; **to be at** ~ **to** tener permiso para; **to take the** ~ **of doing sth** tomarse la libertad de hacer algo.

Libra ['li:brə] n Libra.

librarian [laɪ'brɛərɪən] n bibliotecario/a; **library** ['laɪbrərɪ] n biblioteca.

libretto [lɪ'brɛtəʊ] n libreto.

Libya ['lɪbɪə] n Libia; ~**n** a, n libio/a.

lice [laɪs] pl of **louse.**

licence, license (US) ['laɪsns] n (gen) licencia; (permit) permiso; (also: **driving** ~) carnet m de conducir; (excessive freedom) libertinaje m; ~ **number** n matrícula; ~ **plate** n placa (de matrícula).

license ['laɪsns] n (US) = **licence** // vt autorizar, licenciar; ~**d** a (for alcohol) autorizado para la venta de bebidas alcohólicas.

licensee [laɪsən'si:] n (in a pub) patrón/ona m/f.

licentious [laɪ'sɛnʃəs] a licencioso.

lichen ['laɪkən] n liquen m.

lick [lɪk] vt lamer // n lamedura; **a** ~ **of paint** una mano de pintura.

licorice ['lɪkərɪs] n = **liquorice.**

lid [lɪd] n (of box, case) tapa; (of pan) cobertera.

lido ['laɪdəʊ] n piscina.

lie [laɪ] n mentira // vi mentir // vi, pt **lay,** pp **lain** (act) echarse; (state) estar echado, estar acostado; (of object: be situated) estar, encontrarse; **to** ~ **low** (fig) esconderse; **to** ~ **about** vi (things) estar en desorden; (people) gandulear; **to have a** ~-**down** echarse (una siesta); **to have a** ~-**in** quedarse pegado a las sábanas.

lieu [lu:]: **in** ~ **of** prep en lugar de.

lieutenant [lɛf'tɛnənt] n lugarteniente m; (MIL) teniente m.

life [laɪf], pl **lives** n (gen) vida; (way of ~) modo de vivir; (of licence etc) vigencia; ~ **assurance** n seguro de vida; ~**belt** n cinturón m salvavidas; ~**boat** n bote m salvavidas; ~**guard** n vigilante m;

jacket n chaleco salvavidas; ~**less** a sin vida; (dull) soso; ~**like** a natural; ~**line** n cuerda salvavidas; ~**long** a de toda la vida; ~-**saver** n bañero, socorrista m/f; ~ **sentence** n condena perpetua; ~-**sized** a de tamaño natural; ~ **span** n vida; ~ **support system** n (MED) respirador m artificial; ~**time** n: **in his** ~**time** durante su vida; **once in a** ~**time** una vez en la vida.

lift [lɪft] vt levantar; (steal) robar // vi (fog) levantarse, disiparse // n (elevator) ascensor m; **to give sb a** ~ llevar a uno en el coche; ~-**off** n despegue m.

ligament ['lɪgəmənt] n ligamento.

light [laɪt] n (gen) luz f; (flame) lumbre f; (lamp) luz f, lámpara; (daylight) luz del día; (headlight) faro; (rear ~) luz trasera; (for cigarette etc): **have you got a** ~? ¿tiene fuego? // vt, pt, pp **lighted** or **lit** (candle, cigarette, fire) encender; (room) alumbrar // a (colour) claro; (not heavy, also fig) ligero; (room) alumbrado; **to** ~ **up** vi (smoke) encender un cigarrillo; (face) iluminarse // vt (illuminate) iluminar, alumbrar; ~ **bulb** n bombilla; ~**en** vi (grow) clarear // vt (give light to) iluminar; (make lighter) aclarar; (make less heavy) aligerar; ~**er** n (also: **cigarette** ~**er**) encendedor m, mechero; ~-**headed** a (dizzy) mareado; (excited) exaltado; (by nature) casquivano; ~-**hearted** a alegre; ~**house** n faro; ~**ing** n (act) iluminación f; (system) alumbrado; ~**ly** ad (touch) ligeramente; (thoughtlessly) a la ligera; (slightly) levemente; (not seriously) con poca seriedad; **to get off** ~**ly** ser castigado con poca severidad; ~ **meter** n (PHOT) fotómetro; ~**ness** n claridad f; (in weight) ligereza.

lightning ['laɪtnɪŋ] n relámpago, rayo; ~ **conductor** n pararrayos m inv.

light: ~**weight** a (suit) ligero // n (BOXING) peso ligero; ~ **year** n año luz.

like [laɪk] vt (person) querer, tener cariño a; (things) gustarle a uno // prep como // a parecido, semejante // n: **the** ~ semejante m/f; **his** ~**s and dislikes** sus gustos y aversiones; **I would** ~, **I'd** ~ me gustaría; (for purchase) quisiera; **would you** ~ **a coffee?** ¿te apetece un café?; **to be** or **look** ~ sb/sth parecerse a alguien/algo; **that's just** ~ **him** es muy de él, es característico de él; **it is nothing** ~... no tiene parecido alguno con...; ~**able** a simpático, agradable.

likelihood ['laɪklɪhʊd] n probabilidad f; **likely** [-lɪ] a probable; **he's likely to leave** es probable que se vaya.

like-minded [laɪk'maɪndɪd] a de la misma opinión.

liken ['laɪkən] vt: **to** ~ **sth to sth** comparar algo con algo.

likewise ['laɪkwaɪz] ad igualmente.

liking ['laɪkɪŋ] n: **to his** ~ para su gusto.

lilac ['laɪlɔk] n lila // a (colour) de color lila.

lily ['lɪlɪ] n lirio, azucena; ~ **of the valley** n lirio de los valles.

limb [lɪm] n miembro.

limber ['lɪmbə*]: **to ~ up** vi (fig) entrenarse; (SPORT) desentumecerse.

limbo ['lɪmbəu] n: **to be in ~** (fig) caer en el olvido.

lime [laɪm] n (tree) limero; (fruit) lima; (GEO) cal f.

limelight ['laɪmlaɪt] n: **to be in the ~** (fig) ser el centro de atención.

limerick ['lɪmərɪk] n quintilla humorística.

limestone ['laɪmstəun] n piedra caliza.

limit ['lɪmɪt] n límite m // vt limitar; ~**ation** [-'teɪʃən] n limitación f; ~**ed** a limitado; **to be ~ed to** limitarse a; ~**ed (liability) company (Ltd)** n sociedad f anónima; ~**less** a sin límites.

limousine ['lɪməzi:n] n limusina.

limp [lɪmp] n: **to have a ~** tener cojera // vi cojear // a flojo.

limpet ['lɪmpɪt] n lapa.

limpid ['lɪmpɪd] a límpido, cristalino.

line [laɪn] n (gen) línea; (straight ~) raya; (rope) cuerda; (for fishing) sedal m; (wire) hilo; (row, series) fila, hilera; (of writing) renglón m; (on face) arruga; (specialty) rama // vt (SEWING) forrar (with de); **to ~ the streets** ocupar las aceras; **in ~ with** de acuerdo con; **to ~ up** vi hacer cola // vt alinear, poner en fila; ~**d** a (face) arrugado; (paper) rayado.

linear ['lɪnɪə*] a lineal.

linen ['lɪnɪn] n ropa blanca; (cloth) lino.

liner ['laɪnə*] n vapor m de línea, transatlántico.

linesman ['laɪnzmən] n (SPORT) juez m de línea.

line-up ['laɪnʌp] n alineación f.

linger ['lɪŋgə*] vi retrasarse, tardar en marcharse; (smell, tradition) persistir.

lingerie ['lænʒəri:] n ropa interior (de mujer).

lingering ['lɪŋgərɪŋ] a persistente; (death) lento.

lingo ['lɪŋgəu], pl ~**es** n (pej) jerga.

linguist ['lɪŋgwɪst] n lingüista m/f; ~**ic** a lingüístico; ~**ics** n lingüística.

lining ['laɪnɪŋ] n forro.

link [lɪŋk] n (of a chain) eslabón m; (connection) conexión f; (bond) vínculo, lazo // vt vincular, unir; ~**s** npl campo sg de golf; **to ~ up** vt acoplar // vi unirse; ~**-up** n (gen) unión f; (in space) acoplamiento.

lino ['laɪnəu], **linoleum** [lɪ'nəuliəm] n linóleo.

lintel ['lɪntl] n dintel m.

lion ['laɪən] n león m; ~**ess** n leona.

lip [lɪp] n labio; (of jug) pico; (of cup etc) borde m; ~**read** vi leer los labios; ~**service** n: **to pay ~ service to sth** alabar algo pero sin hacer nada; ~**stick**

n lápiz m labial, barra de labios.

liquefy ['lɪkwɪfaɪ] vt liquidar.

liqueur [lɪ'kjuə*] n licor m.

liquid ['lɪkwɪd] a, n líquido.

liquidate ['lɪkwɪdeɪt] vt liquidar; **liquidation** [-'deɪʃən] n liquidación f; **liquidator** n liquidador/a m/f.

liquidize ['lɪkwɪdaɪz] vt (CULIN) licuar.

liquor ['lɪkə*] n licor m, bebidas alcohólicas fpl.

liquorice ['lɪkərɪs] n regaliz m.

lisp [lɪsp] n ceceo.

list [lɪst] n lista; (of ship) inclinación f // vt (write down) hacer una lista de; (enumerate) catalogar // vi (ship) inclinarse.

listen ['lɪsn] vi escuchar, oír; (pay attention) atender; ~**er** n oyente m/f.

listless ['lɪstlɪs] a apático, indiferente.

lit [lɪt] pt, pp of **light.**

litany ['lɪtənɪ] n letanía.

literacy ['lɪtərəsɪ] n capacidad f de leer y escribir; ~ **campaign** campaña de alfabetización.

literal ['lɪtərl] a literal; ~**ly** ad literalmente.

literary ['lɪtərərɪ] a literario.

literate ['lɪtərət] a que sabe leer y escribir; (fig) culto.

literature ['lɪtərɪtʃə*] n literatura; (brochures etc) folletos mpl.

lithe [laɪð] a ágil.

litigation [lɪtɪ'geɪʃən] n litigio.

litre, liter (US) ['li:tə*] n litro.

litter ['lɪtə*] n (rubbish) basura; (paper) papel m tirado; (young animals) camada, cría; (stretcher) camilla; ~ **bin** n papelera; ~**ed** a: ~**ed with** (scattered) esparcido con; (covered with) lleno de.

little ['lɪtl] a (small) pequeño; (not much) poco; often translated by suffix: eg ~ **house** casita // ad poco; **a** ~ un poco (de); ~ **by** ~ poco a poco.

liturgy ['lɪtədʒɪ] n liturgia.

live [lɪv] vi vivir // vt (a life) llevar; (experience) vivir // a [laɪv] (animal) vivo; (wire) conectado; (broadcast) en directo; (shell) cargado; **to ~ down** vt hacer olvidar; **to ~ on** vt fus (food) vivirse de, alimentarse de; **to ~ up to** vt fus (fulfil) cumplir con; (justify) justificar.

livelihood ['laɪvlɪhud] n sustento.

lively ['laɪvlɪ] a (gen) vivo; (talk) animado; (pace) rápido; (party, tune) alegre.

liver ['lɪvə*] n (ANAT) hígado; ~**ish** a (fig) rezongón(ona).

livery ['lɪvərɪ] n librea.

lives [laɪvz] pl of **life.**

livestock ['laɪvstɔk] n ganado.

livid ['lɪvɪd] a lívido; (furious) furioso.

living ['lɪvɪŋ] a (alive) vivo // n: **to earn** or **make a ~** ganarse la vida; ~ **conditions** npl condiciones fpl de vida; ~ **room** n sala (de estar); ~ **standards** npl nivel m de vida; ~ **wage** n sueldo suficiente para vivir.

lizard ['lɪzəd] n lagartija.
llama ['lɑːmə] n llama.
load [ləud] n (gen) carga; (weight) peso // vt: **to ~ (with)** cargar (con); (fig) colmar (de); **a ~ of, ~s of** (fig) (gran) cantidad de, montones de; **~ed** a (dice) cargado; (question, word) intencionado; (col: rich) forrado (de dinero); (: drunk) trompa.
loaf [ləuf], pl **loaves** n (barra de) pan m // vi (also: **~ about, ~ around**) holgazanear.
loan [ləun] n préstamo; (COMM) empréstito // vt prestar; **on ~** prestado.
loath [ləuθ] a: **to be ~ to do sth** estar poco dispuesto a hacer algo.
loathe [ləuð] vt aborrecer; (person) odiar; **loathing** n aversión f; odio; **it fills me with loathing** me da asco.
loaves [ləuvz] pl of **loaf**.
lobby ['lɔbɪ] n vestíbulo, sala de espera; (POL: pressure group) grupo de presión // vt presionar.
lobe [ləub] n lóbulo.
lobster ['lɔbstə*] n langosta; (large) bogavante m.
local ['ləukl] a local // n (pub) bar m; **the ~s** npl los vecinos, los del lugar; **~ity** [-'kælɪtɪ] n localidad f; **~ly** [-kəlɪ] ad en la vecindad.
locate [ləu'keɪt] vt (find) localizar; (situate) colocar.
location [ləu'keɪʃən] n situación f; **on ~** (CINEMA) en exteriores, fuera del estudio.
loch [lɔx] n lago.
lock [lɔk] n (of door, box) cerradura; (of canal) esclusa; (stop) tope m; (of hair) mechón m // vt (with key) cerrar con llave; (immobilize) inmovilizar // vi (door etc) cerrarse con llave; (wheels) bloquearse, trabarse.
locker ['lɔkə*] n casillero.
locket ['lɔkɪt] n medallón m.
lockout ['lɔkaut] n paro patronal, lockout m.
locomotive [ləukə'məutɪv] n locomotora.
locum ['ləukəm] n (MED) (médico) interino.
locust ['ləukəst] n langosta.
lodge [lɔdʒ] n casa del guarda; (porter's) portería; (FREEMASONRY) logia // vi (person): **to ~ (with)** alojarse (en casa de) // vt (complaint) presentar; **lodger** n huésped/a m/f.
lodgings ['lɔdʒɪŋz] npl alojamiento sg; (house) casa sg de huéspedes.
loft [lɔft] n desván m.
lofty ['lɔftɪ] a alto; (haughty) orgulloso.
log [lɔg] n (of wood) leño, tronco; (book) = **logbook**.
logarithm ['lɔgərɪðəm] n logaritmo.
logbook ['lɔgbuk] n (NAUT) diario de a bordo; (AVIAT) libro de vuelo; (of car) documentación f (del coche).
loggerheads ['lɔgəhɛdz] npl: **at ~ (with)** de pique (con).
logic ['lɔdʒɪk] n lógica; **~al** a lógico.

logistics [lɔ'dʒɪstɪks] n logística.
loin [lɔɪn] n (CULIN) lomo, solomillo; **~s** npl lomos mpl; **~ cloth** n taparrabo.
loiter ['lɔɪtə*] vi perder el tiempo; (pej) merodear.
loll [lɔl] vi (also: **~ about**) repantigarse.
lollipop ['lɔlɪpɔp] n pirulí m; (iced) polo; **~ man/lady** n persona encargada de ayudar a los niños a cruzar la calle.
London ['lʌndən] n Londres; **~er** n londinense m/f.
lone [ləun] a solitario.
loneliness ['ləunlɪnɪs] n soledad f, aislamiento; **lonely** [-lɪ] a solitario, solo.
loner ['ləunə*] n solitario.
long [lɔŋ] a largo // ad mucho tiempo, largamente // vi: **to ~ for sth** anhelar o suspirar por algo; **in the ~ run** a la larga; **so** or **as ~ as** mientras, con tal que; **don't be ~!** ¡no tardes!, ¡vuelve pronto!; **how ~ is the street?** ¿cuánto tiene la calle de largo?; **how ~ is the lesson?** ¿cuánto dura la lección?; **6 metres ~** que mide 6 metros, de 6 metros de largo; **6 months ~** que dura 6 meses, de 6 meses de duración; **all night ~** toda la noche; **~ before** mucho antes; **before ~** (+ future) dentro de poco; (+ past) poco tiempo después; **at ~ last** al fin, por fin; **~distance** a (race) de larga distancia; (call) interurbano; **~-haired** a de pelo largo; **~-hand** n escritura (corriente); **~ing** n anhelo, ansia; (nostalgia) nostalgia // a anhelante.
longitude ['lɔŋgɪtjuːd] n longitud f.
long: ~ jump n salto de longitud; **~-lost** a desaparecido hace mucho tiempo; **~-playing record (L.P.)** n elepé m, disco de larga duración; **~-range** a de gran alcance; **~-sighted** a (fig) previsor(a); **~-standing** a de mucho tiempo; **~-suffering** a sufrido; **~-term** a a largo plazo; **~ wave** a de onda larga; **~-winded** a prolijo.
loo [luː] n (col) wáter m.
loofah ['luːfə] n esponja de lufa.
look [luk] vi mirar; (seem) parecer; (building etc): **to ~ south/on to the sea** dar al sur/al mar // n mirada; (glance) vistazo; (appearance) aire m, aspecto; **~s** npl físico, apariencia; **to ~ like sb** parecerse a alguien; **to ~ after** vt fus cuidar a; **to ~ at** vt fus mirar; (consider) considerar; **to ~ back** vi mirar hacia atrás; **to ~ down on** vt fus (fig) despreciar, mirar con desprecio; **to ~ for** vt fus buscar; **to ~ forward to** vt fus esperar con ilusión; **to ~ into** vt investigar; **to ~ on** vi mirar (como espectador); **to ~ out** vi (beware): **to ~ out (for)** tener cuidado (de); **to ~ out for** vt fus (seek) buscar; (await) esperar; **to ~ round** vi volver la cabeza; **to ~ to** vt fus ocuparse de; (rely on) contar con; **to ~ up** vi mirar hacia arriba; (improve) mejorar // vt (word) buscar; (friend) visitar; **to ~ up to** vt fus admirar; **~-out**

n (*tower etc*) puesto de observación; (*person*) vigía *m*; **to be on the ~-out for sth** estar al acecho de algo.

loom [luːm] *n* telar *m* // *vi* asomarse; (*threaten*) amenazar.

loony ['luːnɪ] *n* (*col*) loco/a; **~ bin** *n* (*col*) manicomio.

loop [luːp] *n* lazo; (*bend*) vuelta, recodo; (*contraceptive*) espiral *f*; **~hole** *n* escapatoria.

loose [luːs] *a* (*gen*) suelto; (*not tight*) flojo; (*wobbly etc*) movedizo; (*clothes*) ancho; (*morals, discipline*) relajado; **to be at a ~ end** no saber qué hacer; **~ly** *ad* libremente, aproximadamente; **loosen** *vt* (*free*) soltar; (*untie*) desatar; (*slacken*) aflojar.

loot [luːt] *n* botín *m* // *vt* saquear; **~ing** *n* pillaje *m*.

lop [lɔp]: **to ~ off** *vt* cortar; (*branches*) podar.

lop-sided ['lɔp'saɪdɪd] *a* desequilibrado.

lord [lɔːd] *n* señor *m*; **L~** Smith Lord Smith; **the L~** el Señor; **the (House of) L~s** la Cámara de los Lores; **~ly** *a* señorial; (*arrogant*) arrogante; **~ship** *n*: **your L~ship** su señoría.

lore [lɔː*] *n* saber *m* popular, tradiciones *fpl*.

lorry ['lɔrɪ] *n* camión *m*; **~ driver** *n* camionero.

lose [luːz] *pt, pp* **lost** *vt* perder // *vi* perder, ser vencido; **to ~ (time)** (*clock*) atrasarse; **loser** *n* perdedor/a *m/f*.

loss [lɔs] *n* pérdida; **to be at a ~** no saber qué hacer; **to be a dead ~** ser completamente inútil.

lost [lɔst] *pt, pp* de **lose** // *a* perdido; **~ property** *n* objetos *mpl* perdidos.

lot [lɔt] *n* (*at auctions*) lote *m*; (*destiny*) suerte *f*; **the ~** el todo, todos; **a ~** mucho, bastante; **a ~ of, ~s of** mucho(s) (*pl*); **to draw ~s (for sth)** echar suertes (para decidir algo); **I read a ~** leo bastante.

lotion ['ləuʃən] *n* loción *f*.

lottery ['lɔtərɪ] *n* lotería.

loud [laud] *a* (*voice*) alto; (*shout*) fuerte; (*noisy*) estrepitoso; (*gaudy*) chillón/ona // *ad* (*speak etc*) en alta voz; **~hailer** *n* megáfono; **~ly** *ad* (*noisily*) ruidosamente; (*aloud*) en alta voz; **~speaker** *n* altavoz *m*.

lounge [laundʒ] *n* salón *m*, sala (de estar) // *vi* reposar, holgazanear; **~ suit** *n* traje *m* de calle.

louse [laus], *pl* **lice** [laɪs] *n* piojo.

lousy ['lauzɪ] *a* (*fig*) vil, asqueroso.

lout [laut] *n* gamberro.

lovable ['lʌvəbl] *a* amable, simpático.

love [lʌv] *n* amor *m* // *vt* amar, querer; **to ~ to do** gustar(le a uno) mucho hacer; **to be in ~ with** estar enamorado de; **to make ~** hacer el amor; **for the ~ of** por amor de; **'15 ~'** (*TENNIS*) 15 a cero; **I ~ paella** me gusta mucho la paella; **'with ~'** con cariño; **~ affair** *n* aventura

sentimental; **~ letter** *n* carta de amor; **~ life** *n* vida sentimental.

lovely ['lʌvlɪ] *a* (*delightful*) precioso, encantador(a); (*beautiful*) hermoso.

lover ['lʌvə*] *n* amante *m/f*; (*amateur*): **a ~ of** un aficionado a *o* un amante de.

lovesong ['lʌvsɔŋ] *n* canción *f* de amor.

loving ['lʌvɪŋ] *a* amoroso, cariñoso.

low [ləu] *a, ad* bajo // *n* (*METEOROLOGY*) área de baja presión // *vi* (*cow*) mugir; **to feel ~** sentirse deprimido; **to turn (down) ~** *vt* bajar; **~-cut** *a* (*dress*) escotado.

lower ['ləuə*] *vt* bajar; (*reduce*) reducir // *vr*: **to ~ o.s. to** (*fig*) rebajarse a.

low: **~-grade** *a* de baja calidad; **~ly** *a* humilde; **~-lying** *a* de bajo nivel.

loyal ['lɔɪəl] *a* leal; **~ty** *n* lealtad *f*.

lozenge ['lɔzɪndʒ] *n* (*MED*) pastilla.

L.P. *n abbr of* **long-playing record.**

L-plates ['ɛlpleɪts] *npl* placa de aprendiz de conductor.

Ltd *abbr of* **limited company** S.A.

lubricant ['luːbrɪkənt] *n* lubricante *m*; **lubricate** [-keɪt] *vt* lubricar, engrasar.

lucid ['luːsɪd] *a* lúcido; **~ity** ['sɪdɪtɪ] *n* lucidez *f*.

luck [lʌk] *n* suerte *f*; **bad ~** mala suerte; **good ~!** ¡que tengas suerte!, ¡suerte!; **~ily** *ad* afortunadamente; **~y** *a* afortunado.

lucrative ['luːkrətɪv] *a* lucrativo.

ludicrous ['luːdɪkrəs] *a* absurdo.

ludo ['luːdəu] *n* parchís *m*.

lug [lʌg] *vt* (*drag*) arrastrar; (*pull*) tirar de.

luggage ['lʌgɪdʒ] *n* equipaje *m*; **~ rack** *n* (*in train*) rejilla, redecilla; (*on car*) vaca, portaequipajes *m inv*.

lukewarm ['luːkwɔːm] *a* tibio, templado.

lull [lʌl] *n* tregua // *vt* (*child*) acunar; (*person, fear*) calmar.

lullaby ['lʌləbaɪ] *n* canción *f* de cuna.

lumbago [lʌm'beɪgəu] *n* lumbago.

lumber ['lʌmbə*] *n* (*junk*) trastos viejos *mpl*; (*wood*) maderos *mpl*; **~jack** *n* maderero.

luminous ['luːmɪnəs] *a* luminoso.

lump [lʌmp] *n* terrón *m*; (*fragment*) trozo; (*in sauce*) grumo; (*in throat*) nudo; (*swelling*) bulto // *vt* (*also*: **~ together**) amontonar; **a ~ sum** suma global; **~y** *a* (*sauce*) lleno de grumos.

lunacy ['luːnəsɪ] *n* locura.

lunar ['luːnə*] *a* lunar.

lunatic ['luːnətɪk] *a, n* loco/a; **~ asylum** *n* manicomio.

lunch [lʌntʃ] *n* almuerzo, comida // *vi* almorzar; **~ time** *n* hora del almuerzo *o* de comer.

luncheon ['lʌntʃən] *n* almuerzo; **~ meat** *n* pastel *m* de carne.

lung [lʌŋ] *n* pulmón *m*; **~ cancer** *n* cáncer *m* de pulmón.

lunge [lʌndʒ] *vi* (*also*: **~ forward**) abalanzarse; **to ~ at** arremeter contra.

lurch [ləːtʃ] *vi* dar sacudidas // *n* sacudida;

to leave sb in the ~ dejar a uno plantado.

lure [luə*] n (bait) cebo; (decoy) señuelo // vt atraer, seducir.

lurid ['luərɪd] a (light) misterioso; (dress) chillón(ona); (account) sensacional; (detail) horrible.

lurk [lə:k] vi (hide) esconderse; (wait) estar al acecho.

luscious ['lʌʃəs] a delicioso.

lush [lʌʃ] a exuberante.

lust [lʌst] n lujuria; (greed) codicia; **to ~ after** vt fus codiciar; **~ful** a lascivo, lujurioso.

lustre, luster (US) ['lʌstə*] n lustre m, brillo.

lusty ['lʌstɪ] a robusto, fuerte.

lute [lu:t] n laúd m.

Luxembourg ['lʌksəmbə:g] n Luxemburgo.

luxuriant [lʌg'zjuərɪənt] a exuberante.

luxurious [lʌg'zjuərɪəs] a lujoso; **luxury** ['lʌkʃərɪ] n lujo // cpd de lujo.

lying ['laɪɪŋ] n mentiras fpl // a mentiroso.

lynch [lɪntʃ] vt linchar; **~ing** n linchamiento.

lynx [lɪnks] n lince m.

lyre ['laɪə*] n lira.

lyric ['lɪrɪk] a lírico; **~s** npl (of song) letra sg; **~al** a lírico.

M

m. abbr of **metre; mile; million.**

M.A. abbr of **Master of Arts** licenciado en letras.

mac [mæk] n impermeable m.

macaroni [mækə'rəʊnɪ] n macarrones mpl.

mace [meɪs] n (BOT) macis f.

machine [mə'ʃi:n] n máquina // vt (dress etc) coser a máquina; **~ gun** n ametralladora; **~ry** n maquinaria; (fig) mecanismo; **machinist** n operario (de máquina).

mackerel ['mækrl] n, pl inv caballa.

mackintosh ['mækɪntɒʃ] n impermeable m.

mad [mæd] a (gen) loco; (crazed) demente; (angry) furioso.

madam ['mædəm] n señora.

madden ['mædn] vt volver loco.

made [meɪd] pt, pp of **make**; **~-to-measure** a hecho a la medida.

madly ['mædlɪ] ad locamente.

madman ['mædmən] n loco.

madness ['mædnɪs] n locura.

magazine [mægə'zi:n] n revista; (MIL: store) almacén m; (of firearm) recámara.

maggot ['mægət] n gusano.

magic ['mædʒɪk] n magia // a mágico; **~al** a mágico; **~ian** [mə'dʒɪʃən] n mago; (conjurer) prestidigitador m.

magistrate ['mædʒɪstreɪt] n juez m/f (municipal).

magnanimous [mæg'nænɪməs] a magnánimo.

magnate ['mægneɪt] n magnate m.

magnet ['mægnɪt] n imán m; **~ic** [-'nɛtɪk] a magnético; **~ism** n magnetismo.

magnification [mægnɪfɪ'keɪʃən] n aumento.

magnificence [mæg'nɪfɪsns] n magnificencia; **magnificent** [-nt] a magnífico.

magnify ['mægnɪfaɪ] vt aumentar; (fig) exagerar; **~ing glass** n lupa.

magnitude ['mægnɪtjuːd] n magnitud f.

magnolia [mæg'nəʊlɪə] n magnolia.

magpie ['mægpaɪ] n urraca.

mahogany [mə'hɒgənɪ] n caoba // cpd de caoba.

maid [meɪd] n criada; **old ~** (pej) solterona.

maiden ['meɪdn] n doncella // a (aunt etc) solterona; (speech, voyage) inaugural; **~ name** n nombre m de soltera.

mail [meɪl] n correo; (letters) cartas fpl // vt (post) echar al correo; (send) mandar por correo; **~box** n (US) buzón m; **~-order** n pedido postal; (business) venta por correo.

maim [meɪm] vt mutilar, lisiar.

main [meɪn] a principal, mayor // n (pipe) cañería maestra; **the ~s** (ELEC) la red eléctrica; **in the ~** en general; **~land** n continente m; **~stay** n (fig) pilar m; **~stream** n corriente f principal.

maintain [meɪn'teɪn] vt mantener; (keep up) conservar (en buen estado); (affirm) sostener; **maintenance** ['meɪntənəns] n mantenimiento.

maisonette [meɪzə'nɛt] n apartamento de dos pisos.

maize [meɪz] n maíz m.

majestic [mə'dʒɛstɪk] a majestuoso; **majesty** ['mædʒɪstɪ] n majestad f.

major ['meɪdʒə*] n (MIL) comandante m // a principal; (MUS) mayor.

Majorca [mə'jɔːkə] n Mallorca.

majority [mə'dʒɒrɪtɪ] n mayoría.

make [meɪk] pt, pp **made** vt hacer; (manufacture) hacer, fabricar; (cause to be): **to ~ sb sad** hacer o poner triste a alguien; (force): **to ~ sb do sth** obligar a uno a hacer algo; (equal): **2 and 2 ~ 4** 2 y 2 son 4 // n marca; **to ~ do with** contentarse con; **to ~ for** vt fus (place) dirigirse a; **to ~ out** vt (decipher) descifrar; (understand) entender; (see) distinguir; **to ~ up** vt (invent) inventar; (parcel) envolver // vi reconciliarse; (with cosmetics) maquillarse; **to ~ up for** vt fus compensar; **~-believe** a fingido; **maker** n fabricante m/f; **~-shift** a improvisado; **~-up** n maquillaje m.

making ['meɪkɪŋ] n (fig): **in the ~** en vías de formación.

malaise [mæ'leɪz] n malestar m.

malaria [mə'lɛərɪə] n malaria.

Malay [mə'leɪ] a, n malayo/a.

Malaysia [mə'leɪzɪə] n Malaysia.

male [meɪl] n (BIOL, ELEC) macho // a (sex, attitude) masculino; (child etc) varón.

malevolent [mə'lɛvələnt] a malévolo.

malfunction [mæl'fʌŋkʃən] n funcionamiento defectuoso.

malice ['mælɪs] n (ill will) malevolencia; (rancour) rencor m; **malicious** [mə'lɪʃəs] a malévolo; rencoroso.

malign [mə'laɪn] vt difamar, calumniar // a maligno.

malignant [mə'lɪgnənt] a (MED) maligno.

malingerer [mə'lɪŋgərə*] n enfermo fingido.

malleable ['mælɪəbl] a maleable.

mallet ['mælɪt] n mazo.

malnutrition [mælnju:'trɪʃən] n desnutrición f.

malpractice [mæl'præktɪs] n falta profesional.

malt [mɔ:lt] n malta.

Malta ['mɔ:ltə] n Malta; **Maltese** [-'ti:z] a, n, pl inv maltés/esa m/f.

maltreat [mæl'tri:t] vt maltratar.

mammal ['mæml] n mamífero.

mammoth ['mæməθ] n mamut m // a gigantesco.

man [mæn], pl **men** n hombre m; (CHESS) pieza // vt (NAUT) tripular; (MIL) guarnecer; **an old ~** un viejo; **~ and wife** marido y mujer.

manacle ['mænəkl] n manilla; **~s** npl grillos mpl.

manage ['mænɪdʒ] vi arreglárselas, ir tirando // vt (be in charge of) dirigir; (person etc) manejar; **~able** a manejable; **~ment** n dirección f, administración f; **manager/ess** n director/a m/f; (SPORT) entrenador/a m/f; **managerial** [-ə'dʒɪərɪəl] a directivo; **managing director** n director m general.

mandarin ['mændərɪn] n (also: **~ orange**) mandarina; (person) mandarín m.

mandate ['mændeɪt] n mandato.

mandatory ['mændətərɪ] a obligatorio.

mandolin(e) ['mændəlɪn] n mandolina.

mane [meɪn] n (of horse) crin f; (of lion) melena.

manfully ['mænfəlɪ] ad violentemente.

mangle ['mæŋgl] vt mutilar, magullar // n rodillo.

mango ['mæŋgəu], pl **~es** n mango.

mangy ['meɪndʒɪ] a roñoso, sarnoso.

manhandle ['mænhændl] vt maltratar.

manhole ['mænhəul] n pozo de visita.

manhood ['mænhud] n edad f viril.

man-hour ['mæn'auə*] n hora-hombre f.

manhunt ['mænhʌnt] n caza de hombre.

mania ['meɪnɪə] n manía; **maniac** ['meɪnɪæk] n maníaco; (fig) maniático.

manicure ['mænɪkjuə*] n manicura // vt (person) hacer la manicura a; **~ set** n estuche m de manicura.

manifest ['mænɪfɛst] vt manifestar, mostrar // a manifiesto; **~ation** [-'teɪʃən] n manifestación f.

manifesto [mænɪ'fɛstəu] n manifiesto.

manipulate [mə'nɪpjuleɪt] vt manipular, manejar.

mankind [mæn'kaɪnd] n la humanidad, el género humano.

manly ['mænlɪ] a varonil.

man-made ['mæn'meɪd] a artificial.

manner ['mænə*] n manera, modo; (behaviour) conducta, manera de ser; (type) clase f; **~s** npl modales mpl, educación f; **bad ~s** mala educación; **~ism** n hábito, peculiaridad f.

manoeuvre, maneuver (US) [mə'nu:və*] vt, vi maniobrar // n maniobra.

manor ['mænə*] n (also: **~ house**) casa solariega.

manpower ['mænpauə*] n mano f de obra.

mansion ['mænʃən] n palacio, casa grande.

manslaughter ['mænslɔ:tə*] n homicidio no premeditado.

mantelpiece ['mæntlpi:s] n repisa, chimenea.

mantle ['mæntl] n manto; (fig) capa.

manual ['mænjuəl] a manual // n manual m; (MUS) teclado.

manufacture [mænju'fæktʃə*] vt fabricar // n fabricación f; **manufacturer** n fabricante m/f.

manure [mə'njuə*] n estiércol m, abono.

manuscript ['mænjuskrɪpt] n manuscrito.

Manx [mæŋks] a de la Isla de Man.

many ['mɛnɪ] det muchos(as) // pron muchos/as; **a great ~** muchísimos, buen número de; **~ a time** muchas veces.

map [mæp] n mapa m // vt trazar el mapa de; **to ~ out** vt proyectar.

maple ['meɪpl] n arce m.

mar [mɑ:*] vt estropear.

marathon ['mærəθən] n maratón m.

marauder [mə'rɔ:də*] n merodeador m; (intruder) intruso.

marble ['mɑ:bl] n mármol m; (toy) canica.

March [mɑ:tʃ] n marzo.

march [mɑ:tʃ] vi (MIL) marchar; (fig) caminar con resolución // n marcha; (demonstration) manifestación f, marcha; **~-past** n desfile m.

mare [mɛə*] n yegua.

margarine [mɑ:dʒə'ri:n] n margarina.

margin ['mɑ:dʒɪn] n margen m; **~al** a marginal.

marigold ['mærɪgəuld] n caléndula.

marijuana [mærɪ'wɑ:nə] n marijuana.

marina [mə'ri:nə] n marina.

marine [mə'ri:n] a marino // n soldado de marina.

marital ['mærɪtl] a matrimonial; **~ status** estado civil.

maritime ['mærɪtaɪm] a marítimo.

marjoram ['mɑ:dʒərəm] n orégano.

mark [mɑ:k] n marca, señal f; (imprint) huella; (stain) mancha; (SCOL) puntuación f, nota; (currency) marco // vt marcar;

manchar; (*SCOL*) calificar; **to ~ time** marcar el paso; **to ~ out** *vt* trazar; **~ed** *a* marcado, acusado; **~er** *n* (*sign*) marcador *m*; (*bookmark*) registro.

market ['mɑ:kɪt] *n* mercado // *vt* (*COMM*) vender; **black ~** mercado negro; **Common M~** Mercado Común; **~ day** *n* día de mercado; **~ garden** *n* (*Brit*) huerto; **~ing** *n* márketing *m*, mercadotecnia; **~-place** *n* mercado; **~ research** *n* análisis *m inv* de mercados.

marksman ['mɑ:ksmən] *n* tirador *m*; **~ship** *n* puntería.

marmalade ['mɑ:məleɪd] *n* mermelada (de naranjas).

maroon [mə'ru:n] *vt* (*fig*): **to be ~ed** (*shipwrecked*) naufragarse; (*fig*) quedar abandonado // *a* marrón.

marquee [mɑ:'ki:] *n* entoldado.

marquess, marquis ['mɑ:kwɪs] *n* marqués *m*.

marriage ['mærɪdʒ] *n* (*state*) matrimonio; (*wedding*) boda; (*act*) casamiento; **~ bureau** *n* agencia matrimonial; **~ certificate** *n* partida de casamiento.

married ['mærɪd] *a* casado; (*life, love*) conyugal.

marrow ['mærəʊ] *n* médula; (*vegetable*) calabacín *m*.

marry ['mærɪ] *vt* casarse con; (*subj: father, priest etc*) casar // *vi* (*also:* **get married**) casarse.

marsh [mɑ:ʃ] *n* pantano; (*salt* ~) marisma.

marshal ['mɑ:ʃl] *n* (*MIL*) mariscal *m*; (*at sports meeting etc*) oficial *m* // *vt* (*facts*) ordenar; (*soldiers*) formar.

marshmallow [mɑ:ʃ'mæləʊ] *n* malvavisco.

marshy ['mɑ:ʃɪ] *a* pantanoso.

martial ['mɑ:ʃl] *a* marcial; **~ law** *n* ley *f* marcial.

martyr ['mɑ:tə*] *n* mártir *m/f* // *vt* martirizar; **~dom** *n* martirio.

marvel ['mɑ:vl] *n* maravilla, prodigio // *vi*: **to ~ (at)** maravillarse (de); **~lous, ~ous** (*US*) *a* maravilloso.

Marxism ['mɑ:ksɪzəm] *n* marxismo; **Marxist** [-sɪst] *a, n* marxista *m/f*.

marzipan ['mɑ:zɪpæn] *n* mazapán *m*.

mascara [mæs'kɑ:rə] *n* rímel *m*.

mascot ['mæskət] *n* mascota.

masculine ['mæskjʊlɪn] *a* masculino; **masculinity** [-'lɪnɪtɪ] *n* masculinidad *f*.

mash [mæʃ] *n* (*mix*) mezcla; (*pulp*) amasijo; **~ed potatoes** puré *m* de patatas.

mask [mɑ:sk] *n* máscara // *vt* enmascarar.

masochist ['mæsəʊkɪst] *n* masoquista *m/f*.

mason ['meɪsn] *n* (*also:* **stone~**) albañil *m*; (*also:* **free~**) masón *m*; **~ic** [mə'sɒnɪk] *a* masónico; **~ry** *n* masonería; (*building*) mampostería.

masquerade [mæskə'reɪd] *n* baile *m* de máscaras; (*fig*) farsa // *vi*: **to ~ as** disfrazarse de, hacerse pasar por.

mass [mæs] *n* (*people*) muchedumbre *f*; (*PHYSICS*) masa; (*REL*) misa; (*great quantity*)

montón *m* // *vi* reunirse; (*MIL*) concentrarse; **the ~es** las masas.

massacre ['mæsəkə*] *n* masacre *f* // *vt* masacrar.

massage ['mæsɑ:ʒ] *n* masaje *m* // *vt* dar masaje a.

masseur [mæ'sɜ:*] *n* masajista *m*; **masseuse** [-'sɜ:z] *n* masajista *f*.

massive ['mæsɪv] *a* (*solid*) sólido; (*head etc*) grande; (*support, intervention*) masivo.

mass media ['mæs'mi:dɪə] *npl* medios *mpl* de comunicación masiva.

mass-production ['mæsprə'dʌkʃən] *n* fabricación *f* en serie.

mast [mɑ:st] *n* (*NAUT*) mástil *m*; (*RADIO etc*) torre *f*.

master ['mɑ:stə*] *n* maestro; (*landowner*) señor *m*, amo; (*in secondary school*) profesor *m*; (*title for boys*): **M~ X** Señorito X // *vt* dominar; (*learn*) aprender a fondo; **~ key** *n* llave *f* maestra; **~ly** *a* magistral; **~mind** *n* inteligencia superior // *vt* dirigir, planear; **M~ of Arts** *n* Licenciado en Letras; **~piece** *n* obra maestra; **~ plan** *n* plan *m* rector; **~ stroke** *n* golpe *m* maestro; **~y** *n* maestría.

masturbate ['mæstəbeɪt] *vi* masturbarse; **masturbation** [-'beɪʃən] *n* masturbación *f*.

mat [mæt] *n* estera; (*also:* **door~**) felpudo // *a* = **matt**.

match [mætʃ] *n* cerilla; (*game*) partido; (*fig*) igual *m/f* // *vt* emparejar; (*go well with*) hacer juego con; (*equal*) igualar, ser igual a // *vi* hacer juego; **to be a good ~** hacer una buena pareja; **~box** *n* caja de cerillas; **~ing** *a* que hace juego; **~less** *a* sin par, incomparable.

mate [meɪt] *n* compañero; (*assistant*) ayudante *m/f*; (*CHESS*) mate *m*; (*in merchant navy*) segundo de a bordo // *vi* acoplarse, parearse // *vt* acoplar, parear.

material [mə'tɪərɪəl] *n* (*substance*) materia; (*equipment*) material *m*; (*cloth*) tela, tejido; (*data*) datos *mpl* // *a* material; (*important*) importante; **~s** *npl* materiales *mpl*; **~istic** [-ə'lɪstɪk] *a* materialista; **~ize** *vi* materializarse.

maternal [mə'tɜ:nl] *a* maternal.

maternity [mə'tɜ:nɪtɪ] *n* maternidad *f*; **~ dress** *n* vestido premamá; **~ hospital** *n* hospital *m* de maternidad.

mathematical [mæθə'mætɪkl] *a* matemático; **mathematician** [-mə'tɪʃən] *n* matemático; **mathematics** [-tɪks], **maths** [mæθs] *n* matemáticas *fpl*.

matinée ['mætɪneɪ] *n* función *f* de tarde.

mating ['meɪtɪŋ] *n* apareamiento; **~ call** *n* llamada del macho; **~ season** *n* época de celo.

matriarchal [meɪtrɪ'ɑ:kl] *a* matriarcal.

matrices ['meɪtrɪsi:z] *pl of* **matrix.**

matrimonial [mætrɪ'məʊnɪəl] *a* matrimonial.

matrimony ['mætrɪmənɪ] *n* matrimonio.

matrix ['meɪtrɪks], *pl* **matrices** *n* matriz *f*.

matron ['meɪtrən] n (in hospital) enfermera jefe; (in school) ama de llaves; ~ly a de matrona; (fig: figure) corpulento.

matt [mæt] a mate.

matted ['mætɪd] a enmarañado.

matter ['mætə*] n cuestión f, asunto; (PHYSICS) sustancia, materia; (content) contenido; (MED: pus) pus m // vi importar; **it doesn't** ~ no importa; **what's the** ~? ¿qué pasa?; **no** ~ **what** pase lo que pase; **as a** ~ **of course** por rutina; **as a** ~ **of fact** de hecho; ~**-of-fact** a prosaico, práctico.

mattress ['mætrɪs] n colchón m.

mature [mə'tjuə*] a maduro // vi madurar; **maturity** n madurez f.

maudlin ['mɔːdlɪn] a llorón(ona).

maul [mɔːl] vt magullar.

mausoleum [mɔːsə'lɪəm] n mausoleo.

mauve [məuv] a de color malva.

maxim ['mæksɪm] n máxima.

maxima ['mæksɪmə] pl of **maximum**.

maximum ['mæksɪməm] a máximo // n, pl **maxima** máximo.

May [meɪ] n mayo.

may [meɪ] vi (conditional: **might**) (indicating possibility): **he** ~ **come** puede que venga; (be allowed to): ~ **I smoke?** ¿puedo fumar?; (wishes): ~ **God bless you!** que Dios le bendiga.

maybe ['meɪbiː] ad quizá(s).

mayday ['meɪdeɪ] n S.O.S. m (llamada de socorro internacional).

mayhem ['meɪhɛm] n mutilación f criminal.

mayonnaise [meɪə'neɪz] n mayonesa.

mayor [mɛə*] n alcalde m; ~**ess** n alcaldesa.

maypole ['meɪpəul] n mayo.

maze [meɪz] n laberinto.

M.D. abbr of **Doctor of Medicine**.

me [miː] pron me; (stressed, after prep) mí; **with** ~ conmigo; **it's** ~ soy yo.

meadow ['mɛdəu] n prado, pradera.

meagre, meager (US) ['miːgə*] a escaso, pobre.

meal [miːl] n comida; (flour) harina; ~ **time** n hora de comer.

mean [miːn] a (with money) tacaño; (unkind) mezquino, malo; (shabby) humilde, vil; (of poor quality) inferior; (average) medio // vt, pt, pp **meant** (signify) querer decir, significar; (intend): **to** ~ **to do sth** pensar o pretender hacer algo // n medio, término medio; ~**s** npl medio sg, manera sg; (resource) recursos mpl, medios mpl; **by** ~**s of** mediante, por medio de; **by all** ~**s!** ¡naturalmente!, ¡claro que sí!; **do you** ~ **it?** ¿lo dices en serio?; **what do you** ~? ¿qué quiere decir?

meander [mɪ'ændə*] vi (river) serpentear; (person) vagar.

meaning ['miːnɪŋ] n significado, sentido; ~**ful** a significativo; ~**less** a sin sentido.

meanness ['miːnnɪs] n (with money)

tacañería; (shabbiness) vileza, bajeza; (unkindness) maldad f, mezquindad f.

meant [mɛnt] pt, pp of **mean**.

meantime ['miːntaɪm], **meanwhile** ['miːnwaɪl] ad (also: **in the** ~) mientras tanto.

measles ['miːzlz] n sarampión m; **German** ~ rubéola.

measly ['miːzlɪ] a (col) miserable.

measure ['mɛʒə*] vt medir; (for clothes etc) tomar las medidas a; (consider) pesar // vi medir // n medida; (ruler) regla; ~**d** a moderado; (tone) mesurado; ~**ments** npl medidas fpl.

meat [miːt] n carne f; **cold** ~ fiambre m; ~**ball** n albóndiga; ~ **pie** n pastel m de carne; ~**y** a carnoso; (fig) sustancioso.

mechanic [mɪ'kænɪk] n mecánico; ~**s** n mecánica // npl mecanismo sg; ~**al** a mecánico.

mechanism ['mɛkənɪzəm] n mecanismo.

mechanization [mɛkənaɪ'zeɪʃən] n mecanización f.

medal ['mɛdl] n medalla; ~**lion** [mɪ'dælɪən] n medallón m; ~**list**, ~**ist** (US) n (SPORT) ganador/a m/f.

meddle ['mɛdl] vi: **to** ~ **in** entrometerse en; **to** ~ **with sth** manosear algo; ~**some** a entrometido.

media ['miːdɪə] npl medios mpl de comunicación.

mediaeval [mɛdɪ'iːvl] a = **medieval**.

mediate ['miːdɪeɪt] vi mediar; **mediation** [-'eɪʃən] n mediación f; **mediator** n intermediario, mediador/a m/f.

medical ['mɛdɪkl] a médico // n reconocimiento médico.

medicated ['mɛdɪkeɪtɪd] a medicinal.

medicinal [mɛ'dɪsɪnl] a medicinal.

medicine ['mɛdsɪn] n medicina; (drug) medicamento; ~ **chest** n botiquín m.

medieval [mɛdɪ'iːvl] a medieval.

mediocre [miːdɪ'əukə*] a mediocre; **mediocrity** [-'ɔkrɪtɪ] n mediocridad f.

meditate ['mɛdɪteɪt] vi meditar; **meditation** [-'teɪʃən] n meditación f.

Mediterranean [mɛdɪtə'reɪnɪən] a mediterráneo; **the** ~ **(Sea)** el (Mar) Mediterráneo.

medium ['miːdɪəm] a mediano, regular // n (pl **media**: **means**) medio; (pl **mediums**: person) médium m/f.

medley ['mɛdlɪ] n mezcla; (MUS) popurrí m.

meek [miːk] a manso, dócil.

meet [miːt] pt, pp **met** vt (gen) encontrar; (accidentally) encontrarse con, tropezar con; (by arrangement) reunirse con; (for the first time) conocer; (go and fetch) ir a buscar; (opponent) enfrentarse con; (obligations) cumplir // vi encontrarse; (in session) reunirse; (join: objects) unirse; (get to know) conocerse; **to** ~ **with** vt fus reunirse con; (face: difficulty) tropezar con; ~**ing** n encuentro; (session: of club etc) reunión f; (interview) entrevista; (COMM) junta, sesión f; (POL) mitin m.

megalomaniac [mɛgələu'meɪnɪæk] a, n megalómano/a.

megaphone ['mɛgəfəun] n megáfono.

melancholy ['mɛlənkɒlɪ] n melancolía // a melancólico.

melee ['mɛleɪ] n refriega.

mellow ['mɛləu] a (sound) dulce; (colour) suave; (fruit) maduro // vi (person) madurar.

melodious [mɪ'ləudɪəs] a melodioso.

melodrama ['mɛləudrɑːmə] n melodrama m.

melody ['mɛlədɪ] n melodía.

melon ['mɛlən] n melón m.

melt [mɛlt] vi (metal) fundirse; (snow) derretirse; (fig) ablandarse // vt (also: ~ **down**) fundir; **to** ~ **away** vi desvanecerse; ~**ing point** n punto de fusión; ~**ing pot** n (fig) crisol m.

member ['mɛmbə*] n (gen) miembro; (of club) socio; **M~ of Parliament (M.P.)** diputado; ~**ship** n (members) número de miembros; **to seek** ~**ship of** pedir el ingreso a; ~**ship card** carnet m de socio.

membrane ['mɛmbreɪn] n membrana.

memento [mə'mɛntəu] n recuerdo.

memo ['mɛməu] n apunte m, nota.

memoirs ['mɛmwɑːz] npl memorias fpl.

memorable ['mɛmərəbl] a memorable.

memorandum [mɛmə'rændəm], pl **-da** [-də] n apunte m, nota; (POL) memorándum m.

memorial [mɪ'mɔːrɪəl] n monumento conmemorativo // a conmemorativo.

memorize ['mɛməraɪz] vt aprender de memoria.

memory ['mɛmərɪ] n memoria; (recollection) recuerdo.

men [mɛn] pl of **man.**

menace ['mɛnəs] n amenaza // vt amenazar; **menacing** a amenazador(a).

menagerie [mɪ'nædʒərɪ] n casa de fieras.

mend [mɛnd] vt reparar, arreglar; (darn) zurcir // vi reponerse // n (gen) remiendo; (darn) zurcido; **to be on the** ~ ir mejorando; ~**ing** n reparación f; (clothes) ropa por remendar.

menial ['miːnɪəl] a doméstico; (pej) bajo // n criado.

meningitis [mɛnɪn'dʒaɪtɪs] n meningitis f.

menopause ['mɛnəupɔːz] n menopausia.

menstruate ['mɛnstrueɪt] vi menstruar; **menstruation** [-'eɪʃən] n menstruación f.

mental ['mɛntl] a mental; ~**ity** [-'tælɪtɪ] n mentalidad f.

mention ['mɛnʃən] n mención f // vt mencionar; (speak of) hablar de; **don't** ~ **it!** ¡de nada!

menu ['mɛnjuː] n (set ~) menú m; (printed) carta.

mercenary ['mɔːsɪnərɪ] a, n mercenario.

merchandise ['mɔːtʃəndaɪz] n mercancías fpl.

merchant ['mɔːtʃənt] n comerciante m/f; ~ **bank** n banco comercial; ~ **navy** n marina mercante.

merciful ['mɔːsɪful] a compasivo; (fortunate) afortunado.

merciless ['mɔːsɪlɪs] a despiadado.

mercury ['mɔːkjurɪ] n mercurio.

mercy ['mɔːsɪ] n compasión f; (REL) misericordia; **at the** ~ **of** a la merced de.

mere [mɪə*] a simple, mero; ~**ly** ad simplemente, sólo.

merge [mɔːdʒ] vt (join) unir; (mix) mezclar; (fuse) fundir // vi unirse; (COMM) fusionarse; **merger** n (COMM) fusión f.

meridian [mə'rɪdɪən] n meridiano.

meringue [mə'ræŋ] n merengue m.

merit ['mɛrɪt] n mérito // vt merecer.

mermaid ['mɔːmeɪd] n sirena.

merriment ['mɛrɪmənt] n alegría.

merry ['mɛrɪ]38 a alegre; ~**-go-round** n tiovivo.

mesh [mɛʃ] n malla; (TECH) engranaje m // vi (gears) engranar.

mesmerize ['mɛzməraɪz] vt hipnotizar.

mess [mɛs] n (gen) confusión f; (of objects) revoltijo; (tangle) lío; (MIL) comedor m; **to** ~ **about** vi (col) perder el tiempo; (pass the time) entretenerse; **to** ~ **about with** vt fus (col) (play with) divertirse con; (handle) manosear; **to** ~ **up** vt (disarrange) desordenar; (spoil) estropear; (dirty) ensuciar.

message ['mɛsɪdʒ] n recado, mensaje m.

messenger ['mɛsɪndʒə*] n mensajero/a.

messy ['mɛsɪ] a (dirty) sucio; (untidy) desordenado.

met [mɛt] pt, pp of **meet.**

metabolism [mɛ'tæbəlɪzəm] n metabolismo.

metal ['mɛtl] n metal m; ~**lic** [-'tælɪk] a metálico; ~**lurgy** [-'tælədʒɪ] n metalurgia.

metamorphosis [mɛtə'mɔːfəsɪs], pl **-ses** [-siːz] n metamorfosis f inv.

metaphor ['mɛtəfə*] n metáfora.

metaphysics [mɛtə'fɪzɪks] n metafísica.

mete [miːt]: **to** ~ **out** vt fus (gen) repartir; (punishment) imponer.

meteor ['miːtɪə*] n meteoro.

meteorological [miːtɪərə'lɒdʒɪkl] a meteorológico; **meteorology** [-'rɔlədʒɪ] n meteorología.

meter ['miːtə*] n (instrument) contador m; (US) = **metre.**

method ['mɛθəd] n método; ~**ical** [mɪ'θɒdɪkl] a metódico.

Methodist ['mɛθədɪst] a, n metodista m/f.

meths [mɛθs], **methylated spirit** ['mɛθɪleɪtɪd-] n alcohol m metilado o desnaturalizado.

meticulous [mɛ'tɪkjuləs] a meticuloso.

metre, meter (US) ['miːtə*] n metro.

metric ['mɛtrɪk] a métrico.

metronome ['mɛtrənəum] n metrónomo.

metropolis [mɪ'trɒpəlɪs] n metrópoli f.

mettle ['mɛtl] n (spirit) valor m, ánimo; (tone) temple m.

mew [mjuː] vi (cat) maullar.

mews [mjuːz] n: ~ **cottage** casa

acondicionada en antiguos establos o cocheras.

Mexican ['mɛksɪkən] *a, n* mejicano/a, mexicano/a (*AM*).

Mexico ['mɛksɪkəu] *n* Méjico, México (*AM*).

mezzanine ['mɛtsəniːn] *n* entresuelo.

miaow [miː'au] *vi* maullar.

mice [maɪs] *pl of* **mouse**.

microbe ['maɪkrəub] *n* microbio.

micro... [maɪkrəu] *pref* micro...; ~**film** *n* microfilm *m*; ~**phone** *n* micrófono; ~**processor** *n* microprocesador *m*; ~**scope** *n* microscopio; ~**scopic** [-'skɔpɪk] *a* microscópico; ~**wave** *a* de microonda.

mid [mɪd] *a*: **in** ~ **May** a mediados de mayo; **in** ~ **afternoon** a media tarde; **in** ~ **air** en el aire; ~**day** *n* mediodía *m*.

middle ['mɪdl] *n* medio, centro; (*half*) mitad *f*; (*waist*) cintura // *a* medio; (*quantity, size*) mediano; ~-**aged** *a* de mediana edad; **the M**~ **Ages** *npl* la Edad Media; ~-**class** *a* de clase media; **M**~ **East** *n* Oriente *m* Medio; ~**man** *n* intermediario; ~ **name** *n* segundo nombre.

middling ['mɪdlɪŋ] *a* mediano.

midge [mɪdʒ] *n* mosca.

midget ['mɪdʒɪt] *n* enano // *a* minúsculo.

Midlands ['mɪdləndz] *npl* la región central de Inglaterra.

midnight ['mɪdnaɪt] *n* medianoche *f*.

midriff ['mɪdrɪf] *n* diafragma *m*.

midst [mɪdst] *n*: **in the** ~ **of** entre, en medio de.

midsummer [mɪd'sʌmə*] *n*: **a** ~ **day** un día de pleno verano.

midway [mɪd'weɪ] *a, ad*: ~ (**between**) a mitad de camino, a medio camino (entre).

midweek [mɪd'wiːk] *ad* entre semana.

midwife ['mɪdwaɪf], *pl* -**wives** [-waɪvz] *n* comadrona, partera; ~**ry** [-wɪfərɪ] *n* partería.

midwinter [mɪd'wɪntə*] *n*: **in** ~ en pleno invierno.

might [maɪt] *vb*: **he** ~ **be there** podría estar allí, puede que está allí; **I** ~ **as well go** más vale que vaya; **you** ~ **like to try** podría intentar // *n* fuerza, poder *m*; ~**y** *a* fuerte, poderoso.

migraine ['miːgreɪn] *n* jaqueca.

migrant ['maɪgrənt] *n* (*bird*) ave *f* migratoria; (*person*) emigrante *m/f*; (*fig*) nómada *m/f* // *a* migratorio; (*worker*) emigrante.

migrate [maɪ'greɪt] *vi* emigrar; **migration** [-'greɪʃən] *n* emigración *f*.

mike [maɪk] *n abbr of* **microphone** micro.

mild [maɪld] *a* (*character*) pacífico; (*climate*) templado; (*slight*) ligero; (*taste*) suave; (*illness*) benigno, leve.

mildew ['mɪldjuː] *n* moho.

mildness ['maɪldnɪs] *n* (*softness*) suavidad *f*; (*gentleness*) dulzura; (*quiet character*) apacibilidad *f*.

mile [maɪl] *n* milla; ~**age** *n* número de

millas; (*AUT*) kilometraje *m*; ~**stone** *n* mojón *m*.

milieu ['miːljə:] *n* medio, medio ambiente.

militant ['mɪlɪtnt] *a, n* militante *m/f*.

military ['mɪlɪtərɪ] *a* militar.

militate ['mɪlɪteɪt] *vi*: **to** ~ **against** militar contra.

militia [mɪ'lɪʃə] *n* milicia.

milk [mɪlk] *n* leche *f* // *vt* (*cow*) ordeñar; (*fig*) chupar; ~**man** *n* lechero; ~ **shake** *n* batido de leche; ~**y** *a* lechoso; **M**~**y Way** *n* Vía Láctea.

mill [mɪl] *n* (*windmill etc*) molino; (*coffee* ~) molinillo; (*factory*) fábrica; (*spinning* ~) hilandería // *vt* moler // *vi* (*also*: ~ *about*) moverse por todas partes, apiñarse.

millennium [mɪ'lɛnɪəm], *pl* ~**s** *or* -**ia** [-nɪə] *n* milenio, milenario.

miller ['mɪlə*] *n* molinero.

millet ['mɪlɪt] *n* mijo.

milli... ['mɪlɪ] *pref*: ~**gram(me)** *n* miligramo; ~**litre** *n* mililitro; ~**metre** *n* milímetro.

milliner ['mɪlɪnə*] *n* modista de sombreros; ~**y** *n* sombrerería.

million ['mɪljən] *n* millón *m*; **a** ~ **times** un millón de veces; ~**aire** *n* millonario.

millstone ['mɪlstəun] *n* piedra de molino.

milometer [maɪ'lɔmɪtə*] *n* cuenta-kilómetros *m inv*.

mime [maɪm] *n* mímica; (*actor*) mimo // *vt* remedar // *vi* actuar de mimo.

mimic ['mɪmɪk] *n* imitador/a *m/f* // *a* mímico // *vt* remedar, imitar; ~**ry** *n* imitación *f*.

min. *abbr of* **minute(s)**; **minimum**.

minaret [mɪnə'rɛt] *n* alminar *m*.

mince [mɪns] *vt* picar // *vi* (*in walking*) andar con pasos menudos // *n* (*CULIN*) carne *f* picada, picadillo; ~**meat** *n* conserva de fruta picada; ~ **pie** *n* empanadilla rellena de fruta picada; **mincer** *n* máquina de picar carne.

mind [maɪnd] *n* (*gen*) mente *f*; (*intellect*) inteligencia; (*contrasted with matter*) espíritu // *vt* (*attend to, look after*) ocuparse de, cuidar; (*be careful of*) tener cuidado con; (*object to*): **I don't** ~ **the noise** no me importa el ruido; **it is on my** ~ me preocupa; **to my** ~ en mi opinión; **to be out of one's** ~ estar fuera de juicio; **never** ~! ¡es igual!, ¡no importa!; (*don't worry*) ¡no se preocupe!; **to bear sth in** ~ tomar o tener algo en cuenta; **to make up one's** ~ decidirse; '~ **the step'** cuidado con el escalón; ~**ful** *a*: ~**ful of** consciente de; ~**less** *a* estúpido.

mine [maɪn] *pron* (el) mío/(la) mía *etc* // *a*: **this book is** ~ este libro es mío // *n* mina // *vt* (*coal*) extraer, explotar; (*ship, beach*) minar; ~**field** *n* campo de minas; **miner** *n* minero.

mineral ['mɪnərəl] *a* mineral // *n* mineral *m*; ~**s** *npl* (*soft drinks*) aguas *fpl* minerales, gaseosa *sg*.

minesweeper ['maɪnswiːpə*] n dragaminas m inv.

mingle ['mɪŋgl] vi: to ~ with mezclarse con.

mingy ['mɪndʒɪ] a (col) tacaño.

miniature ['mɪnətʃə*] a (en) miniatura // n miniatura.

minibus ['mɪnɪbʌs] n microbús m.

minicab ['mɪnɪkæb] n microtaxi m.

minim ['mɪnɪm] n (MUS) blanca.

minimal ['mɪnɪml] a mínimo.

minimize ['mɪnɪmaɪz] vt minimizar.

minimum ['mɪnɪməm] n, pl **minima** ['mɪnɪmə] mínimo // a mínimo.

mining ['maɪnɪŋ] n explotación f minera // a minero.

miniskirt ['mɪnɪskɜːt] n minifalda.

minister ['mɪnɪstə*] n (POL) ministro; (REL) pastor m // vi atender; ~ial [-'tɪərɪəl] a (POL) ministerial.

ministry ['mɪnɪstrɪ] n ministerio.

mink [mɪŋk] n visón m; ~ coat n abrigo de visón.

minnow ['mɪnəu] n pececillo (de agua dulce).

minor ['maɪnə*] a menor; (unimportant) sin importancia; (inferior) secundario; (MUS) menor // n (LAW) menor m/f de edad.

minority [maɪ'nɔrɪtɪ] n minoría; (age) minoridad f.

minster ['mɪnstə*] n catedral f.

minstrel ['mɪnstrəl] n juglar m.

mint [mɪnt] n (plant) menta, hierbabuena; (sweet) caramelo de menta // vt (coins) acuñar; **the (Royal) M**~ la (Real) Casa de la Moneda; **in ~ condition** en perfecto estado.

minuet [mɪnju'et] n minué m.

minus ['maɪnəs] n (also: ~ sign) signo de menos // prep menos.

minute ['mɪnɪt] n minuto; (fig) momento; ~s npl actas fpl // a [maɪ'njuːt] diminuto; (search) minucioso; **at the last** ~ a última hora.

miracle ['mɪrəkl] n milagro; **miraculous** [mɪ'rækjuləs] a milagroso.

mirage ['mɪrɑːʒ] n espejismo.

mirror ['mɪrə*] n espejo; (in car) retrovisor m // vt reflejar.

mirth [mɜːθ] n alegría; (laughter) risa, risas fpl.

misadventure [mɪsəd'ventʃə*] n desgracia, accidente m.

misanthropist [mɪ'zænθrəpɪst] n misántropo.

misapprehension ['mɪsæprɪ'henʃən] n equivocación f.

misbehave [mɪsbɪ'heɪv] vi portarse mal; **misbehaviour** n mala conducta.

miscalculate [mɪs'kælkjuleɪt] vt calcular mal; **miscalculation** [-'leɪʃən] n error m (de cálculo).

miscarriage ['mɪskærɪdʒ] n (MED) aborto; (failure) fracaso; ~ **of justice** error m judicial.

miscellaneous [mɪsɪ'leɪnɪəs] a vario(s), diverso(s).

mischance [mɪs'tʃɑːns] n desgracia, mala suerte f.

mischief ['mɪstʃɪf] n (naughtiness) travesura; (harm) mal m, daño; (maliciousness) malicia; **mischievous** [-ʃɪvəs] a travieso; dañoso; (playful) malicioso.

misconception ['mɪskən'sepʃən] n concepto erróneo, equivocación f.

misconduct [mɪs'kɔndʌkt] n mala conducta; **professional** ~ falta profesional.

miscount [mɪs'kaunt] vt, vi contar mal.

misdeed [mɪs'diːd] n delito.

misdemeanour, misdemeanor (US) [mɪsdɪ'miːnə*] n delito, ofensa.

misdirect [mɪsdɪ'rekt] vt (person) informar mal; (letter) poner señas incorrectas en.

miser ['maɪzə*] n avaro/a.

miserable ['mɪzərəbl] a (unhappy) triste, desgraciado; (wretched) miserable; (despicable) despreciable.

miserly ['maɪzəlɪ] a avariento, tacaño.

misery ['mɪzərɪ] n (unhappiness) tristeza, sufrimiento; (wretchedness) miseria, desdicha.

misfire [mɪs'faɪə*] vi fallar.

misfit ['mɪsfɪt] n (person) inadaptado/a, desplazado/a.

misfortune [mɪs'fɔːtʃən] n desgracia.

misgiving(s) [mɪs'gɪvɪŋ(z)] n(pl) (mistrust) recelo; (apprehension) presentimiento.

misguided [mɪs'gaɪdɪd] a equivocado.

mishandle [mɪs'hændl] vt (treat roughly) maltratar; (mismanage) manejar mal.

mishap ['mɪshæp] n desgracia, contratiempo.

mishear [mɪs'hɪə*] (irg: like **hear**) vt oír mal.

misinform [mɪsɪn'fɔːm] vt informar mal.

misinterpret [mɪsɪn'tɜːprɪt] vt interpretar mal.

misjudge [mɪs'dʒʌdʒ] vt juzgar mal.

mislay [mɪs'leɪ] (irg: like **lay**) vt extraviar, perder.

mislead [mɪs'liːd] (irg: like **lead**) vt llevar a conclusiones erróneas; ~ing a engañoso, erróneo.

mismanage [mɪs'mænɪdʒ] vt administrar mal; ~ment n mala administración f.

misnomer [mɪs'nəumə*] n nombre m inapropiado o equivocado.

misogynist [mɪ'sɔdʒɪnɪst] n misógino.

misplace [mɪs'pleɪs] vt (lose) extraviar, perder.

misprint ['mɪsprɪnt] n errata, error m de imprenta.

mispronounce [mɪsprə'nauns] vt pronunciar mal.

misread [mɪs'riːd] (irg: like **read**) vt leer mal.

misrepresent [mɪsrɛprɪ'zɛnt] vt falsificar.

miss [mɪs] vt (train etc) perder; (fail to hit) errar, fallar; (regret the absence of): **I ~ him** (yo) le echo de menos o a faltar // vi fallar // n (shot) tiro fallido o perdido; (fig): **that was a near ~** (near accident) faltó poco para que chocáramos; **to ~ out** vt omitir.

Miss [mɪs] n Señorita.

missal ['mɪsl] n misal m.

misshapen [mɪs'ʃeɪpən] a deforme.

missile ['mɪsaɪl] n (AVIAT) mísil m; (object thrown) proyectil m.

missing ['mɪsɪŋ] a (pupil) ausente; (thing) perdido; (MIL) desaparecido; **to go ~** desaparecer.

mission ['mɪʃən] n misión f; **~ary** n misionero.

misspent ['mɪs'spɛnt] a: **his ~ youth** su juventud disipada.

mist [mɪst] n (light) neblina; (heavy) niebla; (at sea) bruma // vi (also: **~ over, ~ up**) empañarse.

mistake [mɪs'teɪk] n error m // vt (irg: like take) entender mal, equivocarse sobre; **to ~ A for B** confundir A con B; **mistaken** a (idea etc) equivocado; **to be mistaken** equivocarse, engañarse.

mister ['mɪstə*] n (col) señor m; see **Mr.**

mistletoe ['mɪsltəu] n muérdago.

mistook [mɪs'tuk] pt of **mistake**.

mistreat [mɪs'triːt] vt maltratar; **~ment** n maltrato.

mistress ['mɪstrɪs] n (lover) amante f; (of house) señora (de la casa); (in primary school) maestra; (in secondary school) profesora; see **Mrs.**

mistrust [mɪs'trʌst] vt desconfiar de, dudar de.

misty ['mɪstɪ] a nebuloso, brumoso; (day) de niebla; (glasses) empañado.

misunderstand [mɪsʌndə'stænd] vt, vi (irg: like **understand**) vt, vi entender mal; **~ing** n malentendido.

misuse [mɪs'juːs] n mal uso; (of power) abuso // vt [mɪs'juːz] abusar de; (funds) malversar.

mitigate ['mɪtɪgeɪt] vt mitigar.

mitre, miter (US) ['maɪtə*] n mitra; (CARPENTRY) inglete m.

mitt(en) ['mɪt(n)] n mitón m.

mix [mɪks] vt (gen) mezclar; (combine) unir // vi mezclarse; (people) llevarse bien // n mezcla; **to ~ up** vt mezclar; (confuse) confundir; **~ed** a (assorted) variado, surtido; (school etc) mixto; **~ed-up** a (confused) confuso, revuelto; **~er** n (for food) licuadora; (person) persona sociable; **~ture** n mezcla; **~-up** n confusión f.

moan [məun] n gemido // vi gemir; (col: complain): **to ~ (about)** quejarse (de).

moat [məut] n foso.

mob [mɔb] n multitud f; (pej): **the ~** el populacho // vt acosar.

mobile ['məubaɪl] a móvil // n móvil m; **~ home** n caravana.

mobility [məu'bɪlɪtɪ] n movilidad f.

mobilize ['məubɪlaɪz] vt movilizar.

moccasin ['mɔkəsɪn] n mocasín m.

mock [mɔk] vt (make ridiculous) ridiculizar; (laugh at) burlarse de // a fingido; **~ery** n burla; **~ing** a burlón(ona); **~-up** n maqueta.

mode [məud] n modo; (fashion) moda.

model ['mɔdl] n (gen) modelo; (ARCH) maqueta; (person: for fashion, ART) modelo m/f // a modelo // vt modelar // vi servir de modelo; **~ railway** ferrocarril m de juguete; **to ~ clothes** pasar modelos, ser modelo.

moderate ['mɔdərət] a, n moderado/a // (vb: [-reɪt]) vi moderarse, calmarse // vt moderar; **moderation** [-'reɪʃən] n moderación f.

modern ['mɔdən] a moderno; **~ize** vt modernizar.

modest ['mɔdɪst] a modesto; **~y** n modestia.

modicum ['mɔdɪkəm] n: **a ~ of** un mínimo de.

modification [mɔdɪfɪ'keɪʃən] n modificación f; **modify** ['mɔdɪfaɪ] vt modificar.

modulation [mɔdju'leɪʃən] n modulación f.

mohair ['məuheə*] n moer m.

moist [mɔɪst] a húmedo; **~en** ['mɔɪsn] vt humedecer; **~ure** ['mɔɪstʃə*] n humedad f; **~urizer** ['mɔɪstʃəraɪzə*] n crema hidratante.

molar ['məulə*] n muela.

molasses [məu'læsɪz] n melaza.

mole [məul] n (animal) topo; (spot) lunar m.

molecule ['mɔlɪkjuːl] n molécula.

molehill ['məulhɪl] n topera.

molest [məu'lɛst] vt importunar.

mollusc ['mɔləsk] n molusco.

mollycoddle ['mɔlɪkɔdl] vt mimar.

molten ['məultən] a fundido; (lava) líquido.

moment ['məumənt] n momento; **~ary** a momentáneo; **~ous** [-'mɛntəs] a trascendental, importante.

momentum [məu'mɛntəm] n momento; (fig) ímpetu m; **to gather ~** cobrar velocidad.

monarch ['mɔnək] n monarca m/f; **~y** n monarquía.

monastery ['mɔnəstərɪ] n monasterio.

monastic [mə'næstɪk] a monástico.

Monday ['mʌndeɪ] n lunes m.

monetary ['mʌnɪtərɪ] a monetario.

money ['mʌnɪ] n dinero; **to make ~** ganar dinero; **~lender** n prestamista m/f; **~ order** n giro.

mongol ['mɔŋgəl] a, n (MED) mongólico.

mongrel ['mʌŋgrəl] n (dog) perro cruzado.

monitor ['mɔnɪtə*] n (SCOL) monitor m; (also: **television ~**) receptor m de control // vt controlar.

monk [mʌŋk] n monje m.

monkey ['mʌŋkɪ] n mono; **~ nut** n

cacahuete *m*; ~ **wrench** *n* llave *f* inglesa.
mono... [ˈmɒnəu] *pref*: ~**chrome** *a* monocromo.
monocle [ˈmɒnəkl] *n* monóculo.
monogram [ˈmɒnəgræm] *n* monograma *m*.
monologue [ˈmɒnəlɒg] *n* monólogo.
monopoly [məˈnɒpəlɪ] *n* monopolio.
monorail [ˈmɒnəureɪl] *n* monorriel *m*.
monosyllabic [mɒnəusɪˈlæbɪk] *a* monosilábico.
monotone [ˈmɒnətəun] *n* monotonía; **to speak in a** ~ hablar en un solo tono.
monotonous [məˈnɒtənəs] *a* monótono; **monotony** [-nɪ] *n* monotonía.
monsoon [mɒnˈsuːn] *n* monzón *m/f*.
monster [ˈmɒnstə*] *n* monstruo.
monstrosity [mɒnsˈtrɒsɪtɪ] *n* monstruosidad *f*.
monstrous [ˈmɒnstrəs] *a* (*huge*) enorme; (*atrocious*) monstruoso.
montage [mɒnˈtɑːʒ] *n* montaje *m*.
month [mʌnθ] *n* mes *m*; ~**ly** *a* mensual // *ad* mensualmente // *n* (*magazine*) revista mensual.
monument [ˈmɒnjumənt] *n* monumento; ~**al** [-ˈmɛntl] *a* monumental.
moo [muː] *vi* mugir.
mood [muːd] *n* humor *m*; **to be in a good/bad** ~ estar de buen/mal humor; ~**y** *a* (*variable*) de humor variable; (*sullen*) melancólico.
moon [muːn] *n* luna; ~**beam** *n* rayo de luna; ~**light** *n* luz *f* de la luna; ~**lit**: **a** ~**lit night** una noche de luna.
moor [muə*] *n* páramo // *vt* (*ship*) amarrar // *vi* echar las amarras.
Moor [muə*] *n* moro/a.
moorings [ˈmuərɪŋz] *npl* (*chains*) amarras *fpl*; (*place*) amarradero *m*.
Moorish [ˈmuərɪʃ] *a* moro; (*architecture*) árabe, morisco.
moorland [ˈmuələnd] *n* páramo, brezal *m*.
moose [muːs] *n*, *pl inv* alce *m*.
mop [mɒp] *n* fregona; (*of hair*) greña, melena // *vt* fregar; **to** ~ **up** *vt* limpiar.
mope [məup] *vi* estar o andar deprimido.
moped [ˈməupɛd] *n* (*Brit*) ciclomotor *m*.
moral [ˈmɒrl] *a* moral // *n* moraleja; ~**s** *npl* moralidad *f*, moral *f*.
morale [mɒˈrɑːl] *n* moral *f*.
morality [məˈrælɪtɪ] *n* moralidad *f*.
morass [məˈræs] *n* pantano.
morbid [ˈmɔːbɪd] *a* (*depressed*) melancólico; (MED) mórbido; **don't be** ~! ¡no seas morboso!
more [mɔː*] *det*, *ad* más; **once** ~ otra vez, una vez más; **I want** ~ quiero más; ~ **dangerous than** más peligroso que; ~ **or less** más o menos; ~ **than ever** más que nunca.
moreover [mɔːˈrəuvə*] *ad* además, por otra parte.
morgue [mɔːg] *n* depósito de cadáveres.
moribund [ˈmɒrɪbʌnd] *a* moribundo.
Mormon [ˈmɔːmən] *n* mormón/ona *m/f*.

morning [ˈmɔːnɪŋ] *n* (*gen*) mañana; (*early* ~) madrugada; **good** ~ buenas días; **in the** ~ por la mañana; **7 o'clock in the** ~ las 7 de la mañana; **tomorrow** ~ mañana por la mañana.
Moroccan [məˈrɒkən] *a*, *n* marroquí *m/f*.
Morocco [məˈrɒkəu] *n* Marruecos *m*.
moron [ˈmɔːrɒn] *n* imbécil *m/f*; ~**ic** [məˈrɒnɪk] *a* imbécil.
morose [məˈrəus] *a* hosco, malhumorado.
morphine [ˈmɔːfiːn] *n* morfina.
Morse [mɔːs] *n* (*also*: ~ **code**) (alfabeto) morse.
morsel [ˈmɔːsl] *n* (*of food*) bocado.
mortal [ˈmɔːtl] *a*, *n* mortal *m/f*; ~**ity** [-ˈtælɪtɪ] *n* mortalidad *f*.
mortar [ˈmɔːtə*] *n* argamasa; (*dish*) mortero.
mortgage [ˈmɔːgɪdʒ] *n* hipoteca // *vt* hipotecar.
mortify [ˈmɔːtɪfaɪ] *vt* mortificar, humillar.
mortuary [ˈmɔːtjuərɪ] *n* depósito de cadáveres.
mosaic [məuˈzeɪɪk] *n* mosaico.
Moscow [ˈmɒskəu] *n* Moscú *m*.
Moslem [ˈmɒzləm] *a*, *n* = **Muslim.**
mosque [mɒsk] *n* mezquita.
mosquito [mɒsˈkiːtəu], *pl* ~**es** *n* mosquito.
moss [mɒs] *n* musgo.
most [məust] *det* la mayor parte de, la mayoría de // *pron* la mayor parte, la mayoría // *ad* el más; (*very*) muy; **the** ~ (*also*: + *adjective*) el más; ~ **of them** la mayor parte de ellos; **I saw the** ~ yo vi el que más; **at the (very)** ~ a lo sumo, todo lo más; **to make the** ~ **of** aprovechar (al máximo); ~**ly** *ad* en su mayor parte, principalmente; **a** ~ **interesting book** un libro interesantísimo.
MOT *n abbr of* **Ministry of Transport: the** ~ (**test**) inspección (anual) obligatoria de coches y camiones.
motel [məuˈtɛl] *n* motel *m*.
moth [mɒθ] *n* mariposa nocturna; (*clothes* ~) polilla; ~**ball** *n* bola de naftalina; ~**-eaten** *a* apolillado.
mother [ˈmʌðə*] *n* madre *f* // *a* materno // *vt* (*care for*) cuidar (como una madre); ~**hood** *n* maternidad *f*; ~**-in-law** *n* suegra; ~**ly** *a* maternal; ~**-of-pearl** *n* nácar *m*; ~**-to-be** *n* futura madre; ~ **tongue** *n* lengua materna.
motif [məuˈtiːf] *n* motivo; (*theme*) tema *m*.
motion [ˈməuʃən] *n* movimiento; (*gesture*) ademán, señal *f*; (*at meeting*) moción *f* // *vt*, *vi*: **to** ~ (**to**) **sb to do sth** hacer señas a uno para que haga algo; ~**less** *a* inmóvil; ~ **picture** *n* película.
motivated [ˈməutɪveɪtɪd] *a* motivado; **motivation** [-ˈveɪʃən] *n* motivación *f*.
motive [ˈməutɪv] *n* motivo // *a* motor (*f*: motora, motriz).
motley [ˈmɒtlɪ] *a* variado.
motor [ˈməutə*] *n* motor *m*; (*col: vehicle*) coche *m*, automóvil *m* // *a* motor (*f*:

motora, motriz); ~**bike** n moto f; ~**boat** n lancha motora; ~**car** n coche m, automóvil m; ~**cycle** n motocicleta; ~**cyclist** n motorista m/f; ~**ing** n automovilismo; ~**ist** n conductor/a m/f, automovilista m/f; ~ **oil** n aceite m de coche; ~ **racing** n carreras fpl de coches, automovilismo; ~ **scooter** n moto f; ~ **vehicle** n automóvil m; ~**way** n (Brit) autopista.

mottled ['mɔtld] a abigarrado, multicolor.

motto ['mɔtəu], pl ~**es** n lema m; (watchword) consigna.

mould, mold (US) [məuld] n molde m; (mildew) moho // vt moldear; (fig) formar; ~**er** vi (decay) decaer; ~**ing** n moldura; ~**y** a enmohecido.

moult, molt (US) [məult] vi mudar (la piel/la pluma).

mound [maund] n montón m, montículo.

mount [maunt] n monte m; (horse) montura; (for jewel etc) engaste m; (for picture) marco // vt montar, subir a // vi (also: ~ **up**) subirse, montarse.

mountain ['mauntin] n montaña // cpd de montaña; ~**eer** [-'niə*] n alpinista m/f, montañero/a; ~**eering** [-'niəriŋ] n alpinismo, montañismo; **to go** ~**eering** hacer alpinismo; ~**ous** a montañoso; ~**side** n ladera de la montaña.

mourn [mɔ:n] vt llorar, lamentar // vi: **to** ~ **for** llorar la muerte de, lamentarse por; ~**er** n pariente m/f/amigo del difunto; ~**ful** a triste, lúgubre; ~**ing** n luto // cpd (dress) de luto; **in** ~**ing** de luto.

mouse [maus], pl **mice** n ratón m; ~**trap** n ratonera.

moustache [məs'tɑ:ʃ] n bigote m.

mousy ['mausi] a (person) tímido; (hair) pardusco.

mouth [mauθ], pl ~**s** [-ðz] n boca; (of river) desembocadura; ~**ful** n bocado; ~ **organ** n armónica; ~**piece** n (of musical instrument) boquilla; (spokesman) portavoz m; ~**wash** n enjuague m; ~**-watering** a apetitoso.

movable ['mu:vəbl] a movible.

move [mu:v] n (movement) movimiento; (in game) jugada; (: turn to play) turno; (change of house) mudanza // vt mover; (emotionally) conmover; (POL: resolution etc) proponer // vi (gen) moverse; (traffic) circular; (also: ~ **house**) trasladarse, mudarse; **to** ~ **sb to do sth** mover a uno a hacer algo; **to get a** ~ **on** darse prisa; **to** ~ **about** vi ir de acá para allá; (travel) viajar; **to** ~ **along** vi avanzar, adelantarse; **to** ~ **away** vi alejarse; **to** ~ **back** vi retroceder; **to** ~ **forward** vi avanzar // vt adelantar; **to** ~ **in** vi (to a house) instalarse (en una casa); **to** ~ **on** vi ponerse en camino; **to** ~ **out** vi (of house) abandonar (una casa); **to** ~ **up** vi subir; (employee) ser ascendido.

movement ['mu:vmənt] n movimiento; (TECH) mecanismo.

movie ['mu:vi] n película; **to go to the** ~**s** ir al cine; ~ **camera** n cámara cinematográfica.

moving ['mu:viŋ] a (emotional) conmovedor(a); (that moves) móvil.

mow [məu], pt **mowed**, pp **mowed** or **mown** vt (grass) cortar; (corn: also: ~ **down**) segar; ~**er** n segadora; (for lawn) cortacéspedes m inv.

M.P. n abbr of **Member of Parliament.**

m.p.h. abbr of **miles per hour.**

Mr ['mistə*] n: ~ **Smith** (el) Sr. Smith.

Mrs ['misiz] n: ~ **Smith** (la) Sra. Smith.

Ms [miz] n = **Miss** or **Mrs**: ~ **Smith** (la) Sa. Smith.

M.Sc. abbr of **Master of Science.**

much [mʌtʃ] det mucho // ad, n or pron mucho; (before pp) muy; **how** ~ **is it?** ¿cuánto es?, ¿cuánto cuesta?; **too** ~ demasiado; **it's not** ~ no es mucho; **as** ~ **as** tanto como; **however** ~ **he tries** por mucho que se esfuerce.

muck [mʌk] n (dirt) suciedad f; (fig) porquería; **to** ~ **about** vi (col) perder el tiempo; (enjoy o.s.) entretenerse; **to** ~ **up** vt (col: ruin) arruinar, estropear; ~**y** a (dirty) sucio.

mucus ['mju:kəs] n moco.

mud [mʌd] n barro, lodo.

muddle ['mʌdl] n desorden m, confusión f; (mix-up) embrollo, lío // vt (also: ~ **up**) embrollar, confundir; **to** ~ **through** vi salir del paso sin saber cómo.

mud: ~**dy** a fangoso, cubierto de lodo; ~**guard** n guardabarros m inv; ~**pack** n mascarilla (de belleza); ~**-slinging** n injurias fpl, difamación f.

muff [mʌf] n manguito // vt (chance) desperdiciar; (lines) estropear.

muffin ['mʌfin] n mollete m.

muffle ['mʌfl] vt (sound) amortiguar; (against cold) embozar; ~**d** a sordo, apagado.

mufti ['mʌfti] n: **in** ~ vestido de paisano.

mug [mʌg] n (cup) taza (alta, sin platillo); (: for beer) jarra; (col: face) jeta; (: fool) bobo // vt (assault) asaltar; ~**ging** n asalto.

muggy ['mʌgi] a bochornoso.

mule [mju:l] n mula.

mull [mʌl]: **to** ~ **over** vt meditar sobre.

mulled [mʌld] a: ~ **wine** vino calentado y con especias.

multi... [mʌlti] pref multi...; ~**coloured, ~colored** (US) a multicolor.

multifarious [mʌlti'fɛəriəs] a múltiple.

multiple ['mʌltipl] a, n múltiplo; ~ **sclerosis** n esclerosis f múltiple; ~ **store** n (cadena de) grandes almacenes.

multiplication [mʌltipli'keiʃən] n multiplicación f; **multiply** ['mʌltiplai] vt multiplicar // vi multiplicarse.

multitude ['mʌltitju:d] n multitud f.

mum [mʌm] n mamá // a: **to keep** ~ callarse.

mumble ['mʌmbl] *vt, vi* hablar entre dientes, refunfuñar.

mummy ['mʌmi] *n* (*mother*) mamá; (*embalmed*) momia.

mumps [mʌmps] *n* paperas *fpl.*

munch [mʌntʃ] *vt, vi* mascar.

mundane [mʌn'deɪn] *a* mundano.

municipal [mju:'nɪsɪpl] *a* municipal; ~**ity** [-'pælɪtɪ] *n* municipio.

munitions [mju:'nɪʃənz] *npl* municiones *fpl.*

mural ['mjuərl] *n* (pintura) mural *m.*

murder ['mɔːdə*] *n* asesinato; (*in law*) homicidio // *vt* asesinar, matar; (*spoil*) estropear; ~**er** *n* asesino; ~**ess** *n* asesina; ~**ous** *a* homicida.

murky ['mɔːkɪ] *a* oscuro; (*fig*) tenebroso.

murmur ['mɔːmə*] *n* murmullo // *vt, vi* murmurar.

muscle ['mʌsl] *n* músculo; (*fig: strength*) fuerza (muscular); **to ~ in** *vi* introducirse por fuerza; **muscular** ['muskjulə*] *a* muscular; (*person*) musculoso.

muse [mju:z] *vi* meditar // *n* musa.

museum [mju:'zɪəm] *n* museo.

mushroom ['mʌʃrum] *n* (*gen*) seta, hongo; (*food*) champiñón *m* // *vi* (*fig*) crecer de la noche a la mañana.

mushy ['mʌʃi] *a* triturado; (*pej*) sensiblero.

music ['mju:zɪk] *n* música; ~**al** *a* melodioso; (*person*) musical // *n* (*show*) (comedia) musical; ~**al instrument** *n* instrumento musical; ~ **hall** *n* teatro de variedades; ~**ian** [-'zɪʃən] *n* músico/a.

musket ['mʌskɪt] *n* mosquete *m.*

Muslim ['mʌzlɪm] *a, n* musulmán/ana *m/f.*

muslin ['mʌzlɪn] *n* muselina.

mussel ['mʌsl] *n* mejillón *m.*

must [mʌst] *auxiliary vb* (*obligation*): **I ~ do it** debo hacerlo, tengo que hacerlo; (*probability*): **he ~ be there by now** ya debe estar allí // *n* necesidad *f*; **it's a ~** es imprescindible.

mustard ['mʌstəd] *n* mostaza.

muster ['mʌstə*] *vt* juntar, reunir.

mustn't ['mʌsnt] = **must not.**

musty ['mʌstɪ] *a* mohoso, que huele a humedad.

mute [mju:t] *a, n* mudo/a.

muted ['mju:tɪd] *a* callado; (*MUS*) apagado.

mutilate ['mju:tɪleɪt] *vt* mutilar; **mutilation** [-'leɪʃən] *n* mutilación *f.*

mutinous ['mju:tɪnəs] *a* (*troops*) amotinado; (*attitude*) rebelde.

mutiny ['mju:tɪnɪ] *n* motín *m* // *vi* amotinarse.

mutter ['mʌtə*] *vt, vi* murmurar, hablar entre dientes.

mutton ['mʌtn] *n* carne *f* de cordero.

mutual ['mju:tʃuəl] *a* mutuo; (*gen: shared*) común; ~**ly** *ad* mutuamente.

muzzle ['mʌzl] *n* hocico; (*protective device*) bozal *m*; (*of gun*) boca // *vt* amordazar; (*dog*) poner un bozal a.

my [maɪ] *a* mi // *interj*: ~**!** ¡caramba!

mynah bird ['maɪnə*] *n* mainat *m.*

myopic [maɪ'ɒpɪk] *a* miope.

myself [maɪ'sɛlf] *pron* (*reflexive*) me; (*emphatic*) yo mismo; (*after prep*) mí (mismo).

mysterious [mɪs'tɪərɪəs] *a* misterioso; **mystery** ['mɪstəri] *n* misterio.

mystic ['mɪstɪk] *a, n* místico/a; ~**al** *a* místico.

mystify ['mɪstɪfaɪ] *vt* (*perplex*) dejar perplejo; (*disconcert*) desconcertar.

myth [mɪθ] *n* mito; ~**ical** *a* mítico; ~**ological** [mɪθə'lɒdʒɪkl] *a* mitológico; ~**ology** [mɪ'θɒlədʒɪ] *n* mitología.

N

nab [næb] *vt* (*col: grab*) coger; (*: catch out*) pillar.

nag [næg] *n* (*pej: horse*) rocín *m* // *vt* (*scold*) regañar; (*annoy*) fastidiar; ~**ging** *a* (*doubt*) persistente; (*pain*) continuo // *n* quejas *fpl.*

nail [neɪl] *n* (*human*) uña; (*metal*) clavo // *vt* clavar; (*fig: catch*) coger, pillar; **to ~ sb down to doing sth** comprometer a uno a que haga algo; ~**brush** *n* cepillo para las uñas; ~**file** *n* lima para las uñas; ~ **polish** *n* esmalte *m* o laca para las uñas; ~ **scissors** *npl* tijeras *fpl* para las uñas.

naïve [naɪ'i:v] *a* ingenuo; (*simple*) sencillo.

naked ['neɪkɪd] *a* (*nude*) desnudo; (*fig*) inerme, indefenso; (*flame*) expuesto al aire; ~**ness** *n* desnudez *f.*

name [neɪm] *n* (*gen*) nombre *m*; (*surname*) apellido; (*reputation*) fama, renombre *m* // *vt* (*child*) poner nombre a; (*criminal*) dar el nombre de; (*appoint*) nombrar; **by ~** de nombre; **maiden ~** nombre de soltera; **in the ~ of** en nombre de; **what's your ~?** ¿cómo se llama?; **to give one's ~ and address** dar las señas; ~**less** *a* anónimo, sin nombre; ~**ly** *ad* a saber; ~**sake** *n* tocayo/a.

nanny ['nænɪ] *n* niñera; ~ **goat** *n* cabra.

nap [næp] *n* (*sleep*) sueñecito, siesta.

napalm ['neɪpɑːm] *n* nápalm *m.*

nape [neɪp] *n*: **the ~ of the neck** la nuca, el cogote.

napkin ['næpkɪn] *n* (*also*: **table ~**) servilleta; (*Brit: for baby*) pañal *m.*

nappy ['næpi] *n* pañal *m*; ~ **liner** *n* gasa; ~ **rash** *n* prurito.

narcissus [nɑː'sɪsəs], *pl* -**si** [-saɪ] *n* narciso.

narcotic [nɑː'kɒtɪk] *a, n* narcótico.

narrate [nə'reɪt] *vt* narrar, contar; **narrative** ['nærətɪv] *n* narrativa // *a* narrativo; **narrator** *n* narrador/a *m/f.*

narrow ['nærəu] *a* estrecho, angosto; (*fig*) de miras estrechas, intolerante // *vi* estrecharse, angostarse; (*diminish*) reducirse; **to ~ down the possibilities to** reducir las posibilidades a; ~**ly** *ad* (*miss*) por poco; ~**-minded** *a* de miras estrechas.

nasal ['neɪzl] *a* nasal.

nastiness ['nɑːstɪnɪs] *n* (*malice*)

malevolencia; (*rudeness*) grosería.
nasty ['nɑːstɪ] *a* (*unpleasant: remark*) feo,
horrible; (: *person*) antipático; (*malicious*)
rencoroso; (*rude*) grosero; (*revolting: taste,
smell*) asqueroso, repugnante; (*wound,
disease etc*) peligroso, grave.
nation ['neɪʃən] *n* nación *f*.
national ['næʃənl] *a*, *n* nacional *m/f*;
~**ism** *n* nacionalismo; ~**ist** *a*, *n*
nacionalista *m/f*; ~**ity** [-'nælɪtɪ] *n*
nacionalidad *f*; ~**ization** [-aɪ'zeɪʃən] *n*
nacionalización *f*; ~**ize** *vt* nacionalizar;
~**ly** *ad* (*nationwide*) en escala nacional;
(*as a nation*) nacionalmente, como nación.
nationwide ['neɪʃənwaɪd] *a* en escala *o* a
nivel nacional.
native ['neɪtɪv] *n* (*local inhabitant*) natural
m/f, nacional *m/f*; (*in colonies*) indígena
m/f, nativo/a // *a* (*indigenous*) indígena;
(*of one's birth*) natal; (*innate*) natural,
innato.
NATO ['neɪtəu] *n abbr of* North Atlantic
Treaty Organization OTAN (Organización del Tratado del Atlántico del
Norte).
natter ['nætə*] *vi* charlar.
natural ['nætʃrəl] *a* natural; (*unaffected:
manner*) inafectado, sin afectación; ~**ist**
n naturalista *m/f*; ~**ize** *vt*: to become
~**ized** (*person*) naturalizarse; (*plant*)
aclimatarse; ~**ly** *ad* naturalmente; (*of
course*) desde luego, por supuesto;
(*instinctively*) por instinto, por naturaleza;
~**ness** *n* naturalidad *f*.
nature ['neɪtʃə*] *n* naturaleza; (*group, sort*)
género, clase *f*; (*character*) carácter *m*,
genio; **by** ~ por *o* de naturaleza.
naughty ['nɔːtɪ] *a* (*child*) travieso, (*story,
film*) verde, escabroso.
nausea ['nɔːsɪə] *n* náusea; **nauseate**
[-sɪeɪt] *vt* dar náuseas a; (*fig*) dar asco a;
nauseating [-sɪeɪtɪŋ] *a* nauseabundo; (*fig*)
asqueroso.
nautical ['nɔːtɪkl] *a* náutico, marítimo;
(*mile*) marino.
naval ['neɪvl] *a* naval, de marina; ~
officer *n* oficial *m/f* de marina.
nave [neɪv] *n* nave *f*.
navel ['neɪvl] *n* ombligo.
navigable ['nævɪgəbl] *a* navegable.
navigate ['nævɪgeɪt] *vt* (*guide*) gobernar;
(*sail along*) navegar por; (*fig*) guiar // *vi*
navegar; **navigation** [-'geɪʃən] *n* (*action*)
navegación *f*; (*science*) náutica;
navigator *n* navegador/a *m/f*, navegante
m/f.
navvy ['nævɪ] *n* peón *m* caminero.
navy ['neɪvɪ] *n* marina de guerra; (*ships*)
armada, flota; ~**(-blue)** *a* azul marino.
Nazi ['nɑːtsɪ] *n* nazi *m/f*; **nazism** *n*
nazismo.
neap tide [niːp-] *n* marea muerta.
near [nɪə*] *a* (*place*) cercano, vecino;
(*time*) próximo; (*relation*) estrecho, íntimo
// *ad* cerca // *prep* (*also*: ~ **to**) (*space*)
cerca de, junto a; (*time*) cerca de, casi //
vt acercarse a, aproximarse a; ~**by**

[nɪə'baɪ] *a* cercano, próximo // *ad* cerca;
N~ **East** *n* Cercano Oriente *m*; ~**ly** *ad*
casi, por poco; **I** ~**ly fell** por poco me
caigo; ~**miss** *n* tiro cercano; ~**ness** *n*
proximidad *f*, cercanía; (*relationship*)
intimidad *f*; ~**side** *n* (*AUT: in Britain*) lado
izquierdo; (: *in Spain*) lado derecho;
~**sighted** *a* miope, corto de vista.
neat [niːt] *a* (*place*) bien arreglado *o*
cuidado; (*person*) pulcro, esmerado;
(*skilful*) diestro; (: *plan*) hábil, ingenioso;
(*spirits*) solo.
nebulous ['nebjuləs] *a* nebuloso; (*fig*)
vago, confuso.
necessarily ['nesɪsrɪlɪ] *ad* nece-
sariamente.
necessary ['nesɪsrɪ] *a* necesario, preciso;
he did all that was ~ hizo todo lo
necesario.
necessitate [nɪ'sesɪteɪt] *vt* necesitar,
exigir.
necessity [nɪ'sesɪtɪ] *n* (*thing needed*)
necesidad *f*, requisito; (*compelling
circumstances*) la necesidad; **necessities**
npl artículos *mpl* de primera necesidad.
neck [nek] *n* (*ANAT*) cuello; (*of animal*)
pescuezo // *vi* besuquearse, abrazarse; ~
and ~ parejos; **to stick one's** ~ **out**
arriesgarse.
necklace ['neklɪs] *n* collar *m*.
neckline ['neklaɪn] *n* escote *m*.
necktie ['nektaɪ] *n* corbata.
née [neɪ] *a*: ~ **Scott** de soltera Scott.
need [niːd] *n* (*lack*) escasez *f*, falta;
(*necessity*) necesidad *f*; (*thing needed*)
requisito, necesidad *f* // *vt* (*require*)
necesitar; **I** ~ **to do it** tengo que *o* debo
hacerlo, hay que hacerlo; **you don't** ~ **to
go** no hace falta que vayas.
needle ['niːdl] *n* aguja // *vt* (*fig: fam*)
picar, fastidiar.
needless ['niːdlɪs] *a* innecesario, inútil; ~
to say huelga decir que.
needlework ['niːdlwɜːk] *n* (*activity*)
costura, labor *f* de aguja.
needy ['niːdɪ] *a* necesitado.
negation [nɪ'geɪʃən] *n* negación *f*.
negative ['negətɪv] *n* (*PHOT*) negativo;
(*answer*) negativa // *a* negativo.
neglect [nɪ'glekt] *vt* (*one's duty*) faltar a,
no cumplir con; (*child*) descuidar,
desatender // *n* (*gen*) negligencia,
abandono; (*personal*) dejadez *f*; (*of duty*)
incumplimiento.
negligee ['neglɪʒeɪ] *n* (*nightdress*) salto de
cama; (*housecoat*) bata.
negligence ['neglɪdʒəns] *n* negligencia,
descuido; **negligent** [-ənt] *a* (*careless*)
descuidado, negligente; (*forgetful*)
olvidadizo.
negligible ['neglɪdʒɪbl] *a* insignificante,
despreciable.
negotiable [nɪ'gəʊʃɪəbl] *a* (*cheque*)
negociable; (*road*) transitable.
negotiate [nɪ'gəʊʃɪeɪt] *vi* negociar // *vt*
(*treaty*) negociar; (*transaction*) gestionar,
tramitar; (*obstacle*) franquear;

negotiation [-'eɪʃɔn] n negociación f, gestión f; **negotiator** n negociador/a m/f.

Negress ['niːgrɪs] n negra.

Negro ['niːgrəu] a, n negro.

neigh [neɪ] n relincho // vi relinchar.

neighbour, neighbor (US) ['neɪbə*] n vecino/a; ~**hood** n (place) vecindad f, barrio; (people) vecindario; ~**ing** a vecino; ~**ly** a amistoso, de buen vecino.

neither ['naɪðə*] a ni // conj: **I didn't move and ~ did John** no me he movido, ni Juan tampoco // pron ninguno // ad: ~ **good nor bad** ni bueno ni malo.

neo... [niːəu] pref neo-.

neon ['niːɔn] n neón m; ~ **light** n lámpara de neón.

nephew ['nɛvjuː] n sobrino.

nerve [nəːv] n (ANAT) nervio; (courage) valor m; (impudence) descaro, frescura; ~-**racking** a que crispa los nervios; ~**s** npl (fig: anxiety) nerviosidad f, nerviosismo.

nervous ['nɔːvɔs] a (anxious, ANAT) nervioso; (timid) tímido, miedoso; ~ **breakdown** n crisis f nerviosa; ~**ly** ad nerviosamente; tímidamente; ~**ness** n nerviosidad f, nerviosismo; timidez f.

nest [nɛst] n (of bird) nido; (of wasp) avispero // vi anidar.

nestle ['nɛsl] vi: **to ~ up to sb** arrimarse a uno.

net [nɛt] n (gen) red f; (fig) trampa // a (COMM) neto, líquido // vt coger con red; (SPORT) marcar; ~**ball** n básquet m.

Netherlands ['nɛðələndz] npl: **the ~** los Países Bajos.

nett [nɛt] a = **net.**

netting ['nɛtɪŋ] n red f, redes fpl.

nettle ['nɛtl] n ortiga.

network ['nɛtwəːk] n red f.

neurosis [njuə'rəusɪs], pl **-ses** [-siːz] n neurosis f; **neurotic** [-'rɔtɪk] a, n neurótico/a.

neuter ['njuːtə*] a (sexless) castrado, sin sexo; (LING) neutro // vt castrar, capar.

neutral ['njuːtrəl] a (person) neutral; (colour etc, ELEC) neutro // n (in AUT) punto muerto; ~**ity** [-'trælɪti] n neutralidad f.

neutron ['njuːtrɔn] n neutrón m; ~ **bomb** n bomba de neutrones.

never ['nɛvə*] ad nunca, jamás; **I ~ went** no fui nunca; ~ **in my life** jamás en la vida; ~-**ending** a interminable, sin fin; ~**theless** [nɛvəðə'lɛs] ad sin embargo, no obstante.

new [njuː] a (brand ~) nuevo; (recent) reciente; (different) nuevo, distinto; (inexperienced) tierno, nuevo; ~-**born** a recién nacido; ~-**comer** ['njuːkʌmə*] n recién venido o llegado; ~**ly** ad nuevamente, recién; ~ **moon** n luna nueva; ~**ness** n novedad f; (fig) inexperiencia.

news [njuːz] n noticias fpl; **a piece of ~** una noticia; **the ~** (RADIO, TV) las noticias fpl, telediario; ~ **agency** n agencia de noticias; ~**agent** n vendedor/a m/f de periódicos; ~**caster** n presentador/a m/f

de noticias; ~ **flash** n noticia de última hora; ~**letter** n hoja informativa, boletín m; ~**paper** n periódico, diario; ~**reel** n noticiario; ~ **stand** n quiosco o puesto de periódicos.

New Year ['njuː'jɪə*] n Año Nuevo; ~'**s Day** n Día m de Año Nuevo; ~'**s Eve** n Nochevieja.

New York ['njuː'jɔːk] n Nueva York.

New Zealand [njuː'ziːlənd] n Nueva Zelanda.

next [nɛkst] a (in space) próximo, vecino; (in time) próximo, siguiente // ad (place) después; (time) después, luego; ~ **time** la próxima vez; ~ **year** el año próximo o que viene; ~ **door** ad en la casa de al lado // a vecino, de al lado; ~-**of-kin** n pariente(s) m(pl) cercano(s); ~ **to** prep junto a, al lado de.

N.H.S. n abbr of **National Health Service.**

nib [nɪb] n plumilla.

nibble ['nɪbl] vt mordisquear, mordiscar; (ZOOL) roer.

nice [naɪs] a (likeable) simpático, majo; (kind) amable; (pleasant) agradable; (attractive) bonito, mono; (subtle) fino, preciso; ~-**looking** a atractivo, guapo; ~**ly** ad amablemente, bien.

niche [niːʃ] n nicho.

nick [nɪk] n (wound) rasguño; (cut, indentation) mella, muesca // vt (col) birlar, robar; **in the ~ of time** a última hora.

nickel ['nɪkl] n níquel m.

nickname ['nɪkneɪm] n apodo, mote m // vt apodar.

nicotine ['nɪkətiːn] n nicotina.

niece [niːs] n sobrina.

Nigeria [naɪ'dʒɪərɪə] n Nigeria; ~**n** a, n nigeriano/a.

niggardly ['nɪgədlɪ] a (person) avaro, tacaño; (amount) miserable.

niggling ['nɪglɪŋ] a (trifling) nimio, insignificante; (annoying) molesto.

night [naɪt] n (gen) noche f; (evening) tarde f; **last ~** anoche; **the ~ before last** anteanoche; **good ~!** ¡buenas noches!; **at** o **by ~** de noche, por la noche; ~**cap** n (drink) resopón m; ~ **club** n cabaret m; ~**dress** n camisón m; ~**fall** n anochecer m; ~**ie** ['naɪtɪ] n camisón m.

nightingale ['naɪtɪŋgeɪl] n ruiseñor m.

nightly ['naɪtlɪ] a de noche, nocturno // ad todas las noches, cada noche.

night: ~**mare** n pesadilla; ~ **school** n clase(s) f(pl) nocturna(s); ~ **shift** n turno nocturno o de noche; ~-**time** n noche f; ~ **watchman** n sereno.

nil [nɪl] n cero, nada.

nimble ['nɪmbl] a (agile) ágil, ligero; (skilful) diestro.

nine [naɪn] num nueve; ~**teen** num diecinueve, diez y nueve; ~**ty** num noventa.

ninth [naɪnθ] a noveno.

nip [nɪp] vt (pinch) pellizcar; (bite) morder // n (drink) trago, gota.

nipple ['nɪpl] n (ANAT) pezón m; (of bottle) tetilla; (TECH) boquilla, manguito.

nippy ['nɪpɪ] a (person) ágil, rápido; (taste) picante.

nitrate ['naɪtreɪt] n nitrato.

nitrogen ['naɪtrədʒən] n nitrógeno.

no [nəu] ad no // a ninguno, no ... alguno // n no.

nobility [nəuˈbɪlɪtɪ] n nobleza.

noble ['nəubl] a (person) noble; (title) de nobleza; (generous) noble; ~man n noble m, aristócrata m.

nobody ['nəubədɪ] pron nadie.

nod [nɔd] vi saludar con la cabeza; (in agreement) decir que sí con la cabeza; (doze) cabecear // vt inclinar // n inclinación f de cabeza; to ~ off vi cabecear.

noise [nɔɪz] n ruido; (din) escándalo, estrépito; **noisily** ad ruidosamente; **noisy** a (gen) ruidoso; (child) escandaloso.

nomad ['nəumæd] n nómada m/f; ~ic [-'mædɪk] a nómada.

nominal ['nɔmɪnl] a nominal.

nominate ['nɔmɪneɪt] vt (propose) proponer; (appoint) nombrar; **nomination** [-'neɪʃən] n propuesta; nombramiento.

nominee [nɔmɪ'niː] n candidato/a.

non... [nɔn] pref no, des..., in...; ~**-alcoholic** a no alcohólico; ~**-aligned** a no alineado; ~**-committal** ['nɔnkə'mɪtl] a (reserved) reservado; (uncommitted) evasivo; ~**conformist** a no conformista; ~**descript** ['nɔndɪskrɪpt] a indeterminado; (pej) mediocre.

none [nʌn] pron (person) nadie; (thing) ninguno, nada // ad de ninguna manera.

nonentity [nɔ'nentɪtɪ] n cero a la izquierda, nulidad f.

nonetheless [nʌnðə'lɛs] ad sin embargo, no obstante.

non: ~**-fiction** n literatura no novelesca; ~**plussed** a perplejo.

nonsense ['nɔnsəns] n tonterías fpl, disparates mpl.

non-stop ['nɔn'stɔp] a continuo; (RAIL) directo // ad sin parar.

noodles ['nuːdlz] npl tallarines mpl.

nook [nuk] n rincón m; ~s **and crannies** escondrijos mpl.

noon [nuːn] n mediodía m.

no-one ['nəuwʌn] pron = **nobody.**

noose [nuːs] n lazo corredizo; (hangman's) dogal m.

nor [nɔː*] conj = **neither** // ad see **neither.**

norm [nɔːm] n norma.

normal ['nɔːml] a (usual) normal; (ordinary) corriente, regular; ~**ly** ad normalmente.

north [nɔːθ] n norte m // a del norte, norteño // ad al o hacia el norte; **N~ America** n América del Norte; ~**-east** n nor(d)este m; ~**ern** ['nɔːðən] a norteño,

del norte; **N~ern Ireland** n Irlanda del Norte; **N~ Pole** n Polo Norte; **N~ Sea** n Mar m del Norte; ~**ward(s)** ['nɔːθwəd(z)] ad hacia el norte; ~**-west** n nor(d)oeste m.

Norway ['nɔːweɪ] n Noruega; **Norwegian** [-'wiːdʒən] a, n noruego/a.

nose [nəuz] n (ANAT) nariz f; (ZOOL) hocico; (sense of smell) olfato // vi: to ~ **about** curiosear; ~**bleed** n hemorragia nasal; ~**dive** n (deliberate) picado vertical; (involuntary) caída de narices; ~**y** a curioso, fisgón(ona).

nostalgia [nɔs'tældʒɪə] n nostalgia; **nostalgic** a nostálgico.

nostril ['nɔstrɪl] n ventana de la nariz; ~**s** npl narices fpl.

nosy ['nəuzɪ] a = **nosey.**

not [nɔt] ad no; ~ **at all** no ... en absoluto; ~ **that...** no es que...; ~ **yet** todavía no; ~ **now** ahora no; **why** ~? ¿por qué no?

notable ['nəutəbl] a notable.

notary ['nəutərɪ] n notario.

notch [nɔtʃ] n muesca, corte m.

note [nəut] n (MUS) nota; (banknote) billete m; (letter) nota, carta; (record) nota, apunte m; (fame) importancia, renombre m; (tone) tono // vt (observe) notar, observar; (write down) apuntar, anotar; ~**book** n libreta, cuaderno; ~**case** n cartera, billetero; ~**d** ['nəutɪd] a célebre, conocido; ~**paper** n papel m para cartas.

nothing ['nʌθɪŋ] n nada; (zero) cero; **for** ~ (free) gratis, sin- pago; (in vain) en balde.

notice ['nəutɪs] n (announcement) anuncio; (attention) atención f, interés m; (warning) aviso; (dismissal) despido; (resignation) dimisión f; (period of time) plazo // vt (observe) notar, observar; **to take** ~ **of** tomar nota de, prestar atención a; **at short** ~ a corto plazo, con poco anticipación; **until further** ~ hasta nuevo aviso; ~**able** a evidente, obvio; ~**board** n (Brit) tablón m de anuncios.

notification [nəutɪfɪ'keɪʃən] n aviso; **notify** ['nəutɪfaɪ] vt avisar, notificar.

notion ['nəuʃən] n noción f, concepto; (opinion) opinión f.

notorious [nəu'tɔːrɪəs] a notorio, célebre.

notwithstanding [nɔtwɪθ'stændɪŋ] ad no obstante, sin embargo; ~ **this** a pesar de esto.

nougat ['nuːgɑː] n turrón m.

nought [nɔːt] n cero.

noun [naun] n nombre m, sustantivo.

nourish ['nʌrɪʃ] vt nutrir, alimentar; (fig) fomentar, nutrir; ~**ing** a nutritivo, rico; ~**ment** n alimento, sustento.

novel ['nɔvl] n novela // a (new) nuevo, original; (unexpected) insólito; ~**ist** n novelista m/f; ~**ty** n novedad f.

November [nəu'vɛmbə*] n noviembre m.

novice ['nɔvɪs] n principiante m/f, novato/a; (REL) novicio/a.

now [nau] ad (at the present time) ahora; (these days) actualmente, hoy día; **right**

~ ahora mismo; ~ **and then,** ~ **and again** de vez en cuando; **from** ~ **on** de ahora en adelante; ~**adays** ['nauədeɪz] *ad* hoy (en) día, actualmente.

nowhere ['nəuwɛə*] *ad* (*direction*) a ninguna parte; (*location*) en ninguna parte.

nozzle ['nɔzl] *n* (*gen*) boquilla; (*TECH*) tobera, inyector *m*.

nuance ['njuːɑːns] *n* matiz *m*.

nuclear ['njuːklɪə*] *a* nuclear.

nucleus ['njuːklɪəs], *pl* **-lei** [-lɪaɪ] *n* núcleo.

nude [njuːd] *a, n* desnudo/a; **in the** ~ desnudo.

nudge [nʌdʒ] *vt* dar un codazo a.

nudist ['njuːdɪst] *n* nudista *m/f*.

nudity ['njuːdɪtɪ] *n* desnudez *f*.

nuisance ['njuːsns] *n* molestia, fastidio; (*person*) pesado, latoso; **what a** ~! ¡qué lata!

null [nʌl] *a*: ~ **and void** nulo y sin efecto; ~**ify** ['nʌlɪfaɪ] *vt* anular, invalidar.

numb [nʌm] *a* entumecido; (*fig*) insensible // *vt* entumecer, entorpecer.

number ['nʌmbə*] *n* número; (*numeral*) número, cifra // *vt* (*pages etc*) numerar, poner número a; (*amount to*) sumar, ascender a; **to be** ~**ed among** figurar entre; **a** ~ **of** varios, algunos; **they were ten in** ~ eran diez; ~ **plate** *n* placa de matrícula.

numbness ['nʌmnɪs] *n* entumecimiento; (*fig*) insensibilidad *f*.

numeral ['njuːmərəl] *n* número, cifra.

numerical ['njuːˈmɛrɪkl] *a* numérico.

numerous ['njuːmərəs] *a* numeroso, muchos.

nun [nʌn] *n* monja, religiosa.

nurse [nəːs] *n* enfermero/a; (*nanny*) niñera // *vt* (*patient*) cuidar, atender; (*baby*) criar, amamantar; (*fig*) guardar; **wet** ~ nodriza.

nursery ['nəːsərɪ] *n* (*institution*) guardería infantil; (*room*) cuarto de los niños; (*for plants*) criadero, semillero; ~ **rhyme** *n* canción *f* infantil; ~ **school** *n* parvulario, escuela de párvulos; ~ **slope** *n* (*SKI*) cuesta para principiantes.

nursing ['nəːsɪŋ] *n* (*profession*) profesión *f* de enfermera; (*care*) asistencia, cuidado; ~ **home** *n* clínica de reposo.

nut [nʌt] *n* (*TECH*) tuerca; (*BOT*) nuez *f*; ~**s** *a* (*col*) loco; ~**case** *n* (*col*) loco/a, chalado/a; ~**crackers** *npl* cascanueces *m inv*; ~**meg** ['nʌtmɛg] *n* nuez *f* moscada.

nutrient ['njuːtrɪənt] *n* nutrimento.

nutrition [njuːˈtrɪʃən] *n* nutrición *f*, alimentación *f*; **nutritious** [-ʃəs] *a* nutritivo, rico.

nutshell ['nʌtʃɛl] *n* cáscara de nuez; **in a** ~ en resumidas cuentas.

nylon ['naɪlɔn] *n* nilón *m* // *a* de nilón; ~**s** *npl* medias *fpl* (de nilón).

nymph [nɪmf] *n* ninfa.

O

oaf [əuf] *n* zoquete *m*.

oak [əuk] *n* roble *m* // *a* de roble.

O.A.P. *abbr of* **old-age pensioner.**

oar [ɔː*] *n* remo; **oarsman** *n* remero.

oasis [əuˈeɪsɪs], *pl* **-ses** [-siːz] *n* oasis *m*.

oath [əuθ] *n* juramento; (*swear word*) palabrota; **on** ~ bajo juramento.

oatmeal ['əutmiːl] *n* harina de avena.

oats [əuts] *n* avena.

obedience [əˈbiːdɪəns] *n* obediencia; **in** ~ **to** de acuerdo con; **obedient** [-ənt] *a* obediente.

obesity [əuˈbiːsɪtɪ] *n* obesidad *f*.

obey [əˈbeɪ] *vt* obedecer; (*instructions, regulations*) cumplir.

obituary [əˈbɪtjuərɪ] *n* necrología.

object ['ɔbdʒɪkt] *n* (*gen*) objeto; (*purpose*) objeto, propósito; (*LING*) complemento // *vi* [əbˈdʒɛkt]: **to** ~ **to** (*attitude*) protestar contra; (*proposal*) oponerse a; **I** ~! ¡yo protesto!; ~**ion** [əbˈdʒɛkʃən] *n* protesta; **I have no** ~**ion to...** no tengo inconveniente en que...; ~**ionable** [əbˈdʒɛkʃənəbl] *a* (*gen*) desagradable; (*conduct*) censurable; ~**ive,** *a, n* objetivo; ~**ivity** [ɔbdʒɪkˈtɪvɪtɪ] *n* objetividad *f*; ~**or** *n* objetor/a *m/f*.

obligation [ɔblɪˈgeɪʃən] *n* obligación *f*; (*debt*) deber *m*; **without** ~ sin compromiso.

obligatory [əˈblɪgətərɪ] *a* obligatorio.

oblige [əˈblaɪdʒ] *vt* (*force*): **to** ~ **sb to do sth** forzar *o* obligar a uno a hacer algo; (*do a favour for*) complacer, hacer un favor a; **I should be** ~**d if...** le agradecería que...; **obliging** *a* servicial, atento.

oblique [əˈbliːk] *a* oblicuo; (*allusion*) indirecto.

obliterate [əˈblɪtəreɪt] *vt* borrar.

oblivion [əˈblɪvɪən] *n* olvido; **oblivious** [-ɪəs] *a*: **oblivious of** inconsciente de.

oblong ['ɔblɔŋ] *a* rectangular // *n* rectángulo.

obnoxious [əbˈnɔkʃəs] *a* odioso, detestable; (*smell*) nauseabundo.

oboe ['əubəu] *n* oboe *m*.

obscene [əbˈsiːn] *a* obsceno; **obscenity** [-ˈsɛnɪtɪ] *n* obscenidad *f*.

obscure [əbˈskjuə*] *a* oscuro // *vt* oscurecer; (*hide: sun*) esconder; **obscurity** *n* oscuridad *f*.

obsequious [əbˈsiːkwɪəs] *a* obsequioso.

observance [əbˈzəːvns] *n* observancia, cumplimiento; (*ritual*) práctica.

observant [əbˈzəːvnt] *a* observador(a).

observation [ɔbzəˈveɪʃən] *n* observación *f*; (*by police etc*) vigilancia; (*MED*) examen *m*.

observatory [əbˈzəːvətrɪ] *n* observatorio.

observe [əbˈzəːv] *vt* (*gen*) observar; (*rule*) cumplir; **observer** *n* observador/a *m/f*.

obsess [əbˈsɛs] *vt* obsesionar; ~**ion** [əb-

'sɛʃən] n obsesión f, idea fija; ~**ive** a obsesivo, obsesionante.

obsolescence [ɔbsə'lɛsns] n caída en desuso; **obsolete** ['ɔbsəliːt] a (que está) en desuso.

obstacle ['ɔbstəkl] n obstáculo; (nuisance) estorbo; ~ **race** n carrera de obstáculos.

obstetrician [ɔbstə'trɪʃən] n obstétrico; **obstetrics** [-'stɛtrɪks] n obstetricia.

obstinate ['ɔbstɪnɪt] a terco, porfiado; (determined) tenaz.

obstruct [əb'strʌkt] vt (block) obstruir; (hinder) estorbar, obstaculizar; ~**ion** [əb'strʌkʃən] n obstrucción f; estorbo, obstáculo.

obtain [əb'teɪn] vt (get) obtener; (achieve) conseguir; ~**able** a asequible.

obtrusive [əb'truːsɪv] a (person) importuno, entrometido; (building etc) demasiado visible.

obvious ['ɔbvɪəs] a (clear) obvio, evidente; (unsubtle) poco sutil; ~**ly** ad evidentemente, naturalmente.

occasion [ə'keɪʒən] n (gen) oportunidad f, ocasión f; (reason) motivo; (time) ocasión f, vez f; (event) acontecimiento // vt ocasionar, causar; ~**ally** ad de vez en cuando.

occult [ɔ'kʌlt] a (gen) oculto.

occupant ['ɔkjupənt] n (of house) inquilino/a; (of car) ocupante m/f.

occupation [ɔkju'peɪʃən] n (of house) tenencia; (job) trabajo; (: calling) oficio; **unfit for** ~ (house) inhabitable; ~**al hazard** n riesgo profesional.

occupier ['ɔkjupaɪə*] n inquilino/a.

occupy ['ɔkjupaɪ] vt (gen) ocupar; (house) habitar, vivir en; (time) emplear, pasar; (attention) entretener; **to ~ o.s. with** or **by doing** (as job) dedicarse a hacer; (to pass time) pasar el tiempo haciendo.

occur [ə'kəː*] vi pasar, suceder; **to ~ to sb** ocurrírsele a uno; **it ~s to me that...** se me ocurre que...; ~**rence** n (event) acontecimiento; (existence) existencia.

ocean ['əuʃən] n océano; ~**-going** a de alta mar; ~ **liner** n transatlántico.

o'clock [ə'klɔk] ad: **it is 5** ~ son las 5.

octagonal [ɔk'tægənl] a octagonal.

octane ['ɔkteɪn] n octano.

octave ['ɔktɪv] n octava.

October [ɔk'təubə*] n octubre m.

octopus ['ɔktəpəs] n pulpo.

odd [ɔd] a (strange) extraño, raro; (number) impar; (left over) sobrante, suelto; **60-** ~ 60 y pico; **at** ~ **times** de vez en cuando; **to be the** ~ **one out** estar de más; ~**ity** n rareza; (person) excéntrico; ~-**job man** n hombre m que hace de todo; ~ **jobs** npl bricolaje m; ~**ly** ad curiosamente, extrañamente; ~**ments** npl (COMM) retales mpl; ~**s** npl (in betting) puntos mpl de ventaja; **it makes no** ~**s** no importa, lo mismo da; **at** ~**s** reñidos(as).

ode [əud] n oda.

odious ['əudɪəs] a odioso.

odour, odor (US) ['əudə*] n olor m; (perfume) perfume m; ~**less** a inodoro.

of [ɔv, əv] prep de; **a friend** ~ **ours** un amigo nuestro; **3** ~ **them** 3 de ellos; **the 5th** ~ **July** el 5 de julio; **a boy** ~ **10** un niño de 10 años; **made** ~ **wood** hecho de madera.

off [ɔf] a, ad (engine) desconectado; (light) apagado; (tap) cerrado; (food: bad) pasado, malo; (milk) cortado; (cancelled) anulado // prep de; **to be** ~ (to leave) irse, marcharse; **to be 5 km** ~ estar a 5 kilómetros; **a day** ~ un día libre o sin trabajar; **to have an** ~ **day** tener un día malo; **he had his coat** ~ se había quitado el abrigo; **10%** ~ (COMM) (con el) 10% de descuento; **5 km** ~ **(the road)** a 5 km (de la carretera); ~ **the coast** frente a la costa; **on the** ~ **chance** por si acaso.

offal ['ɔfl] n (CULIN) menudencias fpl.

off-colour ['ɔf'kʌlə*] a (ill) indispuesto.

offence, offense (US) [ə'fɛns] n (crime) delito; (insult) ofensa; **to take** ~ **at** ofenderse por.

offend [ə'fɛnd] vt (person) ofender; ~**er** n delincuente m/f; (against regulations) infractor/a m/f.

offensive [ə'fɛnsɪv] a ofensivo; (smell etc) repugnante // n (MIL) ofensiva.

offer ['ɔfə*] n (gen) oferta, ofrecimiento; (proposal) propuesta // vt ofrecer; (opportunity) facilitar; **'on** ~' (COMM) 'en oferta'; ~**ing** n ofrenda; ~**tory** n (REL) ofertorio.

offhand [ɔf'hænd] a informal // ad de improviso.

office ['ɔfɪs] n (place) oficina; (room) despacho; (position) carga, oficio; **to take** ~ entrar en funciones; ~ **block** n bloque m de oficinas; ~ **boy** n mozo (de oficina); **officer** n (MIL etc) oficial m; (of organization) director m; (also: **police officer**) agente m/f de policía; ~ **worker** n oficinista m/f.

official [ə'fɪʃl] a (authorized) oficial, autorizado // n funcionario, oficial m; ~**dom** n burocracia.

officious [ə'fɪʃəs] a oficioso.

offing ['ɔfɪŋ] n: **in the** ~ (fig) en perspectiva.

off: ~-**licence** n (Brit: shop) bodega, tienda de vinos y bebidas alcohólicas; ~-**peak** a de temporada de poca actividad; ~-**putting** a que desanima; ~-**season** a, ad fuera de temporada.

offset ['ɔfsɛt] (irg: like **set**) vt (counteract) contrarrestar, compensar // n (also: ~ **printing**) offset m.

offshore [ɔf'ʃɔː*] a (que está) cerca de la costa.

offside ['ɔf'saɪd] a (SPORT) fuera de juego.

offspring ['ɔfsprɪŋ] n descendencia, descendientes mpl or fpl.

off: ~-**stage** ad entre bastidores; ~-**the-peg** ad confeccionado; ~-**white** a blanco grisáceo.

often ['ɔfn] ad a menudo, con frecuencia.

ogle ['əugl] vt echar miradas a.
oil [ɔil] n aceite m; (petroleum) petróleo // vt (machine) engrasar; ~**can** n lata de aceite; ~**field** n campo petrolífero; ~**fired** a que quema aceite combustible; ~ **painting** n pintura de óleo; ~ **refinery** n refinería de petróleo; ~ **rig** n torre f de perforación; ~**skins** npl impermeables mpl de hule, chubasquero sg; ~ **tanker** n petrolero; ~ **well** n pozo (de petróleo); ~**y** a aceitoso; (food) grasiento.
ointment ['ɔintmənt] n ungüento.
O.K., okay ['əu'kei] excl O.K., ¡está bien!, ¡vale! // a bien // vt dar el visto bueno a.
old [əuld] a viejo; (former) antiguo; **how ~ are you?** ¿cuántos años tienes?, ¿qué edad tienes?; **he's 10 years ~** tiene 10 años; ~**er brother** hermano mayor; ~ **age** n la vejez; ~**-age pensioner (O.A.P.)** n jubilado/a; ~**-fashioned** a anticuado, pasado de moda.
olive ['ɔliv] n (fruit) aceituna; (tree) olivo // a (also: ~**-green**) verde oliva; ~ **oil** n aceite m de oliva.
Olympic [əu'limpik] a olímpico; **the ~ Games, the ~s** los Juegos Olímpicos.
omelet(te) ['ɔmlit] n tortilla (de huevo).
omen ['əumən] n presagio.
ominous ['ɔminəs] a de mal agüero, amenazador(a).
omission [əu'miʃən] n omisión f; (error) descuido.
omit [əu'mit] vt omitir; (by mistake) olvidar, descuidar.
on [ɔn] prep en, sobre // ad (machine) conectado, (light, radio) encendido; (tap) abierto; **is the meeting still ~?** ¿todavía hay reunión?; **when is this film ~?** ¿cuándo van a poner esta película?; ~ **the wall** en la pared, colgado de la pared; ~ **television** en la televisión; ~ **horseback** a caballo; ~ **seeing this** al ver esto; ~ **arrival** al llegar; ~ **the left** a la izquierda; ~ **Friday** el viernes; **a week ~ Friday** el viernes en ocho días; **to have one's coat ~** tener el abrigo puesto; **to go ~** seguir adelante; **it's not ~!** ¡eso no se hace!
once [wʌns] ad una vez; (formerly) antiguamente // conj una vez que; **at ~** en seguida, inmediatamente; (simultaneously) a la vez; ~ **a week** una vez por semana; ~ **more** otra vez; ~ **and for all** de una vez por todas; ~ **upon a time** érase una vez.
oncoming ['ɔnkʌmiŋ] a (traffic) que viene de frente.
one [wʌn] det, num un, uno, una // pron uno; (impersonal) se // a (sole) único; (same) mismo; **this ~** éste/a; **that ~** ése/a, aquél/aquella; ~ **by ~** uno por uno; ~ **never knows** nunca se sabe; ~ **another** el uno al otro; ~**-man** a (business) individual; ~**-man band** n un hombre-orquesta; ~**self** pron uno mismo; (after

prep, also emphatic) sí (mismo/a); '~**-way**' 'dirección única'.
ongoing ['ɔngəuiŋ] a continuo.
onion ['ʌnjən] n cebolla.
onlooker ['ɔnlukə*] n espectador/a m/f.
only ['əunli] ad solamente, sólo // a único, solo // conj solamente que, pero; **an ~ child** un hijo único; **not ~ ... but also...** no sólo ... sino también... .
onset ['ɔnsɛt] n (beginning) comienzo; (attack) ataque m.
onslaught ['ɔnslɔ:t] n ataque m, embestida.
onto ['ɔntu] prep = **on to**.
onus ['əunəs] n responsabilidad f.
onward(s) ['ɔnwəd(z)] ad (move) (hacia) adelante; **from this time ~** de ahora en adelante.
onyx ['ɔniks] n ónice m, onyx m.
ooze [u:z] vi rezumar.
opal ['əupl] n ópalo.
opaque [əu'peik] a opaco.
open ['əupn] a abierto; (car) descubierto; (road, view) despejado; (meeting) público; (admiration) manifiesto // vt abrir // vi (flower, eyes, door, debate) abrirse; (book etc: commence) comenzar; **to ~ on to** vi fus (subj: room, door) dar a; **to ~ up** vt abrir; (blocked road) despejar // vi abrirse, empezar; **in the ~ (air)** al aire libre; ~**ing** n abertura, comienzo; (opportunity) oportunidad f, vacante f; (job) puesto vacante, vacante f; ~**ly** ad abiertamente; ~**-minded** a imparcial; ~**-necked** a sin corbata.
opera ['ɔpərə] n ópera; ~ **glasses** npl gemelos mpl; ~ **house** n teatro de la ópera.
operate ['ɔpəreit] vt (machine) hacer funcionar; (company) dirigir // vi funcionar; (drug) hacer efecto; **to ~ on sb** (MED) operar a uno.
operatic [ɔpə'rætik] a de ópera.
operating ['ɔpəreitiŋ]: ~ **table** n mesa de operaciones; ~ **theatre** n sala de operaciones.
operation [ɔpə'reiʃən] n (gen) operación f; (of machine) funcionamiento; **to be in ~** estar en funcionamiento o funcionando; ~**al** a operacional, en buen estado.
operative ['ɔpərətiv] a (measure) en vigor.
operator ['ɔpəreitə*] n (of machine) maquinista m/f, operario; (TEL) operador/a m/f, telefonista m/f.
operetta [ɔpə'rɛtə] n opereta; (in Spain) zarzuela.
ophthalmic [ɔf'θælmik] a oftálmico.
opinion [ə'piniən] n (gen) opinión f; (point of view) parecer m, juicio; ~**ated** a testarudo; ~ **poll** n encuesta, sondeo.
opium ['əupiəm] n opio.
opponent [ə'pəunənt] n adversario/a, contrincante m/f.
opportune ['ɔpətju:n] a oportuno; **opportunist** [-'tju:nist] n oportunista m/f.
opportunity [ɔpə'tju:niti] n oportunidad f.

oppose [ə'pəuz] vt oponerse a; **to be ~d to sth** oponerse a algo, resistirse a aceptar algo; **opposing** a (side) opuesto, contrario.

opposite ['ɔpəzit] a opuesto; (house etc) de enfrente // ad en frente // prep en frente de, frente a // n lo contrario.

opposition [ɔpə'zifən] n oposición f.

oppress [ə'prɛs] vt oprimir; ~**ion** [ə'prɛʃən] n opresión f; ~**ive** a opresivo.

opt [ɔpt] vi: **to ~ for** elegir; **to ~ to do** optar por hacer; **to ~ out of** optar por no hacer.

optical ['ɔptikl] a óptico.

optician [ɔp'tiʃən] n óptico.

optimism ['ɔptimizəm] n optimismo.

optimist ['ɔptimist] n optimista m/f; ~**ic** [-'mistik] a optimista.

optimum ['ɔptiməm] a óptimo.

option ['ɔpʃən] n opción f; **to keep one's ~s open** (fig) mantener las opciones abiertas; ~**al** a facultativo, discrecional.

opulent ['ɔpjulənt] a opulento.

or [ɔ:*] conj o; (before o, ho) u; (with negative): **he hasn't seen ~ heard anything** no ha visto ni oído nada; ~ **else** si no.

oracle ['ɔrəkl] n oráculo.

oral ['ɔ:rəl] a oral // n examen m oral.

orange ['ɔrindʒ] n (fruit) naranja // a color naranja.

oration [ɔ:'reiʃən] n oración f; **orator** ['ɔrətə*] n orador/a m/f.

orbit ['ɔ:bit] n órbita // vt, vi orbitar.

orchard ['ɔ:tʃəd] n huerto.

orchestra ['ɔ:kistrə] n orquesta; **orchestral** [-'kɛstrəl] a orquestral.

orchid ['ɔ:kid] n orquídea.

ordain [ɔ:'dein] vt (REL) ordenar, decretar; (decide) mandar.

ordeal [ɔ:'di:l] n experiencia penosa.

order ['ɔ:də*] n orden m; (command) orden f; (type, kind) clase f; (state) estado; (COMM) pedido, encargo // vt (also: **put in ~**) arreglar, poner en orden; (COMM) encargar, pedir; (command) mandar, ordenar; **in ~** (of document) en regla; **in ~ to do** para hacer; **to ~ sb to do sth** mandar a uno hacer algo; ~**ly** n (MIL) ordenanza m; (MED) enfermero (auxiliar) // a (room) en orden, ordenado; (person) ordenado.

ordinary ['ɔ:dnri] a corriente, normal; (pej) ordinario, vulgar; **out of the ~** fuera de lo común.

ordnance ['ɔ:dnəns] n (MIL: unit) artillería; **O~ Survey** n servicio oficial de topografía y cartografía.

ore [ɔ:*] n mineral m.

organ ['ɔ:gən] n órgano; ~**ic** [ɔ:'gænik] a orgánico.

organism ['ɔ:gənizəm] n organismo.

organist ['ɔ:gənist] n organista m/f.

organization [ɔ:gənai'zeiʃən] n organización f; **organize** ['ɔ:gənaiz] vt organizar; **organizer** ['ɔ:gənaizə*] n organizador/a m/f.

orgasm ['ɔ:gæzəm] n orgasmo.

orgy ['ɔ:dʒi] n orgía.

Orient ['ɔ:riənt] n Oriente m; **oriental** [-'ɛntl] a oriental.

orientate ['ɔ:riənteit] vt orientar.

origin ['ɔridʒin] n origen m; (point of departure) procedencia.

original [ə'ridʒinl] a original; (first) primero; (earlier) primitivo // n original m; ~**ity** [-'næliti] n originalidad f; ~**ly** ad (at first) al principio; (with originality) con originalidad.

originate [ə'ridʒineit] vi: **to ~ from or in** surgir de, tener su origen en.

ornament ['ɔ:nəmənt] n adorno; (trinket) chuchería; ~**al** [-'mentl] a decorativo, de adorno.

ornate [ɔ:'neit] a muy ornado, vistoso.

ornithologist [ɔ:ni'θɔlədʒist] n ornitólogo; **ornithology** [-dʒi] n ornitología.

orphan ['ɔ:fn] n huérfano // vt: **to be ~ed** quedar huérfano; ~**age** n orfelinato.

orthodox ['ɔ:θədɔks] a ortodoxo; ~**y** n ortodoxia.

orthopaedic, orthopedic (US) [ɔ:θə'pi:dik] a ortopédico; ~**s** n ortopedia.

oscillate ['ɔsileit] vi oscilar; (person) vacilar.

ostensibly [ɔs'tensibli] ad aparentemente.

ostentatious [ɔsten'teiʃəs] a pretencioso, aparatoso; (person) ostentativo.

osteopath ['ɔstiəpæθ] n osteópata m/f.

ostracize ['ɔstrəsaiz] vt condenar al ostracismo.

ostrich ['ɔstritʃ] n avestruz m.

other ['ʌðə*] a otro; ~ **than** (in another way) de otra manera que; (apart from) aparte de; ~**wise** ad, conj de otra manera; (if not) si no.

otter ['ɔtə*] n nutria.

ought [ɔ:t], pt ought auxiliary vb: **I ~ to do it** debería hacerlo; **this ~ to have been corrected** esto debiera de haberse corregido; **he ~ to win** (probability) debe o debiera ganar.

ounce [auns] n onza (28.35g).

our ['auə*] a nuestro; ~**s** pron (el) nuestro/(la) nuestra etc; ~**selves** pron pl (reflexive, after prep) nosotros; (emphatic) nosotros mismos.

oust [aust] vt desalojar.

out [aut] ad fuera, afuera; (not at home) fuera (de casa); (light, fire) apagado; ~ **there** allí, allí fuera; **he's ~** (absent) no está, ha salido; **to be ~ in one's calculations** equivocarse (en sus cálculos); **to run ~** salir corriendo; ~ **loud** en alta voz; ~ **of** (outside) fuera de; (because of: anger etc) por; ~ **of petrol** sin gasolina; "~ **of order**" "no funciona"; ~**-of-the-way** (fig) insólito.

outback ['autbæk] n interior m.

outboard ['autbɔ:d] a: ~ **motor** motor m de fuera de borda.

outbreak ['autbreik] n (of war) comienzo;

(of disease) epidemia; (of violence etc) arranque m.

outburst ['autbə:st] n explosión f, arranque m.

outcast ['autkɑ:st] n paria m/f.

outcome ['autkʌm] n resultado.

outcry ['autkraɪ] n protesta ruidosa.

outdated [aut'deɪtɪd] a anticuado, fuera de moda.

outdo [aut'du:] (irg: like do) vt exceder.

outdoor [aut'dɔ:*] a, ~s ad al aire libre.

outer ['autə*] a exterior, externo; ~ **space** n el espacio.

outfit ['autfɪt] n equipo; (clothes) traje m; ~**ter's** n camisería.

outgoing ['autgəʊɪŋ] a (character) extrovertido; ~**s** npl gastos mpl.

outgrow [aut'grəʊ] (irg: like grow) vt: **he has** ~ **in his clothes** su ropa le queda pequeña ya.

outing ['autɪŋ] n excursión f, paseo.

outlandish [aut'lændɪʃ] a estrafalario.

outlaw ['autlɔ:] n proscrito // vt (person) declarar fuera de la ley; (practice) declarar ilegal.

outlay ['autleɪ] n inversión f.

outlet ['autlet] n salida; (of pipe) desagüe m; (for emotion) desahogo; (also: **retail** ~) lugar m de venta.

outline ['autlaɪn] n (shape) contorno, perfil m; (of plan) trazado; (sketch) esbozo, idea general.

outlive [aut'lɪv] vt sobrevivir.

outlook ['autluk] n perspectiva; (opinion) punto de vista.

outlying ['autlaɪɪŋ] a remoto, aislado.

outmoded [aut'məudɪd] a anticuado, pasado de moda.

outnumber [aut'nʌmbə*] vt exceder en número.

outpatient ['autpeɪʃənt] n paciente m/f de consulta externa.

outpost ['autpəust] n puesto avanzado.

output ['autput] n (volumen m de) producción f, rendimiento.

outrage ['autreɪdʒ] n (scandal) escándalo; (atrocity) atrocidad f // vt ultrajar; ~**ous** [-'reɪdʒəs] a monstruoso.

outright [aut'raɪt] ad completamente // a ['autraɪt] completo.

outset ['autset] n principio.

outside [aut'saɪd] n exterior m; (surface) superficie f; (aspect) aspecto // a exterior, externo // ad fuera // prep fuera de; (beyond) más allá de; **at the** ~ (fig) a lo sumo; ~ **lane** n (AUT: in Britain) carril m de la derecha; ~-**left** n (FOOTBALL) extremo izquierdo; **outsider** n (stranger) extraño, forastero.

outsize ['autsaɪz] a (clothes) de talla grande.

outskirts ['autskɔ:ts] npl alrededores mpl, afueras fpl.

outspoken [aut'spəukən] a muy franco.

outstanding [aut'stændɪŋ] a excepcional, destacado; (unfinished) pendiente.

outstay [aut'steɪ] vt: **to** ~ **one's welcome** quedarse más tiempo de lo indicado.

outstretched [aut'stretʃt] a (hand) extendido.

outward ['autwəd] a (sign, appearances) externo; (journey) de ida; ~**ly** ad por fuera.

outweigh [aut'weɪ] vt pesar más que.

outwit [aut'wɪt] vt ser más listo que, burlar.

oval ['əʊvl] a ovalado // n óvalo.

ovary ['əʊvərɪ] n ovario.

ovation [əu'veɪʃən] n ovación f.

oven ['ʌvn] n horno; ~**proof** a refractario.

over ['əʊvə*] ad encima, por encima // a (or ad) (finished) terminado // prep (por) encima de; (above) sobre; (on the other side of) al otro lado de; (more than) más de; (during) durante; ~ **here** (por) aquí; ~ **there** (por) allí o allá; **all** ~ (everywhere) por todas partes; ~ **and** ~ (**again**) una y otra vez; ~ **and above** más de; **to ask sb** ~ invitar a uno; **to bend** ~ inclinarse.

over... [əʊvə*] pref sobre..., super...; ~**abundant** a superabundante.

overall ['əʊvərɔ:l] a (length) total; (study) de conjunto // ad [əʊvər'ɔ:l] en conjunto; ~**s** npl mono sg o bata sg (de trabajo).

overbalance [əʊvə'bæləns] vi perder el equilibrio.

overbearing [əʊvə'beərɪŋ] a autoritario, imperioso.

overboard ['əʊvəbɔ:d] ad (NAUT) por la borda; **man** ~! ¡hombre al agua!

overcast ['əʊvəkɑ:st] a encapotado.

overcharge [əʊvə'tʃɑ:dʒ] vt: **to** ~ **sb** cobrar un precio excesivo a uno.

overcoat ['əʊvəkəut] n abrigo, sobretodo.

overcome [əʊvə'kʌm] (irg: like come) vt (gen) vencer; (difficulty) superar.

overcrowded [əʊvə'kraudɪd] a atestado de gente; (country) superpoblado.

overdo [əʊvə'du:] (irg: like do) vt exagerar; (overcook) cocer demasiado.

overdose ['əʊvədəus] n dosis f excesiva.

overdraft ['əʊvədrɑ:ft] n saldo deudor.

overdrawn [əʊvə'drɔ:n] a (account) en descubierto.

overdue [əʊvə'dju:] a retrasado; (recognition) tardío.

overestimate [əʊvər'estɪmeɪt] vt sobreestimar.

overexcited [əʊvərɪk'saɪtɪd] a sobreexcitado.

overexpose [əʊvərɪk'spəuz] vt (PHOT) sobreexponer.

overflow [əʊvə'fləu] vi desbordarse // n ['əʊvəfləu] (excess) exceso; (of river) desbordamiento; (also: ~ **pipe**) cañería de desagüe m.

overgrown [əʊvə'grəun] a (garden) cubierto de hierba.

overhaul [əʊvə'hɔ:l] vt revisar, repasar // n ['əʊvəhɔ:l] revisión f.

overhead [əʊvə'hed] ad por lo alto // a

['əuvəhɛd] de arriba; (*railway*) elevado, aéreo; **~s** *npl* gastos *mpl* generales.

overhear [əuvə'hiə*] (*irg: like* **hear**) *vt* oír por casualidad.

overjoyed [əuvə'dʒɔid] *a* encantado, lleno de alegría.

overland ['əuvəlænd] *a, ad* por tierra.

overlap [əuvə'læp] *vi* traslaparse // *n* ['əuvəlæp] traslapo.

overleaf [əuvə'li:f] *ad* al dorso.

overload [əuvə'ləud] *vt* sobrecargar.

overlook [əuvə'luk] *vt* (*have view on*) dar a, tener vistas a; (*miss: by mistake*) pasar por alto; (: *deliberately*) no hacerse caso de; (*forgive*) perdonar.

overnight [əuvə'nait] *ad* durante la noche; (*fig*) de la noche a la mañana // a de noche; **to stay ~** pasar la noche.

overpass ['əuvəpɑ:s] *n* paso superior.

overpower [əuvə'pauə*] *vt* dominar; **~ing** a (*heat, stench*) abrumador(a).

overrate [əuvə'reit] *vt* sobreestimar.

override [əuvə'raid] (*irg: like* **ride**) *vt* (*order, objection*) no hacer caso de; **overriding** a predominante.

overrule [əuvə'ru:l] *vt* (*decision*) anular; (*claim*) denegar.

overseas [əuvə'si:z] *ad* en ultramar; (*abroad*) en el extranjero // a (*trade*) exterior; (*visitor*) extranjero.

overseer ['əuvəsiə*] *n* (*in factory*) superintendente *m/f*; (*foreman*) capataz *m*.

overshadow [əuvə'ʃædəu] *vt* (*fig*) eclipsar.

overshoot [əuvə'ʃu:t] (*irg: like* **shoot**) *vt* excederse.

oversight ['əuvəsait] *n* descuido.

oversleep [əuvə'sli:p] (*irg: like* **sleep**) *vi* despertarse (muy) tarde.

overspend [əuvə'spɛnd] (*irg: like* **spend**) *vi* gastar demasiado.

overspill ['əuvəspil] *n* exceso de población.

overstate [əuvə'steit] *vt* exagerar; **~ment** n exageración f.

overt [əu'və:t] a abierto.

overtake [əuvə'teik] (*irg: like* **take**) *vt* sobrepasar; (*AUT*) adelantar; **overtaking** n (*AUT*) adelantamiento.

overthrow [əuvə'θrəu] (*irg: like* **throw**) *vt* (*government*) derrocar.

overtime ['əuvətaim] *n* horas *fpl* extraordinarias.

overtone ['əuvətəun] *n* (*fig*) sugestión f, alusión f.

overture ['əuvətʃuə*] *n* (*MUS*) obertura; (*fig*) propuesta.

overturn [əuvə'tə:n] *vt, vi* volcar.

overweight [əuvə'weit] *a* demasiado gordo *o* pesado.

overwhelm [əuvə'wɛlm] *vt* aplastar; **~ing** a (*victory, defeat*) arrollador(a); (*desire*) irresistible.

overwork [əuvə'wə:k] *n* trabajo excesivo // *vt* hacer trabajar demasiado // *vi* trabajar demasiado.

overwrought [əuvə'rɔ:t] a sobreexcitado.

owe [əu] *vt* deber; **to ~ sb sth, to ~ sth to sb** deber algo a uno; **owing to** *prep* debido a, por causa de.

owl [aul] *n* búho, lechuza.

own [əun] *vt* tener, poseer // a propio; **a room of my ~** una habitación propia; **to get one's ~ back** tomar revancha; **on one's ~** solo, a solas; **to ~ up** *vi* confesar; **~er** *n* dueño; **~ership** *n* posesión f.

ox [ɔks], *pl* **~en** ['ɔksn] *n* buey *m*.

oxide ['ɔksaid] *n* óxido.

oxtail ['ɔksteil] *n*: **~ soup** sopa de rabo de buey.

oxygen ['ɔksidʒən] *n* oxígeno; **~ mask/tent** máscara/tienda de oxígeno.

oyster ['ɔistə*] *n* ostra.

oz. *abbr of* **ounce(s).**

ozone ['əuzəun] *n* ozono.

P

p [pi:] *abbr of* **penny, pence.**

p.a. *abbr of* **per annum.**

pa [pɑ:] *n* (*col*) papá *m*.

pace [peis] *n* paso; (*rhythm*) ritmo // *vi*: **to ~ up and down** pasarse de un lado a otro; **to keep ~ with** llevar el mismo paso que; (*events*) mantenerse a la altura de *o* al corriente de; **~maker** *n* (*MED*) regulador *m* cardíaco, marcapasos *m inv*.

pacific [pə'sifik] a pacífico // n: **the P~ (Ocean)** el (Océano) Pacífico.

pacifist ['pæsifist] *n* pacifista *m/f*.

pacify ['pæsifai] *vt* (*soothe*) apaciguar; (*country*) pacificar.

pack [pæk] *n* (*gen*) paquete *m*; (*of hounds*) jauría; (*of thieves etc*) manada, bando; (*of cards*) baraja; (*bundle*) fardo; (*back ~*) mochila // *vt* (*wrap*) empaquetar; (*fill*) llenar; (*in suitcase etc*) meter *o* poner (en maleta); (*cram*) llenar, atestar; (*fig: meeting etc*) llenar de partidarios; **to ~ sb off** despachar a uno; **~ it in!** (*col*) ¡déjalo!; **to ~ one's case** hacerse la maleta.

package ['pækidʒ] *n* paquete *m*; (*bulky*) bulto; (*also:* **~ deal**) acuerdo global; **~ tour** n viaje *m* todo incluido.

packet ['pækit] *n* paquete *m*; (*NAUT*) paquebote *m*.

packing ['pækiŋ] *n* embalaje *m*; (*external*) envase *m*; (*internal*) relleno; **~ case** n cajón *m* de embalaje.

pact [pækt] *n* pacto.

pad [pæd] *n* (*of paper*) bloc *m*; (*cushion*) cojinete *m*; (*launching ~*) plataforma (de lanzamiento); (*foot*) pata; (*col: flat*) casa // *vi* andar (sin hacer ruido); **~ding** n relleno; (*fig*) paja.

paddle ['pædl] *n* (*oar*) canalete *m* // *vt* impulsar con canalete // *vi* (*with feet*) chapotear; **~ steamer** *n* vapor *m* de ruedas; **paddling pool** n estanque *m* de juegos.

paddock ['pædək] *n* corral *m*.

paddy field ['pædɪ-] n arrozal m.
padlock ['pædlɔk] n candado // vt cerrar con candado.
padre ['pɑːdrɪ] n capellán m.
paediatrics, pediatrics (US) [piːdɪ'ætrɪks] n pediatría.
pagan ['peɪɡən] a, n pagano/a.
page [peɪdʒ] n (of book) página; (of newspaper) plana; (also: ~ **boy**) paje m // vt (in hotel etc) buscar a (uno) llamando su nombre.
pageant ['pædʒənt] n (procession) desfile m; (show) espectáculo; ~**ry** n pompa.
pagoda [pə'ɡəʊdə] n pagoda.
paid [peɪd] pt, pp of **pay** // a (work) remunerado; (official) asalariado; **to put** ~ **to** acabar con.
pail [peɪl] n cubo, balde m.
pain [peɪn] n dolor m; **to be in** ~ sufrir; **on** ~ **of death** so pena de muerte; **to take** ~**s to do sth** tomarse trabajo en hacer algo; ~**ed** a (expression) afligido; ~**ful** a doloroso; (difficult) penoso; (disagreeable) desagradable; ~**fully** ad (fig: very) terriblemente; ~**killer** n calmante m; ~**less** a que no causa dolor; **painstaking** ['peɪnzteɪkɪŋ] a (person) concienzudo, esmerado.
paint [peɪnt] n pintura // vt pintar; **to** ~ **one's face** pintarse (la cara); **to** ~ **the door blue** pintar la puerta de azul; ~**brush** n (artist's) pincel m; (decorator's) brocha; ~**er** n pintor/a m/f; ~**ing** n pintura.
pair [pɛə*] n (of shoes, gloves etc) par m; (of people) pareja; **a** ~ **of scissors** unas tijeras; **a** ~ **of trousers** unos pantalones, un pantalón.
pajamas [pɪ'dʒɑːməz] npl (US) pijama m.
Pakistan [pɑːkɪ'stɑːn] n Paquistán m; ~**i** a, n paquistaní.
pal [pæl] n (col) compinche m/f, compañero/a.
palace ['pæləs] n palacio.
palatable ['pælɪtəbl] a sabroso; (acceptable) aceptable.
palate ['pælɪt] n paladar m.
palaver [pə'lɑːvə*] n (fuss) lío; (hindrances) molestias fpl.
pale [peɪl] a (gen) pálido; (colour) claro; **to grow** ~ palidecer; **to be beyond the** ~ estar excluido; ~**ness** n palidez f.
Palestine ['pælɪstaɪn] n Palestina; **Palestinian** [-'tɪnɪən] a, n palestino/a.
palette ['pælɪt] n paleta.
paling ['peɪlɪŋ] n (stake) estaca; (fence) valla.
palisade [pælɪ'seɪd] n palizada.
pall [pɔːl] n (of smoke) capa (de humo) // vi perder el sabor.
pallid ['pælɪd] a pálido.
palm [pɑːm] n (gen) palma; (also: ~ **tree**) palmera, palma // vt: **to** ~ **sth off on sb** (col) encajar algo a uno; ~**ist** n quiromántico/a; **P**~ **Sunday** n Domingo de Ramos.
palpable ['pælpəbl] a palpable.

palpitation [pælpɪ'teɪʃən] n palpitación f; **to have** ~**s** tener vahídos.
paltry ['pɔːltrɪ] a (insignificant) baladí; (miserable) vil.
pamper ['pæmpə*] vt mimar.
pamphlet ['pæmflət] n folleto.
pan [pæn] n (also: **sauce**~) cacerola, cazuela; (also: **frying** ~) sartén m; (of lavatory) taza // vi (CINEMA) tomar una vista panorámica.
panacea [pænə'sɪə] n panacea.
Panama ['pænəmɑː] n Panamá m.
pancake ['pænkeɪk] n panqueque m.
panda ['pændə] n panda m/f; ~ **car** n coche m de la policía.
pandemonium [pændɪ'məʊnɪəm] n (noise) estruendo; (mess) caos m.
pander ['pændə*] vi: **to** ~ **to** complacer a.
pane [peɪn] n cristal m.
panel ['pænl] n (of wood) panel m; (of cloth) paño; (RADIO, TV) tablero; ~**ling**, ~**ing** (US) n paneles mpl, entrepaños mpl.
pang [pæŋ] n: ~**s of conscience** remordimiento sg; ~**s of hunger** dolores mpl del hambre.
panic ['pænɪk] n (terror) pánico // vi aterrarse; ~**ky** a (person) asustadizo; ~**stricken** a preso de pánico.
pannier ['pænɪə*] n (on bicycle) cartera; (on mule etc) alforja.
panorama [pænə'rɑːmə] n panorama m.
pansy ['pænzɪ] n (BOT) pensamiento; (col) maricón m.
pant [pænt] vi jadear.
panther ['pænθə*] n pantera.
panties ['pæntɪz] npl bragas fpl, pantis mpl.
pantomime ['pæntəmaɪm] n revista musical representada en Navidad, basada en cuentos de hadas.
pantry ['pæntrɪ] n despensa.
pants [pænts] n (woman's) bragas fpl; (man's) calzoncillos mpl; (US: trousers) pantalones mpl.
papal ['peɪpəl] a papal.
paper ['peɪpə*] n papel m; (also: **news**~) periódico, diario; (study, article) artículo; (exam) examen m // a de papel // vt empapelar; (identity) ~**s** npl papeles mpl, documentos mpl; ~**back** n libro de bolsillo; ~ **bag** n saco de papel; ~ **clip** n grapa; ~ **hankie** n pañuelo de papel; ~ **money** n papel moneda; ~**weight** n pisapapeles m inv; ~**work** n trabajo administrativo; (pej) papeleo.
papier-mâché ['pæpɪeɪ'mæʃeɪ] n cartón m piedra.
paprika ['pæprɪkə] n pimienta húngara o roja.
par [pɑː*] n par f; (GOLF) par m; **to be on a** ~ **with** correr parejas con.
parable ['pærəbl] n parábola.
parachute ['pærəʃuːt] n paracaídas m inv // vi lanzarse en paracaídas; ~ **jump** n salto en paracaídas.
parade [pə'reɪd] n desfile m // vt (gen)

recorrer, desfilar por; (*show off*) hacer alarde de // *vi* desfilar; (*MIL*) pasar revista.

paradise ['pærədaɪs] *n* paraíso.

paradox ['pærədɔks] *n* paradoja; ~**ical** [-'dɔksɪkl] *a* paradójico.

paraffin ['pærəfɪn] *n*: ~ (**oil**) petróleo.

paragraph ['pærəgrɑːf] *n* párrafo.

parallel ['pærəlɛl] *a* en paralelo; (*fig*) semejante // *n* (*line*) paralela; (*fig, GEO*) paralelo.

paralysis [pə'rælɪsɪs] *n* parálisis *f*; **paralyze** ['pærəlaɪz] *vt* paralizar.

paramount ['pærəmaunt] *a*: **of** ~ **importance** de la mayor importancia, primordial.

paranoia [pærə'nɔɪə] *n* paranoia; **paranoiac** *a* paranoico.

paraphernalia [pærəfə'neɪlɪə] *n* (*gear*) avíos *mpl*.

paraplegic [pærə'pliːdʒɪk] *n* parapléjico.

parasite ['pærəsaɪt] *n* parásito.

parasol [pærə'sɔl] *n* sombrilla, quitasol *m*.

paratrooper ['pærətruːpə*] *n* paracaidista *m/f*.

parcel ['pɑːsl] *n* paquete *m* // *vt* (*also*: ~ **up**) empaquetar, embalar.

parch [pɑːtʃ] *vt* secar, resecar; ~**ed** *a* (*person*) muerto de sed.

parchment ['pɑːtʃmənt] *n* pergamino.

pardon ['pɑːdn] *n* perdón *m*; (*LAW*) indulto // *vt* perdonar; indultar; ~! ¡perdone!; ~ **me!, I beg your** ~! ¡perdone Usted!; (**I beg your**) ~? ¿cómo?

parent ['pɛərənt] *n* padre *m*/madre *f*; ~**s** *npl* padres *mpl*; ~**al** [pə'rɛntl] *a* paternal/maternal.

parenthesis [pə'rɛnθɪsɪs], *pl* **-theses** [-θɪsiːz] *n* paréntesis *m inv*.

Paris ['pærɪs] *n* París.

parish ['pærɪʃ] *n* parroquia; ~**ioner** [pə'rɪʃənə*] *n* feligrés/esa *m/f*.

Parisian [pə'rɪzɪən] *a, n* parisino/a, parisiense *m/f*.

parity ['pærɪtɪ] *n* paridad *f*, igualdad *f*.

park [pɑːk] *n* parque *m* // *vt* estacionar // *vi* aparcar, estacionarse; ~**ing** *n* aparcamiento, estacionamiento; **'no** ~**ing'** 'prohibido estacionarse'; ~**ing lot** *n* (*US*) parking *m*; ~**ing meter** *n* parquímetro.

parliament ['pɑːləmənt] *n* parlamento; (*Spanish*) Cortes *mpl*; ~**ary** [-'mɛntərɪ] *a* parlamentario.

parlour, parlor (*US*) ['pɑːlə*] *n* sala de recibo, salón *m*.

parochial [pə'rəukɪəl] *a* parroquial; (*pej*) de miras estrechas.

parody ['pærədɪ] *n* parodia // *vt* parodiar.

parole [pə'rəul] *n*: **on** ~ libre bajo palabra.

parquet ['pɑːkeɪ] *n*: ~ **floor(ing)** parquet *m*.

parrot ['pærət] *n* loro, papagayo; ~ **fashion** *ad* mecánicamente.

parry ['pærɪ] *vt* parar.

parsimonious [pɑːsɪ'məunɪəs] *a* parco.

parsley ['pɑːslɪ] *n* perejil *m*.

parsnip ['pɑːsnɪp] *n* (*parish*) chirivía.

parson ['pɑːsn] *n* (*parish*) párroco; (*gen*) cura *m*.

part [pɑːt] *n* (*gen, MUS*) parte *f*; (*bit*) trozo; (*of machine*) pieza; (*THEATRE etc*) papel *m*; (*of serial*) entrega // *ad* = **partly** // *vt* dividir; (*break*) partir // *vi* (*people*) separarse; (*roads*) bifurcarse; (*crowd*) apartarse; (*break*) romperse; **to take** ~ **in** participar *o* tomar parte en; **to take sth in good** ~ tomar algo en buena parte; **to take sb's** ~ defender a uno; **for my** ~ por mi parte; **for the most** ~ en la mayor parte; **to** ~ **with** *vt fus* ceder, entregar; (*money*) pagar; (*get rid of*) deshacerse de; **in** ~ **exchange** como parte del pago; **spare** ~ pieza de recambio.

partial ['pɑːʃl] *a* parcial; **to be** ~ **to** ser aficionado a; ~**ly** *ad* en parte.

participant [pɑː'tɪsɪpənt] *n* (*in competition*) concursante *m/f*; **participate** [-peɪt] *vi*: **to participate in** participar en; **participation** [-'peɪʃən] *n* participación *f*.

participle ['pɑːtɪsɪpl] *n* participio.

particle ['pɑːtɪkl] *n* partícula; (*of dust*) grano; (*fig*) pizca.

particular [pə'tɪkjulə*] *a* (*special*) particular; (*concrete*) concreto; (*given*) determinado; (*detailed*) detallado, minucioso; (*fussy*) quisquilloso, exigente; ~**s** *npl* (*information*) datos *mpl*, detalles *mpl*; (*details*) pormenores *mpl*; ~**ly** *ad* especialmente, en particular.

parting ['pɑːtɪŋ] *n* (*act of*) separación *f*; (*farewell*) despedida; (*in hair*) raya // *a* de despedida.

partisan [pɑːtɪ'zæn] *a, n* partidario/a.

partition [pɑː'tɪʃən] *n* (*POL*) división *f*; (*wall*) tabique *m* // *vt* dividir; dividir con tabique.

partly ['pɑːtlɪ] *ad* en parte.

partner ['pɑːtnə*] *n* (*COMM*) socio/a; (*SPORT, at dance*) pareja; (*spouse*) cónyuge *m/f*; (*friend etc*) compañero/a // *vt* acompañar; ~**ship** *n* (*gen*) asociación *f*; (*COMM*) sociedad *f*.

partridge ['pɑːtrɪdʒ] *n* perdiz *f*.

part-time ['pɑːt'taɪm] *a, ad* de medio tiempo *o* media jornada.

party ['pɑːtɪ] *n* (*POL*) partido; (*celebration*) fiesta; (*group*) grupo; (*LAW*) parte *f*, interesado // *a* (*POL*) de partido; (*dress etc*) de fiesta, de gala.

pass [pɑːs] *vt* (*time, object*) pasar; (*place*) pasar por; (*exam*) aprobar; (*overtake, surpass*) rebasar; (*approve*) aprobar // *vi* pasar; (*SCOL*) aprobar, ser aprobado // *n* (*permit*) permiso; (*membership card*) carnet *m*; (*in mountains*) puerto, desfiladero; (*SPORT*) pase *m*; (*SCOL: also*: ~ **mark**): **to get a** ~ **in** aprobar en; **to** ~ **sth through sth** pasar algo por algo; **to** ~ **away** *vi* fallecer; **to** ~ **by** *vi* pasar //

vt (*ignore*) pasar por alto; **to ~ for** pasar por; **to ~ out** *vi* desmayarse; **to ~ up** *vt* renunciar a; **~able** *a* (*road*) transitable; (*work*) pasable.

passage ['pæsidʒ] *n* (*also*: **~way**) pasillo; (*act of passing*) tránsito; (*fare, in book*) pasaje *m*; (*by boat*) travesía; (*MECH, MED*) tubo.

passenger ['pæsindʒə*] *n* pasajero, viajero.

passer-by [pɑːsə'bai] *n* transeúnte *m/f*.

passing ['pɑːsiŋ] *a* (*fleeting*) pasajero; **in ~** de paso.

passion ['pæʃən] *n* pasión *f*; (*anger*) cólera; **~ate** *a* apasionado; colérico.

passive ['pæsiv] *a* (*also LING*) pasivo.

Passover ['pɑːsəuvə*] *n* Pascua (de los judíos).

passport ['pɑːspɔːt] *n* pasaporte *m*.

password ['pɑːswɜːd] *n* santo y seña.

past [pɑːst] *prep* (*further than*) más allá de; (*later than*) después de // *a* pasado; (*president etc*) ex, antiguo // *n* el pasado; (*antecedents*) antecedentes *mpl*; **he's ~ forty** tiene más de cuarenta años; **for the ~ few/3 days** durante los últimos/3 días; **to run ~** pasar a la carrera por.

pasta ['pæstə] *n* pastas *fpl*.

paste [peist] *n* (*gen*) pasta; (*glue*) engrudo // *vt* (*stick*) pegar; (*glue*) engomar.

pastel ['pæstl] *a* pastel; (*painting*) al pastel.

pasteurized ['pæstəraizd] *a* pasteurizado.

pastille ['pæstl] *n* pastilla.

pastime ['pɑːstaim] *n* pasatiempo.

pastor ['pɑːstə*] *n* pastor *m*.

pastoral ['pɑːstərl] *a* pastoral.

pastry ['peistri] *n* pasta; (*cakes*) pastas *fpl*, pasteles *mpl*.

pasture ['pɑːstʃə*] *n* (*grass*) pasto; (*land*) prado, pasto.

pasty ['pæsti] *n* empanada // *a* ['peisti] pastoso; (*complexion*) pálido.

pat [pæt] *vt* dar una palmadita a; (*dog etc*) acariciar // *n* (*of butter*) pastelillo; **to give sb a ~ on the back** felicitar a uno.

patch [pætʃ] *n* (*of material*) parche *m*; (*piece*) pedazo; (*mend*) remiendo; (*of land*) terreno // *vt* (*clothes*) remendar; **to ~ up** *vt* (*mend temporarily*) componer de modo provisional; (*quarrel*) hacer las paces con; **~work** *n* labor *m* de retazos; **~y** *a* desigual.

pâté ['pætei] *n* pastel *m* de carne.

patent ['peitnt] *n* patente *f* // *vt* patentar // *a* patente, evidente; **~ leather** *n* charol *m*.

paternal [pə'tɜːnl] *a* paternal; (*relation*) paterno; **paternity** [-niti] *n* paternidad *f*.

path [pɑːθ] *n* senda, sendero; (*trail, track*) pista; (*of missile*) trayectoria.

pathetic [pə'θetik] *a* (*pitiful*) patético, lastimoso; (*very bad*) malísimo; (*moving*) conmovedor(a).

pathologist [pə'θɔlədʒist] *n* patólogo; **pathology** [-dʒi] *n* patología.

pathos ['peiθɔs] *n* patetismo, lo patético.

pathway ['pɑːθwei] *n* sendero, vereda.

patience ['peiʃns] *n* paciencia; (*CARDS*) solitario.

patient ['peiʃnt] *n* paciente *m/f* // *a* paciente, sufrido.

patio ['pætiəu] *n* patio.

patriot ['peitriət] *n* patriota *m/f*; **~ic** [pætri'ɔtik] *a* patriótico.

patrol [pə'trəul] *n* patrulla // *vt* patrullar por; **~ car** *n* coche *m* patrulla; **~man** *n* (*US*) policía *m*.

patron ['peitrən] *n* (*in shop*) cliente *m/f*; (*of charity*) patrocinador/a *m/f*; **~ of the arts** mecenas *m*; **~age** ['pætrənidʒ] *n* mecenazgo, protección *f*; **~ize** ['pætrənaiz] *vt* (*shop*) ser cliente de; (*business*) patrocinar; (*look down on*) tratar con condescendencia; **~ saint** *n* patrono.

patter ['pætə*] *n* golpeteo; (*of feet*) pasos *mpl* ligeros; (*sales talk*) jerga // *vi* andar con pasos ligeros; (*rain*) tamborilear.

pattern ['pætən] *n* modelo; (*SEWING*) patrón *m*; (*design*) dibujo; (*sample*) muestra.

paunch [pɔːntʃ] *n* panza, barriga.

pauper ['pɔːpə*] *n* pobre *m/f*.

pause [pɔːz] *n* pausa; (*interval*) intérvalo // *vi* hacer una pausa.

pave [peiv] *vt* pavimentar; **to ~ the way for** preparar el terreno para.

pavement ['peivmənt] *n* (*Brit*) acera.

pavilion [pə'viliən] *n* pabellón *m*; (*for band etc*) quiosco; (*SPORT*) caseta.

paving ['peiviŋ] *n* pavimento, enlosado; **~ stone** *n* losa.

paw [pɔː] *n* pata; (*of cat*) garra // *vt* tocar con la pata; (*touch*) tocar, manosear; (*amorously*) sobar.

pawn [pɔːn] *n* (*CHESS*) peón *m*; (*fig*) instrumento // *vt* empeñar; **~broker** *n* prestamista *m/f*; **~shop** *n* monte *m* de piedad.

pay [pei] *n* paga; (*wage etc*) sueldo // (*vb*: *pt, pp* **paid**) *vt* pagar; (*debt*) liquidar; (*visit*) hacer; (*respect*) ofrecer // *vi* pagar; (*be profitable*) rendir; **to ~ attention (to)** prestar atención (a); **to ~ back** *vt* (*money*) devolver; (*person*) pagar; **to ~ for** *vt* pagar por; **to ~ in** *vt* ingresar; **to ~ off** *vt* liquidar; **to ~ up** *vt* pagar (de mala gana); **~able** *a* pagadero; **~ day** *n* día *m* de paga; **~ee** *n* portador/a *m/f*; **~ing** *a* provechoso; **~ment** *n* pago; **advance ~ment** anticipo; **monthly ~ment** mensualidad *f*; **~ packet** *n* sobre *m* de paga; **~roll** *n* nómina; **~ slip** *n* hoja de paga.

p.c. *abbr of* **per cent**.

pea [piː] *n* guisante *m*; **sweet ~** guisante de olor.

peace [piːs] *n* paz *f*; (*calm*) paz *f*, tranquilidad *f*; **~able** *a* pacífico; **~ful** *a* (*gentle*) pacífico; (*calm*) tranquilo, sosegado; **~-keeping** *n* pacificación *f*; **~ offering** *n* prenda de paz.

peach [piːtʃ] *n* melocotón *m*, durazno (*AM*).

peacock ['piːkɔk] *n* pavo real.

peak [pi:k] n (of mountain: top) cumbre f, cima; (: point) pico; (of cap) visera; (fig) cumbre f; ~ **hours** npl horas fpl punta.

peal [pi:l] n (of bells) repique m, toque m de campanas; ~ **of laughter** carcajada.

peanut ['pi:nʌt] n cacahuete m, maní m (AM); ~ **butter** n manteca de cacahuete.

pear [pɛə*] n pera; ~ **tree** n peral m.

pearl [pɜ:l] n perla; **mother-of-~** n nácar m.

peasant ['pɛznt] n campesino/a.

peat [pi:t] n turba.

pebble ['pɛbl] n guijarro.

peck [pɛk] vt (also: ~ **at**) picotear; (food) comer sin ganas // n picotazo; (kiss) beso ligero; ~**ing order** n orden m de jerarquía; ~**ish** a (col) con hambre.

peculiar [pɪ'kju:lɪə*] a (odd) extraño, raro; (typical) propio, característico; (marked) especial; ~ **to** propio de; ~**ity** [pɪkju:lɪ'ærɪtɪ] n peculiaridad f; (feature) característica; (oddity) rareza, singularidad f.

pedal ['pɛdl] n pedal m // vi pedalear.

pedantic [pɪ'dæntɪk] a pedante.

peddle ['pɛdl] vt vender (de puerta en puerta); **peddler** n vendedor/a m/f ambulante.

pedestal ['pɛdəstl] n pedestal m.

pedestrian [pɪ'dɛstrɪən] n peatón m // a pedestre; ~ **crossing** n paso de peatones.

pedigree ['pɛdɪgri:] n genealogía; (of animal) raza // cpd (animal) de raza, de casta.

peek [pi:k] vi mirar a hurtadillas.

peel [pi:l] n piel f; (of orange, lemon) peladuras fpl // vt pelar // vi (paint etc) desconcharse; (wallpaper) despegarse, desprenderse.

peep [pi:p] n (look) mirada furtiva; (sound) pío // vi piar; **to** ~ **out** vi asomar la cabeza; ~**hole** n mirilla.

peer [pɪə*] vi: **to** ~ **at** mirar con ojos de miope // n (noble) par m; (equal) igual m; ~**age** n nobleza; ~**less** a sin par.

peeved [pi:vd] a enojado.

peevish ['pi:vɪʃ] a malhumorado.

peg [pɛg] n clavija; (for coat etc) gancho, colgadero; (also: **clothes** ~) pinza; (tent ~) estaca // vt (prices) fijar; **off the** ~ ad de confección.

pejorative [pɪ'dʒɔrətɪv] a peyorativo.

pekingese [pi:kɪ'ni:z] a pequinés/esa m/f.

pelican ['pɛlɪkən] n pelícano.

pellet ['pɛlɪt] n bolita; (bullet) perdigón m.

pelmet ['pɛlmɪt] n galería.

pelt [pɛlt] vt: **to** ~ **sb with sth** tirar algo a uno // vi (rain) llover a cántaros // n pellejo.

pelvis ['pɛlvɪs] n pelvis f.

pen [pɛn] n pluma; (for sheep) redil m; **play**~ parque m de niño; ~ **name** n seudónimo.

penal [pi:nl] a penal; ~**ize** vt penar; (SPORT) castigar.

penalty ['pɛnltɪ] n (gen) pena; (fine) multa; (SPORT) castigo; ~ **(kick)** n (FOOTBALL) penalty m.

penance ['pɛnəns] n penitencia.

pence [pɛns] pl of **penny**.

pencil ['pɛnsl] n lápiz m; (for eyebrows) lapiz de cejas; **propelling** ~ lapicero; ~ **sharpener** n sacapuntas m inv.

pendant ['pɛndnt] n pendiente m.

pending ['pɛndɪŋ] prep antes de // a pendiente.

pendulum ['pɛndjuləm] n péndulo.

penetrate ['pɛnɪtreɪt] vt penetrar; **penetrating** a penetrante; **penetration** [-'treɪʃən] n penetración f.

penfriend ['pɛnfrɛnd] n amigo/a por correspondencia.

penguin ['pɛŋgwɪn] n pingüino.

penicillin [pɛnɪ'sɪlɪn] n penicilina.

peninsula [pə'nɪnsjulə] n península.

penis ['pi:nɪs] n pene m.

penitence ['pɛnɪtns] n penitencia; **penitent** [-nt] a (gen) arrepentido; (REL) penitente.

penitentiary [pɛnɪ'tɛnʃərɪ] n (US) cárcel f, presidio.

penknife ['pɛnnaɪf] n navaja.

pennant ['pɛnənt] n banderola.

penniless ['pɛnɪlɪs] a sin dinero.

penny ['pɛnɪ], pl **pennies** ['pɛnɪz] or **pence** [pɛns] n penique m.

pension ['pɛnʃən] n (gen) pensión f; (old-age) jubilación f; (MIL) retiro; ~**er** n jubilado; ~ **fund** n caja de jubilaciones.

pensive ['pɛnsɪv] a pensativo; (withdrawn) preocupado.

pentagon ['pɛntəgən] n pentágono.

Pentecost ['pɛntɪkɔst] n Pentecostés m.

penthouse ['pɛnthaus] n ático.

pent-up ['pɛntʌp] a (feelings) reprimido.

penultimate [pɛ'nʌltɪmət] a penúltimo.

people ['pi:pl] npl gente f; (citizens) pueblo sg, ciudadanos mpl // n (nation, race) pueblo, nación f // vt poblar; **several** ~ **came** vinieron varias personas; ~ **say that...** dice la gente que... .

pep [pɛp] n (col) energía; **to** ~ **up** vt animar.

pepper ['pɛpə*] n pimienta; (vegetable) pimiento // vt (fig) salpicar; ~**mint** n menta; (sweet) pastilla de menta.

peptalk ['pɛptɔ:k] n (col) palabras fpl para levantar los ánimos.

per [pə:*] prep por; ~ **day/person** por día/persona; ~ **cent** por ciento; ~ **annum** al año.

perceive [pə'si:v] vt percibir; (realize) darse cuenta de.

percentage [pə'sɛntɪdʒ] n porcentaje m.

perception [pə'sɛpʃən] n percepción f; (insight) perspicacia; **perceptive** [-'sɛptɪv] a perspicaz.

perch [pə:tʃ] n (fish) perca; (for bird) percha // vi posarse.

percolator ['pə:kəleɪtə*] n cafetera filtradora.

percussion [pə'kʌʃən] n percusión f.

peremptory [pə'rɛmptərɪ] a perentorio; (person: imperious) imperioso.

perennial [pə'rɛnɪəl] a perenne.

perfect ['pə:fɪkt] a perfecto // n (also: ~ tense) perfecto // vt [pə'fɛkt] perfeccionar; ~**ion** [-'fɛkʃən] n perfección f; ~**ionist** n perfeccionista m/f.

perforate ['pə:fəreɪt] vt perforar; ~**d** a (stamp) dentado; **perforation** [-'reɪʃən] n perforación f.

perform [pə'fɔ:m] vt (carry out) realizar, cumplir; (concert etc) representar; (piece of music) interpretar // vi (animal) hacer trucos; (THEATRE) actuar; (TECH) funcionar; ~**ance** n (of task) cumplimiento, realización f; (of an artist) representación f; (of player etc) actuación f; (of car, engine) funcionamiento; (of function) desempeño; ~**er** n (actor) actor/actriz m/f; (MUS) interprete m/f; ~**ing** a (animal) amaestrado.

perfume ['pə:fju:m] n perfume m // vt perfumar.

perhaps [pə'hæps] ad quizá(s), tal vez.

peril ['pɛrɪl] n peligro, riesgo.

perimeter [pə'rɪmɪtə*] n perímetro.

period ['pɪərɪəd] n período; (HISTORY) época; (time limit) plazo; (SCOL) clase f; (full stop) punto; (MED) regla, reglas fpl // a (costume, furniture) de época; ~**ic** [-'ɔdɪk] a periódico; ~**ical** [-'ɔdɪkl] n periódico; ~**ically** [-'ɔdɪklɪ] ad de vez en cuando, cada cierto tiempo.

peripheral [pə'rɪfərəl] a periférico; **periphery** [-rɪ] n periferia.

periscope ['pərɪskəup] n periscopio.

perish ['pɛrɪʃ] vi perecer; (decay) echarse a perder, deteriorar(se); ~**able** a perecedero; ~**ing** a (col: cold) helado, glacial.

perjure ['pə:dʒə*] vt: to ~ o.s. perjurarse; **perjury** n (LAW) perjurio.

perk [pə:k] n pago encima del sueldo; to ~ up vi (cheer up) animarse; (in health) sentirse mejor; ~**y** a (cheerful) alegre, despabilado.

perm [pə:m] n permanente f.

permanent ['pə:mənənt] a permanente.

permissible [pə'mɪsɪbl] a permisible, lícito.

permission [pə'mɪʃən] n permiso; (authorization) licencia.

permissive [pə'mɪsɪv] a permisivo.

permit ['pə:mɪt] n permiso, licencia // vt [pə'mɪt] permitir; (authorize) autorizar; (accept) tolerar.

permutation [pə:mju'teɪʃən] n permutación f.

pernicious [pə:'nɪʃəs] a nocivo; (MED) pernicioso.

perpendicular [pə:pən'dɪkjulə*] a perpendicular.

perpetrate ['pə:pɪtreɪt] vt cometer.

perpetual [pə'pɛtjuəl] a perpetuo.

perpetuate [pə'pɛtjueɪt] vt perpetuar.

perplex [pə'plɛks] vt dejar perplejo.

persecute ['pə:sɪkju:t] vt (pursue)

perseguir; (harass) acosar; **persecution** [-'kju:ʃən] n persecución f.

persevere [pə:sɪ'vɪə*] vi persistir.

Persian ['pə:ʃən] a, n persa m/f.

persist [pə'sɪst] vi: to ~ (in doing sth) persistir (en hacer algo); ~**ence** n empeño; (of disease) pertinacia; ~**ent** a persistente; (determined) porfiado; (disease) pertinaz.

person ['pə:sn] n persona; ~**able** a atractivo; ~**al** a personal; (private) particular; (visit) en persona; (TEL) persona a persona; (column) de anuncios personales; ~**ality** [-'nælɪtɪ] n personalidad f; ~**ally** ad personalmente; ~**ify** [-'sɔnɪfaɪ] vt encarnar.

personnel [pə:sə'nɛl] n personal m.

perspective [pə'spɛktɪv] n perspectiva.

perspex ['pə:spɛks] n plexiglás m.

perspiration [pə:spɪ'reɪʃən] n transpiración f, sudor m; **perspire** [-'spaɪə*] vi transpirar, sudar.

persuade [pə'sweɪd] vt persuadir; **persuasion** [-'sweɪʒən] n persuasión f; (persuasiveness) persuasiva; (creed) creencia; **persuasive** [-'sweɪsɪv] a persuasivo.

pert [pə:t] a impertinente, fresco.

pertaining [pə:'teɪnɪŋ]: ~ to prep relacionado con.

pertinent ['pə:tɪnənt] a pertinente, a propósito.

perturb [pə'tə:b] vt perturbar.

Peru [pə'ru:] n el Perú.

peruse [pə'ru:z] vt leer con detención, examinar.

Peruvian [pə'ru:vjən] a, n peruano/a.

pervade [pə'veɪd] vt impregnar, saturar.

perverse [pə'və:s] a perverso; (stubborn) terco; (wayward) travieso; **perversion** [-'və:ʃən] n perversión f.

pervert ['pə:və:t] n pervertido/a // vt [pə'və:t] pervertir.

pessary ['pɛsərɪ] n pesario.

pessimism ['pɛsɪmɪzəm] n pesimismo; **pessimist** [-mɪst] n pesimista m/f; **pessimistic** [-'mɪstɪk] a pesimista.

pest [pɛst] n plaga; (insect) insecto nocivo; (fig) lata, molestia.

pester ['pɛstə*] vt molestar, acosar.

pesticide ['pɛstɪsaɪd] n pesticida m.

pet [pɛt] n animal doméstico; (favourite) favorito // vt acariciar // vi (col) besuquearse, sobarse.

petal ['pɛtl] n pétalo.

peter ['pi:tə*]: to ~ out vi agotarse, acabarse.

petite [pə'ti:t] a chiquita.

petition [pə'tɪʃən] n petición f.

petrified ['pɛtrɪfaɪd] a (fig) pasmado, horrorizado; **petrify** vt petrificar; (frighten) pasmar.

petrol ['pɛtrəl] n (Brit) gasolina; (for lighter) bencina.

petroleum [pə'trəulɪəm] n petróleo.

petrol: ~ **pump** n (in car) bomba de

gasolina; (in garage) surtidor m de gasolina; ~ **station** n gasolinera; ~ **tank** n depósito de gasolina.

petticoat ['petikəut] n enagua; (slip) combinación f.

pettiness ['petinis] n mezquindad f.

petty ['peti] a (mean) mezquino; (unimportant) nimio; ~ **cash** n dinero suelto; ~ **officer** n contramaestre m.

petulant ['petjulənt] a malhumorado.

pew [pju:] n banco.

pewter ['pju:tə*] n peltre m.

phallic ['fælik] a fálico.

phantom ['fæntəm] n fantasma m.

Pharaoh ['fɛərəu] n Faraón m.

pharmacist ['fɑ:məsist] n farmacéutico; **pharmacy** [-si] n farmacia.

phase [feiz] n fase f // vt: to ~ sth in/out introducir/reducir algo por etapas.

Ph.D. abbr of **Doctor of Philosophy.**

pheasant ['feznt] n faisán m.

phenomenon [fə'nɔminən], pl -**mena** [-minə] n fenómeno.

phial ['faiəl] n ampolla.

philanthropist [fi'lænθrəpist] n filántropo/a.

philately [fi'lætəli] n filatelia.

Philippines ['filipi:nz] npl (also: **Philippine Islands**) (Islas) Filipinas fpl.

philosopher [fi'lɔsəfə*] n filósofo; **philosophical** [filə'sɔfikl] a filosófico; **philosophy** [-fi] n filosofía.

phlegm [flɛm] n flema; ~**atic** [flɛg-'mætik] a flemático.

phobia ['fəubjə] n fobia.

phone [fəun] n teléfono // vt telefonear, llamar (por teléfono); **to be on the** ~ tener teléfono; (be calling) estar llamando; **to** ~ **back** vt, vi devolver la llamada.

phonetics [fə'nɛtiks] n fonética.

phoney ['fəuni] a falso; (person) insincero // n (person) farsante m/f.

phosphate ['fɔsfeit] n fosfato.

phosphorus ['fɔsfərəs] n fósforo.

photo ['fəutəu] n fotografía.

photo... ['fəutəu] pref: ~**copier** n fotocopiador m; ~**copy** n fotocopia // vt fotocopiar; ~**genic** [-'dʒɛnik] a fotogénico; ~**graph** n fotografía // vt fotografiar; ~**grapher** [fə'tɔgrəfə*] n fotógrafo; ~**graphic** [-'græfik] a fotográfico; ~**graphy** [fə'tɔgrəfi] n fotografía; ~**stat** ['fəutəustæt] n fotóstato.

phrase [freiz] n frase f // vt expresar; ~**book** n libro de frases.

physical ['fizikl] a físico.

physician [fi'ziʃən] n médico.

physicist ['fizisist] n físico.

physics ['fiziks] n física.

physiology [fizi'ɔlədʒi] n fisiología.

physiotherapy [fiziəu'θerəpi] n fisioterapia.

physique [fi'zi:k] n físico.

pianist ['pi:ənist] n pianista m/f.

piano [pi'ænəu] n piano; **grand** ~ piano de cola.

pick [pik] n (tool: also: ~-**axe**) pico, piqueta // vt (select) elegir, escoger; (gather) recoger; (lock) forzar; **take your** ~ escoja lo que quiera; **the** ~ **of** lo mejor de; **to** ~ **one's teeth** limpiarse los dientes; **to** ~ **pockets** ratear, ser carterista; **to** ~ **off** vt (kill) matar de un tiro; **to** ~ **on** vt fus (person) meterse con; **to** ~ **out** vt escoger; (distinguish) lograr ver; **to** ~ **up** vi (improve) reponerse // vt (from floor) recoger; (telephone) descolgar; (buy) comprar; (find) encontrar; (learn) aprender; **to** ~ **up speed** acelerarse; **to** ~ **o.s. up** levantarse.

picket ['pikit] n (in strike) guardia, piquete m // vt piquetear; ~ **line** n línea de huelgistas.

pickle ['pikl] n (also: ~**s**: as condiment) escabeche m; (fig: mess) apuro // vt encurtir; (in vinegar) conservar en vinagre.

pickpocket ['pikpɔkit] n carterista m/f.

pickup ['pikʌp] n (on record player) pickup m; (small truck) furgoneta.

picnic ['piknik] n picnic m, merienda de campo // vi merendar en el campo.

pictorial [pik'tɔ:riəl] a pictórico; (magazine etc) ilustrado.

picture ['piktʃə*] n cuadro; (painting) pintura; (photograph) fotografía; (film) película // vt pintar; **the** ~**s** el cine; ~ **book** n libro de imágenes.

picturesque [piktʃə'rɛsk] a pintoresco.

pidgin ['pidʒin] a: ~ **English** el inglés macarrónico.

pie [pai] n pastel m; (open) tarta; (of meat) empanada.

piebald ['paibɔ:ld] a pío.

piece [pi:s] n pedazo, trozo; (of land) terreno; (of cake) porción f; (item): a ~ **of furniture/advice** un mueble/un consejo // vt: **to** ~ **together** juntar; (TECH) montar; **to take to** ~**s** desmontar; ~**meal** ad poco a poco; ~**work** n trabajo a destajo.

pier [piə*] n muelle m; (jetty) embarcadero, malecón m.

pierce [piəs] vt penetrar, atravesar; (puncture) pinchar.

piercing ['piəsiŋ] a (cry) penetrante.

piety ['paiəti] n piedad f.

pig [pig] n cerdo, puerco; (fig) cochino.

pigeon ['pidʒən] n paloma; (as food) pichón m; ~**hole** n casilla.

piggy bank ['pigibæŋk] n hucha en forma de cerdito.

pigheaded ['pig'hedid] a terco, testarudo.

pigment ['pigmənt] n pigmento; ~**ation** [-'teiʃən] n pigmentación f.

pigmy ['pigmi] n = **pygmy.**

pigsty ['pigstai] n pocilga.

pigtail ['pigteil] n (girl's) trenza; (Chinese) coleta.

pike [paik] n (spear) pica; (fish) lucio.

pilchard ['piltʃəd] n sardina arenque.

pile [pail] n (heap) montón m; (of carpet)

pelo; (of cloth) pelillo // (vb: also: ~ **up**) vt amontonar; (fig) acumular // vi amontonarse.

piles [paɪlz] npl (MED) almorranas fpl, hemorroides mpl.

pile-up ['paɪlʌp] n (AUT) accidente m múltiple.

pilfer ['pɪlfə*] vt ratear; ~ing n ratería.

pilgrim ['pɪlgrɪm] n peregrino/a; ~age n peregrinaje m, romería.

pill [pɪl] n píldora; **the** ~ la píldora.

pillage ['pɪlɪdʒ] n saqueo, pillaje m.

pillar ['pɪlə*] n (gen) pilar m; (concrete) columna; ~ **box** n (Brit) buzón m.

pillion ['pɪljən] n (of motor cycle) asiento de atrás.

pillory ['pɪlərɪ] vt poner en ridículo.

pillow ['pɪləu] n almohada; ~**case** n funda.

pilot ['paɪlət] n piloto m/f (scheme etc) piloto // vt pilotar; (fig) guiar, conducir; ~ **light** n piloto.

pimp [pɪmp] n alcahuete m, chulo.

pimple ['pɪmpl] n grano.

pin [pɪn] n alfiler m; (TECH) perno; (: wooden) clavija // vt prender (con alfiler); sujetar con perno; ~**s and needles** hormigueo sg; **rolling/ safety** ~ rodillo/imperdible m; **to** ~ **sb down** (fig) hacer que uno concrete; **to** ~ **sth on sb** (fig) acusar (falsamente) a uno de algo.

pinafore ['pɪnəfɔ:*] n delantal m; ~ **dress** n mandil m.

pinball ['pɪnbɔ:l] n billar m automático.

pincers ['pɪnsəz] npl pinzas fpl, tenazas fpl.

pinch [pɪntʃ] n pellizco; (of salt etc) pizca // vt pellizcar; (col: steal) birlar; (: arrest) coger, pescar // vi (shoe) apretar; **to feel the** ~ pasar apuros.

pincushion ['pɪnkuʃən] n acerico.

pine [paɪn] n (also: ~ **tree**) pino // vi: **to** ~ **for** suspirar por; **to** ~ **away** languidecer.

pineapple ['paɪnæpl] n piña, ananás m.

ping [pɪŋ] n (noise) tintineo; (of bullet through air) subido; ~-**pong** n pingpong m.

pink [pɪŋk] a rosado, color de rosa // n (colour) color m de rosa; (BOT) clavel m, clavellina.

pinnacle ['pɪnəkl] n cumbre f.

pinpoint ['pɪnpɔɪnt] vt poner el dedo en.

pint [paɪnt] n pinta (0.57 litros); **to go for a** ~ ir a tomar una cerveza.

pin-up ['pɪnʌp] n fotografía de mujer bonita.

pioneer [paɪə'nɪə*] n pionero.

pious ['paɪəs] a piadoso, devoto.

pip [pɪp] n (seed) pepita; (time signal on radio) señal f.

pipe [paɪp] n tubo, caño; (for smoking) pipa // vt conducir en cañerías; ~**s** npl (gen) cañería sg; (also: **bag**~**s**) gaita sg; **to** ~ **down** vi (col) callarse; ~ **dream** n sueño imposible; ~**line** n tubería, cañería; (for oil) oleoducto; (for gas) gasoducto; **piper** n

(gen) flautista m/f; (with bagpipes) gaitero.

piping ['paɪpɪŋ] ad: ~ **hot** bien caliente.

piquant ['pi:kənt] a picante.

pique [pi:k] n pique m, resentimiento.

pirate ['paɪərət] n pirata m; ~ **radio** n emisora ilegal.

pirouette [pɪru'ɛt] n pirueta // vi piruetear.

Pisces ['paɪsi:z] n Piscis m.

piss [pɪs] vi (col) mear; ~**ed** a (col: drunk) trompa.

pistol ['pɪstl] n pistola.

piston ['pɪstən] n pistón m, émbolo.

pit [pɪt] n hoyo; (also: **coal** ~) mina; (in garage) foso de inspección; (also: **orchestra** ~) platea; (quarry) cantera // vt: **to** ~ **A against B** oponer A a B; ~**s** npl (AUT) box m.

pitch [pɪtʃ] n (throw) lanzamiento; (MUS) tono; (SPORT) campo, terreno; (tar) brea; (in market etc) puesto // vt (throw) arrojar, lanzar // vi (fall) caer(se); (NAUT) cabecear; **to** ~ **a tent** armar una tienda (de campaña); ~-**black** a negro como boca de lobo; ~**ed battle** n batalla campal.

pitcher ['pɪtʃə*] n cántaro, jarro.

pitchfork ['pɪtʃfɔ:k] n horca.

piteous ['pɪtɪəs] a lastimoso.

pitfall ['pɪtfɔ:l] n escollo, peligro.

pith [pɪθ] n (of orange) médula; (fig) meollo.

pithy ['pɪθɪ] a jugoso.

pitiable ['pɪtɪəbl] a lastimoso.

pitiful ['pɪtɪful] a (touching) lastimoso, conmovedor(a); (contemptible) lamentable, miserable.

pitiless ['pɪtɪlɪs] a despiadado.

pittance ['pɪtns] n miseria.

pity ['pɪtɪ] n (compassion) compasión f, piedad f; (shame) lástima // vt tener lástima a, compadecer(se de); **what a** ~! ¡qué lástima!

pivot ['pɪvət] n eje m // vi: **to** ~ **on** girar sobre; (fig) depender de.

pixie ['pɪksɪ] n duende m.

placard ['plækɑ:d] n (sign) letrero; (in march etc) pancarta.

placate [plə'keɪt] vt apaciguar.

place [pleɪs] n lugar m, sitio; (rank) rango; (seat) plaza, asiento; (post) puesto; (home): **at/to his** ~ en/a su casa // vt (object) poner, colocar; (identify) reconocer, ubicar; (find a post for) dar un puesto a, colocar; **to take** ~ tener lugar; **to be** ~**d** (in race, exam) colocarse; **out of** ~ (not suitable) fuera de lugar; **in the first** ~ en primer lugar; **to change** ~**s with sb** trocarse con uno.

placid ['plæsɪd] a apacible.

plagiarism ['pleɪdʒjərɪzm] n plagio.

plague [pleɪg] n plaga; (MED) peste f // vt (fig) acosar, atormentar; **to** ~ **sb** fastidiar a uno.

plaice [pleɪs] n, pl inv platija.

plaid [plæd] n (material) tela a cuadros; (pattern) plaid m.

plain [pleɪn] a (clear) claro, evidente; (simple) sencillo, llano; (frank) franco, abierto; (not handsome) sin atractivo; (pure) natural, puro // ad claro, claramente // n llano, llanura; **in ~ clothes** (police) de paisano; **~ly** ad claramente, evidentemente; (frankly) francamente, con franqueza; **~ness** n claridad f; sencillez f; franqueza.

plaintiff ['pleɪntɪf] n demandante m/f.

plait [plæt] n trenza // vt trenzar.

plan [plæn] n (drawing) plano, (scheme) plan m, proyecto; (schedule) programa m // vt (think in advance) proyectar; (prepare) planear, planificar // vi hacer proyectos; **to ~ to do** proponerse hacer.

plane [pleɪn] n (AVIAT) avión m; (tree) plátano; (tool) cepillo; (MATH) plano.

planet ['plænɪt] n planeta m; **~arium** [-'tɛərɪəm] n planetario.

plank [plæŋk] n tabla; (POL) punto.

planner ['plænə*] n planificador/a m/f.

planning ['plænɪŋ] n planificación f; **family ~** planificación familiar.

plant [plɑːnt] n (gen) planta; (machinery) maquinaria; (factory) fábrica // vt plantar; (field) sembrar; (bomb) colocar; (fam) colocar a escondidas.

plantation [plæn'teɪʃən] n plantación f; (estate) hacienda.

plaque [plæk] n placa.

plasma ['plæzmə] n plasma m.

plaster ['plɑːstə*] n (for walls) yeso; (also: **sticking ~**) curitas m inv, parche m // vt enyesar; (cover): **to ~ with** llenar o cubrir de; **~ed** a (col) trompa; **~er** n yesero.

plastic ['plæstɪk] n plástico // a de plástico.

plasticine ['plæstɪsiːn] n plasticina.

plastic surgery ['plæstɪk'sɜːdʒərɪ] n cirujía plástica.

plate [pleɪt] n (dish) plato; (metal, in book) lámina; (PHOT, dental) placa.

plateau ['plætəʊ], pl **~s** or **~x** [-z] n meseta, altiplanicie f.

plateful ['pleɪtful] n plato.

plate glass [pleɪt'glɑːs] n vidrio cilindrado.

platform ['plætfɔːm] n (RAIL) andén m; (stage) plataforma; (at meeting) tribuna; (POL) programa m electoral; **~ ticket** n billete m de andén.

platinum ['plætɪnəm] n platino.

platitude ['plætɪtjuːd] n lugar m común, tópico.

platoon [plə'tuːn] n pelotón m.

platter ['plætə*] n fuente f, platón m.

plausible ['plɔːzɪbl] a verosímil, admisible; (person) convincente.

play [pleɪ] n (gen) juego; (also: **~time**) recreo; (THEATRE) obra, comedia // vt (game) jugar; (instrument) tocar; (THEATRE) representar; (: part) hacer (el papel de); (fig) desempeñar // vi jugar;

(amuse o.s.) divertirse; (frolic) juguetear; **to ~ down** vt quitar importancia a; **to ~ up** vt (cause trouble to) fastidiar a; **~-acting** n teatro; **~er** n jugador/a m/f; (THEATRE) actor/actriz m/f; (MUS) músico/a; **~ful** a juguetón(ona); **~ground** n (in park) parque m de juegos; (in school) patio de recreo; **~group** n jardín m de niños; **~ing card** n naipe m, carta; **~ing field** n campo de deportes; **~mate** n compañero de juego; **~-off** n (SPORT) partido de desempate; **~pen** n corral m; **~thing** n juguete m; **~wright** n dramaturgo.

plea [pliː] n (request) súplica, petición f; (excuse) pretexto, disculpa; (LAW) alegato, defensa.

plead [pliːd] vt (LAW) interceder; (give as excuse) poner como pretexto // vi (LAW) declarar; (beg): **to ~ with sb** suplicar o rogar a uno.

pleasant ['plɛznt] a agradable; (surprise) grato; (person) simpático; **~ness** n (of person) simpatía, amabilidad f; (of place) lo agradable; **~ries** npl (polite remarks) cortesías fpl.

please [pliːz] vt (give pleasure to) dar gusto a, agradar; (get on well with) caer en gracia a // vi (think fit): **do as you ~** haga lo que quiera o lo que le da la gana; **~!** ¡por favor!; **~ yourself!** ¡como Usted guste!, ¡como quiera!; **~d** a (happy) alegre, contento; **~d (with)** satisfecho (de); **pleasing** a (gen) agradable; (surprise) grato; (flattering) halagüeño.

pleasure ['plɛʒə*] n placer m, gusto; (will) voluntad f // cpd de recreo; **'it's a ~'** el gusto es mío; **it's a ~ to see him** da gusto verle.

pleat [pliːt] n pliegue m.

plebs [plɛbz] npl (pej) la plebe.

plectrum ['plɛktrəm] n plectro.

pledge [plɛdʒ] n (object) prenda; (promise) promesa, voto // vt (pawn) empeñar; (promise) prometer.

plentiful ['plɛntɪful] a copioso, abundante.

plenty ['plɛntɪ] n abundancia; **~ of** (enough) bastante; (many) muchos.

pleurisy ['plʊərɪsɪ] n pleuresía.

pliable ['plaɪəbl] a flexible; (fig) manejable.

pliers ['plaɪəz] npl alicates mpl, tenazas fpl.

plight [plaɪt] n condición f, situación f difícil.

plimsolls ['plɪmsɔlz] npl zapatos mpl de tenis.

plod [plɔd] vi caminar penosamente; (fig) trabajar laboriosamente; **~der** n empollón/ona m/f; **~ding** a laborioso.

plonk [plɔŋk] (col) n (wine) vino corriente // vt: **to ~ sth down** dejar caer algo (pesadamente).

plot [plɔt] n (scheme) complot m, conjura; (of story, play) argumento; (of land) terreno // vt (mark out) trazar; (conspire) tramar, urdir // vi conspirar; **~ter** n conspirador/a m/f.

plough, plow (*US*) [plau] *n* arado // *vt* (*earth*) arar; **to ~ back** *vt* (*COMM*) reinvertir; **to ~ through** *vt fus* (*crowd*) abrirse paso por la fuerza.

ploy [plɔɪ] *n* truco, estratagema.

pluck [plʌk] *vt* (*fruit*) coger; (*musical instrument*) puntear; (*bird*) desplumar // *n* valor *m*, ánimo; **to ~ up courage** hacer de tripas corazón; **~y** *a* valiente, valeroso.

plug [plʌg] *n* tapón *m*; (*ELEC*) enchufe *m*, clavija; (*AUT: also:* **sparking ~**) bujía // *vt* (*hole*) tapar; (*col: advertise*) dar publicidad a.

plum [plʌm] *n* (*fruit*) ciruela // *a* (*col: job*) breva, chollo.

plumage ['plu:mɪdʒ] *n* plumaje *m*.

plumb [plʌm] *ad* (*exactly*) exactamente, en punto // *vt* sondar, sondear.

plumber ['plʌmə*] *n* fontanero; **plumbing** [-mɪŋ] *n* (*trade*) fontanería; (*piping*) instalación *f* de cañerías.

plume [plu:m] *n* (*gen*) pluma; (*on helmet*) penacho.

plummet ['plʌmɪt] *vi:* **to ~ (down)** caer a plomo.

plump [plʌmp] *a* rechoncho, rollizo // *vt:* **to ~ sth (down) on** dejar caer algo en; **to ~ for** (*col: choose*) optar por.

plunder ['plʌndə*] *n* pillaje *m*; (*loot*) botín *m* // *vt* pillar, saquear; (*tomb*) robar.

plunge [plʌndʒ] *n* (*dive*) salto; (*submersion*) zambullida; (*bath*) baño // *vt* sumergir, hundir // *vi* (*fall*) caer; (*dive*) saltar; (*person*) arrojarse; (*sink*) hundirse; **to take the ~** resolverse; **plunger** *n* émbolo; **plunging** *a* (*neckline*) escotado.

pluperfect [plu:'pə:fɪkt] *n* pluscuamperfecto.

plural ['pluərl] *n* plural *m*.

plus [plʌs] *n* (*also:* **~ sign**) signo más // *prep* más, y, además de; **ten/twenty ~** diez/veinte y pico.

plush [plʌʃ] *a* de felpa.

ply [plaɪ] *vt* (*a trade*) ejercer // *vi* (*ship*) ir y venir; (*for hire*) ofrecerse (para alquilar); **three ~** (*wool*) de tres cordones; **to ~ sb with drink** ofrecer bebidas a alguien muchas veces; **~wood** *n* madera contrachapada.

P.M. *abbr of* **Prime Minister.**

p.m. *ad abbr of* **post meridiem** de la tarde o noche.

pneumatic [nju:'mætɪk] *a* neumático.

pneumonia [nju:'məunɪə] *n* pulmonía.

poach [pəutʃ] *vt* (*cook*) escalfar; (*steal*) cazar en vedado // *vi* cazar/pescar en finca ajena; **~ed** *a* (*egg*) escalfado; **~er** *n* cazador *m* furtivo; **~ing** *n* caza/pesca furtiva.

pocket ['pɔkɪt] *n* bolsillo; (*of air, GEO, fig*) bolsa; (*BILLIARDS*) tronera // *vt* meter en el bolsillo; (*steal*) embolsar; (*BILLIARDS*) entronerar; **to be out of ~** salir perdiendo; **~book** *n* (*US. wallet*) cartera; **~ knife** *n* navaja; **~ money** *n* dinero para gastos personales.

pod [pɔd] *n* vaina.

podgy ['pɔdʒɪ] *a* gordinflón(ona).

poem ['pəuɪm] *n* poema *m*.

poet ['pəuɪt] *n* poeta *m/f*; **~ess** *n* poetisa; **~ic** [-'etɪk] *a* poético; **~ laureate** *n* poeta laureado; **~ry** *n* poesía.

poignant ['pɔɪnjənt] *a* conmovedor(a); (*sharp*) agudo.

point [pɔɪnt] *n* (*gen*) punto; (*tip*) punta; (*purpose*) fin *m*, finalidad *f*; (*use*) utilidad *f*; (*significant part*) lo significativo; (*characteristic*) rasgo; (*also:* **decimal ~**): **2 — 3 (2.3)** dos punto tres // *vt* (*show*) subrayar; (*gun etc*): **to ~ sth at sb** apuntar algo a uno // *vi* señalar con el dedo; **~s** *npl* (*AUT*) contactos *mpl*; (*RAIL*) agujas *fpl*; **to make a ~ of** no dejar de; **to get the ~** comprender; **to come to the ~** ir al grano; **there's no ~ (in doing)** no hay para qué (hacer); **to ~ out** *vt* señalar; **to ~ to** indicar con el dedo; (*fig*) indicar, señalar; **~-blank** *ad* (*also:* **at ~-blank range**) a quemarropa; **~ed** *a* (*shape*) puntiagudo, afilado; (*remark*) directo, enfático; **~edly** *ad* directamente, con énfasis; **~er** *n* (*stick*) puntero; (*needle*) aguja, indicador *m*; **~less** *a* (*useless*) inútil; (*senseless*) sin sentido; (*motiveless*) sin motivo; **~ of view** *n* punto de vista.

poise [pɔɪz] *n* (*balance*) equilibrio; (*of head, body*) aire *m*, porte *m*; (*calmness*) confianza.

poison ['pɔɪzn] *n* veneno // *vt* envenenar; **~ing** *n* envenenamiento; **~ous** *a* venenoso; (*fumes etc*) tóxico; (*fig*) pernicioso.

poke [pəuk] *vt* (*fire*) hurgar, atizar; (*jab with finger, stick etc*) empujar; (*put*): **to ~ sth in(to)** introducir algo en // *n* (*to fire*) hurgonada; (*push*) empujón *m*; (*with elbow*) codazo; **to ~ about** *vi* fisgar.

poker ['pəukə*] *n* badila, atizador *m*; (*CARDS*) póker *m*; **~-faced** *a* de cara impasible.

poky ['pəukɪ] *a* estrecho.

Poland ['pəulənd] *n* Polonia.

polar ['pəulə*] *a* polar; **~ bear** *n* oso polar.

polarize ['pəuləraɪz] *vt* polarizar.

pole [pəul] *n* palo; (*GEO*) polo; (*TEL*) poste *m*; (*flag~*) asta; (*tent ~*) mástil *m*.

Pole [pəul] *n* polaco/a.

pole vault ['pəulvɔ:lt] *n* salto con pértiga.

police [pə'li:s] *n* policía // *vt* mantener el orden en; **~ car** *n* coche-patrulla *m*; **~man** *n* policía *m*, guardia *m*; **~ state** *n* estado policíaco; **~ station** *n* comisaría; **~woman** *n* mujer *f* policía.

policy ['pɔlɪsɪ] *n* política; (*also:* **insurance ~**) póliza.

polio ['pəulɪəu] *n* polio *f*.

Polish ['pəulɪʃ] *a, n* polaco.

polish ['pɔlɪʃ] *n* (*for shoes*) betún *m*; (*for floor*) cera (de lustrar); (*for nails*) esmalte *m*; (*shine*) brillo, lustre *m*; (*fig: refinement*) cultura, urbanidad *f* // *vt* (*shoes*) limpiar;

(*make shiny*) pulir, sacar brillo a; (*fig: improve*) refinar, repasar; **to ~ off** *vt* (*work*) terminar; (*food*) despachar; **~ed** a (*fig: person*) culto; (: *manners*) fino.

polite [pə'laɪt] a cortés, atento; (*formal*) correcto; **~ness** n cortesía.

politic ['pɒlɪtɪk] a prudente; **~al** [pə'lɪtɪkl] a político; **~ian** [-'tɪʃən] n político; **~s** npl política sg.

polka ['pɒlkə] n polca; **~ dot** n punto.

poll [pəʊl] n (*votes*) votación f, votos mpl; (*also*: **opinion ~**) sondeo, encuesta // *vt* (*votes*) recibir, obtener.

pollen ['pɒlən] n polen m.

pollination [pɒlɪ'neɪʃən] n polinización f.

polling ['pəʊlɪŋ]: **~ booth** n cabina de votar; **~ day** n día m de elecciones; **~ station** n centro electoral.

pollute [pə'luːt] *vt* contaminar; **pollution** [-'luːʃən] n polución f, contaminación f.

polo ['pəʊləʊ] n (*sport*) polo; **~-neck** a de cuello vuelto.

polyester [pɒlɪ'estə*] n poliéster m.

polygamy [pɒ'lɪgəmɪ] n poligamia.

Polynesia [pɒlɪ'niːzɪə] n Polinesia.

polytechnic [pɒlɪ'teknɪk] n politécnico, escuela de formación profesional.

polythene ['pɒlɪθiːn] n politeno.

pomegranate ['pɒmɪgrænɪt] n granada.

pommel ['pɒml] n pomo // *vt* dar de puñetazos.

pomp [pɒmp] n pompa.

pompous ['pɒmpəs] a pomposo.

pond [pɒnd] n (*natural*) charca; (*artificial*) estanque m.

ponder ['pɒndə*] *vt* meditar; **~ous** a pesado.

pontiff ['pɒntɪf] n pontífice m.

pontificate [pɒn'tɪfɪkeɪt] *vi* (*fig*): **to ~** (*about*) pontificar (sobre).

pontoon [pɒn'tuːn] n pontón m; (*card game*) veintiuna.

pony ['pəʊnɪ] n poney m, jaca; **~tail** n cola de caballo; **~ trekking** n excursión f a caballo.

poodle ['puːdl] n perro de lanas.

pool [puːl] n (*of rain*) charca; (*pond*) estanque m; (*also*: **swimming ~**) piscina; (*billiards*) trucos mpl // *vt* juntar; (*football*) **~s** n quinielas fpl.

poor [puə*] a pobre; (*bad*) de baja calidad // npl: **the ~** los pobres; **~ly** a mal, enfermo.

pop [pɒp] n ¡pum!; (*sound*) ruido seco; (*MUS*) pop m; (*US*: *col*: *father*) papá m; (*lemonade*) gaseosa // *vt* (*put*) poner // *vi* reventar; (*cork*) saltar; **to ~ in** *vi* entrar de sopetón; **to ~ out** *vi* salir un momento; **to ~ up** *vi* aparecer inesperadamente; **~ concert** n concierto pop; **~corn** n palomitas fpl.

pope [pəʊp] n papa m.

poplar ['pɒplə*] n álamo.

poplin ['pɒplɪn] n popelina.

poppy ['pɒpɪ] n amapola.

populace ['pɒpjʊləs] n pueblo, plebe f.

popular ['pɒpjʊlə*] a popular; (*fashionable*) de moda; **~ity** [-'lærɪtɪ] n popularidad f; **~ize** *vt* popularizar; (*disseminate*) vulgarizar.

populate ['pɒpjʊleɪt] *vt* poblar; **population** [-'leɪʃən] n población f.

populous ['pɒpjʊləs] a populoso.

porcelain ['pɔːslɪn] n porcelana.

porch [pɔːtʃ] n pórtico, entrada.

porcupine ['pɔːkjʊpaɪn] n puerco espín.

pore [pɔː*] n poro // *vi*: **to ~ over** estar absorto en.

pork [pɔːk] n carne f de cerdo.

pornographic [pɔːnə'græfɪk] a pornográfico; **pornography** [-'nɔgrəfɪ] n pornografía.

porous ['pɔːrəs] a poroso.

porpoise ['pɔːpəs] n marsopa.

porridge ['pɒrɪdʒ] n avena.

port [pɔːt] n (*harbour*) puerto; (*NAUT*: *left side*) babor m; (*wine*) (vino de) oporto.

portable ['pɔːtəbl] a portátil.

portend [pɔː'tend] *vt* presagiar, anunciar; **portent** ['pɔːtent] n presagio, augurio.

porter ['pɔːtə*] n (*for luggage*) mozo; (*doorkeeper*) portero, conserje m.

porthole ['pɔːthəʊl] n portilla.

portion ['pɔːʃən] n porción f; (*helping*) ración f.

portly ['pɔːtlɪ] a corpulento.

portrait ['pɔːtreɪt] n retrato.

portray [pɔː'treɪ] *vt* retratar; (*in writing*) describir, representar; **~al** n representación f.

Portugal ['pɔːtjʊgl] n Portugal m.

Portuguese ['pɔːtjuː'giːz] a portugués(esa) // n, pl inv portugués/esa m/f; (*LING*) portugués m.

pose [pəʊz] n postura, actitud f; (*pej*) afectación f, pose f // *vi* posar; (*pretend*): **to ~ as** darse tono de // *vt* (*question*) plantear.

posh [pɒʃ] a (*col*) elegante, de lujo.

position [pə'zɪʃən] n posición f; (*job*) puesto // *vt* colocar.

positive ['pɒzɪtɪv] a positivo; (*certain*) seguro; (*definite*) definitivo.

posse ['pɒsɪ] n (*US*) pelotón m.

possess [pə'zes] *vt* poseer; **~ion** [pə'zeʃən] n posesión f; **~ive** a posesivo.

possibility [pɒsɪ'bɪlɪtɪ] n posibilidad f; **possible** ['pɒsɪbl] a posible; **as big as possible** lo más grande posible; **possibly** ['pɒsɪblɪ] ad (*perhaps*) posiblemente, tal vez; **I cannot possibly come** me es imposible venir.

post [pəʊst] n (*letters, delivery*) correo; (*job, situation*) puesto; (*pole*) poste m // *vt* (*send by post*) echar al correo; (*MIL*) apostar; (*bills*) fijar, pegar; (*appoint*): **to ~ to** enviar a; **~age** n porte m, franqueo; **~al** a postal, de correos; **~al order** n giro postal; **~box** n buzón m; **~card** n tarjeta postal.

postdate [pəʊst'deɪt] *vt* (*cheque*) poner fecha adelantada a.

poster ['pɔustə*] n cartel m.
posterior [pɔs'tiəriə*] n (col) culo, trasero.
posterity [pɔs'tɛritɪ] n posteridad f.
postgraduate ['pɔust'grædjuət] n postgraduado.
posthumous ['pɔstjuməs] a póstumo.
post: ~**man** n cartero; ~**mark** n matasellos m inv; ~**master** n administrador/a m/f de correos.
post-mortem [pɔust'mɔːtəm] n autopsia.
post office ['pɔustɔfɪs] n (building) correos f; (organization) Administración General de Correos; ~ **box (P.O. box)** n apartado postal.
postpone [pɔs'pɔun] vt aplazar; ~**ment** n aplazamiento.
postscript ['pɔustskrɪpt] n posdata.
postulate ['pɔstjuleɪt] vt postular.
posture ['pɔstʃə*] n postura, actitud f.
postwar [pɔust'wɔː*] a de posguerra.
posy ['pɔuzɪ] n ramillete m (de flores).
pot [pɔt] n (for cooking) olla; (for flowers) maceta; (for jam) tarro, pote m; (col: marijuana) mota // vt (plant) poner en tiesto; (conserve) conservar.
potato [pə'teɪtəu], pl ~**es** n patata, papa (AM).
potent ['pɔutnt] a potente, poderoso; (drink) fuerte.
potential [pə'tɛnʃl] a potencial, en potencial // n potencial m, potencialidad f.
pothole ['pɔthəul] n (in road) bache m; (underground) caverna; **potholer** n espeleólogo; **potholing** n: **to go potholing** dedicarse a la espeleología.
potion ['pɔuʃən] n poción f, pócima.
potluck [pɔt'lʌk] n: **to take** ~ contentarse con lo que haya.
potshot ['pɔtʃɔt] n: **to take a** ~ **at sth** tirar a algo sin apuntar.
potted ['pɔtɪd] a (food) en conserva; (plant) en tiesto o maceta.
potter ['pɔtə*] n (artistic) ceramista m/f; (artisan) alfarero // vi: **to** ~ **around,** ~ **about** ocuparse en fruslerías; ~**y** n cerámica; alfarería.
potty ['pɔtɪ] a (col: mad) chiflado // n orinal m de niño.
pouch [pautʃ] n (ZOOL) bolsa; (for tobacco) petaca.
pouf(fe) [puːf] n pouf m.
poultice ['pɔultɪs] n cataplasma, emplasto.
poultry ['pɔultrɪ] n aves fpl de corral; (dead) pollos mpl; ~ **farm** n granja avícola.
pounce [pauns] vi: **to** ~ **on** precipitarse sobre // n salto, ataque m.
pound [paund] n (gen) libra; (for dogs) corral m; (for cars) depósito // vt (beat) golpear; (crush) machacar // vi (beat) dar golpes; ~ **sterling** n (libra) esterlina.
pour [pɔː*] vt echar; (tea) servir // vi correr, fluir; (rain) llover a cántaros; **to** ~ **away** or **off** vt vaciar, verter; **to** ~ **in** vi (people) entrar en tropel; **to** ~ **out** vi (people) salir en tropel // vt (drink) echar, servir; ~**ing** a: ~**ing rain** lluvia torrencial.
pout [paut] vi hacer pucheros.
poverty ['pɔvətɪ] n pobreza, miseria; (fig) falta, escasez f; ~**-stricken** a necesitado.
powder ['paudə*] n polvo; (face ~) polvos mpl; (gun~) pólvora // vt polvorear; **to** ~ **one's face** empolvarse; ~ **compact** n polvera; ~ **room** n aseos mpl; ~**y** a polvoriento.
power ['pauə*] n (gen) poder m; (strength) fuerza; (nation) potencia; (ability, POL: of party, leader) poder m, poderío; (drive) empuje m; (TECH) potencia; (ELEC) fuerza, energía // vt impulsar; ~ **cut** n apagón m; ~**ed** a: ~**ed by** impulsado por; ~**ful** a poderoso; (engine) potente; (build) fuerte; (emotion) intenso; ~**less** a impotente, ineficaz; ~ **line** n línea de conducción eléctrica; ~ **point** n enchufe m; ~ **station** n central f eléctrica.
p.p. abbr of per procurationem: ~ **J. Smith** p.p. (por poder de) J. Smith.
practicable ['præktɪkəbl] a (scheme) factible.
practical ['præktɪkl] a práctico; ~ **joke** n broma pesada; ~**ly** ad (almost) prácticamente.
practice ['præktɪs] n (habit) costumbre f; (exercise) práctica, ejercicio; (training) adiestramiento; (MED) clientela // vi, vi (US) = **practise; in** ~ (in reality) en la práctica; **out of** ~ desentrenado.
practise, practice (US) ['præktɪs] vt (carry out) practicar; (be in the habit of) tener por costumbre; (profession) ejercer; (train at) hacer ejercicios de // vi ejercer (profession); (train) entrenar, adiestrarse; **practising** a (Christian etc) practicante; (lawyer) que ejerce.
practitioner [præk'tɪʃənə*] n practicante m/f; (MED) médico/a.
pragmatic [præg'mætɪk] a pragmático.
prairie ['prɛərɪ] n pradera, pampa.
praise [preɪz] n alabanza, elogio, alabanzas fpl, elogios mpl; ~**worthy** a loable, digno de elogios.
pram [præm] n cochecito de niño.
prance [prɑːns] vi (horse) hacer cabriolas.
prank [præŋk] n travesura.
prattle ['prætl] vi parlotear; (child) balbucear.
prawn [prɔːn] n gamba; (small) quisquilla.
pray [preɪ] vi rezar; ~**er** n oración f, rezo; (entreaty) ruego, súplica; ~**er book** n devocionario, misal m.
preach [priːtʃ] vi predicar; ~**er** n predicador/a m/f; (US) pastor m.
preamble [prɪ'æmbl] n preámbulo.
prearranged [prɪːə'reɪndʒd] a arreglado de antemano.
precarious [prɪ'kɛərɪəs] a precario.
precaution [prɪ'kɔːʃən] n precaución f.
precede [prɪ'siːd] vt, vi preceder.
precedence ['prɛsɪdəns] n precedencia;

(*priority*) prioridad *f*; **precedent** [-ənt] *n* precedente *m*.

preceding [prɪ'si:dɪŋ] *a* precedente.

precept ['pri:sept] *n* precepto.

precinct ['pri:sɪŋkt] *n* recinto; **~s** *npl* contornos *mpl*; **pedestrian** ~ zona reservada para peatones; **shopping** ~ zona comercial.

precious ['prɛʃəs] *a* precioso; (*stylized*) afectado.

precipice ['prɛsɪpɪs] *n* precipicio, despeñadero.

precipitate [prɪ'sɪpɪtɪt] *a* (*hasty*) precipitado, apresurado // *vt* [prɪ'sɪpɪteɪt] (*hasten*) acelerar; (*bring about*) causar; **precipitation** [-'teɪʃən] *n* precipitación *f*.

precipitous [prɪ'sɪpɪtəs] *a* (*steep*) escarpado.

precise [prɪ'saɪs] *a* preciso, exacto; (*person*) escrupuloso; **~ly** *ad* exactamente, precisamente; **precision** [-'sɪʒən] *n* precisión *f*.

preclude [prɪ'klu:d] *vt* excluir.

precocious [prɪ'kəʊʃəs] *a* precoz.

preconceived [pri:kən'si:vd] *a* (*idea*) preconcebido.

precursor [pri:'kɜ:sə*] *n* precursor/a *m/f*.

predator ['prɛdətə*] *n* animal *m* de rapiña; **~y** *a* rapaz, de rapiña.

predecessor ['pri:dɪsɛsə*] *n* antecesor/a *m/f*.

predestination [pri:dɛstɪ'neɪʃən] *n* predestinación *f*.

predetermine [pri:dɪ'tə:mɪn] *vt* predeterminar.

predicament [prɪ'dɪkəmənt] *n* apuro.

predict [prɪ'dɪkt] *vt* pronosticar; **~ion** [-'dɪkʃən] *n* pronóstico.

predominant [prɪ'dɒmɪnənt] *a* predominante; **predominate** [-neɪt] *vi* predominar.

pre-eminent [pri:'ɛmɪnənt] *a* preeminente.

pre-empt [pri:'ɛmt] *vt* apropiarse de antemano.

preen [pri:n] *vt*: **to ~ itself** (*bird*) limpiarse (las plumas); **to ~ o.s.** pavonearse.

prefab ['pri:fæb] *n* casa prefabricada.

prefabricated [pri:'fæbrɪkeɪtɪd] *a* prefabricado.

preface ['prɛfəs] *n* prefacio.

prefect ['pri:fɛkt] *n* (*Brit: in school*) tutor *m*, monitor *m*.

prefer [prɪ'fə:*] *vt* preferir; **~able** ['prɛfrəbl] *a* preferible; **~ably** ['prɛfrəblɪ] *ad* de preferencia; **~ence** ['prɛfrəns] *n* preferencia, prioridad *f*; **~ential** [prɛfə'rɛnʃəl] *a* preferente.

prefix ['pri:fɪks] *n* prefijo.

pregnancy ['prɛgnənsɪ] *n* embarazo; **pregnant** [-ənt] *a* embarazada; **to be pregnant** estar encinta; **pregnant with** preñado de.

prehistoric ['pri:hɪs'tɒrɪk] *a* prehistórico.

prejudge [pri:'dʒʌdʒ] *vt* prejuzgar.

prejudice ['prɛdʒudɪs] *n* (*bias*) prejuicio; (*harm*) perjuicio // *vt* (*predispose*) predisponer; (*harm*) perjudicar; **~d** *a* (*person*) predispuesto, con prejuicios; (*view*) parcial, interesado.

prelate ['prɛlət] *n* prelado.

preliminary [prɪ'lɪmɪnərɪ] *a* preliminar.

prelude ['prɛlju:d] *n* preludio.

premarital ['pri:'mærɪtl] *a* premarital.

premature ['prɛmətʃuə*] *a* prematuro.

premeditated [pri:'mɛdɪteɪtɪd] *a* premeditado.

premier ['prɛmɪə*] *a* primero, principal // *n* (*POL*) primer ministro.

première ['prɛmɪɛə*] *n* estreno.

premise ['prɛmɪs] *n* premisa; **~s** *npl* local *m*; (*house*) casa *sg*; (*shop*) tienda *sg*; **on the ~s** en el local.

premium ['pri:mɪəm] *n* premio; (*COMM*) prima; **to be at a** ~ ser muy solicitado.

premonition [prɛmə'nɪʃən] *n* presentimiento.

preoccupation [pri:ɔkju'peɪʃən] *n* preocupación *f*; **preoccupied** [-'ɔkjupaɪd] *a* (*worried*) preocupado; (*absorbed*) absorto.

prep [prɛp] *n* (*SCOL: study*) deberes *mpl*; ~ **school** *n* = **preparatory school**.

prepaid [pri:'peɪd] *a* con porte pagado.

preparation [prɛpə'reɪʃən] *n* preparación *f*; **~s** *npl* preparativos *mpl*.

preparatory [prɪ'pærətərɪ] *a* preparatorio, preliminar; ~ **to con miras a**; ~ **school** *n* escuela preparatoria.

prepare [prɪ'pɛə*] *vt* preparar, disponer // *vi*: **to ~ for** prepararse o disponerse para; (*make preparations*) hacer preparativos para; **~d to** dispuesto a.

preponderance [prɪ'pɒndərəns] *n* preponderancia, predominio.

preposition [prɛpə'zɪʃən] *n* preposición *f*.

preposterous [prɪ'pɒstərəs] *a* absurdo, ridículo.

prerequisite [pri:'rɛkwɪzɪt] *n* requisito (previo).

prerogative [prɪ'rɒgətɪv] *n* prerrogativa.

presbyterian [prɛzbɪ'tɪərɪən] *a*, *n* presbiteriano/a.

preschool ['pri:'sku:l] *a* preescolar.

prescribe [prɪ'skraɪb] *vt* prescribir; (*MED*) recetar.

prescription [prɪ'skrɪpʃən] *n* prescripción *f*; (*MED*) receta.

presence ['prɛzns] *n* presencia; (*attendance*) asistencia; ~ **of mind** *n* presencia de ánimo.

present ['prɛznt] *a* (*in attendance*) presente; (*current*) actual // *n* (*gift*) regalo; (*actuality*) actualidad *f*, presente *m* // *vt* [prɪ'zɛnt] (*introduce*) presentar; (*expound*) exponer; (*give*) presentar, dar, ofrecer; (*THEATRE*) representar; **at** ~ actualmente; **~able** [prɪ'zɛntəbl] *a* presentable; ~ **ation** [-'teɪʃən] *n* presentación *f*; (*gift*) obsequio; (*of case*) exposición *f*; (*THEATRE*) representación *f*;

~**-day** a actual; ~**ly** ad (*soon*) dentro de poco.

preservation [prɛzə'veɪʃən] n conservación f.

preservative [prɪ'zɜːvətɪv] n preservativo.

preserve [prɪ'zɜːv] vt (*keep safe*) preservar, proteger; (*maintain*) conservar; (*food*) hacer una conserva de; (*in salt*) salar // n (*for game*) coto, vedado; (*often pl: jam*) conserva, confitura.

preside [prɪ'zaɪd] vi presidir.

presidency ['prɛzɪdənsɪ] n presidencia; **president** [-ənt] n presidente m/f; **presidential** [-'dɛnʃl] a presidencial.

press [prɛs] n (*tool, machine, newspapers*) prensa; (*printer's*) imprenta; (*crowd*) apiñamiento, agolpamiento; (*of hand*) apretón m // vt (*push*) empujar; (*squeeze*) apretar; (*clothes: iron*) planchar; (*TECH*) prensar; (*harry*) acosar; (*insist*): **to ~ sth on sb** insistir en que uno acepte algo // vi (*squeeze*) apretar; (*pressurize*) ejercer presión; **we are ~ed for time** tenemos poco tiempo; **to ~ on** vi avanzar; (*hurry*) apretar el paso; ~ **agency** n agencia de prensa; ~ **conference** n conferencia de prensa; ~ **cutting** n recorte m (de periódico); ~**ing** a apremiante; ~ **stud** n botón m de presión.

pressure ['prɛʃə*] n presión f; (*urgency*) apremio, urgencia; (*influence*) influencia; (*MED*) tensión f nerviosa; ~ **cooker** n olla a presión; ~ **gauge** n manómetro; ~ **group** n grupo de presión; **pressurized** a a presión.

prestige [prɛs'tiːʒ] n prestigio; **prestigious** [-'tɪdʒəs] a prestigioso.

presumably [prɪ'zjuːməblɪ] ad se supone que, cabe presumir que.

presume [prɪ'zjuːm] vt presumir, suponer; **to ~ to do** (*dare*) atreverse a; (*set out to*) pretender.

presumption [prɪ'zʌmpʃən] n suposición f; (*pretension*) pretensión f; (*boldness*) atrevimiento.

presuppose [priːsə'pəʊz] vt presuponer.

pretence, pretense (US) [prɪ'tɛns] n (*claim*) pretensión f; (*display*) ostentación f; (*pretext*) pretexto; (*make-believe*) fingimiento; **on the ~ of** so pretexto de.

pretend [prɪ'tɛnd] vt (*feign*) fingir // vi (*feign*) fingir; (*claim*): **to ~ to sth** pretender a algo.

pretension [prɪ'tɛnʃən] n (*presumption*) presunción f; (*claim*) pretensión f.

pretentious [prɪ'tɛnʃəs] a presumido; (*ostentacious*) ostenso, aparatoso.

pretext ['priːtɛkst] n pretexto.

pretty ['prɪtɪ] a (*gen*) hermoso; (*person*) guapo; (*dress*) bonito; (*sum*) importante // ad (*quite*) bastante; (*nearly*) casi.

prevail [prɪ'veɪl] vi (*win*) imponerse; (*be current*) imperar; (*be in fashion*) estar de moda; (*be usual*) prevalecer; (*persuade*): **to ~ (up)on sb to do sth** persuadir a uno a hacer algo; ~**ing** a (*dominant*)

imperante; (*usual*) corriente.

prevalent ['prɛvələnt] a (*dominant*) predominante; (*usual*) corriente; (*fashionable*) en boga; (*present-day*) actual.

prevent [prɪ'vɛnt] vt: **to ~ (sb) from doing sth** impedir (a uno) hacer algo; ~**able** a evitable; ~**ative** a preventivo; ~**ion** [-'vɛnʃən] n prevención f; ~**ive** a preventivo.

preview ['priːvjuː] n (*of film*) preestreno; (*fig*) anticipo.

previous ['priːvɪəs] a previo, anterior; (*hasty*) prematuro; ~**ly** ad previamente, con anticipación; (*in earlier times*) antes.

prewar [priː'wɔː*] a de preguerra, prebélico.

prey [preɪ] n presa // vi: **to ~ on** vivir a costa de; (*feed on*) alimentarse de; (*plunder*) robar, pillar; **it was ~ing on his mind** le agobiaba, le preocupaba.

price [praɪs] n precio // vt (*goods*) fijar el precio de; ~**less** a inapreciable.

prick [prɪk] n pinchazo; (*with pin*) alfilerazo; (*sting*) picadura // vt pinchar; picar; **to ~ up one's ears** aguzar el oído.

prickle ['prɪkl] n (*sensation*) escozor m; (*BOT*) espina; (*ZOOL*) púa; **prickly** a espinoso; (*fig: person*) malhumorado; (*touchy*) quisquilloso.

pride [praɪd] n orgullo; (*pej*) soberbia // vt: **to ~ o.s. on** enorgullecerse de, ufanarse de.

priest [priːst] n sacerdote m; ~**ess** n sacerdotisa; ~**hood** n (*practice*) sacerdocio; (*priests*) clero.

prig [prɪg] n presumido/a, pedante m/f.

prim [prɪm] a (*formal*) estirado; (*affected*) remilgado; (*prudish*) gazmoño.

primarily ['praɪmərɪlɪ] ad (*above all*) ante todo; (*firstly*) en primer lugar.

primary ['praɪmərɪ] a primario; (*first in importance*) principal; ~ **school** n escuela primaria.

primate ['praɪmɪt] n (*REL*) primado // n ['praɪmeɪt] (*ZOOL*) primate m.

prime [praɪm] a primero, principal; (*basic*) fundamental; (*excellent*) selecto, de primera clase // vt (*gun, pump*) cebar; (*fig*) preparar, aprestar; **in the ~ of life** en la flor de la vida; ~ **minister** n primer ministro; **primer** n (*book*) libro de texto; (*paint*) pintura de base.

primitive ['prɪmɪtɪv] a primitivo; (*crude*) rudimentario; (*uncivilized*) inculto.

primrose ['prɪmrəʊz] n primavera, prímula.

primus (stove) ['praɪməs] n hornillo de campaña a presión.

prince [prɪns] n príncipe m.

princess [prɪn'sɛs] n princesa.

principal ['prɪnsɪpl] a principal, mayor // n director/a m/f.

principality [prɪnsɪ'pælɪtɪ] n principado.

principle ['prɪnsɪpl] n principio.

print [prɪnt] n (*impression*) marca, impresión f; (*letters*) letra de molde; (*fabric*) estampado; (*ART*) estampa, grabado; (*PHOT*) positiva // vt (*gen*) imprimir; (*on mind*) grabar; (*write in capitals*) escribir en letras de molde; **out of** ~ agotado; **~ed matter** n impresos mpl; **~er** n impresor/a m/f; **~ing** n (*art*) imprenta; (*act*) impresión f; (*quantity*) tirada; **~ing press** n (prensa de) imprenta.

prior ['praɪə*] a anterior, previo // n prior m; ~ **to doing** antes de o hasta hacer.

priority [praɪ'ɔrɪtɪ] n prioridad f.

prise [praɪz] vt: **to ~ open** abrir con palanca.

prism ['prɪzəm] n prisma m.

prison ['prɪzn] n cárcel f, prisión f // a carcelario; **~er** n (*in prison*) preso; (*under arrest*) detenido; (*in dock*) acusado.

privacy ['prɪvəsɪ] n (*seclusion*) aislamiento, soledad f; (*intimacy*) intimidad f.

private ['praɪvɪt] a (*personal*) particular; (*confidential*) secreto, reservado; (*intimate*) privado, íntimo; (*sitting etc*) a puertas cerradas // n soldado raso; '~' (*on envelope*) 'privado'; (*on door*) 'uso particular o privado'; **in ~** en privado; ~ **enterprise** n la empresa privada; ~ **eye** n detective m privado; **~ly** ad en privado; (*in o.s.*) en el fondo.

privet ['prɪvɪt] n alheña.

privilege ['prɪvɪlɪdʒ] n privilegio; (*prerogative*) prerrogativa; **~d** a privilegiado.

privy ['prɪvɪ] a: **to be ~ to** estar enterado de; **P~ Council** n Consejo Privado.

prize [praɪz] n premio // a premiado; (*first class*) de primera clase // vt apreciar, estimar; **~-giving** n distribución f de premios; **~ winner** n premiado/a.

pro [prəu] n (*SPORT*) profesional m/f; **the ~s and cons** los pros y los contras.

probability [prɔbə'bɪlɪtɪ] n probabilidad f; **probable** ['prɔbəbl] a probable; (*plausible*) verosímil; **probably** ['prɔbəblɪ] ad probablemente.

probation [prə'beɪʃən] n: **on ~** (*employee*) de prueba; (*LAW*) en libertad condicional.

probe [prəub] n (*MED, SPACE*) sonda; (*enquiry*) encuesta, sondeo // vt sondar; (*investigate*) indagar.

problem ['prɔbləm] n problema m; **~atic** [-'mætɪk] a problemático.

procedure [prə'si:dʒə*] n (*ADMIN, LAW*) procedimiento; (*method*) proceder m; (*bureaucratic*) trámites mpl.

proceed [prə'si:d] vi proceder; (*continue*): **to ~ (with)** continuar o seguir (con); **~ings** npl acto sg, actos mpl; (*LAW*) medidas fpl; (*meeting*) función f; (*records*) actas fpl; **~s** ['prəusi:dz] npl ganancias fpl, ingresos mpl.

process ['prəusɛs] n proceso; (*method*) método, sistema m; (*proceeding*) procedimiento // vt tratar, elaborar; **in ~** en curso; **~ing** n elaboración f.

procession [prə'sɛʃən] n desfile m; **funeral ~** cortejo fúnebre.

proclaim [prə'kleɪm] vt proclamar; (*announce*) anunciar; **proclamation** [prɔklə'meɪʃən] n proclamación f; (*written*) proclama.

procreation [prəukrɪ'eɪʃən] n procreación f.

procure [prə'kjuə*] vt conseguir, obtener.

prod [prɔd] vt (*push*) empujar; (*with elbow*) dar un codazo a; (*jab*) pinchar // n empuje m; codazo; pinchazo.

prodigal ['prɔdɪgl] a pródigo.

prodigious [prə'dɪdʒəs] a prodigioso.

prodigy ['prɔdɪdʒɪ] n prodigio.

produce [prə'dju:s] n (*AGR*) productos mpl agrícolas // vt [prə'dju:s] (*gen*) producir; (*profit*) rendir; (*show*) presentar, mostrar; (*THEATRE*) presentar, poner en escena; (*offspring*) dar a luz; **producer** n (*THEATRE*) director/a m/f; (*AGR, CINEMA*) productor/a m/f.

product ['prɔdʌkt] n (*thing*) producto; (*result*) fruto, resultado.

production [prə'dʌkʃən] n (*act*) producción f; (*thing*) producto; (*THEATRE*) representación f, obra; ~ **line** n línea o cadena de montaje.

productive [prə'dʌktɪv] a productivo; **productivity** [prɔdʌk'tɪvɪtɪ] n productividad f.

profane [prə'feɪn] a profano; (*language etc*) fuerte.

profess [prə'fɛs] vt profesar; (*regret*) manifestar.

profession [prə'fɛʃən] n profesión f; **~al** n profesional m/f; (*expert*) perito // a profesional; perito, experto; (*by profession*) de oficio.

professor [prə'fɛsə*] n catedrático/a.

proficiency [prə'fɪʃənsɪ] n pericia, habilidad f; **proficient** [-ənt] a perito, hábil.

profile ['prəufaɪl] n perfil m.

profit ['prɔfɪt] n (*COMM*) ganancia; (*fig*) provecho // vi: **to ~ by** o **from** aprovechar o sacar provecho de; **~ability** [-ə'bɪlɪtɪ] n rentabilidad f; **~able** a (*ECON*) rentable; (*useful*) provechoso; **~eering** [-'tɪərɪŋ] n (*pej*) ganancias fpl excesivas.

profound [prə'faund] a profundo.

profuse [prə'fju:s] a profuso, pródigo; **~ly** ad profusamente, pródigamente; **profusion** [-'fju:ʒən] n profusión f, abundancia.

progeny ['prɔdʒɪnɪ] n progenie f, prole f.

programme, program (*US*) ['prəugræm] n programa m // vt programar; **programming, programing** (*US*) n programación f.

progress ['prəugrɛs] n progreso; (*development*) desarrollo // vi [prə'grɛs] progresar, avanzar; desarrollarse; **in ~** en marcha; **~ion** [-'grɛʃən] n progresión f; **~ive** [-'grɛsɪv] a progresivo; (*person*) progresista m/f.

prohibit [prə'hɪbɪt] vt prohibir; **to ~ sb from doing sth** prohibir a uno hacer algo; **~ion** [prəʊɪ'bɪʃən] n (US) prohibicionismo; **~ive** a (price etc) excesivo.

project ['prɔdʒɛkt] n proyecto // (vb: [prə'dʒɛkt]) vt proyectar // vi (stick out) salir, sobresalir.

projectile [prə'dʒɛktaɪl] n proyectil m.

projection [prə'dʒɛkʃən] n proyección f; (overhang) saliente m.

projector [prə'dʒɛktə*] n proyector m.

proletarian [prəʊlɪ'tɛərɪən] a, n proletario/a; **proletariat** [-rɪət] n proletariado.

proliferate [prə'lɪfəreɪt] vi proliferar, multiplicarse; **proliferation** [-'reɪʃən] n proliferación f.

prolific [prə'lɪfɪk] a prolífico.

prologue ['prəʊlɔg] n prólogo.

prolong [prə'lɔŋ] vt prolongar, extender.

prom [prɔm] n abbr of **promenade** baile m de gala.

promenade [prɔmə'nɑːd] n (by sea) paseo marítimo; **~ concert** n concierto (en que parte del público permanece de pie).

prominence ['prɔmɪnəns] n (fig) eminencia, importancia; **prominent** [-ənt] a (standing out) saliente; (important) eminente, importante.

promiscuous [prə'mɪskjuəs] a (sexually) libertino.

promise ['prɔmɪs] n promesa // vt, vi prometer; **promising** a prometedor(a).

promontory ['prɔməntrɪ] n promontorio.

promote [prə'məʊt] vt (gen) promover; (new product) hacer propaganda por; (MIL) ascender; **promoter** n (of sporting event) promotor/a m/f; **promotion** [-'məʊʃən] n (gen) promoción f; (MIL) ascenso.

prompt [prɔmpt] a pronto // ad (punctually) puntualmente // vt (urge) mover, incitar; (THEATRE) apuntar; **to ~ sb to do sth** mover a uno a hacer algo; **~er** n (THEATRE) apuntador/a m/f; **~ly** ad (punctually) puntualmente; (rapidly) rápidamente; **~ness** n puntualidad f; rapidez f.

prone [prəʊn] a (lying) postrado; **~ to** propenso a.

prong [prɔŋ] n diente m, púa.

pronoun ['prəʊnaʊn] n pronombre m.

pronounce [prə'naʊns] vt pronunciar; (declare) declarar // vi: **to ~ (up)on** pronunciarse sobre; **~d** a (marked) marcado; **~ment** n declaración f.

pronunciation [prənʌnsɪ'eɪʃən] n pronunciación f.

proof [pruːf] n prueba; (of alcohol) graduación f normal // a: **~ against** a prueba de; **~reader** n corrector/a m/f de pruebas.

prop [prɔp] n apoyo, (fig) sostén m // vt (also: **~ up**) apoyar; (lean): **to ~ sth against** apoyar algo contra.

propaganda [prɔpə'gændə] n propaganda.

propagate ['prɔpəgeɪt] vt propagar.

propel [prə'pɛl] vt impulsar, propulsar; **~ler** n hélice f; **~ling pencil** n lapicero.

proper ['prɔpə*] a (suited, right) propio; (exact) justo; (apt) apropiado, conveniente; (timely) oportuno; (seemly) correcto, decente; (authentic) verdadero; (col: real) auténtico.

property ['prɔpətɪ] n (gen) propiedad f; (goods) bienes mpl; (estate) hacienda; **it's their ~** es suyo, les pertenece.

prophecy ['prɔfɪsɪ] n profecía; **prophesy** [-saɪ] vt profetizar; (fig) predecir.

prophet ['prɔfɪt] n profeta m/f; **~ic** [prə'fɛtɪk] a profético.

proportion [prə'pɔːʃən] n proporción f; (share) parte f, porción f; **~al** a proporcional; **~ate** a proporcionado.

proposal [prə'pəʊzl] n propuesta; (offer) oferta; (plan) proyecto; (of marriage) declaración f; (suggestion) sugerencia.

propose [prə'pəʊz] vt proponer; (offer) ofrecer // vi declararse; **to ~ to do** proponerse hacer.

proposition [prɔpə'zɪʃən] n propuesta, proposición f.

proprietor [prə'praɪətə*] n propietario, dueño.

propulsion [prə'pʌlʃən] n propulsión f.

pro rata [prəʊ'rɑːtə] ad a prorrateo.

prosaic [prəʊ'zeɪɪk] a prosaico.

prose [prəʊz] n prosa.

prosecute ['prɔsɪkjuːt] vt (LAW) procesar; **prosecution** [-'kjuːʃən] n procesa, causa; (accusing side) parte f actora; **prosecutor** n acusador/a m/f; (also: **public prosecutor**) fiscal m.

prospect ['prɔspɛkt] n (view) vista; (chance) posibilidad f; (outlook) perspectiva; (hope) esperanza // (vb: [prə'spɛkt]) vt explorar // vi buscar; **~s** npl (for work etc) perspectivas fpl; **~ing** n prospección f; **~ive** a (possible) probable, esperado; (certain) futuro; (heir) presunto; (legislation) en perspectiva; **~or** n explorador/a m/f.

prospectus [prə'spɛktəs] n prospecto.

prosper ['prɔspə*] vi prosperar; **~ity** [-'spɛrɪtɪ] n prosperidad f; **~ous** a próspero.

prostitute ['prɔstɪtjuːt] n prostituta.

prostrate ['prɔstreɪt] a postrado; (fig) abatido.

protagonist [prə'tægənɪst] n protagonista m/f.

protect [prə'tɛkt] vt proteger; **~ion** n protección f; **~ive** a protector(a); **~or** n protector/a m/f.

protégé ['prəʊteʒeɪ] n protegido.

protein ['prəʊtiːn] n proteína.

protest ['prəʊtɛst] n protesta // (vb: [prə'tɛst]) vi protestar // vt (affirm) afirmar, declarar.

Protestant ['prɔtɪstənt] a, n protestante m/f.

protocol ['prəʊtəkɔl] n protocolo.

prototype ['prəʊtətaɪp] n prototipo.

protracted [prə'træktɪd] a prolongado.

protrude [prə'truːd] *vi* salir fuera, sobresalir.

proud [praud] *a* orgulloso; (*pej*) soberbio, altanero; (*imposing*) imponente.

prove [pruːv] *vt* probar; (*verify*) comprobar; (*show*) demostrar // *vi*: **to ~ correct** resultar correcto; **to ~ o.s.** ponerse a prueba.

proverb ['prɔvɜːb] *n* refrán *m*; **~ial** [prə'vɜːbiəl] *a* proverbial.

provide [prə'vaid] *vt* proporcionar, dar; **to ~ sb with sth** proveer a uno de algo; **to ~ for** *vt* (*person*) mantener a; (*emergency*) prevenir; **~d (that)** *conj* con tal que, siempre que.

providing [prə'vaidiŋ] *conj* a condición de que, siempre que.

province ['prɔvins] *n* provincia; (*fig*) esfera; **provincial** [prə'vinʃəl] *a* de provincia; (*pej*) provinciano.

provision [prə'viʒən] *n* (*gen*) provisión *f*; (*supply*) suministro; (*supplying*) abastecimiento; **~s** *npl* (*food*) comestibles *mpl*; **~al** *a* provisional; (*temporary*) interino.

proviso [prə'vaizəu] *n* condición *f*, estipulación *f*.

provocation [prɔvə'keiʃən] *n* provocación *f*.

provocative [prə'vɔkətiv] *a* provocativo; (*stimulating*) sugestivo.

provoke [prə'vəuk] *vt* (*arouse*) provocar, incitar; (*cause*) causar, producir; (*anger*) irritar.

prow [prau] *n* proa.

prowess ['prauis] *n* (*skill*) destreza, habilidad *f*; (*courage*) valor *m*.

prowl [praul] *vi* (*also*: **~ about, ~ around**) rondar // *n*: **on the ~** de ronda; **~er** *n* rondador/a *m/f*; (*thief*) ladrón/ona *m/f*.

proximity [prɔk'simiti] *n* proximidad *f*.

proxy ['prɔksi] *n* poder *m*; (*person*) apoderado/a; **by ~** por poder o poderes.

prudence ['pruːdns] *n* prudencia; **prudent** [~ənt] *a* prudente.

prudish ['pruːdiʃ] *a* gazmoño.

prune [pruːn] *n* ciruela pasa // *vt* podar.

pry [prai] *vi*: **to ~ into** entrometerse en.

psalm [sɑːm] *n* salmo.

pseudo- [sjuːdəu] *pref* seudo...; **~nym** *n* seudónimo.

psychiatric [saiki'ætrik] *a* psiquiátrico; **psychiatrist** [-'kaiətrist] *n* psiquiatra *m/f*; **psychiatry** [-'kaiətri] *n* psiquiatría.

psychic ['saikik] *a* (*also*: **~al**) psíquico // *n* medium *m/f*.

psychoanalyse [saikəu'ænəlaiz] *vt* psicoanalizar; **psychoanalysis** [-kəu'nælisis] *n* psicoanálisis *m inv*; **psychoanalyst** [-'ænəlist] *n* psicoanalista *m/f*.

psychological [saikə'lɔdʒikl] *a* psicológico.

psychologist [sai'kɔlədʒist] *n* psicólogo; **psychology** [-dʒi] *n* psicología.

psychopath ['saikəupæθ] *n* psicópata *m/f*.

psychosomatic ['saikəusə'mætik] *a* psicosomático.

psychotic [sai'kɔtik] *a*, *n* psicótico.

pub [pʌb] *n abbr of* **public house** pub *m*, taberna.

puberty ['pjuːbəti] *n* pubertad *f*.

public ['pʌblik] *a*, *n* público.

publican ['pʌblikən] *n* tabernero.

publication [pʌbli'keiʃən] *n* publicación *f*.

public: **~ convenience** *n* aseos *mpl* públicos; **~ house** *n* bar *m*, pub *m*.

publicity [pʌb'lisiti] *n* publicidad *f*.

publicly ['pʌblikli] *ad* públicamente, en público.

public: **~ opinion** *n* opinión *f* pública; **~ relations** *n* relaciones *fpl* públicas; **~ school** *n* (*Brit*) escuela privada; **~-spirited** *a* de buen ciudadano.

publish ['pʌbliʃ] *vt* publicar; **~er** *n* editor/a *m/f*; **~ing** *n* (*industry*) la industria editorial.

puce [pjuːs] *a* de color pardo rojizo.

pucker ['pʌkə*] *vt* (*pleat*) arrugar; (*brow etc*) fruncir.

pudding ['pudiŋ] *n* pudín *m*; (*sweet*) postre *m*; **black ~** morcilla.

puddle ['pʌdl] *n* charco.

puff [pʌf] *n* soplo; (*from mouth*) bocanada; (*sound*) resoplido; (*also*: **powder ~**) borla // *vt*: **to ~ one's pipe** chupar la pipa // *vi* (*gen*) soplar; (*pant*) jadear; **to ~ out smoke** echar humo; **to ~ up** *vt* hinchar, inflar; **~ed** *a* (*col*: *out of breath*) sin aliento.

puffin ['pʌfin] *n* frailecillo.

puffy ['pʌfi] *a* hinchado.

pull [pul] *n* (*tug*): **to give sth a ~** dar un tirón a algo; (*fig*: *advantage*) ventaja; (: *influence*) influencia // *vt* tirar de; (*tug*) jalar; (*muscle*) torcerse; (*haul*) tirar, arrastrar // *vi* tirar, dar un tirón; **to ~ a face** hacer muecas; **to ~ to pieces** hacer pedazos; **to ~ one's punches** no emplear toda la fuerza; **to ~ one's weight** hacer su parte; **to ~ o.s. together** serenarse; **to ~ sb's leg** tomarle el pelo a uno; **to ~ apart** *vt* (*break*) romper (en dos); **to ~ down** *vt* (*house*) derribar; **to ~ in** *vi* (*AUT*: *at the kerb*) parar (junto a la acera); (*RAIL*) llegar (al andén); **to ~ off** *vt* (*deal etc*) cerrar, concluir con éxito; **to ~ out** *vi* irse, marcharse; (*AUT*: *from kerb*) salir // *vt* sacar, arrancar; **to ~ through** *vi* salir (de un apuro); (*MED*) recobrar la salud; **to ~ up** *vi* (*stop*) parar // *vt* (*uproot*) arrancar, desarraigar; (*stop*) parar.

pulley ['puli] *n* polea.

pullover ['puləuvə*] *n* jersey *m*.

pulp [pʌlp] *n* (*of fruit*) pulpa; (*for paper*) pasta.

pulpit ['pulpit] *n* púlpito.

pulsate [pʌl'seit] *vi* pulsar, latir.

pulse [pʌls] *n* (*ANAT*) pulso; (*of music, engine*) pulsación *f*; (*BOT*) legumbre *f*.

pulverize ['pʌlvəraiz] *vt* pulverizar; (*fig*) hacer polvo.

puma ['pju:mə] n puma.
pummel ['pʌml] vt dar de puñetazos.
pump [pʌmp] n bomba; (shoe) zapato de tenis // vt sacar con una bomba; (fig: col) sonsacar; **to ~ up** vt inflar.
pumpkin ['pʌmpkɪn] n calabaza.
pun [pʌn] n juego de palabras.
punch [pʌntʃ] n (blow) golpe m, puñetazo; (tool) punzón m; (for tickets) taladro; (drink) ponche m // vt (hit): **to ~ sb/sth** dar un puñetazo o golpear a uno/algo; (make a hole in) punzar; **~card** n tarjeta perforada; **~line** n palabras que rematan un chiste; **~up** n (col) riña.
punctual ['pʌŋktjuəl] a puntual; **~ity** [-'ælɪtɪ] n puntualidad f.
punctuate ['pʌŋktjueɪt] vt interrumpir; **punctuation** [-'eɪʃən] n puntuación f.
puncture ['pʌŋktʃə*] n pinchazo // vt pinchar.
pundit ['pʌndɪt] n sabio.
pungent ['pʌndʒənt] a acre.
punish ['pʌnɪʃ] vt castigar; **~ment** n castigo.
punt [pʌnt] n (boat) batea.
punter ['pʌntə*] n (gambler) jugador/a m/f.
puny ['pju:nɪ] a débil.
pup [pʌp] n cachorro.
pupil ['pju:pl] n alumno/a.
puppet ['pʌpɪt] n títere m.
puppy ['pʌpɪ] n cachorro, perrito.
purchase ['pɜːtʃɪs] n compra; (grip) pie m firme // vt comprar; **purchaser** n comprador/a m/f.
pure [pjuə*] a puro.
purée ['pjuəreɪ] n puré m.
purge [pɜːdʒ] n (MED) purgante m; (POL) purga // vt purgar.
purification [pjuərɪfɪ'keɪʃən] n purificación f, depuración f; **purify** ['pjuərɪfaɪ] vt purificar, depurar.
purist ['pjuərɪst] n purista m/f.
puritan ['pjuərɪtən] n puritano/a; **~ical** [-'tænɪkl] a puritano.
purity ['pjuərɪtɪ] n pureza.
purl [pɜːl] n punto del revés.
purple ['pɜːpl] a purpúreo; (bruise) morado.
purport [pɜː'pɔːt] vi: **to ~ to be/do** dar a entender que es/hace.
purpose ['pɜːpəs] n propósito; **on ~** a propósito, adrede; **~ful** a resuelto, determinado.
purr [pɜː*] n ronroneo // vi ronronear.
purse [pɜːs] n monedero; (bag) bolsa // vt fruncir.
purser ['pɜːsə*] n (NAUT) contador m de navío.
pursue [pə'sju:] vt seguir, perseguir; (profession) ejercer; **pursuer** n perseguidor/a m/f.
pursuit [pə'sju:t] n (chase) caza; (persecution) persecución f; (occupation) carrera; (pastime) pasatiempo.
purveyor [pə'veɪə*] n proveedor/a m/f.

pus [pʌs] n pus m.
push [puʃ] n (gen) empuje m; (shove) empujón m; (attack) ataque m; (advance) avance m // vt empujar; (button) apretar; (promote) promover; (thrust): **to ~ sth (into)** meter algo a la fuerza (en) // vi empujar; (fig) hacer esfuerzos; **to ~ aside** vt apartar con la mano; **to ~ off** vi (col) largarse; **to ~ on** vi (continue) seguir adelante; **to ~ through** vt (measure) despachar; **to ~ up** vt (total, prices) hacer subir; **~chair** n sillita de ruedas; **~ing** a emprendedor(a), enérgico; **~over** n (col): **it's a ~over** está tirado; **~y** a (pej) agresivo.
puss [pus], **pussy(-cat)** ['pusɪ(kæt)] n minino.
put [put], pt, pp put vt (place) poner, colocar; (~ into) meter; (say) declarar, expresar; (a question) hacer; (estimate) calcular; **to ~ about** vi (NAUT) virar // vt (rumour) diseminar; **to ~ across** vt (ideas etc) comunicar; **to ~ away** vt (store) guardar; **to ~ back** vt (replace) devolver a su lugar; (postpone) posponer; **to ~ by** vt (money) guardar; **to ~ down** vt (on ground) poner en el suelo; (animal) sacrificar; (in writing) apuntar; (suppress: revolt etc) sofocar; (attribute) atribuir; **to ~ forward** vt (ideas) presentar, proponer; (date) adelantar; **to ~ in** vt (application, complaint) presentar; **to ~ off** vt (postpone) aplazar; (discourage) desanimar; **to ~ on** vt (clothes, lipstick etc) ponerse; (light etc) encender; (play etc) presentar; (weight) ganar; (brake) echar; (attitude) adoptar postura de; **to ~ out** vt (fire, light) apagar; (one's hand) alargar; (news, rumour) sacar a luz, diseminar; (tongue etc) sacar; (person: inconvenience) molestar, fastidiar; **to ~ up** vt (raise) levantar, alzar; (hang) colgar; (build) construir; (increase) aumentar; (accommodate) alojar; **to ~ up with** vt fus aguantar.
putrid ['pju:trɪd] a podrido.
putt [pʌt] vt golpear con poca fuerza // n put m, golpe m corto; **~er** n (GOLF) putter m; **~ing green** n campo de golf en miniatura.
putty ['pʌtɪ] n masilla.
puzzle ['pʌzl] n (riddle) acertijo; (jigsaw) rompecabezas m inv; (crossword) crucigrama m; (mystery) misterio, problema m // vt dejar perplejo, confundir // vi devanarse los sesos; **puzzling** a misterioso, enigmático.
pygmy ['pɪgmɪ] n pigmeo.
pyjamas [pɪ'dʒɑːməz] npl pijama m.
pylon ['paɪlən] n pilón m, poste m.
pyramid ['pɪrəmɪd] n pirámide m.
python ['paɪθən] n pitón m.

Q

quack [kwæk] *n* (*of duck*) graznido; (*pej: doctor*) curandero // *vi* graznar.

quad [kwɔd] *abbr of* **quadrangle; quadruplet.**

quadrangle ['kwɔdrængl] *n* (*courtyard: abbr:* **quad**) patio.

quadruple [kwɔ'drupl] *a* cuádruple // *n* cuádruplo // *vt, vi* cuadruplicar.

quadruplets [kwɔ:'dru:plɪts] *npl* cuatrillizos *mpl.*

quagmire ['kwægmaɪə*] *n* lodazal *m*, cenegal *m.*

quail [kweɪl] *n* (*bird*) codorniz *f* // *vi* amedrentarse.

quaint [kweɪnt] *a* curioso; (*picturesque*) pintoresco.

quake [kweɪk] *vi* temblar // *n* *abbr of* **earthquake.**

Quaker ['kweɪkə*] *n* cuáquero/a.

qualification [kwɔlɪfɪ'keɪʃən] *n* (*reservation*) reserva; (*modification*) modificación *f*; (*act*) calificación *f*; (*degree*) título; **qualified** ['kwɔlɪfaɪd] *a* (*trained*) cualificado; (*fit*) apto, competente; (*limited*) limitado; (*professionally*) con título.

qualify ['kwɔlɪfaɪ] *vt* calificar; (*capacitate*) capacitar; (*modify*) modificar; (*limit*) moderar // *vi* (*SPORT*) clasificarse; **to ~ (as)** calificarse (de), graduarse (en); **to ~ (for)** reunir los requisitos (para).

quality ['kwɔlɪtɪ] *n* calidad *f*; (*moral*) cualidad *f.*

qualm [kwɑ:m] *n* escrúpulo.

quandary ['kwɔndrɪ] *n*: **to be in a ~** estar en un dilema.

quantity ['kwɔntɪtɪ] *n* cantidad *f.*

quarantine ['kwɔrntɪn] *n* cuarentena.

quarrel ['kwɔrl] *n* (*argument*) riña; (*fight*) pelea // *vi* reñir; pelearse; **~some** *a* pendenciero.

quarry ['kwɔrɪ] *n* (*for stone*) cantera; (*animal*) presa.

quart [kwɔ:t] *n* cuarto de galón = *1.136 litros.*

quarter ['kwɔ:tə*] *n* cuarto, cuarta parte *f*; (*of year*) trimestre *m*; (*district*) barrio // *vt* dividir en cuartos; (*MIL: lodge*) alojar; **~s** *npl* (*barracks*) cuartel *m*; (*living ~s*) alojamiento *sg*; **a ~ of an hour** un cuarto de hora; **~ final** *n* cuarto de final; **~ly** *a* trimestral // *ad* cada 3 meses, trimestralmente; **~master** *n* (*MIL*) comisario, intendente *m* militar.

quartet(te) [kwɔ:'tɛt] *n* cuarteto.

quartz [kwɔ:ts] *n* cuarzo.

quash [kwɔʃ] *vt* (*verdict*) anular.

quasi- ['kweɪzaɪ] *pref* cuasi.

quaver ['kweɪvə*] *n* (*MUS*) corchea // *vi* temblar.

quay [ki:] *n* (*also:* **~side**) muelle *m.*

queasy ['kwi:zɪ] *a* (*sickly*) delicado.

queen [kwi:n] *n* (*gen*) reina; (*CARDS etc*)

dama; **~ mother** *n* reina madre.

queer [kwɪə*] *a* (*odd*) raro, extraño; (*suspect*) sospechoso // *n* (*col*) maricón *m.*

quell [kwɛl] *vt* calmar; (*put down*) sofocar.

quench [kwɛntʃ] *vt* apagar.

query ['kwɪərɪ] *n* (*question*) pregunta; (*doubt*) duda; (*fig*) interrogante *f* // *vt* preguntar; poner en duda.

quest [kwɛst] *n* busca, búsqueda.

question ['kwɛstʃən] *n* pregunta; (*matter*) asunto, cuestión *f* // *vt* (*gen*) preguntar; (*doubt*) dudar de; (*interrogate*) interrogar, hacer preguntas a; **beyond ~** fuera de toda duda; **out of the ~** imposible, ni hablar; **~able** *a* discutible; (*doubtful*) dudoso; **~ mark** *n* punto de interrogación; **~naire** [-'nɛə*] *n* cuestionario.

queue [kju:] *n* cola // *vi* hacer cola.

quibble ['kwɪbl] *vi* sutilizar.

quick [kwɪk] *a* rápido; (*temper*) vivo; (*agile*) ágil; (*mind*) listo; (*eye*) agudo; (*ear*) fino; **be ~!** ¡date prisa!; **~en** *vt* dar prisa // *vi* apresurarse, darse prisa; **~ly** *ad* rápidamente, de prisa; **~ness** *n* rapidez *f*, agilidad *f*; (*liveliness*) viveza; **~sand** *n* arenas *fpl* movedizas; **~step** *n* (*dance*) fox-trot *m*, quickstep *m*; **~-witted** *a* perspicaz.

quid [kwɪd] *n*, *pl inv* (*Brit: col*) libra.

quiet ['kwaɪət] *a* tranquilo; (*silent*) callado; (*ceremony*) discreto // *n* silencio, tranquilidad *f*; **keep ~!** ¡cállate!, ¡silencio!; **~en** (*also:* **~en down**) *vi* (*grow calm*) calmarse; (*grow silent*) callarse // *vt* calmar; hacer callar; **~ly** *ad* (*gen*) tranquilamente; (*silently*) silenciosamente; **~ness** *n* (*silence*) silencio; (*calm*) tranquilidad *f.*

quilt [kwɪlt] *n* edredón *m*; (**continental**) **~** *n* edredón *m.*

quin [kwɪn] *abbr of* **quintuplet.**

quinine [kwɪ'ni:n] *n* quinina.

quintet(te) [kwɪn'tɛt] *n* quinteto.

quintuplets [kwɪn'tju:plɪts] *npl* quintillizos *mpl.*

quip [kwɪp] *n* pulla.

quirk [kwɜ:k] *n* peculiaridad *f.*

quit [kwɪt], *pt, pp* **quit** *or* **quitted** *vt* dejar, abandonar; (*premises*) desocupar // *vi* (*give up*) retirarse; (*go away*) irse; (*resign*) dimitir; (*stop work*) abandonar (una empresa).

quite [kwaɪt] *ad* (*rather*) bastante; (*entirely*) completamente; **~ a few of them** un buen número de ellos; **~ (so)!** ¡así es!, ¡exactamente!

quits [kwɪts] *a*: **~ (with)** en paz (con).

quiver ['kwɪvə*] *vi* estremecerse // *n* (*for arrows*) carcaj *m.*

quiz [kwɪz] *n* (*game*) concurso; (*questioning*) interrogatorio // *vt* interrogar; **~zical** *a* burlón(ona).

quoits [kwɔɪts] *npl* juego de aros.

quorum ['kwɔ:rəm] *n* quórum *m.*

quota ['kwəʊtə] *n* cuota.

quotation [kwəʊ'teɪʃən] *n* cita; (*estimate*)

presupuesto; ~ **marks** *npl* comillas *fpl.*

quote [kwəʊt] *n* cita *f* // *vt* (*sentence*) citar; (*price*) fijar // *vi*: **to ~ from** citar de.

quotient [ˈkwəʊʃənt] *n* cociente *m.*

R

rabbi [ˈræbaɪ] *n* rabino.

rabbit [ˈræbɪt] *n* conejo; ~ **hole** *n* hura (de conejos); ~ **hutch** *n* conejera.

rabble [ˈræbl] *n* (*pej*) chusma, populacho.

rabies [ˈreɪbiːz] *n* rabia.

RAC *n abbr of* **Royal Automobile Club.**

raccoon [rəˈkuːn] *n* mapache *m.*

race [reɪs] *n* (*gen*) carrera; (*species*) raza, estirpe *f* // *vt* (*horse*) presentar (en carrera); (*engine*) acelerar // *vi* (*compete*) competir; (*run*) correr; (*pulse*) latir a ritmo acelerado; ~ **course** *n* hipódromo; ~ **horse** *n* caballo de carreras; ~ **track** *n* hipódromo; (*for cars*) autódromo.

racial [ˈreɪʃl] *a* racial; ~ **ism** *n* racismo; ~ **ist** *a, n* racista *m/f.*

racing [ˈreɪsɪŋ] *n* carreras *fpl;* ~ **car** *n* coche *m* de carreras; ~ **driver** *n* corredor/a *m/f* de coches.

racist [ˈreɪsɪst] *a, n* (*pej*) racista *m/f.*

rack [ræk] *n* (*also:* **luggage** ~) rejilla; (*shelf*) estante *m;* (*also:* **roof** ~) baca, portaequipajes *m inv;* (*clothes* ~) percha // *vt* (*cause pain to*) atormentar.

racket [ˈrækɪt] *n* (*for tennis*) raqueta; (*noise*) ruido, estrépito; (*swindle*) estafa, timo.

racoon [rəˈkuːn] *n* = **raccoon.**

racquet [ˈrækɪt] *n* raqueta.

racy [ˈreɪsɪ] *a* picante, salado.

radar [ˈreɪdɑː*] *n* radar *m.*

radiance [ˈreɪdɪəns] *n* brillantez *f,* resplandor *m;* **radiant** [-ənt] *a* brillante, resplandeciente.

radiate [ˈreɪdɪeɪt] *vt* (*heat*) radiar, irradiar // *vi* (*lines*) extenderse.

radiation [reɪdɪˈeɪʃən] *n* radiación *f.*

radiator [ˈreɪdɪeɪtə*] *n* radiador *m;* ~ **cap** *n* tapón *m* de radiador.

radical [ˈrædɪkl] *a* radical.

radio [ˈreɪdɪəʊ] *n* radio *f;* **on the** ~ por radio; ~ **station** *n* emisora.

radio... [ˈreɪdɪəʊ] *pref:* ~ **active** *a* radioactivo; ~ **activity** *n* radioactividad *f;* ~ **controlled** *a* teledirigido; ~ **graphy** [-ˈɔɡrəfɪ] *n* radiografía; ~ **logy** [-ˈɔlədʒɪ] *n* radiología; ~ **telephone** *n* radioteléfono; ~ **therapy** *n* radioterapia.

radish [ˈrædɪʃ] *n* rábano.

radius [ˈreɪdɪəs], *pl* **radii** [-ɪaɪ] *n* radio.

raffia [ˈræfɪə] *n* rafia.

raffle [ˈræfl] *n* rifa, sorteo *f* // *vt* rifar.

raft [rɑːft] *n* (*also:* **life** ~) balsa.

rafter [ˈrɑːftə*] *n* viga.

rag [ræg] *n* (*piece of cloth*) trapo; (*torn cloth*) harapo; (*pej: newspaper*) periodicucho; (*for charity*) actividades estudiantiles benéficas // *vt* tomar el pelo a; ~**s** *npl* harapos *mpl;* ~**-and-bone man**

n trapero; ~ **doll** *n* muñeca de trapo.

rage [reɪdʒ] *n* (*fury*) rabia, furor *m;* (*fashion*) boga // *vi* (*person*) rabiar, estar furioso; (*storm*) bramar.

ragged [ˈrægɪd] *a* (*edge*) desigual, mellado; (*cuff*) roto; (*appearance*) andrajoso, harapiento; (*coastline*) accidentado.

raid [reɪd] *n* (*MIL*) incursión *f;* (*criminal*) asalto; (*attack*) ataque *m;* (*by police*) redada // *vt* invadir, atacar; asaltar; ~ **er** *n* invasor/a *m/f;* (*criminal*) asaltante *m/f.*

rail [reɪl] *n* (*on stair*) barandilla, pasamanos *m inv;* (*on bridge, balcony*) pretil *m;* (*of ship*) borda; (*for train*) riel *m,* carril *m;* ~**s** *npl* vía *sg;* **by** ~ por ferrocarril; ~ **ing(s)** *n(pl)* verja *sg,* enrejado *sg;* ~ **road** (*US*), ~ **way** *n* ferrocarril *m,* vía férrea; ~ **wayman** *n* ferroviario; ~ **way station** *n* estación *f* de ferrocarril.

rain [reɪn] *n* lluvia // *vi* llover; **in the** ~ bajo la lluvia; **it's** ~ **ing** llueve, está lloviendo; ~ **bow** *n* arco iris; ~ **coat** *n* impermeable *m;* ~ **drop** *n* gota de lluvia; ~ **fall** *n* lluvia; ~ **y** *a* lluvioso.

raise [reɪz] *n* aumento // *vt* (*lift*) levantar; (*build*) erigir, edificar; (*increase*) aumentar; (*doubts*) suscitar; (*a question*) plantear; (*cattle, family*) criar; (*crop*) cultivar; (*army*) reclutar; (*funds*) reunir; (*loan*) obtener; **to ~ one's voice** alzar la voz.

raisin [ˈreɪzn] *n* paso de Corinto.

rake [reɪk] *n* (*tool*) rastrillo; (*person*) libertino // *vt* (*garden*) rastrillar; (*fire*) hurgar; (*with machine gun*) barrer.

rakish [ˈreɪkɪʃ] *a* (*suave*) gallardo; **at a** ~ **angle** echado al lado.

rally [ˈrælɪ] *n* (*POL etc*) reunión *f,* mitin *m;* (*AUT*) rallye *m;* (*TENNIS*) peloteo // *vt* reunir; (*encourage*) reanimar // *vi* reunirse; (*sick person, Stock Exchange*) recuperarse; **to ~ round** *vt fus* (*fig*) dar apoyo a.

ram [ræm] *n* carnero; (*TECH*) pisón *m* // *vt* (*crash into*) dar contra, chocar con; (*tread down*) apisonar.

ramble [ˈræmbl] *n* caminata, excursión *f* en el campo // *vi* (*pej: also:* ~ **on**) divagar; **rambler** *n* excursionista *m/f;* (*BOT*) trepadora; **rambling** *a* (*speech*) divagador(a); (*BOT*) trepador(a) // *n* excursionismo.

ramp [ræmp] *n* rampa.

rampage [ræmˈpeɪdʒ] *n:* **to be on the** ~ desbocarse // *vi:* **they went rampaging through the town** corrieron como locos por la ciudad.

rampant [ˈræmpənt] *a* (*disease etc*) violento.

rampart [ˈræmpɑːt] *n* terraplén *m;* (*wall*) muralla.

ramshackle [ˈræmʃækl] *a* destartalado.

ran [ræn] *pt of* **run.**

ranch [rɑːntʃ] *n* hacienda, estancia; ~ **er** *n* ganadero.

rancid ['rænsɪd] a rancio.

rancour, rancor (US) ['ræŋkə*] n rencor m.

random ['rændəm] a fortuito, sin orden // n: **at ~** al azar.

randy ['rændɪ] a (col) cachondo.

rang [ræŋ] pt of **ring.**

range [reɪndʒ] n (of mountains) cadena, cordillera; (of missile) alcance m; (of voice) extensión f; (series) serie f; (of products) surtido; (MIL: also: **shooting ~**) campo de tiro; (also: **kitchen ~**) fogón m // vt (place) colocar; (arrange) arreglar // vi: **to ~ over** (wander) recorrer; (extend) extenderse por; **to ~ from ... to...** oscilar entre ... y...; **ranger** n guardabosques m inv.

rank [ræŋk] n (row) fila; (MIL) rango; (status) categoría; (also: **taxi ~**) parada // vi: **to ~ among** figurar entre // a (stinking) fétido, rancio; **the ~ and file** (fig) la base.

rankle ['ræŋkl] vi (insult) doler.

ransack ['rænsæk] vt (search) registrar; (plunder) saquear.

ransom ['rænsəm] n rescate m; **to hold sb to ~** (fig) poner a uno entre la espada y la pared.

rant [rænt] vi divagar, desvariar; **~ing** n lenguaje m declamatorio.

rap [ræp] n golpecito, golpe m seco // vt tocar, dar un golpecito en.

rape [reɪp] n violación f // vt violar.

rapid ['ræpɪd] a rápido; **~s** npl (GEO) rápidos mpl; **~ity** [rə'pɪdɪtɪ] n rapidez f.

rapist ['reɪpɪst] n violador m.

rapport [ræ'pɔ:*] n armonía, relación f amistosa.

rapture ['ræptʃə*] n éxtasis m, rapto; **rapturous** a extático; (applause) entusiasta.

rare [reə*] a raro, poco común; (CULIN: steak) poco hecho.

rarely ['reəlɪ] ad rara vez.

rarity ['reərɪtɪ] n rareza.

rascal ['rɑːskl] n pillo, pícaro.

rash [ræʃ] a imprudente, precipitado // a (MED) salpullido, erupción f (cutánea).

rasher ['ræʃə*] n lonja.

rasp [rɑːsp] n (tool) escofina.

raspberry ['rɑːzbərɪ] n frambuesa; **~ bush** n frambueso.

rasping ['rɑːspɪŋ] a: **a ~ noise** un ruido áspero.

rat [ræt] n rata.

ratchet ['rætʃɪt] n (TECH) trinquete m.

rate [reɪt] n (ratio) razón f; (percentage) tanto por ciento; (price) precio; (: of hotel) tarifa; (of interest) tipo; (speed) velocidad f // vt (value) tasar; (estimate) estimar; **to ~ as** ser considerado como; **~s** npl (Brit) impuesto sg municipal; (fees) tarifa sg; **~able value** n valor m impuesto; **~payer** n contribuyente m/f.

rather ['rɑːðə*] ad antes, más bien; (in speech) mejor dicho; **it's ~ expensive** es algo caro; (too much) es demasiado caro;

there's ~ a lot hay bastante; **I would** or **I'd ~ go** preferiría ir.

ratify ['rætɪfaɪ] vt ratificar.

rating ['reɪtɪŋ] n (valuation) tasación f; (value) valor m; (standing) posición f; (NAUT. category) clase f; (: sailor) marinero.

ratio ['reɪʃɪəu] n razón f; **in the ~ of 100 to 1** a razón de 100 a 1.

ration ['ræʃən] n ración f; **~s** npl víveres mpl // vt racionar.

rational ['ræʃənl] a racional; (solution, reasoning) lógico, razonable; (person) cuerdo, sensato; **rationale** [-'nɑːl] n razón f fundamental; **~ize** vt organizar lógicamente, racionalizar; **~ly** ad racionalmente; (logically) lógicamente.

rationing ['ræʃnɪŋ] n racionamiento.

rattle ['rætl] n golpeteo; (of train etc) traqueteo; (of hail) tamborileo; (object: of baby) sonaja, sonajero; (: of sports fan) matraca; (of snake) cascabel m // vi sonar, golpear; traquetear; tamborilear; (small objects) castañetear // vt agitar, sacudir; **~snake** n serpiente f de cascabel.

raucous ['rɔːkəs] a estridente, ronco.

ravage ['rævɪdʒ] vt hacer estragos, destrozar; **~s** npl estragos mpl.

rave [reɪv] vi (in anger) encolerizarse; (with enthusiasm) entusiasmarse; (MED) delirar, desvariar.

raven ['reɪvən] n cuervo.

ravenous ['rævənəs] a hambriento, famélico.

ravine [rə'viːn] n barranco.

raving ['reɪvɪŋ] a: **~ lunatic** loco de atar.

ravioli [rævɪ'əulɪ] n raviolis mpl.

ravish ['rævɪʃ] vt encantar; **~ing** a encantador(a).

raw [rɔː] a (uncooked) crudo; (not processed) bruto; (sore) vivo; (inexperienced) novato, inexperto; **~ material** n materia prima.

ray [reɪ] n rayo; **~ of hope** (rayo de) esperanza.

rayon ['reɪɔn] n rayón m.

raze [reɪz] vt arrasar.

razor ['reɪzə*] n (open) navaja; (safety ~) máquina de afeitar; **~ blade** n hoja de afeitar.

Rd abbr of **road.**

re [riː] prep con referencia a.

reach [riːtʃ] n alcance m; (BOXING) envergadura; (of river etc) extensión f entre dos recodos // vt alcanzar, llegar a; (achieve) lograr; (stretch out) alargar, extender // vi alcanzar, extenderse; **within ~** (object) al alcance (de la mano); **out of ~** fuera del alcance; **to ~ out for sth** alargar o tender la mano para tomar algo.

react [riː'ækt] vi reaccionar; **~ion** [-'ækʃən] n reacción f; **~ionary** [-'ækʃənrɪ] a, n reaccionario/a.

reactor [riː'æktə*] n reactor m.

read [riːd], pt, pp **read** [rɛd] vi leer // vt

leer; (*understand*) entender; (*study*) estudiar; **to ~ out** *vt* leer en alta voz; **~able** *a* (*writing*) legible; (*book*) que merece leerse; **~er** *n* lector/a *m/f*; (*book*) libro de lecturas; (*at university*) profesor/a *m/f*; **~ership** *n* (*of paper etc*) número de lectores.

readily ['rɛdɪlɪ] *ad* (*willingly*) de buena gana; (*easily*) fácilmente; (*quickly*) en seguida.

readiness ['rɛdɪnɪs] *n* buena voluntad; (*preparedness*) preparación *f*; **in ~** (*prepared*) listo, preparado.

reading ['ri:dɪŋ] *n* lectura; (*understanding*) comprensión *f*; (*on instrument*) indicación *f*.

readjust [ri:ə'dʒʌst] *vt* reajustar // *vi* (*person*): **to ~ to** reorientarse a.

ready ['rɛdɪ] *a* listo, preparado; (*willing*) dispuesto; (*available*) disponible // *ad*: **~-cooked** listo para comer // *n*: **at the ~** (MIL) listo para tirar; **~-made** *a* confeccionado; **~ reckoner** *n* libro de cálculos hechos.

reaffirm [ri:ə'fɔ:m] *vt* reafirmar.

real [rɪəl] *a* verdadero, auténtico; **in ~ terms** en términos reales; **~ estate** *n* bienes *mpl* raíces; **~ism** *n* (*also* ART) realismo; **~ist** *n* realista *m/f*; **~istic** [-'lɪstɪk] *a* realista.

reality [ri:'ælɪtɪ] *n* realidad *f*; **in ~** en realidad.

realization [rɪəlaɪ'zeɪʃən] *n* comprensión *f*; (COMM) realización *f*.

realize ['rɪəlaɪz] *vt* (*understand*) darse cuenta de; (*a project, COMM: asset*) realizar.

really ['rɪəlɪ] *ad* verdaderamente, realmente; **~?** ¿de veras?

realm [rɛlm] *n* reino; (*fig*) esfera.

reap [ri:p] *vt* segar; (*fig*) cosechar, recoger; **~er** *n* segadora.

reappear [ri:ə'pɪə*] *vi* reaparecer; **~ance** *n* reaparición *f*.

reapply [ri:ə'plaɪ] *vi*: **to ~ for** aplicar de nuevo.

rear [rɪə*] *a* trasero // *n* parte *f* trasera // *vt* (*cattle, family*) criar // *vi* (*also*: **~ up**) (*animal*) encabritarse; **~-engined** *a* (AUT) con motor trasero; **~guard** *n* retaguardia.

rearm [ri:'ɑ:m] *vt, vi* rearmar; **~ament** *n* rearme *m*.

rearrange [ri:ə'reɪndʒ] *vt* ordenar *o* arreglar de nuevo.

rear-view ['rɪəvju:] *a*: **~ mirror** (AUT) espejo retrovisor.

reason ['ri:zn] *n* (*gen*) razón *f*; (*cause*) motivo, causa; (*sense*) sensatez *f* // *vi*: **to ~ with sb** alegar razones para convencer a uno; **it stands to ~ that** es lógico que; **~able** *a* razonable; (*sensible*) sensato; **~ably** *ad* razonablemente; **~ed** *a* (*argument*) razonado; **~ing** *n* razonamiento, argumentos *mpl*.

reassemble [ri:ə'sɛmbl] *vt* (*machine*) montar de nuevo // *vi* reunirse de nuevo.

reassure [ri:ə'ʃuə*] *vt* tranquilizar,

alentar; **to ~ sb of** tranquilizar a uno diciendo que; **reassuring** *a* alentador(a).

rebate ['ri:beɪt] *n* (*on product*) rebaja; (*on tax etc*) descuento.

rebel ['rɛbl] *n* rebelde *m/f* // *vi* [rɪ'bɛl] rebelarse, sublevarse; **~lion** *n* rebelión *f*, sublevación *f*; **~lious** *a* rebelde; (*child*) revoltoso.

rebirth [ri:'bɔ:θ] *n* renacimiento.

rebound [rɪ'baund] *vi* (*ball*) rebotar // *n* ['ri:baund] rebote *m*.

rebuff [rɪ'bʌf] *n* desaire *m*, rechazo // *vt* rechazar.

rebuild [ri:'bɪld] (*irg: like* **build**) *vt* reconstruir.

rebuke [rɪ'bju:k] *n* reprimenda // *vt* reprender.

recalcitrant [rɪ'kælsɪtrənt] *a* reacio.

recall [rɪ'kɔ:l] *vt* (*remember*) recordar; (*ambassador etc*) retirar // *n* aviso, llamada.

recant [rɪ'kænt] *vi* retractarse.

recap ['ri:kæp] *vt, vi* recapitular.

recapture [ri:'kæptʃə*] *vt* (*town*) reconquistar; (*atmosphere*) hacer revivir.

recede [rɪ'si:d] *vi* retroceder; **receding** *a* (*forehead, chin*) huidizo.

receipt [rɪ'si:t] *n* (*document*) recibo; (*act of receiving*) recepción *f*; **~s** *npl* (COMM) ingresos *mpl*.

receive [rɪ'si:v] *vt* recibir; (*guest*) acoger; (*wound*) sufrir; **receiver** *n* (TEL) auricular *m*; (*of stolen goods*) receptador/a *m/f*; (COMM) recibidor/a *m/f*.

recent ['ri:snt] *a* reciente; **~ly** *ad* recién, recientemente.

receptacle [rɪ'sɛptɪkl] *n* receptáculo.

reception [rɪ'sɛpʃən] *n* (*gen*) recepción *f*; (*welcome*) acogida; **~ desk** *n* recepción *f*; **~ist** *n* recepcionista *m/f*.

receptive [rɪ'sɛptɪv] *a* receptivo.

recess [rɪ'sɛs] *n* (*in room*) hueco; (*for bed*) nicho; (*secret place*) escondrijo; (POL etc: *holiday*) vacaciones *fpl*; **~ion** *n* recesión *f*.

recharge [ri:'tʃɑːdʒ] *vt* (*battery*) recargar.

recipe ['rɛsɪpɪ] *n* receta.

recipient [rɪ'sɪpɪənt] *n* recibidor/a *m/f*; (*of letter*) destinatario/a.

reciprocal [rɪ'sɪprəkl] *a* recíproco.

recital [rɪ'saɪtl] *n* recital *m*.

recite [rɪ'saɪt] *vt* (*poem*) recitar; (*complaints etc*) enumerar.

reckless ['rɛkləs] *a* temerario, imprudente; (*speed*) excesivo, peligroso; **~ly** *ad* imprudentemente; de modo peligroso.

reckon ['rɛkən] *vt* (*count*) contar; (*consider*) considerar; (*think*): **I ~ that...** me parece que...; **~ing** *n* (*calculation*) cálculo; **the day of ~ing** el día del juicio (final).

reclaim [rɪ'kleɪm] *vt* (*land*) recuperar; (: *from sea*) rescatar; (*demand back*) reclamar; **reclamation** [rɛklə'meɪʃən] *n* recuperación *f*; rescate *m*.

recline [rɪ'klaɪn] *vi* reclinarse; (*lean*) apoyarse; **reclining** *a* (*seat*) reclinable.

recluse [rɪ'klu:s] n recluso.

recognition [rɛkəg'nɪʃən] n reconocimiento; **transformed beyond** ~ tan transformado que resulta irreconocible.

recognizable ['rɛkəgnaɪzəbl] a: ~ **(by)** reconocible (por).

recognize ['rɛkəgnaɪz] vt reconocer, conocer; **to** ~ **by/as** reconocer de/por.

recoil [rɪ'kɔɪl] vi (gun) retroceder; (person): **to** ~ **from doing sth** sentir repugnancia por hacer algo.

recollect [rɛkə'lɛkt] vt recordar, acordarse de; ~**ion** [-'lɛkʃən] n recuerdo.

recommend [rɛkə'mɛnd] vt recomendar; ~**ation** [-'deɪʃən] n recomendación f.

recompense ['rɛkəmpɛns] vt recompensar // n recompensa.

reconcile ['rɛkənsaɪl] vt (two people) reconciliar; (two facts) conciliar; **to** ~ **o.s. to sth** resignarse a algo, conformarse a algo; **reconciliation** [-sɪlɪ'eɪʃən] n reconciliación f.

reconnaissance [rɪ'kɒnɪsns] n (MIL) reconocimiento.

reconnoitre, reconnoiter (US) [rɛkə'nɔɪtə*] vt, vi (MIL) reconocer.

reconsider [ri:kən'sɪdə*] vt repensar.

reconstitute [ri:'kɒnstɪtju:t] vt reconstituir.

reconstruct [ri:kən'strʌkt] vt reconstruir; ~**ion** [-kʃən] n reconstrucción f.

record ['rɛkɔ:d] n (MUS) disco; (of meeting etc) relación f; (register) registro, partida; (file) archivo; (also: **police** ~) antecedentes mpl; (written) expediente m; (SPORT) récord m // vt [rɪ'kɔ:d] (set down) registrar; (relate) hacer constar; (MUS: song etc) grabar; **in** ~ **time** en un tiempo récord; **off the** ~ a no oficial // ad confidencialmente; ~ **card** n (in file) ficha; ~**er** n (MUS) flauta de pico; (TECH) contador m; ~ **holder** n (SPORT) recordman m; ~**ing** n (MUS) grabación f; ~ **player** n tocadiscos m inv.

recount [rɪ'kaunt] vt contar.

re-count ['ri:kaunt] n (POL: of votes) segundo escrutinio // vt [ri:'kaunt] volver a contar.

recoup [rɪ'ku:p] vt: **to** ~ **one's losses** recuperar las pérdidas.

recourse [rɪ'kɔ:s] n recurso; **to have** ~ **to** recurrir a.

recover [rɪ'kʌvə*] vt recobrar, recuperar; (rescue) rescatar // vi (from illness) reponerse; (from shock) sobreponerse; ~**y** n recuperación f; rescate m; (MED) mejora.

recreate [ri:krɪ'eɪt] vt recrear.

recreation [rɛkrɪ'eɪʃən] n recreación f; (play) recreo; ~**al** a de recreo.

recrimination [rɪkrɪmɪ'neɪʃən] n recriminación f.

recruit [rɪ'kru:t] n recluta m/f // vt reclutar; ~**ment** n reclutamiento.

rectangle ['rɛktæŋgl] n rectángulo; **rectangular** [-'tæŋgjulə*] a rectangular.

rectify ['rɛktɪfaɪ] vt rectificar.

rector ['rɛktə*] n (REL) párroco; (SCOL) rector/a m/f; ~**y** n casa del párroco.

recuperate [rɪ'ku:pəreɪt] vi reponerse, restablecerse.

recur [rɪ'kə:*] vi repetirse; (opportunity) producirse de nuevo; ~**rence** n repetición f; ~**rent** a repetido.

red [rɛd] n rojo // a rojo; **to be in the** ~ deber dinero; **R**~ **Cross** n Cruz f Roja; ~**currant** n grosella; ~**den** vt enrojecer // vi enrojecerse; ~**dish** a (hair) rojizo.

redecorate [ri:'dɛkəreɪt] vt decorar de nuevo; **redecoration** [-'reɪʃən] n renovación f.

redeem [rɪ'di:m] vt (gen) redimir; (sth in pawn) desempeñar; (fig, also REL) rescatar; ~**ing** a: ~**ing feature** rasgo bueno o favorable.

redeploy [ri:dɪ'plɔɪ] vt (resources) disponer de nuevo.

red: ~**-haired** a pelirrojo; ~**-handed** a: **to be caught** ~**-handed** cogerse con las manos en la masa; ~**head** n pelirrojo/a; ~**-hot** a candente.

redirect [ri:daɪ'rɛkt] vt (mail) reexpedir.

redness ['rɛdnɪs] n lo rojo; (of hair) rojez f.

redo [ri:'du:] (irg: like **do**) vt rehacer.

redouble [ri:'dʌbl] vt: **to** ~ **one's efforts** intensificar los esfuerzos.

redress [rɪ'drɛs] n reparación f // vt reajustar.

red tape n (fig) trámites mpl, papeleo.

reduce [rɪ'dju:s] vt reducir; (lower) rebajar; '~ **speed now**' (AUT) 'reduzca la velocidad'; **at a** ~**d price** (of goods) (a precio) rebajado; **reduction** [rɪ'dʌkʃən] n reducción f; (of price) rebaja; (discount) descuento.

redundancy [rɪ'dʌndənsɪ] n desempleo.

redundant [rɪ'dʌndnt] a (worker) parado, sin trabajo; (detail, object) superfluo; **to be made** ~ quedarse sin trabajo.

reed [ri:d] n (BOT) junco, caña; (MUS: of clarinet etc) lengüeta.

reef [ri:f] n (at sea) arrecife m.

reek [ri:k] vi: **to** ~ **(of)** oler o heder a.

reel [ri:l] n (gen) carrete o la, bobina; (of film) rollo, película // vt (TECH) devanar; (also: ~ **in**) cobrar // vi (sway) tambalear.

re-election [ri:ɪ'lɛkʃən] n reelección f.

re-enter [ri:'ɛntə*] vt reingresar en; **re-entry** n reingreso.

ref [rɛf] n (col) abbr of **referee**.

refectory [rɪ'fɛktərɪ] n refectorio, comedor m.

refer [rɪ'fə:*] vt (send) remitir; (ascribe) referir a, relacionar con // vi: **to** ~ **to** (allude to) referirse a, aludir a; (apply to) relacionarse con; (consult) remitirse a.

referee [rɛfə'ri:] n árbitro; (for job application) persona que recomienda a otro // vt arbitrar.

reference ['rɛfrəns] n (mention) referencia; (sending) remisión f; (relevance) relación f; (for job application: letter) referencia, carta de recomendación; **with ~ to** con referencia a; (*comm: in letter*) me remito a; **~ book** *n* libro de consulta.

referendum [rɛfə'rɛndəm], *pl* **-da** [-də] *n* referéndum *m*.

refill [riː'fil] *vt* rellenar // *n* ['riːfil] repuesto, recambio.

refine [ri'fain] *vt* (*sugar, oil*) refinar; **~d** a (*person, taste*) refinado, culto; **~ment** *n* (*of person*) cultura, educación *f*; **~ry** *n* refinería.

reflect [ri'flɛkt] *vt* (*light, image*) reflejar // *vi* (*think*) reflexionar, pensar; **it ~s badly/well on him** le perjudica/le hace honor; **~ion** [-'flɛkʃən] *n* (*act*) reflexión *f*; (*image*) reflejo; (*criticism*) reproche *m*, crítica; **on ~ion** pensándolo bien; **~or** *n* (*also AUT*) captafaros *m* inv, reflector *m*.

reflex ['riːflɛks] a, *n* reflejo; **~ive** [ri'flɛksiv] a (*LING*) reflexivo.

reform [ri'fɔːm] *n* reforma // *vt* reformar; **the R~ation** [rɛfə'meiʃən] *n* la Reforma; **~er** *n* reformador/a *m/f*; **~ist** *n* reformista *m/f*.

refrain [ri'frein] *vi*: **to ~ from doing** abstenerse de hacer // *n* estribillo.

refresh [ri'frɛʃ] *vt* refrescar; **~er course** *n* curso de repaso; **~ments** *npl* (*drinks*) refrescos *mpl*.

refrigeration [rifridʒə'reiʃən] *n* refrigeración *f*; **refrigerator** [-'fridʒəreitə*] *n* refrigeradora, nevera.

refuel [riː'fjuəl] *vi* repostar combustible.

refuge ['rɛfjuːdʒ] *n* refugio, asilo; **to take ~ in** refugiarse en.

refugee [rɛfjuˈdʒiː] *n* refugiado/a.

refund ['riːfʌnd] *n* reembolso // *vt* [ri'fʌnd] devolver, reembolsar.

refurbish [riː'fɔːbiʃ] *vt* restaurar, renovar.

refusal [ri'fjuːzəl] *n* negativa; **first ~** primera opción.

refuse ['rɛfjuːs] *n* basura // (*vb*: [ri'fjuːz]) *vt* (*reject*) rehusar; (*say no to*) negarse a // *vi* negarse; (*horse*) resistirse; **~ bin** *n* cubo de la basura; **~ tip** *n* vertedero.

refute [ri'fjuːt] *vt* refutar, rebatir.

regain [ri'gein] *vt* recobrar, recuperar.

regal ['riːgl] a regio, real.

regalia [ri'geiliə] *n, npl* insignias *fpl* reales.

regard [ri'gɑːd] *n* (*gaze*) mirada; (*aspect*) respecto; (*attention*) atención *f*; (*esteem*) respeto, consideración *f* // *vt* (*consider*) considerar; (*look at*) mirar; **'with kindest ~s'** con muchos recuerdos; **~ing, as ~s, with ~ to** con respecto a, en cuanto a; **~less** *ad* a pesar de todo.

regatta [ri'gætə] *n* regata.

regent ['riːdʒənt] *n* regente *m/f*.

régime [rei'ʒiːm] *n* régimen *m*.

regiment ['rɛdʒimənt] *n* regimiento // *vt* reglamentar; **~al** [-'mɛntl] a militar; **~ation** [-'teiʃən] *n* regimentación *f*.

region ['riːdʒən] *n* región *f*; **in the ~ of** (*fig*) alrededor de; **~al** a regional.

register ['rɛdʒistə*] *n* (*gen*) registro; (*list*) lista // *vt* registrar; (*birth*) declarar; (*letter*) certificar; (*subj: instrument*)

marcar, indicar // *vi* (*at hotel*) registrarse; (*sign on*) inscribirse; (*make impression*) producir impresión; **~ed** a (*design*) registrado; (*letter*) certificado.

registrar ['rɛdʒistrɑː*] *n* secretario (del registro civil).

registration [rɛdʒis'treiʃən] *n* (*act*) inscripción *f*; (*AUT: also: ~ number*) matrícula.

registry ['rɛdʒistri] *n* registro, archivo; **~ office** *n* registro civil; **to get married in a ~ office** casarse por lo civil.

regret [ri'grɛt] *n* sentimiento, pesar *m*; (*remorse*) remordimiento // *vt* sentir, lamentar; (*repent of*) arrepentirse de; **~fully** *ad* con pesar, sentidamente; **~table** a lamentable; (*loss*) sensible.

regroup [riː'gruːp] *vt* reagrupar // *vi* reagruparse.

regular ['rɛgjulə*] a (*gen*) regular; (*usual*) corriente, normal; (*soldier*) de línea; (*intensive*) verdadero // *n* (*client etc*) cliente *m/f* habitual; **~ity** [-'læriti] *n* regularidad *f*; **~ly** *ad* con regularidad.

regulate ['rɛgjuleit] *vt* regular; (*TECH*) arreglar, ajustar; **regulation** [-'leiʃən] *n* (*rule*) regla, reglamento; (*adjustment*) ajuste *m*.

rehabilitation ['riːhəbili'teiʃən] *n* rehabilitación *f*.

rehearsal [ri'hɔːsəl] *n* ensayo; **rehearse** *vt* ensayar.

reign [rein] *n* reinado; (*fig*) dominio // *vi* reinar; (*fig*) imperar; **~ing** a (*monarch*) reinante, actual; (*predominant*) imperante.

reimburse [riːim'bɔːs] *vt* reembolsar; **~ment** *n* reembolso.

rein [rein] *n* (*for horse*) rienda; **to give ~ to** dar rienda suelta a.

reincarnation [riːinkɑː'neiʃən] *n* reencarnación *f*.

reindeer ['reindiə*] *n, pl inv* reno.

reinforce [riːin'fɔːs] *vt* reforzar; **~d** a (*concrete*) armado; **~ment** *n* (*action*) reforzamiento; **~ments** *npl* (*MIL*) refuerzos *mpl*.

reinstate [riːin'steit] *vt* (*worker*) reintegrar a su puesto.

reiterate [riː'itəreit] *vt* reiterar, repetir.

reject ['riːdʒɛkt] *n* (*comm*) artículo defectuoso // *vt* [ri'dʒɛkt] rechazar; (*plan*) desechar; (*solution*) descartar; **~ion** [ri'dʒɛkʃən] *n* rechazo.

rejoice [ri'dʒɔis] *vi*: **to ~ at or over** regocijarse o alegrarse de.

rejuvenate [ri'dʒuːvəneit] *vt* rejuvenecer.

rekindle [riː'kindl] *vt* reencender; (*fig*) despertar.

relapse [ri'læps] *n* (*MED*) recaída; (*into crime*) reincidencia.

relate [ri'leit] *vt* (*tell*) contar, relatar; (*connect*) relacionar // *vi* relacionarse; **~d** a afín, conexo; (*person*) emparentado; **~d to** con referencia a, relacionado con; **relating to** *prep* acerca de.

relation [ri'leiʃən] *n* (*person*) pariente *m/f*; (*link*) relación *f*; **~ship** *n* relación *f*;

(*personal ties*) relaciones *fpl*; (*also:* **family ~ship**) parentesco.

relative ['relətiv] *n* pariente *m/f*, familiar *m/f // a* relativo.

relax [ri'læks] *vi* descansar; (*person: unwind*) relajarse // *vt* relajar; (*mind, person*) descansar; **~ation** [riːlæk'seiʃən] *n* (*rest*) descanso; (*ease*) relajación *f*, relax *m*; (*amusement*) recreo; (*entertainment*) diversión *f*; **~ed** *a* relajado; (*tranquil*) tranquilo; **~ing** *a* enervante.

relay ['riːlei] *n* (*race*) carrera de relevos // *vt* (*message*) retransmitir.

release [ri'liːs] *n* (*from prison, obligation*) liberación *f*, libertad *f*; (*of shot*) disparo; (*of gas etc*) escape *m*; (*of film etc*) estreno // *vt* (*prisoner*) poner en libertad; (*book, film*) estrenar; (*report, news*) publicar; (*gas etc*) despedir, arrojar; (*free: from wreckage etc*) soltar; (TECH. *catch, spring etc*) desenganchar; (*let go*) soltar, aflojar.

relegate ['relǝgeit] *vt* relegar; (SPORT): **to be ~d** descender.

relent [ri'lent] *vi* ablandarse, ceder; **~less** *a* implacable.

relevance ['relǝvǝns] *n* relación *f*; **relevant** [-ǝnt] *a* relacionado; (*fact*) pertinente; (*apt*) oportuno.

reliable [ri'laiǝbl] *a* (*person, firm*) de confianza, de fiar; (*method, machine*) seguro; (*news*) fidedigno; **reliably** *ad*: **to be reliably informed that...** saber de fuente fidedigna que... .

reliance [ri'laiǝns] *n*: **~ (on)** dependencia (de).

relic ['relik] *n* (REL) reliquia; (*of the past*) vestigio.

relief [ri'liːf] *n* (*from pain, anxiety*) alivio, desahogo; (*help, supplies*) socorro, ayuda; (ART. GEO) relieve *m*.

relieve [ri'liːv] *vt* (*pain, patient*) aliviar; (*bring help to*) ayudar, socorrer; (*burden*) aligerar; (*take over from: gen*) sustituir a; (: *guard*) relevar; **to ~ sb of sth** quitar algo a uno; **to ~ o.s.** hacer sus necesidades.

religion [ri'lidʒǝn] *n* religión *f*; **religious** *a* religioso.

relinquish [ri'liŋkwiʃ] *vt* abandonar; (*plan, habit*) renunciar a.

relish ['reliʃ] *n* (CULIN) salsa, condimento; (*enjoyment*) entusiasmo; (*flavour*) sabor *m*, gusto // *vt* (*food etc*) saborear; **to ~ doing** gustar de hacer.

reload [riː'lǝud] *vt* recargar.

reluctance [ri'lʌktǝns] *n* renuencia; **reluctant** [-ǝnt] *a* renuente; **reluctantly** [-ǝntli] *ad* con renuencia.

rely [ri'lai]: **to ~ on** *vt fus* confiar en, fiarse de; (*be dependent on*) depender de.

remain [ri'mein] *vi* (*survive*) quedar; (*be left*) sobrar; (*continue*) quedar(se), permanecer; **~der** *n* resto; **~ing** *a* sobrante; **~s** *npl* restos *mpl*; (*leftovers*) desperdicios *mpl*.

remand [ri'mɑːnd] *n*: **on ~** detenido (en espera del juicio) // *vt*: **to ~ in custody**

reencarcelar, mantener bajo custodia; **~ home** *n* reformatorio.

remark [ri'mɑːk] *n* comentario // *vt* comentar; (*notice*) observar, notar; **~able** *a* notable; (*outstanding*) extraordinario.

remarry [riː'mæri] *vi* casarse por segunda vez.

remedial [ri'miːdiǝl] *a* (*tuition, classes*) de niños atrasados.

remedy ['remǝdi] *n* remedio // *vt* remediar, curar.

remember [ri'membǝ*] *vt* recordar, acordarse de; (*bear in mind*) tener presente; **remembrance** *n* (*memory*) memoria; (*souvenir*) recuerdo.

remind [ri'maind] *vt*: **to ~ sb to do sth** recordar a uno que haga algo; **to ~ sb of sth** recordar algo a uno; **she ~s me of her mother** me recuerda a su madre; **~er** *n* advertencia; (*souvenir*) recuerdo.

reminisce [remi'nis] *vi* recordar viejas historias; **reminiscent** *a*: **to be reminiscent of sth** recordar algo.

remiss [ri'mis] *a* descuidado; **it was ~ of him** fue un descuido suyo.

remission [ri'miʃǝn] *n* remisión *f*; (*of debt, sentence*) perdón *m*.

remit [ri'mit] *vt* (*send: money*) remitir, enviar; **~tance** *n* remesa, envío.

remnant ['remnǝnt] *n* resto; (*of cloth*) retazo.

remorse [ri'mɔːs] *n* remordimientos *mpl*; **~ful** *a* arrepentido; **~less** *a* (*fig*) implacable, despiadado.

remote [ri'mǝut] *a* (*distant*) lejano; (*person*) distante; **~ control** *n*,telecontrol *m*; **~ly** *ad* remotamente; (*slightly*) levemente; **~ness** *n* alejamiento; distancia.

remould ['riːmǝuld] *vt* (*tyre*) recauchutar.

removable [ri'muːvǝbl] *a* (*detachable*) amovible, separable.

removal [ri'muːvǝl] *n* (*taking away*) el quitar; (*from house*) mudanza; (*from office: sacking*) destitución *f*; (MED) extirpación *f*; **~ van** *n* camión *m* de mudanzas.

remove [ri'muːv] *vt* quitar; (*employee*) destituir; (*name: from list*) borrar; (*doubt, abuse*) disipar; (TECH) retirar, separar; (MED) extirpar; **removers** *npl* (*company*) agencia de mudanzas.

remuneration [rimjuːnǝ'reiʃǝn] *n* remuneración *f*.

rend [rend], *pt, pp* **rent** *vt* rasgar, desgarrar.

render ['rendǝ*] *vt* (*give*) dar, prestar; (*hand over*) entregar; (*reproduce*) reproducir; (*make*) hacer, volver; (*return*) devolver; **~ing** *n* (MUS *etc*) interpretación *f*.

rendez-vous ['rɔndivuː] *n* cita.

renegade ['renigeid] *n* renegado.

renew [ri'njuː] *vt* renovar; (*resume*) reanudar; (*loan etc*) prorrogar; (*negotiations*) volver a; (*acquaintance*) entablar de nuevo; ~al *n* renovación *f*; reanudación *f*; prórroga.

renounce [rɪ'nauns] *vt* renunciar a; (*disown*) renunciar.

renovate ['rɛnəveɪt] *vt* renovar; **renovation** [-'veɪʃən] *n* renovación *f*.

renown [rɪ'naun] *n* renombre *m*; ~ed *a* renombrado.

rent [rɛnt] *pt, pp of* rend // *n* alquiler *m*, arriendo // *vt* alquilar; ~al *n* (*for television, car*) alquiler *m*.

renunciation [rɪnʌnsɪ'eɪʃən] *n* renuncia.

reorganize [riː'ɔːɡənaɪz] *vt* reorganizar.

rep [rɛp] *n abbr of* **representative; repertory.**

repair [rɪ'pɛə*] *n* reparación *f*, compostura; (*patch*) remiendo // *vt* reparar, componer; (*shoes*) remendar; **in good/bad** ~ en buen/mal estado; ~ **kit** *n* caja de herramientas para reparaciones.

repartee [rɛpɑː'tiː] *n* dimes y diretes.

repay [riː'peɪ] (*irg: like pay*) *vt* (*money*) devolver, reembolsar; (*person*) pagar; (*debt*) liquidar; (*sb's efforts*) devolver, corresponder a; ~**ment** *n* reembolso, devolución *f*; (*of debt*) pago.

repeal [rɪ'piːl] *n* (*of law*) abrogación *f*; (*of sentence*) anulación *f* // *vt* abrogar, revocar.

repeat [rɪ'piːt] *n* (RADIO, TV) retransmisión *f* // *vt* repetir // *vi* repetirse; ~**edly** *ad* repetidas veces.

repel [rɪ'pɛl] *vt* (*lit, fig*) repugnar; ~**lent** *a* repugnante // *n*: **insect** ~**lent** crema/loción *f* anti-insectos.

repent [rɪ'pɛnt] *vi*: **to** ~ (**of**) arrepentirse (de); ~**ance** *n* arrepentimiento.

repercussion [riːpə'kʌʃən] *n* (*consequence*) repercusión *f*; **to have** ~**s** repercutir.

repertoire ['rɛpətwɑː*] *n* repertorio.

repertory ['rɛpətərɪ] *n* (*also*: ~ **theatre**) teatro de repertorio.

repetition [rɛpɪ'tɪʃən] *n* repetición *f*.

repetitive [rɪ'pɛtɪtɪv] *a* (*movement, work*) reiterativo; (*speech*) lleno de repeticiones.

replace [rɪ'pleɪs] *vt* (*put back*) devolver a su sitio; (*take the place of*) reemplazar, sustituir; ~**ment** *n* (*gen*) reemplazo; (*act*) reposición *f*; (*person*) suplente *m/f*.

replenish [rɪ'plɛnɪʃ] *vt* (*glass*) rellenar; (*stock etc*) reponer; (*with fuel*) repostar.

replete [rɪ'pliːt] *a* repleto; (*well-fed*) lleno.

replica ['rɛplɪkə] *n* copia, reproducción *f*.

reply [rɪ'plaɪ] *n* respuesta, contestación *f* // *vi* contestar, responder.

report [rɪ'pɔːt] *n* informe *m*; (PRESS *etc*) reportaje *m*; (*also*: **school** ~) nota; (*of gun*) estallido // *vt* informar sobre; (PRESS *etc*) hacer un reportaje sobre; (*bring to notice: occurrence*) dar cuenta de // *vi* (*make a report*) presentar un informe; (*present o.s.*): **to** ~ (**to sb**) presentarse (ante uno); ~**er** *n* periodista *m/f*.

reprehensible [rɛprɪ'hɛnsɪbl] *a* reprensible, censurable.

represent [rɛprɪ'zɛnt] *vt* representar; (*fig*) hablar en nombre de; (COMM) ser agente de; ~**ation** [-'teɪʃən] *n* representación *f*; (*petition*) petición *f*; ~**ations** *npl* (*protest*) quejas *fpl*; ~**ative** *n* representante *m/f* // *a* representativo.

repress [rɪ'prɛs] *vt* reprimir; ~**ion** [-'prɛʃən] *n* represión *f*; ~**ive** *a* represivo.

reprieve [rɪ'priːv] *n* (LAW) indulto; (*fig*) alivio // *vt* indultar, suspender la pena de.

reprimand ['rɛprɪmɑːnd] *n* reprimenda // *vt* reprender.

reprint ['riːprɪnt] *n* reimpresión *f* // *vt* [riː'prɪnt] reimprimir.

reprisal [rɪ'praɪzl] *n* represalia.

reproach [rɪ'prəutʃ] *n* reproche *m* // *vt*: **to** ~ **sb with sth** reprochar algo a uno; **beyond** ~ intachable; ~**ful** *a* lleno de reproches.

reproduce [riːprə'djuːs] *vt* reproducir // *vi* reproducirse; **reproduction** [-'dʌkʃən] *n* reproducción *f*; **reproductive** [-'dʌktɪv] *a* reproductor(a).

reprove [rɪ'pruːv] *vt*: **to** ~ **sb for sth** reprender algo a uno.

reptile ['rɛptaɪl] *n* reptil *m*.

republic [rɪ'pʌblɪk] *n* república; ~**an** *a, n* republicano/a.

repudiate [rɪ'pjuːdɪeɪt] *vt* (*accusation*) rechazar; (*friend*) repudiar; (*obligation*) desconocer.

repugnant [rɪ'pʌɡnənt] *a* repugnante.

repulse [rɪ'pʌls] *vt* rechazar, repulsar; **repulsive** *a* repulsivo.

reputable ['rɛpjutəbl] *a* (*make etc*) de toda confianza; (*person*) formal.

reputation [rɛpju'teɪʃən] *n* reputación *f*.

repute [rɪ'pjuːt] *n* reputación *f*, fama; ~**d** *a* supuesto; ~**dly** *ad* según dicen o se dice.

request [rɪ'kwɛst] *n* petición *f*; (*formal*) solicitud *f* // *vt*: **to** ~ **sth of** *or* **from sb** pedir algo a uno; (*formally*) solicitar algo a uno.

requiem ['rɛkwɪəm] *n* réquiem *m*.

require [rɪ'kwaɪə*] *vt* (*need: subj: person*) necesitar, tener necesidad de; (: *thing, situation*) exigir; (*want*) pedir; (*order*) insistir en que; ~**ment** *n* requisito; (*need*) necesidad *f*.

requisite ['rɛkwɪzɪt] *n* requisito // *a* preciso, imprescindible; **toilet** ~**s** artículos *mpl* de aseo personal.

requisition [rɛkwɪ'zɪʃən] *n*: ~ (**for**) solicitud *f* (de) // *vt* (MIL) requisar.

reroute [riː'ruːt] *vt* (*train etc*) desviar.

resale [riː'seɪl] *n* reventa.

rescue ['rɛskjuː] *n* rescate *m* // *vt* rescatar; **to** ~ **from** librar de; ~ **party** *n* expedición *f* de salvamento; **rescuer** *n* salvador/a *m/f*.

research [rɪ'sɜːtʃ] *n* investigaciones *fpl* // *vt* investigar; ~**er** *n* investigador/a *m/f*; ~ **work** *n* investigación *f*.

resell [riː'sɛl] *vt* revender.

resemblance [rɪ'zɛmbləns] *n* parecido; **to**

bear a ~ to parecerse a; **resemble** vt
parecerse a.
resent [rɪ'zɛnt] vt resentirse de; ~**ful** a
resentido; ~**ment** n resentimiento.
reservation [rɛzə'veɪʃən] n (gen) reserva;
(on road: also: **central** ~) faja intermedia.
reserve [rɪ'zəːv] n reserva; (SPORT)
suplente m/f; (game ~) coto // vt (seats
etc) reservar; ~**s** npl (MIL) reserva sg; **in**
~ de reserva; ~**d** a reservado.
reservoir ['rɛzəvwɑː*] n (large) embalse
m; (small) depósito.
reshape [riː'ʃeɪp] vt (policy) reformar,
rehacer.
reshuffle [riː'ʃʌfl] n: **Cabinet** ~ (POL)
reconstrucción f del gabinete.
reside [rɪ'zaɪd] vi residir, vivir.
residence ['rɛzɪdəns] n residencia;
(formal: home) domicilio; (length of stay)
permanencia; **resident** [-ənt] n vecino; (in
hotel) huésped/a m/f // a (population)
permanente; (doctor) interno; **residential**
[-'dɛnʃəl] a residencial.
residue ['rɛzɪdjuː] n resto, residuo; (COMM)
saldo.
resign [rɪ'zaɪn] vt (one's post) renunciar a
// vi dimitir; **to** ~ **o.s. to** (endure)
resignarse a; ~**ation** [rɛzɪg'neɪʃən] n
renuncia; (state of mind) resignación f;
~**ed** a resignado.
resilience [rɪ'zɪlɪəns] n (of material)
elasticidad f; (of person) resistencia;
resilient [-ənt] a (person) resistente.
resin ['rɛzɪn] n resina.
resist [rɪ'zɪst] vt resistir, oponerse a;
~**ance** n resistencia.
resolute ['rɛzəluːt] a resuelto.
resolution [rɛzə'luːʃən] n (gen) resolución
f; (purpose) propósito.
resolve [rɪ'zɔlv] n resolución f; (purpose)
propósito // vt resolver // vi resolverse; **to**
~ **to do** resolver hacer; ~**d** a resuelto.
resonant ['rɛzənənt] a resonante.
resort [rɪ'zɔːt] n (town) centro de turismo;
(recourse) recurso // vi: **to** ~ **to** recurrir
a; **in the last** ~ en último caso.
resound [rɪ'zaund] vi resonar, retumbar;
the room ~**ed with shouts** los gritos
resonaron en el cuarto; ~**ing** a sonoro;
(fig) clamoroso.
resource [rɪ'sɔːs] n recurso; ~**s** npl
recursos mpl; ~**ful** a inventivo, ingenioso.
respect [rɪs'pɛkt] n (consideration)
respeto; (relation) respecto; ~**s** npl
recuerdos mpl, saludos mpl // vt respetar;
with ~ **to** con respecto a; **in this** ~ en
cuanto a eso; ~**ability** [-ə'bɪlɪtɪ] n
respetabilidad f; ~**able** a respetable;
(large) apreciable; (passable) tolerable;
~**ful** a respetuoso.
respective [rɪs'pɛktɪv] a respectivo; ~**ly**
ad respectivamente.
respiration [rɛspɪ'reɪʃən] n respiración f.
respiratory [rɛs'pɪrətərɪ] a respiratorio.
respite ['rɛspaɪt] n respiro; (LAW)
prórroga.

resplendent [rɪs'plɛndənt] a
resplandeciente.
respond [rɪs'pɔnd] vi responder; (react)
reaccionar; **response** [-'pɔns] n respuesta;
reacción f.
responsibility [rɪspɔnsɪ'bɪlɪtɪ] n
responsabilidad f.
responsible [rɪs'pɔnsɪbl] a (liable): ~
(**for**) responsable (de); (character) serio,
formal; (job) de confianza.
responsive [rɪs'pɔnsɪv] a sensible.
rest [rɛst] n descanso, reposo; (MUS) pausa,
silencio; (support) apoyo; (remainder)
resto // vi descansar; (be supported): **to** ~
on posar(se) en // vt (lean): **to** ~ **sth
on/against** apoyar algo en o
sobre/contra.
restart [riː'stɑːt] vt (engine) volver a
arrancar; (work) volver a empezar.
restaurant ['rɛstərən] n restorán m,
restaurante m; ~ **car** n coche-comedor
m.
restful ['rɛstful] a descansado, reposado.
rest home n residencia para jubilados.
restitution [rɛstɪ'tjuːʃən] n: **to make** ~
to sb for sth indemnizar a uno por algo.
restive ['rɛstɪv] a inquieto; (horse)
rebelón(ona).
restless ['rɛstlɪs] a inquieto; ~**ly** ad
inquietamente.
restoration [rɛstə'reɪʃən] n restauración
f; **restore** [rɪ'stɔː*] vt (building) restaurar;
(sth stolen) devolver; (health) restablecer.
restrain [rɪs'treɪn] vt (feeling) contener,
refrenar; (person): **to** ~ (**from doing**)
disuadir (de hacer); ~**ed** a (style)
moderado; ~**t** n (restriction) freno,
control m; (moderation) moderación f; (of
style) reserva.
restrict [rɪs'trɪkt] vt restringir, limitar;
~**ion** [-kʃən] n restricción f, limitación f;
~**ive** a restrictivo.
rest room n (US) aseos mpl.
result [rɪ'zʌlt] n resultado // vi: **to** ~ **in**
terminar en, dar por resultado; **as a** ~ **of**
a consecuencia de.
resume [rɪ'zjuːm] vt, vi (work, journey)
reanudar.
résumé ['reɪzjuːmeɪ] n resumen m.
resumption [rɪ'zʌmpʃən] n reanudación f.
resurgence [rɪ'səːdʒəns] n resurgimiento.
resurrection [rɛzə'rɛkʃən] n resurrección
f.
resuscitate [rɪ'sʌsɪteɪt] vt (MED)
resucitar; **resuscitation** [-'teɪʃn] n
resucitación f.
retail ['riːteɪl] n venta al por menor // cpd
al por menor // vt vender al por menor o
al detalle; ~**er** n detallista m/f.
retain [rɪ'teɪn] vt (keep) retener,
conservar; (employ) contratar; ~**er** n
(servant) criado; (fee) anticipo.
retaliate [rɪ'tælɪeɪt] vi: **to** ~ (**against**)
tomar represalias (contra); **retaliation**
[-'eɪʃən] n represalias fpl.
retarded [rɪ'tɑːdɪd] a retrasado.
retch [rɛtʃ] vi dar arcadas.

retentive [rɪˈtɛntɪv] a (*memory*) retentivo.
reticent [ˈrɛtɪsnt] a reservado.
retina [ˈrɛtɪnə] n retina.
retinue [ˈrɛtɪnjuː] n séquito, comitiva.
retire [rɪˈtaɪə*] vi (*give up work*) jubilarse; (*withdraw*) retirarse; (*go to bed*) (ir a) acostarse; ~d a (*person*) jubilado; ~ment n (*state*) retiro; (*act*) jubilación f; **retiring** a (*leaving*) saliente; (*shy*) retraído.
retort [rɪˈtɔːt] n (*reply*) réplica // vi contestar.
retrace [riːˈtreɪs] vt: **to ~ one's steps** volver sobre sus pasos, desandar lo andado.
retract [rɪˈtrækt] vt (*statement*) retirar; (*claws*) retraer; (*undercarriage, aerial*) replegar // vi retractarse; ~**able** a replegable.
retrain [riːˈtreɪn] vt reeducar; ~**ing** n readaptación f profesional.
retreat [rɪˈtriːt] n (*place*) retiro; (*act*) retraimiento; (*MIL*) retirada // vi retirarse; (*flood*) bajar.
retribution [rɛtrɪˈbjuːʃən] n desquite m.
retrieve [rɪˈtriːv] vt (*gen*) recobrar; (*situation, honour*) salvar; (*error, loss*) recuperar; **retriever** n perro cobrador, perdiguero.
retrospect [ˈrɛtrəspɛkt] n: **in ~** retrospectivamente, mirando hacia atrás; ~**ive** [-ˈspɛktɪv] a (*law*) retroactivo.
return [rɪˈtɜːn] n (*going or coming back*) vuelta, regreso; (*of sth stolen etc*) devolución f; (*recompense*) recompensa f; (*FINANCE: from land, shares*) ganancia, ingresos mpl; (*report*) informe m // cpd (*journey*) de regreso; (*ticket*) de ida y vuelta; (*match*) de vuelta // vi (*person etc: come or go back*) volver, regresar; (*symptoms etc*) reaparecer // vt devolver; (*favour, love etc*) corresponder a; (*verdict*) declarar; (*POL: candidate*) elegir; ~**s** npl (*COMM*) ingresos mpl; **in ~** en cambio; **many happy ~s (of the day)!** ¡muchas felicidades!, ¡feliz cumpleaños!
reunion [riːˈjuːnɪən] n reunión f.
reunite [riːjuːˈnaɪt] vt reunir; (*reconcile*) reconciliar.
rev [rɛv] n abbr of **revolution** (*AUT*) // (vb: also: ~ **up**) vt girar (el motor de) // vi acelerarse.
reveal [rɪˈviːl] vt (*make known*) revelar; ~**ing** a revelador(a).
reveille [rɪˈvælɪ] n (*MIL*) diana.
revel [ˈrɛvl] vi: **to ~ in sth/in doing sth** deleitarse en algo/en hacer algo.
revelation [rɛvəˈleɪʃən] n revelación f.
reveller [ˈrɛvlə*] n jaranero, juergista m/f; **revelry** [-rɪ] n jarana, juerga.
revenge [rɪˈvɛndʒ] n venganza; (*in sport*) revancha; **to take ~ on** vengarse de.
revenue [ˈrɛvənjuː] n ingresos mpl, renta; (*on investment*) rédito; (*profit*) ganancia.
reverberate [rɪˈvɜːbəreɪt] vi (*sound*) resonar, retumbar; **reverberation** [-ˈreɪʃən] n retumbo, eco.
revere [rɪˈvɪə*] vt reverenciar, venerar;

reverence [ˈrɛvərəns] n reverencia; **reverent** [ˈrɛvərənt] a reverente.
reverie [ˈrɛvərɪ] n ensueño.
reversal [rɪˈvɜːsl] n (*of order*) inversión f; (*of direction*) cambio completo; (*of decision*) revocación f.
reverse [rɪˈvɜːs] n (*opposite*) contrario; (*back: of cloth*) revés m; (: *of coin*) reverso, (: *of paper*) dorso; (*AUT: also:* ~ **gear**) marcha atrás, contramarcha // a (*order*) inverso; (*direction*) contrario // vt (*turn over*) volver al revés; (*invert*) invertir; (*change: opinion*) cambiar (completamente) de // vi (*AUT*) poner en marcha atrás.
revert [rɪˈvɜːt] vi: **to ~ to** volver a.
review [rɪˈvjuː] n (*magazine, MIL*) revista; (*of book, film*) reseña; (*examination*) repaso, examen m // vt repasar, examinar; (*MIL*) pasar revista a; (*book, film*) reseñar; ~**er** n crítico/a.
revile [rɪˈvaɪl] vt injuriar, vilipendiar.
revise [rɪˈvaɪz] vt (*manuscript*) corregir; (*opinion*) modificar; (*study: subject*) repasar; (*look over*) revisar; **revision** [rɪˈvɪʒən] n corrección f; modificación f; repaso; revisión f.
revitalize [riːˈvaɪtəlaɪz] vt revivificar.
revival [rɪˈvaɪvəl] n (*recovery*) restablecimiento; (*of interest*) renacimiento; (*THEATRE*) reestreno; (*of faith*) despertar m.
revive [rɪˈvaɪv] vt (*gen*) resucitar; (*custom*) restablecer; (*hope, courage*) reanimar; (*play*) reestrenar // vi (*person*) volver en sí, restablecerse; (*from faint*) revivir; (*activity*) recobrarse.
revoke [rɪˈvəʊk] vt revocar.
revolt [rɪˈvəʊlt] n rebelión f, sublevación f // vi rebelarse, sublevarse // vt dar asco a, repugnar; ~**ing** a asqueroso, repugnante.
revolution [rɛvəˈluːʃən] n revolución f; ~**ary**, a, n revolucionario/a; ~**ize** vt revolucionar.
revolve [rɪˈvɒlv] vi dar vueltas, girar.
revolver [rɪˈvɒlvə*] n revólver m.
revolving [rɪˈvɒlvɪŋ] a (*chair etc*) giratorio; ~ **door** n puerta giratoria.
revue [rɪˈvjuː] n (*THEATRE*) revista.
revulsion [rɪˈvʌlʃən] n asco, repugnancia.
reward [rɪˈwɔːd] n premio, recompensa // vt: **to ~ (for)** recompensar o premiar (por); ~**ing** a (*fig*) provechoso, valioso.
rewire [riːˈwaɪə*] vt (*house*) renovar el alambrado de.
reword [riːˈwɜːd] vt expresar en otras palabras.
rewrite [riːˈraɪt] (*irg: like write*) vt volver a escribir o redactar.
rhapsody [ˈræpsədɪ] n (*MUS*) rapsodia; (*fig*) transporte m (de admiración).
rhetoric [ˈrɛtərɪk] n retórica; ~**al** [rɪˈtɒrɪkl] a retórico.
rheumatic [ruːˈmætɪk] a reumático; **rheumatism** [ˈruːmətɪzəm] n reumatismo, reúma.

Rhine [raɪn] *n*: the ~ el (río) Rin.
rhinoceros [raɪˈnɔsərəs] *n* rinoceronte *m*.
rhododendron [rəudəˈdɛndrn] *n* rododendro.
Rhone [rəun] *n*: the ~ el (río) Ródano.
rhubarb [ˈruːbɑːb] *n* ruibarbo.
rhyme [raɪm] *n* rima; (*verse*) poesía.
rhythm [ˈrɪðm] *n* ritmo; ~ **method** método de Ojino; ~**ic(al)** *a* rítmico.
rib [rɪb] *n* (ANAT) costilla // *vt* (*mock*) tomar el pelo a.
ribald [ˈrɪbəld] *a* escabroso.
ribbon [ˈrɪbən] *n* cinta; **in** ~**s** (*torn*) hecho trizas.
rice [raɪs] *n* arroz *m*; ~**field** *n* arrozal *m*; ~ **pudding** *n* arroz *m* con leche.
rich [rɪtʃ] *a* rico; (*banquet*) suntuoso; (*soil*) fértil; (*food*) fuerte; (: *sweet*) empalagoso; **the** ~ los ricos; ~**es** *npl* riqueza *sg*; ~**ness** *n* riqueza; suntuosidad *f*; fertilidad *f*.
rickets [ˈrɪkɪts] *n* raquitismo.
rickety [ˈrɪkɪtɪ] *a* desvencijado; (*shaky*) tambaleante.
rickshaw [ˈrɪkʃɔː] *n* rikisha.
ricochet [ˈrɪkəʃeɪ] *n* rebote *m* // *vi* rebotar.
rid [rɪd], *pt, pp* **rid** *vt*: **to** ~ **sb of sth** librar a uno de algo; **to get** ~ **of** deshacerse o desembarazarse de.
ridden [ˈrɪdn] *pp of* **ride**.
riddle [ˈrɪdl] *n* (*conundrum*) acertijo; (*mystery*) enigma *m*, misterio; (*sieve*) criba // *vt*: **to be** ~**d with** ser lleno o plagado de.
ride [raɪd] *n* (*gen*) paseo; (*on horse*) cabalgata; (*distance covered*) viaje *m*, recorrido // (*vb: pt* **rode**, *pp* **ridden**) *vi* (*as sport*) montar; (*go somewhere: on horse, bicycle*) dar un paseo, pasearse; (*journey: on bicycle, motor cycle, bus*) viajar // *vt* (*a horse*) montar a; (*distance*) viajar; **to** ~ **a bicycle** ir en bicicleta; **to** ~ **at anchor** (NAUT) estar al ancla; **to take sb for a** ~ (*fig*) engañar a uno; ~**r** *n* (*on horse*) jinete *m*; (*on bicycle*) ciclista *m/f*; (*on motorcycle*) motociclista *m/f*.
ridge [rɪdʒ] *n* (*of hill*) cresta; (*of roof*) caballete *m*; (*wrinkle*) arruga.
ridicule [ˈrɪdɪkjuːl] *n* irrisión *f*, mofa // *vt* poner en ridículo, mofarse de; **ridiculous** [-ˈdɪkjuləs] *a* ridículo.
riding [ˈraɪdɪŋ] *n* montar *m* a caballo; ~ **school** *n* escuela de equitación.
rife [raɪf] *a*: **to be** ~ ser muy común; **to be** ~ **with** abundar en.
riffraff [ˈrɪfræf] *n* gentuza.
rifle [ˈraɪfl] *n* rifle *m*, fusil *m* // *vt* saquear; ~ **range** *n* campo de tiro; (*at fair*) tiro al blanco.
rift [rɪft] *n* (*fig: disagreement: between friends*) desavenencia; (: *in party*) escisión *f*.
rig [rɪg] *n* (*also:* **oil** ~) torre *f* de perforación // *vt* (*election etc*) falsificar los resultados de; **to** ~ **out** *vt* ataviar de;

to ~ **up** *vt* armar; ~**ging** *n* (NAUT) aparejo.
right [raɪt] *a* (*true, correct*) correcto, exacto; (*suitable*) indicado, debido; (*proper*) apropiado, propio; (*just*) justo; (*morally good*) bueno; (*not left*) derecho // *n* (*title, claim*) derecho; (*not left*) derecha // *ad* (*correctly*) bien, correctamente; (*straight*) derecho, directamente; (*not on the left*) a la derecha; (*to the* ~) hacia la derecha // *vt* enderezar // *excl* ¡bueno!, ¡está bien!; **to be** ~ (*person*) tener razón; **all** ~! ¡está bien!; (*enough*) ¡basta!; ~ **now** ahora mismo; ~ **in the middle** justo en medio, en pleno centro; ~ **away** en seguida; **by** ~**s** en justicia; **on the** ~ a la derecha; ~ **angle** *n* ángulo recto; ~**eous** [ˈraɪtʃəs] *a* justado, honrado; (*anger*) justificado; ~**eousness** [ˈraɪtʃəsnɪs] *n* justicia; ~**ful** *a* (*heir*) legítimo; ~**-hand** *a* por la derecha; ~**-handed** *a* (*person*) que usa la mano derecha; ~**ly** *ad* correctamente, debidamente; (*with reason*) con razón; ~**-wing** *a* (POL) derechista.
rigid [ˈrɪdʒɪd] *a* rígido; (*principle*) inflexible; ~**ity** [rɪˈdʒɪdɪtɪ] *n* rigidez *f*, inflexibilidad *f*.
rigmarole [ˈrɪgmərəul] *n* galimatías *m*.
rigorous [ˈrɪgərəs] *a* riguroso.
rigour, rigor (US) [ˈrɪgə*] *n* rigor *m*, severidad *f*.
rig-out [ˈrɪgaut] *n* (*col*) atuendo.
rile [raɪl] *vt* irritar.
rim [rɪm] *n* borde *m*; (*of spectacles*) aro; (*of wheel*) aro, llanta.
rind [raɪnd] *n* (*of bacon*) piel *f*; (*of lemon etc*) cáscara; (*of cheese*) costra.
ring [rɪŋ] *n* (*of metal*) aro; (*on finger*) anillo; (*of people, objects*) círculo, grupo; (*of spies*) camarilla; (*for boxing*) cuadrilátero; (*of circus*) pista; (*bull*~) ruedo, plaza; (*sound of bell*) toque *m*; (*telephone call*) llamada // (*vb: pt* **rang**, *pp* **rung**) *vi* (*on telephone*) llamar por teléfono; (*large bell*) repicar; (*also:* ~ **out:** *voice, words*) sonar; (*ears*) zumbar // *vt* (TEL: *also:* ~ **up**) llamar; (*bell etc*) hacer sonar; (*doorbell*) tocar; **to** ~ **back** *vt, vi* (TEL) devolver la llamada; **to** ~ **off** *vi* (TEL) colgar, cortar la comunicación; ~**ing** *n* (*of large bell*) repique *m*; (*in ears*) zumbido; ~**leader** *n* (*of gang*) cabecilla *m/f*.
ringlets [ˈrɪŋlɪts] *npl* rizos *mpl*, tirabuzones *mpl*.
ring road *n* carretera periférica o de circunvalación.
rink [rɪŋk] *n* (*also:* **ice** ~) pista.
rinse [rɪns] *n* (*of dishes*) enjuague *m*; (*of hair*) reflejo // *vt* enjuagar; dar reflejos a.
riot [ˈraɪət] *n* motín *m*, disturbio // *vi* amotinarse; **to run** ~ desmandarse; ~**er** *n* amotinado/a; ~**ous** *a* (*gen*) alborotado; (*party*) bullicioso; (*uncontrolled*) desenfrenado.
rip [rɪp] *n* rasgón *m*, rasgadura // *vt*

rasgar, desgarrar // vi correr; ~cord n cabo de desgarre.

ripe [raɪp] a (fruit) maduro; (ready) listo; ~**n** vt madurar // vi madurarse; ~**ness** n madurez f.

ripple ['rɪpl] n onda, rizo; (sound) murmullo // vi rizarse // vt rizar.

rise [raɪz] n (slope) cuesta, pendiente m; (hill) altura; (increase: in wages) aumento; (: in prices, temperature) subida, alza; (fig: to power etc) ascenso // vi, pt **rose**, pp **risen** ['rɪzn] (gen) elevarse; (prices) subir; (waters) crecer; (river) nacer; (sun) salir; (person: from bed etc) levantarse; (also: ~ up: rebel) sublevarse; (in rank) ascender; **to give** ~ **to** dar lugar o origen a; **to** ~ **to the occasion** ponerse a la altura de las circunstancias.

risk [rɪsk] n riesgo, peligro // vt (gen) arriesgar; (dare) atreverse a; **to take** or **run the** ~ **of doing** correr el riesgo de hacer; **at** ~ en peligro; **at one's own** ~ bajo su propia responsabilidad; ~**y** a arriesgado, peligroso.

risqué ['riːskeɪ] a (joke) subido de color.

rissole ['rɪsəʊl] n croqueta.

rite [raɪt] n rito; **funeral** ~**s** exequias fpl.

ritual ['rɪtjʊəl] a ritual // n ritual m, rito.

rival ['raɪvl] n rival m/f; (in business) competidor/a m/f // a rival, opuesto // vt competir con; ~**ry** n rivalidad f, competencia.

river ['rɪvə*] n río; **up/down** ~ río arriba/abajo; ~**bank** n orilla (del río); ~**bed** n lecho, cauce m; ~**side** n ribera, orilla // cpd (port, traffic) de río, del río.

rivet ['rɪvɪt] n roblón m, remache m // vt remachar; (fig) clavar.

Riviera [rɪvɪ'ɛərə] n: **the (French)** ~ la Costa Azul (Francesa).

road [rəʊd] n (gen) camino; (motorway etc) carretera; (in town) calle f; ~**block** n barricada; ~**hog** n loco del volante; ~**map** n mapa m de carreteras; ~**side** n borde m (del camino) // cpd al lado de la carretera; ~**sign** n señal f (de carretera o calle); ~**user** n usuario de la vía pública; ~**way** n calzada; ~**worthy** a (car) listo para conducir.

roam [rəʊm] vi vagar // vt vagar por.

roar [rɔː*] n (of animal) rugido, bramido; (of crowd) rugido; (of vehicle, storm) estruendo; (of laughter) carcajada // vi rugir, bramar; hacer estruendo; **to** ~ **with laughter** reírse a carcajadas; **to do a** ~**ing trade** hacer buen negocio.

roast [rəʊst] n carne f asada, asado // vt (meat) asar; (coffee) tostar.

rob [rɔb] vt robar; **to** ~ **sb of sth** robar algo a uno; (fig: deprive) quitarle algo a uno; ~**ber** n ladrón/ona m/f; ~**bery** n robo.

robe [rəʊb] n (for ceremony etc) toga; (also: **bath** ~) bata.

robin ['rɔbɪn] n petirrojo.

robot ['rəʊbɔt] n robot m.

robust [rəʊ'bʌst] a robusto, fuerte.

rock [rɔk] n (gen) roca; (boulder) peña, peñasco; (sweet) pirulí // vt (swing gently: cradle) balancear, mecer; (: child) arrullar; (shake) sacudir // vi mecerse, balancearse; sacudirse; **on the** ~**s** (drink) sobre las rocas; (marriage etc) en ruinas; **to** ~ **the boat** (fig) causar perturbaciones; ~ **and roll** n rocanrol m; ~**-bottom** a (fig) por los suelos; ~**ery** n cuadro alpino.

rocket ['rɔkɪt] n cohete m.

rocking ['rɔkɪŋ]: ~ **chair** n mecedora; ~ **horse** n caballo de balancín.

rocky ['rɔkɪ] a (gen) rocoso; (unsteady: table) débil.

rod [rɔd] n vara, varilla; (TECH) barra; (also: **fishing** ~) caña.

rode [rəʊd] pt of **ride**.

rodent ['rəʊdnt] n roedor m.

rodeo ['rəʊdɪəʊ] n rodeo.

roe [rəʊ] n (species: also: ~ **deer**) corzo; (of fish): **hard/soft** ~ hueva/lecha.

rogue [rəʊg] n pícaro, pillo; **roguish** a pícaro.

role [rəʊl] n papel m, rol m.

roll [rəʊl] n rollo; (of banknotes) fajo; (also: **bread** ~) panecillo, bollo; (register) lista, nómina; (sound: of drums etc) redoble m; (movement: of ship) balanceo // vt hacer rodar; (also: ~ **up**: string) enrollar; (: sleeves) arremangar; (cigarettes) liar; (also: ~ **out**: pastry) aplanar // vi (gen) rodar; (drum) redoblar; (in walking) bambolearse; (ship) balancearse; **to** ~ **by** vi (time) pasar; **to** ~ **in** vi (mail, cash) entrar a raudales; **to** ~ **over** vi dar una vuelta; **to** ~ **up** vi (col: arrive) presentarse, aparecer // vt (carpet) arrollar; ~ **call** n acto de pasar lista; ~**er** n rodillo; (wheel) rueda; ~**er skates** npl patines mpl de rueda.

rollicking ['rɔlɪkɪŋ] a alegre, divertido.

rolling ['rəʊlɪŋ] a (landscape) ondulado; ~ **pin** n rodillo (de cocina); ~ **stock** n (RAIL) material m rodante.

Roman ['rəʊmən] a, n romano/a; ~ **Catholic** a, n católico (romano).

romance [rə'mæns] n (love affair) amoríos mpl, aventura sentimental; (charm) lo romántico.

Romanesque [rəʊmə'nɛsk] a románico.

Romania [rəʊ'meɪnɪə] n = **Rumania.**

romantic [rə'mæntɪk] a romántico; **romanticism** [-tɪsɪzəm] n romanticismo.

romp [rɔmp] n retozo, juego // vi (also: ~ **about**) jugar, brincar.

rompers ['rɔmpəz] npl pelele m.

roof [ruːf], pl ~**s** n (gen) techo; (of house) techo, tejado; (of car) baca // vt techar, poner techo a; **the** ~ **of the mouth** el paladar, el cielo de la boca; ~**ing** n techumbre f; ~ **rack** n (AUT) baca, portaequipajes m inv.

rook [ruk] n (bird) graja; (CHESS) torre f.

room [ruːm] n (in house) cuarto, habitación f, pieza; (also: **bed**~) dormitorio; (in school etc) sala; (space) sitio, cabida; ~**s**

npl (*lodging*) alojamiento *sg*; '~s to let' 'se alquilan pisos *o* cuartos'; **single/double** ~ habitación individual/doble *o* para dos personas; ~**mate** *n* compañero/a de cuarto; ~ **service** *n* servicio de habitaciones; ~**y** *a* espacioso.

roost [ru:st] *n* percha // *vi* pasar la noche.

rooster ['ru:stə*] *n* gallo.

root [ru:t] *n* (BOT, MATH) raíz *f* // *vi* (*plant, belief*) arriesgarse; **to** ~ **about** *vi* (*fig*) andar buscando; **to** ~ **for** *vt fus* apoyar a; **to** ~ **out** *vt* desarraigar.

rope [rəup] *n* (NAUT) cable *m* // *vt* (*box*) atar *o* amarrar con (una) cuerda; (*climbers: also:* ~ **together**) encordarse; **to** ~ **sb in** (*fig*) persuadir a uno a tomar parte; **to know the** ~**s** (*fig*) conocer un negocio a fondo; ~ **ladder** *n* escala de cuerda.

rosary ['rəuzərı] *n* rosario.

rose [rəuz] *pt of* **rise** // *n* rosa; (*also:* ~**bush**) rosal *m*; (*on watering can*) roseta // *a* color de rosa.

rosé ['rəuzeı] *n* vino rosado, clarete *m*.

rose: ~**bed** *n* rosaleda; ~**bud** *n* capullo de rosa; ~**bush** *n* rosal *m*.

rosemary ['rəuzmərı] *n* romero.

rosette [rəu'zɛt] *n* rosetón *m*.

roster ['rɔstə*] *n*: **duty** ~ lista de deberes.

rostrum ['rɔstrəm] *n* tribuna.

rosy ['rəuzı] *a* rosado, sonrosado; **a** ~ **future** un futuro prometedor.

rot [rɔt] *n* (*decay*) putrefacción *f*, podredumbre *f*; (*fig: pej*) decadencia *f* // *vt, vi* pudrirse, corromperse.

rota ['rəutə] *n* lista de tandas).

rotary ['rəutərı] *a* rotativo.

rotate [rəu'teıt] *vt* (*revolve*) hacer girar, dar vueltas a; (*change round: crops*) cultivar en rotación; (: *jobs*) alternar // *vi* (*revolve*) girar, dar vueltas; **rotating** *a* (*movement*) rotativo; **rotation** [-'teıʃən] *n* rotación *f*; **in rotation** por turno.

rotor ['rəutə*] *n* rotor *m*.

rotten ['rɔtn] *a* (*decayed*) podrido; (: *wood*) carcomido; (*fig*) corrompido; (*col: bad*) vil, miserable; **to feel** ~ (*ill*) sentirse muy mal.

rotting ['rɔtıŋ] *a* podrido.

rotund [rəu'tʌnd] *a* rotundo.

rouble, ruble (US) ['ru:bl] *n* rublo.

rouge [ru:ʒ] *n* colorete *m*.

rough [rʌf] *a* (*skin, surface*) áspero; (*terrain*) quebrado; (*road*) desigual; (*voice*) bronco; (*person, manner: coarse*) tosco, grosero; (*weather*) borrascoso; (*treatment*) brutal; (*sea*) bravo; (*cloth*) basto; (*plan*) preliminar; (*guess*) aproximado; (*violent*) violento // *n* (*person*) matón *m*; (GOLF): **in the** ~ en las hierbas altas; **to** ~ **it** vivir sin comodidades; **to sleep** ~ pasar la noche al raso; ~-**and-ready** *a* improvisado; ~**en** *vt* (*a surface*) poner áspero; ~**ly** *ad* (*handle*) torpemente; (*make*) toscamente; (*approximately*)

aproximadamente; ~**ness** *n* aspereza; tosquedad *f*; brutalidad *f*.

roulette [ru:'lɛt] *n* ruleta.

Roumania [ru:'meınıə] *n* = **Rumania**.

round [raund] *a* redondo // *n* círculo; (*of toast*) rodaja; (*of policeman*) ronda; (*of milkman*) recorrido; (*of doctor*) visitas *fpl*; (*game: of cards, in competition*) partida; (*of ammunition*) cartucho; (BOXING) asalto; (*of talks*) ronda // *vt* (*corner*) doblar // *prep* alrededor de // *ad:* **all** ~ por todos lados; **the long way** ~ el camino menos directo; **all the year** ~ durante todo el año; **it's just** ~ **the corner** (*fig*) está a la vuelta de la esquina; **to go** ~ **to sb's** (**house**) ir a casa de uno; **to go** ~ **the back** pasar por atrás; **to go** ~ **a house** visitar una casa; **to go the** ~**s** (*story*) divulgarse; **to** ~ **off** *vt* (*speech etc*) acabar, poner término a; **to** ~ **up** *vt* (*cattle*) acorralar; (*people*) reunir; (*prices*) redondear; ~**about** *n* (AUT) glorieta, redondel *m*; (*at fair*) tiovivo // *a* (*route, means*) indirecto; **a** ~ **of applause** una salva de aplausos; **a** ~ **of drinks** una ronda de bebidas; ~**ed** *a* redondeado; (*style*) expresivo; ~**ly** *ad* (*fig*) rotundamente; ~-**shouldered** *a* cargado de espaldas; ~ **trip** *n* viaje *m* de ida y vuelta; ~**up** *n* rodeo; (*of criminals*) redada.

rouse [rauz] *vt* (*wake up*) despertar; (*stir up*) suscitar; **rousing** *a* emocionado, entusiasta.

rout [raut] *n* (MIL) derrota; (*flight*) fuga // *vt* derrotar.

route [ru:t] *n* ruta, camino; (*of bus*) recorrido; (*of shipping*) rumba, derrota; ~ **map** *n* (*for journey*) mapa *m* de carreteras.

routine [ru:'ti:n] *a* (*work*) rutinario // *n* rutina; (THEATRE) número.

roving ['rəuvıŋ] *a* (*wandering*) errante; (*salesman*) ambulante.

row [rəu] *n* (*line*) fila, hilera; (KNITTING) pasada // *n* [rau] (*noise*) estrépito, estruendo; (*racket*) escándalo; (*dispute*) bronca, pelea; (*fuss*) jaleo, follón *m*; (*scolding*) regaño // *vi* (*in boat*) remar // *vi* [rau] reñir(se) // *vt* (*boat*) conducir remando.

rowdy ['raudı] *a* (*person: noisy*) ruidoso; (: *quarrelsome*) pendenciero; (*occasion*) alborotado // *n* pendenciero.

rowing ['rəuıŋ] *n* remo; ~ **boat** *n* bote *m* de remos.

royal ['rɔıəl] *a* real; ~**ist** *a, n* monárquico/a; ~**ty** *n* (~ *persons*) familia real; (*payment to author*) derechos *mpl* de autor.

R.S.V.P. *abbr of* **répondez s'il vous plaît** SRC (Se Ruega Contestación).

rub [rʌb] *vt* (*gen*) frotar; (*hard*) restregar; (*polish*) sacar brillo a // *n* (*gen*) frotamiento; (*touch*) roce *m*; **to** ~ **sb up the wrong way** coger a uno a contrapelo;

to ~ **off** *vi* borrarse; **to ~ off on** influir en; **to ~ out** *vt* borrar.

rubber ['rʌbə*] *n* caucho, goma; (*Brit: eraser*) goma de borrar; ~ **band** *n* goma, gomita; ~ **plant** *n* árbol *m* del caucho, gomero; ~**y** *a* elástico.

rubbish ['rʌbɪʃ] *n* (*from household*) basura; (*waste*) desperdicios *mpl*; (*fig: pej*) tonterías *fpl*; (*trash*) pacotilla; ~ **bin** *n* cubo de la basura; ~ **dump** *n* (*in town*) vertedero, basurero.

rubble ['rʌbl] *n* escombros *mpl*.

ruby ['ru:bɪ] *n* rubí *m*.

rucksack ['rʌksæk] *n* mochila.

ructions ['rʌkʃənz] *npl* lío *sg*, jaleo *sg*.

rudder ['rʌdə*] *n* timón *m*.

ruddy ['rʌdɪ] *a* (*face*) rubicundo, frescote; (*col: damned*) condenado.

rude [ru:d] *a* (*impolite: person*) grosero; (*: word, manners*) rudo, grosero; (*sudden*) repentino; (*shocking*) verde, indecente; ~**ly** *ad* groseramente, toscamente; repentinamente; ~**ness** *n* grosería, tosquedad *f*.

rudiment ['ru:dɪmənt] *n* rudimento; ~**ary** [-'mentərɪ] *a* rudimentario.

rue [ru:] *vt* arrepentirse de; ~**ful** *a* arrepentido.

ruffian ['rʌfɪən] *n* matón *m*, criminal *m*.

ruffle ['rʌfl] *vt* (*hair*) despeinar; (*clothes*) arrugar; (*fig: person*) agitar.

rug [rʌg] *n* alfombra *f*; (*for knees*) manta.

rugby ['rʌgbɪ] *n* (*also:* ~ **football**) rugby *m*.

rugged ['rʌgɪd] *a* (*landscape*) accidentado; (*features, character*) fuerte.

rugger ['rʌgə*] *n* (*col*) rugby *m*.

ruin ['ru:ɪn] *n* ruina // *vt* arruinar; (*spoil*) estropear; ~**s** *npl* ruinas *fpl*, restos *mpl*; ~**ous** *a* ruinoso.

rule [ru:l] *n* (*norm*) norma, costumbre *f*; (*regulation*) regla; (*government*) dominio; (*ruler*) metro // *vt* (*country, person*) gobernar; (*decide*) disponer; (*draw: lines*) trazar // *vi* regir; (*LAW*) fallar; **to ~ out** excluir; **as a ~** por regla general; ~**d** *a* (*paper*) rayado; **ruler** *n* (*sovereign*) soberano; (*for measuring*) regla; **ruling** *a* (*party*) gobernante; (*class*) dirigente // *n* (*LAW*) fallo, decisión *f*.

rum [rʌm] *n* ron *m*.

Rumania [ru:'meɪnɪə] *n* Rumanía; ~**n** *a, n* rumano/a.

rumble ['rʌmbl] *n* retumbo, ruido sordo; (*of thunder*) redoble *m* // *vi* retumbar, hacer un ruido sordo; (*stomach, pipe*) sonar.

rummage ['rʌmɪdʒ] *vi* revolverlo todo.

rumour, rumor (*US*) ['ru:mə*] *n* rumor *m* // *vt*: **it is ~ed that...** se rumorea que... .

rump [rʌmp] *n* (*of animal*) ancas *fpl*, grupa; ~**steak** *n* filete *m* de lomo.

rumpus ['rʌmpəs] *n* (*col*) lío, jaleo; (*quarrel*) pelea, riña.

run [rʌn] *n* carrera; (*outing*) paseo, excursión *f*; (*distance travelled*) trayecto; (*series*) serie *f*; (*THEATRE*) temporada; (*SKI*) pista // (*vb: pt* **ran**, *pp* **run**) *vt*

(*operate: business*) dirigir; (*: competition, course*) organizar; (*: hotel, house*) administrar, llevar; (*to pass: hand*) pasar; (*water, bath*) abrir el grifo (del baño) // *vi* (*gen*) correr; (*work: machine*) funcionar, marchar; (*bus, train: operate*) circular, ir; (*: travel*) ir; (*continue: play*) seguir; (*: contract*) ser válido; (*flow: river, bath*) fluir; (*colours, washing*) desteñirse; (*in election*) ser candidato; **there was a ~ on** (*meat, tickets*) hubo mucha demanda de; **in the long ~** a la larga, a largo plazo; **on the ~** en fuga; **I'll ~ you to the station** te llevaré a la estación en coche; **to ~ a risk** correr un riesgo; **to ~ about** *vi* (*children*) correr por todos lados; **to ~ across** *vt fus* (*find*) dar con, toparse con; **to ~ away** *vi* huir; **to ~ down** *vi* (*clock*) parar // *vt* (*AUT*) atropellar; (*criticize*) criticar; **to be ~ down** estar debilitado; **to ~ off** *vt* (*water*) dejar correr // *vi* huir corriendo; **to ~ out** *vi* (*person*) salir corriendo; (*liquid*) irse; (*lease*) caducar, vencer; (*money*) acabarse; **to ~ out of** *vt fus* quedar sin; **to ~ over** *vt sep* (*AUT*) atropellar // *vt fus* (*revise*) repasar; **to ~ through** *vt fus* (*instructions*) repasar; **to ~ up** *vt* (*debt*) incurrir en; **to ~ up against** (*difficulties*) tropezar con; ~**away** *a* (*horse*) desbocado; (*truck*) sin frenos; (*person*) fugitivo.

rung [rʌŋ] *pp of* **ring** // *n* (*of ladder*) escalón *m*, peldaño.

runner ['rʌnə*] *n* (*in race: person*) corredor/a *m/f*; (*: horse*) caballo; (*on sledge*) patín *m*; (*on curtain*) anillo; (*wheel*) ruedecilla; ~ **bean** *n* (*BOT*) judía escarlata; ~-**up** *n* subcampeón/ona *m/f*.

running ['rʌnɪŋ] *n* (*sport*) atletismo; (*race*) carrera // *a* (*water*) corriente; (*commentary*) continuo; **6 days ~** 6 días seguidos; ~ **board** *n* estribo.

runny ['rʌnɪ] *a* derretido.

run-of-the-mill ['rʌnəvðə'mɪl] *a* común y corriente.

runt [rʌnt] *n* (*also: pej*) redrojo, enano.

runway ['rʌnweɪ] *n* (*AVIAT*) pista de aterrizaje.

rupee [ru:'pi:] *n* rupia.

rupture ['rʌptʃə*] *n* (*MED*) hernia // *vt*: **to ~ o.s.** causarse una hernia, quebrarse.

rural ['ruərl] *a* rural.

ruse [ru:z] *n* ardid *m*.

rush [rʌʃ] *n* ímpetu *m*; (*hurry*) prisa; (*COMM*) demanda repentina; (*BOT*) junco; (*current*) corriente *f* fuerte, ráfaga // *vt* apresurar; (*work*) hacer de prisa; (*attack: town etc*) asaltar // *vi* correr, precipitarse; ~ **hour** *n* horas *fpl* punta.

rusk [rʌsk] *n* bizcocho tostado.

Russia ['rʌʃə] *n* Rusia; ~**n** *a, n* ruso/a.

rust [rʌst] *n* herrumbre *f*, moho // *vi* oxidarse.

rustic ['rʌstɪk] *a* rústico.

rustle ['rʌsl] *vi* susurrar // *vt* (*paper*) hacer crujir; (*US: cattle*) hurtar, robar.

rustproof ['rʌstpruːf] a inoxidable, a prueba de herrumbre.

rusty ['rʌstɪ] a oxidado, mohoso.

rut [rʌt] n rodera, carril m; (ZOOL) celo; **to be in a** ~ ir encarrilado.

ruthless ['ruːθlɪs] a despiadado; ~**ness** n crueldad f, implacabilidad f.

rye [raɪ] n centeno; ~ **bread** n pan de centeno.

S

sabbath ['sæbəθ] n domingo; (Jewish) sábado.

sabbatical [sə'bætɪkl] a: ~ **year** año de licencia.

sabotage ['sæbətɑːʒ] n sabotaje m // vt sabotear.

saccharin(e) ['sækərɪn] n sacarina.

sack [sæk] n (bag) saco, costal m // vt (dismiss) despedir; (plunder) saquear; **to get the** ~ ser despedido; ~**ing** n (material) harpillera.

sacrament ['sækrəmənt] n sacramento.

sacred ['seɪkrɪd] a sagrado, santo.

sacrifice ['sækrɪfaɪs] n sacrificio // vt sacrificar.

sacrilege ['sækrɪlɪdʒ] n sacrilegio.

sacrosanct ['sækrəusæŋkt] a sacrosanto.

sad [sæd] a (unhappy) triste; (deplorable) lamentable; ~**den** vt entristecer.

saddle ['sædl] n silla (de montar); (of cycle) sillín m // vt (horse) ensillar; **to be** ~**d with sth** (col) quedar cargado con algo; ~**bag** n alforja.

sadism ['seɪdɪzm] n sadismo; **sadist** n sadista m/f; **sadistic** [sə'dɪstɪk] a sádico.

sadly ['sædlɪ] ad tristemente; ~ **lacking (in)** muy deficiente (en).

sadness ['sædnɪs] n tristeza.

safari [sə'fɑːrɪ] n safari m.

safe [seɪf] a (out of danger) fuera de peligro; (not dangerous, sure) seguro; (unharmed) a salvo, ileso; (trustworthy) digno de confianza // n caja de caudales, caja fuerte; ~ **and sound** sano y salvo; **(just) to be on the** ~ **side** por mayor seguridad; ~**guard** n protección f, garantía // vt proteger, defender; ~**keeping** n custodia; ~**ly** ad seguramente, con seguridad; (without mishap) sin peligro.

safety ['seɪftɪ] n seguridad f // a de seguridad; ~ **first!** ¡precaución!; ~ **belt** n cinturón m (de seguridad); ~ **pin** n imperdible m.

saffron ['sæfrən] n azafrán m.

sag [sæg] vi aflojarse.

sage [seɪdʒ] n (herb) salvia; (man) sabio.

Sagittarius [sædʒɪ'teərɪəs] n Sagitario.

sago ['seɪgəu] n sagú m.

said [sed] pt, pp of **say**.

sail [seɪl] n (on boat) vela; (trip): **to go for a** ~ tomar un paseo en barco // vt (boat) gobernar // vi (travel: ship) navegar; (: passenger) pasear en barco; (set off)

zarpar; **they** ~**ed into Copenhagen** llegaron a Copenhague; **to** ~ **through** vi, vt fus (fig) hacer con facilidad; ~**boat** n (US) velero, barco de vela; ~**ing** n (SPORT) balandrismo; **to go** ~**ing** salir en balandro; ~**ing ship** n barco de vela; ~**or** n marinero, marino.

saint [seɪnt] n santo; **S**~ **John** San Juan; ~**ly** a santo.

sake [seɪk] n: **for the** ~ **of** por (motivo de).

salad ['sæləd] n ensalada; ~ **bowl** n ensaladera; ~ **cream** n mayonesa; ~ **dressing** n aliño; ~ **oil** n aceite m para ensaladas.

salami [sə'lɑːmɪ] n salami m.

salary ['sælərɪ] n sueldo.

sale [seɪl] n venta; (at reduced prices) liquidación f, saldo; **"grand** ~**"** grandes rebajas; **"for** ~**"** "se vende"; **on** ~ en venta; ~**room** n sala de subastas; **salesman/woman** n vendedor/a m/f; (in shop) dependiente/a m/f; (representative) viajante m/f; **salesmanship** n arte m de vender.

saliva [sə'laɪvə] n saliva.

sallow ['sæləu] a cetrino.

salmon ['sæmən] n, pl inv salmón m.

saloon [sə'luːn] n (US) bar m, taberna; (AUT) (coche m de) turismo; (ship's lounge) cámara, salón m.

salt [sɔːlt] n sal f // vt salar; (put ~ on) poner sal en; ~ **cellar** n salero; ~**water** a de agua salada; ~**y** a salado.

salutary ['sæljutərɪ] a saludable.

salute [sə'luːt] n saludo; (of guns) salva // vt saludar.

salvage ['sælvɪdʒ] n (saving) salvamento, recuperación f; (things saved) objetos mpl salvados // vt salvar.

salvation [sæl'veɪʃən] n salvación f; **S**~ **Army** n Ejército de Salvación.

salve [sælv] n (cream etc) ungüento, bálsamo.

salver ['sælvə*] n bandeja.

same [seɪm] a mismo // ad de la misma forma, igual // pron: **the** ~ el mismo/la misma; **the** ~ **book as** el mismo libro que; **all** or **just the** ~ sin embargo, aun así; **to do the** ~ **(as sb)** hacer lo mismo (que otro); **the** ~ **to you!** ¡igualmente!

sample ['sɑːmpl] n muestra // vt (food, wine) probar.

sanatorium [sænə'tɔːrɪəm], pl **-ria** [-rɪə] n sanatorio.

sanctify ['sæŋktɪfaɪ] vt santificar.

sanctimonious [sæŋktɪ'məunɪəs] a santurrón(ona).

sanction ['sæŋkʃən] n sanción f // vt sancionar.

sanctity ['sæŋktɪtɪ] n (gen) santidad f; (inviolability) inviolabilidad f.

sanctuary ['sæŋktjuərɪ] n (gen) santuario; (refuge) asilo, refugio.

sand [sænd] n arena; (beach) playa // vt enarenar.

sandal ['sændl] n sandalia; (wood) sándalo.

sand: ~**bag** n saco de arena; ~**bank** n banco de arena; ~**castle** n castillo de arena; ~ **dune** n duna; ~**paper** n papel m de lija; ~**pit** n (for children) cajón m de arena; ~**stone** n piedra arenisca.

sandwich ['sændwɪtʃ] n bocadillo, sándwich m // vt (also: ~ **in**) intercalar; ~**ed between** apretujado entre; **cheese/ham** ~ sándwich de queso/jamón; ~ **board** n cartelón m; ~ **course** n curso de medio tiempo.

sandy ['sændɪ] a arenoso; (colour) rojizo.

sane [seɪn] a cuerdo, sensato; (sensible) prudente.

sang [sæŋ] pt of **sing**.

sanitarium [sænɪ'tɛərɪəm] (US) = **sanatorium**.

sanitary ['sænɪtərɪ] a (system, arrangements) sanitario; (clean) higiénico; ~ **towel**, ~ **napkin** (US) n paño higiénico, compresa higiénica.

sanitation [sænɪ'teɪʃən] n (in house) saneamiento; (in town) sanidad f, higiene f.

sanity ['sænɪtɪ] n cordura; (common sense) juicio, sentido común.

sank [sæŋk] pt of **sink**.

Santa Claus [sæntə'klɔːz] n San Nicolás, Papá Noel.

sap [sæp] n (of plants) savia // vt (strength) minar, agotar.

sapling ['sæplɪŋ] n árbol nuevo o joven.

sapphire ['sæfaɪə*] n zafiro.

sarcasm ['sɑːkæzm] n sarcasmo; **sarcastic** [-'kæstɪk] a sarcástico.

sardine [sɑː'diːn] n sardina.

Sardinia [sɑː'dɪnɪə] n Cerdeña.

sari ['sɑːrɪ] n sari m.

sash [sæʃ] n faja.

sat [sæt] pt, pp of **sit**.

Satan ['seɪtn] n Satanás m.

satchel ['sætʃl] n bolsa; (child's) cartera.

satellite ['sætəlaɪt] n satélite m.

satin ['sætɪn] n raso // a de raso.

satire ['sætaɪə*] n sátira; **satirical** [sə'tɪrɪkl] a satírico; **satirize** ['sætɪraɪz] vt satirizar.

satisfaction [sætɪs'fækʃən] n satisfacción f; (of debt) liquidación f; **satisfactory** [-'fæktərɪ] a satisfactorio.

satisfy ['sætɪsfaɪ] vt satisfacer; (pay) liquidar; (convince) convencer; ~**ing** a satisfactorio.

saturate ['sætʃəreɪt] vt: **to** ~ **(with)** empapar o saturar (de); **saturation** [-'reɪʃən] n saturación f.

Saturday ['sætədɪ] n sábado.

sauce [sɔːs] n salsa; (sweet) crema; (fig: cheek) frescura; ~**pan** n perola.

saucer ['sɔːsə*] n platillo.

saucy ['sɔːsɪ] a fresco, descarado; (flirtatious) coqueta.

sauna ['sɔːnə] n sauna.

saunter ['sɔːntə*] vi deambular.

sausage ['sɔsɪdʒ] n salchicha; (cold meat) embutido; ~ **roll** n empanadita.

sauté ['səuteɪ] a salteado.

savage ['sævɪdʒ] a (cruel, fierce) feroz, furioso; (primitive) salvaje // n salvaje m/f // vt (attack) embestir; ~**ry** n ferocidad f; salvajismo.

save [seɪv] vt (rescue) salvar, rescatar; (money, time) ahorrar; (put by) guardar; (avoid: trouble) evitar // vi (also: ~ **up**) ahorrar // n (SPORT) parada // prep salvo, excepto.

saving ['seɪvɪŋ] n (on price etc) economía // a: **the** ~ **grace** of el único mérito de; ~**s** npl ahorros mpl; ~**s bank** n caja de ahorros.

saviour ['seɪvjə*] n salvador/a m/f.

savour, savor (US) ['seɪvə*] n sabor m, gusto // vt saborear; ~**y** a sabroso; (dish: not sweet) no dulce; (: salted) salado.

saw [sɔː] pt of **see** // n (tool) sierra // vt, pt **sawed**, pp **sawed** o **sawn** serrar; ~**dust** n (a)serrín m; ~**mill** n aserradero.

saxophone ['sæksəfəun] n saxófono.

say [seɪ] n: **to have one's** ~ expresar su opinión; **to have a** o **some** ~ **in sth** tener voz o tener que ver en algo // vt, pt, pp **said** decir; **to** ~ **yes/no** decir que sí/no; **that is to** ~ es decir; **that goes without** ~**ing** eso va sin decir; ~**ing** n dicho, refrán m.

scab [skæb] n costra; (pej) esquirol/a m/f; ~**by** a costroso, lleno de costras.

scaffold ['skæfəuld] n (for execution) cadalso, patíbulo; ~**ing** n andamios mpl, andamiaje m.

scald [skɔːld] n escaldadura // vt escaldar; ~**ing** a (hot) hirviendo.

scale [skeɪl] n (gen, MUS) escala; (of fish) escama; (of salaries, fees etc) escalafón m; (of map, also size, extent) escala // vt (mountain) escalar; (tree) trepar; ~**s** npl (small) balanza sg; (large) báscula sg; **on a large** ~ a gran escala; ~ **of charges** tarifa, lista de precios; **social** ~ escala social; ~ **drawing** n dibujo a escala; ~ **model** n modelo a escala.

scallop ['skɔləp] n (ZOOL) venera; (SEWING) festón m.

scalp [skælp] n cabellera // vt escalpar.

scalpel ['skælpl] n escalpelo.

scamp [skæmp] n diablillo, travieso.

scamper ['skæmpə*] vi: **to** ~ **away**, ~ **off** irse corriendo.

scan [skæn] vt (examine) escudriñar; (glance at quickly) dar un vistazo a; (TV, RADAR) explorar, registrar.

scandal ['skændl] n escándalo; (gossip) chismes mpl; ~**ize** vt escandalizar; ~**ous** a escandaloso; (libellous) calumnioso.

Scandinavia [skændɪ'neɪvɪə] n Escandinavia; ~**n** a escandinavo.

scant [skænt] a escaso; ~**y** a escaso.

scapegoat ['skeɪpgəut] n cabeza de turco, chivo expiatorio.

scar [skɑː] n cicatriz f // vt marcar con una cicatriz // vi cicatrizarse.

scarce [skɛəs] a escaso; ~**ly** ad apenas; **scarcity** n escasez f; (shortage) carestía.

scare [skɛə*] n susto, sobresalto; (panic)

pánico // vt asustar, espantar; **to ~ sb
stiff** dejar muerto de miedo a uno; **bomb
~** amenaza de bomba; **~crow** n
espantapájaros m inv; **~d** a: **to be ~d**
asustarse, estar asustado.
scarf [ska:f], pl **scarves** n (long) bufanda;
(square) pañuelo.
scarlet ['ska:lıt] a escarlata; **~ fever** n
escarlatina.
scarves [ska:vz] pl of **scarf.**
scary ['skɛərı] a (col) de miedo.
scathing ['skeıðıŋ] a mordaz.
scatter ['skætə*] vt (spread) esparcir,
desparramar; (put to flight) dispersar // vi
desparramarse; dispersarse; **~brained** a
ligero de cascos; (forgetful) olvidadizo.
scavenger ['skævəndʒə*] n (refuse
collector) basurero; (ZOOL) animal m/ave f
que se alimenta de la carroña.
scene [si:n] n (THEATRE, fig etc) escena; (of
crime, accident) escenario; (sight, view)
vista, perspectiva; (fuss) escándalo; **~ry**
n (THEATRE) decorado; (landscape) paisaje
m; **scenic** a (picturesque) pintoresco.
scent [sɛnt] n perfume m, olor m; (fig:
track) rastro, pista; (sense of smell) olfato
// vt perfumar; (smell) oler; (sniff out)
husmear; (suspect) sospechar.
sceptic, skeptic (US) ['skɛptık] n
escéptico/a; **~al** a escéptico; **~ism**
['skɛptısızm] n escepticismo.
sceptre, scepter (US) ['sɛptə*] n cetro.
schedule ['ʃɛdju:l] n (of trains) horario; (of
events) programa m; (plan) plan m; (list)
lista // vt (timetable) establecer el horario
de; (list) catalogar; (visit) fijar la hora de;
on ~ a la hora, sin retraso; **to be ahead
of/behind ~** estar adelantado/en
retraso.
scheme [ski:m] n (plan) plan m, proyecto;
(method) esquema m; (plot) intriga; (trick)
ardid m; (arrangement) disposición f // vt
proyectar // vi (plan) hacer proyectos;
(intrigue) intrigar; **scheming** a intrigante.
schism ['skızəm] n cisma m.
schizophrenia [skıtsəu'fri:nıə] n
esquizofrenia; **schizophrenic** [-sə'frɛnık]
a esquizofrénico.
scholar ['skɒlə*] n (pupil) alumno/a,
estudiante m/f; (learned person) sabio,
erudito; **~ly** a erudito; **~ship** n erudición
f; (grant) beca.
school [sku:l] n (gen) escuela, colegio; (in
university) facultad f // vt (animal)
amaestrar; **~ age** n edad f escolar;
~book n libro de texto; **~boy** n alumno;
~days npl años mpl del colegio; **~girl** n
alumna; **~ing** n enseñanza;
~master/mistress n (primary)
maestro/a; (secondary) profesor/a m/f;
~room n clase f; **~teacher** n
maestro/a.
schooner ['sku:nə*] n (ship) goleta; (glass)
jarra.
sciatica [saı'ætıkə] n ciática.
science ['saıəns] n ciencia; **~ fiction** n
ciencia-ficción f; **scientific** [-'tıfık] a

científico; **scientist** n científico.
scimitar ['sımıtə*] n cimitarra.
scintillating ['sıntıleıtıŋ] a brillante,
ingenioso.
scissors ['sızəz] npl tijeras fpl; **a pair of
~** unas tijeras.
scoff [skɒf] vt (col: eat) engullir // vi: **to ~
(at)** (mock) mofarse (de).
scold [skəuld] vt regañar.
scone [skɒn] n panecillo.
scoop [sku:p] n cucharón m; (for flour etc)
pala; (PRESS) exclusiva; **to ~ out** vt
excavar; **to ~ up** vt recoger.
scooter ['sku:tə*] n (motor cycle) moto f;
(toy) patinete m.
scope [skəup] n (of plan, undertaking)
ámbito; (reach) alcance m; (of person)
competencia; (opportunity) campo (de
acción).
scorch [skɒtʃ] vt (clothes) chamuscar;
(earth, grass) quemar, secar; **~er** n (col:
hot day) día m abrasador; **~ing** a
abrasador(a).
score [skɔ:*] n (points etc) puntuación f;
(MUS) partitura; (reckoning) cuenta;
(twenty) veinte m, veintena // vt (goal,
point) ganar; (mark) rayar // vi marcar un
tanto; (FOOTBALL) marcar (un) gol; (keep
score) llevar el tanteo; **on that ~** en lo
que se refiere a eso; **to ~ 6 out of 10**
obtener una puntuación de 6 sobre 10;
~board n marcador m; **~card** n (SPORT)
tanteador m; **scorer** n marcador m; (keeping score) tanteador m.
scorn [skɔ:n] n desprecio // vt despreciar;
~ful a desdeñoso, despreciativo.
Scorpio ['skɔ:pıəu] n Escorpión m.
scorpion ['skɔ:pıən] n escorpión m.
Scot [skɒt] n escocés/esa m/f.
scotch [skɒtʃ] vt (rumour) desmentir;
(plan) abandonar; **S~** n whisky m
escocés.
Scotland ['skɒtlənd] n Escocia.
Scots [skɒts] a escocés(esa);
~man/woman n escocés/esa m/f;
Scottish ['skɒtıʃ] a escocés(esa).
scoundrel ['skaundrl] n canalla m/f,
sinvergüenza m/f.
scour ['skauə*] vt (clean) fregar, estregar;
(search) recorrer, registrar; **~er** n
estropajo.
scourge [skɜːdʒ] n azote m.
scout [skaut] n (MIL, also: **boy ~**)
explorador m; **to ~ around** reconocer el
terreno.
scowl [skaul] vi fruncir el ceño; **to ~ at
sb** mirar con ceño a uno.
scraggy ['skrægı] a flaco, descarnado.
scram [skræm] vi (col) largarse.
scramble ['skræmbl] n (climb) subida
(difícil); (struggle) pelea // vi: **to ~
out/through** salir/abrirse paso con
dificultad; **to ~ for** pelear por; **~d eggs**
npl huevos mpl revueltos.
scrap [skræp] n (bit) pedacito; (fig) pizca;
(fight) riña, bronca; (also: **~ iron**)
chatarra, hierro viejo // vt reducir a

chatarra; (discard) desechar, descartar //
vi reñir, armar (una) bronca; ~s npl
(waste) sobras fpl, desperdicios mpl;
~book n álbum m de recortes.

scrape [skreɪp] n (fig) lío, apuro // vt
raspar; (skin etc) rasguñar; (~ against)
rozar // vi: to ~ through pasar con
dificultad; **scraper** n raspador m.

scrap: ~ **heap** n (fig): **on the ~ heap**
desperdiciado; ~ **merchant** n
chatarrero; ~ **paper** n pedazos mpl de
papel; ~**py** a (poor) pobre; (speech)
inconexo; (bitty) fragmentario.

scratch [skrætʃ] n rasguño; (from claw)
arañazo // a: ~ **team** equipo
improvisado // vt (record) rayar; (with
claw, nail) rasguñar, arañar // vi rascarse;
to start from ~ partir de cero, empezar
desde el principio; **to be up to** ~ estar a
la altura (de las circunstancias).

scrawl [skrɔːl] n garabatos mpl // vi hacer
garabatos.

scream [skriːm] n chillido // vi chillar.

screech [skriːtʃ] vi chirriar.

screen [skriːn] n (CINEMA, TV) pantalla;
(movable) biombo; (wall) tabique m; (also:
wind~) parabrisas m inv; (fig) cortina //
vt (conceal) tapar; (from the wind etc)
proteger; (film) proyectar; (candidates etc)
investigar a; ~**ing** n (MED) investigación f
médica; ~ **test** n prueba de pantalla.

screw [skruː] n tornillo; (propeller) hélice f
// vt atornillar; (also: ~ **in**) apretar;
~**driver** n destornillador m; ~**y** a (col)
chiflado.

scribble ['skrɪbl] n garabatos mpl // vt
escribir con prisa.

script [skrɪpt] n (CINEMA etc) guión m;
(writing) escritura, letra.

Scripture ['skrɪptʃə*] n Sagrada Escritura.

scriptwriter ['skrɪptraɪtə*] n guionista
m/f.

scroll [skrəʊl] n rollo.

scrounge [skraʊndʒ] vt (col): **to** ~ **sth
off** or **from sb** obtener algo de otro por
gorronería // vi: **to** ~ **on sb** vivir a costa
de uno; **scrounger** n gorrón/ona m/f.

scrub [skrʌb] n (clean) fregado; (land)
maleza // vt fregar, restregar; (reject)
cancelar, anular.

scruff [skrʌf] n: **by the** ~ **of the neck**
por el pescuezo.

scruffy ['skrʌfɪ] a desaliñado, piojoso.

scruple ['skruːpl] n escrúpulo;
scrupulous a escrupuloso.

scrutinize ['skruːtɪnaɪz] vt escudriñar;
(votes) escrutar; **scrutiny** [-nɪ] n
escrutinio, examen m.

scuff [skʌf] vt desgastar, restregar.

scuffle ['skʌfl] n refriega.

scullery ['skʌlərɪ] n fregadero, trascocina.

sculptor ['skʌlptə*] n escultor m;
sculpture [-tʃə*] n escultura.

scum [skʌm] n (on liquid) nata; (pej:
people) canalla; (fig) heces fpl.

scurry ['skʌrɪ] vi: **to** ~ **off** escabullirse.

scurvy ['skɜːvɪ] n escorbuto.

scuttle ['skʌtl] n (also: **coal** ~) cubo,
carbonera // vt (ship) barrenar // vi
(scamper): **to** ~ **away,** ~ **off**
escabullirse.

scythe [saɪð] n guadaña.

sea [siː] n mar m or f; **on the** ~ (boat) en
el mar; (town) junto al mar; **to be all at**
~ (fig) estar despistado; **out to** or **at** ~
en alta mar; ~ **bird** n ave f marina;
~**board** n litoral m; ~ **breeze** n brisa de
mar; ~**farer** n marinero; ~**food** n
mariscos mpl; ~ **front** n (beach) playa;
(prom) paseo marítimo; ~**going** a (ship)
de alta mar; ~**gull** n gaviota.

seal [siːl] n (animal) foca; (stamp) sello //
vt (close) cerrar; (: with ~) sellar; **to** ~
off obturar; **it** ~**ed his fate** decidió su
destino.

sea level ['siːlevl] n nivel m del mar.

sealing wax ['siːlɪŋwæks] n lacre m.

sea lion ['siːlaɪən] n león m marino.

seam [siːm] n costura; (of metal) juntura;
(of coal) veta, filón m.

seaman ['siːmən] n marinero.

seamless ['siːmlɪs] a sin costura.

seamstress ['sɛmstrɪs] n costurera.

seance ['seɪɒns] n sesión f de espiritismo.

sea: ~**plane** n hidroavión m; ~**port** n
puerto de mar.

search [sɜːtʃ] n (for person, thing) busca,
búsqueda; (of drawer, pockets) registro;
(inspection) reconocimiento // vt (look in)
buscar en; (examine) examinar; (person,
place) registrar // vi: **to** ~ **for** buscar; **to**
~ **through** vt fus registrar; **in** ~ **of** en
busca de; ~**ing** a penetrante; ~**light** n
reflector m; ~ **party** n pelotón m de
salvamento; ~ **warrant** n mandamiento
(judicial).

sea: ~**shore** n playa, orilla del mar;
~**sick** a mareado; ~**side** n playa, orilla
del mar; ~ **side resort** n playa.

season ['siːzn] n (of year) estación f;
(sporting etc) temporada; (gen) época,
período // vt (food) sazonar; ~**al** a
estacional; ~**ing** n condimento, aderezo;
~ **ticket** n billete m de abono.

seat [siːt] n (in bus, train: place) asiento;
(chair) silla; (PARLIAMENT) escaño;
(buttocks) culo, trasero; (of government)
sede f // vt sentar; (have room for) tener
asientos para; **to be** ~**ed** sentarse; ~
belt n cinturón m de seguridad.

sea: ~ **water** n agua m del mar; ~**weed**
n alga marina; ~ **worthy** a marinero, en
condiciones de navegar.

sec. abbr of **second(s).**

secede [sɪ'siːd] vi separarse.

secluded [sɪ'kluːdɪd] a retirado; **seclusion**
[-'kluːʒən] n retiro.

second ['sɛkənd] a segundo // ad (in race
etc) en segundo lugar // n (gen) segundo;
(AUT: also: ~ **gear**) segunda; (COMM)
artículo con algún desperfecto // vt (motion) apoyar; ~**ary** a secundario; ~**ary
school** n escuela secundaria; ~-**class** a
de segunda clase; ~**hand** a de segunda

mano, usado; ~ **hand** *n* (*on clock*) segundero; ~**ly** *ad* en segundo lugar; ~**ment** [sɪˈkɔndmənt] *n* traslado temporal; ~**rate** *a* de segunda categoría.

secrecy [ˈsiːkrəsɪ] *n* secreto; **secret** [-krɪt] *a, n* secreto.

secretarial [sɛkrɪˈtɛərɪəl] *a* de secretario/a.

secretariat [sɛkrɪˈtɛərɪət] *n* secretaría.

secretary [ˈsɛkrətərɪ] *n* secretario/a; **S~ of State** (*Brit: POL*) Ministro (con cartera).

secretive [ˈsiːkrətɪv] *a* reservado, sigiloso.

sect [sɛkt] *n* secta; ~**arian** [-ˈtɛərɪən] *a* sectario.

section [ˈsɛkʃən] *n* sección *f*; (*part*) parte *f*; (*of document*) artículo; (*of opinion*) sector *m*; ~**al** *a* (*drawing*) en corte.

sector [ˈsɛktə*] *n* sector *m*.

secular [ˈsɛkjulə*] *a* secular, seglar.

secure [sɪˈkjuə*] *a* (*free from anxiety*) seguro; (*firmly fixed*) firme, fijo // *vt* (*fix*) asegurar, afianzar; (*get*) conseguir.

security [sɪˈkjuərɪtɪ] *n* seguridad *f*; (*for loan*) fianza; (*: object*) prenda.

sedate [sɪˈdeɪt] *a* (*calm*) tranquilo; (*formal*) serio, formal // *vt* tratar con calmantes.

sedation [sɪˈdeɪʃən] *n* (*MED*) sedación *f*; **sedative** [ˈsɛdɪtɪv] *n* sedante *m*, sedativo.

sedentary [ˈsɛdntrɪ] *a* sedentario.

sediment [ˈsɛdɪmənt] *n* sedimento.

seduce [sɪˈdjuːs] *vt* (*gen*) seducir; **seduction** [-ˈdʌkʃən] *n* seducción *f*; **seductive** [-ˈdʌktɪv] *a* seductor(a).

see [siː], *pt* **saw**, *pp* **seen** *vt* (*gen*) ver; (*accompany*): **to ~ sb to the door** acompañar a uno a la puerta; (*understand*) ver, comprender; (*look at*) mirar // *vi* ver // *n* sede *f*; **to ~ that** (*ensure*) asegurar que; **to ~ about** *vt* atender a, encargarse de; **to ~ off** *vt* despedirse de; **to ~ through** *vt* penetrar (con la vista) // *vt fus* llevar a cabo; **to ~ to** *vt fus* atender a, encargarse de.

seed [siːd] *n* semilla; (*in fruit*) pepita; (*sperm*) semen *m*, simiente *f*; (*fig*) germen *m*; (*TENNIS*) preseleccionado/a; ~**ling** *n* planta de semillero; ~**y** *a* (*shabby*) desaseado, raído.

seeing [ˈsiːɪŋ] *conj*: ~ (**that**) visto que, en vista de que.

seek [siːk], *pt, pp* **sought** *vt* (*gen*) buscar; (*post*) solicitar.

seem [siːm] *vi* parecer; ~**ingly** *ad* aparentemente, según parece.

seen [siːn] *pp of* **see**.

seep [siːp] *vi* filtrarse.

seesaw [ˈsiːsɔː] *n* balancín *m*, columpio.

seethe [siːð] *vi* hervir; **to ~ with anger** enfurecerse.

segment [ˈsɛgmənt] *n* segmento.

segregate [ˈsɛgrɪgeɪt] *vt* segregar; **segregation** [-ˈgeɪʃən] *n* segregación *f*.

seismic [ˈsaɪzmɪk] *a* sísmico.

seize [siːz] *vt* (*grasp*) agarrar, asir; (*take possession of*) secuestrar; (*: territory*) apoderarse de; (*opportunity*) aprovecharse

de; **to ~ (up)on** *vt fus* valerse de; **to ~ up** *vi* (*TECH*) agarrotarse.

seizure [ˈsiːʒə*] *n* (*MED*) ataque *m*; (*LAW*) incautación *f*.

seldom [ˈsɛldəm] *ad* rara vez.

select [sɪˈlɛkt] *a* selecto, escogido // *vt* escoger, elegir; (*SPORT*) seleccionar; ~**ion** [-ˈlɛkʃən] *n* selección *f*, elección *f*; (*COMM*) surtido; ~**ive** *a* selectivo; ~**or** *n* (*person*) seleccionador/a *m/f*.

self [sɛlf] *pron* se; (*after prep*) sí mismo // *n, pl* **selves** uno mismo; **him~/her~** él mismo/ella misma; **the ~** el yo.

self... *pref* auto...; ~**-appointed** *a* autonombrado; ~**-assured** *a* seguro de sí mismo; ~**-catering** *a* sin pensión; ~**-centred** *a* egocéntrico; ~**-coloured** *a* de color natural; (*of one colour*) de un color; ~**-confidence** *n* confianza en sí mismo; ~**-conscious** *a* cohibido; ~**-contained** *a* (*gen*) independiente; (*flat*) con entrada particular; ~**-control** *n* autodominio; ~**-defence** *n* defensa propia; ~**-discipline** *n* autodisciplina; ~**-employed** *a* que trabaja por cuenta propia; ~**-evident** *a* patente; ~**-governing** *a* autónomo; ~**-important** *a* presumido; ~**-indulgent** *a* inmoderado; ~**-interest** *n* egoísmo; ~**ish** *a* egoísta; ~**ishness** *n* egoísmo; ~**lessly** *ad* desinteresadamente; ~**-pity** *n* autocompasión *f*; ~**-portrait** *n* autorretrato; ~**-possessed** *a* sereno, dueño de sí mismo; ~**-preservation** *n* propia conservación *f*; ~**-reliant** *a* independiente, seguro de sí mismo; ~**-respect** *n* amor *m* propio; ~**-righteous** *a* santurrón(ona); ~**-sacrifice** *n* abnegación *f*; ~**-satisfied** *a* satisfecho de sí mismo; ~**-service** *a* de autoservicio; ~**-sufficient** *a* autosuficiente; ~**-taught** *a* autodidacta.

sell [sɛl], *pt, pp* **sold** *vt* vender // *vi* venderse; **to ~ at** *or* **for £10** vender a 10 libros; **to ~ off** *vt* liquidar; **to ~ out** *vi* transigir, transar (*AM*); ~**er** *n* vendedor/a *m/f*; ~**ing price** *n* precio de venta.

sellotape [ˈsɛləuteɪp] *n* cela.

sellout [ˈsɛlaut] *n* traición *f*; (*of tickets*): **it was a ~** fue un éxito de taquilla.

selves [sɛlvz] *pl of* **self**.

semaphore [ˈsɛməfɔ:*] *n* semáforo.

semen [ˈsiːmən] *n* semen *m*.

semi... [sɛmɪ] *pref* semi..., medio...; ~**circle** *n* semicírculo; ~**colon** *n* punto y coma; ~**conscious** *a* semiconsciente; ~**detached (house)** *n* (*casa*) semiseparada; ~**final** *n* semi-final *m*.

seminar [ˈsɛmɪnɑ:*] *n* seminario.

semitone [ˈsɛmɪtəun] *n* (*MUS*) semitono.

semolina [sɛməˈliːnə] *n* sémola.

senate [ˈsɛnɪt] *n* senado; **senator** *n* senador/a *m/f*.

send [sɛnd], *pt, pp* **sent** *vt* mandar, enviar; (*dispatch*) despachar; (*telegram*) poner; **to ~ away** *vt* (*letter, goods*) despachar; **to ~ away for** *vt fus* despachar por; **to ~**

back vt devolver; **to ~ for** vt fus mandar traer; **to ~ off** vt (goods) despachar; (SPORT: player) expulsar; **to ~ out** vt (invitation) mandar; (signal) emitir; **to ~ up** vt (person, price) hacer subir; (parody) parodiar; **~er** n remitente m/f; **~-off** n: **a good ~-off** una buena despedida.

senile ['si:naɪl] a senil; **senility** [sɪ'nɪlɪtɪ] n senilidad f.

senior ['si:nɪə*] a (older) mayor, más viejo; (: on staff) más antiguo; (of higher rank) superior // n mayor m; (in service) miembro más antiguo; **~ity** [-'ɔrɪtɪ] n antigüedad f.

sensation [sɛn'seɪʃən] n sensación f; **~al** a sensacional; **~alism** n sensacionalismo.

sense [sɛns] n sentido; (feeling) sensación f; (good ~) sentido común, juicio; (sentiment) opinión f // vt sentir, percibir; **it makes ~** tiene sentido; **~less** a estúpido, insensato; (unconscious) sin sentido.

sensibility [sɛnsɪ'bɪlɪtɪ] n sensibilidad f; **sensibilities** npl delicadeza sg.

sensible ['sɛnsɪbl] a sensato, juicio; (cautious) prudente; (reasonable) razonable, lógico; (perceptible) apreciable.

sensitive ['sɛnsɪtɪv] a sensible; (touchy) susceptible; **sensitivity** [-'tɪvɪtɪ] n sensibilidad f; susceptibilidad f.

sensual ['sɛnsjuəl] a sensual.

sensuous ['sɛnsjuəs] a sensual.

sent [sɛnt] pt, pp of **send**.

sentence ['sɛntns] n (LING) frase f, oración f; (LAW) sentencia, fallo // vt: **to ~ sb to death/to 5 years** condenar a uno a muerte/a 5 años de cárcel.

sentiment ['sɛntɪmənt] n sentimiento; (opinion) opinión f; **~al** [-'mɛntl] a sentimental; **~ality** [-'tælɪtɪ] n sentimentalismo.

sentry ['sɛntrɪ] n centinela m.

separate ['sɛprɪt] a separado; (distinct) distinto // (vb: ['sɛpəreɪt]) vt separar; (part) dividir // vi separarse; **~ly** ad por separado; **~s** npl (clothes) coordinados mpl; **separation** [-'reɪʃən] n separación f.

September [sɛp'tɛmbə*] n se(p)tiembre m.

septic ['sɛptɪk] a séptico.

sequel ['si:kwl] n consecuencia, resultado; (of story) continuación f.

sequence ['si:kwəns] n sucesión f, serie f; (CINEMA) secuencia.

sequin ['si:kwɪn] n lentejuela.

serenade [sɛrə'neɪd] n serenata // vt dar serenata a.

serene [sɪ'ri:n] a sereno, tranquilo; **serenity** [sə'rɛnɪtɪ] n serenidad f, tranquilidad f.

sergeant ['sɑːdʒənt] n sargento.

serial ['sɪərɪəl] n novela por entregas; **~ize** vt publicar por entregas; **~ number** n número de serie.

series ['sɪərɪːz] n serie f.

serious ['sɪərɪəs] a serio; (grave) grave;

~ly ad en serio; gravemente; **~ness** n seriedad f; gravedad f.

sermon ['sɔːmən] n sermón m.

serrated [sɪ'reɪtɪd] a serrado, dentellado.

serum ['sɪərəm] n suero.

servant ['sɔːvənt] n (gen) servidor/a m/f; (house ~) criado/a; **civil ~** funcionario.

serve [sɔːv] vt (gen) servir; (in shop: goods) servir, despachar; (: customer) atender; (subj: train) pasar por; (treat) tratar; (apprenticeship) hacer; (prison term) cumplir // vi (also TENNIS) sacar; (be useful): **to ~ as/for/to do** servir de/para/para hacer // n (TENNIS) saque m; **to ~ out, ~ up** vt (food) servir.

service ['sɔːvɪs] n (gen) servicio; (REL) misa; (AUT) mantenimiento; (of dishes) vajilla, juego // vt (car, washing machine) mantener; (: repair) reparar; **the S~s** las fuerzas armadas; **to be of ~ to sb** ser útil a uno; **~able** a servible, utilizable; **~ area** n (on motorway) servicios mpl; **~man** n militar m; **~ station** n estación f de servicio.

serviette [sɔːvɪ'ɛt] n servilleta.

servile ['sɔːvaɪl] a servil.

session ['sɛʃən] n (sitting) sesión f; **to be in ~** estar celebrando sesión.

set [sɛt] n juego; (RADIO) aparato; (TV) televisor m; (of utensils) batería; (of cutlery) cubierto; (of books) colección f; (TENNIS) set m; (group of people) grupo; (CINEMA) plató m; (THEATRE) decorado; (HAIRDRESSING) marcado // a (fixed) fijo; (ready) listo; (resolved) resuelto, decidido // (vb: pt, pp **set**) vt (place) poner, colocar; (fix) fijar; (: a time) señalar; (adjust) ajustar, arreglar; (decide: rules etc) establecer, decidir // vi (sun) ponerse; (jam, jelly) cuajarse; (concrete) fraguar; **to be ~ on doing sth** estar empeñado en hacer algo; **to ~ to music** poner música a; **to ~ on fire** incendiar, poner fuego a; **to ~ free** poner en libertad; **to ~ sth going** poner algo en marcha; **to ~ sail** zarpar, hacerse a la vela; **to ~ about** vt fus (task) ponerse a; **to ~ aside** vt poner aparte, dejar de lado; **to ~ back** vt (in time): **to ~ back (by)** retrasar (por); **to ~ off** vi partir // vt (bomb) hacer estallar; (cause to start) poner en marcha; (show up well) hacer resaltar; **to ~ out** vi: **to ~ out to do sth** ponerse a hacer algo // vt (arrange) disponer; (state) exponer; **to ~ up** vt (organization, record) establecer; **to ~ up shop** (fig) establecerse; **~back** n (hitch) revés m, contratiempo.

settee [sɛ'ti:] n sofá m.

setting ['sɛtɪŋ] n (frame) marco; (placing) colocación f; (of sun) puesta; (of jewel) engaste m, montadura.

settle ['sɛtl] vt (argument, matter) componer; (accounts) ajustar, liquidar; (land) colonizar; (MED: calm) calmar, sosegar // vi (dust etc) depositarse; (weather) serenarse; (also: ~ **down**) instalarse, establecerse; **to ~ for sth** convenir en aceptar algo; **to ~ in** vi instalarse; **to ~ on sth** quedar en algo; **to ~ up with sb** ajustar cuentas con uno; **~ment** n (*payment*) liquidación f; (*agreement*) acuerdo, convenio; (*village etc*) pueblo; **settler** n colono/a, colonizador/a m/f.

setup ['sɛtʌp] n (*arrangement*) plan m; (*situation*) situación f.

seven ['sɛvn] num siete; **~teen** num diez y siete, diecisiete; **~th** a séptimo; **~ty** num setenta.

sever ['sɛvə*] vt cortar; (*relations*) romper.

several ['sɛvərl] a, pron varios mpl, algunos mpl; **~ of us** varios de nosotros.

severance ['sɛvərəns] n (*of relations*) ruptura; **~ pay** n paga de despedida.

severe [sɪ'vɪə*] a severo; (*serious*) grave; (*hard*) duro; (*pain*) intenso; **severity** [sɪ'vɛrɪtɪ] n severidad f; gravedad f; intensidad f.

sew [səu], pt sewed, pp sewn vt, vi coser; **to ~ up** vt coser, zurcir.

sewage ['suːɪdʒ] n (*effluence*) aguas fpl residuales; (*system*) alcantarillado.

sewer ['suːə*] n alcantarilla, cloaca.

sewing ['səuɪŋ] n costura; **~ machine** n máquina de coser.

sewn [səun] pp of **sew.**

sex [sɛks] n sexo; **to have ~ with sb** tener sexo con alguien; **~ act** n acto sexual.

sextet [sɛks'tɛt] n sexteto.

sexual ['sɛksjuəl] a sexual.

sexy ['sɛksɪ] a sexy.

shabby ['ʃæbɪ] a (*a person*) desharrapado; (*clothes*) raído, gastado.

shack [ʃæk] n choza, chabola.

shackles ['ʃæklz] npl grillos mpl, grilletes mpl.

shade [ʃeɪd] n sombra; (*for lamp*) pantalla; (*for eyes*) visera; (*of colour*) matiz m, tonalidad f // vt dar sombra a; **in the ~** en la sombra.

shadow ['ʃædəu] n sombra // vt (*follow*) seguir y vigilar; **~ cabinet** n (*POL*) gabinete paralelo formado por el partido de oposición; **~y** a oscuro; (*dim*) indistinto.

shady ['ʃeɪdɪ] a sombreado; (*fig: dishonest*) sospechoso; (: *deal*) turbio.

shaft [ʃɑːft] n (*of arrow, spear*) astil m; (*AUT, TECH*) eje m, árbol m; (*of mine*) pozo; (*of lift*) hueco, caja; (*of light*) rayo.

shaggy ['ʃægɪ] a peludo.

shake [ʃeɪk], pt shook, pp shaken vt sacudir; (*building*) hacer temblar; (*perturb*) inquietar, perturbar; (*weaken*) debilitar; (*surprise*) sorprender, pasmar // vi estremecerse; (*tremble*) temblar // vi (*movement*) sacudida; **to ~ hands with sb** estrechar la mano con uno; **to ~ off** vt sacudirse; (*fig*) deshacerse de; **to ~ up** vt agitar; **shaky** a (*hand, voice*) trémulo; (*building*) inestable.

shall [ʃæl] auxiliary vb: **I ~ go** iré.

shallot [ʃə'lɔt] n chalote m.

shallow ['ʃæləu] a poco profundo; (*fig*) superficial.

sham [ʃæm] n fraude m, engaño // a falso, fingido // vt fingir, simular.

shambles ['ʃæmblz] n confusión f.

shame [ʃeɪm] n vergüenza; (*pity*) lástima // vt avergonzar; **it is a ~ that/to do** es una lástima que/hacer; **what a ~!** ¡qué lástima!; **~faced** a avergonzado; **~ful** a vergonzoso; **~less** a descarado; (*immodest*) impúdico.

shampoo [ʃæm'puː] n champú m // vt lavar el pelo (con champú).

shamrock ['ʃæmrɔk] n trébol m.

shandy ['ʃændɪ] n mezcla de cerveza con gaseosa.

shan't [ʃɑːnt] = **shall not.**

shanty town ['ʃæntɪ-] n barrio de chabolas.

shape [ʃeɪp] n forma // vt formar, dar forma a; (*sb's ideas*) formar; (*sb's life*) determinar // vi (*also: ~ up*) (*events*) desarrollarse; (*person*) formarse; **to take ~** tomar forma; **-shaped** suff: **heart-shaped** en forma de corazón; **~less** a informe, sin forma definida; **~ly** a bien formado o proporcionado.

share [ʃɛə*] n (*part*) parte f, porción f; (*contribution*) cuota; (*COMM*) acción f // vt dividir; (*have in common*) compartir; **to ~ out** (**among** or **between**) repartir (entre); **~holder** n accionista m/f.

shark [ʃɑːk] n tiburón m.

sharp [ʃɑːp] a (*razor, knife*) afilado; (*point*) puntiagudo; (*outline*) definido; (*pain*) intenso; (*MUS*) desafinado; (*contrast*) marcado; (*voice*) agudo; (*person: quick-witted*) astuto; (*dishonest*) poco escrupuloso // n (*MUS*) sostenido // ad: **at 2 o'clock ~** a las 2 en punto; **~en** vt afilar; (*pencil*) sacar punta a; (*fig*) agudizar; **~ener** n (*also:* **pencil ~ener**) afilador m; **~-eyed** a de vista aguda; **~-witted** a listo, perspicaz.

shatter ['ʃætə*] vt hacer añicos o pedazos; (*fig: ruin*) destruir, acabar con // vi hacerse añicos.

shave [ʃeɪv] vt afeitar, rasurar // vi afeitarse // n: **to have a ~** afeitarse; **shaver** n (*also:* **electric shaver**) máquina de afeitar (eléctrica).

shaving ['ʃeɪvɪŋ] n (*action*) el afeitarse, rasurado; **~s** npl (*of wood etc*) virutas fpl; **~ brush** n brocha de afeitar); **~ cream** n crema (de afeitar).

shawl [ʃɔːl] n chal m.

she [ʃiː] pron ella; **~-cat** n gata; *NB: for ships, countries follow the gender of your translation.*

sheaf [ʃiːf], pl sheaves n (*of corn*) gavilla; (*of arrows*) haz m; (*of papers*) fajo.

shear [ʃɪə*], pt sheared, pp sheared or shorn vt (*sheep*) esquilar, trasquilar; **to ~ off** vt cercenar; **~s** npl (*for hedge*) tijeras fpl de jardín.

sheath [ʃiːθ] n vaina; (*contraceptive*) preservativo.

sheaves [ʃiːvz] *pl of* **sheaf.**

shed [ʃed] *n* cobertizo // *vt, pt, pp* **shed** (*gen*) desprenderse de; (*skin*) mudar; (*tears*) derramar.

she'd [ʃiːd] = **she had; she would.**

sheep [ʃiːp] *n, pl inv* oveja; **~dog** *n* perro pastor; **~ish** *a* tímido, vergonzoso; **~skin** *n* piel *f* de carnero.

sheer [ʃiə*] *a* (*utter*) puro, completo; (*steep*) escarpado; (*almost transparent*) diáfano // *ad* verticalmente.

sheet [ʃiːt] *n* (*on bed*) sábana; (*of paper*) hoja; (*of glass, metal*) lámina.

sheik(h) [ʃeɪk] *n* jeque *m.*

shelf [ʃelf], *pl* **shelves** *n* estante *m.*

shell [ʃel] *n* (*on beach*) concha; (*of egg, nut etc*) cáscara; (*explosive*) proyectil *m*, obús *m*; (*of building*) armazón *m* // *vt* (*peas*) desenvainar; (*MIL*) bombardear.

she'll [ʃiːl] = **she will; she shall.**

shellfish [ʃelfɪʃ] *n, pl inv* crustáceo; (*pl: as food*) mariscos *mpl.*

shelter [ʃeltə*] *n* abrigo, refugio // *vt* (*aid*) amparar, proteger; (*give lodging to*) abrigar; (*hide*) esconder // *vi* abrigarse, refugiarse; **~ed** *a* (*life*) protegido; (*spot*) abrigado.

shelve [ʃelv] *vt* (*fig*) aplazar; **~s** *pl of* **shelf.**

shepherd [ʃepəd] *n* pastor *m* // *vt* (*guide*) guiar, conducir; **~ess** *n* pastora *f*; **~'s pie** *n* pastel *m* de carne y patatas.

sheriff [ʃerɪf] *n* sheriff *m.*

sherry [ʃerɪ] *n* jerez *m.*

she's [ʃiːz] = **she is; she has.**

shield [ʃiːld] *n* escudo; (*TECH*) blindaje *m* // *vt*: **to ~ (from)** proteger (contra).

shift [ʃift] *n* (*change*) cambio; (*of place*) traslado; (*of workers*) turno // *vt* trasladar; (*remove*) quitar // *vi* moverse; (*change place*) cambiar de sitio; **~ work** *n* trabajo por turno; **~y** *a* tramposo; (*eyes*) furtivo.

shilling [ʃɪlɪŋ] *n* chelín *m.*

shimmer [ʃɪmə*] *n* reflejo trémulo // *vi* relucir.

shin [ʃɪn] *n* espinilla.

shine [ʃaɪn] *n* brillo, lustre *m* // (*vb: pt, pp* **shone**) *vi* brillar, relucir // *vt* (*shoes*) lustrar, sacar brillo a; **to ~ a torch on** sth dirigir una linterna hacia algo.

shingle [ʃɪŋgl] *n* (*on beach*) guijarras *fpl*; **~s** *n* (*MED*) herpes *mpl* or *fpl.*

shiny [ʃaɪnɪ] *a* brillante, lustroso.

ship [ʃɪp] *n* buque *m*, barco // *vt* (*goods*) embarcar; (*oars*) desarmar; (*send*) transportar o enviar (por vía marítima); **~building** *n* construcción *f* de barcos; **~ment** *n* (*act*) embarque *m*; (*goods*) envío; **~per** *n* exportador/a *m/f*; **~ping** *n* (*act*) embarque *m*; (*traffic*) buques *mpl*; **~shape** *a* en regla; **~wreck** *n* naufragio; **~yard** *n* astillero.

shire [ʃaɪə*] *n* condado.

shirk [ʃəːk] *vt* eludir, esquivar; (*obligations*) faltar a.

shirt [ʃəːt] *n* camisa; **in ~ sleeves** en mangas de camisa.

shiver [ʃɪvə*] *n* temblor *m*, estremecimiento // *vi* temblar, estremecerse.

shoal [ʃəʊl] *n* (*of fish*) banco.

shock [ʃɔk] *n* (*impact*) choque *m*; (*ELEC*) descarga (eléctrica); (*emotional*) conmoción *f*; (*start*) sobresalto, susto; (*MED*) postración *f* nerviosa // *vt* dar un susto a; (*offend*) escandalizar; **~ absorber** *n* amortiguador *m*; **~ing** *a* (*awful*) espantoso; (*improper*) escandaloso; **~proof** *a* a prueba de choques.

shod [ʃɔd] *pt, pp of* **shoe** // *a* calzado.

shoddy [ʃɔdɪ] *a* de pacotilla, de bajísima calidad.

shoe [ʃuː] *n* zapato; (*for horse*) herradura; (*brake ~*) zapata // *vt, pt, pp* **shod** (*horse*) herrar; **~brush** *n* cepillo para zapatos; **~horn** *n* calzador *m*; **~lace** *n* cordón *m*; **~maker** *n* zapatero; **~ polish** *n* betún *m*; **~shop** *n* zapatería.

shone [ʃɔn] *pt, pp of* **shine.**

shook [ʃuk] *pt of* **shake.**

shoot [ʃuːt] *n* (*on branch, seedling*) retoño, vástago // (*vb: pt, pp* **shot**) *vt* disparar; (*kill*) matar (con arma de fuego); (*wound*) herir (con arma de fuego); (*execute*) fusilar; (*film*) rodear, filmar // *vi* (*with gun, bow*): **to ~ (at)** tirar (a); (*FOOTBALL*) chutar; **to ~ down** *vt* (*plane*) derribar; **to ~ in/out** *vi* entrar corriendo/salir disparado; **to ~ up** *vi* (*fig*) subir (vertiginosamente); **~ing** *n* (*shots*) tiros *mpl*; (*HUNTING*) caza con escopeta; **~ing star** *n* estrella fugaz.

shop [ʃɔp] *n* (*workshop*) taller *m* // *vi* (*also*: **go ~ping**) ir de compras; **~ assistant** *n* dependiente/a *m/f*; **~ floor** *a* (*fig*) de la base; **~keeper** *n* tendero/a; **~lifter** *n* mechero/a; **~lifting** *n* mechería; **~per** *n* comprador/a *m/f*; **~ping** *n* (*goods*) compras *fpl*; **~ping bag** *n* bolsa (de compras); **~ping centre, ~ping center** *n* (*US*) zona comercial o de tiendas; **~-soiled** *a* usado; **~ steward** *n* (*INDUSTRY*) enlace *m/f*; **~ window** *n* escaparate *m.*

shore [ʃɔː*] *n* (*of sea, lake*) orilla // *vt*: **to ~ (up)** reforzar.

shorn [ʃɔːn] *pp of* **shear.**

short [ʃɔːt] *a* (*not long*) corto; (*in time*) breve, de corta duración; (*person*) bajo; (*curt*) brusco, seco; (*insufficient*) insuficiente // *vi* (*ELEC*) ponerse en cortocircuito // *n* (*also*: **~ film**) cortometraje *m*; (**a pair of**) **~s** (unos) pantalones *mpl* cortos; **to be ~ of sth** estar falto de algo; **in ~** en pocas palabras; **it is ~ for** es la forma abreviada de; **to cut ~** (*speech, visit*) interrumpir, terminar inesperadamente; **to fall ~ of** resultar (ser) insuficiente; **to stop ~** parar en seco; **to stop ~ of** detenerse antes de; **~age** *n* escasez *f*, falta; **~bread** *n* torta seca y quebradiza; **~circuit** *n* cortocircuito // *vt* poner en cortocircuito // *vi* ponerse en cortocircuito; **~coming** n defecto, deficiencia; **~(crust) pastry** n pasta quebradiza; **~cut** n atajo; **~en** vt acortar; (visit) interrumpir; **~hand** n taquigrafía; **~hand typist** n taquimecanógrafo/a; **~list** n (for job) lista de candidatos escogidos; **~-lived** a efímero; **~ly** ad en breve, dentro de poco; **~ness** n (of distance) cortedad f, (of time) brevedad f; (manner) brusquedad f; **~-sighted** a corto de vista, miope; (fig) imprudente; **~ story** n cuento; **~-tempered** a enojadizo; **~term** a (effect) a corto plazo; **~wave** n (RADIO) onda corta.

shot [ʃɔt] pt, pp of shoot // n (sound) tiro, disparo; (person) tirador/a m/f; (try) tentativa; (injection) inyección f; (PHOT) toma, fotografía; **~gun** n escopeta.

should [ʃud] auxiliary vb: **I ~ go now** debo irme ahora; **he ~ be there now** debe de haber llegado (ya); **I ~ go if I were you** yo en tu lugar me iría; **I ~ like to** me gustaría.

shoulder [ˈʃəuldə*] n hombro; (of road): **hard ~** andén m // vt (fig) cargar con; **~ blade** n omóplato.

shouldn't [ˈʃudnt] = should not.

shout [ʃaut] n grito // vt gritar // vi gritar, dar voces; **to ~ down** vt hundir a gritos; **~ing** n gritería.

shove [ʃʌv] n empujón m // vt empujar; (col: put): **to ~ sth in** meter algo; **to ~ off** vi (NAUT) alejarse del muelle; (fig: col) largarse.

shovel [ˈʃʌvl] n pala; (mechanical) excavadora // vt mover con pala.

show [ʃəu] n (of emotion) demostración f; (semblance) apariencia; (exhibition) exposición f; (THEATRE) función f, espectáculo // (vb: pt showed, pp shown) vt mostrar, enseñar; (courage etc) mostrar, manifestar; (exhibit) exponer; (film) proyectar // vi mostrarse; (appear) aparecer; **to ~ sb in** hacer pasar a uno; **to ~ off** vi (pej) presumir // vt (display) lucir; (pej) hacer gala de; **to ~ sb out** acompañar a uno a la puerta; **to ~ up** vi (stand out) destacar; (col: turn up) presentarse // vt descubrir; (unmask) desenmascarar; **~ business** n el mundo del espectáculo; **~down** n crisis f, momento decisivo.

shower [ˈʃauə*] n (rain) chaparrón m, chubasco; (of stones etc) lluvia; (also: **~bath**) ducha // vi llover // vt: **to ~ sb with sth** colmar a uno de algo; **~proof** a impermeable; **~y** a (weather) lluvioso.

showing [ˈʃəuiŋ] n (of film) proyección f.

show jumping [ˈʃəudʒʌmpiŋ] n hipismo.

shown [ʃəun] pp of show.

show: **~-off** n (col: person) presumido; **~piece** n (of exhibition etc) obra más importante o central; **~room** n sala de muestras.

shrank [ʃræŋk] pt of shrink.

shrapnel [ˈʃræpnl] n metralla.

shred [ʃred] n (gen pl) triza, jirón m // vt hacer trizas; (CULIN) desmenuzar.

shrewd [ʃruːd] a astuto; **~ness** n astucia.

shriek [ʃriːk] n chillido // vt, vi chillar.

shrill [ʃril] a agudo, estridente.

shrimp [ʃrimp] n camarón m.

shrine [ʃrain] n santuario, sepulcro.

shrink [ʃriŋk], pt **shrank**, pp **shrunk** vi encogerse; (be reduced) reducirse // vt encoger; **to ~ from doing sth** no atreverse a hacer algo; **~age** n encogimiento; reducción f.

shrivel [ˈʃrivl] (also: **~ up**) vt (dry) secar; (crease) arrugar // vi secarse; arrugarse.

shroud [ʃraud] n sudario // vt: **~ed in mystery** envuelto en el misterio.

Shrove Tuesday [ˈʃrəuvˈtjuːzdi] n martes m de carnaval.

shrub [ʃrʌb] n arbusto; **~bery** n arbustos mpl.

shrug [ʃrʌg] n encogimiento de hombros // vt, vi: **to ~ (one's shoulders)** encogerse de hombros; **to ~ off** vt negar importancia a.

shrunk [ʃrʌŋk] pp of shrink.

shudder [ˈʃʌdə*] n estremecimiento, escalofrío // vi estremecerse.

shuffle [ˈʃʌfl] vt (cards) barajar; **to ~ (one's feet)** arrastrar los pies.

shun [ʃʌn] vt rehuir, esquivar.

shunt [ʃʌnt] vt (RAIL) maniobrar // vi: **to ~ to and fro** mandar de aquí para allá.

shut [ʃʌt], pt, pp **shut** vt cerrar // vi cerrarse; **to ~ down** vt, vi cerrarse, parar; **to ~ off** vt (supply etc) interrumpir, cortar; **to ~ up** vi (col: keep quiet) callarse // vt (close) cerrar; (silence) callar; **~ter** n contraventana; (PHOT) obturador m.

shuttle [ˈʃʌtl] n lanzadera; (also: **~ service**) servicio de transporte entre dos estaciones.

shuttlecock [ˈʃʌtlkɔk] n volante m.

shy [ʃai] a tímido; (reserved) reservado, cohibido; (unsociable) huraño; **~ness** n timidez f; reserva; lo huraño.

Siamese [saiəˈmiːz] a: **~ cat** gato siamés.

Sicily [ˈsisili] n Sicilia.

sick [sik] a (ill) enfermo; (nauseated) mareado; (humour) negro; (vomiting): **to be ~** vomitar; **to feel ~** estar mareado; **to be ~ of** (fig) estar harto de; **~ bay** n enfermería; **~en** vt dar asco a // vi enfermar; **~ening** a (fig) asqueroso.

sickle [ˈsikl] n hoz f.

sick: **~ leave** n baja por enfermedad; **~ly** a enfermizo; (causing nausea) nauseabundo; **~ness** n enfermedad f, mal m; (vomiting) náuseas fpl; **~ pay** n subsidio de enfermedad.

side [said] n (gen) lado; (of body) costado; (of lake) orilla; (aspect) aspecto; (team) equipo; (of hill) ladera // a (door, entrance) accesorio // vi: **to ~ with sb** tomar el partido de uno; **by the ~ of** al lado de; **~ by ~** juntos(as), lado a lado; **from all ~s** de todos lados; **to take ~s (with)**

tomar partido (con); ~**board** n aparador m; ~**boards**, ~**burns** npl patillas fpl; ~**effect** n efecto secundario; ~**light** n (AUT) luz f lateral; ~**line** n (SPORT) línea lateral; (fig) empleo suplementario; ~**long** a de soslayo; ~ **road** n calle f lateral; ~**saddle** ad a mujeriegas, a la inglesa; ~ **show** n (stall) caseta; (fig) atracción f secundaria; ~**step** vt (fig) esquivar; ~**track** vt (fig) desviar (de su propósito); ~**walk** n (US) acera; ~**ways** ad de lado.

siding ['saɪdɪŋ] n (RAIL) apartadero, vía muerta.

sidle ['saɪdl] vi: **to ~ up (to)** acercarse furtivamente (a).

siege [siːdʒ] n cerco, sitio.

sieve [sɪv] n coladera // vt cribar.

sift [sɪft] vt cribar; (fig: information) escudriñar.

sigh [saɪ] n suspiro // vi suspirar.

sight [saɪt] n (faculty) vista, visión f; (spectacle) espectáculo; (on gun) mira, alza // vt ver, divisar; **in ~** a la vista; **out of ~** fuera de (la) vista; ~**seeing** n excursionismo, turismo; **to go ~seeing** visitar monumentos.

sign [saɪn] n (with hand) señal f, seña; (indication) indicio; (trace) huella, rastro; (notice) letrero; (written) signo // vt firmar; **to ~ sth over to sb** firmar el traspaso de algo a uno; **to ~ up** vi (MIL) alistarse // vt (contract) contratar.

signal ['sɪgnl] n señal f // vi (AUT) señalizar // vt (person) hacer señas a uno; (message) transmitir.

signature ['sɪgnətʃə*] n firma.

signet ring ['sɪgnətrɪŋ] n anillo de sello.

significance [sɪg'nɪfɪkəns] n significado; (importance) trascendencia; **significant** [-ənt] a significativo; trascendente.

signify ['sɪgnɪfaɪ] vt significar.

sign: ~ **language** n la mímica, lenguaje m por señas o de señas; ~**post** n indicador m.

silence ['saɪlns] n silencio // vt hacer callar; (guns) reducir al silencio; **silencer** n (on gun, AUT) silenciador n.

silent ['saɪlnt] a (gen) silencioso; (not speaking) callado; (film) mudo; **to remain ~** guardar silencio.

silhouette [sɪlu'ɛt] n silueta; ~**d against** destacado sobre o contra.

silicon chip ['sɪlɪkən'tʃɪp] n plata de silicio, astilla de silicona.

silk [sɪlk] n seda // a de seda; ~**y** a sedoso.

silly ['sɪlɪ] a (person) tonto; (idea) absurdo.

silt [sɪlt] n sedimento.

silver ['sɪlvə*] n plata; (money) moneda suelta // a de plata, plateado; ~ **paper** n papel m de plata; ~-**plated** a plateado; ~**smith** n platero; ~**y** a plateado.

similar ['sɪmɪlə*] a: ~ **to** parecido o semejante a; ~**ity** [-'lærɪtɪ] n parecido, semejanza; ~**ly** ad del mismo modo.

simmer ['sɪmə*] vi hervir a fuego lento.

simpering ['sɪmpərɪŋ] a afectado; (foolish) bobo.

simple ['sɪmpl] a (easy) sencillo; (foolish, COMM) simple; ~ **ton** n inocentón/ona m/f; **simplicity** [-'plɪsɪtɪ] n sencillez f; (foolishness) ingenuidad f; **simplify** ['sɪmplɪfaɪ] vt simplificar.

simulate ['sɪmjuleɪt] vt simular; **simulation** [-'leɪʃən] n simulación f.

simultaneous [sɪməl'teɪnɪəs] a simultáneo; ~**ly** ad simultáneamente.

sin [sɪn] n pecado // vi pecar.

since [sɪns] ad desde entonces, después // prep desde // conj (time) desde que; (because) ya que, puesto que; ~ **then** desde entonces.

sincere [sɪn'sɪə*] a sincero; **yours** ~**ly** le saluda (afectuosamente); **sincerity** [-'sɛrɪtɪ] n sinceridad f.

sinful ['sɪnful] a (thought) pecaminoso; (person) pecador(a).

sing [sɪŋ], pt **sang**, pp **sung** vt cantar // vi (gen) cantar; (bird) trinar; (ears) zumbar.

singe [sɪndʒ] vt chamuscar.

singer ['sɪŋə*] n cantante m/f.

singing ['sɪŋɪŋ] n (gen) canto; (songs) canciones fpl; (in the ears) zumbido.

single ['sɪŋgl] a único, solo; (unmarried) soltero; (not double) simple, sencillo; (bed, room) individual // n (also: ~ **ticket**) billete m sencillo; (record) single m; ~**s** npl (TENNIS) individual m; **to ~ out** vt (choose) escoger; (point out) singularizar; ~ **bed** n cama individual; **in ~ file** en fila de uno; ~-**handed** ad sin ayuda; ~-**minded** a resuelto, firme; ~ **room** n cuarto individual.

singular ['sɪŋgjulə*] a (odd) raro, extraño; (LING) singular // n (LING) singular m.

sinister ['sɪnɪstə*] a siniestro.

sink [sɪŋk] n fregadero // (vb: pt **sank**, pp **sunk**) vt (ship) hundir, echar a pique; (foundations) excavar; (piles etc): **to ~ sth** fijar algo bajo tierra // vi (gen) hundirse; **to ~ in** vi (fig) penetrar, calar; **a ~ing feeling** un sentimiento de que toda se acaba.

sinner ['sɪnə*] n pecador/a m/f.

sinus ['saɪnəs] n (ANAT) seno.

sip [sɪp] n sorbo // vt sorber, beber a sorbitos.

siphon ['saɪfən] n sifón m; **to ~ off** vt quitar poco a poco.

sir [sə*] n señor m; **S~ John Smith** el Señor John Smith; **yes ~** sí, señor.

siren ['saɪərn] n sirena.

sirloin ['sɜːlɔɪn] n solomillo.

sister ['sɪstə*] n hermana; (nurse) enfermera jefe; ~-**in-law** n cuñada.

sit [sɪt], pt, pp **sat** vi sentarse; (be sitting) estar sentado; (assembly) reunirse // vt (exam) presentarse a; **to ~ down** vi sentarse; **to ~ in on** asistir a; **to ~ up** vi incorporarse; (not go to bed) velar.

site [saɪt] n sitio; (also: **building ~**) solar m // vt situar.

sit-in ['sɪtɪn] n (demonstration)

manifestación f de brazos caídos.

sitting ['sɪtɪŋ] n (of assembly etc) sesión f; (in canteen) turno; ~ **room** n sala de estar.

situated ['sɪtjueɪtɪd] a situado.

situation [sɪtju'eɪʃən] n situación f.

six [sɪks] num seis; ~ **teen** num diez y seis, dieciséis; ~ **th** a sexto; ~ **ty** num sesenta.

size [saɪz] n (gen) tamaño; (extent) extensión f; (of clothing) talla; (of shoes) número; (glue) cola, apresto; **to ~ up** vt formarse una idea de; ~ **able** a importante, considerable.

sizzle ['sɪzl] vi crepitar.

skate [skeɪt] n patín m; (fish: pl inv) raya // vi patinar; ~ **board** n skateboard m; **skater** n patinador/a m/f; **skating** n patinaje m; **skating rink** n pista de patinaje.

skeleton ['skɛlɪtn] n esqueleto; (TECH) armazón m; (outline) esquema m; ~ **key** n llave f maestra; ~ **staff** n personal m reducido.

sketch [skɛtʃ] n (drawing) dibujo; (outline) esbozo, bosquejo; (THEATRE) pieza corta // vt dibujar; esbozar; ~ **book** n libro de dibujos; ~ **pad** n bloc m de dibujo; ~ **y** a incompleto.

skewer ['skju:ə*] n broqueta.

ski [ski:] n esquí m // vi esquiar; ~ **boot** n bota de esquí.

skid [skɪd] n patinazo // vi patinar; ~ **mark** n huella de patinazo.

ski: ~ **er** n esquiador/a m/f; ~ **ing** n esquí m; ~ **jump** n pista para salto de esquí.

skilful ['skɪlful] a diestro, experto.

ski lift n telesilla.

skill [skɪl] n destreza, pericia; ~ **ed** a hábil, diestro; (worker) cualificado.

skim [skɪm] vt (milk) desnatar; (glide over) rozar, rasar // vi: **to ~ through** (book) hojear.

skimp [skɪmp] vt (work) chapucear; (cloth etc) escatimar; ~ **y** a (meagre) escaso; (skirt) muy corto.

skin [skɪn] n (gen) piel f; (complexion) cutis m // vt (fruit etc) pelar; (animal) despellejar; ~ **deep** a superficial; ~ **diving** n natación f submarina; ~ **ny** a flaco, magro; ~ **tight** a (dress etc) muy ajustado.

skip [skɪp] n brinco, salto; (container) cuba // vi brincar; (with rope) saltar a la comba // vt (pass over) omitir, saltar.

ski pants npl pantalones mpl de esquí.

skipper ['skɪpə*] n (NAUT, SPORT) capitán m.

skipping rope ['skɪpɪŋ-] n cuerda (de saltar).

skirmish ['skə:mɪʃ] n escaramuza.

skirt [skə:t] n falda // vt (surround) ceñir, rodear; (go round) ladear; ~ **ing board** n rodapié m.

skit [skɪt] n sátira, parodia.

skittle ['skɪtl] n bolo; ~ **s** n (game) boliche m.

skive [skaɪv] vi (Brit: col) gandulear.

skull [skʌl] n calavera; (ANAT) cráneo.

skunk [skʌŋk] n mofeta; (fig: person) canalla m/f.

sky [skaɪ] n cielo; ~ **blue** a azul celeste; ~ **light** n tragaluz m, claraboya; ~ **scraper** n rascacielos m inv.

slab [slæb] n (stone) bloque m; (flat) losa; (of cake) porción f gruesa.

slack [slæk] a (loose) flojo; (slow) de poca actividad; (careless) descuidado; ~ **s** npl pantalones mpl; ~ **en** (also: ~ **en off**) vi aflojarse // vt aflojar; (speed) disminuir.

slag [slæg] n escoria, escombros mpl; ~ **heap** n escorial m, escombrera.

slalom ['slɑ:ləm] n slalom m.

slam [slæm] vt (door) cerrar de golpe; (throw) arrojar (violentamente); (criticize) hablar mal de // vi cerrarse de golpe.

slander ['slɑ:ndə*] n calumnia, difamación f // vt calumniar, difamar; ~ **ous** a calumnioso, difamatorio.

slang [slæŋ] n argot m; (jargon) jerga; (private language) caló.

slant [slɑ:nt] n sesgo, inclinación f; (fig) punto de vista; ~ **ed**, ~ **ing** a inclinado.

slap [slæp] n palmada; (in face) bofetada; (fig) palmetazo // vt dar una palmada/bofetada a // ad (directly) exactamente, directamente; ~ **dash** a descuidado; ~ **stick** n (comedy) payasadas fpl.

slash [slæʃ] vt acuchillar; (fig: prices) quemar.

slate [sleɪt] n pizarra // vt (fig: criticize) criticar duramente.

slaughter ['slɔ:tə*] n (of animals) matanza; (of people) carnicería // vt matar; ~ **house** n matadero.

Slav [slɑ:v] a eslavo.

slave [sleɪv] n esclavo // vi (also: ~ **away**) sudar tinta; ~ **ry** n esclavitud f; **slavish** a servil.

Slavonic [slə'vɒnɪk] a eslavo.

slay [sleɪ] vt matar.

sleazy ['sli:zɪ] a (fig: place) de mala fama.

sledge [slɛdʒ] n trineo; ~ **hammer** n mazo.

sleek [sli:k] a (gen) lustroso; (neat) pulcro.

sleep [sli:p] n sueño // vi, pt, pp **slept** dormir; **to go to ~** dormirse; **to ~ in** vi (oversleep) dormir tarde; ~ **er** n (person) durmiente m/f; (RAIL: on track) traviesa; (: train) coche-cama m; ~ **ily** ad soñolientamente; ~ **ing bag** n saco de dormir; ~ **ing car** n coche-cama m; ~ **ing pill** n somnífero; ~ **lessness** n insomnio; ~ **walker** n sonámbulo/a; ~ **y** a soñoliento.

sleet [sli:t] n nevisca.

sleeve [sli:v] n manga; (TECH) manguito; ~ **less** a (garment) sin mangas.

sleigh [sleɪ] n trineo.

sleight [slaɪt] n: ~ **of hand** escamoteo.

slender ['slɛndə*] a delgado; (means) escaso.

slept [slɛpt] pt, pp of **sleep.**

slice [slaɪs] n (of meat) tajada; (of bread)

rebanada; (of lemon) rodaja; (utensil) pala // vt cortar, tajar; rebanar.

slick [slɪk] a (skilful) hábil, diestro; (quick) rápido; (astute) astuto // n (also: **oil ~**) masa flotante.

slid [slɪd] pt, pp of **slide**.

slide [slaɪd] n (in playground) tobogán m; (PHOT) diapositiva; (also: **hair ~**) pasador m // (vb: pt, pp **slid**) vt correr, deslizar // vi (slip) resbalarse; (glide) deslizarse; **sliding** a (door) corredizo.

slight [slaɪt] a (slim) delgado; (frail) delicado; (pain etc) leve; (trifling) sin importancia; (small) pequeño // n desaire m // vt (offend) ofender, desairar; **not in the ~est** (ni) en lo más mínimo, en absoluto; **~ly** ad ligeramente, un poco.

slim [slɪm] a delgado, esbelto // vi adelgazar.

slime [slaɪm] n limo, cieno; **slimy** a limoso.

slimming [ˈslɪmɪŋ] n adelgazamiento; a **~ diet** un régimen.

sling [slɪŋ] n (MED) cabestrillo; (weapon) honda // vt, pt, pp **slung** tirar, arrojar.

slip [slɪp] n (slide) resbalón m; (fall) tropezón m; (mistake) descuido; (underskirt) combinación f; (of paper) trozo // vt (slide) deslizar // vi (slide) deslizarse; (stumble) resbalar(se); (decline) decaer; **to give sb the ~** eludir o escaparse de uno; **to ~ away** vi escabullirse; **to ~ in** vt meter // vi meterse; **to ~ out** vi (go out) salir (un momento).

slipper [ˈslɪpə*] n zapatilla.

slippery [ˈslɪpərɪ] a resbaladizo.

slip: ~ road n carretera de acceso; **~shod** a descuidado; **~up** n (error) equivocación f; (by neglect) descuido; **~way** n grada, gradas fpl.

slit [slɪt] n raja; (cut) corte m // vt, pt, pp **slit** rajar, cortar.

slither [ˈslɪðə*] vi deslizarse.

slob [slɔb] n (col) patán m.

slog [slɔg] vi sudar tinta; **it was a ~** costó trabajo (hacerlo).

slogan [ˈsləʊgən] n slogan m, lema m.

slop [slɔp] vi (also: **~ over**) derramarse, desbordarse // vt derramar, verter.

slope [sləʊp] n (up) cuesta, pendiente m; (down) declive m; (side of mountain) falda, vertiente m // vi: **to ~ down** estar en declive; **to ~ up** inclinarse; **sloping** a en pendiente; en declive.

sloppy [ˈslɔpɪ] a (work) descuidado; (appearance) desaliñado.

slot [slɔt] n ranura // vt: **to ~ into** encajar en; **~ machine** n máquina tragaperras.

slouch [slaʊtʃ] vi: **to ~ about** (laze) gandulear.

slovenly [ˈslʌvənlɪ] a (dirty) desaliñado, desaseado; (careless) descuidado.

slow [sləʊ] a lento; (watch): **to be ~** atrasarse // ad lentamente, despacio // vi (also: **~ down, ~ up**) retardar; **'~'** (road sign) 'disminuir velocidad'; **~ly** ad

lentamente, despacio; **in ~ motion** a cámara lenta; **~ness** n lentitud f.

sludge [slʌdʒ] n lodo, fango.

slug [slʌg] n babosa; (bullet) posta; **~gish** a (slow) lento; (lazy) perezoso.

sluice [slu:s] n (gate) esclusa; (channel) canal m.

slum [slʌm] n (area) tugurios mpl; (house) casucha.

slumber [ˈslʌmbə*] n sueño.

slump [slʌmp] n (economic) depresión f // vi hundirse.

slung [slʌŋ] pt, pp of **sling**.

slur [slɜ:*] n calumnia // vt calumniar, difamar; (word) pronunciar indistintamente.

slush [slʌʃ] n nieve f a medio derretir; **~y** a (snow) a medio derretir; (street) fangoso; (fig) sentimental, sensiblero.

slut [slʌt] n marrana.

sly [slaɪ] a (clever) astuto; (nasty) malicioso.

smack [smæk] n (slap) manotada; (blow) golpe m // vt dar una manotada a, golpear con la mano // vi: **to ~ of** saber a, oler a.

small [smɔ:l] a pequeño; **~holder** n granjero, parcelero; **~ish** a más bien pequeño; **~pox** n viruela; **~ talk** n cháchara.

smart [smɑ:t] a elegante; (clever) listo, inteligente; (quick) rápido, vivo // vi escocer, picar; **to ~en up** vi arreglarse // vt arreglar.

smash [smæʃ] n (also: **~-up**) choque m // vt (break) hacer pedazos; (car etc) estrellar; (SPORT: record) romper // vi (collide) chocar; (against wall etc) estrellarse; **~ing** a (col) cojonudo.

smattering [ˈsmætərɪŋ] n: **a ~ of** ligeros conocimientos mpl.

smear [smɪə*] n mancha; (MED) citología // vt untar; (fig) calumniar, difamar.

smell [smel] n olor m; (sense) olfato // (vb: pt, pp **smelt** or **smelled**) vt, vi oler; **it ~s good/of garlic** huele bien/a ajo; **~y** a que huele mal.

smile [smaɪl] n sonrisa // vi sonreír; **smiling** a sonriente.

smirk [smɜ:k] n sonrisa falsa o afectada.

smith [smɪθ] n herrero; **~y** [ˈsmɪðɪ] n herrería.

smock [smɔk] n blusa; (children's) delantal m.

smoke [sməʊk] n humo // vi fumar; (chimney) echar humo // vt (cigarettes) fumar; **~d** a (bacon, glass) ahumado; **smoker** n (person) fumador/a m/f; (RAIL) coche m fumador; **~ screen** n cortina de humo; **smoking** n: **'no smoking'** (sign) 'prohibido fumar'; **smoky** a (gen) humeante; (room) lleno de humo.

smooth [smu:ð] a (gen) liso; (sea) tranquilo; (flat) llano; (flavour, movement) suave; (person) culto, refinado; (: pej) meloso // vt alisar; (also: **~ out**) (creases, difficulties) allanar.

smother ['smʌðə*] vt sofocar; (repress) ahogar.

smoulder ['sməuldə*] vi arder sin llama.

smudge [smʌdʒ] n mancha // vt manchar.

smug [smʌg] a presumido.

smuggle ['smʌgl] vt pasar de contrabando; **smuggler** n contrabandista m/f; **smuggling** n contrabando.

smutty ['smʌti] a (fig) verde, obsceno.

snack [snæk] n bocado; ~ **bar** n cafetería.

snag [snæg] n dificultad f, pero:

snail [sneil] n caracol m.

snake [sneik] n (gen) serpiente f; (harmless) culebra; (poisonous) víbora.

snap [snæp] n (sound) castañetazo; (of whip) chasquido; (click) golpe m seco; (photograph) foto f // a repentino // vt (fingers etc) castañetear; (whip) chasquear; (break) quebrar; (photograph) tomar una foto de // vi (break) quebrarse; (fig: person) contestar bruscamente; (sound) hacer un ruido seco; **to ~ shut** cerrarse de golpe; **to ~ at** vt fus (subj: dog) intentar morder; **to ~ off** vi (break) romperse y quebrar; **to ~ up** vt aprovecharse de, agarrar; ~**shot** n foto f (instantánea).

snare [snɛə*] n trampa // vt cazar con trampa; (fig) engañar.

snarl [snɑːl] n gruñido // vi gruñir.

snatch [snætʃ] n (fig) robo; (small amount): ~**es of** trocitos mpl de // vt (~ away) arrebatar; (grasp) coger, agarrar.

sneak [sniːk] vi: **to ~ in/out** entrar/salir a hurtadillas // n (fam) soplón/ona m/f; ~**y** a furtivo.

sneer [snɪə*] n sonrisa de desprecio // vi sonreír con desprecio; (mock) mofarse.

sneeze [sniːz] n estornudo // vi estornudar.

sniff [snɪf] n (of dog) husmeo; (of person) sorbo (por las narices) // vi sorber (por la nariz) // vt husmear, oler.

snigger ['snɪgə*] n risa disimulada // vi reírse con disimulo.

snip [snɪp] n tijeretazo; (piece) recorte m; (bargain) ganga // vt tijeretear.

sniper ['snaipə*] n francotirador/a m/f.

snippet ['snɪpɪt] n retazo.

snivelling ['snɪvlɪŋ] a (whimpering) llorón(ona).

snob [snɔb] n snob m/f; ~**bery** n snobismo; ~**bish** a snob.

snooker ['snuːkə*] n especie de billar.

snoop [snuːp] vi: **to ~ about** fisgonear; ~**er** n fisgón/ona m/f.

snooty ['snuːtɪ] a presumido.

snooze [snuːz] n siesta // vi echar una siesta.

snore [snɔː*] vi roncar // n ronquido.

snorkel ['snɔːkl] n tubo snorkel.

snort [snɔːt] n bufido // vi bufar.

snout [snaut] n hocico, morro.

snow [snəu] n nieve f // vi nevar; ~**ball** n bola de nieve // vi acumularse; ~**bound** a bloqueado por la nieve; ~**drift** n ventisquero; ~**drop** n campanilla; ~**fall** n nevada; ~**flake** n copo de nieve; ~**man** n figura de nieve; ~**plough**, ~**plow** (US) n quitanieves m inv; ~**storm** n nevada, nevasca; **S~ White** n Blanca Nieves.

snub [snʌb] vt rechazar con desdén // n desaire m, repulsa.

snuff [snʌf] n rapé m.

snug [snʌg] a (sheltered) abrigado; (fitted) ajustado.

snuggle ['snʌgl] vi: **to ~ up to sb** arrimarse a uno.

so [səu] ad (degree) tan; (manner: thus) así, de este modo // conj así que, por tanto; ~ **that** (purpose) para que, a fin de que; (result) de modo que; ~ **do I** yo también; **if ~** de ser así, si es así; **I hope ~** espero que sí; **10 or ~** 10 más o menos; ~ **far** hasta aquí; ~ **long!** ¡hasta luego!; ~ **many** tantos(as); ~ **much** ad, det tanto; ~ **and ~** n Fulano.

soak [səuk] vt (drench) empapar; (put in water) remojar // vi remojarse, estar a remojo; **to ~ in** vi penetrar; **to ~ up** vt absorber.

soap [səup] n jabón m; ~**flakes** npl escamas fpl de jabón; ~ **powder** n jabón en polvo; ~**y** a jabonoso.

soar [sɔː*] vi (on wings) remontarse; (building etc) elevarse.

sob [sɔb] n sollozo // vi sollozar.

sober ['səubə*] a (serious) serio; (sensible) sensato; (moderate) moderado; (not drunk) sobrio; (colour, style) discreto; **to ~ up** vi pasársele a uno la borrachera.

Soc. abbr of **society**.

so-called ['səu'kɔːld] a llamado.

soccer ['sɔkə*] n fútbol m.

sociable ['səuʃəbl] a sociable.

social ['səuʃl] a (gen) social; (sociable) sociable // n velada, fiesta; ~ **climber** n arribista m/f; ~ **club** n club m; ~**ism** n socialismo; ~**ist** a, n socialista m/f; ~**ly** ad socialmente; ~ **science** n ciencias fpl sociales; ~ **security** n seguridad f social; ~ **work** n asistencia social; ~ **worker** n asistente/a m/f social.

society [sə'saiəti] n sociedad f; (club) asociación f; (also: **high** ~) buena sociedad.

sociologist [səusi'ɔlədʒist] n sociólogo.

sociology [-dʒi] n sociología.

sock [sɔk] n calcetín m.

socket ['sɔkit] n (ELEC) enchufe m.

sod [sɔd] n (of earth) césped m; (col!) cabrón/ona m/f.

soda ['səudə] n (CHEM) sosa; (also: ~ **water**) sifón m.

sodden ['sɔdn] a empapado.

sodium ['səudiəm] n sodio.

sofa ['səufə] n sofá m.

soft [sɔft] a (gen) blando; (gentle, not loud) suave; (kind) tierno, compasivo; (weak) débil; (stupid) tonto; ~ **drink** n bebida no alcohólica; ~**en** ['sɔfn] vt ablandar; suavizar; debilitar // vi ablandarse; suavizarse; debilitarse; ~**-hearted** a

compasivo, bondadoso; ∼**ly** *ad*
suavemente; (*gently*) delicadamente, con
delicadeza; ∼**ness** *n* blandura; suavidad *f*;
(*sweetness*) dulzura; (*tenderness*) ternura.

soggy ['sɔgɪ] *a* empapado.

soil [sɔɪl] *n* (*earth*) tierra, suelo // *vt*
ensuciar; ∼**ed** *a* sucio.

solace ['sɔlɪs] *n* consuelo.

solar ['sɔulə*] *a* solar.

sold [sɔuld] *pt, pp* of **sell**; ∼ **out** (*COMM*)
agotado.

solder ['sɔuldə*] *vt* soldar // *n* soldadura.

soldier ['sɔuldʒə*] *n* (*gen*) soldado; (*army
man*) militar *m*.

sole [sɔul] *n* (*of foot*) planta; (*of shoe*) suela;
(*fish: pl inv*) lenguado // *a* único; ∼**ly** *ad*
únicamente, sólo, solamente.

solemn ['sɔləm] *a* solemne.

solicitor [sə'lɪsɪtə*] *n* (*for wills etc*)
notario; (*in court*) abogado.

solid ['sɔlɪd] *a* (*not hollow*) sólido; (*gold etc*)
macizo; (*person*) serio // *n* sólido.

solidarity [sɔlɪ'dærɪtɪ] *n* solidaridad *f*.

solidify [sə'lɪdɪfaɪ] *vi* solidificarse.

solitaire [sɔlɪ'tɛə*] *n* (*game, gem*)
solitario.

solitary ['sɔlɪtərɪ] *a* solitario, solo;
(*isolated*) apartado, aislado; (*only*) único;
∼ **confinement** *n* incomunicación *f*.

solitude ['sɔlɪtjuːd] *n* soledad *f*.

solo ['sɔuləu] *n* solo; ∼**ist** *n* solista *m/f*.

soluble ['sɔljubl] *a* soluble.

solution [sə'luːʃən] *n* solución *f*.

solve [sɔlv] *vt* resolver, solucionar.

solvent ['sɔlvənt] *a* (*COMM*) solvente // *n*
(*CHEM*) solvente *m*.

sombre, somber (*US*) ['sɔmbə*] *a*
sombrío.

some [sʌm] *det* (*a few*) algunos(as);
(*certain*) algún/una; (*a certain number or
amount*) *see phrases below*; (*unspecified*)
algo de // *pron* algunos/as; (*a bit*) algo //
ad: ∼ **10 people** unas 10 personas; ∼
children came vinieron algunos niños;
have ∼ **tea** tome té; **there's** ∼ **milk in
the fridge** hay leche en la refrigeradora; ∼
was left quedaba algo; **I've got** ∼
(*books etc*) tengo algunos; (*milk, money
etc*) tengo algo; ∼**body** *pron* alguien; ∼
day *ad* algún día; ∼**how** *ad* de alguna
manera; (*for some reason*) por una u otra
razón; ∼**one** *pron* = ∼**body**.

somersault ['sʌməsɔːlt] *n* (*deliberate*)
salto mortal; (*accidental*) vuelco // *vi* dar
un salto mortal; dar vuelcos.

something ['sʌmθɪŋ] *pron* algo.

sometime ['sʌmtaɪm] *ad* (*in future*) algún
día, en algún momento; (*in past*): ∼ **last
month** durante el mes pasado.

sometimes ['sʌmtaɪmz] *ad* a veces.

somewhat ['sʌmwɔt] *ad* algo.

somewhere ['sʌmwɛə*] *ad* (*be*) en alguna
parte; (*go*) a alguna parte; ∼ **else** (*be*) en
otra parte; (*go*) a otra parte.

son [sʌn] *n* hijo.

song [sɔŋ] *n* canción *f*; ∼**writer** *n*

compositor/a *m/f* de canciones.

sonic ['sɔnɪk] *a* (*boom*) sónico.

son-in-law ['sʌnɪnlɔː] *n* yerno.

sonnet ['sɔnɪt] *n* soneto.

soon [suːn] *ad* pronto, dentro de poco;
(*early*) temprano; ∼ **afterwards** poco
después; *see also* **as**; ∼**er** *ad* (*time*) antes,
más temprano; (*preference*): **I would
∼er do that** preferiría hacer eso; ∼**er
or later** tarde o temprano.

soot [sut] *n* hollín *m*.

soothe [suːð] *vt* tranquilizar; (*pain*) aliviar.

sophisticated [sə'fɪstɪkeɪtɪd] *a* sofisticado.

soporific [sɔpə'rɪfɪk] *a* soporífero.

sopping ['sɔpɪŋ] *a*: ∼ **wet** totalmente
empapado.

soppy ['sɔpɪ] *a* (*pej*) bobo, tonto.

soprano [sə'prɑːnəu] *n* soprano *f*.

sorcerer ['sɔːsərə*] *n* hechicero.

sordid ['sɔːdɪd] *a* (*dirty*) sucio, asqueroso;
(*wretched*) miserable.

sore [sɔː*] *a* (*painful*) doloroso, que duele;
(*offended*) resentido // *n* llaga; ∼**ly** *ad*: **I
am** ∼**ly tempted** casi estoy por.

sorrow ['sɔrəu] *n* pena, dolor *m*; ∼**ful** *a*
afligido, triste.

sorry ['sɔrɪ] *a* (*regretful*) arrepentido;
(*condition, excuse*) lastimoso; ∼**!** ¡lo
siento!, ¡perdón!, ¡perdone! **to feel** ∼ **for
sb** sentir lástima por uno; **I feel** ∼ **for
him** me da lástima.

sort [sɔːt] *n* clase *f*, género, tipo // *vt* (*also:
∼ **out**: *papers*) clasificar; (: *problems*)
arreglar, solucionar; ∼**ing office** *n*
oficina de distribución de correos.

SOS *n abbr of* **save our souls.**

so-so ['səusəu] *ad* regular, así-así.

soufflé ['suːfleɪ] *n* suflé *m*.

sought [sɔːt] *pt, pp* of **seek.**

soul [sɔul] *n* alma *m*; ∼**destroying** *a*
embrutecedor(a); ∼**ful** *a* lleno de
sentimiento; ∼**less** *a* desalmado.

sound [saund] *a* (*healthy*) sano; (*safe, not
damaged*) firme, sólido; (*secure*) seguro;
(*reliable, not superficial*) formal, digno de
confianza; (*sensible*) sensato, razonable //
ad: ∼ **asleep** profundamente dormido //
n (*noise*) sonido, ruido; (*GEO*) estrecho //
vt (*alarm*) sonar; (*also:* ∼ **out**: *opinions*)
consultar, sondear // *vi* sonar, resonar;
(*fig: seem*) parecer; **to** ∼ **like sonar a**; ∼
barrier *n* barrera del sonido; ∼ **effects**
npl efectos *mpl* sonoros; ∼**ing** *n* (*NAUT etc*)
sondeo; ∼**ly** *ad* (*sleep*) profundamente;
(*beat*) completamente; ∼**proof** *a* a
prueba de sonidos; ∼**track** *n* (*of film*)
banda sonora.

soup [suːp] *n* (*thick*) sopa; (*thin*) caldo; **in
the** ∼ (*fig*) en apuros; ∼**spoon** *n* cuchara
sopera.

sour ['sauə*] *a* agrio; (*milk*) cortado; (*fig*)
desabrido, acre.

source [sɔːs] *n* fuente *f*.

south [sauθ] *n* sur *m* // *a* del sur // *ad* al
sur, hacia el sur; **S**∼ **Africa** *n* África del
Sur; **S**∼ **African** *a, n* sudafricano/a; **S**∼
America *n* América (del Sur); **S**∼

American a, n sudamericano/a; **~-east** n sudeste m; **~erly** ['sʌðəlɪ] a sur; (from the ~) del sur; **~ern** ['sʌðən] a del sur, meridional; **S~ Pole** n Polo Sur; **~ward(s)** ad hacia el sur; **~-west** n suroeste m.

souvenir [suːvəˈnɪə*] n recuerdo.

sovereign ['sɔvrɪn] a, n soberano; **~ty** n soberanía.

soviet ['səʊvɪət] a soviético; **the S~ Union** la Unión Soviética.

sow [sau] n cerda, puerca // vt [səu], pt **sowed**, pp **sown** [səun] (gen) sembrar; (spread) esparcir.

soy [sɔɪ] n: ~ **sauce** salsa de soja.

soya bean ['sɔɪəbiːn] n semilla de soja.

spa [spɑː] n (spring) baños mpl térmicos; (town) balneario.

space [speɪs] n (gen) espacio; (room) sitio // vt (also: ~ **out**) espaciar; **~craft** n nave f espacial; **~man/woman** n astronauta m/f, cosmonauta m/f; **spacing** n espaciamiento.

spacious ['speɪʃəs] a amplio.

spade [speɪd] n (tool) pala, laya; **~s** npl (CARDS: British) picos mpl; (: Spanish) espadas fpl.

spaghetti [spə'gɛtɪ] n espaguetis mpl, fideos mpl.

Spain [speɪn] n España.

span [spæn] n (of bird, plane) envergadura; (of hand) palmo; (of arch) luz f; (in time) lapso // vt extenderse sobre, cruzar; (fig) abarcar.

Spaniard ['spænjəd] n español/a m/f.

spaniel ['spænjəl] n perro de aguas.

Spanish ['spænɪʃ] a español(a) // n (LING) español m, castellano.

spank [spæŋk] vt zurrar.

spanner ['spænə*] n llave f (inglesa).

spar [spɑː*] n palo, verga // vi (BOXING) entrenarse.

spare [spɛə*] a (free) desocupado; (surplus) sobrante, de más; (available) disponible // n (part) pieza de repuesto // vt (do without) pasarse sin; (afford to give) tener de sobra; (refrain from hurting) perdonar; (be grudging with) escatimar; ~ **part** n pieza de repuesto; ~ **time** n ratos mpl de ocio, tiempo libre.

sparing ['spɛərɪŋ] a: **to be ~ with** ser parco en; **~ly** ad escasamente.

spark [spɑːk] n chispa; (fig) chispazo; **~(ing) plug** n bujía.

sparkle ['spɑːkl] n centelleo, destello // vi centellear; (shine) relucir, brillar; **sparkling** a centelleante; (wine) espumoso.

sparrow ['spærəu] n gorrión m.

sparse [spɑːs] a esparcido, escaso.

spasm ['spæzəm] n (MED) espasmo; (fig) arranque m, acceso; **~odic** [-'mɔdɪk] a espasmódico.

spastic ['spæstɪk] n espástico/a.

spat [spæt] pt, pp of **spit**.

spate [speɪt] n (fig): ~ **of** torrente m de; **in ~** (river) crecido.

spatter ['spætə*] vt salpicar, rociar.

spatula ['spætjulə] n espátula.

spawn [spɔːn] vi desovar, frezar // n huevas fpl.

speak [spiːk], pt **spoke**, pp **spoken** vt (language) hablar; (truth) decir // vi hablar; (make a speech) intervenir; **to ~ to sb/of** or **about sth** hablar con uno/de o sobre algo; ~ **up!** ¡habla fuerte!; **~er** n (in public) orador/a m/f; (also: **loud~er**) altavoz m, parlante m; (POL): **the S~er** el Presidente del Congreso.

spear [spɪə*] n lanza; (for fishing) arpón m // vt alancear; arponear; **~head** n punta de lanza.

special ['spɛʃl] a especial; (edition etc) extraordinario; (delivery) urgente; **take ~ care** ponga un cuidado especial; **~ist** n especialista m/f; **~ity** [spɛʃɪ'ælɪtɪ] n especialidad f; **~ize** vi: **to ~ize (in)** especializarse en; **~ly** ad sobre todo, en particular.

species ['spiːʃiːz] n especie f.

specific [spə'sɪfɪk] a específico; **~ally** ad específicamente.

specification [spɛsɪfɪ'keɪʃən] n especificación f; **~s** npl presupuesto; **specify** ['spɛsɪfaɪ] vt, vi especificar, precisar.

specimen ['spɛsɪmən] n ejemplar m, espécimen m.

speck [spɛk] n grano, mota.

speckled ['spɛkld] a moteado.

specs [spɛks] npl (col) gafas fpl.

spectacle ['spɛktəkl] n espectáculo; **~s** npl gafas fpl, anteojos mpl; **spectacular** [-'tækjulə*] a espectacular; (success) impresionante.

spectator [spɛk'teɪtə*] n espectador/a m/f.

spectre, specter (US) ['spɛktə*] n espectro, fantasma m.

spectrum ['spɛktrəm], pl **-tra** [-trə] n espectro.

speculate ['spɛkjuleɪt] vi especular; (try to guess): **to ~ about** especular sobre; **speculation** [-'leɪʃən] n especulación f.

speech [spiːtʃ] n (faculty) habla, palabra; (formal talk) discurso; (talk) palabras fpl; (language) idioma m, lenguaje m; **~less** a mudo, estupefacto.

speed [spiːd] n velocidad f, rapidez f; (haste) prisa; (promptness) prontitud f; **at full** or **top** ~ a máxima velocidad; **to ~ up** vi acelerarse // vt acelerar; **~boat** n lancha motora; **~ily** ad rápido, rápidamente; **~ing** n (AUT) exceso de velocidad; **~ limit** n límite m de velocidad, velocidad f máxima; **~ometer** [spɪ'dɔmɪtə*] n velocímetro; **~way** n (SPORT) carreras fpl de moto; **~y** a (fast) veloz, rápido; (prompt) pronto.

spell [spɛl] n (also: **magic ~**) encanto, hechizo; (period of time) rato, período; (turn) turno // vt, pt, pp **spelt** or **spelled** (also: ~ **out**) deletrear; (fig) anunciar, presagiar; **to cast a ~ on sb** hechizar a uno; **he can't** ~ no sabe escribir bien, sabe poco de ortografía; ~**bound** *a* embelesado, hechizado; ~**ing** *n* ortografía.

spend [spɛnd], *pt*, *pp* **spent** [spɛnt] *vt* (*money*) gastar; (*time*) pasar; (*life*) dedicar; ~**thrift** *n* derrochador/a *m/f*, pródigo/a.

sperm [spə:m] *n* esperma; ~ **whale** *n* cachalote *m*.

spew [spju:] *vt* vomitar, arrojar.

sphere [sfɪə*] *n* esfera; **spherical** ['sfɛrɪkl] *a* esférico.

sphinx [sfɪŋks] *n* esfinge *f*.

spice [spaɪs] *n* especia // *vt* especiar; **spicy** *a* especiado; (*fig*) picante.

spider ['spaɪdə*] *n* araña.

spike [spaɪk] *n* (*point*) punta; (*zool*) pincho, púa; (*bot*) espiga.

spill [spɪl], *pt*, *pp* **spilt** *or* **spilled** *vt* derramar, verter // *vi* derramarse; **to** ~ **over** desbordarse.

spin [spɪn] *n* (*revolution of wheel*) vuelta, revolución *f*; (*aviat*) barrena; (*trip in car*) paseo (en coche) // (*vb*: *pt*, *pp* **spun**) *vt* (*wool etc*) hilar; (*wheel*) girar // *vi* girar, dar vueltas; **to** ~ **out** *vt* alargar, prolongar.

spinach ['spɪnɪtʃ] *n* espinaca; (*as food*) espinacas *fpl*.

spinal ['spaɪnl] *a* espinal; ~ **cord** *n* columna vertebral.

spindly ['spɪndlɪ] *a* zanquivano.

spin-drier [spɪn'draɪə*] *n* secador *m* centrífugo.

spine [spaɪn] *n* espinazo, columna vertebral; (*thorn*) espina; ~**less** *a* (*fig*) débil, flojo.

spinning ['spɪnɪŋ] *n* (*of thread*) hilado; (*art*) hilandería; ~ **top** *n* peonza; ~ **wheel** *n* rueca, torno de hilar.

spinster ['spɪnstə*] *n* soltera; (*pej*) solterona.

spiral ['spaɪərl] *n* espiral *m* // *a* en espiral; ~ **staircase** *n* escalera de caracol.

spire ['spaɪə*] *n* aguja, chapitel *m*.

spirit ['spɪrɪt] *n* (*gen*) espíritu *m*; (*soul*) alma *m*; (*ghost*) fantasma *m*; (*humour*) humor *m*; (*courage*) valor *m*, ánimo; ~**s** *npl* (*drink*) alcohol *m*, bebidas *fpl* alcohólicas; **in good** ~**s** alegre, de buen ánimo; ~**ed** *a* enérgico, vigoroso; ~ **level** *n* nivel *m* de aire.

spiritual ['spɪrɪtjʊəl] *a* espiritual // *n* (*also*: **Negro** ~) canción *f* religiosa, espiritual *m*; ~**ism** *n* espiritualismo.

spit [spɪt] *n* (*for roasting*) asador *m*, espetón *m* // *vi*, *pt*, *pp* **spat** escupir; (*sound*) chisporrotear.

spite [spaɪt] *n* rencor *m*, ojeriza // *vt* causar pena a, mortificar; **in** ~ **of** a pesar de, pese a; ~**ful** *a* rencoroso, malévolo.

spittle ['spɪtl] *n* saliva, baba.

splash [splæʃ] *n* (*sound*) chapoteo; (*of colour*) mancha // *vt* salpicar de // *vi* (*also*: ~ **about**) chapotear.

spleen [spli:n] *n* (*anat*) bazo.

splendid ['splɛndɪd] *a* espléndido; **splendour**, **splendor** (*us*) [-də*] *n* esplendor *m*; (*of achievement*) brillo, gloria.

splint [splɪnt] *n* tablilla.

splinter ['splɪntə*] *n* (*of wood*) astilla; (*in finger*) espigón *m* // *vi* astillarse, hacer astillas.

split [splɪt] *n* hendedura, raja; (*fig*) división *f*; (*pol*) escisión *f* // (*vb*: *pt*, *pp* **split**) *vt* partir, rajar; (*party*) dividir; (*work, profits*) repartir // *vi* (*divide*) dividirse, escindirse; **to** ~ **up** *vi* (*couple*) separarse; (*meeting*) acabarse.

splutter ['splʌtə*] *vi* chisporrotear; (*person*) balbucear.

spoil [spɔɪl], *pt*, *pp* **spoilt** *or* **spoiled** *vt* (*damage*) dañar; (*mar*) estropear, echar a perder; (*child*) mimar, consentir; ~**s** *npl* despojo *sg*, botín *m*; ~**sport** *n* aguafiestas *m inv*.

spoke [spəʊk] *pt of* **speak** // *n* rayo, radio.

spoken ['spəʊkn] *pp of* **speak**.

spokesman ['spəʊksmən] *n* vocero, portavoz *m*.

sponge [spʌndʒ] *n* esponja; (*cake*) pastel *m* // *vt* (*wash*) lavar con esponja // *vi*: **to** ~ **on** sb vivir a costa de uno; ~ **bag** *n* esponjera; ~ **cake** *n* bizcocho, pastel *m*; **spongy** *a* esponjoso.

sponsor ['spɔnsə*] *n* (*radio*, *tv*) patrocinador/a *m/f*; (*for membership*) padrino; (*comm*) fiador/a *m/f* // *vt* patrocinar; apadrinar; (*idea etc*) presentar, promover; ~**ship** *n* patrocinio.

spontaneous [spɔn'teɪnɪəs] *a* espontáneo.

spool [spu:l] *n* carrete *m*; (*of sewing machine*) canilla.

spoon [spu:n] *n* cuchara; ~**feed** *vt* dar de comer con cuchara; (*fig*) tratar como a niño; ~**ful** *n* cucharada.

sporadic [spə'rædɪk] *a* esporádico.

sport [spɔ:t] *n* deporte *m*; (*person*) buen perdedor *m*; ~**ing** *a* deportivo; ~**s car** *n* coche *m* sport; ~**s jacket** *n* chaqueta sport; **sportsman** *n* deportista *m*; **sportsmanship** *n* deportividad *f*; **sportswear** *n* trajes *mpl* de deporte *o* sport; **sportswoman** *n* deportista; ~**y** *a* deportivo.

spot [spɔt] *n* sitio, lugar *m*; (*dot: on pattern*) punto, mancha; (*pimple*) grano; (*freckle*) peca; (*small amount*): **a** ~ **of** un poquito de // *vt* (*notice*) notar, observar; **on the** ~ en el acto, acto seguido; (*in difficulty*) en un aprieto; ~ **check** *n* reconocimiento rápido; ~**less** *a* nítido, perfectamente limpio; ~**light** *n* foco, reflector *m*; ~**ted** *a* (*pattern*) de puntos; ~**ty** *a* (*face*) con granos.

spouse [spaʊz] *n* cónyuge *m/f*.

spout [spaʊt] *n* (*of jug*) pico; (*pipe*) caño // *vi* chorrear.

sprain [spreɪn] *n* torcedura // *vt*: **to** ~ **one's ankle** torcerse el tobillo.

sprang [spræŋ] *pt of* **spring**.

sprawl [sprɔːl] vi tumbarse.

spray [spreɪ] n rociada; (of sea) espuma; (container) atomizador m; (of paint) pistola rociadora; (of flowers) ramita f // vt rociar; (crops) regar.

spread [sprɛd] n extensión f; (distribution) diseminación f, propagación f; (col: food) comilona // (vb: pt, pp **spread**) vt extender; diseminar; (butter) untar; (wings, sails) desplegar; (scatter) esparcir // vi extenderse; diseminarse; untarse; desplegarse; esparcirse.

spree [spriː] n: **to go on a** ~ ir de juerga.

sprightly ['spraɪtlɪ] a vivo, enérgico.

spring [sprɪŋ] n (leap) salto, brinco; (coiled metal) resorte m; (season) primavera; (of water) fuente f, manantial f // vi, pt **sprang**, pp **sprung** (arise) brotar, nacer; (leap) saltar, brincar; **to** ~ **up** vi nacer de repente, aparecer repentinamente; ~**board** n trampolín m; ~**-clean** n (also: ~**-cleaning**) limpieza general; ~**time** n primavera; ~**y** a elástico; (grass) muelle.

sprinkle ['sprɪŋkl] vt (pour) rociar; **to** ~ **water on,** ~ **with water** rociar o salpicar de agua; ~**d with** (fig) sembrado o salpicado de.

sprint [sprɪnt] n sprint m // vi (gen) correr a toda velocidad; (SPORT) sprintar; ~**er** n sprinter m/f, corredor/a m/f.

sprite [spraɪt] n duende m.

sprout [spraut] vi brotar, retoñar; (**Brussels**) ~**s** npl colecillos mpl de Bruselas.

spruce [spruːs] n (BOT) pícea // a aseado, pulcro.

sprung [sprʌŋ] pp of **spring.**

spry [spraɪ] a ágil, activo.

spun [spʌn] pt, pp of **spin.**

spur [spɔː*] n espuela; (fig) estímulo, aguijón m // vt (also: ~ **on**) estimular, incitar; **on the** ~ **of the moment** de improviso.

spurn [spɔːn] vt desdeñar, rechazar.

spurt [spɔːt] n esfuerzo supremo; (of energy) arrebato // vi hacer un esfuerzo supremo.

spy [spaɪ] n espía m/f // vi: **to** ~ **on** espiar a // vt (see) divisar, lograr ver; ~**ing** n espionaje m.

sq. abbr of **square.**

squabble ['skwɔbl] n riña, pelea // vi reñir, pelear.

squad [skwɔd] n (MIL, POLICE) pelotón m, escuadra.

squadron ['skwɔdrn] n (MIL) escuadrón m; (AVIAT, NAUT) escuadra.

squalid ['skwɔlɪd] a vil, miserable, escuálido.

squall [skwɔːl] n (storm) chubasco; (wind) ráfaga.

squalor ['skwɔlə*] n miseria.

squander ['skwɔndə*] vt (money) derrochar, despilfarrar; (chances) desperdiciar.

square [skwɛə*] n cuadro; (in town) plaza // a cuadrado; (col: ideas, tastes) pasota //

vt (arrange) arreglar; (MATH) cuadrar; **all** ~ igual(es); **a** ~ **meal** una comida abundante; **2 metres** ~ 2 metros en cuadro; **1** ~ **metre** un metro cuadrado; ~**ly** ad en cuadro; (fully) de lleno.

squash [skwɔʃ] n (drink): **lemon/orange** ~ zumo de limón/naranja; (SPORT) squash m, frontenis m // vt aplastar; **to** ~ **together** apiñar.

squat [skwɔt] a achaparrado // vi agacharse, sentarse en cuclillas; ~**ter** n persona que ocupa ilegalmente una casa.

squawk [skwɔːk] vi graznar.

squeak [skwiːk] n chirrido, rechinamiento; (of shoe) crujido; (of mouse) chillido // vi chirriar, rechinar; crujir; chillar.

squeal [skwiːl] vi chillar, dar gritos agudos.

squeamish ['skwiːmɪʃ] a delicado, remilgado.

squeeze [skwiːz] n (gen) estrujón m; (of hand) apretón m; (in bus etc) apiñamiento // vt estrujar, apretar; (hand, arm) apretar; **to** ~ **out** vt exprimir; (fig) excluir; **to** ~ **through** abrirse paso con esfuerzos.

squelch [skwɛltʃ] vi aplastar, despachurrar.

squid [skwɪd] n calamar m.

squint [skwɪnt] vi bizquear, ser bizco // n (MED) estrabismo; **to** ~ **at sth** mirar algo de soslayo.

squirm [skwəːm] vi retorcerse, revolverse.

squirrel ['skwɪrəl] n ardilla.

squirt [skwəːt] vi salir a chorros.

Sr abbr of **senior.**

St abbr of **saint; street.**

stab [stæb] n (with knife etc) puñalada; (of pain) pinchazo; (col: try): **to have a** ~ **at (doing) sth** intentar (hacer) algo // vt apuñalar.

stability [stə'bɪlɪtɪ] n estabilidad f; **stabilize** ['steɪbəlaɪz] vt estabilizar // vi estabilizarse; **stable** ['steɪbl] a estable // n cuadra, caballeriza.

stack [stæk] n montón m, pila // vt amontonar, apilar.

stadium ['steɪdɪəm] n estadio.

staff [stɑːf] n (work force) personal m, plantilla; (stick) bastón m // vt proveer de personal.

stag [stæg] n ciervo, venado.

stage [steɪdʒ] n escena; (profession): **the** ~ el escenario, el teatro; (point) etapa; (platform) plataforma // vt (play) poner en escena, representar; (demonstration) montar, organizar; (fig: perform: recovery etc) llevar a cabo; ~**coach** n diligencia; ~ **door** n entrada de artistas; ~ **manager** n director/a m/f de escena.

stagger ['stægə*] vi tambalear // vt (amaze) asombrar; (hours, holidays) escalonar; ~**ing** a (amazing) asombroso, pasmoso.

stagnant ['stægnənt] a estancado; **stagnate** [-'neɪt] vi estancarse.

stag party n fiesta de solteros.

staid [steɪd] *a* serio, formal.

stain [steɪn] *n* mancha; (*colouring*) tintura // *vt* manchar; (*wood*) teñir; **~ed glass window** *n* vidriera de colores; **~less** *a* (*steel*) inoxidable.

stair [stɛə*] *n* (*step*) peldaño, escalón *m*; **~s** *npl* escaleras *fpl*; **~case**, **~way** *n* escalera.

stake [steɪk] *n* estaca, poste *m*; (*BETTING*) apuesta // *vt* apostar; **to be at ~** estar en juego.

stalactite ['stæləktaɪt] *n* estalactita.

stalagmite ['stæləgmaɪt] *n* estalagmita.

stale [steɪl] *a* (*bread*) duro; (*food*) no fresco, pasado.

stalemate ['steɪlmeɪt] *n* tablas *fpl* (por ahogado); (*fig*) estancamiento.

stalk [stɔ:k] *n* tallo, caña // *vt* acechar, cazar al acecho; **to ~ off** irse con paso airado.

stall [stɔ:l] *n* (*in market*) puesto; (*in stable*) casilla (de establo) // *vt* (*AUT*) parar // *vi* (*AUT*) pararse; (*fig*) buscar evasivas; **~s** *npl* (*in cinema, theatre*) butacas *fpl*.

stallion ['stæliən] *n* caballo padre, semental *m*.

stalwart ['stɔ:lwət] *n* (*in build*) fornido; (*in spirit*) valiente.

stamina ['stæmɪnə] *n* resistencia.

stammer ['stæmə*] *n* tartamudeo, balbuceo // *vi* tartamudear, balbucir.

stamp [stæmp] *n* sello, estampilla; (*mark, also fig*) marca, huella; (*on document*) timbre *m* // *vi* patear // *vt* patear, golpear con el pie; (*in dance*) zapatear; (*letter*) poner sellos en; (*with rubber ~*) marcar con estampilla; **~ album** *n* álbum *m* para sellos; **~ collecting** *n* filatelia.

stampede [stæm'pi:d] *n* estampida.

stance [stæns] *n* postura.

stand [stænd] *n* (*position*) posición *f*, postura; (*for taxis*) parada; (*hall ~*) perchero; (*music ~*) atril *m*; (*SPORT*) tribuna; (*news ~*) quiosco // (*vb: pt, pp* **stood**) *vi* (*be*) estar, encontrarse; (*be on foot*) estar de pie; (*rise*) levantarse; (*remain*) quedar en pie // *vt* (*place*) poner, colocar; (*tolerate, withstand*) aguantar, soportar; (*cost*) pagar; (*invite*) invitar; **to make a ~** resistir; (*fig*) aferrarse a un principio; **to ~ for parliament** presentarse como candidato al parlamento; **to ~ by** *vi* (*be ready*) estar listo // *vt fus* (*opinion*) aferrarse a; **to ~ for** *vt fus* (*defend*) apoyar; (*signify*) significar; (*tolerate*) aguantar, permitir; **to ~ in for** *vt fus* suplir a; **to ~ out** *vi* (*be prominent*) destacarse; **to ~ up** *vi* (*rise*) levantarse, ponerse de pie; **to ~ up for** *vt fus* defender; **to ~ up to** *vt fus* hacer frente a.

standard ['stændəd] *n* patrón *m*, norma; (*flag*) estandarte *m*; (*degree*) grado // *a* (*size etc*) normal, corriente, stándard; **~s** *npl* (*morals*) valores *mpl* morales; **~ize** *vt* estandarizar; **~ lamp** *n* lámpara de pie; **~ of living** *n* nivel *m* de vida.

stand-by ['stændbaɪ] *n* (*alert*) alerta, aviso; **to be on ~** estar sobre aviso; **~ ticket** *n* (*AVIAT*) billete *m* standby.

stand-in ['stændɪn] *n* suplente *m/f*; (*CINEMA*) doble *m/f*.

standing ['stændɪŋ] *a* (*upright*) derecho; (*on foot*) de pie, en pie // *n* reputación *f*; **of many years'** que lleva muchos años; **~ order** *n* (*at bank*) giro bancario; **~ orders** *npl* (*MIL*) reglamento *sg* general; **~ room** *n* sitio para estar de pie.

stand: **~-offish** *a* reservado, poco afable; **~point** *n* punto de vista; **~still**: **at a ~still** paralizado, en paro; **to come to a ~still** pararse, quedar paralizado.

stank [stæŋk] *pt of* **stink**.

staple ['steɪpl] *n* (*for papers*) grapa // *a* (*food etc*) corriente // *vt* unir con grapa, engrapar; **stapler** *n* grapadora.

star [sta:*] *n* estrella; (*celebrity*) estrella, astro // *vi*: **to ~ in** ser la estrella *o* el astro de.

starboard ['sta:bəd] *n* estribor *m*.

starch [sta:tʃ] *n* almidón *m*; **~ed** *a* (*collar*) almidonado; **~y** *a* feculento.

stardom ['sta:dəm] *n* estrellato, calidad *f* de estrella.

stare [stɛə*] *n* mirada fija // *vt*: **to ~ at** mirar fijo.

starfish ['sta:fɪʃ] *n* estrella de mar.

stark [sta:k] *a* (*bleak*) severo, escueto // *ad*: **~ naked** en cueros, en pelota.

starlight ['sta:laɪt] *n*: **by ~** a la luz de las estrellas.

starling ['sta:lɪŋ] *n* estornino.

starry ['sta:rɪ] *a* estrellado; **~-eyed** *a* (*innocent*) inocentón(ona), ingenuo.

start [sta:t] *n* (*beginning*) principio, comienzo; (*departure*) salida; (*sudden movement*) salto, sobresalto; (*advantage*) ventaja // *vt* empezar, comenzar; (*cause*) causar; (*found*) fundar; (*engine*) poner en marcha // *vi* (*begin*) comenzar, empezar; (*with fright*) asustarse, sobresaltarse; (*train etc*) salir; **to ~ off** *vi* empezar, comenzar; (*leave*) salir, ponerse en camino; **to ~ up** *vi* comenzar; (*car*) ponerse en marcha // *vt* comenzar; (*car*) poner en marcha; **~er** *n* (*AUT*) botón *m* de arranque; (: *runner*) corredor/a *m/f*; (*CULIN*) entrada; **~ing point** *n* punto de partida.

startle ['sta:tl] *vt* asustar, sobrecoger; **startling** *a* alarmante.

starvation [sta:'veɪʃən] *n* hambre *f*; (*MED*) inanición *f*; **starve** *vi* pasar hambre; (*to death*) morir de hambre // *vt* hacer pasar hambre; (*fig*) privar; **I'm starving** estoy muerto de hambre.

state [steɪt] *n* estado // *vt* (*say, declare*) afirmar; (*a case*) presentar, exponer; **the S~s** los Estados Unidos; **to be in a ~** estar agitado; **~ly** *a* majestuoso, imponente; **~ment** *n* afirmación *f*; (*LAW*) declaración *f*; **statesman** *n* estadista *m*.

static ['stætɪk] *n* (*RADIO*) parásitos *mpl* // *a* estático; **~ electricity** *n* estática.

station ['steɪʃən] n (gen) estación f; (place) puesto, sitio; (RADIO) emisora; (rank) posición f social // vt colocar, situar; (MIL) apostar.

stationary ['steɪʃnərɪ] a estacionario, fijo.

stationer's (shop) ['steɪʃənəz] n papelería; **stationery** [-nərɪ] n papel m de escribir.

station master n (RAIL) jefe m de estación.

station wagon n (US) break m.

statistic [stə'tɪstɪk] n estadística; ~s npl (science) estadística sg; ~al a estadístico.

statue ['stætju:] n estatua.

stature ['stætjə*] n estatura; (fig) talla.

status ['steɪtəs] n condición f, estado; (reputation) reputación f, státus m; the ~ quo el statu quo; ~ symbol n símbolo de prestigio.

statute ['stætju:t] n estatuto, ley f; **statutory** a estatutario.

staunch [stɔ:ntʃ] a firme, incondicional.

stave [steɪv] vt: to ~ off (attack) rechazar; (threat) evitar.

stay [steɪ] n (period of time) estancia // vi (remain) quedar, quedarse; (as guest) hospedarse; (spend some time) pasar (un) tiempo; to ~ put seguir en el mismo sitio; to ~ the night pasar la noche; to ~ behind vi quedar atrás; to ~ in vi (at home) quedarse en casa; to ~ on vi quedarse; to ~ out vi (of house) no volver a casa; to ~ up vi (at night) velar, no acostarse; ~ing power n resistencia.

steadfast ['stɛdfɑ:st] a firme, resuelto.

steadily ['stɛdɪlɪ] ad (firmly) firmemente; (unceasingly) sin parar; (fixedly) fijamente; (walk) normalmente; (drive) a velocidad constante.

steady ['stɛdɪ] a (constant) constante, fijo; (unswerving) firme; (regular) regular; (person, character) sensato, juicioso; (diligent) trabajador; (calm) sereno // vt (hold) mantener firme; (stabilize) estabilizar; (nerves) calmar; to ~ o.s. on or against sth afirmarse en algo.

steak [steɪk] n (gen) filete m; (beef) bistec m.

steal [sti:l], pt stole, pp stolen vt, vi robar.

stealth [stɛlθ] n: by ~ a escondidas, sigilosamente; ~y a cauteloso, sigiloso.

steam [sti:m] n vapor m; (mist) vaho, humo // vt empañar; (CULIN) cocer al vapor // vi echar vapor; (ship) to ~ along avanzar, ir avanzando; ~ engine n máquina de vapor; ~er n vapor m; ~roller n apisonadora; ~y a vaporoso; (room) lleno de vapor; (window) empañado.

steel [sti:l] n acero // a de acero; ~works n (fábrica) siderúrgica.

steep [sti:p] a escarpado, abrupto; (stair) empinado; (price) exorbitante, excesivo // vt empapar, remojar.

steeple ['sti:pl] n aguja, campanario; ~chase n carrera de obstáculos; ~jack

n reparador m de chimeneas.

steer [stɪə*] vt conducir, dirigir // vi conducir; ~ing n (AUT) dirección f; ~ing wheel n volante m.

stellar ['stɛlə*] a estelar.

stem [stɛm] n (of plant) tallo; (of glass) pie m; (of pipe) cañón m // vt detener; (blood) restañar; to ~ from vt fus proceder de.

stench [stɛntʃ] n hedor m.

stencil ['stɛnsl] n (typed) cliché m, clisé m; (lettering) plantilla // vt hacer un cliché de.

step [stɛp] n paso; (sound) paso, pisada; (stair) peldaño, escalón m // vi: to ~ forward dar un paso adelante; ~s npl = ~ladder; to ~ down vi (fig) retirarse; to ~ off vt fus bajar de; to ~ on vt fus pisar; to ~ over vt fus pasar por encima de; to ~ up vt (increase) aumentar; ~brother n hermanastro; ~daughter n hijastra; ~father n padrastro; ~ladder n escalera de tijera o doble; ~mother n madrastra; ~ping stone n pasadera; ~sister n hermanastra; ~son n hijastro.

stereo ['stɛrɪəu] n estereo // a (also: ~phonic) estereo(fónico).

stereotype ['stɪərɪətaɪp] n estereotipo // vt estereotipar.

sterile ['stɛraɪl] a estéril; **sterility** [-'rɪlɪtɪ] n esterilidad f; **sterilization** [-'zeɪʃən] n esterilización f; **sterilize** ['stɛrɪlaɪz] vt esterilizar.

sterling ['stə:lɪŋ] a esterlina; (silver) de ley; (fig) auténtico.

stern [stə:n] a severo, austero // n (NAUT) popa.

stethoscope ['stɛθəskəup] n estetoscopio.

stew [stju:] n cocido, estofado; (fig: mess) apuro // vt, vi estofar, guisar; (fruit) cocer.

steward ['stju:əd] n (gen) camarero; ~ess n azafata.

stick [stɪk] n palo; (as weapon) porra; (walking ~) bastón m // (vb: pt, pp stuck) vt (glue) pegar; (thrust): to ~ sth into clavar o hincar algo en; (col: put) meter; (col: tolerate) aguantar, soportar // vi pegar, pegarse; (come to a stop) quedarse parado; (in mind etc) atascarse; (pin etc) clavarse; to ~ out, to ~ up vi sobresalir; to ~ up for vt fus defender; ~er n etiqueta engomada.

stickler ['stɪklə*] n: to be a ~ for dar mucha importancia a.

stick-up ['stɪkʌp] n asalto, atraco.

sticky ['stɪkɪ] a pegajoso; (label) engomado; (fig) difícil.

stiff [stɪf] a rígido, tieso; (hard) duro; (difficult) difícil; (person) inflexible; (price) exorbitante; ~en vt hacer más rígido; (limb) entumecer // vi endurecerse; (grow stronger) fortalecerse; ~ness n rigidez f, tiesura; dificultad f; (character) frialdad f.

stifle ['staɪfl] vt ahogar, sofocar; **stifling** a (heat) sofocante, bochornoso.

stigma ['stɪgmə], pl (BOT, MED, REL) ~ta [-tə], (fig) ~s n estigma m.

stile [staɪl] *n* escalera para pasar una cerca.

stiletto [stɪ'letəu] *n* (*also*: ~ **heel**) tacón *m* de aguja.

still [stɪl] *a* inmóvil, quieto // *ad* (*up to this time*) todavía; (*even*) aún; (*nonetheless*) sin embargo, aun así; ~**born** *a* nacido muerto; ~ **life** *n* naturaleza muerta.

stilt [stɪlt] *n* zanco; (*pile*) pilar *m*, soporte *m*.

stilted ['stɪltɪd] *a* afectado.

stimulant ['stɪmjulənt] *n* estimulante *m*.

stimulate ['stɪmjuleɪt] *vt* estimular; **stimulating** *a* estimulante; **stimulation** [-'leɪʃən] *n* estímulo.

stimulus ['stɪmjuləs], *pl* **-li** [-laɪ] *n* estímulo, incentivo.

sting [stɪŋ] *n* (*wound*) picadura; (*pain*) escozor *m*, picazón *m*; (*organ*) aguijón *m* // (*vb*: *pt*, *pp* **stung**) *vt* picar // *vi* picar, escocer.

stingy ['stɪndʒɪ] *a* tacaño.

stink [stɪŋk] *n* hedor *m*, tufo // *vi*, *pt* **stank**, *pp* **stunk** heder, apestar; ~**ing** *a* hediondo, fétido.

stint [stɪnt] *n* tarea, destajo; **to do one's** ~ hacer su parte // *vi*: **to** ~ **on** escatimar.

stipend ['staɪpend] *n* (*of vicar etc*) estipendio, sueldo.

stipulate ['stɪpjuleɪt] *vt* estipular, poner como condición; **stipulation** [-'leɪʃən] *n* estipulación, condición *f*.

stir [stə:*] *n* (*fig*: *agitation*) conmoción *f* // *vt* (*tea etc*) remover; (*fire*) atizar; (*move*) mover; (*fig*: *emotions*) conmover // *vi* moverse, menearse; **to** ~ **up** *vt* excitar; (*trouble*) fomentar; ~**ring** *a* conmovedor(a).

stirrup ['stɪrəp] *n* estribo.

stitch [stɪtʃ] *n* (*SEWING*) puntada; (*KNITTING*) punto; (*MED*) punto (de sutura); (*pain*) punzada // *vt* coser; (*MED*) suturar.

stoat [stəut] *n* armiño.

stock [stɔk] *n* (*COMM*: *reserves*) existencias *fpl*, stock *m*; (: *selection*) surtido; (*AGR*) ganado, ganadería; (*CULIN*) caldo; (*fig*: *lineage*) estirpe *f*; (*FINANCE*) capital *m*; (: *shares*) acciones *fpl* // *a* (*fig*: *reply etc*) clásico, acostumbrado // *vt* (*have in* ~) tener (en existencia o almacén); (*supply*) proveer, abastecer; **to take** ~ **of** (*fig*) asesorar, examinar; **to** ~ **up with** *vt* abastecerse de; ~**s** *npl* cepo *sg*; ~**s and shares** acciones y valores.

stockade [stɔ'keɪd] *n* estacada.

stockbroker ['stɔkbrəukə*] *n* agente *m/f* o corredor/a *m/f* de bolsa.

stock exchange *n* bolsa.

stocking ['stɔkɪŋ] *n* media.

stock market *n* bolsa (de valores).

stockpile ['stɔkpaɪl] *n* reserva // *vt* acumular, almacenar.

stocktaking ['stɔkteɪkɪŋ] *n* (*COMM*) inventario, balance *m*.

stocky ['stɔkɪ] *a* (*strong*) robusto; (*short*) achaparrado.

stodgy ['stɔdʒɪ] *a* indigesto, pesado.

stoical ['stəuɪkəl] *a* estoico.

stoke [stəuk] *vt* cargar, cebar.

stole [stəul] *pt of* **steal** // *n* estola.

stolen ['stəuln] *pp of* **steal**.

stomach ['stʌmək] *n* (*ANAT*) estómago; (*belly*) vientre *m*; (*appetite*) apetito // *vt* tragar, aguantar; ~ **ache** *n* dolor *m* de estómago.

stone [stəun] *n* piedra; (*in fruit*) hueso; (*weight*) medida de peso (*6.348kg*) // *a* de piedra // *vt* apedrear; ~**-cold** *a* helado; ~**-deaf** *a* totalmente sordo; ~**work** *n* (*art*) cantería; (*stones*) piedras *fpl*; **stony** *a* pedregoso; (*glance*) glacial.

stood [stud] *pt*, *pp of* **stand**.

stool [stu:l] *n* taburete *m*.

stoop [stu:p] *vi* (*also*: **have a** ~) ser cargado de espaldas; (*bend*) inclinarse, encorvarse.

stop [stɔp] *n* parada, alto; (*in punctuation*) punto // *vt* parar, detener; (*break off*) suspender; (*block*) tapar, cerrar; (*also*: **put a** ~ **to**) terminar, poner término a // *vi* pararse, detenerse; (*end*) acabarse; **to** ~ **doing sth** dejar de hacer algo; **to** ~ **dead** *vi* pararse en seco; **to** ~ **off** *vi* interrumpir el viaje; **to** ~ **up** *vt* (*hole*) tapar; ~**gap** *n* recurso (temporal); ~**lights** *npl* (*AUT*) luces *fpl* de detención; ~**over** *n* parada intermedia.

stoppage ['stɔpɪdʒ] *n* (*strike*) paro; (*temporary stop*) interrupción *f*; (*of pay*) suspensión *f*; (*blockage*) obstrucción *f*.

stopper ['stɔpə*] *n* tapón *m*.

stopwatch ['stɔpwɔtʃ] *n* cronómetro.

storage ['stɔ:rɪdʒ] *n* almacenaje *m*.

store [stɔ:*] *n* (*stock*) provisión *f*; (*depot, large shop*) almacén *m*; (*reserve*) reserva, repuesto; ~**s** *npl* víveres *mpl* // *vt* almacenar; (*keep*) guardar; **to** ~ **up** *vt* acumular; ~**room** *n* despensa.

storey, story (*US*) ['stɔ:rɪ] *n* piso.

stork [stɔ:k] *n* cigüeña.

storm [stɔ:m] *n* tormenta; (*wind*) vendaval *m*; (*fig*) tempestad *f* // *vi* (*fig*) rabiar // *vt* tomar por asalto, asaltar; ~ **cloud** *n* nubarrón *m*; ~**y** *a* tempestuoso.

story ['stɔ:rɪ] *n* historia, relato; (*joke*) cuento, chiste *m*; (*plot*) argumento; (*lie*) cuento, embuste *m*; (*US*) = **storey**; ~**book** *n* libro de cuentos; ~**teller** *n* cuentista *m/f*.

stout [staut] *a* (*strong*) sólido, macizo; (*fat*) gordo, corpulento // *n* cerveza negra.

stove [stəuv] *n* (*for cooking*) cocina; (*for heating*) estufa.

stow [stəu] *vt* meter, poner; (*NAUT*) estibar; ~**away** *n* polizón/ona *m/f*.

straddle ['strædl] *vt* montar a horcajadas.

straggle ['strægl] *vi* (*wander*) vagar en desorden; (*lag behind*) rezagarse; **straggler** *n* rezagado; **straggling, straggly** *a* (*hair*) desordenado.

straight [streɪt] *a* recto, derecho; (*honest*) honrado; (*frank*) franco, directo; (*simple*) sencillo; (*in order*) en orden // *ad* derecho, directamente; (*drink*) sin mezcla; **to put**

or **get sth ~ off** (*at once*) en seguida; **~ away, ~ off** (*at once*) dejar algo en claro; **~ en** *vt* (*also*: **~en out**) enderezar, poner derecho; **~-faced** *a* solemne, sin expresión; **~forward** *a* (*simple*) sencillo; (*honest*) honrado, franco.

strain [streɪn] *n* (*gen*) tensión *f*; (*TECH*) esfuerzo; (*MED*) torcedura; (*breed*) raza // *vt* (*back etc*) torcerse; (*tire*) cansar; (*stretch*) estirar; (*filter*) filtrar // *vi* esforzarse; **~s** *npl* (*MUS*) son *m*; **~ed** *a* (*muscle*) torcido; (*laugh*) forzado; (*relations*) tenso; **~er** *n* colador *m*.

strait [streɪt] *n* (*GEO*) estrecho; **~-jacket** *n* camisa de fuerza; **~-laced** *a* mojigato, gazmoño.

strand [strænd] *n* (*of thread*) hebra; (*of hair*) trenza; (*of rope*) ramal *m*; **~ed** *a* abandonado (sin recursos), desamparado.

strange [streɪndʒ] *a* (*not known*) desconocido; (*odd*) extraño, raro; **stranger** *n* desconocido/a; (*from another area*) forastero/a.

strangle ['stræŋgl] *vt* estrangular; (*sobs etc*) ahogar; **~hold** *n* (*fig*) dominio completo; **strangulation** [-'leɪʃən] *n* estrangulación *f*.

strap [stræp] *n* correa; (*of slip, dress*) tirante *m* // *vt* atar con correa; (*punish*) azotar.

strapping ['stræpɪŋ] *a* robusto, fornido.

strata ['strɑːtə] *pl of* **stratum**.

stratagem ['strætɪdʒəm] *n* estratagema.

strategic [strə'tiːdʒɪk] *a* estratégico.

strategy ['strætɪdʒɪ] *n* estrategia.

stratum ['strɑːtəm], *pl* **-ta** *n* estrato.

straw [strɔː] *n* paja; (*drinking ~*) caña, pajita.

strawberry ['strɔːbərɪ] *n* fresa.

stray [streɪ] *a* (*animal*) extraviado; (*bullet*) perdido; (*scattered*) disperso // *vi* extraviarse, perderse.

streak [striːk] *n* raya; (*fig: of madness etc*) vena // *vt* rayar // *vi* **to ~ past** pasar como un rayo; **~y** *a* rayado.

stream [striːm] *n* riachuelo, arroyo; (*jet*) chorro; (*current*) corriente *f*; (*of people*) oleada // *vt* (*SCOL*) dividir en grupos por habilidad // *vi* correr, fluir; **to ~ in/out** (*people*) entrar/salir en tropel.

streamer ['striːmə*] *n* serpentina.

streamlined ['striːmlaɪnd] *a* aerodinámico.

street [striːt] *n* calle *f* // *a* callejero; **~car** *n* (*US*) tranvía; **~ lamp** *n* farol *m*.

strength [strεŋθ] *n* fuerza; (*of girder, knot etc*) resistencia; **~en** *vt* fortalecer, reforzar.

strenuous ['strεnjuəs] *a* (*tough*) arduo; (*energetic*) enérgico; (*determined*) tenaz.

stress [strεs] *n* (*force, pressure*) presión *f*; (*mental strain*) tensión *f*; (*accent*) énfasis *m*, acento; (*TECH*) tensión *f*, carga // *vt* subrayar, recalcar.

stretch [strεtʃ] *n* (*of sand etc*) trecho, tramo // *vi* estirarse; (*extend*): **to ~ to** *or* **as far as** extenderse hasta // *vt* extender,

estirar; (*make demands of*) exigir el máximo esfuerzo a; **to ~ out** *vi* tenderse // *vt* (*arm etc*) extender; (*spread*) estirar.

stretcher ['strεtʃə*] *n* camilla.

strewn [struːn] *a*: **~ with** cubierto *o* sembrado de.

stricken ['strɪkən] *a* (*wounded*) herido; (*ill*) enfermo.

strict [strɪkt] *a* (*person*) severo, riguroso; (*precise*) estricto, exacto; **~ly** *ad* (*exactly*) estrictamente; (*totally*) terminantemente; (*severely*) rigurosamente; **~ness** *n* exactitud *f*; rigor *m*, severidad *f*.

stride [straɪd] *n* zancada, tranco // *vi*, *pt* **strode**, *pp* **stridden** ['strɪdn] dar zancadas, andar a trancos.

strident ['straɪdnt] *a* estridente; (*colour*) chillón(ona).

strife [straɪf] *n* lucha.

strike [straɪk] *n* huelga; (*of oil etc*) descubrimiento; (*attack*) ataque *m*; (*SPORT*) golpe *m*. // (*vb*: *pt*, *pp* **struck**) *vt* golpear, pegar; (*oil etc*) descubrir; (*obstacle*) topar con // *vi* declarar la huelga; (*attack*) atacar; (*clock*) dar la hora; **to ~ a match** encender un fósforo; **to ~ down** *vt* derribar; **to ~ out** *vt* borrar, tachar; **to ~ up** *vt* (*MUS*) empezar a tocar; (*conversation*) entablar; (*friendship*) trabar; **~breaker** *n* rompehuelgas *m/f inv*; **striker** *n* huelgista *m/f*; (*SPORT*) delantero; **striking** *a* impresionante; (*nasty*) chocante; (*colour*) llamativo.

string [strɪŋ] *n* (*gen*) cuerda; (*row*) hilera // *vt*, *pt*, *pp* **strung**: **to ~ together** ensartar // *vi*: **to ~ out** extenderse; **the ~s** *npl* (*MUS*) los instrumentos de cuerda; **to pull ~s** (*fig*) mover palancas; **~ bean** *n* judía verde, habichuela; **~(ed) instrument** *n* (*MUS*) instrumento de cuerda.

stringent ['strɪndʒənt] *a* riguroso, severo.

strip [strɪp] *n* tira; (*of land*) franja; (*of metal*) cinta, lámina // *vt* desnudar; (*also*: **~ down**: *machine*) desmontar // *vi* desnudarse; **~ cartoon** *n* tira cómica.

stripe [straɪp] *n* raya; (*MIL*) galón *m*; **~d** *a* a rayas, rayado.

stripper ['strɪpə*] *n* artista de striptease.

striptease ['strɪptiːz] *n* striptease *m*.

strive [straɪv], *pt* **strove**, *pp* **striven** ['strɪvn] *vi*: **to ~ to do sth** esforzarse *o* luchar por hacer algo.

strode [strəud] *pt of* **stride**.

stroke [strəuk] *n* (*blow*) golpe *m*; (*MED*) ataque *m* fulminante; (*caress*) caricia; (*of pen*) trazo // *vt* acariciar, frotar suavemente; **at a ~** de golpe.

stroll [strəul] *n* paseo, vuelta // *vi* dar un paseo *o* una vuelta.

strong [strɔŋ] *a* fuerte; **they are 50 ~** son 50; **~box** *n* caja fuerte; **~hold** *n* fortaleza; (*fig*) baluarte *m*; **~ly** *ad* fuertemente, con fuerza; (*believe*) firmemente; ~**room** n cámara acorazada.

strove [strəuv] pt of **strive**.

struck [strʌk] pt, pp of **strike**.

structural ['strʌktʃərəl] a estructural; **structure** n estructura; (building) construcción f.

struggle ['strʌgl] n lucha // vi luchar.

strum [strʌm] vt (guitar) rasguear.

strung [strʌŋ] pt, pp of **string**.

strut [strʌt] n puntal m // vi pavonearse.

stub [stʌb] n (of ticket etc) talón m; (of cigarette) colilla; **to ~ out** vt apagar; **to ~ one's toe** dar con el dedo contra algo.

stubble ['stʌbl] n rastrojo; (on chin) barba (de pocos días).

stubborn ['stʌbən] a terco, testarudo.

stuck [stʌk] pt, pp of **stick** // a (jammed) atascado; ~**up** a engreído, presumido.

stud [stʌd] n (shirt ~) botón m; (of boot) taco; (of horses) caballeriza; (also: ~ **horse**) caballo padre o semental // vt (fig): ~**ded with** sembrado de.

student ['stju:dənt] n estudiante m/f // a estudiantil.

studio ['stju:diəu] n estudio; (sculptor's) taller m.

studious ['stju:diəs] a aplicado; (studied) calculado; ~**ly** ad (carefully) con esmero.

study ['stʌdi] n (gen) estudio // vt estudiar; (examine) examinar, escudriñar // vi estudiar.

stuff [stʌf] n materia; (cloth) tela; (substance) material m, sustancia // vt llenar; (CULIN) rellenar; (animals) disecar; ~**ing** n relleno; ~**y** a (room) mal ventilado; (person) de miras estrechas.

stumble ['stʌmbl] vi tropezar, dar un traspié; **to ~ across** (fig) tropezar con; **stumbling block** n tropiezo, obstáculo.

stump [stʌmp] n (of tree) tocón m; (of limb) muñón m // vt: **to be ~ed** quedar perplejo.

stun [stʌn] vt dejar sin sentido.

stung [stʌŋ] pt, pp of **sting**.

stunk [stʌŋk] pp of **stink**.

stunning ['stʌnɪŋ] a (fig) pasmoso.

stunt [stʌnt] n proeza excepcional; (AVIAT) vuelo acrobático; (publicity) ~ truco publicitario; ~**ed** a enano, achaparrado; ~**man** n doble m.

stupefy ['stju:pɪfaɪ] vt dejar estupefacto.

stupendous [stju:'pendəs] a estupendo, asombroso.

stupid ['stju:pɪd] a estúpido, tonto; ~**ity** [-'pɪdɪtɪ] n estupidez f; ~**ly** ad estúpidamente.

stupor ['stju:pə*] n estupor m.

sturdy ['stə:dɪ] a robusto, fuerte.

stutter ['stʌtə*] n tartamudeo // vi tartamudear.

sty [staɪ] n (for pigs) pocilga.

style [staɪl] n (MED) orzuelo.

style [staɪl] n estilo; **stylish** a elegante, a la moda.

stylus ['staɪləs] n (of record player) aguja.

suave [swɑ:v] a cortés, fino.

sub... [sʌb] pref sub...; ~**conscious** a subconsciente // n subconsciente m; ~**divide** vt subdividir; ~**division** n subdivisión f.

subdue [səb'dju:] vt sojuzgar; (passions) dominar; ~**d** a (light) tenue; (person) sumiso, manso.

subject ['sʌbdʒɪkt] n súbdito; (SCOL) tema m, materia // vt [səb'dʒɛkt]: **to ~ sb to sth** someter a uno a algo; (law) estar sujeto a; ~**ion** [-'dʒɛkʃən] n sometimiento, sujeción f; ~**ive** a subjetivo; ~ **matter** n materia; (content) contenido.

subjugate ['sʌbdʒugeɪt] vt subyugar.

sublet [sʌb'lɛt] vt subarrendar.

sublime [sə'blaɪm] a sublime.

submachine gun ['sʌbmə'ʃi:n-] n metralleta.

submarine [sʌbmə'ri:n] n submarino.

submerge [səb'mə:dʒ] vt sumergir; (flood) inundar // vi sumergirse.

submission [səb'mɪʃən] n sumisión f; **submissive** [-'mɪsɪv] a sumiso.

submit [səb'mɪt] vt someter // vi someterse.

subnormal [sʌb'nɔ:məl] a anormal; (backward) retrasado.

subordinate [sə'bɔ:dɪnət] a, n subordinado.

subpoena [səb'pi:nə] (LAW) n comparendo, citación f // vt mandar comparecer.

subscribe [səb'skraɪb] vi suscribir; **to ~ to** (opinion, fund) suscribir, aprobar; (newspaper) suscribirse a; **subscriber** n (to periodical, telephone) abonado/a.

subscription [səb'skrɪpʃən] n abono, suscripción f.

subsequent ['sʌbsɪkwənt] a subsiguiente, posterior; ~**ly** ad después, más tarde.

subside [səb'saɪd] vi hundirse; (flood) bajar; (wind) amainar; **subsidence** [-'saɪdns] n hundimiento; (in road) socavón m.

subsidiary [səb'sɪdɪərɪ] n sucursal f, filial f.

subsidize ['sʌbsɪdaɪz] vt subvencionar; **subsidy** [-dɪ] n subvención f.

subsistence [səb'sɪstəns] n subsistencia; (allowance) dietas fpl.

substance ['sʌbstəns] n sustancia; (fig) esencia.

substandard [sʌb'stændəd] a inferior.

substantial [səb'stænʃl] a sustancial, sustancioso; (fig) importante; ~**ly** ad sustancialmente.

substantiate [səb'stænʃieɪt] vt comprobar.

substitute ['sʌbstɪtju:t] n (person) suplente m/f; (thing) sustituto // vt: **to ~ A for B** sustituir B por A, reemplazar A por B; **substitution** [-'tju:ʃən] n sustitución f, reemplazo.

subterfuge ['sʌbtəfju:dʒ] n subterfugio.

subterranean [sʌbtə'reɪnɪən] a subterráneo.

subtitle ['sʌbtaɪtl] n subtítulo.
subtle ['sʌtl] a sutil; ~**ty** n sutileza.
subtract [səb'trækt] vt sustraer, restar; ~**ion** [-'trækʃən] n sustracción f, resta.
suburb ['sʌbəːb] n arrabal m, suburbio; ~**an** [sə'bəːbən] a suburbano; (train etc) de cercanías.
subversive [səb'vəːsɪv] a subversivo.
subway ['sʌbweɪ] n (Brit) paso subterráneo o inferior; (US) metro.
succeed [sək'siːd] vi (person) tener éxito; (plan) salir bien // vt suceder a; **to ~ in doing** lograr hacer; ~**ing** a (following) sucesivo, seguido.
success [sək'sɛs] n éxito; (gain) triunfo; ~**ful** a (venture) de éxito; **to be ~ful (in doing)** lograr (hacer); ~**fully** ad con éxito.
succession [sək'sɛʃən] n (series) sucesión í, serie f; (descendants) descendencia; **successive** [-'sɛsɪv] a sucesivo, consecutivo; **successor** [-'sɛsə*] n sucesor/a m/f.
succinct [sək'sɪŋkt] a sucinto.
succulent ['sʌkjulənt] a suculento.
succumb [sə'kʌm] vi sucumbir.
such [sʌtʃ] a, det tal, semejante; (of that kind): ~ **a book** un libro parecido; ~ **books** tales libros; (so much): ~ **courage** tanto valor; ~ **a long trip** un viaje tan largo; ~ **a lot of** tanto; ~ **as** (like) tal como; **a noise ~ as** to un ruido tal que; **as ~** ad como tal // pron los/las que; ~**-and-**~ det tal o cual; **until ~ time as** hasta que.
suck [sʌk] vt chupar; (bottle) sorber; (breast) mamar; ~**er** n (BOT) serpollo; (ZOOL) ventosa; (col) bobo, primo.
suckle ['sʌkl] vt amamantar.
suction ['sʌkʃən] n succión f.
sudden ['sʌdn] a (rapid) repentino, súbito; (unexpected) imprevisto; **all of a ~**, ~**ly** ad de repente; (unexpectedly) inesperadamente.
suds [sʌdz] npl jabonaduras fpl.
sue [suː] vt demandar.
suede [sweɪd] n ante m.
suet ['sʊɪt] n sebo.
suffer ['sʌfə*] vt sufrir, padecer; (bear) aguantar; (allow) permitir, tolerar // vi sufrir, padecer; ~**er** n víctima m/f; (MED) enfermo; ~**ing** n sufrimiento, padecimiento; (pain) dolor m.
suffice [sə'faɪs] vi bastar, ser suficiente.
sufficient [sə'fɪʃənt] a suficiente, bastante; ~**ly** ad suficientemente.
suffix ['sʌfɪks] n sufijo.
suffocate ['sʌfəkeɪt] vi ahogarse, asfixiarse; **suffocation** [-'keɪʃən] n sofocación f, asfixia.
suffrage ['sʌfrɪdʒ] n sufragio; (vote) derecho de votar.
sugar ['ʃʊgə*] n azúcar m // vt echar azúcar a; ~ **beet** n remolacha; ~ **cane** n caña de azúcar; ~**y** a azucarado.
suggest [sə'dʒɛst] vt sugerir; (advise) aconsejar; ~**ion** [-'dʒɛstʃən] n sugerencia;

(hypnotic) sugestión f; ~**ive** a sugestivo; (pej) indecente.
suicidal [sʊɪ'saɪdl] a suicida; **suicide** ['sʊɪsaɪd] n suicidio; (person) suicida m/f.
suit [suːt] n (man's) traje m; (woman's) conjunto; (LAW) litigio, pleito; (CARDS) palo // vt (gen) convenir; (clothes) sentar a, ir bien a; (adapt): **to ~ sth to** adaptar o ajustar algo a; ~**able** a conveniente; (apt) indicado; ~**ably** ad convenientemente, en forma debida.
suitcase ['suːtkeɪs] n maleta.
suite [swiːt] n (of rooms) grupo de habitaciones; (MUS) suite f; (furniture): **bedroom/dining room ~** (juego de) dormitorio/comedor m.
suitor ['suːtə*] n pretendiente m.
sulk [sʌlk] vi tener mohíno; ~**y** a con mohino.
sullen ['sʌlən] a hosco, malhumorado.
sulphur, sulfur (US) ['sʌlfə*] n azufre m.
sultan ['sʌltən] n sultán m.
sultana [sʌl'tɑːnə] n (fruit) pasa de Esmirna.
sultry ['sʌltrɪ] a (weather) bochornoso; (seductive) seductor(a).
sum [sʌm] n (gen) suma; (total) total m; **to ~ up** vt recapitular // vi hacer un resumen.
summarize ['sʌməraɪz] vt resumir.
summary ['sʌmərɪ] n resumen m // a (justice) sumario.
summer ['sʌmə*] n verano // a de verano; ~**house** n (in garden) cenador m, glorieta; ~**time** n (season) verano; ~**time** n (by clock) hora de verano.
summit ['sʌmɪt] n cima, cumbre f; ~ **(conference)** n conferencia cumbre.
summon ['sʌmən] vt (person) llamar; (meeting) convocar; (LAW) citar; **to ~ up** vt cobrar; ~**s** n llamamiento, llamada // vt citar, emplazar.
sump [sʌmp] n (AUT) cárter m.
sumptuous ['sʌmptjuəs] a suntuoso.
sun [sʌn] n sol m; ~**bathe** vi tomar el sol; ~**burn** n (painful) quemadura; (tan) bronceado; ~**burnt** a (tanned) bronceado; (painfully) quemado por el sol.
Sunday ['sʌndɪ] n domingo.
sundial ['sʌndaɪəl] n reloj m de sol.
sundry ['sʌndrɪ] a varios, diversos; **all and ~** todos y cada uno; **sundries** npl géneros mpl diversos.
sunflower ['sʌnflauə*] n girasol m.
sung [sʌŋ] pp of **sing**.
sunglasses ['sʌnglɑːsɪz] npl gafas fpl de sol.
sunk [sʌŋk] pp of **sink**.
sun: ~**light** n luz f del sol; ~**lit** a iluminado por el sol; ~**ny** a soleado; (day) de sol; (fig) alegre; ~**rise** n salida del sol; ~**set** n puesta del sol; ~**shade** n (over table) sombrilla; ~**shine** n sol m; ~**spot** n mancha solar; ~**stroke** n insolación f; ~**tan** n bronceado; ~**tan oil** n bronceador m, crema bronceadora.
super ['suːpə*] a (col) bárbaro.

superannuation [suːpərænjuˈeɪʃən] n jubilación f.

superb [suːˈpəːb] a magnífico, espléndido.

supercilious [suːpəˈsɪlɪəs] a (disdainful) desdeñoso; (haughty) altanero.

superficial [suːpəˈfɪʃəl] a superficial.

superfluous [suˈpəːfluəs] a superfluo, de sobra.

superhuman [suːpəˈhjuːmən] a sobrehumano.

superimpose [ˈsuːpərɪmˈpəuz] vt sobreponer.

superintendent [suːpərɪnˈtɛndənt] n superintendente m/f; (POLICE) subjefe m.

superior [suˈpɪərɪə*] a superior; (smug) desdeñoso // n superior m; ~ity [-ˈɔrɪtɪ] n superioridad f; desdén m.

superlative [suˈpəːlətɪv] a, n superlativo.

superman [ˈsuːpəmæn] n superhombre m.

supermarket [ˈsuːpəmɑːkɪt] n supermercado.

supernatural [suːpəˈnætʃərəl] a sobrenatural.

superpower [ˈsuːpəpauə*] n (POL) superpotencia.

supersede [suːpəˈsiːd] vt suplantar.

supersonic [ˈsuːpəˈsɔnɪk] a supersónico.

superstition [suːpəˈstɪʃən] n superstición f; **superstitious** [-ʃəs] a supersticioso.

supertanker [ˈsuːpətæŋkə*] n superpetrolero.

supervise [ˈsuːpəvaɪz] vt supervisar; **supervision** [-ˈvɪʒən] n supervisión f; **supervisor** n supervisor/a m/f.

supper [ˈsʌpə*] n cena; **to have** ~ cenar.

supple [ˈsʌpl] a flexible.

supplement [ˈsʌplɪmənt] n suplemento // vt [sʌplɪˈmɛnt] suplir; ~ary [-ˈmɛntərɪ] a suplementario.

supplier [səˈplaɪə*] n suministrador/a m/f; (COMM) distribuidor/a m/f.

supply [səˈplaɪ] vt (provide) suministrar, facilitar; (equip): **to** ~ **(with)** abastecer (de) // n suministro, provisión f; (supplying) abastecimiento // a (teacher etc) suplente; **supplies** npl (food) víveres mpl; (MIL) pertrechos mpl; ~ **and demand** la oferta y la demanda.

support [səˈpɔːt] n (moral, financial etc) apoyo; (TECH) soporte m // vt apoyar; (financially) mantener; (uphold) sostener; ~**er** n (POL etc) partidario/a; (SPORT) aficionado/a.

suppose [səˈpəuz] vt, vi (gen) suponer; (imagine) imaginarse; **to be** ~**d to do sth** deber hacer algo; ~**dly** [səˈpəuzɪdlɪ] ad que se supone, según cabe suponer; **supposing** conj en caso de que; **supposition** [sʌpəˈzɪʃən] n suposición f.

suppository [səˈpɔzɪtərɪ] n supositorio.

suppress [səˈprɛs] vt suprimir; (yawn) ahogar; ~**ion** [səˈprɛʃən] n represión f.

supremacy [suˈprɛməsɪ] n supremacía.

supreme [-ˈpriːm] a supremo.

surcharge [ˈsəːtʃɑːdʒ] n sobrecarga; (extra tax) recargo.

sure [ʃuə*] a (gen) seguro; (definite, convinced) cierto; (aim) certero; ~**!** (of course) ¡claro!, ¡por supuesto!; ~**-footed** a de pie firme; ~**ly** ad (certainly) seguramente.

surety [ˈʃuərətɪ] n garantía, fianza; (person) fiador/a m/f.

surf [səːf] n olas fpl.

surface [ˈsəːfɪs] n superficie f // vt (road) revestir // vi salir a la superficie.

surfboard [ˈsəːfbɔːd] n plancha (de surfing), acuaplano.

surfeit [ˈsəːfɪt] n: **a** ~ **of** exceso de.

surfing [ˈsəːfɪŋ] n surfing m.

surge [səːdʒ] n oleada, oleaje m // vi avanzar a tropel.

surgeon [ˈsəːdʒən] n cirujano; **dental** ~ odontólogo.

surgery [ˈsəːdʒərɪ] n cirugía; (room) consultorio; **to undergo** ~ operarse; ~ **hours** npl horas fpl de consulta.

surgical [ˈsəːdʒɪkl] a quirúrgico; ~ **spirit** n alcohol m.

surly [ˈsəːlɪ] a hosco, malhumorado.

surmount [səːˈmaunt] vt superar, sobreponerse a.

surname [ˈsəːneɪm] n apellido.

surpass [səːˈpɑːs] vt superar, exceder.

surplus [ˈsəːpləs] n (gen) excedente m; (COMM) superávit m // a excedente, sobrante.

surprise [səˈpraɪz] n (gen) sorpresa; (astonishment) asombro // vt sorprender; asombrar; **surprising** a sorprendente; asombroso.

surrealist [səˈrɪəlɪst] a surrealista.

surrender [səˈrɛndə*] n rendición f, entrega // vi rendirse, entregarse.

surreptitious [sʌrəpˈtɪʃəs] a subrepticio.

surround [səˈraund] vt rodar, circundar; (MIL etc) cercar; ~**ing** a circundante; ~**ings** npl alrededores mpl, cercanías fpl.

surveillance [səːˈveɪləns] n vigilancia.

survey [ˈsəːveɪ] n inspección f, examen m; (inquiry) encuesta // vt [səːˈveɪ] (gen) examinar, inspeccionar; (look at) mirar, contemplar; (make inquiries about) hacer una encuesta sobre; ~**or** n agrimensor m.

survival [səˈvaɪvl] n supervivencia; **survive** vi sobrevivir; (custom etc) perdurar // vt sobrevivir a; **survivor** n superviviente m/f.

susceptible [səˈsɛptəbl] a: ~ **(to)** susceptible o sensible (a).

suspect [ˈsʌspɛkt] a, n sospechoso // vt [səsˈpɛkt] sospechar.

suspend [səsˈpɛnd] vt suspender; ~**er belt** n portaligas m inv; ~**ers** npl ligas fpl; (US) tirantes mpl.

suspense [səsˈpɛns] n incertidumbre f, duda; (in film etc) suspense m.

suspension [səsˈpɛnʃən] n (gen, AUT) suspensión f; (of driving licence) privación f; ~ **bridge** n puente m colgante.

suspicion [səsˈpɪʃən] n (gen) sospecha; (distrust) recelo; (trace) traza; **suspicious**

[-ʃəs] a (suspecting) receloso; (causing ~) sospechoso.

sustain [səs'teɪn] vt sostener, apoyar; (suffer) sufrir, padecer; ~ed a (effort) sostenido.

sustenance ['sʌstɪnəns] n sustento.

swab [swɔb] n (MED) algodón m, torunda.

swagger ['swægə*] vi pavonearse.

swallow ['swɔləu] n (bird) golondrina; (of food etc) trago // vt tragar; **to ~ up** (savings etc) consumir.

swam [swæm] pt of **swim.**

swamp [swɔmp] n pantano, ciénaga // vt abrumar, agobiar; ~**y** a pantanoso.

swan [swɔn] n cisne m.

swap [swɔp] n canje m, intercambio // vt: **to ~ (for)** canjear (por).

swarm [swɔːm] n (of bees) enjambre m; (gen) multitud f // vi hormiguear, pulular.

swarthy ['swɔːðɪ] a moreno.

swastika ['swɔstɪkə] n suástika, cruz f gamada.

swat [swɔt] vt aplastar.

sway [sweɪ] vi mecerse, balancearse // vt (influence) mover, influir en.

swear [swɛə*], pt **swore**, pp **sworn** vi jurar; **to ~ to sth** declarar algo bajo juramento; ~**word** n taco, palabrota.

sweat [swɛt] n sudor m // vi sudar.

sweater ['swɛtə*] n suéter m.

sweaty ['swɛtɪ] a sudoroso.

swede [swiːd] n nabo.

Swede [swiːd] n sueco/a; **Sweden** n Suecia; **Swedish**, a, n (LING) sueco.

sweep [swiːp] n (act) barredura; (of arm) golpe m; (range) extensión f, alcance m; (also: **chimney** ~) deshollinador m // (vb: pt, pp **swept**) vt barrer; (mines) rastrear // vi barrer; **to ~ away** vt barrer; (rub out) borrar; **to ~ past** vi pasar rápidamente; (brush by) rozar; **to ~ up** vi recoger la basura; ~**ing** a (gesture) dramático; (generalized) generalizado.

sweet [swiːt] n (candy) dulce m, caramelo; (pudding) postre m // a dulce; (sugary) azucarado; (fresh) fresco, nuevo; (fig) dulce, amable; ~**corn** n maíz m; ~**en** vt endulzar; (add sugar to) poner azúcar a; ~**heart** n novio/a; (in speech) amor; ~**ly** ad dulcemente; (gently) suavemente; ~**ness** n (gen) dulzura; (amount of sugar) lo dulce, lo azucarado; ~ **pea** n guisante m de olor.

swell [swɛl] n (of sea) marejada, oleaje m // a (col: excellent) estupendo, excelente // (vb: pt **swelled**, pp **swollen** or **swelled**) vt hinchar, inflar // vi hincharse, inflarse; ~**ing** n (MED) hinchazón m.

sweltering ['swɛltərɪŋ] a sofocante, de mucho calor.

swept [swɛpt] pt, pp of **sweep.**

swerve [swəːv] vi (in car) desviarse bruscamente.

swift [swɪft] n (bird) vencejo // a rápido, veloz; ~**ness** n rapidez f, velocidad f.

swig [swɪg] n (col: drink) trago.

swill [swɪl] n bazofia // vt (also: ~ out, ~

down) lavar, limpiar con agua.

swim [swɪm] n: **to go for a** ~ ir a nadar // (vb: pt **swam**, pp **swum**) vi nadar; (head, room) dar vueltas // vt pasar a nado; ~**mer** n nadador/a m/f; ~**ming** n natación f; ~**ming baths** npl piscina sg; ~**ming cap** n gorro de baño; ~**ming costume** n bañador m, traje m de baño; ~**ming pool** n piscina; ~**suit** n bañador m, traje m de baño.

swindle ['swɪndl] n estafa // vt estafar; **swindler** n estafador/a m/f.

swine [swaɪn] n, pl inv cerdos mpl, puercos mpl; (col!) canalla sg.

swing [swɪŋ] n (in playground) columpio; (movement) balanceo, vaivén m; (change of direction) viraje m; (rhythm) ritmo // (vb: pt, pp **swung**) vt balancear; (on a ~) columpiar; (also: ~ **round**) voltear bruscamente // vi balancearse, columpiarse; (also: ~ **round**) volver bruscamente; **to be in full** ~ estar en plena marcha; ~ **bridge** n puente m giratorio; ~ **door** n puerta giratoria.

swipe [swaɪp] n golpe m fuerte // vt (hit) golpear fuerte; (col: steal) guindar.

swirl [swəːl] vi arremolinarse.

Swiss [swɪs] a, n, pl inv suizo/a.

switch [swɪtʃ] n (for light, radio etc) interruptor m; (change) cambio; (of hair) trenza postiza // vt (change) cambiar de; **to ~ off** vt apagar; (engine) parar; **to ~ on** vt encender, prender; (engine, machine) arrancar; ~**board** n (TEL) central f de teléfonos.

Switzerland ['swɪtsələnd] n Suiza.

swivel ['swɪvl] vi (also: ~ **round**) girar.

swollen ['swəulən] pp of **swell.**

swoon [swuːn] vi desmayarse, desvanecerse.

swoop [swuːp] n (by police etc) redada // vi (also: ~ **down**) calarse, precipitarse.

swop [swɔp] = **swap.**

sword [sɔːd] n espada; ~**fish** n pez m espada.

swore [swɔː*] pt of **swear.**

sworn [swɔːn] pp of **swear.**

swot [swɔt] vt, vi empollar.

swum [swʌm] pp of **swim.**

swung [swʌŋ] pt, pp of **swing.**

sycamore ['sɪkəmɔː*] n sicomoro.

syllable ['sɪləbl] n sílaba.

syllabus ['sɪləbəs] n programa m de estudios.

symbol ['sɪmbl] n símbolo; ~**ic(al)** [-'bɔlɪk(l)] a simbólico; ~**ism** n simbolismo; ~**ize** vt simbolizar.

symmetrical [sɪ'mɛtrɪkl] a simétrico; **symmetry** ['sɪmɪtrɪ] n simetría.

sympathetic [sɪmpə'θɛtɪk] a compasivo; (pleasant) simpático; ~**ally** ad con compasión.

sympathize ['sɪmpəθaɪz] vi: **to ~ with sb** compadecerse de uno; **sympathizer** n (POL) simpatizante m/f.

sympathy ['sɪmpəθɪ] n (pity) compasión f; (liking) simpatía; **with our deepest** ~

nuestro más sentido pésame; ~ **strike** n huelga por solidaridad.

symphony ['sɪmfənɪ] n sinfonía; ~ **orchestra** n orquesta sinfónica.

symposium [sɪm'pəuzɪəm] n simposio.

symptom ['sɪmptəm] n síntoma m, indicio; ~**atic** [-'mætɪk] a sintomático.

synagogue ['sɪnəgɔg] n sinagoga.

synchronize ['sɪŋkrənaɪz] vt sincronizar // vi: **to** ~ **with** sincronizarse con.

syndicate ['sɪndɪkɪt] n (gen) sindicato; (of newspapers) cadena.

syndrome ['sɪndrəum] n síndrome m.

synonym ['sɪnənɪm] n sinónimo; ~**ous** [sɪ'nɔnɪməs] a: ~**ous (with)** sinónimo (con).

synopsis [sɪ'nɔpsɪs], pl **-ses** [-siːz] n sinopsis f inv.

syntax ['sɪntæks] n sintáxis f.

synthesis ['sɪnθəsɪs], pl **-ses** [-siːz] n síntesis f inv.

synthetic [sɪn'θetɪk] a sintético.

syphilis ['sɪfɪlɪs] n sífilis f.

syphon ['saɪfən] = **siphon.**

Syria ['sɪrɪə] n Siria; ~**n** a, n sirio/a.

syringe [sɪ'rɪndʒ] n jeringa.

syrup ['sɪrəp] n jarabe m, almíbar m.

system ['sɪstəm] n (gen) sistema; (method) método; (ANAT) organismo; ~**atic** [-'mætɪk] a sistemático; metódico; ~**s analyst** n analista m/f de sistemas.

T

ta [tɑː] excl (Brit: col) gracias.

tab [tæb] n (gen) lengüeta; (label) etiqueta; **to keep** ~**s on** (fig) vigilar.

tabby ['tæbɪ] n (also: ~ **cat**) gato atigrado.

table ['teɪbl] n mesa; (of statistics etc) cuadro, tabla // vt (motion etc) presentar; **to lay** or **set the** ~ poner la mesa; ~**cloth** n mantel m; ~ **d'hôte** [tɑːbl'dəut] n menú m; ~**mat** n mantel m individual; ~**spoon** n cuchara grande; (also: ~**spoonful**: as measurement) cucharada.

tablet ['tæblɪt] n (MED) tableta, pastilla; (for writing) bloc m; (of stone) lápida.

table: ~ **tennis** n ping-pong m, tenis m de mesa; ~ **wine** n vino de mesa.

taboo [tə'buː] n tabú m // a tabú.

tacit ['tæsɪt] a tácito.

taciturn ['tæsɪtɜːn] a taciturno.

tack [tæk] n (nail) tachuela, chincheta; (stitch) hilván m; (NAUT) bordada // vt (nail) clavar con chinchetas; (stitch) hilvanar // vi virar.

tackle ['tækl] n (gear) equipo; (also: **fishing** ~) aparejo; (for lifting) polea; (RUGBY) atajo // vt (difficulty) enfrentar; (grapple with) agarrar; (RUGBY) atajar.

tacky ['tækɪ] a pegajoso.

tact [tækt] n tacto, discreción f; ~**ful** a discreto, diplomático; ~**fully** ad discretamente.

tactical ['tæktɪkl] a táctico; **tactics** [-tɪks] n, npl táctica sg.

tactless ['tæktlɪs] a indiscreto, falto de tacto; ~**ly** ad indiscretamente.

tadpole ['tædpəul] n renacuajo.

tag [tæg] n (label) etiqueta; (loose end) cabo; **to** ~ **along with sb** acompañar a uno.

tail [teɪl] n (gen) cola; (ZOOL) rabo; (of shirt, coat) faldón m // vt (follow) seguir los talones a; **to** ~ **away, ~ off** vi (in size, quality etc) ir disminuyendo; ~ **coat** n frac m; ~ **end** n cola, parte f final; ~**gate** n puerta trasera.

tailor ['teɪlə*] n sastre m; ~**ing** n (cut) corte m; (craft) sastrería; ~**-made** a hecho a la medida; (fig) especial.

tailwind ['teɪlwɪnd] n viento de cola.

tainted ['teɪntɪd] a (food) pasado; (water, air) contaminado; (fig) manchado.

take [teɪk], pt **took**, pp **taken** vt (gen) tomar; (grab) coger; (gain: prize) ganar; (require: effort, courage) exigir, hacer falta; (tolerate) aguantar; (hold: passengers etc) tener cabida para; (accompany, bring, carry) llevar; (exam) presentarse a; **to** ~ **sth from** (drawer etc) sacar algo de; (person) coger algo a; **I** ~ **it that...** supongo que...; **to** ~ **after** vt fus parecerse a; **to** ~ **apart** vt desmontar; **to** ~ **away** vt (remove) quitar; (carry off) llevar; **to** ~ **back** vt (return) devolver; (one's words) retractar; **to** ~ **down** vt (building) demoler; (letter etc) poner por escrito; **to** ~ **in** vt (deceive) engañar; (understand) entender; (include) abarcar; (lodger) acoger, recibir; **to** ~ **off** vi (AVIAT) despegar // vt (remove) quitar; (imitate) imitar; **to** ~ **on** vt (work) emprender; (employee) contratar; (opponent) desafiar; **to** ~ **out** vt sacar; (remove) quitar; **to** ~ **over** vt (business) tomar posesión de // vi: **to** ~ **over from sb** relevar a uno; **to** ~ **to** vt fus (person) coger simpatía a; (activity) aficionarse a; **to** ~ **up** vt (a dress) acortar; (occupy: time, space) ocupar; (engage in: hobby etc) dedicarse a; ~**away** a (food) para llevar; ~**-home pay** n salario neto; ~**off** n (AVIAT) despegue m; ~**over** n (COMM) absorción f; ~**over bid** n oferta de compra.

takings ['teɪkɪŋz] npl (COMM) ingresos mpl.

talc [tælk] n (also: ~**um powder**) talco.

tale [teɪl] n (story) cuento; (account) relación f; **to tell** ~**s** (fig: lie) chismear.

talent ['tælnt] n talento; ~**ed** a talentoso, de talento.

talk [tɔːk] n (gen) charla; (gossip) habladurías fpl; (chatter) chismes mpl; (conversation) conversación f // vi (speak) hablar; (chatter) charlar; **to** ~ **about** hablar de; **to** ~ **sb into doing sth** convencer a uno de que debe hacer algo; **to** ~ **sb out of doing sth** disuadir a uno de algo; **to** ~ **shop** hablar de asuntos profesionales; **to ~ over** vt hablar de; **~ative** a hablador(a).

tall [tɔːl] a (gen) alto; (tree) grande; **to be 6 feet ~** medir 6 pies, tener 6 pies de alto; **~boy** n cómoda alta; **~ness** n altura; **~ story** n historia inverosímil.

tally ['tælɪ] n cuenta // vi: **to ~ (with)** corresponder (con).

talon ['tælən] n garra.

tambourine [tæmbə'riːn] n pandereta.

tame [teɪm] a (mild) manso; (tamed) domesticado; (fig: story, style) soso.

tamper ['tæmpə*] vi: **to ~ with** entrometerse en.

tampon ['tæmpən] n tampón m.

tan [tæn] n (also: **sun~**) bronceado // vt broncear // vi ponerse moreno // a (colour) marrón.

tandem ['tændəm] n tándem m.

tang [tæŋ] n sabor m fuerte.

tangerine [tændʒə'riːn] n mandarina.

tangible ['tændʒəbl] a tangible.

tangle ['tæŋgl] n enredo; **to get in(to) a ~** enredarse.

tango ['tæŋgəu] n tango.

tank [tæŋk] n (water ~) depósito, tanque m; (for fish) acuario; (MIL) tanque m.

tanker ['tæŋkə*] n (ship) petrolero; (truck) camión m cisterna o tanque.

tanned [tænd] a (skin) moreno, bronceado.

tantalizing ['tæntəlaɪzɪŋ] a tentador(a).

tantamount ['tæntəmaunt] a: **~ to** equivalente a.

tantrum ['tæntrəm] n rabieta.

tap [tæp] n (on sink etc) grifo; (gentle blow) golpecito; (gas ~) llave f // vt dar golpecitos; (resources) utilizar, explotar; **~-dancing** n zapateado.

tape [teɪp] n cinta; (also: **magnetic ~**) cinta magnética; (sticky ~) cinta adhesiva // vt (record) grabar (en cinta); **~ measure** n cinta métrica, metro.

taper ['teɪpə*] n cirio // vi afilarse.

tape recorder ['teɪprɪkɔːdə*] n grabadora.

tapered ['teɪpəd], **tapering** ['teɪpərɪŋ] a afilado.

tapestry ['tæpɪstrɪ] n (object) tapiz m; (art) tapicería.

tapioca [tæpɪ'əukə] n tapioca.

tar [tɑː] n alquitrán m, brea.

tarantula [tə'ræntjulə] n tarántula.

target ['tɑːgɪt] n (gen) blanco; **~ practice** tiro al blanco.

tariff ['tærɪf] n tarifa.

tarmac ['tɑːmæk] n (on road) alquitranado; (AVIAT) pista de aterrizaje.

tarnish ['tɑːnɪʃ] vt quitar el brillo a.

tarpaulin [tɑː'pɔːlɪn] n alquitranado.

tarragon ['tærəgən] n estragón m.

tart [tɑːt] n (CULIN) tarta; (col: pej: woman) fulana // a (flavour) agrio, ácido.

tartan ['tɑːtn] n tartán m, escocés m // a de tartán.

tartar ['tɑːtə*] n (on teeth) sarro; **~(e) sauce** n salsa tártara.

task [tɑːsk] n tarea; **to take to ~** reprender; **~ force** n (MIL, POLICE) destacamento especial.

tassel ['tæsl] n borla.

taste [teɪst] n sabor m, gusto; (also: **after~**) dejo; (sip) sorbo; (fig: glimpse, idea) muestra, idea // vt probar // vi: **to ~ of or like** (fish etc) saber a; **you can ~ the garlic (in it)** se nota el sabor a ajo; **can I have a ~ of this wine?** ¿puedo probar el vino?; **to have a ~ for sth** ser aficionado a algo; **in good/bad ~** de buen/mal gusto; **~ful** a de buen gusto; **~fully** ad con buen gusto; **~less** a (food) insípido; (remark) de mal gusto; **tasty** a sabroso, rico.

tattered ['tætəd] a see **tatters**.

tatters ['tætəz] npl: **in ~** (also: **tattered**) hecho jirones.

tattoo [tə'tuː] n tatuaje m; (spectacle) espectáculo militar // vt tatuar.

tatty ['tætɪ] a (col) raído.

taught [tɔːt] pt, pp of **teach**.

taunt [tɔːnt] n burla // vt burlarse de.

Taurus ['tɔːrəs] n Tauro.

taut [tɔːt] a tirante, tenso.

tawdry ['tɔːdrɪ] a cursi, de mal gusto.

tawny ['tɔːnɪ] a leonado.

tax [tæks] n impuesto // vt gravar (con un impuesto); (fig: test) abrumar; (: patience) agotar; **direct ~** contribución directa; **~ation** [-'seɪʃən] n impuestos mpl; **~collector** n recaudador/a m/f; **~-free** a libre de impuestos.

taxi ['tæksɪ] n taxi m // vi (AVIAT) rodar en suelo.

taxidermist ['tæksɪdəːmɪst] n taxidermista m/f.

taxi: ~ driver n taxista m/f; **~ rank, ~ stand** n parada de taxis.

tax: ~ payer n contribuyente m/f; **~ return** n declaración f de ingresos.

TB abbr of **tuberculosis**.

tea [tiː] n té m; (snack) merienda; **high ~** merienda-cena; **~ bag** n bolsa de té; **~ break** n descanso para el té; **~cake** n bollo.

teach [tiːtʃ], pt, pp **taught** vt: **to ~ sb sth, ~ sth to sb** enseñar algo a uno // vi enseñar; (be a teacher) ser profesor/a; **~er** n (in secondary school) profesor/a m/f; (in primary school) maestro/a m/f; **~ing** n enseñanza.

tea: ~ cosy n cubretetera; **~cup** n taza para té.

teak [tiːk] n (madera de) teca.

tea leaves npl hojas fpl de té.

team [tiːm] n equipo; (of animals) pareja; **~ work** n trabajo de equipo.

teapot ['tiːpɔt] n tetera.

tear [tɛə*] n rasgón m, desgarrón m // n [tɪə*] lágrima // (vb: pt **tore**, pp **torn**) vt romper, rasgar // vi rasgarse; **in ~s** llorando; **to burst into ~s** deshacerse en lágrimas; **to ~ along** vi (rush) precipitarse; **~ful** a lloroso; **~ gas** n gas m lacrimógeno.

tearoom ['ti:ru:m] n salón m de té, cafetería.

tease [ti:z] n bromista m/f // vt bromear, tomar el pelo a.

tea: ~ **set** n juego de té; ~**spoon** n cucharilla; (also: ~**spoonful:** as measurement) cucharadita.

teat [ti:t] n (of bottle) tetina.

tea: ~**time** n hora del té; ~ **towel** n trapo de cocina.

technical ['tɛknɪkl] a técnico; ~**ity** [-'kælɪtɪ] n detalle m técnico; ~**ly** ad técnicamente.

technician [tɛk'nɪʃn] n técnico.

technique [tɛk'ni:k] n técnica.

technological [tɛknə'lɔdʒɪkl] a tecnológico; **technology** [-'nɔlədʒɪ] n tecnología.

teddy (bear) ['tɛdɪ] n osito de felpa.

tedious ['ti:dɪəs] a pesado, aburrido.

tee [ti:] n (GOLF) tee m.

teem [ti:m] vi abundar, pulular; **to** ~ **with** rebosar de; **it is** ~**ing (with rain)** llueve a mares.

teenage ['ti:neidʒ] a (fashions etc) de o para los jóvenes; **teenager** n joven m/f (de 13 a 19 años).

teens [ti:nz] npl: **to be in one's** ~ ser un adolescente, no haber cumplido los 20.

tee-shirt ['ti:ʃə:t] n = **T-shirt**.

teeter ['ti:tə*] vi balancearse.

teeth [ti:θ] pl of **tooth**.

teethe [ti:ð] vi echar los dientes.

teething ['ti:ðɪŋ]: ~ **ring** n mordedor m; ~ **troubles** npl (fig) dificultades fpl iniciales.

teetotal ['ti:'təutl] a (person) abstemio.

telecommunications ['tɛlɪkəmju:nɪ'keɪʃənz] n telecomunicaciones fpl.

telegram ['tɛlɪgræm] n telegrama m.

telegraph ['tɛlɪgrɑ:f] n telégrafo; ~**ic** [-'græfɪk] a telegráfico; ~ **pole** n poste m de telégrafos.

telepathic [tɛlɪ'pæθɪk] a telepático; **telepathy** [tə'lɛpəθɪ] n telepatía.

telephone ['tɛlɪfəun] n teléfono // vt (person) llamar por teléfono; (message) telefonear; ~ **booth**, ~ **box** n cabina telefónica; ~ **call** n llamada (telefónica); ~ **directory** n guía (telefónica); ~ **exchange** n central f telefónica; ~ **number** n número de teléfono; **telephonist** [tə'lɛfənɪst] n telefonista m/f.

telephoto ['tɛlɪ'fəutəu] a: ~ **lens** n teleobjetivo.

teleprinter ['tɛlɪprɪntə*] n teletipo.

telescope ['tɛlɪskəup] n telescopio; **telescopic** [-'skɔpɪk] a telescópico.

televise ['tɛlɪvaɪz] vt televisar.

television ['tɛlɪvɪʒən] n televisión f; ~ **set** n televisor m.

telex ['tɛlɛks] n telex m.

tell [tɛl], pt, pp **told** vt decir; (relate: story) contar; (distinguish): **to** ~ **sth from** distinguir algo de // vi (have effect) tener

efecto; **to** ~ **sb to do sth** mandar a uno que haga algo; **to** ~ **sb off** reñir o regañar a uno; ~**er** n (in bank) cajero; ~**ing** a (remark, detail) revelador(a); ~**tale** a (sign) indicador(a).

telly ['tɛlɪ] n (col) abbr of **television**.

temerity [tə'mɛrɪtɪ] n temeridad f.

temper ['tɛmpə*] n (nature) carácter m; (mood) humor m; (bad ~) genio, mal genio; (fit of anger) cólera, (of child) rabieta // vt (moderate) moderar; **to be in a** ~ estar de mal humor; **to lose one's** ~ perder la paciencia.

temperament ['tɛmprəmənt] n (nature) temperamento; ~**al** [-'mɛntl] a temperamental.

temperance ['tɛmpərns] n moderación f; (in drinking) sobriedad f.

temperate ['tɛmprət] a moderado; (climate) templado.

temperature ['tɛmprətʃə*] n temperatura; **to have** or **run a** ~ tener fiebre.

tempered ['tɛmpəd] a (steel) templado.

tempest ['tɛmpɪst] n tempestad f.

temple ['tɛmpl] n (building) templo; (ANAT) sien f.

tempo ['tɛmpəu], pl ~**s** or **tempi** [-pi:] n tempo; (fig: of life etc) ritmo.

temporal ['tɛmpərl] a temporal.

temporarily ['tɛmpərərɪlɪ] ad temporalmente.

temporary ['tɛmpərərɪ] a provisional, temporal; (passing) transitorio; (worker) temporero.

tempt [tɛmpt] vt tentar; **to** ~ **sb into doing sth** tentar o inducir a uno a hacer algo; ~**ation** [-'teɪʃən] n tentación f; ~**ing** a tentador(a).

ten [tɛn] num diez.

tenable ['tɛnəbl] a sostenible.

tenacious [tə'neɪʃəs] a tenaz; **tenacity** [-'næsɪtɪ] n tenacidad f.

tenancy ['tɛnənsɪ] n alquiler m; (of house) inquilinato; **tenant** n (rent-payer) inquilino; (occupant) habitante m/f.

tend [tɛnd] vt cuidar // vi: **to** ~ **to do sth** tener tendencia a hacer algo.

tendency ['tɛndənsɪ] n tendencia.

tender ['tɛndə*] a tierno, blando; (delicate) delicado; (sore) sensible, dolorido; (affectionate) tierno, cariñoso // n (COMM: offer) oferta; (money): **legal** ~ moneda de curso legal // vt ofrecer; ~**ize** vt (CULIN) ablandar; ~**ness** n ternura; (of meat) blandura.

tendon ['tɛndən] n tendón m.

tenement ['tɛnəmənt] n casa de pisos.

tennis ['tɛnɪs] n tenis m; ~ **ball** n pelota de tenis; ~ **court** n pista de tenis; ~ **racket** n raqueta de tenis.

tenor ['tɛnə*] n (MUS) tenor m.

tenpin bowling ['tɛnpɪn-] n los bolos mpl.

tense [tɛns] a tenso; (stretched) tirante; (stiff) rígido, tieso // n (LING) tiempo; ~**ness** n tensión f.

tension ['tɛnʃən] n tensión f.

tent [tɛnt] n tienda (de campaña).
tentacle ['tɛntəkl] n tentáculo.
tentative ['tɛntətɪv] a experimental; (conclusion) provisional.
tenterhooks ['tɛntəhuks] npl: **on** ~ sobre ascuas.
tenth [tɛnθ] a décimo.
tent: ~ **peg** n (clavija, estaquilla); ~ **pole** n mástil m.
tenuous ['tɛnjuəs] a tenue.
tenure ['tɛnjuə*] n posesión f, tenencia f.
tepid ['tɛpɪd] a tibio.
term [tɜːm] n (limit) límite m; (COMM) plazo; (word) término; (period) período; (SCOL) trimestre m // vt llamar; ~**s** npl (conditions) condiciones fpl; (COMM) precio, tarifa; **in the short/long** ~ a corto/largo plazo; **to be on good** ~**s with sb** llevarse bien con uno; **to come to** ~**s with** (person) llegar a un acuerdo con; (problem) adaptarse a.
terminal ['tɜːmɪnl] a terminal; (disease) mortal // n (ELEC) borne m; (also: **air** ~) terminal f; (also: **coach** ~) estación f terminal.
terminate ['tɜːmɪneɪt] vt terminar // vi: **to** ~ **in** acabar por; **termination** [-'neɪʃən] n terminación f; (of contract) conclusión f.
terminology [tɜːmɪ'nɔlədʒɪ] n terminología.
terminus ['tɜːmɪnəs], pl **-mini** [-mɪnaɪ] n término, estación f terminal.
termite ['tɜːmaɪt] n termita.
terrace ['tɛrəs] n terraza; (row of houses) hilera de casas adosadas; **the** ~**s** (SPORT) gradas fpl; ~**ed** a (garden) escalonado; (house) adosado.
terrain [tɛ'reɪn] n terreno.
terrible ['tɛrɪbl] a terrible, horrible; (fam) malísimo; **terribly** ad terriblemente; (very badly) malísimamente.
terrier ['tɛrɪə*] n terrier m.
terrific [tə'rɪfɪk] a fantástico, fenomenal; (wonderful) maravilloso.
terrify ['tɛrɪfaɪ] vt aterrorizar.
territorial [tɛrɪ'tɔːrɪəl] a territorial.
territory ['tɛrɪtərɪ] n territorio.
terror ['tɛrə*] n terror m; ~**ism** n terrorismo; ~**ist** n terrorista m/f; ~**ize** vt aterrorizar.
terse [tɜːs] a (style) conciso; (reply) brusco.
test [tɛst] n (trial, check) prueba, ensayo, (: of goods in factory) control m; (of courage etc, CHEM) prueba; (MED) examen m; (exam) examen m, test m; (also: **driving** ~) examen m de conducir // vt probar, poner a prueba.
testament ['tɛstəmənt] n testamento; **the Old/New T**~ el Antiguo/Nuevo Testamento.
testicle ['tɛstɪkl] n testículo.
testify ['tɛstɪfaɪ] vi (LAW) prestar declaración; **to** ~ **to sth** atestiguar algo.
testimonial [tɛstɪ'məunɪəl] n (reference) recomendación f; (gift) obsequio.

testimony ['tɛstɪmənɪ] n (LAW) testimonio, declaración f.
test: ~ **match** n (CRICKET, RUGBY) partido internacional; ~ **pilot** n piloto de pruebas; ~ **tube** n probeta.
testy ['tɛstɪ] a irritable.
tetanus ['tɛtənəs] n tétano.
tether ['tɛðə*] vt atar (con una cuerda) // n: **at the end of one's** ~ a punto de perder la paciencia.
text [tɛkst] n texto; ~**book** n libro de texto.
textiles ['tɛkstaɪlz] npl textiles mpl, tejidos mpl.
texture ['tɛkstʃə*] n textura.
Thai [taɪ] a, n tailandés/esa m/f; ~**land** n Tailandia.
Thames [tɛmz] n: **the** ~ el (río) Támesis.
than [ðæn, ðən] conj que; (with numerals): **more** ~ **10/once** más de 10/una vez; **I have more/less** ~ **you** tengo más/menos que tú.
thank [θæŋk] vt dar las gracias a, agradecer; ~ **you (very much)** muchas gracias; ~**s** npl gracias fpl; ~**s to** prep gracias a; ~**ful** a: ~**ful (for)** agradecido por; ~**less** a ingrato; **Thanksgiving (Day)** n día m de acción de gracias.
that [ðæt, ðət] conj que // det ese/esa; (more remote) aquel/aquella // pron ése/ésa; aquél/aquélla; (neuter) eso; aquello; (relative: subject) que; (: object) que, el cual/la cual etc; (with time): **on the day** ~ **he came** el día que vino // ad: ~ **high** tan alto, así de alto; **it's about** ~ **high** es más o menos así de alto; ~ **one** ése/ésa; aquél/aquélla; **what's** ~? ¿qué es eso?; **who's** ~? ¿quién es?; **is** ~ **you?** ¿eres tú?; (formal) ¿es Usted?; ~**'s what he said** eso es lo que dijo; **all** ~ todo eso; **I can't work** ~ **much** no puedo trabajar tanto.
thatched [θætʃt] a (roof) de paja; ~ **cottage** casita con tejado de paja.
thaw [θɔː] n deshielo // vi (ice) derretirse; (food) descongelarse // vt (food) descongelar.
the [ðiː, ðə] def art el/la; (pl) los/las; (neuter) lo; ~ **sooner** ~ **better** cuanto antes mejor.
theatre, theater (US) ['θɪətə*] n teatro; ~-**goer** n aficionado al teatro.
theatrical [θɪ'ætrɪkl] a teatral.
theft [θɛft] n robo.
their [ðɛə*] a su; ~**s** pron (el) suyo/(la) suya etc; **a friend of** ~**s** un amigo suyo.
them [ðɛm, ðəm] pron (direct) los/las; (indirect) les; (stressed, after prep) ellos/ellas; **I see** ~ los veo; **give** ~ **the book** dales el libro.
theme [θiːm] n tema m; ~ **song** tema (musical).
themselves [ðəm'sɛlvz] pl pron (subject) ellos mismos/ellas mismas; (complement) se; (after prep) sí (mismos/as).
then [ðɛn] ad (at that time) entonces; (next) pues; (later) luego, después; (and also)

además // *conj* (*therefore*) en ese caso, entonces // *a*: **the ~ president** el entonces presidente; **from ~ on** desde entonces.

theological [θɪə'lɔdʒɪkl] *a* teológico; **theology** [θɪ'ɔlədʒɪ] *n* teología.

theorem ['θɪərəm] *n* teorema *m*.

theoretical [θɪə'rɛtɪkl] *a* teórico; **theorize** ['θɪəraɪz] *vi* elaborar una teoría; **theory** ['θɪərɪ] *n* teoría.

therapeutic(al) [θɛrə'pjuːtɪk(l)] *a* terapéutico.

therapist ['θɛrəpɪst] *n* terapeuta *m/f*; **therapy** *n* terapia.

there [ðɛə*] *ad* allí, allá, ahí; ~, ~! ¡cálmate!; **it's ~** está ahí; ~ **is, ~ are** hay; ~ **he is** ahí está; **on/in ~** allí encima/dentro; ~ **abouts** *ad* por ahí; ~**after** *ad* después; ~**fore** *ad* por lo tanto; ~'s = ~ **is**; ~ **has**.

thermal ['θəːml] *a* termal.

thermometer [θə'mɔmɪtə*] *n* termómetro.

Thermos ['θəːmɔs] *n* termo.

thermostat ['θəːmoustæt] *n* termostato.

thesaurus [θɪ'sɔːrəs] *n* tesoro.

these [ðiːz] *pl det* estos/as // *pl pron* éstos/as.

thesis ['θiːsɪs], *pl* **-ses** [-siːz] *n* tesis *f*.

they [ðeɪ] *pl pron* ellos/ellas; (*stressed*) ellos (mismos)/ellas (mismas); ~ **say that...** (*it is said that*) se dice que...; ~'**d** = **they had; they would;** ~'**ll** = **they shall, they will;** ~'**re** = **they are;** ~'**ve** = **they have**.

thick [θɪk] *a* espeso; (*fat*) grueso; (*dense*) denso, espeso; (*stupid*) torpe // *n*: **in the ~ of the battle** en plena batalla; **it's 20 cm ~** tiene 20 cm de espesor; ~**en** *vi* espesarse // *vt* (*sauce etc*) espesar; ~**ness** *n* espesor *m*, grueso; ~**set** *a* rechoncho; ~**skinned** *a* (*fig*) insensible.

thief [θiːf], *pl* **thieves** [θiːvz] *n* ladrón/ona *m/f*.

thieving [θiːvɪŋ] *n* robo.

thigh [θaɪ] *n* muslo.

thimble ['θɪmbl] *n* dedal *m*.

thin [θɪn] *a* (*gen*) delgado; (*watery*) aguado; (*light*) tenue; (*hair, crowd*) escaso; (*fog*) poco denso // *vt*: **to ~ (down)** (*sauce, paint*) diluir.

thing [θɪŋ] *n* (*gen*) cosa; (*object*) objeto, artículo; (*matter*) asunto; (*mania*) manía; ~**s** *npl* (*belongings*) efectos *mpl* (personales); **the best ~ would be to...** lo mejor sería...; **how are ~s?** ¿qué tal?

think [θɪŋk], *pt, pp* **thought** *vi* pensar // *vt* pensar, creer; (*imagine*) imaginar; **what did you ~ of them?** ¿qué te parecieron?; **to ~ about sth/sb** pensar en algo/alguien; **I'll ~ about it** lo pensaré; **to ~ of doing sth** pensar en hacer algo; **I ~ so/not** creo que sí/no; **to ~ well of sb** tener buen concepto de alguien; **to ~ over** *vt* reflexionar sobre, meditar; **to ~ up** *vt* imaginar; ~**ing** *a* pensante.

thinly ['θɪnlɪ] *ad* (*cut*) en lonchas finas; (*spread*) con una capa fina.

thinness ['θɪnnɪs] *n* delgadez *f*.

third [θəːd] *a* tercer(a) // *n* tercero; (*fraction*) tercio; (*scol: degree*) de tercera clase; ~**ly** *ad* en tercer lugar; ~ **party insurance** *n* seguro contra terceras personas; ~~**rate** *a* (de calidad) mediocre; **the T~ World** *n* el Tercer Mundo.

thirst [θəːst] *n* sed *f*; ~**y** *a* (*person*) sediento; **to be ~y** tener sed.

thirteen ['θəː'tiːn] *num* trece.

thirty ['θəːtɪ] *num* treinta.

this [ðɪs] *det* este/esta // *pron* éste/ésta; (*neuter*) esto; ~ **is what he said** esto es lo que dijo; ~ **high** así de alto.

thistle ['θɪsl] *n* cardo.

thong [θɔŋ] *n* correa.

thorn [θɔːn] *n* espina; ~**y** *a* espinoso.

thorough ['θʌrə] *a* (*search*) minucioso; (*knowledge, research*) profundo; ~**bred** *a* (*horse*) de pura sangre; ~**fare** *n* calle *f*; '**no ~fare**' "prohibido el paso"; ~**ly** *ad* minuciosamente; profundamente, a fondo.

those [ðəuz] *pl pron* esos/esas; (*more remote*) aquellos/as // *pl det* ésos/ésas; aquéllos/as.

though [ðəu] *conj* aunque // *ad* sin embargo.

thought [θɔːt] *pt, pp of* **think** // *n* pensamiento; (*opinion*) opinión *f*; (*intention*) intención *f*; ~**ful** *a* pensativo; (*considerate*) considerado; ~**less** *a* desconsiderado.

thousand ['θauzənd] *num* mil; **two ~** dos mil; ~**s of** miles de; ~**th** *a* milésimo.

thrash [θræʃ] *vt* apalear; (*defeat*) derrotar; **to ~ about** *vi* revolcarse; **to ~ out** *vt* discutir largamente.

thread [θrɛd] *n* hilo; (*of screw*) rosca // *vt* (*needle*) enhebrar; ~**bare** *a* raído.

threat [θrɛt] *n* amenaza; ~**en** *vi* amenazar // *vt*: **to ~en sb with sth/to do** amenazar a uno con algo/ con hacer.

three [θriː] *num* tres; ~~**dimensional** *a* tridimensional; ~**fold** *ad*: **to increase** ~**fold** triplicar; ~~**piece suit** *n* traje *m* de tres piezas; ~~**piece suite** *n* tresillo; ~~**ply** *a* (*wool*) triple; ~~**wheeler** *n* (*car*) coche *m* de tres ruedas.

thresh [θrɛʃ] *vt* (*AGR*) trillar.

threshold ['θrɛʃhəuld] *n* umbral *m*.

threw [θruː] *pt of* **throw**.

thrift [θrɪft] *n* economía; ~**y** *a* económico.

thrill [θrɪl] *n* (*excitement*) emoción *f*; (*shudder*) estremecimiento // *vt* emocionar; estremecer; **to be ~ed** (*with gift etc*) estar encantado; ~**er** *n* película/novela de suspense.

thrive [θraɪv], *pt* **thrived** *or* **throve** [θrəuv], *pp* **thrived** *or* **thriven** ['θrɪvn] *vi* (*grow*) crecer; (*do well*) prosperar; **thriving** *a* próspero.

throat [θrəut] *n* garganta; **to have a sore ~** tener dolor de garganta.

throb [θrɔb] *n* (*of heart*) latido; (*of engine*)

vibración f // vi latir; vibrar; (pain) dar punzadas.

throes [θrəuz] npl: **in the ~ of** en medio de.

thrombosis [θrɔm'bəusɪs] n trombosis f.

throne [θrəun] n trono.

throttle ['θrɔtl] n (AUT) acelerador m // vt ahogar.

through [θru:] prep por, a través de; (time) durante; (by means of) por medio de, mediante; (owing to) gracias a // a (ticket, train) directo // ad completamente, de parte a parte; **to put sb ~ to sb** (TEL) poner a alguien (en comunicación) con alguien; **to be ~** (TEL) tener comunicación; (have finished) haber terminado; **"no ~ way"** "calle sin salida"; **~out** prep (place) por todas partes de, por todo; (time) durante todo, en todo // ad por o en todas partes.

throw [θrəu] n tirada, tiro; (SPORT) lanzamiento // vt, pt **threw**, pp **thrown** tirar, echar; (SPORT) lanzar; (rider) derribar; (fig) desconcertar; **to ~ a party** dar una fiesta; **to ~ away** vt tirar; **to ~ off** vt deshacerse de; **to ~ out** vt tirar; **to ~ up** vi vomitar; **~away** a para tirar, desechable; **~-in** n (SPORT) saque m.

thru [θru:] (US) = **through**.

thrush [θrʌʃ] n zorzal m, tordo.

thrust [θrʌst] n (TECH) empuje m // vt, pt, pp **thrust** empujar; (push in) introducir.

thud [θʌd] n golpe m sordo.

thug [θʌg] n (criminal) criminal m/f; (pej) bruto.

thumb [θʌm] n (ANAT) pulgar m, dedo gordo (col) // vt (book) hojear; **to ~ a lift** hacer dedo o autostop; **~tack** n (US) chinche m.

thump [θʌmp] n golpe m; (sound) porrazo // vi, vt golpear.

thunder ['θʌndə*] n (gen) trueno; (sudden noise) tronido; (of applause etc) estruendo // vi tronar; (train etc): **to ~ past** pasar como un trueno; **~bolt** n rayo; **~clap** n trueno; **~storm** n tormenta; **~struck** a pasmado; **~y** a tormentoso.

Thursday ['θɔːzdɪ] n jueves m.

thus [ðʌs] ad así, de este modo.

thwart [θwɔːt] vt frustrar.

thyme [taɪm] n tomillo.

thyroid ['θaɪrɔɪd] n tiroides m.

tiara [tɪ'ɑːrə] n tiara, diadema.

tic [tɪk] n tic m.

tick [tɪk] n (sound: of clock) tictac m; (mark) palomita; (ZOOL) garrapata; (col): **in a ~** en un instante // vi hacer tictac // vt marcar; **to ~ off** vt marcar; (person) poner como un trapo.

ticket ['tɪkɪt] n billete m, tíquet m; (for cinema) entrada; (in shop: on goods) etiqueta; (for library) tarjeta; **~ collector** n revisor m; **~ office** n taquilla.

tickle ['tɪkl] n cosquillas fpl // vt hacer cosquillas a; **ticklish** a que tiene cosquillas.

tidal ['taɪdl] a de marea; **~ wave** n maremoto.

tiddlywinks ['tɪdlɪwɪŋks] n juego de la pulga.

tide [taɪd] n marea; (fig: of events) curso, marcha.

tidiness ['taɪdɪnɪs] n (good order) buen orden m; (neatness) limpieza, aseo.

tidy ['taɪdɪ] a (room) ordenado; (dress, work) limpio; (person) (bien) arreglado // vt (also: **~ up**) poner en orden.

tie [taɪ] n (string etc) atadura; (also: **neck~**) corbata; (fig: link) vínculo, lazo; (SPORT: draw) empate m // vt atar // vi (SPORT) empatar; **to ~ in a bow** hacer un lazo; **to ~ a knot in sth** hacer un nudo a algo; **to ~ down** vt atar; (fig): **to ~ sb down** to obligar a uno a; **to ~ up** vt (parcel) envolver; (dog) atar; (boat) amarrar; (arrangements) concluir, despachar; **to be ~d up** (busy) estar ocupado.

tier [tɪə*] n grada; (of cake) piso.

tiger ['taɪgə*] n tigre m/f.

tight [taɪt] a (rope) tirante; (money) escaso; (clothes) ajustado; (budget, programme) apretado; (col: drunk) borracho // ad (squeeze) muy fuerte; (shut) herméticamente; **~s** npl pantimedias fpl; (for gym) malla sg; **~en** vt (rope) estirar; (screw) apretar // vi apretarse, estirarse; **~-fisted** a tacaño; **~ly** ad (grasp) muy fuerte; **~-rope** n cuerda floja.

tile [taɪl] n (on roof) teja; (on floor) baldosa; (on wall) azulejo, baldosín m; **~d** a embaldosado.

till [tɪl] n caja (registradora) // vt (land) cultivar // prep, conj = **until**.

tiller ['tɪlə*] n (NAUT) caña del timón.

tilt [tɪlt] vt inclinar // vi inclinarse.

timber ['tɪmbə*] n (material) madera; (trees) árboles mpl.

time [taɪm] n tiempo; (epoch: often pl) época; (by clock) hora; (moment) momento; (occasion) vez f; (MUS) compás m // vt (gen) calcular o medir el tiempo de; (race) cronometrar; (remark etc) elegir el momento para; **a long ~** mucho tiempo; **for the ~ being** de momento, por ahora; **from ~ to ~** de vez en cuando; **in ~** (soon enough) a tiempo; (after some time) con el tiempo; (MUS) al compás; **in a week's ~** dentro de una semana; **on ~** a la hora; **5 ~s 5** 5 por 5; **what ~ is it?** ¿qué hora es?; **to have a good ~** pasarlo bien, divertirse; **~ bomb** n bomba de efecto retardado; **~keeper** n (SPORT) cronómetro; **~less** a eterno; **~ limit** n (gen) limitación f de tiempo; (COMM) plazo; **~ly** a oportuno; **~ off** n tiempo libre; **timer** n (in kitchen) reloj m programador; **~ switch** n interruptor m; **~table** n horario; **~ zone** n huso horario.

timid ['tɪmɪd] a tímido.

timing ['taɪmɪŋ] n (SPORT) cronometraje

m; (*gen*) elección *f* del momento; **the ~ of his resignation** el momento que eligió para dimitir.

timpani ['tɪmpənɪ] *npl* tímpanos *mpl*.

tin [tɪn] *n* estaño; (*also*: ~ **plate**) hojalata; (*can*) lata; ~ **foil** *n* papel *m* de estaño.

tinge [tɪndʒ] *n* matiz *m* // *vt*: ~**d with** teñido de.

tingle ['tɪŋgl] *n* picotazo // *vi* sentir picazón.

tinker ['tɪŋkə*] *n* calderero; (*gipsy*) gitano; **to ~ with** *vt* manosear.

tinkle ['tɪŋkl] *vi* tintinear // *n* (*col*): **to give sb a ~** dar un telefonazo a alguien.

tinned [tɪnd] *a* (*food*) en lata, en conserva.

tin opener ['tɪnəupnə*] *n* abrelatas *m inv*.

tinsel ['tɪnsl] *n* oropel *m*.

tint [tɪnt] *n* matiz *m*; (*for hair*) tinte *m*.

tiny ['taɪnɪ] *a* minúsculo, pequeñito.

tip [tɪp] *n* (*end*) punta; (*gratuity*) propina; (*for rubbish*) basurero; (*advice*) aviso // *vt* (*waiter*) dar una propina a; (*tilt*) inclinar; (*overturn*: *also*: ~ **over**) dar la vuelta a, volcar; (*empty*: *also*: ~ **out**) vaciar, echar; ~**-off** *n* (*hint*) aviso, advertencia; ~**ped** *a* (*cigarette*) con filtro.

tipsy ['tɪpsɪ] *a* algo borracho, mareado.

tiptoe ['tɪptəu] *n*: **on ~** de puntillas.

tiptop ['tɪp'tɒp] *a*: **in ~ condition** en perfectas condiciones.

tire ['taɪə*] *n* (*US*) = **tyre** // *vt* cansar // *vi* (*gen*) cansarse; (*become bored*) aburrirse; ~**d** *a* cansado; **to be ~d of sth** estar cansado *o* harto de algo; **tiredness** *n* cansancio; ~**less** *a* incansable; ~**some** *a* aburrido; **tiring** *a* cansado.

tissue ['tɪʃu:] *n* tejido; (*paper handkerchief*) pañuelo de papel, kleenex *m*; ~ **paper** *n* papel *m* de seda.

tit [tɪt] *n* (*bird*) herrerillo común; **to give ~ for tat** dar ojo por ojo.

titbit ['tɪtbɪt] *n* (*food*) golosina; (*news*) suceso.

titillate ['tɪtɪleɪt] *vt* estimular, excitar.

titivate ['tɪtɪveɪt] *vt* emperejilar.

title ['taɪtl] *n* título; ~ **deed** *n* (*LAW*) título de propiedad; ~ **role** *n* papel *m* principal.

titter ['tɪtə*] *vi* reírse entre dientes.

titular ['tɪtjulə*] *a* (*in name only*) nominal.

to [tu:, tə] *prep a*; (*towards*) hacia; (*of time*) a, hasta; (*of*) de; **give it ~ me** dámelo; **the key ~ the front door** la llave de la puerta; **the main thing is ~...** lo importante es...; **to go ~ France/school** ir a Francia/al colegio; **a quarter ~ 5** las 5 menos cuarto; **pull/push the door ~** tirar/empujar la puerta; **to go ~ and fro** ir y venir.

toad [təud] *n* sapo; ~**stool** *n* hongo venenoso.

toast [təust] *n* (*CULIN. also*: **piece of ~**) tostada; (*drink, speech*) brindis *m* // *vt* (*CULIN*) tostar; (*drink to*) brindar; ~**er** *n* tostador *m*.

tobacco [tə'bækəu] *n* tabaco; ~**nist's (shop)** *n* estanco.

toboggan [tə'bɒgən] *n* tobogán *m*.

today [tə'deɪ] *ad, n* (*also fig*) hoy *m*.

toddler ['tɒdlə*] *n* niño que empieza a andar.

toddy ['tɒdɪ] *n* ponche *m*.

toe [təu] *n* dedo (del pie); (*of shoe*) punta; **to ~ the line** (*fig*) obedecer, conformarse; ~**nail** *n* uña del pie.

toffee ['tɒfɪ] *n* caramelo; ~ **apple** *n* pirulí *m*.

toga ['təugə] *n* toga.

together [tə'geðə*] *ad* juntos; (*at same time*) al mismo tiempo, a la vez; ~ **with** *prep* junto con; ~**ness** *n* compañerismo.

toil [tɔɪl] *n* trabajo duro, labor *f* // *vi* esforzarse.

toilet ['tɔɪlət] *n* (*lavatory*) servicios *mpl*, wáter *m* // *cpd* (*bag, soap etc*) de aseo; ~ **bowl** *n* palangana; ~ **paper** *n* papel *m* higiénico; ~**ries** *npl* artículos *mpl* de aseo; (*make-up etc*) artículos *mpl* de tocador; ~ **roll** *n* rollo de papel higiénico; ~ **water** *n* agua de tocador.

token ['təukən] *n* (*sign*) señal *f*, muestra; (*souvenir*) recuerdo; (*voucher*) cupón *m*; **book/record ~** vale *m* para comprar libros/discos.

told [təuld] *pt, pp of* **tell.**

tolerable ['tɒlərəbl] *a* (*bearable*) soportable; (*fairly good*) pasable.

tolerance ['tɒlərns] *n* (*also*: TECH) tolerancia; **tolerant** *a*: **tolerant of** tolerante con.

tolerate ['tɒləreɪt] *vt* tolerar; **toleration** [-'reɪʃən] *n* tolerancia.

toll [təul] *n* (*of casualties*) número de víctimas; (*tax, charge*) peaje *m* // *vi* (*bell*) doblar; ~**bridge** *n* puente *m* de peaje.

tomato [tə'mɑ:təu], *pl* ~**es** *n* tomate *m*.

tomb [tu:m] *n* tumba.

tombola [tɒm'bəulə] *n* tómbola.

tomboy ['tɒmbɔɪ] *n* marimacho.

tombstone ['tu:mstəun] *n* lápida.

tomcat ['tɒmkæt] *n* gato.

tomorrow [tə'mɔrəu] *ad, n* (*also fig*) mañana; **the day after ~** pasado mañana; ~ **morning** mañana por la mañana.

ton [tʌn] *n* tonelada; ~**s of** (*col*) montones *mpl* de.

tone [təun] *n* tono // *vi* armonizar; **to ~ down** *vt* (*colour, criticism*) suavizar; (*sound*) bajar; (*MUS*) entonar; **to ~ up** *vt* (*muscles*) tonificar; ~**-deaf** *a* que no tiene oído.

tongs [tɒŋz] *npl* (*for coal*) tenazas *fpl*; (*for hair*) tenacillas *fpl*.

tongue [tʌŋ] *n* lengua; ~ **in cheek** *ad* irónicamente; ~**-tied** *a* (*fig*) mudo; ~**-twister** *n* trabalenguas *m inv*.

tonic ['tɒnɪk] *n* (*MED*) tónico; (*MUS*) tónica; (*also*: ~ **water**) (agua) tónica.

tonight [tə'naɪt] *ad, n* esta noche.

tonnage ['tʌnɪdʒ] *n* (*NAUT*) tonelaje *m*.

tonsil ['tɒnsl] *n* amígdala, anginas *fpl* (*col*); ~**litis** [-'laɪtɪs] *n* amigdalitis *f*, (inflamación *f* de las) anginas.

too [tu:] *ad* (*excessively*) demasiado; (*very*) muy; (*also*) también; ~ **much** *ad* demasiado; ~ **many** *det* demasiados/as.

took [tuk] *pt of* **take.**

tool [tu:l] *n* herramienta; ~ **box** *n* caja de herramientas.

toot [tu:t] *n* (*of horn*) bocinazo; (*of whistle*) silbido // *vi* (*with car-horn*) tocar la bocina.

tooth [tu:θ], *pl* **teeth** *n* (ANAT, TECH) diente *m*; (*molar*) muela; ~**ache** *n* dolor *m* de muelas; ~**brush** *n* cepillo de dientes; ~**paste** *n* pasta de dientes; ~**pick** *n* palillo.

top [tɔp] *n* (*of mountain*) cumbre *f*, cima; (*of head*) coronilla; (*of ladder*) lo alto; (*of cupboard, table*) superficie *f*; (*lid: of box, jar*) tapa, tapadera; (*: of bottle*) tapón *m*; (*of list etc*) cabeza; (*toy*) peonza // *a* más alto; (*in rank*) principal, primero; (*best*) mejor // *vt* (*exceed*) exceder; (*be first in*) ir a la cabeza de; **on ~ of** sobre, encima de; **from ~ to toe** de pies a cabeza; **to ~ up** *vt* llenar; ~**coat** *n* sobretodo; ~ **hat** *n* sombrero de copa; ~**-heavy** *a* (*object*) desequilibrado.

topic ['tɔpik] *n* tema *m*, tópico; ~**al** *a* actual.

top: ~**less** *a* (*bather etc*) con el pecho al descubierto, topless; ~**-level** *a* (*talks*) al más alto nivel; ~**most** *a* más alto.

topple ['tɔpl] *vt* volcar, derribar // *vi* caerse.

topsy-turvy ['tɔpsi'tə:vi] *a, ad* patas arriba.

torch [tɔ:tʃ] *n* antorcha; (*electric*) linterna.

tore [tɔ:*] *pt of* **tear.**

torment ['tɔ:mɛnt] *n* tormento // *vt* [tɔ:'mɛnt] atormentar; (*fig: annoy*) fastidiar.

torn [tɔ:n] *pp of* **tear.**

tornado [tɔ:'neidəu], *pl* ~**es** *n* tornado.

torpedo [tɔ:'pi:dəu], *pl* ~**es** *n* torpedo.

torrent ['tɔrnt] *n* torrente *m*; ~**ial** [-'rɛnʃl] *a* torrencial.

torso ['tɔ:səu] *n* torso.

tortoise ['tɔ:təs] *n* tortuga; ~**shell** ['tɔ:təʃɛl] *a* de carey.

tortuous ['tɔ:tjuəs] *a* tortuoso.

torture ['tɔ:tʃə*] *n* tortura // *vt* torturar; (*fig*) atormentar.

Tory ['tɔ:ri] *a, n* conservador/a *m/f*.

toss [tɔs] *vt* tirar, echar; (*head*) sacudir (la cabeza); **to ~ a coin** echar a cara o cruz; **to ~ up for sth** jugar a cara o cruz algo; **to ~ and turn in bed** dar vueltas en la cama.

tot [tɔt] *n* (*drink*) copita; (*child*) nene/a *m/f*.

total ['təutl] *a* total, entero // *n* total *m*, suma // *vt* (*add up*) sumar; (*amount to*) ascender a.

totalitarian [təutælɪ'tɛərɪən] *a* totalitario.

totem pole ['təutəm-] *n* poste *m* totémico.

totter ['tɔtə*] *vi* tambalearse.

touch [tʌtʃ] *n* (*gen*) tacto; (*contact*) contacto; (FOOTBALL) fuera de juego // *vt* (*gen*) tocar; (*emotionally*) conmover; **a ~ of** (*fig*) una pizca *o* un poquito de; **to get**

in ~ with sb ponerse en contacto con uno; **to lose ~** (*friends*) perder contacto; **to ~ on** *vt fus* (*topic*) aludir (brevemente) a; **to ~ up** *vt* (*paint*) retocar; ~**-and-go** *a* arriesgado; ~**down** *n* aterrizaje *m*; (*on sea*) amerizaje *m*; ~**ed** *a* conmovido; (*col*) chiflado; ~**ing** *a* conmovedor(a); ~**line** *n* (SPORT) línea de banda; ~**y** *a* (*person*) susceptible.

tough [tʌf] *a* (*gen*) duro; (*difficult*) difícil; (*resistant*) resistente; (*person*) fuerte; (*: pej*) bruto // *n* (*gangster etc*) gorila *m*; ~**en** *vt* endurecer; ~**ness** *n* dureza; dificultad *f*; resistencia; fuerza.

toupee ['tu:pei] *n* peluca.

tour ['tuə*] *n* viaje *m*, vuelta; (*also: package ~*) viaje *m* organizado; (*of town, museum*) visita // *vt* viajar por; ~**ing** *n* viajes *mpl* turísticos, turismo.

tourism ['tuərizm] *n* turismo.

tourist ['tuərist] *n* turista *m/f* // *cpd* turístico; ~ **office** *n* oficina de turismo.

tournament ['tuənəmənt] *n* torneo.

tousled ['tauzld] *a* (*hair*) despeinado.

tout [taut] *vi*: **to ~ for** solicitar clientes para // *n*: **ticket ~** revendedor/a *m/f*.

tow [təu] *vt* remolcar; **'on ~'** (AUT) "a remolque".

toward(s) [tə'wɔ:d(z)] *prep* hacia; (*of attitude*) respecto a, con; (*of purpose*) para.

towel ['tauəl] *n* toalla; ~**ling** *n* (*fabric*) felpa; ~ **rail** *n* toallero.

tower ['tauə*] *n* torre *f*; ~ **block** *n* rascacielos *m inv*; ~**ing** *a* muy alto, imponente.

town [taun] *n* ciudad *f*; **to go to ~** ir a la ciudad; (*fig*) hacer con entusiasmo; ~ **clerk** *n* secretario del Ayuntamiento; ~ **council** *n* consejo municipal; ~ **hall** *n* ayuntamiento; ~ **planning** *n* urbanismo.

towrope ['təurəup] *n* cable *m* de remolque.

toxic ['tɔksik] *a* tóxico.

toy [tɔi] *n* juguete *m*; **to ~ with** *vt fus* jugar con; (*idea*) acariciar; ~**shop** *n* juguetería.

trace [treis] *n* rastro // *vt* (*draw*) trazar, delinear; (*follow*) seguir la pista de; (*locate*) encontrar.

track [træk] *n* (*mark*) huella, pista; (*path: gen*) camino, senda; (*: of bullet etc*) trayectoria; (*: of suspect, animal*) pista, rastro; (RAIL) vía; (*on tape, SPORT*) pista // *vt* seguir la pista de; **to keep ~ of** mantenerse al tanto de, seguir; **to ~ down** *vt* (*prey*) averiguar el paradero de; (*sth lost*) buscar y encontrar; ~ **suit** *n* chandal *m*.

tract [trækt] *n* (GEO) región *f*; (*pamphlet*) folleto.

tractor ['træktə*] *n* tractor *m*.

trade [treid] *n* comercio, negocio; (*skill, job*) oficio, empleo // *vi* negociar, comerciar; **to ~ in** *vt* (*old car etc*) ofrecer como parte del pago; ~**-in price** *n* valor *m* de un objeto usado que se descuenta del precio de otro nuevo; ~**mark** *n* marca de fábrica; ~ **name** *n* marca registrada;

trader n comerciante m/f; **tradesman** n (shopkeeper) tendero; ~ **union** n sindicato; ~ **unionism** n sindicalismo; **trading** n comercio; **trading estate** n zona comercial.

tradition [trə'dɪʃən] n tradición f; ~**al** a tradicional.

traffic ['træfɪk] n (gen, AUT) tráfico, circulación f; (air ~ etc) tránsito // vi: **to** ~ **in** (pej: liquor, drugs) traficar en; ~ **circle** n (US) cruce m giratorio; ~ **jam** n embotellamiento; ~ **lights** npl semáforo sg; ~ **warden** n guardia m/f de tráfico.

tragedy ['trædʒədɪ] n tragedia.

tragic ['trædʒɪk] a trágico.

trail [treɪl] n (tracks) rastro, pista; (path) camino, sendero; (wake) estela // vt (drag) arrastrar; (follow) seguir la pista de; (follow closely) vigilar // vi arrastrarse; **to** ~ **behind** vi quedar a la zaga; ~**er** n (AUT) remolque m; (US) caravana; (CINEMA) trailer m, avance m.

train [treɪn] n tren m; (of dress) cola; (series) serie f; (followers) séquito // vt (educate) formar; (teach skills to) adiestrar; (sportsman) entrenar; (dog) amaestrar; (point: gun etc): **to** ~ **on** apuntar a // vi (SPORT) entrenarse; (be educated) recibir una formación; ~**ed** a (worker) cualificado, adiestrado; (teacher) diplomado; (animal) amaestrado; ~**ee** [treɪ'niː] n persona que está aprendiendo; (in trade) aprendiz a m/f; ~**er** n (SPORT) entrenador/a m/f; (of animals) domador/a m/f; ~**ing** n formación f; adiestramiento; entrenamiento; **in** ~**ing** (SPORT) en forma; ~**ing college** n (for teachers) escuela normal; (gen) colegio de formación profesional.

traipse [treɪps] vi andar con desgana.

trait [treɪt] n rasgo.

traitor ['treɪtə*] n traidor/a m/f.

tram [træm] n (also: ~car) tranvía m.

tramp [træmp] n (person) vagabundo // vi andar con pasos pesados.

trample ['træmpl] vt: **to** ~ (**underfoot**) pisotear.

trampoline ['træmpəliːn] n trampolín n.

trance [trɑːns] n trance m; (MED) catalepsia.

tranquil ['træŋkwɪl] a tranquilo; ~**lity** n tranquilidad f; ~**lizer** n (MED) tranquilizante m.

transact [træn'zækt] vt (business) tramitar; ~**ion** [-'zækʃən] n transacción f, negocio.

transatlantic ['trænzət'læntɪk] a transatlántico.

transcend [træn'sɛnd] vt trascender.

transcript ['trænskrɪpt] n copia; ~**ion** [-'skrɪpʃən] n transcripción f.

transept ['trænsɛpt] n crucero.

transfer ['trænsfə*] n (gen) transferencia; (SPORT) traspaso; (picture, design) calcomanía // vt [træns'fə:*] trasladar, pasar; **to** ~ **the charges** (TEL) llamar a cobro revertido; ~**able** [-'fɔːrəbl] a trans-ferible; '**not** ~**able**' "intransferible".

transform [træns'fɔːm] vt transformar; ~**ation** [-'meɪʃən] n transformación f; ~**er** n (ELEC) transformador m.

transfusion [træns'fjuːʒən] n transfusión f.

transient ['trænzɪənt] a transitorio.

transistor [træn'zɪstə*] n (ELEC) transistor m; ~ **radio** n radio f a transistores.

transit ['trænzɪt] n: **in** ~ de tránsito, de paso.

transition [træn'zɪʃən] n transición f; ~**al** a transitorio.

transitive ['trænzɪtɪv] a (LING) transitivo.

transitory ['trænzɪtərɪ] a transitorio.

translate [trænz'leɪt] vt traducir; **translation** [-'leɪʃən] n traducción f; **translator** n traductor/a m/f.

transmission [trænz'mɪʃən] n transmisión f.

transmit [trænz'mɪt] vt transmitir; ~**ter** n transmisor m; (station) emisora.

transparency [træns'pɛərnsɪ] n (PHOT) diapositiva.

transparent [træns'pærnt] a transparente.

transplant [træns'plɑːnt] vt transplantar // n ['trænsplɑːnt] (MED) transplante m.

transport ['trænspɔːt] n (gen) transporte m; (also: **road/rail** ~) transportes mpl // vt [-'pɔːt] transportar; (carry) acarrear; ~**ation** [-'teɪʃən] n transporte m; ~ **café** n cafetería de carretera.

transverse ['trænzvɔːs] a transversal.

transvestite [trænz'vɛstaɪt] n travesti m/f.

trap [træp] n (snare, trick) trampa; (carriage) cabriolé m // vt coger en una trampa; (immobilize) bloquear; (jam) atascar; ~ **door** n escotilla.

trapeze [trə'piːz] n trapecio.

trappings ['træpɪŋz] npl adornos mpl.

trash [træʃ] n (pej: goods) pacotilla; (: nonsense) basura; ~ **can** n (US) cubo de la basura.

trauma ['trɔːmə] n trauma m; ~**tic** [-'mætɪk] a traumático.

travel ['trævl] n viaje m // vi viajar // vt (distance) recorrer; ~ **agency** n agencia de viajes; ~**ler**, ~**er** (US) n viajero/a; ~**ler's cheque** n cheque m de viajero; ~**ling**, ~**ing** (US) n los viajes mpl, el viajar; ~ **sickness** n mareo.

traverse ['trævəs] vt atravesar, cruzar.

travesty ['trævəstɪ] n parodia.

trawler ['trɔːlə*] n barco rastreador o de rastra.

tray [treɪ] n (for carrying) bandeja; (on desk) cajón m.

treacherous ['trɛtʃərəs] a traidor(a); **treachery** n traición f.

treacle ['triːkl] n melaza.

tread [trɛd] n (step) paso, pisada; (sound) ruido de pasos; (of tyre) banda de rodadura // vi (pt **trod**, pp **trodden**) pisar; **to** ~ **on** vt fus pisar sobre.

treason ['triːzn] n traición f.

treasure ['trɛʒə*] n tesoro // vt (value) apreciar, valorar; ~ **hunt** n caza del tesoro.

treasurer ['trɛʒərə*] n tesorero.

treasury ['trɛʒərɪ] n: **the T~** (POL) el Ministerio de Hacienda.

treat [tri:t] n (present) regalo; (pleasure) placer m // vt tratar: **to ~ sb to sth** invitar a uno a algo.

treatise ['tri:tɪz] n tratado.

treatment ['tri:tmənt] n tratamiento.

treaty ['tri:tɪ] n tratado.

treble ['trɛbl] a triple // n (MUS) triple m // vt triplicar // vi triplicarse.

tree [tri:] n árbol m; ~ **trunk** n tronco de árbol.

trek [trɛk] n (long journey) viaje m largo y peligroso; (tiring walk) caminata; (as holiday) excursión f.

trellis ['trɛlɪs] n enrejado.

tremble ['trɛmbl] vi temblar; **trembling** n temblor m // a tembloroso.

tremendous [trɪ'mɛndəs] a tremendo; (enormous) enorme; (excellent) estupendo.

tremor ['trɛmə*] n temblor m; (also: **earth ~**) temblor m de tierra.

trench [trɛntʃ] n trinchera.

trend [trɛnd] n (tendency) tendencia; (of events) curso; (fashion) moda; ~**y** a (idea) según las tendencias actuales; (clothes) a la última moda.

trepidation [trɛpɪ'deɪʃən] n agitación f; (fear) ansia.

trespass ['trɛspəs] vi: **to ~ on** entrar sin permiso en; **"no ~ing"** "prohibido el paso".

tress [trɛs] n trenza.

trestle ['trɛsl] n caballete m; ~ **table** n mesa de caballete.

trial ['traɪəl] n (LAW) juicio, proceso; (test: of machine etc) prueba; (hardship) desgracia; **by ~ and error** por tanteo.

triangle ['traɪæŋgl] n (MATH, MUS) triángulo; **triangular** [-'æŋgjulə*] a triangular.

tribal ['traɪbəl] a tribal.

tribe [traɪb] n tribu f; **tribesman** n miembro de una tribu.

tribulation [trɪbju'leɪʃən] n tribulación f, sufrimiento.

tribunal [traɪ'bju:nl] n tribunal m.

tributary ['trɪbjutərɪ] n (river) afluente m.

tribute ['trɪbju:t] n homenaje m; (payment) tributo; **to pay ~ to** rendir homenaje a.

trice [traɪs] n: **in a ~** en un santiamén.

trick [trɪk] n trampa; (deceit) truco; (joke) broma; (CARDS) baza // vt engañar; **to play a ~ on sb** gastar una broma a uno; ~**ery** n astucia.

trickle ['trɪkl] n (of water etc) hililo // vi gotear.

tricky ['trɪkɪ] a difícil, delicado.

tricycle ['traɪsɪkl] n triciclo.

trifle ['traɪfl] n bagatela; (CULIN) dulce m

de bizcocho, fruta y natillas // ad: **a ~ long** un poquito largo; **trifling** a insignificante.

trigger ['trɪgə*] n (of gun) gatillo; **to ~ off** vt desencadenar.

trigonometry [trɪgə'nɔmətrɪ] n trigonometría.

trill [trɪl] n (of bird) trino.

trim [trɪm] a (elegant) aseado; (house, garden) en buen estado; (figure) con buen tipo // n (haircut etc) recorte m; (on car) tapicería // vt arreglar; (cut) recortar; (decorate) adornar; (NAUT: a sail) orientar; ~**mings** npl decoraciones fpl; (cuttings) recortes mpl.

Trinity ['trɪnɪtɪ] n: **the ~** la Trinidad.

trinket ['trɪŋkɪt] n chuchería; (piece of jewellery) baratija.

trio ['tri:əu] n trío.

trip [trɪp] n viaje m; (excursion) excursión f; (stumble) traspié m // vi (also: ~ **up**) tropezar; (go lightly) andar a paso ligero // vt poner la zancadilla a.

tripe [traɪp] n (CULIN) callos mpl; (pej: rubbish) bobadas fpl.

triple ['trɪpl] a triple.

triplets ['trɪplɪts] npl trillizos/as m/fpl.

triplicate ['trɪplɪkət] n: **in ~** por triplicado.

tripod ['traɪpɔd] n trípode m.

trite [traɪt] a gastado, trillado.

triumph ['traɪʌmf] n triunfo // vi: **to ~ (over)** vencer; ~**ant** [-'ʌmfənt] a triunfante.

trivia ['trɪvɪə] npl trivialidades fpl.

trivial ['trɪvɪəl] a insignificante; (commonplace) trivial; ~**ity** [-'ælɪtɪ] n trivialidad f.

trod [trɔd], **trodden** ['trɔdn] pt, pp of **tread**.

trolley ['trɔlɪ] n carrito; ~ **bus** n trolebús m.

trombone [trɔm'bəun] n trombón m.

troop [tru:p] n grupo, banda; ~**s** npl (MIL) tropas fpl; **to ~ in/out** vi entrar/salir en grupo; ~**er** n (MIL) soldado de caballería.

trophy ['trəufɪ] n trofeo.

tropic ['trɔpɪk] n trópico; ~**al** a tropical.

trot [trɔt] n trote m // vi trotar; **on the ~** (fig: col) de corrido.

trouble ['trʌbl] n problema m, dificultad f; (worry) preocupación f; (bother, effort) molestia, esfuerzo; (unrest) inquietud f; (MED): **stomach ~** problemas mpl gástricos // vt molestar; (worry) preocupar, inquietar // vi: **to ~ to do sth** molestarse en hacer algo; ~**s** npl (POL etc) conflictos mpl; **to be in ~** estar en un apuro; **to go to the ~ of doing sth** tomarse la molestia de hacer algo; **what's the ~?** ¿qué pasa?; ~**d** a (person) preocupado; (epoch, life) agitado; ~**maker** n elemento perturbador; (child) niño alborotado; ~**shooter** n (in conflict) conciliador m; ~**some** a molesto, inoportuno.

trough [trɔf] n (also: **drinking ~**)

abrevadero; (also: **feeding** ~) comedero; (channel) canal m.

troupe [tru:p] n grupo.

trousers ['trauzǝz] npl pantalones mpl.

trousseau ['tru:sǝu], pl ~**x** or ~**s** [-z] n ajuar m.

trout [traut] n, pl inv trucha.

trowel ['trauǝl] n paleta.

truant ['truǝnt] n: **to play** ~ hacer novillos.

truce [tru:s] n tregua.

truck [trʌk] n camión m; (RAIL) vagón m; ~ **driver** n camionero; ~ **farm** n (US) huerto de hortalizas.

truculent ['trʌkjulǝnt] a agresivo.

trudge [trʌdʒ] vi andar con dificultad o pesadamente.

true [tru:] a verdadero; (accurate) exacto; (genuine) auténtico; (faithful) fiel.

truffle ['trʌfl] n trufa.

truly ['tru:lı] ad auténticamente; (truthfully) verdaderamente; (faithfully) fielmente; **yours** ~ (in letter) (le saluda) atentamente.

trump [trʌmp] n triunfo; ~**ed-up** a inventado.

trumpet ['trʌmpıt] n trompeta.

truncheon ['trʌntʃǝn] n porra.

trundle ['trʌndl] vt, vi: **to** ~ **along** rodar haciendo ruido.

trunk [trʌŋk] n (of tree, person) tronco; (of elephant) trompa; (case) baúl m; ~**s** npl (also: **swimming** ~**s**) bañador m; ~ **call** n (TEL) llamada interurbana.

truss [trʌs] n (MED) braguero; **to** ~ **(up)** vt atar.

trust [trʌst] n confianza; (COMM) trust m, cartel m; (obligation) responsabilidad f; (LAW) fideicomiso // vt (rely on) tener confianza en; (entrust): **to** ~ **sth to sb** confiar algo a uno; ~**ed** a de confianza; ~**ee** [trʌs'ti:] n (LAW) depositario, fideicomisario; (of school etc) administrador/a m/f; ~**ful**, ~**ing** a confiado; ~**worthy** a digno de confianza; ~**y** a fiel.

truth [tru:θ], pl ~**s** [tru:ðz] n verdad f; ~**ful** a (person) que dice la verdad; ~**fully** ad sinceramente; ~**fulness** n veracidad f.

try [traı] n tentativa, intento; (RUGBY) ensayo // vt (LAW) juzgar, procesar; (test: sth new) probar, someter a prueba; (attempt) intentar; (strain) hacer sufrir // vi probar; **to** ~ **to do sth** intentar hacer algo; **to** ~ **on** vt (clothes) probarse; **to** ~ **out** vt probar, poner a prueba; ~**ing** a penoso, cansado.

tsar [zɑ:*] n zar m.

T-shirt ['ti:ʃǝ:t] n camiseta.

tub [tʌb] n cubo; (bath) tina, bañera.

tuba ['tju:bǝ] n tuba.

tubby ['tʌbı] a regordete.

tube [tju:b] n tubo; (underground) metro; (for tyre) cámara de aire; ~**less** a sin cámara.

tuberculosis [tjubǝ:kju'lǝusıs] n tuberculosis f.

tube station n estación f de metro.

tubing ['tju:bıŋ] n tubería; **a piece of** ~ un trozo de tubo.

tubular ['tju:bjulǝ*] a tubular; (furniture) de tubo.

TUC n abbr of **Trades Union Congress.**

tuck [tʌk] n (SEWING) pliegue m // vt (put) poner; **to** ~ **away** vt esconder; **to** ~ **in** vt meter; (child) arropar // vi (eat) comer con mucho apetito; **to** ~ **up** vt (child) arropar; ~ **shop** n tienda de golosinas.

Tuesday ['tju:zdı] n martes m.

tuft [tʌft] n mechón m; (of grass etc) manojo.

tug [tʌg] n (ship) remolcador m // vt remolcar; ~**-of-war** n lucha de la cuerda.

tuition [tju:'ıʃǝn] n enseñanza; (private ~) clases fpl particulares.

tulip ['tju:lıp] n tulipán m.

tumble ['tʌmbl] n (fall) caída // vi caerse, tropezar // vt tirar; ~**down** a destartalado; ~ **dryer** n secador m de ropa automático.

tumbler ['tʌmblǝ*] n vaso.

tummy ['tʌmı] n (col: belly) barriga; (: stomach) vientre m.

tumour ['tju:mǝ*] n tumor m.

tumult ['tju:mʌlt] n tumulto; ~**uous** [-'mʌltjuǝs] a tumultuoso.

tuna ['tju:nǝ] n, pl inv (also: ~ **fish**) atún m.

tune [tju:n] n (melody) melodía // vt (MUS) afinar; (RADIO, TV, AUT) sintonizar; **to be in/out of** ~ (instrument) estar afinado/desafinado; (singer) cantar bien/ mal; **to be in/out of** ~ **with** (fig) armonizar/desentonar con; **to** ~ **up** vi (musician) afinar (su instrumento); ~**ful** a melodioso; **tuner** n (radio set) sintonizador m; **piano tuner** afinador m de pianos.

tunic ['tju:nık] n túnica.

tuning ['tju:nıŋ] n sintonización f; (MUS) afinación f; ~ **fork** n diapasón m.

Tunisia [tju:'nızıǝ] n Tunez m.

tunnel ['tʌnl] n túnel m; (in mine) galería // vi construir un túnel/una galería.

tunny ['tʌnı] n atún m.

turban ['tǝ:bǝn] n turbante m.

turbine ['tǝ:baın] n turbina.

turbulence ['tǝ:bjulǝns] n (AVIAT) turbulencia; **turbulent** a turbulento.

tureen [tǝ'ri:n] n sopera.

turf [tǝ:f] n turba; (clod) césped m // vt poner césped; **to** ~ **out** vt (col) echar a la calle.

turgid ['tǝ:dʒıd] a (speech) pesado.

Turk [tǝ:k] n turco/a.

turkey ['tǝ:kı] n pavo.

Turkey ['tǝ:kı] n Turquía; **Turkish** a, n turco; **Turkish bath** n baño turco.

turmoil ['tǝ:mɔıl] n desorden m, alboroto.

turn [tǝ:n] n turno; (in road) curva; (tendency: of mind, events) disposición f, propensión f; (*THEATRE*) número; (*MED*) desmayo // vt girar, volver; (*collar, steak*) dar la vuelta a; (*change*): **to ~ sth into** convertir algo en // vi volver; (*person: look back*) volverse; (*reverse direction*) dar la vuelta; (*milk*) cortarse; (*change*) cambiar; (*become*) convertirse en; **a good ~** un favor; **it gave me quite a ~** me dio un susto (bastante grande); **'no left ~'** (*AUT*) 'prohibido girar a la izquierda'; **it's your ~** te toca a ti; **in ~** por turnos; **to take ~s** turnarse; **to ~ about** vi dar una vuelta completa; **to ~ away** vi volver la cabeza; **to ~ back** vi volverse atrás; **to ~ down** vt (*refuse*) rechazar; (*reduce*) bajar; (*fold*) doblar (hacia abajo); **to ~ in** vi (*col: go to bed*) acostarse // vt (*fold*) doblar hacia dentro; **to ~ off** vi (*from road*) desviarse // vt (*light, radio etc*) apagar; (*engine*) parar; **to ~ on** vt (*light, radio etc*) encender; (*engine*) poner en marcha; **to ~ out** vt (*light, gas*) apagar // vi: **to ~ out to be...** resultar ser...; **to ~ up** vi (*person*) llegar, presentarse; (*lost object*) aparecer // vt (*gen*) subir; **~ing in** (*in road*) vuelta; **~ing point** n (*fig*) momento decisivo.

turnip ['tə:nɪp] n nabo.

turnout ['tə:naut] n asistencia, número de asistentes.

turnover ['tə:nəuvə*] n (*COMM. amount of money*) cifra de negocios; (: *of goods*) movimiento.

turnpike ['tə:npʌɪk] n (*US*) autopista de peaje.

turnstile ['tə:nstaɪl] n torniquete m.

turntable ['tə:nteɪbl] n (*on record player*) plato.

turn-up ['tə:nʌp] n (*on trousers*) vuelta.

turpentine ['tə:pəntaɪn] n (*also: turps*) trementina.

turquoise ['tə:kwɔɪz] n (*stone*) turquesa // a color turquesa.

turret ['tʌrɪt] n torrecilla.

turtle ['tə:tl] n tortuga marina.

tusk [tʌsk] n colmillo.

tussle ['tʌsl] n (*fight*) lucha; (*scuffle*) pelea.

tutor ['tju:tə*] n (*gen*) profesor/a m/f; **~ial** [-'tɔ:rɪəl] n (*SCOL*) seminario.

T.V. [ti:'vi:] n abbr of **television**.

twaddle ['twɔdl] n tonterías fpl, bobadas fpl.

twang [twæŋ] n (*of instrument*) punteado; (*of voice*) timbre m nasal // vi vibrar // vt (*guitar*) puntear.

tweed [twi:d] n tweed m.

tweezers ['twi:zəz] npl pinzas fpl de depilar.

twelfth [twelfθ] a duodécimo; **T~ Night** n Día de Reyes.

twelve [twelv] num doce.

twentieth ['twentɪɪθ] a vigésimo.

twenty ['twentɪ] num veinte.

twerp [twə:p] n (*col*) imbécil m/f.

twice [twaɪs] ad dos veces; **~ as much** dos veces más.

twig [twɪg] n ramita // vi (*col*) caer en la cuenta.

twilight ['twaɪlaɪt] n crepúsculo, ocaso.

twin [twɪn] a, n gemelo/a // vt tener como gemelo.

twine [twaɪn] n bramante m // vi (*plant*) enroscarse.

twinge [twɪndʒ] n (*of pain*) punzada; (*of conscience*) remordimiento.

twinkle ['twɪŋkl] n centelleo // vi centellear; (*eyes*) parpadear.

twirl [twə:l] n giro // vt dar vueltas a // vi girar rápidamente.

twist [twɪst] n (*action*) torsión f; (*in road, coil*) vuelta; (*in wire, flex*) enroscadura; (*in story*) cambio imprevisto // vt torcer, retorcer; (*weave*) entrelazar; (*roll around*) enrollar; (*fig*) deformar // vi serpentear.

twit [twɪt] n (*col*) tonto.

twitch [twɪtʃ] n sacudida; (*nervous*) tic m nervioso // vi moverse nerviosamente.

two [tu:] num dos; **to put ~ and ~ together** (*fig*) atar cabos; **~-door** a (*AUT*) de dos puertas; **~-faced** a (*pej: person*) falso; **~-fold** ad: **to increase ~fold** duplicar; **~-piece** (*suit*) n traje m de dos piezas; **~-piece** (*swimsuit*) n dos piezas m inv, bikini m; **~-seater** n (*plane*) avión m biplaza; (*car*) coche m de dos plazas; **~some** n (*people*) pareja; **~-way** a: **~-way traffic** circulación f en ambas direcciones.

tycoon [taɪ'ku:n] n: (**business**) magnate m.

type [taɪp] n (*category*) tipo, género; (*model*) modelo; (*TYP*) tipo, letra // vt (*letter etc*) escribir a máquina; **~-cast** a (*actor*) encasillado; **~script** n texto mecanografiado; **~writer** n máquina de escribir; **~written** a mecanografiado.

typhoid ['taɪfɔɪd] n tifoidea.

typhoon [taɪ'fu:n] n tifón m.

typhus ['taɪfəs] n tifus m.

typical ['tɪpɪkl] a típico; **typify** [-faɪ] vt ser típico de.

typing ['taɪpɪŋ] n mecanografía; **typist** n mecanógrafa.

tyranny ['tɪrənɪ] n tiranía.

tyrant ['taɪərənt] n tirano/a.

tyre, tire (*US*) ['taɪə*] n neumático, llanta.

tzar [zɑ:*] n = **tsar.**

U

U-bend ['ju:'bɛnd] n (*in pipe*) recodo.

ubiquitous [ju:'bɪkwɪtəs] a ubicuo, omnipresente.

udder ['ʌdə*] n ubre f.

UFO ['ju:fəu] n abbr of **unidentified flying object** O.V.N.I. m (objeto volante no identificado).

ugliness ['ʌglɪnɪs] n fealdad f; **ugly** a feo; (*dangerous*) peligroso.

U.K. n abbr of **United Kingdom.**

ulcer ['ʌlsə*] n úlcera.

Ulster ['ʌlstə*] n Úlster m, Irlanda del Norte.

ulterior [ʌl'tɪərɪə*] a ulterior; ~ **motive** motivo oculto.

ultimate ['ʌltɪmət] a último, final; (authority) supremo; ~**ly** ad (in the end) por último, al final; (fundamentally) en el fondo.

ultimatum [ʌltɪ'meɪtəm] n ultimátum m.

ultraviolet ['ʌltrə'vaɪəlɪt] a ultravioleta.

umbilical cord [ʌmbɪ'laɪkl-] n cordón m umbilical.

umbrella [ʌm'brelə] n paraguas m inv.

umpire ['ʌmpaɪə*] n árbitro // vt arbitrar.

umpteen [ʌmp'tiːn] a tantísimos; **for the** ~**th time** por enésima vez.

UN, UNO abbr of **United Nations (Organization)**.

unable [ʌn'eɪbl] a: **to be** ~ **to do sth** ser incapaz o no poder hacer algo.

unabridged [ʌnə'brɪdʒd] a íntegro.

unaccompanied [ʌnə'kʌmpənɪd] a no acompañado.

unaccountably [ʌnə'kauntəblɪ] ad inexplicablemente.

unaccustomed [ʌnə'kʌstəmd] a: **to be** ~ **to** no tener costumbre de.

unaided [ʌn'eɪdɪd] a sin ayuda, por sí solo.

unanimous [juː'nænɪməs] a unánime; ~**ly** ad unánimemente.

unarmed [ʌn'ɑːmd] a (without a weapon) desarmado; (defenceless) inerme.

unassuming [ʌnə'sjuːmɪŋ] a modesto, sin pretensiones.

unattached [ʌnə'tætʃt] a (person) libre; (part etc) suelto, separable.

unattended [ʌnə'tɛndɪd] a (car, luggage) sin vigilancia.

unattractive [ʌnə'træktɪv] a poco atractivo.

unauthorized [ʌn'ɔːθəraɪzd] a desautorizado.

unavoidable [ʌnə'vɔɪdəbl] a inevitable.

unaware [ʌnə'weə*] a: **to be** ~ **of** ignorar, no darse cuenta de; ~**s** ad de improviso.

unbalanced [ʌn'bælənst] a desequilibrado; (mentally) trastornado.

unbearable [ʌn'beərəbl] a insoportable.

unbeatable [ʌn'biːtəbl] a (team) imbatible; (price) inmejorable.

unbeaten [ʌn'biːtn] a imbatido.

unbeknown(st) [ʌnbɪ'nəʊn(st)] ad: ~ **to me** sin saberlo yo.

unbelievable [ʌnbɪ'liːvəbl] a increíble.

unbend [ʌn'bend] (irg: like bend) vi suavizarse // vt (wire) enderezar.

unblock [ʌn'blɔk] vt (pipe) desatascar.

unborn [ʌn'bɔːn] a sin nacer.

unbounded [ʌn'baundɪd] a ilimitado, sin límite.

unbreakable [ʌn'breɪkəbl] a irrompible.

unbridled [ʌn'braɪdld] a (fig) desenfrenado.

unbroken [ʌn'brəʊkən] a (seal) intacto;

(series) continuo; (record) imbatido; (spirit) indómito.

unburden [ʌn'bɔːdn] vr: **to** ~ **o.s.** desahogarse.

unbutton [ʌn'bʌtn] vt desabrochar.

uncalled-for [ʌn'kɔːldfɔː*] a gratuito, inmerecido.

uncanny [ʌn'kænɪ] a extraño, extraordinario.

unceasing [ʌn'siːsɪŋ] a incesante.

uncertain [ʌn'sɔːtn] a incierto; (character) indeciso; ~**ty** n incertidumbre f.

unchanged [ʌn'tʃeɪndʒd] a sin cambiar o alterar.

uncharitable [ʌn'tʃærɪtəbl] a poco caritativo.

uncharted [ʌn'tʃɑːtɪd] a inexplorado.

unchecked [ʌn'tʃɛkt] a desenfrenado.

uncivil [ʌn'sɪvɪl] a grosero.

uncle ['ʌŋkl] n tío.

uncomfortable [ʌn'kʌmfətəbl] a incómodo; (uneasy) molesto.

uncommon [ʌn'kɔmən] a poco común, raro.

unconcerned [ʌnkən'sɔːnd] a indiferente, despreocupado.

unconditional [ʌnkən'dɪʃənl] a incondicional.

unconscious [ʌn'kɔnʃəs] a sin sentido; (unaware) inconsciente // n: **the** ~ el inconsciente; ~**ly** ad inconscientemente.

uncontrollable [ʌnkən'trəʊləbl] a (temper) ingobernable; (laughter) incontenible.

uncouth [ʌn'kuːθ] a grosero, inculto.

uncover [ʌn'kʌvə*] vt (gen) descubrir; (take lid off) destapar.

undecided [ʌndɪ'saɪdɪd] a (character) indeciso; (question) no resuelto, pendiente.

undeniable [ʌndɪ'naɪəbl] a innegable.

under ['ʌndə*] prep debajo de; (less than) menos de; (according to) según, de acuerdo con // ad debajo, abajo; ~ **there** allí abajo; ~ **repair** en reparación.

under... [ʌndə*] pref sub; ~**-age** a menor de edad; ~**carriage** n tren m de aterrizaje; ~**clothes** npl ropa sg interior; ~**coat** n (paint) primera mano; ~**cover** a clandestino; ~**current** n corriente f submarina; (fig) tendencia oculta; ~**cut** vt irg rebajar los precios para competir con; ~**developed** a subdesarrollado; ~**dog** n desvalido; ~**done** a (CULIN) poco hecho; ~**estimate** vt subestimar; ~**exposed** a (PHOT) subexpuesto; ~**fed** a subalimentado; ~**foot** ad bajo los pies; ~**go** vt irg sufrir; (treatment) recibir; ~**graduate** n estudiante m/f; ~**ground** n (railway) metro; (POL) movimiento clandestino // a subterráneo; ~**growth** n maleza; ~**hand(ed)** a (fig) turbio; ~**lie** vt irg estar debajo de; (fig) ser la razón fundamental de; ~**line** vt subrayar; ~**ling** ['ʌndəlɪŋ] n (pej) subalterno; ~**mine** vt socavar, minar; ~**neath** [ʌndə'niːθ] ad debajo // prep debajo de, bajo; ~**paid** a mal pagado; ~**pants** npl

(*Brit*) calzoncillos *mpl*; ~**pass** *n* paso subterráneo; ~**price** *vt* vender demasiado barato; ~**privileged** *a* desamparado; ~**rate** *vt* menospreciar, subestimar; ~**side** *n* parte *f* inferior, revés *m*; ~**skirt** *n* enaguas *fpl*.

understand [ʌndə'stænd] (*irg: like* **stand**) *vt, vi* entender, comprender; (*assume*) sobreentender; ~**able** *a* comprensible; ~**ing** *a* comprensivo // *n* comprensión *f*, entendimiento; (*agreement*) acuerdo.

understatement [ʌndə'steɪtmənt] *n* descripción *f* insuficiente; (*quality*) modestia (excesiva).

understood [ʌndə'stud] *pt, pp of* **understand** // *a* entendido; (*implied*) sobreentendido.

understudy ['ʌndəstʌdɪ] *n* suplente *m/f*.

undertake [ʌndə'teɪk] (*irg: like* **take**) *vt* acometer; **to** ~ **to do sth** comprometerse a hacer algo.

undertaker ['ʌndəteɪkə*] *n* director *m* de pompas fúnebres, sepulturero.

undertaking [ʌndə'teɪkɪŋ] *n* empresa; (*promise*) promesa.

underwater [ʌndə'wɔːtə*] *ad* bajo el agua // *a* submarino.

underwear ['ʌndəwɛə*] *n* ropa interior.

underweight [ʌndə'weɪt] *a* de peso insuficiente; (*person*) demasiado delgado.

underworld ['ʌndəwəːld] *n* (*of crime*) hampa, inframundo.

underwriter ['ʌndəraɪtə*] *n* (*INSURANCE*) (re)asegurador/a *m/f*.

undesirable [ʌndɪ'zaɪərəbl] *a* indeseable.

undies ['ʌndɪz] *npl* (*col*) paños *mpl* menores.

undignified [ʌn'dɪgnɪfaɪd] *a* indecoroso.

undisputed [ʌndɪ'spjuːtɪd] *a* incontestable.

undo [ʌn'duː] (*irg: like* **do**) *vt* deshacer; ~**ing** *n* ruina, perdición *f*.

undoubted [ʌn'dautɪd] *a* indudable; ~**ly** *ad* indudablemente, sin duda.

undress [ʌn'drɛs] *vi* desnudarse.

undue [ʌn'djuː] *a* indebido, excesivo.

undulating ['ʌndjuleɪtɪŋ] *a* ondulante.

unduly [ʌn'djuːlɪ] *ad* excesivamente, demasiado.

unearth [ʌn'əːθ] *vt* desenterrar.

unearthly [ʌn'əːθlɪ] *a* (*hour*) inverosímil.

uneasy [ʌn'iːzɪ] *a* intranquilo; (*worried*) preocupado.

uneconomic(al) ['ʌniːkə'nɔmɪk(l)] *a* antieconómico.

uneducated [ʌn'ɛdjukeɪtɪd] *a* sin educación, inculto.

unemployed [ʌnɪm'plɔɪd] *a* parado, sin trabajo // *n*: **the** ~ los parados; **unemployment** [-'plɔɪmənt] *n* paro, desempleo.

unending [ʌn'ɛndɪŋ] *a* interminable.

unenthusiastic [ʌnɪnθuːzɪ'æstɪk] *a* poco entusiasta.

unerring [ʌn'əːrɪŋ] *a* infalible.

uneven [ʌn'iːvn] *a* desigual; (*road etc*) quebrado, accidentado.

unexpected [ʌnɪk'spɛktɪd] *a* inesperado.

unfair [ʌn'fɛə*] *a*: ~ **(to)** injusto (con); ~**ly** *ad* injustamente.

unfaithful [ʌn'feɪθful] *a* infiel.

unfamiliar [ʌnfə'mɪlɪə*] *a* nuevo, desconocido.

unfashionable [ʌn'fæʃnəbl] *a* pasado *o* fuera de moda.

unfasten [ʌn'fɑːsn] *vt* desatar.

unfavourable, unfavorable (*US*) [ʌn'feɪvərəbl] *a* desfavorable.

unfeeling [ʌn'fiːlɪŋ] *a* insensible.

unfinished [ʌn'fɪnɪʃt] *a* incompleto, sin terminar.

unfit [ʌn'fɪt] *a* con mala salud, enfermo; (*incompetent*) incompetente, incapaz; ~ **for work** no apto para trabajar.

unflagging [ʌn'flægɪŋ] *a* incansable.

unfold [ʌn'fəuld] *vt* desdoblar; (*fig*) revelar // *vi* abrirse; revelarse.

unforeseen ['ʌnfɔː'siːn] *a* imprevisto.

unforgettable [ʌnfə'gɛtəbl] *a* inolvidable.

unforgivable [ʌnfə'gɪvəbl] *a* imperdonable.

unfortunate [ʌn'fɔːtʃnət] *a* desgraciado; (*event, remark*) inoportuno; ~**ly** *ad* desgraciadamente.

unfounded [ʌn'faundɪd] *a* infundado.

unfriendly [ʌn'frɛndlɪ] *a* antipático.

unfurnished [ʌn'fəːnɪʃt] *a* desamueblado.

ungainly [ʌn'geɪnlɪ] *a* desgarbado.

unhappiness [ʌn'hæpɪnɪs] *n* tristeza; **unhappy** *a* (*sad*) triste; (*unfortunate*) desgraciado; (*childhood*) infeliz; **unhappy with** (*arrangements etc*) poco contento con, descontento de.

unharmed [ʌn'hɑːmd] *a* ileso; (*col*) sano y salvo.

unhealthy [ʌn'hɛlθɪ] *a* (*gen*) malsano; (*person*) enfermizo, con poca salud.

unheard-of [ʌn'həːdɔv] *a* inaudito, sin precedente.

unhook [ʌn'huk] *vt* desenganchar; (*from wall*) descolgar; (*dress*) desabrochar.

unhurt [ʌn'həːt] *a* ileso.

unidentified [ʌnaɪ'dɛntɪfaɪd] *a* no identificado.

uniform ['juːnɪfɔːm] *n* uniforme *m* // *a* uniforme; ~**ity** [-'fɔːmɪtɪ] *n* uniformidad *f*.

unify ['juːnɪfaɪ] *vt* unificar, unir.

unilateral [juːnɪ'lætərəl] *a* unilateral.

unintentional [ʌnɪn'tɛnʃənəl] *a* involuntario.

union ['juːnjən] *n* unión *f*; (*also*: **trade** ~) sindicato // *a* sindical; **U~ Jack** *n* bandera del Reino Unido.

unique [juː'niːk] *a* único.

unison ['juːnɪsn] *n*: **in** ~ en armonía.

unit ['juːnɪt] *n* unidad *f*; (*team, squad*) grupo; **kitchen** ~ mueble *m* de cocina.

unite [juː'naɪt] *vt* unir // *vi* unirse; ~**d** *a* unido; **U~d Kingdom** (**U.K.**) *n* Reino Unido; **U~d Nations** (**Organization**) (**UN, UNO**) *n* (Las) Naciones Unidas *fpl* (O.N.U.); **U~d States** (**of America**)

(US, USA) n (Los) Estados Unidos mpl (EE.UU.).

unity ['ju:nɪtɪ] n unidad f.

universal [ju:nɪ'vɜːsl] a universal.

universe ['ju:nɪvɜːs] n universo.

university [ju:nɪ'vɜːsɪtɪ] n universidad f.

unjust [ʌn'dʒʌst] a injusto.

unkempt [ʌn'kempt] a descuidado; (hair) despeinado.

unkind [ʌn'kaɪnd] a poco amable; (comment etc) cruel.

unknown [ʌn'nəʊn] a desconocido.

unladen [ʌn'leɪdn] a (ship, weight) vacío.

unleash [ʌn'li:ʃ] vt soltar; (fig) desencadenar.

unless [ʌn'les] conj a menos que, a no ser que; ~ he comes a menos que venga; ~ otherwise stated salvo indicación contraria.

unlike [ʌn'laɪk] a distinto // prep a diferencia de.

unlikely [ʌn'laɪklɪ] a improbable.

unlimited [ʌn'lɪmɪtɪd] a ilimitado.

unload [ʌn'ləʊd] vt descargar.

unlock [ʌn'lɒk] vt abrir (con llave).

unlucky [ʌn'lʌkɪ] a desgraciado; (object, number) que da mala suerte; to be ~ tener mala suerte.

unmarried [ʌn'mærɪd] a soltero.

unmask [ʌn'mɑːsk] vt desenmascarar.

unmistakable [ʌnmɪs'teɪkəbl] a inconfundible.

unmitigated [ʌn'mɪtɪgeɪtɪd] a no mitigado, absoluto.

unnatural [ʌn'nætʃrəl] a (gen) antinatural; (manner) afectado; (habit) perverso.

unnecessary [ʌn'nesəsərɪ] a innecesario, inútil.

unnoticed [ʌn'nəʊtɪst] a: to go ~ pasar desapercibido.

unobtainable [ʌnɒb'teɪnəbl] a inconseguible.

unoccupied [ʌn'ɒkjupaɪd] a (seat etc) libre.

unofficial [ʌnə'fɪʃl] a no oficial; (strike) espontáneo, sin la aprobación de la central.

unorthodox [ʌn'ɔːθədɒks] a poco ortodoxo.

unpack [ʌn'pæk] vi deshacer las maletas.

unpalatable [ʌn'pælətəbl] a (truth) desagradable.

unparalleled [ʌn'pærəleld] a (unequalled) sin par; (unique) sin precedentes.

unpleasant [ʌn'pleznt] a (disagreeable) desagradable; (person, manner) antipático.

unplug [ʌn'plʌg] vt desenchufar, desconectar.

unpopular [ʌn'pɒpjulə*] a poco popular.

unprecedented [ʌn'presɪdəntɪd] a sin precedentes.

unpredictable [ʌnprɪ'dɪktəbl] a imprevisible.

unproductive [ʌnprə'dʌktɪv] a improductivo.

unqualified [ʌn'kwɒlɪfaɪd] a (teacher) sin

título, no cualificado; (success) total, incondicional.

unravel [ʌn'rævl] vt desenmarañar.

unreal [ʌn'rɪəl] a irreal.

unrealistic [ʌnrɪə'lɪstɪk] a poco realista.

unreasonable [ʌn'ri:znəbl] a poco razonable; (demand) excesivo.

unrelated [ʌnrɪ'leɪtɪd] a sin relación; (family) sin parentesco.

unrelenting [ʌnrɪ'lentɪŋ] a implacable.

unreliable [ʌnrɪ'laɪəbl] a (person) informal; (machine) de poca confianza.

unrelieved [ʌnrɪ'li:vd] a (monotony) monótono.

unrepeatable [ʌnrɪ'pi:təbl] a (offer) irrepetible.

unrepresentative [ʌnreprɪ'zentətɪv] a poco representativo o característico.

unrest [ʌn'rest] n inquietud f, malestar m; (POL) disturbios mpl.

unroll [ʌn'rəʊl] vt desenrollar.

unruly [ʌn'ru:lɪ] a indisciplinado.

unsafe [ʌn'seɪf] a (journey) peligroso; (car etc) inseguro.

unsaid [ʌn'sed] a: to leave sth ~ dejar algo sin decir.

unsatisfactory ' ['ʌnsætɪs'fæktərɪ] a insatisfactorio.

unsavoury, unsavory (US) [ʌn'seɪvərɪ] a (fig) repugnante.

unscathed [ʌn'skeɪðd] a ileso.

unscrew [ʌn'skru:] vt destornillar.

unscrupulous [ʌn'skru:pjuləs] a sin escrúpulos.

unsettled [ʌn'setld] a inquieto, inestable; (weather) variable.

unshaven [ʌn'feɪvn] a sin afeitar.

unsightly [ʌn'saɪtlɪ] a feo.

unskilled [ʌn'skɪld] a: ~ worker obrero no cualificado.

unspeakable [ʌn'spi:kəbl] a indecible; (bad) horrible.

unsteady [ʌn'stedɪ] a inestable.

unstuck [ʌn'stʌk] a: to come ~ despegarse; (fig) fracasar.

unsuccessful [ʌnsək'sesful] a (attempt) infructuoso; (writer, proposal) sin éxito; to be ~ (in attempting sth) no tener éxito, fracasar; ~ly ad en vano, sin éxito.

unsuitable [ʌn'su:təbl] a inconveniente, inapropiado.

unsure [ʌn'fuə*] a inseguro, poco seguro.

unsuspecting [ʌnsə'spektɪŋ] a confiado.

unswerving [ʌn'swɜːvɪŋ] a inquebrantable.

untangle [ʌn'tæŋgl] vt desenredar.

untapped [ʌn'tæpt] a (resources) sin explotar.

unthinkable [ʌn'θɪŋkəbl] a inconcebible, impensable.

untidy [ʌn'taɪdɪ] a (room) desordenado, en desorden; (appearance) descuidado.

untie [ʌn'taɪ] vt desatar.

until [ʌn'tɪl] prep hasta // conj hasta que; ~ he comes hasta que venga; ~ then hasta entonces.

untimely [ʌnˈtaɪmlɪ] a inoportuno; (*death*) prematuro.
untold [ʌnˈtəuld] a (*story*) inédito; (*suffering*) indecible; (*wealth*) incalculable.
untoward [ʌntəˈwɔːd] a desfavorable.
unused [ʌnˈjuːzd] a sin usar, nuevo.
unusual [ʌnˈjuːʒuəl] a insólito, poco común.
unveil [ʌnˈveɪl] vt (*statue*) descubrir.
unwavering [ʌnˈweɪvərɪŋ] a inquebrantable.
unwelcome [ʌnˈwɛlkəm] a (*at a bad time*) inoportuno; (*unpleasant*) desagradable.
unwell [ʌnˈwɛl] a: to feel ~ estar indispuesto; to be ~ estar enfermo.
unwieldy [ʌnˈwiːldɪ] a difícil de manejar.
unwilling [ʌnˈwɪlɪŋ] a: to be ~ to do sth estar poco dispuesto a hacer algo; ~ly ad de mala gana.
unwind [ʌnˈwaɪnd] (*irg: like wind*) vt desenvolver // vi (*relax*) relajarse.
unwitting [ʌnˈwɪtɪŋ] a inconsciente.
unworthy [ʌnˈwɜːðɪ] a indigno.
unwrap [ʌnˈræp] vt desenvolver.
up [ʌp] prep: to go/be ~ sth subir/estar encima de algo // ad hacia arriba, arriba; ~ there allí arriba; ~ above encima, allí arriba; to be ~ (*out of bed*) estar levantado; it is ~ to you Ud. decide/tú decides; what is he ~ to? ¿qué es lo que quiere?, ¿qué está tramando?; he is not ~ to it no es capaz de hacerlo; ~-and-coming a prometedor(a); ~s and downs npl (*fig*) altibajos mpl.
upbringing [ˈʌpbrɪŋɪŋ] n educación f.
update [ʌpˈdeɪt] vt poner al día, modernizar; (*contract etc*) actualizar.
upgrade [ʌpˈgreɪd] vt ascender; (*job*) revalorizar.
upheaval [ʌpˈhiːvl] n trastorno, conmoción f.
uphill [ʌpˈhɪl] a cuesta arriba; (*fig: task*) penoso, difícil // ad: to go ~ ir cuesta arriba.
uphold [ʌpˈhəuld] (*irg: like hold*) vt sostener.
upholstery [ʌpˈhəulstərɪ] n tapicería.
upkeep [ˈʌpkiːp] n mantenimiento.
upon [əˈpɔn] prep sobre.
upper [ˈʌpə*] a superior, de arriba // n (*of shoe*) pala; ~-class a de clase alta; ~most a el más alto; what was ~most in my mind lo que me preocupaba más.
upright [ˈʌpraɪt] a vertical; (*fig*) honrado.
uprising [ˈʌpraɪzɪŋ] n sublevación f.
uproar [ˈʌprɔː*] n tumulto, escándalo.
uproot [ʌpˈruːt] vt desarraigar.
upset n [ˈʌpsɛt] n (*to plan etc*) revés m, contratiempo; (*MED*) trastorno // vt [ʌpˈsɛt] (*irg: like set*) (*glass etc*) volcar; (*spill*) derramar; (*plan*) alterar; (*person*) molestar, perturbar // a [ʌpˈsɛt] preocupado, perturbado; (*stomach*) trastornado.
upshot [ˈʌpʃɔt] n resultado.
upside-down [ˈʌpsaɪddaun] ad al revés.

upstairs [ʌpˈstɛəz] ad arriba // a (*room*) de arriba // n el piso superior.
upstart [ˈʌpstɑːt] n advenedizo.
upstream [ʌpˈstriːm] ad río arriba.
uptake [ˈʌpteɪk] n: he is quick/slow on the ~ es muy listo/ algo torpe.
up-to-date [ˈʌptəˈdeɪt] a moderno, actual.
upturn [ˈʌptɜːn] n (*in luck*) mejora.
upward [ˈʌpwəd] a ascendente; ~(s) ad hacia arriba.
uranium [juəˈreɪnɪəm] n uranio.
urban [ˈɜːbən] a urbano.
urbane [ɜːˈbeɪn] a cortés.
urchin [ˈɜːtʃɪn] n pilluelo, golfillo.
urge [ɜːdʒ] n (*force*) impulso; (*desire*) deseo // vt: to ~ sb to do sth incitar a uno a hacer algo.
urgency [ˈɜːdʒənsɪ] n urgencia; (*of tone*) insistencia; **urgent** a urgente.
urinal [ˈjuərɪnl] n urinario.
urinate [ˈjuərɪneɪt] vi orinar; **urine** n orina, orines mpl.
urn [ɜːn] n urna; (*also: tea* ~) tetera.
us [ʌs] pron nos; (*after prep*) nosotros/as.
US, USA n abbr of **United States (of America)**.
usage [ˈjuːzɪdʒ] n uso, costumbre f.
use [juːs] n uso, empleo; (*usefulness*) utilidad f // vt [juːz] usar, emplear; she ~d to do it (ella) solía hacerlo; in ~ en uso; out of ~ anticuado, que ya no se usa; to be of ~ servir; it's no ~ (*pointless*) es inútil; (*not useful*) no sirve; to be ~d to estar acostumbrado a; to ~ up vt agotar, consumir; ~d a (*car*) usado; ~ful a útil; to be ~ful servir; ~less a inútil; **user** n usuario/a.
usher [ˈʌʃə*] n ujier m, portero; ~ette [-ˈrɛt] n (*in cinema*) acomodadora.
USSR n: the ~ la U.R.S.S.
usual [ˈjuːʒuəl] a normal, corriente; ~ly ad normalmente.
usurp [juːˈzɜːp] vt usurpar.
utensil [juːˈtɛnsl] n utensilio; **kitchen** ~s batería sg de cocina.
uterus [ˈjuːtərəs] n útero.
utilitarian [juːtɪlɪˈtɛərɪən] a utilitario.
utility [juːˈtɪlɪtɪ] n utilidad f; ~ **room** n trascocina.
utilize [ˈjuːtɪlaɪz] vt utilizar.
utmost [ˈʌtməust] a mayor // n: to do one's ~ hacer todo lo posible.
utter [ˈʌtə*] a total, completo // vt pronunciar, proferir; ~ance n palabras fpl, declaración f; ~ly ad completamente, totalmente.
U-turn [ˈjuːˈtɜːn] n viraje m en U.

V

v. abbr of **verse**; **versus**; **volt**; **vide** véase.
vacancy [ˈveɪkənsɪ] n (*job*) vacante f; (*room*) cuarto libro; **vacant** a desocupado, libre; (*expression*) distraído; **vacate**

[və'keɪt] vt (house) desocupar; (job) salir de; (throne) renunciar a.
vacation [və'keɪʃən] n vacaciones fpl.
vaccinate ['væksɪneɪt] vt vacunar; **vaccination** [-'neɪʃən] n vacunación f.
vaccine ['væksi:n] n vacuna.
vacuum ['vækjum] n vacío; ~ **cleaner** n aspiradora; ~ **flask** n termo.
vagabond ['vægəbɔnd] n vagabundo.
vagina [və'dʒaɪnə] n vagina.
vagrant ['veɪgrnt] n vagabundo.
vague [veɪg] a vago; (blurred: memory) borroso; (uncertain) incierto, impreciso; (person) distraído; ~**ly** ad vagamente.
vain [veɪn] a (conceited) vanidoso; (useless) vano, inútil; **in** ~ en vano.
vale [veɪl] n valle m.
valentine ['vælɔntaɪn] n: **V**~'**s Day** Día m de los Enamorados.
valid ['vælɪd] a válido; (ticket) valedero; (law) vigente; ~**ity** [-'lɪdɪtɪ] n validez f; vigencia.
valley ['vælɪ] n valle m.
valour, valor (US) ['vælə*] n valor m, valentía.
valuable ['væljuəbl] a (jewel) de valor; (time) valioso; ~**s** npl objetos mpl de valor.
valuation [vælju'eɪʃən] n tasación f, valuación f.
value ['vælju:] n valor m; (importance) importancia // vt (fix price of) tasar, valorar; (esteem) apreciar; (cherish) tener en mucho; ~ **added tax (VAT)** n tasa al valor añadido o agregado; ~**d** a (appreciated) apreciado.
valve [vælv] n (gen) válvula; (MED) valva.
vampire ['væmpaɪə*] n vampiro/vampiresa.
van [væn] n (AUT) furgoneta; (RAIL) furgón m (de equipajes).
vandal ['vændl] n vándalo; ~**ism** n vandalismo; ~**ize** vt dañar, destruir.
vanilla [və'nɪlə] n vainilla.
vanish ['vænɪʃ] vi desvanecerse, esfumarse.
vanity ['vænɪtɪ] n vanidad f; ~ **case** n neceser m.
vantage point ['vɑ:ntɪdʒ-] n posición f ventajosa.
vapour, vapor (US) ['veɪpə*] n vapor m; (steam) vaho.
variable ['vεərɪəbl] a variable.
variance ['vεərɪəns] n: **to be at** ~ (**with**) desentonar (con), estar en desacuerdo (con).
variation [vεərɪ'eɪʃən] n variedad f; (in opinion) variación f.
varicose ['værɪkəus] a: ~ **veins** varices fpl.
varied ['vεərɪd] a variado.
variety [və'raɪətɪ] n variedad f, diversidad f; (quantity) surtido; ~ **show** n variedades fpl.
various ['vεərɪəs] a varios(as), diversos(as).

varnish ['vɑ:nɪʃ] n (gen) barniz m; (nail ~) esmalte m // vt (gen) barnizar; (nails) pintar (con esmalte).
vary ['vεərɪ] vt variar; (change) cambiar // vi variar; (disagree) discrepar; (deviate) desviarse; ~**ing** a diversos(as).
vase [vɑ:z] n florero.
vaseline ['væsɪli:n] n vaselina.
vast [vɑ:st] a enorme; (success) abrumador(a); ~**ness** n inmensidad f.
vat [væt] n tina, tinaja.
VAT [væt] n abbr of **Value Added Tax.**
Vatican ['vætɪkən] n: **the** ~ el Vaticano.
vault [vɔ:lt] n (of roof) bóveda; (tomb) tumba; (in bank) sótano // vt (also: ~ over) saltar (por encima de).
veal [vi:l] n ternera.
veer [vɪə*] vi virar.
vegetable ['vedʒtəbl] n (BOT) vegetal m; (edible plant) legumbre f, hortaliza; ~**s** npl (cooked) verduras fpl // a vegetal; ~ **garden** n huerto.
vegetarian [vedʒɪ'tεərɪən] a, n vegetariano/a.
vegetate ['vedʒɪteɪt] vi vegetar.
vegetation [vedʒɪ'teɪʃən] n vegetación f.
vehement ['vi:mənt] a vehemente; (impassioned) apasionado.
vehicle ['vi:ɪkl] n vehículo.
veil [veɪl] n velo // vt velar.
vein [veɪn] n vena; (of ore etc) veta.
velocity [vɪ'lɔsɪtɪ] n velocidad f.
velvet ['velvɪt] n terciopelo // a aterciopelado.
vendetta [ven'detə] n vendetta.
vending machine ['vendɪŋ-] n distribuidor m automático.
vendor ['vendə*] n vendedor/a m/f.
veneer [və'nɪə*] n chapa, enchapado; (fig) barniz m, apariencia.
venereal [vɪ'nɪərɪəl] a: ~ **disease (VD)** n enfermedad f venérea.
Venetian blind [vɪ'ni:ʃən-] n persiana.
Venezuela [venε'zweɪlə] n Venezuela; ~**n** a, n venezolano/a.
vengeance ['vendʒəns] n venganza; **with a** ~ (fig) con creces.
venison ['venɪsn] n carne f de venado.
venom ['venəm] n veneno; ~**ous** a venenoso.
vent [vent] n (opening) abertura; (air-hole) respiradero; (in wall) rejilla (de ventilación) // vt (fig: feelings) desahogar.
ventilate ['ventɪleɪt] vt ventilar; **ventilation** [-'leɪʃən] n ventilación f; **ventilator** n ventilador m.
ventriloquist [ven'trɪləkwɪst] n ventrílocuo.
venture ['ventʃə*] n empresa // vt aventurar; (opinion) ofrecer // vi arriesgarse, lanzarse.
venue ['venju:] n lugar m; (meeting place) lugar m de reunión.
veranda(h) [və'rændə] n terraza; (with glass) galería.
verb [və:b] n verbo; ~**al** a verbal.

verbatim [vɔː'beɪtɪm] a. ad palabra por palabra.

verbose [vɔː'bəus] a prolijo.

verdict ['vɔːdɪkt] n veredicto, fallo; (fig) opinión f, juicio.

verge [vɔːdʒ] n borde m, margen m; **to be on the ~ of doing sth** estar a punto de hacer algo; **to ~ on** vt fus rayar en.

verify ['verɪfaɪ] vt comprobar, verificar.

vermin ['vɔːmɪn] npl (animals) bichos mpl; (insects, fig) sabandijas fpl.

vermouth ['vɔːməθ] n vermut m.

vernacular [vɔ'nækjulə*] n vernáculo.

versatile ['vɔːsətaɪl] a (person) de talentos variados; (machine, tool etc) que tiene muchos usos; (mind) ágil, flexible.

verse [vɔːs] n versos mpl, poesía; (stanza) estrofa; (in bible) versículo.

versed [vɔːst] a: (well-)~ **in** versado en, conocedor de.

version ['vɔːʃən] n versión f.

versus ['vɔːsəs] prep contra.

vertebra ['vɔːtɪbrə], pl ~**e** [-briː] n vértebra; **vertebrate** [-brɪt] n vertebrado.

vertical ['vɔːtɪkl] a vertical.

vertigo ['vɔːtɪgəu] n vértigo.

very ['verɪ] ad muy // a: **the ~ book which** el mismo libro que; **the ~ last** el último (de todos); **at the ~ least** al menos; **~ much** muchísimo.

vespers ['vespəz] npl vísperas fpl.

vessel ['vesl] n (ANAT, NAUT) vaso; (container) vasija.

vest [vest] n camiseta; (US: waistcoat) chaleco; **~ed interests** npl (COMM) intereses mpl creados.

vestibule ['vestibjuːl] n vestíbulo.

vestige ['vestɪdʒ] n vestigio, rastro.

vestry ['vestrɪ] n sacristía.

vet [vet] n abbr of **veterinary surgeon** // vt repasar, revisar.

veteran ['vetərn] n veterano; **~ car** n coche m antiguo.

veterinary ['vetrɪnərɪ] a veterinario; **~ surgeon** n veterinario.

veto ['viːtəu], pl ~**es** n veto // vt vetar, vedar.

vex [veks] vt (irritate) fastidiar; (make impatient) impacientar; **~ed** a (question) batallón(ona), controvertido.

via ['vaɪə] prep por, por vía de.

viable ['vaɪəbl] a viable.

viaduct ['vaɪədʌkt] n viaducto.

vibrate [vaɪ'breɪt] vi vibrar; **vibration** [-'breɪʃən] n vibración f.

vicar ['vɪkə*] n párroco; **~age** n parroquia.

vice [vaɪs] n (evil) vicio; (TECH) torno de banco.

vice- [vaɪs] pref vice; **~chairman** n vicepresidente m.

vice versa ['vaɪsɪ'vɔːsə] ad viceversa.

vicinity [vɪ'sɪnɪtɪ] n (area) vecindad f; (nearness) proximidad f.

vicious ['vɪʃəs] a (violent) violento; (depraved) depravado; (cruel) cruel;

(bitter) rencoroso; **~ness** n violencia; depravación f; crueldad f; rencor m.

victim ['vɪktɪm] n víctima m/f; **~ization** [-'zeɪʃən] n (gen) persecución f; (in strike) represalias fpl; **~ize** vt (strikers etc) tomar represalias contra.

victor ['vɪktə*] n vencedor/a m/f.

Victorian [vɪk'tɔːrɪən] a victoriano.

victorious [vɪk'tɔːrɪəs] a vencedor(a).

victory ['vɪktərɪ] n victoria.

video ['vɪdɪəu] cpd video; **~(-tape) recorder** n video-grabadora.

vie [vaɪ] vi: **to ~ with** competir con.

Vienna [vɪ'enə] n Viena.

view [vjuː] n vista, perspectiva; (landscape) paisaje m; (opinion) opinión f, criterio // vt (look at) mirar; (examine) examinar; **on ~** (in museum etc) expuesto; **in full ~ (of)** en plena vista (de); **in ~ of the fact that** en vista del hecho de que; **~er** n (small projector) visionadora; (TV) televidente m/f; **~finder** n visor m de imagen; **~point** n punto de vista.

vigil ['vɪdʒɪl] n vigilia; **to keep ~** velar; **~ance** n vigilancia; **~ant** a vigilante.

vigorous ['vɪgərəs] a enérgico, vigoroso; **vigour, vigor** (US) n energía, vigor m.

vile [vaɪl] a (action) vil, infame; (smell) asqueroso.

vilify ['vɪlɪfaɪ] vt vilipendiar.

villa ['vɪlə] n (country house) casa de campo; (suburban house) chalet m.

village ['vɪlɪdʒ] n aldea; **villager** n aldeano/a.

villain ['vɪlən] n (scoundrel) malvado; (criminal) maleante m/f.

vindicate ['vɪndɪkeɪt] vt vindicar, justificar.

vindictive [vɪn'dɪktɪv] a vengativo.

vine [vaɪn] n vid f.

vinegar ['vɪnɪgə*] n vinagre m.

vineyard ['vɪnjɑːd] n viña, viñedo.

vintage ['vɪntɪdʒ] n (year) vendimia, cosecha; **~ wine** n vino añejo.

vinyl ['vaɪnl] n vinilo.

violate ['vaɪəleɪt] vt violar; **violation** [-'leɪʃən] n violación f.

violence ['vaɪələns] n violencia; **violent** a (gen) violento; (intense) intenso.

violet ['vaɪələt] a violado, violeta // n (plant) violeta.

violin [vaɪə'lɪn] n violín m; **~ist** n violinista m/f.

VIP n abbr of **very important person.**

viper ['vaɪpə*] n víbora.

virgin ['vɔːdʒɪn] n virgen m/f // a virgen; **the Blessed V~** la Santísima Virgen; **~ity** [-'dʒɪnɪtɪ] n virginidad f.

Virgo ['vɔːgəu] n Virgo.

virile ['vɪraɪl] a viril; **virility** [vɪ'rɪlɪtɪ] n virilidad f; (fig) machismo.

virtually ['vɔːtjuəlɪ] ad (almost) virtualmente.

virtue ['vɔːtjuː] n virtud f; **by ~ of** en virtud de.

virtuoso [vɔːtju'əuzəu] n virtuoso.

virtuous ['vɔːtjuəs] a virtuoso.

virulent ['virulənt] a virulento.

virus ['vaiərəs] n virus m.

visa ['viːzə] n visado, visa (AM).

vis-à-vis [viːzə'viː] prep respecto de.

visibility [vizi'biliti] n visibilidad f.

visible ['vizəbl] a visible; **visibly** ad visiblemente.

vision ['viʒən] n (sight) vista; (foresight, in dream) visión f; **~ary** n visionario.

visit ['vizit] n visita // vt (person) visitar, hacer una visita a; (place) ir a, (ir a) conocer; **~or** n (gen) visitante m/f; (to one's house) visita; (tourist) turista m/f; (tripper) excursionista m/f; **~ors' book** n libro de visitas.

visor ['vaizə*] n visera.

vista ['vistə] n vista, panorama.

visual ['vizjuəl] a visual; **~ize** vt imaginarse; (foresee) prever.

vital ['vaitl] a (essential) esencial, imprescindible; (important) de suma importancia; (crucial) crítico; (person) enérgico, vivo; (of life) vital; **~ity** [-'tæliti] n energía, vitalidad f; **~ly** ad: **~ly important** de primera importancia.

vitamin ['vitəmin] n vitamina.

vivacious [vi'veiʃəs] a vivaz, alegre.

vivid ['vivid] a (account) gráfico; (light) intenso; (imagination) vivo.

vivisection [vivi'sekʃən] n vivisección f.

V-neck ['viːnek] n cuello de pico.

vocabulary [vəu'kæbjuləri] n vocabulario.

vocal ['vəukl] a vocal; (noisy) ruidoso; **~ chords** npl cuerdas fpl vocales; **~ist** n cantante m/f.

vocation [vəu'keiʃən] n vocación f; **~al** a vocacional.

vociferous [və'sifərəs] a vocinglero.

vodka ['vɔdkə] n vodka.

vogue [vəug] n boga, moda.

voice [vɔis] n voz f // vt (opinion) expresar.

void [vɔid] n vacío; (hole) hueco // a (gen) vacío; (vacant) vacante; (null) nulo, inválido.

volatile ['vɔlətail] a volátil.

volcanic [vɔl'kænik] a volcánico; **volcano** [-'keinəu], pl **-es** n volcán m.

volley ['vɔli] n (of gunfire) descarga; (of stones etc) lluvia; (TENNIS etc) voleo; **~ball** n balonvolea, vol(e)ibol m (AM).

volt [vəult] n voltio; **~age** n voltaje m.

voluble ['vɔljubl] a locuaz, hablador(a).

volume ['vɔljuːm] n (gen) volumen m; (book) tomo.

voluntarily ['vɔləntrili] ad libremente, de su propia voluntad.

voluntary ['vɔləntəri] a voluntario, espontáneo; (unpaid) (a título) gratuito.

volunteer [vɔlən'tiə*] n voluntario // vi ofrecerse (de voluntario).

voluptuous [və'lʌptjuəs] a voluptuoso.

vomit ['vɔmit] n vómito // vt, vi vomitar.

vote [vəut] n voto; (votes cast) votación f; (right to ~) derecho de votar; (franchise) sufragio // vt (chairman) elegir // vi votar,

ir a votar; **voter** n votante m/f; **voting** n votación f.

vouch [vautʃ]: **to ~ for** vt garantizar, responder de.

voucher ['vautʃə*] n (for meal, petrol) vale m.

vow [vau] n voto // vi hacer voto.

vowel ['vauəl] n vocal f.

voyage ['vɔiidʒ] n (journey) viaje m; (crossing) travesía.

vulgar ['vʌlgə*] a (rude) ordinario, grosero; (in bad taste) de mal gusto; **~ity** [-'gæriti] n grosería; mal gusto.

vulnerable ['vʌlnərəbl] a vulnerable.

vulture ['vʌltʃə*] n buitre m.

W

wad [wɔd] n (of cotton wool, paper) bolita; (of banknotes etc) fajo.

waddle ['wɔdl] vi anadear.

wade [weid] vi: **to ~ through** caminar por el agua; (fig: a book) leer con dificultad.

wafer ['weifə*] n (biscuit) galleta, barquillo; (REL) oblea.

waffle ['wɔfl] n (CULIN) buñuelo, panqueque m // vi meter paja.

waft [wɔft] vt hacer flotar // vi flotar.

wag [wæg] vt menear, agitar // vi moverse, menearse.

wage [weidʒ] n (also: **~s**) sueldo, salario // vt: **to ~ war** hacer la guerra; **~ claim** n demanda de aumento de sueldo; **~ earner** n asalariado/a; **~ freeze** n congelación f de salarios.

wager ['weidʒə*] n apuesta // vt apostar.

waggle ['wægl] vt menear, mover.

wag(g)on ['wægən] n (horse-drawn) carro; (truck) camión m; (RAIL) vagón m.

wail [weil] n gemido // vi gemir.

waist [weist] n cintura, talle m; **~coat** n chaleco; **~line** n talle m.

wait [weit] n espera; (interval) pausa // vi esperar; **to lie in ~ for** acechar a; **I can't ~ to** (fig) estoy deseando; **to ~ for** esperar (a); **to ~ on** vt fus servir a; **'no ~ing'** (AUT) 'prohibido aparcar'; **~er** n camarero; **~ing list** n lista de espera; **~ing room** n sala de espera; **~ress** n camarera.

waive [weiv] vt renunciar a.

wake [weik], pt **woke** or **waked**, pp **woken** or **waked** vt (also: **~ up**) despertar // vi (also: **~ up**) despertarse // n (for dead person) vela, velatorio; (NAUT) estela; **waken** vt, vi = **wake**.

Wales [weilz] n País m de Gales.

walk [wɔːk] n paseo; (hike) excursión f a pie, caminata; (gait) paso, andar m; (in park etc) paseo, alameda // vi andar; (for pleasure, exercise) pasearse // vt (distance) recorrer a pie, andar; (dog) sacar de paseo, pasear; **10 minutes' ~ from here** desde aquí hay 10 minutos a pie; **people from all ~s of life** gente de todas las esferas; **~er** n (person) paseante *m/f*, caminante *m/f*; ~**ie-talkie** ['wɔːkɪ'tɔːkɪ] *n* walkie-talkie *m*, transmisor-receptor *m* (portátil); ~**ing** *n* el andar; ~**ing shoes** *npl* zapatos *mpl* para andar; ~**ing stick** *n* bastón *m*; ~**out** *n* (*of workers*) huelga sorpresa; ~**over** *n* (*col*) triunfo fácil; ~**way** *n* paseo.

wall [wɔːl] *n* pared *f*; (*exterior*) muro; (*city* ~ *etc*) muralla; ~**ed** *a* (*city*) amurallado; (*garden*) con tapia.

wallet ['wɔlɪt] *n* cartera.

wallflower ['wɔːlflauə*] *n* alhelí *m*; **to be a** ~ (*fig*) comer pavo.

wallop ['wɔləp] *vt* (*col*) zurrar.

wallow ['wɔləu] *vi* revolcarse.

wallpaper ['wɔːlpeɪpə*] *n* papel *m* pintado.

walnut ['wɔːlnʌt] *n* nuez *f*; (*tree*) nogal *m*.

walrus ['wɔːlrəs], *pl* ~ *or* ~**es** *n* morsa.

waltz [wɔːlts] *n* vals *m* // *vi* bailar el vals.

wand [wɔnd] *n* (*also*: **magic** ~) varita (mágica).

wander ['wɔndə*] *vi* (*person*) vagar, deambular; (*thoughts*) divagar; (*get lost*) extraviarse // *vt* recorrer, vagar por; ~**er** *n* vagabundo; ~**ing** *a* errante; (*thoughts*) distraído.

wane [weɪn] *vi* menguar.

wangle ['wæŋgl] *vt* (*col*): **to** ~ **sth** agenciarse algo.

want [wɔnt] *vt* (*wish for*) querer, desear; (*demand*) exigir; (*need*) necesitar; (*lack*) carecer de // *n*: **for** ~ **of** por falta de; ~**s** *npl* (*needs*) necesidades *fpl*; **to** ~ **to do** querer hacer; **to** ~ **sb to do sth** querer que uno haga algo; ~**ing** *a* falto, deficiente; **to be found** ~**ing** no estar a la altura de las circunstancias.

wanton ['wɔntn] *a* (*playful*) juguetón(ona); (*licentious*) lascivo.

war [wɔː*] *n* guerra; **to make** ~ hacer la guerra.

ward [wɔːd] *n* (*in hospital*) sala; (*POL*) distrito electoral; (*LAW: child*) pupilo; **to** ~ **off** *vt* desviar, parar; (*attack*) rechazar.

warden ['wɔːdn] *n* (*of institution*) director *m*; (*of park, game reserve*) guardián *m*; (*also*: **traffic** ~) guardia *m/f*.

warder ['wɔːdə*] *n* guardián *m*, carcelero.

wardrobe ['wɔːdrəub] *n* (*cupboard*) armario; (*clothes*) guardarropa.

warehouse ['wɛəhaus] *n* almacén *m*, depósito.

wares [wɛəz] *npl* mercancías *fpl*.

war: ~**fare** *n* guerra; ~**head** *n* cabeza armada.

warily ['wɛərɪlɪ] *ad* con cautela, cautelosamente.

warlike ['wɔːlaɪk] *a* guerrero.

warm [wɔːm] *a* caliente; (*thanks*) efusivo; (*clothes etc*) cálido; (*welcome, day*) caluroso; **it's** ~ hace calor; **I'm** ~ tengo calor; **to** ~ **up** *vi* (*person, room*) calentarse; (*athlete*) hacer ejercicios de calentamiento; (*discussion*) acalorarse // *vt* calentar; ~-**hearted** *a* afectuoso; ~**ly** *ad* afectuosamente; ~**th** *n* calor *m*.

warn [wɔːn] *vt* avisar, prevenir; ~**ing** *n* aviso, advertencia; ~**ing light** *n* luz *f* de advertencia.

warp [wɔːp] *vi* diformarse.

warrant ['wɔrnt] *n* (*guarantee*) garantía; (*LAW*) mandato judicial.

warranty ['wɔrəntɪ] *n* garantía.

warren ['wɔrən] *n* (*of rabbits*) madriguera; (*house*) conejera.

warrior ['wɔrɪə*] *n* guerrero.

warship ['wɔːʃɪp] *n* buque *m o* barco de guerra.

wart [wɔːt] *n* verruga.

wartime ['wɔːtaɪm] *n*: **in** ~ en tiempos de guerra, en la guerra.

wary ['wɛərɪ] *a* cauteloso, cauto.

was [wɔz] *pt of* **be.**

wash [wɔʃ] *vt* lavar // *vi* lavarse // *n* (*clothes etc*) lavado; (*bath*) baño; (*of ship*) estela; **to have a** ~ lavarse; **to** ~ **away** *vt* (*stain*) quitar lavando; (*subj: river etc*) llevarse; (*fig*) regar; **to** ~ **off** *vt* quitar lavando; **to** ~ **up** *vi* fregar los platos; ~**able** *a* lavable; ~**basin** *n* lavabo; ~**er** *n* (*TECH*) arandela; ~**ing** *n* (*dirty*) ropa sucia; (*clean*) colada; ~**ing machine** *n* lavadora; ~**ing powder** *n* jabón *m* en polvo; ~**ing-up** *n* fregado, platos *mpl* (para fregar); ~**out** *n* (*col*) fracaso; ~**room** *n* servicios *mpl*.

wasn't ['wɔznt] = **was not.**

wasp [wɔsp] *n* avispa.

wastage ['weɪstɪdʒ] *n* desgaste *m*; (*loss*) pérdida; **natural** ~ desgaste natural.

waste [weɪst] *n* derroche *m*, despilfarro; (*wastage*) desgaste *m*; (*of time*) pérdida; (*food*) sobras *fpl*; (*rubbish*) basura, desperdicios *mpl* // *a* (*material*) de desecho; (*left over*) sobrante; (*land*) baldío // *vt* (*squander*) malgastar, derrochar; (*time*) perder; (*opportunity*) desperdiciar; (*use up*) consumir; **to** ~ **away** *vi* consumirse; ~**bin** *n* cubo de la basura; ~ **disposal unit** *n* triturador *m* de basura; ~**ful** *a* derrochador(a); (*process*) antieconómico; ~ **ground** *n* terreno baldío; ~**paper basket** *n* papelera; ~ **pipe** *n* tubo de desagüe.

watch [wɔtʃ] *n* reloj *m*; (*act of watching*) vigilia; (*vigilance*) vigilancia; (*guard*: MIL) centinela *m*; (NAUT: *spell of duty*) guardia // *vt* (*look at*) mirar, observar; (: *match, programme*) ver; (*spy on, guard*) vigilar; (*be careful of*) cuidarse de, tener cuidado de // *vi* ver, mirar; (*keep guard*) montar guardia; **to** ~ **out** *vi* cuidarse, tener cuidado; ~**dog** *n* perro guardián; ~**ful** *a* vigilante, observador(a); ~**maker** *n* relojero; ~**man** *n* guardián *m*; (*also*: **night** ~**man**) sereno; (*in factory*) vigilante *m* nocturno; ~ **strap** *n* pulsera (de reloj); ~**word** *n* lema *m*.

water ['wɔːtə*] *n* agua // *vt* (*plant*) regar; **to** ~ **down** *vt* (*milk*) aguar; ~ **closet** *n* wáter *m*; ~-**colour** *n* acuarela; ~**cress** *n* berro; ~**fall** *n* cascada, salto de agua; ~**hole** *n* charco; ~**ing can** *n* regadera; ~

level n nivel m del agua; ~ **lily** n nenúfar m; ~**line** n (NAUT) línea de flotación; ~**logged** a empapado; ~ **main** n cañería del agua; ~**mark** n (on paper) filigrana; ~**melon** n sandía; ~ **polo** n polo acuático; ~**proof** a impermeable; ~**shed** n (GEO) cuenca; (fig) momento crítico; ~**skiing** n esquí m acuático; ~ **tank** n depósito de agua; ~**tight** a hermético; ~**works** npl central f depuradora; ~**y** a (colour) desvaído; (coffee) aguado; (eyes) lloroso.

watt [wɔt] n vatio.

wave [weɪv] n ola; (of hand) ademán m, señal f; (RADIO) onda; (in hair) ondulación f; (fig) oleada // vi agitar la mano; (flag) ondear // vt (handkerchief) agitar; (weapon) blandir; (hair) ondular; ~**length** n longitud f de onda.

waver ['weɪvə*] vi oscilar; (person) vacilar.

wavy ['weɪvɪ] a ondulado.

wax [wæks] n cera // vt encerar // vi (moon) crecer; ~**works** npl museo sg de cera.

way [weɪ] n (gen) camino; (distance) trayecto, recorrido; (direction) dirección f, sentido; (manner) modo, manera; (habit) costumbre f; (condition) estado; **which ~?** ¿por dónde?, ¿en qué dirección?; **to be on one's ~** estar en camino; **to be in the ~** bloquear el camino; **to go out of one's ~ to do sth** desvivirse por hacer algo; **to lose one's ~** extraviarse; **in a ~** en cierto modo o sentido; **by the ~** a propósito; **'~ out'** 'salida'; **the ~ back** el camino de vuelta; **give ~' (AUT)** 'ceda el paso'.

waylay [weɪ'leɪ] (irg: like **lay**) vt acechar.

wayward ['weɪwəd] a (wilful) voluntarioso; (capricious) caprichoso; (naughty) travieso.

W.C. ['dʌblju'si:] n wáter m.

we [wi:] pl pron nosotros/as.

weak [wi:k] a (gen) débil, flojo; (tea) claro; ~**en** vi debilitarse; (give way) ceder // vt debilitar; (lessen) disminuir; ~**ling** n persona débil o delicada; ~**ness** n debilidad f; (fault) punto débil.

wealth [wɛlθ] n (money, resources) riqueza; (of details) abundancia; ~**y** a rico.

wean [wi:n] vt destetar.

weapon ['wɛpən] n arma.

wear [wɛə*] n (use) uso; (deterioration through use) desgaste m; (clothing): **sports/baby~** ropa de deportes/para niños // (vb: pt **wore**, pp **worn**) vt (clothes) llevar; (shoes) calzar; (put on) ponerse; (damage: through use) gastar, usar // vi (last) durar; (rub through etc) desgastarse; ~ **and tear** n desgaste m; **to ~ away** vt gastar // vi desgastarse; **to ~ down** vt gastar; (strength) agotar; **to ~ off** vi (pain etc) pasar, desaparecer; **to ~ out** vt desgastar; (person, strength) agotar.

weariness ['wɪərɪnɪs] n cansancio; (boredom) aburrimiento, hastío.

weary ['wɪərɪ] a (tired) cansado; (dispirited) abatido // vt cansar // vi: **to ~ of** cansarse de, aburrirse de.

weasel ['wi:zl] n (ZOOL) comadreja.

weather ['wɛðə*] n tiempo // vt (storm, crisis) hacer frente a; ~**beaten** a curtido; ~ **cock** n veleta; ~ **forecast** n boletín m meteorológico; ~ **vane** n = ~**cock**.

weave [wi:v], pt **wove**, pp **woven** vt (cloth) tejer; (fig) entretejer; ~**r** n tejedor/a m/f; **weaving** n tejeduría.

web [wɛb] n (of spider) telaraña; (on foot) membrana; (network) red f; ~**bed** a (foot) palmeado; ~**bing** n (on chair) cinchas fpl.

wed [wɛd], pt, pp **wedded** vt casar // vi casarse // n: **the newly-~s** los recién casados.

we'd [wi:d] = **we had; we would.**

wedded ['wɛdɪd] pt, pp of **wed.**

wedding ['wɛdɪŋ] n boda, casamiento; **silver/golden ~** bodas fpl de plata/de oro; ~ **day** n día m de la boda; ~ **dress** n traje m de novia; ~ **present** n regalo de boda; ~ **ring** n anillo de boda.

wedge [wɛdʒ] n (of wood etc) cuña; (of cake) porción f // vt acuñar; (pack tightly) apretar.

wedlock ['wɛdlɔk] n matrimonio.

Wednesday ['wɛdnzdɪ] n miércoles m.

wee [wi:] a (Scottish) pequeñito.

weed [wi:d] n mala hierba, maleza // vt escardar, desherbar; ~**-killer** n herbicida m.

week [wi:k] n semana; ~**day** n día m laborable; ~**end** n fin m de semana; ~**ly** ad semanalmente, cada semana // a semanal // n semanario.

weep [wi:p], pt, pp **wept** vi, vt llorar; ~**ing willow** n sauce m llorón.

weigh [weɪ] vt, vi pesar; **to ~ down** vt sobrecargar; (fig: with worry) agobiar; **to ~ up** vt pesar; ~**bridge** n báscula-puente f.

weight [weɪt] n peso; (on scale) pesa; **to lose/put on ~** adelgazarse/engordarse; ~**lessness** n ingravidez f; ~ **lifter** n levantador m de pesos; ~**y** a pesado.

weir [wɪə*] n presa.

weird [wɪəd] a raro, extraño.

welcome ['wɛlkəm] a bienvenido // n bienvenida // vt dar la bienvenida a; (be glad of) alegrarse de; **welcoming** a acogedor(a); (speech) de bienvenida.

weld [wɛld] n soldadura // vt soldar; ~**er** n (person) soldador m; ~**ing** n soldadura.

welfare ['wɛlfɛə*] n bienestar m; (social aid) asistencia social; ~ **state** n estado de bienestar.

well [wɛl] n fuente f, pozo // ad bien // a: **to be ~** estar bien (de salud) // excl ¡vaya!, ¡bueno!; **as ~** también; **as ~ as** igual que; ~ **done!** ¡bien hecho!; **get ~ soon!** ¡que te mejores pronto!; **to do ~** ir o salir bien; **to ~ up** vi brotar.

we'll [wi:l] = **we will, we shall.**

well: ~-**behaved** a bien educado, formal; ~-**being** n bienestar m; ~-**built** a (person) fornido; ~-**deserved** a merecido; ~-**developed** a bien desarrollado; ~-**dressed** a bien vestido; ~-**heeled** a (col: wealthy) rico; ~-**informed** a enterado.

wellingtons ['welɪŋtənz] n (also: **wellington boots**) botas fpl de goma.

well: ~-**known** a (person) conocido; ~-**mannered** a educado; ~-**meaning** a bienintencionado; ~-**off** a pudiente, con dinero; ~-**read** a culto; ~-**to-do** a acomodado; ~-**wisher** n admirador/a m/f, amigo.

Welsh [welʃ] a galés // n (LING) galés m; ~ **man/woman** n galés/esa m/f.

went [went] pt of **go**.

wept [wept] pt, pp of **weep**.

were [wə:*] pt of **be**.

we're [wɪə*] = **we are**.

weren't [wə:nt] = **were not**.

west [west] n oeste m // a occidental, del oeste // ad hacia el o al oeste; **the W~** n el Oeste, el Occidente; **the W~ Country** n el suroeste de Inglaterra; ~**erly** a (situation) oeste; (wind) del oeste; ~**ern** a occidental // n (CINEMA) película del oeste; **W~ Germany** n Alemania Occidental; **W~ Indies** npl Antillas fpl; ~**ward(s)** ad hacia el oeste.

wet [wet] a (damp) húmedo; (~ through) mojado; (rainy) lluvioso; **to get** ~ mojarse; '~ **paint**' 'recién pintado'; **to be a** ~ **blanket** (fig) ser un/una aguafiestas; ~**ness** n humedad f; ~ **suit** n traje m de buzo.

we've [wi:v] = **we have**.

whack [wæk] vt dar un buen golpe a; ~**ed** a (col: tired) reventado.

whale [weɪl] n (ZOOL) ballena.

wharf [wɔ:f], pl **wharves** [wɔ:vz] n muelle m.

what [wɔt] excl ¡qué!, ¡cómo! // det que // pron (interrogative) ¿qué?, ¿cómo?; (relative, indirect: object) lo que; (: subject) el/la que; ~ **are you doing?** ¿qué haces?; **I saw** ~ **you did** he visto lo que hiciste; ~ **a mess!** ¡que lío!; ~ **is it called?** ¿cómo se llama?; ~ **about me?** ¿y yo?; ~**ever** det: ~**ever book you choose** cualquier libro que elijas // pron: **do** ~**ever is necessary** haga lo que sea necesario; **no reason** ~**ever** or ~**soever** ninguna razón sea la que sea; **nothing** ~**ever** nada en absoluto.

wheat [wi:t] n trigo.

wheel [wi:l] n rueda; (AUT. also: **steering** ~) volante m; (NAUT) timón m // vt (pram etc) empujar // vi (also: ~ **round**) dar la vuelta, girar; ~**barrow** n carretilla; ~**chair** n silla de ruedas; ~**house** n timonera.

wheeze [wi:z] n respiración f ruidosa // vi resollar.

when [wen] ad cuándo // conj cuando; (whereas) mientras; **on the day** ~ **I met**

him el día que le conocí; ~**ever** conj cuando, todas las veces que; (every time that) siempre que.

where [wɛə*] ad dónde // conj donde; **this is** ~ **aquí es donde; ~abouts** ad ¿dónde? // n: **nobody knows his** ~**abouts** nadie conoce su paradero; ~**as** conj visto que, mientras; **wherever** [-'evə*] ad dondequiera que; (interrogative) ¿dónde?; ~ **withal** n recursos mpl.

whet [wet] vt estimular.

whether ['weðə*] conj si; **I don't know** ~ **to accept or not** no sé si aceptar o no; ~ **you go or not** vayas o no vayas.

which [wɪtʃ] det (interrogative) ¿qué?, ¿cuál?; ~ **one of you?** ¿cuál de vosotros?; ~ **picture do you want?** ¿qué cuadro quieres? // pron (interrogative) ¿cuál?; (relative: subject) que, lo que; (: object) el que etc, el cual etc, lo cual; **I don't mind** ~ no me importa cuál; **the apple** ~ **is on the table** la manzana que está sobre la mesa; **the chair on** ~ **you are sitting** la silla sobre la que estás sentado; **he said he knew,** ~ **is true** el dijo que sabía, lo cual es cierto; **in** ~ **case** en cuyo caso; ~**ever** det: **take** ~**ever book you prefer** coja el libro que prefiera; ~**ever book you take** cualquier libro que coja.

whiff [wɪf] n bocanada.

while [waɪl] n rato, momento // conj durante; (as long as) mientras; (although) aunque; **for a** ~ durante algún tiempo.

whim [wɪm] n capricho.

whimper ['wɪmpə*] n (weeping) lloriqueo; (moan) quejido // vi lloriquear; quejarse.

whimsical ['wɪmzɪkl] a (person) caprichoso; (look) extraño.

whine [waɪn] n (of pain) gemido; (of engine) zumbido // vi gemir; zumbar.

whip [wɪp] n látigo; (for riding) fusta; (Brit: POL) oficial disciplinario del partido // vt azotar; (snatch) arrebatar; ~**ped cream** n crema batida; ~-**round** n colecta.

whirl [wə:l] n remolino // vt hacer girar, dar vueltas a // vi girar, dar vueltas; (leaves, water etc) arremolinarse; ~**pool** n remolino; ~**wind** n torbellino.

whirr [wə:*] vi rechinar, zumbar.

whisk [wɪsk] n (CULIN) batidor m // vt batir; **to** ~ **sth away from sb** arrebatarle algo a uno; **to** ~ **sb away** or **off** llevar rápidamente a uno.

whisker ['wɪskə*] n: ~**s** (of animal) bigotes mpl; (of man) patillas fpl.

whisk(e)y ['wɪskɪ] n whisky m.

whisper ['wɪspə*] n cuchicheo; (rumour) rumor m; (fig) susurro, murmullo // vi cuchichear, hablar bajo; (fig) susurrar.

whist [wɪst] n whist m.

whistle ['wɪsl] n (sound) silbido; (object) silbato // vi silbar.

white [waɪt] a blanco; (pale) pálido // n blanco; (of egg) clara; ~**collar worker** n oficinista m/f; ~ **elephant** n (fig) maula; ~ **lie** n mentira piadosa; ~**ness** n blancura; ~ **paper** n (POL) libro rojo; ~**wash** n (paint) jalbegue m, cal f // vt enjalbegar; (fig) encubrir.

whiting ['waitiŋ] n, pl inv (fish) pescadilla.

Whitsun ['witsn] n pentecostés m.

whittle ['witl] vt: **to ~ away, ~ down** reducir poco a poco.

whizz [wiz] vi: **to ~ past** or **by** pasar a toda velocidad; ~ **kid** n (col) prodigio, portento.

who [hu:] pron (relative) que, el que etc, quien; (interrogative) ¿quién?; (pl) ¿quiénes?; ~**ever** pron: ~**ever finds it** cualquiera o quienquiera que lo encuentre; **ask** ~**ever you like** pregunta a quien quieras; ~**ever se marries** no importa con quién se case.

whole [həul] a (complete) todo, entero; (not broken) intacto // n (total) total m; (sum) conjunto; **the ~ of the town** toda la ciudad, la ciudad entera; **on the ~, as a ~** en general; ~**hearted** a sincero, cordial; ~**sale** n venta al por mayor // a al por mayor; (destruction) sistemático; ~**saler** n mayorista m/f; ~**some** a sano; **wholly** ad totalmente, enteramente.

whom [hu:m] pron que, a quien; (interrogative) ¿a quién?

whooping cough ['hu:piŋkɔf] n tos f ferina.

whopper ['wɔpə*] n cosa muy grande; (lie) bola; **whopping** a (col: big) enorme.

whore [hɔ:*] n (col: pej) puta.

whose [hu:z] det: ~ **book is this?** ¿de quién es este libro?; **the man** ~ **son you rescued** el hombre cuyo hijo salvaste; **the girl** ~ **sister you were speaking to** la chica con cuya hermana estabas hablando // pron: ~ **is this?** ¿de quién es esto?; **I know** ~ **it is** yo sé de quien es.

why [wai] ad por qué; (interrogative) ¿por qué?, ¿para qué? // excl ¡toma!, ¡cómo!; **tell me** ~ dime por qué, dime la razón; ~**ever** ad por qué.

wick [wik] n mecha.

wicked ['wikid] a malvado, cruel.

wicker ['wikə*] n (also: ~**work**) artículos mpl de mimbre.

wicket ['wikit] n (CRICKET) palos mpl.

wide [waid] a ancho; (region, knowledge) vasto, grande; (choice) grande // ad: **to open** ~ abrir de par en par; **to shoot** ~ errar el tiro; (fig) despabilado; ~**ly** ad (different) muy; **it is** ~**ly believed that...** hay una convicción general de que...; **widen** vt ensanchar; ~**ness** n anchura; ~**open** a abierto de par en par; ~**spread** a (belief etc) extendido, general.

widow ['widəu] n viuda; ~**ed** a viudo; ~**er** n viudo.

width [widθ] n anchura; (of cloth) ancho.

wield [wi:ld] vt (sword) manejar; (power) ejercer.

wife [waif], pl **wives** [waivz] n mujer f, esposa.

wig [wig] n peluca.

wiggle ['wigl] vt menear (rápidamente) // vi menearse.

wild [waild] a (animal) salvaje; (plant) silvestre; (rough) furioso, violento; (idea) disparatado, descabellado; (person) loco; ~**s** npl regiones fpl salvajes, tierras fpl vírgenes; ~**erness** ['wildənis] n desierto; ~**life** n fauna; ~**ly** ad (roughly) violentamente; (foolishly) locamente; (rashly) descabelladamente.

wilful ['wilful] a (person) voluntarioso; (action) deliberado; (obstinate) testarudo; (child) travieso.

will [wil] auxiliary vb: **he** ~ **come** vendrá // vt, pt, pp **willed: to** ~ **sb to do sth** desear que alguien haga algo; **he** ~**ed himself to go on** con gran fuerza de voluntad, continuó // n voluntad f; (testament) testamento; ~**ing** a (with goodwill) de buena voluntad; (submissive) complaciente; ~**ingly** ad con mucho gusto; ~**ingness** n buena voluntad.

willow ['wiləu] n sauce m.

will power n fuerza de voluntad.

wilt [wilt] vi marchitarse.

wily ['waili] a astuto.

win [win] n (in sports etc) victoria, triunfo // (vb: pt, pp **won**) vt ganar; (obtain) conseguir, lograr // vi ganar, tener éxito; **to** ~ **over, ** ~ **round** vt atraerse.

wince [wins] vi estremecerse.

winch [wintʃ] n torno.

wind [wind] n viento; (MED) flatulencia; (breath) aliento // (vb: [waind], pt, pp **wound**) vt enrollar; (wrap) envolver; (clock, toy) dar cuerda a // vi (road, river) serpentear // vt [wind] (take breath away from) dejar sin aliento a; **to** ~ **up** vt (clock) dar cuerda a; (debate) concluir, terminar; ~**break** n abrigada; ~**fall** n golpe m de suerte; ~**ing** a (road) tortuoso; ~ **instrument** n (MUS) instrumento de viento; ~**mill** n molino de viento.

window ['windəu] n ventana; (in car, train) ventanilla; (in shop etc) escaparate m; ~**box** n jardinera (de ventana); ~ **cleaner** n (person) limpiacristales m inv; ~ **ledge** n alféizar m; ~ **pane** n cristal m; ~**sill** n alféizar m.

windpipe ['windpaip] n tráquea.

windscreen ['windskri:n], **windshield** ['windʃi:ld] (US) n parabrisas m inv; ~ **washer** n lavaparabrisas m inv; ~ **wiper** n limpiaparabrisas m inv.

windswept ['windswept] a azotado por el viento.

windy ['windi] a de mucho viento; **it's** ~ hace viento.

wine [wain] n vino; ~ **cellar** n bodega; ~ **glass** n copa (para vino); ~ **list** n lista de vinos; ~ **merchant** n vinatero; ~ **tasting** n degustación f de vinos.

wing [wiŋ] n (gen) ala; (AUT) aleta, guardabarros m inv; ~**s** npl (THEATRE) bastidores mpl; ~**er** n (SPORT) extremo.

wink [wiŋk] n guiño, pestañeo // vi guiñar,

pestañear; (*light etc*) parpadear.

winner ['wɪnə*] *n* ganador/a *m/f.*

winning ['wɪnɪŋ] *a* (*team*) ganador(a); (*goal*) decisivo; ~**s** *npl* ganancias *fpl;* ~ **post** *n* meta.

winter ['wɪntə*] *n* invierno // *vi* invernar; ~ **sports** *npl* deportes *mpl* de invierno.

wintry ['wɪntrɪ] *a* invernal.

wipe [waɪp] *n*: **to give sth a** ~ pasar un trapo sobre algo // *vt* limpiar; **to** ~ **off** *vt* limpiar con un trapo; **to** ~ **out** *vt* (*debt*) liquidar; (*memory*) borrar; (*destroy*) destruir.

wire ['waɪə*] *n* alambre *m*; (*ELEC*) cable *m* (eléctrico); (*TEL*) telegrama *m* // *vt* (*house*) instalar el alambrado de; (*also:* ~ **up**) conectar // *vi* poner un telegrama.

wireless ['waɪəlɪs] *n* radio *f.*

wiring ['waɪərɪŋ] *n* instalación *f* eléctrica, alambrado.

wiry ['waɪərɪ] *a* nervioso, nervudo.

wisdom ['wɪzdəm] *n* sabiduría, saber *m*; (*good sense*) cordura; (*care*) prudencia; ~ **tooth** *n* muela del juicio.

wise [waɪz] *a* sabio; (*sensible*) cuerdo; (*careful*) prudente.

...wise [waɪz] *suff*: **time**~ en cuanto a *o* respecto al tiempo.

wisecrack ['waɪzkræk] *n* broma.

wish [wɪʃ] *n* (*desire*) deseo // *vt* desear; (*want*) querer; **best** ~**es** (*on birthday etc*) felicidades *fpl*; **with best** ~**es** (*in letter*) saludos *mpl*, recuerdos *mpl*; **to** ~ **sb goodbye** despedirse de uno; **he** ~**ed me well** me deseó mucha suerte; **to** ~ **to do/sb to do sth** querer hacer/que alguien haga algo; **to** ~ **for** desear; **it's** ~**ful thinking** es un espejismo.

wisp [wɪsp] *n* mechón *m*; (*of smoke*) voluta.

wistful ['wɪstful] *a* pensativo.

wit [wɪt] *n* (*wittiness*) ingenio, gracia; (*intelligence*) entendimiento; (*person*) chistoso/a.

witch [wɪtʃ] *n* bruja; ~**craft** *n* brujería.

with [wɪð, wɪθ] *prep* con; ~ **red** ~ **anger** rojo de cólera; **the man** ~ **the grey hat** el hombre del sombrero gris; **to be** ~ **it** (*fig*) estar al tanto *o* a la moda; **I am** ~ **you** (*I understand*) te entiendo.

withdraw [wɪθ'drɔː] (*irg: like draw*) *vt* retirar, sacar // *vi* retirarse; (*go back on promise*) retractarse; **to** ~ **money (from the bank)** retirar fondos (del banco); ~**al** *n* retirada; ~**n** *a* (*person*) reservado, introvertido.

wither ['wɪðə*] *vi* marchitarse; ~**ed** *a* marchito.

withhold [wɪθ'hould] (*irg: like hold*) *vt* (*money*) retener; (*decision*) aplazar; (*permission*) negar; (*information*) ocultar.

within [wɪð'ɪn] *prep* dentro de // *ad* dentro; ~ **reach** al alcance de la mano; ~ **sight of** a la vista de; ~ **the week** antes de acabar la semana.

without [wɪð'aut] *prep* sin.

withstand [wɪθ'stænd] (*irg: like stand*) *vt* resistir a.

witness ['wɪtnɪs] *n* (*person*) testigo; (*evidence*) testimonio // *vt* (*event*) presenciar; (*document*) atestiguar la veracidad de; ~ **box**, ~ **stand** (*US*) *n* tribuna de los testigos.

witticism ['wɪtɪsɪzm] *n* dicho ingenioso.

witty ['wɪtɪ] *a* ingenioso, salado.

wives [waɪvz] *pl of* **wife.**

wizard ['wɪzəd] *n* hechicero.

wk *abbr of* **week.**

wobble ['wɔbl] *vi* tambalearse; (*chair*) ser poco firme.

woe [wəu] *n* desgracia.

woke [wəuk], **woken** ['wəukən] *pt, pp of* **wake.**

wolf [wulf], *pl* **wolves** [wulvz] *n* lobo.

woman ['wumən], *pl* **women** *n* mujer *f*; ~**ly** *a* femenino.

womb [wuːm] *n* (*ANAT*) matriz *f*, útero.

women ['wɪmɪn] *pl of* **woman.**

won [wʌn] *pt, pp of* **win.**

wonder ['wʌndə*] *n* maravilla, prodigio; (*feeling*) asombro // *vi*: **to** ~ **whether** preguntarse si; **to** ~ **at** asombrarse de; **to** ~ **about** pensar sobre *o* en; **it's no** ~ **that** no es de extrañarse que; ~**ful** *a* maravilloso; ~**fully** *ad* maravillosamente, estupendamente.

won't [wəunt] = **will not.**

woo [wuː] *vt* (*woman*) cortejar.

wood [wud] *n* (*timber*) madera; (*forest*) bosque *m*; ~ **carving** *n* escultura de madera; ~**ed** *a* arbolado; ~**en** *a* de madera; (*fig*) inexpresivo; ~**pecker** *n* pájaro carpintero; ~**wind** *n* (*MUS*) instrumentos *mpl* de viento de madera; ~**work** *n* carpintería; ~**worm** *n* carcoma.

wool [wul] *n* lana; **to pull the** ~ **over sb's eyes** (*fig*) dar a uno gato por liebre; ~**len**, ~**en** (*US*) *a* de lana; ~**lens** *npl* géneros *mpl* de lana; ~**ly**, ~**y** (*US*) *a* lanudo, de lana; (*fig: ideas*) confuso.

word [wəːd] *n* palabra; (*news*) noticia; (*message*) aviso // *vt* redactar; **in other** ~**s** en otras palabras; **to break/keep one's** ~ faltar a la palabra/cumplir la promesa; ~**ing** *n* redacción *f.*

wore [wɔː*] *pt of* **wear.**

work [wɔːk] *n* (*gen*) trabajo; (*job*) empleo, trabajo; (*ART, LITERATURE*) obra // *vi* trabajar; (*mechanism*) funcionar, marchar; (*medicine*) ser eficaz, surtir efecto // *vt* (*clay, wood etc*) tallar; (*mine etc*) explotar; (*machine*) manejar, hacer funcionar; (*cause*) producir; **to be out of** ~ estar parado, no tener trabajo; ~**s** *n* (*factory*) fábrica // *npl* (*of clock, machine*) mecanismo *sg*; **to** ~ **loose** *vi* (*part*) desprenderse; (*knot*) aflojarse; **to** ~ **on** *vt fus* trabajar en, dedicarse a; (*principle*) basarse en; **to** ~ **out** *vi* (*plans etc*) salir bien, funcionar // *vt* (*problem*) resolver; (*plan*) elaborar; **got it** ~ **out?** ¿da resultado?; **it** ~**s out at £100** suma 100 libras; **to get** ~**ed up** exaltarse; ~**able** *a* (*solution*) práctico, factible; ~**er** *n* trabajador/a, obrero; ~**ing class** *n* clase

f obrera; ~**-ing-class** a de clase obrera;
in ~**ing order** en funcionamiento;
~**man** n obrero; ~**manship** n (art)
hechura, arte m; (skill) habilidad f,
trabajo; ~**shop** n taller m; ~**-to-rule** n
huelga de celo.

world [wɔːld] n mundo // cpd (champion)
del mundo; (power, war) mundial; **to think
the** ~ **of sb** (fig) tener un concepto muy
alto de uno; ~**ly** a mundano; ~**-wide** a
mundial, universal.

worm [wɔːm] n gusano; (earth~) lombriz f.

worn [wɔːn] pp of **wear** // a usado; ~**-out**
a (object) gastado; (person) rendido,
agotado.

worried ['wʌrɪd] a preocupado.

worry ['wʌrɪ] n preocupación f // vt
preocupar, inquietar // vi preocuparse;
~**ing** a inquietante.

worse [wɔːs] a, ad peor, inferior // n el
peor, lo peor; **a change for the** ~ un
empeoramiento; **worsen** vt, vi empeorar;
~ **off** a (fig): **you'll be** ~ **off this way**
de esta forma estarás peor que nunca.

worship ['wɔːʃɪp] n culto; (act) adoración f
// vt adorar; **Your W~** (to mayor) señor
alcalde; (to judge) señor juez; ~**per** n
devoto/a.

worst [wɔːst] a (el/la) peor // ad peor // n
lo peor; **at** ~ en lo peor de los casos.

worth [wɔːθ] n valor m // a: **to be** ~
valer; **it's** ~ **it** vale o merece la pena;
~**less** a sin valor; (useless) inútil;
~**while** a (activity) que merece la pena,
(cause) loable.

worthy [wɔːðɪ] a (person) respetable;
(motive) honesto; ~ **of** digno de.

would [wud] auxiliary vb: **she** ~ **come**
ella vendría; **he** ~ **have come** él hubiera
venido; ~ **you like a biscuit?** ¿quieres
una galleta?; **he** ~ **go on Mondays** solía
ir los lunes; ~**-be** a (pej) presunto,
aspirante.

wound [waund] pt, pp of **wind** // n [wuːnd]
herida // vt [wuːnd] herir.

wove [wɔuv], **woven** ['wɔuvən] pt, pp of
weave.

wrangle ['ræŋgl] n riña // vi reñir.

wrap [ræp] n (stole) chal m; (cape) capa //
vt (also: ~ **up**) envolver; ~**per** n (of
book) cubierta, tapa; ~**ping paper** n
papel m de envolver.

wrath [rɔθ] n cólera.

wreath [riːθ], pl ~**s** [riːðz] n (funeral ~)
corona; (of flowers) guirnalda.

wreathe [riːð] vt ceñir.

wreck [rɛk] n naufragio; (ship) restos mpl
del barco; (pej: person) ruina // vt
destruir, hundir; (fig) arruinar; ~**age** n
restos mpl; (of building) escombros mpl.

wren [rɛn] n (ZOOL) reyezuelo.

wrench [rɛntʃ] n (TECH) llave f inglesa;
(tug) tirón // vt arrancar; **to** ~ **sth
from sb** arrebatar algo violentamente a
uno.

wrestle ['rɛsl] vi: **to** ~ **(with sb)** luchar
(con o contra uno); **wrestler** n luchador m

(de lucha libre); **wrestling** n lucha libre;
wrestling match n partido de lucha
libre.

wretched ['rɛtʃɪd] a miserable.

wriggle ['rɪgl] n (gen) culebreo // vi (gen)
serpentear.

wring [rɪŋ], pt, pp **wrung** vt torcer,
retorcer; (wet clothes) escurrir; (fig): **to** ~
sth out of sb sacar algo por la fuerza a
uno.

wrinkle ['rɪŋkl] n arruga // vt arrugar //
vi arrugarse.

wrist [rɪst] n muñeca; ~ **watch** n reloj m
de pulsera.

writ [rɪt] n mandato judicial; **to issue a** ~
against sb demandar a uno (en juicio).

write [raɪt], pt **wrote**, pp **written** vt, vi
escribir; **to** ~ **down** vt escribir; (note)
apuntar; **to** ~ **off** vt (debt) borrar (como
incobrable); (depreciate) depreciar; **to** ~
out vt escribir; **to** ~ **up** vt redactar;
~**-off** n pérdida total; **the car is a** ~**-off**
el coche es pura chatarra; **writer** n
escritor/a m/f.

writhe [raɪð] vi retorcerse.

writing ['raɪtɪŋ] n escritura; (hand-~)
letra; (of author) obra; **in** ~ por escrito;
~ **paper** n papel m de escribir.

written ['rɪtn] pp of **write**.

wrong [rɔŋ] a (bad) malo; (unfair) injusto;
(incorrect) equivocado, incorrecto; (not
suitable) inoportuno, inconveniente // ad
mal; equivocadamente // n mal m; (injustice) injusticia // vt ser injusto con;
(hurt) agraviar; **you are** ~ **to do it** estás
equivocado en hacerlo, cometes un error
al hacerlo; **you are** ~ **about that,
you've got it** ~ en eso, estás equivocado;
to be in the ~ no tener razón, tener la
culpa; **what's** ~? ¿qué pasa?; **to go** ~
(person) equivocarse; (plan) salir mal;
(machine) tener una avería; ~**ful** a
injusto; ~**ly** ad injustamente.

wrote [rɔut] pt of **write**.

wrought [rɔːt] a: ~ **iron** hierro forjado.

wrung [rʌŋ] pt, pp of **wring**.

wry [raɪ] a irónico.

wt. abbr of **weight**.

X

Xmas ['ɛksməs] n abbr of **Christmas**.

X-ray [ɛks'reɪ] n radiografía; ~**s** npl rayos
mpl X // vt hacer una radiografía a.

xylophone ['zaɪləfəun] n xilófono.

Y

yacht [jɔt] n yate m; ~**ing** n (sport)
balandrismo; **yachtsman** n balandrista m.

Yank [jæŋk] n (pej) yanqui m/f.

yap [jæp] vi (dog) aullar.

yard [jɑːd] n patio; (measure) yarda;
~**stick** n (fig) criterio, norma.

yarn [jɑːn] n hilo; (tale) cuento, historia.

yawn [jɔːn] n bostezo // vi bostezar.

yd. *abbr of* **yard(s).**

year [jɪɔ*] *n* año; **to be 8 ~s old** tener 8 años; **~ly** *a* anual // *ad* anualmente, cada año.

yearn [jɔːn] *vi*: **to ~ for sth** añorar *o* suspirar por algo; **~ing** *n* ansia, añoranza.

yeast [jiːst] *n* levadura.

yell [jɛl] *n* grito, alarido // *vi* gritar.

yellow [ˈjɛləu] *a, n* amarillo.

yelp [jɛlp] *n* aullido // *vi* aullar.

yeoman [ˈjəumən] *n*: **Y~ of the Guard** alabardero de la Casa Real.

yes [jɛs] *ad, n* sí *m*.

yesterday [ˈjɛstədɪ] *ad, n* ayer *m*.

yet [jɛt] *ad* todavía // *conj* sin embargo, a pesar de todo; **it is not finished ~** todavía no está acabado; **the best ~** el mejor hasta ahora; **as ~** hasta ahora, todavía.

yew [juː] *n* tejo.

Yiddish [ˈjɪdɪʃ] *n* judío.

yield [jiːld] *n* producción *f*; (*AGR*) cosecha; (*COMM*) rendimiento // *vt* (*gen*) producir; (*profit*) rendir // *vi* rendirse, ceder.

yoga [ˈjəugə] *n* yoga.

yog(h)ourt, yog(h)urt [ˈjəugət] *n* yogur *m*.

yoke [jəuk] *n* (*of oxen*) yunta; (*on shoulders*) balancín *m*; (*fig*) yugo // *vt* acoplar.

yolk [jəuk] *n* yema (de huevo).

yonder [ˈjɔndə*] *ad* allá (a lo lejos).

you [juː] *pron* tú; (*pl*) vosotros; (*polite form*) usted; (*: pl*) ustedes; (*complement*) te; (*: pl*) os; (*after prep*) tí; (*: pl*) vosotros; (*: formal*) le/la; (*: pl*) les; (*after prep*) usted; (*: pl*) ustedes; (*one*): **~ never know** uno nunca sabe; (*impersonal*): **~ can't do that** eso no se hace.

you'd [juːd] = **you had; you would.**

you'll [juːl] = **you will, you shall.**

young [jʌŋ] *a* joven // *npl* (*of animal*) la cría *sg*; (*people*): **the ~** los jóvenes, la juventud *sg*; **~er** *a* (*brother etc*) menor; **~ish** *a* bastante joven; **~ster** *n* joven *m/f*.

your [jɔː*] *a* tu; (*pl*) vuestro; (*formal*) su.

you're [juɔ*] = **you are.**

yours [jɔːz] *pron* tuyo; (*: pl*) vuestro; (*formal*) suyo; **is it ~?** ¿es tuyo *etc*?; **~ sincerely** *or* **faithfully** le saluda atentamente.

yourself [jɔːˈsɛlf] *pron* (*reflexive*) tú mismo; (*complement*) te; (*after prep*) tí (mismo); (*formal*) usted mismo; (*: complement*) se; (*: after prep*) sí (mismo); **yourselves** *pl pron* vosotros mismos; (*after prep*) vosotros (mismos); (*formal*) ustedes (mismos); (*: complement*) se; (*: after prep*) sí mismos.

youth [juːθ] *n* juventud *f*; (*young man*: *pl* **~s** [juːðz]) joven *m*; **~ful** *a* juvenil; **~ hostel** *n* albergue *m* de juventud.

you've [juːv] = **you have.**

Yugoslav [ˈjuːgəuˈslaːv] *a, n* yugoeslavo/a; **~ia** *n* Yugoeslavia.

Yuletide [ˈjuːltaɪd] *n* Navidad *f.*

Z

zany [ˈzeɪnɪ] *a* tonto.

zeal [ziːl] *n* celo, entusiasmo; **~ous** [ˈzɛləs] *a* celoso, entusiasta.

zebra [ˈziːbrə] *n* cebra; **~ crossing** *n* paso de peatones.

zenith [ˈzɛnɪθ] *n* cénit *m*.

zero [ˈzɪərəu] *n* cero.

zest [zɛst] *n* ánimo, vivacidad *f*.

zigzag [ˈzɪgzæg] *n* zigzag *m* // *vi* zigzaguear.

zinc [zɪŋk] *n* cinc *m*, zinc *m*.

Zionism [ˈzaɪənɪzm] *n* sionismo; **Zionist** *n* sionista *m/f.*

zip [zip] *n* (*also*: **~ fastener, ~per**) cremallera // *vt* (*also*: **~ up**) cerrar la cremallera de.

zodiac [ˈzəudɪæk] *n* zodiaco.

zombie [ˈzɔmbɪ] *n* (*fig*): **like a ~** como un sonámbulo.

zone [zəun] *n* zona.

zoo [zuː] *n* (jardín *m*) zoológico.

zoological [zuəˈlɔdʒɪkl] *a* zoológico.

zoologist [zuˈɔlədʒɪst] *n* zoólogo.

zoology [zuːˈɔlədʒɪ] *n* zoología.

zoom [zuːm] *vi*: **to ~ past** pasar zumbando; **~ lens** *n* zoom *m*.

SPANISH VERB TABLES

1 Gerund. *2* Imperative. *3* Present. *4* Preterite. *5* Future. *6* Present subjunctive. *7* Imperfect subjunctive. *8* Past participle. *9* Imperfect.
Etc indicates that the irregular root is used for all persons of the tense, e.g. **oír**: *6* oiga, oigas, oigamos, oigáis, oigan.

acertar *2* acierta *3* acierto, aciertas, acierta, aciertan *6* acierte, aciertes, acierte, acierten

acordar *2* acuerda *3* acuerdo, acuerdas, acuerda, acuerdan *6* acuerde, acuerdes, acuerde, acuerden

advertir *1* advirtiendo *2* advierte *3* advierto, adviertes, advierte, advierten *4* advirtió, advirtieron *6* advierta, adviertas, advierta, advirtamos, advirtáis, adviertan *7* advirtiera *etc*

agradecer *3* agradezco *6* agradezca *etc*

aparecer *3* aparezco *6* aparezca *etc*

aprobar *2* aprueba *3* apruebo, apruebas, aprueba, aprueban *6* apruebe, apruebes, apruebe, aprueben

atravesar *2* atraviesa *3* atravieso, atraviesas, atraviesa, atraviesan *6* atraviese, atravieses, atraviese, atraviesen

caber *3* quepo *4* cupe, cupiste, cupo, cupimos, cupisteis, cupieron *5* cabré *etc* *6* quepa *etc* *7* cupiera *etc*

caer *1* cayendo *3* caigo *4* cayó, cayeron *6* caiga *etc* *7* cayera *etc*

calentar *2* calienta *3* caliento, calientas, calienta, calientan *6* caliente, calientes, caliente, calienten

cerrar *2* cierra *3* cierro, cierras, cierra, cierran *6* cierre, cierres, cierre, cierren

COMER *1* comiendo *2* come, comed *3* como, comes, come, comemos, coméis, comen *4* comí, comiste, comió, comimos, comisteis, comieron *5* comeré, comerás, comerá, comeremos, comeréis, comerán *6* coma, comas, coma, comamos, comáis, coman *7* comiera, comieras, comiera, comiéramos, comierais, comieran *8*

comido *9* comía, comías, comía, comíamos, comíais, comían

conocer *3* conozco *6* conozca *etc*

contar *2* cuenta *3* cuento, cuentas, cuenta, cuentan *6* cuente, cuentes, cuente, cuenten

costar *2* cuesta *3* cuesto, cuestas, cuesta, cuestan *6* cueste, cuestes, cueste, cuesten

dar *3* doy *4* di, diste, dio, dimos, disteis, dieron *7* diera *etc*

decir *2* di *3* digo *4* dije, dijiste, dijo, dijimos, dijisteis, dijeron *5* diré *etc* *6* diga *etc* *7* dijera *etc* *8* dicho

despertar *2* despierta *3* despierto, despiertas, despierta, despiertan *6* despierte, despiertes, despierte, despierten

divertir *1* divirtiendo *2* divierte *3* divierto, diviertes, divierte, divierten *4* divirtió, divirtieron *6* divierta, diviertas, divierta, divirtamos, divirtáis, diviertan *7* divirtiera *etc*

dormir *1* durmiendo *2* duerme *3* duermo, duermes, duerme, duermen *4* durmió, durmieron *6* duerma, duermas, duerma, durmamos, durmáis, duerman *7* durmiera *etc*

empezar *2* empieza *3* empiezo, empiezas, empieza, empiezan *4* empecé *6* empiece, empieces, empiece, empecemos, empecéis, empiecen

entender *2* entiende *3* entiendo, entiendes, entiende, entienden *6* entienda, entiendas, entienda, entiendan

ESTAR *2* está *3* estoy, estás, está, están *4* estuve, estuviste, estuvo, estuvimos, estuvisteis, estuvieron *6* esté, estés, esté, estén *7* estuviera *etc*

HABER *3* he, has, ha, hemos, han *4* hube, hubiste, hubo, hubimos, hubisteis, hubieron *5* habré *etc 6* haya *etc 7* hubiera *etc*

HABLAR *1* hablando *2* habla, hablad *3* hablo, hablas, habla, hablamos, habláis, hablan *4* hablé hablaste, habló, hablamos, hablasteis, hablaron *5* hablaré, hablarás, hablará, hablaremos, hablaréis, hablarán *6* hable, hables, hable, hablemos, habléis, hablen *7* hablara, hablaras, hablara, habláramos, hablarais, hablaran *8* hablado *9* hablaba, hablabas, hablaba, hablábamos, hablabais, hablaban

hacer *2* haz *3* hago *4* hice, hiciste, hizo, hicimos, hicisteis, hicieron *5* haré *etc 6* haga *etc 7* hiciera *etc 8* hecho

instruir *1* instruyendo *2* instruye *3* instruyo, instruyes, instruye, instruyen *4* instruyó, instruyeron *6* instruya *etc 7* instruyera *etc*

ir *1* yendo *2* ve *3* voy, vas, va, vamos, vais, van *4* fui, fuiste, fue, fuimos, fuisteis, fueron *6* vaya, vayas, vaya, vayamos, vayáis, vayan *7* fuera *etc 8* iba, ibas, iba, íbamos, ibais, iban

jugar *2* juega *3* juego, juegas, juega, juegan *4* jugué *6* juegue *etc*

leer *1* leyendo *4* leyó, leyeron *7* leyera *etc*

morir *1* muriendo *2* muere *3* muero, mueres, muere, mueren *4* murió, murieron *6* muera, mueras, muera, muramos, muráis, mueran *7* muriera *etc 8* muerto

mostrar *2* muestra *3* muestro, muestras, muestra, muestran *6* muestre, muestres, muestre, muestren

mover *2* mueve *3* muevo, mueves, mueve, mueven *6* mueva, muevas, mueva, muevan

negar *2* niega *3* niego, niegas, niega, niegan *4* negué *6* niegue, niegues, niegue, neguemos, neguéis, nieguen

ofrecer *3* ofrezco *6* ofrezca *etc*

oír *1* oyendo *2* oye *3* oigo, oyes, oye, oyen *4* oyó, oyeron *6* oiga *etc 7* oyera *etc*

oler *2* huele *3* huelo, hueles, huele,
huelen *6* huela, huelas, huela, huelan

parecer *3* parezco *6* parezca *etc*

pedir *1* pidiendo *2* pide *3* pido, pides, pide, piden *4* pidió, pidieron *6* pida *etc 7* pidiera *etc*

pensar *2* piensa *3* pienso, piensas, piensa, piensan *6* piense, pienses, piense, piensen

perder *2* pierde *3* pierdo, pierdes, pierde, pierden *6* pierda, pierdas, pierda, pierdan

poder *1* pudiendo *2* puede *3* puedo, puedes, puede, pueden *4* pude, pudiste, pudo, pudimos, pudisteis, pudieron *5* podré *etc 6* pueda, puedas, pueda, puedan *7* pudiera *etc*

poner *2* pon *3* pongo *4* puse, pusiste, puso, pusimos, pusisteis, pusieron *5* pondré *etc 6* ponga *etc 7* pusiera *etc 8* puesto

preferir *1* prefiriendo *2* prefiere *3* prefiero, prefieres, prefiere, prefieren *4* prefirió, prefirieron *6* prefiera, prefieras, prefiera, prefiramos, prefiráis, prefieran *7* prefiriera *etc*

querer *2* quiere *3* quiero, quieres, quiere, quieren *4* quise, quisiste, quiso, quisimos, quisisteis, quisieron *5* querré *etc 6* quiera, quieras, quiera, quieran *7* quisiera *etc*

reír *2* ríe *3* río, ríes, ríe, ríen *4* rió, rieron *6* ría, rías, ría, riamos, riáis, rían *7* riera *etc*

repetir *1* repitiendo *2* repite *3* repito, repites, repite, repiten *4* repitió, repitieron *6* repita *etc 7* repitiera *etc*

rogar *2* ruega *3* ruego, ruegas, ruega, ruegan *4* rogué *6* ruegue, ruegues, ruegue, roguemos, roguéis, rueguen

saber *3* sé *4* supe, supiste, supo, supimos, supisteis, supieron *5* sabré *etc 6* sepa *etc 7* supiera *etc*

salir *2* sal *3* salgo *5* saldré *etc 6* salga *etc*

seguir *1* siguiendo *2* sigue *3* sigo, sigues, sigue, siguen *4* siguió, siguieron *6* siga *etc 7* siguiera *etc*

sentar *2* sienta *3* siento, sientas,

sienta, sientan *6* siente, sientes, siente, sienten

sentir *1* sintiendo *2* siente *3* siento, sientes, siente, sienten *4* sintió, sintieron *6* sienta, sientas, sienta, sintamos, sintáis, sientan *7* sintiera *etc*

SER *2* sé *3* soy, eres, es, somos, sois, son *4* fui, fuiste, fue, fuimos, fuisteis, fueron *6* sea *etc* *7* fuera *etc* *9* era, eras, era, éramos, erais, eran

servir *1* sirviendo *2* sirve *3* sirvo, sirves, sirve, sirven *4* sirvió, sirvieron *6* sirva *etc* *7* sirviera *etc*

soñar *2* sueña *3* sueño, sueñas, sueña, sueñan *6* sueñe, sueñes, sueñe, sueñen

tener *2* ten *3* tengo, tienes, tiene, tienen *4* tuve, tuviste, tuvo, tuvimos, tuvisteis, tuvieron *5* tendré *etc* *6* tenga *etc* *7* tuviera *etc*

traer *1* trayendo *3* traigo *4* traje, trajiste, trajo, trajimos, trajisteis, trajeron *6* traiga *etc* *7* trajera *etc*

valer *2* val *3* valgo *5* valdré *etc* *6* valga *etc*

venir *2* ven *3* vengo, vienes, viene, vienen *4* vine, viniste, vino, vinimos, vinisteis, vinieron *5* vendré *etc* *6* venga *etc* *7* viniera *etc*

ver *3* veo *6* vea *etc* *8* visto *9* veía *etc*

vestir *1* vistiendo *2* viste *3* visto, vistes, viste, visten *4* vistió, vistieron *6* vista *etc* *7* vistiera *etc*

VIVIR *1* viviendo *2* vive, vivid *3* vivo, vives, vive, vivimos, vivís, viven *4* viví, viviste, vivió, vivimos, vivisteis, vivieron *5* viviré, vivirás, vivirá, viviremos, viviréis, vivirán *6* viva, vivas, viva, vivamos, viváis, vivan *7* viviera, vivieras, viviera, viviéramos, vivierais, vivieran *8* vivido *9* vivía, vivías, vivía, vivíamos, vivíais, vivían

volver *2* vuelve *3* vuelvo, vuelves, vuelve, vuelven *6* vuelva, vuelvas, vuela, vuelvan *8* vuelto.

VERBOS IRREGULARES EN INGLÉS

present	pt	pp	present	pt	pp
arise	arose	arisen	eat	ate	eaten
awake	awoke	awaked	fall	fell	fallen
be (am,	was,	been	feed	fed	fed
is, are;	were		feel	felt	felt
being)			fight	fought	fought
bear	bore	born(e)	find	found	found
beat	beat	beaten	flee	fled	fled
become	became	become	fling	flung	flung
befall	befell	befallen	fly	flew	flown
begin	began	begun	forbid	forbade	forbidden
behold	beheld	beheld	forecast	forecast	forecast
bend	bent	bent	forget	forgot	forgotten
beset	beset	beset	forgive	forgave	forgiven
bet	bet,	bet,	forsake	forsook	forsaken
	betted	betted	freeze	froze	frozen
bid	bid	bid	get	got	got, (US)
bind	bound	bound			gotten
bite	bit	bitten	give	gave	given
bleed	bled	bled	go	went	gone
blow	blew	blown	(goes)		
break	broke	broken	grind	ground	ground
breed	bred	bred	grow	grew	grown
bring	brought	brought	hang	hung,	hung,
build	built	built		hanged	hanged
burn	burnt,	burnt,	have	had	had
	burned	burned	hear	heard	heard
burst	burst	burst	hide	hid	hidden
buy	bought	bought	hit	hit	hit
can	could	(been able)	hold	held	held
cast	cast	cast	hurt	hurt	hurt
catch	caught	caught	keep	kept	kept
choose	chose	chosen	kneel	knelt,	knelt,
cling	clung	clung		kneeled	kneeled
come	came	come	know	knew	known
cost	cost	cost	lay	laid	laid
creep	crept	crept	lead	led	led
cut	cut	cut	lean	leant,	leant,
deal	dealt	dealt		leaned	leaned
dig	dug	dug	leap	leapt,	leapt,
do (3rd	did	done		leaped	leap
person;			learn	learnt,	lea
he/she/				learned	
it/does)			leave	left	
draw	drew	drawn	lend	lent	
dream	dreamed,	dreamed,	let	let	
	dreamt	dreamt	lie	lay	s
drink	drank	drunk	(lying)		
drive	drove	driven	light		spea
dwell	dwelt	dwelt			

present	pt	pp	present	pt	pp
lose	lost	lost	speed	sped,	sped,
make	made	made		speeded	speeded
may	might	—	spell	spelt,	spelt,
mean	meant	meant		spelled	spelled
meet	met	met	spend	spent	spent
mistake	mistook	mistaken	spill	spilt,	spilt,
mow	mowed	mown,		spilled	spilled
		mowed	spin	spun	spun
must	(had to)	(had to)	spit	spat	spat
pay	paid	paid	split	split	split
put	put	put	spoil	spoiled,	spoiled,
quit	quit,	quit,		spoilt	spoilt
	quitted	quitted	spread	spread	spread
read	read	read	spring	sprang	sprung
rend	rent	rent	stand	stood	stood
rid	rid	rid	steal	stole	stolen
ride	rode	ridden	stick	stuck	stuck
ring	rang	rung	sting	stung	stung
rise	rose	risen	stink	stank	stunk
run	ran	run	stride	strode	strode
saw	sawed	sawn	strike	struck	struck,
say	said	said			stricken
see	saw	seen	strive	strove	striven
seek	sought	sought	swear	swore	sworn
sell	sold	sold	sweep	swept	swept
send	sent	sent	swell	swelled	swollen,
set	set	set			swelled
shake	shook	shaken	swim	swam	swum
shall	should	—	swing	swung	swung
shear	sheared	shorn,	take	took	taken
		sheared	teach	taught	taught
shed	shed	shed			
shine	shone	shone	tear	tore	torn
shoot	shot	shot	tell	told	told
show	showed	shown	think	thought	thought
shrink	shrank	shrunk	throw	threw	thrown
shut	shut	shut	thrust	thrust	thrust
sing	sang	sung	tread	trod	trodden
sink	sank	sunk	wake	woke,	woken,
sit	sat	sat		waked	waked
slay	slew	slain	wear	wore	worn
sleep	slept	slept	weave	wove,	woven,
slide	slid	slid		weaved	weaved
sling	slung	slung	wed	wedded,	wedded,
slit	slit	slit		wed	wed
...ell	smelt,	smelt,	weep	wept	wept
	smelled	smelled	win	won	won
	sowed	sown,	wind	wound	wound
		sowed	wring	wrung	wrung
	spoke	spoken	write	wrote	written

404

LOS NÚMEROS

NUMBERS

un, uno(a)/primer, primero(a)	1	one/first
dos/segundo(a)	2	two/second
tres/tercer, tercero(a)	3	three/third
cuatro/cuarto(a)	4	four/fourth
cinco/quinto(a)	5	five/fifth
seis/sexto(a)	6	six/sixth
siete/séptimo(a)	7	seven/seventh
ocho/octavo(a)	8	eight/eighth
nueve/noveno(a)	9	nine/ninth
diez/décimo(a)	10	ten/tenth
once/undécimo(a)	11	eleven/eleventh
doce/duodécimo(a)	12	twelve/twelfth
trece/decimotercio(a)	13	thirteen/thirteenth
catorce/decimocuarto(a)	14	fourteen/fourteenth
quince/decimoquinto(a)	15	fifteen/fifteenth
dieciséis/decimosexto(a)	16	sixteen/sixteenth
diecisiete/decimoséptimo(a)	17	seventeen/seventeenth
dieciocho/decimooctavo(a)	18	eighteen/eighteenth
diecinueve/decimonoveno(a)	19	nineteen/nineteenth
veinte/vigésimo(a)	20	twenty/twentieth
veintiuno	21	twenty-one
veintidós	22	twenty-two
treinta	30	thirty
treinta y uno(a)	31	thirty-one
treinta y dos	32	thirty-two
cuarenta	40	forty
cuarenta y uno(a)	41	forty-one
cincuenta	50	fifty
cincuenta y uno(a)	51	fifty-one
sesenta	60	sixty
sesenta y uno(a)	61	sixty-one
setenta	70	seventy
setenta y uno(a)	71	seventy-one
setenta y dos	72	seventy-two
ochenta	80	eighty
ochenta y uno(a)	81	eighty-one
noventa	90	ninety
noventa y uno(a)	91	ninety-one
cien, ciento/centésimo(a)	100	a hundred, one hundred/hundredth
ciento uno(a)	101	a hundred and one
doscientos(as)	200	two hundred
doscientos(as) uno(a)	201	two hundred and one
trescientos(as)	300	three hundred
trescientos(as) uno(a)	301	three hundred and one
quatrocientos(as)	400	four hundred
quinientos(as)	500	five hundred
seiscientos(as)	600	six hundred
setecientos(as)	700	seven hundred
ochocientos(as)	800	eight hundred
novecientos(as)	900	nine hundred

milésimo(a)	1000	a thousand, one thousand/thousandth
mil dos	1002	a thousand and two
cinco mil	5000	five thousand
un millón	1,000,000	a million, one million

Ejemplos	**Examples**
va a llegar el 7 (de mayo)	he's arriving on the 7th (of May)
vive en el número 7	he lives at number 7
el capítulo/la página 7	chapter/page 7
llegó séptimo	he came in 7th
1º(1ª), 2º(2ª), 3º(3ª), 4º(4ª), 5º(5ª)	1st, 2nd, 3rd, 4th, 5th

N.B. In Spanish the ordinal numbers from 1 to 10 are commonly used; from 11 to 20 rather less; above 21 they are rarely written and almost never heard in speech. The custom is to replace the forms for 21 and above by the cardinal number.

LA HORA

THE TIME

¿qué hora es?	*what time is it?*
es/son	*it's o it is*
¿a qué hora?	*(at) what time?*
a	*at*
medianoche, las doce (de la noche)	midnight
la una (de la madrugada)	one (o'clock) (a.m. *o* in the morning), 1 a.m.
la una y diez	ten past one
la una y cuarto *or* quince	a quarter past one, one fifteen
la una y media *or* treinta	half past one, one thirty
las dos menos cuarto, la una cuarenta y cinco	a quarter to two, one forty-five
la dos menos diez, la una cincuenta	ten to two, one fifty
mediodía, las doce (de la tarde)	twelve (o'clock), midday, noon
la una (de la tarde), las trece (horas)	one (o'clock) (p.m. *o* in the afternoon)
las siete (de la tarde), las diecinueve (horas)	seven (o'clock) (p.m. *o* at night)
las nueve y media (de la noche), las veintiuna (horas) y media	nine thirty (p.m. *o* at night)